1996

MOROCCO & TUNISIA HANDBOOK

with Algeria, Libya and Mauritania

Editors *Anne and Keith McLachlan*
Cartographer *Sebastian Ballard*

If you want to be a traveller, have always
the eyes of a falcon, the ears of an ass,
the face of an ape, the mouth of a hog,
the shoulder of a camel, the legs of a stag,
and see that you never want two bags very full,
that is one of patience and another of money.
John Florio (1553–1625)

TRADE & TRAVEL
Handbooks

Trade & Travel Publications Ltd
6 Riverside Court, Lower Bristol Road, Bath BA2 3DZ, England
Telephone 01225 469141   Fax 01225 469461
Email 100660.1250@compuserve.com

©Trade & Travel Publications Ltd., September 1995

ISBN 0 900751 67 3   ISSN 1358-3301

CIP DATA: A catalogue record for this book is available from the British Library

In North America, published and distributed by

PASSPORT BOOKS
a division of *NTC Publishing Group*

4255 West Touhy Avenue, Lincolnwood (Chicago), Illinois 60646-1975, USA
Telephone 708-679-5500   Fax 708-679-2494   Email NTCPUB2@AOL.COM

ISBN 0-8442-8889-6

Library of Congress Catalog Card Number 95-69401

Passport Books and colophon are registered trademarks of NTC Publishing Group

IMPORTANT: While every endeavour is made to ensure that the facts printed in this book are correct at the time of going to press, travellers are cautioned to obtain authoritative advice from consulates, airlines, etc, concerning current travel and visa requirements and conditions before embarking. The publishers cannot accept legal responsibility for errors, however caused, that are printed in this book.

MAPS – Publisher's note: a number of frontiers in the area covered by this Handbook are disputed and the subject of territorial claims by various countries in the region. Neither the coloured nor the black and white maps in this book are intended to have any political significance or purport to show authenticated international boundaries.

Cover illustration by Suzanne Evans

Printed and bound in Great Britain by Clays Ltd., Bungay, Suffolk

CONTENTS

PREFACE	5
INTRODUCTION AND HINTS	7
Before you go	7
Getting there	8
When you arrive	9
Where to stay	11
Food and drink	12
Getting around	13
Communications	13
HEALTH INFORMATION	15
REGIONAL INTRODUCTION	24
History of North Africa	24
Travelling in Islamic countries	37
Political risks for travellers	40
Handling the local bureaucracy	43
Travel and survival in the desert	45
Wildlife	49
Dress in North Africa	52
Jewellery of North Africa	56
Language for travel	59
MOROCCO	65
Introduction	65
Land and life	65
Culture	69
History	70
Modern Morocco	71
Rabat and Environs	76
Tanger, Mediterranean Coast and The Rif	92
Northern and Central Atlantic Coast	118
Meknes, Fes and Central Morocco	139
Marrakech, The High and Middle Atlas	172
Southern Morocco	198
Information for visitors	226
MAURITANIA	240
Introduction	240
Land and life	240
Culture	244
History	245
Modern Mauritania	247
Nouakchott and Environs	251
The North	256
The South	265
Information for visitors	270
ALGERIA	278
Introduction	278
Land and life	278
Culture	283
History	286
Modern Algeria	287
Algiers and Environs	291
The East	304
The Northwest	324
The South	334
Information for visitors	354
TUNISIA	361
Introduction	361
Land and life	361
Culture	366
History	367
Modern Tunisia	368
Tunis	372
Cap Bon Peninsula	397
Northern Tunisia	405
Central Tunisia	423
The Djerid	450
Southern Tunisia	461
Information for visitors	478
LIBYA	489
Introduction	489
Land and life	489
Culture	493
History	495
Modern Libya	496
Tripoli	502
Benghazi	534
Fezzan	550
Al-Khalij	559
Information for Visitors	569
GLOSSARY	581
INDEXES	585

THE EDITORS

Anne McLachlan

Anne McLachlan has travelled extensively for many years in North Africa, the Middle East and the Mediterranean, living for a time in Turkey, Iran and Spain. Frequent travel to the North African region has given a broad perspective. Recent visits gathering material for the *Handbooks* include a return to northern Morocco to look in detail at Tanger and the Mediterranean coast, at the Rif mountains and Fes and its environs; northern Tunisia from Bizerte to the Algerian border. She has also been on three fact-finding journeys to Egypt, preparing material for the new *Egypt Handbook*, out in January 1996. The first, travelling by 4WD to the oases of the Western Desert of Egypt, the second, returning to her well-trodden paths in Cairo and the Nile Delta and the third to Sinai.

Iberia is her second home where she lives for part of each year in Andalucía, the heart of Moorish Spain, with easy access to Morocco and the countries of Maghrebi North Africa.

Keith McLachlan

Keith McLachlan has been a professional observer and traveller in the area covered by this *Handbook* for many years. He made his first trans-Saharan voyage as early as 1958, travelling from Al-Khoms on the Mediterranean across the mountains and deserts deep into southern Libya. Since then he has visited each of the countries of North Africa on a regular basis, spending long periods each year in travel. Once again he has journeyed to Libya, Morocco, and Tunisia gathering material for the *Handbook*, as well as Egypt for the *Egypt Handbook*.

His position as professor at the School of Oriental and African Studies involves him in regular research visits to North Africa and he has a long acquaintance with the quirks of travel in this area. He also advises North African governments on their international border disputes and has a constant professional involvement in problems of oil and economic development in the region.

PREFACE

The new ***Morocco and Tunisia Handbook 1996*** concentrates its coverage on the classical Maghreb or western reaches of the Islamic world – Morocco, Mauritania, Algeria, Tunisia and Libya. The traveller can use the *Morocco and Tunisia Handbook* to obtain a unitary view of this fascinating quadrant of the Mediterranean-North West Africa. The common strands of history, architecture and popular culture can be traced along with the great wealth of regional variety.

A range of new and up-dated information for the traveller has been incorporated. Considerable detail has been developed on the region of northern and central Morocco. Morocco offers continuing high value for travellers with its topographic splendours in the High Atlas, a wonderful range of accommodation and delights of low cost transport facilities. Similarly the potentials for the traveller in the much-undervalued northern hill and coastal lands of Tunisia are newly explored in the *Handbook*. Information on travel in Libya has been extended and brought up-to-date, including details on local transport.

The variety of attractions for the visitor in North Africa is considerable. Scenery is infinitely varied from the flat deserts of Saharan Libya and coastal plains of the Tunisian Sahel to the high passes of the Moroccan Atlas and the immense peaks of the Algerian Tells. Desert travel is increasingly catered for throughout North Africa and adventure itineraries in the S of Libya, Tunisia and Morocco are available using 'all-terrain' vehicles. The pre-historic cave painting of the Akasus remain open to and a great treat for the more experienced visitor.

Understanding in the western indus-trial countries of religious and political life in North Africa has always been rather weak. Much has been made of the growth of Islamic fundamentalism and political dissent without realising that ferment of this kind has always been a feature of the region but rarely affects the foreign traveller, who can expect a hospitable and warm welcome in most parts of North Africa. Of course, some caution is necessary but those travellers who are inoffensive and appreciative of the values of local Islamic cultures will find few problems. Morocco is visitor-friendly and is increasingly a venue for international events. The continuing embargo on air transport has made a journey to Libya most likely to begin in Tunisia, adding opportunites to extend the visit but making no problems within the country itself.

Algeria is a clear exception to this rule as the political situation remains uncertain with all foreigners extremely vulnerable. Travel to Algeria only after taking advice on the current situation.

For this edition we have received considerable assistance from Derek Alderton who travelled all over eastern Tunisia, Stephano Ciarli who covered much of Libya by public transport, St John Gould who made many visits to Morocco to collect fresh information and Diana Stone who updated Mauritania. We are also grateful to the many travellers who during the last year have sent us corrections, suggestions and new material. They are acknowledged at the end of each *Information for visitors* section. For their production expertise our thanks to Joanne Morgan, Ann Griffiths and Lorraine Horler.

Anne & Keith McLachlan
The Editors, London

6

MAP SYMBOLS

International Border	— · ◥	State, Regional Capital	□
Disputed Border	— — — ◥	Other Towns	○
State / Province Border	—·—·—	Bus Station	B
Main Road (National Highway)	R 15	Car Park	P
Other Road	————	Hospital	H
Jeepable Road, Track, Trek, Path, Ferry	·— — — ··	Post Office	PO
Railway, Station	┼┼┼■┼┼ T	Key Numbers	27
		Airport	◰
Contours (approx)	〰	Bridge	⊨
River	*River Nile*	Mountain	⩜
Fortified Wall	▲ ▲ ▲		
Built Up Area	▨	Oasis	𝓎
Lake, Reservoir	🗺	National Park, Wildlife Park, Bird Sanctuary	♦
Salt Lake	〰	Church / Cathedral	✝
National Park, Garden, Stadium	▦	Mosque	🕌
Sand Bank, Beach	▦		

MTH0

INTRODUCTION AND HINTS

CONTENTS	
Before you go	7
Getting there	8
When you arrive	9
Where to stay	11
Food and drink	12
Getting around	13
Communications	13

General note The advice given below represents a regional summary of more detailed information provided in the *Information for visitors* section of each country entry.

Before you go

Documents

● Passports

All foreign tourists are recommended to have a passport that is valid for the whole of the period of stay. This avoids unnecessary contact with the bureaucracy. Many countries require visas. Details are given in each country section.

● Special permits

Certain zones, particularly adjacent to borders and in areas of conflict have restricted access and travel there is permitted only with military approval. Details of sensitive areas are given in the relevant country section.

● Identity & membership cards

If you are in full-time education you will be entitled to an International Student Identity Card (ISIC), which is distributed by student travel offices and travel agencies in 77 countries. The ISIC gives you special prices on all forms of transport (air, sea, rail etc) and access to a variety of other concessions and services. Contact ISIC, Box 9048, 1000 Copenhagen, Denmark, T (+45) 33939303.

Health

See main section, page 15

Money

● Travellers' cheques

TCs can be honoured in most banks and *bureaux de change*. US$ are the easiest to exchange particularly if they are well-known like Visa, Thomas Cook or American Express. There is always a transaction charge so it is a balance between using high value cheques and paying one charge and carrying extra cash or using lower value cheques and paying more charges. A small amount of cash, again in US$, is useful in an emergency.

Some countries have a fixed exchange

EXCHANGE RATES (23 JUNE 1995)					
	US$	£	Ffr	DM	Ptas
Algeria (Dinar)	46.11	73.96	9.49	33.23	0.38
Libya (Dinar)	0.35	0.57	0.07	0.26	0.003
Mauritania (Ouguiya)	125.28	200.96	25.79	90.28	1.04
Morocco (Dirham)	8.34	13.38	1.72	6.01	0.07
Tunisia (Dinar)	0.93	1.49	0.08	0.67	0.008

rate – wherever the transaction is carried out. Other countries have a varied exchange rate and, to a greater or lesser degree, a black market. See the appropriate country sections and be sure you know what you are doing before you get involved.

What to take

Travellers tend to take more than they need though requirements vary with the destination and the type of travel that is to be undertaken. Laundry services are generally cheap and speedy. A travel-pack, a hybrid backpack/suitcase, rather than a rigid suitcase, covers most eventualities and survives bus boot, roof rack and plane/ship hold travel with ease. Serious trekkers will need a framed backpack.

Clothing of light cotton or cotton/polyester with a a woollen sweater for evenings, more northern regions, higher altitudes and the clear desert nights. Comfortable shoes with socks as feet may swell in hot weather. Modest dress for women including (see page 9) a sunhat and headscarf. See hints in country sections.

● **Checklist:**
Air cushions for hard seating
Bumbag
Earplugs
Eye mask
Insect repellent and/or mosquito
   net, electric mosquito mats, coils
Neck pillow
International driving licence
Photocopies of essential documents
Plastic bags
Short wave radio
Spare passport photographs
Sun hat
Sun protection cream
Sunglasses
Swiss Army knife
Tissues/toilet paper
Torch
Umbrella (excellent protection from
   sun and unfriendly dogs)

Wipes (*Damp Ones*, *Baby Wipes*)
Zip-lock bags

Those intending to stay in budget accommodation might also include:
Cotton sheet sleeping bag
Money belt
Padlock (for hotel room and pack)
Soap
Student card
Towel
Toilet paper
Universal bath plug

● **Health kit**
Antiacid tablets
Anti-diarrhoea tablets
Anti-malaria tablets
Anti-infective ointment
Condoms
Contraceptives
Dusting powder for feet
First aid kit and disposable needles
Flea powder
Sachets of rehydration salts
Tampons
Travel sickness pills
Water sterilizing tablets

Getting there

Air

It is possible to fly direct to several destinations within the countries of the *Handbook* (other than Libya which is currently suffering a UN embargo on international flights) from Europe, from the Middle East and most adjacent African countries and additionally into Morocco from USA, Canada and Brazil and into Egypt from USA. More details are given in the *Information for Visitors* sections. General airline restrictions apply with regard to luggage weight allowances before surcharge; normally 30 kg for first class and 20 kg for business and economy class. An understanding of the term 'limited' with regard to amount of hand luggage varies greatly. The major destinations are the national capitals and, particularly in Morocco and

Tunisia, the tourist airports. The scheduled flying times from London are Rabat 2½ hrs, Tanger 2 hrs, Tunis 2½ hrs, and from Paris are Nouakchott 5 hrs, Algiers 2½ hrs. Package tours which frequently offer cheaper flight-only deals generally operate smaller planes which take longer.

● **Discounts**

It is possible to obtain significantly cheaper tickets by avoiding school vacation times, by flying at night, by shopping around and by booking early to obtain one of the quota of discounted fares. Group discounts apply in many instances.

● **Airline security**

International airlines vary in their arrangements and requirements for security over electrical items such as radios, tape recorders and lap-top computers (as does the interest of the customs officials on arrival and departure). Check in advance if you can, carry the items in your hand luggage for convenience and have them wrapped for safety but available for inspection. Note that internal airlines often have different rules from the international carriers.

● **Note**

This *Handbook* outlines further details on air links to and from each country, arrival and departure regulations, airport taxes, customs regulations and secu-

rity arrangements for air travel in the relevant *Information for visitors* sections.

Sea

Ferries Numerous ferries operate across the Mediterranean carrying both vehicles and foot passengers. Prices vary according to the season. Details are given in the country sections along with rail and road entry points.

When you arrive

Appearance

There is a natural prejudice in all countries against travellers who ignore personal hygiene and have a generally unkempt appearance. Observation of the local people will show, where they can afford it, their attention to cleanliness and neatness. The men attend the office in suits with a white shirt and tie or a newly pressed native garment and the women beneath their veil are very well dressed. All persons other than manual workers will be fully dressed. Scantily clad visitors, other than round the hotel pool, show insufficient consideration for their host country. In a hot climate it is eminently sensible and certainly more comfortable to copy the locals and cover the body.

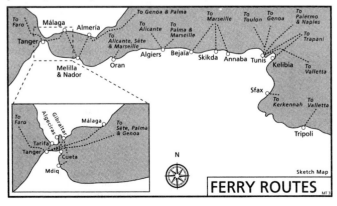

FERRY ROUTES

Bargaining

Bargaining is expected in the bazaars. Start lower than you would expect to pay, be polite and good humoured, enjoy the experience and if the final price doesn't suit – walk away. There are plenty more shops. Once you have gained confidence, try it on the taxi drivers and when negotiating a room.

Beggars

Beggars are a fact of life. It is unlikely that they will be too persistent. Have a few very small coins ready. You will be unable to help many and your donation will most probably be passed on to the syndicate organizer! In the most visited areas of Morocco the tourist police move the mobile beggars on.

Confidence tricksters

The most common 'threat' to tourists is found where people are on the move, at ports and railway and bus stations, selling 'antiques', 'gems', offering extremely favourable currency exchange rates and spinning 'hard luck' stories. Confidence tricksters are, by definition, extremely convincing and persuasive. Be warned – if the offer seems too good to be true that is probably what it is.

Courtesy

Politeness is always appreciated. You will notice a great deal of hand shaking, kissing, clapping on backs on arrival and departure from a group. There is no need to follow this to the extreme but handshakes, smiles and thank yous go a long way. Be patient and friendly but firm when bargaining for items and avoid displays of anger. Be very careful never to criticize as officials, waiters and taxi drivers can understand more than you think. See page 43 on how to deal with the bureaucracy. **However** when it comes to getting onto public transport, forget it all and be ready to push.

Drugs

Ignore all offers of drugs. The Rif area of Morocco is one area particularly noted for this. It is more than likely that the 'pusher', if successful, will report you to the police.

Firearms

Firearms including hunting guns may not be taken into any of the countries covered in this book without prior permission.

Mosques

Visitors to mosques (where permitted) and other religious buildings will normally be expected to remove their shoes and cover-all garments will be available for hire to enable the required standard of dress to be met.

Personal security

Travellers in North Africa are unlikely to experience threats to personal security. On the contrary, followers of Islam are expected to honour the stranger in their midst. However basic common sense is needed for the protection of personal property, money and papers. Use hotel safes for valuable items as hotel rooms cannot be regarded as secure and when travelling, carry valuables as close to the body as possible, and where convenient, in more than one place. External pockets on bags and clothing should never be used for carrying valuables. Bag snatching and pick pocketing is more common in crowded tourist areas. It is obviously unwise to lay temptation in the way of a man whose annual income is less than the cost of your return airfare. **NB** It is wise to keep a record of your passport number, TCs number and air ticket number somewhere separate from the actual items.

Police

Report any incident which involves you or your possessions. An insurance claim of any size will require the backing of a police report. If involvement with the police is more serious, for instance a driving accident, remain calm, read the section on how to deal with the bureaucracy (see page 43) and contact the nearest consular office without delay.

Prisoners Abroad

Prisoners Abroad, a UK charity, was formed to help people who fall foul of the law in foreign countries, where sentencing can be much harsher than at home. If you or a friend do get into trouble, you can contact Prisoners Abroad at 72-82 Rosebury Ave, London EC1R 4RR, T 071 833 3467, F 071 833 3467 (F +4471 833 3467 if outside the UK).

Tipping

Tipping in Morocco and Tunisia is a way of life – everyone expects a coin for services rendered or supposed. Many get no real wage and rely on tips. In Algeria, on the contrary, the practice is not widespread. In hotels and restaurants the service has probably been included so a tip to the waiter is an optional extra. It does no harm to round up the taxi fare, and a handful of small coins eases the way. Check in the relevant country section for what is expected.

Women travelling alone

Women face greater difficulties than men or couples. Young Muslim women rarely travel without the protection of a male or older female, hence a single Western woman is regarded as strange and is supposed to be of easy virtue – a view perpetuated by Hollywood. To minimise the pestering that will certainly occur, dress modestly, the less bare flesh the better (see page 37), steadfastly ignore rude and suggestive comments directed at you but aimed at boosting the caller's ego, avoid any behaviour which would aggravate the situation, and keep a sense of humour. Single men often attract greater attention from customs officials and are more liable to receive unwelcome propositions.

Where to stay

Hotels

There is a very wide range of accommodation in North Africa. In the major cities and the popular tourist resorts, the top quality hotel chains are represented. The best offer top class accommodation with the full range of personal and business facilities while the cheapest are spartan and most frequently sordid. Availability of accommodation for visitors varies from country to country. While Morocco and Tunisia are organized in this respect, the traveller in Libya, Algeria and Mauritania will experience greater problems in finding a place to lay his head. The peak season when there is greatest pressure on accommodation varies on the country and the latitude and the relevant country section gives details.

Prices for the top class hotels are on a par with prices in Europe while medium range hotels are generally cheaper in comparison. In almost every case, the advertised room price, that charged to the individual traveller, is higher than that paid by the package tourist and it may be worth bargaining. The six categories used in this *Handbook* are graded as accurately as possible by cost converted to American dollars. Our hotel price range is based on a double room with bath/shower in high season and includes any relevant taxes and service charges but no meals. Normally the following facilities will be available and are therefore not repeated in the descriptions.

Abbreviations in the listings: a/c = air conditioning, T = telephone, Tx = Telex, F = Facsimile. Bath denotes bath and/or shower.

AL US$90+ This is an international class luxury hotel as found in the capital, large cities and major tourist centres.

Good management ensures that all facilities for business and leisure travellers are of the highest international standard.

A US$75-90 An international hotel with choice of restaurants, coffee shop, shops, bank, travel agent, swimming pool, some business facilities, some sports facilities, air conditioned rooms with WC, bath/shower, TV, phone, mini-bar, daily clean linen.

B US$60-75 Offers most of the facilities in **A** but without the luxury, reduced number of restaurants, smaller rooms, limited range of shops and sport. Offers pool and air conditioned rooms with WC, shower/bath.

C US$40-60 These are the best medium range hotels found in the smaller towns and less popular areas of larger cities. Usually comfortable, bank, shop, pool. Best rooms have air conditioning, own bath/shower and WC.

D US$20-40 Might be the best you can find in a small town. Best rooms may have own WC and bath/shower. Depending on management will have room service and choice of cuisine in restaurant.

E US$10-20 Simple provision. Perhaps fan cooler. May not have restaurant. Shared WC and showers with hot water (when available).

F under US$10 Very basic, shared toilet facilities, variable in cleanliness, noise, often in dubious locations.

Ungraded hotels – too primitive to reach the standard of **F** – but may be cleaner and more interesting than **F**.

Camping

Provision varies. It is permitted at certain hostels; enlightened countries have both government and private sites, often with guards; beach camping depends on location and/or gaining permission. Often the difference between a cheap hotel and paying for a campsite is minimal. Assess the security of any site you choose and where possible ask permission to avoid any unpleasantness.

Youth hostels

These are found in most North African countries as part of the International Youth Hostel Federation. They differ according to location and size, provide a common room, sleeping provision in dormitories, a self-catering kitchen and often budget meals. There is no maximum age limit, persons under 15 should be accompanied by an adult and in some hostels only male guests are accepted. Permission is necessary to stay more than 3 days in one hostel. Most hostels are open 1000-1200 and 1700-2200. Prices are given in the country sections.

Food and drink

Food

Restaurants   Given the variations in price of food on any menu our restaurants are divided where possible into three simple grades – ♦♦♦ expensive, ♦♦ average and ♦ cheap. Bearing in mind the suggestions in the Health section (page 18) on food best avoided in uncertain conditions, a wide choice still remains. Forget the stories of sheep's eyes and enjoy the selection of filling, spicy and slightly unusual meals. For the less adventurous, Western style food (other than pork) can be found in most hotels.

Drink

The most common drink is tea without milk, in a small glass, probably with mint. Coffee is generally available too. Bottled soft fizzy drinks are found even in small settlements and are safer than water. *Alcohol* is officially forbidden in Libya but other countries sell beer and local wine. Where available imported wine and spirits are very expensive. *Bottled water* is an essential part of every traveller's baggage.

Water

Be prepared for shortage or restriction of water, never regard tap water safe to drink. Bottled water is cheap and easily available. See Health, page 18.

Getting around

Air

Domestic airlines link the main towns and run to published but infinitely variable schedules. They are especially recommended to cover the considerable distances in Algeria and to avoid hot dusty rides. Safety records vary. Don't use internal airlines in Libya for this reason. See country sections for times and availability.

Road

Conditions vary from excellent dual carriageways to rural roads and unnerving one vehicle wide and farflung roads which are a rough, unsurfaced *piste*. Problems include blockage by snow in winter, floods in spring and sand at any time.

Buses, the main mode and cheapest means of transport, link nearly all the towns. Air-conditioned coaches connect the biggest cities and keep more strictly to the timetable. Smaller private vehicles require greater patience and often work on the 'leave when full' principle. Book in advance wherever possible. Orderly queues become a jostling mass when the bus arrives. Inner city buses are usually dirty and crowded and getting off can be more difficult than getting on. Sorting out the routes and the fares makes taking a taxi a better option.

Taxis The larger, long distance taxis are good value, sometimes following routes not covered by service buses and almost always more frequent. They run on the 'leave when full' principle and for more space or a quicker departure the unoccupied seats can be purchased. In general these taxis are 25% more expensive than the bus. Inner city taxis are smaller, may have a working meter, and

can also be shared.

Car hire

Cars can be hired, with varying degrees of difficulty. They are not cheap and the condition of the vehicles often leaves much to be desired. The problems of driving your own or a hired car are two fold – other drivers and pedestrians.

Hitchhiking

This is really only a consideration in outlying places not served by the very cheap public transport. Here, eventually, a place on a truck or lorry will be available, for which a charge is made.

Train

Rail networks are limited, are slow and generally more expensive than the alternative – the bus. First class is always more comfortable; offering air-conditioning and sometimes sleeping accommodation. Cheaper carriages can be crowded and none too clean. Train travel offers the advantage of views available only from the track.

Communications

Language

While Arabic is the official language in all the countries of North Africa, many people have as their first language one of the many dialects. French is widely spoken in Morocco, Algeria, Tunisia and Mauritania and in all tourist areas some English or French will be understood. Spanish is useful in parts of Morocco. See Language for Travel, page 59 for a simple vocabulary.

Short wave radio guide

The BBC World Service (London) broadcasts throughout the region. Frequencies are shown in the accompanying table overpage.

RADIO FREQUENCIES

Country	KHz	Transmission times (GMT) Summer	Winter
Algeria, Morocco and Tunisia	17705	0900-1615	0700-1615
	15070	0700-2315	0700-2030
	12095	1500-2315	1500-2315
Libya	21470	0430-1615	0430-1615
	17640	0800-1515	0800-1515
	15070	0600-2030	0600-2030
	12095	0400-0730	0400-0730
	12095	1600-2215	1600-2030
Mauritania	17790	0700-1530	0700-1530
	15400	0430-1130	0445-1130
	15400	1500-2315	1500-2315
	15070	1500-2315	1500-2030

WEIGHTS AND MEASURES

Metric

Weight:
1 kilogram (kg) = 2.205 pounds
1 metric tonne = 1.102 short tons
= 0.984 long ton

Length:
1 millimetre (mm) = 0.03937 inch
1 metre = 3.281 feet
1 kilometre (km) = 0.621 mile

Area:
1 hectare = 2.471 acres
1 square km (km^2) = 0.386 sq mile

Capacity:
1 litre = 0.220 Imperial gallon
= 0.264 US gallon

Volume:
1 cubic metre (m^3) = 35.31 cubic feet
= 1.31 cubic yards

British and US

1 pound (lb) = 454 grams
1 short tonne (2,000lb) = 0.907 metric ton
1 long tonne (2,240lb) = 1.016 metric tonnes

1 inch = 25.417 millimetres
1 foot (ft) = 0.305 metre
1 mile = 1.609 kilometres

1 acre = 0.405 hectare
1 square mile (sq mile) = 2,590 km^2

1 Imperial gallon = 4.546 litres
1 US gallon = 3.785 litres
(5 Imperial gallons are approximately equal to 6 US gallons)

1 cubic foot (cu ft) = 0.028 m^3
1 cubic yard (cu yd) = 0.765 m^3

HEALTH INFORMATION

CONTENTS

Before you go   15
Common problems   17
When you return home   21
Further information   21

The following information has been prepared by Dr David Snashall, Senior Lecturer in Occupational Health, United Medical Schools of Guy's and St Thomas' Hospitals and Chief Medical Officer, Foreign and Commonwealth Office, London.

The traveller to North Africa is inevitably exposed to health risks not encountered in North America or Western Europe. Despite the countries being part of Africa where one expects to see much tropical disease this is not actually the case, although malaria remains a problem in some areas. Because much of the area is economically under-developed, infectious diseases still predominate in the same way as they did in the W some decades ago. There are obvious health differences between each of the countries of North Africa and in risks between the business traveller who tends to stay in international class hotels in large cities and the backpacker trekking through the rural areas. There are no hard and fast rules to follow; you will often have to make your own judgements on the healthiness or otherwise of your surroundings.

There are many well qualified doctors in the area, a large proportion of whom speak English or French but the quality and range of medical care is extremely variable from country to country and diminishes very rapidly away from big cities. In some countries, such as Mauritania, there are systems and traditions of medicine rather different from the Western model and you may be confronted with unusual modes of treatment based on local beliefs. At least you can be reasonably sure that local practitioners have a lot of experience with the particular diseases of their region. If you are in a city it may be worthwhile calling on your Embassy to obtain a list of recommended doctors.

If you are a long way from medical help, a certain amount of self medication may be necessary and you will find that many of the drugs that are available have familiar names. However, always check the date stamping and buy from reputable pharmacists because the shelf life of some items, especially vaccines and antibiotics is markedly reduced in hot conditions. Unfortunately many locally produced drugs are not subjected to quality control procedures and can be unreliable. There have, in addition, been cases of substitution of inert materials for active drugs.

With the following precautions and advice you should keep as healthy as usual. Make local enquiries about health risks if you are apprehensive and take the general advice of European and North American families who have lived or are living in the area.

Before you go

Take out medical insurance. You should have a dental check up, obtain a spare glasses prescription and, if you suffer from a longstanding condition such as diabetes, high blood pressure, heart/lung disease or a nervous disorder, arrange for a check up with your doctor who can at the same time provide you with a letter explaining details of your disability (in English and French). Check the current practice for malaria prophylaxis (prevention) for the countries you intend to visit.

For a simple list of 'Health Kit' to take with you, see page 8.

Inoculations

Smallpox vaccination is no longer required. Neither is cholera vaccination, despite the fact that the disease is endemic in Mauritania and Algeria and also occurs in Morocco and Tunisia. Yellow fever vaccination is only required for Mauritania although in the other countries, particularly Algeria and Libya, you may be asked for a certificate if you have been in an area (Sub-Saharan Africa for example) affected by yellow fever immediately before travelling to North Africa. Cholera vaccine is not effective which is the main reason for not recommending it but occasionally travellers from South America, where cholera is presently raging, or from parts of South Asia where the disease is endemic may be asked to provide evidence of vaccination. The following vaccinations are recommended:

Typhoid (*monovalent*): one dose followed by a booster in 1 month's time. Immunity from this course lasts 2-3 years. Other injectable types are now becoming available as are oral preparations marketed in some countries.

Poliomyelitis: this is a live vaccine, generally given orally and the full course consists of three doses with a booster in tropical regions every 3-5 years.

Tetanus: one dose should be given with a booster at 6 weeks and another at 6 months and 10 yearly boosters thereafter are recommended.

Children: should, in addition, be properly protected against diphtheria, whooping cough, mumps and measles. Teenage girls, if they have not yet had the disease, should be given rubella (German measles) vaccination. Consult your doctor for advice on BCG inoculation against tuberculosis. The disease is still common in the region. North Africa lies mainly outside the meningitis belt and the disease is probably no more common than at home so vaccination is not indi-

cated except during an epidemic.

Infectious hepatitis (jaundice)

This is common throughout North Africa. It seems to be frequently caught by travellers probably because, coming from countries with higher standards of hygiene, they have not contracted the disease in childhood and are therefore not immune like the majority of adults in developing countries. The main symptoms are stomach pains, lack of appetite, nausea, lassitude and yellowness of the eyes and skin. Medically speaking there are two types: the less serious, but more common, is hepatitis A for which the best protection is careful preparation of food, the avoidance of contaminated drinking water and scrupulous attention to toilet hygiene. Human normal immunoglobulin (gammaglobulin) confers considerable protection against the disease and is particularly useful in epidemics. It should be obtained from a reputable source and is certainly recommended for travellers who intend to live rough. The injection should be given as close as possible to your departure and, as the dose depends on the likely time you are to spend in potentially infected areas, the manufacturer's instructions should be followed. A new vaccination against hepatitis A is now generally available and probably provides much better immunity for 10 years but is more expensive, being three separate injections.

The other more serious version is hepatitis B which is acquired as a sexually transmitted disease, from a blood transfusion or injection with an unclean needle or possibly by insect bites. The symptoms are the same as hepatitis A but the incubation period is much longer.

You may have had jaundice before or you may have had hepatitis of either type before without becoming jaundiced, in which case it is possible that you could be immune to either hepatitis A or B. This immunity can be tested for before you travel. If you are not immune to hepatitis B already, a vaccine is available (three shots over 6 months) and if you are not immune to hepatitis A already then you should consider vaccination (or gamma globulin if you are not going to be exposed for long).

Meningitis

This is a 'significant risk' in Mauritania. Protection against meningococcal meningitis A and C is conferred by a vaccine which is freely available.

AIDS

In North Africa AIDS is probably less common than in most of Europe and North America but is presumably increasing in its incidence, though not as rapidly as in Sub-Saharan Africa, South America or Southeast Asia. Having said that, the spread of the disease has not been well documented in the North African region; the real picture is unclear. The disease is possibly still mainly confined to the well known high risk sections of the population i.e. homosexual men, intravenous drug abusers, prostitutes and children of infected mothers. Whether heterosexual transmission outside these groups is common or not, the main risk to travellers is from casual sex, heterosexual or homosexual. The same precautions should be taken as when encountering any sexually transmitted disease. In some of these countries there is widespread female prostitution and a higher proportion of this population is likely to be HIV antibody positive. In other parts, especially high class holiday resorts, intravenous drug abuse is prevalent and in certain cities, homosexual, transsexual and transvestite prostitution is common and again this part of the population is quite likely to harbour the HIV virus in large measure. The AIDS virus (HIV) can be passed via unsterile needles which have been previously used to inject an HIV positive patient but the risk of this is very small indeed. It would, however, be sensible to check that nee-

dles have been properly sterilized or disposable needles used. The chance of picking up hepatitis B in this way is much more of a danger. Be wary of carrying disposable needles yourself. Custom officials may find them suspicious. The risk of receiving a blood transfusion with blood infected with the HIV virus is greater than from dirty needles because of the amount of fluid exchanged. Supplies of blood for transfusion are now largely screened for HIV in all reputable hospitals so the risk must be very small indeed. Catching the AIDS virus does not necessarily produce an illness in itself; the only way to be sure if you feel you have been put at risk is to have a blood test for HIV antibodies on your return to a place where there are reliable laboratory facilities. The results may not be ready for many weeks.

Common problems

Altitude

Mountain sickness is hardly likely to occur in North Africa, even in the High Atlas. A not-too-rapid ascent is the sure way to prevent it. Other problems experienced at moderate altitude are: sunburn, excessively dry air causing skin cracking, sore eyes (it may be wise to leave your contact lenses out, especially in windy and dusty areas) and stuffy noses. Many travellers, as long as they are physically fit, enjoy travelling in the mountains where it is generally cooler and less humid and there are fewer insects.

Heat and cold

Full acclimatisation to high temperatures takes about 2 weeks and during this period it is normal to feel a degree of apathy, especially if the relative humidity is high. Drink plenty of water (up to 15 litres a day are required when working physically hard in hot, dry conditions), use salt on your food and avoid extreme exertion. Tepid showers are more cooling than hot or cold ones. Large hats do not cool you down but prevent sunburn. Remember that, especially in the mountains, there can be a large and sudden drop in temperature between sun and shade and between night and day so dress accordingly. Clear desert nights can prove astoundingly cold with a rapid drop in temperature as the sun goes down. Loose fitting cotton clothes are still the best for hot weather; warm jackets and woollens are essential after dark in some desert areas, and especially at high altitude.

Insects

These can be a great nuisance. Some, of course, are carriers of serious diseases such as malaria and yellow fever. The best way of keeping insects away at night is to sleep off the ground with a mosquito net and to burn mosquito coils containing Pyrethrum. Aerosol sprays or a 'flit' gun may be effective as are insecticidal tablets which are heated on a mat which is plugged into the wall socket (if taking your own check the voltage of the area you are visiting so that you can take an appliance that will work. Similarly check that your electrical adaptor is suitable for the repellent plug).

You can use personal insect repellent, the best of which contain a high concentration of Diethyltoluamide. Liquid is best for arms and face (take care around eyes and make sure you do not dissolve the plastic of your spectacles). Aerosol spray on clothes and ankles deters mites and ticks. Liquid DET suspended in water can be used to impregnate cotton clothes and mosquito nets. Wide mesh mosquito nets are now available impregnated with an insecticide called Permethrin and are generally more effective, lighter to carry and more comfortable to sleep in. If you are bitten, itching may be relieved by cool baths and anti-histamine tablets (care with alcohol or driving) corticosteroid creams (great care – never use

if any hint of sepsis) or by judicious scratching. Calamine lotion and cream have limited effectiveness and anti-histamine creams have a tendency to cause skin allergies and are therefore not generally recommended. Bites which become infected (commonly in dirty and dusty places) should be treated with a local antiseptic or antibiotic cream such as Cetrimide as should infected scratches. Skin infestations with body lice, crabs and scabies are unfortunately easy to pick up. Use Gamma benzene hexachloride for lice and Benzyl benzoate for scabies. Crotamiton cream (Eurax) alleviates itching and also kills a number of skin parasites. Malathion lotion 5% is good for lice but avoid the highly toxic full strength Malathion used as an agricultural insecticide.

Intestinal upsets

Practically nobody escapes this one so be prepared for it. Some of these countries lead the world in their prevalence of diarrhoea. Most of the time intestinal upsets are due to the insanitary preparation of food. Do not eat uncooked fish or vegetables or meat (especially pork), fruit with the skin on (always peel your fruit yourself) or food that is exposed to flies. Tap water is generally held to be unsafe or at least unreliable throughout North Africa with the exception of large cities in Morocco. Filtered or bottled water is generally available. If your hotel has a central hot water supply this is safe to drink after cooling. Ice for drinks should be made from boiled water but rarely is, so stand your glass on the ice cubes, instead of putting them in the drink. Dirty water should first be strained through a filter bag (available from camping shops) and then boiled or treated. Bringing the water to a rolling boil at sea level is sufficient but at high altitude you have to boil the water for longer to ensure that all the microbes are killed. Various sterilising methods can be used and there are proprietary preparations containing chlorine or iodine compounds. Pasteurized or heat treated milk is now widely available as is ice cream and yoghurt produced by the same methods. Unpasteurized milk products including cheese and yoghurt are sources of tuberculosis, brucellosis, listeria and food poisoning germs. You can render fresh milk safe by heating it to 62°C for 30 mins followed by rapid cooling or by boiling it. Matured or processed cheeses are safer than fresh varieties.

Diarrhoea is usually the result of food poisoning, occasionally from contaminated water (including seawater when swimming near sewage outfalls). There are various causes – viruses, bacteria, protozoa (like amoeba) salmonella and cholera organisms. It may take one of several forms coming on suddenly, or rather slowly. It may be accompanied by vomiting or by severe abdominal pain and the passage of blood or mucus when it is called dysentery. How do you know which type you have and how do you treat it?

All kinds of diarrhoea, whether or not accompanied by vomiting, respond favourably to the replacement of water and salts taken as frequent small sips of some kind of rehydration solution. There are proprietary preparations consisting of sachets of powder which you dissolve in water or you can make your own by adding half a teaspoonful of salt (3.5 grams) and four tablespoonfuls of sugar (40 grams) to a litre of boiled water. If you can time the onset of diarrhoea to the minute, then it is probably viral or bacterial and/or the onset of dysentery. The treatment, in addition to rehydration, is Ciprofloxacin 500 mgs every 12 hrs. The drug is now widely available as are various similar ones.

If the diarrhoea has come on slowly or intermittently, then it is more likely to be protozoal i.e. caused by amoeba or giardia and antibiotics will have no effect. These cases are best treated by a doctor, as is any outbreak of diarrhoea continuing for more than 3 days. If there are severe stomach cramps, the following drugs may help: Loperamide (Imodium, Arret) and Diphenoxylate with Atropine (Lomotil).

The lynchpins of treatment for diarrhoea are rest, fluid and salt replacement, antibiotics such as Ciprofloxacin for the bacterial types and special diagnostic tests and medical treatment for amoeba and giardia infections. Salmonella infections and cholera can be devastating diseases and it would be wise to get to a hospital as soon as possible if these were suspected. Fasting, peculiar diets and the consumption of large quantities of yoghourt have not been found useful in calming travellers diarrhoea or in rehabilitating inflamed bowels. Oral rehydration has on the other hand, especially in children, been a lifesaving technique. As there is some evidence that alcohol and milk might prolong diarrhoea, they should probably be avoided during and immediately after an attack. There are ways of preventing travellers diarrhoea for short periods of time when visiting these countries by taking antibiotics but these are ineffective against viruses and, to some extent, against protozoa, so this technique should not be used other than in exceptional circumstances. Some preventives such as Enterovioform can have serious side effects if taken for long periods.

Malaria

This disease occurs in all the regions covered by this book, with the exception of Tunisia. The disease is, however, only common in Mauritania and Libya with some limited transmission occurring, seasonally in coastal Morocco and central Algeria. Despite being nowhere near so common as in Sub-Saharan Africa, malaria remains a serious disease and you are advised to protect yourself against mosquito bites as described above and to take prophylactic (preventive) drugs where and when there is a risk. Start taking the tablets a few days before exposure and continue to take them 6 weeks after leaving the malarial zone. Remember to give the drugs to babies and children and pregnant women also.

The subject of malaria prevention is becoming more complex as the malaria parasite becomes immune to some of the older drugs. This phenomenon, at the time of writing, has not occurred in North African countries other than Mauritania and so the more traditional drugs can be taken with some confidence. Protection with Proguanil (Paludrine) two tablets per day, or Chloroquine two tablets per week will suffice and at this dose will not cause any side effects. In Mauritania where there is Chloroquine resistance, both drugs should be taken. You will have to find out locally the likelihood of malaria and perhaps be prepared to receive conflicting advice on how to prevent yourself from catching it. You can catch malaria even when taking prophylactic drugs, although it is unlikely. If you do develop symptoms (high fever, shivering, severe headache, sometimes diarrhoea) seek medical advice immediately. The risk of the disease is obviously greater the further you move from the cities into rural areas with limited facilities and standing water.

Psychological disorders

First time exposure to countries where sections of the population live in extreme poverty or squalor and may even be starving can cause odd psychological reactions in visitors. So can the incessant pestering, especially of women which is unfortunately common in some of these countries. Simply be prepared for this and try not to over react.

Snake and other bites & stings

If you are unlucky enough to be bitten by a venomous snake, spider, scorpion, lizard, centipede or sea creature try (within limits) to catch the animal for identification. The reactions to be expected are fright, swelling, pain and bruising around the bite, soreness of the regional lymph glands, nausea, vomiting and fever. If in addition any of the following symptoms supervene, get the victim to a doctor without delay: numbness, tingling of the face, muscular spasms, convulsions, shortness of breath or haemorrhage. Commercial snake bite or scorpion sting kits may be available but are only useful for the specific type of snake or scorpion for which they are designed. The serum has to be given intravenously, so is not much good unless you have had some practice in making injections into veins. If the bite is on a limb, immobilise it and apply a tight bandage between the bite and body, releasing it for 90 secs every 15 mins. Reassurance of the bitten person is very important because death by snake bite is in fact very rare. Do not slash the bite area and try and suck out the poison because this kind of heroism does more harm than good. Hospitals usually hold stocks of snake bite serum. Best precaution: do not walk in snake territory with bare feet, sandals or shorts.

If swimming in an area where there are poisonous fish such as stone or scorpion fish (also called by a variety of local names) or sea urchins on rocky coasts, tread carefully or wear plimsolls. The sting of such fish is intensely painful and this can be helped by immersing the stung part in water as hot as you can bear for as long as it remains painful. This is not always very practical and you must take care not to scald yourself but it does work. Avoid spiders and scorpions by keeping your bed away from the wall and look under lavatory seats and inside your shoes in the morning. In the rare event of being bitten, consult a doctor.

Sunburn and heat stroke

The burning power of the sun in North Africa is phenomenal, especially at high altitude. Always wear a wide-brimmed hat and use some form of sun cream or lotion on untanned skin. Normal temperate zone suntan lotions (protection factor up to seven) are not much good. You need to use the types designed specifically for the tropics or for mountaineers or skiers with a protection factor (against UVA) between seven and 15. Certain creams also protect against UVB and you should use these if you have a skin prone to burning. Glare from the sun can cause conjunctivitis so wear sunglasses, especially on the beach.

There are several varieties of heat stroke. The most common cause is severe dehydration. Avoid this by drinking lots of non-alcoholic fluid and adding some salt if you wish.

Other afflictions

Athletes foot and other fungal infections are best treated by exposure to sunshine and a proprietary preparation such as Tolnaftate.

Dengue fever is not common in North Africa but there have been cases of this virus transmitted by mosquito bites producing severe headache and body pains. There is no treatment: you must just avoid mosquito bites.

Filariasis causing such diseases as elephantiasis occurs in Mauritania and again is transmitted by mosquito.

Hydatid disease is quite common in Algeria but can be avoided by keeping well clear of dogs, which is good advice in any case.

Intestinal worms do occur in insanitary areas and the more serious ones, such as hook-worm, can be contracted by walking bare foot on infested earth or beaches.

Leishmaniasis causing a skin ulcer which will not heal is also present in most of the North African countries. It is transmitted by sand flies.

Prickly heat is a common itchy rash avoided by frequent washing and by wearing loose clothing. It can be helped by the regular use of talcum powder to allow the skin to dry thoroughly after washing.

Schistosomiasis (bilharzia) occurs particularly in Morocco and can easily be avoided because it is transmitted by snails which live in fresh water lakes so do not swim in such places or in canals.

Rabies is endemic throughout North African countries. If you are bitten by a domestic animal try to have it captured for observation and see a doctor at once. Treatment with human diploid vaccine is now extremely effective and worth seeking out if the likelihood of having contracted rabies is high. A course of anti-rabies vaccine might be a good idea before you go.

When you return home

Remember to take your anti-malarial tablets for 6 weeks. If you have had attacks of diarrhoea, it is worth having a stool specimen tested in case you have picked up amoebic dysentery. If you have been living rough, a blood test may be worthwhile to detect worms and other parasites.

Further health information

The following organisations give information regarding well-trained English speaking physicians throughout the world: International Association for Medical Assistance to Travellers, 745 Fifth Avenue, New York, 10022; Intermedic, 777 3rd Avenue, New York, 10017.

Information regarding country by country malaria risk can be obtained from the World Health Organisation (WHO) or the Ross Institute, The London School of Hygiene and Tropical Medicine, Keppel Street, London WC1E 7HT which publishes a strongly recommended book entitled *The Preservation of Personal Health in Warm Climates*. The organisation MASTA, (Medical

Advisory Service to Travellers Abroad), also based at The London School of Hygiene and Tropical Medicine, T 0171 6314408, F 0171 4365389, will provide country by country information on up-to-date health risks.

Further information on medical problems overseas can be obtained from Dawood, Richard (ed), *Travellers Health, How to Stay Healthy Abroad*, Oxford University Press, 1992, costing £7.99. We strongly recommend this revised and updated edition, especially to the intrepid traveller heading for the more out of the way places.

General advice is also available in *Health Advice for Travellers* published jointly by the Department of Health and the Central Office of Information (UK) and available free from your Travel Agent.

REGIONAL INTRODUCTION

CONTENTS

History of North Africa   24
Travelling in Islamic countries   37
Political risks for travellers   40
Handling the local bureaucracy   43
Travel and survival in the desert   45
Wildlife   49
Dress in North Africa   52
Jewellery of North Africa   56
Language for travel   59

THE HISTORY OF NORTH AFRICA

The Sahara began to dessicate some 10,000 years ago and divided the Caucasoid populations of North Africa from the Negroid populations of W and Equatorial Africa. The original agricultural mode of production which had been the basis of settlement there was gradually replaced by nomadic pastoralism which, by around 4000 BC, had become the preserve of two groups, the Libyan-Berbers in the E part and the ancestors of the modern Touareg in the W. North African populations, all classified as part of the Hamito-Semitic group which stretched E into Arabia, soon became sub-divided into the Berbers in the W, the Egyptians in the E.

Greeks and Phoenicians

The North African coastal area became the arena for competition between those Mediterranean civilizations which had acquired a naval capacity – the Greeks and the Phoenicians. Indeed, this became the future pattern and resulted in the history of the region being described in the terms of its conquerers.

We do know, however, that the Greek and Phoenician settlements on the coast provoked a response from the nomadic communities of the desert – the Garamantes around the Fezzan in Libya, the Nigritae around Tuwat in modern Algeria and the Pharusii who were located in the Western Sahara. These communities appear to have specialized in warfare based on charioteering and they began to raid the new coastal settlements. At the same time, they also controlled trans-Saharan commerce – one of the major reasons why the Phoenicians, at least, were so interested in North Africa. As a result, they also engaged in trade with the new coastal communities, particularly those created by the Phoenicians.

The Greeks had begun to colonize the Egyptian and eastern Libyan coastline as part of their attempt to control Egyptian maritime trade. Cyrene, the first of five Greek colonies in Cyrenaica in Libya, was founded about 625 BC and, a little earlier, three Phoenician colonies were created in western Libya, on the coast of what is today Tripolitania – hence the name – in order to exploit new commercial opportunities, for the Phoenicians were first-and-foremost traders. More important, however, was the major Phoenician settlement at Carthage, on the coast of northern Tunisia, close to the modern capital of Tunis, which was founded in 814 BC, in order to control access to Sicily.

Greeks and Phoenicians competed for control of the coastal areas in Libya and eventually created an uneasy division of the region between themselves. The Greeks took over Egypt after the creation of the Ptolemaic Kingdom on the death of Alexander the Great in 323 BC and incorporated Cyrenaica into the new kingdom. The Phoenicians, by now being harried in their original Lebanese home base of Tyre by the Assyrians and Persians, created a new and powerful maritime commercial empire based on Carthage, with outlying colonies to the W, right round to the Atlantic coast at Lixus (Larache).

The Roman Empire

Control of North Africa passed on once again, this time to the rapidly expanding city-state of Rome. Control of the Ptolemaic Kingdom of Egypt passed to Rome because of Roman interest in its agricultural produce and Egypt became a province of Rome in 30 BC. Cyrenaica had become a Roman province in 74 BC. Conflict with Carthage had begun much earlier because of its interest in Sicily which, for Rome, was of vital strategic importance. Although Carthage was expelled from Sicily in 201 BC, Rome still feared Carthaginian power and the city was eventually razed to the ground in 146 BC, after 3 years of warfare. The fertile plains around the city, a hinterland which had been its agricultural base and part of the Carthaginian Empire, were then converted into the Roman province of Africa.

The difficult problem of border security for Roman administrators was solved by creating the *limes*, a border region along the desert edge which was settled with former legionaries as a militarized agriculturalist population. Thus, although the border region was permeable to trade, resistance to tribal incursion could be rapidly mobilized from the resident population, while regular forces were brought to the scene. The limes spread W from Egypt as far as the Moroccan Atlantic coast. In S Tunisia, the limes were reinforced by a ditch – the *fossia regia*.

By the beginning of the Christian era, North Africa had been organized into four Roman provinces: Proconsular Africa, Numidia, Mauritania Caesariana and Mauritania Tingitania. It had also become a major source of food for Rome and a major centre of Roman culture as the sedentary Berber populations themselves were Romanised. North Africa had, in short, ceased to be culturally part of Africa and was, instead, now part of the Mediterranean world. In addition to the commercial and cultural interpenetration of North Africa and Rome, this cultural interaction was intensified by two other factors. First, the region had long been in contact with Greek culture and, indeed, through the Phoenicians, with the culture of the Levant. Secondly, as a result of the destruction of the kingdom of Judea in 70 AD, large numbers of

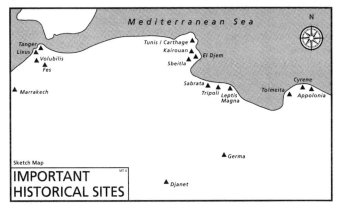

Sketch Map

IMPORTANT HISTORICAL SITES

Jews migrated into North Africa and Judaism intermixed with Berber culture to a significant extent, as contemporary Jewish traditions in Morocco and Tunisia make clear.

Christian North Africa

North African Christianity became the major focus of the development of Christian doctrine. The Coptic Church became the major proponent of Monophysitism after the Council of Chalcedon in 451 AD; Donatism dominated Numidia; and Tunisia was the home of the greatest of the early Christian fathers, St Augustine. At the same time, official Christianity in Egypt – the Melkite Church – combined with the Coptic Church to convert areas to the S of Egypt to Christianity.

Political evolution, however, did not mirror the growth of Christian influence. In the 5th century, as the Roman Empire crumbled, North Africa was invaded by a Teutonic tribe based in Spain, the Vandals, who by 429 AD, had conquered as far as E Cyrenaica.

Byzantine control, of Tunisia at least, was restored by the Emperor Justinian and his general, Belisarius, in 533 AD. However it was unpopular, not least because of the onerous taxation system necessary to cover Byzantium's heavy military expenditure as it tried to confront the Sassanids in Asia as well as maintain its position in the Mediterranean. Hence when, a little more than a century later, Byzantine rule in Africa was threatened by the expansion of Islam, there was little enthusiasm to support its continuation in northern Africa.

The Islamic period

In 642 AD, 10 years after the death of the Prophet Mohammad, Arab armies, acting as the vanguard of Islam, conquered Egypt. To secure his conquest, the Arab commander, Amr bin al-As, immediately decided to move W into Cyrenaica where the local Berber population submitted to the new invaders. Despite a constant pattern of disturbance, the Arab conquerers of Egypt and their successors did not ignore the potential of the region to the S. Nubia was invaded in 641-42 AD and again 10 years later. Arab merchants and, later, bedouin tribes from Arabia were able to move freely throughout the S. However, until 665 AD, no real attempt was actually made to complete the conquest, largely because of internal problems within the new world of Islam. Then, after two feints SW towards the Fezzan, an army under Uqba bin Nafi conquered Tunisia and set up the first Arab centre there at Kairouan in 670 AD. 4 years later, the Arabs in Kairouan were able to persuade Kusayla, the leader of the Berber confederation which spread right across Tunisia and modern Algeria as far as the Muluwiya River in Morocco, to convert to Islam. Shortly afterwards, Uqba bin Nafi, in a famous expeditionary raid to scout the unsubmitted areas to the W, swept across North Africa along the northern edge of the Sahara desert as far as the Atlantic coast of Morocco, into the land of the Sanhadja Berbers who dominated the major Western trans-Saharan trade routes.

These early conquests were ephemeral, being based on two mistaken assumptions. The first was that the new conquerers could afford to ignore the isolated Byzantine garrisons along the North African coast, because they would eventually collapse due to their isolation. The Byzantine navy, in fact, supplied them by sea. The second was that the Ommayyad Arab commanders and administrators now imposed on North Africa ignored the promises of equality of treatment given to Berber converts and thus encouraged a major rebellion, led by Kusayla. Arab control of Kairouan was lost and the Arab conquest of the Maghreb had to be undertaken again.

The first Arab move was against Kusayla, who was killed in 688 or 689 AD.

Then after a further delay caused, once again, by unrest in the Levant, a new army moved northwards against Byzantine centres in Carthage and Bizerta, where the last remaining garrison was defeated in 690 AD. The Arab conquest came up against determined Berber resistance, this time in the Algerian Aurés where the core of the Berber Zenata confederation was led by al-Kahina, a Judaized or Christianised Berber priestess. Once again the Arabs retreated to Cyrenaica, returning to the attack only in 693 AD. In 697 AD, al-Kahina was killed and her forces defeated in a battle at Tubna in the Aurés which marked the start of a permanent Arab presence in North Africa.

The city of Tunis was founded to prevent further Byzantine encroachment at neighbouring Carthage and, under Musa bin Nusayr, Arab armies swept westwards to conquer Tanger in 704 AD. There they came to terms with the sole remaining Byzantine governor in North Africa, Julian of Ceuta, a Christian potentate who paid tribute to the new Muslim governor of neighbouring Tanger, Ziyad bin Tariq, in order to be confirmed in his post. 7 years later, Ziyad, with help from Julian who had maintained links with the Visigoth rulers of Spain, organized the Muslim invasion of the Iberian peninsula, starting at Gibraltar. By 732 AD, Muslim forces had conquered virtually all of Spain and Portugal and had even crossed the Pyrenees. The Muslim advance was stopped at or near to Poitiers by Charles Martel and, although, for the next 4 years, large parts of Provence were ravaged by marauding Muslim armies, the Muslim presence in Europe effectively ceased at the Pyrenees.

The early Islamic period

Despite their victory, the Ommayyads soon became very unpopular in North Africa where the egalitarian and revolutionary doctrines of the *kharejite* movement – that the caliphate should be elective, that a caliph who failed to uphold Islamic principle could be dismissed by the Muslim community and that sin automatically disqualified those involved from being considered to be Muslims – began to take root. Kharejite missionaries arrived in Kairouan in 719 AD and, within 30 years, the Berbers had become such enthusiastic supporters that they launched a rebellion against the Ommayyads at Tanger in 739-40 AD.

Although the rebellion was crushed, *kharajism* survived and, given the difficulties facing the Ommayyads in the Middle East where they were threatened by a new opposition, North Africa was left to its own devices. Ibadi kharajism gained the upper hand in Tripolitania and Sufri kharajism became dominant in southern Tunisia, while the core of Tunisia was left in the hands of the Fihrids, an Ommayyad Arab military caste now effectively abandoned by the Ommayyad caliphate in Damascus. The Ibadis eventually expanded their control throughout Tunisia and forced the Sufris westwards in 758 AD.

In 750 AD, the Ommayyad caliphate was destroyed by the Abbasids who rejected Ommayyad ideas of Arab superiority and supported the early Shi'a schismatic movement against the Sunni Muslim majority. 8 years later, the new Abbasid caliphate reconquered the old Arab province of *Ifriquiya* (modern Tunisia), but was unable to extend its authority further westward. In any case, the Abbasids did not have the resources to maintain a close control on such far-flung provinces and, by 800 AD, the Abbasid caliph in Baghdad, Harun al-Rashid allowed his governor in Ifriquiya, Ibrahim bin al-Aghlab, virtual autonomy. In effect, therefore, the Aghlabids became an independent dynasty in Tunisia until their downfall in 909 AD. The Aghlabids brought prosperity and high culture to Tunisia and, in 827 AD, began the Muslim conquest of Sicily.

The Aghlabids had to share North

Africa with three other separate political authorities. After being expelled from Tripolitania, the Ibadis set up a separate state under Ibn Rustam at Tahert in central Algeria, which maintained close links with the Ibadi centre of Basra in southern Iraq. The Sufri Berbers of the Banu Midrar established their own state, based on their control of trans-Saharan trade, at Sijilmassa in southern Morocco. In the heartland of Morocco the Idrisids appeared, a new dynasty which, although not kharejite in belief, nevertheless was able to capture Berber support by claiming to be directly descended from the Prophet Mohammad. But, because they had supported a Shi'a rebellion against the Abbasids (who, once they had won control of the caliphate, rapidly abandoned Shi'ism in order to gain support for the Sunni majority) they had been forced to flee westwards into North Africa, an area outside Abbasid control. The founder of the dynasty, Idris bin Abdullah, arrived there in 788 AD. His son, Idris II, founded Fes in 809 AD and the dynasty survived until it was crushed by the Fatimids in 921 AD. Nonetheless, the Idrisids are the original founders of the modern Moroccan state and thus still have an influence even today.

The great dynasties and their successors

The failure of the Abbasid caliphate to retain control of North Africa paved the way for a series of local dynasties to take control.

(1) The Fatimids The first of the great dynasties that was to determine the future of North Africa did not, however, originate inside the region. Instead it used North Africa as a stepping stone towards its ambitions of taking over the Muslim world and imposing its own variant of Shi'a Islam. North Africa, because of its radical and egalitarian Islamic traditions, appears to have been the ideal starting point. The group concerned

were the Isma'ilis who split off from the main body of Shi'a Muslims in 765 AD.

The Fatimids took control over what had been Aghlabid Ifriquiya, founding a new capital at Mahdia in 912 AD. Fatimid attention was concentrated on Egypt and, in 913-14 AD, a Fatimid army temporarily occupied Alexandria. The Fatimids also developed a naval force and their conquest of Sicily in the mid-10th century provided them with a very useful base for attacks on Egypt.

After suppressing a kharejite-Sunni rebellion in Ifriquiya between 943 AD and 947 AD, the Fatimids were ready to plan the final conquest of Egypt. This took place in 969 AD when the Fatimid general, Jawhar, finally subdued the country. The Fatimids moved their capital to Egypt, where they founded a new urban centre, al-Qahira (from which the modern name, Cairo, is derived) next to the old Roman fortress of Babylon and the original Arab settlement of Fustat.

The Fatimids' main concern was to take control of the Middle East. This meant that Fatimid interest in North Africa would wane and leave an autonomous Emirate there which continued to recognize the authority of the Fatimids, although it abandoned support for Shi'a Islamic doctrine.

(2) The Hillalian invasions Despite Fatimid concerns in the Middle East, the caliph in Cairo decided to return North Africa to Fatimid control. Lacking the means to do this himself, he used instead two tribes recently displaced from Syria and at that time residing in the Nile Delta – the Banu Sulaim and the Banu Hillal – as his troops. The invasions took place slowly over a period of around 50 years, starting in 1050 or 1051 AD, and probably involved no more than 50,000 individuals.

The Banu Sulaim settled in Cyrenaica, although, 2 centuries later, factions of the tribe also moved westwards towards Tripolitania and Tunisia.

The Banu Hillal continued westwards, defeating and destroying the Zirids in a major battle close to Gabés in 1052.

The Hillalian invasions were a major and cataclysmic event in North Africa's history. They destroyed organized political power in the region and ensured the break up of the political link between Muslim North Africa and the Middle East. They also damaged the trading economy of the region. There was a major cultural development too for the Hillalian invasions, more than any other event, ensured that Arabic eventually became the majority language of the region.

(3) The Almoravids The power vacuum left in the wake of the Hillalian invasions was filled by religious revivalism amongst the Lamtuna tribe, under the influence of a religious scholar, Abdullah ibn Yasin. He transformed the lackadaisical religious observance into a dynamic, inspiring, fully integrated and committed Islamic community. He called his new community the *dar al-murabitun* – the House of the people of the *ribat* (the Muslim equivalent of a monastic retreat, dedicated to preparation for *jihad*), now corrupted to 'Almoravid'.

Religious committment spurred them on. Ibn Yasin was succeeded by Yusuf Ibn Tashfin who led the Almoravids to victory over most of western North Africa as far as Algiers and over the southern half of Spain between 1060 AD and the end of the century. The Almoravids managed, however, to offend established religious leaders and the *Sufi* orders (mystical religious orders) of North Africa by their religious intolerance and rigidity. They also failed to check Christian expansionism in Spain. As a result, when a major rebellion against their authority began close to their capital of Marrakech in 1125 AD, it was not long before they were overthrown.

(4) The Almohads The Almohads (from *al-muwahhidun* – the unitarians) also be-gan as a religious revivalist movement, this time amongst the Masmouda Berbers of the High Atlas close to Marrakech. They were inspired by a religious leader from the Hargha tribe of the Masmouda, located in the Anti-Atlas mountains, Muhammad ibn Tumart, who was born in 1080 AD. He studied in Spain and the Middle East before returning to Morocco, where he sought support for a revivalist movement designed to purify Islamic doctrine and practice.

The Almohads were organized on a tribal basis and, when Ibn Tumart died in 1130 AD, the most capable tribal leader, Abd al-Mumin, took over. In 1145 AD Abd al-Mumin crushed the Almoravids and, 2 years later, occupied the two leading cities of Fes and Marrakech, the latter of which became the Almohad capital.

The Almohads first moved against the Christian *Reconquista* in Spain, where they held the Christian advance towards Granada and Sevilla, although the ruler of Murcia managed to remain independent until 1172 AD. The more important move was against the growing threat of the Normans in the central Mediterranean. By 1160 AD, the Almohads had expelled the Normans from North Africa and had united the region under a single political authority.

The Almohad state was sapped by its essentially tribal political structure. In 1207 in Ifriquiya, the son of the Almohad governor, Abu Hafs Umar, a close associate of Ibn Tumart, created an independent Hafsid state which governed Tunisia until the Ottoman occupation in the 16th century. In a similar fashion, control of the Central Maghreb devolved on the Banu Zayyan clan of the Banu Abd al-Wad in 1233 AD. However it was the Banu Marin, who created the Marinid state in Morocco, who sealed the fate of the Almohads. The Banu Marin were a Zenata Berber tribe of pastoralists located in the lower Moulouya valley and around Figuig.

(5) The successor states The disappearance of the Almohads brought the era of the great unifying North African dynasties to an end. Thereafter power would reflect the division of the region, rather than its unity. There would also be a change in direction and influence, for now Christianity and Europe would increasingly dominate the North African horizon, as would the Mediterranean as a zone of conflict. Yet the experience of the Fatimids, the Hillalian invasions, the Almoravids and the Almohads did leave an important monument behind.

The Marinids Marinid expansionism was related to two factors: first a desire to take complete control of Trans-Saharan trade, for the Moroccan route was losing importance to those routes to the E, and, second, to counter growing Christian influence in Spain and in the Mediterranean. In 1291 AD, during the Marinid period, Castilla and Aragón came to an agreement to divide the North African world between them, in terms of commercial and diplomatic penetration. Castilla concerned itself exclusively with Morocco, while Aragón, by now the dominant trading power in the western Mediterranean, handled the Hafsids and the Zayyanids. The Marinids feared that they would not be able to exclude direct Castillian interference nor protect the remnants of the Muslim Empire in Spain. Indeed, all that was left was the Nasrid state in Granada which had been founded in 1238 AD and was to provide a final flowering of Islamic art in Spain. The Nasrid state was a useful buffer for the Marinids, although the Nasrids themselves were very ambivalent about Marinid support and often allied themselves with Christian powers for protection.

In the end, the Marinid state could not support such expansionist policies and their internal quarrelling made them easy prey for Portuguese aggressiveness. When Portugal occupied Ceuta in 1415 AD, Marinid prestige immediately declined and over the next 50 years the situation worsened as the Marinids faced threats from the Portuguese and their successors, the Wattasids (their former *viziers*).

They also had to face a new development in Morocco, the rapid growth of the *Sufi* cults which had developed in power and prestige after the discovery of the tomb of Idris II in 1437 AD. Political legitimisation now increasingly became a function of Sharifian descent (genealogical descent from the Prophet Mohammad) or of attachment to a *Sufi* order. The Marinids and the Wattasids failed both tests and, when the Portuguese occupied Ksar al-Kabir in 1458 AD, Tanger in 1471 AD, Larache in 1473 AD and Azzemour in 1486 AD, the final collapse of the dynasty was merely a matter of time. The Marinid role as defenders of the state had been taken up by Sharifian and *Sufi* groups. It was the latter who ultimately took over the state.

The Hafsids The new Hafsid state saw itself as the legitimate successor to the Almohads and its ruler as caliph. The claim was widely accepted, even in the Middle East, because the foundation of the Hafsid state coincided with the Mongol invasions which destroyed Baghdad and the last vestiges of the Abbasid caliphate in 1250 AD. But in reality, the Hafsid state lacked the social and political cohesion of its predecessor. Thus its long history was marked by the constant interplay of internal conflict between different members of the Hafsid family and with Arab and other tribal leaders who sought supreme power. Like the Marinid state, it also had to integrate increasing numbers of Muslims and Jews emigrating from al-Andalus.

It had to deal with an ever greater Christian threat. This came in two forms: direct aggression, such as the 8th crusade, led by the French King Louis IX, which beseiged Tunis unsuccessfully in

1270 AD, and commercial penetration. In the early part of the 13th century, the great Italian trading cities of Pisa, Genoa and Venice, together with the French of Provence, obtained trading and residence rights in Ifriquiya. The most important example of commercial penetration came from Aragón. The Aragonese had created a major trading empire in the Western Mediterranean and, after 1246 AD, Aragón had an ambassador in Tunis, the Hafsid capital. This was followed by mercantile representation after 1253 AD. After Aragón annexed Sicily in 1282 AD, this commercial hegemony was backed by military dominance as well.

By 1318 AD Aragonese influence was on the wane and Hafsid fortunes revived. The Hafsid state was, nonetheless, a Mediterranean state rather than one with its attention directed towards Africa or the Middle East. Its finances increasingly depended on piracy. By the end of the 15th century Hafsid influence had declined once again. Spain, the new threat to the Mediterranean Muslim world, annexed Tripoli in Libya and Bejaïa in Western Algeria in 1510 AD, as the first move in a widening penetration into the Maghreb. The Hafsids lingered on until 1574 AD, when the Ottoman Turks destroyed their state.

The Zayyanids The Zayyanid state, based at Tlemcen, was always a buffer between the Hafsids and the Marinids. It suffered from internal struggles for leadership among the three Zenata tribes that dominated it; it controlled a major trans-Saharan trade route; and it was dominated, first by the Marinids and later by the Hafsids. The Zayyanids, like the Hafsids, could not resist the Ottoman invasion of North Africa and disappeared at the start of the 16th century.

The Ottomans in North Africa

The arrival of the Ottomans in North Africa was the last invasion of the region

before the colonial period began in the 19th century.

Events in Morocco

The 16th century was dominated by events outside the Ottoman sphere of control. The Marinid state in Morocco eventually collapsed when confronted with a Sharifian Dynasty, the Saadians, who conquered Marrakech in 1525 and Fes 29 years later. They were able to resist too close an Ottoman embrace, particularly after Portuguese influence was eliminated. Morocco became, under the Sadis, a powerful Muslim state entering into close relations with other nations, even in Europe, where a close relationship developed with Elizabethan England.

The Saadian Dynasty fell into decline and political power in Morocco was seized by a series of powerful *Sufi* orders. The result was the growth of a series of petty states ultimately overwhelmed by the Alawite Dynasty. The Alawites were a Sharifian community that had been living in Sijilmassa since the 13th century.

Mawlay Isma'il, who reigned until 1727, set the Alawite state on firm foundations. He removed the European presence from the Moroccan coastline, except in Ceuta and Melilla, and forced back Turkish incursions from the E. He based his claim to power on his Sharifian status, a claim which has been astutely exploited by his predecessors to underpin their legitimacy, even when much of Morocco – the *bilad as-siba* – lay outside the area under their control – the *bilad al-makhzan*. The Alawite success was to be enduring, for the dynasty still rules Morocco today.

During the remainder of the 18th century, the Alawites concentrated on retaining their power. The Sultanate had to ensure that Turkish ambitions to expand into eastern Morocco were curbed and come to terms with the growth of European power. By the start of the 19th century, the Sultanate abandoned its traditional support for corsairing, banned in 1817, just 1 year after the last Christian slaves had been released. A few years later came France's invasion of Algeria and, in 1844, Morocco was defeated by French troops pursuing the great Algerian resistance leader, the Emir Abd al-Qadir. The defeat was a tremendous shock to Morocco, as its leaders realised they could no longer ignore the European threat. From their base in Tangier, the European consuls made ever greater demands on the Sultanate for commercial contact and, in 1856, Britain and Morocco signed an open-door treaty.

Spain, still present in her enclaves of Ceuta and Melilla, resented British influence over the Sultanate and 4 years later, on the pretext of tribal incursions into its territory, successfully fought a short border war with Morocco. Although the Sultanate survived, in 1880 it was forced to permit extra-territorial rights to Moroccan citizens employed by the European powers – the so-called 'protégé' system.

By the start of the 20th century, events accelerated as Morocco incurred foreign debt and mortgaged its customs revenues to pay off the loans. France, at that stage, began a slow penetration into Moroccan territory. Touat was occupied in 1902, Casablanca in 1907 and Fes in 1911. In every case, furious tribal resistance to French moves only provoked further French advances. Spain, too, began to move into northern Morocco, a zone allocated to her by a secret agreement with France in 1904. The Treaty of Fes of 1912 instituted a Franco-Spanish 'protectorate' over the state.

The Ottoman occupation

The Ottoman occupation of North Africa was a by-product of Ottoman-Venetian competition for control of the Mediterranean, itself part of the boundless expansionism of the Ottomans once they had conquered Constantinople in 1453.

The Ottoman attack was 2-pronged, involving their newly acquired maritime power to establish a foothold and then backing it up with the janissary, land based forces that formed the empire's troops. The decrepit Mamluk Dynasty in Egypt fell to the Ottomans in 1517 and a new, centralized Ottoman administration was established there.

Ottoman interests were soon attracted westward and a maritime campaign was launched on the North African coastline. It was carried out mainly by privateers, attracted both by the religious confrontation between Christian powers in Southern Europe and Islam in North Africa and by the growing practice of corsairing. In the wake of the *Reconquista* in 1492, Spain began to prepare for a veritable crusade against North Africa. 2 years later Spain and Portugal, with Papal blessing, divided their future spheres of influence in North Africa between them and, 3 years later, the Spanish occupation began with the conquest of Melilla.

The Ottoman moves on North Africa were precipitated by the privateering activities of the Barbarossa brothers, Uruj and Khayr al-Din. The Ottomans eventually occupied Tunis permanently in 1574. Before this, however, they had gained a hold over Libya. Khayr al-Din Barbarossa occupied Tajura, on the coast close to Tripoli, in 1531 and was consequently able to threaten the precarious hold of the Knights of the Order of St John of Jerusalem on Tripoli itself. They had just occupied Tripoli and Malta at the request of Charles V of Spain, but were forced out of Tripoli altogether by the Ottomans in 1551. For 270 years North Africa, except for Morocco, was an Ottoman preserve.

The Barbary regencies

Direct control from Istanbul did not last long. The North African coastline was divided into a series of administrative units, with power divided among the *bashas*, sent from Istanbul, the *deys* who were in charge of the permanent janissary garrisons and, in Algiers at least, the *taifa*, the captains of the corsairing privateers that continued to operate.

Tripoli

At the beginning of the 18th century, the final formal links with Istanbul were broken. In 1711 a dynasty was founded in Tripoli by Ahmad Karamanli, who seized power in the temporary absence of the Ottoman governor and then massacred the leaders of the janissaries. The new autonomous government eventually controlled Tripolitania and the coastal regions of Cyrenaica. After a tussle for influence in Tripoli between Britain and France, the Ottoman Empire reoccupied the Regency of Tripoli and ejected the Karamanlis in 1835.

Algiers

In Algeria, the Ottomans organized a military administration which soon forced the Spanish out of their enclaves at Wahran (Oran) and Tlemcen. This new Ottoman possession suffered from continual struggles between the janissaries and the *taifa*. In 1671, the *taifa* turned on the janissaries, assassinating the *agha*. In his place they elected a *dey* who shared formal power with the Sultan's *basha*. Algiers, too, had effectively broken away from Istanbul's control.

The Regency of Algiers became a major corsairing centre during the 18th century. The more powerful European states expressed their displeasure by raiding North African corsairing ports, while their weaker colleagues bought immunity by paying tributes.

In 1827, the Dey of Algiers, enraged at the insolence of the French consul during an argument over debt, struck him with a fly whisk. In 1830 Charles X, the last Bourbon ruler of France, casting around for some way of distracting the military elite from threatening his régime's survival, recalled the incident of the *insult to French dignity* and ordered the invasion of Algiers. After an unopposed landing at Sidi Fredj, close to Algiers, the city was occupied without a fight and the Regency of Algiers came to an end.

Tunis

Once the Spaniards had been driven out of Tunisia and the remnants of the Hafsid Dynasty had been eliminated, the Ottoman commander, Sinan Pasha, organized an administration similar to that in Algiers. By 1591, a system of janissary leadership through the *dey* was imposed on the Ottoman-appointed *basha* but rural administration was entrusted to another official, the *bey*, a post which soon rivalled the power of the *dey*. In 1702 the two offices were combined. After defeating an attempt by the Regency of Algiers to conquer Tunisia in 1705, Husayn bin Ali became *bey* and initiated the Husaynid Dynasty that ruled Tunisia until 1957. Following his accession to power, Tunisia effectively became independent of Istanbul and was known as the Regency of Tunis.

By the 19th century, the rule of the *bey* had become corrupt and remote. European interference in Tunisian affairs had become more intrusive resulting in a growing European population which enjoyed extra-territorial rights under the 'Capitulations' system, and European consuls who became ever more powerful. Domestic unrest increased and in 1860, the *bey*, in desperation, granted Tunisians the Arab world's first constitution, the *Destour*. By 1868 the economic crisis had worsened and European powers insisted on a debt commission being instituted to handle Tunisia's finances in order to ensure repayment.

In 1878, the Congress of Berlin decided that Tunisia should fall under French influence. Then, in 1881, on the grounds that the Khroumir border tribe had been raiding into French-controlled Algeria, France invaded Tunisia and, in a rapid campaign, took control of the country.

Colonialism in North Africa

The colonial experience throughout North Africa took many different forms. It involved four European states: Britain after WW2, in part of Libya; Italy in Libya up to WW2, together with residual interests in Tunisia; Spain in northern Morocco and in the Sahara desert to the S of the country; and France, which controlled Tunisia, Algeria and most of Morocco, as well as the southern part of Libya after WW2. Colonialism took different forms, as well. In Algeria and Libya full colonial occupation was instituted, with a degree of integration into the administration and political structures of the metropolitan power. In Tunisia and Morocco, a form of protectorate was instituted whereby the colonial power was present as a tutor, with the object of modernising political structures and the economy before restoring full Independence.

The colonial period in Libya

The reimposition of Ottoman rule in Libya in 1835 marked an end to the corsairing economy of the Regency of Tripoli. Ottoman control was never fully applied throughout the country.

The Sanusi Order, which was named after its Algerian founder, Sayyid Muhammad bin Ali al-Sanusi was an Islamic revivalist movement. It chose the Sahara for its arena and settled amongst the Cyrenaican tribes, where it was welcomed for its piousness and for its ability to arbitrate tribal disputes. Later on, the Order also coordinated tribal resistance throughout the Sahara to French colonial penetration. The Order also began to control the eastern trade routes across the Sahara and, as a result, effectively became, an autonomous government of the central Saharan region. In Cyrenaica its power was so great that, outside the major urban settlements such as Benghazi, the Ottomans accepted it as the de facto government and a Turkish-Sanusi

condominium developed.

The Ottoman administration in Tripoli had to cope with continuing European pressure, particularly from Italy and Malta. British and French influence led to the end of the slave trade towards the end of the 19th century, while the economy of Tripoli became increasingly integrated into the global economy of the Mediterranean region. By the start of the 20th century Italy's intention to colonize Tripolitania, Cyrenaica and the Fezzan became clear.

Fighting broke out between tribes backed by dissident Ottoman officers and the Italian army. The outbreak of WWI allowed the Ottoman Empire to provide military aid to the resistance and eventually a peace agreement was signed between Italy and the Sanusi at Akrama in Apr 1917. In 1922, with the Fascists in power, Italy again decided to occupy Libya. The second Italo-Sanusi war was between the Italians and the bedouin of Cyrenaica, for resistance in Tripolitania and the Fezzan was quickly broken. The ferocious struggle continued to 1930 when the last remnants of resistance were wiped out and Italy finally occupied the vast Libyan desert hinterland.

The Fascist victory was short-lived, for the Italian army was forced out of Libya during WW2 and British military administrations took over in Cyrenaica and Tripolitania with the French in Fezzan. Under the Italians, Libya had acquired the basic elements of a communications infrastructure and some modernisation of the economy. It had also acquired a 50,000 strong Italian settler population, a substantial portion of whom remained until they were expelled by the Ghadhafi régime in 1970.

The situation of Libya posed problems. By the end of WW2 it had acquired strategic significance for Britain and, after the Cold War began, for the USA as well. Britain had promised Cyrenaica that Italian control would never be restored. A series of proposals were made including Soviet Union trusteeship over Libya and the Bevin-Sforza Plan, whereby Britain would take a mandate for Cyrenaica, Italy for Tripolitania and France for the Fezzan for a period of 10 years, after which the country would be granted Independence. These were clearly unacceptable to the Libyans themselves, and the whole issue was dropped in the lap of the newly created United Nations in 1949.

The United Nations' special commissioner was able to convince all the Libyan factions that the only solution was a federal monarchy, bringing the provinces of Cyrenaica, Tripolitania and the Fezzan together under the Sanusi monarchy of Sayyid Idris. In Dec 1951, the independent kingdom of Libya came into being.

Colonialism in the Maghreb

Algeria

The French conquest of Algiers in 1830 drew the army ever further into the interior. French forces fanned out westward, and came into contact with the forces of the Amir Abd al-Qadir, who had created a major tribal confederacy to resist further French advances. In 1847, after a brutal campaign of repression under General Bugeaud and a short border war with Morocco, culminating in the Moroccan defeat at the battle of Isly in 1844, Abd al-Qadir was forced into exile. By that time French forces had conquered the eastern region around Constantine and were moving into the vast reaches of the Sahara.

Settler colonization was encouraged and soon there was a substantial European population living in Algeria with an administration tied into that of France. Emperor Napoleon III's attempt to create a pattern of indirect administration which would allow Algerian society to survive its colonial experience collapsed in 1871 and by the end of the 19th century Algeria was fully integrated into France from an administrative point of view.

Algeria was required to contribute heavily to the French war effort in WW1, particularly in the provision of manpower. This led to demands for a reform of the relationship between Algeria and France. In the event, the French government reneged on promises to reform it had made during the war. The 1930s were a period of political stagnation and economic deprivation, as the Great Depression hit North Africa. The result was massive rural depopulation and severe economic hardship which resulted in serious famine. Some minor reforms were introduced but there was no evidence at all that real change would ever occur.

WW2 changed the picture, for France's defeat at the hands of the Germans destroyed the myth of French invincibility. The disappointment of Algerians who had served during the hostilities and returned home expecting radical change, resulted in the development of a new strand in Algerian nationalism. Many of its founding members had also had experience of army service in French colonies. They envisaged a secret organization that would launch a guerrilla campaign against the French presence in Algeria and thereby obtain popular support.

The War of Independence raged for the next 8 years. Although the French army eventually contained the war within Algeria, the measures it used only stimulated popular support for Independence and for the FLN that they had been designed to crush. At the same time, settler anxieties over the vacillations of governments in Paris led to a combined army-settler revolt in Algiers in 1958 which brought General Charles de Gaulle to power in France. De Gaulle eventually accepted the Evian Accords which, in 1962, gave Algeria complete Independence.

Tunisia

In the immediate aftermath of the installation of the French Protectorate, Tunisian resistance was confined to tribal groups in the S of the country. Opposition to colonial occupation gradually began to gather strength reflecting popular opposition to the growing and predominantly Italian European settler colony in Tunisia, a colony totalling around 100,000 people and controlling some 800,000 ha of Tunisia's best agricultural land.

The opposition was led by a young, French-trained lawyer, Habib Bourguiba, who wanted a far more radical approach towards the French presence. In 1934, Habib Bourguiba took over the movement, now renamed the neo-Destour. French reaction to this radicalisation was very repressive until WW2 when Tunisia was eventually occupied by Allied forces. In the wake of the war, it became clear that some concessions to nationalist sentiment would have to be made.

Before this was done, France tried to enforce its position in Tunisia by requiring the Bey to accept the idea of 'co-sovereignty', whereby France would gain permanent rights to Tunisian territory. Following this attempt by France in 1950 to gain a firmer foothold inside North Africa, the nationalist movement under Habib Bourguiba took on the characteristics of a mass movement. As a result, Habib Bourguiba was able to negotiate autonomy for Tunisia in 1955 and in 1956, when Morocco was granted Independence, Tunisia soon followed suit.

Morocco

Colonialism came to Morocco far later than it did to its two Maghrebi partners. Indeed, the colonial period only lasted 44 years in Morocco and the country was not fully pacified until 1934, just 22 years before Independence was granted. In addition, the initial colonial experience was less severe in Morocco than in either Tunisia or Algeria, largely because it was carefully controlled by one man, Marshall Hubert Lyautey. Apart from a short

break during WWI, he remained in charge of Morocco until his final recall in 1925. Lyautey was determined to preserve traditional Moroccan political institutions whilst modernising them and tried to avoid major violence in pacifying tribal rural Morocco, preferring instead a mixture of coercion and persuasion.

Northern Morocco, was occupied by Spain and the Spanish army experienced serious difficulties in controlling the Rif. In 1921, a major anti-colonial war broke out under Abd al-Karim, which eventually required a combined Franco-Spanish army of 500,000 to suppress it in 1926.

In the aftermath of the Rif War, the first stirrings of nationalist resistance appeared. The movement sprang into public prominence in 1930. WW2 and the Allied occupation of Morocco in 1942 had ended the myth of French omnipotence and in 1944, with secret support from the Sultanate, *Istiqlal*, a movement demanding full Independence, was formed.

Riots in Casablanca in 1947 persuaded Sultan Mohammed V openly to support Istiqlal; which he did during a speech in Tanger. Popular support for Independence and for the Sultan as the symbol of Morocco's political integrity burgeoned, and in Mar 1956, Morocco became an independent state. Spain hurried to follow the French example, retaining control only of its towns on Morocco's Mediterranean coast, the enclave of Sidi Ifni (which it abandoned in 1969) and the colony of the Western Sahara which, it claimed, had never formed part of Morocco historically.

Mauritania

Until 1960, Mauritania had had no independent national existence. Instead it was traditionally divided between the nomadic populations of the Sahara desert and the sedentary populations of the Senegal River valley. Population pressures in the Sahara had, however, consistently forced excess population northwards into Morocco. Indeed, as with the Lamtuna in the 11th century, these northward migrations could have profound political significance, for it generated the empire of the Almoravids. The Zenata Berber tribes of the Sahara were intermingled from the 13th century onwards with Arab migrants, particularly the Banu Hassan. These Arab tribes effectively Arabised the Saharan populations and gave them their characteristics as the Moors of Mauritania. By the 17th century, the Arab tribes dominated their Berber neighbours and in 1674, the latter were symbolically subjugated to their Arab victors as *Zawaya* tribes.

For the history of the region after Independence, see individual country entries: (Morocco, see page 70; Mauritania, page 245; Algeria, page 286; Tunisia, page 367; and Libya, page 495).

TRAVELLING IN ISLAMIC COUNTRIES

The people of North Africa principally follow Islam, which is similar to Judaism and Christianity in its philosophical content and Muslims recognise that these three revealed religions (religions of the book *Ahl Al-Kitab*) have a common basis. Even so, there are considerable differences in ritual, public observance of religious customs and the role of religion in daily life. When travelling through Islamic countries it as well to be aware that this is the case. The Islamic revivalist movement has in recent years become strongly represented in North African countries, particularly in Algeria, though it is important elsewhere too.

Travel, tourism and foreign workers are common throughout the region so that the sight of outsiders is not unusual. Tourists attract particular hostility, however. They are seen as voyeuristic, short-term and unblushingly alien. Tourists have become associated with the evils of modern life – loose morals, provocative dress, mindless materialism and degenerate/Western cultural standards. In many cases these perceptions are entirely justified and bring a sense of infringed Islamic values among many local people, most of whom are conservative in bent. Feelings are made worse by apparent differences in wealth between local peoples whose per head income ranges from US$6,800 in Libya to US$530 in Mauritania and foreign tourists living on an average of US$17,500 per head in the industrialized states. Tourists, whose way of life for a few weeks a year is dedicated to conspicuous consumption, attract dislike and envy. Muslims might wonder why a way of life in Islam, seen as superior to all other forms of faith, gives poor material rewards vis-à-vis the hordes of infidels who come as tourists.

The areas where sensitivity can best be shown are:

The dress code

Daily dress for most North Africans is governed by considerations of climate and weather. Other than labourers in the open, the universal reaction is to cover up against heat or cold. The classic case is Libya, where the traditional dress, the *barakan*, is a successor of the Roman toga made up of 5 or more metres length by 2m width of woven wool material which wraps round the head and body. For males, therefore, other than the lowest of manual workers, full dress is normal. Men breaching this code will either be young and regarded as of low social status or very rich and westernized. When visiting mosques (where this is allowed), *medressa* or other shrines/tombs/ religious libraries, men wear full and normally magnificently washed and ironed traditional formal wear. In the office, men will be traditionally dressed or in Western suits/shirt sleeves. The higher the grade of office, the more likely the Western suit. At home people relax in loose *jallabah*. North Africans will be less constrained on the beach where Ber-

THE PRACTICE OF ISLAM: LIVING BY THE PROPHET

Islam is an Arabic word meaning 'submission to God'. As Muslims often point out, it is not just a religion but a total way of life. The main Islamic scripture is the Koran or Quran, the name being taken from the Arabic *al-qur'an* or 'the recitation'. The Koran is divided into 114 *sura*, or 'units'. Most scholars are agreed that the Koran was partially written by the Prophet Mohammad. In addition to the Koran there are the hadiths, from the Arabic word *hadith* meaning 'story', which tell of the Prophet's life and works. These represent the second most important body of scriptures.

The practice of Islam is based upon five central tenets, known as the Pillars of Islam: Shahada (profession of faith), Salat (worship), Zakat (charity), *saum* (fasting) and Haj (pilgrimage). The mosque is the centre of religious activity. The two most important mosque officials are the *imam* – or leader – and the *khatib* or preacher – who delivers the Friday sermon.

The **Shahada** is the confession, and lies at the core of any Muslim's faith. It involves reciting, sincerely, two statements: 'There is no god, but God', and 'Mohammad is the Messenger [Prophet] of God'. A Muslim will do this at every **Salat**. This is the prayer ritual which is performed five times a day, including sunrise, midday and sunset. There is also the important Friday noon worship. The Salat is performed by a Muslim bowing and then prostrating himself in the direction of Mecca (Arabic *qibla*). In hotel rooms throughout the Muslim world there is nearly always a little arrow, painted on the ceiling – or sometimes inside a wardrobe – indicating the direction of Mecca and labelled qibla. The faithful are called to worship by a mosque official. Beforehand, a worshipper must wash to ensure ritual purity. The Friday midday service is performed in the mosque and includes a sermon given by the *khatib*.

A third essential element of Islam is **Zakat** – charity or alms-giving. A Muslim is supposed to give up his 'surplus' (according to the Koran); through time this took on the form of a tax levied according to the wealth of the family. Good Muslims are expected to contribute a tithe to the Muslim community.

The fourth pillar of Islam is **saum** or fasting. The daytime month-long fast of Ramadan is a time of contemplation, worship and piety – the Islamic equivalent of Lent. Muslims are expected to read one-thirtieth of the Koran each night. Muslims who are ill or on a journey have dispensation from fasting, but otherwise they are only permitted to eat during the night until "so much of the dawn appears that a white thread can be distinguished from a black one".

The **Haj** or Pilgrimmage to the holy city of Mecca in Saudi Arabia is required of all Muslims once in their lifetime if they can afford to make the journey and are physically able to. It is restricted to a certain time of the year, beginning on the 8th day of the Muslim month of Dhu-l-Hijja. Men who have been on the Haj are given the title *Haji*, and women *Hajjah*.

The Koran also advises on a number of other practices and customs, in particular the prohibitions on usury, the eating of pork, the taking of alcohol, and gambling.

The application of the Islamic dress code varies across North Africa. It is least used in the larger towns and more closely followed in the rural areas.

muda shorts and swimming trunks are the norm, especially in the Maghreb states.

For women the dress code is more important than for men. Quite apart from dress being tell-tale of social status among the ladies of Fes or of tribal/regional origin, decorum and religious sentiment dictates full covering of body, arms and legs. The veil is increasingly common for women moving in public as a reflection of growing Islamic revivalist views. There are many women who do not conform, including those with modern attitudes towards female emancipation, professional women trained abroad and, remarkably, many Berber women or women with genuinely nomadic or semi-nomadic lives such as the Touareg. The religious minorities – Jews in Morocco for example – do not wear the veil. Jewellery (see page 56) is another major symbol in women's dress especially heavy gold necklaces (see the Dar Cherait Museum at Tozeur in Tunisia for an excellent set of displays of women's dress (see page 455).

The role of dress within Islamic and social codes is clearly a crucial matter for the people of North Africa. While some latitude in dress is given to foreigners, good guests are expected to conform to the broad lines of the practice of the house. Thus, except on the beach or 'at home' in the hotel (assuming it is a tourist rather than local establishment), modesty in dress pays off. This means jeans or slacks for men rather than shorts together with a shirt or tee-shirt. In Islamic places such as mosques or *medressa*, hire *jallabah* at the door. For women, modesty is slightly more demanding. In public wear comfortable clothes that at least cover the greater part of the legs and arms. If the opportunity arises to visit a mosque or *medersa* open to tourists such as the Grand Mosque in Kairouan, *jallabah* and slippers are available for hire at the doors. Elsewhere full covering of arms and legs and a head scarf is neces-

sary. Offend against the dress code – and most Western tourists in this area do to a greater or lesser extent – and risk antagonism and alienation from the local people who are increasingly fundamentalist in their Islamic beliefs and observances.

Forbidden places

Do not enter mosques in Morocco, except the new mosque in Casablanca. In other countries do not enter mosques during a service. In other places dedicated to religious purposes behave with decorum – refrain from shouting, unseemly laughter and take photographs only when permitted. Outsiders have spent much time and ingenuity in penetrating Islam's holiest shrines. In North Africa this is not worth the effort since the most interesting sites are open to visitors in any case, except in Morocco. People who are clearly non-Muslim will be turned away by door keepers from places where they are not wanted. Those who try to slip past the guardians should be sure they can talk their way out of trouble !

Good manners

Islam has its codes of other practices and taboos but few will affect the visitor unless he or she gains entry to local families or organisations at a social level. A few rules are worth observing in any case by all non-Muslims when in company with Muslim friends. (i) Do not use your left hand for eating since it is ritually unclean. If knives and forks are used, then both hands can be used. (ii) Do not accept or ask for alcohol unless your host clearly intends to imbibe. (iii) If eating in traditional style from a common dish, use your right hand only and keep your feet tucked under your body away from the food. (iv) Never offer pork or its derivatives to a Muslim visitor. Buy *hallal* meat killed in accordance with Muslim ritual and/or provide a non-meat dish. Do not provide alcoholic drink.

Religious festivals and holidays

The Islamic year (Hejra/Hijra/Hegira)

is based on 12 lunar months which are 29 or 30 days long depending on the sighting of the new moon. The lengths of the months vary therefore from year to year and from country to country depending on its position and the time at sunset. Each year is also 10 or 11 days shorter than the Gregorian calendar. The Islamic holidays are based on this Hejarian calendar and determining their position is possible only to within a few days.

Ramadan is a month of fasting (see below). The important festivals which are public holidays (with many variations in spelling) are *Ras el Am*, the Islamic New Year; *Eïd al-Fitr* (also called Aïd es Seghir), the celebration at the end of Ramadan; Eïd al-Adha (also called Aïd el Kebir), the celebration of Abraham's willingness to sacrifice his son and coinciding with the culmination of the Haj in Mecca; *Mouloud*, the birthday of the Prophet Mohammad.

The day of rest for Muslims is Fri. Observance of Fri as a religious day is general in the public sector though privately owned shops may open for limited hours. The main exception is tourism where all systems remain operative other than in Libya and areas of Algeria. Holy days and feast days are taken seriously throughout the North African region. Approximate dates for 1996:

21 Jan Beginning of Ramadan
22 Feb End of Ramadan
29 Apr Festival of Sacrifice
20 May Islamic New Year
        (Anno Hegira 1417)
29 Jul Prophet's Birthday

Ramadan, the 9th month of the Muslim calendar, is a month of fasting for Muslims. The faithful abstain from eating between dawn and sunset for the period until an official end is declared to the fast and the start of the festival of the Eïd Al-Fitr. During the fast, especially if the weather is difficult or there are political problems affecting the Arab world, people can be depressed or irritable. The pace of activity in official offices slows down markedly. Travellers have to manage in these conditions by leaving even more time to achieve their aims and being even more patient than usual. If you have a choice, stay out of North Africa during Ramadan and the Eïd Al-Fitr. Travel, services and the atmosphere are all better at other times of year. Travel facilities immediately before and immediately after Ramadan are often very congested since families like to be together especially for the Eïd Al-Fitr.

POLITICAL RISKS FOR TRAVELLERS

Political risks are not necessarily higher in North Africa than in other parts of the 'developing world' but they do exist. To an extent the situation of security in each state in the area is tolerable for the individual traveller for most of the time. The following section gives a brief résumé of the situation in the countries covered by the *Handbook* and what signs of difficulty can be spotted to give advance warning of problems.

Checklist

Be prepared for a real threat to personal safety and/or disruption of travel/banking/commercial services if:
1. There are truck loads of armed police parked in side streets near the main thoroughfares, *suqs*, mosques, schools and universities.
2. Traffic is very light and the streets clear of pedestrians.
3. Armoured vehicles are seen or heard moving in urban areas.
4. The local radio/TV plays non-stop martial music or its normal programmes are disrupted.
5. Shooting/explosions can be heard, however distant.
6. Streets are thronged by chanting or stone-throwing groups.

What to do if unrest occurs

It is wise in circumstances of political

uncertainty for a foreigner to be very discreet:

1. Stay in your hostel or hotel.
2. If the telephones are working, get in touch with your embassy or consulate so that your location is known.
3. Conserve any rations you might have.
4. Do not join in any action by locals. Your motives could be misunderstood.
5. Make contact in your hostel or hotel with other foreigners so that you can form a mutual-assistance group.
6. Listen carefully to the advice given by local hostel or hotel officials.

There is no real science for assessing political risks. Any traveller who intends to be travelling in North Africa for a protracted period should check with his/her national authorities on the advisability of visiting the area. In the UK, the relevant Foreign and Commonwealth Office T 0171 2333000 desk will give you the latest assessment from their embassies overseas. If you are deeply concerned, where possible phone your national embassy direct and ask for the press/information officer. Otherwise, take an interest in trends in the countries you intend to visit before leaving home. Some newspapers can be very helpful in this area notably the *Financial Times*, *Le Monde*, and the *International Herald Tribune*. Otherwise be aware of the key risks for the individual countries using the thumb-nail political assessment below. A summary of what professional risk assessors thought likely is given below :

Political risk in North Africa

Estimates Mar 1996

Relative scores for stability out of 100: the more points, the less the risk

USA	82
Morocco	78
Tunisia	76
Libya	68
Algeria	58
Mauritania	N/A

Source: International Country Risk Guide

Key factors affecting political risks

Much of North Africa is at risk of sudden and violent change because governments are either entirely unrepresentative of the people or have only partial political legitimacy. Most authorities are repressive in policies, relying on secret police, threats against their opponents or even crude tactics of imprisonment and torture. There is thus a constant undercurrent of repressed political strife within North African communities, though each country is different in situation and practice.

Algeria

Algeria faces a set of economic and political changes in the years ahead in a process that could be difficult and at times violent. The conservative elements in the régime have been in power for some 30 years and, despite their failures, are loath to give up authority and privilege. They wish to control transition to a democratic structure, which is a contradiction. Particularly they do not wish to see the secular and socialist traditions of the party which won the struggle for Independence against France put aside by an incoming government of Islamic fundamentalists. The fundamentalists meanwhile clearly have a sense of moral victory in view of the régime's cancellation of the spring elections in 1992 and represent a strong and well organized political opposition which uses violent confrontation as a tool in its attempt to take over power. Meanwhile, other forces for change – intellectual, political and social in origin – create further elements of ferment.

Algeria's political uncertainties are made worse by its economic problems. Living standards are depressed and welfare is deteriorating as the government struggles with the difficulties of high foreign debts, poor oil revenues and low domestic output. The combination of economic and political problems will make Algeria relatively unstable. Violence is already considerable, directed against the régime and the security forces but also specifically against 'foreigners' and 'those from the W'. Precipitate alterations in the political climate are likely and travellers should as a matter of course check with their government agencies before entering the country.

Libya

Libya is a political oddity. In a general sense there are few domestic risks to the stability of the régime. There is negligible organized political opposition. Colonel Ghadhafi has a certain populist appeal which should not be underestimated. The security services and Colonel Ghadhafi's bodyguard battalions are relatively very powerful. The main risks in Libya are that Colonel Ghadhafi, who is the undisputed and sole centre of power, is removed by natural or other means or that there is a palace coup d'état. The Libyan state is so bound with personalities and so weak in national institutions that change could bring comparative anarchy for a period.

The main risks for foreigners are from capricious alterations in Libyan government policies on visas, internal movements and taxation on foreigners. Decisions are taken overnight by the ruling personalities and implemented without due notification to the public. A second area of risk is the actions of foreign governments against Libya. Libya is believed in some Western countries to be involved in state terrorism. The Lockerbie incident is currently at the centre of attention but other issues of a similar kind also exist. The bombing of Tripoli by the USA in 1986 was not notified in advance while the cessation of international air traffic in 1992 was. Measures of this latter kind are more of an inconvenience to travellers than an absolute block. But the tensions that go with failures in diplomatic relations mean that foreign visitors should be highly sensitive to personal risks. Care in taking photographs and asking questions needs to be doubled in Libya. Some European governments and the US administration advise their nationals to take care when visiting Libya but the realities on the ground suggest that travellers are suffering no problems other than those arising through the UN embargo on air transport to/from Libya.

Mauritania

The political fate of Mauritania is closely linked to that of its neighbours, particularly Morocco and the issue of the Western Sahara. A continuing weakness of Polisario will diminish strains on Mauritania from the threat of Saharois ascendancy. Internally, Mauritania is in the course of democratisation which seems to be partially succeeding. The main coastal sites offer the traveller only problems normal in developing countries. Inland, security is less absolute.

Morocco

It is an irony that the monarchy in Morocco is in its way far more legitimate as a government than other so-called popular régimes in the region. The king stands as a successor to a powerful tradition of leadership within Islam. The issue of fundamentalism in Islam has less damaging and possibly less serious implications in Morocco than elsewhere in the region. The king transcends the sectional interests of Arabs and Berbers and has separate lines of appeal to the common man and the bourgeoisie. Morocco is none the less politically a vigorous country and opposition movements are also strong. In so far as the king is able to co-opt powerful political interests to his side or to balance rival factions one against the other, he survives. He has acute dilemmas which are causes of instability. The question of the Western Sahara is unsettled, awaiting a UN referendum to gauge self-determination by the inhabitants of the area. Any hint of a loss of the area would be unsettling. The king has to co-operate with the industrialised countries, notably the USA, in order to secure arms, financial aid and diplomatic support. Yet the USA has policies towards the Arabs, including the Iraqis, which are deeply unpopular with the Moroccan masses. Similarly, the régime has to maintain good relations with Western Europe to ensure the flow of investment funds and tourists at a time when some European countries are pursuing policies against their Moroccan migrant workers. Within Morocco, government success or otherwise in job-creation and lifting the standard of living, while also managing to keep foreign creditors and the demands of the IMF satisfied, creates constant strains.

Deep tensions exist, therefore. Riots over costs of food occurred in 1984. There were (mainly orderly) mass street demonstrations in major cities in 1990 at the time of the UN Desert Storm operation against Iraq in Kuwait. Several assassination attempts have been made against the king, though some years ago. Morocco can thus be described as being in a state of stable equilibrium but one where, because of the key role of one individual, the king, rapid change is always possible. In sum, the political risk for the traveller in Morocco is comparatively small if the guidelines above are followed.

Tunisia

Tunisia is wracked by many of the problems experienced in Algeria – transition from an established highly centralized and increasingly unrepresentative régime to new structures which have a stamp of democratic legitimacy but at a time when Islamic revivalism is deeply affecting society. The current régime has established itself, though at the expense of becoming more hardline against the Islamic groups. It is in control of the fundamentalists to a large extent and seems to have been accepted fairly widely by the population at large. The govern-

ment's economic difficulties are substantial but are being handled well, assisted by acting as a gateway to Libya during that country's international isolation. The government has repaired its relations with the USA and Europe in the wake of the Gulf Crisis and is experiencing a return of its important tourist trade. Overall, Tunisia seems to have survived a difficult few years and has remained for the most part a pleasant, mannerly and cultured society with a fair prospect for political stability. The future is inevitably slightly uncertain, however, since changes in adjacent states could adversely affect Tunisia. For the traveller, Tunisia is less immediately threatening than Algeria since the Tunisians generally recognize their dependence for jobs and income on tourism and will be most unlikely to attack foreigners.

HANDLING THE LOCAL BUREAUCRACY/ POLICE/SECURITY

North Africa is Islamic in religion, oriental in civilization and despotic in political tradition. Governments rule by fear, a culture of populism and political manipulation. They are changed most often by force and violence (see political risks, page 40). Travellers in North Africa should remember these facts in dealing with the local civil and military administrations.

Travellers will not be put off by these 'facts of life'. It is important, though, to adapt to the local ethos and to learn to live with it wherever you are. The quality of the civil service varies greatly throughout the region:

Civil Service
The higher the score the better the service

USA	100
Morocco	55
Tunisia	50
Algeria	35
Libya	35
Mauritania	35

There are a number of quite clear rules in handling situations in these areas:

Avoid trouble The main areas of difficulty affect relations with the bureaucrats, police and other officials. To avoid trouble bear in mind:

(i) Documents: do not lose your passport and ensure that all travel documents are in order. Passports are lost but they are also traded for cash/drugs and officials can be very unsympathetic. Long and often expensive delays can occur while documents are replaced, especially in Libya where there is no diplomatic help for US, British, Venezuelan and several other nationals. Keep all forms such as landing cards and currency documents together with bank receipts for foreign exchange transactions.

(ii) Prices: understand what prices are being asked for taxis, meals and hotels. Do not accept 'favours', like 'free lunches' they do not exist. In Tunisia and Morocco, for example, shop owners will attempt to give you gifts. At best these are used as a lever to get you buy other items expensively or can lead to disputes over alleged non-payment for goods. It is also a matter of discretion how you handle friendly relations with locals who invite you home for a meal/visit. In Libya, only hospitality will be involved and the same will largely be true in Algeria. But in Morocco and Tunisia in particular, commercial or other motives might arise in the form of pressure to buy a carpet, to deal in drugs or to pledge help for a visa to Europe. Be genial but firm in these situations. Or use local ways out – promise to look at the matter *ba'd bokhra enshallah*, ie later!

(iii) Drugs: do not get involved in buying and selling drugs. It is an offence in all the countries in this Handbook to handle drugs. Penalties can be severe including jail sentences in dismal prison conditions. In Morocco especially *agents provocateurs* can sell drugs and then inform the police.

(iv) Politics: keep clear of all political activities. Nothing is so sensitive in North Africa as opposition to the régimes. By all means keep an interest in local politics but do not become embroiled as a partisan. The *mokharbarat* (secret services) in North Africa are singularly unforgiving and unbridled in taking action against political dissent.

(v) Black Market: make use of black market currency only when it is private and safe. Some countries such as Libya and Algeria have tight laws against currency smuggling and illegal dealing.

(vi) Driving: keep to driving regulations and have an appropriate international licence. Bear in mind that the incidence of traffic accidents in North Africa is high and that personal rescue in the event of an accident can be protracted and not necessarily expert.

(vii) Antiquities: trading in antiquities is everywhere illegal. Most items for sale such as 'Roman lamps' and ancient coins are fakes. Real artifacts are expensive and trading in them can lead to confiscation and/or imprisonment.

Keep cool Remain patient and calm whatever the provocation. Redress against officials is next to impossible. Keep the matter from becoming serious by giving no grounds for offence to officials. Be genial and low key. Aggression and raised voices do little to help. Where you feel you are right, be smilingly persistent but not to the point of a break down in relations.

Get help Getting help can often be cheap or free. Start off with agencies used to foreigners, namely travel agents, airline offices and hotels. They will have met your problem before and might offer an instant or at least painless solution on the basis of past experience. They will know the local system and how it works. They act as free translators. Friends who are either locals or who live locally can act as translators and helpers. They will often have networks of family and acquaintances to break through the bureaucratic logjams. Last, and only last, turn to your embassy or consulate. Embassies are there principally to serve the needs of the home country and the host government, not the demands of travellers, though they have ultimate responsibility for official travel documents and, at their own discretion, for repatriation in cases of distress. Treat embassy and consular officials calmly and fairly. They have different priorities and do not necessarily feel themselves to be servants for travellers in trouble.

TRAVEL AND SURVIVAL IN THE DESERT

Travellers and the nature of deserts

For those travellers staying in well regulated accommodation in good hotels, the realities of the desert can be disguised for as long as electricity and pure water supplies are sustained. Much of the information in the following section can thus be ignored, though not with total impunity. Trips into the desert even by the most careful of tour operators carry some of the hazards and a knowledge of good practice might be as helpful on the beach or tourist bus as for the full-blooded desert voyager.

There is a contemporary belief that the problems of living and travelling in deserts have been solved. Much improved technology in transport together with apparent ease of access to desert areas has encouraged these comfortable ideas. The very simplicity of the problems of deserts, lack of water and high temperatures, make them easy to underestimate. In reality, deserts have not changed and problems still arise when travelling in them, albeit with less regularity than 20 or so years ago. One aspect of the desert remains unchanged – mistakes and misfortune can too easily be fatal.

Desert topography is varied. Excel-lent books such as Allan JA & Warren A (1993) *Deserts: a conservation atlas*, Mitchell Beazley, show the origins and constant development of desert scenery. In North Africa, desert and semi-desert is the largest single surface area and so has an importance for travellers rarely met with elsewhere. Its principal features and their effects on transport are best understood before they are met on the ground. The great *ergs* or sandseas comprise mobile dunes and shifting surface sands over vast areas. Small mobile *bark-hans*, which are crescent shaped, can often be driven round on firm terrain but the larger transverse and longitudinal dunes can form large surfaces with thick ridges of soft sand. They constantly change their shape as the wind works across them. While not impassible, they can be crossed only slowly and with difficulty. The major sand seas such as those at Calanscio, Murzuq, and Brak should be treated as no-go areas for all but fully equipped and locally supported expeditions. Similar conclusions apply to the extensive outcrops of rocky desert as exemplified by the Jabal As-Sawda in Libya or the rougher parts of the S Atlas zones of Algeria and Morocco. The *wadi* beds which penetrate much of the Sahara, *serirs* and gravel plains provide good access for all-terrain vehicles.

The main characteristic of the desert is its **aridity**. Aridity is calculable and those navigating deserts are advised to understand the term so that the element of risk can be appraised and managed with safety. CW Thornthwaite's aridity index shows water deficiency relative to water need for a given area. There is a gradient from N to S throughout the region, of rising temperatures, diminishing rainfall and worsening aridity. Aridity of the desert is thus very variable, ranging from the Mediterranean sub-tropical fringe to a semi-arid belt to the S and a fully arid desert interior. In basic terms, the further S you are the more dangerous the environment. Do not assume that conditions on the coast properly prepare you for the deep S. The Sahara is also very varied in its topography, climate and natural difficulties posed for the traveller. Rapid transition from rough stone terrain to sand sea to salt flat has to be expected and catered for.

For practical purposes, aridity means **no moisture and very high temperatures**. The world's highest temperatures are experienced in the Sahara – over 55°C. Averages in the S desert run in summer at more than 50°C in the shade at midday. In full sun very much higher figures are reached. High temperatures are not the only difficulty. Each day has a large range of temperature, often of more than 20°C, with nights being intensely cold, sometimes below freezing. In winter, air temperatures can be very low despite the heat of the sun and temperatures drop very rapidly either when the sun goes down or when there is movement from sunlight to shade, say in a deep gorge or a cave.

Increasing aridity means greater **difficulty in water availability**. Scientists define the problem in terms of water deficits. North Africa as a whole and the deep Sahara in particular are very serious water deficit areas. Surface waters are lacking almost everywhere. Underground water is scarce and often available only at great depths. Occasional natural see pages of water give rise to oases and/or palmeries. They are, however, rare. Since water is the key to sustaining life in deserts, travellers have always to assume that they must be self-sufficient or navigate from one known water source to another.

Isolation is another feature of the Sahara. Travellers' tales tend to make light of the matter, hinting that bedouin Arabs will emerge from the dunes even in the most obscure corner of the desert. This is probably true of the semi-desert and some inland *wadi* basins but not a correct assumption on which to build a journey in the greater part of the Sahara. Population numbers in the desert are very low, only one person per 20 km sq in Al-Kufrah in SE Libya, for example, and most of these are concentrated in small oasis centres. Black top road systems are gradually being extended into and through the Sahara but they represent a few straggling lines across areas for the most part without fixed and maintained highways. The very fact that oil exploration has been so intense in the Sahara has meant that the surface of the desert is criss-crossed with innumerable tracks, making identification of all routes other than black top roads extremely difficult. Once off the main roads, travellers can part from their escorts and find no fixed topography to get them back on course. Vanishing individuals and vehicles in the Sahara are too frequent to be a joke. To offset this problem read on.

The most acute difficulty with off-road emergencies is finding the means of raising assistance because of isolation. Normal preventative action is to ensure that your travel programme is known in advance by some individual or an institution to whom regular check-in is made from points on the route. Failure to contact should automatically raise the alarm. Two vehicles are essential and often obviate the worst problems of break-down and the matter of isolation. Radio communication from your vehicle is an expensive but useful aid if things go wrong.

Bear in mind the enormous distances involved in bringing help even where the location of an incident in the desert is known. Heavy rescue equipment and/or paramedical assistance will probably be 500 km or more distant. Specialist transport for the rescuers is often not instantly available, assuming that local telecommunications systems work and local administrators see fit to help.

Living with the climate

Living with desert environments is not difficult but it does take discipline and adherence to sensible routines at all times. It is an observed fact that health problems in hot and isolated locations take on a greater seriousness for those involved than they would in temperate climates. It is still common practice with Western oil companies and other commercial organisations regularly engaged at desert sites to fly ill or injured persons home as a first measure in the knowledge that most will recover more rapidly without the psychological and environmental pressures of a desert site. Most health risks in the desert are avoidable. The rules, evolved over many years, are simple and easy to follow:

1. Allow time to acclimatise to full desert conditions. Conserve your energy at first rather than acting as if you were still in a temperate climatic régime. Most people take a week or more to adjust to heat conditions in the deep Sahara.

2. Stay out of direct sunlight whenever possible, especially once the sun is high. Whenever you can, do what the locals do, move from shade to shade.

3. Wear clothes to protect your skin from the sun, particularly your head and neck. Use a high Sun Protection Factor (SPF) cream, preferably as high as SPF15 (94%) to minimize the effects of Ultraviolet-B. Footwear is a matter of choice though many of those from the temperate parts of the world will find strong, light but well ventilated boots ideal for keeping sand, sun, venomous livestock and thorns off the feet. Slip on boots are best of all since they are convenient if visiting Arab encampments/housing/religious sites, where shoes are not worn.

4. Drink good quality water regularly and fully. It is estimated that 10-15 litres per day are needed by a healthy person to avoid water deficiency in desert conditions, even if there is no actual feeling of thirst. The majority of ailments arising in the desert relate to water deficiency and so it is worth the small effort of regular drinking of water. Too much alcoholic drink has the opposite effect in most cases and is not, unfortunately, a substitute for water!

5. Be prepared for cold nights by having some warm clothes to hand.

6. Stay in your quarters or vehicle if there is a **sand storm**.

7. Refrain from eating dubious foods. Deserts and stomach upsets have a habit of going hand in hand – 'gyppy-tummy' and 'Tripoli-trots' give a taste of the problem! Choose hot cooked meals in preference to cold meats and tired salads. Peel all fruit and uncooked fresh vegetables. Do not eat 'native' milk-based items or drink untreated water unless you are absolutely sure of its good quality.

8. Sleep off the ground if you can. There are very few natural dangers in the desert but scorpions, spiders and snakes are found (but are rarely fatal) and are best avoided.

Transport and common sense in the desert

The key to safe travel in desert regions is reliable and well equipped transport. Most travellers will simply use local bus and taxi services. For the motorist, motorcyclist or pedal cyclist there are ground rules which, if followed, will help to reduce risks. In normal circumstances travellers will remain on black top roads and for this need only a well prepared 2WD vehicle. Choose a machine which is known for its reliability and for which spares can be easily obtained. Across the whole of North Africa only Peugeot and Mercedes are found with adequate spares and servicing facilities. If you have a different type of car/truck, make sure that you take spares with you or have the means of getting spares sent out. Bear in mind that transport of spares to and from Libya might be tediously long. Petrol/benzene/gas is everywhere available though diesel is equally well distributed except in the smallest of southern settlements. 4WD transport is useful even for the traveller who normally remains on the black top highway. Emergencies, diversions and unscheduled visits to off the road sites become less of a problem with all-terrain vehicles. Off the road, 4WD is essential, normally with two vehicles travelling together. A great variety of 4WD vehicles are in use in the region, with Toyota and Land Rover probably found most widely.

All vehicles going into the S areas of North Africa should have basic equipment as follows:

1. Full tool kit, vehicle maintenance handbook and supplementary tools such as clamps, files, wire, spare parts kit supplied by car manufacturer, jump leads.
2. Spare tyre/s, battery driven tyre pump, tyre levers, tyre repair kit, hydraulic jack, jack handle extension, base plate for jack.
3. Spare fuel can/s, spare water container/s, cool bags.

For those going off the black top roads other items to include are:

4. Foot tyre pump, heavy duty hydraulic or air jack, power winch, sand channels, safety rockets, comprehensive first aid kit, radio-telephone where permitted.
5. Emergency rations kit/s, matches, Benghazi burner (see page 49).
6. Maps, compasses, latest road information, long term weather forecast, guides to navigation by sun and stars.

Driving in the desert is an acquired skill. Basic rules are simple but crucial.

1. If you can get a local guide who perhaps wants a lift to your precise destination, use him.
2. Set out early in the morning after first light, rest during the heat of the day and use the cool of the evening for further travel.
3. Never attempt to travel at night or when there is a sandstorm brewing or in progress.

4. Always travel with at least two vehicles which should remain in close visual contact.

Other general hints include not speeding across open flat desert in case the going changes without warning and your vehicle beds deeply into soft sand or a gully. Well maintained corrugated road surfaces can be taken at modest pace but rocky surfaces should be treated with great care to prevent undue wear on tyres. Sand seas are a challenge for drivers but need a cautious approach – ensure that your navigation lines are clear so that weaving between dunes does not disorientate the navigator. Especially in windy conditions, sight lines can vanish, leaving crews with little knowledge of where they are. Cresting dunes from dip slope to scarp needs care that the vehicle does not either bog down or overturn. Keep off salt flats after rain and floods especially in the winter and spring when water tables can rise and make the going hazardous in soft mud. Even when on marked and maintained tracks beware of approaching traffic. One of the editor's friend's car was hit by the only vehicle which passed him that day on a 500 km drive in S Libya!

Emergencies

The desert tends to expose the slightest flaw in personnel and vehicles. Emergency situations are therefore to be expected and planned for. There is no better security than making the schedule of your journey known in advance to friends or embassy/consulate officials who will actively check on your arrival at stated points. Breakdowns and multiple punctures are the most frequent problem. On the highway the likelihood is always that a passing motorist will give assistance, or a lift to the nearest control post or village. In these situations it is best simply remain with your vehicle until help arrives making sure that your are clear of the road and that you are protected from other traffic by a warning triangle and/or rocks on the road to rear and front.

Off the road, breakdowns, punctures and bogging down in soft sand are the main difficulties. If you have left your travel programme at your last stop you will already have a fall back position in case of severe problems. If you cannot make a repair or extricate yourself, remain with your vehicle in all circumstances. Unless you can clearly see a settlement (not a mirage) stay where you are with water, food and shelter. The second vehicle can be used to search for help but only after defining the precise location of the incident. In the case of getting lost, halt, conserve fuel while you attempt to get a bearing on either the topography or the planets/stars and work out a traverse to bring you back to a known line such as a highway, mountain ridge or coastline. If that fails, take up as prominent a position as possible for being spotted from the air. Build a fire to use if and when y ou hear air activity in your vicinity. Attempt to find a local source of water by digging in the nearest wadi bed, collecting dew from the air at night. If you have fuel to spare it can be used with great care both as a means of attracting attention and a way of boiling untreated water. A *Benghazi burner*, two crude metal cones welded together to give a water jacket and space for a fire in the centre can achieve this latter purpose. As ever in North Africa, be patient and conserve your energy.

WILDLIFE

The area covered by the book divides itself into two climatic regions, the Mediterranean and the Desert, with transitional areas between the two extremes. Within these zones, however, is a wide variety of habitats. The sea areas may be enclosed like the Mediterranean, or subject to tidal influences as in Morocco. Coastal wetlands include deltas, salt marsh and estuaries, while inland lakes and reservoirs provide freshwater sites. The *maquis* and the *garrigue* contrast with the agricultural areas, while mountain ranges such as the Atlas provide their own climate, delaying flowering and shortening seasons. Even the desert areas provide contrasts with the sands (*erg*), gravels (*reg*) and rock (*hammada*) interspersed with the occasional oasis.

Many of the habitats mentioned above are under threat, either from pollution, urbanisation, desertification or advanced farming techniques. Fortunately, in some countries such as Morocco and Tunisia, the conservation movement is gaining pace and many National Parks and Nature Reserves have been created and programmes of environmental education set up. In other countries, regrettably, wildlife is still regarded as a resource to be exploited, either for food or sport.

In both the Mediterranean and Desert regions, wildlife faces the problem of adapting to drought and the accompanying heat. The periods without rain may vary from 4 months on the shores of the Mediterranean to several years in some parts of the Sahara. Plants and animals have, therefore, evolved numerous methods of coping with drought and water loss. Some plants have extensive root systems; others have hard, shiny leaves or an oily surface to reduce water loss through transpiration. Plants such as the *broom* have small, sparse leaves, relying on stems and thorns to attract sunlight and produce food. Animals such as the *addax* and *gazelle* obtain all their moisture requirements from vegetation and never need to drink. Where rain is a rare occurrence, plants and animals have developed a short life cycle combined with years of dormancy. When rain does arrive, the desert can burst into life, with plants seeding, flowering and dispersing within a few weeks or even days. Rain will also stimulate eggs to hatch which have lain dormant for years. Many animals in the desert areas are nocturnal, taking advantage of the cooler night temperatures, their tracks and footprints revealed in the morning. Another adaption is provided by the *sandfish*, which is a type of skink (lizard) which 'swims' through the sand in the cooler depths during the day. Perhaps the most remarkable example of adaption is shown by the *camel* (see box, page 262). Apart from its spreading feet which enable it to walk on sand, the camel is able to adjust its body temperature to prevent sweating, reduce urination fluid loss and store body fat to provide food for up to 6 months.

Mammals

Mammals have a difficult existence throughout the area, due to human disturbance and the fact that many of the species are not well adapted to drought. Many have, therefore, become nocturnal and their presence may only be indicated by droppings and tracks. Some mammals common in northern Europe can, nevertheless, be seen in the Mediterranean environments and these include *fox*, *rabbit*, *hare*, Red, Fallow and Roe *deer* and at least three species of *hedgehog*. Despite widespread hunting, *wild boar* are common wherever there is enough cover in deciduous woodlands. *Hyenas* and *jackals* still thrive in many areas of North Africa, but the attractive *fennec*, whilst still fairly common in Tunisia and northern Algeria, is frequently illegally trapped. Typical woodland species include the *red squirrel* (the grey variety from North America has not been introduced), *garden dormouse*, which readily hibernates in houses, *pine* and *beech martens* and the *polecat*. The cat family, once common, is now rare, but the *lynx* hangs on in some areas. The *leopard*, formerly common in North Africa, is now extremely rare, but is occasionally seen in some isolated regions, to the panic of local people. There are at least three species of *gazelle* in North Africa, the Dorcas Gazelle preferring the steppes, the Mountain Gazelle

inhabiting locations over 2,000m especially where there is juniper forest, and the Desert Gazelle locating in the *reg* of the northern Sahara. The latter is often hunted by horse or vehicle, its only defence being its speed. There are over 30 species of *bat* in the area, all but one – the Egyptian Fruit Bat – being insectivorous. Recent ringing has shown that bats will migrate according to the season and to exploit changing food sources. Many species of bat have declined disastrously in recent years due to the increased use of insecticides and disturbance of roosting sites. Desert rodents include the large-eyed *sand rat*, the *gerbil* and the *jerboa*. Many, sadly, find themselves in pet shops.

Reptiles and amphibians

Tortoises are widespread in North Africa. The best distributed is *Hermanns tortoise* which can reach a maximum size of 30 cm. *Pond terrapins* are small fresh water tortoises and can be found in all the Mediterranean habitats. Both tortoises and terrapins are taken in large numbers for the pet trade. There are over thirty species of lizard in the area, the most common being the *wall lizard*, which often lives close to houses. *Sand racers* are frequently seen on coastal dunes, while *sand fish* and *sand swimmers* take advantage of deep sand to avoid predators and find cooler temperatures in the desert *reg*. The *ocellated lizard* is impressive in size, growing to 20 cm. *Geckoes* are plump, soft-skinned, nocturnal lizards with adhesive pads on their toes and are frequently noted near houses. The *chameleon* is a reptile with a prehensile tail and a long sticky tongue for catching insects. Although basically green, it can change colour to match its surroundings. *Snakes* are essentially legless lizards. There are some thirty species in the Mediterranean areas alone, but only the viperine types are dangerous. These can be identified by their triangular heads, short plump bodies and zig-zag markings. The *horned viper* lies just below the surface of sand, with its horns projecting, waiting for prey. *Sand boas* stay underground most of the time, while other species twine themselves around the branches of trees. Most snakes will instinctively avoid contact with human beings and will only strike if disturbed or threatened. For what to do if you are bitten by a snake (see page 20).

Marine life

The Mediterranean is a land-locked sea and it is only in the extreme W near the Straits of Gibraltar that there is any significant tidal range. Without strong tides and currents bringing nutrients, the Mediterranean is somewhat impoverished in terms of marine life. Fish and shell fish, nevertheless, have figured prominently in the diet of the coastal people for centuries, with *sardines, anchovies, mullet, sole, squid* and *prawns* being particularly popular. *Tuna* and *swordfish* are also widely caught. Over-fishing, leading to the depletion of stocks, has become increasingly problematic. Marine mammals, such as the *common dolphin* and *porpoise* are frequently seen in the Straits of Gibraltar. Some whales are occasionally found in the western Mediterranean, having strayed through from the Atlantic. These are most likely to be *minke* or *fin whales*.

The North Atlantic Ocean marking the western boundary of Morocco and Mauritania is, due to a strong upwelling movement, a mixture of warm surface water and the cold Canaries current. This mixture attracts both tropical and cold water fish, and in addition to the *sardines* and *tuna* on which the fishing industry is based there are *sea bream, skate, red mullet, tarpon, sea bass* and *conger eel*. Dolphins are a common sight.

Butterflies and moths

Because of the lack of vegetation on which to lay eggs, butterflies are scarce in the steppe and desert areas. The Mediterranean fringe of North Africa, in contrast, are often rich in species, some quite exotic. The life cycle – mating, egg production, caterpillar, pupa, butterfly – can be swift, with some species having three cycles in 1 year. some of the butterflies are large and colourful, such as the *swallowtail* and the *two-tailed pasha*. The most common butterflies in the early spring are the *painted ladies*, which migrate from North Africa northwards, often reaching as far as Britain. Other familiar species include the *Moroccan orange tip, festoon, Cleopatra* and *clouded yellow*. Moths are also widely represented, but as they are largely nocturnal they are rarely seen. Day flying moths include the *Burnet* and *hummingbird hawk moths*. The largest moth of the area is the *giant peacock moth*, with a wingspan of up to 15 cm.

Birds

Neither the Mediterranean nor the desert areas are particularly rich in resident bird species, but both can be swollen temporarily by birds on passage. Four categories of birds may be noted. Firstly, there are the **resident** birds which are found throughout the year, such as the *crested lark* and the *Sardinian warbler*. Secondly, there are the **summer visitors**, such as the *swift* and *swallow*, which spend the winter months S of the Equator. **Winter visitors**, on the other hand, breed in northern Europe but come S to escape the worst of the winter and include many varieties of wader and wildfowl. **Passage migrants** fly through the area northwards in spring and then return southwards in increased numbers after breeding in the autumn. Small birds tend to migrate on a broad front, often crossing the desert and the Mediterranean Sea without stopping. Such migrants include the *whitethroat*, plus less common species such as the *nightjar* and *wryneck*. Larger birds, including *eagles, storks* and *vultures*, must adopt a different strategy, as they depend on soaring, rather than sustained flight. As they rely on thermals created over land, they must opt for short sea crossings. One route uses the narrow Straits of Gibraltar, while the more easterly route follows the Nile Valley, Turkey and the Bosphorus. A third, lesser-used, route runs via Tunisia, Malta and Sicily, where birds run the gauntlet of the guns of so-called 'sportsmen'.

Within North Africa there is a number of typical habitats each with its own assemblage of birds. The Mediterranean itself has a poor selection of sea birds, although the rare *Audouins gull* always excites 'twitchers'. Oceanic birds such as *gannets* and *shearwaters*, however, enter the Mediterranean during the winter. Wetland areas, such as Lake Ichkeul in Tunisia (see page 411) contain numerous varieties of the heron family such as the *night heron* and *squacco heron*, while *spoonbill*, *ibis* and both *little* and *cattle egrets* are common.

Flamingoes breed in a number of locations when conditions are right. Waders such as the *avocet* and *black winged stilt* are also typical wetland birds. The wetland species are augmented in the winter by a vast collection of wildfowl. Resident ducks, however, are confined to specialities such as the *white-headed duck*, *marbled teal* and *ferruginous duck*. On roadsides, the *crested lark* is frequently seen, while overhead wires often contain *corn buntings*, with their jangling song, and the colonial *bee-eaters*. Mountain areas are ideal for searching out raptors. There are numerous varieties of *eagle*, including *Bonelli's*, *booted*, *short toed* and *golden*. Of the *vultures*, the *griffon* is the most widely encountered. The *black kite* is more catholic in its choice of habitat, but the *Montagu's harrier* prefers open farmland.

The desert and steppe areas have their own specialist resident birds which have developed survival strategies. Raptors include the *long-legged buzzard* and the *lanner*, which prefer mountain areas. Among the ground-habitat birds are the *Houbura bustard* and the *cream coloured courser*. *Dupont's lark* is also reluctant to fly, except during its spectacular courtship display. The *trumpeter finch* is frequently seen at oases, while the insectivorous *desert wheatear* is a typical bird of the *erg* and *reg* regions.

We are grateful to Rowland Mead for providing us with this information.

DRESS IN NORTH AFRICA

First time visitors to the countries of North Africa will be fascinated by the variety and colour of the garments worn as 'everyday' wear. This section, contributed by Jennifer Scarce, Curator of Eastern Cultures, National Museums of Scotland, sketches in the background and attempts an explanation of what is being worn and why.

The dress traditions of North Africa are striking and colourful evidence of a rich cultural heritage. Here, as in all societies, dress is a powerful form of cultural expression, a visual symbol which reveals a wealth of information about the wearer. Dress also reflects historical evolution and the cumulative effects of religious, ethnic and geographical factors on a society.

It is hardly surprising that the many influences which have shaped North African history have produced an equally diverse dress culture in which elements from antiquity, the Islamic world and Europe are found. The heritage from earlier times is a rich blending of decorative motifs and drapery. Carthaginian material culture drew upon local tradtions of colourful geometric ornament, which is still seen in Berber clothing and textiles. Greek and Roman fashions have survived in the striking dress of the inhabitants of the deserts and mountains of Morocco, Algeria and Tunisia where draped and folded garments are fastened with elaborate jewelled pins (see Jewellery page 56) and buckles. The Arabs introduced a different dress tradition, influenced by the styles of Egypt and Syria. Here the main features were loose flowing robes and cloaks, wrapped turbans and headcovering which combined a graceful line, comfort and modest concealment. The establishment of Islamic cities encouraged a diverse range of professions and occupations – civil and religious authorities, merchants, craftsmen – all with their distinctive dress. Within cities such as Fes, Marrakech, Algiers and Tunis specialist trades in textiles, leather and jewellery supported dress production. Widening political and commercial relations stimulated new elements in dress. Jewish and Muslim immigrants from Andalucía in the 15th century introduced styles influenced by Spanish tradition which survived in the full-skirted tight-waisted dresses of Moroccan Jewish women.

The Ottoman Turks introduced another feature into city dress, in the form of jackets, trousers and robes of flamboyant cut and lavishly embroidered decoration. Finally European fashion, with emphasis on tailored suits and dresses entered the North African scene.

One of the more rewarding pleasures of a visit to North Africa is the opportunity to see the intricate pattern of mixed dress styles which reflect an adjustment to economic and social change.

The widest range is seen in urban environments where European styles mingle with interpretations of local dress and the clothing of regional migrants. Men have adopted European dress in varying degrees. The wardrobes of civil servants, professional and business men include well-cut sober coloured European suits, which are worn with toning shirts, ties and smart shoes. Seasonal variations include fabrics of lighter weight and colour and short-sleeved shirts and 'safari' jackets. Casual versions of this dress code, including open-necked shirts, are seen in more modest levels of urban society. Blue jeans, blouson jackets, T shirts and trainers may be worn equally by manual workers and students.

Men's city dress alternates between European and local garments according to taste and situation. Traditional dress is based on a flexible combination of loose flowing garments and wraps which gives considerable scope for individuality. One of the most versatile garments is the *jallabah*, an ankle length robe with long straight sleeves and a neat pointed hood, made in fabrics ranging from fine wool and cotton in dark and light colours to rough plain and striped homespun yarn. Elegant versions in white may be beautifully cut and sewn and edged with plaited silk braid. A modern casual version has short sleeves and a V-shaped neck and is made of poly-cotton fabric in a range of plain colours. Professional men may change from a suit into a *jallabah* at home, while working class men may wear a plain or striped *jallabah* in the street over European shirt and trousers.

The more traditional interpretation of dress can be seen in the medinas. Here the *jallabah* is worn with the hood folded at the the back or pulled up and draped over the head. In the past a fez or turban was worn under the hood and a white cotton high-necked shirt with long sleeves and loose white trousers gathered just below the knee were worn under the *jallabah*. In Tunisia and Algeria trousers of a more exaggerated voluminous style were worn as a result of Ottoman Turkish influence.

A handsome and dignified garment worn by high ranking state and religious officials is the *caftan*, another long robe with very wide sleeves and a round neck. The cut and detail, such as the use of very fine braid around the neck and sleeves and along the seams, are more formal than those of the *jallabah*. The modern *caftan* has narrower sleeves and is worn in public by men of an older and more conservative generation.

Traditional dress may be completed with the addition of drapery. Examples include the *selham* or *burnous*, a wide semicircular cloak with a pointed hood and the *ksa*, a length of heavy white woollen cloth which is skilfully folded and wrapped around the head and body in a style resembling that of the classical Roman toga.

Headcoverings are a revealing indication of status and personal choice. A close fitting red wool felt pillbox cap, a *fez* or *chechia*, was normally worn alone or neatly wrapped with a turban length. Such caps were a major product of the souk of Tunis and were widely exported. Currently they are seen more often on older men both in traditional and European dress.

Footwear is a distinctive product of North Africa's longstanding leather industry. Shoes (see page 178) usually in bright yellow or white, are made of fine leather. They are close fitting, have a long pointed toe and are worn with the back folded under at the heel.

Women's town dress is also a mixture of traditional and modern European forms and depends on wealth, status and personal taste. In the larger cities where women are employed in business and professions, European clothes are worn, cleverly accessorised with scarves and jewellery. Longer skirts and long-sleeved blouses are worn, being a more modest form of European dress.

Traditional dress is remarkably enduring especially in the cities of Morocco among women of all classes. The most important garments are the *caftan* and *jallabah* of the same basic cut and shape as those for men. The *caftan*, as worn in the past by wealthy women, was a sumptuous garment of exaggerated proportions made of rich velvet or brocaded silk embroidered with intricate designs in gold thread. The modern *caftan* is usually made of brightly coloured and patterned light-weight fabric and edged with plaited braid. The shape is simple and unstructured with a deep slit at each side from waist to hem. Variations can be found in texture and colour of fabric, changes in proportions of sleeves and length of side slits. The *caftan* in its many variations is always worn as indoor dress and can suit all occasions. Traditionally it is worn as an everyday garment belted over a long underskirt. A light shawl may be draped around the neck and the hair tied up with a patterned scarf. Women who normally wear European dress to work often change into a *caftan* at home. Very chic versions of the *caftan*, combined with modern hairstyles and accessories, are worn as evening wear at private and official functions.

Outdoor dress varies across North Africa and Morocco and Tunisia offer different solutions to the traditional requirements of modesty and concealment. Moroccan women wear a long straight *jallabah*, in a variety of materials and colours and usually slit from knee to ankle, over a *caftan*. There are two versions of the hood, a small one neatly folded at the back which functions more as a collar, or a large one which is pulled tightly over the face over a rectangular veil which conceals nose, mouth and chin. This traditional outdoor dress is worn with backless soft leather slippers or European sandal style shoes. In comparison the Tunisian outdoor dress is less structured and may be worn over European clothes. Here the basic garment is the *sifsari*, a length of white fabric which is folded in half and secured around the waist. The top half is then pulled up over the head and draped according to the required degree of facial concealment.

While the balance between contrasting dress codes is subject to subtle changes of emphasis in everyday life, the rituals of *marriage* still require a conspicuous display of traditional dress, jewellery and cosmetics for both bride and female guests. The city of Fes offers one of the most distinctive wedding ceremonies where the bride, robed in layers of magnificent brocaded garments and shawls and adorned with a gold crown hung with strings of pearls and with intricate patterns drawn with henna on her hands, is transformed into a splendid icon.

Regional dress, though less varied than in the past, is a striking visual record of the complex ethnic patterns and harsh living conditions of the rural areas. Particularly in Morocco, the tradition of the Berber tribes both settled and nomadic, is still retained in their handsome and brilliantly coloured draped garments. Extremes of heat and cold mean that adjustable layers of loose clothing and protective headgear such as a swathed turban or a straw hat are essential.

In rural areas the men's hooded *jallabah* is the most common, usually of homespun wool in unbeached white, blue or beige and brown stripes. It may be worn over another *jallabah*. Head coverings may be a closefitting knitted cap, a loosely wrapped white turban, or a tall pointed hat with a wide flat brim plaited from reeds, palm fibre or dried grass. Berber men used to drape a *haik*, a heavy cloak in coarse plain or striped wool, over their garments. In the S, the Touareg men still wear brilliant blue robes and conceal their heads and faces with turbans and veils as an extreme precaution against the sun, wind and sand.

Women's dress is considerably more varied and depends on a combination of colourful drapes. The basic garment of the Berber women is an *izar*, a long straight piece of cotton or wool in a series of colours ranging from white or black through to vivid reds, purples and yellows. The *izar*, worn over a *caftan*, is folded in half to envelope the body and is fastened at the shoulders with heavy silver pins or brooches. (See Jewellery, page 56). It can then be further draped, belted and adorned according to local usage. Striped woollen cloaks may be worn over the *izar*. Large turbans bound with cords and scarves, elaborately plaited and coiled hair, and much chunky silver jewellery traditionally complete this form of dress. Some of the most spectacular examples of Berber female dress are seen among the tribes in the High Atlas mountains, where heavy striped cloaks, are worn together with towering head-dresses adorned with skeins of wool and silk threaded with silver chains and pendants. The effect is completed by boldly tattooed and rouged faces.

Other easily identifiable forms of regional dress include the large black *haiks* with which women in the S conceal themselves and the red and white striped skirts and shawls and large straw hats of the country women of Chaouen in Morocco.

In their different ways, **state ceremonies** and tourism encourage the survival of local dress. The soldiers guarding the tomb of King Mohammed V in Rabat wear a dashing scarlet uniform based on Turkish style jackets and trousers worn with a swirling *burnous*. In Tunisia officials wear traditional dress on state occasions, thus supporting the makers of *chechias* and other garment makers.

In tourist areas doormen, porters and waiters are garbed in white *jallaba* and scarlet *fez*, watersellers in traditional dress and gaily decorated broadbrimmed hats roam the streets, displays of Berber dancing are arranged and tourists are encouraged to purchase 'local garments' and participate in versions of local festivals. The souks in these resorts are festooned with *caftans* and leather slippers.

At another level, North Africa's impressive cultural heritage is taken very seriously and many museums have displays of traditional dress which can be enjoyed by both local and foreign visitors (see Dar Cherait Museum, Tozeur, page 455).

THE JEWELLERY OF NORTH AFRICA

North Africa today boasts a distinctive culture whose abundance of styles of dress and adornment almost defies description. The dynamic history of the region has produced imaginative tradititional designs mixed with foreign elements leading to a range of decoration few regions in the world can rival. Influences from the Phoenicians, Greeks and Romans, Arabs and Andalusians have each contributed subtly to the immense range of jewellery found in this part of the world.

Although some urban dwellers have adopted Western attitudes to dress and decoration, at times of festivals and especially for marriage ceremonies, traditional dress and elaborate jewellery that has changed little since the Middle Ages is still worn. The increase of tourism, while in some cases destroying traditional values, is in fact promoting and preserving crafts, especially jewellery making, by providing an eager and lucrative market for ornaments that was rapidly declining. Unfortunately, with the changes of cultural values, changes in fashion and style also occur and in North Africa large quantities of old, exquisite silver jewellery have been destroyed to provide raw materials for new pieces.

Throughout North Africa there is a division of tastes and wealth between towns where gold is favoured and the countryside where silver predominates. Basically, traditional styles continue to be popular and, especially in the Maghreb, jewellery tends to become more traditional the further S one goes. A general shift can be discerned away from silver towards gold which is now believed to be a better investment.

Despite a whole field of inspiration being forbidden to Muslim jewellers, that of the human form, they developed the art of decorating jewellery in ways that eventually merged to become a distinctive 'Islamic' style. Using floral (arabesque), animal, geometric and calligraphic motifs fashioned on gold and silver with precious and semi-precious gems, coral and pearls they worked their magic.

According to Islamic law, silver is the only pure metal recommended by the Prophet Mohammad. For the majority of Muslims this sanction is felt to apply only to men who do not, as a rule, wear any jewellery other than a silver wedding ring or seal ring.

Every town has its own jewellery *suq* with larger centres providing a greater range of jewellery. There is almost always a distinction between the goldsmiths and the silversmiths and there are also shops, which produce jewellery in brass or gold plate on brass for the cheap end of the market.

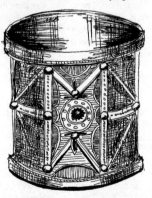

Bracelets from the Maghreb

Jewellers also sell silver items in the cheaper end of the tourist market which

One of the many styles of Khamsa or Hand of Fatima

North African anklets or *Khul-Khal* (always worn in pairs)

is very popular as 'ethnic' jewellery. Gold and silver jewellery is usually sold by weight and, although there might be an additional charge for more intricate craftmanship, this means the buyer must judge quality very carefully.

The **earring** is by far the most popular and convenient ornament throughout North Africa. It appears in an infinite variety of styles with the crescent moon shape being the most common. This is closely followed by the **bracelet** or **bangle** which is also very much part of a woman's everyday wardrobe.

Most of the jewellery is worn both as an **adornment** and as an indication of social status or rank. It generally has some symbolic meaning or acts as a charm. Jewellery is usually steeped in tradition and is often received in rites of passage like puberty, betrothal and marriage. In North Africa, women receive most of their jewellery upon marriage. This is usually regarded as their sole property and is security against personal disaster.

Many of the **symbols** recurrent in North African jewellery have meanings or qualities which are thought to be imparted to the wearer. Most of the discs appearing in the jewellery represent the *moon* which is considered to be the embodiment of perfect beauty and femininity. The greatest compliment is to liken a woman to the full moon. Both the moon and the fish are considered as *fertility symbols*. The cresent is the symbol of Islam but its use actually predates Islam. It is the most common symbol throughout the region and acquires greater Islamic significance with the additon of a *star* inside. Other symbols frequently seen are the *palm* and the *moving lizard* both of which signify life and the *snake* which signifies respect.

Amulets are thought to give the wearer protection from the unknown, calamities and threats. They are also reckoned to be curative and to have power over human concerns such as longevity, health, wealth, sex and luck. Women and children wear amulets more frequently as their resistance to evil is considered to be weaker than that of a man.

The most popular amulets are the *Hirz*, the Eye which has always had mystical connotations and the *Khamsa* or hand.

Silver fibula from Algeria, inset with coral

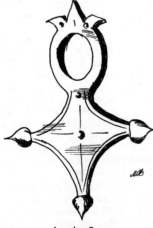

Agades Cross

The *Hirz* is a silver box containing verses of the Koran. The *Khamsa* is by far the most widespread of the amulets. It comes in a multitude of sizes and designs of a stylized hand and is one of the most common components of jewellery in the region. This hand represents the 'Hand of Fatima', Mohammad's favourite daughter. Koranic inscriptions also form a large section of favoured pendants and are usually executed in gold and also heavily encrusted with diamonds and other precious stones.

Coins or *mahboub* form the basis of most of the traditional jewellery, seen in the spectacular festival and marriage ensembles worn in the Mahgreb. Each area, village or tribe has its own unique and extraordinary dress of which jewellery, be it hundreds of coins or huge amber beads, forms a fundamental part.

Among the more interesting items are **anklets** called *khul khal*, worn in pairs and found in a great variety of styles. They are mostly of solid silver fringed with tiny bells. Fine examples are expensive due to their weight. They are losing popularity among the younger generation as they are cumbersome to wear with shoes and because of their undertones of subservience and slavery.

Characteristic **Libyan** jewellery is gold plated silver though both silver and gold are common. The predominant motif, a tiny version of the 'Hand of Fatima', appears on every piece. In **Tunisia** and other countries of the Maghreb, look out for *fibulae* and *pectorals* used to secure women's capes. They occur in various styles and are usually of silver, sometimes inlaid with coral. The two most distinctive styles of jewellery in **Algeria** belong to the Kabyles of the High Atlas and coastal plain and to the Saharan tribes like the Touareg. Kabyle jewellery is distinguished by its colourful *enamelling* in bright yellow, violet and turquoise, while that of the Touareg is generally made of leather and engraved silver. The most well known *Touareg* piece is the *Agades Cross (tanaghilit)* which comes in many variations of the basic style. **Moroccan** jewellery, especially that of Fes and Tanger, shows a clear Andalusian influence in the intricate flowing *floral/leafy patterns*. Floral networks of filigree enhanced with enamelling are a speciality of Essaouira, while more geometric designs are found in Meknes.

Today the main jewellery bazaars in North Africa are *Suq al-Mushir* in Tripoli (page 504) and *Souk el-Berka* in Tunis, (page 386). In Algeria the suqs of Tamanrasset, Bou Saada Ghardaïa and Biskra have good jewellery. In Morocco *Essaouira* and the Imperial cities are all jewellery centres and *Tiznit* is the place to find Berber jewellery.

Marie-Claire Bakker contributed the text and illustrations for this section.

LANGUAGE FOR TRAVEL – ARABIC, FRENCH AND SPANISH

Arabic It is impossible to indicate in the Latin script how Arabic should be pronounced so we have opted for a very simplified transliteration which will give the user a sporting chance of uttering something that can be understood by an Arab. An accent has been placed to show where the stress falls in each word of more than two syllables.

For both Spanish and French the gender of nouns has been given in brackets. In Spanish masculine is *el* and feminine *la* with plurals *los* and *las*. In French the plural of both *le* (masculine) and *la* (feminine) is *les*.

Spanish is spoken more or less as it appears. Bear in mind that *z*, and *c* before *e* and *i* are a soft *th*, *h* is silent, *ll* is pronounced *y* as in million, *ñ* as in *ny* in onion and *v* almost like the English *b*.

French unlike Spanish, does not have the final letter of the word pronounced unless accented as in *marché*.

Numbers

	Arabic	French	Spanish
0	sífr	zéro	cero
1	wáhad	un (m) une (f)	uno (m) una (f)
2	tnéen	deux	dos
3	taláata	trois	tres
4	árba	quatre	cuatro
5	khámsa	cinq	cinco
6	sítta	six	seis
7	sába	sept	siete
8	tamánia	huit	ocho
9	tíssa	neuf	nueve
10	áshra	dix	diez
11	ahdásh	onze	once
12	itnásh	douze	doce
13	talatásh	treize	trece
14	arbatásh	quatorze	catorce
15	khamstásh	quinze	quince
16	sittásh	seize	dieciséis
17	sabatásh	dix-sept	diecisiete
18	tmantásh	dix-huit	dieciocho
19	tissatásh	dix-neuf	diecinueve
20	ishréen	vingt	veinte
30	tlaatéen	trente	treinta

	Arabic	French	Spanish
40	arba'éen	quarante	cuarenta
50	khamséen	cinquante	cincuenta
60	sittéen	soixante	sesenta
70	saba'éen	soixante-dix	setenta
80	tmanéen	quatre-vingts	ochenta
90	tissa'éen	quatre-vingt dix	noventa
100	mía	cent	cien
200	miatéen	deux cents	doscientos
300	tláata mia	trois cents	trescientos
1000	alf	mille	mil

ARABIC NUMERALS

١	1	١٠	10	١٩	19	٨٠	80
٢	2	١١	11	٢٠	20	٩٠	90
٣	3	١٢	12	٢١	21	١٠٠	100
٤	4	١٣	13	٢٢	22	٢٠٠	200
٥	5	١٤	14	٣٠	30	٣٠٠	300
٦	6	١٥	15	٤٠	40	٤٠٠	400
٧	7	١٦	16	٥٠	50	١٠٠٠	1000
٨	8	١٧	17	٦٠	60		
٩	9	١٨	18	٧٠	70		

Greetings

	Arabic	French	Spanish
Hello!	assálamu aláikum	bonjour	buenos días
How are you?	keef hálek?	comment ça va?	¿como está?
Well!	kwáyes	très bien	muy bien
Good bye!	bisaláma	au revoir	adiós
Go away!	ímshi, barra	allez vous en!	¡márchese!
God willing!	inshállah	si Dieu le veut	si Dios quiere
Never mind	ma'lésh	ne t'inquiète pas	no se preocupe
Thank God!	hamdulilláh!	Dieu merci!	¡Gracias a Dios!
Yes/no	naam, áiwa/la	oui/non	sí/no
Please	min fádlek	s'il vous plaît	por favor
Thank you	shukran	merci	muchas gracias
OK	kwáyes	d'accord	vale
Excuse me	ismáh-lee	excusez-moi	perdón

Days

	Arabic	French	Spanish
Sunday	al-áhad	dimanche	domingo
Monday	al-itnéen	lundi	lunes
Tuesday	at-taláta	mardi	martes
Wednesday	al-árba	mercredi	miércoles
Thursday	al-khemées	jeudi	jueves
Friday	al-júma	vendredi	viernes
Saturday	as-sébt	samedi	sábado

Food

	Arabic	French	Spanish
banana	mouz	banane (f)	plátano (m)
beer	bírra	bière (f)	cerveza (f)

	Arabic	**French**	**Spanish**
bread	khubz	pain (m)	pan (m)
breakfast	futóor	petit déjeuner (m)	desayuno (m)
butter	zíbda	beurre (m)	mantequilla (f)
cheese	jíbna	fromage (m)	queso (m)
coffee	qáhwa	café (m)	café (m)
dessert	hélwa	dessert (m)	postre (m)
dinner	ásha	dîner (m)	cena (f)
drink	mashróob	boisson (f)	bebida (f)
egg	baid	oeuf (m)	huevo (m)
fish	sámak	poisson (m)	pescado (m)
food	akl	nourriture (f)	comida (f)
fruit	fawákih	fruit (m)	frutas (f)
lemonade	gazóoza	limonade (f)	limonada (f)
lunch	gháda	déjeuner (m)	comida (f)
meat	láhma	viande (f)	carne (f)
menu (fixed price)	ká'ima	menu (à prix fixe)	menu (del día) (m)
milk	lában	lait (m)	leche (f)
olive	zeitóon	olive (f)	olivo (m)
restaurant	restaurán	restaurant (m)	restaurante (m)
salt	méleh	sel (m)	sal (m)
soup	shórba	potage (m)	sopa (f)
sugar	súkar	sucre (m)	azúcar (m)
tea (tea bag)	shay (shay kees)	thé (m)	té (m)
water (bottled)	móyyah (botri)	l'eau (f) (en bouteille)	agua (f) (embotellada)
wine	khamr	vin (m)	vino (m)

Travel

	Arabic	**French**	**Spanish**
airport	al-matár	aéroport (m)	aeropuerto (m)
arrival	wusóol	arrivée (f)	llegada (f)
bicycle	bisiclét/darrája	vélo (m)	bicicleta (f)
birth (date of)	youm al-meelád	date de naissance(f)	fecha de nacimiento (f)
bus	autobées	autobus (m)	autobús (m)
bus station	maháttat al-autobées	gare routière (f)	estación de autobuses (f)
car	sayára	voiture (f)	coche (m)
car hire	sayárat-ujra	location de voitures (f)	alquilar de coches
customs	júmruk/gúmruk	douane (f)	aduana (f)
departure	khuróoj	départ	salida (f)
duty (excise)	daréebat	droit (m)	derechos (m)
duty free	bidóon daréeba	hors-taxe	libre de impuestos
engine	motúr	moteur (m)	motor (m)
fare	ujrat as-safr	prix du billet (m)	precio del billete (m)
ferry (boat)	má'diya	ferry/bac (m)	barca (f)
garage	garáge	garage (m)	taller (m)
here/there	héna/henák	ici/là	aquí/allí
left/right	yesáar/yeméen	à gauche/droite	a la izquierda/derecha
left luggage	máktab éeda al-afsh	consigne (f)	consigna (f)
map	kharéeta	carte (f)	mapa (m)
oil (engine)	zeit	huile (f)	aceite (m)
papers (documents)	watá'iq	papiers d'identité(m)	documentación (f)
parking	máwkif as-sayyarát	parking (m)	aparcamiento (m)
passport	jawáz	passeport (m)	pasaporte (m)

	Arabic	**French**	**Spanish**
petrol	benzéen	essence (f)	gasolina (f)
port	méena	port (m)	puerto (m)
puncture	tókob	crevaison (f)	pinchazo (m)
quickly	sarée'an	vite	de prisa
railway	as-sikka al-hadeedíya	chemin de fer (m)	ferrocarril (m)
road	trik	route (f)	carretera (f)
slowly	shwai shwai	lentement	despacio
station	mahátta	gare (f)	estacíon de trenes (f)
straight on	alatóol	tout droit	todo recto
surname	lákab	nom de famille (m)	apellido (m)
taxi	taxi	taxi (m)	taxi (m)
taxi rank	maháttat at-taxiyát	station de taxis (f)	parada de taxis (f)
ticket	tázkara	billet (m)	billete (m)
ticket (return)	tázkara dhaháb wa-eeyáb	billet de retour (m)	billete de ida y vuelta (m)
what time is it?	is-sa'a kam?	quelle heure est-il?	¿qué hora es?
train	tren	train (m)	tren (m)
tyre	itár	pneu (m)	neumático (m)
visa	fisa, ta'shéera	visa (m)	visado (m)

Common words

	Arabic	**French**	**Spanish**
after	bá'ad	après	después
afternoon	bá'ad az-zohr	après-midi	tarde (f)
Algeria	Aljazáyer	Algérie (f)	Argelia (f)
America	Amréeka	Amérique (f)	América (f)
and	wa	et	y
bank	bank	banque (f)	banco (m)
bath	hammám	bain (m)	baño (m)
beach	sháti al-bahr	plage (f)	playa (f)
bed	seréer	lit (m)	cama (f)
before	qabl	avant	antes de
Belgium	Belg	Belgique (f)	Bélgica (f)
big	kebéer	grand	grande
black	áswad	noir	negro
blue	ázrag	bleu	azul
camp site	mukháyyam	terrain de camping (m)	camping (m)
castle	kál'ah	château (m)	castillo (m)
cheap	rakhées	bon marché	barato
chemist shop	saidalíya	pharmacie (f)	farmacia (f)
church	kenéesa	église (f)	iglesia (f)
closed	múglaq	fermé	cerrado
cold/hot	bárid/sukhna	froid/chaud	frío/caliente
consulate	consulíya	consulat (m)	consulado (m)
day/night	youm/lail	jour (m)/nuit (f)	día (m)/noche (f)
desert	sahra	désert (m)	desierto (m)
doctor	tebeeb	médecin (m)	médico (m)
Egypt	Masr	Egypte (f)	Egipto (m)
embassy	sifára	ambassade (f)	embajada (f)
England	Ingiltérra	Angleterre (f)	Inglaterra (f)
enough	bás	assez	bastante
entrance	dukhóol	entrée (f)	entrada (f)
evening	mássa	soir (m)	tarde (f)
exchange (money)	tabdéel	change (m)	cambio (m)
exit	khuróoj	sortie (f)	salida (f)

	Arabic	**French**	**Spanish**
expensive (too)	kteer	cher (trop)	caro (demasiado)
film	feelm	pellicule (f)	película (f)
forbidden	mamnóoh	défendu	prohibido
France	France/Francia	France (f)	Francia (f)
full	melyán	complet	lleno
Germany	Almáni	Allemagne (f)	Alemania (f)
good (very good)	táyeb, kwáyes	bien (très bien)	bien (muy bien)
great	ákbar	formidable	magnífico
green	khádra	vert	verde
he/she	húwa/híya	il/elle	él/ella
house	mánzel	maison (f)	casa (f)
hospital	mustáshfa	hôpital (m)	hospital (m)
hostel	bait ash-shebáb	auberge (f)	hostal (m)
hotel	fúnduq/hotéel	hôtel (m)	hotel (m)
how far to..?	kam kilometri...	... est à combien de km?	¿Cuántos km a..?
how much?	bikám	c'est combien?	¿cuánto es?
I/you	ána/inta	je/vous	yo/usted
information	malumát	renseignements (m)	información (f)
is there/are there?	hinák	y a-t-il un ..?	¿hay un ..?
Italy	Itálya	Italie (f)	Italia (f)
key	miftáh	clef (m)	llave (f)
later	ba'déen	plus tard	más tarde
Libya	Líbiya	Libye (f)	Libia (f)
light	nour	lumière (f)	luz (f)
little	sghéer	petit	pequeño
market	sook	marché (m)	mercado (m)
me	ána	moi	me
money	flóos	argent (m)	dinero (m)
more/less	áktar/akál	plus/moins	más/menos
morning	sobh	matin	mañana (f)
Morocco	al-Maghreb	Maroc	Marruecos (m)
mosque	mesjéed	mosquée (f)	mezquita (f)
near	karéeb	près	cerca
Netherlands (Dutch)	Holánda	Pays-Bas (m) (hollandais)	Países Bajos (m) (holandés)
newspaper	jaréeda	journal (m)	periódico (m)
new	jedéed	nouveau	nuevo
not	mush	ne...pas	no
now	al-án	maintenant	ahora
oil (heating)	naft	mazout (m)	aceite combustible(m)
open	maftooh	ouvert	abierto
pharmacy (see chemist)			
photography	taswéer	photographie (f)	fotografía (f)
police	bulées/shurta	gendarmerie (f)	policia (f)
post office	máktab al-baréed	poste	correos (m)
price	si'r	prix (m)	precio (m)
red	áhmar	rouge	rojo
river	wádi, wed	rivière (f),fleuve (m)	río (m)
roof	sat'h	toit (m)	techo (m)
room	górfa	chambre (f)	habitación (f)
sea	bahr	mer (f)	mar (f)
shop	dukkán	magasin (m)	tienda (f)
shower	doosh	douche (f)	ducha (f)
small	sghéer	petit	pequeño
Spain	Espánya	Espagne (f)	España (f)
square	maidán	place (f)	plaza (f)

	Arabic	French	Spanish
stamp	tábi'	timbre poste (m)	sello (m)
street	shári	rue (f)	calle (f)
Sudan	as-Sóodan	Soudan (m)	Sudán (m)
Switzerland	Esswízi	Suisse (f)	Suiza (f)
synagogue	kenées	synagogue (f)	sinagoga (f)
telephone	teleefóon	téléphone (m)	teléfono (m)
today	al-yóom	aujourd'hui	hoy
toilet	tualét	toilette (f)	servicio (m)
tomorrow	búkra	demain	mañana
tower	qasr	tour (f)	torre (m)
Tunisia	Toónis	Tunisie (f)	Túnez (m)
United States	al-wilayát al-muttáhida	Etats-Unis (m)	Estados Unidos (m)
washbasin	tusht	évier (m)	lavabo (m)
water(hot)	móyya (sukhna)	eau (chaude)	agua (caliente) (f)
week/year	usboo'/sána	semaine (f)/an (m)	semana (f)/año (m)
what?	shenu?	quoi?	¿qué?
when?	ímta?	quand?	¿cuándo?
where (is)?	wain?	oú (est)?	¿dónde (está)?
white	ábyad	blanc	blanco
why	laih	pourquoi	¿por qué?
yellow	ásfar	jaune	amarillo
yesterday	ams	hier	ayer

MOROCCO

INTRODUCTION

Morocco is certainly Europe's nearest African neighbour with glimpses of settlements and traffic clearly visible across the Straits of Gibraltar. Yet Morocco is a very different world. In its 703,000 sq km there are long, sandy beaches for the sun-loving watersports enthusiasts, towering snow capped mountain ranges with ski resorts, expanses of barren desert for the intrepid traveller, ancient cave drawings and striking Roman ruins for the historian along with crowded, colourful weekly markets, troglodyte dwellings, primitive pastoral agriculture and quaint mud-built *ksour*. There is the pink Morocco of the spring almond blossom, the green Morocco of the geometric olive tree plantations, the creamy/white dwellings and the deep black Morocco of the Saharan night. The senses record the mixed spices in the *souq*, the smell of mint tea and of donkeys, and taste of *tagine* and the sound of the *muezzin* calling the faithful to prayer. Morocco is not a place to look at, it is a country to be absorbed.

CONTENTS

Introduction	65
Land and life	65
Culture	69
History	70
Modern Morocco	71
Rabat and Environs	76
Tanger, Mediterranean Coast and The Rif	92
Northern and Central Atlantic Coast	118
Meknes, Fes and Central Morocco	139
Marrakech, The High and Middle Atlas	172
Southern Morocco	198
Information for visitors	226

MAP

Morocco	66

Basics

OFFICIAL NAME al-Mamlakah al-Maghribiyah (kingdom of Morocco)

NATIONAL FLAG Red background with a green pentacle in the centre

OFFICIAL LANGUAGE Arabic

OFFICIAL RELIGION Islam

INDICATORS *Population*: 26.5 million. *Urban population*: 49%. *Religion*: Muslim (mainly Sunni) 98.7%, Christian 1.1%. *Birth rate*: 29 per 1,000. *Death rate*: 6.3 per 1,000. *Life expectancy*: 66 men, 70 women. *GNP per Capita*: US$1,030.

Land and life

Geography

Morocco at 458,730 sq km is only a fifth the surface area of Algeria or Libya and is slightly smaller than Spain. Morocco has 703,000 sq km if the Moroccan controlled territory of Western Sahara is included.

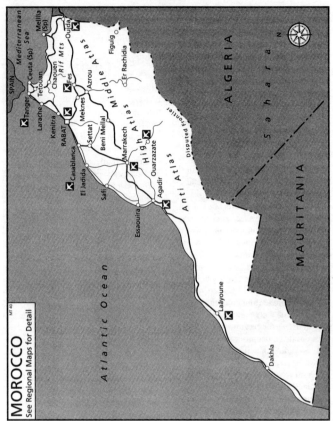

Borders

Morocco has a 1,835 km coastline from Saidia on the Algerian frontier to La Gouera on the border with Mauritania, of which a fifth lies on the Mediterranean and the rest faces the Atlantic. Border problems affect both the Western Sahara where Moroccan occupation is challenged by the Saharois and the SE where the line with Algeria in the region of Tindouf is not firmly settled. Morocco itself has long-standing claims to the Spanish enclaves of Melilla and Ceuta. The border disputes periodically affect

freedom of transit for travellers, through military action in the Western Sahara and occasional but temporary frictions elsewhere.

Main regions

Morocco is a country of great variety of topography in which huge mountain chains lying SW to NE dominate the relief (see map, page 66). The Rif rises sheer from the Mediterranean, few areas lying below 1,500m and the limestone peaks rising to 2,458m in Jbel Tidiguin. Together with its outlier, the Jebala, these mountains all but seal off the rest of Morocco from coastal North Africa. To the S lie the Atlas Mountains in three great chains – the Middle Atlas, the High Atlas and, in the S, the Anti-Atlas.

The Middle Atlas attains heights of 3,290m and in parts is well wooded and fertile. The great mass of the High Atlas begins in a series of well watered hills on the Atlantic coast but rapidly achieves altitudes of 2,000m and peaks in the Jbel Toubkal at 4,165m high to the S of Marrakech. The country's richest agricultural area is in the plain of the Gharb and the inland basins around Fes and Oujda. The coastal region aligned along the Atlantic between Rabat and Essaouira and limited to the E by the High and Middle Atlas forms a broken plateau of 210m average height. To the E of the High Atlas and S of the Middle Atlas is the W fringe of the High Plateau which run in fuller form through Algeria. To the S of the Anti-Atlas is the Sahara desert.

The chains of the Atlas Mountains both by scale and height tend to present problems for communications. Travellers should plan their journeys through the limited number of passes such as those at Tizi-n-Test and Tizi-n-Tichka in daylight to maximize enjoyment of the scenery. Heavy snows and landslides can disrupt transport through these passes from time to time in the winter and early spring. In most years mountain snows melt away by Jun.

Traditional regional loyalties are influenced largely by the topographic divisions of the country and comprise (1) The Rif mountains in the N, (2) the agriculturally rich Rharb plain with Meknes and Fes, (3) the Haouz (region) of Marrakech, (4) the Sous which takes in the valley of the Oued Sous and the adjacent lands of the Anti-Atlas and (5) the Tafilalt desertic areas of E Morocco. Racial, tribal, linguistic and historical elements give these regions distinctive flavours among which there is both rivalry and co-operation.

The average altitude for the country as a whole is 800m above sea level, making Morocco the most mountainous in North Africa.

There is a complex set of river systems, the majority running to the sea from the high mountain zone. In the NE the Oued Moulouya takes its origins in the Middle Atlas and collects the streams of the E Rif before reaching the Mediterranean at Saidia. The Rif proper is drained by a series of fast flowing streams to the Mediterranean such as the Oued Bou Frah and the Oued M'Ter but to the S, surface water runs to the Sebou and its tributary the Ouerrha and thence to the Atlantic near Kenitra. The Jebala is drained by the Loukkos and its tributaries to the Atlantic coast at Larache. The Oum er Rbia drains the vast areas of the Middle Atlas around Beni Mellal and the coastal plateau with the Oued Tensift taking flows from the area immediately to the S from the Marrakech basin. In the S of the country two important rivers, the Sous and the Draa run from sources in the High Atlas towards the Atlantic. On the E side of the High Atlas, streams such as the Rhéris and the Guir run S to inland drainage basins.

There are considerable variations in flows of streams in Morocco depending on the level of rain and snow fall in winter. The larger streams drawing their sources in the higher mountain areas flow for most of the year with snow melt persisting through as late as Jul but many oueds elsewhere are short-lived.

Climate

As is to be expected with a country as large as Morocco, there is a wide range of climatic types. The N coast falls into the Mediterranean climatic zone, though the usual régime of mild wet winters and warm dry summers is affected by the proximity of the Atlantic from which depressions move across N Morocco, bringing heavier and more reliable rainfall than in much of the rest of the Mediterranean basin. The Atlantic coast in the S feels the moderating influence of the ocean even in summer thanks to the cold Canaries current which drifts S along the littoral.

Away from the coasts, high altitudes and the influence of the Sahara make for a complex set of microclimates. In general, movement S and E brings the effect of the Sahara nearer, including higher daytime and lower night temperatures together with greater aridity. Increasing altitude in the Atlas reduces temperatures and also means very cold nights in exposed areas and higher risks of rain and snow in the months of Nov-Mar. Winters can be bitterly cold and wet throughout the Middle and High Atlas. Marrakech averages only 16°C in Jan but 33°C in Jun. Rabat on the coast has temperatures in Jan of 19°C against 25°C in Jun. Rainfall has great importance since the majority of people still rely on agriculture for a living. The rains in recent years have been above average and agriculture has thrived but periods of extreme drought are frequent and mean disaster for rural peoples. Rabat on the Atlantic coast receives an average of 530 mm of rain while Marrakech, further S and in the foothills of the High Atlas, receives only 230 mm. In the SE arid desertic conditions prevail. Rain is often in the form of heavy showers, some with intense thunder and lightning which can occur in the N at any season of the year. In Apr 1995, for example, there was an entire week in the Rif punctuated by thunder storms. During storms there is a high risk of flash floods, with oued beds carrying violent spates for short periods.

The prevailing winds are from the Atlantic Ocean and variably W. Occasional S winds from the desert known as the *shergui* bring high temperatures, very low relative humidity and dust storm conditions, a miserable combination for the traveller. In the Tanger area and the Straits of Gibraltar a 'levanter' wind from the E can bring misty and cold conditions at any time of the year.

Flora and fauna

Morocco has a wide variety of environments, so offering an interesting range of flora and fauna. Semi desert scrub is widespread, and vivid desert flowers appear after rain in contrast to the heavily wooded mountain areas and scented Mediterranean *maquis*. Migratory birds crossing the narrow Gibraltar Straits include huge storks and vultures and smaller (in comparison) buzzards and eagles. Distinctive coloured flamingoes, bee-eaters and hoopoes are found in many areas. Snakes and lizards are common and scorpions too on the drier areas. Larger mammals such as antelopes and gazelle are delightful sightings, the wild boars of the Rif and the Barbary Apes of the Middle Atlas perhaps less so.

Agriculture

Land use

Morocco, excluding Western Sahara, has proportionately more economically useable land than any other country of North Africa. Land use in 1991 was given as:

Land use	(%)
Arable and orchard	22.1
Meadow and pasture	46.8
Forest and woodland	17.7
Other uses	13.4
Total	100.0

Source: *Encyclopaedia Britannica*

The 10,200,000 ha of land under cultivation carry crops of cereals, including wheat, barley and maize, sugar beet, citrus fruits, potatoes, tomatoes, olives and beans. Hill areas of the interior are intricately terraced for agricultural purposes, otherwise the main areas of cultivation are the plains and river valleys.

Land tenure

Moroccan land tenure conditions are

dominated by large landlords, communal lands and religiously endowed land known in Morocco as *habous*. The landlord class is well entrenched politically and largely coopted by the régime with support and favour. No reform of tenure conditions has been attempted and large estates farmed by landlords using daily-paid labour or share croppers are the norm except for pockets of small landlords in the Sous and other limited areas. The land is very densely populated, forms of tenure apart, and more than 40% of people still live off farming. The country has experienced a steady drift of people from the land for some years, especially from the Rif and Atlas mountain zones where farming is made difficult by the hostile environment and limited material rewards. The above average rainfall of recent years had eased some of the strains in these communities but the respite will not be permanent, as the drought conditions of 1995 indicate.

Potential

Morocco has a number of important advantages over other countries of North Africa. It is comparatively well-watered over large areas. It has a vigorous and innovating agricultural community. The climate is generally kind, with potential for growing a wide range of crops such as citrus, flowers and early vegetables in demand in nearby Western Europe. The climate, varied terrain and rich heritage also open up possibilities for tourism. The endowment of raw materials is generous, giving Morocco a substantial role as a producer of phosphates, semi-precious stones and non-ferrous minerals. All these resources offer the basis for industrial processing. In many ways Morocco is currently in the throes of urbanization and modernization and seeking to make the best of its natural advantages to accommodate a 26.5 million population rapidly increasing at 2.4% each year and support a US$20,975mn foreign debt.

Culture

People

The **population** of Morocco was estimated in 1994 at 26.5 million, of which half was male. Although the crude birth rate has fallen sharply in recent years to 29 per 1,000 population, potential fertility is high, as improved medical facilities enable improvements in the child survival rate. At the same time, death rates are also down to 6 per 1,000 and life expectancy, now 68 years on average, will improve to swell the total population.

Morocco is an intermixture of Arab and Berber peoples. The two sections have intermarried over many centuries so that there are few pure residual groups. Differentiation at the present day is more linguistic that ethnic. The principal Berber-speaking areas are clustered in the mountainous areas of the country, reflecting the retreat of the Berbers to regions of refuge during the Arab invasions. For convenience there are three main Berber areas where somewhat different forms of Berber are spoken – *Rifian* in the N mountain zone, *Amazigh* among the communities in the Middle Atlas and *Chleuh* in the Sous and adjacent areas of the High Atlas Mountains. The Arab inhabitants came in waves of adventurers and conquerors in the long period of invasions, including those of the Beni Hillal and Beni Sulaim between the 7th and 12th centuries. The important Jewish community, some locally based among rural Berbers, was reinforced from Iberia during the flight of Jews after the *reconquista* by highly educated and talented urban groups. Many Jews left Morocco after the foundation of the Jewish state of Israel in 1948. Trade with trans-Saharan Africa in goods and slaves introduced Negro blood, while Morocco's Mediterranean connection brought in traders from as far away as Malta and, in the late 19th century and 20th century, settlers from France, Germany and Spain.

Much of the population is concentrated in the coastal cities and plains. Approximately half the population now lives in cities, the great concentrations being in Casablanca with 2.2 million, Rabat with 520,000, Fes with 450,000 and Marrakech with 440,000 (1988 official figures). Areas of heavily settled land with 60-95 people per sq km are found round the Mediterranean and N Atlantic shores, notably in the Rif, Jebala, the Rharb plain and the coastal plateaux and valleys as far S as the Sous. Densities decline rapidly inland. Other than the great cities of Marrakech, Meknes and Fes, the inland area carries low population densities, averaging between 20-60 per sq km. The E and S of the country is sparsely settled with less than 20 people per sq km.

The population is fairly young on average. More than 40% of people are under the age of 15 and a mere 6% over 60. Educational progress has increased adult literacy rates to 50%. Some 37% of Moroccans enjoy the benefits of secondary and 1% tertiary education. Morocco is the poorest of the Maghreb states with average personal incomes estimated at US$1,030 in 1993. National income is maldistributed. The income of rural people is very low – less than US$250 per year in many cases and the urban poor, crowded in shanty areas, are little better off. Nutrition levels are improving, however, and aided by continued good rainfall there is a fragile air of prosperity to the country at the present time.

History since Independence

Morocco became independent on 3 March 1956 through the efforts of Sultan Mohammed V, who was determined that the Sultanate should be the supreme political power within independent Morocco. The only competitor

for control of the newly independent country was the Istiqlal party. Although Istiqlal formed the first government of independent Morocco, the monarchy sought to widen political representation to balance its influence. The Royal Palace favoured the Mouvement Populaire, a rural-based, pro-Berber and royalist movement but continued to collaborate with Istiqlal until, in 1959, the party itself split, with a new, more radical wing becoming a separate political party, the Union Nationale des Forces Populaires, under Mehdi Ben Barka. This provided the monarchy with the opportunity to dominate the political process by arbitrating among the different political parties.

The government had to contend with a series of rural rebellions. The most serious of these which occurred in the Rif was crushed by Morocco's new army. Central government distrust of the Rif as a result of the rebellion still persists today.

King Mohammed V died unexpectedly in 1961 and was succeeded by his eldest son, Crown Prince Hassan. The new king had long been groomed for government, with an education both in Arabic in Morocco and in French at Bordeaux and with experience of government, both as an army commander and as premier in the period just before his father's death. Although the Sultanate has been traditionally powerful because of the religious legitimization of its occupant as Amir Al-Muminin (Commander of the Faithful), King Hassan II, like all new Sultans, faced immediate threats to his survival on the grounds of his personal competence. The new monarch sought to introduce limited parliamentary democracy within a constitutional monarchy. The experiment was not very successful and came to an end in Nov 1963, only a few months after it had been begun.

For the next 7 years King Hassan ruled without parliament, and Morocco was placed under a 5 year state of emergency. A new constitution, designed to increase the role of pro-Royalist parties, was promulgated in 1970 but the parliament elected in the subsequent elections was dissolved. A coup attempt against the king took place on the king's birthday on 10 July, 1971, involving an army-backed attack against him and his guests at his summer palace of Skhirat, just outside Rabat, and a simultaneous military attempt to take over the government. Both prongs of the plan failed, in the case of the attack on the king, largely because of his personal courage. The ringleaders were killed or later executed and widescale purges of army and government took place.

The coup highlighted the serious problems of growing corruption and ostentatious amassing of wealth within the administration. Economic conditions inside Morocco had also worsened. The government attempted to respond to both types of complaint, but on 26 August, 1972, units of the airforce attempted unsuccessfully to shoot down the king's aircraft. Once again, King Hassan survived largely because of his personal bravery. On this occasion it was established that the person responsible for both this attack and the coup attempt the preceding year was the minister of defence, General Mohammed Oufkir.

The Western Sahara issue

King Hassan tried to rally support throughout Morocco for the monarchy by reviving Morocco's claim to the Western Sahara. In 1974 Morocco began a diplomatic campaign to force Spain to evacuate the region. Inside the Western Sahara, a national movement, the *Polisario Front*, founded in 1973, had widespread support. Morocco persuaded the UN to place the competing claims for the Western Sahara before the International Court of Justice in The Hague. The Court determined in 1975 that Morocco did not have a sustainable claim

of full territorial sovereignty. Morocco nonetheless assumed that the Court had backed its claim and, in a massive display of popular support, organized the **Green March**, a demonstration involving 350,000 Moroccans, to the border of the Western Sahara. Spain acquiesced in a secret deal and created a temporary tripartite administration in the Western Sahara between Morocco, Mauritania and Spain itself. The Polisario Front with Algerian and Libyan support was not prepared to accept Moroccan occupation and moved around 30,000 Sahrawi into refugee camps in Algeria and undertook a guerrilla war to liberate the Western Sahara. Although the Polisario Front succeeded in forcing Mauritania to abandon its occupation in 1978 (Morocco simply moved forces in instead) and in forcing Moroccan forces back into the major towns, it was not able to end Morocco's hold on the region. Starting in 1980, Morocco slowly won back control over virtually all the territory.

By the end of the decade, the UN had stepped in, with a proposal for a referendum over self-determination which was formally accepted by both sides. Morocco, however, made it clear that it would not abandon control of the Western Sahara.

Modern Morocco

Government

Morocco remains officially a constitutional monarchy. The system in use is one chamber, a House of Representatives, which is summoned and dissolved by the king at will. In theory, the House of Representatives can bring forward its own legislative programme but this can effectively be vetoed by the king who can also issue laws for endorsement through popular referendum. The king is commander of the armed forces. Four main political parties exist but those which fail to accept the central role of the monarchy are suppressed. The palace has attempted to recruit more support among the previously alienated intellectual classes and universities aided by improvements in living standards and promises of political liberalization.

The autocracy of the centre has been somewhat modified recently by the grant of limited autonomy to local administrations – city, town and region – and to the regional offices of the ministries so that decision-making can genuinely reflect local sentiments. Governors are appointed by the king. Administration in the Western Sahara is in the hands of the military.

Despite successes in foreign policy, King Hassan has not yet been able to democratize the political system without endangering the position of the monarchy. It remains to be seen to what degree he will be prepared to relinquish power after the forthcoming elections, in the face of considerable domestic political pressure to do so. The king's position has been rendered more malleable by the misjudgement of the popular mood his government had made during the war against Iraq in 1991. Moroccans generally had opposed the US-led Multinational Coalition, although the Moroccan government had initially supported it. Nonetheless, King Hassan has proved to be a consummately skilful political operator in the past and will, no doubt, show an equal sureness of touch in dealing with current problems.

Economy

Traditional agriculture
Almost 40% of the labour force in Morocco is engaged in agriculture, by far the majority in traditional farming. In the traditional sector there are many peasant proprietors with smallholdings but most are tenant farmers. It is estimated that 33% of farmland is owned by 3% of the farmers. Much of the area of private land is under traditional tenancies with holdings of less than 10 ha. Forms of nomadism persist in a few areas but there is an increasing tendency for livestock to be herded by shepherds rather than entire families on the move and for former nomadic groups to become settled. Similarly, the traditional valley cultivation areas of the high mountains are being deserted as the low returns and high demands on manual labour are rejected by people seeking higher incomes in the towns. Despite these changes, traditional farming remains the backbone of the economy, heavily involved with cereal growing and vegetable production in which the country, unusual for North Africa, is mainly self-sufficient. Peasant farmers and herders also own the bulk of the country's 16.3 million sheep, 4.7 million goats and 2.9 million cattle and a heavy concentration of fodder production results from this.

Modern agriculture
Modern farming is limited to the fertile plains of the Gharb, Marrakech and other smaller areas, much originally developed as medium-to-large scale enterprises by French settlers. The French have now been replaced by Moroccan owners, some of whom have also invested in reclaiming land elsewhere to take advantage of new irrigation water or modern farming methods. Most large scale farms produce export crops with concentration on citrus, where Morocco has been successful in breaking into Western European markets, sugar beet and specialist early vegetables such as potatoes and soft fruits. The modern farms have taken the largest share of newly provided irrigation water and state credits to the detriment of the small traditional units. There are some 9 million ha under cultivation with approximately 800,000 ha under irrigation. Farm output has expanded in recent years, helped by good rainfall:

Agricultural Output

('000 tonnes)	1993
Sugar beet	3,162
Wheat	1,573
Barley	1,027
Oranges	860
Potatoes	869
Olives	550

Source: *FAO*

Morocco has a major *fishing* industry, the 1993 catch being 607,000 tonnes and efforts are being made to develop the industry with foreign aid. Morocco is the world's largest producer of sardines. The over-exploited *forests* yielded 2,356,000 cu m of timber in 1992 though a great deal of indiscriminate cutting is used to produce firewood.

Energy/petroleum

Morocco has very poor domestic sources of fuel. Its small reserves of oil in the Rharb are being run down very rapidly and, despite intensive exploration, few discoveries have been made. Oil production was 83,600 barrels in 1992 with natural gas at 23,987,000 cu m. There is some generally low grade coal available, 1990 output being 526,000 tonnes. Other than natural gas, internal output is inadequate to satisfy demand of 1,791,000 tonnes of coal and 47,500,000 billion barrels of oil, the balance of which is imported. Increasing use is being made of hydroelectric power to support a total electricity consumption of 11,257,000,000 kwh. Much hydroelectric potential remains to be developed. The Meskala gas fields remain underexploited as a result of cash shortages and technical difficulties.

Economic policies and plans

Morocco has put little reliance on economic planning and its experiences have been generally negative. In the 1960s there was an attempt in the national plan to foster rapid industrialization, mainly using state monopoly agencies. Other plans have tended at various times to be sectoral, providing for agriculture, industry or energy as separate entities but rarely extending, as was claimed, to an integrated national economic plan on the French model on which they were supposedly based. The indicative 1988-92 development plan achieved economic growth at 4% per year in real terms (see also Economic Trends, page 74). Current policies are designed to cultivate privatization of state enterprises, private investment in modern industry, transport and communications. Special incentives apply to investment by foreign interests in Morocco for which tax holidays and preferential treatment are offered.

A key element in Moroccan economic policy is alignment towards the EU. This arose originally from the close relationship between Morocco and France but has since been widened to include Germany, Spain and UK and the EU as an entity. Morocco has sought special terms of association with the EU to gain access for its products and labour. The anti-North Africa sentiment in France and elsewhere has not deterred the Moroccan government from continuing to look for closer commercial links with the EU.

Industry

Is now as important a contributor to national income as agriculture, being valued at MD44,636 million in 1990. It provides only a modest proportion of employment, however, with 15.5% against 39.2% in agriculture. A large segment of industry is still French-owned despite an accelerated programme of Moroccanization. Processing of agricultural products is a major activity, including olive pressing, flour milling, vegetable and fruit canning and milk treatment. There has been increasing success with using phosphates and other minerals as raw materials for domestic industrial use rather than simply for export. Phosphates in particular are the basis for a set of industrial developments related to phosphoric acid and other chemicals. Construction materials, above all cement, form another area of rapidly growing industrial activity. There is a strong traditional craft manufacturing industry located in the major cities, especially Marrakech, Meknes, Fes and Tanger. World famous for design and quality are leather goods, hand-woven rugs and textiles, pottery and metalwork.

Industrial Production 1992

	(tonnes)
Cement	6,036,000
Wheat products	3,162,000
Carpets (sq m)	1,642,900*
Tyres (units)	1,002,500*
Refined sugar	520,000**

Source: *Encyclopaedia Britannica*
* 1989 figure ** 1993 figure

Economic trends

The war in the Western Sahara contributed towards Morocco's growing economic crisis. The government had, in 1976, decided to make an accelerated push for development in the hope of diffusing the growing social tensions which had contributed so much to the domestic political unrest of the early 1970s. Morocco pushed ahead with ambitious development plans using borrowed funds. However, by 1983, the costs of development, together with those of the war, had created an impossible situation.

Economic Structure 1993

	(%)
Agriculture	14.3
Mining	2.0
Manufacturing	18.0
Utilities	7.7
Other services	53.3
Construction	4.7
Total	100.0

In Sep 1983, Morocco had to reschedule its debt in the face of a worsening economic crisis and, despite the likelihood of the need to impose severe austerity measures, turned to the IMF for help. It had already had to face growing domestic discontent and there was every sign that this would recur. Indeed, the IMF economic restructuring plans, which insisted on the removal of consumer price subsidies on staples, such as sugar, flour and cooking oil, produced precisely that effect in Jan 1984. Riots swept the country and the government was forced to rein in its planned austerity measures. Since then the Moroccan government has plotted a very careful economic course, balancing off the need to satisfy its foreign creditors against domestic tensions. Its foreign debt rose from US$11bn in 1983 to around US$21bn in 1992. Morocco has also benefited from aid from the World Bank and from official aid donors, mainly in Europe. The result has been that the economy has been liberalized, the state sector is being dismantled and many observers now expect Morocco to begin slightly more rapid economic growth.

Symbolic of Morocco's desire for modernization has been a privatization programme, in which US$2bn of state companies will be handed over to private enterprise by 1995. Convertibility of the dihram for international transactions began in 1994. In Apr 1994 the GATT (General Agreement on Tariffs and Trade) annual meeting was held in Marrakesh when Morocco officially joined the organization. Despite some criticism that membership of GATT will impede domestic economic growth, accession to membership was seen as endorsing Morocco's growing maturity as a developing economy.

Main economic indicators

Despite a brief surge in the value of national output in the late 1980s, the Moroccan economy is now growing only modestly at 4% per year. Personal incomes have tended nonetheless to stagnate. Unemployment is officially put at 11% but, with seasonal unemployment and underemployment taken into account, a much larger number is less than gainfully employed. Inflation rose sharply in 1990-92 to close on 5% per year. Morocco's trade performance has been dismal, with a large deficit on current account.

ECONOMIC INDICATORS			
	1989	**1991**	**1993**
GDP (MD billion)	140	...	247
Imports (MD billion)	48	56	62
Exports (MD billion)	35	38	34
Balance of Trade (MD billion)	-14	-13	-29
Inflation (1985=100)	117.9	138.1	153.6
Foreign Debt (US$ billion)	19.9	21.2	...
Source: IMF, *Encyclopaedia Britannica*			

RABAT AND ENVIRONS

CONTENTS

Rabat	76
Places of interest	81
Local information	85
Sale	89
Excursions from Rabat	91

MAPS

Rabat and Sale	78-79
Rabat Medina	83

Rabat and Sale may lack for travellers the exotic appeal of Fes, Marrakech or Tanger, but these two cities have an impressive architectural legacy which reflects their long and turbulent histories. The massive but incomplete Hassan Tower, the Kasbah des Oudaias overlooking the river and sea, the ruins of the Merinid necropoli of Chellah, and the Abul Hassan Medersa with its intricate carving, are some of the most important and rewarding sites in Morocco. The medinas of Rabat and Sale are small and easy to explore, with beautiful houses and public buildings, and interesting markets and shops. The French built *ville nouvelle* (new town) retains much of the ambience of the colonial capital city, and has a surprisingly relaxed atmosphere. It is a comfortable and convenient place to stay, and perhaps a better first-stop than Casablanca.

> "They call Rabat the Pearl of Morocco. It stands high on the steep southern bank of the Bouragrag where the green river lashes the blue sea, above cactus-grown ochre rocks, a long rambling line of white and yellow, everywhere dominated by the huge grey Tower of Hassan."
> Rankin, Reginald, *In Morocco* (1908).

RABAT

Pop 518,816 (1982). *Alt* 65m. *Best season* Fine all year round, as the humid summer, with high Jul and Aug peak temperatures, is relieved by sea breezes.

History

City of Old and New
The name 'Rabat', a shortened and corrupted form of 'Ribat al-Fath', literally a 'monastery of conquest', indicates an initial role as a religious retreat and fortification. The city, located on the bank of the Oued Bou Regreg, with the kasbah on a promontory overlooking both the Atlantic Ocean and the estuary, lies opposite its historic rival, Sale. Rabat, capital since 1912, is Morocco's second largest city. The ambitiously extensive city walls laid out by the third Almohad Sultan Abu Yusuf Ya'qub al-Mansur now enclose, with the river and the sea on the remaining sides, the kasbah, the old medina, and the core of the *ville nouvelle*, the old and new directly alongside each other unlike the more common French pattern found in Fes, Marrakech and Meknes, where the new

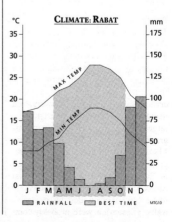

CLIMATE: RABAT

RAINFALL   BEST TIME   MTG10

town was built some distance from the medina.

Early origins
Sala Colonia and the Ribat The first settlement of this area was probably outside the present city walls, on the site of the later Merinid mausoleum of **Chellah**. There is conjecture of prior Phoenician and Carthaginian settlement, but it is with the Roman **Sala Colonia** that Rabat's proven urban history began. Accorded municipal privileges, Sala Colonia was the most southwesterly town of the Roman Empire for the 2 centuries they ruled it, a trading post on the Oued Bou Regreg (which has since changed course), and a defensive settlement, located close to the line of frontier outposts, running through the modern-day suburbs to the S of the city.

Sala Colonia was then occupied by Berbers from the 8th to the 10th century, but their heretic Kharajite beliefs represented a challenge to the orthodoxy of the inland Muslims. In the 10th century the Zenata tribe built a fortified monastery, or *ribat*, on the site of the current **Kasbah des Oudaias**, as a base from which to challenge the heretics on both sides of the river, and their supporters, the powerful Berghouata tribe. This led eventually to the abandonment of Sala Colonia.

Rabat under the Almohads
The *ribat* was used by the Almoravid Dynasty, but it was the Almohad Sultan Abd al-Mumin who redeveloped the settlement in 1150, transforming it into a permanent fortress town with palaces, the main mosque which still stands, reservoirs, and houses for followers, and using it as an assembly point for the large Almohad army. However, it was his grandson, Ya'qub al-Mansur, who from 1184 carried out the most ambitious programme of development, with his dream of Rabat as one of the great imperial capitals. He ordered an enormous city to be built, surrounded by extensive walls. These walls were probably completed by 1197, and ran along two sides of the city, broken by four gates, most notably the **Bab er Rouah**. A grid of broad streets, residential quarters, a covered market, public baths, hotels, workshops and fountains were built, along with a new gateway to the medina. A bridge to Sale, and its **Grand Mosque**, were also constructed.

Yet the most impressive monument from this period, the Hassan Mosque, was never completed. Projected to be the largest mosque in western Islam, the vast minaret never reached its full height, and little more than pillars remain of the rest. Ya'qub al-Mansur's death in 1199 led to the abandonment of the project. Rabat then fell into decline, some of it destroyed in fighting between the Almohads and Merinids, so that Leo Africanus, visiting in 1500, found only 100 or so houses, two or three inhabited quarters, and very few shops. As Rabat declined under the Merinids, Sale prospered. The dynasty's most noteworthy contribution to Rabat was the funeral quarter on the **Chellah** site, with its impressive mausoleums, but even that was eventually neglected.

Piracy and Andalusians
Rabat's fortunes did not revive until the 17th century, when the Atlantic Ocean became more important to international trade, and corsairing, or piracy, boomed. For a time Rabat was the centre of this piracy, with 'the Sallee Rovers' of historical repute more likely to have been based here than in present-day Sale. Robinson Crusoe was a fictional captive of 'a Turkish rover of Salle'.

Rabat also benefited from the flow of Muslims leaving Spain during the Inquisition. First rejected by Sale, the Hornacheros settled in the Rabat kasbah in 1609, and the other Andalusians in the Rabat medina in 1610. The medina they settled in was considerably smaller than the city Ya'qub al-Mansur had envisaged, as indicated by the 17th century rampart, which, when built, demarcated the extent of the settlement, and now runs between the medina and the *ville nouvelle*. The area beyond this rampart was used for agricultural purposes, and most of it remained undeveloped until the arrival of the French. The Andalusian influence can be observed in the medina, in the regularity of the street plan, in the motifs on doors, and in the past and present styles of decorative arts and crafts.

A fierce rivalry existed between the Hornacheros and the Andalusians, both of which had set up autonomous city-states, and the period 1610 to 1666 was marked by intermittent strife between the three towns of the Bou Regreg estuary. By 1627 these were united under the control of the Hornacheros as the Republic of the Bou Regreg, a control against which the Andalusians frequently

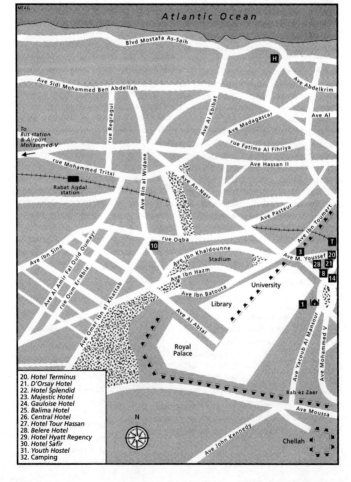

20. Hotel Terminus
21. D'Orsay Hotel
22. Hotel Splendid
23. Majestic Hotel
24. Gauloise Hotel
25. Balima Hotel
26. Central Hotel
27. Hotel Tour Hassan
28. Belere Hotel
29. Hotel Hyatt Regency
30. Hotel Safir
31. Youth Hostel
32. Camping

rebelled, most notably in 1636. The Republic lost its independence in 1638. In 1641 the three cities were united, and in 1666 were brought under the authority of the Alawite Sultanate, when Moulay al-Rachid captured the estuary.

The principal background to these conflicts was the struggle for control over the gains from piracy, a profitable activity. Piracy was a form of trade, but also fed off trade, and the legal, illegal and govern-mental aspects were often closely linked. Rabat was popular with corsairs, many of whom originated in the Mediterranean, because, unlike several other ports, it had not been occupied by Europeans.

Alawite Capital

Under the Alawites, Rabat changed considerably. Trade and piracy were taken over as official functions, the profits

RABAT & SALE MT 41R

1. Grand Mosque (Sunna)
2. Cathedral of Saint Pierre
3. Bab er Rouah
4. Hassan Tower
5. Mohammed V Mausoleum
6. Museum of Moroccan Arts
7. Museum of Traditional Arts
8. Post Office Museum
9. Archaeological Museum
10. Ibn Yassine Hall
11. Post Office
12. Tourist Office
13. Mohamed V Theatre
14. Saidoune Restaurant
15. El Bahia Restaurant
16. Café Maure
17. Caravelle Restaurant
18. Mona Lisa Restaurant
19. Saadi Restaurant

going to the state. The port declined, replaced initially by Mogador (Essaouira). Moulay al-Rachid took over the kasbah, expelling its residents and strengthening the walls, and built the **Qishla** fortification to overlook and control the medina. However Sultan Moulay Ismail, most closely associated with Meknes, ignored Rabat, and broke the power of the corsairs.

From 1768, Mohammed Ibn Abdellah had a palace built in Rabat, and since then the Alawite Sultans have maintained a palace there, making the city one of their capitals. Increased trade with Europe in the 19th century temporarily revitalized Rabat's role as a port, but it was gradually supplanted, perhaps because of the shallow mouth of the Bou Regreg and the poor harbour facilities which were inadequate for larger boats, but also because newer towns and cities, notably Casablanca, were more easily controlled by Europeans. In 1832 the rebellious Oudaia tribe were settled in the abandoned kasbah, giving it its current name, whilst the kasbah continued to be administered separately from the medina until the 20th century.

Rabat in the Twentieth Century

The French landed in Rabat in 1907, and occupied it until 1912, when the Protectorate was officially declared. Fes was initially chosen as the capital, but as it remained a centre of dissidence and rebellion, and the inland areas remained insecure, Rabat was its replacement, formally confirmed in 1913. The first Resident-General, Lyautey, with his architect Henri Prost, planned and built the majority of the new capital, the *ville nouvelle*, both within and outside Ya'qub al-Mansur's walls, leaving the medina much as they found it. Rabat's economy today is primarily based on its role as Morocco's capital, with massive numbers on the government pay-roll. The economic growth of the city has continued to attract migrants from the countryside, with population growth outstripping the supply of housing. Thus Rabat today is a city of extremes, with streets of ostentatious and luxurious villas not far from crowded, decrepit and insanitary tin-shack slums, or *bidonvilles*.

ACCESS Air Regular buses from **Airport Mohammed V** in Casablanca to Rabat, taking 90 mins, cost MD50. Tickets are sold at the booth outside the front entrance of the airport, from where the buses depart, to both Casablanca and Rabat. The buses arrive in Rabat outside the *Hotel Terminus*, Ave Mohammed V, beside the station. Grand-taxis, which also leave just outside the airport, are expensive as they cannot be shared. The local **Rabat-Sale airport**, T 727393, 10 km from Rabat off the P1 Sale to Meknes road, has daily flights from Casablanca and Paris and a weekly flight (Fri) from Tetouan. For the town centre follow the signs to Sale, cross the river and continue up Ave Hassan II. There is a train service into town from the new station.

Train The main railway station, **Rabat Ville**, T 767353, is on Ave Mohammed V, in the city centre, close to the main hotels. There are luggage lockers, but they are often all occupied. There is another station, **Rabat Agdal**, T 772385, in rue Abderrahman El Ghafiki, closer to the university, the newer ministry buildings and residential areas, but otherwise not convenient. All trains from Marrakech, Oued Zem, El Jadida and Casablanca stop at both stations, as do some of those from Tanger, Meknes, Fes and Oujda.

Road From Tanger and N the P2 brings the traveller through Sale, as does the P1 from Meknes, Fes and E. To get to Rabat, from the roundabout near the Bab Mrisa, cross the Pont Moulay Hassan and turn right, up to Ave Hassan II. From Casablanca and the S on the P36, turn right along Ave An-Nasr, and into the walled city via Bab er Rouah. **Bus** The principal bus terminal, for both CTM buses and those of the private lines, is inconveniently located at Place Zerktouni, 3 km out from the centre. Catch a No 30 bus to Ave Hassan II, or a petit-taxi for about MD15.

Places of interest

Routes through the city

The *Kasbah des Oudaias*, the *medina* and the *Chellah* have to be explored on foot. Start at the kasbah, carry along Tarik al Marsa to the *Hassan Tower* (4) and the *Mohammed V Mausoleum* (5). From there follow Blvd Bou Regreg, Ave Tariq Ibn Ziad and Ave Moussa Ibn Nossair to the *Chellah*. Enter the *ville nouvelle* by *Bab ez Zaer* to the *Sunna Mosque* (1). Turn along Ave Moulay Hassan and through *Bab er Rouah* (3) to view it from the outside. Pass down Ave Ibn Toumert, past *Bab el Had* to *Bab el Alou*, and right into the medina. Turn right down Blvd Mohammed V and carry on through the medina to Ave Hassan II. Those with transport must park here and explore the medina and the *ville nouvelle*. Blvd Mohammed V is the only drivable road in the medina, Ave Mohammed V in the *ville nouvelle* is one way S from Ave Hassan II to the post office.

The Walls and Gates

Rabat has three sets of walls: the *Almohad* wall around the kasbah, the 5 km of *Almoravid* wall around much of the city centre dating from the 12th century, and the wall now separating the *medina* and the *ville nouvelle* built by the Andalusians in the early 17th century. The walls are mainly built of *pisé* or *pisé*-cement and, whilst they have inevitably been considerably repaired, strengthened and adapted, they are much as they were originally. There are four gates still standing in the Almoravid wall: **Bab el Alou**, **Bab el Had**, **Bab er Rouah** and **Bab ez Zaer**. **Bab er Rouah** is the most important and impressive of these, but **Bab el Had** is worth seeing. Located at the intersection of Ave Hassan II and Ave Ibn Toumert, the substantially remodelled **Bab el Had** has a blind arch and is flanked by two 5-sided stone towers. Currently you pass through two chambers, at different levels. A number of traditional scribes work in this area.

Bab er Rouah, at Place An-Nasr, can best be approached along Ave An-Nasr from outside the walled city, when its scale and beauty is most obvious. The gate is now used as a gallery, and is only open when exhibitions are being held, so it is well worth taking any opportunity to see inside it. The arch of the gate is framed by a rectangular band of Kufic inscription. Between the arch and the frame there is a floral motif, with the scallop symbol on either side. The arch itself, with an entrance restored by the Alawites with small stones, is made up of three different patterns, of great simplicity, producing the overall effect of a sunburst confined within a rectangle. The entrance passage inside follows a complex double elbow. This, combined with the two flanking bastions outside, indicate that the gate was defensive as well as ceremonial.

Kasbah des Oudaias

The Kasbah des Oudaias, originally a fortified *ribat*, later settled by Andalusians, is both beautiful and peaceful, and well worth a visit. It can be reached along rue de Consuls through the medina, Blvd el Alou along the N of the medina, or by Tarik al Marsa along beside the Oued Bou Regreg. There is a number of entrances to the kasbah, but the best is by the imposing **Bab al-Kasbah** gateway at the top of the hill. At this point avoid the unofficial guides as the kasbah is very small and quiet and easily explored without assistance.

Bab al-Kasbah was located close to the **Souq el-Ghezel**, the main mediaeval market, whilst the original palace was just inside. The gateway was built by Ya'qub al-Mansur in about 1195, inserting it into the earlier kasbah wall built by Abd al-Mumin, and it did not have the same defensive role as the **Bab er Rouah**. The gate has a pointed *outrepassé* arch surrounded by a cusped, blind arch. Around this there is a wide band of geometric carving, the common *darj w ktaf*. The two corner areas between this band and the rectangular frame are composed of floral decoration, with, as in the **Bab er Rouah**, a scallop or palmette in each. Above this are more palmettes, a band of Koranic lettering, and on top a wide band of geometric motifs. There would originally have been a porch roof. The entrance to the kasbah is via stairs and through two rooms, a third room being closed to the public. The inside of the gate is also decorated, though more simply.

Inside the gate, the main street, rue al-Jama, runs past the **Kasbah Mosque**, dating from 1150, the oldest in Rabat. It leads to the semaphore platform, where there is a carpet factory. This gives an excellent view over the sea, the Oued Bou Regreg with its natural sand-bar defence, and Sale. Steps down from the platform lead to the *Caravelle Restaurant*, in a small fort built by an English renegade, and the popular, but not too clean, kasbah beach.

Coming back from the platform take the second on the left, rue Bazzo. This narrow and cobbled street with steps winds down through the whitewashed Andalusian-style houses to the bottom of the kasbah, directly into the *Café Maure* alongside which is a small but beautiful Andalusian style garden, developed by the French, which is also a pleasant place for a rest. On the other side of the garden is a section of the **Museum of Moroccan Arts** exhibiting traditional dress from many regions of Morocco. In the building of a 17th century palace, where Moulay Ismail once lived, is the main **Museum of Moroccan Art** (0830-1200, 1500-1830, except Tues) entrance fee MD10, with arms, instruments, jewels and carpets. This is worth seeing just for the interior, and the decoration of the building. There are a number of reception rooms around a central courtyard, in particular seek out the palace baths, the *hammam*.

The Medina

Most of the buildings in the medina date at the earliest from the arrival of the Andalusian Muslims in the 17th century. The Andalusian character of the buildings and decoration sets the medina apart from those such as Marrakech. Whilst Rabat medina is smaller and more limited in the range of markets, shops and buildings than Fes, Marrakech and Meknes, and less distinct in its way of life, its accessability, size and the simplicity of its grid-like street pattern make it a good first experience of Moroccan medinas. Physically close to the *ville nouvelle*, the medina is very different in the design of buildings and open space, and the nature of commerce and socialization. It as an interesting and safe place to wander, with little risk of getting lost or hassled. Blvd Mohammed V is one of the major arteries of the medina, but the second right, **rue Souika**, and its continuation **Souq es Sebbat**, are the main shopping streets, with an unusually wide range of shops for such a small area. The **Grand Mosque**, on rue Souika, is much restored Merinid. Just opposite the **Grand Mosque**, on a side turning, is the interesting stone façade of a fountain, now a bookshop, but dating from the 14th century reign of the Merinid Sultan Abu Faris Abd al-Aziz.

Souq es Sebbat leads down to the river, past the *mellah* on the right. The *mellah* is the former Jewish area, still the poorest area of the medina, with small cramped houses and shops, and narrow streets. It is a triangular zone, bound by rue Ouqasson (the continuation of rue des Consuls), the medina wall, and the river. As in many Islamic cities, Jews were kept in one area, for both protection and control, and so that they would be easily accessible to the seat of power to carry out tasks Muslims could not

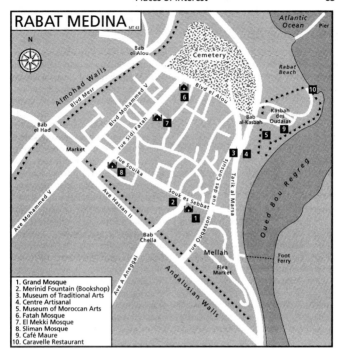

RABAT MEDINA MT 43

N

Atlantic Ocean
Pier

Bab el Alou

Cemetery

Almohad Walls

Blvd Mesr

Blvd el Alou

Rabat Beach

Blvd Mohammed V

rue Sidi Fatah

[6]

[7]

10

Kasbah des Oudaias

Bab al-Kasbah

[9]

Bab el Had

Market

[5]

rue Souika

[8]

[3] [4]

Souk es Sebbat

Tarik al Marsa

Oued Bou Regreg

Ave Mohammed V

Ave Hassan II

[2]

[1]

rue Oudaïon rue des Consuls

Bab Chella

Mellah

Foot Ferry

Ave A Aneggaï

Andalusian Walls

Flea Market

1. Grand Mosque
2. Merinid Fountain (Bookshop)
3. Museum of Traditional Arts
4. Centre Artisanal
5. Museum of Moroccan Arts
6. Fatah Mosque
7. El Mekki Mosque
8. Sliman Mosque
9. Café Maure
10. Caravelle Restaurant

perform. There are few Jews left in the *mellah*, most having emigrated to Israel. The streets around here now support an interesting *joutia*, or flea market.

Turning left off **Souq es Sebbat** one can follow the rue des Consuls to the kasbah. This road was where many European consuls and important merchants once lived. Rue des Consuls is now lined with the more expensive shops selling leather work and carpets. There is a carpet market on the street on Tues and Thur mornings. Turn right at the end of rue des Consuls and you are in Tarik al Marsa. On the left is the **Museum of Traditional Arts**, with crafts and arts. Opposite is the **Centre Artisanal**, with fixed prices for looking at, or buying, craft products. Open 0830-1200, 1500-1830, entrance fee MD10.

The Hassan Tower and Mohammed V Mausoleum

The Almohad **Hassan Tower** dominates the skyline of Rabat, and even unfinished it is an impressive building, testimony to Ya'qub al-Mansur's unfulfilled vision of his imperial capital. It overlooks the Oued Bou Regreg and Sale, and can be reached most easily by Blvd Bou Regreg, or by turning right at the end of Ave Hassan II.

The building of the mosque was abandoned on Ya'qub al-Mansur's death in 1199, leaving most of the minaret, but just part of the columns and walls. All the portable parts, tiles, bricks and the roofing material, have been taken for use in other buildings. The remains of the mosque were excavated and reconstructed by the French and Moroccans.

The mosque would have followed a T-shape, with the main green-tile roof section between the minaret and the modern mausoleum. The *mihrab* (prayer niche) would have been in the S *qibla* wall, where the mausoleum is, and therefore was not properly orientated towards Mecca. It is also unusual to find the minaret opposite the *qibla* wall.

The incomplete minaret of the Hassan Mosque stands at 45m. When completed, it would have been 64m, four times as high as it was wide, with the lantern making it 80m, five times as high. This is in keeping with the classic North African minaret style, as with the **Koutoubia** in Marrakech (page 173). It is decorated with geometric designs, there being no inscription or floral decoration, but their scale and clarity of execution makes them clearly discernible from a distance. Each of the faces has a different composition, interweaving designs, arches and windows. The common Moroccan motif of *darj w ktaf*, resembling a tulip or a truncated *fleur de lys*, and formed by intersecting arcs with superimposed rectangles, is present, notably on the N and S upper registers.

Adjacent to the **Hassan Tower** is the **Mohammed V Mausoleum**, dedicated to the first king of independent Morocco and father of the current king, and dating from 1971. The tomb chamber, but not the mausoleum's mosque, is open to non-Muslims, and shows a number of traditional Moroccan motifs and techniques of religious architecture, with a carved and painted ceiling, the carved marble tomb, and the *zellij* tiles (mosaic) on the walls. Open 0800-1830 daily, entrance free.

The Chellah

The Chellah is reached by going past the main **Sunna Mosque** in the *ville nouvelle*, and carrying on S down Ave Yacoub al Mansour and through the **Bab ez Zaer**. This walled Merinid necropolis was built between 1310 and 1334, ap-proximately on the site of the Roman town of **Sala Colonia**. The second Merinid Sultan, Abu Yusuf Ya'qub built a mosque and Abul Hassan then built the enclosure wall and the gate. The Roman ruins at the bottom of the **Chellah** enclosure have been excavated, and include a forum, baths, shops and a temple.

The gate is smaller and less impressive than the Almohad **Bab er Rouah**. It is decorated with carving, and coloured marble and tiles, with an octagonal tower on either side. The entrance is on the elbow pattern and you turn right through three chambers, before walking out into a wild and lush garden. To get to the mausoleum take the wide path to the bottom, where it stands on the right, the Roman ruins on the left. On the far right are the tombs of local saints, surrounding a pool.

The door into the Merinid mausoleum, facing the Roman ruins, opens into the mosque of Abu Yusuf Yaqub, which consists of a small courtyard, followed by a 3-aisled sanctuary. The arched doorway on the left has the remains of floral and geometric *zellij* in five colours. Entering the sanctuary the *mihrab*, is straight ahead. A door to the right leads to an area including the remains of the mosque's minaret, and a pool. From this one enters the area of tombs, including those of Abul Hassan and his wife Shams al-Dawha. The remaining area of the mausoleum is taken up with the *zawia*, or mosque-monastery, of Abul Hassan. This includes a minaret, and a ruined funerary chapel, with very intricate carving, notably on the exterior of the S wall. The main part of the *zawia* is a rectangular courtyard with a small mosque at one end, and surrounded by small cells. It had a pool surrounded by a columned arcade, the bases of the columns still discernible. The *mihrab* has some intricate stucco carving. The tiles on the upper portion of the minaret are perhaps recent, but the original effect would have been a bright tiled structure.

The Ville Nouvelle

This contains some fine examples of French colonial architecture, which in Morocco incorporated an element of local design tradition, and is called *Mauresque*. Note particularly the main post office (PTT Centrale) and the Bank al-Maghrib, both on Ave Mohammed V. This main boulevard is wide and particularly impressive in the evening, when it is crowded with people out for a stroll. Off to the left, opposite the railway station, is the **Catholic Cathedral of Saint Pierre**. Below the station is the Parliament building. Just past the *Hotel Terminus* is a small postal museum exhibiting stamps. The 18th century but much restored **Sunna Mosque** dominates the view up Ave Mohammed V. To the left of the mosque is the **Archaeological Museum** (open 0830-1200, 1430-1800, closed Tues), which has a small but impressive collection, particularly of Roman bronzes, mainly from Volubilis. To the right of the **Sunna Mosque** is the vast palace complex, where King Hassan II spends part of the year. It is not possible to go beyond this point up the central avenue of the complex.

Festivals

Rabat is the best place for the state festivals, the *Coronation* on 3 Mar, the *Green March* on 6 Nov and *Independence Day* on 18 Nov.

Local information

● **Accommodation**

Price guide:			
AL	US$90+	D	US$20-40
A	US$75-90	E	US$10-20
B	US$60-75	F	under US$10
C	US$40-60		

In summer hotels can fill up early. There are not many good, cheap hotels in Rabat. The budget hotels in the medina, for which prices can be very flexible, are in general best avoided. The centre of the *ville nouvelle* provides a wide range of good hotels. **AL** *Hotel Hyatt Regency*, Aviation Souissi, T 771234, F 773039, 220 rm, 28 suites, former Hilton, luxurious, set in an extensive park on the road out past the **Chellah**, rather far from the city centre, but offers everything, including a business centre, mini golf-course, art gallery, pool and *hammam*; **AL** *Hotel de la Tour Hassan*, 26 Ave de Chellah, T 733816, F 725408, 158 rm, convenient location, a Protectorate period building which is perhaps the most atmospheric but least modernized of the top class hotels, excellent restaurants, conference room, popular nightclub and bar, no pool; **AL** *Hotel Safir*, Place Sidi Makhlouf, T 731091, F 725408, convenient, at end of Ave Hassan II overlooking the river and Sale, built around a courtyard in an approximation of a Moroccan palace, quite luxurious, pool, most other facilities and services.

C *Hotel Belere*, 33 Ave Moulay Youssef, T/F 769901, 763749, conveniently located nr the station.

D *Hotel Balima*, 173 Ave Mohammed V, BP 173, across from the station, T 707755, 708625, Tx 31738M, popular café-bar, restaurant, snack bar, salon de thé, nightclub, formerly top hotel in Rabat, a faded grandeur, reasonably priced; **D** *Hotel d'Orsay*, 11 Ave Moulay Youssef, nr station, T 761319, convenient, less interesting than *Balima*.

E *Hotel Central*, 2 rue Al Basra, T 767356, beside the *Balima*, well-run hotel, very good and crazily decorated double rooms, singles not so good, one of the best cheap options for sharers; **E** *Hotel des Oudaias*, 132 Blvd el Alou, nr the kasbah, T 732371, convenient for sightseeing, and well-fitted, one of the few respectable hotels in the medina; **E** *Hotel Gauloise*, 1 rue Hims, off Ave Mohammed V, T 723022, 59 tatty rm; **E** *Hotel Majestic*, 121 Ave Hassan II, T 722997, cheap and rec; **E** *Hotel de la Paix*, 2 rue Ghazza, T 722926,

732031, not very friendly, some rooms no bath, no communal shower; **E** *Hotel Splendid*, 24 rue Ghazza, T 723283, good rooms, friendly staff, pleasant courtyard with meals from restaurant opp.

F *Hotel Berlin*, 261 Ave Mohammed V, T 703435, cheapest in the *ville nouvelle*. There are a number of small, cheap hotels in the medina; **F** *Hotel des Voyageurs*, best of these three, and *Hotel du Marché* and *Hotel Alger*, are all on rue Souq Semara, second left off Ave Mohammed V, tatty; **F** *Maghreb al Jedid*, *Hotel El Alam*, best of these three, and *Hotel Marrakech*, all on rue Sebbahi, right off Ave Mohammed V, tatty and cheap.

● **Youth hostel**

43 rue Marassa, Bab el Had, T 725769, 60 beds, bed/breakfast MD35 for IYHA members, kitchen, basic and friendly, you can make an identity card here, with a photograph and your passport. Train 1.2 km and bus 150m.

● **Camping**

Is an inconvenient option in Rabat, the two nearest sites being Sale and Temara (see pages 91 and 91).

● **Places to eat**

Price guide:
♦♦♦Expensive; ♦♦average; ♦cheap.

Most higher quality restaurants are located within the walled *ville nouvelle*. A range of fairly cheap restaurants is to be found throughout the city, but the budget options, small Moroccan canteens and café-restaurants, are located in the medina, along Ave Mohammed V, rue Souika, rue Sidi Fatah and adjacent streets. This is also a good area to wander and sample juices, pâtisseries, snacks and sandwiches, particularly from the *laiteries* that make sandwiches to order.

♦♦♦*Justine's*, in *Hotel Hyatt Regency*, Souissi, T 771234, reservations required, very expensive, prestigious, with a large range of European dishes; *El Andalous*, in *Hotel Hyatt Regency*, Souissi, T 771234, reservations required, vast selection of Moroccan dishes, live music; *La Couronne* in *Hotel de la Tour Hassan*, 26 Ave de Chellah, T 721402, reservations rec, high standard international cuisine, good value and very good service, music in the evening; *El Mansur*, in *Hotel de la Tour Hassan*, 26 Ave de Chellah, T 721402, reservations rec, very good Moroccan food, particularly the *pastilla* and the *tagines*, with the option of eating at low tables, Moroccan

music accompanies the meal; *Kanoun Grill*, in *Hotel Chellah*, 2 rue d'Ifni, T 764052, reservations rec, a big menu of good Moroccan food, particularly grilled.

♦♦*Le Relais du Père Louis*, Zankat Ibn Haoqual, behind the *Hotel Balima*, T 769629, good Moroccan and French food, licensed; *Les Fouquets*, 285 Ave Mohammed V, T 708007, good Moroccan food and service, specializes in fish, licensed; *Hotel Balima*, 173 Ave Mohammed V, continental cuisine on the terrace or inside, but better for drinks; *La Mamma*, 1 Zankat Tanto, Italian food; *Café Restaurant Saadi*, 81 bis Ave Allal Ben Abdellah, T 769903, good Moroccan meals, licensed; *Hong Kong*, 261 Ave Mohammed V, Vietnamese/Chinese food.

♦*Café Anaouil*, Ave Moulay Abdellah, good *tagines*, salads and juices, European food also; *Mona Lisa*, Passage Derby, 258 Ave Mohammed V, reasonable *tagines*, Moroccan food, salads; *Restaurant Saidoune*, mall off Ave Mohammed V, opp *Hotel Terminus*, very good value Lebanese restaurant, friendly, and with some tasty dishes; *Restaurant El Bahia*, Ave Hassan II, in the wall nr junction with Ave Mohammed V, Moroccan food in a courtyard, good value, erratic service; *Restaurant de l'Union*, 260 Ave Mohammed V, medina, cheap but unexciting meals; *Restaurant de la Jeunesse*, Ave Mohammed V, medina, cheap snacks and meals; *Elfarah Restaurant*, 10 Zankat Sidi Mohammed El Ghazi, third right off Ave Mohammed V, medina, Moroccan canteen: cheap, basic, clean and good, set lunch, *harira* and *brochettes* in the evening; *Café Taghzout*, rue Sebbahi, similar as above in nearby street.

● **Bars**

Piccadilly Piano Bar, in *Hotel Hyatt Regency* popular for those who can afford it, nightly jazz band; *Hassan Bar*, in *Hotel de la Tour Hassan*, 22 Ave de Chellah, similarly expensive, with dated charm; *Hotel Balima*, 173 Ave Mohammed V, one of the most popular places to drink a beer or coffee, particularly during the evening promenade; *Baghdad Bar*, Zankat Tanto, belly-dancing awaits you.

● **Cafés, Pâtisseries and Glaceries**

There are many good cafés, pâtisseries and glaceries on or nr Ave Mohammed V, two of the best being *Lina* (a smoke-free café with excellent pâtisseries), at the top of Ave Allal Ben Abdellah, and *Le Petit Poucet*, on Ave Mohammed V. The *Café Maure* in the Kasbah des Oudaias serves mint tea and pastries, good views, waiters in traditional dress, a pleasant place to while away the time. There are excellent stand-up juice bars in the medina.

● **Banks & money changers**
ABM, 19 Ave Allal Ben Abdellah, T 724907; **Banque al Maghrib**, Ave Mohammed V, T 763009; **Banque Marocaine de Commerce Exterieur (BMCE)**, 241 Ave Mohammed V, T 721798, the best for change (cash, TCs and VISA/Mastercard) for which it has a separate door (open 0800-2000 weekdays, 1000-1200 and 1600-2000 weekends); **BMAO**, Ave Allal Ben Abdellah, T 769980; **Credit du Maroc**, Ave Allal Ben Abdellah, T 721961; **Wafabank**, Ave Mohammed V, T 721181/82.

● **Embassies & consulates**
Algeria, 46 rue Tarik Ibn Ziad, T 765591; **Austria**, 2 rue Tiddas, T 764003; **Belgium**, 6 Ave de Marrakech, T 764746; **Canada**, 13 bis rue Jaafar Assadik, T 771375/7; **Denmark**, 4 rue de Khemisset, T 767986; **Egypt**, 31 Ave d'Alger, T 731833; **France**, rue Sahnoun, T 777822; **Germany**, 7 rue Madnine, T 765474; **Greece**, 23 rue d'Oujda, T 723839; **Italy**, 2 rue Idriss El Azhar, T 766598; **Libya**, Zankat Chouaib Doukally, T 766863; **Mauritania**, 6 rue Thami Lamdour, off Ave John Kennedy, T 770912, 756817; **Netherlands**, 40 rue de Tunis, T 733512/3; **Norway**, 4 Zankat Jaafar As-Sadik, Agdal, T 773871/2; **Portugal**, 5 rue Thami Lamdouar, T 756446; **Senegal**, rue Cadi Ben Hammadi Senhadji, T 754171; **Spain**, 3 rue Madnine, T 768988; **Sweden**, 159 Ave John Kennedy, T 759303/759308; **Switzerland**, Square Berkane, T 766974; **Sudan**, 9 rue de Tedders, T 761368; **Tunisia**, 6 Ave de Fes, T 730636/37; **UK** (also used by **Australia, Ireland** and **New Zealand**), 17 Blvd de la Tour Hassan, T 720905/06; **USA**, 2 Ave de Marrakech, T 762265.

● **Entertainment**
Rabat has little of the entertainments one might expect in a capital city, particularly late at night.

Art galleries: *Galerie Arcanes*, 130 Blvd el Alou, T 735890; *Galerie L'Atelier*, 16 rue Annaba; *Galerie Le Mamoir*, 7 rue Baitlahm; *Galerie Marsam*, 6 rue Oskofiah.

Cinemas: the four biggest cinemas are easily found, three in Ave Mohammed V, and one at the junction of Ave Allal Ben Abdellah and al-Mansur ad-Dahbi which has perhaps the best range of films. Most films are in French.

Discos and nightclubs: the most rec is *Queen's Club, Hotel de la Tour Hassan*, 22 Ave de Chellah, very popular, open from 2230, entrance MD50; otherwise try *Biba* or *Jefferson* in Ave Patrice Lumumba, or the *Balima* in Ave Mohammed V.

Theatres and concert halls: *Theatre Mohammed V*, rue Al Kahira, has a range of plays and concerts. The various national cultural centres, such as the Russian Cultural Centre in Ave Moulay Abdellah and the British Council in rue Tanger, advertise and promote events. Check *Al Bayane, L'Opinion* or *Le Matin* newspapers for other listings.

● **Hammams (Public baths)**
On Ave Hassan II, beside the *Rex*, or for residents at the *Hyatt Regency*.

● **Hospitals & medical services**
Ambulance: T 15.
Chemists: *Pharmacie du Chellah*, Place de Melilla, T 724723, and another on rue Moulay Slimane, if not, look in a newspaper or T 726150 for the name of the night chemist. **Hospital**: *Hôpital Avicenne*, Ave Ibn Sina, T 773194, 774411.

● **Laundry**
Most hotels will do your laundry for you for an arranged price. Otherwise try *Rabat Pressing*, 67 Ave Hassan II.

● **Post & telecommunications**
PTT Centrale, Ave Mohammed V, 0800-1200, 1400-1830. Rue al-Mansur ad-Dahbi, just off Ave Mohammed V, opposite the post office has a permanent facility for telephoning and collecting letters. Check with staff that previous call is cleared before using cabin.

● **Places of worship**
Catholic: Cathedrale Saint Pierre, rue Abou Inan, T 722301.
Jewish: Synagogue Talmuch Torah, 9 Ave Moulay Ismail, information, T 724504.
Protestant: Temple, 44 Ave Moulay Abdellah, service: 0945.

● **Shopping**
Books & maps: the *American Bookshop* at the American Language Center in rue Tanger has a very useful selection of novels, guidebooks and books on Islam and Morocco, all in English. There is an English language bookshop at 7 Zankat Alyamama, behind the railway station, which sells a large selection of secondhand paperbacks. For books in French there are a number of well-stocked bookshops in

Ave Mohammed V, such as *Kahla wa Dimna*, and Ave Allal Ben Abdellah. Bookshops in Ave Mohammed V stock simple maps of Rabat or Morocco. For hiking maps go to the **Division de la Cartographie**, 31 Ave Moulay al Hassan, which sells official maps if it is not being too bureaucratic.

Libraries: *British Council*, 36 rue Tanger, BP427, T 760836, free entry, reference books, novels, some books on Morocco, magazines and newspapers, Sky News on the TV, small café; *George Washington Library*, 35 Ave el Fahs, also has some newspapers.

Markets: local markets are on Thur at Sale, Fri at Bouznika, Sat at Temara, Sun at Bouknadel and Skhirat. In Rabat medina the vegetable market is best on Sun, and carpets in rue des Consuls on Tues and Thur morning. In the *ville nouvelle* there is an underground vegetable and fruit market at Place Moulay al Hassan, with excellent flower sellers above ground outside.

Modern shops: there are a range of large shops on Ave Mohammed V and Ave Allal Ben Abdellah. It should be possible to get most things you need here.

Moroccan shops: use the **Centre Artisanal (Coopartim)** in Tarik al Marsa to get an idea of the range, then go out and bargain in the small boutiques in the medina, on or just off Ave Mohammed V, rue Souika, **Souq es Sebbat** and rue des Consuls. There are a number of larger shops, in the *ville nouvelle*, on Ave Mohammed V, or in the malls just off, where the high prices may be negotiable.

Newspapers & magazines: there are three or four boutiques on the pavements of Ave Mohammed V stocking a full range of British, American, French and international newspapers and magazines. However the best is perhaps inside the main railway station. The international edition of *The Guardian* arrives in Rabat about 1800.

● **Sport**

Flying: *Aéro-Club Royal Aerodrome*, T 751335.

Golf: *Royal Golf Dar Es Salam*, 12 km from Rabat on rue de Zaers, T 754692, is the largest and most famous course in Morocco, with 45 holes, Red course 6,825m par 73, Blue course 6,205m par 72, Green course (nine holes) 2,150m par 32, fees approx MD500 per day; there is also the smaller Golf Club du Souissi, T 750359. For information: *Moroccan Royal Federation of Golf*, 2 rue Moulay Slimane,

T 731693.

Horse-riding & polo: the *Royal Polo Equestrian Club* is at the Royal Golf Dar Es Salam, rue de Zaers, T 754692.

Swimming: the main beach in Rabat is that below the kasbah, which is popular but not too clean. That at Sale is similar, and both have dangerous currents from the river. It may be worth going further afield, to the Plage des Nations, Temara or Skhirat (see page 91 and page 91). Try the pools at Royal Golf Dar Es Salam, the *Hotel Hyatt Regency* or the *Hotel Safir*.

Tennis: *Club des Cheminots*, Agdal, T 770048; *Club El Wifak*, rue de Zaers, T 754539; *Olympique Marocain*, 2 rue Ibn Khaldoun, T 771872, seven courts; *Riad Club*, rue Abdelaziz Boutaleb, Agdal, T 722776, six courts; *Stade Marocain*, Ave Haroun Rachid, T 771903, seven courts.

Walking & climbing: information from Alpine Club 19, Blvd de la Resistance, T 727220.

Watersports: Yacht Club de Rabat, Quai de la Tour Hassan, T 720254; Fath Union Sport, Port de Rabat, T 733679; Olympique Marocain, Quai Léon Petit, T 725123; information from Yachting Federation, Ave Ibn Yassine Bellevue, Agdal, BP332, T 771782.

● **Tourist offices**

Office du Tourisme, 22 Ave d'Alger, T 730562; Syndicat d'Initiative, Ave Patrice Lumumba, T 723272, not very useful.

● **Tour companies & travel agents**

Afric Voyages, 28 bis Ave Allal Ben Abdellah, T 709646/47, 706833; *First International Tours*, 32 Ave Ben Khattab, T 775060; *Gharb Voyages*, 289 Ave Mohammed V, T 767311; *La Royale*, Immeuble Montfavet, Place Mohammed V, T 707031; *North Africa Tours*, Residence El Minzah, rue Kadira, T 769747, F 762298; *Rainbow Travel*, 1 rue Derna, Place Pietri, T 762563, 762568; *Wagons-Lit Tourisme*, 1 Ave Moulay Abdellah, T 769625; *Welcome Voyages*, 29 Ave d'Alger, T 702871/72, F 702873. *Air France*, 281 Ave Mohammed V, T 767066; *Iberia* 104 Ave Mohammed V; *Royal Air Maroc* Ave Mohammed V, T 709766, 9 rue Abou Faris Almarini, T 709700, reservations: T 708076, 709710.

● **Useful addresses**

Fire: T 15.

Garages: *Concorde*, 6 Ave Allal Ben Abdellah; *Garage Citroen* (SIMA), at the junction of rue de Congo and rue de Senegal.

Language centres: *American Language Center*, rue Tanger, it may also be possible to arrange Arabic lessons here; *British Council*, 36 rue Tanger, BP427, T 760836.

Motoring club: 45 Ave Patrice Lumumba.

Police: rue Soekarno, behind the PTT Centrale, T 19.

● **Transport**

Local Buses: run all over the city, many originating from Ave Hassan II, nr **Bab el Had**, or just past Parc du Triangle de Vue. Six and 12 go to Sale, 17 to Temara, 1, 2 and 4 for the **Chellah**, get off at **Bab Zaer**. **Petit-taxis**: in Rabat are blue. They are some of the best in Morocco, nearly always metered, and often shared. They can be picked up anywhere, most easily at the stand on Ave Hassan II, close to the junction with Ave Mohammed V. Alternatively, T 720518, 730311. A Rabat petit-taxi cannot take you to Sale, which has its own taxis. **Car hire**: Avis, 7 Zankat Abou Faris El Marini, T 767503, 769759, Tx 31029, also at Rabat-Sale Airport; **Budget**, Rabat-Ville Railway Station, T 767689; **Hertz**, 467 Ave Mohammed V, T 709227, 707366, Tx: 31977, also at Rabat-Sale Airport; **Holiday Car**, 1 bis Ave Ibn Sina, T 771684, 771351; **Inter Rent-Europcar**, 25 bis rue Patrice Lumumba; **La Royale**, Immueble Montfavet, Place Mohammed V, T 763031.

Air Buses to Airport Mohammed V run from in front of *Hotel Terminus*, Ave Mohammed V. Tickets can be bought at the kiosk for MD50. Departures: 0500, 0630, 0830, 1000, 1230, 1530 and 1830, journey time 90 mins. For Rabat-Sale airport, T 727393, 730316, follow the P1 Sale-Meknes road. Daily direct flights to Paris and Casablanca, 1 a week to Tetouan (Fri).

Train Rabat Ville station, T 767353, Ave Mohammed V, departures – Casablanca: 35 daily between 0437 and 2337; **Marrakech**: 8 daily between 0437 and 2337; **El Jadida**: 1957, **Oued Zem**: 0815, 1527, 1930; **Meknes and Fes**: 9 daily between 0752 and 2349, **Taza** and **Oujda**: 1047, 1522, 2141, 2349; **Tanger**: 0748, 1327, 1656 and 0155; **Aeroport Mohammed V**: 11 daily between 0512 and 1900. **Rabat Agdal** station, T 772385, rue Abderrahman El Ghafiki, departures – Casablanca, Marrakech, El Jadida and Oued Zem: as above, 4-6 mins later, Meknes, Fes, Oujda and Tanger: as above 6-8 mins earlier.

Road Bus: the main bus terminal for all buses is at Place Zerktouni, 3 km from the centre. Catch a petit-taxi there, or a No 30 bus from

Ave Hassan II. Current buses – Casablanca: 10 a day (1½ hrs), Tanger: 2 a day (5 hrs), Meknes: 3 a day (4 hrs), Fes: 6 a day (5½ hrs). **Grand-taxi**: shared between six passengers, run from the bus station for distant locations, and for local locations, such as Temara, Skhirat, Sale and Bouknadel, from the stand on Ave Hassan II, just past the Parc du Triangle de Vue.

SALE

History

Sale, pronounced and often written as Salé, is Sala or Sla in Arabic, after the Roman Sala Colonia. Sale was founded in the 11th century, and its Great Mosque dates from 1163-1184. The town was embellished and fortified by the Merinids in the 13th century, becoming an important commercial centre. Great rivalry, even armed conflict, has existed between Rabat and Sale, although they were united in the Republic of the Bou Regreg. Up until the 17th century Sale had enjoyed long periods as the more important of the two cities, being known for religious learning and piety. In the 20th century Rabat has outstripped Sale, the latter becoming more and more a dormitory settlement for the former, with little of its own economic activities. Sale is worth a day-trip from Rabat to visit the beautiful **Abul Hassan Medersa** and explore the medina and the *souqs*, which are far more traditional than those of Rabat, and less visited by tourists than Fes or Meknes.

Places of interest

Bab Mrisa means 'Gate of the Little Harbour'. This was originally the sea gate of the medina, as there was once a channel running to it from the river. The gate is easily found, dominating the approach to Sale from Rabat, on the left side. This gate is very large, its *outrepassé* arch opening of 11m in height sufficient to allow access to the sailing boats of the day. Bab Mrisa was built by the Merinid Sultan Abu Yusuf in the 1270s. However in style it is closer to the Almohad gates, with the triangular space between the arch and the frame covered with floral decoration centred on the palmette, with the use of the *darj w ktaf* motif down the sides. Originally it had a porch. Alongside the tower there are two tall defensive towers. It may be possible to get access to the top of the gate. A custodian guards a small door on the left, inside the gate, which gives access to a small garden leading to a round tower. From this tower walk back along the top of the rampart to the gate. There is another similar sea gate, the next gate around the wall to the left.

Abul Hassan Medersa This *medersa*, or religious school (open 0800-1200, 1430-1800), is the most important building to visit in Sale, being the only *medersa* in this region. It was built by the Merinid Sultan Abul Hassan and finished in 1342. To reach it follow the city walls around to the left from Bab Mrisa to a small square at Bab Bou Hajar, alongside a park. Just beyond this there is an area where cars should be parked. Take the small lane off to the far right at the end of this area. Take the first left, then the first right. 200m later, just after the lane passes under a house, turn left. The particularly large **Grand Mosque** in front was built by the Almohad Sultan Abu Yusuf Ya'qub in the late 12th century, although the minaret and door are both modern. Just beyond the mosque is the tomb of Sale's patron saint, Sidi Abdellah bin Hassun. The *medersa* is to the left of the mosque.

Note at the entrance the intricate decorations, with complex designs of inscription around a cusped, interlaced arch, below a green tiled roof resting on cedar. The *medersa* is quite small, with a courtyard surrounded by a gallery, its columns decorated with *zellij* mosaic tiling. The walls above the columns are decorated with geometric and floral motifs, whilst the ceilings of the ground floor have panelled wood in geometric patterns. There has been restoration to

both wood carving and stucco, but much is original, and in good condition. The decoration which covers almost all the *medersa*, is finely executed. To reach the upper floors, return to the entrance and climb the stairs. These are the students' cells, which seem tiny and ill-lit, but give an insight into the nature of *medersa* life. From the roof is a view of Sale, and beyond it, Rabat.

The Medina Sale medina is small and easy to explore. Walking in any direction you are likely to arrive at the *souqs*, the **Grand Mosque** and **Abul Hassan Medersa**, or the city walls. The **Mausoleum of Sidi Bin Ashir at-Tabib** is located close to the W wall of the cemetery that lies between the medina and the sea. This 14th century Muslim saint was famous for curing people, and the sick still visit his tomb for its curative powers. The building is comparatively tall, and in stark white.

The **Fondouk al Askour** is worth seeing for its decorated portal. From **Bab Bou Hajar** follow rue Bab al-Khabbaz, and take the fourth lane on the left past the park, which is obstructed by three concrete posts. This leads to a textile *souq*. After 120m the **souq** passes under an arch. On the right is the *fondouk*. It was originally built in about 1350 as a *medersa* by Abu Inan, son of Abul Hassan. It was later a merchants' hostel. The door is surrounded by a partially restored *zellij* mosaic of the *darj w ktaf* pattern. Above this is a panel of *zellij* with the traditional eight pointed star motif, and above that a row of nine niches carved into a plaster panel. Inside there is a courtyard with two storeys of arcades around it.

In this area there are some interesting *souqs*, which are perhaps more traditional than those of Rabat, and worth exploring. This textile market is **Souq el-Merzouk**, while **Souq el-Ghezel** is the wool market. There are stone-masons and carpenters in rue Kechachine, and blacksmiths and brassworkers in rue Haddadine. The **Sidi Marzouq Souq** is noted for its jewellery and embroidery. The medina of Sale is also noted for a procession of candles, or thick poles bearing various representations, which occurs every year on the afternoon before the Prophet's birthday, Moulid an-Nabi. This proceeds through the town, culminating at the **Tomb of Sidi Abdellah bin Hassun**. The seafaring past of the city is particularly visible in this event, with the men in pirate costumes.

Local information
● **Accommodation & places to eat**
Very few travellers stay in Sale, as there are few hotels, and the city is easily accessible from Rabat. There is the cheap **E** *Hotel des Saadiens*, by the bus station. *Camping de la Plage* is by the river and the sea, with toilets, showers and a shop. There are a number of small and cheap café-restaurants just inside both main gates, and along rue Kechachin. *Café Marhaba* nr the SGMB bank is also rec.

● **Transport**
Local Bus: to get to Sale take a bus No 6 or 12 from Ave Hassan II in Rabat, a grand-taxi from the stop on the same street, or walk down to the quay below the kasbah and take a rowing boat across the river, from where you can walk up to **Bab Bou Hajar**. Rabat petit-taxis are not allowed to cross the river. Once in Sale it should be possible to explore most of the centre on foot, but if not, the city has its own petit-taxis. If you have your own transport, go along Tarik al Marsa, Ave Hassan II or Blvd du Bou Regreg and cross the bridge below the **Hassan Tower**. It is possible to walk this route in about half an hour.

EXCURSIONS FROM RABAT

Northwards
The **Mamora Forest** is a peaceful area of cork and eucalyptus trees, a pleasant change after Rabat. It lies off the road to Meknes. Turn off left at Sidi Allal Bahroui. Return via the P2 and P29.

The **Jardins Exotiques** are about 20 km from Rabat, on the P2, and the 28 bus route. They are the work of a French horticulturalist, François, in the 1950s. There are many species of plants from Morocco and all over the world, laid out with pools, bridges and summerhouses, often in the manner of one particular area. They are well-worth a visit and are open from 0900-1830.

The **Plage des Nations** is at Sidi Bouknadel, about 30 km of Rabat. It is very popular with the affluent, and more a family beach than those of Rabat-Sale, but the currents can be dangerous. Take the bus No 28 from Sale, and walk the 1 km from the turning, or share a grand-taxi, also from Sale. The **C** *Hotel Firdaous*, T 780407, has a bar, restaurant, pool and is rec. Further on Mehdia and Kenitra can be visited as an excursion from Rabat, by train, bus or car (see page 122).

Southwards
Temara is 16 km from Rabat, off the P36. Bus 17 from Ave Hassan II goes to the town and the ruins of a kasbah. The beach is a 4 km walk to the W. There are two hotels, **D** *Hotel La Feloque*, T 744388, 23 rm, restaurant, bar, pool, tennis, and **E** *Hotel Casino*, as well as *Camping de Temara*, the first from Rabat on the coastal road. There are also a number of popular discos. Temara Zoo is open from 1000 to sunset.

Skhirat is 31 km from Rabat and is clearly signposted off the P36, P1 and RP36. There are two trains from Rabat-Ville each day, at 0730 and 1855, taking 17 mins. Skhirat town has little of interest itself beyond a Sun *souq*. The palace near the beach was the scene of a bloody but unsuccessful *coup* attempt in Jul 1971. Skhirat beach is upmarket, as are the restaurants and hotels nearby, incl **C** *La Kasbah*, Rose Marie Plage, T 749133, F 749116, 42 rm, pool, tennis, restaurant, bar, parking, and the rec **D** *Amphitrite Hotel*, Km 28, route de Rabat, T 742317, 36 rm, restaurant, bar, pool, tennis.

TANGER, MEDITERRANEAN COAST AND THE RIF

CONTENTS

Tanger	92
Ceuta	103
Tetouan and Environs	104
Chaouen and the Northern Rif	108
The Mediterranean Coast	112
Ouezzane and the Southern Rif	116

MAPS

Tanger	94
Tanger Medina	96
Mediterranean Coast & The Rif	102
Tetouan	105
Chaouen	109

Tanger (Tangier) is a city which reflects its position at the crossroads of Africa and Europe, the Mediterranean Sea and the Atlantic Ocean, as well as its historical experience as an international zone. It is a shabby and bustling city, full of character. Ceuta and Melilla are Spanish enclaves, other towns such as Chaouen, Ouezzane and Tetouan reflect the Andalusian input into the area, whilst Al Hoceima is a more recent Spanish input, that of the 20th century protectorate. The Mediterranean Sea coast is a succession of large, characterless resort complexes and small, isolated, idyllic fishing villages. The Rif, inland, is a wild mountain range with a history of rebellion and a controversial role in hashish production.

TANGER

(*Pop* 266,346 (1982); *Alt* 75m) Tanger has a highly individual character, a product of its location at the gate to the Mediterranean Sea and at the meeting point of Africa and Europe, and of its recent historical past, notably as an international city from 1923 to 1956, when its tax-free status and reputation attracted many writers, artists and other famous Westerners, as well as a sizeable banking industry. Tanger also had fame as a gay resort. It remains today a lively city, popular with travellers, including those arriving or just visiting from Spain, interesting to explore, and with a wide range of restaurants and entertainments. A recent cleansing of the city when the King proposed a visit has improved the area. The beach is popular and the resort area extends E adjacent to the new promenade. The city is now an important passenger port and tourist resort. Tanger is well worth a visit, particularly for the **Kasbah**, former residence of Sultans, and the **Medina**, a small and complex maze of houses, shops and narrow, steep streets.

In Tanger it is almost impossible not to recall the numerous celebrated figures that once visited the city. They are part of the official and unofficial hard-sell, and are closely bound up in the history and the buildings. Visitors include English diarist Samuel Pepys, film stars Marlene Dietrich and Errol Flynn, writers Oscar Wilde, Brion Gysin, Allen Ginsberg, Joe Orton (*Entertaining Mr Sloane*), Paul Bowles (author of *The Sheltering Sky* and numerous short stories set in North Africa), Ian Fleming, Jack Kerouac, William Burroughs, Richard Hughes (*High Wind in Jamaica*), James Leo Herlihy (*Midnight Cowboy*), Tennessee Williams, painter Francis Bacon, and French composer Camille Saint-

Saën, as well as the Woolworth heiress Barbara Hutton, Truman Capote, Winston Churchill, Ronnie Kray, Gertrude Stein and the photographer Cecil Beaton. The French painter Eugène Delacroix visited in 1832, and Henri Matisse in 1912, both completing many paintings of Tanger. This expatriate population has since declined, and Tanger can now seem to be resting on its former glories and notoriety.

Early History

Perhaps the oldest city in Morocco, Tanger was active as early as 1600 BC. There was a Phoenician settlement here. Roman mythology ascribes its founding to the Greek giant Anteus, son of Poseidon, god of the earth, and Gaia, goddess of the earth. Anteus challenged Hercules, Hercules killing the giant and having a child by the widow, Tingis. Hercules pulled apart Spain and Africa to give this son, Sophix, a city protected by the sea. King Sophix named his city Tingis. Tanger was known to the Phoenicians, Romans, Vandals and Byzantines and has always been important in view of its strategic location commanding the Straits of Gibraltar. The Romans made it at one point capital of their North African provinces, and controlled it until 429 AD. Later, the Vandals and Byzantines struggled to control the city. Arabs took the city in 706 AD. Tanger remained at the centre of conflict between the major Arab and Berber Dynasties.

Mediaeval History

Tanger achieved commercial importance in the Mediterranean sphere during the 1300s. It was conquered by the Portuguese in 1471, became Spanish in 1578 and Portuguese in 1640. The city was part of English King Charles II's dowry when marrying the Portuguese Catherine of Braganza in 1661, but the English departed in 1684, destroying the kasbah as they left. Sultan Moulay Ismail rebuilt the town after the English left.

Modern History

In the 19th century Tanger became a popular base for European merchants and housed a large European colony, as well as the focus of political competition between expansionist European powers. In 1923 the city became a tax-free International Zone controlled by a 30 member international committee. The city was reunited with Morocco in Oct 1956 but its tax-free status was maintained until 1960. Since Independence, Tanger has declined in international economic importance, but has also rapidly developed its tourist industry.

NB Hassle and guides

A drawback of Tanger is that the hassling of tourists for business can be constant and very skilled. If you need a guide, it is better to wait until you can get to the Tourist Office or one of the larger hotels to arrange an official guide. This should keep away the unofficial guides who will otherwise approach at any opportunity. However if you are accompanied by an official guide (or indeed an unofficial guide) you will pay an undeclared commission every time you purchase something. There is also considerable pressure to buy hashish,

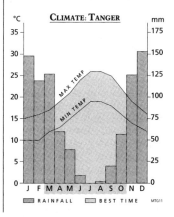

CLIMATE: TANGER

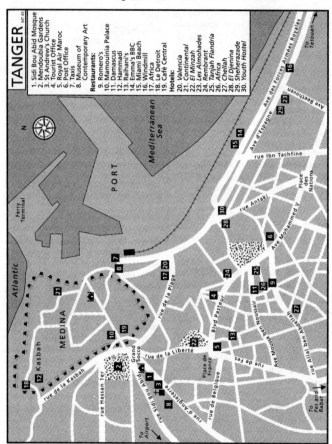

TANGER MT 45

1. Sidi Bou Abid Mosque
2. Mendoubia Gardens
3. St Andrew's Church
4. Tourist Office
5. Royal Air Maroc
6. Post Office
7. Taxis
8. Museum of Contemporary Art

Restaurants:
9. Romero's
10. Mamouinia Palace
11. Damascus
12. Hammadi
13. Raihani's
14. Emma's BBC
15. Miami Beach
16. Windmill
17. Africa
18. Le Detroit
19. Café Central

Hotels:
20. Valencia
21. Continental
22. El Minzah
23. Les Almohades
24. Rembrant
25. Tanjah Flandria
26. Africa
27. Chellah
28. El Djenina
29. Sheherazade
30. Youth Hostel

grown in the nearby Rif mountains. It is unadvisable to succumb to this pressure, in view of the often close links between the dealers and the police. Deterring the attentions of unofficial guides, drug dealers or others will take incredible patience, politeness and firmness. A much more minor problem is that a number of streets have two names: the original and still widely used French name and the newer Arabic name found on the street signs. A few have a third

Spanish name.

ACCESS Air Tanger's Boukhalef airport is 15 km SW of the city, T 935129, 934717, on the P2 road to Rabat. Entry formalities slow as tourists and nationals are not separated. Catch bus 17 or 70 from the terminal to the Grand Socco (Place de 19 Avril 1947), or take a grand-taxi MD70 by day MD105 after 2100 in winter and 2200 in summer. (Rates displayed on wall by customs.)

Train Arriving by train from Marrakech, Casablanca, Rabat, Meknes and Fes the traveller stops first at Tanger Ville, and then at Tanger Port. The former is convenient for the city and its main hotels.

Road The P2 from Rabat brings the driver into Tanger along rue de Fes. The S704 from Ceuta twists along the coast and feeds into Ave Mohammed V, as does the P38 from Tetouan. **Bus**: CTM buses arrive at the terminal in Ave des Forces Armées Royales, adjacent to the port gates and Tanger Ville railway station. Private lines arrive at the terminal at the end of rue de Fes.

Sea Transmediterranea and Limadet, T 933626, jointly run the car/passenger ferry service from Algeciras, Spain. Hopefully passports will have been stamped on the boat. In the terminal there is a *bureau de change* for cash and TCs, as well as a ticket office for trains. Hydrofoils from Algeciras and more traditional ferries from Gibraltar dock close by. Just outside the terminal is Tanger Port railway station for immediate departure to Asilah, Meknes, Fes, Oujda, Rabat, Casablanca and Marrakech, as well as a rank for both kinds of taxis. Negotiation over prices will be necessary but hard.

Places of interest

The Kasbah is constructed on the highest point of the medina. Follow rue d'Italie and rue de la Kasbah and enter by Porte de la Kasbah. From the medina, follow rue des Chrétiens from the Petit Socco, and then rue Sidi Ben Rassouli to Bab el Assa.

There has been a similar construction on the site of the kasbah since Roman days, and it was the traditional residence in Tanger of the Sultan and his harem. It was burnt to the ground by the English as they left in 1685. More recently, during the hey-day of Tanger as an international city, the kasbah was considered a fashionable address for people such as the novelist Richard Hughes (who lived at 'Numéro Zero, Le Kasbah, Tanger').

The **Musée de la Kasbah**, T 932097, open 0930-1300, 1500-1800, closed Tues, is in the former palace of the kasbah, the **Dar al-Makhzen**, and includes Moroccan arts and antiquities. The palace was built by the Sultan Moulay Ismail in the 18th century, and was used as the Sultan's palace up until 1912, when Sultan Mawlay Hafid, exiled to Tanger, lived there, alongside his extensive harem. The museum has a wide range of carved and painted woods, carpets and textiles. The palace is itself worth seeing, with an impressive central courtyard, whilst the rooms off it have intricate wall and ceiling carving, particularly in the Fes room, which has ceramics from Fes and Meknes. The garden of the palace is worth exploring, a beautiful mature Andalusian arrangement, with fragrant plants. As you leave the palace stop at *Le Detroit* for a drink and pastries, and an impressive view of the city and sea.

To the left of the palace is the **Museum of Ethnography and Archaeology**. In front of the palace is the Place de la Kasbah, where criminals were once punished or executed. Note the **Grand Mosque** adjacent to the port. In the sea wall a gate leads out onto a belvedere with excellent views of the seascape. On the other side of the Place de la Kasbah, just outside the kasbah gate on rue Sidi Hassani, is the **Musée International d'Art Contemporain**. Also nearby is **Villa Sidi Hosni**, former residence of Barbara Hutton, the American heiress whose Tanger life is famous.

The Medina Lying below the kasbah, and running from the Grand Socco (Place de 19 Avril, 1947) down to the port, the medina is focused on the Petit Socco, and is full of narrow, twisting streets and old houses, many of which are now shops, hotels or restaurants catering for tourists. It is a quarter which has captured the imagination of numerous European and American writers, with the stories of Paul Bowles amongst the most evocative. It is easy to get lost here, so it might be advisable for the visitor with limited time to take an official guide. Unaccompanied, unofficial guides will hawk for business continuously.

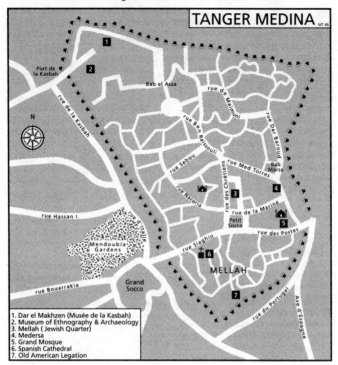

TANGER MEDINA MT 46

1. Dar el Makhzen (Musée de la Kasbah)
2. Museum of Ethnography & Archaeology
3. Mellah (Jewish Quarter)
4. Medersa
5. Grand Mosque
6. Spanish Cathedral
7. Old American Legation

The Grand Socco is where the medina begins. Nowadays it is a busy place, but no longer a thriving market square with street entertainers and food stalls. It now has a few fruit shops, cheap restaurants, and several cafés. Note the tiled minaret of the **Sidi Bou Abid Mosque** (1917) on the corner of the Grand Socco and rue Sidi Bou Abid. On Thur and Sun Rifi Berber women sell all sorts of wares in rue de la Plage (rue Salah Eddine El Ayoubi). Along rue d'Angleterre they also sell woven blankets. On the rue Bourrakia side of the Grand Socco, the arch with Arabic on it leads in to the **Mendoubia Gardens**, quiet but unimpressive, and normally closed. The **Mendoubia Palace** is the former residence of the Sultan's representatives.

Rue Siaghin, the old silversmiths' street, running from the Grand Socco to the Petit Socco, is still an important commercial area of the medina, and the easiest route by which to enter the main area of the medina. To the right of rue Siaghin, is the *mellah*, the Jewish quarter. One also passes the **Spanish Cathedral**, now boarded up. Rue Siaghin leads into the Petit Socco, which lies at the heart of the medina. This market square was once bigger, but now seems strangely cramped. It is surrounded by a number of famous but primitive *pensiones*, and the *Café Central*, formerly a café-bar attracting the likes of William Burroughs, Allen Ginsberg and Jack Kerouac, but now with no alcohol sold in the medina it is just a fairly ordinary café with a pleasant terrace to watch life pass by.

Below the Petit Socco, the **Grand Mosque** lies in between rue de la Marine and rue des Postes. This is built on the site of a Portuguese cathedral, although that had been predated by a mosque and, probably, a Roman temple. Opposite is a 14th century *medersa*. Also on rue des Postes (rue Mokhtar Ahardan) is the *Pensión Palace*, where Bertolucci filmed *The Sheltering Sky*, based on the Paul Bowles' novel.

The **Old American Legation**, 8 Zankat d'Amerique, T 935904, open 0930-1200, 1600-1830, is the oldest American diplomatic property, given to the US by the Moroccan Sultan in 1821 and used as a Consulate until 1961. From rue des Postes turn right after the *Hotel Mamora* into rue Ikiredj, through a confusing region at the heart of the medina, into rue de Four, right into rue Haybender, and left into rue d'Amerique. It is now a museum and study centre, with a good collection of prints. Note also the building's classic architecture.

Tanger's *ville nouvelle* has little of great interest but it is a pleasant place to explore. Place de France (Place de Faro) has a good view of the bay, with the famous *Café de France* alongside, where wartime agents met and made deals. Blvd Pasteur is the main shopping and business street of the new town. Rue de la Liberté is also worth wandering along, perhaps stopping off at the *Centre Culturel Français*'s Galerie Delacroix if it has an exhibition.

At 50 rue d'Angleterre, **St Andrew's** is an Anglican Church consecrated in 1905, with architecture and internal decoration modelled on Moorish Granada. The key is kept by the friendly and helpful groundsman, Mustapha, who will unlock the church and give you a guided tour. Note the Arabic inscriptions of the Lord's Prayer and Gloria at the altar end. Memorials and graves, both inside and outside, feature a number of important former residents of Morocco, including 19th century British consul Sir John Drummond Hay, early 20th century *Times* correspondent Walter Harris, Caid Sir Harry McLean, Scottish adviser to Sultan Mawlay Abd al-Aziz, and Emily Keane, 19th century wife of the Sherif of Ouezzane.

Nearby, the **Musée d'Art Contemporain de la Ville de Tanger**, 52 rue d'Angleterre, T 938436, has a wide selection of the more important painters of Morocco, but is not very impressive on the whole, entrance MD10. Originally this was the English consulate.

Forbes Magazine Museum of Military Miniatures, Palais Mendoub, rue Shakespeare, just W of the stadium, T 933606, open 1000-1700, entry free, closed Thur. Malcolm Forbes, American magazine owner, set up this museum of over 115,000 toy soldiers in a former residence of the Moroccan Sultan. There is a vast collection of miniatures, some arranged in historical reconstructions of famous battles, with a number of Arab figures. Essential for the enthusiast, a pleasant change for others. The gardens are magnificent.

The **beach** and the clubs alongside it were previously known as an expatriate zone where anything was permissable and a good time easily available. The clubs are a shadow of what they once were but still offer a range of drinking, eating and dancing opportunities. Try *Emma's BBC*, *The Windmill* or *Miami Beach*. The beach is popular, particularly with Moroccans in Jul and Aug. There is no shortage of more relaxing, less crowded and cleaner beaches either way along the coast.

Tanger is a splendid place for watching the birds which migrate across the Straits of Gibraltar – the easiest crossing place between Europe and Africa. Literally hundreds of species make use of the thermals to cross N in spring and S in autumn, the flocks of huge storks and vultures being the most impressive sight.

Local information

NB There is a shortage of water in Tanger due to poor rainfall. Be prepared for the supply to be cut at any time.

● **Accommodation**

AL *Hotel El Minzah*, 85 rue de la Liberté (Zankat el Houria), T 935885, F 934546, 100 rm with bath, pricey but central, dates from the 1930s, beautiful gardens set around an Andalusian courtyard, convenient for exploring the medina, two restaurants, wine bar, coffee bar, tea room, mini-golf, tennis, pool, extensions in progress will increase to 153 rm and improve facilities; **AL** *Hotel Les Almohades*, Ave des Forces Armées Royales, T 940431, F 946317, 138 rm, nr the beach, most with sea views, luxurious, 4 restaurants, bar, nightclub 'Up 2000', pool, sauna.

B *Hotel Rembrandt*, Ave Mohammed V, T 937870/2, centre of the new town, luxurious and prestigious, restaurant and popular bar, garden, pool.

C *Africa Hotel*, 17 rue Moussa Ben Noussair, T 935511, 86 rm, comfortable and lively, bar, pool, restaurant, nightclub; **C** *Hotel Sheherazade*, Ave des Forces Armées Royales, T 940500, 140 rm, close to the sea, pool, private beach, bar and terrace; **C** *Tanjah Flandria Hotel*, 6 Ave Mohammed V, T 931231/936285, F 934347, centre of the new town, 170 rm, comfortable, 2 restaurants, piano bar, disco (2100-0300), sauna (men: 1200-1400, 1900-2100, women: 1000-1200), art gallery, bank, pool.

D *Chellah Hotel*, 47-49 rue Allal Ben Abdellah, T 943389, 180 rm not all with a/c, good value, disco, tea room; **D** *Hotel Marco Polo*, Ave d'Espagne, T 938213, 9 rm, German run, restaurant and bar, overlooking the sea.

E *Continental Hotel*, 36 rue Dar Baroud, in the medina, T 931024, Tx 33086, by far the best cheap option, has fallen on hard times but is being renovated, convenient, with a sea view, historic decoration, restaurant; **E** *Hotel El Djenina*, 8 rue El Antaki (rue Grotius), just off Ave d'Espagne, T 936075, 21 rm, rec; **E** *Hotel El Muniria*, rue Magellan, incl the *Tanger Inn Bar*, both popular, numbering William Burroughs, Kerouac and Ginsberg among former residents; opp is the **E** *Hotel Ibn Batouta*, 8 rue Magellan, T 937170, with restau-

rant; **E** *Mansora Hotel*, 19 rue des Postes, T 934105, only good hotel in the centre of the medina; **E** *Valencia*, 72 Ave d'Espagne, junction with rue de la Plage (Zankat Salah Eddine el Ayoubi), T 930770, 45 rm, clean but basic, no restaurant.

F *Hotel Grand Socco*, rue Imam Layti, behind the Grand Socco, is cheap, dirty and noisy, but convenient; **Petit Socco** (Place Souq Dakhil) is the heart of the medina and its *pensiones* have a history, but they may be poorly equipped, try **F** *Pensión Mauritania*, T 934671, which has a cold shower; or just off, on rue des Postes (Ave Mokhtar Ahardan) **F** *Pensión Palace* is good; in the *ville nouvelle* there are cheap and basic *pensiones* in rue de la Plage, where prices do not seem to be fixed, but many do not have showers, incl **F** *Royal*, *Madrid*, *Le Detroit*, *Playa* and *Atou*, the last being particularly cheap, whilst *Le Detroit* is rec.

● **Youth hostel**

T 46127, 8 rue El Antaki, Ave d'Espagne, 60 beds, overnight fee, MD20-25, advanced booking essential, station 800m, bus 100m. Good reports given on this hostel.

● **Camping**

Camping sites are not much cheaper than a budget hotel and rather far from the city. *Camping Miramonte*, T 937138, is 3 km W from the city, on bus routes 1, 2 and 21. *Camping-Caravaning Tingis*, T 940191, is 6 km E, well-equipped but 2 km from the beach. *Robinson Plage Camping*, 8 km E by Caves of Hercules, good but far, take the *Boughaz* minibus.

● **Places to eat**

◆◆◆ *El Erz*, Hotel El Minzah, 85 rue de la Liberté, T 935885, reservations rec, popular restaurant with a wide range of European dishes, often with music; *El Korsan*, Hotel El Minzah, 85 rue de la Liberté, T 935885, reservations rec, Moroccan food amid traditional decor and music.

◆◆ *Brenda's*, Ave du Prince Moulay Abdellah, is a cheap English restaurant; *Restaurant Chez Bernard*, off Blvd Pasteur nr the *Hotel Rembrandt*, Spanish menu dominated by fish; *Damascus*, 2 bis Ave du Prince Moulay Abdellah, T 934730, Moroccan food, bar and tea room; *Dar Tajine*, rue du Commerce, high-class Moroccan meals, some tour parties; *Restaurant El Mabrouk*, rue Ahmed Chaouki, off Place de France, has very reasonably-priced set menus with good Moroccan food; further up the same road *Raihani's*, T 934866, also has reasonable menus with excellent Moroccan cuisine, *Restaurant le Detroit*, Ave du Prince Moulay Abdellah, Spanish food, cheaper than nearby Romero's; *Restaurant Hammadi*, 2 rue de la Kasbah, opp junction with Paseo del Docteur Cenarro, T 934514, Moroccan meals in 'authentic' surroundings; *L'Ibis*, rue Khalid Ibn Oualid, nr Place de France (Place de Faro), moderately priced but unexciting French restaurant/bar; *Restaurant Mamounia Palace*, 6 rue Semmarin, Petit Socco, T 935099, set menus of Moroccan food with authentic decor and folklore/music; *Negresso*, rue Mexique, a bar, snack-bar and restaurant, offers French, English and Moroccan drinks and food; *Romero's*, 12 Ave du Prince Moulay Abdellah, T 932277, highly rec Spanish cuisine, fair prices but not cheap; try also *Emma's BBC*, Ave d'Espagne, famous and cheap beachside bar-restaurant, open summer only; *La Presse Salon de Thé/Restaurant*, Blvd Pasteur; *Miami Beach*, Ave des Forces Armées Royales, T 943401, 1000-1800, beachside bar-restaurant, gay bar and disco at night; *Windmill*, Ave des Forces Armées Royales, T 940907, oldest beachside restaurant patronized by writer Joe Orton, fish, Moroccan and Spanish food.

♦*Restaurant Africa*, 83 rue de la Plage (rue Salah Eddine El Ayoubi), T 935436, a good cheap option; *Dallas* is a cheap fish restaurant in rue El Moutanabi; *Restaurant Hassi Baida* and *Restaurant Cleopatre* are in the same road and similar; the Grand Socco has several cheap places to eat and the *Café-Restaurant Ataif*, in the medina, there are a number of cheap, basic restaurants, such as *Mauritania* and *Assalam* in rue de la Marine, and *Aladin*, *Grece* and *Andaluz* in rue du Commerce. The latter, at No 7, is particularly good.

● **Bars**

Patio Wine Bar, *Hotel El Minzah*, 85 rue de la Liberté, T 935885, a wine bar in which to explore the wines of Morocco and overseas, a little pricey; *The Pub*, 4 rue Sorolla, T 934789, food, beer and other drinks in a pub atmosphere; *Caid's Bar*, *Hotel El Minzah*, 85 rue de la Liberté, T 935885, Moroccan decoration and expensive drinks in an atmospheric and celebrated bar; *Tanger Inn*, 1 rue Magellan, T 935337, small bar popular with expatriates; *Emma's BBC*, Ave d'Espagne, beachside bar; *Number One*, 1 Ave Mohammed V, T 931817, popular with gays.

● **Cafés**

As you leave the palace in the kasbah, stop at the *Salon de Thé/Restaurant le Detroit*, T 938080, which is pricey for food, but good for tea, coffee, pastries and a view of the palace, kasbah and the sea, established by the writer Brion Gysin. *Café de France*, 1 Place de France, has a history as a meeting place of the important and famous, popular with Francis Bacon, William Burroughs, Tennessee Williams and Truman Capote. The *Café Central*, in the Petit Socco, has a similar history, but is now just a nice place to watch the hustle and bustle of the medina.

● **Banks & money changers**

BMCE, Blvd Pasteur, with a *bureau de change*. BMCI 8 Place de France, T 935553. Banque du Maroc, 78 Ave Mohammed V, T 935553. Credit du Maroc, Agence Grand Socco, rue de l'Italie. Banks are open 0830-1130 and 1430-1630.

American Express: c/o Voyages Schwartz, 54 Blvd Pasteur, T 933459, 0900-1230 and 1500-1900 Mon-Fri, 0900-1230 Sat.

● **Cultural & language centres**

American Language Center, 1 rue M'Sallah; Centre Culturel Français, rue de la Liberté.

● **Embassies & consulates**

Belgium, 5A Immeuble Jawara, Place Al Medina, T 943234; Denmark, 3 rue Ibn Rochd, T 938183; France, Place de France, T 932039; Germany, 47 Ave Hassan II, T 938700; Italy, 35 rue Assad Ibn Forrat, T 937647; Netherlands, 47 Ave Hassan II, T 931245; Norway, 3 rue Henri Regnault, T 931245; Portugal, 9 Place des Nations, T 931708; Spain, rue Sidi Bouabid, T 937000, 935625; Sweden, 31 Ave Prince Heritier, T 938730; Switzerland, rue Henri Regnault, T 934721; UK, 9 rue d'Amerique du Sud, T 935895; USA, 29 rue El Achouak, T 935904.

● **Entertainment**

Art galleries: *Galerie Delacroix*, rue de la Liberté; *Tanjah Flandria Art Gallery*, rue Ibn Rochd, behind the *Hotel Flandria*, T 933000.

Cinemas: *Ciné Alcazar*, junction of rue de l'Italie and rue Ibn Al Abbar (Paseo del Doctor Cenarro); *Cinema Rif*, Grand Socco, not very good looking. Preferably look around Blvd Pasteur.

Discos and nightclubs: the continuation of rue Mexique, rue Sanlucar (Zankat El Moutanabi), has a number of clubs/discos incl

Churchill's, *Scott's* and *Koutoubia Dancing*. Also try the more upmarket *Up 2000* in *Hotel les Almohades*, Ave des Forces Armées Royales, T 940431, built on the roof of a hotel; or *Ali Baba* at *Chellah Hotel*, 47-49 rue Allal Ben Abdellah. *Morocco Palace*, 11 Ave du Prince Moulay Abdellah, T 938614, has belly-dancing until 0100, when it becomes a disco.

● **Hospitals & medical services**

Ambulance: T 15.

Chemists: *Pharmacie de Fes*, 22 rue de Fes, T 932619, 24 hrs a day; *Pharmacie Pasteur*, Place de France, T 932422.

Dentist: Dr Ibrahim Filali, 53 Ave du Prince Moulay Abdellah, T 931268, speaks English.

Doctor: Dr Joseph Hirt, 8 rue Sorolla, T 935729, speaks English, and will pay calls to hotels.

Hospital: emergencies: T 934242; Hôpital Al Kortobi, rue Garibaldi, T 931073; Hôpital Español, T 931018.

● **Post & telecommunications**

Area code: 9. All numbers are six figs in most cases beginning with the area code.

Post Office: the main post office (PTT) is at 33 Ave Mohammed V, T 935657 (0830-1200, 1430-1800, Mon-Fri, 0830-1200 Sat).

Telephone: international phone (24 hrs) far right of post office. Also telephone from the PTT at the junction of rue El Msala and rue Belgique.

● **Places of worship**

Anglican: St Andrew's Episcopal Church, 50 rue d'Angleterre, T 934633, services on Sun 0830 and 1100 and Wed.

Interdenominational Protestant: American Church, 34 rue Hassan Ibn Ouezzane (rue Léon l'Africain), T 932755, service on Sun 1100.

● **Shopping**

Food: there is a food market between rue d'Angleterre and rue Sidi Bou Abid. The stalls along rue d'Angleterre are not very impressive. There are numerous fruit sellers along rue de la Plage and its side streets. Just off, on rue El Oualili, is another food market.

Handicrafts & antiques: Tanger is not the best place to buy handicrafts, for although it has a large selection, Marrakech and Fes have better access to the different production regions, and prices will be lower. The pressure to buy in Tanger is intense, with bazaarists and hawkers used to gullible day-trippers and weekend visitors from Spain. The cheapest

shops and stalls, with the most flexible prices, will be found in the medina. Shops in the *ville nouvelle* may claim fixed prices but in most this is just another ploy. *Coopartim, Ensemble Artisanal*, rue de Belgique, T 931589, is a good place to start, a government controlled fixed price shop with a vast range of goods from all over the country, where one can get an idea of prices. Also try *Sahara*, 30 rue des Almouahidine; *Bazaar Chaouen*, 116 rue de la Plage; and in the medina, *Marrakech la Rouge*, 50 rue es Siaghin. For crafts and antiques see the amazing *Galerie Tindouf*, 64 rue de la Liberté, T 931525.

Library: Tanger Book Club, the Old American Legation, 8 rue d'Amerique, the medina, T 935317 (0930-1200, Tues-Sat).

Newspapers & books: foreign newspapers can be brought from shops in rue de la Liberté or outside the post office in Ave Mohammed V. For books in French, and a few in other languages, go to *Librairie des Colonnes*, 54 Blvd Pasteur, T 936955.

● **Sport**

Flying: *Royal Flying Club*, Boukhalef Airport, T 935720.

Golf: *Royal Club de Golf*, Boubana, T 938925, 18 hole, 5,529m par 72, fees MD450 per day.

Riding: *Country L'Etrier*, Boubana.

Tennis: *M'Sallah Garden Tennis Courts*, rue de Belgique, T 935203; *Municipale*, Ave de la Paix, T 943324.

Yachting: *Tanger Yacht Club*, the Port, T 938575.

● **Tourist offices**

Office du Tourisme, 29 Blvd Pasteur, T 938239/40 open 0800-1400, Mon-Sat; **Syndicat d'Initiative**, 11 rue Khalid Ibn El Oualid, T 935486.

● **Tour companies & travel agents**

Holiday Service, 84 Ave Mohammed V, T 933362; *Wagons-Lit Tourisme*, rue de la Liberté. *Air France*, 20 Blvd Pasteur; *GB Airways*, 83 rue de la Liberté, T 935877; *Iberia*, 35 Blvd Pasteur, T 936177; *Royal Air Maroc*, Place de France, T 935501/2.

● **Useful addresses**

Fire: T 15.

Garage: Tanjah Auto, 2 Ave de Rabat.

Police (general): rue Ibn Toumert, T 19; **Police** (traffic): T 177.

● **Transport**

Local Bus: T 946682, Tanger is fairly small and thus it is unlikely that you will want to use local buses. If you do they can be picked up in the Grand Socco or in Ave des Forces Armées Royales outside the port gates. Boughaz mini-buses, from just outside the port gate, may be useful to get to the private bus station, or on excursions from Tanger westwards. **Bicycle & motorcycle hire**: Mesbahi, 7 rue Ibn Tachfine, just off Ave des Forces Armées Royales, T 940974, renting bicycles, 50cc and 125cc motorbikes, deposit required for 3 days or more. **Car hire**: Avis, 54 Blvd Pasteur, T 938960, 933031, and at the airport; Budget, 7 Ave du Prince Moulay Abdellah, T 937994, and at the airport; Europcar, 87 Ave Mohammed V, T 938271; Hertz, 36 Ave Mohammed V, T 933322, 934179, and at the airport; Leasing Cars, 24 rue Henri Regnault, and at the airport, a little cheaper. **Grand-taxis**: can be picked up from the Grand Socco or in front of **Tanger Ville** railway station, to destinations within or outside of the city. You will need to set a fare with the driver. Tanger's **petit-taxis**, turquoise with yellow stripe, may be cheaper, although that will depend on your skill as the meters are not always operated. For a taxi T 935517.

Air Tanger's Boukhalef airport is 15 km from the city along the P2, T 935129, 934717. Catch bus 17 or 70 from Grand Socco or a grand-taxi. Arrive 1½-2 hrs early. There are direct flights to Agadir, Al Hoceima and Casablanca and direct international flights to European cities including Amsterdam, Barcelona, Brussels, Frankfurt, Gibraltar, London, Madrid and Paris.

Train There are two stations in Tanger, very close together. All trains go from **Tanger Ville**, T 931201, on Ave des Forces Armées Royales in the town centre, some leave just before from **Tanger Port**, beside the ferry terminal. Departures – **Rabat and Casablanca**: 0850, 1700, 2345; **Marrakech**: 0850, 2345; **Meknes, Fes and Oujda**: 1100, 0130. All trains stop at Asilah.

Road Bus: information: T 932415. CTM buses depart from the ticket office near the entrance to the port in Ave des Forces Armées Royales. Current departure times – Kenitra, **Rabat and Casablanca**: 1100, 2230, 2330, 2400; **Souq El Arba du Gharb, Ksar el Kebir, Larache, Asilah**: 1100, 1630, 1800, 2230, 2330, 2400; **Sidi Kacem, Meknes, Fes**: 1800;

Agadir, Tiznit: 1630; **Paris**: 0500. Private buses, running from the terminal at the end of rue de Fes, go to most destinations and are generally cheaper. Departures: **Tetouan** every 15 mins (1 hr); **Asilah** 0915, 0945, 1100 (30 mins; Larache every hour (90 mins); **Meknes** 0700, 1000, 1300, 1600 (5 hrs); **Fes** 1000, 1600; (6 hrs); **Chaouen** 0545, 0800, 1045, 1300, 1330, 1815 (2½ hrs); **Ceuta** 0730, 0945, 1245 (2 hrs); **Ouezzane** 0900, 1400 (4 hrs). To get to the terminal take a petit-taxi or a Boughaz minibus. **Taxi**: to many destinations take a shared grand-taxi from the bus terminal at the end of rue de Fes. To Tetouan and Ceuta this is a quick, practical and not too expensive option. For excursions from Tanger to the Caves of Hercules or Cap Malabata negotiate for a grand-taxi in rue de Hollande.

Sea Ferry tickets to **Algeciras** can be bought at the Limadet Agents in Ave du Prince Moulay Abdellah, just off Blvd Pasteur, T 933626, at travel agents in Blvd Pasteur, or at the ferry terminal. Transmediterranea and Limadet jointly operate this car and passenger service 3 or 4 times a day in the summer and 2 in the winter. Passengers from MD196, cars from MD8500. Check in at least 1 hr early, to allow time to collect an embarkation card, complete a departure card, and have your passport stamped. For tickets for the Bland's Line ferry to **Gibraltar** go to Med Travel, 22 Ave Mohammed V, T 935872/3, or to the port. Departures Mon 0930, Wed, Thur and Fri 1430, Mon and Fri 1830 and Sun 1630, single: MD250 (£20), return: MD360 (£27). Day trip MD400. Motos and bicycles MD200. Vehicles up to 6m MD600. Journey takes 1 hr on hydrofoil and 2-2½ hrs on traditional ferry. **NB** Holding a return ticket for a specific sailing is no guarantee you will be allowed on the boat – Bland's excursion customers come first. Tickets to **Sete** can be bought from Voyages Comanov, 43 Ave Abou El Alaâ El Maâri, T 932649, F 932320. There is a ferry every 3-4 days. Passenger tickets from MD2720. Car and van passengers from MD3740. **NB** At the port avoid all touts selling embarkation cards which are free from the officals. Exchange your ticket for a boarding card at the ticket desk.

Atlantic beach, the Caves of Hercules and ancient Cotta

The excursion W is a rewarding experience, with a dramatic drive en route. The

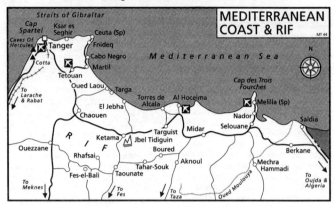

Straits of Gibraltar

MEDITERRANEAN COAST & RIF   MT 44

Cap Spartel, Ksar es Seghir, Ceuta (Sp), Caves Of Hercules, Tanger, Fnideq, Cotta, Cabo Negro, Martil, *Mediterranean Sea*, Tetouan, To Larache & Rabat, Oued Laou, Targa, Cap des Trois Fourches, El Jebha, Torres de Alcala, Al Hoceima, Melilla (Sp), Chaouen, Nador, Selouane, Saïdia, Targuist, Midar, R I F, Ketama, Jbel Tidiguin, Ouezzane, Boured, Berkane, Rhafsai, Aknoul, Mechra Hammadi, Tahar-Souk, Taounate, Oued Moulouya, To Oujda & Algeria, Fes-el-Bali, Taza, To Meknes, To Fes, Oued Moulouya

options are to negotiate a round-trip price with a grand-taxi driver in rue d'Angleterre, take a Boughaz minibus from the port gates, or in your own transport, follow rue Sidi Bou Abid and rue Sidi Amar on to the S701. This goes past Montagne, an exclusive suburb of royal palaces and villas. 11 km from Tanger is **Cap Spartel**, the extreme NW corner of Africa, with a notable lighthouse, and the *Café-Bar Sol*. This is followed by the long and wild Atlantic (or Robinson) Beach. This is a dramatic place, and swimmers should exercise caution. Nearby is the **C** *Hotel Les Grottes d'Hercules*, T 938765; and the **E** *Hotel Robinson*; as well as *Camp Robinson* and the *Robinson Café-Restaurant*.

The **Caves of Hercules** are natural formations which have been extended by quarries for millstones up to the 1920s. Later prostitutes worked here, and a number of Tanger's rich and famous held parties. The natural rock chambers are open from 1000 to sunset, for a nominal charge. From a window shaped like Africa which overlooks the sea there is an impressive view.

After the Caves of Hercules take a rough farm track off the road to the **Ancient Cotta**. This is a small site, less impressive than Volubilis, centred around a factory for *garum*, or anchovy paste. Also note remains of the temple.

Cap Malabata, Ksar Es Seghir

From Tanger, E along the S704 road around **Cap Malabata**, are large tourist developments, including the *Club Mediterranée* complex, numerous cafés as well as some excellent beaches used by the people from Tanger. By the Oued Melaleh estuary is an old Portuguese settlement. Further on the **Chateau Malabata** is a Gothic folly, inhabited by a Moroccan family.

Ksar es Seghir is a small seaside town 37 km E of Tanger, dominated by the ruined Portuguese castle. The town was named Ksar Masmuda under the Almohads, and Ksar al Majaz under the Merinids, who added walls and gates in 1287. The Portuguese took the town in 1458. The floor of the *hammam* and mosque should be noted, as well as the intact sea gate arch. The **F** *Café Restaurant Hotel Kassar al Majaz Tarik Ibn Ziad*, is basic. There are other cafés and restaurants, including the recommended *Restaurant Caribou*, *Café Dakhla* to W of town, *Café Dahlia* to E and *Café Lachiri* on bridge (sea food), possibilities for camping, and a splendid beach. Onwards, between Ksar es Seghir and Ceuta, there is a string of beautiful and often deserted beaches. Bus 15 from Grand Socco, Tanger, serves this route. This road is busy on a Sun and very busy in summer. Out of season many places are closed.

Gibraltar/Algeciras

Excursions take only 75 mins. Day trips cost MD360 to Gibraltar, MD250 to Algeciras. See transport details, page 101.

CEUTA

Ceuta is a Spanish enclave within Morocco, administered not as a colony but as an integral part of Spain, with a mixed population of Spaniards, Spanish Moroccans and Moroccan immigrant workers. Ceuta was a strategic site for the Phoenicians, Romans, Vandals and Byzantines. It was taken by the Portuguese in 1415, and passed to the Spanish in 1580, who have occupied it ever since. Morocco makes periodic claims for Ceuta and the other enclave, Melilla, pointing out the parallel with Spanish claims for Gibraltar. Its contemporary role is as a military base, a passenger and car port and a duty free zone. Ceuta, which straddles the isthmus between Mt Hacho and mainland, is a convenient alternative arrival point in Africa to Tanger, with less hassle.

ACCESS **Road** From Ceuta follow the signposts to Morocco. The frontier post is on the S side of the peninsula, a little way out. Petrol is cheaper in Ceuta than Morocco. For those without transport, pick up a Spanish taxi or take bus 7 from Plaza de la Constitución. There are some long distance Spanish buses, from the bus station on the S coast road in Ceuta, to Casablanca, Al Hoceima and Nador. Tetouan is a better option for finding bus services. Arriving from Morocco, drive through Fnideq to the frontier. There are bus and grand-taxi services between Fnideq and Tetouan, and between Fnideq and Tanger. Between the frontier and Fnideq there is a grand-taxi, currently costing MD3. **The Frontier**: passports have to be checked and stamped by Moroccan officials both ways, and there are often lengthy queues. Travellers with their own transport have to have their vehicles registered and their papers, including insurance, registration and licence, checked. This can take some time. Cash can be exchanged on the Moroccan side of the frontier at the Banque Populaire booth.

Sea The Algeciras-Ceuta ferries are cheaper and quicker than those between Algeciras and Tanger, with passengers from MD130 and cars from MD645, taking 80 mins. There are normally six services a day Mon-Sat, five each Sun generally with refreshments available. Tickets can be bought from Transmediterranea in Cañonero Dato, T 509496, F 509530; from Isleña de Navegación, in the port building, T 509139/40; or from the numerous travel agents around the town centre. The port is in the centre of the town and the main destinations are clearly signposted. The hydrofoil service to Algeciras should be booked in advance at 6 Muelle Cañonero Dato, T 516041.

Places of interest

Our Lady of Africa is the 18th century town cathedral in Plaza de Africa on the site of a former mosque, large but not very interesting, with a small museum. Wander around the older quarters of town centre, around Paseo del Revellin and Calle Real. The **Museo Municipal**, Paseo del Revellin, has a collection of archaeological exhibits and maps closed Sun. The **Museo de la Legión**, Paseo de Colón, open 1100-1400 and 1600-1800, Sat and Sun, entry free, includes a large collection of exhibits relating to the Spanish Foreign Legion.

The town leads on to a tree-covered hill, at the end of the peninsula, the Monte Hacho, a pleasant place for a stroll. At the far E edge is an old Portuguese fort. Stop off at the **Ermida de San Antonio**, a convent rebuilt in the 1960s. In the fort there is a small military museum, 5 rm, the **Museo Militar del Castillo del Desnarigado** includes such attractions as Franco's cape. Absolutely fascinating if you can read Spanish and have a knowledge of Spanish history. Open 1100-1400 and 1600-1800, Sat and

Sun. Fortifications and walls separating isthmus from mainland on way to port.

Local information
● Accommodation
The best and most expensive hotel is the parador **AL** *Gran Hotel la Muralla*, 15 Plaza Virgen de Africa, opp the Cathedral, T 514940, 106 rm, pool, bar, nightclub. Similarly expensive is the **AL** *Hotel Ulises*, 5 Calle Cameons, T 514540, 124 rm, with pool.

The main area to try for cheaper hotels is Paseo del Revellin, Calle Cameons and Calle Real. In Calle Real, try **C** *Pensión Real*, 11 rm; **C** *Pensión La Perla*, 7 rm; **C** *Atlante*, 1 Paseo de las Palmeras, T 513548.

Also very good in Calle Real is **D** *C H Rociera*. At the foot of Paseo del Revellin, opp the Banco Popular Español, is the **D** *Pensión Revellin*, 16 rm, No 2, T 516267; and **D** *Bohemia* in Calle Cameons, clean, rec.

● Youth hostel
27 Plaza Viejo, T 515148, only open in Jul and Aug. Often crowded but the cheapest place in summer.

● Camping
Camping Marguerita, T 523706, is located 3 km W of the town. Take the Benzu road and then turn left, at the signs, just after a bar. We have received comments regarding poor facilities and high charges here and have been rec another site closer to the town.

● Places to eat
◆◆◆ Try the expensive and rec *La Torre*, 15 Plaza de Africa; *Casa Silva*, 3 Almirante Lobo, T 513715, expensive array of Spanish fish and seafood dishes, as well as good wine; *El Sombrero de Copa*, 4 Padilla, T 518284, seafood specialists; or *Casa Fernando*, at the Benitez Beach, T 514082, good for seafood.

◆ For a cheaper option, sample some of the *tapas* in a number of the bars.

● Banks & money changers
Banco de España, Plaza de España; Banco Popular Español, 1 Paseo de Revellin.

● Beaches
Either avoid the rubbish on the town beaches, or head out W to the more pleasant beach at Benzu.

● Entertainment
Discos: *Bogoteca*, Calle Real; *Coconut*, Carretara del Jaral; *San Antonio*, Monte Hacho.

Festivals: Fiesta de Nuestra Patrona, La Virgen d'Africa, 5 Aug; **Carnival** in Feb.

● Post & telecommunications
Plaza de España, T 509275.

● Shopping
There are numerous shops selling duty-free goods, but the savings are not enormous but shop around for bargains, especially spirits. Fuel is cheaper here than in Morocco. For travellers heading on to Morocco, stock up on Spanish cheese and wine from the local supermarkets. Excellent fresh fish and shell fish.

● Tourist offices
Oficina de Información de Turismo, Muelle Cañonero Dato, by the port, T 509275.

● Transport
Local Taxis: in Ceuta T 505406, 505407, 505408. **Ferry**: Ceuta to Algeciras takes 1½ hrs, 1,750 Ptas.

TETOUAN AND ENVIRONS

Tetouan is the first major centre along the P28 from the border with Ceuta. There is a number of appealing resorts between Ceuta and Tetouan and also further round the coast which can be visited en route, or as an excursion from Tetouan.

Tetouan

Tetouan with a population of 200,000 has a striking location, between the Rif and the Mediterranean Sea. The city is dramatically beautiful with the white buildings of the medina heavily influenced by Andalusian Islamic architecture, often with balconies and tiled lintels. Some impressive colonial architecture is found in the more recent Spanish town. The city is an interesting place to explore, albeit with more noise and hassle than Chaouen and Ouezzane to the S.

Tetouan was founded in the 3rd century BC as Tamuda, but destroyed by the Romans in 42 AD. The Merinid ruler Sultan Abou Thabit built a kasbah at Tetouan in 1307. Sacked by Henry III of

Castille in 1399 to disperse the corsairs based there, Tetouan was neglected until it was taken over by Muslims from Granada in 1484, bringing with them the distinctive forms and traditions of Andalusian Islamic architecture, still observable in the medinas of Granada and Cordoba. Many of the Andalusians worked as corsairs continuing the tradition. In 1913 Tetouan was chosen as the capital of the Spanish Protectorate in N Morocco which influenced its character and has remained an important regional centre in independent Morocco.

WARNING Tourists to Tetouan must be careful as hashish dealers, pickpockets,

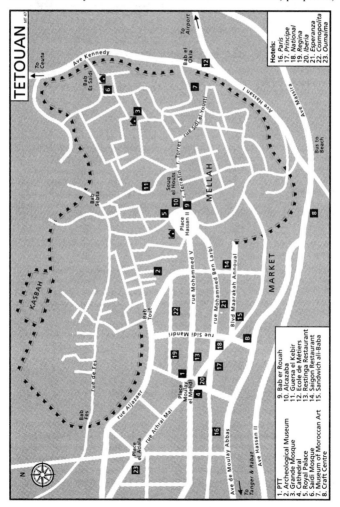

TETOUAN

Hotels:
16. Paris
17. Principe
18. National
19. Regina
20. Iberia
21. Esperanza
22. Cosmopolita
23. Oumaima

1. PTT
2. Archeological Museum
3. Grande Mosque
4. Cathedral
5. Saidi Mosque
6. Royal Palace
7. Museum of Moroccan Art
8. Craft Centre
9. Bab er Rouah
10. Alcazaba
11. Guersa el Kebir
12. Ecole de Métiers
13. Restinga Restaurant
14. Saigon Restaurant
15. Sandwich ali-Baba

and unofficial guides are out in force. It is advisable to pay great attention to one's personal belongings and preferably to avoid having any dealings with people operating in this manner. The tourist office and the larger hotels can arrange official guides.

ACCESS Air Tetouan's airport, used for internal flights from Rabat, Al Hoceima and Casablanca, is Aéroport Saniat R'Mel, T 971233, 5 km from the city. It is currently being redeveloped. Take a grand-taxi into the city. **Road** The P38 from Tanger, and the P28 from Ceuta to the N and Chaouen, Meknes and Fes to the S, both feed into Ave Hassan I, from where the medina and the centre of the *ville nouvelle* are clearly signposted. **Bus** CTM and most private line bus services arrive at the bus station at the corner of Ave Hassan I and rue Sidi Mandri, close to both Place Moulay el Mehdi and Place Hassan II. The ONCF coach service, for passengers leaving the rail network at Tnine Sidi Lyamani, arrives at Place el Adala. Local buses from the beaches normally drop passengers on Ave Massira or outside the main bus station.

Places of interest

A good point to start is **Place Hassan II**, the focal point of the city and former market, and the best place to stroll or sit in a café terrace in the evening. It is dominated by the gleaming **Royal Palace** (5), originally from the 17th century but much added to recently, as the place has been redeveloped. Unfortunately parts have been cordoned off and it has lost some of its atmosphere. The other major centre in the *ville nouvelle* is Place Moulay el Mehdi, along Blvd Mohammed V from Place Hassan II dominated by an impressive golden-yellow **Cathedral** (4).

Bab er Rouah, in the corner of Place Hassan II, leads into the medina. The **medina** of Tetouan is a confusing maze of streets and *souqs*, well worth exploring, although perhaps with the assistance of an official guide. In the *souqs* look out for artifacts with Tetouan's favoured red colouration. Rue Terrafin is

a good route through the medina, leading into rue Torres and rue Sidi el Yousti, and out at Bab el Okla. North of rue Sidi el Yousti is an area with some of the larger and more impressive houses.

Souq el Houts, with pottery, meat and fish is to the left of rue Terrafin behind the palace. Behind the *souq* is a small 15th century fortress, the **Alcazaba** (10), now taken over by a cooperative. Take the left-hand of the two N-bound lanes from the **Souq el Houts** and on the right is **Guersa el Kebir** (11), a textile *souq*, selling in particular the type of striped woven blanket worn by Rifi women. Further on from this *souq*, leading up to Bab Sebta, is a number of specialist craft *souqs* and shops. Running between Bab Sebta and Bab Fes is rue de Fes, a more general commercial area, although with a number of *souqs* around. From Bab Sebta the road out of the city passes through a large cemetery. Above the medina is the crumbling kasbah, closed to visitors, and nearby a vantage point providing stunning views over the city.

On Place Hassan II, the first alleyway S of Bab er Rouah leads on to the main street of the *mellah*, the 19th century Jewish quarter, where there is a number of abandoned synagogues but few of the original inhabitants. The previous *mellah* is near the Grand Mosque.

The Archaeological Museum, Blvd Aljazaer, near Place Hassan II (0900-1200 and 1400-1800, except Tues), contains a small archaeological collection from the Phoenician, Roman and Muslim periods, notably exhibits of mosaics and statues from **Lixus**, near Larache. Note particularly the Roman coins and mosaics. There is also an extensive Spanish library.

The Musée d'Art Marocain/Musée Ethnographique (open 0830-1200 and 1430-1730 Mon-Fri, 0830-1200 Sat), Bab el Okla, contains traditional domestic exhibits and local costume, weapons and Andalusian musical instruments, with an Andalusian garden. Nearby, the **Ecole de Métiers** (Artisan School) (open 0900-1200, 1430-1730, except Tues and Sat), has craftsmen and students at work on *zelij* tiles, leatherwork, carpentry and pottery.

Local information
● Accommodation

Tetouan has *Hotel Champs* to E of town and *Hotel Malaga* to W of town, both at the more expensive end of the market. **C** *Hotel Safir Tetouan*, Ave Kennedy, T 970144, frequented by package tours, garden, pool, tennis, restaurant, nightclub (2300-0300).

The budget hotels or *pensiones*, in and nr the medina and Place Hassan II, are often primitive and unhygienic. **E** *Hotel Oumaima*, rue Achra Mai, T 963473, central, convenient and respectable; **E** *Hotel National*, 8 rue Mohammed Torres, T 963290, rec and not too expensive, with a café; **E** *Paris Hotel*, 11 rue Chakib Arsalane, T 966750, similar, with garage; **E** *Hotel Principe*, 20 Ave de la Resistance, T 962795, large, clean, not all rooms have hot water; **E** *Hotel Regina*, 8 rue Sidi Mandri, T 962113, a cheaper hotel in the *ville nouvelle*, all 58 rm with bath, no hot water.

F *Pensión Iberia*, above BMCE, Place Moulay el Mehdi, small and cheap with hot water; also good are **F** *Pensión Esperanza*, Ave Mohammed V; and **F** *Pensión Cosmopolita*, 5 Blvd General Franco.

● Camping
A number of camping sites at a little distance from Tetouan along the coast, the nearest by the river and beach at Martil.

● Places to eat
Tetouan does not have any exceptional restaurants. The city is known for its sweets.

◆◆◆ *Hotel Safir Tetouan*, Ave Kennedy, T 967044, well-rec and reliable.

◆◆*La Restinga*, 21 rue Mohammed V, good well-priced Moroccan food with good *tagines*; *Restaurant Marrakech de Tetouan*, in the medina, has good Moroccan food and music, busy at lunch time; *Restaurant Saigon*, rue Mourakah Anual, Moroccan and Spanish food; *Zarhoun*, 7 Ave Mohammed Torres, nr the bus station, Moroccan decor and music, and set Moroccan meals, bar.

◆ *Café-Restaurant Moderne*, 1 Pasaje Achaach, nr the bus station, cheap Moroccan food; *Sandwich Ali Baba*, rue Mourakah Anual, is a popular place for cheap local food; also try the places around rue Luneta and Bab er Rouah.

● Banks & money changers
Banque Marocaine, Place Moulay el Mehdi; **BMCE**, 11 Ave Mohammed Ibn Aboud (0800-2000 Mon-Fri, 0900-1300 and 1500-2000 Sat-Sun); **BMCI**, 18 rue Sidi Mandri.

● Post & telecommunications
Area code: 9.
Post Office: Place Moulay el Mehdi, T 966798.

● Shopping
Try the *souqs*, or the *Ensemble Artisanal*, the government fixed-price shop on Ave Hassan I.

● Tourist offices
Office du Tourisme (ONMT), 30 rue Mohammed V, T 967009.

● Useful addresses
Police: Blvd General Franco, T 19.

● Transport
Local Much of Tetouan can be reached on foot. A petit-taxi is a cheap alternative.

Air Aéroport de Sania R'Mel, 5 km away, T 971233, services to Rabat, Al Hoceima and Casablanca; Royal Air Maroc, 5 Ave Mohammed V, T 961260.

Road Bus: the bus station, at the corner of Ave Hassan I and rue Sidi Mandri, T 966263, has both CTM and private line services to most major destinations. Services to **Fnideq** (for Ceuta, 30 mins), **Chaouen** (1½ hrs), **Tanger** (1½ hrs), **Meknes** (8 hrs) and **Fes** (6 hrs). ONCF also operates a coach service to link up with the rail network at Tnine Sidi Lyamani. Through tickets can be bought from the office at Place el Adala, where the coach also departs from each day at 0650 and 1555. Buses to Martil, Cabo Negro and Mdiq leave from near the old railway station on Ave Massira, those for Oued Laou from the main bus station. **Taxi**: much of Tetouan is quite manageable on foot, but a cheap and reasonable alternative is a petit-taxi. Grand-taxis to Tanger, Fnideq (for Ceuta), Chaouen, the beaches and other places, leave from Blvd Maarakah Annoual or nearby.

Around Tetouan: the beaches

From Fnideq to Tetouan, the P28 passes through a flat strip of beaches and marshes, and a number of tourist developments. **Restinga Smir**, 22 km from Tetouan, has a long beach and a correspondingly long line of holiday complexes, hotels, bungalows and camping areas. It incl a *Club Méditerranée*, **D** *Hotel Carabo*, T 977070, 24 rm, bar, restaurant, pool, tennis and disco, the rec restaurant *Nuevo Le Chariot* with a sea view and fine sea food, *Al Fraia* campsite or *Camping Andalus* though there are many good campsites to choose from, and the small marina/pleasure port of **Marina Smir**. After Restinga Smir the road passes through **Kabila**, another beach and marina, and **Mdiq**, a small fishing port with some traditional boat construction. Accommodation ranges from **A** *Hotel Golden Beach*, T 975077, F 975096, 86 rm, on beach side opp bus station; **A** *Kabila Hotel*, T 975013, 96 rm, to **E** *Hotel Playa*, T 975166, and a campsite, as well as the *Restaurant du Port* and *Restaurant Al Khayma* in centre of town. After Mdiq turn for **Cabo Negro** which is 3.5 km off the P28. At Cabo Negro is another large *Club Méditerranée* adjacent to the golf course; as well as **D** *Hotel Petit Merou*, T 978115/6, 23 rm, restaurant, bar, disco. The *Restaurant La Ferma*, T 968075, with French food is only 1 km from main road. Horses for hire here.

Martil, Tetouan's former port, and a pirate base, it is now another resort, with a popular beach. Stay at the **E** *Hotel Etoile de la Mer*, Ave Mawlay al Hassan, T 6776, 30 rm; **E** *Hotel Nuzha*, rue Miramar; *Camping Martil*, by the river or *Camping Oued La Malah* clearly signed further out of town. *Hotel/Café Addiyafa* on right towards Tetouan, is recommended. Buses from Tetouan to Martil, Cabo Negro and Mdiq leave from Ave Massira, near the old railway station.

Oued Laou is 44 km from Tetouan, along the spectacular coastal road, the S608. It is a relaxed fishing village with an excellent beach but only basic facilities. Stay at **F** *Hotel-Café Oued Laou*; **F** *Hotel-Restaurant Laayoune*; or *Camping Laayoune*. Eat at the hotels or food stalls. Note the tiled octagonal mosque. An option from Oued Laou is to drive inland or take a bus to Chaouen.

The road continues along the coast through the villages of **Targa**, **Steha**, **Bou Hamed**, and **Dar M'Ter**. Possibly a more convenient place to stop is the final settlement, **El Jebha**, built by the Spanish. It is another fishing village and beach, with a *souq* on Tues morning. Stay at the **F** *Grand Hotel* or the **F** *Petit Hotel*, neither very good. It is served by buses from Tetouan and Chaouen. A tortuous mountain road, the 8500, takes the intrepid traveller to meet the P39 W of Ketama.

CHAOUEN AND THE NORTHERN RIF

Chaouen

(Pop 23,563 (1982); Alt 600m) Chaouen, 60 km from Tetouan, also called Chefchaouen, is a beautiful blue and whitewashed Andalusian town in the Rif, set above the Oued Laou valley. Chaouen lies below the twin peaks, Jbel ech-Chaouen, that have given it its name 'the horns'. Just nearby is the P28, N to Tetouan and S to Ouezzane, and the P39 E through the Rif to Al Hoceima. Lying within easy reach of Ceuta or Tanger, it is an excellent and peaceful introduction to Morocco. The selling of hashish is a big business here, but persistent refusal should rid travellers of unwanted attentions.

Here you may have your first sighting of the distinctive garments of the women of the Rif, the *fouta* or overskirt usually of red and white vertical stripes and the very large conical straw hat with woollen tassels.

Chaouen was founded in 1471 by Sherif Moulay Ali Ben Rachid, a follower of Moulay Abd es-Salam Ben Mchich, the patron saint of the local

Djeballa area whose tomb is nearby, in order to halt expansion further S of the Spanish and Portuguese. The city's population was later supplemented by Muslims and Jews expelled from Spain, particularly from Granada, and for a time the rulers of Chaouen controlled much of N Morocco, whilst the town also grew in importance as a pilgrimage centre.

From 1576 Chaouen was in conflict with, and isolated from, the surrounding area, with the gates locked each night. Prior to 1920 only three Christians had braved its forbidding walls, the Frenchman de Foucauld disguised as a *rabbi* in 1883, Walter Harris, Times correspondent and author of *Morocco that Was*, in 1889, and the American William Summers, poisoned in Chaouen in 1892. In 1920 Chaouen was taken over by the Spanish as part of their protectorate, when they found Jews still speaking 15th century Andalusian Spanish. The Spanish were thrown out from 1924 to 1926, by Abd al-Karim's Rifian resistance movement, but then returned to stay until Independence in 1956.

ACCESS Buses and grand-taxis will drop travellers on Ave Al Khattabi. Walk up through the market alongside to reach Ave Hassan II, then turn right to reach Bab el Aïn and the medina. There are many one-way streets which can be confusing for the motorist.

Places of interest

The Spanish-built new town of Chaouen is small and not very spectacular, but a pleasant and relaxing place. The centre is Place Mohammed V, with its small Andalusian garden. Ave Hassan II leads to Bab el Aïn and the medina. The market is down some steps from Ave Hassan II, on Ave Al Khattabi. Normally a food market, there is a local *souq* on Mon and Thur.

The Medina of Chaouen is one of the most rewarding to explore, sufficiently small not to get lost, but with intricate Andalusian architecture, arches, arcades and porches, white or blue-washed houses and clean, quiet cobbled streets. By car, park in Place el Makhzen and explore the rest on foot. Approaching the medina on foot, enter by Bab el Aïn. From Bab el Aïn a small road leads

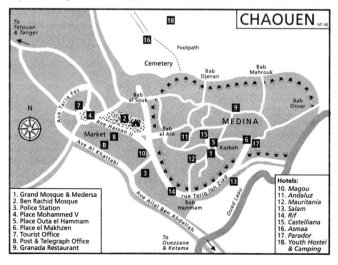

CHAOUEN MT 48

1. Grand Mosque & Medersa
2. Ben Rachid Mosque
3. Police Station
4. Place Mohammed V
5. Place Outa el Hammam
6. Place el Makhzen
7. Tourist Office
8. Post & Telegraph Office
9. Granada Restaurant

Hotels:
10. *Magou*
11. *Andaluz*
12. *Mauritania*
13. *Salam*
14. *Rif*
15. *Castelliana*
16. *Asmaa*
17. *Parador*
18. *Youth Hostel & Camping*

through to Place Uta el Hammam. This is the main square, lively at night, and surrounded by a number of stalls and café-restaurants, popular with *kif* (hashish) smokers.

The square is dominated by the 15th century kasbah, now the **Musée de Chefchaouen** (including the **Centre d'Etudes et de Recherches Andaluses**) (open 1000-1200 and 1400-1900, 0900-1700 in Ramadan). As a prison it housed the Rifi leader Abd al-Karim from 1926. The museum has an unremarkable exhibition of local costume, tools and instruments, but it is an interesting building, worth climbing to the top for a good view of the town from the roof, and exploring the dungeons and prison cells below. There is a quiet garden to relax in. Note the beautiful **Grand Mosque**, with its octagonal minaret, beside the kasbah, dating from the 15th century, but restored in the 17th and 18th. Next door is a 16th century **medersa**, unfortunately closed. Opposite the *Restaurant Kasbah*, at No 34, is an old *caravanserai*.

Further on, Place el Makhzen, the picturesque second square, has stalls along the top side, the **Ensemble Artisanal** at the end. Chaouen has a large number of artisans employed in metalwork, leatherwork, pottery and woodwork, amongst other crafts, and is particularly known for weaving the striped Rifi blankets, as seen on country women. It is well worth exploring the *souqs*, many of which are in the alleys S of Place Outa el Hammam.

For swimming there are several popular pools down in the Oued Laou, either walk or get a taxi. A pleasant pool to visit, and rest in a nearby café, is Ras el Ma, above the medina. Leave Place el Makhzen and head out above Bab Onsar.

Chaouen is a good base for *mountain walks*, with some spectacular scenery and plentiful animal and bird-life. Either take a guide or buy a map in Rabat. Expect suspicious questioning, and be prepared for a long and strenuous day.

Local information
● Accommodation

B *Hotel Parador*, Place el Makhzen, T 986324, 35 rm, bar, restaurant, pool, the best in Chaouen, a wonderful central location, comfortable and well-equipped, reservations needed.

C *Hotel Asmaa*, T/F 987158, 94 rm, placed insensitively on a hill above the town, but with an excellent view of the medina and the valley beyond, pool, bar, 2 tearooms, restaurant.

D *Hotel Magou*, 23 rue Moulay Idriss, outside Bab el Aïn, T 986257, 986275, 32 rm with bath, clean and rec.

E *Hotel Ibiza*, rue Sidi Mandri, T 986323, on the entry to the town from Tetouan, a small hotel which is highly rec; **E** *Hotel Rif*, 29 rue Tarik Ibn Ziad, T 986207, bar and restaurant, a friendly hotel with a restaurant and a good view from higher rooms; **E** *Hotel Salam*, 38 rue Tarik Ibn Ziad, T 986239, just below the medina, clean rooms with hot water, breakfast.

The cheap hotels and *pensiones* in Chaouen are often very good, basic but clean and very reasonably priced. The **F** *Andaluz* is clean and friendly with hot water, a few minutes walk from Place Outa el Hammam, follow signs; the **F** *Pensión Castilliana*, signposted just off the main square; and **F** *Auberge Granada*, up rue Targhi from Place Uta El Hammam, are also cheap; **F** *Pensión Mauritania*, 20 Kadi Alami, below the square, is a friendly place with music and a café; **F** *Pensión Ibn Batouta*, clean and quiet, just off the road between Bab el Aïn and Place Outa el Hammam.

● Youth hostel
T 986031, with 30 beds, meals available, kitchen, overnight fee MD20 and **Camping Municipal** are together, 2 km above the town nr the *Hotel Asmaa*. Follow the signs from the road in from Tetouan, or walk (diplomatically) through the cemetery above the medina. there is a small café, a shop, simple toilets and showers, tents amongst the trees, good view of the valley.

● Places to eat
♦♦ *Restaurant de l'Hotel Magou*, 23 rue Moulay Idriss, rec Moroccan food. More up-market are the *Hotel Asma* and the *Hotel Parador*, the latter with an extensive French-Moroccan menu.

◆There are several cafés and restaurants on the main square, Place Uta el Hammam such as *Restaurant Azhar*, rue Moulay Idris, friendly restaurant nr the *Hotel Magou*; *Restaurant Kasbah*; also try *Restaurant Tissemlal*, 22 rue Targhi, with excellent Moroccan food; *Restaurant Zouar*, rue Moulay Ali Ben Rachid, nr the main square, wide range of cheap Spanish dishes incl fish; *Restaurant La Plaza Grande Kazba*, rue Targhi, cheap Moroccan food nr the main Place Uta el Hammam. For a modestly priced licensed restaurant go to *Restaurant-Bar Omo Rabi*, on rue Tarik Ibn Ziad. *Pâtisserie Magou*, Ave Hassan II, is good for bread and cakes; the *Hotel Parador* and *Hotel Asma* are good for a drink and view.

● **Banks & money changers**
Banque Populaire, Ave Hassan II; BMCE, Ave Hassan II.

● **Hospitals & medical services**
Chemist: beside the *Hotel Magou*.

● **Post & telecommunications**
Area code: 09.
Post Office: PTT, Ave Hassan II.

● **Tourist offices**
Syndicat d'Initiative, Place Mohammed V, open mornings.

● **Transport**
Road Bus: CTM is just down from Bab el Aïn. Private line buses run from the station next to the market, on Ave Al Khattabi. Buses are often through services and can thus be full. There are several buses a day for **Ouezzane**, 2 daily for **Meknes** (5 hrs), 1 per day for **Fes** (6 hrs), several a day for **Tetouan**, 2 daily for **Al Hoceima** (8 hrs), 2 a week for **El Jebha** (7 hrs). **Grand-taxis**: leave from the bus station on Ave Al Khattabi to most destinations.

The Northern Rif

The P39 from Chaouen to Al Hoceima is one of Morocco's most dramatic journeys, a route through a succession of small villages with stunning views over the remote valleys and towards the snow-capped Rif Mountains. Care must be taken on this narrow, hill-top road which may be closed by snow in winter. Traditionally this was an area of unrest against central authorities, notably in the Rif rebellion of Abd el-Krim against

the Spanish from 1921 to 1926, whilst more recently bandits have preyed on travellers. Today the situation has improved, and the main dilemma is how to replace the production of *kif* (hashish) as the principal economic activity. Despite government programmes and pressures from Europe, production continues. Along this road it will be assumed that all travellers are there for the sole purpose of buying *kif* (hashish), and the numerous vendors are unlikely to believe anything else, and can be aggressive, so do not stop. There is often close cooperation between the police and the vendors, and sentences can be stiff.

Ketama is the centre of hashish growing and selling, although it had a previous importance as a walking resort. Although it has little else of interest and can be a stressful place to stay, it is perhaps the most comfortable along this road, with the **C** *Hotel Tidighine* in the town centre, 67 rm, an old Spanish hotel with tennis, pool, bar and restaurant. Cheaper options are the **F** *Café-Hotel Saada* and **F** *California*.

The S302 runs S from Ketama to Taounate, Aïn Aicha and Fes with views of deep valleys and forested slopes. This road, the *Route de l'Unité*, was built just after Independence by voluntary labour battalions, to link the Spanish Protectorate of the N with the French Protectorate to the S.

E of Ketama, along the P39, the Rif becomes increasingly barren. After 12 km 8500 branches off to the left, a 61 km drive to the small coastal resort of El Jebha (see page 108). 30 km further there is another road, the 8501 to Torres de Alcala, a tiny fishing village, with some basic café-hotels. Just E of Torres de Alcala is the site of the port of Badis, destroyed in 1564, and offshore, the small island of Penon de Velez de la Gomera, still owned by the Spanish. 4 km W of Torres de Alcala is a campsite near Kalah Iris one of the most beautiful Mediterranean beaches.

Back on the P39 the next stop is Targuist by the Oued Rhis, a more peaceful alternative to Ketama, and a safer place from which to explore the mountains. There are many walks and rides in the cedar forests here. This is where Abd al-Karim finally surrendered. Stop at **F** *Hotel Chaab* or **F** *Hotel Café-Restaurant El Mostakbel* by the square where the buses stop. Visit the small handicraft centre. There are fairly regular buses and grand-taxis to Al Hoceima.

THE MEDITERRANEAN COAST

Al Hoceima

(*Pop* 41,662; Tanger 300 km, Melilla 170 km, Algerian border 250 km) Al Hoceima (previously Alhucemas), is a beautiful though not overly developed resort. The *Club Méditerranée* lies about 10 mins E of the town, and the Maroc-Touriste complex is down from the centre by the beach. The beauty of its location, above a clear blue bay, makes a visit worthwhile though the difficulty of approach by road reduces the flow of casual visitors. The character of the centre is distinctly Spanish, reflecting input in the protectorate years. Established by the Spanish in 1926 as Villa Sanjurjo, it was built as a garrison to control the Beni Ouriaghel tribe, of which Abd al-Karim was the chief, immediately after the Rif rebellion. To the E of Al Hoceima is the long and less busy beach of the Alhumecas bay, offshore is Peñon de Alhumecas, a remarkable idiosyncrasy of history. This small rocky island, topped by a few buildings and a church, is owned and occupied by Spain and apparently used as a prison. It is completely dependent on Melilla for supplies and even water, and has no contact with the Moroccan mainland, off which it sits like a ship at anchor.

Places of interest

View the vibrant Place du Rif, from the crazily decorated *Florido Café*. The souq, busiest on Tues, is unremarkable. The new town of Al Hoceima is dominated by Ave Mohammed V (banks and cafés) which leads down to the rather characterless Place du Marche Verte. Rue Tarik Ibn Ziad to the left has some crumbling Spanish colonial buildings while to the right a road curves down to the main beach (note on the left the intricate and colourful old Spanish school) and the port. The beach is dominated by the *Hotel Quemado* complex, open to non-residents, offers watersports, scuba diving, busy in the summer. There is no shortage of good beaches nearby. Visit the port area, which includes a fishing port (some good fish restaurants) as well as a naval port closed to visitors. A relaxed place to wander.

Local information

● **Accommodation**

D *Hotel Quemado*, reservations by Maroc Tourist in Rabat T 763915, an ugly complex but with an ideal beach location, comfortable rooms, bungalows and villas, restaurant, bar, nightclub, tennis; **D** *Hotel Maghreb El Jadid*, Ave Mohammed V, T 982504, 40 good rm, restaurant, the best option in the town.

E *Hotel Karim*, 25 Ave Hassan II, T 982184, clean and reasonable establishment, bar and restaurant; **E** *Hotel National*, 23 Rue Tetouan, T 982141, 16 a/c rm with bath, telephone, breakfast room and TV room.

F *Hotel Florido*, 40 Place du Rif (Sahat Rif), T 982235, a stylish pink and white Spanish building dominating the main square, once the town's casino, friendly, clean, best rooms overlook the square, cold showers, restaurant, café; or as a fall-back the **F** *Hotel de Station*, Place du Rif, basic, cold showers, friendly, convenient for buses; **F** *Rif Hotel*, rue Sultan Moulay Youssef, also rec; or at the camping sites, *El Jamil*, T 982009, 2 km E; *Kalah Iris*, nearby and cheaper.

● **Places to eat**

There are few top eating options in Al Hoceima but try ◆◆◆ *Hotel Maghreb El Jadid*, Ave Mohammed V, T 982504, with a mixed French, Spanish and Moroccan menu, or *Hotel*

Karim, 25 Ave Hassan II, T 982184, French and Spanish cuisine, good for fish. At the port there are several good **fish restaurants** incl ◆◆ *Restaurant Karim*, T 982310, licensed; *Restaurant Scorpio Sahara*, T 4410, *Restaurant Chez Mimoune*, and the rougher, licensed ◆ *Bar-Restaurant des Poissons*, most do not speak French. Other economic options in town are *Restaurant Mabrouk* or *Restaurant Al Hoceima* in rue Izzemounen just off Place du Rif, both serving *tagines*.

● **Banks & money changers**
Mainly on Ave Mohammed V, incl **Banque Populaire** (at No 47), BMCE, BMC and SGMB.

● **Hospital & medical services**
Hôpital Mohammed V, Ave Hassan II, nearby to a number of pharmacists.

● **Shopping**
Markets: Souq is on Tues, fish market each morning.

● **Tourist offices**
Délégation Regionale du Tourisme, Immeuble Cabalo, rue Tarik Ibn Ziad off Place Marche Verte, T 982830 (0830-1200 and 1400-1800), small but friendly.

● **Transport**
Local The town is small enough to explore on foot but for the port or beaches hail one of the blue and beige petit-taxis.

Air The airport, Aéroport Côte du Rif is at Charif al Idrissi, 17 km from Al Hoceima, T 982063, with flights to **Amsterdam** (2 a week) and **Brussels** (1 a week), **Tanger** and **Casablanca** (2 a week) and **Tetouan** and **Rabat** (1 a week).

Road Bus: all buses leave from Place du Rif, which has ticket booths for the different companies. Most buses leave early in the morning. CTM (T 982273) services to **Casablanca** (2000: 10 hrs), **Nador** (0500, 1230: 7 hrs), **Tetouan** (3 per day), **Targuist** (3 per day); private line services to **Tetouan** (0700, 0800, 1900, 10 hrs), **Nador** (0600, 0955, 1315, 1400, 1530, 1745), **Targuist** (0315, 0700, 0815, 0945, 1900), **Tanger** (0800), **Oujda** (1100, 5 hrs), **Fes** (0315, 0945, 12 hrs), **Ketama** (0315, 0945). **Taxi**: grand-taxis leave from just off Place du Rif, to **Nador**, **Taza** and **Targuist**, amongst other destinations.

Nador

Between Al Hoceima and Nador the P39

winds inland through the foothills of the Rif, which are fairly deserted. One can stop at two roadside towns, **Drouiche** with the basic **F** *Hotel Es-Salam*, and **Mont Aroui**, with the similar **F** *Hotel Hassan*. At **Selouane**, a small mining and industrial settlement, the P39 continues inland to Nador and Melilla, whilst the P27 leads off to Berkane, Ahfir, Oujda and Algeria.

Nador (*Pop* 62,040), is a relaxed settlement with the atmosphere, commerce and transport of a border town, and it is most likely that travellers will pass through only en route or from Melilla. This modern city is now a major port and industrial centre and has a university. It is not a typical Moroccan town. There is a pleasant walk by the lagoon on Blvd Zerktoun, the cafés and evening promenade are on Ave Mohammed V, where the banks and travel agents are located.

20 km round the lagoon to the E is a good beach at Qariat Arkmane, where there are also some good fish restaurants, the *Karia Plage* camping site and birdwatching opportunities. Some continue to Ras el Ma for birdwatching.

Local information
● **Accommodation**
C *Hotel Rif*, 1 Ave Youssef Ben Tachfine, T 603635, at seaside, restaurant, nightclub, pool and tennis, large and well-equipped; **C** *Hotel Ryad*, Ave Mohammed V, BP60, T 607715, F 607719, 41 rm, 18 suites, lavish decor, restaurant with Moroccan and international cuisine, 2 bars, café, 24 hrs room service.

D *Hotel Mediterranée*, 2-4 rue Youssef Ben Tachfine, opp *Rif*, T 602611, restaurant.

E *Hotel Annoual*, pleasant but over-priced; **E** *Hotel le Marche Verte* also called *Hotel al Massira Khadra*, 106 rue Ibn Rochd, T 606721, an excellent option in the lower-price bracket. The cheap hotels are in and around Ave Youssef Ben Tachfine.

● **Places to eat**
◆◆ *Hotel Rif*, T 606535, and *Hotel Ryad*, T 607715, both have international and Moroccan cuisine.

♦♦ Slightly less expensive, with good fish dishes, is *Restaurant Romero*, on the corner of Ave Hassan II and Ave Yacoub El Mansour.

♦There are cheap reasonable restaurants serving Moroccan food in Ave Hassan II, try *Restaurant Centrale* or *Restaurant Kanaria*. The best cafés are on Ave Mohammed V.

● **Tourist offices**
80 Blvd Ibn Rochd, T 606518.

● **Transport**
Road The bus station, a noisy, busy, dirty place is at the end of Ave Hassan II, near the junction with Ave des Forces Armées Royales. CTM buses run to **Tetouan** (0930, 1800), **Al Hoceima** (0900, 1645), **Oujda** (0600, 0800, 0900, 1500) and **Casablanca** (2000); private lines run to **Ras El Ma** (1130, 1400), **Kariat Arekmane** (0900, 1230, 1730), **Guercif** (1220), **Oujda** (14 from 0600-1830), **Tanger** (0415, 1600, 1700, 2130), **Tetouan** (0415, 0530, 0800, 1700, 1800, 1900), **Ceuta** (1700), **Chaouen** (0415, 1115, 1700), **Targuist** (0415, 1115, 1700), **Al Hoceima** (10 between 0415-1700), **Casablanca** (1600, 1700, 1800, 2000, 2030), **Rabat** (1900, 2000), **Meknes** (0500, 1030, 1730), **Fes** (0000, 0500, 0630, 0800, 1200, 1730), **Taza** (1300, 1340), **Taourirt** (1345, 1500, 1515), **Berkane** (1130, 1330), and to **Ketama** and **Bab Taza**. ONCF, the railway company, run a bus at 2000 to **Taourirt** to connect with the trains to **Fes**, **Meknes**, **Rabat** and **Casablanca**. **Taxi**: grand-taxis from beside the bus station, with numerous destinations including **Ahfir** (over 1 hr) and from there to **Saïdia**, to the border with **Spanish Melilla** (MD4), to **Al Hoceima** (MD50), **Meknes** and **Fes**. **Boat**: there is a Comanov car and passenger ferry service from Nador to Séte in France, every 4 days from Jun to Sep, tickets and information from Comanov Passages, Immeuble Lazaar Beni Enzar, BP 89, T 06608538, or from the same company in Casablanca, 43 Ave des Forces Armées Royales, T 03310015/6.

Melilla

Melilla, just beyond Nador, has been a Spanish enclave since 1497. As with the larger Ceuta, although it has North African influences, it is clearly European, and a change for those on a long visit to Morocco, but is a declining and unexciting town.

The old quarter of **Medina Sidonia**, separated from the new town by the garden of the Plaza de España, and on an outcrop beside the ferry terminal, is an interesting quarter to explore, with a mixture of Moroccan and Spanish architectural influences and narrow winding streets, contained within the 16th century citadel walls. Enter by **Puerta de Santiago** on Paseo General Macias or **Fosa de Hornabeque** by the port. Whilst in the citadel find time to visit the **Iglesia de la Concepción**, a church, and the **Museo Municipal** (open 0900-1300 and 1500-1800), with coins, maps and historical archives, and Roman pottery.

Construction of the new town began in the 19th century, with many buildings designed by the modernist architect Enrique Nieto, but like Ceuta it is an uninspiring town. Ave de Juan Carlos I is the most popular street in the evening. There is a bull-ring at the Plaza de Toros.

Local information
● **Accommodation**
A *Parador Don Pedro de Estopina*, T 684940, with 27 rm.

B *Hôtel Nacional*, T 684540, 10 Avda Primo de Rivera.

C *Hostal Residencia Miramar*, Paseo General Macias.

D *Hostal España*, T 684645, Avda de Juan Carlos I, homely and reasonable; **D** *Pensión Numéro 7*, Ave de Generalisimo. There is also a camping site.

● **Places to eat**
For those missing Moroccan food already, or impatient to try it, go to *Le Marrakech*, nr the port. For reasonably-priced Spanish food try *Bar El Rincón*, rue Lopez Moreno; or *El Mesón de Comidas*, at 9 Calle Castelon, a good street for bars and restaurants, incl also *Bodegas Madrid*. A selection of *tapas* in some of the bars is a good option. Food can turn out quite a lot more expensive than in Morocco. After the disappointing ice-creams of Morocco, *Heladeria Alaska*, Ave du Generalisimo, may come as a welcome relief.

● **Banks & money changers**
Banks: are on Avda de Juan Carlos I.

● **Shopping**

Duty free: as with Ceuta there is a range of duty-free shops, with unimpressive prices, and Moroccan *bazaars*, best wait for the genuine thing.

● **Tourist offices**

20 Calle del General Aizpura (open 0900-1400 and 1600-1800, Mon-Fri, 1000-1200, Sat).

● **Transport**

Air There are several flights a day for Málaga.

Road Buses to near the **border** with Morocco run from Plaza de España. From the other side take a grand-taxi, or one of the regular buses, into Nador. **NB** The border into Morocco will take time and patience to cross. Hire cars cannot be taken across.

Sea Ferry services connect Melilla with Almería (Mon-Sat in the summer, 3 per week in the winter, 8 hrs) and Málaga (daily Mon-Sat, 10 hrs). Buy tickets from the RENFE office on Calle Gen O'Donnel, Transmediterranea on Calle Gen Marina or from the ferry terminal.

Eastwards towards Algeria

From just S of Nador, at Selouane, the P27 branches off the P39, leading to the Algerian border at Ahfir, 91 km to the E a pleasant if undramatic journey through the Rif foothills. From Berkane, 79 km from Nador, an interesting diversion to the S takes travellers through the **Zegzel Gorges**, dramatic both in the rock formations and the vegetation on the slopes and terraces. It is an exhilarating place for a walk, and quite trouble-free after the hashish producing areas. Those without their own transport can also visit the area by taking a grand-taxi to Taforalt and another from there through the gorges. Stop off at the unlit **Grotte du Chameau cave**, just before the gorges, for the stalactites and hot stream, but be careful not to get lost in the tunnels. Back on the P27 the next town after Berkane is Ahfir, a quiet border town. From here there are three options, N to the nearby resort of Saïdia about 20 km, E into Algeria or S through the Col de Guerbouss with good views, and the flat Plains des Angads into Oujda.

Saïdia

The road to Saïdia runs parallel to the Algerian border, at one point through a narrow gorge when all that separates the traveller from Algeria is the narrow but ironically named Oued Kiss. Saïdia is a pleasant resort popular with Moroccans, which has not been overly developed, and perhaps lacks some comforts. It is packed in the summer, with no shortage of places to eat, but limited and expensive hotels, some of which are closed in winter, when the place is fairly deserted. There is a 12 km long attractive sandy beach, views of the Spanish held Islas Chafarinas and of Algeria, and a still occupied 19th century kasbah. It is an easy place to walk around, with a grid of brightly coloured houses, restaurants and hotels parallel to the beach.

● **Accommodation** Hotel options are limited, particularly as many are closed out of season, but try **C** *Hotel Hannour*, rue Sidi Mohammed, T 615115, a large, ugly place, good for a meal or drink. **D** *Hotel Select*, rue Sidi Mohammed, similar to *Hannour*, T 615110. **E** *Hotel Al Kalaa*, rue Laayoune, by the beach, T 615123, 33 rm, small restaurant and bar; and **E** *Hotel Medierannée*, rue Laayoune, cold showers, best of basic hotels. There are also several camp sites: *Camping du Sit* for families, *Camping Caravaning Al Mansur*, and *Camping Tours*. Saïdia is well-connected with Oujda by bus and grand-taxi.

● **Places to eat** Several standard restaurants on rue Sidi Mohammed, open all year round, incl ◆*Café Restaurant Plus*. Try ◆*Café Bleu* in rue Laayoune, relaxed and friendly atmosphere.

● **Transport** Grand-taxis leave from rue Laayoune or from the tree-lined road behind and parallel to rue Sidi Mohammed, to **Ahfir** (20 mins), and on to **Oujda**, **Berkane** and **Nador**.

OUEZZANE AND THE SOUTHERN RIF

An alternative route follows the P28 through the cork oaks and coniferous forest from Chaouen to Ouezzane. Look out for Pont de Loukkos, the old border post with café and stalls. However, whilst Ouezzane is a memorable town imbued with the atmosphere of an historic pilgrimage centre, and the scenery E is impressive, the opportunities for visitors are sparse.

Ouezzane

Ouezzane with a population of 41,000 is 60 km S of Chaouen along the P28, and like the latter has a dramatic hillside location, with impressive views of the rugged Rif Mountains and the verdant valleys between. It is worth visiting en route from Chaouen to Meknes or Fes.

The town was founded in 1727 by Moulay Abdellah Sherif founder of the Tabiya Islamic order. This brotherhood achieved great national prominence from the 18th century when the *zaouia*, or monastery, they had founded in Ouezzane, became the focus of extensive pilgrimage activity. Ouezzane had close links with the Sultan's court, which was often dependent on the *zaouia* and its followers for support.

Ironically, in view of the veneration Muslims accorded the *sherifs*, the then *Sherif* of Ouezzane married the Englishwoman Emily Keane in 1877 in an Anglican service, after they had met at the house of the American Consul where Keane was governess, although she later separated from him to live out her dotage in Tanger, where she is now buried in the Anglican Church. The *zaouia's* importance was destroyed by the *sherif's* growing connection with the French.

Ouezzane has importance today in the production of olive oil, and because of its *souq* on Thur, drawing in local farmers and tradesmen.

ACCESS Road The P28 to the N leads to Chaouen and Tetouan, S to Meknes. The P26 is to Fes and the P23 to Rabat and Casablanca. These roads meet at Place de l'Indépendence, the main square. There are numerous grand-taxis to Chaouen, and others to Souq El Arba du Gharb and Meknes. Buses to Chaouen (80 mins), Meknes (4 hrs) and Fes (5½ hrs) pass through Ouezzane, calling at Place de l'Indépendence.

Places of interest

The **medina** of Ouezzane has some of the most interesting architecture in the Rif, with the picturesque tiled roof houses along winding cobbled streets. The focus of the town is the 18th century *zaouia*, on rue de la Zaouia, a distinctive green-tiled building with an octagonal minaret. Non-Muslims should not approach too close. Nearby are old lodgings for the pilgrims and the decaying Sherifian palace.

Place de l'Indépendence, the centre of the medina, is busiest during the town *souq* on Thur. To get to the permanent craft *souqs*, centred around Place Bir Inzarane, follow rue Abdellah Ibn Lamlih up from Place de l'Indépendence. Ouezzane is particularly known for woollen carpets woven in the weavers' *souq* at the top of the town. The smiths' *souq* is along rue Haddadine. There is a **Centre Artisanale** on Place de l'Indépendence, and another on Ave Hassan II, open 0800-1900.

● **Accommodation** Ouezzane is very limited for hotels, and is perhaps best visited in passing or as an excursion from Chaouen. Choose between F *Marhaba*; F *Horloge*; and F *El Elam*, on Place de l'Indépendence; or the more basic F *Grand Hotel* on Ave Mohammed V, although none of these is an attractive option. Eat at the basic café-restaurants on Place de l'Indépendence. *Café Africa*, 10 km N is a good place to stop.

East of Ouezzane

From Ouezzane, the P26 goes SE as far as Fes-el-Bali. This Rifian village is on the site of the ruined Almoravid 11th century city, the walls of which can still be seen, along with the *hammam*. From here the P26 continues S, 84 km to Fes a long winding route on an adequate road, good surface but poor camber. There are excellent views and a scattering of settlements, their tree lined approach indicating the French influence, providing the essential petrol and drinks, best S of Port du Sebou. Construction of a new barrage on the Oued Ouerrha N of Fes-el-Bali causes some delays. Of note, and perhaps the only reason to take this route, are the unique *white villages* where all the buildings and the straw stacks are plastered with lime and local clay and merge into the landscape. Difficult to photograph. A daily bus from Ouezzane to Fes follows this route. The S304 weaves E through the Rif, 17 km to Ourtzargh, where a side road takes intrepid drivers to the village of Rafsai (Ghafsai), an olive market, from where a track leads to Jbel Lalla Outka, a 1,595m mountain from which there are extensive views over much of the Rif.

The next stopping point is Taounate, an uninteresting town with a large *souq* on Fri. From here it is possible to continue N to Ketama and S to Fes on the S302 (the **Route de l'Unité**). It is a long and tortuous drive to Aknoul from which there is a 39 km drive N to the P39 between Al Hoceima and Nador, and 53 km S to Taza on P1, with grand-taxis.

NORTHERN AND CENTRAL ATLANTIC COAST

CONTENTS

The Northern Coast   118
Casablanca and Environs   123
El Jadida and Environs   131
Central Atlantic Coast   134

MAPS

North & Central Atlantic Coast   118
Casablanca   125
Casablanca Medina   126
Casablanca Centre   128
El Jadida   133
Essaouira   137

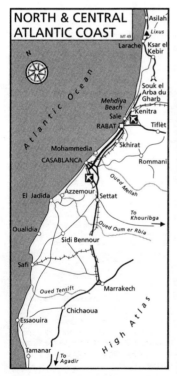

NORTH & CENTRAL
ATLANTIC COAST MT 49

The Atlantic Coast has a wide variety of environments, reflecting its great length. At its centre is the immense axis of cities which dominate the country demographically, industrially, economically and politically, from Kenitra in the N, through Sale, Rabat, Mohammedia, to Casablanca in the S. This massive city, the second largest in Africa, has many of the facilities and problems of cities elsewhere in the Third World and is just as typical of modern Morocco as Fes or Marrakech. Elsewhere are a series of walled cities, initially built by the Portuguese, and now often relaxed beach resorts, including Asilah, El Jadida, Safi and Essaouira.

THE NORTHERN COAST

Asilah

"Surrounded by the still imposing zone of its old, ruinous grey ramparts, covered with lichen that preys upon them, the ancient town, so often captured and recaptured, is quietly dying away in the proud sepulchre of its lofty decaying walls ...."
Montbard, George, *Among the Moors* (1894).

With a population of 19,000 (1982), Asilah is a striking fishing port and coastal town of white and blue houses, surrounded by ramparts and lying alongside an extensive beach. As the first stopping point S of Tanger by road or rail, it provides an excellent introduction to Morocco, in spite of the extent to which tourism dominates. If it is possible, visit in Aug for the cultural festival, the *International Festival of Asilah*.

History

The site of Asilah was occupied by the Phoenicians, who called it *Silis*, and later by the Carthaginians, Byzantines and Romans. After destruction by the Romans, the town was rebuilt in 966 by El Hakim II, ruler of Cordoba. It was the last stronghold of the Idrissid Dynasty. The Portuguese occupied Asilah from 1471, and built the town's impressive fortifications, and in 1578 King Sebastian landed there on his way to defeat in the *Battle of the Three Kings*. This defeat led to the Spanish absorption of Portugal, and thus of Asilah, but the Portuguese influence on the town is still quite discernible.

The Moroccans recovered Asilah in 1691, under Moulay Ismail. In 1826 Austria bombarded Asilah, then a base of piracy, as did the Spanish in 1860. In the late 19th and early 20th century Ahmed al-Rasouli, the bandit chief who terrorized much of the NW of Morocco, was based in the town, as described by his one time hostage and later friend, Walter Harris, in *Morocco That Was*. Al-Rasouli built his palace in the medina, and from it exercised power over much of the region, being for a time its governor. The Spanish took Asilah in 1911, as part of their protectorate of N Morocco.

ACCESS Train The train station is just to the N of the town, a distance which can be walked, or if heavily laden, travelled in a taxi or local bus. There are frequent trains from Tanger, so this is a practical day excursion. **Road** Just off the P2 from Tanger to Rabat. Buses arrive in the town centre, 5 mins walk from the medina. Grand-taxis take an hour from Tanger, and drop passengers a short walk from the medina, near the bus station.

Places of interest

The **medina** is the main interest of Asilah, a quarter of predominately white and blue buildings, reflecting in their design the influences of Portuguese and Spanish occupation. Note the modern murals on some of the houses in the medina, painted by artists during the festival. The ramparts were built by the Portuguese in the 15th century, and are broken by a number of important gates, including **Bab el Kasbah**, **Bab el Bahar**, 'the sea gate', **Bab el Hamar** 'the land gate', an impressive structure topped with the eroded Portuguese coat of arms, as well as **Bab el Jbel**, 'the mountain gate', and **Bab Ihoumer**. At points it is possible to climb the fortifications for impressive views of the town and along the coast. Within the medina, **Le Palais de la Culture** is a cultural centre converted from the former residence of the brigand Ahmed al-Rasouli, built in 1909 right beside the sea. It is difficult to gain access except during the festival, but it is quite possible to visualize those who incurred al-Rasouli's wrath being made to walk the plank from the palace windows over the cliff front.

The Souq The Thur market attracts farmers from the surrounding area. In addition to the sale of the usual fruit, spices and vegetables, handicrafts distinctive of the Rif region are also on display.

The International Festival of Asilah, a cultural festival which has taken place in Asilah since 1978, involves performers from all over the world. Events throughout the town each Aug attract many spectators.

The **beach** is often windy, frequented by bathers, men touting camel rides, and fishermen, but at times can be quite perfect. The beach stretches beyond the building works to the N of the city, and to the S.

Local information
● Accommodation

C *Hotel Al Khaima*, Route de Tanger, BP 101, T 917230, F 917566, 113 rm with bath, on edge of town with restaurant, disco, bar, pool, tennis.

D *Hotel Ouad El Makhazine*, Ave Melilla, T 917090, 917500, 29 rm with a/c, no showers, best hotel in the town centre, restaurant, bar and café, but with unexciting atmosphere and decor; **D** *Hotel Mansur*, 49 Ave Mohammed V, T 917390, 8 rm with bath, is a reliable choice.

E *Hotel l'Oasis*, 8 Place des Nations Unies, T 917186, 12 rm, an old palace with restaurant and bar.

F *Hotel Asilah*, 79 Ave Hassan II, T 917286, 11 rm, reasonable, friendly and central; **F** *Hotel Marhaba*, 9 rue Zallakah, T 917144, nr the medina, adequate and cheap, rooms poorly sound-proofed but with colourful decor; **F** *Hotel Nasr*, Place Zallakah, cheap and basic; **F** *Hotel Sahara*, 9 rue Tarfaya, T 917185, 24 rm, not very exciting.

● **Camping**
There are numerous camping sites just N of the town along the road to Asilah, incl *Camping International*, with full facilities; *Camping Ocean*; *Camping Atlas*; *Camping Echrigui*, T 917182, with a shop and restaurant; and the adjacent *As Saadi* which is rec.

● **Places to eat**
♦♦ *La Alcazaba*, 2 Place Zallakah outside the ramparts, T 917012, an excellent Italian/Spanish restaurant concentrating on fish and seafood dishes; *Casa Garcia*, rue Ya'qub al-Mansur, is also rec for similar food. ♦ *El Espignon* and *El Oceano* are both on Place Zallach just outside the ramparts. Several places here sell excellent and very fresh fish dishes.

● **Banks & money changers**
Banque Hispano-Marocaine, Place Mohammed V, T 917321.

● **Hospitals & medical services**
Chemist: *Pharmacie Loukili*, Ave de la Liberté, T 917278.
Hospital: Ave du 2 Mars, T 917318.

● **Post & telecommunications**
PTT, Place des Nations Unies.

● **Useful addresses**
Police: Ave de la Liberté, T 19 or 917089.

● **Transport**
Train Asilah railway station is just outside the town alongside the P2 to Tanger, T 987320, and can be reached by local bus, by either petite or grand-taxi from Place Mohammed V. There are six trains daily to Tanger; 4 daily to Meknes, Fes and Oujda and 2 daily to Rabat and Casablanca.

Road Bus: the bus station is on Ave de la Liberté, T 987354. There are regular bus links with Tanger, Ouezzane, Tetouan, Meknes, Rabat and Casablanca. Taxi: grand-taxis which are particularly convenient for Tanger, leave from Place Mohammed V.

Larache

Although with less appeal than Asilah, Larache is a relaxed, faded seaside town, with a good beach and not too many tourists, a halfway house between Spanish and Moroccan urban life. The town is easily reached by the P2 from either Tanger or Rabat. The bus station is just off Ave Hassan II.

Larache is called El Araish in Arabic, a name which refers to the vine arbours of the Beni Arous, a local tribe. The occupation of the area dates back to the Phoenician, Carthaginian and Roman settlement of nearby **Lixus**. Larache was occupied by the Spanish from 1610 to 1689, and as part of their protectorate, from 1911. They then added the harbour and the new town, using it as the principal port of their N Morocco zone. Larache has fruit processing and exporting activities, as well as fishing, but has lost its status as a major port. Amongst a small foreign population a former resident of Larache was Jean Genet, French playwright, now buried in the Spanish graveyard.

Places of interest

On the way into Larache from Rabat, travellers pass **La Cigogne** (also called Castillo de las Ciguenas or Al Fath), a large fort built either by Moulay Ahmed al-Mansur and his Christian slaves in 1578, or during the subsequent Spanish occupation. The 16th century **Kebibat Fortress** is near the port, seeming to rise out of the sea, and now used as a hospital. Ave Mohammed V is the main street of the new town, with gardens on either side as well as a castle on the right and the **Iglesia de Nuestra Señora del Pilar** on the left (as heading to the centre). The circular Place de la Liberation with a fountain, is the heart of the town, lying between the medina and the new town.

Bab el Khemis leads off Place de la Liberation to the medina, a poor quarter but with some architectural appeal. Just inside is the Spanish built market square. There is a number of *souqs* in the medina, notably **Socco de la Alcaiceria**, the cloth market, a picturesque sight, in an otherwise unexciting old town. At the edge of the medina is the **Moroccan National Academy of Music**, built by the Spanish in 1915, near to an **Archaeological Museum**, open 0900-1200 and 1500-1730, Wed-Sun, which includes some items from Lixus. The medina is surrounded by a thick rampart. Through this **Bab el Kasbah** leads through to the ruined mediaeval kasbah.

For the main beach take town bus No 4, or a boat across the estuary. This is an extensive strip of fine beach, with a number of cafés nearby.

Local information
● Accommodation

D *Hotel Riad*, Ave Moulay Mohammed Ben Abdallah, T 912626/29, Tx 33803, a converted former residence of the Duchess of Guise, large well-maintained gardens, good restaurant and bar, tennis and pool, 24 rm, half-board required.

E *Gran Hotel España*, 6 Ave Hassan II/Place de la Liberation, T 913195, is the best cheap option.

F *Hotel Cervantes*, Place de la Liberation, a rather dismal place; the *pensiones* just off Ave Moulay Mohammed Ben Abdallah, **F** *Pensión Es-Saada*; **F** *Pensión Amal*, T 912788; and **F** *Pensión Palmera*; and *Pensión Atlas* in the medina.

● Places to eat

♦♦*Restaurant Al Khozama*, 114 Ave Mohammed V, T 914454.

♦Cheaper eating options are *La Grotte de Pêche*, 7 rue Tarik Ibn Ziad, a fish restaurant; *Le Medina*, a small Moroccan place in the medina; *Restaurant Oscar*, just off Ave Mohammed V; and *Restaurant Larache*, on Ave Moulay Mohammed Ben Abdallah.

● Shopping

Ensemble Artisanal is on the road out to Rabat.

● Tourist offices

There is a **Syndicat d'Initiative** on Ave Mohammed V, T 913532.

Excursion to ancient Lixus

Lixus is perhaps the second most important Roman site in Morocco after Volubilis, and lies just N of Larache on the right bank of the Oued Loukkos. Immediately after the bridge look out for a sign to Plage Las Rimmel. Some writers located at Lixus the Garden of Hesperides, with the golden apples harvested by Hercules to gain his place on Mt Olympus more likely to have been oranges. There was a Phoenician and Carthaginian settlement here, and the Romans made it a colony, with particular importance under the Emperor Claudius, when it exported salt, olives and fish. Lixus had a strategic position on the road from Tingis (Tanger) to Sala Colonia (Rabat) and was occupied until the 5th century AD.

To reach the site follow the Tanger road out of the town, take a bus across from the town, or bus No 4. The site is open during daylight hours. It is not enclosed, entry is free. If you wander in someone will come and offer to show you round. The lower town includes several salt factories. The upper town includes an acropolis complex, with temples dating back as far as the 7th century BC, and a Christian basilica. Between the two parts of the site are a bath house with mosaics of Neptune and shellfish, an amphitheatre and theatre.

Beyond Lixus the road to the beach has picnic and camping areas, salt flats and traditional shipbuilding.

Ksar el Kebir, Arbaoua, Souq el Arba du Gharb and Moulay Bousselham

Ksar el Kebir means the 'Great Fortress'. An 11th century settlement here was expanded and fortified by Ya'qub al-Mansur in the late 12th century. Near the town in 1578 was fought the famous Battle of Three Kings, where King Sebastian of Portugal, Saadian Sultan Abd al-Malek, and a claimant to the throne, former Sultan El Mutawakkil, all died. Moulay Ismail destroyed much of the town in the 17th century. The Spanish occupied Ksar el Kebir in 1911, rebuilding it and calling it Alcazarquivir, and developing it as a military centre. There is a large regional market (Sun) outside the station, as well as permanent *souqs* throughout the town, and a tannery. The town has an Almohad **Grand Mosque**, near to a Merinid *medressa*. **Accommodation F** *Café-Hotel Andaluz*, very basic. *Getting there*: there are six trains a day to Tanger, 4 a day to Fes, Meknes and Oujda, 4 a day to Rabat and Casablanca, and 2 a day to Marrakech.

Arbaoua lies to the W of the P2, the trees providing shade for a popular picnic area in summer, although mosquitoes can be a nuisance. **E** *Hotel Route de France*, T (07) 902668, 26 rm with bath, restaurant serves medium range meals, speciality is rabbit. A splendid lunch stop.

Souq el Arba du Gharb is an important market town, with a *souq* each Wed, at the centre of the rich agricultural region of the Gharb, which extends as far N as Larache, and as far S as Kenitra. This region has been important for cereal, and then citrus and vegetable, production.

● **Accommodation E** *Hotel Gharb*, Route de Rabat-Tanger, T 902203, 902441, with a restaurant and bar; also a number of basic hotels and restaurants, but little else.

● **Transport** There are regular trains to Tanger, Meknes, Fes, Oujda, Rabat, Casablanca and to Marrakech, as well as regular buses and grand taxis to Ouezzane and Moulay Bousselham.

Moulay Bousselham is a small beach resort with a relaxed atmosphere and rough swimming conditions. Although easily reached from Souq el Arba du Gharb, Moulay Bousselham is bypassed by most tourists. The place is named after a 10th century saint, who is commemorated in a nearby *koubba*, and a festival, or *moussem*, in Jul. The beach is spectacular but dangerous for swimming, al-

though not bad for fishing. The lagoon, Merja Zerja, is safer for swimming, and attracts a number of species of birds, notably flamingos. Those who want to birdwatch can hire boats from local fishermen. Bargain firmly. **Accommodation D** *Hotel le Lagon*, T 902603, with restaurant, bar, nightclub and pool; at the cafés; or at the basic *Camping Moulay Bousselham*. Eat at *L'Ocean*.

Kenitra

Kenitra (*Pop* 188,194 (1982)) is an industrial and military centre of importance within Morocco, but perhaps of little attraction to the traveller. Kenitra was a small Moroccan military fort until 1913 when the French built a new town, as well as an artificial harbour used as a military port and to export citrus fruit and other products from the rich agricultural areas of the surrounding Gharb region. The port was developed to replace Larache, in the Spanish zone, and Tanger, in the International Zone. In 1933 the French renamed Kenitra Port Lyautey, after their first Resident-General of the Moroccan Protectorate. US troops landed here in Nov 1942 as part of Operation Torch, and experienced heavy casualties under fire from the port at Mehdiya, but from 1947 the USA returned to establish an important naval base, which they used until 1977. After Independence Port Lyautey was renamed Kenitra. Kenitra is still important as military centre and port. It lies on the P2 from Rabat to Tanger, close to the beach at Mehdiya.

● **Accommodation C** *Hotel Safir*, Place Administrative, T 365600, Tx 91995, good but unexciting, from an established chain with restaurant, bar, nightclub and pool. **D** *Hotel Mamora*, Ave Hassan II, T 363007, 365006, with a good restaurant and bar, nightclub and pool. **E** *Hotel la Rotonde*, 50 Ave Mohammed Diouri, T 363343/4, with a restaurant and bar; as well as cheaper hotels along Ave Mohammed V.

● **Camping**   Camping   la   Chenaie,

T 363373, with a restaurant and shop.

● **Places to eat** There is no shortage of restaurants on Ave Hassan II and Ave Mohammed V. *Hotel Mamora* and *Hotel la Rotonde* are rec as places to eat and drink.

● **Post & telecommunications Post Office**: Ave Mohammed V.

● **Sports Horse riding**: at *Club Equestre de la Mamora*, the Hippodrome. **Tennis**: at the *Tennis Club de Kenitra*, Ave des Sports, BP 131, T 363160, which has six courts. **Watersports**: wind surfing and yachting organized through *Union Athlétique de Kenitra*, Clos Dublin Kenitra, T 362012.

● **Tourist offices** Syndicat d'Initiative on Ave Mohammed V, T (07) 162277.

● **Transport Train** From the railway station, T 365095, 363402, trains leave regularly to Asilah, Tanger, Meknes, Fes, Oujda and Marrakech, and there are almost hourly services to Rabat and Casablanca between 0400 and 2309. **Road** The bus station is on Ave Mohammed V.

Mehdiya

This is the beach for Kenitra, noted for windsurfing but more interesting to visit for its kasbah, and the nearby **nature reserve** around Lac de Sidi Bourhaba. Mehdiya is 11 km from Kenitra, with plentiful grand-taxis.

The **kasbah** was built by the Portuguese, and changed greatly by Moulay Ismail. In the 17th century it was used as a governor's palace, but was damaged by the US troops during their 1942 landing. The nature reserve is an extensive area focused on the **Lac de Sidi Bourhaba**, popular for birdwatching, and in the summer, for picnicking. The *koubba* has a festival in Aug.

● **Accommodation D** *Hotel Atlantique*, 21 rm, with a popular nightclub featuring live music; **F** *Auberge de la Forêt*; and *Camping Mehdia*, T 4849, open in the summer with pool, restaurant and shop.

● **Places to eat** There are cafés nr the beach. *Restaurant-Café Dauphine* is rec for fish meals.

CASABLANCA AND ENVIRONS

Mohammedia

Just to the N of Casablanca, stands Mohammedia, population 105,120 (1982), one of Morocco's major ports since the opening of an oil refinery in 1961. Industrial activities are centred around a rock salt factory. Its sandy beaches makes it a popular recreational area for the people of Casablanca.

● **Accommodation A** *Hotel Miramar*, rue de Fes, T 322021, F 324613, 188 rm, a luxurious place with restaurant, bar, nightclub, tennis and pool. **C** *Hotel Samir*, Blvd Moulay Youssef, T 310770/4, F 323330, 154 rm, good value with all facilities. **F** *Hotel Castel* and **F** *Hotel Voyageurs* are much more basic. There is a camping site, the *Camping International Loran*, T 322957, with pool, restaurant and shop.

● **Places to eat** ♦♦♦The restaurant in *Hotel Samir* is good, but expensive; *Le Frégate*, rue Oued Zem, particularly good for fish; *Auberge des Grands Zenata*, T 352102, midway between Casablanca and Mohammedia, sea food specialities, pricey.

● **Sport** Mohammedia is very well equipped for sports. **Golf**: the course, T 322052, with 18 holes is one of the best in Morocco, despite the high winds, 5,909m, par 73, fees MD450. **Horse riding**: *Club Equestre* on Blvd Moulay Youssef. **Tennis**: *Tennis Club de Mohammedia*, nine courts, T 322037. **Watersports**: a number of yachting regattas between Oct and May through the *Yacht Club de Mohammedia*, Port de Mohammedia, T 322331, well-equipped club-house. A watersports centre at the *Ibn Batouta Nautic Base de Mohammedia*. Water skiing is popular here. The beach is good, despite its proximity to Casablanca.

● **Tourist offices** At 14 rue Al Jahid, T 324299.

● **Transport Train** There are regular trains from Mohammedia to Rabat between 0707 and 0107, to Casablanca Port between 0547 and 2306, and to Casablanca Voyageurs between 0526 and 0033, as well as to all other major destinations. **Road Bus/taxi**: there are frequent bus and grand-taxi services into Casablanca.

Casablanca

Pop 2,150,000 (1982), unofficial est 6 million; *Alt* 50m; *Best Season* Any time of year except Jul-Aug which can be humid. Casablanca is also known as El-Dar-el-Beida, both names meaning 'the white house'. The city is the economic capital of Morocco, the centre for trade, industry and finance, a major port handling a wide range of commodities including phosphates, and by far the largest city in the country, the second largest in Africa after Cairo. Travelling through the city its immense size is impressive, less so the sprawling *bidonvilles*, tin-shack slums, which house much of the city's rapidly expanding population. Casablanca is a city where extreme poverty and wealth co-exist uncomfortably, where crime, prostitution and unrest are more evident than elsewhere in the country. The city does not have the historic monuments of Rabat, Fes and Marrakech, and has a noisy westernized air that is unlikely to appeal to many travellers. However, as Morocco's largest city it is an interesting place to see, and is as representative as any of contemporary society.

History

There is believed to have been a Phoenician settlement at Casablanca, and a later Berber town. It was conquered by the Almohads in 1188, and developed by Sultan Abd el-Moumen as a port. In the 14th century the Portuguese established a settlement here on the site of the village of Anfa, but when it became a pirates' base in 1468, they destroyed it, repeating this act in 1515. The Portuguese reestablished themselves in the late 16th century, renaming the town Casa Blanca, staying until 1755, when an earthquake destroyed the settlement. The town was rebuilt at the end of the 18th century by Sultan Mohammed Ibn Abdellah, including the construction of the **Grand Mosque**, but it declined in the early 19th century.

In the 19th century, European traders settled at Casablanca, and at the beginning of the 20th century the French obtained permission from Sultan Abd al-Aziz to construct an artificial harbour, which marked the beginning of Casablanca's rapid expansion. The French occupied Casablanca in 1907, and expanded and developed the medina, which from 1918 until the establishment of Israel, became a largely Jewish quarter. In 1915 the French resident-general, Lyautey, and his chief architect, Henri Prost, planned the new city centre which bears a heavy imprint of French planning, with a grid of wide boulevards, large white commercial and residential constructions, and key state buildings designed in a style amalgamating European and Moroccan traditions, known as *Mauresque*. The city has subsequently sprawled far beyond this core, with vast planned projects and unplanned *bidonvilles*. Anfa was the site of the Casablanca Conference of Allied leaders in Jan 1943. Moroccan trade unions developed in Casablanca during the French protectorate, and were important in the nationalist struggle, notably in the riots of 1952 and insurrection from 1953-5.

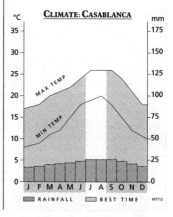

CLIMATE: CASABLANCA

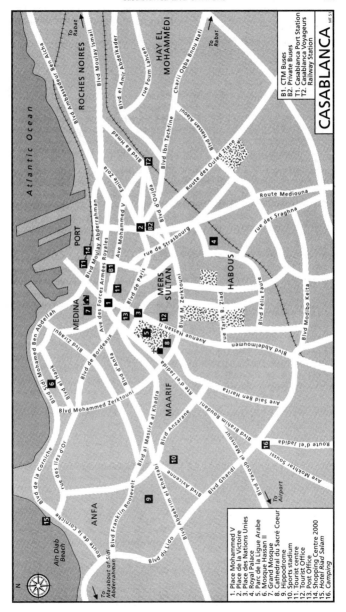

CASABLANCA

MT 51

B1. CTM Buses
B2. Private Buses
T1. Casablanca Port Station
T2. Casablanca Voyageurs
Railway Station

1. Place Mohammed V
2. Place de la Victoire
3. Place des Nations Unies
4. Royal Palace
5. Parc de la Ligue Arabe
6. Mosque Hassan II
7. Grand Mosque
8. Cathedral du Sacré Coeur
9. Hippodrome
10. Sports stadium
11. Tourist centre
12. Tourist Office
13. Post Office
14. Shopping Centre 2000
15. Hotel Riad Salam
16. Camping

No part of the Warner Bros 1942 production 'Casablanca' was filmed here.

ACCESS Air Aéroport Mohammed V, T 339100, for most international flight arrivals and the centre of Royal Air Maroc's national network is 30 km to the S of the city at Nouasseur, and there are regular buses price MD25 to the city centre, arriving at the CTM terminal on rue Leon l'Africain. There are also expensive *grand-taxis* costing MD150, MD200 before 0700 and after 2000 and taking 1 hr. The airport has a BMCE bureau de change, open most hours, car hire agencies, and desks for the major hotel chains, as well as a bar, restaurant and post office. An express train direct to Casablanca Ville or Casablanca Port takes 20 mins and costs MD30 economy class.

Train The city has two main stations: Casablanca Port, at the end of Blvd Houphouet Boigny, which is most convenient for the city centre; Casablanca Voyageurs, at the end of Ave Mohammed V, which has more services; and the small suburban station of Aïn Sebaa, to the E of the city.

Road Casablanca is well connected by road, with the P36 from Rabat and the N entering the city centre via Blvd Emile Zola, which leads into Ave Mohammed V; the P8 from Agadir and El Jadida enters via Blvd Brahim Roudani; the P7 from Marrakech via Ave Hassan II. **Bus:** CTM buses arrive at the terminal on rue Leon l'Africain, off Ave des Forces Armées Royales, private line services at the square near Place de le Victoire, from here it will be necessary to get a petit-taxi.

Places of interest

There is some confusion with street names as the French is being translated into Arabic but transliterated into Latin script. In general, despite this, streets are still referred to in French.

The City Centre of Casablanca is a bustling place full of life, an example of the diversity of Moroccan society. The buildings are large, dirty, white constructions with balconies and shutters, revealing the predominate French influence on the design, and indeed it has the feel of a European Mediterranean

CASABLANCA MEDINA
1. Grand Mosque
2. Chleuh Mosque
3. Koubba of Sidi Bou Smara
4. Youth Hostel

city. The centre piece is the Place des Nations Unies, surrounded by major state buildings designed by the French in the *Mauresque* style, an amalgam of European and Moroccan architecture. This has a square and fountain popularized by western and Moroccan tourists, with crazily-dressed water-sellers wandering through the crowd. There is a lights display, 3 nights a week, which brings the city centre to life. Near the square is the pleasant Parc de la Ligue Arabe, and adjacent to that is the exuberant design of **Cathedral de Sacré Coeur**, built in 1930 and now used as a school.

The Medina the site of the old city, is a ramshackle, tatty quarter, dating primarily from the 19th century, and occupied for a while by a Jewish population. It can easily be explored in a couple of hours, entering from Place Mohammed V. The **Grand Mosque** was built by Sultan Sidi Mohammed Ibn Abdellah at the end of the 19th century. The medina is a good place to shop, although real bargains or high quality handicrafts are difficult to find.

The Port was constructed at the beginning of the 20th century, and is now a massive complex used for fishing, phosphates, commerce and industry, pleasure boats and cruise ships. There is a shopping centre, Centre 2000, and a number of fish restaurants, beside the port.

Grand Mosque Hassan II was inaugurated Aug 1993, the culmination of 5 years of intensive labour by over 30,000 workers and craftsmen. Apart from 50 chandeliers, all the materials and labour is Moroccan. This exceptionally beautiful new mosque has a highly decorative minaret, a landmark in the city. It is huge, in terms of covered area the largest in the world, and has space for 80,000 worshippers as well as a library and a museum. It is built out over the sea, the water washing against the windows of the ablutions room, the bay windows of the prayer hall (which has a mobile roof allowing it to be opened to the sky) looking over the Atlantic Ocean. The costly operation has been paid for by public subscription. Now support is required for the maintenance and day to day running costs. Non-Muslims may enter as part of a guided tour. The easiest way to get there is by petit-taxi.

Aïn Diab is the beach quarter, along which the Corniche sweeps. To get to it take Bus 9 from the centre. The beach is not clean, but there are some interesting beach clubs along the Corniche, with cafés, restaurants and bars, most of which charge an entrance fee. The **Marabout of Sidi Abderrahman**, 3 km further W, still visited by Muslims, dedicated to an ascetic from Baghdad, said to have miraculous powers of healing, is on a rock off the coast.

The New Medina, an area also called the **Quartier Habous**, was built in the 1930s. It was an interesting attempt by the French to solve a housing problem and incorporate features of traditional Moroccan house design and community layout with modern streets and utilities. Perhaps they failed, but it is an appealing area nevertheless. Take Bus 4 or 40 from the bus station at the junction of Blvd de Paris and Ave des Forces Armées Royales. Incidentally, the Quartier Habous sells excellent pickles and olives.

Local information
● Accommodation

Price guide:			
AL	US$90+	**D**	US$20-40
A	US$75-90	**E**	US$10-20
B	US$60-75	**F**	under US$10
C	US$40-60		

Hotels in Casablanca are often booked up early in the day. The lower range hotels are often more expensive than elsewhere in Morocco and unusually can often be of a lower standard of cleanliness. **AL** *Hotel El Mansur*, 27 Ave des Forces Armées Royales, T 313011/2, F 314818, 170 rm, 2 restaurants, coffee bar, bar, health club and pool, overlooked by the new mosque; **AL** *Hotel Hyatt Regency*, Place Mohammed V, T 261234, F 220180, 300 rm, one of the centre-pieces of the town, 5 restaurants, bar, nightclub, health club, art gallery, squash courts and pool; **AL** *Hotel Sheraton*, 100 Ave des Forces Armées Royales, T 317878, F 315136, 306 spotless and well-equipped rm, helpful reception, 5 restaurants, 3 bars, high quality business centre, special meeting room, health club, *hammam* and nightclub.

A *Hotel Riad Salam Meridien*, Blvd de la Corniche, T 363535, Tx 24692, 140 rm, the best place by the beach, with health facilities, restaurant, bar, nightclub, tennis and pool; **A** *Hotel Safir*, 160 Ave des Forces Armées Royales, T 311212, Tx 24896/7, 310 pleasantly decorated and well-equipped rm, 4 restaurants, 2 bars, nightclub and heated pool.

B *Los Almohades*, Ave Hassan I, T 220505, Moroccan style hotel, takes tour groups.

C *Basma*, 30 Ave Moulay Hassan I, T 223323, modern, comfortable.

D *Hotel du Centre*, 1 rue Sidi Belyout, T 312448, fair prices, clean and convenient; *Hotel Excelsior*, 2 rue Nolly, T 200048, 54 rm, 32 with bath, central, with a more illustrious past; **D** *Hotel Plaza*, 18 Blvd Houphouet Boigny, T 221262, 27 rm, satisfactory place with restaurant and bar; **D** *Hotel Windsor*, 93 Place Oued El Makhazin, T 278274, 32 good rm, no restaurant, bar.

E *Hotel Guynemer*, 2 rue Pegoud, T 275764, a friendly, good and clean hotel in a quiet but central location; **E** *Hotel Rialto*, 9 rue Claude, T 275122, fine; **E** *Hotel Touring*, 87 rue Allal

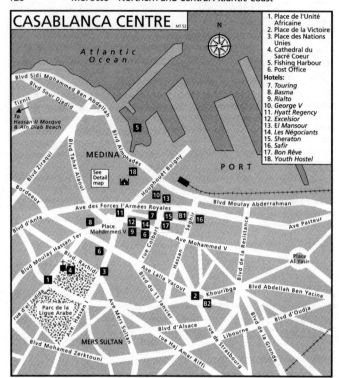

CASABLANCA CENTRE   MT 52   N

1. Place de l'Unité Africaine
2. Place de la Victoire
3. Place des Nations Unies
4. Cathedral du Sacré Coeur
5. Fishing Harbour
6. Post Office

Hotels:

7. Touring
8. Basma
9. Rialto
10. George V
11. Hyatt Regency
12. Excelsior
13. El Mansour
14. Les Négociants
15. Sheraton
16. Safir
17. Bon Rêve
18. Youth Hostel

Ben Abdullah, T 310216, very good large rooms often with balconies, fills up early.

F *Hotel Bon Reve*, rue Allal Ben Abdullah, similar; **F** *Hotel du Perigord*, 56 rue de Foucauld, not very clean but could be worse; **F** *Hotel Genève*, 44 rue du Marché aux Grains, in the medina, is clean and basic; **F** *Hotel Les Négociants*, rue Allal Ben Abdullah, good and cheap.

● **Youth hostel**

6 Place Amiral Philibert, T 220551, a square in the medina off Blvd des Almohades, 80 beds, meals available, overnight fee MD30-40 incl breakfast, bus and train 350m, renovated, friendly.

● **Camping**

Camping de l'Oasis, Ave Mermoz, T 253367, this is the nearest, in the direction of El Jadida, take Bus 31; in the same direction are *Camp-*ing *Tamaris*; and *Camping Desserte des Plages*, both at rue Azemmour, Km 16.

● **Places to eat**

Price guide:
♦♦♦Expensive; ♦♦average; ♦cheap.

♦♦♦ *Al Mounia*, 95 rue du Prince Moulay Abdullah, T 222669, Moroccan food; *Andalus Restaurant* and *Sakura* both in *Hotel Sheraton*, 100 Ave des Forces Armées Royales, T 311194, for local or Japanese food; *Dar Beida*, *Hotel Hyatt Regency*, Place Mohammed V, T 261234, reservations needed, sumptuous restaurant with all Moroccan specialities and music; *La Cambuse* at Aïn Diab, T 367105, noted for fish dishes; *Ma Bretagne*, Sidi Abderrahman beyond Aïn Diab, T 362111, excellent fish and good wine cellar, sea view; *Oriental Restaurant*, *Hotel El Mansour*, 27 Ave des Forces Armées Royales,

T 313011, excellent Moroccan specialities; *Restaurant Wong Kung*, Hotel Hyatt Regency, T 261234, the best Chinese restaurant in Morocco, incl excellent seafood dishes.

◆◆*Restaurant de l'Etoile Maroccaine*, 107 rue Allah Ben Abdullah, adjacent to market, no alcohol; *La Corrida*, 59 rue Guy Lussac, Spanish food; *La Marignan*, 63 rue Mohammed Smiha, excellent Japanese food; *La Tajine*, Centre 2000, by the port, good Moroccan food; *Las Delicias*, 18 Ave Mohammed V, good Spanish restaurant; *Le Petit Poucet*, 8 Ave Mohammed V, licensed French restaurant; *Maharaja Restaurant*, 46 rue Mohammed El Qorri, T 273780, a very good Indian restaurant with alcohol; *Restaurant Saigon*, 40 rue Colbert, T 286007, good Asian food; *Taverne du Dauphin*, Blvd Houphouet Boigny, T 221200, good for seafood.

◆A cheap area for eating is around rue Colbert and rue Allal Ben Abdullah, try *Café Restaurant Anwal*, 116 rue Allal Ben Abdullah, T 319630, standard Moroccan fare; *Café Intissar*, rue Allal Ben Abdullah, reliable; another cheap area is in the medina, with the *Restaurant Widad* a good choice.

● Bars
Rick's Bar, in the Hotel Hyatt Regency on Place Mohammed V, is not the original, but has marginal curiosity value; *Le Sphinx*, Ave Mohammed V, is a cheaper option; the *Churchill Club*, rue Pessac, Aïn Diab is an expatriate club for English speakers.

● Cafés and pâtisseries
Casablanca's reputation for ice-cream is quite without foundation, but for exotic combinations try *Olivier's*, Ave Hassan II. There are some good cafés along Ave Mohammed V, and a popular scene around Place Mohammed V.

● Airline offices
Air Afrique, Tour des Habous, Ave des Forces Armées Royales, T 312866; Air France, 15 Ave des Forces Armées Royales, T 294040; British Airways (Tour Atlas), 57 Place Zellaqa, T 307607; Iberia, 17 Ave des Forces Armées Royales, T 294003, Aéroport Mohammed V, T 339260; KLM, 6 Blvd Mohammed El Hansali, T 203232; Lufthansa, Tour des Habous, Ave des Forces Armées Royales, T 312371; Libyan Airlines, Tour des Habous, Ave des Forces Armées Royales, T 311500; Royal Air Maroc, Airport T 912000, 44 Ave des Forces Armées Royales, T 311122, 90 Ave Mers Sultan, T 268712, 44 Place Mohammed V, T 203270,

reservations, T 314141; Swissair, Tour des Habous, Ave des Forces Armées Royales, T 313280; Tunis Air, Direction 10, Ave des Forces Armées Royales, T 273914.

● Banks & money changers
ABM, Place du 16 Novembre, T 221275; Banque du Maroc, Blvd de Paris, T 224110; BMAO, 115 Blvd d'Anfa, T 278828; Credit du Maroc, 48-58 Ave Mohammed V; GMB, 55 Blvd Abd el-Moumen, T 224134; SMDC, 79 Ave Hassan II, T 224114.

American Express: Voyages Schwartz, Ave Moulay Abdellah.

● Consulates
Algeria, 159 Blvd Moulay Idriss I, T 804175; Austria, 45 Ave Hassan II, T 266904; Belgium, 13 Blvd Rachidi, T 222904; Denmark, 30 rue Sidi Belyout, T 316656; France, rue Prince Moulay Abdellah, T 265355; Germany, 42 Ave des Forces Armées Royales, T 314872; Greece, 48 Blvd Rachidi, T 277142; Italy, 21 Ave Hassan Souktani, T 277558; Japan, 22 rue Charam Achaykh, T 253264; Netherlands, 26 rue Nationale, T 221820; Norway, 44 rue Mohamed Smiha, T 305961; Portugal, 104 Blvd de Paris, T 220214; Russia, 31 rue Soumaya, T 255708; Spain, 29 rue d'Alger, T 220752; Sweden, 88 Blvd Lalla Yacout, T 319003; Switzerland (Visa Office), 43 Blvd d'Anfa, T 205856; UK, 60 Blvd d'Anfa, T 221653, 223185; USA, 8 Blvd Moulay Youssef, T 264550, 224149.

● Entertainment
Discos & nightclubs: *La Fontaine*, Blvd Houphouet Boigny, has belly dancing and music; *La Cage*, by the port, popular with the youth; *Le Balcon*, Aïn Diab, a good disco; also try *Caesar's* in the Hotel Sheraton, 100 Ave des Forces Armées Royales, T 311194.

● Hospitals & medical services
Ambulance: T 15.
Chemists: *Pharmacie de Nuit*, Place Mohammed V, T 269491.
Doctors: Dr A El Kouhen, 24 rue Nolly, T 275343, speaks English; *Croissant Rouge*, T 340914.

● Laundry
Pressing Mers Sultan, 116 Ave Mers Sultan, T 264194.

● Post & telecommunications
Area code: 02.
Post Office: the main PTT is on Place des Nations Unies, for collecting *poste restante* and

good for telephoning, there is another PTT on Ave Mohammed V.

● **Places of worship**

Anglican: Church, 24 rue Guedj, T 365104 (1030, Sun).

Catholic: Eglise Notre-Dame de Lourdes, Rond Point d'Europe, T 220852; Eglise Saint-François d'Assise, 2 rue de l'Eglise, T 300930; Eglise d'Anfa, 13 Ave Jeanne d'Arc, T 361913.

Jewish: Temple Beth-El 67, rue Verlet-Hanus; Synagogue Téhila Le David, Blvd du 11 Janvier; Synagogue Benarrosh, rue de Lusitania.

Protestant: Temple, 33 rue d'Azilal, T 301922.

● **Shopping**

Books: *English Forum*, 27 rue Clemenceau; *American Language Center Bookshop*, Blvd Moulay Youssef.

Food: there is a large covered market on Ave Mohammed V which has some excellent and cheap foodstuffs for sale.

Handicrafts: the best fixed price shop, and a friendly place just to look, is the government-run *Coopartim* in the Grande Arcade Complexe Commerciale, just off Place des Nations Unies, T 269444. There are smaller shops in the medina and along Blvd Houphouet Boigny.

Newspapers: stalls, some selling European papers, on Place Mohammed V and along Ave Mohammed V.

● **Sport**

Archery: *Archery Les Compagnons de l'Arc*, 25 rue des Flamants, T 277981.

Bowls: *La Boule Fédérale*, Parc de la Ligue Arabe, T 272868.

Boules: *La Boule Fédérale*, Parc de la Ligue Arabe, T 272868.

Golf: *Royal Golf d'Anfa*, nine holes, T 251026, 10 mins from the centre of the city, a prestigious course with a luxurious club-house and a restaurant.

Horse Riding: *L'Etrier*, Quartier des Stades, Route d'El Jadida; *Club Equestre Bayard*, rue Schuman; CAFC, Quartier des Stades, Route d'El Jadida, T 259779, 255005.

Hunting: *Club La Gazelte de la Chaouia*, 21 rue d'Oudin le Romon, T 252911.

Rowing: *RUC*, Jetée Moulay Youssef.

Swimming: the beach is an unadvisable option, there are, however, pools in the Aïn Diab area, try the *Miami* beach club.

Tennis: *Cercle Athlétique de Casablanca*, Ave Jean Mermoz, T 254342, 18 courts; *Cercle Municipal de Casablanca*, Parc de la Ligue Arabe, T 279621, six courts; *Racing Universitaire de Casablanca*, Clos d'Aviation, Route d'El Jadida, T 254572; *Stade Olympic* Casablancais, Route d'El Jadida, T 254023, eight courts; *Union Sportive Marocaine/Tennis Club de Casablanca*, Parc de la Ligue Arabe, T 275429, eight courts.

Watersports: *Water Skiing Federation*, Port de Casablanca, T 227775.

Yachting: *Société Nautique de Casablanca*, Jetée de Delure, T 225721; Centre National de Voile, Royal Naval Club.

● **Tour companies & travel agents**

Comanov Voyages, 7 Blvd de la Resistance, T 303012, 302006; *Discover Morocco*, 62 rue de Foucauld, T 273519; *Gibmar Travel*, 8 rue Nolly; *Menara Tours*, 57 Place Zellaqa, T 307607, 307629; *Olive Branch Tours*, 35 rue de Foucauld, T 223919; *Sun Tours and Travel*, 75 rue Driss Lahrizi, T 200196; *Transalpino*, 98 Ave Mers Sultan, T 270096; *Wagons-Lit Tourisme*, 60 rue de Foucauld, T 203051.

● **Tourist offices**

Office du Tourisme, 55 rue Omar Slaoui, T 271177, F 205929; **Syndicat d'Initiative**, 98 Ave Mohammed V, T 221524, 274904.

● **Useful addresses**

Chamber of Commerce: Chambre Brittanique, 185 Blvd Zerktouni, T 256920.

Fire: rue Poggi, T 15.

Garage: Renault-Maroc, Place de Bandoeng, T 15.

Motoring Club: Touring Club de Maroc, 3 Ave des Forces Armées Royales (0900-1200 and 1500-1830, Mon-Fri).

Police: Blvd Brahim Rodani, T 19; **Traffic police**: 177.

● **Transport**

Local Bus: the local bus station is at the junction of Blvd de Paris and Ave des Forces Armées Royales, take No 9 for Aïn Diab, No 4 and No 40 for the Habous quarter, No 31 for *Camping Oasis*. **Car hire**: Avis, 19 Ave des Forces Armées Royales, T 312424, 311135, and at Aéroport Mohammed V, T 339072; **Euro Rent**, 3 rue Assaâd Ibnou Zarara, T 254033; **Hertz**, 25 rue de Foucauld, T 312223, Airport T 339181; **Inter-Rent Europcar**, Tour des Habous, Ave des Forces Armées Royales, T 313737; **Inter-Voyages**, 4 Ave des Forces Armées Royales; **Leasing Cars**, 110 Blvd Zerktouni, Y 265331, a cheap option. **Taxi**: Casablanca's red petit-taxis are numerous, efficient and usually metered, hail them anywhere or T 255030. Nowhere in city should cost more than MD12.

Air Aéroport Mohammed V, T 339100 S of the city at Nouasseur connected by trains from Casablanca Voyageurs and Casablanca Port and by buses from inside the CTM terminal on rue Leon l'Africain and grand-taxis outside. Buses leave CTM terminal at 0530, 0630 then hourly from 0700 to 2200. There are flights to/from Casablanca to **Agadir** (at least 2 daily), **Al Hoceima** (2 weekly), **Dakhla** (weekly), **Fes** (daily), **Laayoune** (daily), **Marrakech** (2 daily), **Ouarzazate** (4 weekly), **Oujda** (daily), **Rabat** (daily), **Tanger** (daily), **Tan-Tan** (weekly) and **Tetouan** (weekly). Most major world cities are connected to Morocco through Casablanca. Internal transfers to other cities are not always at convenient times.

Train Departures from **Casablanca Port**, T 223011, 271837, to **Rabat** almost hourly between 0645 and 2035; **Meknes** and **Fes**: 0700, 1850, 2035; **Taza** and **Oujda**: 2035; **Tanger**: 0645; **Aeroport Mohammed V**: 12 a day between 0510 and 2000. Departures from **Casablanca Voyageurs**, T 243818, 240800 to **Rabat** almost hourly between 0754 and 0017; **Marrakech**: 0600, 0730, 0914, 1156, 1455, 1652, 1912, 0140; **El Jadida**: 0845, 2055; **Oued Zem** 1000, 1710, 2030; **Meknes** and **Fes**: 0945, 1047, 1225, 1400, 1730, 2235; **Taza** and **Oujda**: 0945, 1400, 2235; **Tanger**: 1225, 1555, 0045; **Aeroport Mohammed V**: 12 a day between 0522 and 2012.

Road Bus: the CTM terminal is at 23 rue Léon l'Africain, off rue Colbert and Ave des Forces Armées Royales, T 268061-7; daily services to Essaouira (5 hrs), El Jadida, Agadir, Tiznit, Beni Mellal, Marrakech, Fes, Tanger and Rabat. Private line buses leave from the terminal on rue Strasbourg, near Place de le Victoire. The following destinations are served daily: **Rabat** (51), **El Jadida** (32), **Mohammedia** (22), **Agadir, Fes** (11), **Meknes** (10), **Essaouira** (9), **Marrakech** (6), **Tafraoute** (5), **Ouarzazate** (4), **Azzemour, Inezgane, Tiznit** (3), **Khenifra, Khouribga, Oued Zem, Kasbah Tadla, Safi, Taza Tetouan, Sefrou** (2), **Nador, Taroudant, Oujda, Kenitra, Larache** (1). Call 'Allo CTM' on (02) 449424 for full details of all services. **Taxi**: grand-taxi to Mohammedia and Rabat from by the CTM terminal.

Sea Boat: Marinasmir, has 7 km of quay, and places for 454 private boats with draught up to 65m, T 306066.

EL JADIDA AND ENVIRONS

Azzemour

With a population of 24,774 (1982), Azzemour, still partly surrounded by ochre ramparts, is located at the mouth of the Oued Oum er Rbia, 15 km N of El Jadida. The white medina built alongside the river is striking, and the beach one of the best, but the town attracts few visitors. There is a train from here to Casablanca and Rabat at 0827, and buses and grand-taxis to and from El Jadida, and is best visited as an excursion, although there is the **F** *Hotel de la Victoire*, 308 Ave Mohammed V.

There was a trading post here called Azama in the Carthaginian period. In the 15th century Azzemour was an important trading port on the routes between Portugal and West Africa. The Portuguese occupied Azzemour in 1513 as a base from which to attack Marrakech, but under opposition from the Saadians had to withdraw in 1541. The town assumed regional importance under the Saadians, but soon lost ground to the growth of its near neighbour, El Jadida. Azzemour is known for embroidery. The town is sometimes referred to as Moulay Bou Chaib, after its patron saint, who has a *zaouia* above the town.

The walls of the old medina can be explored by the rampart walk, with excellent views of the town. Enter the medina, with its clear Portuguese architectural influences and impressive wooden doors, by **Bab es-Souq** and visit the *kissaria*, or covered market, the **Sanctuary of Moulay Abdellah Ben Ahmed**, and the **kasbah**, which also had a role as a *mellah*, or Jewish quarter. In the kasbah, visit the **Dar el Baroud** building. Climb its tower for a view of the town. Outside the town is the popular beach of Haouzia, a walk away, with the usual cafés.

El Jadida

El Jadida (*Pop* 81,500 (1982)), is a popular beach resort, particularly for Moroccans, and has a faded elegance rather like some English seaside towns. The main historic site of the walled citadel is, however, distinctly Portuguese in character.

El Jadida is a contraction of '*Al Brija al Jadida*', meaning 'the new little port', but before Independence was known as Mazagao, or Mazagan. The town was the site of an Almohad *ribat*, or fortress, later abandoned. The Portuguese founded a town at Mazagan in 1515, and it became one of their most important bases, holding it after the fall of their other enclaves. Sultan Mohammed Ibn Abdellah retook the town in 1769, and it expanded beyond the walls of the Portuguese city. There was a significant influx of Jews from Azzemour in the 19th century, and the town was further developed by the French, as the chief town of the Doukkala region. The town has an important port, with involvement in sardine fishing. The major deep-water port is just to the S of the town, at Jorf Lasfar. Each summer there is an influx of Moroccan tourists, particularly from Marrakech.

ACCESS Train The train station lies to the NW of El Jadida, and trains are met by a local bus to carry people in the town. **Road** The bus station is S of the centre, along Ave Mohammed V. From here it is a 5-10 mins walk to Place Mohammed V, the focus of the town.

Places of interest

The Citadel was built by the Portuguese from 1513, and its distinctive character was maintained after their departure in 1769 by European and Jewish merchants who settled here from 1815. The quarter is small and relaxed, and very easily explored. The ramparts, access from the right of the main gates, which are surmounted by the escutcheons of the Portuguese kings, were completed in 1541. The gates are broken on the coastal side by the **Porte de la Mer**, from where the Portuguese finally left. The old walled city includes a chapel, hospital, prison and Governor's palace, a lighthouse converted into the **Grand Mosque**. The **Church of Our Lady of the Assumption**, a Portuguese construction, was restored by the French in 1921, and later converted into a mosque. The citadel's prison was converted into a synagogue.

The Cistern, a most distinctive feature of the citadel, underground on Praça do Terreiro (open 0800-1200 and 1400-1800), dates from the 16th century and was designed originally to store munitions. It served as a fencing school before being used as a tank to store water for times of shortage. The symmetrical construction has a vaulted roof supported by 25 pillars, with just one window. The floor is covered with water, which produces a remarkable effect of the shimmering reflection of the roof in the half-light of the cistern. Orson Welles used it in his film of Othello.

The **beach** of El Jadida has a long elegant corniche, flanked by cafés, restaurants and beach clubs but the beach itself is not always clean.

Local information
● Accommodation

Hotels are often heavily booked in the summer, so ring ahead if possible, particularly if arriving late at night. The best are **C** *Hotel Club Salam Doukkala*, Ave Al Jamia al-Arabi, T 343737, Tx 78014, 85 rm, a modern, well-equipped, unexciting hotel, restaurant, bar, nightclub, tennis, pool, and a sea view.

D *Hotel le Palais Andalous*, Ave de la Nouie, T 343745, Tx 78001, charming hotel from the Protectorate period, a good restaurant and excellent bar.

E *Hotel de Bruxelles*, 40 Ave Ibn Khaldoun, T 342072, clean and reasonable doubles with bath; **E** *Hotel Royal*, 108 Ave Mohammed V, T 342839, Tx 78968, a comfortable establishment with restaurant and bar; **E** *Hotel Suisse*, 145 rue Zerktouni, T 342816, reasonable value and quiet.

F *Hotel de la Plage*, Ave Al Jamia al-Arabi, T 342648, cheap and reliable; **F** *Hotel de*

Provence, 42 Ave Fkih Errafi, T 342347, a good value and friendly place with restaurant and bar; **F** *Hotel du Maghreb*, rue Lescoul, just off Place Mohammed V, basic and convenient.

● Camping
Camping International, Ave des Nations Unies, T 342547, with a restaurant, shop and pool.

● Places to eat
◆◆*Restaurant du Port*, nr the *Provence*, 42 Ave Fkih Errafi, T 342347, French meals.

◆*Restaurant Chahrazad*, 38 Place el Hansali, off rue Zerktouni, reasonable Moroccan food; *Café des Amis*, Place el Hansali; *Chez Chiquito*, fish by the port.

● Bars
One of the best is at *Hotel le Palais Andalous*, Ave de la Nouie, T 343904, 343745; also try *Hotel de la Plage*, Ave Al Jamia al-Arabi.

● Post & telecommunications
PTT Centrale, Place Mohammed V.

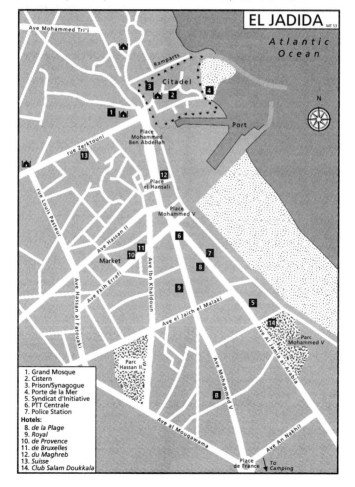

EL JADIDA MT 53

Ave Mohammed Tri'i

Atlantic Ocean

Ramparts

Citadel

N

rue Zerktouni

Place Mohammed Ben Abdellah

Port

rue Louis Pasteur

Place el Hansali

Place Mohammed V

Ave Hassan II

Market

Ave Hassan al Fatouaki

Ave Fkih Errafi

Ave Ibn Khaldoun

Ave el Jaich el Malaki

Parc Mohammed V

Ave Al Jabia al Arabia

Parc Hassan II

Ave Mohammed V

Ave al Mouqawama

Ave An Nakhil

Place de France → To Camping

1. Grand Mosque
2. Cistern
3. Prison/Synagogue
4. Porte de la Mer
5. Syndicat d'Initiative
6. PTT Centrale
7. Police Station
Hotels:
8. de la Plage
9. Royal
10. de Provence
11. de Bruxelles
12. du Maghreb
13. Suisse
14. Club Salam Doukkala

● **Shopping**

The main traditional shops and stalls are around Ave Zerktouni. A *souq* is held near the lighthouse on Wed.

● **Sport**

Horse Riding: *Real Club Equestre S/C de Tribunal Regional*.
Tennis: *Tennis Club Jedidi*, Parc Hassan II, T 342775, five courts.
Yachting: *Association Nautique d'El Jadida*, Port d'El Jadida, T 342718.

● **Tourist offices**

Office du Tourisme, Immeuble Chambre du Commerce, Ave Ibn Khaldoun, T 332724; **Syndicat d'Initiative**, Ave Al Jamia al-Arabi, T 342080.

● **Transport**

Train Trains leave to Casablanca and Rabat at 0815 and 0800. The train station is far out of the town, and will entail a trip in a petit-taxi, or in the bus which leaves from in front of the citadel ramparts.
Road The bus station is in Ave Mohammed V, with regular services to Azzemour, Casablanca, Safi, Settat, Essaouira and Agadir.

Excursion to the beaches and Moulay Abdellah (Tit)

The beaches S of El Jadida on the S121 are reached by bus No 2 and grand-taxis. First is Sidi Ouafi and after the more developed Sidi Bouzid, with a bar, café-restaurants and a camp site. **Moulay Abdellah (Tit)** is a fishing village with an attached site of religious importance, lying 10 km from El Jadida. Tit, meaning 'the source', was founded by Ismail Amghar, an ascetic from Arabia, who settled here in the 11th century. The minaret of Ismail Amghar dates from the Almoravid period, and is almost intact. The place was renamed Moulay Abdellah, after a son of Ismail Amghar who founded a *zaouia* and another mosque here, and built the fortifications. The Almohad *zaouia* attracts many pilgrims to its annual *moussem*, or festival, in Aug.

CENTRAL ATLANTIC COAST

Oualidia

The coastal road from El Jadida to Safi with its 40 km long chain of lagoons is popular with bird watchers during the spring and autumn migrations, particularly at Sidi Moussa and Cap Beddouza. The main reason, however, to take this road, is Oualidia, an attractive port village, with a beach and kasbah, 78 km S of El Jadida, 64 km N of Safi. The town has a market (Sat), and good opportunities for sailing, surfing and fishing.

● **Accommodation D** *Hotel Hippocampe*, T 346499, small, very relaxed, good restaurant, bar, tennis and pool, beautiful setting above lagoon. **E** *Hotel Auberge de la Lagune*, T 346477, even smaller, has town's best restaurant and bar. **Camping** *Camping Municipal* and *Camping International de Oualidia* sites.

Safi

With a population of 197,309 (1982), Safi is a port and an important industrial centre. While not the most attractive of the coastal resorts, there is a **medina** worth visiting, and it is a convenient stopping point on the way down the coast. Its harbour has been important since pre-Roman times and it was one of the first areas of Morocco to receive Islam. Later it was the site of a *ribat*, or holy fortress. The Almohads surrounded the city with ramparts and built the **Zaouia of Sheikh Mohammed Saleh**. During their reign, Safi had an active intellectual and religious life. The Portuguese occupied the city in 1508, built a citadel and repaired the Moroccan kasbah, before leaving in 1541. The Saadians developed the city's trading role, notably in sugar, and built the **Grand Mosque** in the medina. The Alawites added further buildings and restored the medina. In the 17th century, European countries had a significant trading presence in Safi, and Moulay Ismail was instrumental in developing the city in the early 18th century. Safi had importance as the base of a large sardine fishing fleet, which continues to this day.

The French developed it as a port for exporting phosphate rock, connecting it by rail to the mines around Youssoufia, and from 1964 a new processing complex enabled the export of phosphate fertilizers, as well as unprocessed phosphates, and established Safi as one of the largest ports. The city also has important fish processing industries, and a reputation for producing some of the best pottery of the country.

ACCESS Both the railway station, on rue de R'bat, and the bus terminal, on Ave du President Kennedy, are to the S of the town centre, which is easily reached by local bus or petit-taxi. Trains run from Benguerir, which is on the line from Marrakech to Settat. The town is on the S121 coastal road from El Jadida and the P12 from Marrakech. Approaching on the main P8 from Casablanca and El Jadida to Essaouira and Marrakech turn along the P12 from Tleta de Sidi Bougedra.

Places of interest

The Medina with its ramparts and large towers, can be entered by the main gate, **Bab Chaaba**. The main thoroughfare is rue du Socco, around which are located the main *souqs*. Just off this street is the **Grand Mosque** with a notable minaret, and behind it a ruined Gothic church built by the Portuguese, and originally intended as part of a larger cathedral. There is also an interesting old *medressa*. On the E flank of the medina is the **Kachla** (open 0900-1200 and 1500-1900), a large kasbah built by the Saadians, clearly identifiable with its towers and green-tiled roofs. On the right of its entrance is a large round tower built by the Portuguese, and within the **Kachla** is the **Bahia Palace**, an 18th century governor's residence surrounded by gardens. There are good views from the fortress.

Dar el Bahar Just outside the medina ramparts, overlooking the sea, is the Dar el Bahar fort and prison (open 0900-1200 and 1400-1600, Mon-Fri), built by the Portuguese in 1523, and used by them as the governor's residence. It is worth entering the building, if only for the view. There are also some 17th century cannons.

The Potters' Quarter at **Bab Chaaba** is worth a visit to watch the craftsmen at work, using traditional processes and materials. The predominate Safi colours are blue and white. Safi also produces the green tiles which are found on many major buildings throughout Morocco.

Beaches

The best local beach is Sidi Bouzid, just N of the town and on the No 15 bus route, with cafés and the very good *Le Refuge* seafood restaurant. Further afield is the Lalla Fatma beach, just past Cap Safi.

Local information
● Accommodation

C *Hotel Atlantide*, 50 rm, rue Chaouki, T 462160/1, Tx 71724, restaurant, bar; **C** *Hotel Safir*, Ave Zerktouni, T 464299, Tx 71071, 90 rm, a modern place from an established chain with restaurant, bar, nightclub, tennis and pool.

D *Hotel les Mimosas*, rue Ibn Zeidoune, T 463208, Tx 71765, restaurant, bar.

E *Hotel Assif*, Ave de la Liberté, T 462311, friendly place with restaurant.

F *Hotel Majestic*, Ave Moulay Youssef, friendly and clean; there are other cheap places around the medina.

● Camping

Camping de Sidi Bouzid, 3 km N of Safi at Sidi Bouzid, T 462871, shop.

● Places to eat

Restaurant in *Hotel les Mimosas*, rue Chaouki, T 462160, is rec; as is *Restaurant Calypso*, nr Place de l'Indépendence; and *Restaurant de Safi*, 3 rue de la Maraine; cheaper places are around the medina.

● Banks & money changers

BMCE, Place Ibnou Sina.

● Post & telecommunications

PTT, Place de l'Indépendence.

● **Shopping**

The best bargain in Safi is pottery, for which the town is celebrated.

● **Sport**

The beach at Sidi Bouzid is known for surfing. There is horse riding at *Club Equestre*, Route de Sidi Ouassel.

● **Tourist offices**

Rue Imam Malek, T 464553.

● **Transport**

Local Car hire: Europcar, Place Ibnou Sina, T 462935.

Train The railway station is to the S of the town, on rue de R'bat, T 463375, 462176, there are trains to Benguerir at 0530 and 1730 connecting with trains to Marrakech and Casablanca.

Road There are regular buses to Marrakech, El Jadida and to Essaouira, the latter takes 3 hrs. The bus terminal is on Ave du President Kennedy.

Essaouira

(*Pop* 42,000 (1982)) Essaouira is one of the most relaxed of the coastal resorts, with little of the large scale tourist infrastructure found elsewhere, but is understandably popular with independent travellers and surfers. It has a friendly, peaceful atmosphere and an interesting medina.

There was a small Phoenician settlement at Essaouira, previously called Magdoura or Mogador, a corruption of the Berber word *Amegdul*, meaning 'well-protected'. The Romans were interested in the purple dye produced from shellfish, which they used to colour the robes of the rich. Mogador was occupied by the Portuguese in the 15th century who built the fortifications around the harbour. The town was one of their three most important bases, but was abandoned in 1541, from when it went into decline. Visited by Sir Francis Drake, Christmas 1577. In 1765, the Alawite Sultan Sidi Mohammed Ibn Abdellah transformed Mogador into an open city, enticing overseas businessmen in with trade concessions, and it soon became a major commercial port, with a large foreign and Jewish popula-

tion establishing the town as a major centre of trade. The Sultan employed the French architect Cornut to design the city and its fortifications. Mogador was shelled by the French in 1844.

Orson Welles stayed here for some time, filming part of Othello at the **Skala**. From Independence the town was called Essaouira, a local name meaning 'little fortress'. In the 1960s Essaouira had a brief reputation as a 'happening place', which attracted hippies, notably the rock star Jimi Hendrix. Essaouira now seems to be emerging from several decades of decline, for on top of fishing, fish processing, a small market and handicraft industries, particularly woodwork, the town is attracting greater numbers of tourists, notably surfers.

ACCESS Essaouira is connected to Marrakech via the P10, and lies just to the W of the P8 from Casablanca to Agadir. The new bus station is to the N of **Bab Doukkala**, and it is worth taking a *calèche* or petit-taxi as far as the gate to the medina or Ave Mohammed V.

Places of interest

The Medina is Essaouira's major attraction. Entering from **Bab Doukkala** the main thoroughfare is rue Mohammed Zerktouni, which leads into Ave de l'Istiqlal, where there is the **Grand Mosque**, and just off, on Darb Laalouj, the **Museum of Sidi Mohammed Ibn Abdellah** (open 0830-1200 and 1430-1800, except Tues), which has an interesting collection of weapons, as well as handicrafts such as woodwork and carpets, and the **Ensemble Artisanal**. Ave de l'Istiqlal leads into Ave Okba Ibn Nafi, on which is located the small **Galerie des Arts Frederic**, at the end of the street a gate on the right leads into Place Moulay Hassan, the heart of the town's social life and although recently repaved and modernized, still with character. The town's *souqs*, are mainly located around the junction between rue Mohammed Zerktouni and rue Mohammed El Gorry, although there is an area of woodworkers inside the **Skala** walls to the N of Place Moulay Hassan, where some fine pieces can be picked up with some good-natured bargaining.

The Harbour and Skala Off Place Moulay Hassan is the small but vibrant harbour, which principally supports a fishing fleet, and is worth a visit. Adjacent to the harbour and continuing along the coastal side of the medina is the **Skala**, an old Portuguese sea defence and battery, with cannons still in position. Just to the N of Place Moulay Hassan it is possible to go on to walls, from where there is an impressive view along the coast and other to the islands.

This part is separated from that by the port, which can also be visited.

Cemeteries Outside the walls is the Consul's cemetery for British officials who died there converting Mogador into a trading post with strong UK links. Across the road in the Jewish cemetery – if you can find the man with the key – is the resting place of Leslie Hore-Belisha who invented the first pedestrian crossing light.

The **beach** at Essaouira is very beautiful, isolated but fiercely windy. The wind, known as the *alizee*, stirs up a lot of sand, and it is cold for swimming, but

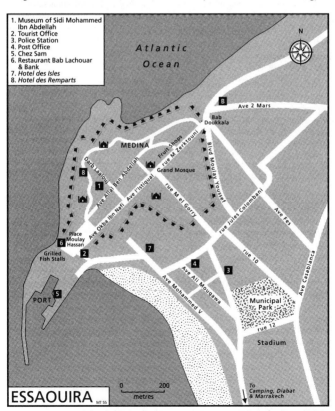

1. Museum of Sidi Mohammed Ibn Abdellah
2. Tourist Office
3. Police Station
4. Post Office
5. Chez Sam
6. Restaurant Bab Lachouar & Bank
7. *Hotel des Isles*
8. *Hotel des Remparts*

Atlantic Ocean

N

MEDINA

Fruit Shops

Bab Doukkala

Ave 2 Mars

Darb Laalouj

Ave Allal Ben Abdellah

rue M Zerktouni

Grand Mosque

Blvd Moulay Youssef

Ave l'Istiqual

rue M el Gorry

Ave Oqba Ibn Nafi

rue Jules Colombani

Ave Fes

Place Moulay Hassan

Grilled Fish Stalls

Ave Casablanca

Ave Ali Mouqawa

rue 10

Ave Mohammed V

Municipal Park

PORT

rue 12

Stadium

To Camping, Diabat & Marrakech

ESSAOUIRA MT 55

0   200
metres

ideal for surfing. When walking far along the beach it should be noticed that the incoming tide makes the small stream below Diabat into an impassable river.

Diabat The ruined palace/pavilion below Diabat is worth a detour from a beach walk, just after the stream which crosses it, but the village of Diabat is dreadfully miserable.

Isles des Purpuraires These islands are a bird sanctuary, particularly for White Falcons. It is possible to visit the main island and the ruins of a prison, by contacting the Tourist Information Office on Place Moulay Hassan. They will direct the visitor to the Province office off Ave Mohammed V where a permit can be obtained for MD50, and will arrange a boat for transport, for a negotiable price.

Local information
● Accommodation
For hotels in Essaouira it is important to get a well ventilated room with windows, and preferably a view of the sea, for the others can be dark, claustrophobic and damp. **C** *Hotel des Iles*, Ave Mohammed V, T 472329/74, Tx 71042, 65 rm, an historic hotel with tasteful period decoration, restaurant, bar, nightclub and pool.

D *Hotel Tafoukt*, 98 Ave Mohammed V, BP 38, T 472504/5, Tx 71022, 40 rm, a reasonable hotel, with tea rooms, bar and restaurant, try and get a sea view.

E *Hotel Mechouar*, Ave Okba Ibn Nafi, T 472018, 24 rm, a bit cheaper; **E** *Hotel Sahara*, Ave Okba Ibn Nafi in the medina, T 472292, 70 rm, comfortable and central.

F *Hotel Beau Rivage*, on Place Moulay Hassan, central, overlooking main square and friendly, double rooms with bath, very damp; **F** *Hotel des Remparts*, 18 rue Ibn Rochd, a popular place with friendly staff and a spectacular view from the roof terrace, but damp and with poor utilities; **F** *Hotel du Tourisme*, rue Mohammed Ben Messaoud is cheap but poorly-equipped and very damp; **F** *Hotel Smara*, just inside the ramparts N from Place Moulay Hassan, is by far the best cheap option, clean and friendly, although make sure the room is one of those with a stunning sea view, the others are damp, good roof terrace.

● Camping
Camping Municipal d'Essaouira, along Ave

Mohammed V from the medina.

● Places to eat
◆◆◆*Chalet de la Plage*, 1 Ave Mohammed V, T 472158, good fish dishes but a wide range of other fishes; *Chez Sam*, in the harbour, a fish and seafood restaurant and bar, with good food and drink and a distinctive atmosphere, particularly good lobster; *Restaurant Riad*, Ave Allal Ben Abdellah, a wide range of Moroccan dishes.

◆◆*Restaurant El Khaima*, Place Moulay Hassan, a good licensed restaurant with Moroccan specialities; also try *Restaurant Bab Lachouar*, on Place Moulay Hassan.

◆By far the best cheap eating option is to sample the freshly caught fish grilled at open air restaurants between Place Moulay Hassan and the port; accompanied by a tomato salad this makes a delicious meal at a reasonable, negotiated price. There are also a series of so-called Berber Cafés off to the left of rue Mohammed Zerktouni as walking towards Bab Doukkala. Other good cheap options incl *Café-Restaurant Essalam*, Place Moulay Hassan; and *Mustafa's*, on Ave Allal Mohammed Ben Abdellah. The latter street has a number of cheap places.

● Bars
Try *Chez Sam*, in the harbour; or *Hotel des Isles*; and *Hotel Tafoukt*, both on Ave Mohammed V.

● Cafés
The best cafés are on Place Moulay Hassan, particularly *Chez Driss*, a good place to have breakfast, or watch the evening social life pass by. There are several beachside cafés, ideal for a rest from the wind.

● Banks & money changers
Place Moulay Hassan.

● Post & Telecommunications
The PTT is on Ave Lalla Aicha, back from the seafront and Ave Mohammed V.

● Tourist offices
Place Moulay Hassan.

● Transport
Local Bus: CTM and private line bus services operate from the terminal N of Bab Doukkala, with connections to Casablanca, Safi, Marrakech and Agadir. An ONCF service to Marrakech, to connect with onward trains to Casablanca and Rabat leaves at 0620. **Taxi**: grand-taxis operate from a parking lot beside the bus terminal.

MEKNES, FES AND CENTRAL MOROCCO

CONTENTS	
Meknes and Environs	139
Fes and Environs	151
Taza and Environs	167
Oujda and on to Algeria	169

MAPS	
Central Morocco	139
Meknes	144
Meknes Medina	145
Volubilis	149
Fes	153
Fes El Bali	155
Fes El Jedid	161
Fes Ville Nouvelle	162

The region of Central Morocco is the pivotal strategic region of the country, through which military and trade routes have always passed, as well as a productive agricultural area. It is thus a region in which power has often been concentrated, and some of the greatest urban settlements have evolved.

Under the Romans power was, for a time, concentrated at the site of **Volubilis**, still the best preserved and most informative site of the period. Nearby, Moulay Idriss, the father of the Moroccan state is honoured in the pilgrimage town of the same name, a memorable settlement, with houses cascading down hills on either side of a large sanctuary. Moulay Idriss founded **Fes** which went on to become an imperial capital, and the undisputed intellectual, spiritual and cultural centre of the country. Today it is full of stunning examples of different periods of Islamic architecture, as well as *souqs*, each with its own speciality, still functioning at the heart of the city. **Meknes**, 522m, lying to the W of Fes, is a quieter city with a pleasant medina and the ruins of Sultan Moulay Ismail's vast capital. To the E of Fes, towards Algeria, Taza and Oujda are regional centres which have held vital strategic roles. To the S of Fes and Meknes lie the Middle Atlas mountains, with peaceful small towns amidst attractive wooded valleys.

MEKNES AND ENVIRONS

From Rabat to Meknes the P1 passes through the Mamora Forest and a belt of fertile, relatively prosperous and unexciting countryside. The only major town en route is Khemisset, with a *souq* on Tues, and a reputation for the best *brochettes* in the small restaurants along the main street. The former imperial capital of Meknes lies between the

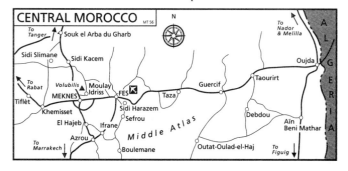

Middle Atlas and the Cheraga hills. It is an essential stop en route to Fes, with a traditional medina and the ruins of Moulay Ismail's vast imperial city on either side of the huge and brightly tiled **Bab Mansur**. The shrine town of Moulay Idriss and the ruins of the Roman capital of Volubilis, the best ancient site in Morocco, are easy excursions from Meknes.

Meknes

History

Meknes is one of the great historic cities of Morocco, pre-eminent during the reign of Moulay Ismail when its vast, and now mostly ruined, imperial city was built. This is memorable more for the impressive size and feeling of space than for the architecture. Another distinct part of Meknes is the historic medina which includes the intricately decorated **Bou Inania Medersa**, the traditional but vibrant *souqs*, and numerous mosques. The *ville nouvelle* was built by the French on the opposite bank of the Oued Boufekrane, commanding impressive views over the medina and the imperial city. It has a relaxed atmosphere, a calm place to drink a coffee or tea and watch the evening *promenade* pass by.

Early origins Meknes was originally a kasbah from the 8th century, used by the Kharajite Berbers against the Arabs. The town itself was founded by the Zenata Berber tribe called Meknassa in the 10th century and then destroyed by the Almoravids in 1069. A later kasbah was destroyed by the Almohad Sultan Abd el-Moumen in order to build a new grid-patterned medina, some features of which still remain. This city was ruined during the conflict between the Almohads and the Merinids, but was partially rebuilt and repopulated in 1276 under Sultan Moulay Youssef. The Merinids also built the *medersa*.

The Reign of Moulay Ismail The reign of the Alawite Sultan, Moulay Ismail (1672-1727) witnessed the peak of Meknes' glory, as the dynamic Sultan used his immense power as *pasha* to develop the city before his succession to the imperial throne. Meknes was chosen as his capital rather than the rebellious and self-important rivals of Fes and Marrakech. Moulay Ismail is renowned for his ruthless violence, but many of the stories recounted by the guides may be apocryphal. What is certain is that he made a great impression on the visitors to the court from Europe, and Meknes became a kind of Moroccan Versailles, indeed, some suggest that the Sultan was trying to rival Louis XIV, who was building his French palace at the same time. Moulay Ismail conquered and then controlled Morocco and left his mark all over the country, particularly with the kasbahs built by his troops as they pacified the numerous rebellious tribes, but also with an array of mosques, public buildings and medinas.

Moulay Ismail's vision of Meknes was vast, and although much of the *pisé* cement city is in ruins, those walls still standing are testimony to its original scale. The city was built by a massive army of slaves, both Moroccan and Christian, and the Sultan was in particular famed for his barbaric treatment of these people, supposedly interring them in the walls. He built several palaces to accommodate his wives, concubines, children and court, as well as quarters for his army of Abids, black slaves, which was the instrument of his power. The city contained within it all that was necessary for such a large population and military machine, with store houses, stables, armouries, exercise areas, gardens and ponds.

After Moulay Ismail After Moulay Ismail's death Meknes gradually declined. His huge court and army could not be held together without his authority, and his successors Moulay Abdellah and Sidi

Mohammed returned the emphasis to Fes and Marrakech. Furthermore the earthquake of 1755 destroyed many of Moulay Ismail's creations. The French revitalized Meknes, appreciating its strategic position in the corridor linking E Morocco and Algeria with the coastal belt around Rabat and Casablanca. They built their *ville nouvelle* apart from the medina and the Imperial City, on the E bank of the Oued Boufekrane, as part of their policy of separate development of Moroccan and European quarters. Meknes was an important army base for the French, and was not neglected in the way that Fes or Marrakech were.

Although Meknes is perhaps overshadowed by its near neighbour Fes, with a population of 319,783 (1982) it is today the fifth largest city in Morocco with both tourism and industrial activities, and the centre of a highly productive agricultural region, noted particularly for its wines which are the best in the country.

ACCESS Train: the main railway station is at Ave de la Basse, T 520017, 520689, but most trains also call at the Al Amir Abdelkader station, E of Ave Mohammed V, both in the *ville nouvelle*. **Road**: coming in from the E from Rabat along the P1, the principal route skirts the medina, crossing the Oued Boufekrane and reaching the *ville nouvelle* at the junction of Ave Moulay Ismail and Ave des Forces Armées Royales. Another route continues into the medina via Bab Khemis. From Fes and the E the P1 leads into Ave de Fes in the *ville nouvelle*. The P6 from Tanger and the N brings the traveller into the *ville nouvelle* along rue de Yougoslavie (Ave Al Moutahadia). **Bus**: CTM buses arrive at the terminal at 47 Ave Mohammed V, T 522583. Private line buses call at the terminal below Bab Mansur.

Places of interest

Guides Meknes is one of the easiest imperial cities to explore independently but there is no shortage of *faux guides* offering their services, often aggressively, in Place el Hedim and nearby. If

you need assistance, obtain an official guide from the tourist office or one of the larger hotels. MD100 is a realistic fee.

The Medina: Place el Hedim (the Square of Destruction), opposite **Bab Mansur** is the centre of Meknes' old city, and the best starting point for exploration. Despite its name this is a quiet area, other than the *faux guides* plying their trade, recently paved, set out with unremarkable fountains and surrounded by a few handicraft stalls and cafés. It is a pleasant place to sit. To the left of the square is a crowded, covered food market with vast displays of vegetables and pickles. On the right-hand corner of the square down a few steps is **Dar Jamai**, a 19th century palace, owned by officials at the court of Sultan Moulay Hassan, now the Museum of Moroccan Arts open 0900-1200 and 1500-1800, entrance MD10. Exploring the house gives an insight into the houses and life of the 19th century Muslim élite, with an interesting exhibition of craftwork and antique household items, porcelain, jewellery and carpets mixing Berber and Andalusian influences, including pottery from Meknes and Fes, and carpets from the Middle Atlas. Note also the wall tiles and jewellery. The upstairs includes a furnished reception room.

The souqs Meknes has a number of traditional *souqs*, which whilst not quite of the order of those in Marrakech or Fes, are worth exploring. Immediately to the left of the **Dar Jamai** a small entrance leads to the *souqs*. The alley bends around to the right behind Dar Jamai past some undistinguished clothes shops. Just before a carpet shop turn left. The passage, now covered, widens slightly, and continues past a range of shops selling modern goods, a bank, and various minor side turnings. At the junction, on the left, is **Souq Nejjarin** (see below). **Souq Sebbat** is the right hand turning including sellers of *baboushes*, modern clothes and *kaftans*, several tourist and handicraft shops, a *fondouk* on the right, and another on the left before the **Bou Inania Medersa**. A turning on the right opposite the *medersa* leads directly onto rue Dar Smen, a good alternative route to remember.

Bou Inania Medersa The Merinid Bou Inania *Medersa* (open 0900-1200 and 1500-1800), dating from 1345, is the most important building to visit in the medina. It is best approached from Souq Sebbat. The door to the *medersa*, part of a cedar screen, is just past a dome, notable for its ribbed design.

This religious school has 40 cells for its students, on both floors, around an oblong courtyard including a pool, with arcades surrounded by a screened passageway. As with many of the *medressa* there is a good range of decoration, the *zellij* tiling catching the eye, whilst the carving on the beams and screens are also skilfully and beautifully executed. There is a plentiful display of intricate Koranic inscription executed in a range of materials around the walls and pillars.

Turn right to the green and yellow tiled prayer hall. The door is ornamented with *zellij* tiling, as well as the customary and perhaps a little over-the-top stalactite style plasterwork. Note the inscriptions by the *mihrab*. Climb up onto the roof for a view of the medina, including the domed roof of the Great Mosque, the minaret of the Nejjarin Mosque, and other minarets.

Beyond the *medersa* bear right then second left passing a number of handicraft shops, notably selling iron pots and figures decorated with beaten silver thread, to **El Mansur Palace**, a former palace now a carpet shop and called the *Palais des Idrissides*. It is worth entering to see the impressive stucco and wood carving, and ceiling painting. From here the energetic can continue on into the northern medina.

Souq Nejjarin, includes sellers of textiles, and carpenters, another entrance to the carpet *souq*, and a *fondouk* hardly changed since it was built. This route passes the Almoravid **Nejjarin Mosque**. At the end one can turn left towards the *mellah* or Place el Hedim or right into the dusty and noisy **Souq Sraira**, just inside the city walls, used by carpenters and metalworkers. At the very end, on left, is the 12th century Almohad **Bab Jedid** gate, around which are some interesting stalls selling musical instruments. **Souq Cherchira**, initially occupied by tentmakers runs parallel to Souq Sraira but outside the city walls.

The Mellah To the W of Place El Hedim through a street popular with hawkers of household goods turn left into Ave de Mellah. On the left is the *mellah* a quarter built by Moulay Ismail in 1682 for his large Jewish community, walled off from the Muslim medina. The **Bab Berrima Mosque** dates from the 18th century when the *mellah* was becoming increasingly Muslim, as the Jews were moved further downhill into the medina.

Heading SW towards Rabat the city wall is broken by **Bab El Khemis (Bab Rih)**, built by Moulay Ismail, with a range of different arches, decoration and calligraphy. Through this the Blvd Circulaire leads past the 18th century tomb of Sidi Mohammed Ben Aissa, founder of the important religious brotherhood of the Aissoua, closed to non-Muslims but worth a look from a respectable distance. The Ben Aissa religious fête is still held on *Mouloud*, but is no longer the ritually violent occasion it once was. The Blvd Circulaire continues round to Bab el-Berdaine, the entrance to the N medina.

The northern medina is less frequented by tourists. Either weave through the medina from the *medersa* or the *souqs*, or more easily, enter from the Blvd Circulaire. **Bab Berdaine**, dates from the 17th century, a decorated building flanked by two immense towers. Inside, on Place el Berdaine, is the **Berdaine Mosque**. Travelling S the streets continue through an area of the traditional medina, less spoilt by the demands of tourism, and indicating more clearly the nature of the Islamic City where private and public space are clearly differentiated, commercial areas zoned by function, with each quarter having its own mosque, *hammam* and *four* (bakers), the three most important facilities in the neighbourhood. Eventually one will pass the **El Mansur Palace**, another 19th century house (see above).

Back on the Blvd Circulaire, the next major gate around towards Oued Boufekrane is Bab Tizmi, near to *Restaurant Zitouna*. Opposite Bab Tizmi is the small and quiet **Parc Zoologique El Haboul** (open 1300-1700 Tues-Thur, 1000-2000 Fri-Sun, closed Mon). This zoo is one part of an area of gardens and recreational facilities in the valley dividing the medina and the *ville nouvelle*.

Bab Mansur Meknes is dominated by the monumental gate at the top of the hill in the medina, opposite Place el Hedim. Bab Mansur dates from the reign of Sultan Moulay Ismail, completed by his son Moulay Abdellah, and marks the entrance to the huge grounds of his Imperial City. The gate is named after one of the Sultan's Christian slaves, Mansur the Infidel. The huge size is more of a testimony to its Sultan than a reflection of defensive strength, as design is more ceremonial, for example the decorated flanking towers do not have firing posts.

The *outrepassé* arch is surrounded by a blind arch including the *darj w ktaf* motif and colourful *zellij* tiling. The frame is a band of *darj w ktaf* and *zellij* surmounted by inscription, and between the arch and the band is a black tiled area with floral patterns. The overall effect of the main gate is an exuberant and powerful display of the architecture of Moulay Ismail's reign. This has come to be a symbol of Meknes.

The Imperial City of Moulay Ismail is a massive area of crumbling walls and ruins well worth taking a day to explore at leisure. Immediately through Bab Mansur from Place el Hedim there is Place Lalla Aouda, a relaxing and pleasant area to rest. In the far corner is the **Lalla Aouda Mosque**, the story being that it was built by Princess Aouda as penance for eating a peach during the Ramadan fast.

Directly opposite Bab Mansur, in the right hand corner of the square, a space in the walls leads through to a second square, the Mechouar. To the right note the domed **Koubat al-Khayyatin** situated in a small park behind a fence, entrance MD10. A plain building with pleasing simple decor. In the 18th century this was used to receive ambassadors, and later to make uniforms. To the right of this building steps lead down to an underground space, variously explained as a prison or a storehouse. In the wall opposite the small park the right hand gate leads to a golf course. This was originally to have been a lake, but was converted into its present usage by the present king. Behind the golf course is a later palace of Moulay Ismail, the **Royal Palace** or **Dar al-Makhzen**, still in use and now heavily restored, closed to visitors.

The Mausoleum of Moulay Ismail can be reached through the gate to the left of that to the golf course. The Mausoleum, inside, opposite some shops selling overpriced handicrafts, contains the tombs of Moulay Ismail, his wife and Moulay Ahmed. Unusually for religious buildings in Morocco, the Mausoleum is open to non-Muslims who can enter as far as an annex to the mosque section and admire from there the plaster stucco, *zellij* tiling and distinctive and exuberant colouring. The guardian normally allows visitors to take photos of the interior of the mosque from the annex. Entrance free. Just past the mausoleum is an entrance to **Dar**

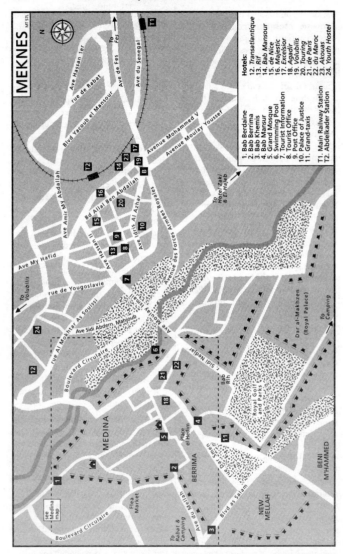

MEKNES MT 575

N

To Fes

Hotels:
12. Transatlantique
13. Rif
14. Bab Mansour
15. de Nice
16. Majestic
17. Excelsior
18. Agadir
19. Volubilis
20. Touring
21. de Paris
22. du Maroc
23. Akouas
24. Youth Hostel

1. Bab Berdaine
2. Bab Berrima
3. Bab Khemis
4. Bab Mansour
5. Grand Mosque
6. Swimming Pool
7. Tourist Information
8. Tourist Office
9. Post Office
10. Palace of Justice
11. Grand-taxis

T1. Main Railway Station
T2. Abdelkader Station

Ave Hassan 1er
rue de Rabat
Ave du Senegal
Blvd Yacoub el Mansour
Ave de Fes

Avenue Mohammed V
Avenue Moulay Youssef

Ave Amir My Abdallah
Bd Allal Ben Abdallah
Ave Idris Al Azhar
Ave II Hassan

Hotel Zaki
& El-Hajeb

Ave My Hafid
rue de Yougoslavie

To Volubilis

Ave Sidi Abderr Mahjoub
Ave Sidi Abderr Mahjoub

Boulevard Circulaire

Avenue des Forces Armees Royales

Dar al-Makhzen
(Royal Palace)

To Camping

rue Sidi Naijan

Bab Rih

Royal Golf
and Parks

MEDINA

BERRIMA

Place
el Hedim

rue des Sarraijine
Ave du Mellah

rue des Sarraijine

Flea Market

To Rabat &
Camping

Blvd as salam

NEW MELLAH

BENI M'HAMMED

Boulevard Circulaire

see
Medina
map

al-Kebira, Moulay Ismail's late 17th century palace. The palace is in ruins, and occupied by squatters in an ironic statement on Morocco's housing situation, but the nature and vast scale of the original basic structure of the building can be easily discerned. Back out on the road pass under the passage of the **Bab ar-Rih**,

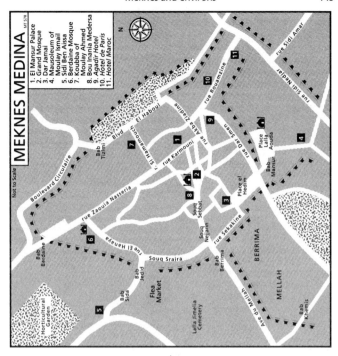

MEKNES MEDINA MT 576

1. El Mansur Palace
2. Grand Mosque
3. Dar Jamai
4. Mausoleum of Moulay Ismail
5. Sidi Ben Aissa
6. Berdaine Mosque
7. Koubba of Moulay Ahmed
8. Bou Inania Medersa
9. Agadir Hotel
10. Hôtel de Paris
11. Hotel Maroc

Not to Scale

a long, arched structure. Follow the walled road, running between the Dar al-Kebira and the Dar al-Makhzen and turn right at the end. Carry straight ahead until the large **Heri as-Souni** building is reached.

Heri as-Souni, open 0830-1200 and 1430-1830, is a large, impressive structure dating from the reign of Moulay Ismail, used variously as a granary, warehouse and water point, to provide for the court, army and followers in either the normal run of events or in case of conflict or drought, and indicating the scale of the imperial city which Moulay Ismail built. The first, long room exhibits typical furniture, decoration and woodwork from the richer Meknes houses. The second room is surrounded by large storerooms and wells, the latter were used with

a donkey-powered system of chain-buckets. Behind this is a vast space originally used as a granary. From the roof there is a good view. To the right is the Agdal basin storing water for irrigation purposes. This is a pleasant location, popular at weekends and summer evenings.

Heri al-Mansur Turn right and then take the second left. On the left is the **Dar al-Baida** built by Sultan Mohammed Ibn Abdellah in the 1790s, now a military academy closed to visitors. He also built the **Rouah Mosque** in 1790, with columns from the **Badia Palace** in Marrakech. To the left is a small *medersa* used as a Koranic school. Nearby is a long canal alongside the massive structure of the **Heri al-Mansur**, also known as the **Rouah**. This ruined building, once the stables, reveals much about the size of the Sultan's retinue.

Local information

● Accommodation

B *Hotel Tikida Transatlantique*, rue El Marinyen, T 525051/6, F 520057, 120 a/c rm, 2 restaurants and a bar, tennis, 2 good pools, an elegant, stylish and well-equipped hotel with excellent view of the medina, dating from the 1930s.

C *Hotel Rif*, rue d'Accra, *ville nouvelle*, T 522591/4, F 524428, 120 rm, new, comfortable, Moroccan decor, lively nightclub (2130-0300), restaurant, good bar, pool; **C** *Hotel Zaki*, Blvd Al Massira, city outskirts, T 520990, Tx 41079, 230 a/c rm, 2 restaurants, 2 bars, nightclub and pool, rec.

D *Akouas Hotel*, 27 rue Emir Abdelkader, T 515967, F 515994, new, 52 rm, 2 restaurants, bar, nightclub (2200-0100); **D** *Hotel Bab Mansur*, 38 rue Emir Abdelkader, T 525239/40, F 510741, 76 rm and 2 suites, new, restaurant, bar, nightclub, in *ville nouvelle*; **D** *Hotel de Nice*, 10 rue d'Accra, T 520318, restaurant, bar, centre of *ville nouvelle*, good rooms; **D** *Hotel Volubilis*, 45 Ave des Forces Armées Royales, T 520102, bar, nightclub, quite old, conveniently located.

E *Hotel Excelsior*, 57 Ave des Forces Armées Royales, T 521900, 42 rm, another cheap *ville nouvelle* option; **E** *Hotel Majestic*, 19 Ave Mohammed V, T 522033, F 527427, 42 clean rm, excellent value, friendly staff; **E** *Hotel Touring*, 34 Ave Allal Ben Abdellah, T 522351, cheap, respectable, large rooms, café.

F *Hotel du Maroc*, 7 Derb Ben Brahim, off rue Rouamzine, T 530075, 28 rm, the best cheap hotel in the medina, quiet, clean and efficient, cold showers; *Hotel Agadir*, 2 rue Dar Smen (on the small square), T 530141, 18 tiny and basic rm in a bizarre, distinctively decorated rabbit-warren; *Hotel de Paris*, 58 rue Rouamzine, 11 good rm but no showers.

The gates on the left of Heri as-Souni lead to the campsite.

● Youth hostel

T 524698, Ave Okba Ibn Nafii, 1000-1200, 1600-1700, near the municipal stadium and *Hotel Transatlantique*, 60 beds, MD25-35 per night, kitchen, meals available, bus 25m, train 1.2 km. This is the YHA headquarters in Morocco and is one of the best and most friendly hostels with dormitories around a garden.

● Camping

Camping Agdal, 2 km from Meknes centre on the road to Rabat, take buses 2 or 3, there is a shop, café and hot showers, and it is clean and well organized.

● Places to eat

♦♦♦*Restaurant Belle Vue* in *Hotel Transatlantique*, rue El Marinyen, T 525051-6, an extensive international menu, good wines, excellent views over Meknes medina from its *ville nouvelle* hilltop location; *La Hacienda*, Route de Fes outside Meknes, T 521092, highly rec excellent French and international food in a farm atmosphere, nightclub below; *Restaurant Zitouna*, 44 Jamaa Zitouna, T 532083, in style of a Moroccan palace in a medina side-street nr Bab Tizmi, with a Moroccan menu, no alcohol.

♦♦*Restaurant Bar Brasserie Metropole*, 12 Ave Hassan II, T 522576, international menu, licensed; *Bar Restaurant La Coupole*, Ave Hassan II, T 522483, French/Moroccan menu, friendly, quiet, reasonable food, licensed; *Café Restaurant Camprinoss*, Ave Omar Ibn El Ass (opp the market in the *ville nouvelle*), T 520258, French, Spanish and Moroccan cuisine, unlicensed; *Le Dauphin*, 5 Ave Mohammed V, T 523423, licensed Moroccan restaurant, seafood; *Pizzeria Le Four*, 1 rue Atlas, T 520857, reasonable international cuisine and moderate pizzas in a pleasant atmosphere, good wine.

♦ *Rôtisserie Karam*, 2 Ave Ghana, good chicken, *brochettes* and salads; *Novelty*, Ave de Paris, T 522156, Moroccan food, licensed; *Restaurant Economique* is perhaps the best of several cheap and basic Moroccan restaurants on rue Dar Smen.

● Bars

Hotel Transatlantique, rue El Marinyen, is an excellent place for a relaxing drink, not least because of the view over the medina; also try the *Hotel de Nice*, 10 rue d'Accra; *La Caravelle*, 6 rue de Marseille; *Bar Continental* and *La Coupole* both in Ave Hassan II.

● Cafés

The aromatic mint tea of Meknes is recommended. Try one of the cafés on rue Dar Smen, or one of the better hotels. In the *ville nouvelle* try *Cremerie-Patisserie Miami*, Ave Mohammed V.

● Banks & money changers

ABM, Angle Blvd Nehru and rue Ali Ben Rahal, T 520015; **Banque du Maroc**, 33 Ave Mohammed V; **BMAO**, 15 Place 2 Septembre;

BMCE, 98 Ave des Forces Armées Royales, T 520352, bureau de change open every day 1000-1400 and 1600-2000; **Credit du Maroc**, 33 Ave Mohammed V; **SGMB**, Place Al Wahda Al Ifriquia, T 527896; **Wafabank**, 11 Ave Mohammed V, T 521151.

● **Cultural Centre**

Centre Culturel Français, Zankat Farhat Hachad, Ave Hassan II, cultural and social programme.

● **Entertainment**

Discos & nightclubs: *Bahia*, *Rif Hotel*, rue d'Accra (2130-0300); *Cabaret Oriental*, *Grand-Hotel Volubilis*, 45 Ave des Forces Armées Royales. Also at *Hotel Zaki*, Blvd Al Massira, *Akouas Hotel*, 27 rue Emir Abdelkader (2200-0100) and *Hotel Bab Mansur*, 38 rue Emir Abdelkader.

● **Hammam**

4 rue Patrice Lumumba.

● **Hospitals & medical services**

Ambulance: T 15.

Chemists: *Pharmacie d'Urgence*, Place Administrative, T 523375, 0830-2030; *Depot de Nuit*: *Medicaments d'Urgence*, *Hotel de Ville*, Place Administrative (2030-0830).

Hospitals: Hôpital Mohammed V, T 521134; Hôpital Moulay Ismail, Ave des Forces Armées Royales, T 522805, 522806.

● **Post & telecommunications**

PTT Centrale, Place Administrative, 0800-1400, T 0800-2100; also the PTT on rue Dar Smen, in the medina.

● **Places of worhsip**

Catholic Church: *Notre Dame des Oliviers*, Place Poereiam, services Sat 1800, Sun 1030.

● **Shopping**

One of the specialities of Meknes is iron work decorated with beaten silver thread. For this and other specialities try the medina, or the *Ensemble Artisanale*, on the road out to Rabat, 0830-1200 and 1530-1830, with a fixed price shop, bank, and an extensive training centre and individual workshops which visitors will be shown on request.

● **Sports**

Golf: *Royal Golf Club*, El Mhancha, T 530753.

Riding: *L'Etrier* (Haras Régional).

Swimming: *Lahboul Park*, Rond-Point Bou Amer, BP 45, T 520415.

Tennis: *Club de Meknes*, Lahboul Park, Rond-Point Bou Amer, BP 45, T 520415.

● **Tourist offices**

Office du Tourisme (ONMT), 27 Place Batha-l'Istiqlal, T 521286, very helpful; **Syndicat d'Initiative**, Palais de la Foire, T 520191.

● **Tour companies & travel agents**

Wagons-Lit Tourisme, 1 rue de Ghana, T 521995; *Wasteels Voyages*, Ave Mohammed V, T 523062. *Royal Air Maroc*, 7 Ave Mohammed V, T 520963.

● **Useful addresses**

Fire: T 15.

Police: T 19.

● **Transport**

Local Bus: buses No 5, 7 and 9 run between the *ville nouvelle* and the medina. **Car hire**: *Stop Car*, 3 rue Essaouira, T 525061; *Zeit*, 4 rue Antsirebe, T 525918. **Taxi**: use the light blue petit-taxis.

Train The main station is at Ave de la Basse, T 520017, 520689. Departures for **Rabat** and **Casablanca**: 0409, 0749, 0954, 1144, 1503, 1655, 1927, 2026, 0242; for **Tanger**: 0459, 1346; for **Fes**: 11 a day between 0547 and 0240; for **Taza** and **Oujda**: 0547, 1344, 1549, 1855, 0031, 0240. Some trains also stop at Meknes El Amir Abdelkader station, just below Ave Mohammed V, and closer to the centre of the *ville nouvelle*.

Road Bus: CTM buses to Rabat, Casablanca and Fes (7 a day), Tanger, Ifrane, Azrou, Ouezzane and Er Rachidia (daily) leave from 47 Ave Mohammed V, T 522583. Private line services go from the terminal below Bab Mansur. **Taxi**: grand-taxis which are a particularly good option to both Fes and Azrou, leave from the car park below Place el Hedim, opposite the private line buses. Ask the drivers hanging around for the destination. Grand-taxis for Moulay Idriss (and then a short walk to Volubilis) leave from rue Yougoslavie.

Excursion to Moulay Idriss and Volubilis

The shrine town of Moulay Idriss is 30 km to the N of Meknes. Leave Meknes by rue de Yougoslavie in the *ville nouvelle*, and follow the P6 as far as Aïn el-Kerna, and from there the P28 to Moulay Idriss. Take a grand-taxi from rue de Yougoslavie, or from the square below Place el Hedim, to Moulay Idriss. There are also regular buses from below Bab Mansur. The last bus back is at 1900. Volubilis is a clearly signposted 5 km drive from Moulay Idriss, a pleasant walk on a nice day, or a short taxi ride. Alternatively, bargain in Meknes for a grand-taxi all the way.

Moulay Idriss

Coming round the last bend from Meknes, Moulay Idriss is a dramatic sight, houses and mosques piled up around two rock outcrops, with the *zaouia*, or sanctuary, in between. The centre of the Jbel Zerhoun region, Moulay Idriss is a pilgrimage centre, including as it does the tomb of its namesake, the great-grandson of the prophet, the town a Mecca in Morocco for those unable to do the ultimate pilgrimage. Moulay Idriss came to Morocco from Arabia, after defeat at the Battle of Fakh in 786. In 788 he was accepted as *Imam* by the Berber Aurora tribe at Volubilis, and went on in his short life in Morocco, before he was poisoned in 791, to win over the loyalty of the tribes to the Idrissid Dynasty he established, and to spread further Islam. This town and Fes were two of his major legacies.

However, the town of Moulay Idriss was mainly developed in the 18th century by Sultan Moulay Ismail, in part using materials lifted from nearby Volubilis, which the Sultan plundered without restraint. Moulay Idriss was closed to non-Muslims until 1912, and even today is primarily a Muslim sanctuary, best visited during the day as an excursion, and although not unfriendly, certainly a place to be treated with cautious respect. A religious festival, or *moussem* is held here in Sep, when the town is transformed by an influx of pilgrims and a sea of tents.

Buses and taxis stop in the main square where there are some basic restaurants and cafés, and below it an open market space. Above it is the **Moulay Idriss Zaouia**, as well as shops for items associated with pilgrimage: rosaries,

scarves, candles, and a delicious array of nougats, candies and nuts, taken by Muslims as souvenirs. The sanctuary itself, with its green-tiled roofs, a succession of prayer halls, ablution areas and tombs, is closed to non-Muslims.

Looking up from the square, the medina clings to the two hills, on the left is Khiba, Tasga on the right. The steep paths through either section pass through a fascinating and largely unaltered area of housing. After the steep climb there is a rewarding view over the sanctuary, showing the courtyards and roofs, and the adjacent royal guesthouse. The road through the town, keeping right, leads to a Roman bath just above the stream. Further on, beyond the road, there is a ruined 18th century palace with a good view of the town.

There are no hotels in Moulay Idriss, but there is a camp-site, *Zermoune Belle Vue*, en route to Meknes, whilst opposite the turning to Volubilis the proprietor of the café allows people to camp. For lunch *Baraka de Zerhoun*, 22 Aïn Smen-Khiber, T 44184, with good Moroccan food at average prices, is recommended.

Volubilis

Volubilis is the most impressive Roman site in Morocco, and whilst much has been removed to adorn other cities over the centuries, or taken to museums such as that in Rabat, the structure of the town, the nature of its society and economy, and the design of the buildings is clearly discernible from the ruins, whilst some floor mosaics are still intact. Lying just below the Jbel Zerhoun and 5 km from Moulay Idriss along the P28, the site which is poorly signed from the road has free parking, a café and ticket office but little else. It can be viewed in a day trip from Meknes but for comfort stay at the **C** *Volubilis*, T (05) 544405/7, F (05) 544408, 52 rm, two restaurants, pool, terrace, excellent views, just to the N of site. In summer start early to avoid the heat. Admission is MD20, and the site is open from 0800 to sunset. On the way in, note the collection of mosaics and sculptures.

Archaeological evidence points to the possibility of a Neolithic settlement at Volubilis, whilst tablets found show there was a 3rd century BC Phoenician settlement. In AD 24 it was the Western capital of the Roman kingdom of Mauritania, and from AD 45 to 285 the capital of the Roman province of Mauretania

Tingitania. Under the Romans the immediate region was rich agriculturally, with significant production of olive oil, and contained scattered villas. However Volubilis was at the SE extremity of the province, connected to Rome through the Atlantic ports, its weak position necessitating the extensive city walls.

Under the Emperor Diocletian, Rome withdrew to the coastal areas, leaving Volubilis at the mercy of

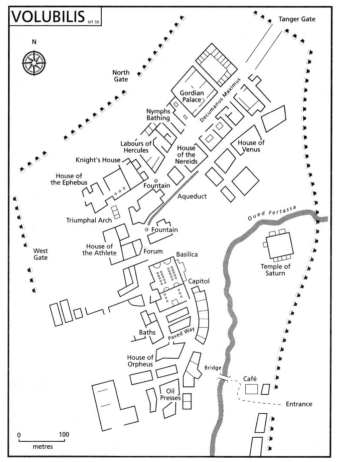

VOLUBILIS MT 59

N

North Gate
Tanger Gate
Gordian Palace
Decumanus Maximus
Nymphs Bathing
Labours of Hercules
House of the Nereids
House of Venus
Knight's House
House of the Ephebus
Fountain
Aqueduct
Triumphal Arch
Oued Fertassa
Fountain
West Gate
House of the Athlete
Forum
Basilica
Temple of Saturn
Capitol
Baths
Paved Way
House of Orpheus
Bridge
Café
Oil Presses
Entrance

0   100
metres

neighbouring tribes, but the city survived with diminished importance, notably with Christian and Jewish inhabitants, and later as the Christian enclave Oualila during the 8th century. Moulay Idriss was proclaimed as Sultan in Volubilis but during his reign he gave greater emphasis to Fes, so the city of Volubilis became totally deserted by the 11th century. Volubilis suffered when Moulay Ismail ransacked it to build Meknes, and further in the earthquake of 1755. French excavations and reconstruction began in 1915. The metal tracks on the site date from this work.

From the ticket office the entrance to the city is by the SE gate. A path, with sculptures and tombstones alongside it, leads down to a bridge across the Oued Fetassa. Up on the other side the first important remains in an area of small houses and industrial units is of an **olive press** complex. The mill stones, for crushing the olive stones, and the tanks for collecting and separating the oil, can be seen. Olive presses can be found through much of the city, as olive oil production was an essential element in its economy, as it is in the area today, where many of the same techniques are still used.

Right of the olive press is the **House of Orpheus**, a large mansion. In this building, as in most, some areas will be clearly roped off, and it is advisable to respect this, to avoid the whistle and wrath of the otherwise very friendly guardian. The first entrance gives access to a room with an intricate dolphin mosaic, to a kitchen with a niche for religious figures, and to a paved bathroom and boiler room. Note the complex heating system. The second entrance leads to an open court with a mosaic of the goddess Amphitrite, with living rooms around, including a dining room with an Orpheus mosaic, showing the hero playing his harp.

Heading further down and then to the right lie the **Baths of Gallienus**,

public baths in the manner of a Moroccan *hammam*. Beyond this the large public square in front of the **Basilica** is the **Forum**. In this area are a number of monuments to leading Roman figures. The **Basilica** is one of the most impressive ruins, with a number of columns intact. This 3rd century building was the court house for the city.

Beside the Basilica is the **Capitol**, also with columns. In the court in front there is an altar, and steps leading up to the temple. This temple is dedicated to Juno, Minerva and Jupiter Optimus Maximus. This building had great state importance, being the place where the council would assemble on great occasions.

Adjacent to the Forum is the **House of the Athlete**, named after the mosaic of an athlete winning a cup. The **Triumphal Arch** dominates the skyline, as well as the **Decumanus Maximus**, the roadway leading to the Tanger Gate. This was built in 217 AD to honour Emperor Caracalla and his mother Julia Domna. Originally topped by nymph fountains, and with medallions honouring its dedication, the arch was heavily reconstructed by the French. **Decumanus Maximus** was lined with a columned arcade with small shops, in front of a series of large houses, some containing interesting mosaics.

Starting on the left, from just beside the **Triumphal Arch**, the **House of the Ephebus** was built around a courtyard with a pool. Note in one of the surrounding public rooms a mosaic of Bacchus in a chariot. Two houses up, the **Knight's House** has an interesting mosaic of Bacchus, Eros, Ariadne and Theseus. The **House of the Labours of Hercules** has a mosaic with individual pictures of Hercules' life, and another of Jupiter. Further up the **House of the Bath of the Nymphs** has a mosaic showing nymphs undressing in front of Pegasus and Acteon. The largest house on this side, the **Gordian Palace**, is fronted by columns but the remains are quite plain. This may have been the governor's residence from the time of Gordian III, with both domestic quarters and offices.

On the right hand side of Decumanus Maximus from the Triumphal Arch there is a large public bath and fountains, fed by an aqueduct. Three houses up is the **House of Nereids** with a pool mosaic. Behind this and one up is the **House of Venus** has one of the best array of mosaics. The central courtyard pool has a mosaic of chariots. There are also mosaics of Bacchus, on the left, and Hylos and two nymphs, on the right. Nearby is a mosaic of Diana and the horned Acteon. From the House of Venus cross back over the Oued Fetassa to the remains of the **Temple of Saturn**, a Phoenician temple before the Romans took it over. From here, follow the path back to the entrance, perhaps for refreshments in the café after the labours in Volubilis.

FES AND ENVIRONS

Fes (also called Fez, and derived from the Arabic word for the pickaxe used in its construction) is a city which will take several days to come to terms with, several days to take in the atmosphere (this does not mean the industrial pollution which hangs over the city although this cannot be ignored), and several days to explore, but is worth giving the time. Spread out over three sites, the two most historic areas are full of memorable buildings, centred around the **Qarawi-**

> Ideas that never change, indeed something resembling an instinct, mean that in Fez there is only one age and one style: that of yesterday. It is the site of a miracle – that of suppressing the passage of time. That has given this city a unique character – unique perhaps in the universe, certainly in the Mediterranean world."
> Tharaud, Jerôme/Tharaud, Jean, *Fez*, (1930).

yin Mosque and some memorable *souqs*. Fes is also a base from which to explore nearby regions, Bhalil and Sefrou to the S and the springs of Sidi Harazem to the SE, as well as sites further afield, the Middle Atlas resorts of Azrou and Ifrane, and the historic sites near Meknes, Volubilis and Moulay Idriss.

Fes

(*Pop* 448,823 (1982); *Alt* 415m)

History of a city at the heart of Morocco

The historic city of Fes lies in the Oued Sebou basin, astride the traditional trade route from the Sahara to the Mediterranean, as well as on the path from Algeria and the Islamic heartland beyond into Morocco. For centuries the dominant axis within Morocco was of Fes and Marrakech, two cities linked by their immense power as well as by their rivalry. Even today, while the coastal belt centred on Rabat and Casablanca dominates the country in demographic, political and economic terms, Fes is still seen as the spiritual and cultural capital, and holds an enduring fascination for visitors, as one of the largest historic medina, full of monuments reflecting the different periods of Morocco's impe-

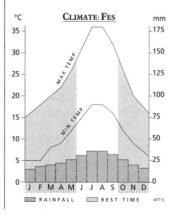

CLIMATE: FES

rial and architectural development. Fes has for long supplied the mercantile and intellectual élite of the country, and the *Fassi* (the people of Fes) are to be found in most towns and cities. The *Fassi* are rightly proud of their city and history, and often have a self-confidence quite beyond that of most Moroccans. Perhaps it does not have the immediate friendliness of the villages and towns of the mountains or the desert, but it is a city well worth giving time.

The Three Cities The city is composed of three distinct parts. On either side of the Oued Fes, a tributary of the Oued Sebou, lies Fes El Bali, the oldest part of the city, a medina divided by the river into Adwa al Andalusiyin (the Andalusian quarter on the E bank) and Adwa al Qarawiyin (the Qarawiyin quarter on the W bank). On a plateau just to the W lies Fes El Jedid, containing the royal palace and the *mellah*, which could be described as the new historic city. To the SW, on another raised area, lies the *ville nouvelle*, the modern city built by the French which has taken over many of the political, administrative and commercial functions of Fes.

Andalusiyin and Qarawiyin The first settlement here was the village Medinat Fes founded in 789/90 by Moulay Idriss, the Sultan and saint commemorated in the shrine town bearing his name near Meknes. However the town proper was founded by his son Idriss II as Al-Aliya in 808/9. Muslim families, refugees from Cordoba and surrounding areas of Andalucía soon took up residence in the Adwa al Andalusiyin quarter. Later 300 families from Kairouan in modern-day Tunisia settled on the opposite bank, forming Adwa al Qarawiyin. The **Qarawiyin Mosque**, perhaps the religious centre of Morocco, is the centre of a university founded in 859, including several important *medressa*, and one of the most prestigious of the Arab World. The **Andalusian Mosque** was also founded in

this period. The minarets of both major mosques date from 955/6.

Almoravids and Almohads The two parts of Fes El Bali were united by the Almoravids in the 11th century, and as the focus of independent Morocco, Fes became one of the major cities of Islam. In the 12th century the Qarawiyin mosque was enlarged to its present form, one of the largest in North Africa and can take up to 22,000 worshippers. The Almohads strengthened the fortifications of the great city. Under both dynasties Fes was in competition with the southern capital of Marrakech.

The Growth of Fes under the Merinids Fes reached its peak in the Merinid period, when the dynasty built the new capital of Fes El Jedid reflecting its power, containing the green-roofed Dar al-Makhzen still occupied by the monarch, the **Grand Mosque** with its distinctive polychrome minaret dating from 1279, and the *mellah*, to which the Jews of Fes El Bali were moved in 1438. The Merinid Sultans Abu Said Uthman and Abu Inan left a particularly notable legacy of public buildings. Among the achievements of the period are the **Bou Inania Medersa** and other *medressa*, several mosques and the **Merinid Tombs**. The **Zaouia of Moulay Idriss**, which holds the tomb of Idriss II was rebuilt in 1437. In the 15th century Fes consolidated its position as a major centre for artisanery and trade.

Saadian and Alawite Fes Under the Saadians Fes declined, with a degree of antagonism between the authorities and the people. Their main act was to refortify the city, adding the **South Borj** and **North Borj** fortresses.

Under the Alawites Fes declined further. In 1889 the French writer Pierre Loti described it as a dead city. However the dynasty had added a number of new *medressa* and mosques, and reconstructed other important buildings. The French entered Fes in 1911, but were unable at first to gain full control of the city and its hinterland and thus abandoned plans to make it their capital, choosing Rabat instead. The *ville nouvelle* was founded in 1916, but dates principally from the 1920s. French policies left the historic quarters intact, preserved in their traditional but perhaps stagnant form.

During the 20th century Fes has been overshadowed by the growth of Rabat and Casablanca, and the medina faces critical conservation problems, which a current programme by UNESCO aims to address. However, there is some controversy over the specific plans, particularly the creation of new openings in the city walls, and the building of two roads into the centre, one up to Talaa Kebira, and the other over the existing course of Oued Fes.

The large and beautiful houses of the historic city are being abandoned by the élite who move to the *ville nouvelle*, or to

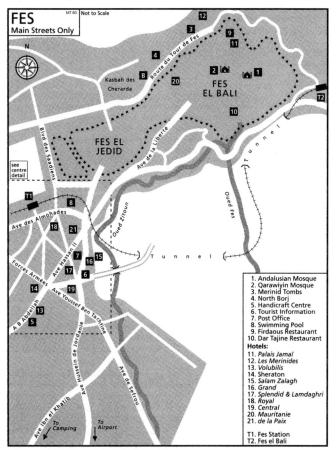

FES
Main Streets Only   MT 60 Not to Scale

Kasbah des Cherarda

Route du Tour de Fes

FES EL BALI

FES EL JEDID

see centre detail

Ave des Almohades

Ave de la Liberté

Oued Zitoun

Oued Fes

Tunnel

Tunnel

Forces Armées

Ave Hassan II

A B Abdellah

Ave Youssef Ben Tachine

Ave Hussein ibn de Jordanie

Ave Ibn el Khatib

Ave de Sefrou

To Camping   To Airport

1. Andalusian Mosque
2. Qarawiyin Mosque
3. Merinid Tombs
4. North Borj
5. Handicraft Centre
6. Tourist Information
7. Post Office
8. Swimming Pool
9. Firdaous Restaurant
10. Dar Tajine Restaurant
Hotels:
11. *Palais Jamaï*
12. *Les Merinides*
13. *Volubilis*
14. Sheraton
15. *Salam Zalagh*
16. *Grand*
17. *Splendid & Lamdaghri*
18. *Royal*
19. *Central*
20. *Mauritanie*
21. *de la Paix*

T1. Fes Station
T2. Fes el Bali

Casablanca and elsewhere, and often being taken over by poor migrants from the country. With rapidly increasing population densities the houses and the infrastructure are crumbling. There are, however, still many impressive houses, and a walk in Fes El Bali is one of the memorable experiences of a visit to Morocco.

ACCESS Air Aéroport Fes Saiss is 15 km to the S of the city, off the P24, T 624712. Take Bus 16 to the railway station.

Train The railway station is at the end of Blvd Chenguit, in the *ville nouvelle*, T 622501, 625132. Head down this road and slightly to the left into Ave de la Liberté. This joins Ave Hassan II, the main street of the new town, at Place de Florence.

Road Fes lies at a crossroads in Morocco, and is an excellent base from which to plan and carry out the next stage of travels. The P1 W from Meknes, Rabat and Casablanca arrives in the city at the corner of the walls of the royal palace, continue straight ahead for the medina (Fes El Bali), or right into Blvd des Saadiens for the *ville nouvelle*, the P26 N to Chaouen, Tetouan and Tanger and the P1 W to Taza, Oujda and Algeria arrive to the N of Fes El Bali, from where gates enter the old quarter, or the Route du Tour de Fes circumnavigates the city, either way, leading to Fes El Jedid and the *ville nouvelle*. The P24 S to Azrou and Marrakech and the P20 S to Sefrou lead into Place de l'Atlas. Turn left into Ave Allal ben Abdellah, and then right into Ave Hassan II. **Warning** On the routes into the city men on motorbikes often drive alongside motorists to tout for unofficial guide work – it is advisable to ignore them. **Bus**: CTM buses arrive at the terminal on Ave Mohammed V, T 622041. Private buses arrive at the new terminal off the Route du Tour de Fes, just below the N Borj.

Places of interest

Fes has so many rewarding and interesting sites that most visitors will have to be selective. If time is limited, go to Fes El Bali and see the **Bou Inania Medersa**, the **Moulay Idriss Zaouia** and the **Qarawiyin Mosque**, as well as a few of

the *souqs* nearby. In Fes El Jedid stroll through the two *mechouars* past the entrance to the **Royal Palace (Dar al-Makhzen)**. Outside the historic heart of the city go to the **Merinid Tombs** or the *Hotel Les Merinides* for a panoramic and memorable view across Fes El Bali. Fes El Bali can only be explored on foot. It has a complex layout, and it may save time to engage the services of an official guide, as long as the balance between sites of interest and expensive shops is agreed to the visitor's preference. Avoid the numerous unofficial guides and 'students' who will offer their services.

Fes El Bali The best approach to Fes El Bali, the oldest part of Fes, is E along Ave des Français from Fes El Jedid between the Alawite wall on the left and on the right the **Boujeloud Gardens** (Jardins de la Marche Verte), open 0900-1800 except Mon. Rue de l'UNESCO leads right to **Dar el Beida**, a late 19th century palace. The **Boujeloud Mosque** is ahead. Behind the mosque a small road leads to the **Dar Batha**, a 19th century palace set in lovely gardens, and now a **Museum of Moroccan Arts and Handicrafts** (0900-1130 and 1500-1800 except Tues), with an excellent display, including particularly fine tapestries, pottery and carved wood and craftsmen at work.

Bab Boujeloud, marks the entrance into the most historic part of Fes, the medina known as Fes El Bali. Bab Boujeloud itself is a large blue-tiled structure which looks misleadingly ancient. An earlier version is just to the left, while the current gate was built in the first few years of the Protectorate. The name is derived from *Abu Juloud*, or 'father of soldiers'.

The region of the medina up on the left of the gate is the Kasbah Filala, originally occupied by people from the Tafilelt who arrived with the early Alawite kings. **Bab Boujeloud** and the two small squares before and after make up busy area with fruit stalls and throngs of people, including persistent *faux guides*, despite the presence of a tourist police post. Just inside the gate is a square with a few small cafés and restaurants which may offer respite before exploring the medina.

The two minarets visible from the square are the 14th century **Bou Inania Medersa** and the nearer 9th century **Sidi Lazzaz Mosque**.

There are two routes onto the main thoroughfares of Fes El Bali. Talaa Seghira leads to the right. Talaa Kebira, leads to the left, directly past the Sidi

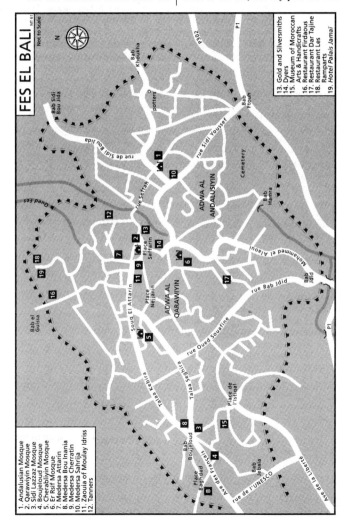

FES EL BALI

Not to Scale

1. Andalusian Mosque
2. Qarawiyin Mosque
3. Sidi Lazzaz Mosque
4. Boujeloud Mosque
5. Cherabliyin Mosque
6. Er Rsif Mosque
7. Medersa Attarin
8. Medersa Bou Inania
9. Medersa Cherratin
10. Medersa Sahrija
11. Zaouia of Moulay Idriss
12. Tanners

13. Gold and Silversmiths
14. Dyers
15. Museum of Moroccan Arts & Handicrafts
16. Restaurant Firdaous
17. Restaurant Dar Tajine
18. Restaurant Les Remparts
19. Hotel Palais Jamaï

Lazzaz Mosque, and the next major building, the Bou Inania Medersa, one of the most important sites in Fes.

Bou Inania Medersa, open 0800-1700 every day except Fri, entrance fee MD10, and one of the most important sites to visit in Fes, was built by the Merinid Sultan Abu Inan. It is a large and particularly impressive example of the architecture of the period, dating from 1350-5, and until the 1960s was used to accommodate students studying at the university, as well as providing some lessons itself. Enter through a highly decorated vestibule roofed by a stalactite dome. Inside the building a channel of water separates the prayer hall from the courtyard. The channel marks the limit for non-Muslims, as the prayer hall is closed, still being used as a mosque. The mosque area has a highly decorated minaret, indicating that it was far more important than most *medressa*, which normally do not have minarets, or even pulpits for the Fri prayer. Indeed, the *medersa* has the status of a Fri mosque, and for a time rivalled the great Qarawiyin Mosque.

The courtyard is decorated with *zellij* tiling, Koranic inscriptions, and some fine carved woodwork, well worth close inspection. Around the courtyard are a number of students' cells, with decorated ceilings, which give an indication of the life led by the students here, studying zealously in often cramped conditions. There are similar cells on the 2nd flr. Take the next flight of stairs up to the roof for a view of the surrounding area and of the minaret.

There used to be a complex water clock built in the wall opposite the *medersa*, dating from the 14th century. This clock is said to have enabled the **Bou Inania Medersa**, visible to both the Qarawiyin Mosque and the Mosque of Fes El Jedid, to signal the correct time for prayer to both. However, as part of the restoration programme this clock was moved to the Qarawiyin. The Mer-inid latrines or ablution halls are currently being repaired but once reopened it is worth seeing the intricate carving.

Talaa Kebira, the main thoroughfare of Fes El Bali, is only a narrow, crowded, alley way, descending steeply through distinct residential and commercial areas, towards the **Moulay Idriss Zaouia** and the **Qarawiyin Mosque**, the spiritual heart of the city. Beware of the heavily-laden mules carrying goods across the city, guided by muleteers crying out 'Balak!' to warn pedestrians. The distinctive character of Talaa Kebira may soon be lost, as a road has been constructed to convey tourists and goods into the heart of the medina. As you descend look out for **Fondouk Talaat Kebira**, still used to sell olives, butter and jam in bulk, and **Fondouk Labatta**, now used by tanners.

Talaa Kebira becomes **rue Cherabliyin** (slippermakers) as it descends, where each afternoon except Fri people hawk secondhand shoes and slippers. The **Cherabliyin Mosque** dates from 1342, the reign of Sultan Abul Hassan, and has a small and attractive minaret tiled in green and white including the *darj w ktaf* motif. On the right is the *Palais des Merinides*, one of the more impressive of the palace restaurants, and worth a look inside even if you cannot afford the food. Note the fountain, and the cedar carving treated with egg white. Further on in rue Cherabliyin is the Aïn Allou area where leather articles are auctioned everyday except Fri. At the bottom of rue Cherabliyin is a crossroads, just before the entrance to Souq El Attarin, the commercial heart of the medina.

Before exploring into Souq El Attarin turn right to an interesting area of *souqs*. On the left is **Souq al Henna**, a small square around two trees which originally specialized in *henna*, the powder used to dye the feet and hands of women. It now also sells other beauty products (perfume, myrrh and amber), traditional medicines, and some pottery and general handicrafts. On its right is **Merstane Sidi Frej**, a hospital built in 1286 by Youssef Ibn Yacoub but not currently open. On the right of this turning is a carpenters' *souq*, followed by the **Souq Sekhatin**, originally dominated by belts and saddles, but now includes a variety of goods including silverwork.

On **Place Nejjarin** (Carpenters' Square) is the 18th century **Fondouk Nejjarin**, a building of impressive tiles and carving, now being restored by UNESCO. In recent years it accommodated students in a similar way to the city's *medressa*. The 18th century tiled **Nejjarin Fountain**, also being carefully restored, has water which was reputed to cure fever. Nearby Place Nejjarin are the **Souq Kashashin**, where metalworkers operate and kitchenware and clocks are sold, and **Hammam Laraïs**, apparently used by grooms and brides before a pre-marriage trip to the Moulay Idriss Zaouia which can be approached from here, or from Souq al Attarin.

Souq El Attarin at the bottom of rue Cherabliyin, was originally just the spice sellers' *souq*, but is now one of the major *souqs* of the city, with a wide range of goods, and the focus of the commercial area of Fes El Bali. The sunlight filtered through the straw covering over the alleyway combines with the sculpted heaps of colourful spices and other goods to create an unforgettable atmosphere. On the *souq* is the *Dar Saada*, a recommended restaurant for lunch. To the left is a number of small *souqs*, including **Souq Tellis**, **Souq el-Haik**, **Souq Selham** and **Souq El Bali**.

To the right of Souq El Attarin is the **Moulay Idriss Zaouia**. Many shops around the *zaouia* sell candles and other artifacts for pilgrims, the distinctive chewy sweets which are taken home as souvenirs of a pilgrimage, and silverware. The *zaouia* itself is prohibited to non-Muslims, but is encircled by a precinct which is open to all visitors and from here parts of the *zaouia* can be seen by tactful glances through the large unscreened door spaces. Each entrance to the precinct is crossed by a wooden bar, which both marks the limit for animals and forces people to bow as they approach the building. The 18th century building contains the 9th century remains of Idriss II and includes a Louis IV clock. The sultan is considered a saint, and numbers amongst his devotees women, who can be seen in one of the rooms opening on to the precinct. On the way round note that the exterior of the sanctuary includes a circular porthole through which offerings are passed, and the ablutions room. The **Zouag Mosque**, now closed, was apparently for travellers who could not wait for prayers in the *zaouia*.

The Kissaria, off the *zaouia*, is a covered market area dating from the 9th century but rebuilt after most of it was destroyed in a fire this century. The *kissaria* is consequently not the most picturesque commercial area of Fes, but for particular goods is probably more reasonably priced and certainly less frantic than the *souqs*. There are distinct areas of the *kissaria* including those devoted to *baboushes*, thread and jewellery. One of the *kissaria* gates is directly opposite the main entrance to the Qarawiyin Mosque.

The Attarin Medersa (open 0900-1200 and 1400-1800), is a remarkably decorated Merinid building dating from 1323, built by Sultan Abu Said, used to accommodate students from the NW of Morocco, and functioning as a constituent college of the Qarawiyin University, which instructed students in religious and related subjects.

The courtyard is one of the most elaborately decorated in Morocco, with carved stucco, cedar wood carving, and *zellij* tiling, surrounded by the arches of the overhanging gallery. The prayer hall has a chandelier bearing the name of the *medersa*'s founder. The niche is on the right, flanked by two pilasters in marble.

As with most *medressa*, the 2nd flr has a succession of student's cells which are interesting to see. From the roof of the *medersa* is one of the best views of the minaret and interior of the Qarawiyin Mosque but at present the terrace is closed.

To the left of the Attarin Medersa is the closed and partially ruined Merinid **Misbahiya Medersa**. On the same route note a cloth *souq*, the central medina's PTT, and the **Fondouk Hayouni**. Opposite the PTT is a branch of *Banque Populaire*, in an historic building with impressive carving and tilework. Further down is the **Tomb of Sidi Muhammad Tijani**, dating from the 13th century, a pilgrimage centre for followers of Tijani, many of whom live in Senegal.

The **Qarawiyin Mosque** at the end of Souq El Attarin, dominates Fes and serves as the focal point of Fes El Bali, the centre of a complex of *medressa*, added mainly by the Merinids, and the most important religious building of Morocco. The mosque was the main building of the Qarawiyin quarter of the city, and owes its original construction to the generosity of a rich emigrant family in 857. It was enlarged in 956 and again most importantly under the Almoravids between 1135 and 1144. The Almohads built a large ablution hall, whilst the Merinids built a timekeeper's room and redecorated the courtyard and minaret, and the Saadians added the pavilion. The original minaret, the oldest in Morocco, dates from 956. There is also the **Borj an-Naffara** tower, used during Ramadan. On the SW side is an Almoravid funeral chapel.

The mosque has 14 doors, 275 pillars and three fountains for ablutions. It includes some elaborate Almohad carving, a 13th century chandelier and an historic wooden pulpit. With space for some 20,000 devotees it is one of the biggest mosques in North Africa. The separate space for women is raised, behind the men. The Qarawiyin was also a very important university, one of the oldest in the Arab world, with professors in law, theology, algebra, mathematics, philosophy, and astronomy. Students often gathered around their teacher in front of a particular pillar. The *medressa* across the city formed part of this university, often accommodating students from a particular part of Morocco, but also from across the Islamic world, attracted by the fame of the university and the reputation and wisdom of individual teachers.

The Qarawiyin Mosque is, however, a frustrating building for the non-Muslim, as it is impossible to get a clear view of the structure, surrounded as it is by the city. Walk around the mosque taking diplomatic glances in where possible, but no photographs.

Behind the mosque, past the stairs used by the *imam* to the Qarawiyin Library, is the 14th century three storey **Fondouk Titouani**, which originally provided accommodation for merchants from Tetouan, now used by artisans and a carpet shop, but worth seeing for its carved and panelled interior and for an insight into the way in which *fondouks* functioned. Both this and the nearby *Palais de Fes* restaurant, apparently a former marriage palace, have an excellent view of the Qarawiyin's courtyard and pavilion.

The triangular **Place Seffarin** (Brassworkers' Square) is marked by a tree that is noticeable in views over Fes El Bali from the N or S Borj. On the right is the **Qarawiyin Library** founded in 1349, still operational and with a valuable and ancient collection of books but closed to non-Muslims. It is an atmospheric place, with the sound of copper and other metals being beaten into large pans and cauldrons and the light filtered through the tree.

On the left is the **Seffarin Medersa**,

the earliest *medersa*, from the 13th century, a partly ruined building in the style of a *Fassi* house, but with some interesting carving and a small minaret.

Cherratin Medersa Continuing off to the right along Sma't El Adoul (Street of Notaries) around the Qarawiyin, one passes the **Sidi Talouk sanctuary**, and then to the right the Alawite Cherratin Medersa, built in 1670 by Sultan Moulay Rashid, and currently being restored. This is a more modern *medersa* with a different design from the Merinid structures, including three storeys, in order to house a greater number of students, and three arches leading from the prayer hall to the courtyard.

Dabbaghin To get to the tanneries turn left at the Fondouk Titouani entrance into Place Seffarin, into Derb Mechattine. This alleyway leads to the tanneries, or **dabbaghin**, where leather is tanned and dyed in ancient pits, as in time immemorial. Although this is somewhat of a dirty and smelly place, it is a memorable experience for the courageous. Two enterprising individuals have turned their tiny houses into viewing terraces for the tanneries. There is no charge to climb up the steep and narrow stairs for a worthwhile view, but of course the owners have provided handicrafts boutiques on the roof, to tempt you before you struggle back down.

As-Sabbaghin At the end of Place Seffarine one passes a *souq* for silverwork, and then can take a right turn to the dyer's area, As-Sabbaghin, still in use to dye huge amounts of wool and other materials in an array of bright colours. It is a highly photogenic area, but those who work there are well aware of the possibilities for tipping. As-Sabbaghin is beside the notoriously dirty Oued Fes, which the UNESCO programme may cover over to provide another road for vehicular access to the central medina. Currently this only reaches as far as Place Rsif just along the river to the right.

The Andalusian Quarter Cross the Oued Bou Khrareb and follow rue Seftah to the **Andalusian Mosque** with its green and white minaret dating from the same period as the Qarawiyin Mosque but smaller and less important. The minaret dates from the 10th century, and the mosque was enlarged in the 13th century, with an architect from Toledo designing the impressive doorway, surmounted by carved wood.

Adjacent is the **Sahrija Medersa** from 1321-3, built for students studying at the mosque. It is a heavily restored building but there is still some memorable *zellij* tiling and wood carving. Note the scallop motif, much in evidence. The white marble basin from the courtyard has been removed. The view from the roof of the *medersa* is recommended. Nearby is the **Sebbayin Medersa**, still in use. If you have a guide you could seek out the small **Fondouk Derb Laamti**, restored by Mawlay Hassan I in the 19th century, and of interest because it is still used for accommodation and storage by trading caravans, and also the **Derb Laamti Fountain**. From here, return to the Qarawiyin quarter by rue Sidi Youssef and the El Aouad bridge, noting the potters at work in the area. Alternatively take the No.18 bus from the **Mosque er Rsif** to Place de la Resistance.

Less grand, but very useful, Bab Ftouh has a large wholesale market and a flea market. Nearby is the **Koubba of Sidi Harazem** which has a *moussem* each spring.

To the N the square **Kasbah des Cherarda** (after the Cherarda tribe), also called the **Kasbah al-Khemis** (after the nearby Thur *souq*). This was built in 1670 by the Alawite Sultan Moulay Rashid, and is now occupied by the Hopital Ibn al-Khatib, university buildings and a school.

View of Fes El Bali There are three

excellent vantage points for viewing Fes El Bali permitting one to piece together the places explored or plan visits.

The Merinid Tombs, best approached from Fes El Jedid by car or petit-taxi date from the 14th century. The tombs are ruins, and much of the ornamentation documented by earlier visitors has not survived. A word of caution – this is not a safe place to go alone. Nearby is *Hotel Les Merinides*, also with an excellent view. It is a good place for a relaxing coffee, gazing out over the rooftops and minarets of Fes El Bali.

The North Borj is a fortress built by the Saadian Sultan Ahmad al-Mansour in 1582, which, though small, is an interesting example of the fortress architecture of the period. There is a good view of parts of Fes El Bali from the roof. It contains an Arms Museum (closed Tues) which exhibits a diverse display of weapons and military paraphernalia from all periods, including an array of European cannons.

The South Borj provides a different view of Fes El Bali. It dates from the 13th century and is used by the military, but visitors can park beside it to admire the scene. Nearby is a **Son et Lumiere** auditorium, providing a spectacular history of Fes El Bali from this panoramic position. This 45 mins show takes place every evening between Feb 15 and Nov 15, entrance MD200. For further information contact the office in Tour Al Wataniya, Ave Hassan II, T 931892-3.

Fes El Jedid This is the Merinid capital, containing the Royal Palace, now a rather quiet area between the hustle and bustle of Fes El Bali and the modern *ville nouvelle*.

The Vieux Mechouar is the larger of the two open spaces in Fes El Bali. The large door on the W leads to the **Makina**, a desolate structure which has seen better days, originally built in the 19th century as an Italian run arms factory and now used for various functions including a rug factory and youth club. The large gate, Bab Dekkakine, leads onto the Petit Mechouar.

The Petit Mechouar is often bustling with people. On the left a gate leads to Ave des Français and Fes El Bali. Directly in front is a gate to the Royal Palace, the **Dar al-Makhzen**, a Merinid building from the 14th century, at the heart of a large estate closed to visitors. To the right a doorway leads into **Moulay Abdellah**, now a normal area of housing but under the Protectorate a red light district. The 18th century mosque built by Moulay Abdellah stands here.

The Waterwheel and the Grande Rue
In the bottom left corner a gate leads into the rest of Fes El Jedid. Just inside this gate steps lead down to a pleasant walk around the perimeter of Fes El Jedid. It passes a bridge by an old, non-operative waterwheel, and the pleasant *Café Restaurant La Nouria* with the Boujeloud Gardens beyond. The Grande Rue de Fes El Jedid is the main marketing street of the area. Although the shops, many of which sell clothes, are less interesting than Fes El Bali, it is perhaps a more relaxing place to wander. The **Grand Mosque** has a minaret with a simple relief design and a tiled section at the top. The taller of the minarets, green with tiles at the top, belongs to the **El Hamra Mosque**, dating from 1339. Surprisingly at this point there is a tree growing in the *souq*. At the end of the street is the 20th century **Bab Semmarin**, opening into rue Bou Khessissat.

The Mellah Rue Bou Khessissat with its balconies of wood and wrought iron leads W towards the *ville nouvelle*, past the 16th century Merinid gates to the Dar al-Makhzen. On the left is the *mellah* which includes a number of old synagogues and Jewish public buildings, although the area is now predominantly Muslim. The **Serfati** and **Fassiyin** synagogues now used for other purposes now. The houses are smaller

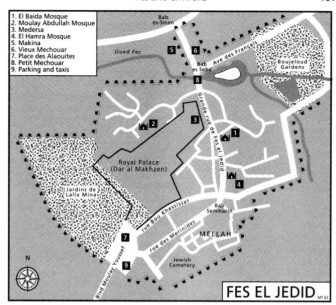

1. El Baida Mosque
2. Moulay Abdullah Mosque
3. Medersa
4. El Hamra Mosque
5. Makina
6. Vieux Mechouar
7. Place des Alaouites
8. Petit Mechouar
9. Parking and taxis

FES EL JEDID MT 62

and have a quite distinct architectural style. Below the *mellah* the Jewish cemetery is being restored. Since the beginning of the peace process in the Middle East, Morocco has opened its doors to Israeli tourists. The Jewish heritage of the *mellah* in Fes is now on the itinerary of many Jewish visitors.

Local information
● Accommodation

AL *Hotel Jnan Palace Fes*, Ave Ahmed Chaouki, T 653965, 193 rm; **AL** *Hotel Les Merinides*, Borj Nord, T 646040, F 645225, 80 rm, 11 suites, pool, restaurant, bar, nightclub, pool, modern, conference room, overlooking the medina with 4 restaurants, 2 bars, the *Nightclub Les Merinides*; **AL** *Hotel Palais Jamaï*, Bab El Guissa, T 634331/3, F 635096, 99 rm, 2 restaurants, bar, popular nightclub, *hammam*, tennis and a pool, a former palace with excellent views of the medina, and a beautiful garden, reservations advisable, this is the best hotel in town but service is slow, breakfast disappointing, certainly not value for money.

A *Hotel Sheraton*, Ave des Forces Armées Royales, T 625002, F 620486, 280 rm, modern, comfortable, in *ville nouvelle*, extensive gardens, 2 restaurants, coffee shop, bar, tennis and pool, used by tour groups hence package tour treatment of all guests, grab your buffet meal before it goes cold, dancer in Moroccan restaurant highly rec.

C *Hotel Sofia*, 3 rue de Pakistan, just off Ave Hassan II, T 624265/7, F 644244, 98 a/c rm and 4 suites, restaurant, bar, nightclub, pool, parking; **C** *Hotel Volubilis*, Ave Allal Ben Abdellah, T 621125, F 621125, restaurant, bar, pool, good hotel from the PLM chain with a pleasant garden.

D *Hotel Batha*, rue de l'Unesco, T 636437/9, recently renovated; **D** *Hotel de la Paix*, 44 Ave Hassan II, T 626880, Tx 51636, stylish, in *ville nouvelle* from the Protectorate period with bar and restaurant, a/c, clean and comfortable; **D** *Le Grand Hotel*, Blvd Chefchaouni, T 625511-2, Tx 51631, a 1930s building in centre of *ville nouvelle* with style and atmosphere, a restaurant, bar, and nightclub; **D** *Hotel Mounia*, 60 rue Asilah, T 624838, Tx 51801, this is a mock kasbah with modern, comfortable rooms, *hammam*, restaurant and a bar; **D** *Moussafir Hotel*, Ave des Almo-

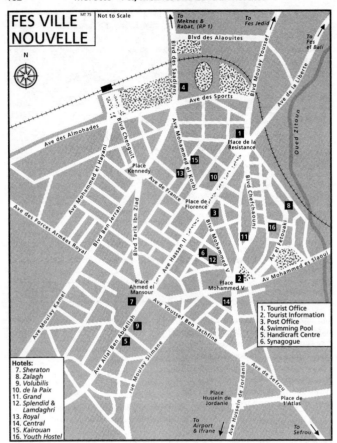

FES VILLE NOUVELLE MT 75   Not to Scale

N

To Meknes & Rabat, (RP 1)
To Fes Jedid
To Fes el Bali

Blvd des Alaouites

Blvd des Saadiens

Ave des Sports

Blvd Moulay Youssef

Ave de la Liberte

Oued Zitoun

Ave des Almohades

Blvd Chenguit

Ave Mohammed el Hayani

Ave Mohammed el Korbi

4

1
Place de la Resistance

Place Kennedy

15
13   10

Ave de France

Blvd Ben Jerrah

Blvd Tarik Ibn Ziad

Ave des Forces Armees Royal

Place de Florence
3

Blvd Chefchaouni

8

16

Ave el Fetouaki

11

Ave Hassan II

6
12

Blvd Mohammed V

Ave Mohammed es Slaoui

Place Ahmed el Mansour

2

Place Mohammed V

Ave Moulay Kamel

7

14

Ave Youssef Ben Tachfine

Ave Alla Ben Abdellah

9

5

rue Moulay Slimane

Ave de Sefrou

Place Hussein de Jordanie

Ave Hussein de Jordanie

Place de l'Atlas

To Airport & Ifrane
To Sefrou

1. Tourist Office
2. Tourist Information
3. Post Office
4. Swimming Pool
5. Handicraft Centre
6. Synagogue

Hotels:
7. Sheraton
8. Zalagh
9. Volubilis
10. de la Paix
11. Grand
12. Splendid & Lamdaghri
13. Royal
14. Central
15. Kairouan
16. Youth Hostel

hades, T 651902, part of the chain attached to the railway company, efficiently run and comfortable, nr the railway station; **D** *Hotel Olympic*, Ave Mohammed V, T 624529, central location, restaurant, reasonable and comfortable; **D** *Splendid Hotel*, 9 rue Abdelkrim El Khattabi, T 622148, 626770, Tx 51763, good pool.

E *Hotel Central*, 50 rue du Nador, T 622333, big and clean rooms, very cheap; **E** *Hotel Kairouan*, 84 rue du Soudan, T 623590, reasonable, nr railway station; **E** *Hotel Lamdaghri*, 10 rue Abasse El Massadi, off Blvd Mohammed V, T 620310, small and highly rec,

around a courtyard, with a restaurant and bar; **E** *Nouzha Hotel*, 7 rue Hassan Dkhissi, off Place Atlas, T 640002, recently opened, clean, efficient staff, café, bar; **E** *Hotel Royal*, 36 rue d'Espagne, T 624656.

F *Hotel Mauritanie*, by the **Bab Boujeloud** gate, one of best in medina, clean and with efficient and friendly management; nearby is the almost as good **F** *Hotel Erraha*, nr the bus station; *Hotel Jardin Publique*, nr the Boujeloud Mosque is a safe bet; in the *ville nouvelle* cheap options are *Hotel Rex*, Place de l'Atlas; *Hotel Regina* and *Hotel Maghrib*, Ave Mohammed es Slaoui.

● **Youth hostel**

18 rue Abdestam Serghini in the *ville nouvelle*, T 624085, 60 beds, kitchen, bus 150m, train 1.2 km, overnight fee MD25, cheap option for those with a YHA card. Unfavourable reports have again been received about a manager here.

● **Camping**

Camping du Diamant Vert, nr Aïn Chkeff, right off the P24, expensive but well-equipped site with shop and restaurant.

● **Places to eat**

◆◆◆ *Fes El Bali* has a number of beautiful palaces converted into restaurants, with elaborate decoration and sumptuous *Fassi* menus, look out for *pastilla*, not all are licensed; *Restaurant Palais Tijani*, 51-3 Derb Ben Chekroune, Lablida, T 633335; a more spectacular setting is *Restaurant Dar Saada*, 21 Souk El Attarin, T 637370-1, convenient for sightseeing; also try *Palais Mnebhi*, 15 Souq Ben Safi Talaa Sghira, T 633893, good Moroccan food; *Dar Tajine*, 15 Ross Rhi, T 634167, fixed Moroccan menus in an exquisitely decorated 19th century palace, try the *pastilla*; *Restaurant Palais des Merinides*, 99 Zkak Roah, T 634028, serves lunch and dinner. Easier to find but pricier are the hotel restaurants: *Al Fassia*, in the *Hotel Palais Jamaï*, Bab El Guissa, T 634331, reservations advisable, one of the best Moroccan restaurants with a vast array of dishes incl quail *tagine*, and traditional Moroccan music; *La Koubba du Ciel*, in *Hotel Les Merinides*, Borj Nord, great cuisine and entertainment with the best view of Fes El Bali.

There are reasonable licensed restaurants in the *ville nouvelle*: ◆◆*Oued de la Biere*, Ave Mohammed V, T 625324, Moroccan and French cuisine, good *tagine de kefta*, clean and relaxed; *Restaurant Mounia*, 11 Blvd Mohammed Slaoui, rue Houceine El Khaddar, T 626661, Moroccan and European food but unlicensed; *Restaurant du Centre*, 106 Ave Mohammed V, T 622823, good Moroccan food; *Restaurant Pizzeria Chez Vittorio*, 21 rue Brahim Roudani, T 624730, good Italian food.

There is no shortage of cheap restaurants in Fes El Bali, particularly nr *Bab Boujeloud*, one of the best is ◆*Restaurant Bouayad*, 26 Bab Boujeloud, T 633432, open 24 hrs, a large and cheap menu incl *pastilla* and excellent *brochettes*. In the *ville nouvelle* one of the best cheap places is *Restaurant Chamonix*, 5 rue

Mokhtar Soussi, off Ave Mohammed V, T 626638, Moroccan, European and pizzas; also try *Croque Burger*, 26 Ave Slaoui, T 654029, take away, delivery and eat in burgers and pizzas; *Fes Mondi Sportif*, Tazi Cherti Abdellah, nr intersection of Ave des Forces Armées Royales and Ave Hassan II; *Marhaba*, 23 Ave Mohammed V, very good *tagines* and salads; *Chawarma Sandwich*, 42 rue Normandie, reasonable and clean.

● **Bars**

A drink in the *Hotel Palais Jamai* is a good break in the medina, the *Hotel des Merinides* has a good view of the city. In the *ville nouvelle* try *Es Saada*, on Ave Slaoui, or *Bar du Centre*, Ave Mohammed V.

● **Cafés**

The best cafés are in the *ville nouvelle*, but the best for watching *Fassi* life are in the medina. In the *ville nouvelle* try *L'Elysée*, 4 rue de Paris; or *Café l'Opéra*.

● **Banks & money changers**

ABM, Ave Hassan II, T 651515; **BMAO**, Immeuble Mamda, Place de Florence, T 650785; **Banque al Maghrib**, Ave de France, T 625596-8; **BMCE**, Place Mohammed V; **Banque Populaire**, Ave Mohammed V; **Credit du Maroc**, Ave Mohammed V; **SGMB**, Ave Lalla Yacout, T 625011; **SMDC**, 3 Blvd Bir Anzarane, T 642611; **Wafabank**, Ave Mohammed V, T 622591.

● **Cultural Centre**

Centre Culturel Français, rue el-Bahrein, T 623921, library and films.

● **Entertainment**

Disco & nightclubs: *Nightclub Les Merinides*, in the *Hotel Les Merinides*, Borj Nord, T 645225 (2130-0300), a fashionable but expensive place, with drinks from MD50; also try *Nightclub* in the *Hotel Palais Jamai*, Bab El Guissa, T 634331 (2200-0300), similarly expensive but popular with those that can afford it.

● **Hospitals & medical services**

Chemists: there is an all night chemist at the Municipalité de Fes, Blvd Moulay Youssef, T 623380 (2000-0800); during the day try *Bahja*, Ave Mohammed V, T 622441; or *Bab Ftouh* at Bab Ftouh, T 649135.

Hospital: Hôpital Ghassani, Quartier Dhar Mehraz, T 622776.

● **Post & telecommunications**

The PTT Centrale is at the junction of Ave

Hassan II and Ave Mohammed V. Telephone facilities are open 0800-2100. There is another post office in the medina, at Place Batha.

● **Shopping**

Books & newspapers: try the *English Bookshop* of Fes, 68 Ave Hassan II, nr Place de la Résistance. Newspapers from the stalls in Ave Mohammed V.

Handicrafts & Moroccan goods: Fes has for long been one of the great trading centres of Morocco. The *souqs*, *kissaria* and boutiques offer a splendid selection for visitors. Many of the boutiques in the hotels, the *ville nouvelle* and near the important tourist attractions charge inflated prices. The further afield you go, the lower the prices are and the more genuine the claims of regional provinence and antiquity. The large carpet shops, have some incredible goods to sell, but have very experienced salesmen. Look for the blue and white pottery, metalwork, jewellery and carpets.

For antique carpets, jewellery and artifacts, *Maison Berbere*, 4 Riad Jouha, nr the Attarin Medersa, T 635686, is normally a wholesaler, but has an excellent selection at low prices. For new carpets in the medina try *Dar Ibn Khaldoun*, 45 Derb Ben Chekroune Lablida, BP 745, T 633335 or *Palais Vizier*, 35 Derb Touil Blida which give an opportunity to see two restored 'palaces'. Two places where one should be very cautious about the prices and products are *Palais Andalous*, 15 Derb Selma, and *La Bahia*, 3 Bouakda, Zkak Rouamane. For new and antique jewellery, metalware and silverware, as well as *kaftans*, you should not miss a visit to *Dar Kairouan*, 6 Derb el Hammam Joutia, T 633735. Another good place to buy antiques is *Aux Merveilles de Fes*, 11 rue Rahabt el Kaïss, opp the Attarin Medersa, T 633632. For smaller items wander in the Souk El Attarin and nearby *souqs*, with *babouches* best bought from the *kissaria*. For most nights the *Coopartim Centre Artisanale*, Blvd Allal Ben Abdellah, T 625654 (0900-1400 and 1600-1900), has a good selection but fixed prices. Fes El Jedid is a quieter but slightly more pricey area to shop in.

● **Sport**

Riding: at *Club Equestre Moulay Idriss*, Hippodrome Moulay Kamel.

Swimming: in the large hotels, mainly *Hotel Salam Zalagh*, rue Mohammed Diouri, or at the municipal pool, Ave des Sports.

Tennis: at *Sporting Club Fassi*, Clos de la Ren-

aissance, 10 rue Moulay Slimane, T 641512, with five courts or *Tennis Club Fassi*, Ave Mohammed El Kori, T 624272, with seven courts.

● **Tourist offices**

Office du Tourisme, Place de la Résistance, T 623460, F 623146; **Syndicat d'Initiative**, Ave Mohammed V, T 625301.

● **Tour companies & travel agents**

Azur Voyage, 3 Ave Lala Meriem, T 625115; *Fes Voyages*, 9 rue de Turquie, T 621776; *Number One*, 41 Ave Slaoui, T 621234; *Tak Voyages*, 41 Ave Mohammed V, T 624550, 622455, F 652736; *Wagons-Lits Tourisme*, Immeuble Grand Hotel, T 654464. *Royal Air Maroc*, 52 Ave Hassan II, T 625516-7, reservations T 620456-7.

● **Useful addresses**

Fire: T 15.

Garages: Fiat, Ave Mohammed V, T 623435; Renault, rue d'Espagne, T 622232.

Police: Ave Mohammed V, T 19.

● **Transport**

Local Bus: these can be a convenient option in Fes. No 1 runs from Place des Alawites to Dar Batha, No 3 from Place des Alawites to Place de la Résistance, No 9 from Place de la Résistance to Dar Batha, No 10 from Bab Guissa to Place des Alaouites and No 18 from Place de la Résistance to Bab Ftouh. **Car hire**: Avis, 50 Blvd Chefchaouni, T 626746; **Budget**, adjacent *Palais Jamaï Hotel*, T 620919; **Europcar-Inter-Rent**, 41 Ave Hassan II, T 626545; **Hertz**, Kissariat de la Foire No 1, Blvd Lalla Meryem, T 622812; airport T 651823; **Holiday Car**, 41 Ave Mohammed V, T 624550, 622455, F 652736; **SAFLOC**, *Hotel Sheraton*, T 931201; **Zeit**, 35 Ave Mohammed Slaoui, T 625510. **Taxis**: red, are a cheap and quick way to get around Fes, can be found around much of the city, and sometimes have meters. Parking can be a problem approaching the medina, so it is perhaps better not to use one's own car.

Air Aéroport Fes Saiss is 15 km from the city, off the P24, T 624712. Flights to Casablanca with connections to internal and international destinations (see page 126), 1 a week to Er Rachidia, as well as direct flights to Marseille (Wed) and Paris (Sun). To get to the airport take Bus 16 from the train station.

Train The train station is at the end of Blvd Chenguit, T 625001. Departures to **Taza** and **Oujda**: 0400, 0640, 1455, 1715, 2020, 0130;

Meknes: 11 a day between 0315 and 0145; **Tanger**: 0410 and 1250; **Rabat** and **Casablanca**: 0315, 0700, 0900, 1040, 1410, 1605, 1835, 1930 and 0145.

Road Bus: CTM buses leave from the station on Ave Mohammed V, T 622041, for Beni Mellal at 0630 and 2300, Marrakech at 0630 and 2100, Tetouan at 0800 and 1100, Tanger at 1100, 1800 and 0030, Taza at 1230 and 1830, Oujda at 1230, Nador at 0130, for Casablanca 8 a day between 0700 and 1900, for Rabat 7 a day between 0930 and 1900, and for Meknes 8 a day between 0700 and 1900. Most other private line buses leave from the new terminal off the Route du Tour de Fes, below the N Borj. Buses for the Middle Atlas leave from the Laghzaoui terminal, rue Ksar el Kebir. **Taxi**: grand-taxis leave from Place Baghdadi, except for Sefrou and Azrou which leave from rue de Normandes.

Excursion to Moulay Yacoub

Moulay Yacoub lies 20 km NW of Fes, a short journey through rolling countryside and some interesting capital intensive irrigated farming. Taxis from Bab Boujeloud stop near the car park above the village and the steep walk down to the pool and hammams has small shops, cafés and a number of cheap lodging. **C** *Hotel Moulay Yacoub*, also called the *Fes Motel*, stands above the village, T 694035, F 694012, 60 rm with TV, bath and terrace, 60 bungalows, restaurant with magnificent views, bar, tennis, pool. A new tree lined road leads down from the hotel to the medical treatment centre using *thermal springs*, with neat gardens, café and practice golf.

Excursions to Sidi Harazem, Bhalil and Sefrou

Sidi Harazem In restaurants all over Morocco the mineral water is almost exclusively from Sidi Ali or Sidi Harazem (see page 195). Sidi Harazem was originally buried in Marrakech. The source and spa centre of that name is an easy day excursion being only 4 km along the P1 from Fes, with buses from the CTM bus station and Bab Bou-

jeloud, and grand-taxis from Bab Ftouh. The area around the thermal baths is still very popular for swimming and picnics but the once impressive water courses, pools and spas have been disappointingly neglected. There is too much concrete and the cafés and trinket sellers are not recommended. There is a 17th century *koubba*, and the PLM chain **C** *Hotel Sidi Harazem*, T 690057, F 690072, 62 a/c rm, with health facilities, restaurant and bar.

Bhalil En route to Sefrou, 5 km before the town off the P20, is Bhalil. This small hill village may have had a Christian population before the coming of Islam. Behind the picturesque village are several troglodyte dwellings, with people still inhabiting the caves. The road takes you round the town, giving excellent views on all sides, and two good clean cafés on the outskirts when approaching from the E.

Sefrou

Sefrou is 32 km S of Fes along the P20. It is unlikely to be reached en route, as the P24/P21, via Ifrane and Azrou, is a better route from Fes to Er Rachidia and the S, but is certainly worth visiting as an excursion from Fes or to stay for a few days, as this is one of the most appealing towns in Morocco, an unspoilt historic walled town lying in a beautiful wooded valley, with a calm and genuinely friendly atmosphere. Both buses and taxis arrive and leave from Place Moulay Hassan, by Bab Taksebt and Bab M'Kam, where the road from Fes meets the old town. Buses from Fes leave from Bab Boujeloud and many go on to Er Rachida. Grand taxis from Fes leave from Bab Ftouh.

Although now bypassed by new roads, Sefrou once lay astride the major caravan routes from Fes and the N, to the S and the Sahara beyond, and is an important market-place for the surrounding agricultural region. Sefrou always had a distinctive character due to its Jewish roots, which predated Moroccan Islam, and although converted to Islam by Moulay Ismail, it returned to its status with the migration of Jews from Tafilalt and Algeria in the 13th century. This characteristic lasted until the emigration of Jews to the large cities, Europe and Israel after WW2 and the 1967 Arab-Israeli War. More than any other equivalent small town it has fascinated Western academics, with the anthropologists Geertz, Rosen and Rabinow carrying out reseach here. Recently Sefrou was created a province in its own right, and received new and badly-needed investment, as it was a town declining into shabby anonymity.

The market place below and E of Ave Mohammed V is a relaxed place to wander, best during the Thur **souq**. The town, which is known for olive and cherry production, has a large **Fête des Cerises** in Jun, and other smaller *fêtes* during the year. There is a *moussem*, or religious gathering, for Sidi Lahcen Lyoussi.

Entering from the N the road curves down to the Oued Aggaï, past the Centre Artisanal (0800-1200 and 1400-1900, except Sun) into the busy Place Moulay Hassan. From here Bab M'Kram is the main entrance to the *medina* which lies N of the river and Bab Taksebt the main entrance, over the bridge, into the *mellah*. Both are small, maze-like quarters, but it is difficult to get seriously lost. The *mellah* can also be entered from the covered market place through Bab M'Rabja. Beside a mosque built into the wall, bend right and down the main street, beside small restaurants, butchers, shops and craftsmen, and then left to reach one of several small bridges over the Oued Aggaï. Alternatively, take one of the small side turnings to discover the cramped design of the *mellah*, now mainly occupied by poorer Muslims, with houses often built over the narrow streets.

In the medina, the **Grand Mosque of El Jamaa Kebir**, restored in the 19th century, lies beside the river, and the *souqs* just upstream. In the *souqs*, where bargaining will be less fierce than in Fes, note the silversmiths and the woodworkers. Past the *souqs* is the **Zaouia of Sidi Lahcen ben Ahmed**. In the medina there is a clearly discernible difference in the design of the quarter, reflecting the strict regulations and conditions under which Jews in the *mellah* lived. Sefrou is quite remarkable, however, in that the *mellah* is as large as the medina.

Ave Moulay Hassan crosses the Oued Aggaï, where there is a *Syndicat d'Initiative*, T 660380, past the Jardin Publique, which has a swimming pool and continues as Ave Mohammed V, the main street of the unexciting new town, with the Post Office, and a few shops and simple café-restaurants, the *rôtisseries*, for grilled chicken, being one of the places. Take time to explore. Turn into rue Ziad by the post office, past hotel Sidi Lahcem Lyoussi and continue uphill on the black top road. Camping is signed to the left but continue up to the koubba of Sidi Bou Ali, white walls and distinctive green tiled roof. There is a café, a few stalls and a magnificent view. Another small excursion beginning S of the river leads W to the small waterfall grandly known as the cascades.

• **Accommodation** The two best places to stay are the **D** *Hotel Sidi Lahcen Lyoussi*, off Ave Moulay Hassan, T 660497, 24 rm, a dated but comfortable place with a restaurant, bar and pool; and **F** *Hotel les Cerises*, Ave Mohammed V, T 661528, a large, impersonal but cheap hotel; there is also the **F** *Hotel Lafrenie*, Route de Fes, T 662030, a small *pensiones*. Follow rue Ziad, by the post office on Ave Mohammed V, to a campsite, *Camping de Sefrou*, T 660001, 2 km from the town, and on a fork off that road, the **F** *Hotel-Café Boualserhim*, by the green-roofed **Koubba of Sidi Bouserghine**, Sefrou's patron saint.

TAZA AND ENVIRONS

Taza

The town is divided into three quite separate parts, the area around the railway and bus station, the *ville nouvelle* around Place de l'Indépendence, and the quiet medina on the hill. Unfortunately its most impressive historic buildings are closed to non-Muslims.

History

Taza (*Pop* 77,216), is a modest market town which has in the past achieved considerable regional importance under successive dynasties. The town has been settled since Neolithic times, and has gained importance with its highly strategic location in the Taza Gap, between the Rif and the Middle Atlas. The town was developed by the Meknassa tribe of Berbers, and was an important but finally unsuccessful fortification against the advance of the Fatimids from the E. The Almohads under Sultan Abd el-Moumen captured the city in 1141-1142, making it their second capital, and used it to attack the Almoravids. The Almohads built a mosque and provided much of the city's fortifications.

Taza was the first city taken by the Merinids, who added considerably to the Almohad city. Its important defensive role continued under the Merinids and the Saadians, and was again pivotal in the rise to power of the Alawites, who further extended and fortified the city, later using it as a defence against the French threat from the E.

The eccentric pretender, Bou Hamra, proclaimed himself as Sultan here in 1902 and controlled much of E Morocco until 1912, when he was caught and killed. He was known as a wandering miracle-maker, travelling Morocco on a donkey. Taza was occupied by the French in 1914, and became an important military centre.

ACCESS Taza is well connected by road and rail. The railway station, private bus station and grand-taxi rank are N from the centre of the *ville nouvelle*, Place de l'Indépendence, beyond walking distance. Buses, taxis and car parking in Place Moulay Hassan in the medina.

Places of interest

The *ville nouvelle* for hotels, restaurants, banks and other services is a quiet place centred around the old French buildings on Place de l'Indépendence.

The older buildings are in the small, attractive medina reached from Ave de la Gare. The focus of the medina is the **Mechouar** which runs parallel to Place Moulay Hassan with its cafés and transport and the souqs which stretch in a line between the two principal mosques. The souqs, noted particularly for jewellery and carpets, refreshingly, are not aimed at tourists, and refreshing to wander in, and include an interesting secondhand section. One can perhaps gain a brief passing glance of the **Zaouia of Sidi Azouz** and note the beautiful wall-basin beside the door. It is difficult to gain a good view of the **Grand Mosque** at the end of the souq. The mosque, including the existing minaret, was built by the Almohads in the second half of the 12th century, with further elaboration by the Merinids in the late 13th century and the Alawites in the late 17th century. The minaret follows the classic proportions of 1:5, as does the **Koutoubia** mosque in Marrakech (see page 176). Only muslims can view the beautiful bronze chandelier bearing 514 oil lamps which lights the mosque. Turning left along the Mechouar the street broadens. On the right note the carved woodwork lintel of the 14th century Merinid **Medersa of Abul Hassan**. The Andalusian mosque, with a small 12th century minaret, requires some neck stretching to see. Behind it, to the right, is the ruined house of Bou Hamra, the early 20th century pretender, and if one can find the doorkeeper it may be possible to get access.

A tour of the ramparts of Taza is recommended. These walls were originally laid out by the Almohads, and repeatedly improved since. Note the Almohad **Bab er Rih** gate facing NNW, and the circular **El Sarasine** tower, also Almohad. There is a large weekly market outside the walls.

Turning left along the Mechouar head towards the 12th century minaret of the Andalusian mosque. Before reaching the mosque note on the right the 14th century **Medersa of Abul Hassan**, named after a Merinid Sultan. This is closed but the exterior shows a carved lintel in cedar wood, and a porch roof overhanging the road. At the end of the Mechouar, in a lane to the right of the mosque, Zankat Dar al-Makhzen, there is the former house of Bou Hamra the pretender.

With its commanding location, a tour of the ramparts of Taza is recommended. These walls were originally laid out by the Almohads, and repeatedly improved since. Note the Almohad **Bab er Rih** gate facing NNW, and the circular **El Sarasine** tower, also Almohad.

Local information
● **Accommodation**

D *Hotel Salam Friouato*, Ave de la Gare, T 672593, 58 rm, top hotel in town, bar, restaurant, tennis and pool, but inconveniently located between the medina and the *ville nouvelle*.

E *Grand Hotel du Dauphine*, at the centre of the town on junction of Ave de la Gare and Place de l'Indépendence, T 673567, 26 rm, some with shower but no communal shower for those without, comfortable, rec bar and restaurant, dating very obviously from the Protectorate period with style and charm.

Cheaper and more basic options incl **F** *Hotel de la Poste*, Place de l'Indépendence, T 672589; and *Hotel Guillaume Tell* on Place de l'Indépendence, basic and not very clean.

● **Camping**
At *Zeitoun*, off Ave de la Gare en route to the medina.

● **Places to eat**
◆◆◆ The *Hotel Salam Friouato*, T 672593, has reasonable, unexciting meals. A better option is the ◆◆*Grand Hotel du Dauphine*, junction of Place de l'Indépendence and Ave de la Gare, T 673567.

◆ *Café Restaurant Majestic*, Ave Mohammed V, Moroccan food, and on same street *Restaurant Azzam* and *Restaurant des Gouts*. Try also Ave de Tetouan.

● **Banks & money changers**
Wafabank, Place Moulay Hassan; **BMCE**, Ave Mohammed V.

● **Post & telecommunications**
Rue Moussa Ibn Noussair, near Place de l'Indépendence.

● **Tourist offices**
Ave Hassan II, T 672737.

● **Tour companies & travel agents**
Taza Voyages, Ave Mohammed V.

● **Transport**
Local Taxi: it is advisable to take one of Taza's light blue petit-taxis between Place de l'Indépendence and the railway station (MD3-5), or the medina (MD5). There are also town buses.

Train To Oujda (3½ hrs): 0339, 0615, 0859, 1715, 1951, 2247; to **Tanger** (8 hrs): 0959, 0141; to **Fes** (2 hrs) and Meknes (3 hrs): 0959, 1329, 1601, 2244, 0048, 0141; to **Rabat** (6 hrs) and **Casablanca** (7 hrs): 1329, 1601, 2244, 0048.

Road Bus: CTM buses leave from their office on Place de l'Indépendence to **Oujda** at 1500 and **Fes** at 0700 and 1500. Other companies operate from near the railway station, turn right at the end of Ave de la Gare. Regular services to **Oujda** at 0600, 0700, 0900, 1000, 1100, 1200, 1300, 1530, 1600 (4 hrs), **Fes** between 0500 and 1800 (2 hrs), **Nador** at 0700, 0800, 1100, 1300, 1400 (4 hrs), other services to **Al Hoceima** (4 hrs), **Aknoul** (1 hr). **Taxi**: grand-taxis leave from the bus station to **Oujda** (2½ hrs), **Fes** (1½ hrs), **Al Hoceima**, **Nador**, amongst other places.

Excursion on the Tazzeka Road
To the S of Taza and the P1 lies the **Jbel Tazzeka National Park** in an area of outstanding mountain scenery. The S311 winds its way through this area from S of Taza, rejoining the P1 31 km

further W. This is an excursion primarily for those with their own transport, but it may be possible to bargain for a grand-taxi part of the way, from the rank by the railway station. En route travellers should stop at the waterfalls, the **Cascades de Ras El Oued**, and further on, the **Dayat Chiker**. Nearby is the **Gouffre du Friouato**, an immense series of caves, dominated by a 180m deep underground bowl, worth exploring with a torch. After the caves, continue on to the Bab Taza pass from which a rough and challenging track goes N up to the Jbel Tazzeka, where there are incredible views of the surrounding mountains. After, or avoiding, the Jbel Tazzeka the road continues through the narrow gorge by the Oued Zireg and back to the P1. Excursions S to Immouzer du Kandar and the Dayats of Aaoua, Afourgan and Ifra see page 197.

OUJDA AND ON TO ALGERIA

Oujda

History

Oujda, with a present population of 260,000, is the most significant city in the E of Morocco, its essential character determined by its location close to the Algerian border. Indeed the city has many Algerians involved in cross-border commerce. There are few visitors enjoying the fairly peaceful, comparatively modern medina or taking a day trip to the Sidi Yahia oasis. It is a convenient stopping point for those crossing the border into Algeria or Spanish Melilla, or planning to journey down S to Figuig, in the Sahara. It is a well-equipped city which can be a useful last stop in relative comfort for the determined Saharan traveller.

Although Roman ruins have been found at Marnia, in 944 Zenata Berbers founded Oujda, strategically located on the main route from Rabat and Meknes to Algeria. It has traditionally been contested by the rulers of Fes, in Morocco, and Tlemcen, in Algeria. Captured by Sultan Youssef Ben Tachfine in 1206, it was a major centre for the Almohads. Later the Ottoman Regency of Algiers gained control of the city, but Moulay Ismail regained it in 1687. Oujda was acknowledged as part of Morocco by treaties with Morocco, but was occupied by French forces in 1844 and 1859. In 1903 Oujda was the centre of the insurgency by Bou Hamra, and was again taken by French forces from Algeria in 1907. The city was a centre of nationalist activity prior to Independence.

ACCESS Air Aéroport Oujda-Les Angad is 15 km from the city, off the P27, T 683261. Take a grand-taxi into town. **Train** Oujda is at the E end of the Moroccan rail network. The railway station is on Place de l'Unité Africaine, at the end of rue Zerktouni not far from the town centre. **Road** Oujda is a long haul over the P1 from Rabat, Fes and Taza to the W, which brings motorists over the Oued Nachaf into Blvd Mohammed ben Lakhdar, along with the P19 from Figuig, a hard drive across the Sahara. The P27 from Melilla, Nador and Ahfir enters Oujda along Blvd Abdellah Chefchaouni. From Ahfir continue to Saïdia and the Mediterranean. East to Algeria along the P1 follow Ave Mohammed V. **Bus**: CTM and other buses run into the Oued Nachef terminal, across the river from the town centre, take a petit-taxi to the town centre. Some CTM buses terminate in Place du 16 Août in the town centre. **Grand-taxis** from Nador, Berkane, Ahfir and the border terminate near Place du Maroc in the town centre, those for Figuig, Bouarfa and Taza stop at the bus station.

Places of interest

Oujda is not a city to visit for sightseeing. Its small medina is surrounded by the *ville nouvelle*, and is not particularly distinct from it, being a primarily 20th century quarter, with no notable buildings, but is pleasant to wander in. At night the streets are deserted and not very inviting. The area is partly surrounded by Merinid ramparts. Place du Maroc and Ave des Marchés are busy commercial areas with stalls, and with *souqs* alongside. From rue de Marrakech **Bab Ouled Amrane** leads into the *mellah*, Oujda's Jewish quarter.

Along Ave des Marchés, **Bab Abd el-Ouahab** is the main gate to the medina, above which the heads of criminals used to be placed on poles. Just inside and outside the gate is an area where people gather, particularly in the evening, to watch and listen to the entertainers, including acrobats, musicians and storytellers, and sample the wares at the food stalls. Inside the gate is a large *kissaria*, or covered market, and a small area of *souqs*, a relaxing place in which to browse and bargain, best on Wed and Sun. The first of these is the busy **Souq el Ma**, or irrigation market, alongside the **Sidi Oqba Mosque**, with a striking minaret. Turn left from the rue des Marchés, past vegetable stalls, into Place Al-Attarine, with the *koubba* of Sidi Abd el-Ouahab, as well as the Merinid **Grand Mosque** and **medressa**, built by Sultan Abu Yaqub. Adjacent to the Place is the kasbah, former residence of government officials. On rue el Ouahda is the **French Cathedral**.

The **Lalla Aisha** gardens are small, pleasant to wander in or relax, but nothing remarkable. They contain the **Lalla Aisha ethnographic museum**, open 0900-1200 and 1430-1730. The city also has the **Lalla Meryem museum**.

Following Blvd de Sidi Yahia 6 km from the medina takes one eventually to the **Shrine of Sidi Yahia**. This is thought to be the tomb of St John the Baptist, and has been revered by Jews, Christians and Muslims. It is a pleasant area of trees around a stream, popular with pilgrims and visitors, with stalls, a few areas reserved for Muslims, and has two *moussems* (religious festivals) in honour of Sidi Yahia, in Aug and Sep. Take a town bus from Bab El Ouahab, they run every 10 mins and take 20 mins, or a petit-taxi to here from the city centre, perhaps for a picnic.

Local information
● Accommodation

C *Hotel al-Massira Salam*, Blvd Maghreb al-Arabi, T 685300-3, Tx 61617, 108 rm, pool, tennis, bar, restaurant, nightclub from 2230, reliable, in the Salam chain; **C** *Hotel Terminus*, Place de l'Unité Africaine, T 683211-2, F 686378, 106 rm, comfortable with a good and popular bar, restaurant, tennis and pool, convenient for the railway station, the best top choice.

D *Grand Hotel*, rue Beni Marine, T 680508, this a good, modern hotel; **D** *Hotel la Concorde*, 57 Ave Mohammed V, T 682328, 70 a/c rm, bar, restaurant, disco; **D** *Hotel Moussafir*, Blvd Abdallah Chefchaouni/Place de la Gare, T 688202, F 688208, 72 rm or suites each with a/c, TV, shower, telephone, restaurant, bar, pool, exchange; **D** *Hotel Oujda*, Ave Mohammed V, T 685600/2, Tx 61062, conveniently situated and comfortable with restaurant, bar and pool.

E *Hotel Lutetia*, 44 Blvd Hassan Loukili, T 683365, 40 rm, convenient and adequate, with a bar; **E** *Hotel Royal*, 13 Blvd Zerktouni, T 682284, 60 good rm, clean and friendly, an efficient management; **E** *Hotel Simon*, Blvd Tarik Ibn Ziad, T 686304, 43 rm, bar and restaurant, changes money.

The best cheap hotel is the **F** *Hotel Zeglel*, nr the bus station, very friendly; **F** *Hotel Afrique* in the medina, nr Bab el Ouahab, is another good cheap option; as is **F** *Hotel du 16 Août*, rue de Marrakech, 23 clean rm, cold showers, mainly used by Algerian traders; whilst **F** *Hotel Majestic*, Ave Hassan II, T 682948, is a basic hotel but without hot water; *Hotel Victoria*, 74 Ave Mohammed V, T 685020, 10 rm, clean; **F** *Hotel Ziri*, Ave Mohammed V, T 684540, good view, 30 basic rm with bath (cold water).

● Youth hostel
11 Ave Allal ben Abdellah, T 680788, 45 beds, kitchen, meals available, bus 100m, train 500m, overnight fee MD20.

● Places to eat
◆◆◆The *Brasserie-Nightclub de France*, 87-89 Ave Mohammed V, T 685981, serves good Spanish, Moroccan and continental food and has an excellent bar; also try the restaurant in *Hotel Terminus*, Place de l'Unité Africaine.

◆◆*La Chaumière*, rue de Marrakech, is good

for French cooking; *Le Dauphin*, nr Blvd Ahfir, is a good Moroccan restaurant known for fish.

♦Try *Restaurant Bab el-Garbi*, nr the gate of that name, for cheap Moroccan food; or *Sandwich Taroudant*, Ave Allal ben Abdellah, with a good range of dishes. Perhaps the best cheap meals can be had at the stalls nr **Bab el Ouahab**.

● **Banks & money changers**
BMCE, 93 Ave Mohammed V; **Credit du Maroc** and **Wafabank** on Place du 16 Août.

● **Consulates**
Algeria, 11 Blvd de Taza, T 683740-1; **France**, 16 rue Imam Lechaf, T 682705.

● **Hospitals & medical services**
Chemist: all night on rue de Marrakech, T 683490.

● **Post & telecommunications**
Post Office: PTT, Ave Mohammed V/Place du Jeddah.

● **Shopping**
More expensive places than the *souqs* in which to shop, but good to sample the range of goods, are the official *Ensemble Artisanat*, Place Dar al-Makhzen; and the *Maison de l'Artisanat*, Blvd Allal ben Abdellah.

● **Sport**
Sporting Tennis Club, T 682545, and **Riding Club**, T 682499.

● **Tourist offices**
Delegation Regionale du Tourisme, Place du 16 Août, BP 424, T 684329 (open 0800-1200 and 1430-1830).

● **Transport**
Local Car hire: Avis, 110 Ave Allal ben Abdellah, T 683993, 684618, and at the airport; **Hertz**, 2 Immeuble El Baraka, Blvd Mohammed V, T 683802, Tx 61639, and at the airport. **Taxis**: petit-taxis are red. Watch out for unofficial red vehicles without signs. Taxi from Ave Mohammed V to Oued Nachaf bus station MD5.

Air There are flights to Casablanca (6 a week), as well as to Amsterdam, Bastia in Corsica, Brussels, Dusseldorf, Frankfurt, Marseille and Paris. Take a grand-taxi from Place du Maroc. **Royal Air Maroc** has an office at the *Hotel Oujda*, Ave Mohammed V, T 683963-4, as does **Air France**.

Train The train station is on Place de l'Unité Africain, T 683133. Departures to **Tanger** (12 hrs): 0610, 2210; **Taza** (3½ hrs); **Fes** (6½ hrs) and **Meknes** (7½ hrs): 0610, 1005, 1230, 1905, 2125, 2210; **Rabat** (9½ hrs) and **Casablanca** (10½ hrs): 1005, 1230, 1905 and 2125. There is also a once weekly train down the E flank of the country into the Sahara. The train leaves on Sat, calling at **Aïn Beni Mathar** (4 hrs) and **Bouarfa** (8½ hrs), and is useful for **Figuig**, 109 km to the SE of the latter station and connected by buses. Trains have run at times to Algiers and Tunis. Check at the station.

Road CTM buses leave from 12 rue Sidi Brahim, just off Place du 16 Août, T 682047, to **Fes** (1100), **Nador** (0500, 1000, 1300, 1530) and **Casablanca** (2000, 2030), and from the Oued Nachaf bus station at Place du 3 Mars to Fes (0500, 1100) and **Nador** (0700, 1000, 1300, 1530). Private line buses leave from the Oued Nachaf bus station, T 682262, to **Casablanca** (0430, 0630, 1600, 1700, 1800, 1930, 2030), Fes (0500, 0830, 1100), **Meknes** (1430), **Taza** (0400, 0730, 0930, 1200, 1300), **Taourirt** (1400, 1500, 1600, 1700, 1730), **Midelt** (0600), **Figuig** (0600, 1000, 1500 – the earlier the better to avoid the heat), **Bouarfa** (0700, 1700), **Nador** (10 between 0200 and 1315: 2 hrs), **Al Hoceima** (1400), **Berkane** (9 between 0740 and 1315), **Saïdia** (0800, 0900, 1330, 1420, 1610), **Ahfir** (regularly from 0635 to 1740). **Taxi**: grand-taxis to Berkane, Ahfir (40 mins) and the border leave from just off Place du Maroc. For Saïdia change at Berkane or, preferably, Ahfir. Grand-taxis to Taza, Figuig and Bouarfa leave from by the bus station.

The Algerian Border

At present travel in Algeria is not recommended.

CONTENTS

Marrakech	172
The High Atlas	188
Beni Mellal and Environs	193
The Middle Atlas	195

MAPS

Marrakech	175
Marrakech Souqs	179
Marrakech Medina	181
High & Middle Atlas	189

An ideal tourist location, Marrakech lies within reach of beautiful High Atlas valleys and arid pre-Saharan plains. The city itself is one of the great Islamic cities of North Africa, with the Koutoubia Mosque a memorable building which dominates the city, and the Djemaa El Fna square, a place of continual activity and entertainment. Around these the medina stretches, its narrow streets and flat-roofed red houses accommodating a way of life which has retained many characteristics from over the centuries. Within easy reach of Marrakech, the Ourika valley and the Toubkal National Park are some of the most popular areas of the High Atlas, and there is excellent skiing at Oukaimeden N of Marrakech, where the Middle Atlas mountain range runs up towards Meknes and Fes, with the relaxed Alpine-style resorts of Azrou and Ifrane.

MARRAKECH

(*Pop* 439,728 (1982); *Alt* 470m)

> "The *souks* of Marrakech seem, more than any others, the central organ of a native life that extends far beyond the city walls into secret clefts of the mountains and far-off oases where plots are hatched and holy wars formented – farther still, to yellow deserts whence negroes are secretly brought across the Atlas to that inmost recess of the bazaar where the ancient traffic in flesh and blood still surreptitiously goes on."
> Wharton, Edith, *In Morocco* (1927).

Along with Fes, Marrakech is the most important historic city in Morocco, with the **Koutoubia Mosque** and **Ben Youssef Medersa** among its most distinctive buildings. Marrakech has a memorable beauty, with its palm-lined streets and red earth walls, surrounding a huge medina of flat-roofed, red houses. The High Atlas mountains, snow-capped until Apr, loom above the city, a venue for numerous excursions. Above all Marrakech is worth visiting because of the vibrant mass of people that mill around in the unique **Djemaa El Fna** square, with its grill-stalls, traders and entertainers, and the vast network of *souqs*, people that come from all over the surrounding plains, the High Atlas and the Sahara. The character of the city owes much to its continuing role as a trading centre and capital for the S of the country. Tourist hassle which deterred some visitors in the past is now much reduced and the predominant atmosphere is very relaxed, best appreciated from a café terrace beside Djemaa El Fna.

The city of Marrakech, or Marrakesh, takes the Arabic form of 'Marrakch', whilst in some early European maps it appears as 'Morocco City'. The location of the city is particularly impressive. It is situated in the Tensift valley, in the rich agricultural Haouz plain, normally called the 'Haouz of Marrakech'. The city is surrounded by extensive palmeries, into which areas of villas and hotels are gradually spreading. Yet there are also sandy, arid areas near, and even within, the city, which give it a semi-Saharan character. The other dominant landform is the mountains. Arriving from Fes or Meknes one crosses the end of the Middle Atlas range, and from Casablanca or Rabat the dry, sparsely populated Bahira Jbilet. But from most points in Marrakech it is the High Atlas which is the visible mountain range, its often snow-covered peaks appearing to rise from just behind the city. Indeed the popular mountain destinations of the Ourika Valley, Oukaimeden, Asni and the Toubkal Park are easily accessible from Marrakech. Marrakech is also an important crossroads, the focal point of the S, linking roads from Fes/Meknes, Rabat/Casablanca, Safi, El Jadida, Essaouira, Agadir, Taroudant and Ouarzazate/the Sahara, whilst it also has an airport and is the S terminus of the railway network.

Marrakech covers a large area, with distinct zones separated by less populated areas. For the visitor this will entail long walks between the main points of interest and utility in the medina, the French built *ville nouvelle*, and the two gardens of Agdal and Menara, or more probably reliance on taxis, *calèches*, buses or their own transport. The long, wide tree-lined boulevards of the *ville nouvelle*, a number of which are focused on the beautiful **Koutoubia Mosque**, give the city an impressive feeling of spaciousness, which contrasts with the equally impressive density of the medina.

Marrakech is Morocco's fourth largest city, with a population including Arab, Berber and mixed elements, whilst many of its residents are immigrants from surrounding rural regions, and further S. The economy of the city includes administrative activities and modern shops and services, whilst it has for many centuries been an important regional market for trade in agricultural produce and other goods. There is still a wide range of handicraft production and small-scale industry, particularly in the medina. There are a number of factories and industrial units, notably in agro-processing. However the city's economy and employment are heavily dependent on tourism, Marrakech being one of the major tourist attractions of Morocco. Furthermore many of the city's large unemployed or under-employed labour force supplement their incomes by casual work with tourists, their unwanted attentions having in the past given Marrakech a bad name.

History

Almoravid origins Although Marrakech has probably been occupied since Neolithic times, it was first founded properly in 1062 by the Almoravids, as a base from which to control the High Atlas mountains. A kasbah, Dar al-Hajar, was built close to

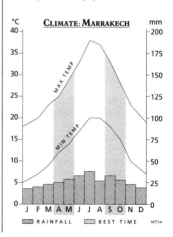

CLIMATE: MARRAKECH

RAINFALL   BEST TIME

the site of the Koutoubia Mosque. Under Youssef Ben Tachfine Marrakech was an important capital and marketing centre, with the building of several mosques, palaces and the city's famous walls, as well as the development of extensive gardens and an irrigation system. The city attracted leading mediaeval thinkers from outside Marrakech.

Marrakech under the Almohads Marrakech was taken by the Almohads in 1147, who almost totally destroyed and then rebuilt the city, making it the capital of their extensive empire. Under the Almohad Sultan Abd el-Moumen the *Koutoubia Mosque* was built on the site of Almoravid buildings, with the minaret added by Ya'qub al Mansur. Under the latter Marrakech gained palaces, gardens and irrigation works, and again became a famous centre for musicians, writers and academics, but on his death it declined and fell into disarray.

Merinid neglect and Saadian revival Whilst the Merinids added several *medressa* to Marrakech, Fes received much of their attention, and was preferred as capital, although from 1374 to 1386 Marrakech was the centre of a separate principality. Marrakech was revitalized by the Saadians from 1524 with the rebuilding of the *Ben Youssef Mosque*, and the construction by Ahmed al-Mansur Ad-Dahbi of the *El Badi Palace* and the *Saadian Tombs*. Marrakech also became an important trading post, due to its location between the Sahara and the Atlantic.

Alawite Marrakech The Alawites took control of Marrakech in 1668. In the early 18th century the city suffered from Moulay Ismail's love of Meknes, with many of the major buildings, notably the *El Badi Palace*, stripped to glorify the new capital, and a significant shift in power and wealth. The destructive effects of this period were compounded by the civil strife following his death. However, under the Alawite Sultan Moulay Hassan I, from 1873, and his

son, Marrakech gained a number of important buildings and reestablished its prestige. From 1898 Thami el-Glaoui and his family controlled the city as a powerful *pasha* with considerable autonomy from central control. A number of leading merchants built palaces in the city.

The French took control of Marrakech and its region in 1912, crushing an insurrection by a claimant to the Sultanate. The French built the *ville nouvelle*, Gueliz, in the 20th century, but Marrakech stagnated in comparison to the coastal cities of Casablanca and Rabat. In recent decades the city has grown enormously, with the authorities developing its tourist appeal and capacity, as well as its role as a conference centre.

ACCESS Air Aéroport Marrakech-Menara, T 430939 and 447903, is 5 km to the SW of the city near the Menara Gardens. It has a *bureau de change* open until 1800. Road 6010 leads to the city, the routes are clearly signposted. There are taxis from the airport, MD50 by day, MD90 after 2100 as well as bus No 11.

Train The railway station is in Gueliz, on Ave Hassan II, T 447768, 447947. There is usually no shortage of taxis waiting for the arrival of trains, although fixing a reasonable rate may be difficult for the new arrival. Most hotels in the *ville nouvelle* or the medina should be reached for MD5-10, and MD8-15 at night. Alternatively take bus No 3 or 8 from outside the station along Ave Hassan II and Ave Mohammed V, to the medina.

Road The P10 from Essaouira and Agadir enters the city along Ave d'Essaouira and Ave Hassan II, into Gueliz, and at Place 16 Novembre turn right along Ave Mohammed V for the medina. On the approach along the P9 from Safi (via the P12) and El Jadida cross the roundabout for the medina, and turn right along Ave Mohammed Abdelkrim Al Khattabi for Gueliz. From the P7 from Rabat and Casablanca turn right along Ave Allal Al Fassi for the medina, for Gueliz continue ahead. The P24 from Fes and Meknes skirts the N ramparts, from Bab Doukkala follow the outside of the walls to reach Djemaa

MARRAKECH MT 64

1. Tourist Office
2. PTT

Restaurants:
3. Le Dragon d'Or
4. Al Fassia
5. Chez Jack'Line
6. Villa Rosa
7. Trattoria de Gian Carlo & Bagatelle
8. La Taverne

Hotels:
9. Borj
10. Es Saadi
11. Safir Marrakech
12. Siaha Safir
13. Imilchil
14. Pacha & Toulousain
15. Koutoubia & Rôtisserie du Café de la Paix
16. Oasis
17. Hotel des Voyageurs
18. Franco Belge
19. Oudaya
20. Pullman
21. Campsite
22. Youth Hostel

El Fna and the centre of the medina, turn along Ave des Nations Unies for Gueliz. From the P31 from Ouarzazate follow the ramparts round to Bab Doukkala. Route 501 from Taroudant reaches Marrakech at a roundabout near Bab Rob, pass through the gate for the medina, turn left for Gueliz. **Bus** All long-distance buses arrive at the Gare Routière at Bab Doukkala, T 433933, from where taxis and bus No 3 or 8 can easily be taken. CTM services for Agadir and Casablanca also call at the office in Gueliz, in Blvd Mohammed Zerktouni. ONCF buses from Laayoune and Agadir arrive at the railway station in Ave Hassan II.

Places of interest

Main areas of interest Marrakech is clearly divided into the large historic city, the medina, and the *ville nouvelle*, Gueliz. The focal point of the medina, and indeed of the whole city, is the **Dje-** **maa el Fna**, an open place full of street entertainers and food sellers, adjacent to which are the most important markets, as well as numerous hotels, restaurants, cafés and shops. This is a good base from which to explore the historic sites of the medina. The gates in the city walls are also important centres, notably **Bab Rob**, **Bab Doukkala** and **Bab el Khemis**. The major thoroughfare of the Gueliz is Ave Mohammed V, and the evening promenade along its length is very popular. There is little to see in the Gueliz but it is a pleasant place to wander or rest in a café. The **Menara Gardens** are to the S of Gueliz, the **Agdal Gardens** directly to the S of the medina. On the E side of Marrakech, across the Oued Issil, is the **Palmery**.

It is worth attempting to coincide a visit to Marrakech with the **National**

Festival of Popular Art, an extravagant mixture of music, dance and folklore displays. The exact date in the summer for this varies annually so check with a tourist office.

Djemaa El Fna The Djemaa El Fna is unique in Morocco, perhaps the greatest pull for tourists, yet still a genuine social area for the Marrakchi people, and those flooding in from the surrounding regions, with much aimed solely at Moroccans. It is a large irregular space full of people hawking their goods or talents and others watching, walking, talking and arguing. Its activity never seems to finish, and at each point of the day has a distinctive character. It is particularly memorable during Ramadan when the day's fast ends. Whatever the time of the day or year, Djemaa El Fna is somewhere that the visitor will return to again and again, responding to the magnetic pull that affects locals as much as tourists, to mingle with the crowd or watch from the terrace of the *Café de France* or *Café-Restaurant Argana*.

Djemaa El Fna means 'assembly of the dead', and may refer to the traditional display of the heads of criminals, executed here until the 19th century. In 1956 the government attempted to close down the square by converting it into a corn market and car park, but soon reverted it to its traditional role. Visit it during the day to explore the stalls and collections of goods spread out on the floor: fruit, herbs and spices, clothes, shoes, electrical goods and handicrafts, as well as the snake charmers and monkey tamers, who pose for photographs. Return in the evening to watch and listen to the folk-healers, dancers, musicians, boxers, acrobats and storytellers that crowd the square, each with a throng of people gathered around. Those with courage may sample the food from the stalls, but it is wise to eat only what is cooked on request. Try the excellent freshly-squeezed orange juice from one of the stalls surrounding the square.

WARNING It is wise to take extreme caution with pickpockets, and to deal patiently with the numerous unofficial guides, 'students', or 'friends' that will seek business.

The Koutoubia Mosque dominates the whole of Marrakech, a landmark throughout much of the medina, and around which the French laid out their road network. It is clearly visible as, unlike the Qarawiyin Mosque in Fes, it is set apart from the dense areas of historic building, and has a tall minaret, of over 65m. According to legend as this structure overlooked the harem, only a blind muezzen was allowed to climb it to call the faithful to prayer. However it is a memorable structure with both elegance and simplicity in the design. The name, meaning the 'Bookseller's Mosque', reflects the trade which used to go on in the immediate surrounds.

The Koutoubia Mosque is at the end of Ave Mohammed V, close to the Djemaa El Fna. In viewing the site it is wise to be extremely careful, as the mosque is closed to non-Muslims and, as the most important in Marrakech, does not welcome close inspection. However it is possible to walk around and through the surrounding areas, where there are some interesting points from which to take photographs.

The site of the mosque is itself historic, with its prior occupation by a late 11th century kasbah, the **Almoravid Fortress**, or **Dar al-Hajar**. This was built by either Youssef Ben Tachfine or Abu Bakr, and formed the focus of the town. The configuration of the walls of this fortress can be seen between the mosque and Ave Mohammed V. The walls consist of 2m wide parts, with a gap down the centre. It is an impressive structure indicating a highly developed indigenous building capability. At the W extremity of the walls are the sites of a S facing gate and a fountain. These were decorated with painted panels from the

Almoravid period which are now in the **El Badi Palace**. The fortress ruins are the oldest Almoravid site in the country, and one of the few remaining in Marrakech.

On the corner of the two sections of the wall is **Bab Ali**, named after the son of Youssef Ben Tachfine. This is the ruins of a tower and entry arch, an entrance into the kasbah. It is suggested that it may have been the place where the Almohads finally defeated the Almoravids.

The successful Almohads destroyed much of the Almoravid city, and in 1147 built a large mosque, located between the kasbah and the later Koutoubia Mosque. The *mihrab* of this mosque was located on its S wall, bordering the existing building, and it is suggested that its location was wrong and led to the mosque's destruction. The two mosques existed for some time together, the bricked-up spaces on the N wall of the Koutoubia Mosque indicating the doors which connected them. However the complex was excessive in size and the older structure fell into disrepair and eventual ruin. The site was excavated from 1948. These excavations also revealed a *maqsura* or screen, in front of the *mihrab*, which could be wound up through the floor to protect the Sultan, and a *minbar*, or pulpit, which was moved into position on wooden rollers. The two cisterns in the centre are probably from a previous Almoravid structure. On the E flank of this mosque was an arcade of which a niche and the remains of one arch remain. Along this arcade runs a paved street where the booksellers worked.

The existing Koutoubia Mosque was built by Abd el-Moumen in 1162, soon after the building of the first mosque. The minaret is 12.5m wide by 67.5m high, and is the mosque's principal feature, rightly ranked along with the later Almohad structure of the **Hassan Tower** in Rabat (see page 83). The minaret, with its 1:5 proportions, had great influence on subsequent buildings in Morocco.

The minaret is composed of six rooms, one on top of the other. The cupola on top of the minaret is a symmetrical, square structure surmounted by a ribbed dome and three golden orbs. These are alleged to have been made from the melted down jewellery of Ya'qub al-Mansur's wife, in penance for having eaten three grapes during Ramadan. The cupola has two windows on each side, above which is a panel of stone-carved *darj w ktaf*. The main tower has a band of hexagonal and square tiles at the top, below which is a different series of arches and windows on each side, including a representation of many Almohad design motifs. The main building itself is fairly plain. Behind the mosque, on rue Sidi Mimoun, is a small tomb to the Almoravid Sultan Youssef Ben Tachfine, the founder of Marrakech.

The Souqs of Marrakech, many of which retain their original function, and the presence of both craftsmen and traders, are worth at least a morning to explore. It is, however, far from a relaxing experience, with traders continually besieging tourists with pleas of 'just for looking' or similar. It is worth getting an idea of prices before choosing a reasonable trader and getting down to serious bargaining. An unofficial guide is likely to be more trouble and expense than he is worth, and certainly one should not believe the 'Berber market, only open today' line, which is used everyday. **NB** It is important to inspect goods closely, especially anything involving gold, silver or gems, as these are often fakes. The increasing business in antiques often involves new products which have been treated.

The main *souqs* lie to the N of Djemaa El Fna. The entrance is to the left of the mosque. Follow this round to the left

NEATLY SHOD

The traditional footwear, *baboushes*, soft leather slippers worn with the heel turned in, vary in design. Men's slippers lined with sheepskin and having stronger, goatskin soles are normally dyed yellow but grey slippers are becoming more common. Women's outdoor slippers are most often black or red leather while the indoor slippers or those for special occasions are of brighter colours, lighter material and heavily decorated in gold or silver thread with stylised designs of leaves, flowers and geometric shapes. When purchasing, look for the craftsman's seal on the heel.

and then turn right in the main thoroughfare of the *souqs*, **Souq Semmarin**. Alternatively enter through the small touristic pottery market, further round to the left on Djemaa El Fna. Souq Semmarin is a busy place, originally the textiles market, and although there are a number of large, expensive tourist shops, there are still some cloth sellers. To the left is a covered *kissaria* selling clothes. The first turning on the right leads past **Souq Larzal**, a wool market, and **Souq Btana**, a sheepskin market, to **Rahba Kedima**, the old corn market, now selling a range of goods including traditional cures and cosmetics, spices, vegetables and cheap jewellery, and with some good carpet shops. Walk back onto the main *souq* via a short alley with wood-carved goods. Here the *souq* forks, into **Souq el Attarin** on the left and **Souq el Kebir** on the right.

To the right of Souq el Kebir is the **Criée Berbère**, where carpets and *jallabahs* are sold. This was where slaves, mainly from across the Sahara, were auctioned until 1912. Further on is the **Souq des Bijoutiers**, with jewellery. To the left of Souq el Kebir is a network of small alleys, the *kissarias*, selling Western goods. Beyond the *kissarias* is the **Souq Cherratin**, with leather goods, somewhere to bargain for camel or cow hide bags, purses and belts.

Continuing back on the other side of the *kissarias* is the **Souq des Baboushes**, a far better place to buy slippers than in the tourist shops. This feeds into **Souq**

el Attarin, the spice and perfume *souq*, which itself leads back into Souq Semmarin. West of the Souq el Attarin is the **Souq Chouari**, with carpenters. From here walk on to a Saadian fountain and the 16th century **Mouassin Mosque**. South of Souq Chouari is the **Souq des Teinturiers**, or dyers' market, where wool recently dyed is festooned over the walkways, the most picturesque area of the medina. Nearby are the blacksmiths' and coppersmiths' *souqs*.

The Almoravid Koubba and Ben Youssef Medersa These buildings are close to each other, to the N of the Djemaa El Fna, see map page 177.

The **Almoravid Koubba (Koubba el-Baroudiyin)** dates from the 11th century, and is a rare example of the architecture of this period, the only complete Almoravid building surviving. It dates from the reign of Ali bin Youssef (1107-43), and perhaps formed part of the toilet and ablutions facilities of the mosque which at the time existed nearby.

At first glance it is a simple building, with a dome surmounting a square structure. The dome is quite decorated, however, with a design of interlocking arches, and a star and chevron motif on top. The arches leading into the *koubba* are different on each side. Climb down the stairs to look at the structure close-up. Inside, the ceiling below the dome is intricately carved. It includes an octagon within an eight pointed star, and the use of a range of Almoravid motifs, including the palmette, pine cone and acanthus. Around the corniche is a dedicatory inscription in cursive script.

Close by the *koubba* is the large 12th century **Ben Youssef Mosque**, rebuilt in the 19th century. On a side street just to the E of the mosque is the Saadian **Ben Youssef Medersa** (open 0900-1200 and 1430-1800, closed Fri), an impressive example of religious architecture of the period, with strong influences from Andalucía. A boarding school for religious students, it was founded in 1564-5 by Sultan Moulay Abdellah, on the site of a previous Merinid *medersa*. The *medersa* is centred around a courtyard containing a pool, and with arcades on two sides. The arcades and walls are comprehensively decorated with a variety of different designs and scripts, with use of *zellij* tiling on the arcade floor, walls and pillars. Inscriptions are in Kufic and cursive lettering, interwoven with floral patterns.

At the far end is the *mihrab*, or prayer hall. Note the stalactite ceiling of the *mihrab*, and the carved stucco walls, in which the pine cone motif is prominent. There are small students' cells on both levels of the building, around separate courtyards. On the second level they often have a tiny sleeping room above, entered by bars on the wall.

On the way out of the *medersa*, the smelly toilets on the right of the vestibule have an elaborate stalactite design on the ceiling. There is also a 10th century Andalusian ablution basin in the vestibule, decorated with eagles and Cordoban floral designs.

To the N of the Ben Youssef Medersa is an area of the medina which is worth exploring for an indication of the structure and working of the traditional Islamic city, unspoiled by the demands of the tourist industry which have so influenced areas closer to Djemaa El Fna. This area includes the **Shrine of Sidi bel-Abbes**, one of the seven saints of Marrakech. He was born in Ceuta in

MARRAKECH SOUQS

1145 and during his life in Marrakech was patronized by Ya'qub al-Mansur. The shrine, recently restored, is strictly closed to non-Muslims. Nearby is the **Zaouia of Sidi Ben Slimane el-Jazuli**, a 14th century *sufi*.

Bab Agnaou, Saadian Tombs and El Badi Palace Bab Agnaou marks the entrance to the kasbah quarter. To get to it, follow rue Bab Agnaou from Djemaa El Fna, or enter the medina at Bab Rob. The kasbah quarter dates from the late 12th century and the reign of the Almohad Sultan Ya'qub al-Mansur. Bab Agnaou is also Almohad. The gateway itself is surrounded by a series of arches within a rectangle of floral designs and a further band of Kufic inscription.

The road from the gate leads to rue de la Kasbah, turn right along this and then along the first left. On this road is the much restored **Kasbah Mosque**, dating from 1190. The minaret has the *darj w ktaf* (*fleur de lis*) and *shabka* (net) motifs on alternate sides, with a background of green tiles, above which is a band of coloured tiles. The minaret is not as impressive as that of the Koutoubia Mosque but is worth noting en route to the Saadian Tombs.

The entrance to these lies directly to the right of the mosque. The late 16th century **Saadian Tombs** (open 0800-1200 and 1400-1800) are the mausoleums for the dynasty's Sultans and their families, and were discovered in 1917, having been sealed off by Moulay Ismail. There is a series of chambers and tombs off a small garden, with carved cedarwood and plasterwork which is in a remarkably good condition. The design is influenced strongly by the Andalusian tradition. The *mihrab* of the first main mausoleum is particularly impressive, and in this room is the tomb of Moulay Yazd. The second room contains the tomb of Ahmed al-Mansur, with finely carved columns. The second and older mausoleum was built for the tombs of Ahmed al-Mansur's mother, Lalla Messaouda, and Mohammed es-Sheikh, founder of the Saadians. In the garden and courtyard are the tombs of numerous princes and household members. As a small site the Saadian Tombs can become crowded with tour groups.

The **El Badi Palace** (open 0900-1200 and 1430-1730) was built by the Saadian Sultan Ahmed al Mansur Ad-Dahbi between 1578 and 1593, following his accession after the Battle of the Three Kings at Ksar el Kebir. To get to it, return to the Bab Agnaou and head right inside the ramparts, and then take the second right. This road leads more or less directly to Place des Ferblantiers. Pass through Bab Berima, the gate on the S side. The entrance to the palace is on the right.

The El Badi Palace was a lavish display of the best craftsmanship of the period, using the most expensive materials, including gold, but was largely destroyed in the 17th century by Moulay Ismail, who stripped it of its decorations and fittings and carried them off to Meknes. Little now remains except the palace's *pisé*-cement walls. The palace probably had a largely ceremonial purpose, being used for receptions. Past the mosque is the central courtyard, built above water channels connecting a number of pools. The largest of these even has an island. The ruins on either side of the courtyard were probably summer houses, that at the far end called the **Koubba el Hamsiniya** after the 50 pillars in its construction. The complex contains a small museum which includes the movable *minbar* from the Koutoubia Mosque. The scattered ruins of the palace, with odd fragments of decoration amidst the debris, include also stables and dungeons. To the S of the El Badi Palace is the **Dar al-Makhzen**, the modern-day Royal Palace, now one of King Hassan II's favourite residences.

Nearby, the **Musée Dar Al Funun Ashaabia**, 154 Derb Sahrige, rue Arste Moussa Riad Zitoune Kedim, T 426632, has audio-visual displays on various themes of Moroccan arts including dance, theatre and the marriage ceremony, each lasting between 20 and 45 mins.

The Southeastern Medina To get to the SE area of the medina follow rue des Banques from just past *Café de France* on the Djemaa El Fna. This leads into rue Zitoun Jedid. Off to the left is the **Dar Si Said** museum (open 0900-1200, 1600-2100 in the summer, 1430-1800 in the winter, closed Tues) is on Riad Zitoun Jedid, T 442464. This palace was built by Si Said, *Visir* under Moulay El Hassan, and half-brother of Ba Ahmed Ben Moussa, who built the El Bahia Palace.

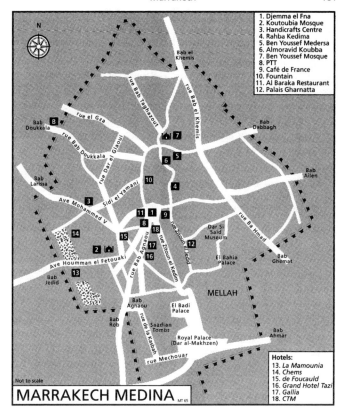

1. Djemma el Fna
2. Koutoubia Mosque
3. Handicrafts Centre
4. Rahba Kedima
5. Ben Youssef Medersa
6. Almoravid Koubba
7. Ben Youssef Mosque
8. PTT
9. Café de France
10. Fountain
11. Al Baraka Restaurant
12. Palais Gharnatta

Bab el
Khemis

rue Bab el Khemis

rue Bab Taghazout

rue el Gza

Bab
Doukkala **B**

rue Bab Doukkala

rue Dar el Giaoui

Bab
Dabbagh

Bab
Allen

Bab
Larissa

10

4

3 Ave Mohammed V Sidi el Yamani

rue Ba Hmad

11 **1** **9**

8 **18**

Dar Si
Said
Museum

14

15

rue Bab Agnaou

rue Zitoun el Jedid

12

2

17

16

Ave Houmman el Fetouaki

El Bahia
Palace

Bab
Ghemat

Bab
Jedid

13

MELLAH

Bab
Agnaou

El Badi
Palace

rue de la Kasbah

Saadian
Tombs

Bab
Rob

Royal Palace
(Dar al-Makhzen)

Bab
Ahmar

rue Mechouar

Not to scale

MARRAKECH MEDINA MT 65

Hotels:
13. *La Mamounia*
14. *Chems*
15. *de Foucauld*
16. *Grand Hotel Tazi*
17. *Gallia*
18. *CTM*

The museum includes pottery, jewellery, leatherwork from Marrakech and a collection of beautiful carpets from Chichaoua. It is particularly strong on Berber artifacts, notably jewellery and arms. The palace itself is small but with a cool and pleasant courtyard.

At 8 rue de la Bahia, between the El Bahia Palace and Dar Si Said, is *Maison Tiskiwin*, T 443335. This includes a shop, a café and a museum, the latter concerned with Moroccan rural culture and society, a collection put together by the art historian Bert Flint. There is an exhibition of craftsmen's materials and techniques from regions as far apart as

the Rif, High Atlas and the Sahara, including jewellery and costume. Note the nomad's tent from the Middle Atlas. The building itself, around a courtyard, is an authentic and well-maintained example of traditional domestic architecture.

Further to the S, the **El Bahia Palace** (open 0800-1200 and 1430-1800) was built in the 19th century by the *Visir* Ba Ahmed Ben Moussa, or Bou Ahmed, a former slave who exercised considerable power under Moulay Hassan and Abd al-Aziz. The palace has the Andalusian-inspired decor of the period, although executed in a garish fashion which does not do justice to the craftsmanship of the city. Bou Ahmed was so hated that, on his death in 1900, his palace was looted and his possessions stolen by slaves, servants and members of his *harem*. The building is centred around a marble courtyard. There is a colourful garden of fruit-trees and flowers.

The *mellah*, the Jewish quarter, was created in 1558. This lies S of the El Bahia Palace and to the W of the El Badi Palace. This is an extensive quarter reflecting the community's historic importance to the city, when they were involved in the sugar trade and banking, as well as providing most of the jewellers, metalworkers and tailors. There were several synagogues, and under the control of their *rabbis*, the area had considerable autonomy. There are now few Jews left, but the quarter is still distinct in the cramped houses and narrow streets. Conditions here remain worse than in much of the medina, with unpaved roads and insanitary drainage. It is worth asking around to be let into one of the synagogues.

The Walls and Gates The extensive ramparts of Marrakech (20 gates and 200 towers stretching for 16 km) are predominantly Almoravid, excepting those around the Agdal Gardens, although extensively restored since. The reconstruction is a continual process as the *pisé*-cement walls, made of the distinctive earth of the Haouz plains, gradually crumble. The ramparts and gates are one of the distinctive sights of Morocco, and a tour in a horse-drawn *calèche* is recommended. All the gates are clearly named.

Bab Rob, near the buses and grand-taxis on the SW side of the medina, is Almohad, and is named after the grape juice which could only be brought through this gate. **Bab Dabbagh** (the Tanners' gate) on the E side, is an intricate defensive gate with a twisted entrance route and wooden gates which could shut off the various parts of the

building for security. From the top of the gate there is a good view of the tanneries. It is possible to look around the tanneries. Note that hides are often laid out to dry on the banks of the nearby *oued*. **Bab el Khemis**, on the NE side, opens into the **Souq el Khemis** (Thur market) and an important area of mechanics and craftsmen. There is a small saint's tomb inside the gate building. **Bab Doukkala**, on the NW side by the bus station is a large gate with an *outrepassé* arch and two towers. The medina side has an *outrepassé* arch and a cusped, blind arch, with a variation on the *darj w ktaf* motif along the top.

The Gardens The **Agdal Gardens**, stretching S of the medina, were established in the 12th century under Abd el-Moumen, and expanded by the Saadians. The vast expanse includes several pools, and extensive areas of olive, orange and pomegranate trees. They are in the main closed when the king is in residence, but are worth visiting at other times. Of the pavilions, the **Dar al-Baida** was used by Sultan Moulay Hassan to house his *harem*. The largest pool, **Sahraj el Hana** receives its coach-loads of tourists, but in between times is a pleasant place to relax, although not to swim.

From the medina and the Agdal Gardens, Ave de la Menara leads past the **Oliveraie de Bab Jedid** to the **Menara Gardens**. This is an olive grove, itself not very interesting but a good place for a picnic. At the centre is a rectangular pool with a good view of the Atlas Mountains, a picture on numerous postcards and brochures. The green-tiled pavilion alongside was built in 1866. Inside, above the small display of carpets and other Berber artifacts, is an impressive painted cedarwood ceiling.

The Jardin Majorelle, also called the **Bou Saf-Saf** (open 0800-1200 and 1400-1700 in the winter, 0800-1200 and 1500-1900 in the summer), is off Ave Ya'qub al-Mansur. This is a small tropical garden laid out by a French artist, Louis Majorelle. The buildings are a vivid blue, but the overall effect is worth seeing. There is also a small **Musée d'Art Islamique** in the grounds.

The Palmery includes around 180,000 trees used mainly for wood. It is a good place for a drive or a *calèche* tour, but is gradually being expropriated by large villa and hotel developments. Take the Route de Palmeraie off the P24 to Fes to explore it.

Local information
● Accommodation

Price guide:			
AL	US$90+	**D**	US$20-40
A	US$75-90	**E**	US$10-20
B	US$60-75	**F**	under US$10
C	US$40-60		

AL *Hotel Es Saadi*, Ave Kadissia, Hivernage, T 448811, similarly luxurious hotel built in 50s style and set in large and pleasant gardens, with a rec restaurant, bar, casino, nightclub, tennis and pool; **AL** *La Mamounia*, Ave Bab Jedid, T 448981, F 444940, is itself a monument, a place to visit, a converted patronized by the rich and famous, recently redecorated to the highest standard, everything completed to perfection, with little touches that will delight the visitor, 171 luxurious rm, 49 normal suites, 8 incredible themed suites, 3 villas, outstanding service, 5 restaurants serving stunning menus of the highest standard, 5 bars, casino, conference room, business centre, shops, fitness and beauty centre, *hammam*, excellent pool, tennis, squash, beautiful flower gardens, if you cannot stay there, visit for a coffee; **AL** *Palmerie Golf Palace*, T 301010, F 305050, in Les Jardins de la Palmerie, 77 ha site, 314 rm, 5 pools, 18 hole golf course, 8 restaurants, 4 bars, nightclub, shopping arcade, conference centre; **AL** *Sheraton Marrakech*, Ave de la Menara, T 448998, F 437843, 291 comfortable a/c rm and suites, Moroccan and international restaurants, pizzeria, pool restaurant, pool, tennis, shops, salon, very friendly atmosphere.

A *Imperial Borj*, 5 Ave Echouhada, T 447322, 187 rm, modern, conference centre, restaurant, bar and popular nightclub; **A** *Hotel Pullman Mansur Eddahbi*, Ave de France, T 448222, 450 rm, restaurant, pool, tennis;

A *Hotel Safir Marrakech*, Ave President Kennedy, T 447400, F 448730, 280 rm, a fully equipped hotel with a disco, 2 tennis courts, bar, restaurant, shops, *hammam* and a pool surrounded with palm trees; **A** *Hotel Semiramis Le Meridien*, Route de Casablanca, BP 525, T 431377, F 447127, restaurant, bar, nightclub, tennis, and an excellent pool.

B *Hotel Tichka*, Route de Casablanca, Semlalia, T 448710, Tx 74855, 138 rm, beautifully designed and decorated, restaurant, bar, nightclub, tennis, good pool.

C *Hotel Chems*, Ave Houmane El Fetouaki, BP 594, T 444813, Tx 72008, small, restaurant, bar and nightclub; **C** *Hotel le Tafilalet*, Ave Mohammed Abdelkrim El Khattabi, T 434518, Tx 72955, mock kasbah style, pleasant room, a good garden; **C** *Hotel Siaha Safir*, Ave President Kennedy, T 448952, F 448730, 243 rm, pool and *hammam*.

D *Hotel Amalay*, Ave Mohammed V, clean and modern; **D** *Hotel de Foucauld*, Ave El Mouahidine, T 445499, 33 rm, a good hotel with restaurant and bar, same management as the *Tazi*; **D** *Hotel Gallia*, 30 rue de la Recette, T 445913, conveniently located just off the Djemaa El Fna (via rue Bab Agnaou), in an old building and some good rooms; **D** *Grand Hotel Imilchil*, Ave Echouhada, T 447653, Tx 74073, modern hotel with pool, restaurant and bar; **D** *Hotel Koutoubia*, 51 Blvd Mansur Eddahbi, T 430921, restaurant, central courtyard with excellent (when in use) pool; **D** *Hotel le Grand Sud*, 25 Blvd Mansur Eddahbi, modern, rec; **D** *Hotel Oudaya*, 147 rue Mohammed El Baqal, T 448512, F 435400, 15 suites, 77 rm, modern hotel with pool, restaurant and bar; **D** *Hotel Pacha*, 33 rue de la Liberté, T 431626/7, highly rec small hotel with dated charm, bar and restaurant, on a quiet street; **D** *Grand Hotel Tazi*, rue Bab Agnaou, T 442152, Tx 74021, memorable rooms with extravagantly painted ceilings and furniture, one of the few bars in the medina, a very good Moroccan restaurant at average prices, and a pleasant pool, strongly rec and very convenient for the sights.

E *Hotel Toulousain*, 44 rue Tarik Ibn Ziad, Gueliz, T 430033, best cheap option in the *ville nouvelle*, quiet location around 2 courtyards; in this area also try *Hotel Oasis*, 50 Ave Mohammed V, T 447179, good but noisy, with restaurant and bar; *Hotel des Voyageurs*, 40 Blvd Mohammed Zerktouni, T 447218, reasonable and central; *Hotel Franco Belge*, 62

Blvd Mohammed Zerktouni, T 448472, similar; **Hotel CTM**, on the Djemaa El Fna, T 442325, good and clean rooms, some with a view of the square, often full.

There are cheap hotels in the medina, on the small alleys between rue Bab Agnaou and rue Zitoun el Kedim, to the S of Djemaa El Fna, of very variable quality. Always ask to see a room. Try **F Hotel Oukaimeden**, a basic place on the Djemaa El Fna; **F Hotel de France**, 197 rue Zitoun el Kedim, T 443067; **F Hotel Central**, **F Hotel Afriquia** with a good patio and roof terrace, and **F Hotel Nouazah** on the first left off rue Bab Agnaou; and **F Hotel El Atlas**, a friendly, efficient place on rue de la Recette.

● **Youth Hostel**
Rue El Jahed, Quartier Industriel, T 4432831, 80 beds, kitchen, meals available, bus 200m, train 700m, overnight fee MD20.

● **Camping**
Camping Municipal is off Ave de France, S of the railway station, T 431844, with shop, showers and café.

● **Places to eat in Gueliz**

Price guide:
♦♦♦Expensive; ♦♦average; ♦cheap.

♦♦♦ **Al Fassia**, 232 Ave Mohammed V, T 434060, reservations rec, an excellent Moroccan restaurant on the main street, delicious desserts; **Le Jacaranda**, 32 Blvd Mohammed Zerktouni, T 447215, French food, strong on fish, closed Tues and Wed lunch time, bar; **La Trattoria du Gian Carlo**, 179 rue Mohammed El Bequal, T 432641, a very good Italian restaurant with an excellent selection of wines, in an art deco villa; **Le Dragon d'Or**, 10 bis Blvd Mohammed Zerktouni, T 433341, Chinese food; **Villa Rosa**, 64 Ave Hassan II, T 430832, a small Italian restaurant with terrace specializing in pasta and fish.

♦♦ **Rotisserie du Café de la Paix**, 68 rue Yougoslavie, Gueliz, T 433118, there is a garden in the summer, and reasonable grilled food all the year round; just opp is **Restaurant Bagatelle**, 101 rue Yougoslavie, T 430274, good French food served in the restaurant and vine shaded courtyard open 1200-1400 and 1900-2300; **Chez Jack'Line**, 63 Ave Mohammed V, T 447547, Italian, French and Moroccan dishes, good for pizzas; **Restaurant La Taverne**, 23 Blvd Mohammed Zerktouni, T 446126, fixed standard menus and a bar.

♦Top of the cheap range in the *ville nouvelle*

is **Brasserie du Regent**, 34 Ave Mohammed V, T 448749; also try **Le Petit Poucet**, Ave Mohammed V, T 448238, bar and restaurant with basic but good French dishes; **Le Sinbad Café**, Place 16 Novembre, basic but tasty meals and breakfasts, good service; or **Café Agdal**, 86 Ave Mohammed V, T 448707, good for chicken, no alcohol.

● **Places to eat in the Medina**
♦♦♦**Restaurant Marocain du Mamounia**, in the *Hotel Mamounia*, Ave Bab Jedid, T 448991, reservations rec, lavishly decorated restaurant with one of the best introductions to élite Moroccan cuisine, an excellent *pastilla* (pigeon dish), music/folklore in the evening; **Restaurant La Calèche**, in the *Hotel Mamounia*, Ave Bab Jedid, T 448991, top-notch French food with a view over the hotel's famous gardens; **La Maison Arabe**, 5 Derb Ferrane, nr Bab Doukkala, T 422604, with a reputation for the best food in Morocco, expensive, reservations necessary; **Restaurant Riad**, rue Arset El Maach, T 425430, in the medina, with expensive but excellent Moroccan meals accompanied by evening entertainment; **Restaurant Relais Al Baraka**, Djemaa el Fna, nr the police station, T 442341, Moroccan meals around a courtyard with fountain, convenient after sightseeing, reservations rec; **Restaurant Palais Gharnatta**, 56 Derb el Arsa, Riad Zitoun Jedid, T 445216, nr the El Bahia Palace, this restaurant offers Moroccan dishes at high prices, clients pay for the supposedly 16th century palace surroundings, reservations rec; **El Bahia**, 1 Riad Zitoun Jedid, similar arrangement with evening entertainment; **Restaurant Stylia**, 34 rue Ksour, T 443587, reservations rec, a 15th century palace, with variations on Moroccan traditional dishes.

♦♦ **Restaurant de Foucauld**, in the *Hotel Foucauld*, Ave El Mouahidine, good *couscous* and *tagines* nr the Djemaa El Fna; **Restaurant Tazi**, in the *Grand Hotel Tazi*, rue Bab Agnaou, similar restaurant run by the same management, the cheapest licensed establishment in the medina; Buffet dinner in *Hotel Ali*, rue Moulay Ismail, nr the Djemaa El Fna massive choice and very reasonably priced; **Café-Restaurant Argana**, Djemaa El Fna, food with a view; **Restaurant Etoile de Marrakech**, rue Bab Agnaou, very good value set meals with view of Djemaa El Fna from the roof.

♦In the medina the most popular option is to eat at the open-air restaurants in the **Djemaa**

El Fna. Each has a different variety of cooked food, some of which tastes very good. The conditions are, however, far from sanitary, and so it is best to go for the food cooked to order whilst waiting, as other dishes may have been around for some time. For a safer meal try the excellent value *Chez Chekrouni*, on Djemaa El Fna, left of the *Café de France*; the somewhat smelly *Café de Fath* which has very good *tagines*; or *Restaurant Toubkal*, in the opp corner. There are a series of cheap restaurants along Bani Marine, in between rue Moulay Ismail and rue Bab Agnaou, such as *Casse-Croûte des Amis*.

● Bars

Piano Bar, at the *Hotel Mamounia*, Ave Bab Jedid, T 448981, 1800-0100, drinks are not cheap but the Western atmosphere and music a pleasant change; *La Renaissance*, Ave Mohammed V, go up the lift to the rooftop bar with the best view of the Gueliz; *Le Petit Poucet*, 56 Ave Mohammed V, no view but fairly cheap drinks; also try *Ambassadeurs*, 6 Ave Mohammed V; or *Haouz*, Ave Hassan II.

● Cafés

One of the best places for a drink is beside the Djemaa El Fna: *Café-Restaurant Argana* has a good terrace view; even better is the *Café de France*, with several levels and an excellent panorama over the square, and the medina beyond, scattered with minarets. In Gueliz Ave Mohammed V and Blvd Mohammed Zerktouni meet at a roundabout with popular cafés on each side, incl the *Brasserie des Négociants* and *Café Renaissance*; *Boule de Neige*, on rue de Yougoslavie just off Ave Mohammed V, is a trendy place for pricey but excellent drinks, ice cream and breakfasts; next door is *Pâtisserie Hilton*, with a full range of Moroccan sweets and cakes; the best is perhaps *Pâtisserie Zohor*, rue de la Liberté. For late night coffees or ice creams (most places close by 2130), try *Café-Glacerie Siroua*. Locals swear by *Café Zohor*, rue de la Liberté; *Café Firdaous*, Ave Mohammed V, also has an authentic local clientele.

● Banks & money changers

ABM, 55 Blvd Zerktouni, T 448912; **Banque Al Maghrib**, Djemaa El Fna, T 442037; **Banque Populaire**, 69 Ave Mohammed V, T 434851; **BCM**, Blvd Zerktouni, T 434805; **BMCI**, Blvd Mohammed Zerktouni, **Credit du Maroc**, Ave Mohammed V, T 434851; **SGMB** 59 rue de Yougoslavie, T 448702; **Uniban**, rue

Moulay Ismail, T 425285; **Wafabank**, 213 Ave Mohammed V, T 433840.

American Express: Voyages Schwartz, Immeuble Moutaouskil, rue Mauritania, T 433321.

● Cultural & language centres

American Language Center, 3 Impasse Moulin du Gueliz, weekly film, small library and bookshop; **Centre Culturel Français**, (open 0830-1200 and 1430-1830, except Mon), Route de la Targa, Gueliz, with a café, library and pleasant garden, has films, exhibitions and other cultural events.

● Entertainment

Casinos: *Grand Casino de la Mamounia*, at the *Mamounia Hotel*, Ave Bab Jedid, T 444570, open from 2000 or 2100; *Hotel Es Saadi*, Ave Kadissia, T 448811.

Cinemas: the major cinemas showing films in French, are the *Colisée*, Blvd Mohammed Zerktouni; the *Regent*, Ave Mohammed V; try also the *Centre Culturel Français*, Route de Targa, Gueliz, T 447063, 446930.

Discos & nightclubs: *Disco Paradise*, at the *Hotel Pullman Mansur Eddahbi*, Ave de France, T 448222, admission MD80, 2200-0700, a large disco with the latest equipment; *Cotton Club*, at the *Hotel Tropicana*, Semlalia, T 433913, admission MD60, 2100-0500; also try *L'Atlas* and *Le Flash* on Ave Mohammed V; *Le Diamant Noir* at the *Hotel Marrakech*, Ave Mohammed V; or *Temple de Musique* at the *Hotel PLM N'Fis*, Ave de France.

● Folklore & fantasia

The *Cappa Club* at the *Hotel Issil*, the *Hotel le Marrakech*, Ave Mohammed V, and the *Club Mediterranée* all have large folklore displays but can be difficult to get into. The best bet is the *Restaurant Riad*. For fantasia, drive or take a taxi to *Chez Ali*, in the **Palmery** after the Tensift bridge, T 448187; *El Borj*, after the Tensift bridge, T 446376, *Zagora* Route de Casablanca, T 445237; *Ancien Casino de Marrakech*, Ave el Kadissia, T 448811, food and extravagant displays from 2100, admission MD100; *Restaurant Chaouia*, nr the airport, T 442915, displays of horsemanship, sword play, dance and music.

● Hammams

Try one of those on rue Zitoun el Kedim; or *Hammam Dar El Bacha*, rue Fatima Zohra, with amazing decor.

● **Hospitals & medical services**
Ambulance: T 15 (private ambulance service: 10 rue Fatima Zohra, T 443724).
Chemists: *Pharmacie Centrale*, 166 Ave Mohammed V, T 430151; *Pharmacie de Paris*, 120 Ave Mohammed V; *Pharmacie Bab Ftouh*, Djemaa El Fna, T 422678. There is an all night chemist, *Pharmacie de Nuit*, at rue Khalid Ben Oualid, T 430415.
Dentists: Dr Hamid Laraqui, 203 Ave Mohammed V, T 433216; and Dr E Gailleres, 112 Ave Mohammed V, both speak English.
Doctors: Dr Ahmed Mansouri, rue de Sebou, T 430754; and Dr Perez, 169 Ave Mohammed V, T 431030, both speak English.
Hospitals: *Hôpital Ibn Tofail*, rue Abdel Ouahab Derraq, T 448011; *Hôpital Avenzoar*, rue Sidi Mimoun, T 422793.

● **Post & telecommunications**
Area code: 4.
Post Office: the Central PTT for post, telegrams, poste restante and telephones is on Place 16 Novembre, Gueliz, the telephone service being particularly inefficient, slow and expensive, open till 2100. There is also a reasonable post/telephone office on the Djemaa El Fna.

● **Places of worship**
Catholic: *Eglise des Saints-Martyrs*, rue El Imam Ali, Hivernage, for information T 430585.
Jewish: *Synagogue Bet-el-Gueliz*, Arset El Maash, for information T 447832, 447976.
Protestant: *Protestant Church*, 89 Blvd Moulay Rachid, T 431479.

● **Shopping**
The *souqs*, N of the Djemaa El Fna, are the best place to search for bargains in carpets and handicrafts, but a visit can be a tiresome experience as the tourist is besieged by traders and misled by absurd prices. Bargaining is a long activity requiring patience, and should be carried out without assistance from guides, whose commission will be added on to any price. *Souq Semmarin* is the main area with the largest boutiques, some with supposedly fixed prices, and can be more expensive. *Rahba Kedima*, off to the right, has some interesting small shops. Leather goods should be bought in *Souq Cherratin*, Moroccan slippers from the *Souq des Baboushes*, where they are often made as well as sold.
Coopartim Ensemble Artisanale, Ave Mohammed V, 5 mins walk from the Koutou-

bia Mosque, T 423835, can be treated as an exhibition of locally-made handicrafts, even some craftsmen working on the premises, but one can also buy at fixed prices.
Marrakech has numerous good jewellers, who sell a variety of traditional jewellery, including bracelets, necklaces and inlaid boxes, antique items, and less attractive European-style gold and silver. Amongst many small but good boutiques is *Tresorie du Sud*, rue El Moissine, T 440439.
Souqs which can be reached by excursion from Marrakech include Ourika (Mon), Amizmiz (Tues), Tahanaoute (Tues), Ouirgane (Thur), Setti Fatma (Thur), Asni (Sat) and Chichaoua (Sun).
Foreign newspapers can be bought from the stands along Ave Mohammed V, and in the large hotels. They normally arrive a day late. Books in French from Ave Mohammed V, particularly *Librairie Chatr Ahmed*, No. 19, T 447997.

● **Spectator sport**
The *Kawkab* (KACM) football club of Marrakech, one of the best in Morocco, can be seen at the **Stade al Harti**, rue Moulay El Hassan, Hivernage.

● **Sport**
Ballooning: take off behind *Oasis Restaurant*, MD2,000 for 1 hr.
Flying: *Royal Flying Club*, Aéroport Marrakech Menara, T 431769.
Go-Karting: at *Kart Hotel*, Sud Quad.
Golf: the *Royal Golf Club*, 6 km S off the Ouarzazate road (P31), T 443441, is a large 18 hole course set in orchards, 4,805m, par 71, fee MD400. *Palmeraie Golf Palace*, 18 hole, par 72, 6,200m, fee MD350, 15 km S of town.
Riding: at *Club de l'Atlas* (Haras Régional), Quartier de la Menara, T 431301; or there is another 4 km along the road to Asni, T 448529.
Skiing: call at *Skiing Club*, Ave Mohammed V, T 434026, the best site is 76 km from Marrakech at Oukaimeden.
Swimming: at the municipal pool in the *Moulay Abd es-Salam Garden*, rue Abou el Abbes, nr the Koutoubia Mosque. The large hotels have pools, the cheapest and most convenient for the medina is the *Grand Hotel Tazi*, on rue Bab Agnaou.
Tennis: *Royal Tennis Club de Marrakech*, eight courts, Jnane El Harti, rue Oued El Makhazine, T 431902. 30 tennis courts in hotels.

● **Tour companies & travel agents**
Menara Tours, 41 rue Yougoslavie, T 446654, has English speaking staff; also try *Atlas Tours*, 40 Ave al-Mansur Ad-Dahbi, T 433858; *Sahara Tours*, 182 Ave Abdelkrim El Khattabi, T 430062; *Comanov Voyages*, 149 Ave Mohammed V, T 430265; *Atlas Voyages*, 131 Ave Mohammed V, T 430333; *Wagons Lits Tourisme*, 122 Ave Mohammed V, T 431687. **Royal Air Maroc**, 197 Ave Mohammed V, T 436205.

● **Tourist offices**
Office du Tourisme, Place Abd el-Moumen Ben Ali, T 448889; **Syndicat d'Initiative**, 176 Ave Mohammed V, T 432097, 434797.

● **Useful addresses**
Fire: rue Khalid Ben Oualid, T 16.
Garages: Peugeot: Toniel S A, rue Tarik Ibn Ziad; **Renault**: CRA, 55-61 Ave Mohammed V, T 432015; others are **Auto Hall**, rue de Yougoslavie; and **Garage Ourika**, 66 Ave Mohammed V, T 430155.
Police: rue Ibn Hanbal, T 19.

● **Transport**
Local Buses: T 433933, can be caught from rue Moulay Ismail, just off the Djemaa El Fna, and elsewhere along Ave Mohammed V and Ave Hassan II. No 1 is the most useful, running from Djemaa El Fna along Ave Mohammed V, No 3 and 8 run from the railway station to the bus station, via Djemaa El Fna, No 10 from Djemaa El Fna to the bus station, No 11 from the Djemaa El Fna to the Menara Gardens. **Bicycle/motorcycle hire**: *Hotel de Foucauld*, Ave El Mouahidine, T 445499; **Peugeot**, 225 Ave Mohammed V; several cheaper places in Bani Marine, the road in between rue Moulay Ismail and rue Bab Agnaou. **Calèches**: green-painted horse-drawn carriages, can be hailed along Ave Mohammed V, or from the stands at Djemaa El Fna and Place de la Liberté. There are fixed prices for tours around the ramparts, other routes are up for negotiation, but they are not normally prohibitively expensive, and this is a pleasant way to see the city. **Car hire**: MD2,000 for 3 days. **Avis**, 137 Ave Mohammed V, T 433727; **Europcar Inter-Rent**, 63 Blvd Mohammed Zerktouni, T 431228 and at the airport; **Euro Rent**, 9 Ave al-Mansur Ad-Dahbi, T 433184; **Hertz**, 154 Ave Mohammed V, T 434680, airport 447230; **La Royale**, 17 rue Mauritanie, T 447548; lesser known firms with more competitive rates are **Concorde Cars**, 154 Ave Mohammed V, T 431114 (speak English) and **SAFLOC**, 221 Ave Mohammed V, T 433388. **Taxis Petit-taxis**: are easy to find around the city, beware as many do not operate meters, and inflate their prices dramatically for tourists. From the medina to Gueliz should cost MD5-10 during the day, and MD8-15 during the late evening and night. Few journeys should cost much more than this. Major ranks are to be found in Djemaa El Fna, at the Gare Routiere by Bab Doukkala, and outside the *marché municipal*, Gueliz. **Grand-taxis**: are normally more expensive, can be found at the railway station and the major hotels. They also run over fixed routes, mainly to outlying suburbs, from Djemaa El Fna and Bab Doukkala.

Air Aéroport Marrakech Menara, T 447862, is 6 km W of the city, by the Menara Gardens, and clearly signposted from the centre. There are flights to Casablanca (2 a day), Ouarzazate (4 a week), Agadir (2 a week), as well as to Brussels (Fri), Geneva (Sun), Paris (Mon and Fri), London (Sat and Tues), and Madrid.

Train The railway station is in Gueliz, on Ave Hassan II, T 447768. Although there are long-term plans for an extension of the line S to Agadir and Laayoune, at present ONCF operates only bus services to the S, connecting with the arrival of the express trains. Express trains for **Casablanca** (3 hrs) and **Rabat** (4hrs) leave at 0900, 1230, 1400 and 1900, and non-express services at 0700, 1705, 2050 and 0130.

Road Buses: run from the Gare Routière at Bab Doukkala, T 433933, which is easily reached by taxis and local buses. There is often a choice between a number of different companies, including CTM, with different prices and times. CTM departures are currently: **Ouarzazate** 0445, 0730, 1300 and 1700; **Er Rachidia** 0445; **M'Hamid** 0730; **Beni Mellal** 0630, 1900 and 2100; **Agadir** 0800 and 1830; **Laayoune** 1900; and **Casablanca** 0630, 1230, 1630 and 1800. There are also private line services to **Beni Mellal** (19 a day), **El Kelaa des Srarhna** (17 a day), **Rabat** (13 a day), **El Jadida** (9 a day), **Essaouira** (6 a day), **Ouarzazate and Skoura** (5 a day), **Agadir** (4 a day), **Safi** (3 a day), **Taroudant** (2 a day), **Fes, Tiznit, Tafraoute, Ouarzazate and Essaouira** (all 1 a day), as well as to Asni, **Oualidia, Khouribga, Ifni** and **Demnate**. It is wise to call at the station the previous day as some services, notably across the High Atlas to **Taroudant** and **Ouarzazate**, leave early in the morning. There are CTM services to Paris every day except Fri and Sun at 1700, cost MD1150. The private line alternative leaves at 1200. CTM services for **Agadir** and **Casablanca** can also be taken from Gueliz, in Blvd Mohammed Zerktouni, but places should be reserved a day in advance. Buses to the **Ourika Valley**, **Asni** and **Moulay Brahim** run from Bab Rob. **Taxi**: grand-taxis running over fixed routes, with fixed prices, leave from a variety of places around the city. For Ourika, Asni and Ourigane leave from Bab Rob. For most other destination, including Chichaoua, Essaouira and Agadir, go to Bab Doukkala.

THE HIGH ATLAS

Marrakech is an ideal base from which to make excursions to the High Atlas, which provide welcome relief both from the hassle and the heat of the city, as well as having a distinct interest of their own. Transport for most of these is by bus or grand-taxi from the rough ground outside Bab Rob.

Chichaoua and Amizmiz

Chichaoua is a small town, 100 km from Essaouira, at the intersection with the road to Agadir. There are garages, café-restaurants and a small Sun *souq* near the crossroads, and a *Centre Cooperative Artisanal* (closed Sun) where the carpets for which the town is well known are exhibited and sold. There are regular buses (MD13) and grand-taxis (MD15) to and from Marrakech. The road from Marrakech is over flat plains and in through the western residential and industrial quarters of the city.

Amizmiz, 55 km from Marrakech at the end of the S507, is known for its acrobatic school which has existed since mediaeval times, and now trains the acrobats which appear in Marrakech and in Europe. It was founded by a *marabout*, Sidi Ahmed. There is also a semi-ruined kasbah, a former *mellah*, and an important Tues morning *souq*, specializing in carpets and pottery. The **F** *Hotel de France*, with attached bar, is adequate. There are regular buses (2½ hrs), and much quicker grand-

taxis, to and from Bab Rob in Marrakech.

Asni, the Toubkal National Park and Ourigane

Asni   There are regular grand-taxis from Bab Rob to Asni, as well as the Taroudant buses which leave from the *gare routière* at Bab Doukkala and call at Bab Rob. En route from Marrakech to Asni the S501 passes through the large village of **Tahanaoute** with a good *souq* on Tues and a *zaouia* to Moulay Brahim, who brings luck to childless women.

Asni, a typical Berber village, has a *souq* on Sat, and is a busy village with houses in dark earth stacked in clusters around the green valley. It is a pleasant place to stop en route to Ourigane, Tin Mal or Taroudant, or on to the Toubkal National Park, if one avoids the attentions of the jewellery sellers.

● **Accommodation**   The main option is the **D** *Grand Hotel de Toubkal*, T Asni 3, a converted kasbah, 19 comfortable rm, celebrated restaurant with local specialities, bar, pool and a delightful garden with fruit trees and rose bushes. **Youth hostel**, T 447713, on Route d'Amlil, through the market and to the left, 40 beds, kitchen, overnight fee MD20.

● **Places to eat**   Limited choice available. Eat expensively at *Grand Hotel de Toubkal* or in the centre of the village at the number of stalls and cafés cooking *harira* soup and *tagines*. This is the last place to stock up on basic supplies for a visit to the Toubkal region.

Toubkal National Park is reached by a track which leads off left in Asni, through the market. For those without transport either hike or negotiate a grand-taxi. It is possible to walk from Asni to *Imlil*, or to *Tachedirt*, which has a *Refuge Club Alpin Français*. In Imlil one can stay and eat at **F** *Café du Soleil*, a tiny and basic place; the **F** *Etoile de Toubkal*; or at the *Refuge Club Alpin Français*, which provides clean but minimal facilities. Mules and guides can be hired in Imlil, most easily in the *Refuge* or at *Ribat Tours*.

● **Walking**   Options include the **Aremd** circuit, a refreshing hike through remote villages

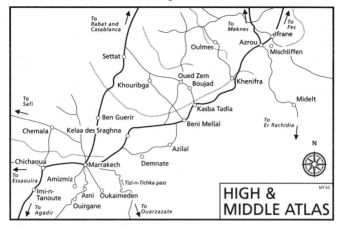

To Rabat and Casablanca

To Meknes

To Fes

Ifrane

Settat

Oulmes

Azrou

Mischliffen

Oued Zem
Boujad

Khouribga

Khenifra

To Safi

Midelt

Kasba Tadla

Ben Guerir

Beni Mellal

To Er Rachidia

Chemaïa

Kelaa des Sraghna

Chichaoua

Azilal

N

To Essaouira

Marrakech

Demnate

Amizmiz

Tizi-n-Tichka pass

Imi-n-Tanoute

Asni

Oukaimeden

To Agadir

Ouirgane

To Ouarzazate

HIGH & MIDDLE ATLAS

MT 63

and past breathtaking views, and a hike to the **Lac d'Ifni**. Another is to walk to **Setti Fatma**, in the Ourika Valley. Much more challenging is to climb **Jbel Toubkal**, the highest mountain in North Africa at 4167m. It is necessary to break the walk at the *Refuge Club Alpin Français* at Neltner, a simple dormitory place with no meals. In winter this is a difficult trek and full equipment is essential. A wise plan is to purchase specialist hiking books, such as Robin Collomb's *Atlas Mountains*, and maps, for the region, before arriving.

Ouirgane is a beautiful village about 1 hr drive from Marrakech in a dramatic valley location, on the S501. It can be reached by bus from Marrakech (the Taroudant service), or by grand-taxi from Asni. The two hotels in Ouirgane offer wonderful food and the opportunity to explore the valley in easy rambles. The **C** *Le Val de La Roseraie*, BP 769, T 432094, F 432095, 23 a/c rm, is a beautiful and peaceful hotel set in extensive and profusely flowering grounds, with two fine restaurants, bar, disco, nightclub, *hammam*, hydrotherapy centre, tennis, horse riding and pool; whilst the **D** *L'Hostellerie au Pont d'Ouirgane 'Auberge Au Sanglier Qui Fume'*, T Ouirgane 9, is an *auberge* run by a Frenchwoman, with 14 old style chalets amidst the gardens, a restaurant serving excellent French country food, a

bar, tennis and a pool in the summer, as well as camping for those who have a meal in the restaurant.

Tin Mal

Tin Mal is a ruined settlement high in the Atlas mountains, off the S501 from Marrakech to Taroudant. It was the holy city of the Almohad Dynasty, and it enables the non-Muslim to see the interior of a major mosque, with examples of 12th century Almohad decor intact amidst the ruins.

Tin Mal is 100 km from Marrakech, just past the village of Ijoujak. From Marrakech drive, or take a Taroudant bus as far as Ijoujak, where there are several basic cafés with rooms. Just after the village, on the right, is the **Talat n-Yacoub Kasbah**, the home of the Goundafis, who formerly ruled the area, and a ruined summer pavilion with a ribbed dome, and further along, on the left, another kasbah of the Goundafi family. Carry on walking, and across the river to the right can be seen the square structure of the **Tin Mal Mosque**. Cross the river on the next bridge (often impassable by car), and walk up past Tin Mal village to the mosque.

The town, the base of the Almohad

HANDMADE CARPETS

The visitor will be surprised at the number of carpets on display in the *souqs* of North Africa. There is a great variety of designs, materials and unusual colours. A carpet is a splendid memento of a holiday in North Africa and a better choice will be made with a little knowledge and by taking your time in making your selection. North African carpets, unlike Persian carpets, are best not considered as investments.

There are two main types of handmade carpet, the flat woven *kilims* and knotted carpets usually of wool on a cotton base.

Kilims are flat woven rugs and include tapestries with woven scenes. They have the great virtue of being cheap, light in weight and easily packed. Very decorative are the thin Bedouin rugs in bright reds and golds, while there are also coarse rag rugs made from scraps of material common in Egypt. Most valuable are the *kilims* made entirely of wool and dyed in natural colours or mixed fibres, some in very bright hues.

Handknotted carpets and rugs are more expensive than *kilims*. The number of knots per square centimetre determines the quality of a handknotted carpet, as does the materials of which it is constructed. The backing (the warp) may be of cotton, wool or silk and the knots of wool or silk. Coarse woollen material is used when knot densities are low, on average about 25 per centimetre, while the fine wools and silks require higher densities of up to 69 knots per centimetre, take longer to make and therefore cost more.

Designs for the handknotted carpets are very varied, though the best usually take their patterns from tile designs from the walls of the famous mosques. Often however designs are adapted from traditional patterns made popular elsewhere in the Middle East – Persian, Turkish and Caucasian being most widespread. Pleasing designs on small rugs follow the classical patterns of the tree of life, formal hunting scenes, the Persian garden, bird carpets and central medallions.

revolt against the Almoravids, became a necropolis for its rulers, with the burial there of Ibn Tumart, Abd el-Moumen, Abu Ya'qub and Abu Youssef. The tombs and the mosque became venerated as a pilgrimage centre, even after the Merinid destruction of 1275-6. The mosque dates from 1153-4, during the reign of Sultan Abd el-Moumen, and was built by the tomb of Ibn Tumart.

The mosque has a rectangular shape, with thick *pisé*-cement and stone and a low minaret of brick, unusually located behind the *mihrab*. The *mihrab* niche, with its stalactite dome, is built into the minaret, in between the door used by the *Imam*, and a room used to store the pulpit. Below the courtyard is a cistern fed by two conduits. The mosque is deco-

rated with plaster applied to the brick facing, and is simple as befits the conservative tastes of the period. The *mihrab* niche has a distinctive shape, accentuated by the configuration of two arches and rectangular frame surrounding it, with rosettes in the spaces between the arch and frame. Around this is a geometric pattern of interlacing 8-pointed stars and rectangles. The three windows above the niche are surmounted by a band of interlacing 6-pointed stars. The stalactite dome above once included plaques of Almohad floral decor, two of which remain in this dome. The remainder of the mosque includes a large number of arches and several areas of stalactite plaster work. Examples of the *darj w ktaf* and palmette motifs can be

Most small rugs were and to an extent are still produced as prayer mats and incorporate a triangular top portion to act as the indicator of the direction to Mecca copied from the *mihrab* in the wall of the mosque.

The most prolific producers of fine carpets and rugs are Egypt, Tunisia and Morocco, all of which have their own favourite colours and designs. It is best to buy a local speciality. The fact that carpets are slightly misshapen is not a sign of poor quality. Handlooms are all different and little credit is given in the traditional as opposed to tourist orientated weaving areas to mathematical accuracy. Indeed, in Morocco some Berber carpets are made deliberately out of square by women who make a portion of their carpet to reflect each separate month of their pregnancy. The nine-strip carpets bulge interestingly towards the central area !

Machine made carpets, normally to be avoided, can be distinguished by the fringe which will often have been sewn on later, or by the sides which are much neater and flatter than handmade rugs, and by the back which does not show the pattern very clearly and is quite smooth. Fold back the carpet for a close examination of the knots and pattern on the rear of the carpet to check the mathematical precision of weaving which gives away the fact that it is factory made.

Each carpet will have to be bargained for with patience and humour. The following pointers will help during this process. In Morocco carpets ought to carry a government seal indicating the price. In official handicraft shops fixed prices are generally the rule, though this might not make them cheaper than the souq for the avid bargainer. In Tunisia and particularly Morocco tourist guides will lead you to carpet shops which will give him a commission on your purchase. This is already included in the price. There is no need to be rushed in your purchase – the tale that the 'shop is closed tomorrow' is often a ploy used to clinch a sale. If possible take your carpet with you rather than let the shop arrange delivery to your hotel or your home address.

found, but little inscription. Stairs up lead to an impressive view over the valley.

The Tizi-n-Test and the road to Taroudant

The S501 from Marrakech to Taroudant, is one of the most spectacular routes in Morocco, winding its way up and then down through the High Atlas mountains, above the beautiful valleys of this region and past isolated villages, eventually reaching the Tizi-n-Test pass, with its breathtaking views across the Sous valley to the Anti Atlas mountains. There are buses between the two cities, although check that they are *par Tizi-n-Test*. Driving has been feasible since the road, a traditional trading route, was

formerly opened in 1928, following the work of French engineers. Some of its sections are a bit scary, but it is a highly recommended experience, particularly when tied in with visits to Asni, Ouirgane and Tin Mal. Signs on the exit to Marrakech will indicate if the pass is open. The S501 joins the P32 from Taroudant to Ouarzazate.

Oukaimeden

Oukaimeden, at 2,600m, the meeting place of the four winds, is Morocco's major ski resort, open Dec-Mar, with an extremely high ski lift up the 3,273m Jbel Oukaimeden. The skiing is reputedly good, with a range of standards, although the slopes often become wet by the afternoon. There are instructors working in the resort, and a skiing shop is located beside the *Hotel de l'Angour*. It is also possible to climb the Jbel Oukaimeden in a day. Another option is to walk the piste which leaves the road S of Oukaimeden, and cross the hills to the S501 to S of Asni. In summer visitors can walk, climb and parasail while in spring the drive through the blossoming walnut and almond trees is breathtaking.

To get to Oukaimeden, follow the S513 from Marrakech, branching off the Ourika valley just before Arhbalou. For accommodation the choice is between the **D** *Hotel Imlil*, T 459132, a comfortable place with restaurant, bar, and *après-ski* nightclub; E *Hotel de l'Angour* (also called *Auberge Chez Juju Oukaimeden*), T 459005, with a good restaurant, bar, half-pension required, but reasonably priced; and the *Refuge de Club Alpin Français* which often has beds for non-members, a restaurant and bar; *Camping Oukaimeden* is open only to caravans.

The Ourika Valley

The Ourika Valley is a beautiful area of green, terraced fields above the winding Oued Ourika, the most popular excursion for Marrakechis, particularly the young who can court here without police harassment. Buses and grand-taxis to Ourika leave from Bab Rob, Marrakech. It is worth going all the way to Setti Fatma, at the head of the valley. Once in Ourika, a good means of transport is a lift in the open top vans and lorries which speed along the valley. **NB** The valley has a problem with flooding, which campers should bear in mind.

Dar Caid Ourika is the first major settlement, with a Mon *souq* often crowded with tourists. Don't be confused by the field of donkeys which are local transport and not for sale. It also has a *zaouia* and a ruined kasbah. Some buses terminate here. The next big village is **Arhbalou**, which has one of the best hotels of the valley, the **C** *Hotel*

Ourika, T 433993, 27 a/c rm, with good food, a pleasant atmosphere, nightclub and pool; also try the **E** *Auberge Ramuntcho*, T 446312, with a good restaurant, bar and pool. Three other good places to eat in Arbalou are *Hotel Restaurant Bar le Lion de l'Ourika*; *Bar Restaurant Amnougour*; and *Bar Restaurant Kasbah de l'Ourika*, all patronized by coach parties. There is also a shop selling antiques, carpets and ceramics, the *Musée d'Aghbalou*, just beyond the village.

The road ends at **Setti Fatma**, noted for its ancient walnut trees, where there is a small market and a number of basic hotels, incl **F** *Hotel Café Atlas*, good rooms; also **F** *Hotel Azrou* and **F** *Hotel Asgaoua*. However the main part of Setti Fatma is further on, entailing a climb along the right hand side of the river. At the main village, cross over to the grassy area where the youth of Marrakech picnic and relax. There are a number of café-restaurants along the bank, **F** *Hotel Café Bouche de la Source*, provides basic rooms and cheap *tagines*; alongside, and marginally better, is **F** *Auberge des Routards/Restaurant les 7 Cascades*; beyond is the *Restaurant des Cascades*. The 7 cascades are 30 mins scramble up from Setti Fatma, following the path up behind the first café. There is a café perched up where the path ends, beside the first waterfall. Setti Fatma is also another good point to start a walking tour, with guides who will accompany tourists the 10 km to Tachedirt, where there is a *Refuge Club Alpin Français*.

Tizi-n-Tichka, Kasbah Telouet and the road to Ouarzazate

The P31 from Marrakech to Ouarzazate, and its Tizi-n-Tichka pass, is a larger road and safer option than the route over the Tizi-n-Test, but is still an exhilarating experience with similarly stunning views, passing through the range of environments, from the Haouz plains, through the verdant foothills, to the barren peaks and the arid regions around Ouarzazate. The route is often lined with mineral and fossil sellers, and there are a number of café stops en route. Before the pass is the village of Taddert, with the French-run **E** *Le Noyer auberge*.

Just past the pass is a turning on the left leading to the **Kasbah Telouet**. This was the base of the el-Glaoui family, who from the late 19th century, under the brothers Madani and Thami controlled much of S Morocco, a dominance which continued under the French, who used them to establish control over the region. Thami el-Glaoui was a ruthless and powerful *pasha* of Marrakech as late as 1956. The kasbah itself is a vast, labyrinthine, decaying place, built by Thami el-Glaoui. A guardian will appear to unlock the door and show groups round part of the building. There are grand-taxis from the village of Irherm to Telouet. From the pass the road sweeps down to Ouarzazate. The kasbah of Aït Benhaddou can be visited en route, or the next day as an excursion, see page 212.

BENI MELLAL AND ENVIRONS

Beni Mellal

This is one of the major centres of central Morocco, with a population of 95,003 (1982), and an important *souq* on Tues. The town is scruffy but relaxed, and with adequate facilities for a pleasant stay. At the entrance to the town is the **Kasbah Bel Kush**, built in the 17th century by Moulay Ismail, but heavily restored in the 19th century. The main thing to do in Beni Mellal is to walk up from the town to the small and quiet gardens, which lie below the ruined **Kasbah de Ras el Aïn**, perched precariously on the cliffside. There is a nice café in the gardens.

● **Accommodation B** *Bassatine*, Route de Ben Salah, T 482227, 61 a/c rm, pool, restaurant. Both **C** *Hotel Ouzoud*, Route de Mar-

rakech, T 483752/3, with restaurant, bar, tennis and pool; and **C** *Chems*, Route de Marrakech, BP 68, T 483460, Tx 24891, 77 rm, with restaurant, bar, nightclub, tennis and pool, are a bit far out from the centre.

The more central options incl **E** *Hotel Gharnata*, Ave Mohammed V, T 483482, 14 comfortable rm, restaurant with European food, and a bar; **E** *Hotel de Paris*, Nouvelle Medina, T 482245, with a restaurant and bar; **E** *Auberge du Vieux Moulin*, Ave Mohammed V, T 482788, 9 rm, good restaurant and a bar. Much cheaper options are the **F** *Hotel des Voyageurs*, Ave Mohammed V, basic but satisfactory; the **F** *Hotel El Amria*, Ave des Forces Armées Royales, T 483531, simple; and the **F** *Hotel de l'Aïn-Asserdoun*, Ave des Forces Armées Royales, T 483493, a modern place with restaurant.

● **Places to eat** There are several cheap restaurants in the town centre, but one of the best places to eat is *Auberge du Vieux Moulin*, Ave Mohammed V; another on the same street is in *Hotel Gharnata*. A good place to drink a tea or coffee, or eat a delicious pastry, is the *Salon de Thé Azouhour*, 241 Ave Mohammed V; similarly good is *Salon de Thé El Afrah*, Place Afrique; there are several other good *laiteries* and *cafés* along the main street.

● **Tourist offices** A tourist office is located on the 1st flr of Immeuble Chichaoui, Ave Hassan II, T 483981.

● **Transport Road** CTM buses leave from the terminal on the Route de Marrakech. There are regular connections with Marrakech and 3 a day for Fes. From the bus station it is a 10 mins walk up Ave des Forces Armées Royales to the town centre.

Excursion to Bin El Ouidane, Azilal and the Cascades d'Ouzoud

This region around Azilal, to the S of Beni Mellal, is predominantly Berber, a forested, mountainous area popular with walkers. The villages clustering around its slopes have adobe houses with added stone and woodwork. Skiing is popular from Feb to Apr, and there is good hiking in the Mgoun mountains. The Taghia ravine is a popular climbing site. There are a number of high altitude refuges.

The **Bin El Ouidane dam** and lake, 38 km S of the P24, is good for fishing, swimming, sailing and wind-surfing. Stay at the **E** *Auberge du Lac*, a clean and reasonable place with a restaurant serving Moroccan and European food, and which hires out boats for use on the lake.

28 km further on is **Azilal**, a small town with a Thur *souq*. Accommodation is available at the **E** *Hotel Tanout*, T 488281, 12 rm, restaurant. Azilal has a tourist office on Ave Hassan II, T 488334, and is connected by buses with Beni Mellal and Marrakech. The **Cascades d'Ouzoud** are 41 km from Azilal, along a turning off the S508. For those without a car hire a grand-taxi from Azilal. The Cascades d'Ouzoud is a picturesque Middle Atlas site which has become very popular, particularly with young Moroccans camping in the summer. Camping is possible at various small sites, whilst there are also rooms at *Hotel Dar es Salam*, which has a reasonable restaurant.

Kasbah Tadla

Kasbah Tadla was built in 1687 by the Alaouite Sultan Moulay Ismail. The town is a military garrison with a relaxed air but little to see. There is the kasbah, now crumbling and squatted by families of soldiers, as well as an old bridge with 10 arches over the Oum er Rbia, also built by Moulay Ismail. The **Jamia Mosque** on the main market square is from the same period. Nearby is a covered market and a small medina. The *souq* is on Mon.

● **Accommodation** The town has one reasonable hotel, the **D** *Hotel Bellevue*, just outside the town off the P24 from Fes to Beni Mellal, T 418731/2/3. There are three basic hotels in the centre: **F** *Hotel des Allies*, Ave Mohammed V, T 418171, is perhaps the best; the others are **F** *Hotel El Atlas*, rue el Majati Obad, T 418046; and **F** *Hotel Oum Rbia*, 26 Blvd Mohammed Zerktouni, with no shower. There are a few basic restaurants in the town centre.

● **Transport Road** CTM buses leave at 1035 for Fes, 1145 for Marrakech, 1335 for Casablanca and 1705 for Beni Mellal, and private line buses from *Agence SLAC* for Beni Mellal at 1300, Boujad and Oued Zem at 1700, and Rabat at 0430, 0730 and 1300. These can all be caught from the agencies on the main street, Blvd Mohammed Zerktouni.

Detour to Boujad, Oued Zem and Khouribga

Boujad has a beautiful and historic medina, with cobbled streets and white houses, and had importance as a pilgrimage centre up to the 19th century, dating from the 16th century establishment of a *zaouia*, although much of the town was destroyed in 1785. The medina is dotted with shrines and mosques, most notably the **Shrine of Sidi Othman** and the **Mosque of Sidi Mohammed Bu'abid ech Cherki**, the town's founder. There is one hotel on the main square, Place du Marché, the **F** *Café-Hotel Essalyn*, and several cheap restaurants nearby. This is also from where regular buses and grand-taxis leave to Kasbah Tadla and Oued Zem.

Oued Zem (*Pop* 58,744 (1982)) is an uninteresting phosphates town with useful railway connections and a busy market in the centre. The **F** *Hotel El Salam*, is very cheap and central; the other option is the **F** *Hotel des Cooperatives*, on rue Rachid II. There are cheap restaurants in the centre. Trains to Casablanca leave at 0720, 0840 and 1500 and take between 2 hrs 15 mins and 3 hrs.

Khouribga is an important and prosperous city with a population of 127,181 (1982), owed much to its central role in the phosphates industry, but is singularly lacking in any charm or appeal. There is one luxury hotel, the **A** *Hotel Safir*, T 492013, 493013, with restaurant, bar, tennis and pool; the best cheap hotel is the excellent value, clean and comfortable **F** *Hotel de Paris*, 18 Ave Mohammed V, T 492716; the only other is **F** *Hotel* *des Hotes*, 1 rue Moulay Ismail, T 493030, a basic and unfriendly place. Around the market, just off the main street, are a number of basic restaurants. Trains to Casablanca, with connections to Marrakech, El Jadida, Safi, Rabat, Fes and Tanger, leave at 0757, 0923, 1540 and to Oued Zem at 1228, 1931 and 2239.

THE MIDDLE ATLAS

Khenifra and environs

El Ksiba Continuing on from Kasbah Tadla, the P24 passes El Ksiba, just off to the S of the road. This is a pleasant place to stay. **E** *Hotel Henri IV*, excellent food, good rooms; or at *Camping Tagh-balout*.

Khenifra is a relaxed Middle Atlas resort with a population of 38,840 (1982). It has a large Wed and Sun *souq*, and a reputation amongst Moroccans as a centre of prostitution. The town was the site of a large defeat for the French in 1914, at the hands of a local *caid*. The top place to stay is **C** *Hotel Hamou Azzayani Salam*, in new town, T 586020, Tx 41932, 60 a/c rm, restaurant, bar, nightclub, tennis and pool; a much cheaper option is the basic but clean **F** *Hotel-Restaurant de France*, Quartier Forces Armées Royales, T 586114; or the **F** *Hotel Voyageurs*, nearby. There is a tourist office at Immeuble Lefraoui, Hay Hamou-Hassan.

A popular excursion from Khenifra is to the tree-lined lake of **Aguelmane Azigza**, 24 km along the 3485. The road continues to the source of the Oued Oum er Rbia and Aïn Leuh, and then back onto the P24 just SW of Azrou. 96 km N of Khenifra, just off the 2516 to Rabat, is **Oulmes-Tarmilate**, a spa from where *Oulmes* sparkling mineral water originates. There is a hotel here, the **D** *Hotel les Thermes*, T 552355, 42 rm, restaurant, bar, and there are waterfalls just below at Lalla Haya. Back on the P24, in between Khenifra and Azrou, is **Mrirt**, with a large and fascinating Thur *souq*.

Azrou

Azrou is a small Berber market town and hill resort named after the rock around which it is built. The town has a relaxed air and good hiking in the wooded vicinity. The ruined kasbah was built by Moulay Ismail. The French built the **Collège Berbère**, which trained many of the civil and military staff of the Protectorate, as part of a divide and rule policy.

All buses, except those of CTM, arrive at a rough patch of land surrounded by food and fruit stalls, in front of the town's distinctive rock. The heart of the town, Place Mohammed V, is to the right on leaving the bus stop. There is a covered market near Place Mohammed V, whilst the *Ensemble Artisanal* (open 0830-1200 and 1430-1800), is situated

---

BOTTLED UP

Travellers can be easily identified by how quickly they take to the bottle.....of water. There are three main brands. *Oulmès*, SW of Meknes gives its name to a spring of naturally gaseous water, with health-promoting trace elements including calcium, magnesium, sodium and iron. *Oulmès* sold in small glass bottles has been on the market for over half a century. From the same area comes the non-gaseous *Sidi Ali*, commonly used as table water and recommended for salt-free diets. It is sold in the ubiquitous semi-transparent blue plastic bottles. This is more recent, first marketed in 1977, and now selling more than 500,000 hectolitres annually. The third source, known since Roman times, is the spring at *Sidi Harazem* just 10 km from Fes. This is also non-gaseous but contains sodium which can be noted in the taste. This too is sold as table water though in less quantities than *Sidi Ali*.

off Ave Mohammed V, with a fixed price shop and a number of craftsmen working on the premises, look out for the Middle Atlas carpets. There is a large Berber *souq* held just above the town on Tues, with vegetables, textiles and some interesting Middle Atlas carpets, as well as traditional entertainment from musicians and others. The town also has a small pool for summer use.

● **Accommodation** A pleasant hotel with a good view is the **D** *Hotel Panorama*, T 562010, 39 rm, rec restaurant and bar, good view. **E** *Hotel Azrou*, Route de Khenifra, T 562116, reasonable, 9 rm, restaurant and noisy bar. Best value for money is **F** *Hotel des Cèdres*, Place Mohammed V, T 562326, a clean establishment with hot water, communal showers and a good restaurant; also try **F** *Hotel Salam*, on a square off Place Mohammed V opp the *Hotel des Cèdres*; alongside the less rec **F** *Hotel Ziz* and **F** *Hotel Beau Séjour*. **Youth hostel** T 563733, Route de Midelt, Azrou, BP147, to get to it follow the signs from Place Mohammed V, and turn left off the road to Midelt, clean and friendly, 40 beds, kitchen, overnight fee MD20.

● **Places to eat** The best meals are in the restaurant of *Hotel Panorama*; at the *Café Restaurant Relais Forestier*; or the restaurant of *Hotel des Cèdres*, both on Place Mohammed V, or at the cheaper places along the road to Marrakech and around the bus stop.

● **Banks & money changers** The Banque Populaire is on Place Mohammed V.

● **Transport Road** CTM buses depart from near Place Mohammed V, at 0730 for Casablanca, 0800 for Midelt, and at 0730 and 0800 for Meknes. There are other CTM or private line services from Azrou to Rissani, Er Rachidia, Marrakech, Khenifra and Fes, and numerous grand-taxis to Khenifra, Ifrane, Immouzer du Kandar, Meknes and Fes.

Aïn Leuh, the waterfalls and Aguelmane Azigza

At 19 km S of Azrou, a turning off the P24 leads to **Aïn Leuh**, a Berber village with a Wed *souq* important to the seminomadic Beni M'Guid tribe, a ruined kasbah from the reign of Moulay Ismail,

and nearby **waterfalls**. 20 km S of this is the source of the Oued Oum er Rbia, with a footpath leading from the road to the numerous and impressive waterfalls, falling from a cliff into a dangerous pool. Further on again is **Aguelmane Azigza**, a crater lake ideal for swimming. The tree-lined spot has its devoted followers amongst Moroccan campers and is an ideal location. There is also accommodation in a café. The road continues to rejoin the P24 at Khenifra.

Detour to Midelt and on to Er Rachidia

Midelt lies in the Atlas mountains, a convenient stopping point en route from Fes, Meknes or Azrou to Er Rachidia and the Sahara, a town with little to recommend except a calm, friendly atmosphere and a large *souq* on Sun. In the town, the minerals and fossils of the region are energetically sold by the young and in shops. Also look out for the town's *excellent carpets*, which have the distinctive vegetable-dyed geometric patterns of the region. These can be found in the permanent market opposite the bus station. They can also be bought at a weaving school, the **Atelier de Tissage**, run by Franciscan sisters in a convent off the road to Tattiouine.

● **Accommodation D** *Hotel Ayachi*, rue d'Agadir, T 582161, 28 rm, quiet, restaurant, nightclub and garden; there are several more basic hotels, the best perhaps are *Hotel Minlal*, on the N entrance to the town, good restaurant; *Hotel Toulouse* in the centre; and *Hotel Roi de la Bière*, nr the S exit. The *Camping Municipal* is on the road to Er Rachidia.

● **Places to eat** *Restaurant de Fes*, 2 Ave Mohammed V, which has very good *couscous*; *Excelsior*, also in the town centre; *Brasserie Chez Aziz*, by the Er Rachidia exit.

A possible excursion is to **Er Rachidia** on the rough pistes of the Cirque Jaffar, to the W of Midelt, signposted from the town, and only possible for part of the year. The P21 continues to Er Rachidia and into the Sahara, past the military fort at Aït Messaoud and the uninteresting village of Rich, before entering the spectacular **Ziz Gorge** and then Er Rachidia.

Ifrane, Mischliffen and an excursion to the Lakes

Ifrane is a mountain resort developed by the French, which now has numerous large villas and chalets, as well as a royal palace and hunting lodge. When this is occupied by the king, the town becomes busy with staff and politicians. From the town there are good walks in the *cedar forests*, and a drivable excursion round the *dayats* (crater lakes). There is *skiing* at the nearby resort of Mischliffen.

● **Accommodation** The most luxurious hotel is the **A** *Hotel Michlifen*, BP 18, T 56607, F 566623, 107 rm, restaurant, bar, nightclub and pool, 2 conference rooms; **D** *Grand Hotel*, Ave de la Marche Verte, T 566407, 33 rm, dated style, comfortable and calm; **D** *Hotel Perce Neige*, rue des Asphodelles, T 566404, 566210, a friendly place, restaurant and bar. The budget alternative is **F** *Hotel Tilleuls*.

● **Camping** *Camping International* is very busy in the summer but open all the year round, signposted from the town centre.

● **Places to eat** Good places to eat are *Café-Restaurant de la Rose*, 7 rue des Erables, T 566215; and *Au Rendez-Vous des Skieurs*, on the main street.

● **Services** There is a Syndicat d'Initiative information centre and a municipal swimming pool in the town, and regular buses from Ifrane to both Azrou and Fes.

Skiing at Mischliffen near Ifrane is from Jan to Mar with good but short slopes, sometimes with patchy snow cover. Hire equipment from the *Chamonix* restaurant in Ifrane and take a taxi to the resort. This is a small area with cafés and ski lifts but little else.

Aaoua, Afourgan and Ifrah Dayats N of Ifrane, leave the P24 to the E for a tour of the *dayats*, lakes formed by solu-

tion of the limestone. There are three lying between the P24 and the P20: Aaoua, Afourgan and Ifrah. Dayat Aaoua could be a scenic place to picnic but at present the lake is less than 25% capacity and there are no boats and few birds. **D** *Hotel Chalet du Lac*, Route de Fes, T Ifrane 0, an atmospheric hotel with French restaurant and bar, adjacent to lake, don't rely on it being open. Due to the lack of rain the other *dayats* are also disappointing.

Immouzer de Kandar

This is a small mountain resort, beautiful in spring with the apple blossom, a lively place during the **Fête des Pommes** in Jul, and with *souq*, Mon, in its ruined kasbah. It is a popular excursion from Fes, from where there are regular buses and grand-taxis. *Aïn Erreggada* is clearly signed to the W of the road, the approach from the centre of town near the taxis being the easier. Unfortunately due to the drought the opportunity to swim in the municipal pool, filled with spa water, is not available and the area currently looks very forlorn.

Just N of Immouzer de Kandar are the popular picnic/camping springs, *Aïn Seban* and *Aïn Chifa* clearly signed to the W of the road. In drought conditions they are less attractive.

● **Accommodation D** *Hotel Royal*, Ave Mohammed V, T/F 663080, 663186, 40 rm, TV lounge, restaurant and bar; the better value **D** *Hotel des Truites*, Ave Mohammed V, T 663002, a small and friendly place with a popular restaurant and bar; **E** *Hotel Chahrazed*, basic, central. **Camping** At *Camping d'Immouzer*, S of town, only in summer.

● **Places to eat** ◆◆*La Chaumière*, nr the southern exit of the town, with moderately-priced European food; the adjacent *Auberge de Chamotte*. ◆*Hotel des Truites*, popular, pleasant atmosphere.

198

SOUTHERN MOROCCO

CONTENTS

Agadir and Environs 198
Taroudant and Environs 205
Ouarzazate and the Draa Valley 209
The Gorges 215
Er Rachidia and the Ziz Valley 217
The Eastern Sahara 219
The Deep South 220

MAPS

Southern Morocco 199
Agadir 201
Taroudant 206
Ouarzazate 211

The S of Morocco is quite different from the centre and N, with the arid areas of the Sahara a great attraction to travellers. Morocco has its dunes, near Zagora and Erfoud, but the most beautiful features of the desert are the oases and fertile valleys, with the distinctive earth-built *ksour* and kasbahs, areas of housing clustered together behind impressive but crumbling fortifications. The Draa, Dades and Ziz valleys are memorable areas in which to explore the date palmeries and small villages, whilst the Dades and Todra gorges are striking natural formations, where the rivers descend from the High Atlas. The Sous valley has the historic town of Taroudant at its centre: at its mouth lies the modern city of Agadir, the most popular tourist destination in Morocco noted for its beach and fine weather conditions. To the S of Agadir there are more remote towns, where travelling becomes harder. The Western Sahara has been incorporated within Morocco, but resistance from the Independence movement Polisario continues around its borders with Algeria and Mauritania. At the moment it is still relatively undeveloped for tourists.

AGADIR AND ENVIRONS

Agadir

(*Pop* 110,479 (1982); *Alt* 20m) The city of Agadir, lying on the Atlantic coast at the mouth of the Sous valley, takes the largest number of tourists in Morocco, and has perhaps the best facilities for them, with a vast number of hotels. Agadir has a vast expanse of sand stretching around the bay, and excellent weather conditions which enable tourists to swim and sunbathe for almost all of the year. Many of these tourists are on package holidays, based in whole or part in one of the larger hotels. Agadir is also an excellent entry point to Morocco, with regular flights arriving at its new airport, and can serve as a good base for exploring nearby regions, the Sous valley, the Sahara, the Atlantic coast, the Anti Atlas and High Atlas mountain ranges. Whilst the city has the relaxed air of beach resort, it has perhaps little which is distinctively 'Moroccan', as the old settlement was almost totally destroyed in the earthquake of 1960, and has been rebuilt and developed around

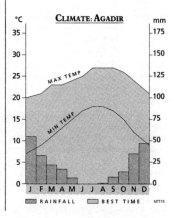

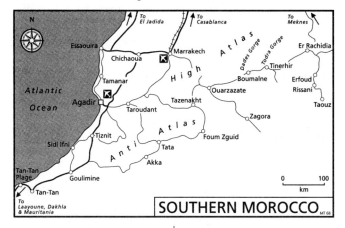

SOUTHERN MOROCCO MT 68

its tourist potential, in the image of a European resort. There are not many places to visit in the city, nor is it a good place to shop, but the onward connections are good, particularly by bus from Agadir or nearby Inezgane.

History

Agadir under the Portuguese and Saadians The name Agadir, a shortened form in this case of Agadir n Irir, refers to the Berber word meaning 'a fortified granary'. Agadir was occupied by the Portuguese who built a fort on the site in 1503 which was known as Santa Cruz de Aguer. The Berber tribes of the Sous valley carried out a *jihad*, or holy war, against the colony, and the Saadian Emir of the Sous, Mohammed Echeikh El Mehdi, captured it in 1541, pre-empting the Portuguese departure from most of their Atlantic strongholds. His son, Moulay Abdellah El Ahalib, built the kasbah on the hill overlooking the city, the ruins of which still stand. With the development by the Saadians of the agricultural potential of the Sous valley, Agadir became an important trading centre in the 17th and 18th centuries, exporting sugar cane, olive oil, gold and spices, both from the immediate hinterland of the Sous valley, and further afield

from the Sahara. However Agadir declined during the reign of Sidi Mohammed Ibn Abdellah, who preferred to develop Essaouira, to the N, and closed down Agadir's port.

Agadir in the 20th century In 1911 an incident occurred offshore, when a German gunboat appeared 'to protect German interests', in spite of the 1906 Algeciras treaty. This crisis was settled by negotiations between the French and Germans, recognizing France's rights in Morocco, in exchange for territorial concessions in the Congo. The French occupied Agadir in 1913. They constructed the port in 1914, and enlarged it in 1930 and 1953. The town was destroyed by the earthquake of February 29 1960. The town was totally rebuilt to the S, planned on a Western influenced layout as a major tourist resort, with distinct functional zones separated by green swathes, with the large hotels kept well apart from the local population. Much of the architecture of the city has the characteristic functional blocks of the period, with little influence of Moroccan design, except in the token embellishment of more recent constructions. The port which escaped total destruction was developed as the base for a large fishing fleet and as the centre of an industrial zone. The city has grown rapidly in size, population and prosperity.

ACCESS Air Agadir Al Massira Aéroport, T 839002, is 28 km from the city. Take a grand-taxi or a bus which will drop you off at Place Salam where a petit-taxi can be hired.

Road From Rabat, Casablanca, El Jadida and Essaouira entrance to Agadir is via the P8, leading into Ave Mohammed V; from Marrakech and the P40 turn left along Blvd Mohammed Cheikh Saadi into the town centre; from the airport and Inezgane, and beyond along the P32 to Taroudant or the P30 to Tiznit and the S, one enters along either Ave Hassan II or Ave Mohammed V. **Bus** There are ONCF buses from Marrakech, connecting with the trains from Rabat and Casablanca, which arrive on rue Ya'qub al-Mansur just off Place Lahcen Tamri, as do CTM and private line services. Some buses, however, go to Inezgane, connected to Agadir by Bus No 5, Bus No 6 or a grand-taxi.

Places of interest

The **beach** is Agadir's main asset, an excellent strip of sand and enjoyable swimming. It is clean and relatively free of hassle, and well provided with cafés. From the city centre walk down Ave du Prince Heritier Sidi Mohammed, turn right along Ave Mohammed V, and then left down to Blvd du 20 Août, which runs parallel to the beach.

The Port To get to the port take a petit-taxi for MD6, or Bus No 1 or walk along from the beach. The main reason for visiting, beyond any curiosity in Moroccan industry, is to sample the wares on offer at the small and excellent fish restaurants to the right of the port's entrance.

The Kasbah was built in 1540 to launch an attack on the Portuguese city, and was retained after the victory as a fortification against local insurrection. Whilst ruined by the 1960 earthquake, the ramparts and entrance way have been maintained in a reasonable condition, as Agadir's one historic site. The kasbah, which has a

good view over Agadir, used to be a densely populated area, but was not re-settled after 1960. It is reached by a winding road to the N of the centre, off Ave Mohammed V.

Architecturally the city is far from memorable, except for the marginal appeal of the modern **Grand Mosque**, on Ave des Forces Armées Royales, and the particularly ugly post office and shopping centre on either side of Ave du Prince Heritier Sidi Mohammed. Off Ave du Prince Moulay Abdellah is the dull **Jardin Ibn Zaidoun**. **The Folk Museum** (open 0930-1300 and 1430-1800), opposite the *Hotel Salam*, has a small but interesting display of local handicrafts from S Morocco, as well as occasional visiting displays. **La Vallée des Oiseaux**, lying between Ave Mohammed V and Blvd du 20 Août is a pleasant place to wander and listen to bird song.

Local information
● Accommodation

AL *Hotel Atlas-Amadil*, Route de l'Oued Sous, T 840620, F 823663, 322 rm, beside the beach but further from the town centre, a reliable place, 3 restaurants, a wine bar, 2 bars, a coffee shop, nightclub, hairdresser, laundry, library, pool, tennis; **AL** *Europa Hotel Safir*, Blvd du 20 Août, T 821212, F 823435, 221 rm, Moroccan-influenced design and decor, 3 restaurants, 2 bars, business centre, art gallery, tennis, pool; **AL** *Sheraton Hotel*, Ave Mohammed V, T 843232, F 844379.

A *Club PLM Dunes d'Or*, on beach, T 840150, Tx 81827, 450 rm, price incl all activities, famous tennis courts which host professional events, sauna, *hammam*, gym, horse riding, volleyball and basketball, 2 pools, 5 restaurants, 6 bars and a nightclub, constant activity, not the place for a rest; **A** *Hotel Sahara Agadir*, Ave Mohammed V, T 840660, F 840738, popular and luxuriously equipped with 300 pleasant rm, 4 restaurants, 2 bars, nightclub, hairdresser, sauna, *hammam*, tennis, horse riding and volleyball, children's and adult's pools; **A** *Hotel Tamlelt-Agador*, Quartier des Dunes d'Or, T 841525, 659 rm, this complex links 2 hotels, the *Tamlelt* inspired by Moroccan medinas, the *Agador* by the kasbahs, luxurious establishment, large gar-

```
AGADIR MT 69
To Marrakech
rue Mokhtar Soussi
To Hospital
N
To Kasbah & Port
Ave du General Kettani
Ave des forces Armées Royales
Blvd Mohammed Cheikh Saadi
Ave du Prince Moulay Abdellah
Avenue Hassan II
rue de 29 Fevrier
rue du President Kennedy
rue du 18 Novembre
Ave Mohammed V
Atlantic Ocean
Stadium
Route de Oued Souss
Avenue Mohammed V
To Hotel Atlas-Amadil
Blvd de 20 Août
```

1. Folk Museum
2. Royal Palace
3. Grand Mosque
4. Synagogue
5. National Tourist Office
6. PTT
7. Royal Air Maroc
8. Tour de Paris Rest.
9. Daffy Restaurant
10. Jardin Ibn Zaidoun

Hotels:
11. Beach Club
12. Dunes d'Or
13. Europa Safir
14. Sahara
15. Atlas
16. Agador
17. Tamlelt
18. Petite Suede
19. Moderne
20. El Bahia & Paris
21. Excelsior, Amenou, Tifout & Sindibad
22. Oumnia
23. Mabrouk
24. Royal
25. Miramar
26. Les Palmiers
27. Ayour
28. Select & La Baie
29. Camping

dens, numerous fountains, 4 restaurants, a nightclub, hairdresser, several bars, 4 pools, not suitable for disabled.

B *Agadir Beach Club*, T 840791, F 825763, 374 rm, luxurious rooms, nightclub, 2 bars, nightclub, laundry, hairdresser, tennis, magnificent pool; **B** *Hotel Oasis*, just off Ave Mohammed V, T 843313-6, F 842260, excellent view, 132 rm, 2 restaurants, 2 bars, pool, sauna, *hammam*, nightclub, tennis and golf.

C *Hotel Atlas*, Ave Mohammed V, T 843232, F 844379, 156 rm, and bungalows amidst the gardens, a rec and reasonably priced option, 2 restaurants, tennis, pool, nightclub; **C** *Hotel Oumnia*, Quartier des Dunes, T 823351, close to the beach, well-equipped and friendly.

D *Hotel Ayour*, 4 rue de l'Entraide, T 824976, modern, comfortable, pool; **D** *Hotel Mabrouk*, Blvd du 20 Août, T 840606, 40 rm, nearer town centre, reasonable place, pool and bar; **D** *Hotel Miramar*, Ave Mohammed V, T 840770, a pleasant, quiet place nr the port,

reasonable restaurant; **D** *Hotel Royal*, Ave Mohammed V, T 840675, 73 rm/bungalows amidst pleasant gardens, with bar, restaurant and pool; **D** *Hotel Sindibad*, Place Lahcen Tamri, T 823477, small and popular place on a busy square with bar and adjoining restaurant.

E *Hotel De La Baie*, rue Allal Ben Abdellah, T 823014, reasonable and convenient; **E** *Hotel El Bahia*, rue El Mehdi Ibn Toumert, T 822724, 823954, breakfast available, the traveller hang-out, very friendly, recently renovated with spotless, well-equipped rooms; **E** *Hotel Excelsior*, rue Ya'qub El Mansur, T 821028, nr the bus station but otherwise not brilliant and rather noisy; **E** *Hotel Moderne*, rue El Mehdi Ibn Toumert, T 823373, quite good and quiet; **E** *Hotel Paris*, Ave Kennedy, T 822694, clean, quiet, recently redecorated, the best value place around; **E** *Hotel Petite Suede*, Ave Hassan II, T 840779, 840057, a friendly place with reasonably priced and comfortable rooms.

F *Hotel Select*, behind *Restaurant Salam*, rue

Allal Ben Abdellah, shower outside, reasonable and convenient; **F** *Hotel Tour Eiffel*, rue Allal Ben Abdellah, small and simple; *Hotel Amenou*, 1 rue Ya'qub al Manour, T 823026, clean and welcoming; *Hotel Tifawt*, rue Ya'qub al-Mansur, T 824375, quite basic.

● **Camping**
Camping Caravaning International d'Agadir, Blvd Mohammed V, T 840374, a well-equipped and reasonably priced place nr the centre, with showers, shops.

● **Places to eat**
♦♦♦*La Tour de Paris*, Ave Hassan II, T 840906, closed Sat, reservations advised, an elegant restaurant in the town centre with *nouvelle cuisine* and traditional French dishes; the *Golden Gate*, Blvd du 20 Août, T 840820, 2 restaurants with excellent fish dishes, a bar.

♦♦*Restaurant Daffy*, rue des Oranges, set menus, incl good value *mechoui*, *pastilla* and *tangia* specialities; *Restaurant Copenhagen*, Prince Moulay Abdellah, Danish food in Agadir may be bizarre but this is the place for it; *Restaurant Marine Heim*, Ave Mohammed V, T 840731, excellent German food and drink centred around fish, friendly and efficient; *Via Veneto*, Ave Hassan II, T 841467, high quality European food and a very popular place, reservations advised; *Restaurant la Tonkinoise*, Ave du Prince Heritier Sidi Mohammed, reasonable Chinese food; the *Miramar*, Italian food; *Le Jardin d'Eau*, Blvd du 20 Août, T 840195, very good French food and Moroccan dishes, particularly the lamb *mechoui*, reasonable prices; *Darkhoum Restaurant Marocain*, Ave du General Kettani, T 840622, reservations advised, below the *Hotel Sud Bahia*, Moroccan decor, food and music; *Restaurant du Port*, T 843708, a seafood restaurant by the port with mixed reports; *Pizzeria Annamunda*, Ave du Prince Heritier Sidi Mohammed, music and Italian food.

♦The *Resto Poissons* restaurants by the port have cheap and excellent fresh fish, open 1230-2030, standards and reasonable prices maintained through hectic competition. Take a petit-taxi there for MD5, or Bus No 1; in another good area try *Restaurant Sindibad*; *Restaurant Mille et Une Nuits*, which has good Moroccan main courses and salads; *Restaurant Chabib*, rec for a cheap *tagine*; or *Restaurant Coq d'Or*, all on Place Lahcen Tamri; nearby there are 2 good fish restaurants on rue du 29 Février; and the satisfactory

Café-Restaurant Select, in *Hotel Select* on rue Allal Ben Abdellah; *Chez Redy*, Ave du Prince Heritier Sidi Mohammed, has standard fare, lots of alcohol and a lively atmosphere.

● **Cafés**
Oufella's, rue Allal Ben Abdellah adjacent to *Hotel Select*, is a *pâtisserie* with a good selection of cakes, sweets and drinks.

● **Bars**
Try *Corniche Restaurant Bar*, by the beach, with bands each night.

● **Banks & money changers**
ABM, Ave Prince Heritier Sidi Mohammed, T 841567; **Banque du Maroc**, Ave du General Kettani, T 840172; **BCM**, rue des Administrations Publiques, T 840808; **BMAO**, Ave Hassan II, T 820425; **SGMB**, Ave du General Kettani, T 840281; **SMDC**, Ave Al Mouquaouma, T 821676; **Wafabank**, 43 Ave du General Kettani, T 840496.

American Express: Voyages Schwartz, Ave Hassan II, T 822894.

● **Consulates**
France, Blvd Mohammed Saadi, T 840826; **Spain**, rue Ibn Batouta, T 822126; **UK**, rue des Administrations Publiques, T 827741.

● **Entertainment**
Discos & nightclubs: are plentiful in the large hotels but they are of variable quality, try the *Tan Tan*, at the *Hotel Almohades*, Blvd 20 Août, T 840233, 840096; the *Byblos*, at the *Club PLM Dunes d'Or*, on the beach front, T 820150 (open 2130-0500), admission MD60, popular and the drinks are reasonable; *Black Jack Disco*, at the *Hotel Agador*, T 841525 (open 2130-0500), admission MD60.

Excursions: *Sahara Tours*, Ave General Kettani, T 840634, 840421, organize a range of excursions outside Agadir starting at MD130, incl visits to Taroudant, Marrakech, Tafraoute and Essaouira, usually incl at least one meal. Other agents in the same building also organize trips to Immouzer des Ida Outanane, Tata and Akka, and imine.

Folklore: *Sahara Tours*, Ave du General Kettani, T 840421, 840634, organize evening meal and folklore excursions out of Agadir, better than the tame displays at the Agadir hotels.

● **Hospitals & medical services**
Ambulance: T 15.

Chemists: *Pharmacie*, Municipalité d'Agadir, T 823349, open all night.

● **Hospital**
Hôpital Hassan II, Route de Marrakech, T 841477.

● **Post & telecommunications**
Area code: 08.
Post Office: the PTT is located on the corner of Ave Prince Heritier Sidi Mohammed and Ave du Prince Moulay Abdellah.

● **Places of worship**
Catholic: *Eglise Saint Anne*, rue de Marrakech, T 822251.
Jewish: *Synagogue Beth-El*, rue Afghanistan.
Protestant: *Temple*, 2 rue Chouhada.

● **Shopping**
Handicrafts: Agadir has no shortage of handicrafts for sale, notably from the traders displaying their wares along the paths and roads leading from the big hotels to the beach. The quality of these goods is, however, questionable, and the prices often exorbitant. Similarly, the fixed price shops, around the shopping centre located between Ave du Prince Moulay Abdellah and Ave Hassan II, and along Ave Sidi Mohammed, are expensive, although their prices are often in fact negotiable. The best display and most reliable, although inflexible, prices, are to be found as with most Moroccan cities, at the *Centre Artisanal Cooperative* in rue du 29 Février.

　　General: for more general shopping try the Moroccan quarter rather than the expensive tourist quarter. Perhaps the best stock is held by the supermarket *Uniprix*, Ave Hassan II, (open 0830-1230 and 1430-1930), which also does handicrafts. There is a number of good beer and wine shops on Ave Mohammed V, right from Ave du General Kettani. European newspapers can be bought from stalls outside the major hotels and on Ave Hassan II. There is a bookshop, the *Crown English Bookshop*, in the shopping centre off Ave du Prince Moulay Abdellah.

　　Souq the best days for Agadir's *souq* are Sat and Sun. It is located on rue Chaïr el Hamra Mohammed ben Brahim, which is left turn off Ave Mohammed V on the S edge of the city. Agadir's souq is not very impressive in comparison with places such as Taroudant.

● **Sports**
Golf: at *Royal Club de Golf*, 12 km from Agadir, between Inezgane and Aït Melloul,

nine holes; *Club Les Dunes*, 27 holes, fees MD550, MD2,500 for 6 days.

Horse riding: at *L'Etrier*, BP 20, Route d'Inezgane, MD150 for 1½ hrs, bring your own hard hat.

Swimming: apart from the sea, a pool by the beach front, turn off Ave Mohammed V by the Syndicat d'Initiative.

Tennis: 120 clay courts at *Royal Tennis Club d'Agadir*, Ave Hassan II, T 23395, 23738, seven courts.

Yachting: *Yacht Motor Club*, Port d'Agadir.

● **Tour companies & travel agents**
Atlas Voyages, rue de l'Hotel de Ville, T 821284; *Comanov Voyages*, 5 bis Ave Mohammed V, T 840669; *Menara Tours*, 341 Ave Hassan II, T 821108; *Wagons-Lits Tourisme*, 26 Ave des Forces Armées Royales, T 823528. **Air France**, 287 Ave Hassan II, T 842546, 825037; **Royal Air Maroc**, Ave du General Kettani, T 840145.

● **Tourist offices**
Office du Tourisme, Immeuble A, Place Prince Heritier Sidi Mohammed, T 822894, 841367 (open Mon-Fri 0800-1500 (Jun-Sep); 0800-1200 and 1430-1830 (Sep-Jun); **Syndicat d'Initiative**, Ave Mohammed V, T 840307.

● **Useful addresses**
Fire: T 15.
Police: rue 18 Novembre, T 19.

● **Transport**
Local Bus: from Blvd Mohammed Cheik Saadi, No 5 and 6 go to Inezgane, Bus No 1 goes to the port. Place Salam is a good place to pick up services. **Bicycle/motorcycle hire**: there are several individuals hiring bicycles, mopeds and motorbikes from Blvd du 20 Août, but they can often be rather expensive. **Car hire**: Afric Car, Ave Mohammed V, T 840750; **Agadir Voitures**, Immeuble Baraka, rue de Paris, T 22426; **Avis**, Ave Hassan II, T 841755, and at the airport, T 840345; **Budget**, Ave Mohammed V, T 840762; **Hertz**, Bungalow Marhaba, Ave Mohammed V, T 839071, and at the airport; **Inter-Rent Europcar**, Ave Mohammed V, T 840367; **Lotus Cars**, Ave Mohammed V, T 840588; **Tiznit Cars**, Ave Hassan II, T 20998; **Tourist Cars**, Ave Mohammed V; **Week-End Cars**, Ave Mohammed V, T 20567.
Taxis: Agadir is quite a wide spread city and therefore its plentiful petit-taxis, painted orange, can be useful, particularly to get to the kasbah or the port.

Air Agadir Al Massira Aéroport is 28 km from the city, on the road to Inezgane, T 839003/6. Take a grand-taxi, or as bus from Place Salam. There are 3 flights a day to Casablanca, 2 a day to Marrakech, 6 a week to Laayoune, 2 a week to Tanger and Las Palmas, 1 a week to Dakhla and Ouarzazate, as well as regularly to European cities. The loudspeakers at the airport are impossible to understand. Watch the departure boards with care.

Road Bus: ONCF buses, T 841207, leave from rue Ya'qub al Mansur, connecting with the trains at **Marrakech**, departures 0440, 0800, 0930, 1930, 2030. CTM and private line services leave from the same place. There are private line services to **Marrakech** (5 a day), **Casablanca** and **Taroudant** (4 a day), **Essaouira** and **Tiznit** (3 a day), **Safi, Tata, Tan-Tan** and **imine** (2 a day), **Akka, Tafraoute, Rabat, Meknes, Fes, Oujda, Taza** and **Tanger**. CTM services also leave from here. Local buses to the airport, **Inezgane** (5 and 6) and **Tarhazoute** (12 and 14) leave from Place Salam. **Taxi**: grand-taxis leave for various destinations, particularly Inezgane and Taroudant, from Place Salam.

Excursion north to Tarhazoute and Immouzer des Ida Outanane

The coast to the N offers the potential for rewarding excursions, and some limited opportunities for staying out of the city. Although this potential is gradually being realized by developers, the area remains idyllic and tranquil, with the **Paradise Beach** and others stretching 30 km to the N of Agadir. To the E the **Paradise Valley** is a beautiful gorge and river basin, dotted with palm trees and waterfalls, leading up into the mountains.

Tarhazoute is the main settlement on this area of the coast, 19 km N of Agadir. The village is being developed with the construction of many homes, but remains a relaxing place to enjoy the superb beach. To get here, catch Bus 12 or 14 from Place Salam in Agadir. It is possible to rent cheap rooms in private houses, normally for a week minimum. The official camp site is to the S, with a café and basic facilities, an official site is

nearby. Near the camp site is the best restaurant, *Taoui-Fik*, other cafés are around the village. 6 km to the S of Tarhazoute is Tamrakht, in a banana grove, and a good place to buy them.

Immouzer des Ida Outanane 12 km N of Agadir, just before Tamrakht, a road turns off to the right. This leads through Paradise Valley for part of the way, through a beautiful gorge with possibilities of camping, although beware of flooding. Stop on the way at *Café-Restaurant Tafrite*, a good restaurant. At the end of this valley, 61 km from Agadir, at an altitude of over 1,000m, is the small market town of Immouzer des Ida Outanane, named after the confederation of Berber tribes in this area. There is a daily bus from Place Lahcen Tamri in Agadir (1400). Camping is possible near the *Café de Miel*, but the best option is the **D** *Auberge des Cascades*, T 16, a wonderful hotel with 18 rm, terrace or balcony, with bath, excellent food in the restaurant, bar, tennis, pool and a garden of fruit and olive trees located above the waterfalls. The village, which has a *souq* on Thur, is known for honey production, with a honey festival in Jul. The celebrated waterfalls lie below the village, and although they have been reduced in volume in recent years, are popular for both sightseeing and bathing. The village is also a good place for bird watching and walking, be it rambles in the immediate surrounds, or more strenuous walks further afield.

Inezgane and Oued Massa

Inezgane (*Pop* 17,592 (1982)) lies 13 km S of Agadir and is almost a suburb of it now. It is primarily a transport hub, with taxis, local buses and coaches to Casablanca, Rabat, Tiznit, Marrakech, Taroudant (1 hr), Ouarzazate and Laayoune, amongst other places, with far more services than Agadir. This is likely to be the main reason for staying overnight, for there is little of interest in the town, and the buses make it extremely noisy. All long-distance buses and grand-taxis stop along the wide, busy main street lined by bus agents, including CTM, small shops and cheap restaurants. At the end of this is the main square, with the local bus stands. Off to the right of the square is a relaxed and mildly interesting covered market, with the main market day on Tues. 42 km S of Agadir the lagoon Oued Massa nature reserve provides a splendid spot for bird watching. The estuary is home to flamingoes, bald ibis, spoonbills and rare herons. A week's visit can be organized for MD1,300.

● **Accommodation** The best hotel lies just outside Inezgane, the **C** *Hotel Club Hacienda*, Route de l'Oued Sous, T 830176, with bar, restaurant, nightclub, tennis, pool and horse riding; also rec is the **D** *Hotel-Restaurant les Pergolas*, T 830841, along the road to Agadir, with 23 rm, a bar and a highly-rec restaurant serving French food; **D** *Hotel Provencal*, nearby, T 831208, 44 rm, bar, restaurant and pool; **D** *Hotel les Pyramides*, Route de l'Oued Sous, T 834705, a quiet place with 20 rm, a pool, restaurant, bar and horse riding; and **D** *Hotel Hagounia*, 9 Ave Mokhtar Sousi, T 830783, with 48 rm, located on the road just before the town centre. Grouped around the main square are nine cheap hotels, preferably choose the **F** *Hotel El Merjane*.

● **Places to eat** There is no shortage of restaurants, but a good inexpensive one is the ◆ *Café-Restaurant Bateau de Marrakech*, on the main square.

● **Transport Road** Between Inezgane and Agadir take Bus 5 or 6, or a grand-taxi.

TAROUDANT AND ENVIRONS

Taroudant

Taroudant (*Pop* 36,000) is nicknamed by the locals 'grandmother of Marrakech', and indeed it has some of the character of the more famous city, although on a smaller scale and with a far more relaxed air. The small medina is enclosed by impressive red earth walls and is focused on two intimate and friendly squares, in between which lie a range of interesting *souqs* selling handicrafts for which Taroudant is famous. Although without any distinctive monuments, the town is well worth a visit, and after Agadir, feels far more 'Moroccan'. Taroudant is also a good base, with Agadir and the coast to the W, the High Atlas and the Tizi-n-Test pass to the N (see page 191), the Saharan oases of Tata and Akka to the S (page 208), and the routes to Ouarzazate and the Draa, Dades and Ziz valleys to the E (see page 209). It is also well provided with good hotels and restaurants, and has a handicrafts and folklore fair in Apr.

Taroudant has always been a major population and marketing centre of the fertile Sous valley and has played a strategic role, although rarely achieving any national prominence. The town was conquered by the Almoravids in 1056, but under the Almohads had greater independence. From 1510 the Saadians gave greater prominence to Taroudant, when their first leader, Mohammed al Quaim, was based here as Emir of the Sous. Even after the Saadians gained control of Morocco, Taroudant remained for a while their capital. Taroudant supported Moulay Ismail's nephew in his rebellion, and when the Sultan overcame the town in 1687 he extracted his revenge by slaughtering the population and destroying much of the town. Decline set in, which continued into the 18th and 19th centuries. In the early years of the French protectorate Taroudant harboured the rebel Sultan El Hiba and was consequently sacked by the colonial forces. The French neglected Taroudant after this, and the town now remains little more than a regional market.

ACCESS Buses from Inezgane, Agadir, Marrakech and Ouarzazate deposit their passengers either at Place Talmoklate or Place Assarag. The town is small enough to walk around, although there are petit-taxis, painted light brown, and horse-drawn *calèches*, around the town.

Places of interest

The Souqs in Taroudant are excellent and this is likely to be an easier place to shop or appreciate handicrafts than the central and northern cities, whilst offering more variety than elsewhere S of Marrakech. The busiest days are Thur and Sun, the *souq* days, bringing in people from the villages, but much of it operates during the week. The *souqs* lead off from Place Assarag, beside the bank, and weave across to Place Talmoklate. Notable specialities of Taroudant amongst its excellent handicrafts are jewellery, some of it antique or mock antique, limestone sculptures, and the excellent carpets of the region. There are numerous small stalls to shop at, as well as bigger tourist shops, of these *Ali Baba*, 95 Joutia, T 852435, is friendly. Off the other side of Place Talmoklate is an area of small stalls, notably selling spices, herbs, medicines and pottery.

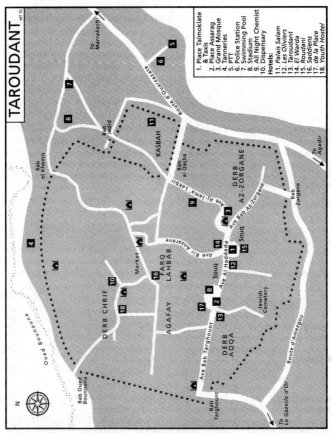

TAROUDANT MT70

1. Place Talmoklate & Taxis
2. Place Assarag
3. Grand Mosque
4. Tanneries
5. PTT
6. Police Station
7. Swimming Pool
8. Stadium
9. All Night Chemist
10. Dispensary

Hotels:
11. Palais Salam
12. Les Oliviers
13. Taroudant
14. El Warda
15. Roudani
16. Saddiens
17. De la Place
18. Youth Hostel

To Marrakech
Route d'Ouarzazate
Bab el Jedid
KASBAH
Bab el Khemis
Bab al Qacba
DERB AZ-ZORGANE
Ave Al-Jama'-Lakbir
Bab Zorgane
To Agadir
Ave Bab Az-Zorgane
Souq
Ave Bir Anzarane
Market
FARQ LAHBAB
Ave Al Haddada
Souq
AGAFAY
Jewish Cemetery
DERB CHRIF
DERB AQQA
Ave Bab Targhount
Route d'Amezgou
Oued Bou Ndouna
Bab Oued Bounouna
Bab Targhount
To La Gazelle d'Or
To Taliouine
N

The Walls and Kasbah The Saadian *pisé* walls interspersed with towers are still intact and are worth following around the town, preferably by *calèche*. They are broken by five gates, at least one of which can be mounted for a view over gardens and olive groves. En route they pass the kasbah, now looking like a more densely-populated and poor area of the town, but in fact it was once a fortress for Moulay Ismail. Outside the walls are the tanneries, left from **Bab el Khemis**, a smelly area understandably located beyond the medina, where skins of a variety of animals are still cured by traditional methods.

Local information
● Accommodation
AL *Hotel la Gazelle d'Or*, Route d'Amezgou, T 852039/48, F 852537, 2 km outside the town, one of the two most luxurious, exclusive and expensive hotels in Morocco, with 30 individual bungalows set amidst beautiful gardens and orange groves, as well as two restaurants, bar, tennis and pool,

C *Hotel Palais Salam*, Route d'Ouarzazate, T 852312, F 852654, 144 rm in a beautiful 18th century palace and bungalows amidst gardens, three restaurants, bar, tennis, pools, car and bicycle hire. We rec this.

D *Hotel Saadiens*, Borj Oumansour/Annasim, T 852589, small and friendly, in the medina with 57 rm, restaurant, bar, tea room, pool, parking.

E *Hotel Taroudant*, Place Assarag, T 852416, old, French run, friendly atmosphere, 37 good rm around a verdant courtyard, with roof-terrace, excellent bar, and a very good restaurant selling reasonably priced and large meals.

F *Hotel de la Place*, Place Talmoklate, cheap, cold water only; **F** *Hotel El Warda*, Place Talmoklate, noisy but cheap; **F** *Hotel les Oliviers*, just off Place Talmoklate, clean, only cold water; **F** *Hotel Roudani*, Place Assarag, reasonable, hot water.

● Camping
There is an unofficial area of camping in front of the police station, Route d'Ouarzazate.

● Places to eat
◆◆◆ *La Gazelle d'Or*, Route d'Amezgou, T 852039, reservations necessary, one of the best Moroccan restaurants, with a diverse

menu incl an excellent pigeon *pastilla* and desserts; *Hotel Palais Salam*, Route d'Ouarzazate, T 852312, reservations rec, for lavish Moroccan cuisine, specialities should be ordered in advance.

◆◆*Hotel Taroudant*, Place Assarag, T 852416, big portions of good French-Moroccan cuisine; *Hotel Roudani*, good Moroccan food; *Hotel Saadiens*, a rec place for reliable Moroccan cuisine.

◆*Restaurant Tout Va Bien*, Place Talmoklate, with good prices and food, particularly *couscous*; *Café-Restaurant Dallas*, Place Assarag, is fine and cheap but with dodgy *couscous*; *Restaurant Sindibad*, Place Assarag, is also good; other cheap places are located between the two main squares.

● Bars
In *Hotel Taroudant*, Place Assarag, T 852416, a small friendly bar with a good atmosphere and low prices; of another class is the cocktail bar at the *Hotel Palais Salam*, Route d'Ouarzazate, T 852312.

● Cafés
In Place Assarag there is a large café with seating on the square, a pleasant place to relax; and several on Place Talmoklate, incl the excellent *Pâtisserie El Ouarda*.

● Bank & money changers
Banque Populaire, Place Assarag.

● Hammams
There is a *hammam*, near the *Hotel Taroudant*, another is off Place Assarag opp.

● Hospitals & medical services
Doctor: Dr Ahmed Iben Jdid, T 852032 (clinic), T 853626 (home).

● Sport
Cycle hire: MD13/hr.
Tennis: *Tennis Roudani*, nr the *Hotel Palais Salam*.

● Tourist offices
Syndicat d'Initiative, Maison de Jeune de Téromo.

● Transport
Road Bus: bus agencies are located on Place Assarag and Place Talmoklate, although some of the services leave early in the morning. There are regular buses to **Inezgane** (1 hr), and other services to **Ouarzazate** (5 a day, 3 hrs), **Tata** (3 a week), **Casablanca** and **Agadir** (4 a day). A bus leaves for **Marrakech** via the spectacular

Tizi-n-Test pass at 0400, taking 9 hrs. There is another service to **Marrakech** via the less impressive route through Agadir. **Taxi**: grand-taxis are a practical option to Inezgane and Agadir, entailing a change at Ouled Teima.

Tioute 33 km from Taroudant on the road S to Tata has a splendid palmery and a newly restored 16th century kasbah overlooking the seven small villages. *Restaurant Kasbah Tioute*, T 851048, is highly recommended for lunch, ask for the chicken tajine served in traditional style.

Detour southwards to Tata and beyond

Just 7 km E of Taroudant, a road leaves the P32, and follows a 171 km route across the Anti Atlas mountains and down into the Sahara at Tata. This is a spectacular journey, rarely travelled by tourists, but worth it for devotees of wilderness, and now passable by car.

THE ARGANE TREE – THE TREE OF THE FLYING GOATS

Visitors to this particular area of Morocco might be forgiven in thinking that the trees are full of flying creatures. The creatures are goats but though they are perched on the extended boughs of the argane tree they climb, they do not fly.

The argane tree is found today only in this small region of Morocco between Agadir and Essaouira and eastwards along the Sous valley beyond Taroudant and in parts of Mexico.

At first glance one could mistakenly think that the area was under olive cultivation. The trees are well spaced and the average height is the same, around 4m, although some specimens reach 20m. The short trunk, however, is thicker, perhaps 8m in girth. In fact it is not one trunk but a fusion of stems and the canopy of clumps of argane can spread to 40m. The trees grow very slowly but live a long time, with an estimated average lifespan of 125 years.

The wood from the tree is extremely hard and makes excellent charcoal and the small pale green leaves set among vicious spines make nutritious fodder. The small greenish flowers are produced in spring and sometimes in autumn and the resulting fruit, something like a wrinkled yellow plum, appears between May and Sep. Don't be tempted to try one. The fruit is much prized. The fleshy cover makes a rich, longlasting cattle cake, while being particularly rich in sugar the juice can be fermented to produce an alcoholic drink.

The oil from the kernels within the hard shell is used by the local population who have acquired the taste. It is honey coloured with a nutty flavour. It is used in cooking, in the preparation of sweets and mixed with almond paste and honey it makes a delicious 'butter'. A bowl of argane oil into which hot bread is dipped is served at most meals.

The goat herders collect the fruits from the ground. Officially they are forbidden to beat the trees to make the fruits fall. Some fruits are dislodged by the feeding goats, in other cases the stones which are spat out by the goats who have eaten the pulp and the stones which have travelled through the animal's digestive system are collected. The nuts can be stored for years, providing food in times of scarcity. The women produce the oil in small quantities because it cannot be stored. They break the shell, roast the kernel often using the shell casing, grind the kernels into a paste which is mixed with tepid water and from this squeeze the oil. The work is tedious and the yield is very low, estimated at about 2 kg of oil for every 100 kg of kernels. The oil's reputation as an aphrodisiac is widespread.

From Tata, the options are to travel E to
Foum-Zguid and Zagora, along the Jbel
Bani mountain range, or W along the
P30 through a series of oases to Bou
Izakarn, and connect with the Agadir-
Tiznit-Laayoune road. There are four
buses a week between Taroudant and
Tata, and daily buses between Tiznit,
Bou Izakarn and Tata. The roads are
passable by car, although spare parts and
petrol are less plentiful in this region. 93
km from Taroudant the road reaches
Irherm, which has a Wed *souq*, a petrol
station, and the *Café de la Jeunesse*, with
basic accommodation.

Tata is the principal town of the region,
a pink settlement built around an oasis.
The oasis, with its scattered housing and
several *ksour*, is cultivated by the Berber-
speaking population who wear distinctly
Saharan clothing. At the centre of the
town is a garden square, and nearby are
all the facilities, the bank, the post office
and basic café-restaurants. The best
place to stay is at the **E** *Hotel de la Renaissance*, 96 Ave des Forces Armées Royales, T 802042, 45 rm, with the town's top
restaurant; the other options are the
F *Hotel Sahara*; and the **F** *Hotel Salam*,
both basic.

East from Tata There are police checks
along this route, and it may be necessary
to get a permit: check with the police in
Tata. Transport is by 4WD vehicle, or by
hitching a lift on a lorry. 70 km E from
Tata, **Tissint** has five *ksour* and is known
for its excellent dates. **Foum-Zguid** has
a Thur *souq*, basic accommodation, and
buses to Ouarzazate. There is a rough
road from Foum-Zguid to Zagora.

West from Tata Akka lies 70 km W of Tata,
a village with an interesting old quarter,
with a history as a trading post, and with
basic accommodation at the **F** *Hotel-Café
Tamdoult*. Further on, **Foum El Hassan** is
another oasis, with rock carvings in the
town centre. 4 km from the town, up the
track into the mountains, are more remarkable carvings of animals.

From the village of **Timoulay Izder**,
a road leads 10 km to **Ifrane de l'Anti
Atlas**, an historic settlement sur-
rounded by a number of *ksour*, spaced
around the slopes of the mountain bowl.
Ifrane had a large Jewish population,
who still revisit the necropolis just to the
N. The village has an interesting *souq* on
Sun morning. There are three places to
stay, marginally the best is the **F** *Hotel
Anti-Atlas*; the others are the **F** *Café-Res-
taurant de la Poste*; and the **F** *Café du
Paix*. Back on the main route, **Bou
Izakarn** lies on the junction with the
Agadir to Laayoune road, with regular
transport to Goulimine and Tiznit, and
a Fri *souq*. The **E** *Hotel Anti-Atlas*,
T 874134, 10 rm, on the road to
Goulimine, has a restaurant, pool and
garden, and is a pleasant place to stay.
From here there are buses and grand-
taxis to Ifrane de l'Anti Atlas.

OUARZAZATE AND THE DRAA VALLEY

The road from Taroudant to Ouarzazate
incorporates all ranges of scenery – intensive oasis agriculture, dry farming,
argane culture, expanses of gravel desert
grazed by goats and camels and extensive views from the winding road
through the Anti Atlas. Stop at **Talioune**
at *Hotel Ibn Touret* or *Café Renaissance*.
Town also has a pharmacy, mechanics
and taxis.

Ouarzazate

(*Pop* 19,000; *Alt* 1,135m) Ouarzazate's
primary attraction is not in the settlement itself, an unexciting town and
military garrison with a crumbling *ksar*,
but as a base for exploring the Saharan
regions, and as a transit point en route
to the desert. For this, it is well-equipped
and a pleasant enough place to stay.

Located at the confluence of three
rivers, Ouarzazate is in a strategic location, and has been garrisoned since the
Almohad period. A tribal war in the late

19th century left Ouarzazate in the hands of the el-Glaoui family, and the kasbah became the power base from which they expanded control over the S. The town was chosen by the French in 1928 as a military garrison and administrative centre – the buildings from this period straggle along the main street. Around and above them are the large hotels, which have been built in recent years, giving Ouarzazate a prosperity unusual in this region. This is compounded by the role of the town and its immediate vicinity as a film location. From the point that *Lawrence of Arabia* was filmed at Aït Benhaddou, this area has become a popular director's choice, and there is now a permanent studio nearby. Ouarzazate hosts a handicrafts fair in May and a *moussem* in Sep. Popular with bird watchers.

ACCESS Air The airport is at Taorirt, NE of Ouarzazate, T 882345. **Road** Access is by the P31 NW from Marrakech; and by the P32 W from Taroudant; E to Boumalne, Tinerhir and Er Rachidia on the P32; and SE on the P31 to Zagora. **Bus** The CTM bus terminal is on a square on the main street, Ave Mohammed V, private line buses arrive at Place 3 Mars, and grand-taxis on Place Mouahidine. Most of the important buildings are located on or near Ave Mohammed V.

Places of interest

The main days for the town market are Sun and Tues, but beyond this the main point of interest in Ouarzazate is the **Kasbah Taorirt**, located E of the town centre along Ave Mohammed V. This was an el-Glaoui kasbah, built in the 19th century, reaching its height of importance in the 1930s. The kasbah would have housed the extended family of the chief, his servants and followers, as well as a community of tradesmen, artisans and cultivators, gathered together in a continuous area of building for common security. The kasbah is partly ruined, but is still occupied, on its rear side, by some of the poorest people in Ouarzazate in a maze of narrow passageways, small houses and shops. The area of the kasbah adjacent to the road has been maintained (open 0830-1200 and 1500-1800 Mon-Fri, 0830-1200 Sat). This would have been the quarters of the family and immediate associates, and includes a courtyard and several reception rooms. Upstairs are a small dining room and salon.

Opposite the kasbah in the *Ensemble Artisanal* (open 0800-1200 and 1300-1800 Mon-Fri, 0830-1200 Sat), which has a number of sculptors working on the premises, as well as a selection of local handicrafts. The local woollen carpets of the Ouzgita Berbers are worth looking out for. In the town centre there is also a *Coopérative Artisanale des Tissages de Tapis*, another fixed price shop. *Atlas Studios*, where film work is regularly in process, is open to public view (0800-2000), and is located 3 km from the centre, along the road to Marrakech. Outside Ouarzazate, to the E, the Barrage al-Mansur, is a large man-made lake with the partly ruined **Tamdaght Kasbah**. To the S, off the P31, lies the **Kasbah Tifoultoutte**, now used as a hotel, with good food, T 882813.

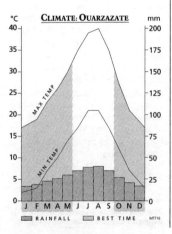

°C   **CLIMATE: OUARZAZATE**   mm

RAINFALL   BEST TIME   MTT16

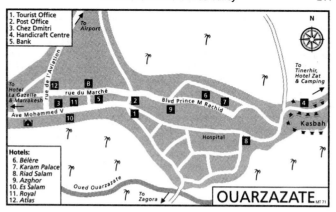

1. Tourist Office
2. Post Office
3. Chez Dmitri
4. Handicraft Centre
5. Bank

Hotels:
6. Bélère
7. Karam Palace
8. Riad Salam
9. Azghor
10. Es Salam
11. Royal
12. Atlas

OUARZAZATE MT 71

Local information
● Accommodation

A *Hotel Bélère*, Ave Moulay Rachid, T 882803, F 883145, 270 rm, a/c, pool, tennis, nightclub, cool, spacious, excellent facilities, helpful manager, second best hotel in town; **A** *Hotel Karam Palace*, Blvd Prince Moulay Rachid, T 882225, luxurious, 150 rm, restaurant, bar and pool, riding, tennis, built in style of kasbah; **A** *Hotel Riad Salam*, Ave Mohammed V, T 882206, 2 converted kasbahs, luxuriously equipped, 14 suites, 63 rm, restaurant, bar, spectacular pool with waterfall, as well as a sauna, massage, horse riding and tennis.

C *Hotel Azghor*, Blvd Prince Moulay Rachid, T 882612, above the town, a good place with 150 rm, a restaurant, bar, nightclub and pleasant pool; **C** *PLM Hotel Zat*, Aït Gief, T 882521, 60 rm, a quieter hotel on the outskirts, with an excellent restaurant, a bar and pool.

D *Hotel la Gazelle*, Ave Mohammed V, T 882151, a good option with 30 rm, an excellent bar-restaurant, small pool, a little out of town on the Marrakesh road.

E *Hotel Es Salam*, Ave Mohammed V, T 882512, a well-run hotel, some of the 50 rm are poorly lit; **E** *Hotel Royal*, 24 Ave Mohammed V, T 882258, a friendly place with good rooms with bath, and fair prices.

F *Hotel Atlas*, 13 rue du Marché, T 882307, behind the main street, cheap and satisfactory.

● Camping
Camping Municipal, T 882578, is on the Tinerhir exit of the town, a friendly place with running water, café and simple restaurant, a bit expensive.

● Places to eat

◆◆◆*PLM Hotel Zat*, Aït Gief, T 882521, a very good restaurant; *Le Palais Vert*, Aït Kdif, opp the *PLM Hotel Zat*, T 882428, with Moroccan decor, specializes in local food. **Chez Dmitri**, on Ave Mohammed V, in the town centre, is an excellent bar-restaurant, once the focus of Ouarzazate, serving excellent European/Italian food, with a good *lasagne*; further out from the centre is the rec restaurant of the *Hotel la Gazelle*, Ave Mohammed V, T 882151.

◆The cheapest places are along rue du Marché and nearby streets, *Restaurant Es-Salam*, Ave du Prince Heritier Sidi Mohammed, is a reasonable cheap option for Moroccan food; *Restaurant El-Helah*, 6 rue du Marché, is a good second choice.

● Bar
The best place for a drink is *Chez Dmitri*, Ave Mohammed V.

● Banks & money changers
Banque Populaire, Ave Mohammed V; BMCE, Ave Mohammed V.

● Hospitals & medical services
Chemist: *Pharmacie de Nuit*, Ave Mohammed V, T 882708.

● Post & telecommunications
The PTT is on Ave Mohammed V.

● Sport
Sporting Club: *Hotel Karam*, T 882225.
Riding Club: to E of town beyond kasbah.

Swimming: at major hotels and municipal pool.

● **Tour companies & travel agents**
Ksour Voyages, Place du 3 Mars, T 882997; *Palmiers Voyages*, Place de la Poste, T 882617; *Top Voyages*, *Hotel Karam*, T 883645, for excursions in the region.

● **Tourist offices**
Ave Mohammed V, opposite the CTM bus terminal, T 882485 (open 0900-1200 and 1430-1830 Mon-Fri). Syndicate d'Initiatives et du Tourisme, Kasbah de Taourirt.

● **Useful addresses**
Fire: T 15.
Police: Ave Mohammed V, T 19.

● **Transport**
Local Car hire: Budget, Ave Mohammed V, on the road to Marrakech, T 882892; **Hertz**, Blvd Mohammed V, T 882048; **Inter-Rent**, Place du 3 Mars, T 882035; other agencies around Place du 3 Mars.

Air There are flights from the Taourirte airport, NE of the city, T 882348, to Casablanca and Marrakech (4 a week) and Agadir (1 a week). International flights to Europe (mainly Paris) in season.

Road Buses: to Marrakech cross the High Atlas by the impressive Tizi-n-Tichka pass. There are also several services a day to **Zagora**, E to **Boumalne**, **Tinerhir**, **Er Rachidia**, and W to **Taroudant** and **Inezgane**. CTM buses leave from the terminal on Ave Mohammed V, private line buses from the nearby Place du 3 Mars. **Taxi**: from Place Mouahidine go to Skoura, Boumalne and Zagora amongst other destinations.

Excursion to Aït Benhaddou

Aït Benhaddou, 30 km from Ouarzazate, is a spectacular village with kasbahs scattered around a dramatic hillside location, their red towers on splendid vantage points. This was a strategic location on the old route from Marrakech to Ouarzazate since the 16th century, but with few people living there now. The village, however, attracts day-trippers from Ouarzazate, because of both its intrinsic appeal and its role in the film industry, with *Lawrence of Arabia* and *Jewel of the Nile* filmed here, as well as *Jesus of Nazareth*, for which part of the settlement was rebuilt. Guides will show tourists around the kasbahs, which have been given UNESCO 'World Heritage' status. They are intricately decorated and well preserved. The village also includes a large *agadir*, or storehouse, on the hill top. *Getting there*: to get to Aït Benhaddou leave Ouarzazate on the Marrakech road, the P32 and then the P31, and turn right after 22 km. The village is a further 10 km. Take a guide or the villagers will claim the streets are private.

● **Accommodation & places to eat** F *Café-Restaurant la Kasbah*, above the village, with 8 dormitory rm and a bar-restaurant; or F *Auberge-Restaurant Al Baraka*, below the village, a small place with a restaurant and 5 rm, or sleeping possibilities on the roof or in the tent in front; there is a camping site nearby. These two places are fine for lunch and adequate for dinner.

Detour to Zagora and the Draa Valley

The Draa Valley The road to Zagora is spectacular, first winding its way across the Jbel Anaouar mountains, and then down along the Draa valley, a strip of intense cultivation of settlement, a band of vivid colour weaving through the desert. The P31 is a good road, with frequent villages en route, but it is worth allowing adequate time and taking sufficient water. There are regular buses and grand-taxis connecting Ouarzazate, Agdz and Zagora, but one's own transport will enable visits to the numerous smaller and less spoilt oases and villages that are passed.

Agdz is the first major settlement of the valley, with a Thur *souq*. The buses, often full, pass through here, and there are grand-taxis. It is possible to stay at the F *Hotel-Café-Restaurant de Draa*, with 17 rm, breakfast provided, a friendly place; or F *Kissane*, Ave Mohammed V, 29 rm. *Camping la Palmeraie*, clean, with showers and a simple restaurant. The village has carpet and pottery shops, and the palmery nearby is a pleasant place to wander.

Zagora

Zagora is the main town of the valley, an administrative centre, the best place to stay and the destination of most tour groups. Unfortunately the influx of tourists has encouraged some inhabitants to be over enthusiastic in their attempts to make sales. It dates from the 13th century when it was founded by an Arab tribe. Although Zagora is itself an unexciting settlement it is an excellent location to explore the nearby areas of the valley, with paths through the date palmeries and to the various *ksour*. Particularly pleasant is the **Amazrou date palm oasis** across the river, where there is also some accommodation. In Amazrou there is a former Jewish kasbah, where their traditions of silverwork are still carried on. Above Zagora and within walking distance are two hills, from where there is an excellent view over the valley and towards the dunes. Nearby are the ruins of an 11th century Almoravid fortress.

During the *mouloud*, there is a major religious festival held in Zagora, the *Moussem of Moulay Abdelkader Jilala*. The town's market days are on Wed and Sun. Look out for the blue cloth worn by the men of the desert tribes, called in the tourist literature 'blue men'. The *souq* is an important place for the exchange of produce and livestock for the surrounding region. *Camel excursions* can be organized, try *La Fibule du Draa*, 2 km to the S in Amazrou.

Local information
● **Accommodation**

For a small town, Zagora has a reasonable selection of hotels. Among the more expensive places, choose between the modern **B** *Pullman Hotel Reda*, T 847079, F 847012, 155 rm, restaurant, bar, tennis and 2 pools.

Also **D** *Grand Hotel Tinsouline*, T 847252, 90 reasonable rm, central position, beautiful gardens, a good restaurant, bar and excellent pool; and the **D** *Hotel-Restaurant Kasbah Asma*, T 113, along the M'Hamid road towards Amazrou; **D** *La Fibule du Draa*,

T 847318, 26 rm, 1 km to the S in Amazrou, an idyllic and relaxing little place with pool and rec restaurant-bar.

The cheaper places incl the **E** *Hotel de la Palmeraie*, Ave Mohammed V, T 847008, friendly with 16 rm, restaurant, popular bar.

F *Hotel Oued Draa*, Ave Mohammed V, T 10, clean hotel with restaurant-bar; **F** *Hotel Vallée du Draa*, Ave Mohammed V, basic but adequate, with restaurant; **F** *Hotel-Café-Restaurant des Amis*, Ave Mohammed V, friendly, clean and with a reasonable restaurant, cold water.

● **Camping**

At *Camping d'Amazrou*, 1 km to the S in Amazrou, basic and friendly; *Camping la Montagne*, further to the S, friendly and with a pool; *Camping Sindibad*, beside the *Grand Hotel Tinsouline*, in a small palmery with a small restaurant and pool.

● **Places to eat**

Incl *Grand Hotel Tinsouline*, T 22; and the cheaper *Hotel de la Palmeraie*, Ave Mohammed V, T 08; *Restaurant Timbuctou*; *Café-Restaurant Essahara*; or *Restaurant l'Afrique*. The best place is a 1 km walk away in Amazrou: *La Fibule du Draa*, reasonably priced and not to be missed. Drink at the *Hotel de la Palmeraie*.

● **Useful addresses**

Ave Mohammed V has most of the town's facilities, incl the grand-taxi park, the bus station, post office, the **Banque Populaire**, *Pharmacie Zagora* and the *souq*. Bicycles can be hired in Ave Hassan II.

Tamegroute lies 20 km SE from Zagora on the left bank of the Oued Draa and is visited mainly because of the *zaouia*, **or monastery**, founded in the 17th century, headquarters of the influential Naciri Islamic brotherhood, which had great importance in the Draa region until recently, and is visited by scholars from the Islamic world. The outer sanctuary and library are open to public view (closed 1200-1500), the latter containing a number of impressively old *korans*. Whilst there, the village is interesting to explore, a close-knit area of old housing typical of the region, with potters at work producing the characteristic green and brown pottery, and a *souq*, main day Sat. It is possible to stay in Tamegroute, at the **F** *Hotel Said Naciri*, a welcoming place; or the **F** *Hotel-Restaurant Riad Dar Nousri*, a reasonable establishment with 18 rm, restaurant, pool and garden. There is a daily bus, and grand-taxis, to Tamegroute. South of Tamegroute are the **Tinfou dunes**, popular with tourists seeking the stereotypical desert view. There is a small inn, the **F** *Auberge du Repos des Sables*, which is popular amongst independent travellers, and boasts an impressive collection of art for sale.

M'Hamid can be reached by bus or by a negotiated grand-taxi from Zagora. It is a 90 km drive S along a reasonable road through the desert, the main reason for the excursion, an impressive view of stony desert interspersed with verdant oases. M'Hamid has basic facilities, cafés and accommodation, a Mon *souq*, and dunes nearby. M'Hamid is a good place from which to arrange short camel rides. There is very poor accommodation and food at **F** *Hotel Sahara*, T 9, 10 rm, separate shower or camping 2 km from the town. A second small hotel is being built. Hire of camel MD275 and Land Rover MD1,200 per day available.

From Zagora to Rissani and Foum-Zguid

Rough tracks exist E from Zagora to Rissani, just S of Erfoud, and W to Foum-Zguid (and then to Tata). **NB** These are difficult journeys only to be undertaken in a 4WD vehicle. Ask at the hotels for details of the vans and lorries covering the routes. There is a better route to Rissani which is generally passable with a sturdy car, but 4WD vehicles are recommended (see page 47). Drive 60 km N from Zagora and turn E across the Oued Draa through the small oases of Nkob (42 km from junction) and Mellal towards Tazarine (75 km from junction) a small settlement which offers

petrol, shop, camping and **F** *Hotel Bougafer*, T 10, 40 rm, restaurant, very basic. Here the black top ends and although there are signs that the old road is being upgraded and in places a new road is under construction there are 31 bumpy, dusty km of *piste* to cross. Back on the smoother surface pass through the tiny oasis settlement of Tiguerna (128 km from junction), the airstrip where anti-locust spray planes are parked before reaching the more major oasis settlement of Alnif with two hotels, **F** *Hotel Restaurant Bougafer*, very basic, fairly clean, well meaning staff and opp the similar **F** *Gazelle du Sud*. Meals provided at both places. Mechanics, petrol and shop available. With just 90 km to go to Rissani, small villages such as Achbarou with shops and a café and after a further 30 km Maoisis with school, petrol and café *Levée de Solei* are passed, before crossing the dry river bed and turning S the last 3 km into Rissani.

The Dades Valley

The Dades valley, 80 km from Ouarzazate has a similar if less dramatic appeal than the Draa valley: a belt of productive agricultural land beside the river, and a series of earth-built and crumbling *ksour* stretching from Skoura to Boumalne, flanked by arid mountains on either side. Skoura and El Kelaa des M'Gouna are practical excursions from Ouarzazate, or can be visited en route to Boumalne and the Gorges du Dades.

The Skoura oasis is more interesting than the village at its centre: a large palmery surrounded by kasbahs and *ksour*. Before the village, to the left of the road, is **Kasbah Amerhidl**, the largest of Skoura's kasbahs, with a particularly decorative design. The village also includes two kasbahs formerly occupied by the el-Glaoui family, **Dar Toundout** and **Dar Lahsoune**. Skoura village has a *souq* on Mon and Thur, a few basic restaurants, and the **F** *Hotel Nakhil*, a somewhat primitive establishment.

El Kelaa des M'Gouna Beyond Skoura, this is another area of *ksour* along the valley, including another el-Glaoui kasbah. The village, which has a Wed *souq*, is known for the production of rose water, with a rose water factory, and a rose festival in late May/early Jun with dances and processions under a shower of rose petals. It is possible to stay at the **C** *Hotel des Roses du Dades*, T 18, 102 rm, above the town at 1,927m, the cool interior gives welcome relief from the heat, reasonable restaurant, bar, tennis, horse riding and a good pool; or the much more basic but friendly **F** *Hotel du Grand Atlas*, Ave Mohammed V, T 37, 12 rm, communal showers.

THE GORGES

Oued Dades and Oued Todra both descend from the High Atlas mountains through narrow and spectacular gorges that are attractive excursions from Boumalne and Tinerhir. Both gorges offer options for walking up into the hills beyond, but most people choose just to walk in the gorge and enjoy the scenery from the pleasant vantage point of the restaurants located nearby.

Boumalne

Boumalne is a small town, with a market on Wed, and a reasonable selection of hotels. The town has grown from a very basic settlement to its current size mainly in the second half of the 20th century. In the Muslim cemetery there is a *koubba* to Sidi Daoud, who is commemorated in an annual festival, when bread is baked from flour left at the grave, and fed to husbands to ensure their fertility.

● **Accommodation** **C** *Hotel Madayeq*, T 04 834031, 100 rm, comfortable, good restaurant, bar and rooftop pool; **E** *Auberge de Soleil Bleu*, off to the right before the *PLM Hotel Madayeq*, T 153, 12 rm with bath, good restaurant; **E** *Hotel-Restaurant Vallée des Oiseaux*, T 04 834138, a new place with 12 comfortable rm and a restaurant; **F** *Hotel-Res-*

taurant Salam, opp the *PLM Hotel Madayeq*, a friendly and helpful place which provides free transport to Aït Oudinar in the gorge, 15 rm, communal showers, heating, rooftop terrace and restaurant with local food; **F** *Hotel Adrar*, opp the *souq*, T 04 830355, 27 rm around a courtyard, with restaurant.

● **Places to eat** The best restaurant in town is at the ◆◆◆*PLM Hotel Madayeq*, T 31, 32; cheaper options are the ◆◆*Hotel-Restaurant Salam*, rec for regional specialities; and the ◆ *Café Atlas*, in the centre, good for for food or just a tea or coffee; just outside Boumalne, on the Er Rachidia road, *Restaurant Chems* is highly rec, with reasonable prices and a pleasant terrace.

● **Transport Road** There are grand-taxis from Boumalne to Tinerhir or Ouarzazate. There is a variety of vehicles available for the journey up into the gorges, including grand-taxis, vans, Land Rovers and lorries. Msemrir, beyond the gorges, is also possible by local transport.

Excursion to the Gorges du Dades

The 6901 leaves the P31 at Boumalne and follows the Oued Dades through limestone cliffs which form the striking Gorges du Dades. The principal destination is the section of the gorges following Aït Oudinar, but the track continues up into the High Atlas, with public transport as far as Msemrir. There are very basic *pistes* into the mountains, and around into the Gorges du Todra.

Just beyond Boumalne is **Aït Arbi**, where there are a series of striking *ksour* above the road. The road continues past areas of unusual rock formations, through Tamnalt and Aït Oudinar, where there is basic accommodation. The valley narrows after Aït Oudinar, creating the most striking area of the gorges, where the cliffs are in vivid shades of red. From Aït Hammou the road continues in theory, linking with the 6902 through the Gorges du Todra, and up into the High Atlas.

● **Accommodation** In Tamnalt accommodation and food are available at the **E** *Hotel-Res-*

taurant Kasbah. But the best place in the gorges is the E *Auberge des Gorges Dades 'Aït Oudinar'*, with a restaurant; there is camping nearby. Further on is the F *Café des Peupliers*, with 3 rm and camping and the E *Kasbah de la Vallée de Dades*, with 6 rm and a restaurant. At Aït Hammou there is the F *Café-Hotel Taghea*, with several rooms but no electricity. Basic accommodation is available at Msemrir.

Tinerhir

Tinerhir is a modern administrative centre alongside a large oasis and older settlement, ideal for visiting the Gorges du Todra, but in itself a pleasant and interesting place to stay. The oasis settlement is a walk away behind the town, and a visit here is recommended. Hire a guide for MD35. The main part of the settlement was previously the Jewish quarter and has olive and fruit trees intercropped with grains and vegetables, and is interspersed with *ksour*. The main population is the Aït Atta tribe, often divided into small clans. Above the town and oasis is the massive ruined **el-Glaoui kasbah**, officially closed but normally possible to enter. There is a Tues *souq*, behind the *Hotel Todgha*. PTT is on Place Principale and the *Banque Populaire* on Ave Mohammed V.

● **Accommodation B** *Hotel Bougafer*, Blvd Mohammed V, T (04) 833200/80, F 833282, 2 km W of town, new, comfortable, clean, good pool, but footsteps and door slamming echo through building; **C** *Hotel Sargho*, T (04) 834181, on the Ouarzazate road, with the appearance of a *ksar*, 62 comfortable rm, a restaurant, bar and pool; **E** *Hotel Todgha*, 32 Ave Hassan II, T (04) 834249, 30 rm, restaurant, over-priced; **F** *Hotel Oasis*, Place Principal, cheap, clean, central, welcoming, upstairs restaurant with good food and views over town; **F** *Hotel El Salam Saada*, Place Principal, basic.

● **Camping** There are three camping sites 8 km along the road leading to the gorges, rec are *Camping Atlas*, small and friendly with a restaurant; *Camping du Lac*, bar, restaurant, more expensive. *Camping Almo* is in centre of town.

● **Places to eat** *Hotel Sargho* has the best

restaurant; *Hotel Todgha*, 32 Ave Hassan II; and *Hotel Oasis*, Place Principal are cheaper; *La Gazelle d'Or*, in the town centre is also good; *La Kasbah*, Ave Mohammed V, T 13, a friendly place with delicious food. A good café is *Chez Habib*.

● **Transport Road** Buses and grand-taxis to all locations, including Ouarzazate, Boumalne and Er Rachidia, leave from Place Principal. *Grand-taxis* and vans run from Place Principal to the gorge. Hotels organize trips to the gorge for MD55.

Excursion to the Gorges du Todra

The Gorges du Todra are more spectacular than the Gorges du Dades, particularly popular in the evening when the rocks are coloured in bands of bright sunlight and dark shadow. There are places to stay near the narrowest part of the gorge, a highly recommended break from the activity of the major towns.

8 km from Tinerhir are the three camping sites already mentioned, in an idyllic location beside a pool and palmery. 6 km further on is the most visited section of the gorge, where the high cliffs leave just enough space for the road and river. It is a particularly photogenic sight at sunset, and is also excellent for birdwatching. Just before the gorge are the three hotels: the **F** *Hotel Restaurant El Mansur* is very basic with shared rooms but is the cheapest option, it also has a restaurant; further on the E *Hotel des Roches* has 10 good rm and a restaurant in a ceremonial tent; the E *Hotel Yasmina*, T (04) 833013, newly extended with 12 'Moroccan' rm, and a large and recommended restaurant in a traditional black tent, often used by tour groups. Camping here by arrangement.

It is possible to continue along the pistes from the gorges, either across to the Gorges du Dades, the road from Tamtatouche to M'semrir being particularly rough, or up into the High Atlas towards Imilchil. **NB** Passable only in 4WD vehicle. Alternatively, try to get a lift from a lorry.

From Tinerhir to Er Rachidia

Buses run from Tinerhir to Er Rachidia, or from Tinejdad, en route, across to Erfoud. There are grand-taxis from Tinerhir to Tinejdad, Tinejdad to mima, and mima to Er Rachidia. **Tinejdad** is a Berber and Haratin town in a large oasis, with some significant kasbahs, notably the **Ksar Asrir**; and the *F Hotel-Restaurant Tizgui*, with basic accommodation and food. **mima** is similar, a large number of *ksour* around a palmery, with a basic town at the centre, a camp site, and the *F Hotel Gheriz*, with reasonable rooms and good food.

ER RACHIDIA AND THE ZIZ VALLEY

Er Rachidia

ACCESS Buses from **Aéroport Er Rachidia**, T 572350, stop at the bus station off Ave Mohammed V, the main street, and the grand-taxi park opposite.

Er Rachidia (*Pop* 27,040), previously known as Ksar Es Souq, was established by the French, initially by the Foreign Legion, as a military and administrative centre, a role it retains today. The town has little of interest for the visitor, beyond a **19th century** *ksar* near the Erfoud exit. However Er Rachidia is a convenient stopping point at the meeting of routes to Ouarzazate, Erfoud, Figuig and Fes, and is such is reasonably well equipped and with a relaxed atmosphere. The town, an important local *souq*, has its biggest market days on Sun, Tues and Thur.

● **Accommodation** C *Hotel Rissani*, Ave de la Marche Verte (direction Erfoud), T 572186, F 572585, pleasant location on the town's outskirts, 60 rm, restaurant, bar, disco, tennis and pool; D *Hotel Oasis*, 4 rue Abou Abdellah, T 572519, a modern place with 46 rm, restaurant and bar; E *Hotel Meski*, Ave Mohammed V, T 572065, 25 comfortable rm with restaurant, café and pool; F *Hotel-Café la Renaissance*, 19 rue Moulay Youssef,

T 572633, 20 clean rm, people are helpful and friendly, good restaurant; F *Hotel des Oliviers*, 25 Place Hassan II, T 572449, satisfactory.

● **Camping** 2 km along the Erfoud road there is a basic camp site with a pool.

● **Places to eat** ♦♦*Hotel Oasis*, 4 rue Abou Abdellah, T 572519, 572526, has a good and clean licensed restaurant serving Moroccan food; *Restaurant Lipton*, Ave Mohammed V, good food throughout the day and night; *Restaurant Imilchil*, Ave Mohammed V, T 572123, good traditional Moroccan food in a licensed establishment. ♦The most economic place is *Restaurant Sijilmassa*, Ave Mohammed V, with a simple but good menu; *Hotel-Café la Renaissance*, 19 rue Moulay Youssef, T 572633, is reliable, with excellent *couscous*. There are other cheap places along Ave Mohammed V.

● **Bank & money changers** Banque Populaire, Ave Mohammed V.

● **Hospitals & medical services Chemist**: (all night) Blvd Moulay Ali Cherif.

● **Post & telecommunications** PTT, just off Ave Mohammed V nr the *Banque Populaire*.

● **Shopping** The *Complexe Artisanal*, nr the bridge, has a selection of fixed-price goods.

● **Tourist offices** Ave Moulay Ali Cherif, T 572733 (open 0830-1200 and 1400-1800).

● **Useful addresses Police**: T 19; **Fire**: T 15.

● **Transport to & from Er Rachidia Air** There is a weekly flight to Fes, and from there to other destinations, from Aéroport Er Rachidia, T 572350. **Road Bus**: buses leave from the bus station off Ave Mohammed V, T 572760, with several a day for Erfoud and Rissani (2 hrs), Midelt (3 hrs), Tinerhir (3^1/$_2$ hrs), Fes (9 hrs), and Meknes (8 hrs), and one each morning to Figuig (8 hrs). **Taxi**: there are frequent grand-taxis to Erfoud, Meski and Tinejdad, the park is opposite the bus station.

Excursion to Meski

Meski, also known as Source Bleu, was developed by the French Foreign Legion. It is a springwater pool surrounded by palms, with the ruined **Meski Ksar** and a popular camp site, the *Camping de la Source Bleu*, T 249, which in the summer has a lively atmosphere but can become overcrowded: its restaurant is not recommended. Lying to the W of the Erfoud road 18 km S of Er Rachidia, **the source** is well worth a visit, and there is frequent transport to and from Er Rachidia.

Detour along the Ziz Valley

The Tafilalt From Meski, the P21 follows the Ziz valley S. This is another of the memorable valleys of the S, a succession of *ksour* alongside a heavily cultivated riverside area, with on either side the vast stony expanses of the Sahara. Many of the settlements of the valley were destroyed in the flood of 1965. The S stretches of the Ziz valley, a region known as the Tafilalt, are particularly fertile, and historically of considerable importance. This was due in part to its location on the trans-Saharan trade routes, with the town of Sijilmassa a major mediaeval population centre, whose rapid decline has not yet been fully explained. In the 8th and 9th centuries the region was a separate kingdom, and became known as a centre of religious unorthodoxy – of the Kharajite Berber heresy and later of Shi'ism. The present Alawite Dynasty of Moroccan Sultans originated in Rissani. From 1916 to 1931 French control of the region was challenged and effectively thwarted by local forces. Nowadays it is a poor date-producing region with a small flow of tourists.

Erfoud is the administrative centre of the Tafilalt, built in the 1930s, and an excellent base for exploring the valley and nearby desert areas. On the other side of the river from the town is the **Borj Est**, a military fort with impressive views. There is a *souq* on Sun in the town centre, and a Date Festival in Oct. A visit to the interesting **Marmar Marble Factory**, near the *Hotel Salam*, is worthwhile.

● **Accommodation C** *Hotel Salam*, Route de Rissani, T 576424, F 576426, modern, well-equipped in traditional style, 100 rm, 45 deluxe suites, bar, a good restaurant, pool (not al-

ways!), gardens, vehicle and driver hire; **C** *Hotel Sijilmassa*, T 576522, modern, fully-equipped. **D** *Hotel Tafilalt*, Ave Moulay Ismail, T 576036, F 576036, 64 a/c rm, bar, restaurant, pool and garden; **D** *Hotel la Gazelle*, Ave Mohammed V, good apart from noisy rooms at the front, a reasonable restaurant. **E** *Hotel Farah Zouar*, Ave Moulay Ismail, T/F 576230, 30 a/c rm, restaurant serving typical Moroccan food. **F** *Hotel-Bar Ziz*, 1 Ave Mohammed V, T 576154, 20 rm some with showers, good licensed restaurant; **F** *Hotel des Palmiers*, 36 Ave Mohammed V, 15 rm, communal shower, cheap restaurant; **F** *Hotel-Restaurant de la Jeunesse*, Ave Mohammed V, basic, with restaurant; there is also **camping** nr the *Hotel Salam*, with basic facilities and a pool, not rec.

● **Places to eat** ♦♦ *Hotel Salam*, Route de Rissani, T 576426 offers the best meals. ♦ There are cheaper meals at the excellent *Hotel-Restaurant de la Jeunesse*; and the rec *Café-Restaurant les Fleurs*; as well as at the *Restaurant-Café du Sud*; *Restaurant Merzouga*; and *Hotel-Bar Ziz*, all in Ave Mohammed V.

● **Services** The post office, a branch of the **Banque Populaire**, and the bus station are located in the town centre on Ave Mohammed V.

● **Telecommunications Area code**: 05.

● **Transport** There is a bus each day to Er Rachidia. Transport onwards to Rissani is by bus, or by a hired Land Rover.

Rissani, 22 km S of Erfoud, birthplace of the Alaouite Dynasty is a modern village close to the site of the ruined town of Sijilmassa. It includes a 17th century *ksar*, housing most of the population, and a street with a bank and cafés. It is possible to stay at the **E** *Hotel-Café- Restaurant Sijilmassa*, Place Massira Khadra, T 5042, 8 rm, modern and clean, nearest to the ruins and the mechanics, overpriced; or the **F** *Hotel El Filala*, good size rooms but often dirty. The village has an interesting *souq* on Sun, Tues and Thur, and there are several handicraft shops.

Sijilmassa was once the Berber capital of the Tafilalt region, and a major trading centre. It was founded in 707 by the Arab leader Musa ben Nasser, and its location on the major Sahel to Europe trade route, from Niger to Tanger, gave it considerable importance and prosperity. The ruins, little of which remain, are between the town and the river. The kasbah was kept up by Moulay Ismail, but the Aït Atta tribe destroyed the town in 1818. The current Alawite Dynasty settled in the surrounding region in the 13th century before gaining the Moroccan Sultanate in the 17th century. The ruins are of historical interest only and the 'guides' are ill informed. The fanciful tales of earthquake destruction must be discounted.

To the SE of Rissani is the **Zaouia of Moulay Ali Sherif**, closed to non-Muslims, where the founder of the Alawites is buried. Adjacent to this is the **Ksar d'Akbar**, a ruined Alawite palace from the 19th century, whilst 2 km to the S is the **Ksar Ouled Abd el-Helim**, a striking structure dating from 1900. *Getting there*: there is a daily bus to Er Rachidia, and a Land Rover taxi each Thur along the rough piste to Zagora. There are lorries and Land Rover taxis from the village centre to Merzouga.

Merzouga, 61 km from Erfoud, has one attraction, the huge dunes called **Erg Chebbi**, a vast pile of sand stretching into the Sahara. There is little else, beside the other tourists and a small village with a Sat *souq*, but then the calm and wilderness is part of the appeal. A short walk across the dunes is a must once there. There are also camel excursions organized by the *Auberge La Grand Dune*, and some good bird watching particularly the pink flamingo in Feb by the adjacent lake. The *piste* continues S to Taouz. A taxi from Rissani, changing at Merzouga will cost MD20.

● **Accommodation** It is possible to stay at Merzouga, although accommodation is often taken early in the day. The options incl the **D** *Auberge-Kasbah Derkaoua*, nr the dunes at Erg Chebbi, BP 64, full board, very good

French-Moroccan licensed restaurant, pool. **F** *Hotel Merzouga*, a friendly place with good food; **F** *Café des Amis*; **F** *Auberge la Grand Dune*; and **F** *Café-Restaurant de Palmeraie*, all basic places with dormitory accommodation.

THE EASTERN SAHARA

Bouarfa

The road from Er Rachidia to Figuig, the P32 as far as Bouarfa, and the P19 from then on, is a long and impressive journey through the relative wilderness of the E Sahara – red mountains and stony desert-scapes, broken only by small villages which are unlikely to detain the traveller for long. At the junction with the P19 from Oujda to Figuig is **Bouarfa**, a small administrative and military town. The town makes some interesting carpets from cloth scraps.

● **Accommodation** **F** *Hotel Tamlatte*; and the **F** *Hotel Hauts Plakas*, on the main street, basic.

● **Transport Train** There is a weekly train from Oujda to Bouarfa, leaving at 2240 on Sat and arriving at 0635 on Sun, and making the return journey to Oujda from 0920 on Sun, arriving at 1701 the same day, this is a useful service for visitors to Figuig. **Road** buses from Oujda to Figuig pass through Bouarfa. There are two buses a day to Er Rachidia.

Figuig

Figuig is a large palm oasis lying on the border with Algeria. This has given it a strategic position, and it has often been fought over between the Moroccan Sultanate and the powers to the E, most recently in 1963 and 1975 between Algerian and Moroccan forces. Nowadays the border is open (see below), and this is a popular place to cross.

ACCESS In Figuig buses stop in front of the *Hotel Sahara* on Ave Hassan II, the ticket office is nearby. There are four buses a day to Oujda, and a daily morning service to Er Rachidia.

Places of interest

The *ksour* of Figuig are distinctly separate, and were more so in the past, when bitter disputes existed, particularly over water. The construction of the *ksour* is thus highly defensive. It is worth visiting one or two of the **ksour**, built with a maze-like system of alleys and houses. **Ksar El Ouadarhir** is to the left of the main street, **Ksar El Maiz** is an attractive area to the right of the street, **Ksar El Hammam el Foukanni**, with a hot spring, beyond that. **Ksar Zenaga** is perhaps the best to visit, a large area with a mosque, and above it a platform from which there is a good view over the oasis.

The oasis has seven distinct *ksour*, with the main street, Ave Hassan II, running through the centre, along which most of the town's facilities are located: the *Banque Populaire*, shops and basic café-restaurants. There is some attractive leatherwork and silverware for sale in Figuig. The oasis, with its clearly discernible community structure and strongly religious nature, is an interesting place to stop for a few days en route to or from Algeria.

● **Accommodation** F *Hotel Camping*, best place, pool, restaurant, satisfactory rooms and a camping area; F *Hotel Meliasse*, a basic place at the entrance to the town; F *Auberge de la Palmeraie*, a good place with a restaurant, at Ksar Zenaga; or the F *Hotel Sahara*, Ave Hassan II, cheap and adequate.

● **Places to eat** *Café El Fath* and *Café Oasis* both on Ave Hassan II, both reasonable.

Algerian Border To go into Algeria it is necessary to get one's passport stamped at the police station (0800-1500) on the main street. From here walk, hitch or drive to the border, where one passes through Moroccan and Algerian checkpoints, and the Algerian customs, before arriving at the small Algerian town of Beni Ounif (see page 338).

THE DEEP SOUTH

Tiznit

To the S of Agadir, is Tiznit, an important garrison and market town, with pinkish brown houses surrounded by large *pisé* walls, well worth a wander after an overnight stop. The town was founded in 1882 by Moulay Hassan, enclosing a number of separate *ksour* within the walls, and was the first base for El Hiba's insurrection against the French from 1912, following the example of his father Ma el Ainin in 1910.

Places of interest
The town *souq* is on the Tafraoute exit, with its main days on Thur and Fri. There is an interesting jewellery *souq*, on the right between Place du Mechouar and the town walls. Along rue de l'Hôpital from the square is the **Grand Mosque** with a minaret reminiscent of the Sahelian style, with protruding perches. Adjacent to this is the **Source Bleu de Lalla Tiznit**, a spring named after the town's saint, a reformed prostitute. From **Bab Targua**, on the N side of the town, it is possible to get onto the walls. There are two religious festivals in Tiznit in Aug, the Moussem of Sidi Abderrahman, and the acrobat's Moussem of Sidi Ahmed ou Moussa.

Local information
● **Accommodation**
The top two hotels in Tiznit are the D *Hotel de Tiznit*, rue Bir Inzaran, on the edge of the town, T 862411, 862119, 40 rm, with the *Anzli Club* nightclub, restaurant, bar and good pool.

E *Hotel de Paris*, Ave Mohammed V, T 862865, 20 rm, fine restaurant.

F *Hotel Atlas*, Place du Mechouar, clean and reasonable, good restaurant; F *Hotel des Amis*, Place du Mechouar, satisfactory; F *Hotel du Bon Acceuil*, Place du Mechouar, clean and basic; F *CTM Hotel*, nr the bus terminal, friendly with bar and restaurant.

● **Places to eat**
There is good food at the ♦♦*Hotel de Tiznit*,

rue Bir Inzaran; and cheaper but still tasty meals at the ◆*Hotel Atlas*, Place du Mechouar; and the *Hotel du Bon Acceuil*, on the same square.

● **Services**

Around the square are a tourist information office, the **Syndicat d'Initiative**, T 869199, a bank and post office, as well as hotels and cafés.

● **Transport**

Road   Most buses and grand-taxis arrive at Place du Mechouar, the focal point of the town. There are private line buses from Place du Mechouar, including several services a day to Tafraoute, Tata, Goulimine, Sidi Ifni and Agadir, and CTM services to Agadir and Laayoune from the nearby **Bab Ouled Jarrar**. Grand-taxis leave from Place du Mechouar, with Land Rover taxis from the Tafraoute road.

West of Tiznit is the beach of **Sidi Moussa d'Aglou**, with a long sand strip, dangerous swimming and a small troglodyte village of fishermen's families. There is good accommodation at the **F** *Motel d'Aglou*; and a camp site; as well as good food at the *Café-Restaurant Ouazize*. Grand-taxis from Tiznit leave from near Place du Mechouar.

Detour to Tafraoute and the Ameln Valley

Tafraoute is the most rewarding town of this area of the Anti Atlas mountains, located in the attractive Ameln Valley, with its unusual granite rock formations and beautiful villages. There are two approaches to Tafraoute, along the 7074 from Tiznit or the S509 from Agadir. The road from Tiznit passes through a series of oases, several with basic accommodation, and the impressive **Col du Kerdous**, at 1,100m. The road from Agadir and Inezgane is also scenic, through a mountain landscape, and including the Wed *souq* of Aït Baha.

Tafraoute is the modern administrative centre of the valley and the best base for exploration. There is a large almond festival here, the Fête des Amandes, in Jan-Feb, and a *souq* on Wed. The town

has a post office and a *Banque Populaire*, both on Place Hassan II, as well as a branch of the *BMCE*. Tafraoute market is an excellent place to pick up handicraft bargains. Visitors should on no account omit a visit to La Maison Touareg, Ave Mohammed V, T 800210, which behind its unprepossessing exterior has an amazing range of carpets and other goods, and very friendly staff. It is also the only place to change money in the evening and at weekends. friendly staff.

● **Accommodation** C *Hotel Les Amandiers* is the most luxurious here, but offers little for the price, located on a rock above the town, T 800088, with 62 rm, a restaurant, bar and pool; **E** *Hotel Tafraoute* in the town centre is the best bargain, with hot water, clean rooms and friendly staff; the nearby **F** *Hotel Redouane* and **F** *Hotel Tanger* are basic places with minimal facilities and hygiene standards, but friendly staff. **Camping** the site along the Tiznit road, is reasonably equipped and has a café.

● **Places to eat** *Hotel les Amandiers* has the best restaurant and the only bar, *Restaurant Etoile du Sud* which caters for large groups, is cheaper and often good; cheaper still are the *Hotel Tanger*; and the *Café Atlas*, the latter with excellent value meals of local specialities. *Snack Sportive* is excellent value in the cheaper range.

● **Transport   Road**   Most buses from Inezgane and the N pass through Tiznit and along the 7074. There are several buses a day from Inezgane and Tiznit, and even one from Casablanca. Grand taxis, often Land Rovers, connect Tafraoute with Tiznit. Transport out to the villages is difficult. There are two buses a day, other options will be hitching, or bargaining with grand taxi drivers.

The Ameln Valley, or Valley of Almonds, is scattered with villages in between areas of irrigated agriculture, producing argane oil (see page 208) and almonds. Many of the men work elsewhere, returning for holidays or retirement, and are known for their participation in the grocery trade. Across the river, reached by bus or taxi, is the village of **Oumesnate**, a large community with some bizarre

BLOOMING TREES

Snow drifts are common in the Atlas massifs but the drifts of blossom in early spring which clothe the slopes for a second time are much more attractive. There are over 12 million almond trees to delight with their pale pink and fragile white blooms in Jan and Feb. Both roads from Marrakech to Agadir, the road from Agadir to Tafraoute and the whole region fed by the Oued Draa are breathtakingly beautiful at this season. These groves of self-seeded almonds have adapted to the environment, are resistant to drought and cold and provide, despite their low yields, an important source of income. While the early almond blossom here is in sharp contrast to the barren earth the blossom on trees in the oasis gardens has a green backcloth. In addition there are almond plantations especially in the Haouz of Marrakech which are equally beautiful and show greater profits. The almond is Morocco's second most important tree crop and Morocco is the world's fifth largest producer of almonds.

house designs, notably a number on stilts. To the W of this are a series of villages, an enjoyable day's exploration. To the S of Tafraoute is **Agard Oudad**, built below a rock named after Napoleon's horse. From here you should get a guide to show you the *'les Pierres Bleus'*. These are rocks and mountain sides painted in various colours by the Belgian landscape artist Jean Verame, known for performing art projects on a massive scale. This is an impressive and vast piece, one of the truly memorable sights of Morocco, even if it has faded a little since 1984.

Goulimine

Goulimine has become a major stop on the tourist network, a regular excursion from Agadir. This is because of its camel *souq*, on Sat morning, which is, however, nowadays geared almost totally towards the demands of the tourist industry, with the nomadic tribesmen distinguished by their blue clothing, the 'blue men', in dutiful attendance. The market is along the road to Tan-Tan. More genuine, however, are the religious festivals, or *moussems*, held in Jun (at Asrir) and Aug, when Touareg nomads are in plentiful supply. From the 8th century Goulimine was an important trading post on a route swapping Saharan salt and West African

gold. From the 12th century the town declined, but still retained some importance, with a large camel market. The town is located in an area of calm wilderness, but it is likely that the traveller will move on fairly quickly. There is a **kasbah** above the market.

● **Accommodation E** *Hotel Salam*, Route de Tan-Tan, T 872057, friendly, 20 rm, bar and restaurant; **F** *L'Ere Nouvelle*, Ave Mohammed V, basic, reasonable restaurant; **F** *Hotel Bir Nazarene*, cheap, cold water only. **Camping** signposted from Place Hassan II, is not rec.

● **Services** In the village there is a bank and post office. Tourist office, 3 Residence Sahara, Blvd d'Agadir, T 872545. The grand-taxi stop is on Place Bir Nazarene, and the café-restaurants on Place Hassan II; nearby is the bus stop.

Detour to Sidi Ifni

Sidi Ifni is one of the strangest towns in Morocco, a crumbling port town with a distinctive Spanish feel, and some unusual architecture. It was occupied by the Spanish from 1476 to 1524, and again from 1860, as a consequence of the Treaty of Tetouan. Sidi Ifni was always an enclave, surrounded by Morocco from 1860-1912 and from 1956-1969, and between 1912 and 1956 by the French Protectorate. The town had a port and an airstrip, and a role as a duty free zone. The economic survival of the town was based on the fact that the border was open to trade. In the 1960s Morocco grew tired of the continuing Spanish presence, and forced Spain into negotiations from 1966. The enclave was returned in 1969. Sidi Ifni is a wonderfully relaxing place to stay and wander for a few days, but after that its ghost town feel can get oppressive.

The **Plaza de España**, renamed Place Hassan II, is the centre of the colonial town, a pleasant garden and fountain surrounded by bizarre Art Deco buildings: the church, which is now the tribunal, the town hall, the Spanish consulate which opens 1 day a month, the *Hotel Belle Vue*, and several others. From there a promenade winds down the cliff to the beach. This is a long and often deserted strip with excellent swimming. To the S is the defunct Spanish port, an odd offshore construction on a concrete island linked to the mainland by a cable car. The Moroccans have built a new port nearby. The main *souq* on Sun is very disappointing. There is a large *moussem* in Jun.

● **Accommodation** E *Hotel Belle Vue*, 9 Place Hassan II, T 875072, an old building, 14 rm in need of decoration, restaurant and bar; E *Hotel Aït Ba Hamran*, rue de Plage, T 875267, 20 rm, restaurant and bar, a sad, dead place; E *Hotel Suerta Loca*, T 875350, is by far the best in town, friendly, clean, excellent food, with some lovely new rooms overlooking the sea, a popular hang-out in the evening, downhill from Place Hassan II; F *Hotel Beau Rivage*, modern, popular bar and restaurant. **Youth hostel** Complex Sportif, T (10) 3402, 40 beds, kitchen, overnight fee MD15. **Camping** Site, signposted from the town centre, is basic.

● **Places to eat** Excellent food at the *Hotel Suerta Loca*, order 2 hrs in advance, otherwise try *Hotel Belle Vue*, *Hotel Beau Rivage*, *Hotel Aït Ba Hamran*, or nr the market, the cheap and basic *Café-Restaurant de la Marine*.

● **Bars** The two bars are at the *Hotel Belle Vue* and the depressing *Hotel Aït Ba Hamran*.

● **Transport** There are regular grand-taxis between Sidi Ifni and either Tiznit or Goulimine, as well as daily buses to Agadir, Tiznit and Goulimine.

Tan-Tan was the starting point for the Green March into the Spanish Sahara, now incorporated into Morocco as the Western Sahara, albeit with an ongoing conflict with the local Independence movement, the Polisario. The town is a dull administrative centre, with duty-free shops and a fishing port. The blue cloth worn by the formerly nomadic inhabitants of this area is sold in the *souq*. There is a beach 25 km away, with some good fish cafés.

● **Accommodation** Travellers who decide to stay have the choice of the E *Hotel Amgala*, Ave de la Jeunesse, T 877308, 29 rm, restaurant; the E *Hotel Etoile du Sahara*, 17 rue El Fida, T 877085, clean, 34 rm, restaurant; or the E *Hotel Dakhla*, Place Tan-Tan, a satisfactory hotel. Camping possible on beach.

● **Places to eat** *Restaurant le Jardin*, Ave Mohammed V, the most popular place in town.

● **Bank & money changers** BMCE, Ave Hassan II, T 877277.

● **Transport Air** There are flights from Aéroport Tan-Tan, Place Blanche, 9 km out of the town, T 877143, 877164, to Laayoune and Casablanca (1 a week). The *Royal Air Maroc* office is on Ave de la Ligue Arabe, T 877259. From Tan-Tan the onward options are to Laayoune, or inland to Smara. **Road** There are buses, grand-taxis and Land Rover taxis on from Tan-Tan.

Tarfaya lies SW of Tan-Tan, just off the road to Laayoune. A grand-taxi from Laayoune to Tarfaya takes 90 mins and costs MD40. On the way into the town several wrecked ships are passed. The town is an oppressively quiet place with a few old sand blown Spanish colonial buildings. Spanish from 1916 as Villa Bens, capital of the S zone of their protectorate of Morocco from 1920 to 1956, and prior to that, between 1878 and 1895, it was a British trading post known as Port Victoria. The post office is the prominent building in the centre. The market is near the mosque. The **Dar Mar**

is a square structure just off the beach, supposedly British. There is also an abandoned church and colonial buildings. There is not much in the way of facilities in Tarfaya, although there are basic cafés, which do snacks and *harira*, and a few shops. **F** *Hotel-Café Tarfaya* is at the end of the main street nr the port.

Laayoune

Laayoune, with a population of 93,875 in 1982 and known before as El Aioun, was the capital of Spanish Sahara, and is the provincial capital under the Moroccans. The Moroccan government, to underline their claim to the region, have carried out an extensive programme of development, establishing facilities and constructing buildings unrivalled S of Agadir, and settling a large population from Morocco in the town, in addition to the big military garrison. Beyond the political curiosity of seeing the effect of post-colonialism, there is little to do in the town. It is, however, a strangely calm place, and not unpleasant to stay in.

ACCESS Hassan I Aéroport is 2 km outside the town, T 893346/7. There are taxis into the town, although it may be necessary to wait a while. For the energetic, it is a manageable walk. The CTM buses arrive on Ave de la Mecque, in the centre, the ONCF buses at the stadium a little further out.

Places of interest

The Place du Mechouar is interesting architecturally, a square with large canopies, with an exhibition space commemorating the Green March in 1975, and the modern **Grand Mosque** alongside. There is also a bird sanctuary, the **Colline des Oiseaux**, a calm place with some interesting species, on rue Okba Ibn Nafi, opposite the *Hotel Parador*. The Malhfa, on Blvd Kairouan, off Ave de la Mecque opposite the *Hotel Massira*, is the main market area. Below the town is the lagoon, a beautiful spot, but not for swimming in. See **Travel agents** below for excursions.

Local information
● Accommodation

A *Hotel Al Massira*, 12 Ave de la Mecque, BP 12, T 894225, Tx 28801, comfortable, 72 rm, restaurants, bar, nightclub, tennis and pool, often taken by tour groups; **A** *Hotel Parador*, rue Okba Ibn Nafih, BP 189, T 894500, Tx 28800, 31 rm, small, luxurious, restaurant, popular bar, tennis, good pool.

C *Hotel Nagjir*, Place Nagjir, a fork on Ave de la Mecque, T 894168/9, Tx 28019, with a bar, restaurant, nightclub.

D *Hotel El Alya*, 193 rue Kadi Ghallaoui, T 893133, Tx 20087, 32 comfortable rm, restaurant; **D** *Hotel Lakouara*, Ave Hassan II, nr the market, T 893378/9, 40 rm in a sleepy faded establishment.

F *Hotel Marhaba*, 36 rm, not very friendly but the best cheap option, clean rooms, hot communal showers, roof-terrace, above a café; **F** *Hotel Rif*, in a square opp rue Cheikh Maalaouine, T 894369;.

● Youth hostel
Complexe Sportif, Sakiat Alhamra, T 3402, 40 beds, kitchen, overnight fee MD20.

● Places to eat
Hotel Parador, rue Okba Ibn Nafih; and the *Hotel Al Massira*, Ave de la Mecque have good restaurants and there are several cheap restaurants on Ave Mohammed V; *Snak Fes* on Ave Hassan II, with reasonable and nourishing food.

● Banks & money changers
Banque Populaire, Ave Mohammed V; BMCE, rue Mohammed Zerktouni; Wafabank, 5 Ave Mohammed V, T 893598.

● Hammam
An experience not to be missed, MD10, spotlessly clean.

● Tour companies & travel agents
Agence Massira Tours International, 20 Ave de la Mecque, BP 85, T 894229, who organize excursions to Tarfaya for fishing, to Laayoune Plas International, 20 Ave de la Mecque, BP 85, T 894229, who organize excursions to Tarfaya for fishing, to Laayoune Plage and to Oasis Lamsaid, and hire out Land Rovers and drivers; *Bureau du Tourisme du Sahara*, Oum Saad, T 894224; *Agence de Voyages Sahara*, rue Kadi Ghellaoui, T 894144. Royal Air Maroc, 7 Place Bir Anzarane, T 894071/77.

● **Tourist offices**
Ave de l'Islam, BP 471, T 892233/75.

● **Transport**
Local Car hire: Comptoir Sakia Al Hamra, Quartier Industriel, Sahat Dchira, T 893345; **Ouled Abdellah**, Assurance Ouled Abdellah, T 893911; **BTS**, T 894224.

Air Hassan I Aéroport is 2 km outside Laayoune, T 893346/7, with flights to Casablanca and Agadir (1 a day), Tan-Tan (1 a week), Las Palmas (2 a week), Dakhla (3 a week).

Road CTM buses leave from Ave de la Mecque, by *Agence Massira Tours International*, services to Boujdour/Dakhla, Smara/Tan-Tan and Agadir/Marrakech. ONCF services to Agadir and Marrakech, from near the stadium. **Taxi**: grand-taxi from the roundabout at the end of Ave Hassan II, by the market, go to Agadir (MD150) and Marrakech (MD220). For grand-taxis to Tarfaya and Tan-Tan go by petit-taxi across the river to the *police controle* on the road out to the N, and pick one up there.

Around the Western Sahara

Laayoune Plage and Port To get to Laayoune Plage, it will probably be necessary to hire a whole grand-taxi, as the regular services go to the port, which is a distance from the beach. However the beach itself is not very clean. It is possible to stay at the **F** *Maison des Pêcheurs*. Laayoune Port, which no longer has ferries to the Canary Islands, is a phosphates port located 25 km from Laayoune, MD6 by grand-taxi. It is a sand-swept settlement with a few semi-operational café-restaurants, but little else.

Smara There is little to draw the traveller along this route, apart from a long desert journey, and one is likely to incur considerable police and army suspicion.

Smara is a garrison with two basic hotels, the **F** *Hotel Erraha*; and the **F** *Hotel Sakia El Houria*, and two flights a week to Laayoune.

Dakhla (*Pop* 6,500) is over 1,000 km S of Agadir and almost on the Tropic of Cancer. For those who wish to continue along the coastal road, there are lorries making the journey to Dakhla, and an ONCF bus service leaving Laayoune at 1200. **Boujdour** has a fishing port and beach. Dakhla is in a beautiful location with impressive beaches and cliffs. It was formerly called Villa Cisneros and was built on a spit protruding from the coast. Today it is a minor military and administrative centre with fishing (sea bass) and surfing.

● **Accommodation** There is only basic accommodation, incl the **F** *Hotel Imlil*, nr the *souq*; also try the *Pensión Atlas* or the *Hotel Bahia*; there are a basic restaurants around the town. Free camping possible on beach opp city entrance, secure. Camping also reported 7 km N of town at hot springs.

● **Services** There is a tourist office at 1 rue Tiris, T 898228, and a travel agent, *Dakhla Tours*, on Ave Mohammed V, T 141. **Bank**: BMCE, Ave Mohammed V. The **Royal Air Maroc** office is on Ave des PTT, BP 191, T 897050.

● **Transport Air** From Aéroport Dakhla, 5 km from the town, T 897049; direct flights to Casablanca, Agadir and Laayoune (1 a week). **Road** Bus from Laayoune.

Mauritanian border There is a road S of Dakhla to the border with Mauritania. All formalities in Dakhla, allow whole day to cross border, camping at border, customs minimal, convoys to border once/twice a week.

INFORMATION FOR VISITORS

CONTENTS

Before you go	226
Entry requirements	226
When to go	227
Health	227
Money	227
Getting there	228
Air; Train; Road; Boat; Customs	
When you arrive	230
Airport information; Airport tax; Conduct/clothing; Hammam; Hours of business; Laundry; Monuments; Official time; Photography; Safety; Shopping; Tipping; Voltage; Weights and measures	
Where to stay	232
Food and drink	233
Getting around	235
Air; Train; Bus; Car hire; Other land transport	
Communications	237
Language; Postal services; Telephone services	
Entertainment	237
Newspapers; Radio; Television; Sport	
Holidays and festivals	238
Further reading	239

Before you go

Entry requirements

● **Visas**

No visas are required for full passport holders of the UK, USA, Canada, Australia, NZ, Canada, Ireland and most EU countries. Obtain a separate passport if the current one has an Israeli or South African stamp in it. On the aeroplane or boat, or at the border, travellers will be required to fill a form with standard personal and passport details, an exercise to be repeated in almost all hotels throughout the country. From the point of entry travellers can stay in Morocco for 3 months.

Visa Extensions will require a visit to the **Immigration** or **Bureau des Etrangers** department at the police station in a larger town,

as well as considerable patience. An easier option is to leave Morocco for a few days, preferably to Spain, if not to Ceuta or Melilla.

● **Vaccinations**

None required unless travelling from a country where yellow fever and/or cholera frequently occurs. It is advised to be up to date with polio, tetanus, typhoid and hepatitis protection. See Health, page 15.

● **Representation overseas**

Algeria, 8 rue des Cèdres, El Mouradia, Algiers; **Australia**, 2 Phillis Lane, N Curl, Sydney, NSW, T 6496019; **Belgium**, Blvd Saint-Michel, 29 Brussels 1040, T 02 7361100; **Canada**, 38 Range Rd, Ottawa, T 2367391; **Denmark**, Oregarrds Allé 19, 2900 Hellerup, Copenhagen, T 624511; **France**, 5 rue le Tasse, 75016, Paris, T 4050 6879; **Germany**, Gotenstrasse 7-9, Badgodesberg 5300, Bonn, T 228 355044; **Netherlands**, Oranje Nassaulaan 1-1075, Amsterdam, T 736215; **Spain**, Serrano 179, Madrid, T 4580950; **Sudan**, PO Box 2042 Amarat, St No 1, Khartoum; **Sweden**, Kungsholmstorg 16, Stockholm, T 544383; **Switzerland**, 22 Chemin François-Lehmann, Grand Saconnex, Geneva, T 981535; **UK**, 49 Queens Gate Gardens, London SW7, T 0171 5815001/4627979; **USA**, 1601 21st St NW, Washington DC 20009, T 202 4627979.- **Consulates Spain**, Ave de Francisco 4, Algeciras, T 56673698 and Ave de Andalucía 63, Málaga, T 52329962; **USA**, 437 Fifth Ave, New York, 10016, T 212 7582625.

● **Information offices**

Many towns have an **Office du Tourisme** (Tourist Office) and a **Syndicat d'Initiative** (Information Office). These are rarely of much use, and will normally only have the fairly general official brochures, and addresses for hotels and restaurants. They may be of most use in arranging excursions and getting the services of an official guide. The national tourist organization, **ONMT**, has offices in **Australia**, 11 West St, Sydney, NSW 2060, T 9576711; **Belgium**, 66 rue du Marché-aux-Herbes, Brussels 1040, T 027361100; **Canada**, 2 Carlton St, Suite 1803, Toronto, Ontario M5B 1K2, T 4165982208; **France**, 161 rue Saint-Honoré, Place du Théâtre-Français, 75001 Paris, T 42604724; **Spain**, Calle Quintana 2 (2°e), Madrid, T 5427431; **Sweden**, Sturegaten 16, Stockholm 11436, T 66099; **Switzerland**, Schifflande, 5, 8001 Zurich, T 2527752; **UK**, 205 Regent St, London, T 0171 4370073; **USA**, 20 East 46th St, Suite 1201, New York NY 10017, T 2125572520.

● **Specialist tour companies**
Alpinschule of Innsbruck, In der Stille 1, A-6161 Natters, Innsbruck, Austria, organize walking tours based on Taroudant. The walks are not too strenuous and participants are taken to and from the walk by Landrover. *Exodus Walking Explorer*, 9 Weir Rd, London SW12 0LT, T 0181 675550. 7-23 day treks supported by guides and mules in the High Atlas. Winter treks in the Jbel Sahro. *Creative Leisure Management*, 4a William St, London SW1 9HL, T 0171 2350123 provide a reliable 'Morocco Made to Measure' service and will arrange whatever is required. *The Best of Morocco*, Seend Park, Seend, Wiltshire, SN12 0NZ, UK, T 380 828533 offer unlimited flexibility using quality hotels. *Nature Trek*, Chautara, Bighton, Hampshire, offer natural history and bird watching tours in S Morocco.

When to go

● **Best time to visit**
This will depend on requirements. Sun seekers congregate in the N between Apr-Oct and move S in the winter to places like Agadir. For sightseeing, from Marrakech S the heat can be oppressive during the day from Jun to Sep. Routes from Tanger are busy in summer with returning migrant workers from Europe in overloaded cars and are best avoided as is Tanger itself with day-trippers from Spain. Worst on Wed.

● **Climate**
In general Morocco is pleasant all the year round. Some of the coastal towns can be humid, particularly near rivers. Desert and pre-desert areas are obviously dry and hot, but from Dec to Feb can get cold at night. Equally, whilst the mountain areas are cold at night and during the winter, they can get quite hot during the summer days. Occasional but heavy showers occur turning the dry river beds into dangerous flash floods and snow blocks the high passes in winter. See Climate, page 67.

Health

● **Staying healthy**
Morocco is well provided with fairly reliable chemists, dentists, doctors and hospitals, although none is free. Addresses are to be found in this guide book, or via larger hotels, the **Syndicat d'Initiative** or the **Office du Tourisme**. For ambulances T 15. Most standard medicines can be obtained in medium and large-sized towns. In general Morocco is a clean and fairly low risk country – the worst experience being diarrhoea. Tap water is generally good, but the short-term visitor may wish to play safe by buying the very cheap bottled mineral water. Some rivers and oases have bilharzia, making drinking or bathing hazardous. Travel insurance, including coverage for health risks, is advised. Tampons can be bought at general stores in towns and cities.

● **Further health information**
Read the section on Health, see page 15 and be prepared for some stomach upsets due to heat and a change of diet.

Money

● **Banking hours**
Are 0830-1130 and 1500-1630. In the summer and during the fast month of Ramadan they are 0830-1400. There are also separate *bureaux de change* in the major cities, mainly of **BMCE**, often open for longer hours (0800-2000), which in theory give the same rates of exchange but charge different amounts of commission. There are several different banks in Morocco, with **BMCE, Credit du Maroc, Wafabank** and **Banque Populaire** all widespread. The latter is often the only bank in southern towns. Banking in Morocco is a slow, tortuous process, with several different desks for different purposes.

● **Cost of living**
It is possible to live in Morocco for US$25-30 a day. Accommodation, food and transport are all cheap, and there is a lot to see and do for free. Imported goods, notably cosmetics, toiletries and electrical goods, are expensive. Top quality hotels, restaurants, nightclubs and bars are similar to Europe. Rabat, Casablanca and Agadir are the most expensive places while goods in remote rural areas cost more. There are plenty of things to buy in Morocco, and the prices, if you bargain, can be quite reasonable. Sample prices: bottled water MD10, beer MD10, tea/coffee MD6.

● **Credit cards**
These are widely accepted at banks, top hotels, restaurants and shops, but it is wise to check first. *American Express* are represented by

Voyages Schwartz in Morocco, with limited services.

● **Currency**
The major unit of currency in Morocco is the **dirham** (in this Handbook: MD). 1 **dirham**=100 **centimes**. There are coins for 1 (very rare), 5, 10, 20 and 50 **centimes**, and for 1 and 5 **dirhams**, as well as notes for 5 (quite rare), 10, 50, 100 and 200 **dirhams**. Currency is labelled in Arabic and French. Most transactions are in cash. To the complete confusion of travellers, many Moroccans refer to **francs**, which equal 1 centime, and **reals**, which equal 5 centimes, but these only exist in speech. For exchange rates for Jun 1995 see page 7.

● **Currency regulations**
Foreign currency may be imported freely.

● **Eurocheques**
These are accepted in Morocco, and can be a good way to make sure one will not run out of money. Try at banks with the *Eurocheque* sticker.

● **Travellers' cheques**
These are usable in Morocco, although the traveller may be sent from bank to bank before the appropriate one is found. Use TCs from a bank/company that will be familiar to the cashiers, and preferably with UK, US, French or German currency, although this is not an absolute rule. Some hotels and shops will exchange TCs.

Getting there

Air

There are numerous scheduled and charter flights to Morocco, and reasonably convenient and quite cheap flights on from Spain or Gibraltar. A number of airlines fly to Morocco, and flights are fairly cheap, but only when bought outside Morocco. The state airline, **Royal Air Maroc**, is a reliable and not overpriced company which has large international and national networks. Its main services go through **Casablanca**.

● **From Europe**
Most of the major European airlines fly to Morocco, including **Air France**, **Iberia** and **British Airways**. The most competitive from UK are normally **KLM** and **Royal Air Maroc** (205 Regent St, London W1, T 0171 4394361). The latter also has flights from Amsterdam,

Athens, Barcelona, Bastia, Bordeaux, Brussels, Copenhagen, Dusseldorf, Frankfurt, Geneva, Lisbon, Madrid, Málaga, Marseille, Milan, Munich, Nice, Paris, Rome, Stockholm, Strasbourg, Toulouse, Vienna and Zurich. **Air France** and **Royal Air Maroc** offer cheap flights from Paris. Charter flights or package holidays bought in Europe can be a cheap alternative, particularly to Tanger or Agadir.

● **Fly-boat**
It is possible to get a flight to Gibraltar, Almería or Málaga, and then continue by boat to Melilla, Ceuta or Tanger. **British Airways** have London-Gibraltar-Morocco flights which can be booked in Morocco at their Tanger office, 83 rue de la Liberté, T 935211, or via **Menara Tours** in either Casablanca or Marrakech. Flights to Málaga are particularly cheap if one shops around and takes a standby.

● **From the Americas**
Royal Air Maroc flies between Casablanca, Montreal and New York.

● **From Africa and the Middle East**
In North Africa all the national carriers fly to Casablanca. **Royal Air Maroc** runs regular services between Casablanca and major cities in the other countries, including 6 a week from **Algiers**, 8 a week from **Tunis** and 4 a week from **Cairo**. From the Canary Isles (Las Palmas) there are direct flights to Agadir and Laayoune. There are 2 flights a week between Casablanca and **Nouakchott**. Elsewhere in Africa there are flights from Casablanca to Abidjan, Bamako, Conakry, Dakar and Libreville, and in the Middle East to Abu Dhabi, Jeddah and Riyadh.

Train

Train travel to Morocco is a relatively cheap option for those under 26, and a convenient way to tie in a visit to Morocco with a short stay in Europe. For those under 26 an **InterRail** ticket bought in any participating European country includes the Moroccan train network, and a reduction on the Algeciras-Tanger ferry. Travelling through Spain often entails extra cost, as there are supplements to be paid on a number of trains. **British Rail International**, London Victoria Railway Station, T 0171 8342345 (enquiries), T 0171 8280892 (tickets), only sell tickets to Algeciras, about £214 return. **Eurotrain**, T 0171 7303402, and **Campus Travel**, their agents for people under 26, T 0171 8284111, sell tickets from London Victoria to Tanger, including both ferry crossings. These are very reasonably priced from £219 return, and enable the traveller to stop off at any point on the fixed route for any length of time within the 2 month validity of the ticket. Rail entry from Europe is only through Tanger. Rail entry from Algeria in more settled times is at Oujda.

Road

● Car

See below for car ferries. It is compulsory to have full and valid Green Card Insurance, and this will be inspected at the border, along with the vehicle registration document and International Driving Licence (or national licences). The car will be entered in the drivers' passport, and checked on leaving the country, to ensure that it has not been sold without full taxes being paid. It should be noted that some car hire companies do not allow customers to take cars into Morocco from Europe. The minimum age of driving is 21. Car entry is not possible from Mauritania. From Algeria the crossing points are Oujda and Figuig.

● Bus

There are regular coach services to Morocco from Paris and other French cities. From London Victoria there is **Eurolines/Iberbus** to Algeciras, which takes 2 days, T 0171 7300202. Leaves Mon and Fri, adult £143 return, under 26 £129 return. Coach services use the Algeciras-Tanger ferry.

Sea

The many sea routes from Europe to Morocco provide relatively cheap travel. The principal passenger arrival point is Tanger. Other scheduled passenger services run to the Spanish enclaves of Ceuta and Melilla, as well as to the Moroccan towns of Mdiq, near Ceuta, and Nador, near Melilla. There is a commercial port at Casablanca, and some cruises stop here but there are no scheduled services.

● Between Algeciras and Tanger

The main ferry route between Spain and Morocco is the Algeciras/Tanger passenger and car service, operated jointly by **Transmediterranea** and **Isleña de Navegación**. This is very convenient for onward rail or bus transport from Tanger. Algeciras has regular bus services from Gibraltar and Málaga, both towns having cheap flights from UK. Algeciras has a train service from Madrid, and tickets can be bought from London to Algeciras or Tanger. The ferry

terminal, near the town centre, has a ticket office and money changing facilities. There are similar facilities in the Tanger terminal. The ferry takes 2-3 hrs, and there are normally between 6 and 10 services a day, either way, with some seasonal variation. **NB** Although services usually leave late one should allow at least an hour to clear the police and customs, particularly in Tanger. Be cautious about scheduling onward journeys on the same day, in view of the delays. The passenger fare one way is currently around MD200 (MD100 for children), with cars from MD600 and bicycles from MD200. It is cheaper to buy a return in Tanger than two singles, if applicable. Tickets can be bought at either terminal or at numerous agents in both towns.

The ferries are often dirty and crowded with the usual bars, restaurants, cafés and lounges, as well as a *bureau de change*. When travelling from Algeciras to Tanger all passengers must have their passports stamped by Moroccan border police whilst on the boat. **NB** This ferry service is booked solid in summer and around Muslim feast days. The conditions on board at that time **would prevent any chance of escape** in an emergency from overcrowded cabins where seats, aisles, corridors and exits are piled high with the passengers' unwieldy baggage.

The **hydrofoil service** runs Mon-Sat and takes 1 hr. Contact **Transtour**, T 956 665200.

● Between Algeciras and Ceuta

The connection between Algeciras and the Spanish enclave of Ceuta, which lies E of Tanger and N of Tetouan, is cheaper and quicker, but onward travel from Ceuta is more difficult than from Tanger, and accommodation is more expensive. Ferries are run by the same companies from the same terminal in Algeciras. There are between six and nine services every day except Sun, when there are five, the journey taking $1\frac{1}{2}$ hrs. Passenger fares are from MD146/2,200 Ptas, children 4-12 half price, car fares from MD600/9,000 Ptas, bicycles and motorbikes from MD150/2,300 Ptas. It is possible to buy tickets at either terminal or from numerous agents. Ceuta is a comfortable if unexciting place to stay, but more expensive than Morocco, except for some duty free goods. There is a reasonable number of transport options from the scruffy town of Fnideq, just in Morocco, and there is a *bureau de change* at the border. It can take a while to pass through the border. There is also a faster (30 mins) but more expensive and slightly less frequent **hydrofoil** (£30/6,000 Ptas return), 6 Mon-Sat, 4 on Sun, between Algeciras and Ceuta. Contact T 956 509139 or **Stirling Travel**, Gibraltar 71787.

● **Between Málaga or Almería and Melilla**
A long distance service from Málaga and Almería, leaving at 1300, plies to the Spanish enclave of Melilla. Fares are from 2,530 Ptas for passengers, 7,300 Ptas for cars, and 2,900 Ptas for bicycles and motorbikes.

● **Between Sète and Nador or Tanger**
Comanov run car and passenger ferry services from Sète in the S of France to Nador, adjacent to Melilla. Passenger fares are from MD1,390 (Nador) and MD1,200 (Tanger), car fares from MD1,700 (Nador) and MD1,340 (Tanger), bicycles and motorbikes from MD620 (Nador) and MD490 (Tanger). These are relatively luxurious services, running every 4 days between Nador and Sète from Jun to Oct, and daily between Tanger (leaving 1800) and Sète (leaving 1900). **Comanov** are at 7 Blvd de la Résistance, Casablanca, T 302412, F 308455; 43 Ave Abou El Alaâ El Maâri, Tanger, T 932649, F 932320; Immeuble Lazaar Beni Enzar, BP 89, Nador, T 608538, F 608667; **SNCM Ferryterranee**, 4 Quai d'Alger, BP 81,34 202 Sète Cedex, France, T 67747055, F 490545; **Compagnie Charles Leborgne**, 6 Quai François Maillol, 34 202 Sète Cedex, France, T 67745055, F 67743304. Bookings also through **Continental Shipping and Travel**, London, T 071 4914968.

Between Gibraltar and Tanger Direct services from Gibraltar run daily and take 2½ hrs. 1995 fares were single MD250/£18, return MD390/£28. Tickets can be purchased in Tanger from **Med Travel**, Ave Mohammed V, T 935872/3, and in Gibraltar from **Exchange Travel**, 241 Main St, T 76151/2, F 76153. Day tour travellers take precedence over booked return tickets – be warned. **NB** See note regarding overcrowding on ferries from Algeciras to Tanger which also applies here.

● **Between Gibraltar and Mdiq**
There is a weekly (Thur) catamaran service in summer between Gibraltar and Mdiq, a small town S of Ceuta, with regular transport to Tetouan. Contact **Seagle**, 9B George's Lane, Gibraltar, T 76763.

● **Between Faro and Tanger**
There are three car and passenger ferries a week from Faro, in Portugal, to Tanger, taking

9-10 hrs. Contact **ACP Viages**, 49A Rua Rosa Araugo, Lisbon, T 01 560382, or **Comanov**, 43 Ave Abou El Alaâ El Maâri, Tanger, T 932649, F 932320.

Customs

Visitors may take in, free of duty, 400 grammes of tobacco, 200 cigarettes or 50 cigars and such personal items as a camera, binoculars, a portable radio receiver, computer or typewriter.

● **Prohibited items**
There are severe penalties for possession of or trade in narcotic drugs: 3 months to 5 years imprisonment and/or fines up to MD240,000.

When you arrive

● **Airport information**
The principal destination is the much improved **Aéroport Mohammed V**, which is at **Nouasseur**, 30 km SE of Casablanca, T 339100. From here there are trains to Casablanca and regular bus services to both Casablanca (40 mins) and Rabat (90 mins). They drop and collect passengers at the CTM terminal in Casablanca, off Ave des Forces Armées Royales, and in Rabat in front of the *Hotel Terminus*, on Ave Mohammed V. There are also more expensive grand-taxi services. The airport terminal includes a restaurant, bar, post office, a **BMCE** *bureau de change* and agencies for the larger hotels, tour companies and car hire companies.

Agadir is the next major destination as large numbers of tourists fly there direct. **Aéroport Agadir Al Massira**, is a modern construction 28 km from the city, T 839002, with connections by bus and grand-taxis.

Other important international airports are: **Aéroport Marrakech Menara**, 6 km from Marrakech, undergoing improvements; **Aéroport Les Angads**, 15 km from Oujda; and **Aéroport Boukhalef**, 15 km from Tanger. There are also some international flights to **Aéroport Charif Al Idrissi**, Al Hoceima; **Aéroport Fes Saiss**, Fes; **Aéroport Hassan I**, Laayoune; **Aéroport Taorirt**, Ouarzazate; and **Aéroport Rabat-Sale**, 10 km from Rabat. All airports are well-connected by buses or grand-taxis.

● **Airport tax**
There are no airport taxes. On entry into Morocco vehicles and larger electronic equipment will be entered in the passport, to prevent

resale without paying taxes which can be as high as 100%.

● **Conduct/clothing**

Morocco is more relaxed than many Muslim countries and therefore it is possible to wear clothing that exposes arms and legs in coastal resorts. However, to minimize hassle, women are advised to cover themselves away from the hotel compounds at social occasions and visits in traditional rural areas. Full coverage of limbs and head is recommended when travelling in the heat. Winter temperatures can be low and night temperatures in the desert and at altitude are low all the year round so carry extra garments.

● **Hammam**

These are public baths where most Moroccans wash, relax and gossip and are worth a visit. The **hammam** is a succession of hot steamy rooms with plentiful water, and masseurs and assistants on hand. Men and women will either have separate premises or hours. Foreigners may be less welcome in some hammams than others – it is worth asking at the hotel, youth hostel or campsite for a recommendation.

● **Hours of business**

Working hours are normally 0900-1200 and 1400-1800. There are different working hours for summer and during Ramadan. On Fri the midday break is normally longer to allow for prayers.

● **Laundry**

Laundries and dry-cleaners are available everywhere, cheapest in the medina, where they are speedy but of varying quality. Hotels are expensive but reliable.

● **Monuments – entry**

Entrance fee to government run sites is always MD10 – except at Volubilis, MD20.

● **Official time**

Morocco follows GMT all year round, 1 hr behind the UK and a surprising 2 hrs behind Spain in summer.

● **Photography**

Many people, including Moroccans, dislike being a subject for a photograph, and it is very unwise to photograph women. People like water-sellers, musicians, animal tamers and camel owners expect to be paid for posing while small children will get in the way and then demand remuneration. Take great care near military or sensitive installations. Protect your camera from the dust and heat. Films are available for purchase in Morocco, but can be of variable quality. If possible purchase where the film has been properly stored or only recently imported. In selecting films and the camera to take remember that the sunlight is bright and the main subjects are likely to be buildings and scenery.

● **Safety**

Security Morocco is neither the most dangerous nor the safest country in the world. If reasonable precautions are taken the risk can be minimized. It is advisable never to carry valuables or large amounts of cash and to carry money and documents securely, ie in a money belt. Camp-sites are notoriously insecure places while hotels are normally much better. Never leave valuables in the car, and preferably entrust the car to a **gardien** for a small fee. Most importantly travellers should trust their personal instincts, and not go anywhere with anyone who seems suspicious or overly keen.

Airports and ports can be chaotic due to complicated bureaucracy and lack of order. Baggage is normally hastily checked. All papers should be correct otherwise even greater delays will occur. The traveller often arrives confused and insecure, particularly at the bustling port of Tanger, and this a favourite time for pickpockets and con-artists to strike. Do not believe a word the latter say, but go immediately to the hotel, railway or coach station already chosen.

Guides Travellers are likely to be hassled by guides often posing as 'students' or 'friends', and extreme caution should be taken in accepting help from these people, as it will lead to considerable expense (whatever the initial fee) and possible personal danger. The worst places are Tanger, Fes, Meknes and Marrakech. These people are often extremely skilled at the job, and have considerable linguistic abilities. Travellers will be well advised to use an official guide from the tourist office or manage without. The only medinas where guides may be necessary are Fes, Meknes and Marrakech. A much less threatening variation on the *faux guides* is the children in S villages who ask for money or presents, or who offer their help in exchange for a small remuneration.

Hashish Throughout Morocco, although particularly in the Rif, travellers will be offered hashish. It should be borne in mind that hashish dealers often tip off the police, and that there are considerable risks involved, despite the attraction of the cheap prices. The charity **Prisoners Abroad** supports a number of travellers who succumbed to the temptation – be warned.

Police Throughout the country the police are normally helpful to tourists, and there is no problem approaching them for directions. The traveller will have more dealings with the grey-uniformed **Sûreté** than the khaki-uniformed **Gendarmerie**.

Women should be careful when travelling in Morocco, and preferably should not travel alone. Hassle from Moroccan men can be quite heavy-duty.

● **Shopping**

Many of the main tourist towns now have fixed price shops, although some of these can be negotiated despite the label. The best is the *Ensemble Artisanal*, run by the government, which is normally a good guide to the range of products available, although it is a bit expensive. The best bargains, and the more authentic experience, are to be had in the *souqs*, the areas of traditional shops found in most historic cities. Similarly cheap and interesting are the markets which are held on a daily or weekly basis in large villages and towns throughout the countryside, as well as specialist markets in larger urban centres.

Best buys include leather goods, pottery. metalwork and woodwork. Essaouira has excellent carved cedarwood products. Pottery is best in Safi and Fes. In leather, belts and *baboushes* (slippers) are cheap. Jewellery was traditionally the preserve of Jews, but despite their emigra-

tion good pieces can still be bought. Carpets are excellent and come in a variety of forms, from basic rugs, to vast silk carpets, and reflect regional traditions. It is worth inspecting the weave closely. Chichaoua and Taroudant are good places to buy.

● **Tipping**

It is normal to tip waiters in cafés, restaurants and bars, who often receive a very low basic pay. In some more expensive restaurants service is included in the bill. Tipping is also advisable for porters on buses and trains and in hotels. It is optional with taxi-drivers, but recommended (10%) when the meter is being used.

Do not tip for taxi journeys where the meter is not being used, as the negotiated price will be generous anyway. For handling baggage in hotels tip around MD2-3, MD3-5 on buses and MD5 on trains and in airports.

● **Electricity**

Most of the country runs at 220V, although some areas are on 110V. International adaptors are a good investment.

● Weights & measures

Morocco uses the metric system. See conversion table on page 14.

Where to stay

● **Hotels**

Rooms are normally easy to find except in some popular places in peak seasons. The most difficult place all year round is Casablanca, where cheap rooms go early in the day. It is wise to

---

CAVEAT EMPTOR – THE ART OF BARGAINING

Most artisanal goods in Morocco are bought by haggling. This is a great skill in Morocco, and quite entertaining to witness, although less entertaining when the purchase price is considered later. There is the potential to be heavily ripped-off. Most dealers recognise the wealth and gullibility of travellers and start at exorbitant prices, so although the final price may seem to have involved the dealer coming down greatly, in fact it is the purchaser who will have paid way above the real price. It is better to be relaxed and get in a conversation with the dealer, taking time and inspecting the good closely. Do not be pressurised, and do not believe anything that the dealer says, such as the price he bought it at, etc. Do not feel guilty about ripping the dealer off, for one can be sure that he will not sell without making a profit. It is wise to compare prices and quality in a number of shops before buying. Walking away from the dealer normally brings the price down rapidly. It may be possible to exchange Western electronic goods or clothing for Moroccan goods and make a good deal.

HOTEL CLASSIFICATIONS

AL US$90+. International class luxury hotel. All facilities for business and leisure travellers are of the highest international standard.

A US$75-90. International hotel with air conditioned rooms with WC, bath/shower, TV, phone, mini-bar, daily clean linen. Choice of restaurants, coffee shop, shops, bank, travel agent, swimming pool, some sport and business facilities.

B US$60-75. As **A** but without the luxury, reduced number of restaurants, smaller rooms, limited range of shops and sport.

C US$40-60. Best rooms have air conditioning, own bath/shower and WC. Usually comfortable, bank, shop, pool.

D US$20-40. Best rooms may have own WC and bath/shower. Depending on management will have room service and choice of cuisine in restaurant.

E US$10-20. Simple provision. Perhaps fan cooler. May not have restaurant. Shared WC and showers with hot water (when available).

F under US$10. Very basic, shared toilet facilities, variable in cleanliness, noise, often in dubious locations.

reserve rooms in the top hotels in most cities. In almost all hotels, the night's accommodation ends at 1200, although some will be flexible in view of travel plans, and most will look after bags between 1200 and a later departure. On arrival at the hotel it will be necessary to fill a form giving name, occupation, address, date of arrival in Morocco, passport details, etc. Hotels in Morocco cover a wide range from the super luxurious hotels like the *Mamounia* in Marrakech and the *Gazelle d'Or* in Taroudant, to absurdly cheap and small establishments that have little more than a bed and ceiling. At the cheapest end the hotels (also called *auberges* and *pensiones* in some places) are basic rather than miserable. Moroccan hotels are classified in a number of starred bands from five down to 1B, with the remainder, the cheapest places, unclassified. It is advisable to see the room before agreeing to stay in all but the five and four star hotels. Unclassified hotels are often found in the old part of town, the medina, where there is often a problem with water. The more expensive hotels are normally in the new town.

● **Youth Hostels (auberges de jeunesse)**
11 in total affiliated to the IYHA, and a cheap option for anyone with a YHA card, are found in the largest cities: Casablanca, Rabat, Fes, Meknes and Marrakech, as well as at Azrou in the Middle Atlas and Asni in the Grand Atlas. The headquarters is in Meknes, in Ave Oqba Ibn Nafi. Overnight charge MD20-40, use of kitchen MD2, maximum stay 3 nights, priority given to people under 30 years of age. Opening hours: summer 0800-1000, 1200-1600 and 1830-2400; winter 0800-1000, 1200-1500 and 1800-2230.

● **Refuges**
In the High Atlas there are a number of refuges run by *Club Alpin Français* which have basic sleeping and cooking facilities.

● **Camping**
Sites are found all over Morocco. Security can be a problem, as can the climate. Sites are often poorly equipped, and far from the town centre, whilst they are often not much cheaper than basic hotels.

Food and drink

RESTAURANT CLASSIFICATIONS

Given the variations in price of food on any menu our restaurants are divided where possible into three simple grades: ♦♦♦ expensive, ♦♦ average and ♦ cheap.

● **Food**
Most Moroccan towns have cafés, some of which offer *croissants*, *petit-pain* and cake, occasionally soup and basic snacks. Restaurants will be divided into **medina** and **ville nouvelle** establishments, the former cheap and basic, the latter normally more expensive. Restaurants may be limited to larger settlements, those with a tourist appeal, or on major roads. Fast food outlets occur in larger cities. **Laiteries** and snack bars will make up sandwiches to order. Beyond these options there are food stalls and open air restaurants in every village, town and city serving various types of soup (normally the standard broth, *harira*), snacks and grilled meat. The best place for the adventurous open air eater is the Djemaa El Fna square in Marrakech, which is full of stalls in the evening. Another good place is near the

port in Essaouira, where fresh fish are grilled. Obviously there is a greater risk of food poisoning with this type of food, so it is better to go for dishes that are cooked as one waits, or that are on the boil.

Moroccan food in restaurants can often be simple, centred around meat, and somewhat dull for vegetarians. Real Moroccan cuisine, in top restaurants, or in houses, is excellent, and worth seeking out. The following are the main specialities:

Couscous is Morocco's most famous speciality, steamed granules of semolina cooked with various combinations of meat and vegetables. In some houses and restaurants this is reserved for Fri, the holy day, a very approximate equivalent of Sun lunch.

Harira: a staple soup, the exact composition varying according to availability of ingredients, normally involves vegetables, meat and chick peas. This is a filling and tasty snack available for a few dirhams in most restaurants and at many stalls or cafés.

Kebab and Kefta: the main meat in cheaper restaurants are *kebabs*, made of beef, mutton or lamb, which are also called *brochettes*. Minced meat, called *kefta*, is also common. These are often served with chips (*frites*).

Mechoui involves mutton roasted on a spit, and is often eaten at festivals. In restaurants order in advance.

Pastilla is most famous in Fes. This sweet layered pastry dish usually made with pigeon, saffron and almonds often has to be ordered in advance.

Salads are good, although risky, (see Health, page 18) in cheaper establishments. The local combination is called, unsurprisingly, *salade marocaine*, there is also *salade verte*, *salade des tomates* and *salade nicoise*. Finely chopped tomato and onion are a popular accompaniment to *kebab* or *kefta*.

Sweets Morocco has good pastries, although the quality varies. Distinctive are the coiled sticky sweets eaten at the daily breaking of the Ramadan fast. Try the yoghourt made in the local *laiterie*. Fresh *fruit* is excellent, and cheap, in season. Oranges are particularly cheap, as are prickly pears, sold off barrows.

With *tagines*, meat, fish or vegetables are stewed in a conical ceramic utensil, with combinations of potatoes, olives, lemon, prunes and spices. This very tasty dish is found in the top restaurants and roadside cafés, and will often involve local ingredients.

The speciality of Marrakech is *Tangia*, a tall ceramic pot in which meat is baked in butter, spices and olives for hours, normally in the embers of the local *hammam*.

● **Drink**

All over Morocco the main drink apart from water is **mint tea** (*thé à la menthe* or *thé marocain*) a cheap, refreshing drink which is made with green tea, fresh mint and masses of white sugar. The latter two ingredients predominate in the taste. **Coffee** is most commonly drunk black and strong, although the preferred strength can be requested. *Café au lait* (with milk) is common. For a half-way version ask for *demi-demi* or *nus-nus*. Prices in cafés are fixed by the government according to the quality. **Fruit juices** are excellent, notably the freshly squeezed orange juice (*jus d'orange*) available in most cafés. Similar, although less common, is grapefruit juice (*jus de pamplemousse*), and lemon juice (*jus de citron*), the latter to be taken with sugar. Altogether different are banana juice (*jus de banane*) and apple juice (*jus de pomme*), as these are in fact a sort of milk shake. Similar, delicious, although a bit less common are almond juice (*jus d'amand*) and avocado juice (*jus d'avocat*). Very good cafés may have strawberry juice (*jus de fraise*), pineapple juice (*jus d'ananas*), raspberry juice (*jus de framboise*), and a mixed cocktail (*panaché* or *mélange*).

Soft drinks are also common and popular, often called collectively *limonades*. There are many varieties, including *Coca-Cola* and *Pepsi-Cola*, both of which seem to taste different in Morocco, and lemonade, such as *7-Up*, *Sprite* and the local *Cigogne*. Still mineral water (*eau naturel*) is almost always *Sidi Harazem* or *Sidi Ali*. There is also fizzy mineral water (*eau gazeuse*).

Despite its Islamic status, Morocco is fairly relaxed about **alcohol** which officially is only for sale to non-Muslims. Imported lager, wine and spirits are readily available. Morocco also makes its own wine and beer, which are of course cheaper. The wine, in red, rosé and white, can often be quite good, particularly *Guerrouane* from Meknes, Morocco's main producing area. There are also some very poor wines. Moroccan beers, *Stork*, *Flag Pils* or *Flag Special* are all inoffensive lagers.

Getting around

Air

Royal Air Maroc and its subsidiary **Royal Air Inter** serves the country's major cities. The head office is at Aéroport Casa-Anfa, Casablanca, T 02 912000, F 02 912397. The network includes Agadir, Al Hoceima, Casablanca, Dakhla, Er-Rachidia, Fes, Laayoune, Marrakech, Ouarzazate, Oujda, Rabat, Smara, Tanger, Tan-Tan and Tetouan.

Train

The **ONCF** rail service is limited by the physical geography and recent development of Morocco. At present the track is single except between Kenitra and Casablanca and delays occur, but in general the service is speedy and reliable, particularly if the traveller picks the special rapid services. Between Casablanca, Kenitra and Rabat there are regular **Trains Navettes Rapides**. For Rabat the train is more convenient than the bus.

The network has three branches from Sidi Kacem; S through Kenitra, Sale, Rabat, Mohammedia, Casablanca, Settat and Marrakech; E through Meknes, Fes, Taza and Oujda; N to Asilah and Tanger. A weekly service uses freight lines from Oujda to Bouarfa, on the E flank of the country, N of the Figuig crossing into Algeria. In addition, **ONCF** buses connect with its trains, from Tnine Sidi Lyamani (just S of Asilah) to Tetouan, from Taourirt (in between Taza and Oujda) to Nador, from Khouribga to Beni Mellal, and from Marrakech to Agadir, Laayoune and Dakhla. Most train stations have *consigne* (left luggage depots) but normally only for locked baggage.

First class compartments are spacious and generally quieter than second class. Second class train fares are little more expensive than the Compagnie de Transporte Marocaine, CTM buses, and compartments are very comfortable. 'Economic' compartments are very basic and crowded, but quite feasible for the budget traveller. The trains normally have a drinks and snacks trolley.

Bus

Morocco has a highly competitive bus service. The government company, **Compagnie de Transporte Marocaine (CTM)**, has a 24 hr information service 'Allo CTM' on (02) 449424 for Casablanca or (02) 449254 for other towns. This company is by far the most reliable and comprehensive. It runs to a fixed timetable. Its buses leave on time and do not dawdle en route. Except for a few so-called 'rapid' services with videos, the private companies are normally cheaper and less comfortable, and far slower. The private companies do however reach some small places which CTM ignores, and will follow more difficult routes, such as the spectacular road over the High Atlas mountains and the famous Tizi-n-Test pass, between Taroudant and Marrakech.

Bus travel is confusing. Some towns have one terminal for all buses while others have separate terminals for CTM and private companies. Others have different terminals for different lines and destinations. Where tickets do not specify seats it is worth being early to avoid competition for the best places. Luggage will be stowed in the boot or on top of the bus, it is normal to tip the man for this job. For early morning buses it is worth buying tickets in advance.

Most larger towns have local urban buses which are very crowded, when pick-pocketing is a great danger. The buses are cheap, but then so are petit-taxis. The buses are perhaps only necessary for getting around Fes, Marrakech, Rabat and Casablanca, and for visiting outlying sites of interest, beaches and airports.

Car hire

Car hire is relatively easy in Morocco. There are international agencies and smaller and local firms, in most large towns. It is possible to arrange one-way hire. Before leaving the agency check that the car is fully equipped with all the necessary spares. Prices begin at MD200 per day plus MD2 per km or MD800 per day unlimited distance. The cheapest car is almost always the *Renault 4*, which is quite suitable for rough Moroccan roads. See Car hire details town by town.

Other land transport

● Bicycles/motorcycles
These can be hired in the larger towns. Cycling is a tough but rewarding option in Morocco, with four mountain ranges to confront, where mountain bicycles are particularly suitable on the pistes. There is no shortage of mechanics for either bicycles or motorbikes, as both are popular with Moroccans. Security will be more of a problem. City centres have **gardiens** who wear blue coats and tin badges and guard cars, motorbikes, mopeds and bicycles, for a small

	Agadir	Al Hoceima	Beni Mellal	Casablanca	El Jadida	Er Rachidia	Essaouira	Fes	Laayoune	Marrakech	Meknes	Nador	Ouarzazate	Oujda	Rabat	Safi	Tanger
Al Hoceima	1019																
Beni Mellal	467	564															
Casablanca	511	536	210														
El Jadida	419	632	271	99													
Er Rachidia	681	616	375	545	506												
Essaouira	173	887	370	351	252	745											
Fes	756	275	291	289	388	364	640										
Laayoune	649	1740	1116	1160	1066	1330	822	1396									
Marrakech	273	758	196	238	197	510	176	485	922								
Meknes	740	335	278	231	328	346	580	60	1389	467							
Nador	1095	175	628	628	727	510	979	339	1736	822	399						
Ouarzazate	375	992	398	442	399	306	380	687	1024	204	652	816					
Oujda	1099	293	632	635	731	514	983	343	1748	826	403	104	820				
Rabat	602	445	260	93	190	482	442	198	1251	321	138	535	528	541			
Safi	294	792	351	256	157	683	129	545	943	157	486	884	361	888	347		
Tanger	880	323	538	369	468	608	720	303	1529	598	287	1086	811	609	278	625	
Tetouan	892	278	536	385	484	602	736	281	1541	675	258	437	820	555	294	641	57

Morocco: distances by road between major cities (Km)

fee (bicycles normally MD1-2). Trains, buses, grand-taxis and trucks will take travellers' bikes for a small fee.

● **Hitchhiking**

Hitchhiking is possible, although it usually involves some payment. This is one of the main ways to get around the more isolated mountain and desert areas. Vans and lorries will pick up passengers for a bargained price. **NB** Hitchhiking is unadvisable for women on their own.

● **Motoring**

Morocco has a good road network, and plentiful petrol stations and mechanics, except in mountainous and desert areas. A 4WD vehicle is advisable for more adventurous exploration off the major roads in the Sahara and the mountains. Mountain roads are narrow and winding and should be approached with caution. The only fast, wide route is the toll road (cars: MD10) between Rabat and Casablanca. Roads are not heavily congested, there are few

private cars, but numerous taxis, buses and lorries that thunder down the roads at dangerous speeds. Driving and parking in town is relatively easy, although some roads within the old medinas are extremely narrow. Employ a **gardien** to guard the car when parking in cities. The only cities with traffic problems similar to western conurbations are Rabat and Casablanca. The overall speed limit is 100 km per hr. Night driving is more dangerous. Always drive with a good spare tyre.

● Taxis

Grand-taxis run over fixed routes within cities, between different towns and cities, or from urban centres to outlying settlements. There is a fixed price for each route, and passengers pay for a place, with six in a Mercedes and nine in a Peugeot. The taxis wait until they are full, but each passenger has the right to pay for the remaining places in order to leave sooner or have more space.

Between towns, grand-taxis are quicker

than trains and buses and normally only a little more expensive. Each town has a taxi rank, where someone will point travellers to the first car leaving for the appropriate destination.

Petit-taxis are used within a town, have a limited range, are normally small or medium sized saloons, and colour coded, blue in Rabat, red in Casablanca and buff in Marrakech. Officially they are metered, with an initial fare (MD1 in Rabat, MD5 in Casablanca) followed by increments for time and distance, and a 50% surcharge in the late evening and during the night. Petit-taxis may pick up to three passengers which makes fare calculation confusing. For taxis that are not metered, it will be necessary to estimate one's own fare. As a general rule most city centre journeys should not be more than MD5. Tipping is welcomed. Taxi drivers have very variable standards of French.

Communications

● Language
The official and predominate language is Arabic. A large minority, particularly in rural regions speak Berber, which has three distinct dialects, based in the Rif, the High Atlas and the Sous valley. Many Arabs and Berbers also speak Spanish and French, the latter being the language in which much business and politics is carried out, and the main vehicle for tourists. Street signs are in Arabic and French, and occasionally in tourist towns in English. English is becoming increasingly popular as a foreign language.

● Postal services
Letters to or from Europe can take up to a week. Posting letters is relatively easy, with the *PTT Centrale* of each town selling the appropriate stamps. It is best to post the letter in the box inside or just outside this building as these are emptied more frequently than those elsewhere. For those without a contact address to receive letters, instruct that they should be addressed clearly, with the surname underlined, to: Poste Restante, PTT Centrale, the town, Morocco. Each *PTT Centrale* will have a **post restante** section, where letters are kept for a number of weeks. There is a small charge on collection. Post offices are open 0800-1200 and 1500-1800 Mon-Fri in the winter, 0800-1500 in the summer. Some travellers use **American Express** offices to collect mail, in Morocco this is c/o *Voyages Schwartz*. Postage costs to Europe are MD3.5 for a letter and

MD3.2 for a post card.

● Telephone services
Telephone call boxes are plentiful. They are often very busy, and sometimes out of order. For internal calls put in several MD1 coins and dial the region code, followed by a 6 figure number. For overseas calls, put in at least 3 MD5 coins, dial 00 and wait for a musical sequence before proceeding. Most call boxes only accept the 'silver all over' coins. Calls can also be made at the **PTT Centrale**, or the *permanence telephonique* cabins where generally the number is given to the telephonist who dials it and then calls out a cabin number where the call is waiting. This is more expensive than the call boxes and can be a lengthy and frustrating process, particularly when dialling overseas. It is simpler but more expensive to phone from a hotel.

Calling Morocco from abroad the code is **212**.

Regional codes:
02 – Casablanca
04 – Marrakech and Safi
05 – Meknes
06 – Fes and Sefrou
07 – Rabat/Sale and Kenitra
08 – Agadir and the south
09 – Tanger

Fax and telex facilities are available from luxury hotels and the main PTT offices.

Entertainment

● Newspapers
Moroccan newspapers are produced in Arabic, French and Spanish. Although some represent opposition parties criticism of the monarchy is rare, as there is strict government control. In French *Le Matin du Sahara* and *Maroc Soir* are the most pro-government, whilst *L'Opinion*, *Liberation* and *Al Bayane* are more independent. These newspapers are cheap and give an insight into Morocco and its politics, but will have limited interest for the traveller. Coverage of overseas news is limited. Foreign newspapers are available in larger towns and cities. *The Guardian* and *Herald Tribune* (International editions) and *Le Monde* reach Rabat and Casablanca in the evening, *Le Figaro*, which is printed in Casablanca, the same morning.

● Radio
BBC World Service Radio broadcasts on short

wave (see page 13 for frequencies), although reception can be difficult in the night and morning. The commercial radio station *MIDI-1* gives news and music in Arabic and French. The state radio service is predominantly in Arabic and French, but has an afternoon slot in English. Northern areas can pick up broadcasts from Gibraltar, Spain and Portugal.

● **Television**

Satellite TV in some hotels provides Sky and other overseas channels. The few houses with TVs receive the state run channel, with programmes in Arabic and French. Others who have a decoder can get the commercial TV station.

● **Sport**

Golf is the favoured sport of the King, and boasts international tournaments. There are excellent courses at Agadir, Rabat, Mohammedia, Marrakech, Casablanca, Meknes and Tanger.

Hiking There are considerable opportunities for climbing and hiking, and in areas such as the Toubkal National Park in the High Atlas, guides are available. Specialist maps and guides will be useful to hikers.

Hunting and Fishing Wild boar in the countryside around Asni and Amizmiz; partridge and quail in the Ourika valley; pike, perch, roach, carp and trout in lakes and rivers.

Riding is a good way to explore the High Atlas. Riding centres are listed for most towns.

Skiing and mountain sports are being developed in Morocco at a number of sites in the Middle and High Atlas mountain ranges. The best places are the Mischliffen resort near Ifrane, in the Middle Atlas just S of Fes, and the skiing centre of Oukaimeden, S of Marrakech in the High Atlas. Both have ski lifts and good slopes, as well as equipment for hire and instruction. Mountain Information Centre of Ministry of Tourism, 1 rue Oujda, Rabat, T 7701280, has details of escorted and individual cross-Atlas treks.

Swimming Large towns have municipal pools but these can be crowded. In the summer the luxury hotels are very tempting, with their pools. There are occasional cheaper establishments with facilities. There is some good sea swimming, but beware of currents.

Tennis Morocco has an international tournament in Agadir, and excellent tennis facilities at larger hotels and tennis clubs.

Watersports centres are found in Agadir and Mohammedia. Essaouira is excellent for surf-

ing. Equipment can normally be hired. Salt and fresh water fishing is popular.

● **Spectator sports**

The major cities have arenas with Basketball, Handball, Athletics and Football. Check the local press for details. Football is seriously popular, with kick-arounds in the most remote locations, and an excellent standard on beaches and in town pitches. The national team qualified for the 1986 and 1994 World Cups. The national league is strong, with particularly strong teams at Casablanca (WIDAD and RAJA) and Marrakech (KACM).

Holidays and festivals

1 Jan:	New Year's Day
3 Mar:	Coronation of King Hassan II – celebrated with processions/ dancing
1 May:	Labour Day
23 May:	National Day
9 Jul:	King's Birthday and Youth Day
14 Aug:	Allegiance Day
6 Nov:	Anniversary of Green March
18 Nov:	Independence Day

The dates of the Islamic holidays and the fast, Ramadan, vary each year, as they are calculated according to the moon. Ramadan is strictly observed by most Moroccans, and it is advisable not to eat or drink in public during this period in the daytime. The breaking of the fast each evening is a very sociable and entertaining time, particularly when invited to a house.

Approximate dates in 1995:

12 Jan:	**Beginning of Ramadan**
21/22 Feb:	**Aïd es Seghir (end of Ramadan)**
29 Apr:	**Aïd el Kebir**
20 May:	**Islamic New Year**
29 Jul:	**Prophet's Birthday**

There are a number of large **moussems**, or religious festivals, each year throughout the country. The following are worth seeing:

Tafraoute	Feb – almonds
Immouzer des Ida Outanane	Apr – honey
Moulay Bousselham	May
Tan-Tan	end May
Goulimine	early Jun
Sefrou	Jun – cherries
Setti Fatma (Ourika)	Jul
Moulay Abdellah (El Jadida)	Aug
Moulay Idriss	Sep
Imilchil	
(Er Rachida)	Sep –Berber engagements

Further reading

● **Books**

Anthropology and society Crapanzano, V (1980) *Tuhami: Portrait of a Moroccan*, University of Chicago Press; Deshen, S (1980) *The Mellah Society*, University of Chicago Press; Dwyer, K (1982) *Moroccan Dialogues: Anthropology in Question*, John Hopkins University Press: Baltimore; Gellner, E (1969) *Saints of the Atlas*, Weidenfeld & Nicolson: London; Mernissi, F *Beyond the Veil*, London, Al-Saqi; Warnock, E *A Street in Marrakech*, Doubleday; Westermarck, E (1926) *Ritual and Belief in Morocco*, MacMillan: London, 1926.

Archaeology and monuments Landau, R (1969) *The Kasbahs of Morocco*, Faber and Faber: London; Burckhardt, T (1992) *Fez: City of Islam*, Islamic Texts Society: Cambridge; Paccard, A, *Traditional Islamic Craft in Moroccan Architecture*, Editions Atelier; Parker, R (1981) *A Practical Handbook to Islamic Monuments in Morocco*, Baraka Press: Virginia.

Food Wolfert, P *Good Food from Morocco*, John Murray.

Historical travelogues Cunninghame-Graham, R B (1898) *Maghreb el Acksa: A Journey in Morocco*; Harris, W (1921) *Morocco That Was*, Eland Books; Ibn Khaldoun (1967) *The Muqaddimah: An Introduction to History*, Routledge, translated from the Arabic, London; Lewis, W (1983) *Journey into Barbary*, Black Sparrow Press: Santa Barbara; Maxwell, G (1983) *Lords of the Atlas* Century; Meakin, B (1901) *The Land of the Moors*, London; Wharton, E (1920) *In Morocco*, MacMillan: London.

History Abun-Nasr, J M (1971) *A History of the Maghreb in the Islamic Period*, Cambridge University Press; Barbour, N (1965) *Morocco*, Thames and Hudson.

Politics Amnesty International (1989) *Morocco File*, Amnesty International: London; Hodges, A (1983) *Western Sahara: the Roots of a Desert War*, Croom Helm; Rogers, P D (Reprinted 1989) *A History of Anglo-Moroccan Relations*, London.

Short stories and novels Bowles, P (1982) *Points in Time*, Arena; Bowles, P *Sheltering Sky*, Granada; Bowles, P *Their Heads are Green and Their Hands Are Blue*, Abacus; Bowles, P *The Spider's House*, Arena; Bowles, P *Two Years Beside the Strait: A Tangier Journal, 1988-89*, Peter Owen; Bowles, P *Without Stopping*, Papermac; Burgess, A *Earthly Powers*, Penguin; Charhadi, D *A Life Full of Holes*, Grove Press; Chraibi, D (1972) *Heirs to the Past*, Heinemann: London; Choukri, M (1987) *For Bread Alone*, Grafton: London; Gysin, B *The Process*, Paladin; Hughes, R (1979) *In the Lap of the Atlas*, Chatto & Windus: London; Jallounn, Tahar Ben (1988) *The Sand Child*, 1988, Quartet.

Travel and hiking Brown, H *Great Walking Adventure*, Oxford Illustrated Press; Collomb, R G (1987) *Atlas Mountains*, Goring: West Col; Peyron, M *Grand Atlas Traverse*, Goring: West Col; Smith, K *Atlas Mountains: A Walker's Guide*, Cicerone Press; Winter, Bert and Mabel (1989) *The Rogues' Guide to Tangier*, Tanger.

Travel accounts Canetti, E (1978) *The Voices of Marrakech*, Marion Boyars; Mayne, P *A Year in Marrakech*, Eland Books.

● **Maps and town plans**

Simple town plans are printed in the brochures available from tourist offices, others are available from street kiosks in Tangier, Rabat, Casablanca, Fes, Meknes, Marrakech and Agadir. Maps of Morocco as a whole are best bought before reaching the country, notably from *Stanfords* in Long Acre, London, T 0171 8361321. Try the *Michelin* or the *Hildebrand* road maps. Topographic maps suitable for hiking are sometimes available from the **Division de Cartographie**, Ave Moulay Al Hassan, Rabat. Others are sold in the hiking base, Imlil.

● **Acknowledgements**

StJohn Gould who was responsible for much of the original material has again updated significant sections. Other acknowledgements to Abdelhamid El Abboubi of Marrakech; Abdelkrim Ouachikh, Regional Delegate for Meknes, and Tawfiq Baddou, Meknes Delegation of the Tourism Ministry; Abdeljalil Badrane and Ouadoui Fouad guides in Fes; Rachid, Fes Delegation of the Tourism Ministry; Royal Air Maroc and Creative Leisure Management for generous travel assistance; Abdellah Bennis at the Moroccan Embassy in London; Dr Mohamed Chtatou of ISESCO in Rabat; Mary Wall of California; Bob Kuehn of New Orleans; A Gandhi of Luton.

MAURITANIA

INTRODUCTION

Most of Mauritania is arid sand desert and most of its small population were until recently nomadic. Today the settled majority live in the two main coastal towns of Nouakchott and Nouadhibou, in scattered desert towns, or in villages in the wetter southern region near the Senegal river. Culturally it is a transitional region being partly Arab and partly African. There is very little physical provision made for the traveller but those who are adventurous enough to place Mauritania on their itinerary will be rewarded with a dramatic travel experience.

Indeed for the intrepid traveller, and desert enthusiasts more generally, Mauritania's austere but visually stunning Saharan-Sahelian setting has much to offer including ancient caravan towns, beautiful oases, Neolithic ruins, wild life sanctuaries and hundreds of kilometres of unspoilt beaches. Moreover, the almost total absence of hustlers, even in the large cities, makes Mauritania a particularly relaxing and safe place to travel, for both men and women.

CONTENTS

Introduction	240
Land and life	240
Culture	244
History	245
Modern Mauritania	247
Nouakchott and Environs	251
The North	256
The South	265
Information for visitors	270

MAPS

Mauritania	241
Nouakchott	252

Basics

OFFICIAL NAME   al-Jumhuriyah al-Islamiyah al-Muritaniyah (Islamic Republic of Mauritania)

NATIONAL FLAG Green field with large yellow crescent and star, placed centrally.

OFFICIAL LANGUAGE Arabic

OFFICIAL RELIGION Islam

INDICATORS *Population*: (1994) 2.1 million. *Urban*: 39%. *Religion*: Muslim 99.4% (mainly Malekite), Christian 0.4%. *Birth rate*: 48 per 1,000. *Death rate*: 16 per 1,000. *Life expectancy*: 45/51. *GNP per capita*: US$530.

Land and life

Geography

Mauritania has a surface area of 1,030,700 sq km, more than twice the size of neighbouring Morocco but half the size of Algeria. It spreads 1,287 km from N to S and 1,255 km from W to E. Its coastline on the Atlantic runs for 666 km from the delta of the Senegal River in the S to Cap Blanc in the N.

Borders

Mauritania has lived uneasily in its na-

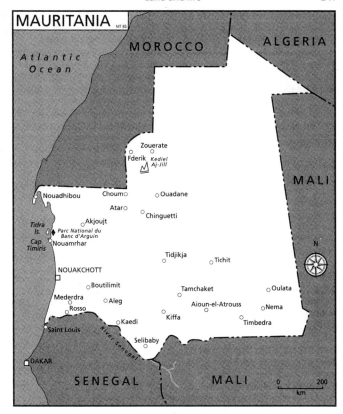

MAURITANIA MT 85

Atlantic
Ocean

MOROCCO

ALGERIA

MALI

Zouerate
Fderik *Kediet*
Aj-Jill

Choum Ouadane
Atar Chinguetti

Nouadhibou

Tidra Is. Akjoujt
Parc National du Banc d'Arguin
Cap Timiris Nouamrhar

Tidjikja
Tichit

NOUAKCHOTT
Boutilimit
Tamchaket
Mederdra Aleg Aioun-el-Atrouss Oulata
Rosso Nema
Kaedi Kiffa
Saint Louis Timbedra
Selibaby
River Senegal

DAKAR

SENEGAL MALI

N

0 200
km

tional borders, surrounded by more powerful neighbours. Morocco is a key influence in the N through its occupation of the western Sahara and until recent years also had territorial claims on Mauritanian territory. Mauritania gave up all claims to, and withdrew from, the western Sahara in 1979. Mauritania has no border disputes with Algeria in the NE, though Morocco has frequently claimed that Saharoui forces have operated from Algerian territory through Mauritania in their guerrilla war. There is a long international border with Mali which is geometric and permeable. In the S, Mauritania's uneasy

border with Senegal runs along the N bank of the Senegal River. The country's position as a residual Saharan territory between North Africa and black Africa is reflected in the uncertain border situation, its poor allocation of resources and the many claims by foreign interests upon its territory.

Major regions

The landscape in Mauritania is unspectacular in respect of altitudes, especially in comparison with Morocco and Algeria. It is formed by three large regions of rather uniform relief. In the N is a vast territory of low altitude, broken only by the occasional rocky ridge and sand covered areas where dune series are aligned roughly NE-SW. The highest point in the region is the peak of **Kediel Aj-Jill** at 915m. In the central zone, extending E to the border with Mali, is a vast basin where the rock series form scarp slopes facing towards the centre separated by gravel plains. Sand dune cover, in places highly ridged and attaining heights of 90m, is general in this area, with low points where salt lakes are found. The interior is at altitudes of little more than 220m with the coastal plains below 45m. The Mauritanian S is a narrow strip made up of the basin of the Senegal River, with richer sedimentary soils. Overall the topography is constrained, with the bulk of the country lying well below 100m.

Rivers

The arid centre and N carry few streams other than temporary *wadis* in spate after storms. Most drainage is internal to salt lakes or indeterminate seepage areas. Very little water reaches the sea. The exception to this is the S where the Senegal River drains the better-watered Mauritanian side of the basin in streams such as the Gorgol Al-Abiad and the Wadi Guélaour. The Senegal River is entirely within Senegalese territory and cannot be counted as a Mauritanian river but is considered as an international resource shared by member states of the OMVS (l'Organisation pour la mise en valeur du fleuve Sénégal), Guinea, Mauritania, Mali and Senegal.

Climate

Other than the region of the Senegal River valley, Mauritania receives negligible rainfall and is profoundly arid. Rainfall at Nouakchott comes erratically but principally between Jul and Sep and is less than 150 mm on average. Further N rainfall is even less, an average of less than 125 mm at Atar and 35 mm at Nouadhibou. In the S, the N rim

of the Senegal valley at sites such as Kiffa, receive 365 mm on average and the immediate river banks such as Selibaby approximately 390 mm. Most rain in the S falls in summer between Jul and Sep.

Temperatures in Mauritania are extreme. The coast benefits to a small extent from proximity to the sea as at Nouakchott, though temperatures of 45°C have been recorded there. In the centre and E, Saharan conditions prevail with very hot daytime temperatures but cold nights. The S has more tropical thermal conditions of the savanna type with less extremes both season to season and between day and night temperatures. Maxima run at 25°C in Dec against 30°C in Jun and minima at 18°C in Dec against 23°C in Jun at Rosso, for example.

The prevailing winds are the NE Trades, which are dry. In summer a shift in wind belts brings South Westerlies to the area and rainfall principally for the S region. Travellers should be ready to cope with the hot dry wind from the E, the **harmattan** in Dec, Jan and Feb, which pushes up temperatures and leads to rapidly diminishing relative humidity.

Flora and fauna

Animal life is, of course, sparse in the desert but look out for leopards, jackals, antelopes, gazelles and ostriches. The most interesting areas are the coast, and for birdlife particularly visit Parc National du Banc d'Arguin.

Agriculture

Mauritania was a country of nomads. Until recent years and the terrible effects of the Sahelian droughts, it is estimated that 85% of the population was traditionally nomads, semi-nomads and seasonally migrating herdsmen. Thus land use is registered in forms of pasture. The S is savanna grasslands with occasional trees, merging gently into the

Sahel, or 'rim' of the Sahara, where thin grasslands and drought resistant shrubs survive eventually fading out N into patchy scrub in areas where annual rainfall averages less than 150 mm per year. Here in the large regions of the centre, N and NE pasture is scant and confined to temporary pastures receiving erratic rainfall or to *wadi* basins. In recent years of drought all the pastures have been depleted by lack of rain and overgrazing.

Land use (1991)	(%)
Arable and orchards	0.2
Forests and woodlands	4.2
Pastures and meadows	38.3
Desert	57.3

Source: *Encyclopaedia Britannica*

Only a tiny proportion of the country is under permanent forms of cultivation – less than one quarter of 1%. The cultivated area is almost entirely in the S region of the Senegal except for pockets of oasis cultivation in the deserts of the centre and N.

Land tenure

In the past the complex land tenure system strongly reflected the hierarchical nature of Mauritanian society. In the case of the nomadic Moors, if pasture was not owned as such, access was determined by the position a given group occupied in the social hierarchy. The dominant warrior tribes collectively controlled most of the nomadic zones, while the few wells that existed were dug and owned by tribes of religious scholars known as *zawaya* who were obliged to provide water for the warriors. A third group, who were mainly herders, paid tribute to the warriors in return for access to water and pasture. The numerous palmeries situated in the oases of Adrar and Tagant were owned by *zawaya* individuals and families, as were the main zones of cultivation under Moorish control in the S. The oases and fields were tended by slaves and ex-slaves (*haratin*), as the Moors disdained physical labour associated with agricultural work. In the

S, in the areas where African groups predominated, elite African lineages owned most of the land.

During the colonial period the tenure system was slightly modified. The French encouraged free access to pasture, and built a large number of wells. The colonial administration did little, however, to change the land ownership system, which persisted into the independence period. Eventually, in 1983, after the devastating droughts of the previous decade, the government introduced sweeping land reforms. These reforms, which were designed to resolve the problems caused by increasing competition over land and water, became the source of considerable inter-ethnic tension.

Potential

Mauritania started its national life at Independence with a very poor and basic economy. However, the raw material resources are promising. In particular iron ore near Zouerate and copper deposits in Akjoujt, could provide the basis for a large scale extractive industrialization programme once political security and management of the economy is improved.

Despite setbacks caused by the drought, and economic mismanagement, the existence of natural resources suggests that the potential for dramatic improvement is considerable. Aside from the resources already mentioned, offshore the fish resources of the Atlantic within the country's economic zone are enormous. At the same time, provision of more reliable water supplies for arable farming offer prospects for the country being able to feed itself. The small population at some 2 million is a constraint on national economies of scale but also means that the state is not yet faced with an insurmountable problem of population growth and numbers.

Culture

People

The **population** of Mauritania was estimated at 2.1 million in 1994 against 1.86 million in the 1988 census. Growth is tending to rise slightly towards 2.8% as the fertility rate goes up. The crude birth rate is rising and the crude death rate is much improved but life expectancy at 45 years for males and 51 years for females remains poor.

Ethnic groups

The country's position on the interface between the Wet Equatorial and Arid Sahara zones is matched by its parallel situation as the meeting point for two worlds: one Arabo-Berber, the other African. Today, the Arabo-Berber Moors—who call themselves *bidan* (the whites)—constitute with the *haratin* (ex-slaves mainly of African origin) the majority of the population. They speak *hassaniyya*, an Arabic dialect, and until recently shared a nomadic way of life.

All Moors belong to a particular tribe in a ranked hierarchy. In the pre-colonial period warrior and raider tribes of Arab descent were supreme and tribute and taxes were paid to them by other social groups in return for protection, access to pasture and passage through territory under warrior control. Another powerful social category, known as *zawaya* (marabouts), was comprised of tribes of religious specialists (Islamic scholars, judges, mystics, saints, healers) of Arab and Berber descent. In addition to religious activities, these tribes owned most of the herds and slaves, organized agricultural enterprises, the caravan trade and were responsible for digging many of the wells. A lower rung in the hierarchy was occupied by tribes of *zenaga*, herding specialists.

The French occupation modified the social hierarchy. From the 1950's, tributary payments ceased and many of the *hassan* became involved in herding or commerce. On the other hand, *zawaya* tribes, with a background in religious learning and trade were the first to take advantage of the colonial education system and the commercial opportunities offered by the introduction of the market economy. Although some warrior tribes have considerable power in Mauritania today, all religious leaders, and most politicians and entrepreneurs come from a *zawaya* background.

Apart from a very small minority of Lebanese traders and professionals, of whom some are Christian, the remainder of Mauritania's present day population is composed of several Muslim African minorities—the Halpulaar, Soninke, Wolof, Peul and Bambara. With the exception of the Peul, who are cattle nomads, all the other African groups are by tradition agriculturalists living mainly in the S of the country, along the Senegal River valley, in Gudimaka and in the regions bordering Mali.

The precise demographic breakdown of the different ethnic groups is hard to establish due to the politically sensitive nature of this question in Mauritania. At Independence the *bidan* and *haratin* together made up about 75% of the population. This proportion has increased in recent years with the expulsion of African Mauritanians, and the return of Moors from Senegal during 1989.

Beyond their cultural and linguistic differences each ethnic group shares an adherence to Sunni Islam and follows the Maliki legal school. This common religious tradition and shared religious identity is emphasized in the naming of Mauritania as an Islamic Republic, and is frequently held up as the one key factor uniting the diverse population within the state. Indeed, although the Arabization policies of the Moor elite have become a source of increasing inter-ethnic tension, inter-ethnic religious alliances have remained important.

Distribution and density of the population

A sign of the effects of the drought and modernization is the growing urbanization of the country, with 48% of the population now living in towns and cities in contrast to a mere 25% some 10 years ago. The main towns are Nouakchott, the capital, with 393,325 people in 1992, Nouadhibou (formerly called Port Etienne) with 72,305, Kaedi 35,241, Kiffa 29,292 (1988) and Rosso 27,783 (1988).

A second feature of population distribution is the concentration of more than 90% of people in the southern zone where rainfall totals more than 100 mm per year – roughly S of the Nouakchott-Nema road. Here densities are comparatively high at five people per km sq but the national average is a mere two people per km sq. There is a slight seasonal bias to population distribution with the semi-nomads gathering in their millet and fruit growing lands of the S for the period of rainfall and agricultural activity but spreading N in search of pasture later in the year. In the N the two plateau areas of Adrar, N of Atar, and Zouerate are centres of small, relatively densely settled, districts.

Age groups

Mauritania, in common with most developing nations, has a youthful population. No less than 45% of Mauritanians are under 15 years of age, 50% in the principal working age group between 15-59 and only 5% 60 years and over.

Literacy

Literacy among adults, probably exaggerated by official statistics, is 34%, with a far greater proportion of men (47%) than women (21%) having had schooling. School participation rates are very low with a mere 10% of children attending at primary level.

Income per head

Mauritania is among the poorest (about 32nd in UN rank) countries of the world with income per head put at US$530 in 1992. While Mauritania seems to have avoided the very worst effects of maldistribution of income, there is a skew that benefits the new urban elite and those of the traditional leadership who also control land and water ownership.

History since Independence

Mauritania became independent in 1960. In many respects, the new state was a French colonial artefact in which different and potentially antagonistic ethnic groups had been thrown together. At the time of Independence the majority Moorish population were divided among themselves: some supported the pre-Moroccan Nahda party, founded in 1958, while others, including the future President Mokhtar Ould Daddah, opposed Moroccan claims on the region and favoured Mauritanian independence. Although a considerable proportion of the African minorities supported Ould Daddah's party, the AJM (l'Association de la Jeunesse Mauritanienne), others pursued an African nationalist line, and looked to the S for their political inspiration.

The Ould Daddah government

Mokhtar Ould Daddah, elected premier in 1959, became president of Mauritania in 1960. He replaced the long standing multiparty system with the PPM (le Parti du Peuple Mauritanienne) which remained the sole legal party until the coup d'état of 1978. Ould Daddah, from a prestigious maraboutic family, was an astute diplomat who, at least initially, attempted to steer a middle course between the demands of Arab and African nationalists. He placed great emphasis on Mauritania as the the link between Arab and African worlds. The first in a series of inter-ethnic conflicts erupted in Nouakchott in 1966 and in sub-sequent years Ould Daddah also faced protests from Moorish students and trade unionists who demanded reforms including nationalization of the mining industry and the creation of a national currency. After serious unrest in 1968, 1969 and 1971, Ould Daddah intro-duced a series of reforms, which met the demand of the protesters, many of whom then joined the PPM.

In foreign affairs, the Ould Daddah régime attempted to pursue a non-aligned stance, and enjoyed good rela-tions with most African states. This position was partly imposed by the re-fusal of virtually every Arab state, except Tunisia, to recognize Mauritania in 1960. By the end of the decade, however, most Arab régimes, including Morocco, had recognized Mauritania, thus paving the way for the latter's entry into the Arab League in 1973. During the 1970s Ould Daddah, who had enjoyed close relations with Algeria, switched alli-ances to support Moroccan claims to the former Spanish Sahara. Indeed, Mauri-tania was persuaded to make its own claim on the S part of the colony – the Rio de Oro or the Tiris Al-Gharbia – and, when Spain withdrew in 1976, Maurita-nia, after a short period of tripartite administration with Spain and Mo-rocco, took over the Tiris Al-Gharbia.

The Polisario Front, the western Saha-ran national liberation movement which, with Algerian backing, was fighting for the right of the western Saharans to self-determination, decided to direct its ma-jor military effort against Mauritania, by far the weaker of the two occupying pow-ers. By 1978, after attacks on Zouerate and even Nouakchott, the Mauritanian government accepted a ceasefire in re-turn for withdrawal from the Tiris Al-Gharbia. The presence of 9,000 Moroccan troops added to the consider-able domestic unrest and, in Jul 1978, Ould Daddah was overthrown by a mili-tary coup led by Lieutenant-Colonel Mustafa Ould Saleck. A succession of governments followed, until Colonel Mohammed Khouna Ould Haidallah took power, initially as Prime Minister in 1979, then as President in 1980.

In mid-1979, after a 9 month truce, the Polisario Front attacked Mauritania again, forcing the Haidallah govern-ment to negotiate a peace agreement – the Algiers Agreement – with the Po-lisario Front's government-in-exile, the Saharan Arab Democratic Republic, re-nouncing all claims to the western Sa-hara. Mauritania did not actually recognize the Republic until 1984, largely because of Moroccan pressure. Morocco, in response, occupied the re-gion itself and began to support Mauri-tanian exile groups.

Tensions between the two countries arose intermittently as Morocco ex-tended its control over the western Sa-hara during the 1980s, particularly when Morocco's defensive wall system abutted against the railway line from Zouerate to Nouadhibou after 1987. Mo-rocco also regularly accused Mauritania of allowing the Polisario Front's guerril-las to use Mauritanian territory in or-ganizing attacks on Moroccan forces. Relations between the two countries were eventually normalized when both joined the Maghreb Arab Union (UMA), a regional unity agreement signed in Marrakech by Morocco, Mau-ritania, Algeria, Tunisia and Libya in early Feb 1989. Earlier, in 1983, Mauri-tania had joined a mutual support treaty arrangement with Algeria and Tunisia.

Internally the Haidallah régime con-tinued to have constant problems. In spite of introducing a number of reforms including the abolition of slavery, the introduction of the Sharia in 1980, land reform in 1983, by 1984 Ould Haidallah had alienated most Mauritanians. In Dec 1984, the chief-of-staff of the armed forces Colonel Maaouiya Ould Sid'Ahmed Taya took power.

Although initially welcomed by Mauritanians, the Ould Taya régime rapidly ran into problems. Several of Ould Taya's plans, the Arabization programme, closer integration into the Maghreb and wider Arab world, permitting Moor entrepreneurs to buy land in the Senegal River valley, were viewed with great disquiet by African Mauritanians. In 1987, a failed coup attempt on the part of Halpulaar army officers led to three executions and life imprisonment for many others. Another alleged coup attempt in 1988 by pro-Iraqi Ba'ath elements in the army was met with further oppression by the régime.

During Ramadan 1989, anti-Moor riots and looting erupted in Senegal. As reports of these reached Mauritania, massacres of Senegalese and other West African nationals took place in Nouakchott and Nouadibou. These in turn led to massacres of Moors and *haratin* in Dakar. The subsequent international airlift repatriated over 200,000 Moors and *haratin* to Mauritania and over 60,000 Senegalese. In the backlash more than 50,000 African Mauritanians, mainly Halpulaar and Peul, took refuge in Senegal. Mauritania and Senegal broke off diplomatic relations, and by early 1990 were on the brink of war. The crisis strengthened the alliance between Mauritania and Iraq, the sole Arab state to lend their unequivocal support to Mauritania during the conflict. In return the Mauritanian government lent its tacit support for Saddam Hussain in the Gulf crisis, a position that led to serious problems with the allies, notably Saudi Arabia and Kuwait who were hitherto principal donors of aid to Mauritania.

In Apr 1991 Ould Taya, in a bid to shore up his credibility, announced, possibly under pressure from France, his decision to implement a series of democratic reforms.

Modern Mauritania

Government

Mauritania is an Islamic republic. A new constitution was adopted following a referendum in Jul 1991 which provided for a two chamber national assembly to replace the military rulers in 1992. The new constitution, which aside from references to Islam was largely inspired by the constitution of the French Republic, was approved overwhelmingly in the referendum, although black and Islamist politicians, who had recommended a boycott, accused the government of falsifying the figures. Nonetheless, political parties were allowed to form and elections were promised for the following year. A general amnesty was announced after the referendum for all political dissidents who had opposed the military régime. In subsequent months more than 10 political parties formed, all of whom, except the Islamist party (Umma), who had opposed the referendum, were granted official recognition. The first open presidential elections were held in 1992, in which Ould Taya, the incumbent, defeated Ould Daddah, the younger brother of the former president. The results were contested by the main opposition parties who boycotted the legislative and senatorial elections, allowing Ould Taya's party to dominate the 2-chamber National Assembly. In spite of continuing to question Ould Taya's legitimacy, the main opposition groups agreed to participate in local municipal elections in Jan 1994 when they did fairly well, particularly in the two major cities.

Despite its obvious flaws, Mauritania's democratization process has had positive effects, notably the creation of a free press, the easing of ethnic tensions and the reconciliation with Senegal, and has been heralded as one of the rare success stories in the region. The French in particular, disturbed by the debacle in Algeria, and instability in Mali, have given support to Ould Taya who they consider a stable force. This French seal of approval has led to the gradual international rehabilitation of Mauritania, which in turn has been a key factor in restoring internal confidence in the Ould Taya regime. Hence, while 1994-95 has witnessed a certain amount of unrest; the arrests in Sep 1994 of the Islamists, and riots in Jan 1995 after a 25% rise in the price of bread followed by the brief arrest of main opposition leaders, such events have posed little real threat to the régime to date.

Economy

Traditional agriculture

As many as 90% of the Moors were engaged in various forms of pastoral nomadism until the early 1970s. During the droughts of the 1970s, many herds, particularly camels, were sold at rock bottom prices to urban based entrepreneurs who hired the former nomads as salaried herders. A fair proportion of the country's 5.4 million sheep, 3.6 million goats, 1.4 million cattle, 990,000 camels and 154,000 asses remain, however, in the hands of nomads. Camel nomads are nowadays mainly found in the N and E, while cattle nomads, mainly Peul, are found in the Assaba and Gorgol regions. The Sahelian drought reduced animal numbers by an estimated 45% but there has since been a recovery. The nomadic herdsmen retain as many animals as they can and dispose of them only when they need money or when the pastures will no longer support the herds. The animal trade can be seen at Kaedi, Kiffa, Timbedra and Nema where the dealers and exporters are centred. In recent years the government has attempted to rehabilitate and modernize the pastoral sector and the World Bank has funded a project for pastoralist associations.

The country is not self-sufficient in grain and the loss of farmers from the land during the drought and the fighting by Polisario in the N made the situation worse. In the S, sedentary rainfed or flood based agriculture is undertaken by *haratin* or African farmers in the Senegal River belt, where the main crops are millet, vegetables and pulses. In the Adrar and Tagant date palm oases continue to produce important harvests. The palmeries are owned by Moors but tended by *haratin* who keep a share of the produce and are nowadays often paid a salary. Farming in the N is possible only with irrigation water withdrawn from cistern water-stores or from wells dug into the beds of *wadis*.

Modern agriculture

Some attempts have been made to improve the quality of pastoralism. The French colonial administration set up wells and fodder points in the N zone to help ensure fewer disputes over land and water. A veterinary service was also set up which brought about significant improvements in the quality of animals. Some small scale development works were attempted in the oases and a rational system of marketing and taxation was established. Some of this structure was lost as a result of Independence and the drought. The new government of Mauritania attempted to pursue food self-sufficiency as a goal and concentrated its efforts on the Senegal River area. Rice became the main crop on the 300,000 ha Golgol project which used water drawn from the Senegal River at Kaedi. The construction of a series of dams in the early 1980s made irrigated agriculture possible on a wide scale and attracted the interest of Moor entrepreneurs. Tensions between the latter and black farmers have been a major source of ethnic unrest in recent years. In spite of the introduction of irrigated agriculture Mauritania still spends over 30% of its available foreign exchange on imported foodstuffs.

Agricultural production 1992

	(tonnes)
Sorghum	50,000
Pulses	19,000
Rice	18,000
Dates	12,000
Vegetables	11,000
Millet	3,000
Maize	2,000

Source: *FAO*

Energy/petroleum

Mauritania produces neither coal nor petroleum and its electricity output of 146 million kwh is produced with imported fuels. A refinery produces 825,000 tonnes per year of petroleum products, inadequate to fulfil domestic demand. Imports of crude oil and products account for 10.7% of the country's total import bill.

Economic plans

A series of economic development plans has been adopted by independent Mauritania, beginning in 1963 with the first 4-year plan. Funds for the plan came from revenues earned from mining operations and from foreign aid, notably from Spain and China. The plan went far from smoothly and by 1966 it became inoperative. In practice, the various plans involved taking on foreign debt and the need for state management of large scale ventures which eventually overwhelmed the abilities of the government. The problems were exacerbated in 1972 by nationalizations of most trade activities. The impact of the Sahelian drought after 1973 brought the economy into an increasingly depressed state. This was worsened by the war in the western Sahara. Aid from the EU and Arab countries did little other than enable the country to survive. Mauritania is presently in the midst of an extensive World Bank/IMF Structural Adjustment programme and in late 1992, the Ougiya was devalued 28%.

Contrary to fears, the devaluation has not led to uncontrollable inflation and, with the resumption of financial aid from Saudi Arabia and the Gulf States, the Mauritanian economy now seems healthier than in recent years.

Industry

The principal industry in Mauritania is mining. The iron ore extracting industry is based on the Kediel Aj-Jill deposits which are limited and reaching exhaustion. Other low grade ores occur E of Zouerate but require large investments in new plant at a time of low profitability for iron ore exports. The iron industry is controlled by SNIM (Société Nationale d'Industrialization Minier). The Akjoujt copper mine began output in 1973 based on modest reserves of 28 million tonnes. Copper concentrate is carried to Nouakchott by a specially constructed road from a mining town at Akjoujt. The company, Somima, was less than successful as a result of internal difficulties and falling prices for copper on the world market. It was also nationalized and amalgamated in the state-owned SNIM. A shut-down occurred in 1978 but the mine has now reopened. Since 1991 gold is also being mined in Akjoujt by the Australian company, Morag. The mining industry produced 9.4 million tonnes of iron ore and 3,240 tonnes of gypsum in 1993. Other small scale industry relies on processing animal and food products.

Economic trends

Growth in the economy has been at about 5.5% per year in the last decade, obviously hindered badly by war, the Sahelian drought and internal mismanagement of the economy. National income was worth only US$1,109mn in 1992 and is still growing inadequately to outstrip the increase in population. Agriculture dominates the economy despite mining and the expansion of government services in recent years.

Structure of GDP	(%)
Agriculture	26.2
Mining	10.6
Manufacturing	8.8
Public Utilities/Construction	6.2
Transport	6.2
Other Services	42.0

Source: *Encyclopaedia Britannica*

Economic Indicators

Most economic indicators are adverse, including inflation at 9.4% (1993) and foreign debt at US$1.86 billion, far exceeding the annual value of total GDP.

ECONOMIC INDICATORS				
	1989	**1990**	**1991**	**1992**
GDP (UM million)	118.0	125.0	135.6	100.2
Inflation (1985=100)	93.8	100.0	105.6	116.3
Exports (UM million)	37.45			37.0
Imports (UM million)	29.17			35.3
Balance of Trade (UM million)	+8.28			+2.3
Foreign Debt (US$ billion)	1.86	0.99		1.86

US$1 = 85.09 Mauritanian Ouguiya

Source: IMF, EIU, *Encyclopaedia Britannica*

CONTENTS	
Nouakchott and Environs	251

MAPS	
Nouakchott	252

Nouakchott, capital since 1958, is located on the Atlantic coast and offers the best access both to the desert and to the Sahel. It struggles against the encroaching Sahara, is the government and administrative centre and has the best hotel, hospital and educational facilities.

Pop 393,325 (1988), more recent estimates vary but are usually between 400,000-500,000. *Alt* 1m.

History

Construction of Nouakchott began in 1958 as an extension of an old **ksar**, or fortified town, and a French military post. It was made capital of the newly independent Mauritania in 1960. Before this the French colony had been governed from St Louis in Senegal. Nouakchott was chosen as capital because it was in a neutral zone situated outside the areas associated with the most powerful Moorish tribes. At that time Nouakchott was some distance from the Sahara, but desertification has brought arid, sandy conditions to the edge of the city. Indeed Nouakchott with its pervasive dust, orange sand dunes, sandy streets and herds of camels gives the impression of a city not just trailing off into the desert but inhabited by it. The general impression is of a yellow haze/fog hanging over the town, particularly to the E. If it wasn't for the pleasant sea breeze that refreshes Nouakchott in the late afternoon, it would be easy to forget that the Atlantic Ocean only lies 6 km away. For the traveller arriving from overseas, Nouakchott is unsophisticated, with very few of the facilities and services normally associated with a capital city. Like the rest of the country, Nouakchott has a somewhat sleepy air, a city waiting for something to happen to it. Do not rely on the few traffic lights being obeyed. Traffic discipline is poor. The city is relaxed, the people are shy but not unfriendly, but has little to occupy the traveller after 2 or 3 days.

Originally designed for 12,000, Nouakchott's population has swollen as drought has forced people to migrate to the capital to escape from the difficult economic conditions prevailing in the interior. As a consequence there are vast areas of shacks on all sides of the city, some made only from waste packaging materials and containers. Many recent migrants use tents. Nouakchott has one of the worst cases of over-urbanization in Africa, with high unemployment and great shortages of basic services and utilities, as well as the housing dilemma. The problem is that Nouakchott has a

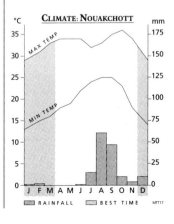

CLIMATE: NOUAKCHOTT

RAINFALL   BEST TIME   MIT17

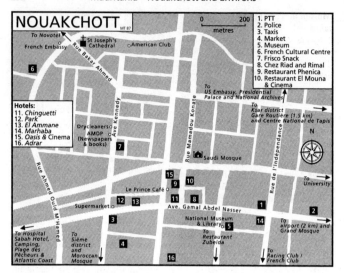

NOUAKCHOTT MT 87

0   200
metres

1. PTT
2. Police
3. Taxis
4. Market
5. Museum
6. French Cultural Centre
7. Frisco Snack
8. Chez Riad and Rimal
9. Restaurant Phenica
10. Restaurant El Mouna & Cinema

To Novotel
French Embassy
Rue Bakar Ahmed
St Joseph's Cathedral
American Club

6

To US Embassy, Presidential Palace and National Archives

To Ksar district Gare Routière (1.5 km) and Centre National de Tapis

Hotels:
11. *Chinguetti*
12. *Park*
13. *El Ammane*
14. *Marhaba*
15. *Oasis & Cinema*
16. *Adrar*

Ave Kennedy

Rue Mamadou Konate

Drycleaners
AMOP (Newspapers & books)

7

Saudi Mosque

N

Rue de l'Independance

To University

Rue Ahmed Ould M'Hamed

15   9   10
Le Prince Café

12   13   11   8
Supermarket
Ave. Gamal Abdel Nasser

1

2

3

National Museum & Library   5

14

To Hospital Sabah Hotel, Camping, Plage des Pêcheurs & Atlantic Coast

To 5ième district and Moroccan Mosque

4

16

To Restaurant Zubeida

To airport (2 km) and Grand Mosque

To Racing Club / French Club

very shallow economic base, with few vigorous economic concerns, perhaps a consequence of its hasty planning and construction.

The city of Nouakchott is located in a flat, sandy area close to the sea, and is centred around an older Moorish town, the ksar, and the modern town centre which has wide streets but few impressive buildings. Most of the larger public buildings are little more than functional. The city is, however, the location of most of the country's important commercial and industrial corporations.

The city has a large and interesting market area, as well as a long and pleasant beach, where travellers can take an invigorating swim or watch local fishermen at work. The construction of a wharf has made Nouakchott the country's second most important port, but in an economic backwater like Mauritania that is not saying much.

ACCESS Air The airport, 3 km to the E, now hosts a newly opened international terminal which has a café, shops and a bank. The old international terminal is now used for domestic flights only and has

minimal facilities, a drinks counter, a small shop, and a *bureau de change* which is occasionally open. There is no airport bus service. Travellers must rely on a taxi to the centre, 10 mins away, which may cost as much as UM300, after hard bargaining.

Road Taxi from Rosso, the SE or the Adrar terminate at the *Gare Routière* in the Ksar area of the city, not far from the airport. Either take a taxi, or ask directions to where the yellow and green minivans labelled *Transports Urbaines* will stop.

LAYOUT The airport and *Gare Routière* are in the Ksar district of the city. Ave Gamal Abdel Nasser is the main thoroughfare running into the centre and on to the sea. The intersection with Ave Kennedy marks the city centre, or what there is of it. Ave Kennedy runs from the government, diplomatic quarters and *quartiers chics* in the N to the market and residential areas in 5ième district to the S.

Places of interest

The City Centre Just off Ave Kennedy is the large covered **Central Market** selling a large variety of goods. It is best to visit here early in the day. There is a women's centre behind the market. Along Ave Général de Gaulle is the

Maison du Parti et de la Culture, containing the **National Museum** (1000-1200 Tues-Sat and 1430-1745 Tues-Sun), with ceramic and historical exhibits. There are few architecturally impressive buildings in Nouakchott. Perhaps one should see the two main mosques, one donated by Saudi Arabia and the other by Morocco but do not attempt to enter mosques uninvited.

The Cinquième district The most interesting area of Nouakchott is the 5ième district, an area of economic housing and popular commerce. A 5 min minibus ride away from the city centre, it is an enjoyable place to wander. The main target will be the market, a rambling area full of stalls selling everything from fruit and vegetables to handicrafts.

The Ksar is the old Moorish town of the Nouakchott area which was destroyed by a 1950 flood and rebuilt. It is a run-down area, with some traders, notably sellers of rugs. There is also a women's rug school, the **Centre National du Tapis**, rue Ghary, perhaps an expensive place to buy carpets but an interesting place to visit. On the road S to Rosso is the **Centre Artisanal**. It is a good place to look at and buy handicrafts. Along this road and the route to the Adrar are large areas of shanty town accommodation.

Tevragh Zeina, which means in hassaniyya 'the most beautiful place', is the area that lies N of Ave Kennedy. It is here, and in the adjoining *quartier chic* of Las Palmas, that the Mauritanian élite have constructed their immense villas, and is worth a visit if only to gain an idea of the huge disparities of wealth that exist in Mauritania.

Local information
● **Accommodation**

Nouakchott's hotels are very expensive, the grades indicating the price and facilities but not the general rundown, shabby conditions which prevail everywhere, and give little opportunity for economizing without misery. The **AL** *Novotel Dar el Barka*, behind the French Embassy, BP 1366, T 53526, is perhaps the best of this limited choice, with pool, bar, restaurant and a/c rooms.

B *Hotel Marhaba*, BP 2391, T 51838, 51686, Marba, a/c rooms with TV, also suites, lunch/dinner at UM1,500-2,000 and breakfast at UM500-800 in the restaurant, as well as a bar, snack bar, *bureau de change*, a small handicrafts stall and a pool.

C *Hotel El Ammane*, Ave Nasser, BP 13, T 52178, F 53765, reasonable rooms, adequate restaurant with breakfast for UM300-400 and meals for UM1,500-2,000; **C** *Park Hotel*, BP 150, T 51444/6, a/c rooms with balconies, a bar selling non-alcoholic drinks, reasonable restaurant with breakfast for UM300; **C** *Sabah Hotel*, BP 452, T 51552, 51564, Tx 821, is located 100m from the beach and 6 km from the town, with 40 reasonable a/c rooms and suites, a covered pool, a poor restaurant, bar, disco, free transport to/from airport (ask at the *Sabah* café), and transport to/from town.

D *Hotel Chinguitti* next to *Restaurant Phenica*, T 53537; **D** *Hotel Oasis*, Ave Général de Gaulle, BP 4, T 52011, restaurant and reasonable but overpriced a/c rooms.

E *Hotel Adrar*, is a dirty, smelly, shabby place doubling as a brothel, which although it is comparatively cheap and quite friendly, is only for the hardened traveller with a streak of madness.

● **Camping**

Camping is possible and permitted on the beach, 6 km W of the city, which is comparatively secure and safe. Camping costs UM500 per person. Huts which sleep five or six available for UM3,000. Common rooms available for lounging in but be very careful as the tea and coffee so readily served is very expensive and causes unpleasant situations.

● **Places to eat**

◆◆◆ Restaurants in the hotels incl *Novotel*, said to serve the best food in the city but is commensurately expensive and certainly not busy; *Hotel El Ammane* serves excellent continental food and is one of the most popular establishments in town; *Le Dragon d'Or*, opp Saudi Mosque, T 53211, serves Chinese food; *Park Hotel* also has a reasonable conventional menu at slightly cheaper prices. ◆◆ *Frisco Snack* serves western food and a few Lebanese dishes, a bit pricey, but clean and friendly with reasonable food; *Restaurant Phenica*, T 525-

75, standard European/Middle Eastern food, reasonably good and popular; *El Mouna* situated opp the *Phenica* is slightly cheaper and less rec; *Rimal*, Ave Gamal Abdel Nasser, serves Lebanese food, has pleasant terrace; *Sindibad*, across from the downtown market, has a wide range of cheap dishes; *Chez Riad* serves reasonable Lebanese food at good prices; *Zubeida* is a good Moroccan restaurant on Ave Gamal ◆ Abdel Nasser, although it is not very cheap. ◆ there are few cheap places to eat, but try along Ave Kennedy where a multitude of cheap Shawarma restaurants has opened in the last 2 years; *Le Palmier*, nr the market is economical; *Le Prince* nr Park Hotel serves good food, popular with locals.

● **Bars**

Are only found at the *Novotel* and the *Hotel Marhaba* where alcohol is not served. Alcohol can only be ordered at the *American Club* and the *Racing Club*.

● **Airline offices**

Air Afrique, BP 51, T 252084; **Air Algérie**, Ave Gamal Abdel Nasser, T 252059; **Air Mauritanie**, Direction Commerciale, Ave Gamal Abdel Nasser, BP 41, T 52211/2, Tx 573 AIRRIM, F 53815; **Iberia**, Ave Gamal Abdel Nasser, BP 727, T 252654; **Royal Air Maroc**, Ave Gamal Abdel Nasser, T 253564; **UTA**, Ave Gamal Abdel Nasser, BP 662, T 253916.

● **Banks & money changers**

Banque Arabe Africaine en Mauritanie (BAAM), Imm. Afarco, Ave Gamal Abdel Nasser, BP 622, T 52826; **Banque Al Baraka Mauritanienne Islamique (BAMIS)**, Ave du Roi Fayçal, BP 650, 4944, T 51424, F 51621; **Banque Arabe Libyenne Mauritanienne (BALM)**, Ave Gamal Abdel Nasser, BP 626, T 52142, F 53382; **Banque Internationale pour la Mauritanie (BIMA)**, Ave des Dunes, BP 210, T 52363; **Société Mauritanienne de Banque (SMB)**, Ave Gamal Abdel Nasser, BP 614, T 52602.

● **Embassies & consulates**

The few embassies in Nouakchott include **Algeria**, T 52182; **Egypt**, BP 176, T 52192; **France**, BP 231, rue Ahmed Ould M'Hamed, T 51740; **Germany**, BP 372, T 51394; **Libya**, T 52552; **Morocco**, BP 621, T 52304; **Senegal**, BP 611, T 52106; **Spain**, BP 232, T 52080; **Tunisia**, T 52124; **USA**, BP 609, T 52068.

The nearest embassies for other countries are in Dakar, Senegal: **Canada**, BP 3373,

T 210290; **Italy**, BP 348, T 220076; **Japan**, BP 3140; and the **UK**, BP 6025, T 217392, Tx 548.

● **Entertainment**

Cinemas: there are three choices for films, normally in French or Arabic, the *Cinéma Oasis*, the *Cinéma El Mouna* opp, and the *SNC Theatre*, nr the post office.

The French Cultural Center also occasionally shows films at its cinematheque, and also has an excellent video lending library. There are numerous video rental stores in Nouakchott, the quality of films, however, is often very poor.

Night life and live music: with the ban on alcohol and the need to get special licenses to hold public events, Nouakchott's night life leaves much to be desired. However, for the visitor who happens to be in town on a public holiday there are usually live concerts that feature Mauritanian and occasionally foreign musicians. These events offer a chance to hear the unusual but haunting music performed by Mauritanian *griots* (hereditary musicians) and meet Mauritanians. Apart from such events, most night life takes place behind closed doors, at weddings, baptisms and private parties which are well worth going to if one is lucky enough to be invited.

● **Hospitals & medical services**

Hospital: T 252135.

● **Laundry & dry cleaners**

Available at *Novotel* and *Hotel Marhaba* are very expensive. Better value from the various *blanchisserie* around the market and the dry cleaner in Immeuble el Mamy on Ave Kennedy.

● **Post & telecommunications**

PTT, Ave Gamal Abdel Nasser (0800-1230 and 1400-1830) for post, poste restante and telex. For telephones use the *Novotel*, the *Hotel Marhaba* or the cheaper *cabine telephonique* found throughout the city. Fax can be sent/received at *Novotel* and many *cabine telephonique*.

● **Shopping**

Books and newspapers: try *Gralicoma* or SLIM nr the market for books, or the boutique in the *Novotel*, or the *AMDP* situated in Immeuble el Mamy on Ave Kennedy for a wide range of press. The AMDP also sells French language books, although prices can be high. The French Cultural Centre sells French books on Mauritania at very reasonable rates, and also has an excellent specialist library on Mauritania. Another useful library collection is located at the Catholic Church.

Food: there are two supermarkets nr the *Hotel El Ammane* in Ave Gamal Abdel Nasser, which sell imported foreign foodstuffs at inflated prices.

Handicrafts: the best place to get bargains is the open market in the Sième district. Look for engraved silverware, beads, neolithic arrow heads, dyed leather cushions, carpets, wood carvings, hand-crafted leather tobacco pouches and local-style pipes. The various markets are also good for buying cloth such as the colourful locally dyed *melafhas* worn by Moorish women and the richly dyed and embroidered *bazin* cottons used to make up the *boubous* worn by Moorish men and African Mauritanians. Buying cloth can also provide an interesting opportunity for meeting Moorish women who run the stalls. Higher quality items can be bought in the *Centre Artisanal*, such as copper and silver jewellery, daggers, carpets, wooden boxes and chests; or from the dealers in front of the *Hotel El Ammane*. *L'Artisanat Feminin* (0800-1100 and 1600-1800 Sat-Thur), opp the central market, is a women's cooperative selling clothes, purses, pillows, leather cushions and tents. *Le Grand Marché* and *Le Souk*, off Ave Gamal Abdel Nasser, sell leather goods. The *Centre National du Tapis* in rue Ghary has a selection of expensive carpets.

● **Sports**

Fishing: the area is good for fishing, but equipment is difficult to find.

Softball: Fri at 0900, ask at the American Embassy.

Swimming: there are pools at the *Novotel*, the *Marhaba* and the *Sabah*, as well as the sea at the Plage des Pêcheurs.

● **Tourist office**

Direction à l'Artisanat et au Tourisme, off Ave General Nasser, BP 246, T 53337, ext'n: 368, 322, 374; **Société Mauritanienne du Tourisme et de l'Hôtellerie (SMTH)**, BP 552, T 2353.

● **Useful addresses**

Car repair: this is most likely to be in the Ksar district of the town. Try *Peyrissac*, on Ave Gamal Abdel Nasser, T 252213.
Police: T 17.

● **Transport**

Local Car hire: Avis, T 51713; **Cotema**, T 52352; **Europcar** T 51136; **Lacombe**, T 52221. **Taxis**: are generally green and yellow,

though there are considerable variations, and some surprisingly decrepit vehicles. Green and yellow minivans, labelled **Transports Urbaines**, run over the city along fixed routes, and are very cheap, often overcrowded and subject to frequent stops by the police. There are no buses from the airport to the town centre, taxis are the only option and will entail serious bargaining.

Air Air Mauritanie has international flights to **Casablanca**, and domestic flights to towns throughout the country. Times are very variable. Check locally. To **Nouadhibou**, daily (UM8,300); also **Aioun-el-Atrouss**, Fri (UM8,500); **Atar**, Sat, Mon, Thur (UM7,100); **Kaedi**, Wed (UM6,100); **Kiffa**, Tues (UM7,200); **Nema**, Fri (UM11,300); **Tidjikja**, Tues (UM8,400); **Selibaby**, Wed (UM7,200); **Zouerate**, Tues, Thur (UM10,100). Return flights are same day and cost double price of single ticket.

Road Transport to **Nouadhibou** is difficult as there is no direct road. The most practical way is by aeroplane. A cheaper option is by truck, which can be picked up from the 5ième district of Nouakchott. Trucks and *bâches* (converted pick-up trucks) leave from this district to Nouadhibou, Atar and Kaedi.

Excursion

Plage des Pêcheurs and the Wharf The Wharf is a small, old port, now mainly used by small-scale fishermen and artisans, with deep sea fishing and facilities available for hire. The best time to visit is around 1600 when the fishing boats return. This is a good place to buy fish. It has recently been developed as a small modern port. The Chinese built port, S of the wharf, is also worth a visit although access can sometimes be difficult. Fishing also takes place at the Plage des Pêcheurs, which is also a pleasant place to wander or swim. After the little sightseeing that Nouakchott has to offer this is the main place to spend time, a long, unspoilt beach stretching into the distance. To get there follow the black top road W from the Ave Kennedy/Ave Gamal Abdel Nasser intersection or get a green Renault taxi costing UM25.

CONTENTS	
The Coast from Nouakchott to Nouadhibou	256
The Adrar Region	259
The Far North	263

The coast N from Nouakchott to Nouadhibou, a distance of 525 km, contains some excellent beaches and some spectacular flora and fauna. It passes Cap Timirist and the *Parc National du Banc d'Arguin*, a huge reserve for migrating birds.

THE COAST FROM NOUAKCHOTT TO NOUADHIBOU

In this unusual country there is no black top road connecting the two main towns. Even the *piste* N from Noukchott to Nouadhibou is frequently undefined. Few vehicles (mainly lorries carrying water/fuel and trucks piled high with goods and passengers, few private cars) make this journey and most (perhaps 20-30 trucks a day) use partly *piste* and, depending on the tide, the 3m band of firm sand exposed on the shore. It is recommended to take a guide if aiming for Nouadhibou as particularly further N there are numerous vehicle tracks over a very wide area and the route to Bou Lanouar where one turns W for Nouadhibou is certainly not as clear as the maps indicate. Only 4WD vehicles stand a chance of completing the journey. It is possible, but quite unnecessary, to do this journey in 2 days. Allow 3 full days with 2 nights camping en route.

Officially one needs an authorization to take a vehicle out of the town and this may be asked for at the road check on the town's outskirts – but not of course if you drive up the beach from beside the *Sabah Hotel*.

Nouamghar, 155 km N of Nouakchott, a collection of about 200 shanties, is the major village of the Imraguen, a group of about 800 coastal dwellers who depend for their livelihood on fish, particularly mullet, the main season for which is Oct-Dec. The sea here is very shallow, the net is positioned into a semi-circle and the fish are driven into the net by hitting the water with large flat boards. The dolphins, frequent visitors to this coast, are always in evidence at this time. While it is romantic to assume that the dolphins are there to assist the fishermen, the more likely explanation is that they are only there for the food. Boats may be hired here but **Iwik** further N is a better place from which to visit the islands for bird watching.

The **Parc National du Banc d'Arguin** is a very significant site for aquatic birds migrating between Africa and Eurasia. They include broad-billed sandpipers, black terns, flamingoes, white pelicans, spoonbills, herons, white herons and cormorants. Some birds remain and breed here in this tranquil and food-rich environment. The birds often inhabit the offshore sand islands, thus a boat is required for proper birdwatching. The main entrance to the park is at Nouamghar. The man who sells the tickets is in one of the smarter shacks. Entrance UM800 per day. Just say for how many days. Once in the park—which is really no more than a strip of coast, much of it quite swampy, backed by a huge area of desert—one is free to ride. We recommend you to take a guide who will navigate across the erg rather than the very poor quality *piste*.

Trips to sail round the islands are best arranged from **Iwik**, another small collection of shacks 60 km N of Nouamghar. The main island is **Tidra** but there are many smaller ones too. It is necessary to consider the weather. The sailing boats can only operate if there is a wind but the birds are only there if it is calm ... so try to book on a day with a light breeze. The boat which can take 4-6 passengers will cost, after some hard bargaining, about UM10,000 for 4-6 hrs. Be firm too about the time scale as the boat owner will return you sooner if he can. There is much to observe without landing. Special permits are required to land on the islands and to walk among the birds. These are only given to genuine ornithologists. Restrictions to protect the birds from visitors in the breeding season do not appear to operate. Permits may be granted at Iwik but make enquiries both at the tourist office in Nouakchott and at the park entrance in case the routine has changed – it is too far to go back. For specialist tours to this area see page 271.

There are some cabins for visitors near the manager's house in Iwik although the two main camping spots are both N of Iwik, at **Cap Tafarit**, noted also for fishing, though jackals can be a problem here and **Cap Tagarit**, only 8 km further N, which is much prettier and has fewer jackals.

Nouadhibou

Pop 59,198 (1988), *Alt* 8m.

History
Nouadhibou, formerly called Port Etienne, is Mauritania's second city and the capital of the Dakhlet-Nouadhibou (Baie du Levrier) region. It is the most northerly settlement in Mauritania, on the coast, on the sheltered side of a peninsula shared with Moroccan western Sahara but administered in the whole by Mauritania. This is a very barren area of coast. Nouadhibou is the country's main port, with economic activities centred around iron ore and fishing, for this is one of the richest fishing grounds in the world. It lies at the terminus of the iron

ore railway line from Zouerate, which brings in vast amounts of this raw material, which is then exported in large ore carriers, from Port Minéralier which is S of the city centre. The state-controlled iron-ore company, *SNIM*, runs the railway, the port and Cansado, an autonomous settlement for company employees, 6 km S of the town on the peninsula tip. There is a substantial West African immigrant population, who arrive in Nouadhibou as the last stop, before the border with Morocco. Many seek to stow away on boats to the Canary Islands or Europe.

ACCESS The train from Choum or Zouerate arrives at Port Minéralier, S of the city centre. Taxis or the police will take travellers from the train into town. Arriving at the rather tumbledown airport (aptly described as just a more level piece of erg between Nouadhibou and La Gouèra), the city centre is a short taxi ride away, taking 5-10 mins and costing UM30-50. Coming in by road there is a customs post about 16 km N of Nouadhibou. It is not always easy to get through here and travellers report that sometimes 'presents' are demanded in return for the car documents.

Places of interest
The town, such as it is, has one main street running NS with minor ones parallel and alleys connecting across. To the

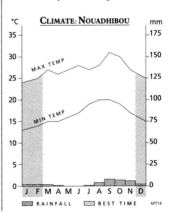

CLIMATE: NOUADHIBOU

°C / mm

J F M A M J J A S O N D

RAINFALL — BEST TIME

MAX TEMP
MIN TEMP

MTT18

N is a large area of shanty dwellings. The town has no real centre except the point on the main road at the taxi stand where there are some 2-storey buildings, banks etc. There are half a dozen restaurants and the liveliest area is around the shops. The town is unusual in Mauritania, because of its mix of ethnic communities, European and Far Eastern workers, particularly Korean, at the port and West Africans looking for work or a passage to Europe. This is reflected in the shops and restaurants around Nouadhibou. The Paris to Dakar rally passes through each Jan. Near the airport are the ruins of Tcherka, formerly occupied by the Canary Islanders. South again are the ports for cargo and fishing while the harbour to the E is noted for its 150 or so rusting hulks out to sea. South again another 6 km is Cansado where Mauritanians and expatriates have beach huts – perhaps slightly less run down than Nouadhibou. Further S again is Port Minéralier where the train line from Zouerate terminates and the iron ore is loaded on to boats.

There is no swimming in the bay to the E as it is polluted. Swim instead off the W coast. Monk seals can be seen off shore here but there are more on the W coast where they come out of the water. Between 50-100 such seals have been counted. Cap Blanc at the southern tip of the peninsula has a lighthouse, and good views.

It is possible to go on the W side of the peninsula where there is a very attractive beach with bays and headlands and a huge wrecked freighter. This attractive area which sometimes gets good surf, at other times provides good swimming. The bottom is very rocky. The Atlantic coast N along the peninsula has some spectacular cliffs. You will need a car to get there. It is not possible to go further N than **La Gouèra**, an old Spanish fishing village, as this is occupied by the Mauritanian army. **Take great care** on the W side of the peninsula. Although the beach itself is not mined do not venture on the dunes behind

the beach or the land as far E of the central border.

There are no maps available of the area but the restaurant *Le Surf* has some amazingly detailed maps of Cap Blanc peninsula on the wall.

Local information
● Accommodation
Nouadhibou has several good hotels, some of which serve alcohol. Try the **B** *Sabah Hotel*, near the airport, BP 285, T 45317/77, F 45499, with pool, disco and bar.

D *Hotel du Maghreb*, Blvd Median, BP 160, with breakfast at UM200 and lunch/dinner at UM1200, and a bar; the more economic **D** *Hotel des Imraguens*, 1 km from the centre, BP 160, T 2272, with 21 rm, restaurant and nightclub; and the **D** *Hotel Niabina*, rue Sonney, BP 146, T 45983. Apparently the Catholic Mission also has accommodation.

In Cansado, the iron ore company runs a good hotel, the **C** *Hotel Oasian*, Cansado, BP 42, T 2700, on coast, views of bay, 36 rm, three suites, TV, phone, frig, with a restaurant, bar and pool.

● Places to eat
Seafood is a popular speciality. Try ◆◆◆*Le Surf* in *Hotel Oasian* for shellfish; ◆◆*Le Marin* is good for fresh fish; *Le Cabana*, in the Port de Pêche, near the town centre, is a good bet for fish and other food. There are a number of bars selling alcohol in Nouadhibou.

● Banks & money changers
Banque Al Baraka Mauritanienne Islamique (BAMIS), BP 205, T 45663/4, F 45665; Banque Arabe Libyenne Mauritanienne (BALM), T 45132, F 45133.

● Sport
Fishing: Nouadhibou has good fishing all year, particularly of sea bass, sea bream, ray, umbrine and trout. Surf casting is very popular and there are fishermen in the port that will take enthusiasts out for a negotiated price. However, serious fishers will want to go to the *Centre de Pêche Sportive*, in the Baie de l'Étoile, 15 km N of Nouadhibou. This is a residential centre, with excellent opportunities for fishing, mainly surf casting, for an immense variety of species. The centre has eight double rooms, a restaurant, vehicles, staff and guides. *Air Afrique* organizes package tours to the centre, including the air ticket, lodging, meals and fishing gear,

from Nouakchott or Paris, and varying in length from a few days to weeks. Contact: Service Tourism, **Air Afrique**, 29 rue du Colisée, F 75008, Paris, T 42257169.

Swimming: there are good beaches on the peninsula.

● **Transport**
The easiest way to get to Nouakchott is by aeroplane, a cheaper way is by truck. However, as there is no road this is a problematic route. **Local** Nouadhibou has taxis to the airport, as well as to Cansado and Port Minéralier.

Air Air services from Nouadhibou include **Air Mauritanie** to Atar, Zouerate, Nouakchott (daily by airbus 300, takes 35 mins, costs UM8,300 single) or Las Palmas, and **Iberia** to Las Palmas. There may also be *Aeroflot* flights.

Train The trains to Choum or Zouerate leave from Port Minéralier.

THE ADRAR REGION

If there is only time for one tour, then perhaps the Adrar should be the destination, as it offers some of the most dramatic scenery and two historic towns.

The Adrar region is a large massif of mountains, plateaux, dunes and canyons in the N of Mauritania, with some breathtaking desert scenery. It is one of the most interesting areas of the country, an historic area of settlement, and a region where nomads have traditionally lived. Indeed, the Adrar has been occupied since Neolithic times, as stone tools and other remains testify. Its warriors were known throughout the area, and it

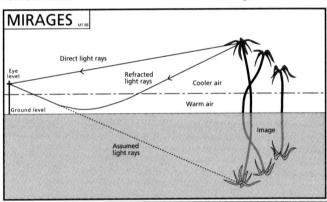

MIRAGES MT 88

Direct light rays

Eye level

Refracted light rays

Cooler air

Warm air

Ground level

Image

Assumed light rays

MIRAGES – ILLUSIONS IN THE DESERT

A mirage is a type of optical illusion caused by the refraction (bending) of rays of light as they pass through air layers of varying temperatures and densities. The most common mirage occurs in the desert where what appears to be a distant pool of water, perhaps surrounded by palm trees turns out, to the disappointment of the thirsty traveller, to be only another area of dry sand.

The rays of light that come directly to the eye show the palm trees in their correct position. The rays of light that travel through the warmer, less dense air travel faster as they meet less resistance and change their direction. They bend nearer to the ground but are assumed to have come directly to the eye so the brain records the trees and the blue sky as reflections in a pool of water.

The rays are real, just misinterpreted, thus a mirage can be photographed but that does not, alas, make the shimmering 'water' available to quench the thirst.

was the base of an Emirate until French colonization. More recently, the Adrar was known as a centre of opposition to the rule of the republic's first president, Ould Daddah. There is a number of oases, several associated with historic sites and towns. In the months of Jul and Aug, many families and individuals originally from the region descend on the oases of Adrar for the date harvest, known as *guetna*, which is a major social occasion not to be missed if you are travelling through Adrar during this period. In the oases and gorges crops are cultivated for local consumption, including millet, sorghum, barley, tomatoes and green vegetables, but dates dominate. However, as in much of Mauritania, the towns and cultivated areas are often threatened by encroaching sand. Cut into the plateaux are some impressive canyons, and there are some interesting ancient rock paintings. Travel to the Adrar can be by aeroplane to Atar (from Nouakchott or Nouadhibou), by taxi or private vehicle from Nouakchott. The only other possibilities, for the adventurous, are the train to Choum and then a taxi to Atar, or across the deep desert from Tidjikja, Nema or Ouadane, in a camel or 4WD vehicle convoy.

Akjoujt, although not actually in the Adrar, is the first town en route from Nouakchott to Atar, and stands at the end of the black top road. The 250 km black top road itself is of a poor quality, but will be passable by most vehicles in about 6-9 hrs. This town, which is the administrative centre of the Inchiri region, is based around the mines for the copper resources discovered in 1941, notably at Guelb Moghrein, which have since closed down. There are shops, tea houses and fuel at Akjoujt. The track from Akjoujt to Atar is not black top, but there are taxis.

Terjit and **Oujeft** could be visited en-route to Adrar, or as an excursion from Atar. Terjit, signposted to the right of the *piste* before Atar, is worth visiting, with its tree-lined hot and cold springs, where swimming is pleasant. A further 35 km S of Terjit is Oujeft, a scenic oasis with verdant palmeries and interesting archaeological relics.

Atar

Pop 16,326 (1976), *Alt* 226m.

This is the capital of the Adrar region, an old oasis settlement lying on the route of the historic salt caravans, and an important marketing centre for the nomads of the region, with an historic core, the ksar. The town has had a considerable colonial influence, and in fact there are still French there, at the Inter-Arab Ecole Militaire, for Atar is also a military base. Atar is a pleasant, relaxed town and a good base for exploring the surrounding region. There is a petrol station and basic provisions shops. Walk along the dike that separates the town from the rural area, and from the beautiful date palm groves that surround the town.

Places of interest

Atar is divided into an interesting **ksar** area with narrow streets, and a modern area of wider streets and bigger buildings. The **market** between has a small selection of things to buy, including leatherware, jewellery and rugs. There are also workshops for leather, jewellery and metal work in the surrounding areas of the town. Near the hotel is a **French fort** dating from WW2, as well as a contemporary military school. Exploration of the date palmery is interesting because of the use of traditional systems of irrigation. The locals enjoy the walk along the dike at sunset. This can be reached from either the town or the palmeries, or from the grounds of the hotel.

Local information
● Accommodation

Atar has a good hotel, the **D** *Hotel des Almoravides*, which has a/c rooms with bath, restaurant and non-alcoholic drinks bar, with a set meal at UM800 and breakfast at UM200. Ask directions from the town centre. There is also a basic and run down rest house near the centre. Apparently it is also possible to stay at the Catholic Mission.

● **Places to eat**

Apart from the hotel, basic meals can be had at establishments in the old part of town. The situation there changes quickly in these cheap places so be selective.

● **Transport**

Air Atar is connected by air with Nouakchott. Flights on Sat, Mon, Thur UM7,100 single. Taxis to/from the airstrip cost UM500.

Road A place in a taxi to Nouakchott costs UM2500, with driving time approximately 8 hrs. There are also taxis to Choum to meet the Zouerate-Nouadhibou trains, along a rough but just passable track. Land Rovers make the run to Chinguetti, these cost UM700 outside and UM1,000 in the cab. They wait till they are full and therefore do not leave every day, but one can take a Land Rover alone and immediately for UM9,000. The journey takes 1 hr. Places are also available on the twice-weekly food lorry to Chinguetti. The track to Chinguetti and on to Ouadane is not an easy one. A car and driver can be hired for 1 day, with the itinerary fixed by the client, for UM15,000. Travellers with their own 4WD vehicle will probably need a guide to get to Amogjar,

Chinguetti or Ouadane. For those with less time, there are some feasible short excursions from Atar. As well as Terjit, Oujeft and Amogjar which can mainly be reached only by personal transport, there are the ruins at **Azougui**, which can be reached by taxi costing UM50/100.

Excursions

Azougui lies along a scenic route, 15 km to the NW of Atar. This oasis has the ruins of a citadel, dating from the Al-moravid period of the 11th and 12th century, when it was capital of the Adrar. This was the base for conquests of the empire of Ghana, notably Aoudaghost, and the establishment of the powerful Moroccan Dynasty that toppled the Idrissids. Close to the citadel is the Al-moravid Imam Hadrami's necropolis.

Amorgar (or Amogjar) is a mountain pass 70 km along the track from Atar to Chinguetti, the summit of the Adrar plateau which has impressive views. A day excursion from Atar is a spectacular experience, passing through dramatic mountain scenery. En route there are fortifications marking Mauritania's period of involvement in the W Sahara war. Near the pass itself, to the left of the track are rock paintings of suns, giraffes, cows and hunters. These are of great antiquity but still discernable. The verdant landscape depicted in the paintings indicates how the environment of the region has changed. 6 km further on, on the right, are some more curious rock paintings. From the rock paintings, return to Atar or continue along the rough *piste* to Chinguetti.

Chinguetti

Mauritania's most famous historic city, Chinguetti dates from the 13th century. Named 'Shinqit' in Arabic, a name also used for the whole country before the French colonization. It is located on the salt caravan route. It was both a Moorish capital and a religious centre famous around the Islamic World, and reckoned

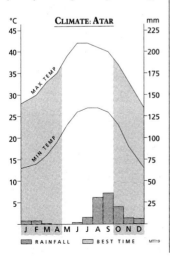

°C — CLIMATE: ATAR — mm

MAX TEMP

MIN TEMP

J F M A M J J A S O N D

▬ RAINFALL   ▭ BEST TIME   MTT19

to be Islam's seventh city. It was the point where the pilgrims from the region gathered for the caravan across Africa to Mecca. Chinguetti was known for its poets and Islamic scholars, and still has an important mosque and libraries. The town is now declining both in status and in physical terms with erosion, being literally worn away by or covered with the sand. The visitor arrives first in the newer area of the town. The fort in Chinguetti, originally occupied by the Foreign Legion, was used in *Fort Saganne*, a French film from the early 1980s. Near the fort there is also a curious non-functional solar demonstration pump, and the police station, where travellers are required to register.

Across the *wadi* is the old town, with its impressive stone buildings. It is still owned today mainly by members of the Idaw'ali and Laghlal *zawaya* tribes. The 16th century mosque is famous and quite striking, but closed to non-Muslims, although views of it from around the town should satisfy the curiosity. Its minaret has five pinnacles, each surmounted by the *oeufs d'autruche* (ostrich eggs). The principal Koranic library has some 1,300 ancient manuscripts, some as old as the 3rd century. The market displays some interesting items to buy, including ancient tools and arrow heads.

● **Accommodation** Accommodation is in the basic **E** *Maison du Bien Etre*, the even more basic *Auberge des Caravanes*, or with local people who will share what little they have. There is nowhere to eat, but food can be bought at the market stalls or shops.

● **Transport** Travel on to Ouadane is over a rough desert *piste* that leaves the *piste* from Atar just before the town. Follow either the 120 km *Piste du Dhar Chinguetti*, or the *Piste du Batha* over sand dunes. Both require a 4WD vehicle, the latter a guide too. There are few vehicles making the journey.

Ouadane

In a country of ruins Ouadane is one of the most impressive, a hillside of stone buildings in a dramatic landscape above a beautiful palmery. It is rewarding at

---

CAMELS – SHIPS OF THE DESERT

There are two kinds of camel, *Camelus Dromedarius*, the Arabian camel with one hump and *Camelus Bactrianus*, the Bactrian which has two. Arabian camels, found in North Africa, though only as domestic animals, are about 3m long and about 2m high at the shoulder. They range in colour from white to black.

They are not the most attractive of creatures, looking particularly ragged and scruffy at the spring moult. Large bare leathery areas on legs and chest look like some serious skin complaint but are normal and act as cushions when the animal kneels down.

Interesting physical characteristics which allow these animals to survive in the desert include hairs inside the ear opening as well as the ability to close the nostrils between breaths, both preventing sand penetration; thick eyebrows to shade the eyes from the sun's glare; a pad of skin between the two large toes on each foot forming a broad, tough 'slipper' which spreads the animal's weight over a larger area and prevents sinking in the loose sand; the ability to store a reserve of fat in the hump and to go for days without water. Each eye has three eyelids, the upper and lower lids have very long eyelashes to protect the eyes from sand whipped up by desert winds, while a third, thinner lid blinks away dust from the eyeball. The skin inside a camel's mouth is so tough that cactus thorns do not penetrate, hence a camel can eat anything, 'even its owner's tent'.

Camels can go for many days without food as the hump can store up to 35 kilos of fat as emergency rations. They can go without water for even longer,

the end of the long journey from Atar via Chinguetti, but only the dedicated travellers will make it. The town of Ouadane dates from either the 9th or the 12th century, according to different accounts. Some of its earliest inhabitants were the Berber Idawalhaj tribe. Today Ouadane is still home to Idawalhaj families as well as members of the Kunta and Amgarish tribes. Ouadane soon became an important and prosperous camel caravan centre, located as it was between the West African states and the trade routes to the N. These caravans were mainly taken up with salt, dates and gold. Even the Portuguese recognized its economic importance, setting up a significant trading post in the 15th century. However, Ouadane's location in the N of Mauritania meant that it suffered more than most places from the conquests of the powerful Moroccan Dynasties, the Saadians and the Alawites.

There are beautiful views from Ouadane's hill location, over the oasis, palm groves and surrounding desert areas. The ruins include a mosque and the Ksar el Klali. Other than basic rest house accommodation in Ouadane, which may be available, travellers will be dependent on the hospitality of the locals.

Tinlabbé

Whilst in Ouadane travellers should not miss the opportunity to visit the cave dwellings and rock paintings of Tinlabbé, 7 km NW of the town. Ask directions in Ouadane. It's a long, hot walk but worth it.

THE FAR NORTH

Mauritania reaches a considerable distance N, its joint border with Algeria and Morocco is parallel with Laayoune in Morocco and In Salah in Algeria. In this immense area of generally low-lying land the massif of Kediel Aj-Jill at 915m is conspicuous. The towns associated with the exploitation of the iron ore in this massif are the only settlements in the region.

depending on the weather and the kind of food available. As camels do not sweat but instead function at a higher body temperature without brain damage, their demands of fluid are less. At a water hole they drink only enough to balance their body moisture content.

Less pleasant characteristics include a most unpredictable nature, especially in the mating season, which includes nasty habits like using its long sharp teeth to bite people and other camels, viciously kicking with the back legs, spitting and being generally awkward. When a camel stands up it moves in a series of violent jerks as it straightens first its hind legs then its front legs. When a camel walks, it moves both the legs at one side at the same time, giving a very rolling motion which can give the rider travel sickness.

Camels are unwilling beasts of burden, grunting and groaning as they are loaded and generally complaining at being made to lie down or stand up. Once underway though, they move without further protest.

These large, strong beasts are used to pull ploughs, turn water wheels and carry large loads for long distances across difficult terrain. They can carry up to 400 kg but usually the load is nearer 200 kg. Despite moving at a mere 5 or 6 km an hour, camels can travel 100 km in a day. They also provide their owners with hair for cloth, rich milk and cheese, dried dung fuel and eventually meat, bones for utensils and hides for shoes, bags and tenting.

The Arabian dromedary, bred for riding and racing, is of a slighter build but can cover 160 km in a day and reach speeds of up to 15 km per hour.

Choum can be reached by a rough, bumpy, but often spectacular taxi journey of 120 km from Atar. The only reason to go to Choum is because of the Zouerate to Nouadhibou train line. Choum has basic tea tents/houses where travellers wait for the train.

Zouerate, 190 km N from Choum, with the associated settlement of Fderik, and formerly Fort Gouraud, used to be on the western caravan route across the Sahara. It has grown to a population of 22,500 (1992), as a town devoted to iron ore mining, the centre of that activity in Mauritania, and at the end of the long iron ore railway to Nouadhibou. There is little of interest in the town, but for those visiting, the mining company runs a hotel and restaurant. Transport runs as far as the town, but onward travel is impossible because of problems in the western Sahara. There are flights to Nouakchott on Tues and Thur, UM10,100 single.

Bir-Moghrein, formerly called Fort Trinquet, used to be a caravan post. It has a rest house and rock paintings which ought not to be missed if you have got so far. Located 400 km N from Zouerate, one needs **permission from the police** in Nouakchott to go this far.

Zouerate, Choum & Nouadhibou

The state iron ore company has a railway line between the iron ore mines at Zouerate and the port at Nouadhibou. It runs two daily trains each way. These trains are, at 2.5 km, the longest in the world. The train consists mainly of open wagons of iron ore. However there is often, but not always, a passenger wagon attached, tickets being reasonably priced, about UM300. Many Mauritanians choose to travel for free on top of the iron ore rubble. Indeed this is the only means when a passenger wagon is not laid on. This is a most dramatic way to travel, perhaps one of the world's memorable journeys, if not just for the serious discomfort of the swirling invasive dust, and at night, the biting cold. Take warm clothes and preferably a blanket or sleeping bag, a plastic sheet to lie on, a scarf to wrap tightly round the mouth and eyes, and food and water. The train also stops at Choum, with one of the services leaving at about 1800 for Nouadhibou. The taxi will take its passengers to the train. The train journey from Choum to Nouadhibou takes about 12 hrs.

THE SOUTH

CONTENTS

The Route de L'Espoir	265
The Tagant Region	267
The Senegal valley	268

Southern Mauritania which experiences winter rains in varied proportions encompasses very diverse regions, dunes and sandstone plateaux with villagers dependent on livestock rearing, small areas of cereal cultivation and bare rock outcrops. In the extreme S the Senegal River valley contains areas of sedentary agriculture, even irrigation.

THE ROUTE DE L'ESPOIR

The Route de l'Espoir, the Road of Hope, was built by the Brazilians. It connects the S and SE of the country to Nouakchott. The building of this road means that it is now significantly quicker for the people of these regions to reach the capital. As a consequence, migration from the rural areas, where livelihoods are difficult to maintain, has rapidly increased to the capital where there is the dream of gainful employment, but the reality of great hardship. Along the road lie a succession of towns, of varying interest, but with the advantage of comparatively frequent transport. It is possible to complete the Route de l'Espoir to Nema in 2 days, but why go so fast? Off the road there are interesting detours to the Tagant region, the Koumbi Saleh archaeological site, and the desert religious centre of Oualata with its beautiful houses.

Boutilimit is the first town along the road, 265 km and 2 hrs from Nouakchott. It was founded in the 19th century by a religious scholar and mystic, and remains today one of the most renowned centres for religious learning in the region with several *medressa* still functioning. This century it had fame as the birthplace of the country's first president, Mokhtar Ould Daddah. The town is now also known as the location of an Institute for Higher Islamic Studies, an important centre in West Africa. Boutilimit has a large **market**, which is worth seeing as the town is known for its craftwork, particularly silverware and rugs.

After **Aleg**, the centre of the Brakna region but an unexpected place where taxis often stop for tea breaks, the next major settlement is **Kiffa**, population: 29,292 (1988), the main town, administrative centre and market of the Assaba region. The town is connected by an air service with Nouakchott each Tues, UM7,200 single. It has little to see except a reasonably interesting market, with some local handicrafts for sale. However the town does have accommodation, at the **D** *Hotel de l'Amitié et du Tourisme à Kiffa*, BP 46, T 233, meals UM200-500, a well-run place with electricity but no air-conditioning, and clean, basic rooms with just a mattress, and a separate shower room. The alternative is to stay with local people.

From Kiffa two routes lead off to the N. It is not a great problem to find transport along the 120 km deviation NE to **Tamchaket** but **Tagdawst**, the archaeological site of the Sanhadja Berber capital of Aoudaghost, 40 km further, is only reachable by those with their own transport. This was a very important trading city, through which passed large caravans of horses and bullocks from Morocco from at least 500 BC, and which attained greater prosperity with the arrival of the camel as a transport animal from the 3rd century AD. The city retained its importance until 1050, when it was captured by the empire of Ghana, and by the Almoravids under Yahya Ibn 'Omar, in 1054. Archaeological excavations have revealed that the town had been rebuilt on successive levels as the sand covered it, notably in the 16th and 17th centuries, but was then abandoned. The site is not very rewarding to the visitor.

The second route N from Kiffa is to Tidjikja – a rough route not to be undertaken lightly. See Tidjikja, page 267.

Aioun-El-Atrouss 210 km E of Kiffa along the main road is a well established town, the administrative centre of the western Hodh area, with a hotel, bank, post office and shops, and some attractive sandstone houses. There are flights from the town's airstrip to Nouakchott Fri morning, contact Air Mauritanie in Nouakchott UM9,500 single, or the distance can be covered by public transport in 2 days. There is accommodation at the **D** *Aioun Hotel*, BP 41, T 90079, 90060, a quiet friendly place, simple rooms with bath, supposed to have electricity and a/c, but both are unreliable.

A wander amongst the houses is pleasant, whilst there are good views from the rocks that ring the town. A very scenic area with some strange rock formations. There is an interesting market with a good line in beads.

The *piste* S from Aioun-El-Atrouss goes to Mali, about 180 km. There is a customs post on the border. Problems are reported of 'fines' of up to US$40 per person for not spending a minimum of UM10,000 per day while in Mauritania. Appeals to the chief of police might save you.

Timbedra, which has an important animal market, lies 170 km E of Aioun-El-Atrouss and it may be possible to get a lift from vehicles en route to Mali. **Koumbi Saleh** is 70 km SE of Timbedra along a quite reasonable track. This is Mauritania's most important archaeological site. Koumbi Saleh was once one of the most populous cities of the world, as capital of the empire of Ghana

from the 3rd century. It included two distinctive settlements, a royal town and a large area of residential districts and mosques, the two connected by further houses. It is the main residential district that is the archaeological site to be seen, revealing impressive stone houses and one of the large mosques.

Nema, 106 km beyond Timbedra, is the capital of the eastern Hodh region, an area of the Kunta people, and known for its use as a place of exile for political prisoners. The town marks the end of the Route de l'Espoir, although there are plans to continue this to Mali. Nema has many houses built from stone and clad with clay, in a similar but less decorative style than Oualta (see below). The town has a petrol station, police, a bank, a post office, shops, a market, and an airstrip with weekly flights to Nouakchott on Fri UM11,300 single. Camel convoys still leave for the Saharan regions to the N, and it is a good place to arrange transport and vehicles. The long taxi journey to Nouakchott will probably have to be taken in sections, perhaps changing vehicles in Aioun-El-Atrouss and Kiffa. There is an occasional and very slow bus which makes the journey to Nouakchott. There is no hotel, but accommodation with the family of Sass Ould Moulay Abdelmalek, Commerçant, BP 27 is recommended, which will probably cost UM550 plus meals, as arranged, ask in the town for 'Maison Sass' or 'Commerçant Sass'. All passport formalities must be carried out at the police station in Nema for entry into Mali or Senegal. At Adel Bagrou there are customs but no problems are encountered there.

Oualata, 95 km N of Nema, is a mediaeval fortified settlement which has had great importance as a Saharan caravan post and Islamic centre, with a famous **Koranic school** that is still running, and includes an important library. The **Muslim cemetery** at Tirzet is nearby. Oualata is built on a high terrace, an impressive location. Most striking in Oualata are the houses, which were traditionally heavily ornamented, with intricate decorations executed in gypsum and different colours of clay. Many of these older houses have been abandoned, and the art has declined. However the interiors and studded wooden doors are impressive. Sensitivity over photography should be borne in mind, as this town is also used for internal exile, and indeed the police must be visited on arrival. There is no accommodation in Oualata other than with families. There are some vehicles which make the journey from Nema, particularly after the flights from Nouakchott arrive.

THE TAGANT REGION

The Tagant Region is a dramatic area of stony plateaux with impressive views, prehistoric rock paintings, archaeological remains, palmeries, and some interesting old forts and towns which are now being over-run by sand. The name itself means 'forest' in the Zenaga language, implying the environment was more verdant in the past. Although very appealing, the Tagant is a difficult region to visit. Travellers will find it easiest to use the weekly flight from Nouakchott to Tidjikja (despite uncertainties about day or time of departure). Public land transport is difficult although the road has recently been repaired, the best option being a *taxi-brousse* from Nouakchott, or closer at hand from Aleg or Magta-Lahjar. For those with their own 4WD vehicles, turn off the Route de l'Espoir at Sangarafa, 20 km E after Magta-Lahjar. From Sangarafa there is a rough sandy track to Tidjikja. The fuel supply is unreliable in the region.

Tidjikja

The capital of Tagant, this is a small town, with a busy market but few facilities for tourists except the airstrip. Flights on Tues to Nouakchott,

UM8,300 single. There is a **French colonial fort** built by Xavier Coppolani, assassinated here in May 1905, and near the town there are remains from the Neolithic period, including arrowheads and pottery. Tidjikja was founded in 1680 by Idaw'ali exiles from the Adrar. The historic area lies on the NE bank of the *wadi*, with an old mosque, housing and Tidjikja's celebrated palm groves dating from the original settlement. Although some of the houses are vacant or ruined, the Tagant region's impressive architecture is highly evident in Tidjikja. The houses are built from stone with clay added. The buildings have flat roofs, palm-trunk waterspouts, narrow rooms and elevated latrines carved into stone. The distinctive features are the decorative niches with carved geometrical designs, and gargoyles on the roofs. The historic quarter is threatened by sand.

To the SW of the *wadi* is the modern area, with a bank, post office, shops, a hospital and a petrol station. Tidjikja has a lake but we do not recommend swimming. 4WD vehicles can be hired in Tidjikja, for a 40 km drive to Rachid, or for the 200 km, more expensive, journey to Tichit. This is the starting point of the 470 km to Atar, only negotiable by high clearance 4WD vehicles in convoy with guides. There is a basic rest house in Tidjikja, otherwise accommodation must be with locals.

Rachid lies 40 km to the N of Tidjikja, and is an impressive fort settlement with rock engravings, ruined buildings and a delightful palmery. In Jul/Aug many natives of Rachid who live elsewhere descend on the town for the *guetna* or date harvest. It was a bedouin citadel built by Kunta in the 18th century, a refuge for those who would rob caravans. Access is mainly by private 4WD vehicle.

Tichit

200 km to the E of Tidjikja, Tichit is very difficult to get to, but fascinating in

architectural and social terms, and worth visiting whilst it struggles on as a functioning settlement, a ghost of its impressive past. Tichit is a fortified caravan town founded around 1150 AD, from when it was a stopping point on the route between West Africa and the Sahel, and Morocco and the Mediterranean, and a large city. It has declined rapidly, with encroaching sand, changing economic circumstances and rapid emigration.

Now only a handful of families remains. These families reflect the traditional complex ethnic diversity of Tichit and its position as a transit point for Moor tribes nomadizing in the region. They include the Masena, blacks who speak Aser; Abid, former slaves often still working in similar situations and Haratin Moors, slaves liberated much earlier.

The old houses are impressive structures built from local rock, often using colouration and carvings, of a similar style but more elaborate than in Tidjikja. Green, white and red stone is used, and the ornamental niches are quite beautiful. There are also distinctive wooden doors. However, many of the houses are partly ruined and poorly maintained. The town mosque is worth seeing, although much of its fabric dates from frequent repairs. The surrounding area has other ruins and ancient rock paintings. There is an archaeological site nearby at Akreijt. Palm groves stretch S from Tichit, with a date harvest in Jul.

• **Transport** From Tidjikja, this is very difficult, with lifts only possible after the arrival of flights at the airstrip. A chartered flight continuation from Tidjikja is an expensive option. For motorists a 4WD vehicle, plentiful petrol (there is none in Tichit) and a guide are essential. The route is straightforward to Leckcheb, and then much more difficult over a bad *piste* and dunes to Tichit. From Tichit those with time and petrol could follow a 400 km long *piste* to Oulata, along an old caravan route.

THE SENEGAL VALLEY

South of the Route de l'Espoir is a more fertile area, firstly dry savanna and bush, and nearer the river Senegal irrigated crop lands, producing rice and millet. The region is mainly populated by black people speaking languages other than Arabic although in recent years the Moor and Haratin populations have increased.

Rosso, with a population of 27,783 (1988), is the administrative centre of the Trarza region, an area of mixed ethnic groups reflecting a diverse environment in which agriculture and cattle-rearing are dominant. It is an uninteresting town, only normally visited for travel to, or from, Senegal. There is a basic rest house/restaurant, the **E** *Hotel Trarza*, with 9 rm, and a Catholic mission. There is a black top road to Nouakchott, which was rebuilt after the floods of 1950, a dull journey, although look out for encampments of nomads. Taxis take approximately 3 hrs to Nouakchott, and can be found at the *Gare Routière*, 500m N out of the town. Horse-drawn *calèches* carry people from the town centre. The airstrip has no scheduled service.

From Rosso there is a ferry to the Senegal bank of the river, every 20 mins from 0700-1230 and 1500-1700, taking 3 mins, with frequent waits due to heavy traffic. There is a black top road from the river to Dakar, with frequent taxis. As relations between Mauritania and Senegal have been strained the border has on occasion been closed.

Mderdra is 20 km from Rosso, reachable for those with 4WD vehicles. Traditionally a gum arabic centre, it is now famous for inlaid wooden chests made for nomads, and silverware.

Keur Massène, W of Rosso, located in the river Senegal delta, close to the ocean. Keur Massène is a village with an eight bungalow *campement de chasse*, or hunting centre, run by *Air Afrique*. This offers surf-casting on the ocean as well as shooting of a wide variety of wildfowl. Contact: Service Tourisme, *Air Afrique*, 29 rue du Colisée, F 75008 Paris, T 42257169, or the Nouakchott office, BP 51, T 52084.

Bogué is an unremarkable town on the river Senegal. However, it is well connected, with a recently constructed paved road covering the 60 km distance S from Aleg on the Route de l'Espoir. A *pirogue*, an open boat, takes foot passengers across the river to the Senegalese Isle à Marfil.

Kaedi, *pop* 30,515 (1988), is the largest town in the Valley region and the economic centre of the E, linked by 100 km of *piste* to Bogué. It has an airstrip with a regular link to Nouakchott on Wed, UM6,100 single, and a rest house. The town is best known for its large market, one of the most interesting in the country and with good handicrafts. Kaedi is the capital of the Gorgol region, an economically diverse area with strong agriculture, fishing and cattle-rearing sectors.

Selibaby is the capital of the Guidimakha region, where the Soninke people live. It is an area of savanna and sub-tropical forest producing a wide variety of crops. The town has an airstrip, with a service to Nouakchott on Wed, UM7,200 single.

INFORMATION FOR VISITORS

CONTENTS

Before you go	270
Entry requirements	270
When to go	271
Health	271
Money	271
Getting there	272
Air; Road; Sea; Customs	
When you arrive	273
Hours of business; Photography; Shopping; Safety; Tipping; Weights and measures	
Where to stay	274
Food and drink	274
Getting around	274
Air; Train; Road; Other land transport	
Communications	276
Language; Postal services; Telephone services	
Entertainment	276
Media; Sports	
Holidays and festivals	276
Further reading	276

Before you go

Entry requirements

● **Visas**

Visas are required for most visitors. Exceptions include France, Italy and some African countries. The difficulty may be finding an embassy. Visas require two forms, two passport photographs and a return air ticket as evidence of intention to limit stay. A letter from your Travel Agent will not do but a letter from a Mauritanian may be useful. In Paris the cost is FF122, one is asked to go in person but postal requests are accepted. Time to process the visa here varies from immediate to 24 hrs, or, alas, a refusal and a suggestion to try in Rabat. There is a problem for overland travellers who may have to buy an air ticket to get the visa then return to the travel agency for a refund. Available also in Bonn, Brussels, Madrid and Rabat (reported to be cheaper than in Paris). Some travellers have obtained visas at the border, but

this a very unreliable option. It is possible to get visas in neighbouring countries such as the Canary Islands and Morocco, but one will need a letter of introduction from one's own embassy. French embassies are often helpful in African countries without a Mauritanian embassy. Mali, for example, does not have a Mauritanian embassy. For visa renewals go to the Commisariat Centrale, on Ave Gamal Abdel Nasser, in Nouakchott.

Entry into Senegal and other African countries Visas for Senegal are not available in Nouakchott or at the river crossing, but are available on arrival at the airport in Dakar. The French embassy in Nouakchott provides visas for a number of Francophone African countries, takes 24 hrs usually with no fuss.

Departure Provided you retain all receipts for financial transactions and are in no great hurry, leaving is no problem.

● **Vaccinations**

Travellers no longer require certificates of immunization against Yellow Fever and Cholera, but protection against these is advisable on health grounds anyway (see **Health** page 16). There are mosquitoes and anti-malarial medication is also recommended.

● **Representation overseas**

Algeria, BP 276, El-Mouradia, Algiers; **Belgium**, Ave Colombie 6, Bruxelles, T 322 6724747; **Egypt**, c/o the Senegal Embassy, 46 Abdel Moneim Riad St; **France**, 69 rue du Cherche Midi, 75006 Paris, T 45482388; **Libya**, BP 4664, Tripoli; **Mali**, BP 135, Bamako; **Morocco**, 30 Ave d'Alger, Rabat; **Senegal**, BP 12019, Dakar; **Spain**, Calle Velázquez 90, Madrid, T 3415757007; **Tunisia**, Route du Hilton, Notre Dame, Tunis; **UK**, nearest is the embassy in Paris; **USA**, 2129 Leroy Place NW, Washington DC 20008, T 2441491. There are also embassies in China, Gabon, Germany, the Ivory Coast, Nigeria, Russia and Zaire.

● **Tourist information**

That little information that there is can be had from either the **Direction à l'Artisanat et au Tourisme**, off Ave Gamal Abdel Nasser, BP 246, Nouakchott, T 53337, ext'n: 368, 322, 374; or the **Société Mauritanienne du Tourisme et de l'Hôtellerie (SMTH)**, BP 552, Nouakchott, T 2353. It is probably better to go to one of the travel agents below.

● **Specialist tour companies**

These include **Agence-Dayna Voyages et Tourisme**, Ave Gamal Abdel Nasser, and **Inter Tour**, Ave Gamal Abdel Nasser, BP 708, T 53217. One of the most helpful is **Adrar Voyages**, BP 926, Nouakchott, T 51717, F 53210 (0800-1230 and 1500-1830 Sat-Wed, 0800-1230 and 1500-1700 Thur). This company offers pre-arranged tours, and tours designed for the customer, primarily centred around desert safaris and watersports, with guides, vehicles, food and accommodation laid on. On a daily basis desert safari costs are approximately: vehicle, driver, food and fuel – UM45,000. A sample week-long tour takes in Nouakchott, Akjoujt, Atar, Chinguetti, Azougui and Terjit. **Adrar Voyages** in conjunction with Sodetour also runs safaris and fishing holidays along the coast, through the Parc National du Banc d'Arguin to Nouadhibou. The company works with a number of travel agents in France, Italy, Switzerland and South America. Staff speak French, Arabic and English.

Encounter Overland, 267 Old Brompton Rd, London SW5, T 0171 3706845; Backerstr 52, Postfach CH8026, Zurich, T 01 2971112; Schipholweg 101, PO Box 360, 2300 Leiden, Netherlands cover Mauritania and the W Desert in their itineraries. **Explorator**, 16 Place de la Madeleine, 75008 Paris, T 42666624 organizes birdwatching in the Parc National du Banc d'Arguin. **Dragoman Overland Expeditions**, T 0728 861133, include Mauritania in their trans-African trips.

When to go

● **Best time to visit**

The heat is most manageable between Nov and Feb, but even then it can be uncomfortable. Avoid Jul to Oct for visiting the Senegal Valley.

● **Climate**

Mauritania has a Saharan climate in the N and centre, hot and very dry with hardly any rain. The rain that does fall comes between Jul and Oct, although it is rarely above 30 mm. The hottest season is May to Sep, with peak temperatures between 40 and 45°C. Night temperatures in the desert can be as low as 13°C in Nouakchott. These cool night temperatures occur mainly in Dec to Feb. The coast is a little, but not much, cooler. The S, near the Senegal River, has a more humid climate.

Health

● **Staying healthy**

Visitors must be immunized against Yellow Fever to enter the country, however, certificates are rarely checked if visitors arrive from Europe or the US. They should also be immunized against polio, typhoid, meningitis, hepatitis B, and take appropriate anti-malarial pills, particularly in the S. Water should be boiled or sterilized. Mineral water is a fairly cheap alternative. On long journeys it is essential to drink sufficient water. Protection from the sun is essential throughout the year. Travel insurance is of course recommended. There is a reasonable hospital in Nouakchott, with French doctors as well as several private medical clinics with French, Russian or Lebanese doctors. For emergency dental care there are several Lebanese dentists with private practices around Ave Gamal Abdel Nasser in Nouakchott.

● **Further health information**

Visitors are recommended to read the section on Health, see page 15

Money

● **Banks**

There are no western banks, but a number of Mauritanian banks: the **Banque Centrale de Mauritanie** (BCM), **Banque Arabe Africaine Mauritanienne** (BAAM), **Société Mauritanienne de Banque** (SMB), **Banque Internationale pour la Mauritanie** (BIMA), **Banque Mauritanienne pour le Développement et le Commerce** (BMDC) and **Banque Arabe Libyenne-Mauritanienne pour le Commerce Extérieur et le Développement** (BALM). Banks are easy to find in Nouakchott and Nouadhibou, but very rare elsewhere except in Atar, Aioun-El-Atrouss, Kaedi, Kiffa, Nema and Rosso. Banks are open 0800-1300 every day except Fri and Sat.

● **Cost of living**

In comparison with Morocco, Egypt or Tunisia, Mauritania is an extremely expensive country. Distances to be covered are long and prices high, with travellers often having to resort to air travel. A day's travel can be upwards of UM2,800. There is little choice in hotels, which are also highly priced, often above UM1,500 for quite basic accommodation. Meals in Nouakchott or Nouadhibou restaurants are similarly exorbitant. Local meals are cheaper.

● **Credit cards**

These are not normally accepted outside the few large hotels, or airlines. American Express has no representation in Mauritania.

● **Currency**

A **currency declaration**, of cash and TCs, must be made at the place of entry. Fill in all financial transactions and keep it safe. It is unwise to be economical with the truth as the fines are steep. Mauritanian currency cannot be taken out of the county. There is no restriction on foreign currency, in fact officially one should have sufficient funds for the duration of the stay and a return journey (or air ticket).

The Mauritanian currency is the Ouguiya (UM), pronounced 'oogeeya', which equals five khoums. It is unlikely that visitors will come across anything other than 5, 10 and 20 UM coins, and 100, 200 and 1000 UM notes.

Regulations and money changing There is no limit, within reason, on bringing foreign currency into the country. Both currency and TCs have to be declared fully on arrival by filling out a form. The receipts from money changing should be kept in case they are needed on departure. As it is difficult to find banks outside the main towns plan well ahead. There are limited possibilities for informal transactions, but not at greatly preferential rates. Most Western currencies are acceptable but it is safest to stick to US, UK, German or, preferably, French, currency as you get 10% more for changing cash than changing TCs. For exchange rates for Jul 1995 (see page 7).

● **Eurocheques and Travellers' cheques**

It is unlikely that these will be usable in Mauritania, so cash is the best option.

Getting there

● **General note**

It is both difficult and expensive to get to Mauritania. European flights are mainly restricted to services from Paris and Las Palmas. There are limited flights from nearby African countries. Overland travel is straightforward from Senegal, difficult from Mali and Morocco and almost impossible from Algeria. There are no scheduled shipping routes.

Air

Mauritania has only two international airports, at Nouakchott and Nouadhibou. Travellers will find the facilities quite primitive. Taxis wait outside both airports for the short trip into the centre – they tend to charge exorbitant prices. There are connecting flights from both these airports to regional airports.

International services are limited, with no direct flights from the Americas. From New York **Air Afrique** flights are via Dakar. There is a service four times a week between Paris and Nouakchott run by **Air Afrique/Air France**, which takes 5 hrs. **Aeroflot** runs an occasional service from Moscow or Budapest to Nouadhibou. **Air Afrique** runs a weekly service between Nouakchott and Jeddah. **Tunis Air** to Nouakchott each Tues.

Within Africa There are services between Nouakchott and Algiers (**Air Algérie**), Banjul and Casablanca (**Royal Air Maroc, Air Mauritanie** and **Gambia Airways**), Conakry (**UTA**), Niamey and Ndjamena (**Air Afrique**), daily to Dakar (**Air Afrique, Air Mauritanie** and **Air Sénégal**, although the last is unreliable) and three times a week to Las Palmas in the Canary Islands (**Air Mauritanie** and **Iberia**). From Nouadhibou there are links with Bissau (**Aeroflot**), Conakry (**UTA**) and twice weekly with Las Palmas (**Air Mauritanie**).

Road

The main road approach is from Dakar in Senegal, across the river Senegal ferry at Rosso. There is a black top road from Dakar to the river. There is a ferry every 20 mins from 0700-1230 and 1500-1700. The crossing takes 3 mins but there can be quite a wait due to heavy traffic. There is also a reasonable black top road from Rosso to Nouakchott. Relations between Mauritania and Senegal are somewhat strained, and the border has on occasion been closed. Along the Senegal riverbank there is a black top road, on the Mauritanian side an unmade track. It is possible to cross at other points up the river, notably between Matam and Sive.

Entry from Mali into Mauritania is quite possible although the roads are of a poor quality. Many travel from Aioun-El-Atrouss, across the border to Nioro. Another route is from Nema to Nara in Mali. Travellers should get their passports stamped in the last Mauritanian town.

Due to the western Saharan conflict it is difficult to enter from Algeria, via Tindouf, the Polisario stronghold, but it is worth checking the current situation at the time of travel.

From Dakhla in Morocco there are one or

two convoys a week to the border where all formalities must be concluded. Camping is available at the border and while the customs are more interested in vehicles than people and are happy to accept 'gifts', no serious problems have been reported. It is advised to hire a guide if driving S to Nouakchott as there is no defined road.

● **Motoring**

Drivers will need to have an **autorisation d'importation** to bring a car into the country. For information contact the Direction des Douanes, BP 183, Nouakchott.

● **Taxi and bus**

By taxi the route from Dakar to Nouakchott, via Rosso, will take about 11 hrs, changing at the border. There are both car and minivan taxis, as well as lorries, running from Rosso to Nouakchott which terminate at the *Gare Routière*. There are also taxis which make the journey from the Malian border.

Sea

There are no regular ferry services to or from Mauritania, but from the major port of Nouadhibou it is occasionally possible to arrange passage on cargo vessels to Las Palmas in the Canary Islands, and further afield to Casablanca and Dakar (Senegal). Contact the Port Autonome de Nouadhibou, BP 236, Nouadhibou, T 2134. Similarly, ask around in Las Palmas, Casablanca or Dakar.

Customs

There are no taxes. Importation of alcohol is strictly banned.

When you arrive

● **Clothing**

The most appropriate clothing is light cotton, covering the whole body, with a scarf to wrap around the face as protection from blowing sand and sun on journeys, sunglasses and headwear. Women should avoid exposing arms and shoulders in respect of religious sensibilities.

● **Hours of business**

Banks are open 0800-1300 Sun-Thur, Government offices 0800-1500 Sat-Wed and 0800-1400 Thur, Private offices 0800-1230 and 1500-1700 Sat-Thur, and shops 0800-1230 and 1500-1700 Sat-Thur.

● **Official time**

Mauritania is in the same time band as Morocco and the UK, always on GMT.

● **Photography**

This is allowed without a permit, but there is sensitivity about official and military buildings and installations. Be discrete when taking photographs in Nouakchott and along the Sengal River. The largest hotels in Nouakchott will sell film but its age must be checked. Better to bring your own supplies.

● **Safety**

Crime in Nouakchott and the rest of the country is relatively scarce. There are frequent roadblocks in Mauritania, when the police attempt to read passports and ask irrelevant questions. There is normally a checkpoint at the entry to each town, and the police will often accompany travellers to the central police station for registration. Some police like to write in one's passport, which can be annoying after several towns. Vehicle searches do occur. Women will find in Mauritania less hassle than in Morocco, although there may be a lot of curiosity. It is perhaps unadvisable to travel alone. Hints: cover hair to minimize unwanted attention, don't offer to shake hands with a man unless he does so first and avoid lying on the back or stomach in public.

● **Shopping**

For handicrafts and many other items, purchase is by haggling, which is usually good natured and less exploitative than in Morocco. Trading in Western goods can get the traveller a good deal. A few shops and cooperatives are listed for Nouakchott. Otherwise the best place to shop is in the markets, which in different areas will reflect the local handicraft and other industries.

Best buys At the upper end of the market are carpets and wooden chests, but prices are much above the usual range in North Africa. Try for jewellery and the colourful cloths that Mauritanian women wear. In some areas interesting Neolithic artifacts, such as tools and arrow heads, are sold.

● **Tipping**

Tipping is rarely demanded and it is up to the client in restaurants and hotels. 10% is reasonable.

● **Weights and measures**

Mauritania uses the metric system. See conversion table on page 14.

Where to stay

● **Hotels**

There are few hotels in Mauritania, particularly outside Nouakchott and Nouadhibou. Few are anything to write home about, and most are over-priced.

HOTEL CLASSIFICATIONS

AL	US$90+. International class luxury hotel. All facilities for business and leisure travellers are of the highest international standard.
A	US$75-90. International hotel with air conditioned rooms with WC, bath/shower, TV, phone, mini-bar, daily clean linen. Choice of restaurants, coffee shop, shops, bank, travel agent, swimming pool, some sport and business facilities.
B	US$60-75. As **A** but without the luxury, reduced number of restaurants, smaller rooms, limited range of shops and sport.
C	US$40-60. Best rooms have air conditioning, own bath/shower and WC. Usually comfortable, bank, shop, pool.
D	US$20-40. Best rooms may have own WC and bath/shower. Depending on management will have room service and choice of cuisine in restaurant.
E	US$10-20. Simple provision. Perhaps fan cooler. May not have restaurant. Shared WC and showers with hot water (when available).
F	under US$10. Very basic, shared toilet facilities, variable in cleanliness, noise, often in dubious locations.

● **Camping**

This is legal in most places, but there are no organized sites.

● **General**

There are no **Youth hostels** in Mauritania. The Peace Corps is mentioned in some guides as a possible source of accommodation. Please note this is NOT the case. Some trainees/volunteers may put people up if they meet them, but this is not a reliable source. The *Maison du Passage* just outside Kiffa does not have accommodation, and that in Chinguetti is closed. Accommodation is occasionally possible at **Catholic Missions**. In many towns the only source of accommodation is local hospitality. Gifts such as biros, lighters, or small Western items are the usual means of recompense.

Food and drink

● **Food**

Travellers should not go to Mauritania expecting a taste sensation. The food, much of which is imported, is often dull. It is often difficult to get fruit and vegetables outside Nouakchott and Nouadhibou, indeed food supplies are difficult in the interior and travellers should be prepared with their own back-up. Mauritanian food is dominated by lamb, beef, camel, chicken, with rice, *couscous* and pasta. Fish and seafood, which is excellent and cheap is available along the coast, look out for Poutarge, mullet eggs, which is a delicacy in France. Dates are easy to find. The fruit in the S is varied and good. Travellers can purchase plenty of expensive imported tinned food in both Nouakchott and Nouadhibou.

RESTAURANT CLASSIFICATIONS

Given the variations in price of food on any menu our restaurants are divided where possible into three simple grades:
♦♦♦ expensive, ♦♦ average and ♦ cheap.

● **Drink**

Mauritanians drink a lot of tea, served sweet in small glasses, which should be drunk quickly so the glass can be passed on for the next person to use, as well as *zrig*, milk mixed with water and sugar. Canned and bottled soft drinks, and mineral water, can be bought in most towns. *Alcohol* is officially banned in Mauritania, but is available in a few large hotels in Nouadhibou, and at the American and French clubs in Nouakchott.

● **Where to eat and drink**

In Nouakchott and Nouadhibou there are restaurants in the hotels and outside, primarily serving European food. Prices can be as expensive as in Europe. Elsewhere there are tents serving basic food, although hygiene is often inadequate.

Getting around

Air

This is one of the best means of getting around the country, with fares only two or three times that of the taxis, whilst the services are, of course, far quicker. **Air Mauritanie** runs a reasonably good network, although services can be cancelled or delayed at short notice. There are daily or twice daily services between Nouakchott and Nouadhibou. There is a weekly service connecting Nouadhibou with Atar, and another with Zouerate. There are three services a week between Atar and Nouakchott, two a week between Zouerate and Nouakchott, two a week connecting Nouakchott with Tidjikja and Kiffa, and another two with Selibaby and Kaedi, and a weekly service between Nouakchott, Aioun-El-Atrouss and Nema. The airline's offices are at Ave Gamal Abdel Nasser, BP 41, Nouakchott, T 52211, and BP 10, Nouadhibou, T 45022.

Train

Mauritania has only one railway line, which runs from the NE iron ore town of Zouerate to the port of Nouadhibou. The train is primarily for transporting iron ore, it is slow and very long. The operating company normally attaches a basic passenger compartment, but many Mauritanians travel for free in the open trucks on top of the piles of iron ore. This is a very cold and extremely dusty way of travelling, so take warm clothing and a scarf to cover the mouth and eyes. There are two trains a day either way. These can be taken from Zouerate or Nouadhibou, or either way from Choum, mid-way along the line, between the Moroccan border and the town of Atar. See also page 260.

Road

The main road in the country is the Route de l'Espoir, from Nouakchott through Kiffa and Aioun-El-Atrouss to Nema, although even this is narrow and pot-holed in parts. There are also adequate roads from Rosso to Nouakchott, Nouakchott to Akjoujt and Aleg to Bogué. There is, incredibly, no black top road from Nouakchott to Nouadhibou, nor for that matter, anywhere else in the country. Consequently public transport is limited, infrequent, very slow and expensive, and driving in one's own vehicle is difficult.

Other land transport

● **Bicycles/motorcycles**
These are totally impractical in Mauritania.

● **Bus**
These run along the Route de l'Espoir, between Nouakchott and Nema. They are very slow, uncomfortable and infrequent, but much cheaper than the shared taxis. Buses leave from the *Gare Routière* in Nouakchott.

● **Car hire**
Car hire in Mauritania is expensive and limited to Nouakchott and Nouadhibou. There is a **Europcar** at Nouakchott airport. In some places, such as Atar, Land Rovers can be hired, with or without a driver.

● **City minibuses**
In Nouakchott the best means of transport, and a fairly cheap one at that, is the green and yellow *transports urbaines* minibuses that hurtle around the city. Travellers will need to ask locals where to wait. Each minibus has a boy hanging out the back door, who takes the money and knows the route.

● **City taxis**
In Nouakchott and Nouadhibou are not as standard in appearance as in many cities, but are usually fairly recognizable. There is a base price, but prices are in general negotiable as there are no meters.

● **Hitchhiking**
Most transport in Mauritania will require payment.

● **Motoring**
It is important to bear in mind that there are very few black top roads in Mauritania. Those in the desert can become hazardous and difficult to follow because of drifting sand, those in the S can become waterlogged because of rain. Coastal routes are dangerous because of sandbanks and tides. Thus a 4WD vehicle, careful planning, and all necessary equipment, are essential prerequisites of a journey. Stock up on petrol, oil, water and food, and carry a first aid kit and shelter at all times, as well as a repair kit with all essential spare parts, shovels, ropes and sand ladders. When one is stuck in sand, let out air from the tyres. In a breakdown, stay near the vehicle. Inform the authorities in each settlement of the route to be followed, and in the deep desert it is preferable to travel in convoy and to hire a guide. Take into account that there is little help on hand for motorists with problems. See main introduction, page 47.

Nouakchott to Atar (8 hrs) is fairly straightforward, as is Nouakchott to Kiffa, Aioun-El-Atrouss and Nema, and Nouakchott to Rosso. The track from Atar to Choum is rough but possible, that from Atar to Chinguetti and Ouadane is very difficult. Nouakchott to Nouadhibou is not black top, indeed it runs along the beach for part of the distance. This route is not advised for the independent motorist.

● **Taxis brousses**

These are normally large Peugeot 504 estates, which take nine passengers. They will leave when nine passengers are assembled. There are standard fares, about which the drivers are normally honest. If in doubt, check with the police. Journeys will be interrupted by frequent tea stops, in addition to the prayer stops. The taxi driver will normally pay for the tea. Drivers and passengers are quite casual about deciding to stop for the night under a tent, and equally casual about transferring passengers from one car to another. It is relatively straightforward to get taxis between Nouakchott and Rosso, Nouakchott and Atar, and along the Route de l'Espoir, between Nouakchott, Kiffa, Aioun-El-Atrouss and Nema. There are also services in the Senegal Valley area.

● **Trucks and Land Rovers**

Off the black top roads, trucks and Land Rovers act as taxis, notably between Nouakchott and Nouadhibou. Trucks and minivans also follow the same routes as the *taxis brousses*, but are less comfortable and slower.

Communications

● **Language**

Arabic is the main language, and has the status of official language. The form of Arabic spoken in Mauritania is Hassaniya. In the S a number of African languages are spoken by a substantial minority, including Wolof, Fula, Pulaar and Soninke. Other languages are spoken by migrants from Mali, Senegal and other West African states. Due to the linguistic diversity of the state French is often used as a language of communication between the different linguistic groups. English is very rarely spoken.

● **Postal services**

There are large *PTTs* (post offices) in Nouakchott and Nouadhibou, and smaller offices in regional centres such as Nema, Aioun-El-Atrouss, Kiffa, Kaedi, Rosso and Atar. Post from and to Mauritania is very slow. Postcards are UM50, letters UM100. Letters can be received *poste restante*, although it is perhaps best to use just Nouakchott *PTT Centrale* for this. DHL have an office next to *Hotel Marhaba* in Nouakchott.

● **Telephone services**

The Mauritanian telephone system is connected by satellite with the international system, but it is not cheap to call overseas. 1 min to the UK costs approximately £1 = UM200. It is easiest to call from the large hotels or *cabine telephonique*.

Entertainment

● **Media**

Daily papers, and some aged international newspapers, are available in Nouakchott. There is an extremely lively local press published in French. The best are '*Mauritanie Novelles*' and '*Le Calame*'. The state owned radio service, run by the *Office de Radiodiffusion et Télévision de Mauritanie*, broadcasts in French, Arabic, Wolof, Toucouleur and Sarakolé. The BBC World Service (Africa) can be picked up for part of the day on long wave frequency. There is a basic TV service broadcast in colour which began in 1984. Finding a TV set may be difficult, with little reward when found.

● **Sports**

There are almost no sporting facilities in Mauritania. The most likely activities are swimming and fishing. The latter is a popular activity because of Mauritania's rich fishing grounds and a great variety of fish is caught by enthusiasts. **Air Afrique** and **Adrar Voyages** organize a number of packages, at, for example, Keur Massène (see page 268), Baie de l'Étoile (see page 258) and Banc d'Arguin (see page 256).

Holidays and festivals

1 Jan: New Year's Day
26 Feb: National Reunification Day
8 Mar: Women's Day
1 May: Labour Day
25 May: Organization of African Unity Day
10 Jul: Armed Forces Day
28 Nov: Independence Day
12 Dec: Restructuration Day

The dates of the Islamic religious holidays and the fast, Ramadan, are celebrated on different dates each year as they are calculated according to the moon (see page 40). Approximate dates for 1996:

21 Jan: Beginning of Ramadan
21 Feb: End of Ramadan
29 Apr: Festival of Sacrifice
20 May: Islamic New Year (Anno Hegira 1417)
29 Jul: Prophet's Birthday

Further reading

● **Books**

Abeille, Barbara (1979) *A Study of Female Life in Mauritania*, USAID: Washington DC – study for American aid organization; Calderini, Simonetta; Cortese, Delia; Webb, James, LA jnr (1992) *Mauritania* (World Bibliographical Series Vol 141), Clio Press: Oxford – a comprehensive bibliography of sources in European languages; de Chassey, Claude (1984) *Mauritania 1900-1975*, L'Harmattan: Paris – introduction to the country; Gerteiny, Alfred G (1981) *Historical Dictionary of Mauritania* (African Historical Dictionaries No 31), Scarecrow Press: Metuchen (NJ) – basic historical facts, people and places; Gerteiny, Alfred G (1967) *Mauritania*, Pall Mall: London – useful summary of Mauritania, its geography, history and people; Handoff, Robert E (ed) (1990) *Mauritania: A Country Study*, US Government Printing Office: Washington DC – official study in this comprehensive series, covers most aspects of the country in some detail; Hudson, Peter (1990) *Travels in Mauritania*, Virgin Books: London – a very readable account of a recent visit to Mauritania; Moorhouse, Geoffrey (1986) *The Fearful Void*, Penguin: Harmondsworth – aborted trans-Saharan journey; Norris, H T (1986) *The Arab conquest of the western Sahara*, Longman: Harlow – draws on local sources to describe the process of Arabization, and the structure of society in the past; Ould Daddah, Mokhtar (1973) *Mauritania: A Land of People*, Centre d'Information et de Formation: Nouakchott – dated and superficial propaganda from the then president; Stewart, C C (1973) *Islam and Social Order in Mauritania: a case study from the nineteenth century*, Clarendon Press: Oxford – a biography of a 19th century sheikh who founded Boutilimit; Stone, Diana, 'The Moors of Mauritania' in Carmichael, P (1991) *Nomads*, Collins and Brown: London – focussing on a group of contemporary camel nomads; Toupet, C, 'Nouadhibou (Port Etienne) and the Economic Development of Mauritania', in Hoyle, B S/Hilling, D (eds) (1970) *Seaports and Development in Tropical Africa*, London – for those with a fascination for ports; Westebbe, Richard M (1971) *The Economy of Mauritania*, Praeger: New York – comprehensive but dated guide to the depressed economics of the country.

● **Maps and town plans**

There are no useful town plans of Nouakchott or Nouadhibou. Other towns are easy to explore in a few minutes. For maps of Mauritania the choice in the UK is limited to a few undetailed large-scale sheets available at well-stocked map specialists. Michelin 953 gives an overall view. The French (IGN) map costing £7.50 (must be ordered from Stanfords bookshop in London) has also been recommended. In Paris, very detailed small scale maps are sold at IGN, 107 Rue la Boétie, 75008 Paris.

ALGERIA

INTRODUCTION

Tourism, until recently, has been Algeria's greatest potential earner of foreign exchange yet those who travelled there did not find the crowds of foreigners so common in Tunisia or Morocco. The country offers a succession of contrasts, an Algiers bursting at the seams and an unpopulated desert; roads made impassable by snow and roads lost under drifting sands; mountain chains reaching over 2,500m and salt lakes below sea-level. To appreciate these, one had to overcome the problems of access and the lack of suitable accommodation. At present more serious problems prevail. **It is a source of great regret that currently the political unrest makes it impossible to recommend travel here.** (See Political Risks page 41 and Safety page 357.)

CONTENTS

Introduction	278
Land and life	278
Culture	283
History	286
Modern Algeria	287
Algiers and Environs	291
The East	304
The Northwest	324
The South	334
Information for visitors	354

MAPS

Algeria	280-281

Basics

OFFICIAL NAME al-Jumhuriyah al-Jaza'iriyah ad-Dimuqratiyah ash-Shabiyah (Democratic and Popular Republic of Algeria).

NATIONAL FLAG Rectangular, with equal green and white fields vertically separated at the centre; a red crescent and star in central position overlapping the two coloured fields.

OFFICIAL LANGUAGE Arabic.

OFFICIAL RELIGION Islam.

INDICATORS *Population*: 27.8 million. *Urban*: 52%. *Religion*: Sunni Muslim 99.5%, Christian 0.5%. *Birth rate*: 30 per 1,000. *Death rate*: 6 per 1,000. *Life expectancy*: 66/68. *GNP per capita*: US$1,650.

Land and life

Geography

The Democratic Republic of Algeria takes its name from Barr Al-Jazair meaning 'lands of the islands'. At 2,381,741 sq km, Algeria is the largest of the three Maghreb countries and the second largest country in Africa. By surface area it is the tenth largest in the world and is the equivalent in size of Western Europe, thus being five times the size of Spain and 10 times the size of the United Kingdom.

The northern frontier runs 1,200 km along the Mediterranean Sea. Land borders straggle for 6,000 km along the eastern border with Libya and Tunisia. Morocco lies to the W and Mali, Niger and Mauritania run along the southern frontier. There are three main physical regions.

The Coastal Hills and Plains

In the N of the country is a fertile, narrow and discontinuous coastal strip where the majority of the population is found. The coast is hilly except for limited reaches of plain on which Algeria's main cities, Algiers, Annaba and Oran, are located. To the immediate S of the coast is the Atlas range, a mountainous region where the main ridges run from SW to NE, more or less parallel to the coast.

The Atlas

The great eroded folds of the Atlas Mountains date from the Tertiary age and comprise three sub-regions. First, the **Tell Atlas** made up of hills, internal basins and valleys runs in the W from the Moroccan frontier to Cap Carbon at Bejaïa in the E. Here the most productive farmlands are to be found in the Mitidja Plain to the S and W of Algiers. Unfortunately, large areas of the plain are being built over as Algiers city expands rapidly. The Bejaïa Plain is another zone of intense agricultural development. Most other basins in the Tell are more arid, lacking reliable irrigation water supplies and suffering from extremes of temperature. The highest points of the Tell are in the Djebel Ouarsenis at 1,985m and the Kef Righa at 1,714m, both now conserved as national parks, together with the Titteri and Djurdjura ranges, which attain almost 3,000m. This is a region of outstanding natural beauty and well worth a prolonged visit.

The second sub-region, the **High Plateaux**, runs from the Moroccan frontier E of the Chott Ech-Chergui on a roughly SW to NE axis to Chott El-Hodna and terminating in the detached basin E of Batna. The area is undulating with altitudes ranging from 1,300m in the W to 400m in the E. The western districts of the High Plateaux are famous for their abundance of esparto grass (see page 442) though the area in general is austere, arid and relatively featureless.

The third sub-region is the **Saharan Atlas** which is a high rim to the immediate S of the plateaux. There are three main chains in the system, the Djebel Amour in the SW, the mountains of the Oulad Nail in the centre and the Monts du Zab in the NE. Rainfall on the Saharan Atlas is higher than on the plateaux and there are extensive ranching pastures.

The Sahara Desert

The Sahara in the S makes up more than 80% of the surface area of the country. It begins as a low flat plain and rises gradually over great distances to the S to become the volcanic Hoggar Massif, 800 km across and 3,000m in altitude. The Hoggar is the geographical centre of the Sahara, its highest peak, Mt Tahat, standing 2,918m. Sand seas and dunes make up a quarter of the region, mainly in the eastern quadrant. The W is characterized by arid gravel and pebble deserts. The deserts contain small pockets of settlement in oases where date production and small scale farming can be carried on using irrigation from shallow wells. In the N is the M'Zab Plateau where esparto grass is the main natural product (see page 442). The M'Zab Plateau is the effective division between the Grand Erg Oriental and the higher Grand Erg Occidental.

NE Algeria differs strongly from the rest of the country. Here the parallel ridges and plateaux are absent and in

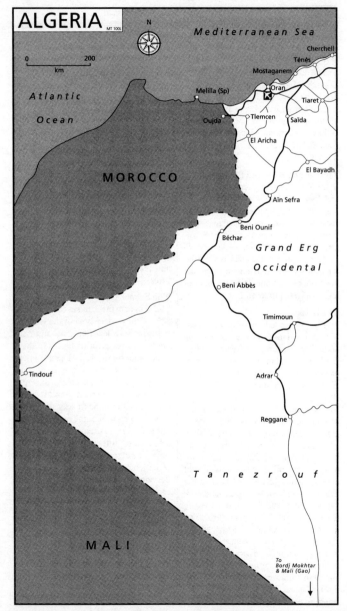

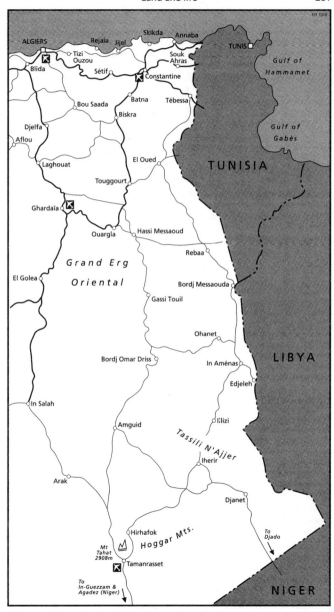

their place is a set of massifs between the Mediterranean coast and a southern line set by the Hodna and Aurés Mountain blocks. The area includes Lesser Kabylia, Constantine and Annaba in a region of tremendous variety of landscape and culture.

Rivers

Most surface streams in Algeria are seasonal. The main rivers are the Chelif, which drains the Tell Atlas over 200 km, and the Soummam, which flows from a source in Grande Kabylia. Other river valleys, notable for providing routeways from N to S, include the Rhumel and the Seybouse, which drain the high plains of Sétif and Constantine. In the E, the streams are short in length with steep gradients and they are harnessed in places to provide hydroelectric power while the longer river systems have dams to provide irrigation. In the height of summer most rivers are no more than a string of pools joined by small trickles of water. In winter, however, stream flow can be violent and it is wise never to camp in a dry river valley. The streams of the High Plateaux are unpredictable while those of the Saharan Tell are seasonal. Many of the streams from these areas drain into the temporary salt lakes and marsh lands such as the Chotts of the High Plateaux and the areas S of the Aurés Mountains. Many of the dry water courses have a subterranean water flow.

Climate

Climate, more so even than terrain, is the important factor for agriculture and settlement. Rainfall diminishes from N to S with as much as 1,000 mm/year on exposed northern mountain slopes, reducing to 130 mm in the sheltered regions and to virtually nil in the deep S. Most rainfall comes in the winter, with little in the summer months. The further S, the less reliable and significant the precipitation becomes and the more arid the conditions. The narrow coastal strip enjoys a Mediterranean climate with warm, wet, westerly winds in winter and hot dry summers as does, to a more limited extent, the N facing slopes of the Tell Atlas. Here the rain falls generally in the 3-4 winter months in many cases as snow in the higher hill ranges. In summer the shade temperature can reach 40°C but averages are 12°C in the winter and 25°C in the summer. High relative humidity can make temperatures feel very high.

The climate in the Tell Atlas is much the same but is slightly modified by the higher altitudes which moderate temperatures and increase the amount of rain as well as the length of the rainy period. The High Plateaux are semi-arid with longer rainless summers and overall very erratic precipitation. Annual average rainfall is generally around 400 mm but can be as low as 200 mm. Temperatures are slightly lower than the High Plateaux. The Saharan S is arid, with precipitation less than 130 mm. Many years are entirely rainless. The average daily range of temperature can be 32°C and maximum recorded shade temperatures have reached 55°C. Travellers should remember that in the Hoggar Mountains, altitude reduces temperatures. Beware of winter snows in the Kabylia Mountains, which can block roads and make travel hazardous or at times impossible.

Westerly winds in winter are pleasantly associated with rainfall but the hot dry winds from the S, known as the *Sirocco* or *Ghibli*, are less welcome. Such winds are common on the High Plateaux where they can occur for as many as 50 days a year though they occur less in the coastal areas of the country where their incidence is down to some 20 days a year. Nevertheless, the fall in relative humidity and increase in temperature and dust in the atmosphere associated with the *Sirocco* can cause distress. In the summer the sea breeze on the coast helps to temper the heat of the day.

Sunshine is experienced in most months of the year and Algeria is among the least cloudy regions of the world even in winter.

Flora and Fauna

Wildlife resembles that of other Mediterranean countries (see page 49) but the fauna of the desert region is very specialized. There are still a few leopard and panther, but the animals most commonly found in the desert are the gazelles, antelopes and hyenas. In the mountains to the N, wild boars and red deer are common. The Sahara has scorpions and reptiles such as snakes, vipers, and Monitor lizards.

There is a wide variety of birds, many of them staying only during the winter months. These include bustard, plover, snipe, heron, pelican, stork, eagles, vultures, hawks and ostriches.

Agriculture

Climate, especially the level of rainfall, is the dominant factor governing agricultural output. In the northern zone a wide range of Mediterranean crops is produced, often with the aid of irrigation. Dry farming is also practised and there are large areas given over to livestock herding. Some forestry and natural product gathering is possible in the cork oak forests.

Land use in 1991 is given as agricultural land 3.2%, meadows and pastures 13.0%, forests 1.7% and desert and other 82.1%. Only 7.5 million ha are suitable for agriculture, and these are of variable quality, approximately 1 million ha concentrated in the narrow fertile coastal strip, 1 million ha in the High Tell and the remaining, often poor lands of 5.5 million ha, situated in the High Plateaux.

Land tenure

Agricultural land holding has been reformed under state direction since the repatriation of most of the French colonists. Approximately one third of all farmed land, including the best agricultural areas, was under French control but was sequestrated after Independence. Until recent years one fifth of the land was held by large and often absentee Algerian landlords and an unsuccessful attempt was recently made to distribute this to peasant farmers. On the remaining farming land, about 47% of the total, small private farmers have a mass of tiny and fragmented holdings. Many plots were assimilated into 'socialist villages' in the 1970s and 1980s. Remarkably, the private sector produces the bulk of cereals, vegetables and meat. Since 1985 the government has tried to develop the private sector to compensate for the virtual failure of the state and co-operative farms. So far, however, little of a serious nature has been done to improve the situation in agriculture and to reduce dependency on imported foodstuffs.

Development potential

The potential for development in Algeria is considerable. Improved provision of irrigation water, better use of existing resources and a positive attitude towards farming from the government would all give the country a better level of farm output. Rapid urbanization and growth of the total population has probably already outstripped the capacity of domestic farmers to feed all Algerians. However the diversity of food available could be much developed despite climate constraints on farming as a whole.

Culture

Total population

The distribution of population is directly related to the amount of rainfall and soil fertility. The majority of people live in the richer, well-watered northern region of the country adjacent to the Mediterranean coast. The population in 1994 was 27,815,000 and is projected to

FUNDAMENTALISM

Islam has been marked over the course of history by the emergence of rigorous revivalist movements. Most have sought a return of the faithful to the fundamentals of Islam – the basic doctrines of the Prophet Mohammad – uncluttered by the interpretations of later Islamic jurists and commentators. Behind the movements was generally the idea that Muslims should go back to the simple basics of their religion. Some, like the Wahhabi movement in Saudi Arabia were puritan in concept, demanding plain lives and an adherence to the tenets of Islam in all daily aspects of life. Others, imposed a rigorous schedule of ritual in prayer and avoidance of the 'unclean' in public life. A good example of this type of reformist tendency was the Senusi Movement in Libya which in the period from the close of the 19th century to 1969 created an educational, commercial and religious society throughout eastern Libya and northern Chad.

Until recent times the fundamentalist movements inside Islam arose from a desire to cleanse the religion of unnecessary ideology and to make all Muslims observe the basic pillars of the Islamic religion – prayer, belief and actions on a consistent and demonstrable basis. In the last 100 years there has been a growing tendency in the Islamic world for revivalist movements to be reactions to political, military and cultural setbacks experienced at the hands of the Western industrialized world. The aim of the reformers has been to make good the disadvantage and backwardness of the Muslim states in contrast with the powerful countries of Europe, America and the Far East. The matter is varied and complex, depending on the particular cases involved, but the clear linkage between an increasingly dominant Western culture and economy and the growth of reactive Islamic movements is inescapable. In North Africa, the power of the Muslim Brotherhood in Egypt was an early form of revivalist movement of this kind. Founded by an

---

be 32,693,000 by the year 2000. This implies a doubling of the population within 29 years, posing immense problems for the future.

Racial composition

The ethnic composition in 1993 was Arabs 83% and Berbers 17%, although there are large overlaps between the two populations where inter-marriage has taken place over many years.

It is estimated that about 82% of the population speak Arabic and the others speak forms of Berber with Arabic as a second language. Many Algerians speak French, but very few speak English. Forms of Berber include Taqbaylit (spoken by the Kabilis in the northern mountains of that name) and Tamashak, spoken by the Touareg nomads of the S. There is still speculation as to the origins of the Touareg tribes. It is suggested

that they came from SW Asia in about 3000 BC. According to Ibn Khaldoun they were only converted to Islam in the 9th century and rejected the faith 14 times. They call themselves Imaghzen, '*the free ones*' and still pursue their independent ways of life. The role of the women is important, and in contrast to the Arab population, the women are unveiled and the men wrapped in long blue scarves, covering all but their eyes. The Kabyles are also an important group of Berber origin. They are thought to have come from Yemen, but again this is only speculation.

Location of population

With 52% of the people living in towns, Algeria is becoming a highly urbanized country. The main concentration of population is in the large towns of the N, with something like 94% of the popu-

Egyptian school teacher, Hassan al-Banna in 1928, it initially tried to take Islam back to its roots and therefore to its perceived strengths but was later taken over by extremists who used its organization for political ends. The development of the Muslim Brotherhood as a clandestine political group and the harnessing of religious fervour to political objectives, including the assassination of political enemies, set the pattern for most later movements of the kind.

The Iranian revolution of 1979, taken over by fundamentalist religious leaders after the overthrow of the Shah, gave a great boost to revivalist Islamic groups by demonstrating that Islam could be used as a means of changing the political system, defying the West and bringing about radical social reform.

In North Africa there was a rapid spread of fundamentalism in the 1980s and early 1990s. In Egypt the Muslim Brotherhood remained the main organization though other smaller sects were also founded. The Iranian model of Islamic revolution was adopted in Algeria where the Fundamentalist Islamic Salvation Front has become a serious contender to take over the established but politically isolated National Liberation Front government. Fundamentalism in Sudan has been adopted as a system of government and many of the attributes of the Iranian revolution have been copied, some with Iranian assistance. Libya has not been threatened by Islamic fundamentalism on the scale experienced elsewhere in the region. The régime in Libya has some Islamic credentials with which to protect itself though a Wahhabi movement did emerge among university students on a small scale in the 1980s. Morocco, although deeply Islamic, has always had its own form of Muslim rule through the royal family, itself of descent from the Prophet Mohammed. Islam in Morocco is also something of a law unto itself with a heavy bias towards vernacular mystical forms, which makes the appeal of puritanical and fundamental Islam less appealing than elsewhere.

lation living in the northern part of the country, covering only 14% of the total area. Greater Algiers, the capital and chief industrial centre, has a population of 3 million and towns like Oran, the second port and an equally important industrial centre has 1 million. Other important northern towns include Constantine, an administrative and commercial centre with a population of 750,000, Annaba 450,000, Tizi Ouzou 350,000, Sétif 200,000, Tlemcen 200,000, and Batna 182,000.

Population densities

The average population density for the country as a whole is given as 11.7 people/sq km (1994). In the northern region it does not fall below 30 people/sq km with some *wilayat* (provinces) reaching 1,100 people/sq km (Tizi Ouzou). The density of population in parts of the Sahara is given in sq km pp rather than people/sq km.

Age groups

The demographic boom has caused a severe imbalance in age structure. In 1993, 42% of the population was under 15 years of age. On the other hand the male-female ratio is stable and was almost at an equal balance in 1993, with 49.86% females. The age breakdown for 1990 was 42.3% under 15, 28.8% between 15 and 29, 23.2% between 30 and 59 and 5.7% over the age of 60.

Literacy

Education remains a big problem with such a large proportion of the population under 25. According to government figures, 85% of children between the age of 6 and 13 attend school. The literacy rate in 1991 was 57.4% for the population over 15 years of age, with male literacy being 69.8% and female 45.5%. In 1989, 38% of the population over 15 had no formal education. Due to lack of infrastructure, some schools operate on an alternate morning and afternoon basis, in order to cater for all the children. Although far from perfect, the system is nevertheless giving a minimum of education to a majority of the children. Universities and technical colleges are found in Oran, Constantine, Annaba, Batna, Tizi-Ouzou, Tlemcen and Algiers.

Income per head

Income/head in Algeria was estimated at US$1,650 in 1993.

Crude birth rates

Algeria's most demanding problem is the huge rate of increase in population. The population which was only 5 million in 1930 was 27.8 million in 1994. The high birth rate and the low death rate give a natural increase of 24.2% against a world average of 16.8%. Life expectancy at 66 years for males is low compared to European standards.

The official number of unemployed stands at 21% of the work force whilst under-employment, though impossible to measure, is estimated to be still greater. Unemployment hits the young particularly hard, the under-25s making up a high proportion of the jobless. Women are also affected but they do not make up an important proportion of the work force. Long term unemployment, of over 2 years, is quite frequent and many qualified workers and university graduates are finding it very difficult to find work. An additional problem is the 400,000 young people each year ending school without any kind of diplomas or skills. These high unemployment figures, particularly within the young population, add to social problems and create a fertile ground for political unrest as well as fuelling the black economy.

History since Independence

For the history of this region before Algeria gained Independence see The History of North Africa (see page 24).

After Independence there was a brief struggle for power which ended with **Colonel Boumedienne**, backed by the FLN, in control. **Ahmed Ben Bella** was elected premier to run Algeria as a revolutionary Arab-Islamic state based on principles of socialism and collective leadership. Co-operative farms were set up on what had been French-owned land and handed over to landless peasants. Yet socialism did not extend so far as to redistribute the lands of wealthy and influential Algerians. The marriage of socialism and Islam was not easy; eg the socialist view of equality for women in the new state conflicted with Islamic principles.

Following the bloodless coup of 1965, Colonel Boumedienne attempted to sort out the problems of under-employment, unemployment and lack of expertise in public administration. Many Algerians found their only source of employment was as guest workers in France despite the racial tensions there. Concentration on industrial development and the loss of French farmers caused agricultural production to fall below pre-revolutionary levels. Attempts were made to distribute more land and to reduce illiteracy. After his death in 1978, Boumedienne was replaced by **Colonel Chadli Benjedid**, who was the head of state until Jan 1992. The 1980s saw the agricultural sector still in poor health, despite its enormous labour force. The **FLN** remained the only political party while the problems of a cumbersome centralized bureaucracy grew acute. Positive attempts were made to reduce dependence on imported goods but the Algerians faced increasing economic hardship, for which they blamed the government. The 1980s also saw the rise of Islamic fundamentalism, leading to riots in 1985 when the government was called a 'band of atheists' by its Islamic opponents.

In 1985 Chadli's new charter removed most of Boumedienne's appointees and reinstated many who had been previously disgraced. Legislation was passed to encourage private sector involvement as government controls and central planning were reduced. But President Chadli moved slowly so as to preserve a political balance. Following the riots of Oct 1988, a new constitution was approved. Under this, the role of the ruling FLN was reduced, political opposition groups were allowed but with some controls, the role of the army was limited to defence and public sector workers were given the right to strike. In Jul 1989, a new law permitted opposition groups to form political parties but with many restrictions, effectively preventing the FLN from losing its dominant role, although in practice many of these restrictions seem to have been later ignored.

In Dec 1991, a **general election** was held, but the second round of the elections was never held due to the resignation of President Chadli. He was pressurized into resignation by the imminent victory of the **Islamic Salvation Front** (FIS) whose political agenda was the creation of an Islamic state. The country is now led by a transitional government the core of which is military men opposed to the FIS.

Algerian foreign policy is anti-imperialist and supports struggles for liberation. Algeria has been noted for its conciliatory efforts in the Iran-Iraq war and in various border disputes between neighbouring states. The country gives support to the Polisario guerrillas in their conflict with Morocco in former Spanish Sahara, though it is phasing out its role in that arena. The Algerian-Morocco border reopened in 1988, but entry points are limited and a full political rapprochement is awaited despite both sides' adherence to the UMA (Maghreb Arab Union).

Modern Algeria

Government

The republic Algeria is a self-declared multiparty republic with one legislative house known as the National People's Assembly which contains 295 members elected by universal adult suffrage. The political system is presidential, the head of state appointing the prime minister and other ministers who meet weekly. In Feb 1989, a new Constitution guaranteeing multi-party democracy was approved by referendum, giving rise to the Dec 1991 parliamentary elections. The Head of State and government was, until Jan 1992, Chadli Benjedid, elected by popular suffrage in 1979 for a period of 5 years and reelected in 1984 and 1989.

Until the Dec 1991 elections, the largest Party was the **National Liberation Front (FLN)** of which the president was secretary-general. The results of the election's first round gave the newly formed Islamic Salvation Front (FIS) some 188 seats and the FLN only 15. The second round of the elections was never held due to the resignation of President Chadli. A group of army officers stepped into power and established the **Higher Council of State (HCS)**. This amounted to a military takeover to prevent the FIS from gaining power as they were certain of victory in the second round of the elections. On Feb 9, a state of emergency was declared and the FIS was banned. In early 1994 a new president was appointed to lead a transitional régime. The new president, Liamine Zeroual, a former senior army officer and minister of defence, is determined to open dialogue with the banned FIS albeit on his own terms. The most likely outcome of the transitional presidency will be a coalition régime leading to new elections under much stricter electoral laws though progress towards this end is very slow.

Provincial administration is executed through 48 *wilayat* (provinces) headed by a wali, an elected member of the central government who runs the province with the assistance of an elected executive council. The *wilayat* are also divided into *dairate*, which are smaller municipal areas. Each town has its municipal council, the Assemblée Populaire Communale, which is elected. Since 1989, the government has been trying to give more independence to the provinces and the push towards decentralization has been welcome.

Economy

The Algerian economy has shifted dramatically from the dominance of agriculture at the time of Independence to dependency on urban services and industry. The confidence and security needed for industrial development were provided by exploitation of oil and natural gas reserves. The economy grew rapidly, with investments in large industrial projects, as well as the extensive development of the hydrocarbon sector.

The 1980s were less successful, falling oil revenues and rising debts reducing the industrial growth. By the early 1990s, Algeria was oil-dependent with large shares of GDP arising in state-funded oil, construction and services. Much economic activity was undertaken in the informal so-called 'black economy' and not necessarily included in official GDP.

Structure of the Economy 1992

Agriculture	12.2
Construction	11.9
Hydrocarbons	25.5
Trade/Transport/ Communications	26.1
Other mining	0.2
Manufacturing	9.7
Other services (incl Defence)	13.3
Public utilities	1.1
Total	100.0

Source: *Encyclopaedia Britannica*

Agricultural production

Agricultural production from what was once termed '*the bread basket of the Roman Empire*' has fallen dramatically since Independence, from 93% self sufficiency to an import dependency of more than 60% of requirements of cereals. Agriculture's contribution to GDP in 1987 was only 15% and a mere 14% of the work force were in farming against twice those proportions 20 years earlier.

The major livestock holdings in 1991 were sheep (13,350,000) with smaller numbers of goats (3,800,000) and cattle (1,443,000). Asses (see box, page 306) are used rather than mules, donkeys or camels and there are 24,000,000 chickens. The supply of red meat has remained constant whereas the rearing of white meat from battery chickens has increased substantially.

Traditional crops

The main crops are **cereals**, such as soft wheat, hard wheat, barley, oats, maize, sorghum and rice, vegetables, including beans, peas, lentils, chick peas, fresh vegetables like potatoes, cucumbers, tomatoes, onions, French beans, carrots, melons and water melons and artichokes, as well as tobacco, sunflower, sugar beet, tomatoes for tinning and sunflower as industrial crops. **Vines** are also grown for grapes and wine. Large numbers of **citrus fruits** are cultivated such as oranges, mandarins, clementines, lemons, and grapefruit.

Most production is for local consumption and the main agricultural exports are olives, figs, the famous *deglet nur dates*, wine and tobacco. Wine has been an increasing problem as freedom of access to the French market has declined and the area under the vine has drastically reduced.

Due to climatic constraints, most products are grown in the northern areas. Citrus fruit comes mainly from the coastal districts where water is available. Olives are grown in the western coastal belt and the Kabylia region and dates are a speciality of the southern oases.

Agriculture is in a poor state as the farmers need more encouragement from the government to improve production. Without more irrigation, water and easier availability of credit to purchase fertilizers and machinery, it is hard to see how they can succeed. Improved storage facilities for crops, as well as better roads and electricity supply are also badly needed. The government has never been seriously interested in agriculture and promises of land reform, privatization and development funds have never been fulfilled. The 5 year plan of 1985, eg aimed to channel 40% of state investment into agriculture, principally for the purchase of farm equipment and fertilizers, but this had little effect due particularly to the decrease in state resources caused by falling oil prices.

The forested area has been much reduced by clearance but the Tell Atlas still has suitable conditions for pines and cork oak. A programme for reafforestation has begun, concentrating on the more drought resistant pines in areas of the High Plateaux.

Fishing

Algeria makes only modest use of its sea coast for fishing. The fish catch in 1992 was 95,274 tonnes.

Primary industry

Primary industries make up 17% of GDP (1988). The main products mined are mercury, iron ore, phosphates, gypsum, barite, zinc and silver. Current output is moderate:

Production of minerals 1990

	(tonnes)
Iron ore	2,350,000
Barite	42,800
Phosphates	1,136,000
Zinc	10,000
Gypsum	275,000
Silver (troy ounces)	96,500

Source: *Encyclopaedia Britannica*

Manufacturing industry

Other than petrochemicals, produces mainly for internal consumption and represents 14% of GDP (1988). The main items are for construction such as cement, bricks, structural steel and basic materials for other industries like ferroalloys and crude steel. There is a growing automobile assembly industry with other light consumer goods and food processing industry in the main towns of the N.

Service industry

This sector represents 36% of GDP (1988). Investment continues in domestic water supply, sewerage, telecommunications and transport infrastructure, all of which are tremendous tasks in so large a country. Unfortunately much of the boom in services has been funded by the central government in non-commercial areas and very large proportions of national wealth are absorbed unproductively in defence and the civil service.

Tourism

Is a trade that is still in its infancy in Algeria. There are no large tourist towns on the coast as in Morocco and Tunisia, adding to the charm of the country. The government intended to develop tourism as a source of foreign currency. In 1990, receipts from tourism were US$149mn. Institutional changes needed to promote tourism such as the loosening of currency restrictions and easier provision of visas are still awaited. The political violence in Algeria makes tourism a poor prospect for short-term development.

Energy

Hydrocarbons earned 87% of foreign currency in 1992, generated 17.7% of GDP and provided 38.1% of government income and this despite a fall in the international price for crude oil in recent years. Proven reserves for petroleum are only 9,200 million barrels, good for only 21 years at present rates of output. Deteriorating crude reserves has led to an effort to concentrate on exploitation of the more abundant natural gas. Published proven reserves of natural gas in 1993 stood at 3,600 million cubic metres enough to last for 71 years at current levels of output. Algeria is a member of Opec and, through it, is pressing for an improved international oil price. Oil and gas are looked on as a source of industrial raw materials and fuel in Algeria rather than simply as primary product exports. A large petrochemical and refining industry has been set up at sites such as Arzew, Bejaïa and Skikda to which natural gas and crude are carried by pipelines from the southern fields. Unfortunately these efforts at industrialization using hydrocarbons have been dogged by inefficiencies and have starved the rest of the economy of resources.

Trends in the economy

Exports, valued at US$11,800mn in 1991, are mainly in the form of mineral fuels and lubricants (98% of GDP) mainly sold to the EU (74%) and the USA (19%). Imports in 1991 were high including raw materials for industry at 6.0%, machinery and equipment at 62.4%, food and beverages at 26.0% and consumer products at 4.6%. These came mainly from EU countries (64%), USA (11.5%) and Japan (5%). Foreign exchange and imports are controlled by the government, so only Algerian goods are available in shops. Since 1991, the government has clamped down on nonessential imports and the total import bill was cut by 20.5%, to the bare minimum needed to keep the economy functioning.

Exposure to **modern communication systems** such as television and telephones remains quite low. In 1990, there was 1 telephone/23 inhabitants and 1 television/16 inhabitants.

The main trends in the economy have been adverse since 1985/86 and markedly so since 1987 after which GDP/head at US$2,752 fell steadily to US$1,650 in 1993. The economic crisis, caused by the sustained fall in oil prices, severe foreign indebtedness and economic mismanagement is having serious effects. Industrial production is down by 5.5%, with industry only working at 57% of capacity. This is due to shortage of spare parts, working capital and trained personnel. Inflation stands at approximately 17% and is worsening as price liberalisation proceeds and the Dinar loses value against foreign currencies. Foreign debt, excluding trade related debt, was estimated at US$24,762mn in 1992. Repayments put great pressure on the country. There is now a new IMF loan of US$1bn and debt rescheduling has taken place. Meanwhile, Algerian workers are finding it difficult to find jobs in Western Europe, reducing the US$274mn/year remittances formerly coming from this source. There are no simple economic solutions for Algeria for as long as the oil price remains low and domestic output so depressed. The government's economic plan calls for growth through increasing the productivity of existing industrial capacity. Tax collection are also being reformed and attempts made to bring the black market under control.

ECONOMIC INDICATORS

	1990	1991	1992	1993
GDP (US$ billion)	51.6	52.3	49.0	44.4
Imports (US$ billion)	10.4	7.7	...	...
Exports (US$ billion)	15.2	11.8	...	...
Balance of Trade (AD billion)	+13.6	+4.1	+4.1	...
Foreign Debt (US$ billion)	24.3	24.0	24.7	26.0
Inflation % (1985=100)	163.0	25.9	45.7	50.0

Sources: IMF, EIU, *Encyclopaedia Britannica*

ALGIERS AND ENVIRONS

CONTENTS

Algiers	291
Places of interest	294
Local information	298
Around Algiers	300

MAPS

Algiers	292-293
Algiers Kasbah	296
Algiers environs	301
Tipasa	302

Because of the immense size of Algeria, many tours do not begin in the capital but fly into a more convenient starting point. However, the region around Algiers in 'just a few short steps' encompasses the essence of Rome's domination (evidenced in the coastal residences of Tipasa), the prosperity of the Ottomans when the large kasbah was constructed, the magnificence of Islam with its variety of mosques and minarets and the more recent French cathedral. Beyond these lie the golden beaches of the Sidi-Fredj complex and, behind, the ski resorts nestling under the 1,510m peak of Chréa. Algiers makes an excellent first stop and the transport network allows easy and speedy departure in any desired direction.

ALGIERS

Pop 2,500,000; Alt 50m.

ACCESS Air The airport is situated 22 km outside the city. The easiest and cheapest way to the city centre is the bus that leaves opposite the terminal building. The trip takes about 40 mins. Buses stop at the Air Algérie air terminal, by the *Hotel Aletti* close to the sea-front. Otherwise, take a taxi, but agree on a price before departure if it does not have a meter. **Trains** From the W stop at Agha station which is S along the sea-front. The main bus station is also on the sea front near the train station. The ferry terminal and main train station are on the quayside, in front of the place Port Saïd, below the street level. There is a lift to the street for a minimal fee. There is also a cheap, no time limit, left-luggage deposit at the station. For information, T 647380. It is an easy 4 mins walk to the town centre from here. **Road** The long distance bus station, *Gare Routière*, is on route de l'Armée de Libération Nationale near where this approaches the Bassin de l'Agha on the quayside, 10 mins walk at most from place du 1er Mai and 15 mins walk SE from the Grande Poste. Buses go to place des Martyrs. Between the long distance bus station and the Grande Poste is the bus station for local buses that serve the suburbs of Algiers and the local area.

History

Algiers, originally known as **Icosium** during the pre-Christian era, was, according to legend, founded by 20 of Hercules' companions who abandoned him during his Mediterranean tour. During the Phoenician and Carthaginian periods, Icosium remained relatively unimportant, not developing until the Arab invasion. In the 10th century, **Bologhine Ibn Ziri** founded the new town named **El Djezaïr**, which rapidly developed into an important commercial centre. The prosperity of the new town was subjected to foreign domination over

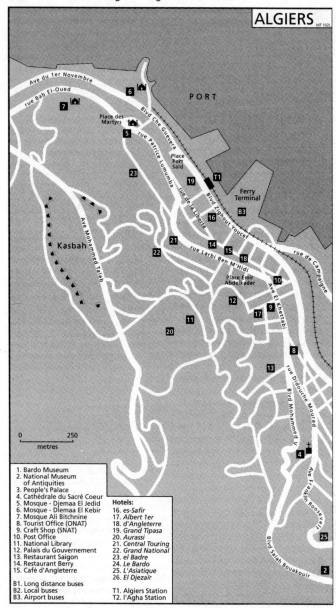

ALGIERS
MT 102L

Ave du 1er Novembre
rue Bab El-Oued

PORT

Place des Martyrs

Blvd Che Guevara

rue Patrice Lumumba

Place Port Said

Ferry Terminal

rue de la Liberté

Blvd Zighout Youcef

rue de Campaigne

Kasbah

Ave Mohammed Taleb

rue Larbi Ben M'Hidi

Place Emir Abdelkader

Ave El Khettabi

Blvd Mohammed V

rue Didouche Mourad

Ave Franklin Roosevelt

Blvd Salah Bouakouir

0   250
metres

1. Bardo Museum
2. National Museum of Antiquities
3. People's Palace
4. Cathédrale du Sacré Coeur
5. Mosque - Djemaa El Jedid
6. Mosque - Djemaa El Kebir
7. Mosque Ali Bitchnine
8. Tourist Office (ONAT)
9. Craft Shop (SNAT)
10. Post Office
11. National Library
12. Palais du Gouvernement
13. Restaurant Saigon
14. Restaurant Berry
15. Café d'Angleterre

Hotels:
16. *es-Safir*
17. *Albert 1er*
18. *d'Angleterre*
19. *Grand Tipasa*
20. *Aurassi*
21. *Central Touring*
22. *Grand National*
23. *el Badre*
24. *Le Bardo*
25. *L'Asiatique*
26. *El Djezaïr*

B1. Long distance buses
B2. Local buses
B3. Airport buses

T1. Algiers Station
T2. l'Agha Station

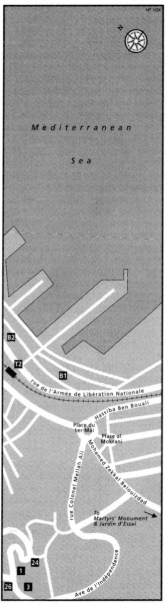

the following years. In 1235 it fell to the Hafsid King **Abou Zakarya** and in the 14th century for a short period to the Merinids. By the start of the 15th century, the Hafsids had retaken the city and at the beginning of the 16th century the **Spanish**, seeking to consolidate their presence in North Africa, seized control of El Djezaïr. In 1516, threatened by the Spanish presence, the inhabitants called on the pirate **Barbarossa** for assistance. The ensuing struggle between Barbarossa and the Spanish lasted 13 years, El Djezaïr eventually falling into the pirates' hands in 1529. Stones from the partially destroyed fort were used to build the harbour's protective walls, and the town was transformed into a pirates' lair. Many unsuccessful attempts were made by the Spanish and the British to dislodge them.

On June 14 1830, a **French** attack on the town, now called Algiers, succeeded and a planned short military action resulted in a full occupation until 1962. During those 132 years, the French made many changes to the town. The walls of the kasbah were razed and large boulevards were built. The town expanded rapidly, and for the first time developed outside its original walls. During WW2, Algiers was an important strategic asset. Charles de Gaulle set up his headquarters of the Free French army there in 1943, and the town kept its military importance until the liberation of France. From early Jan 1957, Algiers was in the forefront of the struggle for Independence and when it was granted in 1962, was the scene of great jubilation. As capital of independent Algeria, Algiers has been faced with the endemic problems of over-population, shortage of housing and traffic congestion. Nevertheless, Algiers has gained an important place within the international community, organizing important conferences, involving the OAU, Opec and the Non-Aligned movement. In 1980, Algiers hosted a conference on the Iraq-Iran war.

Location

Algiers has an idyllic coastal location, overlooking a beautiful bay with a backdrop of steep wooded mountains. The town, once known as White Algiers due to the whitewashed walls, faces E and is at its most beautiful in the morning sun. The present skyline has two important landmarks; to the SE of the centre, the Martyrs' Monument reaching 90m into the sky, and more central, the square shape of the up-market *Hotel Aurassi*. The town is divided into two parts. The old town, known as the kasbah lies on the hill, behind the place des Martyrs. The new town, mostly French built, starts by the waterfront at the S of the kasbah and continues S round the bay. One of the main commercial streets is rue Larbi Ben M'Hidi with the central Post Office at its S end. By the sea front between the kasbah and the Post Office are the train station, the ferry terminal and the Air Algérie air terminal.

Climate

The climate is typically Mediterranean, but with a cooler light wind from the sea. The hottest months are Jun, Jul and Aug while the season from Nov to Feb is mild, sometimes rainy and generally humid.

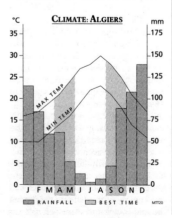

CLIMATE: ALGIERS

Places of interest

Around the city

The *centre ville* is the modern part of the city that stretches more or less from the place Port Saïd to the rue Didouche Mourad. The **rue Larbi Ben M'Hidi** is the main commercial street in Algiers and is now a crowded pedestrian zone. There are a great number of shops, including the *Gallerie Algériennes*, of neo-Moorish style, that should not be missed. A third of the way down is the elegant **place Emir Abdelkader**, with an enormous statue of Abdelkader, the famous resistance fighter. Continuing down the rue Larbi Ben M'Hidi brings you to the **Grande Poste**, a large neo-Moorish building, that is worth a look, even if you do not need to post anything. Opposite the Grande Poste, the Ave El Khettabi leads to the rue Didouche Mourad, another important commercial street, lined with large French style buildings. This street continues up a hill, twisting a little, to the **Cathedral du Sacré Coeur** and to the **Bardo** and **National Antiquity museums**.

The sea front, along the Blvd Che Guevara to the N of the corniche is lined by French buildings with arcades. Behind the sea front, by the Djemaa El Jedid Mosque, is the **place des Martyrs**. This square is the centre of life in the lower part of the kasbah and is extremely lively at all times. Close by, on a square off the rue Amar El-Kama, is the colourful **Chaat market**, selling everything from clothes to fresh fruit and spices.

Most of the mosques and many of the monuments cannot be visited. The hours and days open will be indicated when appropriate. It is important to dress correctly when visiting a mosque. If time is limited, there are a few places that should not be missed. By the sea front, next to the place des Martyrs is the **Djemaa El Jedid mosque**, also known as the Mosquée de la Pêcherie.

Built in 1660 by the Turks of the Hanefite sect, it is surprisingly built in the shape of a cross. Legend has it that the mosque was built by a Christian slave, who paid with his life for his sacrilegious efforts. Two streets away, along the sea front is the **Djemaa El Kebir mosque.** The date of its construction is not clear, but it was built in the place of one of the Christian basilicas and is the oldest mosque in Algiers. The main building was probably erected in the 11th century by Youcef Ben Tachfin, and the minaret in 1324. The main courtyard, with its two fountains gives an overall impression of great simplicity. Originally the mosque had no ornaments on the outside walls, but in 1837, the French took a marble portico from a demolished mosque and added it to the rue Al Mourabitine side of the mosque. Unfortunately neither mosque can be visited by non-Muslims. Going back towards the NW corner of place des Martyrs you can take the rue Bab El Oued, which leads to the **Ali Bitchnine mosque.** Built in 1623 by Piccini, a rich Italian pirate working for the Turks, the mosque follows the plans of Byzantine churches, with a great octagonal dome over a square room. On three sides of this room are galleries, each covered in a small dome. During the French occupation the mosque was converted into a Christian church.

The street on the right side of the Mosque leads to the **Museum of Popular Arts and Traditions**, situated in an old traditional palace built in 1570 by the Turks. In 1830 the palace became the first French town hall and has since been converted into a very interesting museum. The building is as interesting as the exhibits, with beautiful rooms and the ceiling of the main first floor room is particularly attractive. The items displayed include a large variety of regional carpets, highlighting their regional differences, together with jewels, pottery and furniture. On the first floor, rooms have been arranged and decorated in the traditional manner. The museum is situated off the rue Hadj Omar, on the left. Open daily 1000-1200 and 1400-1700, except Fri and Sat.

Going back S along the rue Hadj Omar, on the right, along the small rue Mechtri, is the **Dar Mustapha Pacha**. This was the private residence of Mustapha Pacha, who was Bey of Algiers from 1798 until 1805. The palace was built in 1799. Now it serves as an administrative office, so it is possible to look in during the day. Return along the rue Hadj Omar which leads into the place Cheikh Ben Badis. Before reaching the square, on the right is the **Dar Hassan Pacha**, a winter palace built in 1790, of typical Moorish style. The inside may be visited, as the building now houses government administration.

On the left of place Cheikh Ben Badis is the Dar Aziz Bent El Bey, and the Ketchaoua mosque. The **Dar Aziz Bent El Bey** was built in the 17th century and is one of the few remaining important buildings in the lower part of the kasbah. It is also known as the Princess's palace and was built in the typical Moorish style. The courtyard can be visited. The **Ketchaoua mosque** was built in 1794, but was completely restored in 1845. During the French occupation it was initially converted into a Christian church and later into a cathedral. From here walk up into the kasbah, which starts in the area beyond the rue Amar Ali and the rue Abderrahmane Arbadji. **The kasbah** used to encompass the entire town. It was only towards the end of the 19th century that the town expanded outside its original walls. The French destroyed the walls and a large part of the lower area of the kasbah by the sea, and built large, French-style boulevards and houses. Until the 19th century, the kasbah had been the home of some of the richest families in Algeria, but with the coming of the French, the kasbah became poorer and more decrepit and

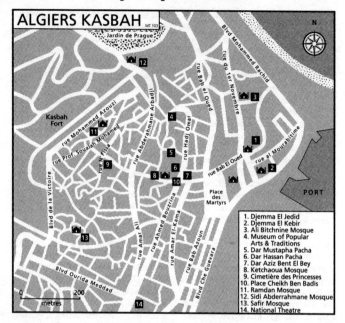

ALGIERS KASBAH MT 103

1. Djemma El Jedid
2. Djemma El Kebir
3. Ali Bitchnine Mosque
4. Museum of Popular Arts & Traditions
5. Dar Mustapha Pacha
6. Dar Hassan Pacha
7. Dar Aziz Bent El Bey
8. Ketchaoua Mosque
9. Cimetière des Princesses
10. Place Cheikh Ben Badis
11. Ramdan Mosque
12. Sidi Abderrahmane Mosque
13. Safir Mosque
14. National Theatre

the wealthy moved out to new, more comfortable, houses. In the 1950s, the colonial government moved half the inhabitants out of the old town, but the kasbah soon refilled with people from the country in search of work. The result was overcrowding, poor living conditions and poorly maintained buildings. For many years the government ignored the problem and it took an important demonstration by the kasbah's inhabitants in 1985 before an organization for the restoration of the kasbah was set up in collaboration with UNESCO. The kasbah has not had a total facelift and problems of overpopulation still exist, but walking around it is still a very interesting experience. The little narrow streets wind up the hill, through arches and short tunnels. The houses are built tightly together and inter-communicate by their roof terraces. If the op-

portunity arises, visit a house and from the roof admire the superb view over the other white terraces and the bay. In the kasbah few streets are named and it is quite easy to get lost, but people will willingly give you directions, and in any case, all roads downhill lead to the harbour.

Do not miss the **Cimetiére des Princess**, off the rue N'fissa, a quiet spot where one can sit in the shade surrounded by Muslim tombstones. The **Kasbah Fort** built in 1592 and once the Bey's palace dominates the town and the bay. It is here the incident later used by the French as a pretext for the 1830 invasion took place (see page 33). Unfortunately, the fort cannot be visited. From the Kasbah Fort take the Blvd de la Victoire, and then the rue Mohammed Azouzi and on the right, down a small street is the **Sidi Ramadan mosque**.

Built in the 16th century before the arrival of the Turks, it is one of the oldest mosques in Algiers but cannot be visited. Take the rue Mohammed Azouzi down some stairs to the **Sidi Abderrahmane Mosque** built between 1696 and 1730. By the entrance is the tomb of a highly venerated 15th century saint. From here you can walk back down the rue Abderrahmane Arbadji to the lower part of the kasbah and the town centre.

To the S there are a number of places of interest. **The Bardo Museum**, 3 Ave Franklin Roosevelt, is at the top of the rue Didouche Mourad: take a bus from in front of the Grande Poste. The museum, set in a beautiful Moorish style mansion has a very large section on the pre-history and ethnography of North Africa. The display of costumes and crafts from the different Algerian ethnic groups is very good. There is also an impressive display of jewellery, especially from Kabylia. On the second floor are displayed objects from the Sahara, in particular from the Hoggar. These include leather goods, camel saddles, clothing and weapons. Open daily except Fri morning and Sat 0900-1200 and 1400-1700.

Further up the hill, in the Parc de la Liberté, is the **National Museum of Antiquities** which has a collection of items including antique mosaics, Roman glass and sculptures and some Islamic art. Open daily except Fri morning and Sat 0900-1200 and 1400-1700. Entry is free on Fri afternoons. The **People's Palace**, is 400m further up the road from the Museum of Antiquities, just off the Ave Franklin Roosevelt. It was the President's residence but in 1987 he gave it to the town of Algiers. It contains a **History Museum**, with a good display of swords and jewellery dating from the Turkish period, and a **Natural History Museum** with a great variety of plants, trees and stuffed animals from around the world. The surrounding park is open daily 0900 to 2100 except Mon. The museums are open 0900-1200 and 1400-1800, and closed on Fri.

Martyrs Monument was built in 1982 and commemorates all those who died in the struggle for Independence. The three stylized palm fronds reach a height of 95m and make the monument hard to miss. On the large esplanade in front of the monument is the massive Riad el-Feth commercial centre. Its three storeys with fountains and patios, include many restaurants and an open-air theatre. Under the Martyrs monument is the **Jihad Museum**, which covers the entire struggle for Independence since 1830. Unfortunately, the period from 1954 to 1962 is covered rather superficially, and most material is in Arabic. Open daily 0900-1700, except Sat and Sun mornings.

On the other side of the esplanade, the **War Museum** is set in a splendid marble-floored building. This museum is to a certain extent the continuation of the Jihad Museum, covering the same period, but without a clear link between the displays. It nevertheless has some interesting displays, such as a plan of Algiers in the 1830s, showing the defensive logic of the architecture, as well as a real guillotine, and various rooms with displays on the struggle for Independence.

The **Museum of Fine Arts**, is opposite the Jardin d'Essai, at the bottom of the hill, under the Martyrs monument. The collection has some interesting paintings from well known European painters, and some from contemporary Algerian artists. Open 0930-1200 and 1430-1700 daily except Fri and Sat.

Opposite the museum is the **Jardin d'Essai**, the National Nature Museum, once a very impressive botanical garden. Open 1000-1800, closed Sat.

Parks

Parc de la Liberté is S of the town, at the S end of the rue Didouche Mourad. This is an attractive park set out in terraces. **Jardin de Prague** situated to the N of the kasbah, behind the Sidi Abderrahmane mosque is a small garden, wonderfully fresh during the warm days. The **War Cemetery** is 500m before Déli-Ibrahim, 10 km to the SW of the city on the N side of the N36. A second area has been dedicated for war graves at the El Alia civil cemetery on the road to El Harrach. It lies to the S side of the W118 from El Harrach.

Local information

CURFEW At time of going to press 2230-0400.

● **Accommodation**

WARNING It can be difficult to find a hotel in Algiers, as the town is overcrowded and many Algerians live in hotels. Start searching early as, after midday, finding a room can be very difficult. Ignore the '*complet*' sign which is often on constant display, as they may well have rooms. Also, do not hesitate to ask for directions, as hotels often only have a sign in Arabic, or even none at all.

A *Hotel El Aurassi*, Ave Frantz Fanon, T 748252, F 632292, 400 rm with excellent views, pool, tennis, good restaurant, booking essential; **A** *Hotel El Djezaïr*, 24 Ave Souidani Boudjemma, T 601010, F 606408, formerly the *Hotel St George* and traditionally the most fashionable hotel in Algiers, delightful Moorish architecture, attractive bars and terrace, large and well appointed restaurant, 155 rm, fine views over city and bay and (limited) parking space, payment by foreign guests in hard currency only, booking essential.

B *Hotel Es-Safir*, 14 Blvd Zighout Youcef on sea-front, T 635040, 150 rm with bath, a/c, some with sea view, good restaurant, payments by foreign guests in hard currency only.

C *Hotel Albert 1er*, 5 Ave Pasteur, one block up Blvd Mohammed Khémisti from the Grande Poste, T 630020-2, F 637368, 69 rm, 116 beds, pleasant bar and restaurant, mainly business

visitors, payment by foreign guests in hard currency only; **C** *Hotel Mouflon d'Or*, BP165, Hydra, T 568225, 60 rm, spacious hotel in very pleasant situation on heights above Algiers, restaurant, bar, shop, pool, garden terrace, car park.

D *Central Touring Hotel*, 9 rue Abane Ramdane, T 635440, 300m to the S of place Port Saïd, all rm with bath; **D** *Hotel d'Angleterre*, 11 Blvd Ben Boulaïd Mustapha, T 636540, a block to E of place Emir Abdelkader; **D** *Hotel Samir*, 74 rue Didouche Mourad, T 643064.

E *Hotel El Badre*, 31 rue Amar el-Kama, in lower part of kasbah, a small street off place Port Saïd, T 620812, clean, well-kept hotel, over 80 rm, rarely full, communal pay shower (hot), in a noisy area; **E** *Grand Hotel Modern*, 7 rue de la Liberté, T 636374; **E** *Grand Hotel National*, 1 rue Patrice Lumumba, T 634173, close to place Port Saïd at the intersection with the rue Larbi Ben M'Hidi; **E** *Grand Hotel Tipaza*, 4 rue Rachid Kessentini, T 630040.

Youth hostels: 213 rue Hassiba-Ben-Bouali, T 670032, open 0800-1200 and 1400-2200, 74 beds, kitchen, laundry, 4 km from bus station and ferry terminus, train 1 km, bus Nos 1, 3, 5, 6 or 9.

Camping: Nearest camping site is at Zeralda, 40 km W of Algiers by the sea, well connected to Algiers, any bus going to Cherchell or Tipasa stops there. The journey takes 1 hr, and the campsite is 2-3 km further on.

● **Places to eat**

♦♦♦*L'Asiatique*, 2 rue François Garnier, off N side (left going up) of the upper end of rue Didouche Mourad, nr Ministry of Information and opp Parc de la Liberté, Chinese and Vietnamese cuisine, good service, pleasant ambiance, chic clientèle, seats 60-70, booking advisable; *Le Bardo*, upper end of rue Didouche Mourad, just below the Musée du Bardo and roughly opp the Ministry of Public Works (Ministère des Travaux Publics), T 607343, currently fashionable with reputation for good expensive food.

♦♦ *Restaurant Café d'Angleterre*, 11 Blvd Mustapha Ben Boulaïd, moderate food, moderate service and tolerably priced; *Restaurant le Berry*, 8 Blvd Mustapha Ben Boulaïd, behind *Hotel Es Safir*, T 633414/633424, range of interesting dishes incl seafood, at reasonable prices served in quiet and rather sober surroundings.

◆For cheap food, the area E of the kasbah is the best place to go. Around the place des Martyrs, and between the place Emir Abdelkader and the place Port Saïd, there are many food stalls and small restaurants selling brochettes, chicken and *merguez* (spicy sausages). In front of the Djemaa El Jedid mosque a small ramp leads to a number of small fish restaurants. **NB** Before ordering any fish, be sure of the price, as this depends on the pre-cooked weight. *Le Simbad*, on the ramp in front of the El Jedid mosque, expensive, one of the best fish restaurants in Algiers; *Restaurant Bassora*, Blvd Che Guevara, towards the place Port Saïd, good and filling food, Moorish decor, restaurant closes at 2200; *Restaurant La Porte de la Mer*, first restaurant on the right, going down the ramp in front of the Djemaa El Jedid mosque, simple but good local food at very cheap prices.

● **Airline offices**
See Information for visitors, see page 355.

● **Banks & money changers**
Banque Central d'Algérie, 8 Blvd Zighout Youcef; **Banque National d'Algérie**, 47 rue Didouche Mourad, Hall Air Algérie, 1 place Audin (open daily 0800-1800 except Fri) and Air terminal, rue Colonel Ben Abderrazak (open daily 0800-1230 and 1330-1900).

● **Embassies & consulates**
See also Information for visitors, see page 354 for Representation overseas. **Australia**, 12 Ave Emile Marquis, Djenane El-Malik, Hydra, T 601965/602846; **Canada**, 27 bis, rue des Frères Benhafid, Hydra, T 606611; **France**, 6 Ave Larbi Alik, Hydra, T 604488; **UK**, 7 chemin Capt Hocine Slimane, T 605038/605411; **USA**, 4 chemin Cheikh Bachir El Ibrahimi, El Biar, T 601186/601425.

● **Entertainment**
Discotheques/nightclubs: these are found at the beach resort hotels. Try *El Djazaïr Hotel* and *Hotel Aurassi*.

● **Hospitals & medical services**
Chemists: all night chemists can be found at 19 rue Abane Ramdane, T 633631 and 2 rue Didouche Mourad, T 634743.
Hospitals: *Hôpital Mustapha*, close to the place du 1er Mai, T 663333.

● **Post & telecommunications**
Area code: 02.

Post Office: the main Post Office is on the Place Grande Poste at the S end of the rue Larbi Ben M'Hidi, open 0800-1900 and Thur 0800-1300, closed Fri.

Telephones: the telephone exchange is by Place Grande Poste on the corner of rue Asselah, open 24 hrs.

● **Shopping**
Bookshops: most bookshops are along the rue Didouche Mourad and rue Larbi Ben M'Hidi, with a couple in the rue Hamani which joins the bottom of rue Didouche Mourad. There is a shop selling mainly books on Berber culture on the Blvd Zighout Youcef as it approaches Square Port Saïd. Most shops tend to sell only books in French and Arabic. Bookshops are also the place to buy town plans of Algiers.

General: the main shopping area with many large stores is in the rue Larbi Ben M'Hidi, and across the place de la Grande Poste, along the rue Didouche Mourad. Crafts can be found in the 3 SNAT (Societé National d'Art et Tradition) stores specializing in local traditional crafts: 2 Blvd Mohammed Khémisti, 1 rue Didouche Mourad and 3 rue Maitre Ali Boumendjel.

● **Sport**
Golf: there is an 18-hole course on Route de Chérage, nr the Olympic Stadium.

Sailing: is available at Moretti and Sidi Fredj.

Skiing: for information about the adjacent skiing resorts, contact Fédération Algérienne de Ski, 30 Blvd Zighout Youcef, Algiers.

Swimming: numerous pools incl Olympic pool on Route de Chérage and many good beaches.

Tennis: Fédération Algérienne de Tennis, 60 rue Larbi Ben M'Hidi.

● **Tourist offices**
ONAT (Office National Algerian de Tourisme): Central Office, 5 Blvd Ben Boulaïd, T 641550 and at 2 rue Didouche Mourad, T 631066 and 4 rue Elisée Reclus, T 663583. There are also branches in the *Hotel Aurassi*, T 640148 and at the airport, T 753367. All ONAT agencies have a travel agency service and sell tickets for all major airlines. They organize interesting half-day tours of the town for which you register the day before.

● **Useful Addresses**
Ambulance: T 623333.
Police: T 17.

● **Transport**
Local Bus: for short distances you will probably need only 1 or 2 routes during your stay

in Algiers. For information, go to the bus station either on the Place Grande Poste or on the Place des Martyrs. **Car hire**: Algérie Auto Tourism, 120 rue Didouche Mourad, T 616456; **Algiers Location Auto**, 14 rue Dr Saadane Cherif, T 636905; **Avis**, 109 rue Didouche Mourad, T 668427; **Central Auto Location**, 54 Blvd Mohammed V, T 636087; **Europacar**, 32 Blvd Mohammed V, T 647793; *ONAT*, 4 rue Elisée Reclus, T 663583. **Taxi**: these are plentiful but there are no taxis stations, so flag them down. Each taxi has a meter, but make sure it is used or else negotiate the price beforehand. It may be difficult to find a taxi in the rush hour.

Air To get to the airport either take a taxi or the bus in front of the *Hotel Es-Safir*, on the Blvd Zighout Youcef. For **international flights** see Information for visitors, page 355. In summer, seats are scarce so book well in advance. In Algiers, you will most probably have to pay with Algerian Dinars changed at the official rate, and proved by a document (*Attestation de Cessation de Devises*). **Internal flights** to Annaba, Béchar, Constantine, Djanet, El-Golea, El-Oued, Ghardaïa, In-Salah, Oran, Tamanrasset and Timimoun.

Train The station is on the quayside by place Port Saïd. Take the lift from the street. For information, T 647380. Trains to Annaba, Bejaïa, Constantine, Souk Ahras, Tizi-Ouzou and Tunis. All other destinations to the W of Algiers incl Oran and Tlemcen leave from the Agha station, which is S along the sea-front, after the Place du Pérou. For information, T 611510.

Road Bus: there are three bus stations in Algiers. The main station for direct buses for the Algerian main towns, incl Béchar, Bejaïa, Ghardaïa, El Oued and Oran, is after the Agha train station, by the water front. From the place des Martyrs the buses go to this bus station. For buses to the W coast to Cherchell, Ténès, Tipasa and Zeralda, the bus station is situated on the sea front, by the Customs House, opposite the place du Pérou. For buses to the E coast the bus station is at the lower level in front of the *Hotel Es-Safir*. **NB** The main station is well organized with all prices and time displayed. Tickets can be bought in advance, and in summer it is recommended to book at least a day in advance. **Taxi**: these leave from the ramp by the main train station, in front of the place Port Saïd to all major cities.

AROUND ALGIERS

The N11 coast road W from Algiers goes through a built up area for the first 30 km with only occasional glimpses of the sea. Beyond Aïn Benian, the road swings inland leaving the coastal strip for tourist development and intensive market gardening.

The coast to the west

Moretti and Sidi Fredj

These are both important seaside resorts, mostly frequented by people from Algiers. Their beautiful beaches make these typical resort towns very pleasant for a day trip out of the capital. Unfortunately there are very few hotels and they all tend to be expensive. **NB** Sidi Fredj is named Sidi-Ferruch on the Michelin map.

    Moretti which is only 25 km away from Algiers via Cheraga along the shorter N41 is particularly accessible for a day trip. **Accommodation C** *Hotel El Minzah*, T 391435, 95 rm, the only hotel in Moretti.

Sidi Fredj

Has a longer history, is strategically placed and has a much larger infrastructure. This is the place where the French landed in 1830 and where the Allied troops sent to liberate North Africa in WW2 began their campaign. Today Sidi Fredj is above all an important and highly successful seaside resort. A very ambitious project has transformed this town into a well-planned, modern tourist complex. There is an excellent yacht harbour, an activity centre and an open air theatre in the old fortress. The beaches, part of the 'Turquoise coast,' are really beautiful and live up to expectations.

● **Accommodation C** *El Manar*, T 783816, 400 rm, pool; **C** *El Riadh*, T 814402, 125 rm, pool; **D** *El Marsa*, T 801315, 100 rm, pool.

● **Transport** There are buses to the airport and Algiers, provided for hotel visitors, but can be used by anyone.

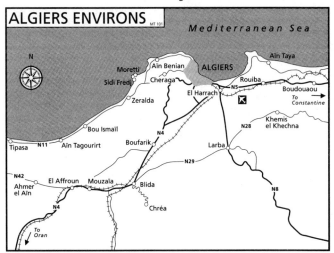

ALGIERS ENVIRONS MT 101

Mediterranean Sea

Zeralda

30 km from Algiers Zeralda is another seaside resort noted for its beach of fine sand and for its peaceful natural park within the neighbouring pine forest. Many facilities are available and this little town makes a nice day trip.

● **Accommodation C** *Les Sables d'Or*, T 396924, Tx 63112, tourist Complex with 258 rm, pool and tennis; **D** *La Résidence*, T 782922; **D** *Mazafran*, T 812614, 200 rm, pool and tennis. **Youth hostels** At Douaouda-Marine 7 km S, open 0800-1200 and 1400-2200, 20 beds, kitchen, laundry.

Further along the N11 coast road, 84 km from Algiers, beyond **Aïn Tagourirt** the W40 leads up to the hill top site of the **Mausoleum of the Mauritanian Royal Family**, confusingly called the Tomb of the Christian Girl. The huge monument, perhaps dating back to 100BC, cylindrical in shape, and decorated with 60 columns, had four fake doors. The actual entrance leads by a devious route into an empty chamber. When 'discovered' in 1865 this was empty. There is a splendid view from here.

Tipasa

71 km from Algiers, Tipasa is both an important archaeological site and a seaside resort. The town has two separate parts, **Tipasa-plage** the tourist complex, and **Tipasa-ville**, where the ruins are situated. The village in itself is quite charming, but the real interest is the ruins.

History

Originally a Phoenician trading post, it became a Roman colony in the 2nd century AD and one of the most important Christian settlements in this area of North Africa. In 430 AD, the Vandals took control of Tipasa and tried to convert the inhabitants to the heretical belief in Arianism. A large proportion of the population fled to Spain, and those who remained were persecuted. Myth has it that their tongues were cut out, but that they still continued to speak. This was hailed as a miracle throughout the Christian world. In 534 AD, the Byzantines retook the town which was already declining in prosperity and falling into ruin. By the time the Arabs

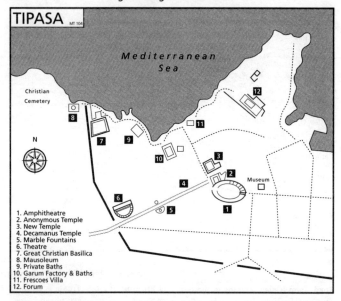

TIPASA MT 104

Mediterranean Sea

Christian Cemetery

N

1. Amphitheatre
2. Anonymous Temple
3. New Temple
4. Decamanus Temple
5. Marble Fountains
6. Theatre
7. Great Christian Basilica
8. Mausoleum
9. Private Baths
10. Garum Factory & Baths
11. Frescoes Villa
12. Forum

Museum

invaded, there was little left. They named it Tefassed, which in Arabic means 'the damaged'.

The site

The site by the sea is magnificent, and still relatively free of tourists. By the entrance are the imposing remains of an amphitheatre. Further along are the **Anonymous Temple** and the **New Temple**, later converted into a Christian Basilica. Between these two temples, lies a well preserved 200m long section of the **Decamanus Maximus**, the ancient road that linked Cherchell to Algiers, at the far end of which stands the **Nyphaeum**, a marble fountain. A little further on are the remains of a **theatre**. By the sea, stands the 4th century AD **Great Christian Basilica**. It is 52m long, 40m wide and has nine naves with mosaic-covered floors. Around the main building are other remains including a **chapel with mosaics**, and a **baptistery**. To the W lies a **large Christian cemetery**. One of the most interesting monu-

ments here is a large round **5th century mausoleum** containing 14 places for sarcophagi and inscriptions indicating the date of construction. Return to the Great Christian Basilica and follow the path to the E which passes some small well-preserved private baths. Further on is the *garum* factory (producing a spicy fish-based sauce) and some smaller baths. By the sea is the **Frescoes Villa**, clearly once owned by a rich inhabitant. Most of the frescoes from here are in the museum.

Continuing E along the coast, the road leads to a very well preserved **Forum**, the oldest area within Tipasa. Open 0900-1200 and 1400-1700 closed Sat. At end of the tour of the site, visit the small, very interesting **museum**. It contains some superb mosaics dating back to the 1st century AD which were found in the Basilica. It is on the left of the road as you leave the site. Entrance AD1. Open 0900-1700.

Local information

CURFEW At time of going to press 2330-0400.

● **Accommodation**

B *Hotel de la Baie* at Tipasa-plage (1½ km W of the village), T 461822, 111 rm, tennis, pool.

C *Hotel de la Résidence* at Tipasa-Plage, T 461824, 352 rm, 4 pools, all sports facilities, garden; **C** *Hotel les Pavilions*, 2-3 km E along the Algiers road, T 461761, 500+ bungalows; **C** *Hotel Simbad*, is the only hotel in the village.

Camping: at Chenoua-plage which lies W of Tipasa. Beyond Tipasa, turn right onto the W109 and Chenoua is reached after about 3 km. Tents for hire or take your own. Has a good beach, but the facilities are far from perfect.

● **Places to eat**

The restaurants nr the entrance to the site are best described as up-market.

◆◆*Le Progrès* is rec as average.

◆Those nearer the port are cheaper.

● **Transport**

Road There are regular buses from and to Algiers and Cherchell.

Chréa and Blida

Chréa, 20 km on the N37 from Blida and 70 km from Algiers via the N1, is a ski resort that lies at 1,500m. In the summer it is equally popular for the many walks around the mountains. The view from the road up to Chréa, back towards Algiers is breathtaking. **Blida** today is an important regional and agricultural centre dealing mainly in olives and citrus fruits. The town was founded by Andalusian immigrants in the 16th century who introduced irrigation in order to grow oranges.

CURFEW At time of going to press 2330-0400.

● **Accommodation E** *Hotel des Cédres*, in Chréa, T 03 14, 30 rm, 1,000m up in the forest; **E** *Hotel El Kebir*, 74 Blvd Laichi Abdellah, in Blida, T 634952; **E** *Hotel Royal*, in Blida, place du 1er Novembre (main square), T 03 492801. **Youth hostels:** Kritli Mokhtar, Blida, T 499601, 40 beds, kitchen, bus 500m, train 1 km.

● **Transport** There are regular buses to/from Algiers. Local buses for Chréa leave from the main street in Blida. Blida train station, directly W of the centre, is on the main line from Algiers and Oran.

THE EAST

CONTENTS

Algiers to Bejaia via the N12	304
Algiers to Bejaia via the N24 Coast Road	308
Bejaia to Jijel	309
Around Constantine	310
Excursions from Constantine	316

MAPS

Kabylia	305
Constantine environs	311
Djemila	313
Constantine	315
Annaba	317
The Aurés	320
Timgad	321

This region, stretching E from Algiers to the border of Tunisia, includes the important towns of Constantine, Annaba, Bejaïa and Sétif, starting point for visits to the ruins of Roman Djemila. Tourists are attracted to the forested Grand and Petit Kabylie ranges, the Djurdjura National Park, a region of outstanding beauty, and the awesome gorges in the Aurés Massif between Batna and Biskra. The forested hills and the intensively cultivated patches of fertile ground, the tiny villages clinging to the mountain sides and the breathtaking views from the tortuously winding roads, make any journey here memorable.

Kabylia

This region extends from Algiers E to Bejaïa. It is often subdivided into the Grande and Petite Kabylies. **Grande Kabylie** is the region around the Djurdjura massif with summits reaching 2,000m. The **Petite Kabylie** is the Bejaïa hinterland also with high mountains,

the Babors, which reach 1,200m. These mountain ranges, well wooded and cut with deep gorges, rise straight from the coast making access difficult.

The landscape, and the inaccessibility of many villages has ensured that the Kabyles have kept a strong and individual identity, the physical isolation encouraging an independent streak amongst the people of the area. They speak Kabyle, a Berber dialect, and it is said that they speak French as a second language and Arabic as a third. Family units are very strong, and women enjoy a greater freedom, unveiled and colourfully clothed.

The landscape of Kabylia is intriguing in the way that remote villages appear to cling to the mountain side. Life here in winter can be very harsh, and many roads are blocked or dangerous to use due to snow.

ALGIERS TO BEJAIA VIA THE N12

The 300 km route crosses the low-lying plain behind Algiers as a dual carriageway, the quickest way to cut through the straggling suburbs. The road makes use of the valleys of the Isser and Oued Sébaou as far as Azazga. Sit on the S side of the coach for the best views of the Djurdjursas. It then twists and winds its way up through the northern ranges of the Grand Kabylie through passes at almost 1,000m before its descent to El Kseur on the Oued Soummam and thence to Bejaïa.

Tizi Ouzou

On the main N5/N12 road from Algiers, Tizi Ouzou is the administrative capital of the *wilaya* of Greater Kabylia. With its population approaching 400,000 and growing fast, it is situated 100 km E of Algiers and mid way between Algiers

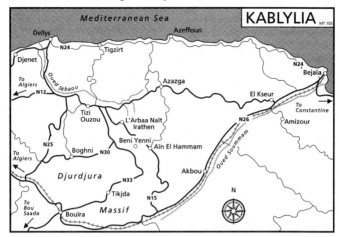

KABLYLIA MT 105

and Bejaïa. It is better as a departure point for those wishing to explore the region than as a place to stay. Being the only town in a remote area, Tizi Ouzou offers both commercial and administrative facilities. It is known for its large market, every Thur.

Local information
● Accommodation
C *Hotel Amraoua*, T 408546, situated at foot of Beloua mountain nr Tala Allam, on NW outskirts of town, most expensive and well appointed hotel in Tizi Ouzou, attractive bar, good restaurant, 154 comfortable (if somewhat gloomy) rm, tennis, pool, splendid terrace, magnificent views; **C** *Hotel Lalla Khedidja*, at the S exit of the town, on the road to Mechtras, 10 mins from station, T 402901, 60 rm.

D *Hotel Beloua*, 16 rue Larbi Ben M'Hidi, T 401990, central location a short walk from the bus station, 60 rm; **D** *Hotel les Andalouses*, by the mosque and the police station.

E *Hotel Olympia*, rue Larbi Ben M'Hidi, central, 10 mins from station.

Youth hostels: is on rue Boulila Amar, BP 456, Tizi Ouzou, T 201212, 50 beds, kitchen, bus 1 km, train 2 km.

● Places to eat
◆◆◆Restaurant at *Hotel Amraoua* serves European and Algerian cuisine in spacious restaurant or on the splendid terrace which can seat 200 and has magnificent views over the town and the mountains of Kabylia to the S.

◆There are two small restaurants at the *Olympic Pool* for cheaper food. Rue Larbi Ben M'Hidi has cheap eating places too.

● Post & telecommunications
Area code: 03.

● Tour companies & travel agents
Air Algérie, 1 rue Larbi Ben M'Hidi, T 406992.

● Tourist offices
ONAT, 3 rue Larbi Ben M'Hidi, T 402711.

● Transport
Road Bus: the bus station, a large blue building on the rue Larbi Ben M'Hidi, the road on the W from Algiers, provides a helpful information desk. Buses run frequently to Algiers (usually 6 daily) and to various points in Kabylia such as Aïn El Hammam, Azazga, Beni Yenni, Dellys, Tigzirt and Tikjda. Local buses also leave from the main bus station or from the streets immediately N of the large roundabout at the E end of rue Larbi Ben M'Hidi. **Taxi**: to the W, these leave from opposite the bus station on rue Larbi Ben M'Hidi. Those to the N, S and SW in Kabylia leave from the other side of the main roundabout and the nearby main square half way down rue Abane Ramdane. Taxis to the E and SE (Aïn El Hammam, Tassaft, etc) leave from the E edge of town.

Excursions from Tizi Ouzou

The steep, winding mountain road N from Tizi Ouzou to **Tigzirt**, 39 km (see page 308), has amazing views over the sea. The **Shrine of Sidi Beloua**, Tizi Ouzou's patron saint, on the summit of the Beloua mountain immediately N of town provides a magnificent panorama of the region for the energetic.

L'Arbaa-Naït-Irathen is on the scenic N15 and has a huge fort, built in the 1850s by the French when controlling the area, which provides commanding views over the valleys on both sides.

Currently it is a craft centre. From here it is only 20 km of scenic road to Aïn El Hammam (see below).

Tala Guilef which in Berber means 'the fountain of the wild boar' at 1,500m is a splendid spot on the N side of the **Djurdjura Range** towards their W end. From Tizi-Ouzou take the N12 to the E, after 6 km take the N30 S and at 53 km from Tizi-Ouzou, after some very winding roads and very beautiful scenery, you arrive at Boghni. From here there are 19 km of narrow road but Tala Guilef is well worth visiting for the walks and

---

ASSES, DONKEYS AND MULES

There is a certain amount of confusion when naming the normally overladen and generally undernourished beasts of burden found in the countries of North Africa and Spain. While there can be no confusion as to what is a **horse**, *Equus caballus*, or even an **ass**, *Equus asinus*, despite the fact that it is most commonly called a **donkey**, except in Spain where it is a **burro**, a **mule** requires some definition.

The term **mule** can refer to any hybrid but as a beast of burden it is the offspring of a male donkey (jack) and a female horse (mare), while the offspring of a male horse (stallion) and a female donkey (jenny) is correctly termed a **hinny**.

A mule is a horse in the middle with a donkey at either end. It has longer ears, and a thinner mane and tail than its mother and carries the typical 'cross' markings on the shoulders and back. The hinny is less popular, being nearer the size of a donkey and has the shorter ears and thicker mane and tail of its father.

A mule is stronger than a horse, has a much longer working life under the right circumstances, can withstand extremes of temperature without long-term ill effects, is less vulnerable to sickness and can survive on a very limited diet. Mules are noted for being surefooted and for being fast and accurate kickers. Mules are generally considered to be infertile though instances of offspring are recorded.

The Algerian wild ass originally roamed the Atlas Ranges. The Romans carefully preserved them on mosaics but are held responsible for their demise. The Nubian wild ass, of a distinctive reddish hue, roamed the semi-desert areas between the River Nile and the Red Sea shores. It survived into the 20th century.

The Egyptians used asses. Illustrations from 2500BC show us that even then these domesticated beasts were carrying loads and passengers out of all proportion to their size. They also had mules which are thought to have first been bred around 1750BC. Models of this hybrid were found in the pyramids and a mule drawing a chariot is depicted on a vase found in Thebes.

The Romans placed heavy reliance on the mule, for riding, to draw carts and farm implements and to carry equipment. To assist copulation they devised a wooden cage with a ramp to enable the shorter jack ass reach the taller mare.

Facts The Food and Agriculture Organization's (FOA) latest figures place Morocco (470,000) and Algeria (160,000) second and third for mule populations in Africa and Spain (129,000) first in Europe.

scrambles in the surrounding forests, plus rock climbing and skiing in season.

● **Accommodation** C *Hotel El Arz*, T 422476-8, built in mid 1970s but still has good reputation, 200 beds in 80 rm with bath and balcony, restaurant with 165 places, bar/café, pool, tennis. **Youth hostels** T 402821, 80 beds, kitchen.

Beni Yenni Kabylia's most famous tribe inhabit a group of seven very interesting mountain villages from which there are amazing panoramic views over the surrounding mountains, particularly beautiful at sunset. Two of the villages, **Aït Larbaa** at 760m and **Taourirt Mimoun** are well known for their traditional jewellery and silverwork, and there are a few shops with fixed prices. Take the N12 E from Tizi Ouzou, after 6 km take the N30/N33 S and at about 38 km from Tizi Ouzou look out for the minor road signed to Aïn El Hammam on the left. Take this but don't miss the spectacular views at this junction, and shortly turn left again to Beni Yenni which is a further 2 km. Complicated but worth it. Buses run from Tizi Ouzou which save all the effort but they don't stop for photographs. **Accommodation** D *Hotel Le Bracelet d'Argent*, T 59, 24 clean rm.

Aïn El Hammam is along a **very** winding road from Beni Yenni. At 1,080m it offers more gorges, peaks and breathtaking views of the Grande Kabylie and for the more energetic a starting point for mountain walks. Another 16 km S beyond Aïn El Hammam, is the Col de Tirourda (1,780m) beyond which the road snakes down to the Oued Sahel. The road is **steep** and liable to be closed for 3 or 4 months in winter. **Accommodation** D *Hotel Djurdjura*, T 409325, small, clean and very pleasant.

Tikjda

With an altitude of 1,600m on the N33, Tikjda is an idyllic spot in the **Djurdjura National Park**, in the very heart of the Djurdjura mountains, in sight of the highest peak, Tamgout n'Lalla Khedidja, 2,308m. It is a popular winter skiing resort for the nearby Akouder and Tigounatine *pistes*, and in summer attracts rock climbers and walkers in the surrounding cedar forests. The road from the pass of Tizi-N'Kouilal to Tikjda is both steep and winding. Just 2 km beyond Tizi-N'Kouilal is **Point de vue du Djurdjura** which speaks for itself and in another 5 km before Tikjda, stop at the **Gouffre de l'Akouker**, for the incredible view. The entire Kabylia lies below and on clear days, the sea can be seen on the horizon. The road from Tikjda to Tizi Ouzou is often closed by snow in winter and by landslides in summer. Be sure to check before a journey. If you only want to visit Tikjda it is straighter and quicker to reach it by bus or taxi from Bouïra via the N5. Numerous buses stop at Bouïra en route from Algiers.

● **Accommodation** C *Hotel Djurdjura*, on N15 in Aïn El Hammam, T 03 527270, pool, 80 rm, 171 beds, restaurant with 160 places, bar, pool; F *Chalet refuge des Cheminots*, in an older chalet style building at foot of the *Hotel Djurdjura*, T 03 527201, originally established for workmen, it is basic but clean with plain, good meals, cheapest place.

Excursions from Tikjda
It is possible to visit the **Takouatz Guerrisséne glacier**, which is on the S flank of the Ras Timedouine mountain. It is about 3-4 km along a track to the N.

The extraordinary **Goulmin lake** cradled high in the mountains to the W is very beautiful, but further away. Follow the Bouïra road for 5 km to the DNC Chalet. Walk from here up the mountain path on the right, allow 4 hrs for the complete walk. The N12 continues E to **Azazga**, noted mainly as a cross roads, to Yakouren and on to El Kseur, a busy town worth stopping at to look at the craft goods in the market.

Yakouren is a small and pleasantly quiet town, on the N12, 11 km E of Azazga, the best jumping off point for exploring the E districts of the Grande Kabylia and the Soummam valley, especially the vast forest of Akfadou which straddles the two.

● **Accommodation** **D** *Hotel Tamgout*, T 0315414, friendly atmosphere, 128 beds in 49 rm, restaurant with 80 places, 2 bars, volley ball, table tennis and children's playground. **Youth hostels** At Bouira 30 km W, T (3) 927503, 50 beds, kitchen, bus and train 1 km.

ALGIERS TO BEJAIA VIA N24 COAST ROAD

This is an option for those with more time and offers splendid ocean views at Cap Blanc (44 km) and Cap Djenet (78 km). Beyond Delly the road surface deteriorates and at Azeffoun it is best to return to the N12 via the W158, as the last 93 km to Bejaïa are really rough.

The first recommended beach E of Algiers is 21 km away at **Aïn Taya**. There are huge quantities of sand and huge crowds from Algiers. **Dellys**, 106 km, is a recommended lunch stop. The cafés on the harbour offer fresh fish meals.

Tigzirt

This is a small coastal town on a sheltered bay protected by a small rocky island. Although advertised as relatively untouched by tourism this is quickly changing. It originates from Roman times when it was known as *Iomnium* and was an important harbour. Today the remains of a **Christian basilica** (5th-6th century) can be seen in the centre of town.

● **Accommodation** **C** *Hotel le Mizrana*, T 03 046, pool, tennis, 30 rm, sea views.

Around Tigzirt

The coast road E leads to many small deserted beaches. The virtually untouched village of **Azzefoun**, clinging to the mountain side, 38 km from Tigzirt along the coast once was an important port for exporting charcoal. Beyond Azzefoun the road towards Bejaïa, 77 km, affords splendid views and passes yet more secluded beaches. The road is only partially surfaced and is not recommended in bad weather. An alternative is to take a minor road, the W43, S up through the hills, and join the main road to Bejaïa.

Bejaïa

ACCESS Air The airport is 4 km S of the town. **Road** Long distance buses stop at the bottom of the town so there is a long uphill walk to the centre. Local buses are available. Ask for place Cherif Medjahed.

(*Pop* 150,000) This is an important regional town with recently developed petrochemical industries. Pipelines carry oil from Hassi Messaoud, 660 km away in the S. The town is situated by the sea, on the side of the Gouraya mountain and protected by Cap Carbon. The town centre and its maze of narrow streets which climb up the hillside are the main points of interest for the visitor. The view over the Gulf of Bejaïa is worth a visit in its own right.

History

The town was established as a trading post by the Phoenicians and then the Romans but today few remains exist. In the 11th century, the Hammamid chief developed it into an important town, En Nassria, and in 1090, his son, El Mancour, made it the capital of his kingdom, and built many impressive monuments. The town prospered during his reign with an important boat-building industry and a population reported at about 100,000. The town fell into the hands of the Almohad leader, Abd El Moumin in 1151 and later into Hafsid hands where its prosperity declined. In the 16th century, the inhabitants turned to piracy. Because of this, the town was attacked and then occupied by the Spanish for 50 years. Next it was taken by the Turks. The French who captured it in 1833 renamed it Bougie (after its importance in candle wax manufacture). By the end of the 19th century the population was reduced to 2,000, and the city had lost all evidence of its glorious past.

Places of interest

The place du 1er Novembre is the lively centre of the town. It is lined by houses with arcades and a magnificent view over the sea. Under the place du 1er Novembre, there is the **Archaeological Museum** with exhibits from the Roman and Hafsid periods. The **Emile Aubry Museum**, rue Youcef Bouchebah, (between the place Abane Ramdane and the kasbah) displays contemporary Algerian paintings. Open 0900-1200 and 1400-1700.

La Réunion **War Cemetery** with 200 graves, mainly British, lies 14 km to the SW along the N12.

Excursions

Cap Carbon, 5 km N of town is definitely worth a visit. From the car park it is another 30 mins walk to the top for a splendid view over the bay and coast. The **Spanish fort**, at an altitude of 660m provides yet another impressive view over the bay. To get there, leave by the Porte du Ravin, pass by the **Pic des Singes** which also provides good views, and continue on to the fort.

Local information

● Accommodation

D Hotel de l'Etoile, place du 1er Novembre, T 920350; **D** Hotel de l'Orient, 7 rue Si-Lahoues, T 921131.

E Hotel Terminus, 22 Ave Ben Boulaïd, T 921049.

Youth hostels: Tichi, 18 km E of Bejaïa, T (5) 231450, open 0800-2200, 40 beds, meals available, family rm.

● Places to eat

◆◆La Brise de Mer on Baie de Sidi Yahia for seafood of course; Le Seville on rue Cheikh Amar Amah, rec for European food.

◆The fish restaurants on rue Si El Haoues.

● Banks & money changers

Main bank on place du 1er Novembre.

● Post & telecommunications

Area code: 05.

Post Office: on place Chérif Medjahed. The **telephone office** is in the same building.

● Tour companies & travel agents

Air Algérie, rue de la Liberté, T 225731.

● Tourist offices

ONAT, place Chérif Medjahed, T 928001.

● Transport

Air The airport is 4 km S of the town with flights to Algiers.

Road Bus: the bus station is to the S of the town, at the bottom of the hill. There are regular buses to Algiers, Constantine, Jijel and Sétif. The bus station is reasonably organized, with a booking office. **Taxi**: for out of town, these leave from the intersection of the Algiers and Jijel road.

BEJAIA TO JIJEL

The Corniche Kabylia from Bejaïa to Jijel, also known as 'the Sapphire Coast', is a scenic road which winds along the coast, clinging on to, and in places cutting into the mountains which drop steeply into the sea. This part of the coast is one of the most beautiful in Algeria. The road starts at Souk et Tnine, about 30 km E of Bejaïa where the N43 continues to follow the coast and the N9 goes inland S through the Kherrata gorges. On the coast, E of Ziama Mansouria, visit an amazing rock cavern, the **Grotte Merveilleuse**. Unfortunately, a new road tunnel cuts out the most impressive views, but it is nevertheless still a grand sight.

Tichi

This small town 17 km E of Bejaïa has been transformed into a tourist complex which is, perhaps, a little too near the petrochemicals of Bejaïa for comfort. It has a beautiful soft sandy beach. A convenient day trip, it is very busy in summer.

● **Accommodation** C Les Hammadites, T 575859, by sea, 140 rm, tennis, watersports; **E** Hotel la Grande Terrace is in the village, 30 rm.

The turning inland on the N9/N43 junction at Souk Et Tnine takes you through the 8 km long **Kherrata gorges**, one of the deepest cuttings in the Atlas Mountains. Its name *Chabet El Akra* means 'Death Ravine'.

Back on the Corniche Kabylia at the fishing village of Zama Mansouria 50 km from Bejaïa, turn right to the Barrage de Merdj-Ez-Erraguene (30 km) along a winding minor road. Turnings to the right and left along forest roads make pleasant detours through the woodlands: a track to the left has a good viewing point at 846m. It is possible, vehicle, weather and road conditions permitting, to return to the Corniche Kabylia down the W137.

Jijel

Is a small, quiet town at the E end of the Corniche Kabylia. Its main attraction is a large sandy beach. It is a convenient and pleasant overnight stop.

● **Accommodation D** *Hotel le Beau Rivage*, Blvd Zighout Youcef, T 964158; **D** *Hotel du Littoral*, Ave du 1er Novembre, T 96507, modern; **E** *Hotel Tindouf*, 14 rue Larbi Ben M'Hidi, T 962071. **Youth hostels** There are 2: *AJ Jijel*, rue de Frères Khecha, T 460980, 50 beds, open 0800-1200 and 1700-2200, kitchen, bus 2 km; and *AJ Taher*, rue de 1er Novembre, T 960427, open 0800-1200 and 1400-2200, 70 beds, kitchen, laundry facilities, bus 500m, reservations required.

● **Places to eat** ♦♦Restaurants in the hotels and along Blvd Zighout Youcef nr *Hotel le Beau Rivage*.

● **Banks & money changers** In the main street, Ave du 1er Novembre.

● **Post & telecommunications Area code**: 05. **Post Office**: Ave du 1er Novembre.

● **Tour companies & travel agents** *Air Algérie*, Ave du 1er Novembre, T 964636.

● **Transport Road** The bus station is about 100m from place de la République. There are regular departures for all the main towns. There are frequent buses to Bejaïa.

AROUND CONSTANTINE

This region extends from Kabylia to the Tunisian border and from the coast to the Aurés mountains with extremely attractive and varied landscape which should not be missed. The main city, Constantine, has a rich historical heritage and an impressive situation by the **Rhumel gorges** while the second city, Annaba, is an important commercial centre with excellent communications. There are Roman sites to visit, the most interesting being **Djemila** one of the most perfectly preserved cities, and **Hippo Regius**.

Sétif

ACCESS Both the bus and the train station are to the SE of the town, no great distance to walk from the centre. Sétif has a bypass to the S so hitch-hikers may have a longer walk to the centre.

Sétif, situated at an altitude of 1,100m which makes it pleasant even in the summer heat, and with a population of 200,000, became important following the French occupation in 1838. The town had existed since the Roman times, but had largely fallen into decay. The French transformed Sétif into a major military garrison, and rebuilt the town in a geometric grid pattern. In 1945, Sétif was drawn to world attention as the scene of a horrible massacre, the result of a nationalistic outburst, in which 84 Europeans were massacred, and over 2,000 Algerians were killed in retaliation by the French army. Today the town is a medium-sized typical colonial town, with a distinct French atmosphere. The main street, Ave du 8 Mai 1945, lined with arcades housing the main shops and banks, is the most lively in the town. Sétif is recommended as a base from which to visit Djemila which has virtually no accommodation.

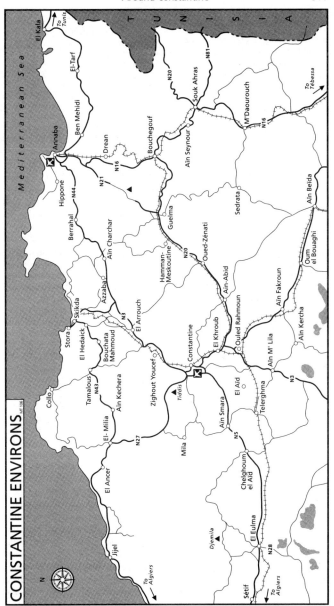

CONSTANTINE ENVIRONS

MT106

Mediterranean Sea

T U N I S I A

To Tunis

El Kala

El-Tarf

Ben Mehidi

Annaba

Hippone

Drean

Bouchegouf

Ain Seynour

Souk Ahras

N20

N81

M'Daourouch

N16

To Tébessa

N20

N16

Berrahal

N44

Ain Charchar

Guelma

Sedrata

Ain Beida

N21

Hamman-Meskoutine

N20

Oued-Zénati

Skikda

Azzaba

N3

El Arrouch

Constantine

El Khroub

Ain-Abid

Ouled Rahmoun

Ain Fakroun

Oum el Bouaghi

Stora

El Hedaick

Bouchata Mahmoud

Zighout Youcef

Tiddis

Ain M' Lila

N3

Ain Kercha

Collo

Tamalous

Ain Kechera

El Aid

Telerghma

Ain Smara

N5

Mila

El-Milia

N27

El Ancer

Chelghoum el Aid

Djemila

El Eulma

N28

Jijel

Sétif

To Algiers

To Algiers

N

Places of interest

The **museum** on rue de la Palestine, has a collection ranging from pre-historic local finds, to Roman, Christian and Muslim remains. The most interesting exhibits are the **Roman mosaics** including the 4th century '*Venus upon a dolphin*', and '*Bacchus' Indian Triumph*'. The museum is open 0900-1200 and 1400-1800, closed Fri morning and Sat. To the N of the place de l'Indépendence on the square Rafaoui is a restored **Roman water tank** and further N are the remains of the **Byzantine walls** and two **basilicas**.

Local information

● **Accommodation**

C *Hotel El Hidab*, Blvd Cheikh Laif, T 904043, 130 rm, central, pool, restaurant.

D *Hotel Mountazeh*, 12 Ave Ben Boulaïd, second street on the right, off Ave du 8 Mai 1945, after the place de l'Indépendence, 72 rm, T 904828.

E *Hotel El Riadh*, 2 rue Frères Meslem, T 907847, 60 rm; **E** *Hotel Port Said*, 6 Ave Ben Boulaïd, T 907183.

● **Places to eat**

◆◆◆*Hotel El Hadab* on Blvd Cheikh Laif.

◆◆*Hotel Riadh* on 2 rue Frères Meslem and adjacent to *Hotel Port Said* on Ave Ben Boulaïd.

● **Banks & money changers**

In the Ave du 8 Mai 1945.

● **Post & telecommunications**

Area code: 05.

Post Office: on Ave du 1er Novembre, a continuation E from the Ave du 8 Mai 1945.

● **Tour companies & travel agents**

Air Algérie, 13 Ave du 8 Mai 1945, T 851818; *Air France*, 14 Ave du 8 Mai 1945, T 903572.

● **Tourist offices**

ONAT, 13 Ave du 8 Mai 1945, T 902502.

● **Transport**

Train Connections to **Algiers** and **Constantine**. Take the third street right off Ave du 1er November after the Post Office, and the station is at the end.

Road The bus station is on the first street right off Ave du 1er November, just after the Post Office. Regular buses to **Algiers**, **Batna**, **Bejaïa**, **Constantine** and **Ghardaïa**. The buses for **Djemila** leave from in front of the train station.

Djemila

ACCESS There are a few, unreliable, direct buses that leave from Sétif, information possibly available from the bus station in Sétif. It is easier to take a bus to Constantine from in front of the train station in Sétif and get off at El Eulma where taxis are readily available to do the remaining 20 km.

The little village of Djemila, 50 km from Sétif, is particularly noted for the remains of **Cuicul**, an important Roman town, one of the most remarkable and well preserved in Algeria.

History

The town, known as Cuicul, was founded in the 1st century AD by the Roman emperor Nerva. It was at first a military garrison, but influenced by the surrounding fertile lands, agriculture became an important activity. By the 2nd century the population had grown to 10,000 and was organized with a central elected administration. By the 3rd century, the town had outgrown the original walls, and the southern ramparts were pulled down to make way for the new forum, which was surrounded with grand monuments. This period was the height of Cuicul's prosperity. By the 4th century, the introduction of Christianity gave a new lease of life to Cuicul with the erection of new monuments, including a church and a baptistery. After the 5th century, Cuicul fell into disuse, and it was not until the French arrived in 1839 that the site was again occupied. Excavations began in 1909.

The site

From the entrance near the museum, the tree-lined path leads past the Grand Baths to the **New Forum**. To the W of the Forum stands the **Triumphal Arch**, dedicated to the Emperor Caracalla, built in AD 216. The road through the arch went originally to Sétif. On the S side of the Forum is the **Septimien Temple**, dedicated to Septimus Severus and built in 229. From the Forum take the

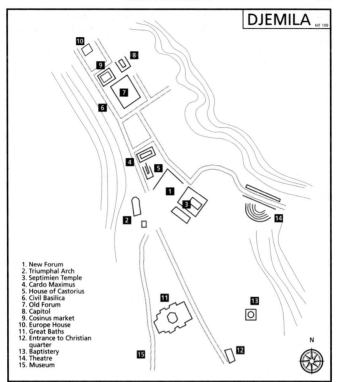

DJEMILA MT 109

1. New Forum
2. Triumphal Arch
3. Septimien Temple
4. Cardo Maximus
5. House of Castorius
6. Civil Basilica
7. Old Forum
8. Capitol
9. Cosinus market
10. Europe House
11. Great Baths
12. Entrance to Christian quarter
13. Baptistery
14. Theatre
15. Museum

N

Cardo Maximus, or main street that leads N from the corner in front of the Arch. On the right stands the **House of Castorius**, noted for its private baths. Further on the left, stands the **civil basilica**, originally used as a Tribunal and trade centre. Up the road, on the right, is the **Old Forum** with its well-preserved original paving stones. To the N stands the **Capitol**, a temple dedicated to the triple cult of Jupiter, Juno and Minerva. To the left of the Capitol is the **Cosinus Market**, named after its donator, Cosinus Primus. The market, entered through an arch on the Cardo Maximus, is one of the most remarkable monuments in Cuicul. The merchants' tables, organized around a central courtyard,

are still in place and well preserved.

After the market, to the N, stands the **Europe House**, named after a mosaic found inside. The house is large and luxurious, with 18 rooms arranged around a central courtyard lined with Ionic columns. The Cardo Maximus leads to the N gate, where the road for Jijel started. To the S of the New Forum lies the Christian part of the town, built in the 4th century. From the New Forum, take the path directly opposite the Cardo Maximus, leading towards the **Great Baths**. The baths, to the SW of the path are in a very good condition and in some rooms it is still possible to see the pipes and double panels where the hot water circulated. To the N of the baths, is a large courtyard, where a good view over the ruins can be enjoyed. The entrance to the Christian quarter is delimited by a great door, at the end of the path coming from the New Forum. Follow the path up the hill to the large circular **Baptistery** which still contains all the original mosaics and is today covered by a restored dome. The **theatre**, built outside the boundaries of the town is situated to the E of the New Forum. It is thought that the theatre was not built within the walls due to the great expansion of the city in the 3rd century and its capacity of 3,000 seats indicates the size of the population at that time. From the theatre there is a wonderful view over the surrounding landscape. Open daily 0700-1800 in summer, 0700-1700 in winter.

The Museum Situated by the entrance to the ruins, it has an impressive collection of mosaics. The three main rooms are covered in mosaics, to an almost overpowering extent. There are also some marble statues as well as small but interesting everyday objects, such as oil lamps and cooking implements. Open 0900-1200 and 1400-1700, closed Sat.

WARNING On arrival at the site, and even long before, you may be offered many 'original' items such as coins or oil lamps. Some of these may be genuine, but be very careful before buying anything. Similarly, on entering the ruins, you will undoubtedly be offered the services of a guide. Most guides are unofficial. If you are interested, it is best to agree on a price beforehand.

Constantine

ACCESS **Air** The airport is 9 km out of town. A bus runs into town. **Train** There are daily trains to Algiers, Skikda, Touggourt and Tunis. **Road** The main bus station is by the river 3-4 km S of the town, so it is possible to walk rather than catch the bus. Constantine is well connected to all the major towns in Algeria.

Constantine is an amazing town of 500,000 inhabitants perched at 694m on the summit of a rock. To the E, the town is built along the rim of the precipitous Rhumel Gorges, some 200m below. The situation is made more dramatic by the four bridges that cross the gorges.

History

Founded by the Phoenicians and called **Cirta**, it was taken over by Massinissa in 203 BC and made the capital of Numidia. During Massinissa's reign, agriculture developed and a strong centralized state system was established and aligned with Rome. In about 154 BC Jugurtha, Massinissa's grandson, tried to rid himself of the Roman tutelage but failed. During the first years of the Christian era, Cirta was part of a confederation of cities in the region, and by the end of the 2nd century it became a colony of Cuicul (Djemila). At this time, the town really prospered, becoming one of the richest cities in North Africa. In AD 311, the town was destroyed by Maxence following an insurrection, but Constantine rebuilt the town and gave it his name, Constantina. In the 8th century, the town was taken by Abou El Mouhajer, coming from Kairouan in present day Tunisia and fell in turn into the hands of the Zirids, Hammadids, Almohads and the Hafsids. In the 16th century, the Turks from Algiers took control of the town. From 1830, the town was effectively independent from Algiers and not taken by the French until 1837, after many unsuccessful attempts. Today, Constantine is a strongly Islamic city where traditions are still important.

Places of interest

The place du 1er Novembre is the centre of town, with a great number of cafés. It extends W into a large esplanade where an amazing view over the gorges can be enjoyed. From here, the rue Larbi Ben M'Hidi, leads into the old town. On the right is the **Great Mosque**, or Djemaa El Kebir. It has a modern façade, was constructed from 'recycled' Roman columns and capitals and was built on the remains of an ancient Temple: 11th century inscriptions have been discovered. The rue Larbi Ben M'Hidi, opens out on to the place Mohammed Tahar Ladjabi, where stands an interesting **neo-Moorish medersa**. There is also a footbridge leading directly to the station on the other side of the gorges. To get to the bridge, there is an elevator on the square that leads directly down to the bridge. At the end of the rue Larbi Ben M'Hidi, the El Kantara bridge spans a distance

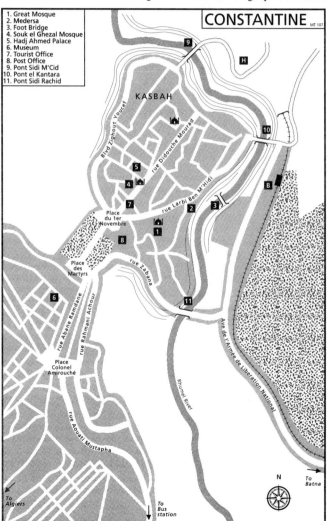

1. Great Mosque
2. Medersa
3. Foot Bridge
4. Souk el Ghezal Mosque
5. Hadj Ahmed Palace
6. Museum
7. Tourist Office
8. Post Office
9. Pont Sidi M'Cid
10. Pont el Kantara
11. Pont Sidi Rachid

CONSTANTINE MT 107

KASBAH

Blvd Zighout Youcef

rue Didouche Mourad

rue Larbi Ben M'Hidi

Place du 1er Novembre

Place des Martyrs

rue Zaabana

rue Abane Ramdane

rue Rahman Achour

Place Colonel Amirouché

rue Aouati Mustapha

Rhumel River

Ave de l'Armée de Libération National

N

To Batna

To Algiers

To Bus station

of 128m at a height of 125m over the Rhumel gorges and there is an excellent view from the bridge.

In the rue Didouche Mourad, the main commercial street in Constantine, is the **Souk El Ghezal mosque**. The mosque was built in 1730 by a Moroccan architect and in 1838 was transformed into a catholic church by the French. The **Hadj Ahmed palace** is situated on the place du Commandant Si El Haoues, off the rue Didouche Mourad. The palace was built in 1835 by the last of the Beys and is luxuriously decorated with marbled columns, painted Italian tiles and frescoes. The rue Didouche Mourad leads to the gorges and on the right, to the impressive **Sid M'Cid suspension bridge**. The bridge was built in 1912 and is 168m long with a most impressive view from the centre of the bridge, towering over the Rhumel, 175m below. The Blvd Zighout Youcef, hugging the side of the cliff leads from the bridge to the place du 1er Novembre. The view from the boulevard, over the cliff, is amazing. The **museum** is behind the place des Martyrs to the S. The most interesting items are the Numidian exhibits and the Roman displays, though these are of less importance. Open 0800-1200 and 1400-1700 except Fri mornings and Sat.

Local information
● **Accommodation**
C *Hotel Cirta*, rue Rahmani Achour, T 9440331, 126 rm; C *Hotel Panoramic*, 59 rue Aouati Mustapha, T 942477, 35 rm, fine views.

E *Grand Hotel*, 2 rue Larbi Ben M'Hidi, T 933047; E *Hotel de Paris* 1 rue Larbi Ben M'Hidi.

Youth hostels: Cité Filali, Constantine, T 695461, 25 beds, bus 500m, train 2 km; Skikda, 87 km N of Constantine, T 743400, 25 beds, kitchen.

● **Places to eat**
◆◆*Hotel Cirta* on rue Rachmani Achour.

◆Continue along this avenue for a selection of cheaper eating places – choose with care.

● **Banks & money changers**
Banque Central d'Algérie, Blvd Zighout Youcef; Banque National d'Algérie, place du 1er Novembre.

● **Post & telecommunications**
Area code: 04.

Post Office: Place du 1er Novembre. Telephone office next to it, open 24 hrs.

● **Tour companies & travel agents**
Air Algérie 1 place des Martyrs, T 937070; *Air France*, 8 rue Abane Ramdane, T 935987; *ONAT*, 6 rue Zabana, T 943954.

● **Tourist offices**
ONAT, 16 rue Didouche Mourad, T 941403. There is also a local office at 32 rue Abane Ramdane, T 932661.

● **Transport**
Air The airport is 9 km out of town. For information contact, T 936962. Flights to **Algiers, Lyon, Marseille Oran, Paris** and **Tamanrasset**.

Train The station is on the E side of the gorge. The quickest way is to take the foot bridge. Trains go to **Algiers, Skikda** and **Touggourt**. There is a daily train to **Tunis**.

Road Bus: there are two bus stations. The first for towns close to Constantine is opp the railway station. The second, and main one, for long distance is situated a few 3-4 km to the S of the town, by the river. There are buses to virtually everywhere in Algeria and a bus every 2 days to Tunis. For long journeys, particularly in summer, places should be booked in advance. **Taxis**: leave from the main bus station, by the river.

EXCURSIONS FROM CONSTANTINE

Tiddis

Take the N2 NW from Constantine for 23 km then turn left at the crossroads, clearly signed. Be prepared to walk from the main road. Amidst the wild flowers on the S facing hillside are the ruins of **Castellum Tidditanorum** with its steep winding mainstreet. The water systems both hot and cold are worth examination. Up the hill beyond the water storage tanks admire the view across the steep Rhumel gorge.

Annaba

ACCESS Air The airport is 12 km out of town. For information, T 828302. Flights to Algiers, El-Oued, Ghardaïa, Lyon, Marseille, Oran and Paris. **Train** Daily trains to Algiers, Constantine and Tunis. The train station is across the square at the S end of the Cours de la Révolution. **Road** The bus station (see map), is just 500m from the train station on Ave de l'Armée. There are frequent buses from all the major Algerian towns and a daily connection with Tunis leaving from the Tunis-S bus station at 0500. **Sea** The port is at the S end of the Cours de la Révolution and the ferry terminal just 100m away – very central.

(*Pop* 450,000) The town of Annaba is situated at sea level on one of the few coastal planes in the E of Algeria. It is a thriving city, with important industries such as the El Hadjar steel works 12 km S and a large busy port. Today, Annaba is the third biggest city in Algeria. The city is of little interest apart from the ruins of Hippo Regius but is nevertheless pleasant enough for a stopover.

History

Annaba, ancient **Hippo Regius** (also known as Hippone, see page 319) was founded by the Phoenicians and allied, until its destruction, to Carthage. For a century Hippo Regius was independent and was one of the favourite residences of the Numidian kings. Due to the war

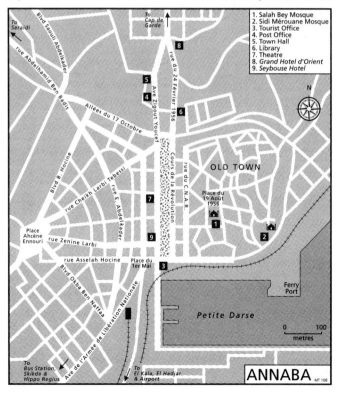

1. Salah Bey Mosque
2. Sidi Mérouane Mosque
3. Tourist Office
4. Post Office
5. Town Hall
6. Library
7. Theatre
8. *Grand Hotel d'Orient*
9. *Seybouse Hotel*

ANNABA MT 108

between Caesar and Pompeii, and the subsequent annexation of Numidia by Caesar, Hippo Regius became a Roman colony in 46 BC. For the following 4 centuries the town prospered until the invasion by the Vandals. At the end of the 4th century, the town was a centre for Christianity, Augustine the Bishop having a great influence throughout the Christian world. He died in 430 during the siege by the Vandals, the town remaining under their control for a century before being taken by the Byzantines who initiated large reconstruction projects, the city having suffered heavily during the Vandal's rule.

In the 7th century, the invading Arabs took little interest in the town and after having pillaged it, decided to build a new town, 2 km away, on the site of the present Annaba. Over the centuries, Annaba, like many other coastal towns was involved in piracy. In 1522 it was occupied briefly by Barbarossa, and then by the Spanish. In 1830 the French attacked the city, but were obliged to retreat, only successfully gaining control of the town 2 years later. During WW1 the town was bombarded by the Germans and in WW2 served as an operation base for the Allied Forces in North Africa. The town was again heavily bombed during the winter of 1942-43.

Places of interest

The best thing to do in Annaba is to stroll along the tree-lined Cours de la Révolution, the main N-S artery, and the main area of social activity with its numerous cafés. The **old town** is to the E of the Cours de la Révolution, with at its centre the place du 19 Août 1956. The square is pleasant, with many cafés and the **Salah Bey mosque** (built in 1790) to the S. To the SE, and dominating the old town and the harbour is the much older **Sidi Bou Mérouane mosque**, built in the 11th century. The new (1900) **Basilica of St Augustine** is on a small hill S of the town. The **war cemetery** with 870

graves adjoins the leisure park. About 5 km W of Annaba on the N44 take the road to Saraidi.

Local information

● **Accommodation**

A *Seybouse International*, rue du 24 Février 1956, T 822125, all rm a/c, good restaurant, splendid views.

D *Grand Hotel d'Orient*, Cours de la Révolution, T 822051; **D** *Hotel Regina*, 6 rue Bakhli Mokhtar, T 823461.

Youth hostels: on rue Abdaoui Mouloud, 23000 Wilaya d'Annaba, T 844983, 38 beds, kitchen, bus 3 km, trains 2 km, ferry 4 km, airport 13 km.

● **Places to eat**

◆◆◆restaurant in *Seybouse International Hotel*.

◆◆Try *Le Bosphorus* on Cours de la Révolution.

◆Select from the cafés in the same street.

● **Banks & money changers**

Banque Centrale d'Algérie, 7 Cours de la Révolution; Banque National d'Algérie, 17 Cours de la Révolution.

● **Post & telecommunications**

Area code: 08.

Post Office: Rue Zighout Youcef.

● **Shopping**

Crafts: there is a state run craft shop, the *SNAT*, at 2 Cours de la Révolution.

● **Tour companies & travel agents**

Air Algérie, Carrefour Sidi Brahim, T 837474 and at 2 Cours de la Révolution, T 820020; *Air France*, 8 bis rue Prosper Dubourg.

Ferry tickets: at the *CNAN*, 2 Cours de la Révolution, T 822230.

● **Tourist offices**

ONAT, 1 rue Tarik Ibn Zaid, T 825886.

● **Transport**

Local Car hire: Algérie Auto Tourisme, 3 Ave Zighout Youcef, T 827288. They also have an office at the airport, T 822330.

Air The airport is 12 km out of town. For information, T 828302. Flights to Algiers, El Oued, Ghardaïa, Lyon, Marseille, Oran, Ouargla and Paris.

Train The railway station is on the place du 1er Mai. There are daily trains to Algiers,

Constantine and Tunis. For information, T 824904.

Road Bus: the bus station is 700m along the Ave de l'Armée de Libération Nationale, which starts to the right of the train station. There are daily buses to all the major towns in Algeria incl **Algiers, Constantine, El-Oued, Ghardaïa, Souk Ahras** and a daily departure for **Tunis**. Tickets should be bought in advance for long distance journeys, especially in summer.

Sea In the summer there are about 4 departures a month for Marseille. The ferry port is at the centre of town, at the S end of the Cours de la Révolution.

Around Annaba

Hippo Regius

The ruins of Hippo Regius (see also page 317) are just 1½-2 km out of town. To get there, take the Ave de l'Armée de Libération National, which starts on the right of the station, and the site is further on the left. In the ruins, the mosaic floor of the **Great Christian Basilica** where St Augustine was bishop is particularly interesting. The **Great Baths** to the N are well preserved, the heating systems visible in the walls. To the SW of the Baths is the imposing **Forum**, built in the 1st century. Open only at 0830, 1030, 1230 and 1430 Wed, Thur and Fri. Be punctual. No photography allowed.

The **museum**, to the S of the ruins, contains some wonderful mosaics as well as everyday objects found during the excavations. Open 0800 to 1100 and 1400 to 1700 except Fri and Sat.

Cap de Garde

12 km to the N of Annaba, offers wonderful views over the sea and coast. On the road leading to the Cap de Garde, 4 km out of Annaba, there is an extensive beach. The village of **Seraidi**, 10 km W of Annaba, is perched at nearly 900m, in the cork oak forest, again with impressive views. It is cool and fresh here in the summer and much frequented by the inhabitants of Annaba. Recommended for birdwatching. To the W the **Massif**

de l'Edough is excellent walking country. Stay in **C** *Hotel El Montazah*, T 822699 in Seraidi. The fishing village of **Chetaïbi** is further W along the coast and gives access to Cap Takouch and Cap de Fer, two headlands extending into the Mediterranean.

El Kala

87 km E from Annaba has a small harbour where fishing is still an important activity. The village is surrounded by forest and looks out towards the sea: there is a good beach. The W166 leads W along the coast to the remains of Vieux El Kala while further inland the W109 beside Lac Oubaïra branches to **Cap Rosa**, takes in a view point towards Annaba, and returns to the main coast road. El Kala is also a good point for getting into Tunisia. The frontier is 36 km away and Tabarka only 45 km.

● **Accommodation** There is one good hotel, **C** *El-Morjane*, T 820242, 100 rm, own beach. **Youth hostels** *AJ El Kala*, Cité du 19 Juin, Wilaya de Tarf 36100, T 650534, 20 beds, free kitchen, bus 2 km, train 2 km.

Souk Ahras on the N16 SE of Annabas is on the best route into Tunisia. There is a choice of the N 20 to the frontier at Ghardimaou on the way to Jendouba, or the minor road W30 to the frontier at Sakiet Sidi Toussef on the way to Le Kef. There is no direct transport into Tunisia but you can take a bus or a taxi to the border and walk across. There is also a daily train for Tunis at about middday, the railway line following the Oued Medjerda.

The Aurés Mountains

The Aurés mountains are part of the Saharan Atlas range, running from the SW to NE across Algeria. The N, around Batna, is climatically cool whilst the S, near Biskra, is virtually Saharan. The landscape varies dramatically and is most impressive. The people of the Aurés mountains, like the Kabyles, have a strong identity. They speak a Berber dialect, are of Berber origin, and are

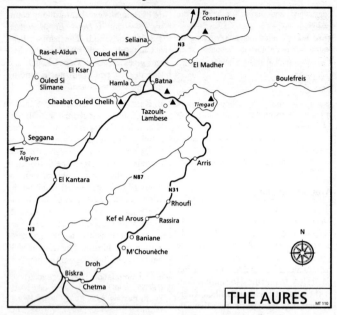

THE AURES

MT 110

known as the Chaouia. One of the interesting local crafts is the weaving of goats' hair carpets. The result is a hard-wearing, though somewhat coarse, material.

There are two main N-S routes from Batna to Biskra. The N3, the quickest, lies to the W of the mountains, leading through some spectacular scenery, particularly at the Défilé, close to the village of El Kantara. This is the main road used by the bus. The other road, the N31, E of the range is the quieter scenic route following the Oued El-Abiod. No direct buses from Batna to Biskra go this way.

Batna

(*Alt* 1,038m) The town was built in 1844 by the French as a military camp for the protection of the road to the Sahara. Today, the town is prosperous and is an important educational and industrial centre. Batna is a good base for reaching the ruins of Timgad or exploring the surrounding area.

● **Accommodation** B *Hotel le Chélia*, 2 allée Ben Boulaïd, T 873362; **C** *Hotel Laverdure*, 3 Ave de l'Indépendence, T 551163; **D** *Hotel Amin*, rue Mohammed Khémisti, T 873404; **D** *Hotel Hyatt*. **Youth hostels** Rue des Abattoirs, T 553807, open 0800-1200, 1400-2200, 30 beds, bus 300m, self catering.

● **Post & telecommunications Area code**: 04.

● **Tour companies & travel agents** *Air Algérie*, rue des Frères Maazouzi, T 552665.

● **Tourist offices** ONAT and car hire, allée Ben Boulaïd, T 559345.

● **Transport Road** The bus station is in the town centre. There are daily buses to **Algiers**, **Annaba**, **Biskra**, **Constantine** and **Timgad**. **Taxi**: the taxi rank is 500m from the bus station.

Timgad

ACCESS There are buses to and from Batna, but the timetable varies. The taxis congregate around the site entrance.

15 km E of Batna, Timgad is famous for the remarkable remains of the ancient Roman town of **Thamugadi**. Being very well preserved by the Sahara sands, the old town gives a very good idea of everyday life virtually 2,000 years ago.

History

The Roman colony of Thamugadi was founded by Trajan in the year 100 AD, and was mainly built by Roman soldiers.

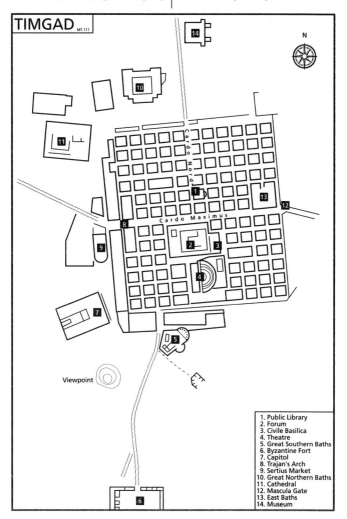

TIMGAD MT 111

N

Cardo Nord

Cardo Maximus

Viewpoint

1. Public Library
2. Forum
3. Civile Basilica
4. Theatre
5. Great Southern Baths
6. Byzantine Fort
7. Capitol
8. Trajan's Arch
9. Sertius Market
10. Great Northern Baths
11. Cathedral
12. Mascula Gate
13. East Baths
14. Museum

The purpose of the town was to provide retired legionnaires with a place to live, where culture and leisure were important. The town was destroyed in the 6th century by the Berbers but soon rebuilt by the Byzantines. It was destroyed and abandoned during the Arab invasion in the 7th century. In 1795 an English traveller rediscovered the site but excavation work only began in 1880.

The site

The town was built in a geometric pattern, with the main axes cutting through from N-S and E-W. From the gate, take the Cardo Nord leading to the **Forum**. The paving stones are still in good condition and wheel ruts are clearly visible. There is evidence of a sophisticated drainage system under the paving stones. On the left, along the Cardo Nord are the remains of the public library. The Cardo Nord meets the Cardo Maximus at right angles. The Cardo Maximus is lined with small arcades, once shops. The Forum, entered by stairs at the S end of the Cardo Nord, is a large rectangular square surrounded by arcades. To the E stands the **Civile Basilica**, where judgments and conferences took place.

To the S of the Forum is the **Theatre**, large enough to seat over 3,000. The **Great Southern Baths** are S, slightly outside the town's perimeter. They were built in the 2nd century and are much smaller than the **Great Northern Baths**. A **Byzantine fort** built in 539, stands 300m to the S of the site. The **Capitol** is at the SW corner of the town, curiously beyond the town's perimeter. The Capitol must have been enormous, with a large flight of 28 steps leading to it. The columns at the front, originally 6, were 14m high with beautiful capitals. For a good view over the entire site, climb up the hill directly S of the Capitol. Marking the entrance to the town, stands one of the main monuments, **Trajan's Arch**, built in the early 3rd century. At the W end of Cardo Maximus is the **Sertius Market**, also 3rd century. **Mescula Gate** stands at the E end of Cardo Maximus. The Market was arranged around the central courtyard, each merchant having his own stand. The slates for displaying food are visible today. To the N outside the perimeter are the **Great Northern Baths**. This enormous building, with over 30 rooms, houses many pools, hotrooms and gymnasiums. Open daily 0700 to sunset.

The Museum

To the left of the main gates holds a collection of very beautiful mosaics, and a number of interesting objects which give a good idea of the sophistication of everyday life. Open 0800-1200 and 1400-1800, closed Sat.

Local information
● **Accommodation**

The best thing to do is to stay in Batna and come for a day trip.

D *Hotel El Kahina*, most rm have a/c, far from perfect.

E *Hotel Timgad*, 70 rm, quiet.

● **Places to eat**

The only places rec are the hotels.

The Oued El-Abiod

The E route to Biskra from Batna by the N31 follows the Oued El-Abiod. The landscape is beautiful. **Arris** (*Alt* 1,171m), 56 km from Batna is a *dechra* village clinging to the mountainside. *Dechras* have been described as earth coloured 'terraced hamlets topped by fortress silos' and are characteristic of the area. The **Museum of Aurés** in Arris has displays of silver jewellery and traditional floor coverings. View the white-sided gorges of Tighanimine before stopping at **Rhoufi**, 90 km from Batna. At Rhoufi, follow the road to the right indicating **le balcon de Rhoufi** where the view over the gorge is fabulous. At the bottom of the gorge, the palm trees provide some respite from the sun and walks besides the river are particularly refreshing. There is a river walk to Baniane taking 2-3 hrs, and on through the gorges to M'Chounèche another 3 hrs for those with stamina. Rhoufi being an important carpet weaving centre for goat hair carpets has hopeful sellers on the road on either side of the village.

El Kantara, is on the N28, the main road from Batna to Biskra. The **Défilé** at El Kantara is really spectacular, dividing the two regions, for S of El Kantara is the desert.

● **Youth Hostels**   T 718532, 50 beds, kitchen, bus and train 1 km.

Biskra

This is the first real oasis town when arriving from the N. It is not as interesting as others further S but is nevertheless an agreeable town. The large oasis contains over 150,000 palm trees producing the famous *deglet nur* dates. The market, best visited in the early morning, is very lively and sells a wide selection of fresh products. The best way to see the oasis is probably by taking a *calèche*, which are better than average and leave from in front of the *Hotel Les Zibans*. Negotiate the price before you step in. The park in the newer part of town is a shaded, colourful walk.

● **Accommodation**   C *Hotel Les Zibans*, route de M'Cid, T 04 713067, pool, tennis, 100 rm, used by tour operators so can be full; E *Hotel Guendouz*, Blvd Emir Abdelkader, T 715769, 60 rm. **Youth hostels**   12 Hadi Tayeb, Vieux Biskra, 1 km S of town, 50 beds, kitchen, family rm, open 0800-1200, 1700-2200, train station 2 km, airport bus.

● **Tour companies & travel Agents**   *Air Algérie*, Ave Benbadis, T 04 715804.

● **Tourist offices**   37 Ave de la République.

● **Transport Air**   The airport is 10 km out of town. For information, T 04 714052. There are flights to **Algiers**. **Train** Daily to **Constantine** and **Touggourt**. **Road** The bus station is 400m to the N of the main street. Daily connections to **Algiers**, **Batna**, **Constantine**, **El Oued**, **Ghardaïa** and **In Aménas**.

CONTENTS	
Algiers to Oran	324
Inland to Tlemcen	329

MAPS	
Northwest Algeria	325
Oran	328
Tlemcen	330

The fertile plain that extends from Algiers W to the Moroccan border offers pleasant and refreshing landscapes. The coast has many attractive beaches and secluded bays but there is a shortage of accommodation. The best itinerary is to follow the coast as far as Oran and then cut inland towards Tlemcen, leaving out the less interesting inland towns. Oran is an important industrial and commercial centre with some remains of French architectural influence but is not an essential visit, whereas Tlemcen should not be missed.

ALGIERS TO ORAN

Cherchell

ACCESS There are frequent buses from Algiers, Blida and Mostaganem which will drop you off at the bus station which is at the W entrance to the town, close to the Roman baths on the road in from Algiers.

30 km W from Algiers, Cherchell is a small seaside town, with a population of 100,000 and is famous historically, with monuments visible in and around the modern town.

History
Founded in the 4th century BC by the Phoenicians it was later named Caesarea by Juba II, a Numidian prince. The town was made capital of Mauritania, but by 40 BC was made a Roman colony. Caesarea became the capital of a large province, stretching as far E as Sétif. It was fortified and prospered greatly accumulating rich monuments and works of art. An aqueduct, over 28 km long, brought water from near Menaceur. In 372 the town was ruined by the Vandals but regained a certain importance under the Byzantines. The Arabs occupied the town in the 10th century. In the 15th century, a great number of Andalusians sought refuge in Cherchell, and in 1518 Barbarossa occupied the town. A number of unsuccessful attempts were made by the French to take the city until in the 1830s, France gradually occupied Algeria and Cherchell finally fell into their hands in 1840.

Places of interest
There have been very few excavations at Cherchell, partly because the new town is built over the ancient city. Some monuments are still visible. The best pieces are in the archaeological **Museum** on the E side of the place des Martyrs, the town's central square. Of note are the copies of **Greek statues** which are incredibly well executed. These statues were probably made in Cherchell and demonstrate the great skills of the local artisans. Of the statues, that of Apollo is a perfect copy of one of Phidias' creations. Also worth a look is the gigantic **statue of Hercules** and another of **Venus**. The mosaics depicting agricultural scenes are recommended too. The **museum** is open 1000-1200 and 1430-1700. Closed Fri mornings and Sat. Photography not allowed.

To the S of the place des Martyrs is the area where remains of the **Forum** and **Civile Basilica** have recently been discovered. Further to the S is the **Roman Theatre**, built in the 1st century but transformed into an amphitheatre in the 3rd century. At the W entrance to Cherchell, stand the **Baths** which have only been partially excavated. Many of the statues in the museum were found here.

A 1 km walk to the E of the town in a magnificent setting on the coast stands a 17th century shrine (*koubba*) containing the tomb of **Sidi Brahim el Ghobrini**, a noted religious teacher.

The road directly S of the town crosses the river and climbs up to give a good view over the settlement.

Local information
● **Accommodation**
C *Hotel Césarée*, place des Martyrs, T 051/467161, 31 rm.

● **Tour companies & travel agents**
Air Algérie 2 rue Abdelhak, T 445800.

● **Tourist offices**
On rue Abdelhak (off place des Martyrs), T 67460.

NORTHWEST ALGERIA

From Cherchell to Ténès

The N11 coast road, the Corniche Dahra from Cherchell to Ténès is 108 km long. It is particularly beautiful, the best part undoubtedly being the 41 km between the river crossing at Damous and Ténès.

Ténès

ACCESS Buses from Algiers, El Asnam and Mostaganem. The nearest airport is at El Asnam, 53 km.

The new town built in a geometric pattern is of very little interest to the traveller but the old town founded in 875 which is 2 km SE out of town along the road to El Asnam, is well worth a visit. Remains of the walls and a door can be seen as well as an interesting mosque constructed from parts taken from older buildings.

● **Accommodation** C *Hotel Cartenna*, route du Phare, T 457510; D *Hotel des Arts*, rue de la Révolution.

Mostaganem

ACCESS Buses from Algiers, Ghardaïa, Mascara and Oran stop in the town centre. The station, trains from Oran and Algiers via Mohammadia lies to the E of the town, too far to walk.

This important fishing port with a certain charm is a pleasant stop-over. Arriving from either E or W, you will end up in the centre of the new town on Ave Benaied Bendehiba and the place du 1er Novembre. The place du 1er Novembre is bordered with arcades and cafés with a good view to the W towards the sea and to the N the old Turkish quarter. From the other end of the Ave Benaied Bendehiba, a bridge links the old town.

● **Accommodation** B *Hotel Royal*, 53 Ave A Cherif, T 262372; D *Hotel Es Sahel*, rue Benguedda Tayeb, T 262433; E *Hotel Albert 1er*, rue Khelifa Mohammed, T 262923, dated, 40 rm some with bath. **Youth hostels** Nearest hostel at Relizane 60 km SE, open 0800-1200, 1400-2200, 50 beds, meals available, train and bus 150m.

● **Post & telecommunications Area code:** 06.

● **Tour companies & travel agents** *Air Algérie*, Ave Benaied Bendehiba, T 212427.

● **Tourist offices** ONAT, 2 Blvd Khémisti, T 266221.

The first 48 km between Mostaganem and Oran are along the N11, a low-lying coast road through agricultural land. The obtrusive oil town of Arzew is best avoided by turning off at Bettioua. The detour to Kristel on the W27 offers a winding, picturesque ride through a narrow gorge and then vineyards to the coast, a view across the bay and access to Oran at the harbour.

Oran

ACCESS **Air** The airport is 22 km away along the motorway at Tafraoui. There are buses to the central square, place 1er November 1954. For information, T 418500. **Train** The train station is at the top of the Blvd Mellah Ali, to the E of the town, a 1 km downhill walk to the central square with trains from Algiers, Mohammadia and Tlemcen. **Road** Buses from Tlemcen and places W terminate near the railway station while all other buses terminate S of the town. **Sea** Ferries from France and Spain dock in the centre of the port, which is about 1 km walk up to the central square.

(*Pop* 800,000; *Alt* 90m) Oran, the second biggest city in Algeria, offers the visitor a lively atmosphere. The town is thriving and renowned for its liberalism and Western outlook.

History

Oran is one of the few Algerian towns which does not seem to have been settled by the Romans, though there are signs of prehistoric life in caves throughout the surrounding area. The town was founded in 937 by Andalusian sailors, prospered under the Zianids and developed good trading relations with the Spanish. It was occupied by the Spanish from 1509 until 1708 when it was taken by the Turks. 24 years later the Spanish retook Oran but left 2 years after the massive 1790 earthquake that destroyed most of the town. At the time the French entered the city in 1831, the population was estimated at 4,000. The town's development suffered in 1849 in a major cholera epidemic. In the second half of the 19th century, French and Spanish settlers introduced a certain European aspect to the town. After Independence, 200,000 Europeans left the city, reducing it to a virtual ghost town. It took some time for Oran to regain its previous vitality, but today it is the second major town in Algeria and an important industrial, cultural and educational centre.

The Nobel prize-winning French writer Albert Camus was born in Oran, the town being the setting for two of his most famous books *The Plague* and *The Stranger*. Fashion designer Yves Saint Laurent was also born here.

Places of interest

The centre of the town is place du 1er Novembre from which the town's main four arteries spring. The **Promenade Ibn Badis** which starts on the left of the Rampe du Commandant Farradj, downhill from the place du 1er Novembre is a garden created by the General Létang in 1847. It contains a collection of exotic trees and plants and has a commanding view over the harbour. On top of the hill

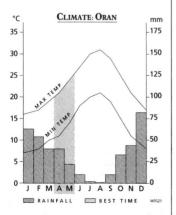

°C CLIMATE: ORAN mm

RAINFALL   BEST TIME   MTG21

behind the Promenade stands the **Chateau Neuf**, a fortress built by the Spanish and subsequently used as a residence by the Spanish governors and Beys. Today it is being transformed into a luxury hotel and cannot be visited. Directly to the S of the Chateau Neuf is the **Great Mosque**, Djemaa el Kebir, built in 1796 to commemorate the departure of the Spanish. Particularly interesting is the **octagonal minaret** which can be climbed, with permission, for a splendid view. The Mosque is open 0800-1200 except Fri.

To the W, the **Marabout Sidi Mohammed El Haouri** built in 1793 has an attractive minaret and is clearly influenced by Andalusian architecture. To the S along the rue Sidi El Haouri, stands the Porte d'Espagne. The **Demaeght Museum** on the Blvd Zabana has three interesting sections. The prehistoric section displays finds from throughout the Maghreb during Palaeolithic and Neolithic times. The ethnographic display on the first floor covers the tribes in the Maghreb and Asia, with a room devoted just to Oran. A natural history display of animals from the Maghreb is situated on the lower ground floor. The museum is open 0900-1200 and 1500-1900 in summer, 0830-1200 and 1430-1800 in winter, closed Fri afternoon and all day Sat.

The present library with stained glass windows and mosaics which depict religious scenes over the doors, was the **Cathedral of Sacré Coeur**. Worth seeing, entrance free.

Le Petit Lac Military Cemetery lies 4 km SE of Oran on the approach road to the airport on the S side of Ave Di Sidi Chami.

Beaches

It is necessary to get right out of Oran to find a decent beach. Go W to Mers El Kebir and beyond along the W84 to **Les Andalouses** 32 km. Here is a lively summer resort with accommodation and watersports.

Local information
● Accommodation
C *Hotel Timgad*, 22 Ave Emir Abdelkader, T 394797, 200 rm, restaurant.

D *Hotel Murdjadjo*, 3 rue Ampère,

T 334568, 68 rm.

E *Hotel de l'Ouest*, 6 Blvd Mellah Ali, T 364698, 43 rm; **E** *Hotel Riadh*, 46 Blvd Mellah Ali, T 363846.

Youth hostels: there are two youth hostels: 3

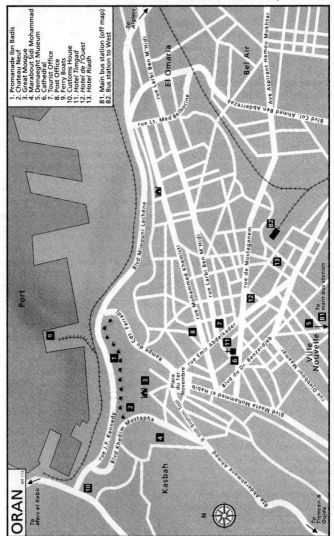

ORAN

MT113

1. Promanade Ibn Badis
2. Chateau Neuf
3. Great Mosque
4. Marabout Sidi Mohammad
5. Demaeght Museum
6. Cathedral
7. Tourist Office
8. Post Office
9. Ferry Boats
10. Customs House
11. Hotel Timgad
12. Hotel de l'Ouest
13. Hotel Riadh

B1. Main bus station (off map)
B2. Bus station to West

rue Benadjila, Lahouari, Seddikia, T 350245, 40 beds, kitchen, 200m from bus and 2 km from train station; and 19 rue Maoued Ahmed, T 398026, 40 beds, 500m from bus and 1 km from train station.

● **Banks & money changers**
Banque Centrale d'Algérie, 13 Blvd de la Soummam; Banque Nationale d'Algérie, 4 Blvd de la Soummam.

● **Hospitals & medical services**
Hospitals: 76 Blvd Ben Zerdeb, T 344311.

● **Post & telecommunications**
Area code: 06.
Post Office: Blvd Mohammed Khémisti.

● **Shopping**
Crafts: *SNAT*, 3 Blvd de la Soummam. Large number of local goods and crafts for sale.

● **Tour companies & travel agents**
Air Algérie, 2 Blvd Emir Abdelkader, T 391555; *Air France*, 5 place Abdelmalek Ramdane, T 336965; *CNAN*, 13 Blvd Abane Ramdane, T 332767, for ferry tickets.

● **Tourist offices**
ONAT, 10 Blvd Emir Abdelkader, T 391611. They issue air tickets and have a car hire service. For local information, 4 rue Mohammed Khémisti, T 335130.

● **Transport**
Air Buses to the airport (22 km) leave from the place du 1er Novembre. For information, T 418500. Flights to Adrar, Algiers, Annaba, Béchar, Constantine, Geneva, Lyon, Marseille, Paris, Tamanrasset, Tindouf, Toulouse and Zürich.

Train There are departures to Algiers, Mohammadia (for Béchar) and Tlemcen. A night train for Algiers leaves at 2200. Be there at least 1 hr before if you want a seat. For information, T 340621.

Road There are two bus stations in Oran. The bus station for the W and Tlemcen is by the train station. Buses to all other main towns leave the main bus station 1½ km beyond the museum on Blvd Zabana.

Sea Ferries leave from directly below the Ramp de Commandant Ferradj. Sailings: Marseille in summer (Jul, Aug, Sep) there are 4 return journeys a month, otherwise there are 2 a month. Alicante in summer 8 return journeys a month, otherwise 4 a month. Sète in summer 3 return journeys a month.

Excursions

Most visitors aiming for Tlemcen, 138 km away, take the direct N2. This road skirts the huge salt sea for 30 km, climbs easily through a rich agricultural landscape to **Aïn-Témouchent** and then winds and turns up to Tlemcen nestling at the foot of the Monts de Tlemcen. Travellers with their own transport are recommended to take instead the N2 W, the corniche to **Mers el Kebir**, with fine sea views and one or two good beaches, in particular Les Andalouses (15 km from Oran) which is just beyond the lighthouse perched on **Cap Falcon**. Aim back to the N2 at Bou-Tlélis or El Amria. Further roads to the W lead down to pleasant beaches and the N35 and Aïn-Témouchent before cutting through the wooded Traras mountain range to **Beni-Saf**, a thriving port. The N22 S goes on to Tlemcen.

INLAND TO TLEMCEN

Tlemcen

ACCESS **Air** The airport is at Zénata, 24 km N. There are buses to the centre of town. For information, T 220314. **Train** From Oran and the Moroccan border trains stop at the station to the E of the town about 15 mins walk. The bus station is on the corner of rue du 1er Novembre and Blvd Gaouar Hocine. The station is well organized. **Road** There are buses from Algiers, Béchar, Oran, Sebdou, Tiaret and the Moroccan border.

(*Pop* 200,000; *Alt* 830m) Tlemcen lies 170 km from Oran and is one of the finest cities in Algeria, noted for its unique cultural and architectural heritage. Despite modern additions on the outskirts it remains a truly beautiful city situated in an equally beautiful region which one must take time to explore and appreciate.

History
The area was inhabited by cave dwellers during prehistoric times, and was also the site of a Roman legionnaire's camp

of which very little remains. In the 8th century, the Arab town, established by Idris I, was named Agadir meaning fortress. The actual town of Tlemcen was founded in the 11th century by the Almoravid Youcef Ben Tachfin, who made it his capital and built the Great Mosque. It reached its peak under the Zianids, or Abd El Ouadites whose leader was the Berber Yaghmoracen, and became the capital of the central Maghreb prospering in trans-Saharan trade. Bitter rivalry between the Zianids in Tlemcen and the Merinids from Fes prompted a struggle for the control of Tlemcen. The first siege was in 1299, when Abou Yacoub, the Merinid leader, built the city of Mansourah, just outside Tlemcen. In 1307, Abou Yakoub was assassinated and Mansourah evacuated. Two subsequent sieges, in 1337 and 1359, took place before the Merinids finally controlled Tlemcen. They established their capital in Mansourah.

During the early 15th century, the Zianid's power decreased and control of the town oscillated between the Mer-

inids and the Hafsids of Tunis. In 1511, the Zianids finally succumbed to Spanish influence from Oran, and in 1555 the Turks ended all Zianid power and took the town which declined during their rule. At this time a new and important ethnic group was formed, the Kouloughlis, descendants of Turkish men and local women. With the French occupation of Algiers in 1830, Tlemcen was divided, the Kouloughlis siding with the French and the Moors and Berbers supporting Emir Abdelkader. The French finally took Tlemcen in 1842 but the seeds of Algerian nationalism were already in place. Ahmed Messali Hadj, born in Tlemcen, founded the first Independence movement in 1924. By 1946, he was head of the MTLD (Mouvement pour le Triomphe des Libertés Démocratiques). Many leaders who came to prominence in the struggle for independence came from this movement.

Places of interest

The centre of town is the place Emir Abdelkader. This is a lively square, with a great number of cafés, most popular in

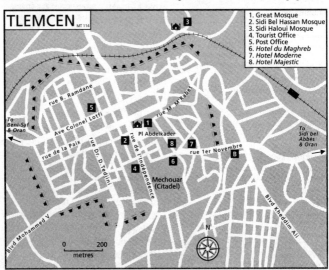

TLEMCEN MT 114

1. Great Mosque
2. Sidi Bel Hassan Mosque
3. Sidi Haloui Mosque
4. Tourist Office
5. Post Office
6. *Hotel du Maghreb*
7. *Hotel Moderne*
8. *Hotel Majestic*

rue B. Ramdane

Ave Colonel Lotfi

rue de la Paix

rue Dr. D.Tedjini

rue de l'Indépendence

rue M. M'Rabti

Pl Abdelkader

rue 1er Novembre

Mechouar
(Citadel)

Blvd Mohammed V

Blvd Khedaim Ali

To
Beni-Saf
& Oran

To
Sidi bel
Abbès
& Oran

N.

0   200
metres

the early evening. To the N of the square is the **Great Mosque**, built in 1082 by Youcef Ben Tachfin. It was embellished by the Almoravid Ali Ben Youcef in 1135 and enlarged a century later by Yaghmoracen. It is styled on the mosque in Córdoba and has 13 naves. The entrance, on the E side, leads straight into the prayer hall. The dome above the *mihrab* is remarkable, the intricate decoration simulating stalactites. The *mihrab* itself is richly and elegantly ornate. The large courtyard, over 20m in length, once covered in onyx, has a central fountain for ablutions, surrounded by benches decorated with multicoloured tiles. In the N corner of the mosque, stands the 35m rectangular minaret added by Yaghmoracen. Open daily 0800-1100 except Fri.

The **Sidi Bel Hassan Mosque**, to the W of the place Emir Abdelkader, has been deconsecrated and transformed into a museum. This mosque was built in honour of Yaghmoracen, in 1296. It is thought that the mosque was named after the famous theologian Abou El Hassan, who started teaching before Yaghmoracen's death. Inside, the mosque is separated into three naves supported by eight onyx columns. The carved plasterwork is noteworthy. The museum's exhibits are displayed in the prayer hall and an adjoining room mainly consisting of intricate mosaics, 12th century carved woodwork, funerary steles, minerals, fossils and pottery. Open daily 0900-1200 and 1400-1800, closed Fri afternoon and Sat all day. Entrance free.

The Hadars, the old Andalusian quarter, starts from the NE of the place Emir Abdelkader. The main street in this area, rue Mohammed M'Rabet, has been turned into a highly commercial pedestrian zone. This quarter, in the morning or late afternoon is incredibly lively and full of atmosphere. One block S of place Emir Abdelkader is the Mechouar, or citadel, mainly recon-structed in the 19th century. To the N of the town, just outside the walls, is the **mosque** dedicated to Sidi Haloui who gave up being a law professor to become a sweet seller, got on the wrong side of the Sultan and was executed in 1337. The mosque was built in 1353 by the Merinid Abou Inane Farés. It stands out white against the surrounding greenery. The prayer hall is divided into five naves held up by eight onyx columns with intricate capitals. The rectangular minaret is decorated with coloured glazed tiles.

Local information
● Accommodation
B *Hotel Les Zianides*, Blvd Kheddim Ali, T 201821, best hotel in town, 10 mins from town centre, garden, pool, tennis.

D *Hotel du Maghreb*, place du Commandant Ferradj, T 203571, 78 rm.

E *Hotel Moderne*, 20 rue du 1er Novembre, T 208796; *Hotel Majestic*, place Cheikh Bahir Ibrahimi, T 200786, no showers.

Youth hostels: Sidi Chaker, Tlemcen 13000, T 263226, open 0800-1200 and 1400-2200, 50 beds, laundry facilities, bus 500m.

Camping: Municipal camp site 2 km to W of town in olive groves, sounds idyllic, actually very basic.

● Banks & money changers
Banque Centrale d'Algérie, Ave Colonel Lotfi (next to Post Office).

● Entertainment
Hammam: on rue 1er November, separate opening times for men and women so check! AD10 incl soap and towel.

Music: Tlemcen is noted for its music making; classical Andalusian music is studied.

● Post & telecommunications
Area code: 07.

Post Office: Ave Colonel Lotfi, open 0800-1830 Sat-Wed, 0800-1600 Thur. Parcel department on left, telephones at rear.

● Shopping
Bargains: fine embroidery, local and imported carpets, leather work and woodwork especially cabinets and inlaid boxes.

● Tour companies & travel agents
Air Algérie rue Dr Damerdji Tedjini, T 266762;

Air France, rue de La Paix, T 203901; *CNAN*, T 200071, rue 1er November for shipping.

● **Tourist offices**

ONAT, 15 rue de l'Indépendance, nr mechouar entrance, T 208801. Travel agency and car hire available. **Local** place du Commandant Ferradj, T 203456. Open 0900-1200 and 1430-1900. Very helpful with good free map.

Around Tlemcen

Visit **Mansourah** about 2 km W of Tlemcen. The town was built in 1302 by the Merinid Abou Yacoub, while holding Tlemcen's first siege. By the end of the 14th century, the town was abandoned and used as a source of building stone for Tlemcen, which accounts for the few remains. Still standing are parts of the walls which were originally 4 km long, reaching a height of 12m and 1½m in thickness, complemented by 80 towers. The best pieces remaining stand to the N and W of the site. The only other ruins include the **mosque** which has virtually disappeared and the minaret, still al-most intact, apart from the S side. The **minaret** has been acknowledged as one of the finest examples of Hispano-Moorish architecture and ranks with the Koutoubia in Marrakech (see page 176) and the Giralda in Sevilla.

At **El Eubbab**, 2 km to the E of the town, is the **Sidi Bou Medine mosque** and tomb. Sidi Bou Medine, was born in Sevilla in 1126. He was highly revered throughout the Maghreb and taught in Sevilla, Fes and Bejaïa after having been to Mecca. He died in Tlemcen on a journey to Marrakech in 1197 and was buried here. The shrine, reached through a splendid columned courtyard, has been frequently added to and restored. The mosque built in 1339 by Merinid Sultan Abou El Hassan Ali, is one of the finest examples of the Hispano-Moorish style, with spectacular arches and carved decorative plasterwork in floral and geometric designs, similar to the Palace of the Alhambra in Granada, and is unique in Algeria. The

THE FRENCH FOREIGN LEGION

The Légion Etrangère was set up in 1831 for service outside France, at that time principally in Algeria. The **Beau Geste** image of the Legion is deserved not simply because of the desert terrain and the colonial wars in which it fought but because conditions of service were and remain extremely tough. The Foreign Legion was deployed in Algeria and Morocco and its buildings, including forts and garrison towns, remain a characteristic symbol of the French occupation of the region. The group's headquarters were at Sidi Bel Abbès in Algeria until 1962 when the French gave Independence to Algeria. The Legion saw bloody but heroic service in Mexico, Spain and Crimea before being sent to Indochina in 1885 where it was a major military element of the French colonial presence. The Legion took part in the splendid but ultimately unsuccessful battle at Dien Bien Phu, after which the French administration ended.

The Legion's officers are French, with few exceptions. The ranks are made up of other mainly European nationalities who have joined the Legion because of its unique record of professionalism and its almost constant involvement in warfare in distant places. The backbone of the Legion has always been made up of an élite often originally trained in national armies and there is little truth in the belief that it was made up of untrained thieves, murderers and n'er do wells.

In recent years the Legion served with distinction not only in Indochina but in the great world wars. France deployed the Foreign Legion in Corsica after the withdrawal from Algeria and it is thus not far away from the North African territories where its legend was created.

minaret which was built at the same time has beautiful designs in brick and tiles. It is possible to climb up to the top where there is a very good view. Next to the mosque, is a once beautiful **medersa**, which unfortunately has suffered neglect over the years. The famous historian and geographer Ibn Khaldoun frequently came here. The *koubba*, mosque and *medersa* are open 0800-1100 every day except Fri.

Beni Bahdel lake 32 km SW along the N22 and W54 over the Col d'Hafrir is surrounded by dense forest.

Cascades d'El Ourit 7 km E along the N7, a 7-layer waterfall from the dam outlet tumbles into the irrigated valley below.

Maghnia, 50 km W of Tlemcen through expanses of vineyards and orchards, is the last town before the border with Morocco, another 13 km on. Be prepared for tedious checking procedures as you cross. Make sure your financial documents are in order.

Nédroma (*Alt* 395m) is a quiet town 37 km N of Maghnia on the W46, which winds through areas of olives and vines before crossing the forested ridge of the Traras range. The Taza pass offers spectacular views. The Great Mosque built by the Almoravids and the remains of battlements recall the town's historic past. Today Nédroma is better known for its pottery and the woven and embroidered garments it produces.

The circuit back to Oran can be completed by taking the eastern route via **Sidi-Bel-Abbès**, a booming town, proud of its new university. For the first 40 km the N7 and the railway keep company, taking turns to cross first under then over as they cut through some pleasant, prosperous farming land with the wooded hills to the S. Sidi-Bel-Abbès was famous as the home of the French Foreign Legion (see box). **Accommodation C** *El Djazaïr* is rec for an overnight stay. The road then follows the (dry) river bed N to Oued Tlélat and the busy motorway into Oran.

THE SOUTH

CONTENTS

Grand Erg Oriental	334
Grand Erg Occidental	338

MAPS

Grand Erg Oriental	335
Grand Erg Occidental	339
Ghardaïa	344
The Hoggar	347
Assekrem Circuit	350
Tassili N'Ajjer	351

The Sahara Desert takes up a massive 85% of the S of Algeria. No wonder 95% of the population lives in the N of the country! The road network is good though many of the roads are not black top and traffic uses the N-S routes through the Grand Ergs Oriental and Occidental to the oases of Djanet, Regganne and In Salah, then on to Tamanrasset. This vast empty space sprawls under clear blue skies and has as its focal point the Hoggar range of mountains reaching 3,000m. It contains the chaotic landscapes of Tassili N'Ajjer, shelters one of the world's richest prehistoric art museums and reveals surprisingly luxuriant oases. For security reasons traffic in the vicinity of oil and gas installations in this area, particularly around El Oued, Ouargla and Illizi, is restricted to oil/gas company employees and local inhabitants.

GRAND ERG ORIENTAL

The Grand Erg Oriental is the immense stretch of sand in the E of Algeria, going right up to the Tunisian and Libyan borders. It is considerably larger than the Grand Erg Occidental.

The Souf

The region in the N of the Grand Erg is known as the Souf and has its own traditions and way of life. First inhabited during the Neolithic period, the region was later settled by Berbers and Arabs, mostly from the Yemen. Today, the Souafas speak a very pure Arabic, only a few Berber words remaining. Despite recent efforts towards settling these people, nomadism still exists and a number of families still spend half the year with their animals, only returning to the oasis for date picking. Traditional activities such as carpet and *burnous* weaving continue wherever the women are. A remarkable aspect of life in the Souf is the ingenious cultivation system. Instead of making the water rise to the ground, the cultivation is done as close to the water table as possible. The 'gardens' are dug in the sands, reaching depth of 3 to 20m. The use of the *bour* circumvents the need for complex irrigation systems as the roots of the palm trees draw water directly from the underground water supply. Nevertheless, the work involved is not any less than in the maintenance of an irrigation system. The sand incessantly fills in the holes and it is a continuous effort to keep it at bay. The architecture of the region illustrates both the need to use any available materials in the building, and the rigours of the environment. All the houses are built to minimize the effect of the heat, with domes to deflect the sun and with few windows, while the thick walls reduce the heat inside.

El Oued

ACCESS Air The airport is 18 km away on the road to Biskra, at Guémar. **Road** Buses stop at the main bus station 3 km N of the town along Ave Mohammed Khémisti.

Known as the town of the Thousand Domes, El Oued is in the centre of the Souf region. In summer, temperatures of 45°C are not uncommon and even 50°C is reached. The town itself is very pleasant, with beautiful architecture and fits perfectly into the surroundings, with its rounded shapes and white walls. El Oued is a good place from which to enter Tunisia. There are taxis to the border and buses from there to Tozeur in Tunisia. There is also a bank on the Algerian side of the border for converting Dinars.

Places of interest

The town centre and major point of interest is the **market place** in the old part of town. The market takes place every day, but is best in the morning or evenings, especially on Fri. It is a colourful and lively market selling fresh vegetables, fruit and local *burnouses* and carpets. Local carpets frequently have a

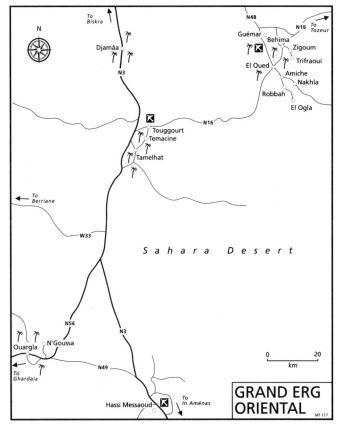

GRAND ERG ORIENTAL

MT 117

brown cross in the design. Prices are a bit lower than in Ghardaïa. Also interesting are *Affanes*, a kind of woollen slipper used by the nomads as protection from cold and from the burning sands. By the side of the road going to Tunisia, there is a market with sheep, horses and camels. From the market, ask to see the **Sidi Salem mosque** from which there is an excellent view over the city. The **museum**, on the Ave Taleb Larbi, by the Tourist Office has only one room, but contains some interesting exhibits. There is a collection of desert animals and insects as well as some sand roses and an explanation of how they are formed. A display of interesting geological finds proves that the Sahara was once a sea. The museum is open 0900-1200 and from 1500-1800, closed Mon. Entry AD1.

Local information
● **Accommodation**

C *Hotel du Souf*, S of the town, T 728523, pool, a/c, and a tower with a good view.

D *Hotel de l'Or Noir*, T 728219, on the outskirts of El Oued on the road to Biskra, 40 rm, pool.

E *Hotel Central*, Ave Taleb Larbi, T 728825; **E** *Hotel Si Moussa*, Ave Mohammed Khémisti, T 728381, slightly out of the centre, close to the bus station, sleep on roof.

Youth hostels: 17 km S at Nakhla, 50 beds, kitchen, bus and train 17 km.

Camping: About 10 km out of El Oued, on the road to Tunisia.

● **Places to eat**

◆◆◆In *Hotel du Souf*.

◆For cheaper meals Ave Mohammed Khémisti is the best bet.

● **Banks & money changers**

There a few banks in the Ave Taleb Larbi, but be careful as they usually close on Fri and Sat. Possible to change money at the *Hotel du Souf*.

● **Post & telecommunications**
Area code: 04.

Post Office: this is in a small street, immediately behind the tourist office.

● **Tour companies & travel agents**

Air Algérie, Ave Mohammed Khémisti, T 728666.

● **Tourist offices**

There are two offices close to each other. The **ONAT** is at 17 rue Talbi Larbi, T 79175. The **Syndicat d'Initiative**, next door is more helpful.

● **Transport**

Local Bus: there is a local bus station in the Ave Taleb Larbi, close to the taxi station. The buses go to the surrounding towns and there is also a minibus service to the main bus station.

Air From Guémar airport to **Algiers** and **Annaba**.

Road Bus: from Ave Mohammed Khémisti to Annaba, Algiers, Biskra, Constantine, Ghardaïa, Ouargla and Touggourt. **Taxis**: leave from Ave Taleb Larbi to Touggourt and the Tunisian border.

Around El Oued

The road SE from El Oued to El Ogla (17 km) is very interesting, especially the village of **Robbah** at 12 km, and beyond where there is an impressive concentration of *bours* for palm tree cultivation and many large dunes. The same road out of El Oued, but forking to the left at Amiche towards El Ogla, leads to **Nakhla** also with some impressive *bours*, and from here a track continues across the Erg to Ghadames in Libya, 450 km away. To the NE from El Oued along the N16 road to Tunisia lies **Z'Goum**, one of the oldest villages in the Souf region. From here you may be able to push on to Trifraoui, but the sand often makes the trip difficult. **Guémar**, on the N48 N from El Oued, is also an important town and has strong local traditions. Visit the *zaouia* and walk around in the streets. Very beautiful, particularly at sunset. The N16 S from El Oued to Touggourt, 95 km, passes through a landscape of impressive dunes.

Touggourt

The town is an important administrative centre. There are a few things that should not be missed. The Mestaoua quarter, W of the place des Martyrs, is an impressive labyrinth of small winding and covered streets. Unfortunately, the area is not being well preserved and is being slowly pulled down, making place for new developments, but it is still worth a look. To the E of the place des Martyrs is the large central market on Fri, which is very lively and has a large choice of fresh fruit and vegetables.

● **Accommodation C** *Hotel de l'Oasis*, S of the town towards the oasis, T 09 726916, pool, tennis; **E** *Hotel de la Paix*, in the centre by the Post Office, sleep on the roof in summer; **E** *Hotel des Bédouins*, 5 km out of town on the road to El Oued, a few bungalows and sleeping under large bedouin tents. **Youth hostels** *AJ Kheir-Eddine*, Touggourt 30200, T 674709, open Sep-Jun incl, 80 beds, kitchen, laundry, meals available, free kitchen, train 100m, bus 150m.

● **Tour companies & travel agents** *Air Algérie*, rue du 1er Novembre, T 09 726096.

● **Transport Air** The airport is 5 km E of the town on the road to El Oued. For information, T 09 766018. Flights to Algiers. **Train** These run daily to Biskra around midnight. **Road Bus**: the bus station is by the train station. There are buses to Algiers, Biskra, Constantine, El Oued, Hassi Messaoud and Ouargla. Most of the buses are just passing through, so getting a seat can be difficult. Be there early. For local buses to Temacine and Tamelhat, the bus stop is further down the road. **Taxi**: the taxi rank is at the start of the El Oued road, slightly out of town. Main destinations are Biskra, El Oued and Ouargla.

Around Touggourt

The oasis to the S of the town is enormous with over 1,300,000 palm trees producing the excellent *deglet nur* dates. Further S, the village of **Temacine** can be reached either along the minor road by the *Hotel de l'Oasis*, but this can be difficult, or more easily by turning left off the N3 road to Ouargla after 12 km. Buses and taxis run there from Touggourt. The village of Temacine looks like a fortress. Inside the walls are beautiful small, winding, covered streets. There is

a good view from the top of the mosque's minaret, built in 1431. **Tamelhat**, 2 km further S, is very similar but seems to have been abandoned or fallen asleep. Inside the village, there are a great number of finely decorated beautiful houses, as well as a few houses badly in need of attention. The tomb and mosque of **Sidi El Hadj Ali** should not be missed. Next to the mosque is the mausoleum, also built in 1284, which has an impressive finely sculpted and coloured plastered dome as well as walls covered in glazed tiles.

Ouargla

This was once an important transit place in the gold and slave trade, with caravans coming up from the Sudan. It was also an important Ibadite city until they were forced to leave by the Almoravids, and went to settle in the M'Zab. Today, the city is an important link in the black gold trade, oil. **Hassi Messaoud** 80 km S has large oil reserves. Ouargla is the closest large town and serves as a necessary link. The result is of little interest for the visitor except for the Saharan museum which has a splendid collection of crafts produced in various Saharan regions including Ouargla. Open 0800-1200 and 1500-800, closed Fri. The market has a good supply of fresh foods as well as a great number of sand roses, many of an impressive size.

● **Accommodation C** *Hotel el Mehri*, T 09 722066, 60 rm, pool, in the centre of town; **D** *Hotel de Tassili*, T 09 703004, slightly out of town to the SW; *Hotel Des Rhimmels*, situated close to Air Algérie. **Youth hostels** There are two youth hostels: *AJ Mostefa-Ben-Boulaïd*, Quartier Emire-Abdel-Kader, Ouargla 3000, open Sep-Jun incl, 40 beds, meals available, laundry, free kitchen, bus 200m, airport bus; and *AJ Rose des Sables*, Av de la Palestine, Route de Ghardaïa, Ouargla, T 703820, open Sep-Jun incl, 40 beds, laundry facilities, airport bus. **Camping** *Camping Tahost* has tents, grass huts and showers.

● **Tour companies & travel agents** *Air Algérie*, rue Chemine Kaddour, T 09 702858.

● **Tourist offices** Ave Emir Abdelkader, close to the market, T 09 705183.

● **Transport Air** The airport is 8 km out of town. For information, T 09 704529. Flights to Algiers, Djanet, **In Aménas** and **Tamanrasset**. **Road** There are buses to Ghardaïa, , Hassi-Messaoud, Touggourt and two buses a week to In Aménas.

THE GRAND ERG OCCIDENTAL

The Grand Erg Occidental is the huge sea of sand in the W of Algeria. Access to this area is easy, as the Erg has a good black top road on both its E and W extremities. This region with particularly impressive dunes and some extremely beautiful oases is a good place to experience the desert without going further S.

Aïn Sefra

ACCESS **Train** The single daily train from N and S stops at the station between the town and the N6. **Road** Buses from Algiers, Béchar, Oran and Tlemcen will drop you in the main square.

430 km S of Oran at an altitude of 1,000m, at the S end of the Saharan Atlas could be your first encounter with the real desert. The golden red sand dunes at the foot of the mountains are most impressive. The N6 actually passes N of the town which in itself is of little interest except for the view over the gorge and the Ksour mountains. There is limited accommodation, except for the **C** *El Mekter Hotel*, T 07 311771, 30 rm, tennis, pool.

Towards Morocco

The N6 continues SW alongside the railway to Beni Ounif (153 km) on the way to Béchar, a further 114 km. Spare time to turn left off the road to the oasis of Moghrar-Tahtani or right at 85 km from Aïn-Sefra towards the Col de Founassa along a rough but picturesque road. The frontier post for Morocco is about 2 km N of Beni Ounif. There is a daily train

from Mohammadia to Béchar and vice versa. Buses to Béchar from the N also go through Beni Ounif. The border crossing is to Figuig, and can take some time to cross on foot. Take a taxi from Beni Ounif to the border. It is then only a short walk across to the Moroccan side. The Algerian Customs officers are renowned for their thorough searches here, so be patient.

Béchar

ACCESS **Air** The airport is about 5 km N of the town and a bus runs to the bus station in the town centre. **Train** The train station lies about 2 km to the W of the town.

(*Alt* 772m) Béchar, the largest town in the Western Sahara, is a modern administrative and commercial centre, of importance to the traveller as a stop on the way S, and a good place to stock up with petrol, water and food and change money. There are shops, a market near the mosque with fresh vegetables and fruit, and a few banks.

Local information
● **Accommodation**
C *Hotel Antar* on Ave du 1er Novembre, T 237161, 100 rm.

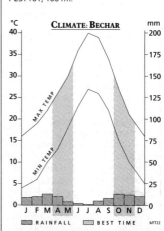

CLIMATE: BECHAR

MAX TEMP

MIN TEMP

J F M A M J J A S O N D

▨ RAINFALL   ▨ BEST TIME   MTT22

D *Hotel de la Saoura*, 24 rue Belahreche, T 235404, 29 rm.

Youth hostels: Cité Riadi, 0800 Béchar, T 810844, open 0800-1200 and 1400-2200, 50 beds, cooking facilities, laundry, 2 km from bus or train.

● **Post & telecommunications**
Area code: 07.

Post Office: this is on the main square, place de la République.

● **Tour companies & travel agents**
Air Algérie, rue Aspirant Djamel, T 836730, also does car hire.

● **Tourist offices**
ONAT, 6 rue Aspirant Djamel, T 235537.

● **Transport**
Air The airport is 5 km N out of town and local buses go there. For information, T 235592. Flights to **Algiers**, **Ghardaïa** and **Oran**.

Train Daily to **Mohammadia**. For information, T 235592.

Road Bus: the bus station is close to the market in the centre. For information, T 235388. It is very busy. There are buses to Algiers, Adrar, Beni Abbès, Ghardaïa, Oran, Taghit, Timimoun and Tlemcen. It is best to book a seat in advance.

Taghit

ACCESS There are buses from Béchar and Beni Abbès, but be sure to check re-

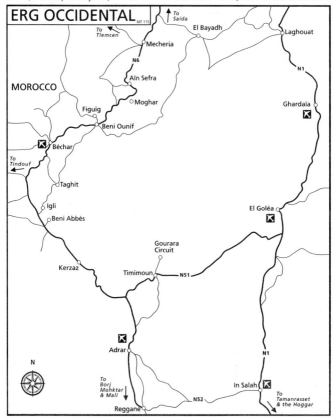

turn times if you wish to avoid a night in Taghit.

92 km S of Béchar, this is a beautiful oasis village, a wonderful place to stop. It has the most amazing views over the dunes of the Grand Erg, particularly at sunrise. The view from the top of the dunes to the E is superb, especially in comparison with the green of the oasis to the W. The houses of the village, built around the ksar, are constructed of brown mud bricks. The only hotel is **C** *Hotel Taghit*, with pool and 40 a/c rm, clean and simple. There are a few shops, a petrol station and a Post Office.

Places of interest 15 km S of Taghit there is a cliff alongside the dry river bed with some Neolithic animal paintings. Worth a visit if you have no opportunity to see the other more famous Neolithic sites.

Beni Abbès

This is a small oasis town 250 km S of Béchar with the advantage of having two hotels and a few shops as well as a very pleasant municipal pool. There are two parts to the town. While the new town is the hub of activity, such as there is, the more interesting part is the old, typically Saharan, mud brick town, which unfortunately is slowly disintegrating. The dunes, rising steeply to the E, are well worth the climb for the amazing view over the seemingly endless sands. The panorama is especially memorable at sunset. The **municipal pool**, by the old town, is shaded by a few trees and is fed by spring water always at a constant 26°C. The **museum** in the new part of town, N of the main square, has a collection of desert fauna, prehistoric fossils and a section on Saharan traditional crafts. Open 0700-1200 and 1400-1700. Closed Fri. Next to the museum, a small **zoo** contains some of the more common Saharan birds and animals.

History
According to a myth, the town of Beni

Abbès was founded in the 11th century by Sidi Othman. He and his companion were on their way to Egypt. While stopping in Beni Abbès, Sidi Othman pushed his stick into the sand and said that when he died, water would spring from the hole. Sidi Othman died that night, and the spring flowed, giving birth to the oasis. The village's development was hampered throughout the years by the feud with the rival Ghenanmas and the Doui Menia from Morocco, until in 1750 the inhabitants of Beni Abbès built a fortress and agreed a truce with their enemies. In 1901 the French troops came, and by 1957 the old town was almost abandoned in favour of the more modern houses in the new part of town.

Places of interest
The **church** of Les Petites Soeurs de Jésus stands on a small rise to the S of the town. Mass is said daily. While the **museum** is worth visiting being surprisingly well organized and informative, the zoo in the adjacent botanical garden is not. The town has a Post Office, a bank, a market and a few shops.

Local information
● **Accommodation**
C *Hotel Rym*, T 07 233224, 40 rm, pool.
E *Hotel Grand Erg*, T 07 233439, 20 rm.
Youth hostels: open 0800-2400, 80 beds AD50, meals, family rm, laundry, watersports, bus 300m.

● **Transport**
Road Buses leave from the bus station in the town centre tom Béchar, Taghit, Timimoun and Adrar.

Kerzaz is situated 120 km S of Beni Abbès on the road to Timimoun. The old village is 2 km along the road on the left, just before the petrol station. The buildings are typical of Saharan architecture, walled with narrow, covered meandering streets. It is very attractive and well worth a stop if only to examine the system of lifting water from the deep wells, but it is not easy to get back on a bus as all those passing through are generally full. Buses go to Adrar, Béchar and Timimoun. There is no accommodation.

Timimoun

This little town is in one of the most beautiful oases in the Algerian Sahara. Built of red mud in a style similar to Sudanese architecture, it is a real delight. The old town has houses built virtually one on top of the other. The narrow winding streets are often covered and very unusual. The new town, built by the French, follows the traditional style very closely making the entire town very pleasant.

Places of interest
The oasis itself is interesting as well as very refreshing. Timimoun has an ingenious system for supplying water by *foggaras*. These are underground tunnels, dug at a slight angle, transporting water from the spring. The tunnels were hand dug and reach distances of over 5 km in length. Vertical access tunnels are situated every 100m or less, to facilitate digging and maintenance. The system, widespread in Iran where they are known as *qanats*, limits the amount of water lost through evaporation and provides a steady and effortless water supply. Produce from the oasis includes a wide variety of vegetables and surprisingly, stoneless dates.

The Gourara circuit
This journey around the dried up lake, with incredible and unforgettable desert landscapes is not to be missed, having come so far. The circuit, about 80 km, does not necessitate a 4WD vehicle but it is wise to take a local with you to spot soft sand. Otherwise, the Tourist Office organizes daily trips. The circuit must be done in a clockwise direction to avoid getting stuck in the sand. Leaving Timimoun to the NE, and pass the village of Massine on the left which specializes in pottery. Shortly after Massine the road forks.

Go right, following the edge of the lake to **El Kef Gabsa**. After this small village, the road starts climbing up to **Badriane**, a village which used to be an assembly point for the start of the pilgrimage to Mecca. The best view is from the small village of Tialet, 1 km further on. At **Izgzer**, there are large caverns where the inhabitants come to seek refuge from the sun and rest during the hot afternoons. From here the road continues with yet more breathtaking views along the ridge to Tindjillet and Semouta, a beautiful village from where the road leads down to the dry lake bed. At **Ouled Said** there is an important oasis with an intricate system of water rationing. The road then returns to Timimoun along the lake bed. About 6 km before Timimoun to the right of the road, sand roses can be dug up.

Local information
● **Accommodation**
C *Le Gourara*, T 234451, 60 rm, view the sunrise/sunset from the roof, tennis, pool. *Hotel Ighzer; Hotel Rouge de l'Oasis*, T 234417.

● **Places to eat**
The restaurant in *Le Gouara* is rec.

● **Banks & money changers**
Banque National d'Algérie, along main street, close to the market.

● **Post & telecommunications**
Area code: 07.

● **Tour companies & travel agents**
Air Algérie on the main square, T 234555.

● **Tourist offices**
In the municipality building.

● **Transport**
Air The airport is 8 km out of town. For information, T 932054. There is one flight a week from **Algiers**.

Road Bus station is on the main street. Most buses only pass through Timimoun and booking is not possible. There are a few that start in Timimoun going to Adrar, Béchar, Ghardaïa where booking may be possible.

Adrar

This regional centre is important for the traveller going to Mali as it is a good place to stock up with fuel and supplies and deal with customs formalities. If you do not have your own transport, it is probably best not to take the bus to Borj-Mokhtar, as it may be very difficult to get a lift from there on. Best to try and get a lift in Adrar.

● **Accommodation**   **C** *Hotel Touat*, T 259933, 125 rm, pool; **E** *Hotel Djemila*, 21 rm.

● **Youth hostels** *Maison de Jeunes de la Wilaya*, 01000 Adrar, T 258284, open 0800-1200 and 1400-2200, 25 beds, cooking facilities, laundry, bus 200m.

● **Post & telecommunications Area code**: 07.

● **Tour companies & travel agents** *Air Algérie*, main square, T 259365.

● **Transport Air** The airport is 13 km out of town. For information, T 259020. Flights to **Algiers**, **Borj-Mokhtar**, **Ghardaïa**, **Oran** and **Tamanrasset**. **Road** The bus station is N of the main square. Booking is available. Buses to **Aoulef**, **Béchar**, **Borj-Mokhtar**, **Ghardaïa** and **In Salah**.

El Goléa (El Meniaa)

About 450 km E from Timimoun, El Goléa is a large oasis, with 200,000 palm trees. It is an important stopover on the route S. The town is pleasant, dominated by the Ksar El Meniaa.

Places of interest

The Ksar El Meniaa, situated on a rocky mound, overlooks the entire region. It is interesting to wander around the deserted ruins. 3 km to the N of the town, is the **tomb of Charles de Foucauld**, buried here in 1929. He set up the hermitage in the Hoggar, but his body was brought to El Goléa for burial. A church was built in these pleasant surroundings. The **museum** of local geological specimens is private but can be visited by specialists in this field. To the

S is the Sebkha El Melah. To get there, take the road to In Salah, and 2 km after El Goléa, take a road on the left, after a large stone road sign. The lake is another 2 km further on. In El Goléa, the **market** on the main square has a large choice of fresh fruit and vegetables. The water here is very good, so if you are driving, stock up here.

Local information

● **Accommodation**

C *Hotel El Boustan*, by the oases, on the road to the Ksar, T 09 736142, pool, tennis.

D *Hotel Vieux Ksar* on the road to In Salah, T 09 733310, 30 rm.

● **Tour companies & travel agents**
Air Algérie, rue de la Liberté, T 09 736100.

● **Transport**
Air The airport is 3 km out of town. For information, T 09 736101. Flights to **Algiers** and **Tamanrasset**.

Road The bus station is in the town centre. Buses go to **Adrar**, **Ghardaïa** and **Timimoun**. Unfortunately, all these buses only pass through El Goléa, and there is no certainty of getting a seat. There is also a bus to **In Salah** every 2 days.

Ghardaïa and the M'Zab

Ghardaïa is the name of the largest town in the centre of the valley known as the **M'Zab** which is one of the most beautiful and interesting areas in the Algerian Sahara and should certainly not be missed. The five towns in the pentapolis were all built by the Mozabites from the Ibadite sect, and are situated by an escarpment alongside the Oued M'Zab. Each is built around a central mosque on a rocky knoll. Ghardaïa, the main town and the centre for tourism with a number of hotels, is the most interesting town to visit, along with Melika (the Queen) and Beni Isquen (Sons of Those Who Keep Their Word). Bou Noura (Father of Light) and El Ateuf (the Turning) are less interesting.

History

The Mozabite sect goes back to the disappearance of the third Caliph in 656. This event created a schism within Islam and the rejection of the authority of Ali, the Prophet's son-in-law. The Kharejites formed their own sect with the belief that any Muslim could become Caliph, as long as he was an example of virtue and fidelity towards the Koran and the Sunna. The Kharejites broke away and soon split again, giving rise to the Ibadite sect, followers of Abdellah Ben Abad. Under the leadership of Ibn Rostem, the Ibadites came to North Africa and founded the prosperous town of Tahert (close to Tiaret in the NW of Algeria). In 911, the inhabitants of Tahert were defeated by the Fatimids and went to settle close to Ouargla. Once again, the prosperity of the town was to cause conflicts and by the 11th century the Ibadites moved to the M'Zab in the hope that nobody would come and find them in such an inhospitable environment. Between 1012 and 1048 they built the five towns, Ghardaïa being the last. The Mozabites today are mostly from Berber origin and speak a dialect very similar to Kabyle. The total population of the M'Zab now exceeds 100,000 people.

Architecture

In the building of the towns, the Mozabites have shown great simplicity, to a certain extent explained by the austere landscape and scarcity of building materials, but also due to the prevailing philosophy that no ornamentation was necessary. The result is absolute beauty and great harmony. The houses are built close together and painted only by white and blue (said to keep the flies away) and the ochre-coloured earth. The houses are softly curved with very few straight walls. The town is built around the central mosque, always situated at a certain height, expanding concentrically from the centre. Every house is near enough to hear the Muezzin. All the streets are built wide enough to enable the passing

of a mule with side packs and each arch is high enough to permit a rider to pass mounted on his mule. The central market place was built outside the main living area, in order to keep outsiders away from the real town. Houses were also built with great thought to privacy. The doors have a wall directly behind them, so hiding the life within the house from the passer-by. The houses are organized around a central room with no external windows, but a hole in the roof provides natural sunlight. The roof is reserved for the women. In the summer, when the heat gets excessive, the families move to the oasis, where they all have a 'summer house' near wells and under the shade of the palm trees.

Ghardaïa

ACCESS Air The airport is 18 km out of town on the road to El Goléa. For information, T 894062. There is a bus from the airport to the town centre which stops in front of the Air Algérie Office. **Road** Buses from all main towns, stop at the main bus station on rue Ahmed Talbi just 2 mins walk from the ONAT office. Local buses from the M'Zab area stop opposite the entrance to the old city.

(*Alt* 441m) Ghardaïa is the main town of

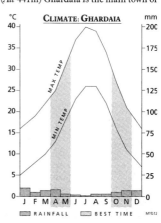

CLIMATE: GHARDAIA

the region with all the facilities and has greatly expanded beyond the old city and its walls. According to a myth, the town was founded by Sheikh Sidi Bou Gdemma who, passing by, saw some smoke coming from a cave. He stopped and saw a beautiful young woman known as Daia, who had been abandoned by all because she was pregnant. He was seduced by her beauty, asked for her hand in marriage and founded the town of Ghardaïa. The town's name in Arabic means Daia's cave (Ghar meaning cave).

Places of interest

The town is divided into the old and new. The new town is centred around the Ave du 1er Novembre, rue Emir Abdelkader and the rue Ahmed Talbi. To reach the old town, take the rue Emir Abdelkader that leads to the rue Ibn Rostem which

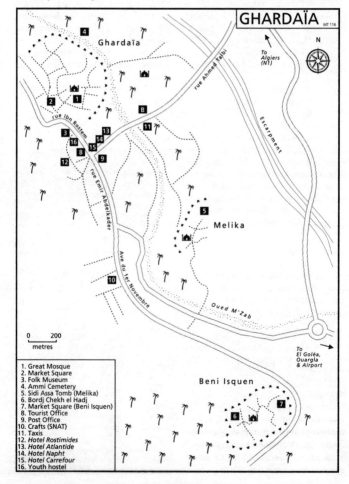

GHARDAÏA MT 116

Ghardaïa

To Algiers (N1)

Escarpment

rue Ahmed Talbi

rue Ibn Rostem

rue Emir Abdelkader

Ave du 1er Novembre

Melika

Oued M'Zab

0   200
metres

To El Goléa, Ouargla & Airport

Beni Isquen

1. Great Mosque
2. Market Square
3. Folk Museum
4. Ammi Cemetery
5. Sidi Assa Tomb (Melika)
6. Bordj Chekh el Hadj
7. Market Square (Beni Isquen)
8. Tourist Office
9. Post Office
10. Crafts (SNAT)
11. Taxis
12. *Hotel Rostimides*
13. *Hotel Atlantide*
14. *Hotel Napht*
15. *Hotel Carrefour*
16. Youth hostel

THE MOZABITES

The Mozabites are still very firmly attached to their traditions and live an austere and, for the women in particular, a secluded life. The austerity of the region forced the inhabitants to turn to trading as their main income, and this generally meant leaving the region for long periods. Trading however was greatly successful, many shops throughout Algeria still being owned by Mozabites. In order to preserve the traditions and shield themselves from outside influences, women were forbidden to leave the M'Zab and men to return with a 'foreign' woman. The women virtually never left their homes. Working on the principal that not to report a fault was as bad as doing it oneself, the society based itself on the two principals of delation (informing against each other) and surveillance. A group of women known as the *laveuses de mort* had the responsibility of washing bodies of the deceased people, but also and more importantly so, keeping an eye on the families whose husbands where absent. Another prevailing law is a kind of egalitarianism, where no external sign of wealth is to be shown, not even an indication that the pilgrimage to Mecca (the Hadj) has been completed, as this can be construed as a sign of wealth.

goes directly to the main market square. The square is lined with arcades, and there is a very colourful **daily market** selling everything from vegetables to carpets and silver trays. The best time is in the morning. On Wed and Sun a traditional **auction market** is held in the NE corner of the square in the Souk El Dellada, very similar to the one held in Beni Isquen. The **Great Mosque** is further up the hill after you go through the Souk El Dellada. The mosque has a very interesting pyramidal minaret and can be visited in the mornings, though you may have to be accompanied by a guide. Reach it from the market place by climbing the series of steps and ramps. To the S of the mosque, a covered street leads to the famous cave that according to the myth was at the origin of the town. It is still venerated by the Mozabite women.

The **Folk Museum** at the entrance to the old town, in the rue Emir Abdelkader, contains various interesting everyday items, but most interesting is the reconstruction of the interior of a traditional Mozabite house. Open daily 0830-1200 and 1500-1830. In winter open every evening 1930-2100.

Local information
● Accommodation
C *El Djanoub*, T 894620/890630, 250 rm, pleasant situation, pool, restaurant.

F *Hotel Atlantide*, Ave Ahmed Talbi, T 892536; **F** *Hotel Es Saada*, place Andalouse, on the square behind *Hotel Napht*, T 891654; **F** *Hotel Napht*, in the first street on the left off Ave Ahmed Talbi, T 890009.

Hotel Carrefour, on corner of rue Emir Abdelkader and rue Ahmed Talbi, T 893179; *Hotel de la Palmeraie*, on the road to the oasis, 1½ km out of town, T 892312; *Hotel le Rym*, Ave du 1er Novembre, T 893202.

Youth hostels: there are two youth hostels: *Maison de Jeunes Dahane Brahim à Metlili*, T 897668, 20 beds, bus 200m; and *Maison de Jeunes Emir Abdelkader*, Ghardaïa Centre, T 894403, 38 beds, bus 500m.

● Banks & money changers
These are in the main street and money can be changed in the *Hotel Rostimedes*.

● Post & telecommunications
Area code: 09.

Post Office: Ave du 1er Novembre.

● Shopping
Ghardaïa is an important centre for carpets but quality can vary greatly. See advice in section on carpets, page 190. Burnouses, a type of wool jallabah, are very good quality but generally very expensive. There are also silver trays (of doubtful quality) and local jewellery. Beauty

products such as khol or henna and spices are found in the central market and in the shops under the arcades.

● **Tour companies & travel agents**
Air Algérie, Ave du 1er Novembre, T 894663.

● **Tourist offices**
ONAT, rue Emir Abdelkader, T 891757.

● **Transport**
Local Bus: to other M'Zab towns leave from opp the entrance to the Old City.

Air The airport is 18 km out of town on the road to El Goléa. There is a bus service that departs from in front of the Air Algérie office. Make sure you have reconfirmed your flight booking and to be on the safe side be there at least 2 hrs before the flight is due to leave. For information, T 894062. Flights to **Algiers**, **Annaba**, **Béchar**, **Djanet**, **In Salah** and **Tamanrasset**.

Road Bus: the main bus station is along the rue Ahmed Talbi. There is a ticket office and it is possible to book. This can be important during busy periods. There are daily buses to all the main towns. **Taxi**: long distance taxis leave from opp the bus station and most go to **Algiers** and **El Goléa**.

Around Ghardaïa

From the bus station, follow the dry river bed to the NW. At about 500m there is the very large **Ammi Said cemetery**. According to tradition, the graves are not marked, and broken pots are left to aid recognition. In the centre of the cemetery there is an interesting mosque which has been dug into the ground. There is also an excellent view over the town of Ghardaïa. To visit the oasis which is 4 km to the NW, take a taxi or bus from the N side of the market. The old reservoir on the Oued M'Zab is very interesting. The river only ever has water once a year, but an ingenious system has been devised in order to distribute the water fairly throughout the oasis. The dam has many openings leading into lined underground tunnels all carrying the water to specific land plots within the oasis. Climb down an opening and take a look. The oasis itself which stretches further to the NW is

very pleasant particularly in the late afternoon. In it there are over 200,000 palm trees which are underplanted with fruit and vegetables. There is a large number of houses here, which are used only in the summer to escape the intense heat.

Melika The closest town to Ghardaïa, 1 km to the SE is situated on the top of a rocky knoll. It was once the religious centre of the M'Zab and is a very attractive town. The two main points of interest are the cemetery and the view over the valley and Ghardaïa. The cemetery is to the N of the town. The tomb of Sidi Aissa and his family is particularly interesting, surrounded by a large prayer area, from which the view towards Ghardaïa is impressive. The other, again unmarked, tombs are covered in broken pottery to assist recognition.

Beni Isguen, situated 2½ km S of Ghardaïa, is the present religious centre of the M'Zab. It is strongly attached to local traditions and customs, trying to limit the outside influence to a minimum. At night the three gates are closed and visits are only permitted with a guide. The town is also closed off from 1200 to 1530 for prayer. The best time to visit is in the late afternoon when activity on the main square increases and the daily market with its auction takes place. To enter the town it is important to be correctly dressed and fulfil a number of other requirements, such as not smoking which are all listed at the entrance. Photographing people is forbidden. The only way to see anything is to take an official guide from by the main gates for a set tour. The tour goes to the **Bordj Cheikh El Hadj** in the E of the town, to admire the view and will probably end in the market place, where if you arrive before 1700 you will see the **auction**. There are also a number of shops selling carpets and other crafts.

Outside the town to the W, is the oasis which is smaller and more pleasant than the one in Ghardaïa. The open streams known as *saggias*, and the long and sinuous reservoir are all part of the important irrigation system.

El Ateuf situated 9 km E of Ghardaïa, was the first of the five towns to be built. When entering the town it may be difficult not to take a guide, so negotiate the price firmly. The town has an unusual mosque. From outside, the **Sidi Brahim mosque** is unimpressive, but once inside it is a delight. The rooms are organized according to the time of day they were used. The coolest, below ground level, was used during the noonday heat. The room on the ground floor opens out with arcades on to a terrace and there is a large courtyard for important events. It is not in use so is open to anyone. The **cemetery** contains more of the strange tomb markers. Both well worth a visit.

The Hoggar

The **Hoggar mountains**, extending 800 km from E to W at the very centre of the Sahara, are one of Algeria's most stunning sights and at the same time, the most inhospitable region in Africa. The landscape is exceptional, with wind-eroded mountains rising to over 2,000m, erupting out of the sun-scorched arid desert plain. At the centre of the Hoggar is the **Ermitage de Père de Foucauld** at 3,800m. Sunrises and sunsets here are some of the most memorable you are ever likely to see.

The Touaregs, a Berber tribe, have, over centuries, remained the dominant population of the region. Local tradition alleges that the Touareg tribes all descend from the Touareg Queen Tin Hanan. She came from Tafilalet with her servant Takamat and settled in Abalessa. Here, according to the mythology, Tin Hanan and Takamat gave birth to two of the main Touareg tribes, the Kel Rela and the Dag Rali. Recently in Abalessa, a woman's skeleton and various jewels dating back to the 4th century were found and it is thought that this was the body of Tin Hanan.

The Touareg tribes developed a system of matrilineal inheritance, names and titles being passed from one generation to the next by the woman, whilst no male ancestors were recognized. This was at a time when the men were largely absent warriors. Traditionally, the Touareg society has been organized as a confederation of tribes with a strong hierarchy, noble tribes being at its centre. The noble tribes were mostly warriors, leaving on long expeditions while the other tribes looked after the lands. The lands were cultivated by slaves brought from the Sudan, as the Touaregs considered working the earth as a lesser task. With the abolition of slavery, the slaves became free men and established themselves as farmers in the oasis, but still working on lands owned by the Touaregs.

Today Touaregs are settling down in houses and working on farms, mines and administrative jobs. Nevertheless, centuries of customs and traditions have not been totally lost, and habits peculiar to the region are still obvious to the visitor, unveiled women still enjoying a large amount of freedom, whereas the men are almost fully veiled, only their eyes showing.

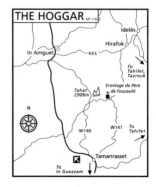

In Salah

This is the main stop on the way S to the Hoggar on the N1 road from El Goléa to Tamanrasset. It appears after 400 km of a flat and seemingly never-ending plateau, an attractive little town built in red bricks, surrounded by golden dunes and a large oasis. The inhabitants have to struggle against three fierce elements; the heat (in summer temperatures reach 60°C and rarely fall below 40°C); frequent sand storms (averaging one a week, the sand is slowly encroaching on the town); and the salty water (unpleasant to drink and making agriculture difficult – In Salah means 'salt spring'). The town was an important trading post, where European goods were exchanged for gold, ivory and slaves from the Sudan. Today the main activity is the production of dates from the 220,000 palm trees in the large oasis to the W of the town. Recently, natural gas was found in the vicinity and work is still being carried out to link this to the existing pipeline. As for the town itself, there is little to do or see here, but if you have brought your own water it is a pleasant place to stop.

There is an Air Algérie office (T 09 730239) and a bank in the main street. The market is just N of Air Algérie, but generally has little to offer. There are two hotels, but choose *Hotel Tidi-Kelt*, T 09 730393, 120 rm, just off the main road from El Goléa to Tamanrasset. In the centre, there is a camping site at the W end of the main street.

● **Transport Air** The airport is 10 km N of the town. For information, T 09 730093. Flights to **Adrar**, **Algiers**, **Ghardaïa** and **Tamanrasset**. **Road** To Tamanrasset it is, in theory, black top all the way, but in reality due to the wear caused by the large numbers of trucks, in many places it is in an awful state. In many sections the piste on the side is often better than the bad road. Stock up with petrol, as you may not find any until Tamanrasset (700 km). Towards Reggane, the piste goes as far as Aoulef (90 km), and from then on it is black

top. The piste is good and well signposted. The bus station is out of town on the main road from El Goléa to Tamanrasset. **Bus**: there are buses to **Adrar**, **Ghardaïa** and **Tamanrasset**. The departures are unpredictable. Tickets have to be bought in advance. Seats are not numbered, so be there early to secure a comfortable place. **Taxi**: main destination is **Aoulef**, from where you can take a bus to Adrar and further N.

Tamanrasset

ACCESS Air The airport is at Aguemar, 12 km N of the town. For information, T 734276. **Road** The bus station is in the N of the town, on the road to In Salah.

(*Pop* 30,000; *Alt* 1377m) Until recently this was a small village: now it is the place where all trans-Saharan travellers stop over and the centre for trips to the Hoggar mountains. Due to its altitude it is never unbearably hot, even in the middle of the summer and can be quite brisk in winter despite the sunshine. Trips into the Hoggar mountains, an opportunity that should not be missed, are organized around the mountains to Assekrem and the Père de Foucauld mountain top hermitage. Try any of the agencies on Ave Emir Abdelkader. As the rental of a 4WD vehicle is expensive, either try to form a group of 6-7 interested people, or ask around for a spare place. Finally, be care-

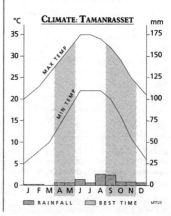

ful when changing money on the black market, as some changers have a tendency to denounce you to the police.

The buildings in Tamanrasset are constructed of brown mud bricks and the walls are plastered with brown mud. Fortunately in the sunshine it glows red and looks splendid. There is nothing specific to see, as this is essentially a modern settlement, apart from the **defensive fort** built by Foucauld and the market off the main street, Ave Emir Abdelkader, where food and Touareg crafts including beautiful jewellery can be bought. **The museum** on Ave Emir Abdelkader, displays Touareg items of leatherwork, weapons and jewellery.

A **livestock market** is held on the dry river bed which cuts through the town. Make an early start to visit this. The town is not unpleasant, and the mixture of people is in itself an attraction. The Touaregs are still present, sometimes seen riding their white camels. Dec is the busy month here when the fair takes place on the Assihar showground. Better to book in advance at that time.

All customs formalities for going on into Niger must be cleared here, including the currency form, but the passport control is done at the border in In Guezzam. If you are hitching, Tamanrasset is a good place to arrange for a lift right through to Niger.

Local information
● Accommodation
C *Hotel Tahat*, SE part of town, after the Customs office, T 734472, 120 a/c rm.

E *Hotel Ilamane*, rue de la Palestine, the road crossing the river, central position, 30 rm; **E** *Hotel Tin Hinane*, Ave Emir Abdelkader, T 734409, opp the ONAT, parts a/c.

Youth hostels: is in Quartier Tahagart, T 734047, 100 beds, kitchen, bus 500m.

Camping: *Les Zéribas*, S of the town, past the *Hotel Tahat*, on the right. Accommodation available in very small and basic local *zeribas* (small huts).

● Banks & money changers
Are in the Ave Emir Abdelkader. Money can

also be changed in the *Hotel Tahat*.

● Embassies & consulates
Niger and Mali have consulates in Tamanrasset. They are situated next to each other, about 500m S of the town centre on the road to the *Hotel Tahat*.

● Post & telecommunications
Area code: 09.

Post Office: Ave Emir Abdelkader, close to Air Algérie.

● Tour companies & travel agents
Air Algérie, Ave Emir Abdelkader, T 734363.

● Tourist offices
ONAT, Ave Emir Abdelkader, T 734117. They organize excursions into the Hoggar, camel treks and 4WD hire as do a number of private tour agents.

● Useful addresses
Customs: the customs office is situated to the S along the same road as the Consulates, before the *Hotel Tahat*.

Visas for Niger: it is necessary to produce three passport photos, have a cholera vaccination stamp and pay AD70. The issuing of the visas can take up to 3 days. For **Mali**, procedures are simple and visas are usually issued immediately.

● Transport
Air The airport is at Aguemar, 12 km N of the town. For information, T 734276. Flights to **Adrar, Algiers, Constantine, El Goléa, Ghardaïa, In Guezzam, In Salah, Oran** and **Ouargla**.

Road The road to In Guezzam is described as black top for first 50 km but it is in a poor state. After that it is piste which is quite good, but be very careful not to lose sight of the stageposts. There is no water between Tamanrasset and In Guezzam, and there may be no petrol in In Guezzam, so stock up. The border is 10 km further S after In Guezzam, and is closed from 1200 to 1600 and after 1800. The road to Djanet via Assekrem is virtually impassable, and certainly should not be ventured without a 4WD vehicle. Go 100 km back up the road to In Salah, and follow the signs to Idelès. **Bus**: the main destination is In Salah with departures on Mon, Wed and Sat at 0400 and tickets have to be booked the evening before. Be there an hour before departure to get a good seat as the trip lasts 20 hrs minimum. There is one departure a week to In Guezzam, but this is of little use as you will still have to hitch across the border.

Around Tamanrasset

Having travelled so far, do not miss **Assekrem** which is generally done as a circuit. The plateau is 80 km NE of Tamanrasset and will take about 3-4 hrs by car. The road E goes between the volcanic peak of **Iharen** and by the **cascades of Imeleoulaouene**, such a panoramic landscape making progress slow as stops are made for photographs. A local guide will enable you to detour to see some ancient rock engravings. The Assekrem plateau summit can only be reached by foot and it is a 30 mins walk up to the top. The **Ermitage de Père de Foucauld** is on the plateau and the area has some of the most amazing scenery, particularly at sunrise. The Hermitage was built in 1910, at an altitude of 2,600m, by Père de Foucauld and is still run by Fathers. Limited accommodation is available (30 beds) in the refuge on the Assekrem pass, but food is not always provided. Returning the W route gives views of Algeria's highest peak **Djebel Tahat** at 2,908m and majestic scenery. Access to the Assekrem plateau is only really possible in a 4WD vehicle which can be hired from the

The ASSEKREM CIRCUIT MT 120

ONAT or any of the travel agencies in Tamanrasset. The hire rate is expensive (around AD1,000 for 24 hrs) but cars will seat 6-7 people. Otherwise, hitch a lift from Tamanrasset, or 'buy' a spare place. The travel agencies also organize the trip to Asskrem by camels. See ONAT or any travel agency.

The Hoggar circuit

The circuit of the Hoggar is more ambitious. Some 6 km before the refuge on the Assekrem pass, a winding track goes N to Hirafok. The volcanic material makes the track very rough and the scenery splendid. The Oued Zerzaoua emerges to the W of the track, its position marked by a thin line of vegetation. **Hirafok village**, where most of the dwellings are constructed of reeds, is surprisingly green. The irrigation water for the fruit and vegetables is lifted by solar energy. A local guide can take you to see more rock engravings about 6 km N of the village. The circuit continues NE to Idelès before turning SE towards **Tazrouk**. The road S crosses the Azrou pass and drops down to Tahifet which stands by a wide dry river bed. The water flowing over the falls at **Tamekrest**, a great improvement on those at Imeleoulaouene, supports beds of reeds and even trees.

Amsel This village is 30 km S of Tamanrasset on the road to In Guezzam, and has a reservoir where it is possible to swim. The village market has cheap fresh fruit and vegetables for sale. Stock up here if going to Niger.

Tassili N'Ajjer

The Tassili N'Ajjer is a huge high plateau, about the size of England which runs along the NE of the Hoggar mountains. The area is particularly striking with unusual landscapes of deep chasms and steep cliffs, as the name implies. No vehicles can reach the centre. It contains a large number of rock paintings, some dating back 8,000 years.

The N3 road from Hassi Messaoud is black top until In Aménas. There is a bus to In Aménas, but nothing onwards to Illizi and Djanet. Without your own transport, the only way of getting there is by taxi, by hitching or by plane. Hitching is difficult from In Aménas down to Djanet, and there is no guarantee that you will find a ride. However the return journey down to Tamanrasset from Djanet is easier, either by hitching or by taxi.

In Aménas The town is modern and built purely for the oil industry. It is of no interest to the traveller, but a good point for stocking up with food, water and petrol. When arriving, it is compulsory to go to the municipal office and give them details of your trip to Djanet. There is only one hotel, the *Hotel Cash*. The airport is 14 km SE of the town. For information, T 09 739375. There are flights to Ouargla. There is one bus a week that goes to Biskra, but no buses going further S.

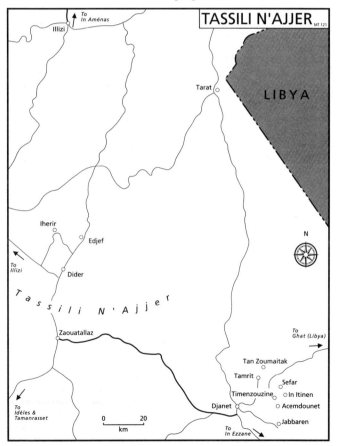

TASSILI N'AJJER MT 121

Illizi

This is a town of very little interest apart from being the main stop on the piste to Djanet. There are a few shops, petrol and a hotel. There is also an airport, 10 km N of the town. For information, T 09 731355. There are flights to Algiers, Djanet and Ghardaïa.

● **Youth hostels** *AJ Tassili*, Illizi 33000, open 0800-1200 and 1400-2200, 50 beds, kitchen, airport 7 km, bus 1 km.

From Illizi to Djanet is about 380 km, the first 100 km of piste is difficult driving, but after Zaouatallaz the road is much better.

Djanet

ACCESS   Air The airport is 15 km out of town, too far to walk and an expensive taxi ride. If you have contacted an agent for touring in the region get him to come and meet you.

This is really a cluster of villages rather than a small town, 700 km from Tamanrasset, situated at an altitude of 1,100m. It is the main settlement in the Tassili N'Ajjer and lies in pleasant surroundings beside an oasis (djanet means garden). It is dominated by a fortress from where there is a good view. It can get very hot here so take precautions.

The main interest of Djanet is in its proximity to the **Tassili National Park** with its large number of rock paintings and marvellous landscape. You can only enter the park if you are accompanied by a guide. The ONAT in Djanet organizes tours, but they are generally expensive and by foot, which entails covering distances of 15 to 20 km a day. If you require a permit to visit the National Park or permission to take photographs there, the office is on place du Marché. They have a small **museum** which exhibits Neolithic tools and has pictures of the wall engravings.

Djanet contains a mixture of people from the surrounding area, Senussi from Libya, Tibu from the Tibesti

mountains and Touareg nomads. Water is drawn from deep wells, generally by animal power and the oasis produces cereals, vegetables and dates. There is a small souk just off the main road.

● **Accommodation** There is one hotel in Djanet, *Hotel Les Zéribas*, where basic accommodation is provided in small huts.

● **Tour companies & travel Agents** all at place du Marché.

● **Tourist offices** ONAT, T 09 735024, place du Marché, on main square.

● **Transport   Air** For information, T 09 735032. Flights to **Algiers**, **Ghardaïa**, **Illizi** and **Ouargla**. **Road** The road to Tamanrasset goes NW for the first 164 km before turning W. It is good until Idelès, but from here it is advisable to take the piste that continues W and joins the main N3 road from In Salah to Tamanrasset. The piste leading up through the Hoggar to Tahifet is very scenic, but should not be tackled without a 4WD vehicle. From Djanet it is also possible to go to Ghat in Libya. NB There are no buses from Djanet, so you will have to hitch, take a plane or a taxi. The taxis run to Tamanrasset but a fair number of vehicles go this way and hitching should be relatively easy. If you want to go on to Ghat in **Libya**, there are expensive taxis that take you for the 300 km ride.

Excursions from Djanet

NB It is not permitted to wander off into the wilderness of the Tassili on your own. For safety reasons it is necessary to obtain a pass – from L'Office du Parc National du Tassili (OPNT) – and for that you must go in person, taking your passport, a day-to-day itinerary with the precise places of overnight stay, name of your guide who must be a local and a valid reason for your visit – and you still won't get a pass unless you have the backing of a local agency. Better to join an organized group.

Be prepared for a deal of walking, and carrying your own provisions which you are advised to bring with you from the N. During the tourist season, Oct to Apr, a camp is set up permanently at **Tamrit**, giving a base from which to see the paintings at **Tan Zoumaitak** on the wall of a huge cave, the floor paintings of elephants at **Timenzouzine** and a visit to the greatest concentration of paintings, those at Séfar, calling in at In Itinen and In Etouham on the way. The paintings were discovered in 1933.

The paintings at **Jabbaren**, including the hunter, legions and warriors and herds of tended cattle can be reached via Alemdounet or by a very strenuous 3 hrs climb over very rough terrain on a day trip from Djanet.

INFORMATION FOR VISITORS

CONTENTS

Before you go	354
Entry requirements	354
When to go	355
Money	355
Getting there	355
Air; train; road; sea; customs.	
When you arrive	356
Banking hours; electricity; hours of business; official time; photography; safety; shopping; tipping; weights and measures.	
Where to stay	357
Food and drink	358
Getting around	358
Air; train; road.	
Communications	359
Language; postal services; telephone services.	
Entertainment	359
Media; sport.	
Holidays and festivals	359
Further reading	359

Before you go

Entry requirements

● Visas

Obtaining a single entry tourist or business visa in advance from Algerian Embassies is easy. It is issued in 2-3 days, requires three passport photos and costs £26 for UK citizens. Multiple entry visas lasting 3 months cost £32. An invitation or reservation from a hotel in Algeria is required to be sent with the application form. All European nationals require visas. German and Dutch travellers may have to wait longer (up to 20 days). The visa is valid for 30 days from date of issue, but is renewable in Algeria. In UK, visas can be obtained at the Algerian Consulate, 6 Hyde Park Gate, London SW7, T 0171 589 6885, open every day 0900-1130 and 1600-1700. US and Canadian visitors must obtain visas through the Embassies in Washington or Ottawa. Australians and New Zealanders

can get their visas free of charge in the UK in 2-3 days. It may be possible to obtain a visa in Tunisia (Tunis) or Morocco (Rabat) but it is better to get it before. **NB** At present, visas will be refused if the passport already contains stamps from Israel or South Africa.

Visas for other African countries In Algiers, most countries to the S have embassies, and it is easy to obtain any necessary visas from them. Both Mali and Niger have Consulates in Tamanrasset and it is easier and quicker to obtain them there. **Burkina Faso**, 23 rue Mouloud Belchouat, T 02 613897; **Cameroon**, 60 Blvd Colonel M'Hamaed Bougara, T 02 788195; **Central African Republic**, 6 Ave Larbi Alik, Hydra, T 02 604488; **Mali**, Cité DNC Villa 15, Chemin Ahmed Kara, Hydra, T 02 606118; **Niger**, 54 rue du Vercos, Bouzareah, T 02 788921; **Nigeria**, 27b rue Ali Boufelgued, T 02 606050.

● Vaccinations

Read the section on Health, see page 16. To enter Algeria no special vaccinations are required, except if arriving from a yellow fever zone. In this case a vaccination certificate is required. When entering from the S, make sure you have a valid International Health certificate, as a cholera vaccination is compulsory. Malaria is virtually non-existent in Algeria and the risk of catching it so small, that it does not justify taking tablets. However, if you are travelling further S it is recommended to have a cholera and yellow fever vaccination, as well as taking anti-malaria tablets. The **water** is safe to drink throughout the country and bottled water is available in most places.

● Representation overseas

Canada, 435 Ave Daly Kin 643 Ottawa, T 613 232 9453; **France**, 11 rue d'Argentine, Paris 75016, T 75016; **Morocco**, 8 rue d'Azrou, Rabat, T 65474; **Spain**, 12 Calle General Oraa, Madrid, T 4116065; **UK**, 54 Holland Park, London W11, T 0171 221 7800; **USA**, 2118 Kalorama Rd NW, Washington, SCN 20008, T 202 3285300.

● Tourist information

Tourist Office (ONAT) Headquarters: 25-27 rue Khalifa Boukhaifa, Algiers, T 02 743376, F 02 743214; **Central Region**: 5 Blvd Ben Boulaïd, Algiers, T 02 631387, F 02 743214; **Western Region**: 6 Blvd Emir Abdelkader, Oran, T 06

398210; **Eastern Region**: 1 rue Tarik Ibn Zaid, Annaba, T 08 825886; **Southern Region**: 2 Blvd Emir Abdelkader, Ghardaïa, T 09 891751; **Hoggar/Tassili Regions**: Blvd Emir Abdelkader, Tamanrasset, T 09 734117.

When to go

● **Best time to visit**

The spring is the best season with autumn the second choice, due to the heat and the dust haze of the summer. The coast is pleasant to visit at any time of the year but humidity can be a problem. The best time to visit the Sahara is of course the winter.

● **Clothing**

Bear in mind the extreme daily range of temperature and take clothing to prevent feeling chilly in the evening, or freezing at high altitudes in the winter and in the clear Saharan night. Also essential are sunglasses, head covering against the sun and a scarf to keep out some of the sand which gets everywhere. Full coverage of limbs and head is always sensible when travelling in the heat. Algeria is a Muslim country and the suggestions in the introduction (see page 37) apply here.

Money

● **Cost of living**

The cost of living is cheaper than UK and has got cheaper with recent devaluations. Travel is particularly cheap. The AD1,000 changed on entering Algeria should last about 3 days if staying at the cheapest hotels. Changing money on the black market alters the situation.

● **Credit cards**

Generally not accepted.

● **Currency**

The currency in Algeria is the Algerian Dinar (AD in this text), divided into notes of 5, 10, 20, 50, 100 and 200. The dinar is divided into 100 centimes. Coins in circulation are 5, 10, 20 and 50 centimes as well as 1, 5 and 10 dinars.

Currency regulations On arrival, all foreign currency (cash and TCs) must be noted down on the **Currency Declaration Form**. The Customs officials often demand to count the money. The form must be carried with you throughout your stay in Algeria, with all official transactions being recorded and it will have to be produced on leaving. The customs officials then check to see that the amount declared on entry adds up to the money left, minus the money spent during the stay. It is obviously very important not to lose this form, as its loss may require you to return to your point of entry and, at the very least face great hassle. If the sums do not balance on departure, you will probably be fined.

Officially, money has to be changed in a bank, or hotel, and the transaction noted down on the Currency Declaration Form. However, there is a thriving black market, and a great number of 'money changers' who will change at rates up to three times better than the official rate. It is generally easy to change money on the black market, but you should be careful of 'changers' coming up to you in the street. Using the black market involves smuggling money in that is not declared on the Currency Declaration Form. In most cases this is relatively easy, but in certain cases when leaving, checks by Customs can be quite thorough. In all cases, be careful to hide the non-declared money very well, or else you risk its confiscation. The best money to change on the black market is the French franc.

On entering, it is also compulsory to change the equivalent of AD1,000 at the official rate. In most border posts you will have to change the money there and then, but there are certain places where no banks are available and money should in theory be changed in the closest bank. In this case it is possible not to change any money on the official market but you run the heavy risk of having to change it on departure and have the AD1,000 confiscated by the Customs officials. Changing excess dinars back into another currency is in theory possible, but generally very difficult in practice. Be careful not to change too much money at a time.

Exchange rates for Jul 1995, see page 7.

● **Travellers' cheques**

The only bank that changes TCs is the **Banque National d'Algérie**, but a few hotels will change them as well.

Getting there

● **Air**

Algeria has four international airports, Algiers, Oran, Constantine and Annaba. Houari Boumedienne 20 km S of Algiers is the main airport, but the others also have international flights to Paris, Lyon and Marseille.

From Europe Flights to Algiers: **Air Algérie** from London Fri and Sun at 1530. Information contact Air Algérie in London, T 0171 4875709; **Air France** from Paris-Orly T (1) 44082222 (T in London 0181 7426600 but getting an answer is almost impossible); **Alitalia** from Rome Mon, Wed, Sat at 1055. **Information contact London T 0171 602 7111, Rome 0665621.**

Air Algérie flies to other European destinations incl Barcelona, Berlin, Brussels, Frankfurt, Geneva, Paris (daily), Rome. Other Airlines that go to Algeria (but not direct from London) are Aeroflot, Egypt Air, Tunisair and Royal Air Maroc.

From USA/Canada There are no direct flights to Algeria. The cheapest and most frequent flights are via Paris and London.

From African countries There are flights to and from Cairo, Casablanca and Tunis.

From Algiers there are good connections to West and Central Africa. Air Algérie flies to Bamako (3 times a week), Dakar, Niamey, Nouakchott and Ouagadougou (once a week).

Check in at least 2 hrs before departure. Keep an eye on your luggage and try to see it is loaded on your plane!

● **Train**
There is a daily train between Tunis and Algiers crossing the border at Ghardimaou. The train leaves Algiers at 1350 and Tunis at 1255 and takes 24 hrs. The train can be boarded at Constantine, Annaba and Souk Ahras.

● **Road**
Entering from **Tunisia** is easy as there are a number of border crossings. The most frequented is between Ghardimaou and Souk Ahras, but the border further N, at Oum-Teboul between Tabarka and El Kala is also good. In the S, the crossing at Bou Aroua between Nefta and El Oued is easy, and generally the customs officials are quite relaxed. **Bus**: there is a daily bus from Tunis to Annaba. The bus leaves Tunis S station at 0700 and Annaba at 0500. Important to book.

To **Morocco**, there is a crossing between Tlemcen and Oujda. At this crossing it may sometimes not be possible to cross by foot, but is never a problem by car. The other crossing is further S, between Figuig and Beni Ounif and is far easier, but customs officials are known to be very thorough.

To **Niger**, the border is 10 km S of In Guezzam, but you still have to go to the custom office in Tamanrasset first. The border is closed to tourists at the time of going to press.

To **Mali**, the border is in Bordj Mokhtar, 600 km S of Reggane. Customs formalities may still have to be done in Reggane. Check before you set out on the 600 km trip, as the border crossing is closed at time of going to press.

To **Mauritania**, the border crossing S of Tindouf is effectively closed to all traffic.

● **Sea**
One of the nicest ways of arriving in Algeria is by ferry, but it is expensive, particularly with a car. In the summer, the boats run behind schedule and tend to be full. Booking early on is very important as well as being at the port of departure well in advance of the sailing time. There are ferries from France and Spain. Fares are cheaper to Tunisia and Morocco, so it may be worth while going via either of these, particularly if you have a car.

From Marseille (France) to Algiers and Oran: winter, every 3 days, summer daily. The crossing takes about 24 hrs. Contact in London, T 0171 4914968. Contact Algerian Ferries, 6 Blvd Khémisti, Algiers, T 632698/638279, Tx 67413.

From Alicante (Spain) to Oran and Algiers: 2 sailings a month in the summer but none in the winter. For information, T +34 6 208333.

From Palma (Majorca) to Algiers: 4 trips a month in the summer and 1 a month in winter. The boats go on to Marseille. For information, T +34 71 727141.

● **Customs**
On entering Algeria you can carry 200 cigarettes, 50 cigars or 400 gm of tobacco, one bottle of spirits and 2 bottles of wine.

WARNING   It is advisable to note down on the Currency Declaration Form (see page 355) any valuable personal effects such as cameras, skis, musical instruments, radios, etc, as some people having not done this, have had them confiscated on departure.

When you arrive

● **Banking hours**
These are 0900-1500, Mon-Thur, with some closing for lunch. In Ramadan the hours are shorter. The larger hotels will change money.

● **Electricity**
220 and in some places 120 volts. Be sure to check before connecting appliances. A continental adaptor plug is essential.

● **Hours of business**

Government offices, Sat-Wed 0800-1200 and 1400-1730, Thur open mornings only. Banks generally Sat-Thur 0900-1500, but some have different hours. Shops tend to close 1200-1500 but there is no set rule on this.

● **Official time**

GMT plus 1 hr.

● **Photography**

Films and camera batteries are on sale everywhere, but check to make sure they are not beyond the sell by date. A good way of getting recent film is to buy it at a source that appears to have a good turnover.

As far as taking pictures there are little restrictions apart from aerodromes, military zones and installations and military personnel. When taking pictures of people, take the usual polite precautions, remembering that women in particular and most people in general object to being the subject of a photography without giving their permission.

People wishing to film on a professional level must have permission from the Ministry of Information or the Algerian Embassy in their home country.

● **Safety**

At present visitors are advised not to travel to Algeria in view of the current security situation. There have been a number of terrorist attacks in recent months and further attacks cannot be ruled out. Those who must make essential visits are advised to take all possible security precautions, limiting movements by road to a minimum and avoiding the densely populated poorer areas in and around Algiers. They should make their whereabouts known to their embassy (see page 299) who can provide further advice if necessary.

● **Shopping**

Best buys are rugs and carpets if you have the space but be sure you know what you want before you start looking. Ghardaïa is a good centre for carpets. Touareg items, some genuine bargains but many made for tourists, can be found in Tamanrasset and El Oued. Bargaining is of course part of the fun and the only way to reduce the inflated asking price to something close to the real value of the article. Take some time to do this negotiation.

● **Tipping**

Tipping is not expected so don't be surprised that no-one rushes to help you carry a case! Service will be incl in meal prices. Give the taxi driver 10%.

● **Weights and measures**

The metric system is used throughout Algeria. For conversion table, see page 14.

Where to stay

● **Hotels**

There tends to be a problem of under-capacity in Algeria, particularly in the large towns such as Algiers. Nevertheless if you start early enough, finding a room in large towns should not be a major problem, as there are a fair number of well run, clean, cheap hotels. When looking for a cheap hotel, do not be put off by the sign '*Complet*' as the hotel will often still have some rm. Top end accommodation is rarer, but generally of a good quality, the only real inconvenience being that many require

HOTEL CLASSIFICATIONS

AL	US$90+. International class luxury hotel. All facilities for business and leisure travellers are of the highest international standard.
A	US$75-90. International hotel with air conditioned rooms with WC, bath/shower, TV, phone, mini-bar, daily clean linen. Choice of restaurants, coffee shop, shops, bank, travel agent, swimming pool, some sport and business facilities.
B	US$60-75. As **A** but without the luxury, reduced number of restaurants, smaller rooms, limited range of shops and sport.
C	US$40-60. Best rooms have air conditioning, own bath/shower and WC. Usually comfortable, bank, shop, pool.
D	US$20-40. Best rooms may have own WC and bath/shower. Depending on management will have room service and choice of cuisine in restaurant.
E	US$10-20. Simple provision. Perhaps fan cooler. May not have restaurant. Shared WC and showers with hot water (when available).
F	under US$10. Very basic, shared toilet facilities, variable in cleanliness, noise, often in dubious locations.

you to show your Currency Declaration Form if you are paying in foreign currency. In the S, many of these hotels have swimming pools (some may be empty!) which can be a real pleasure in the intense heat.

● **Youth hostels**
There are 41 youth hostels and associated youth centres which are usually open 1000-1200 and 1700-2200. The overnight fee is AD40. Some hostels have a free members' kitchen. Maximum stay 3 nights. Self catering is available only in a limited number of hostels.

● **Camping**
This is permitted at some youth hostels.

Food and drink

RESTAURANT CLASSIFICATIONS

Given the variations in price of food on any menu our restaurants are divided where possible into three simple grades:
♦♦♦ expensive, ♦♦ average and ♦ cheap.

● **Food**
Algerian cooking is very similar to Moroccan and Tunisian, but has a few regional specialities.

Chorba – soup served with onions, tomatoes, meat and carrots: it can be very spicy.

Bourek – is a speciality from Algiers. Mince meat, with onions, and fried eggs, rolled in a cigar shape and fried in batter.

Dolma – dishes with a mixture of tomatoes and peppers.

Couscous – chicken or mutton, served on steamed semolina, a traditional dish throughout North Africa.

Méchoui – roasted meat, generally lamb.

Merguez – spicy sausage.

Cakes are very good, generally made from semolina, almonds, dates and honey. Most cakes are served with fresh mint tea.

● **Drink**
Algeria has some quite good wines, generally with a higher alcohol content than European wines. The *Mascara* is the best known, the *Bordjia* is a cooked wine best as an aperitif. Wines tend to be expensive and not always available. Beer is not bad, but by no means cheap whereas spirits are very expensive. Bottled water is found everywhere, but be sure to check that the seal has not been

broken. The best and most refreshing drink is hot mint tea (*thé à la menthe*), but order it with fresh mint leaves, as it is sometimes made with mint syrup.

Getting around

● **Air**
Internal flights are quite cheap, particularly when paid for in black market money, but this is generally very difficult as most Air Algérie offices ask for the Currency Form. 27 towns are listed as having airports. All major cities have regular air links and if going to the S, the plane can save you a lot of time. Flights are generally heavily booked, and reconfirming your booking is essential. Check-in time is a serious 1 hr before take-off. The paperwork always seems to take that long. It is rare for seat numbers to be allocated so be prepared to scramble.

● **Train**
The train runs along the N coast, connecting the main towns of Oran, Algiers, Constantine and Annaba. There is also a line that runs S to Touggourt from Constantine, and a line from Oran to Béchar. The train is slow and a bit more expensive than the bus. It is nevertheless easier to get seats and some trains have couchettes.

● **Road**
Bus The bus service is quite reliable and the best way of getting around. Almost all the towns in Algeria are on a bus route, incl towns in the Sahara. Trips, however can be long and hot. On long distances, it is important to try and make a booking the day before as buses can get very crowded. In any case, be there an hour before the bus leaves.

Car hire It is very difficult to find cars to hire and if you intend to do so, try and arrange it from abroad. The prices are also very expensive, around AD250 a day and most companies **do not take credit cards**. Do not expect the car to be of a high standard or have a spare tyre. Minimum age for hire is 25.

Hitchhiking Relatively easy, particularly in the N. In the S, it is much more difficult, purely because of the large distances. The best is to try and hitch a ride with other tourists. To get a ride, go to a petrol station or restaurant and ask people directly rather than standing in the burning sun. Trucks, all run by the government SNTR are officially not permitted to take passengers, but they generally do. In the S, ask a driver who may then pick you up after the Police control. A small fee is sometimes required. Women hitch-hiking on their own should be careful: it is best to hitch with a male friend.

Motoring If you are bringing your own vehicle, a compulsory insurance has to be purchased at the point of entry. The prices are about AD60 for 10 days and 120 for 30 days. Fuel is quite cheap. When going to the S, always set out with a full tank of fuel and double-check where the next petrol station is.

Taxis Shared taxis are a cheap, popular and efficient means of travel. They are generally only marginally more expensive than the bus. Standard routes link and connect most of Algeria's towns and cities. In most towns the taxi station can be found beside the bus terminal.

Communications

● **Language**

Arabic is the official language throughout Algeria but French is still the language of business and administration. Some people do speak English, but this tends to be more the exception than the rule.

● **Postal services**

The postal system is very slow and it is well to expect letters to or from overseas to take from one to 3 weeks. Posting in a main town speeds the process. Letter Boxes – yellow – are widespread but Post Offices generally offer a more reliable and perhaps speedier collection.

Parcels are best sent if at all from the larger Post Offices. The parcels must be inspected before sealing. It is not possible to give an estimate of the transit time, but parcels sent by air take longer than letters and surface mail takes longer still!

● **Telephone services**

Telephones are not very good, particularly for overseas calls which can take a few hours to get connected. The connections from Algiers are much easier and considerably faster than from the other cities. For local calls, the problem is not the connection but the inevitable long queues. All the telephone exchanges are in, or by, the Post Office and some, as in Algiers are open 24 hrs. Prices to Europe for a 3 mins call are around AD60, every additional minute costing AD20. The international code for Algeria is +213 plus the area code and number.

Entertainment

● **Media**

There are no newspapers in English. The major Arabic newspaper is *El Massaa*. The major French daily newspaper is *El Moudjahid*, which is reported to sell about 350,000 copies a day. The other French newspapers are *El Chaab* and *Horizons 2000* (which has one page in English). A French weekly paper is published in Algiers each Thur, *Algérie-Actualité*.

● **Sport**

In Algerian hotels, facilities are usually available for tennis and swimming. Coastal resorts offer the usual watersports with the added attraction of underwater fishing at Algiers, Oran, Annaba and Jijil organized by the Algerian Federation for Subaquatic Activities. Wild boar hunting excursions into the regions of El Kala, Tlemcen and Kabylia take place in the winter months.

Holidays and festivals

Algeria is a Muslim country and observes all the main Islamic festivals as holidays (see page 40). The dates of the Islamic holidays and the fast, Ramadan, vary each year, as they are calculated according to the moon. Ramadan is strictly observed by most Algerians, and it is advisable not to eat or drink in public during this period in the daytime. In addition several national events are celebrated as holidays. Friday is the day of rest.

1 Jan:	New Year's Day
1 May:	Labour Day
19 Jun:	Commemoration Day: Anniversary of the overthrow of Ben Bella
5 Jul:	Independence Day
1 Nov:	Anniversary of Revolution

Approximate dates for 1996:

21 Jan:	Ramadan begins
21/22 Feb:	Eid al-Fitr
29/30 Apr:	Eid al-Adha
20 May:	Islamic New Year (Anno Hegira 1417)
29 Jul:	Prophet's Birthday

Further reading

● **Books**

Glen, Simon and Jan (1987) *Sahara Handbook*, Lascelles: London 1987; *Guide du Rou-*

tard, Hachette: Paris (French); *Polyglott*, book (German); *Algérie*, Hachette Guides Bleus: Paris 1986.

Dickinson, Matt ed (1991) *Long Distance Walks in North Africa*, Crowood Press; Dumas, Alexandre, *Adventures in Algeria (or Tangiers to Tunis (transl) 1959)*; Eberhardt, Isabelle (1987) *The Passionate Nomad*, Virago: London.

● **Maps**
Michelin 953 offers the best overall coverage, but it covers the whole of North and West Africa, and does not have quite enough detail. The best detailed map is the Michelin 172, covering the N as well as Tunisia, but leaving out an important part of the Sahara.

TUNISIA

INTRODUCTION

Tunisia lying between 30°N and 38°N and 9°E and 12°E extends the furthest N of all the African countries. For the traveller it offers a gentle introduction to North Africa being very Western in character. French is widely spoken. It offers endless reliable sunshine, beautiful beaches, inspiring mountain ranges, palm-fringed oases and in the south, wide expanses of sandy desert. It contains many spectacular Roman monuments, a wide range of Islamic architecture and unusual underground dwellings.

Tunisia is small, by the far the smallest country in N Africa, equal in area to that of England and Wales or half of Italy. Thus the variety of geographical and historical sights as well as the opportunities to relax or be entertained are all easily accessible.

CONTENTS

Introduction	361
Land and life	361
Culture	366
History	367
Modern Tunisia	368
Tunis	372
Cap Bon Peninsula	397
Northern Tunisia	405
Central Tunisia	423
The Djerid	450
Southern Tunisia	461
Information for visitors	478

MAP

Tunisia	362

Basics

OFFICIAL NAME al-Jumhuriyah at-Tunisiyah (Republic of Tunisia).

NATIONAL FLAG Red with a white circle in the centre, bearing a crescent moon and a five point star in red.

OFFICIAL LANGUAGE Arabic.

OFFICIAL RELIGION Islam.

INDICATORS *Population*: 8.5 million. *Urban*: 53%. *Religion*: Sunni Muslim 99.4%, Christian 0.3%, Jewish 0.1%. *Birth rate*: 25 per 1,000. *Death rate*: 6 per 1,000. *Life expectancy*: 66/69. *GNP per capita*: US$1,720.

Land and life

Geography

The Republic of Tunisia has a surface area of 163,610 sq km, equal to that of England and Wales or half of Italy and is by far the smallest country in N Africa. It measures 750 km from N to S and averages 150 km from W to E. There are 1,600 km of coast, 330 km facing N and

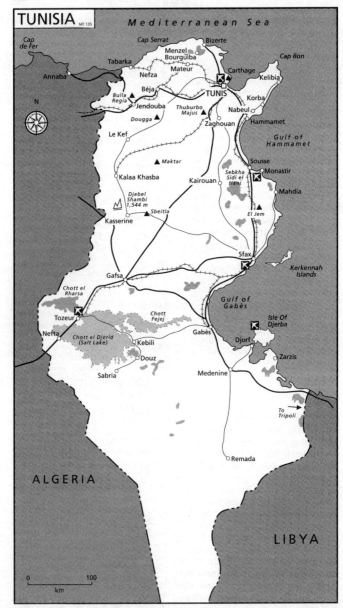

TUNISIA MT 135

Mediterranean Sea

Cap de Fer
Cap Serrat
Bizerte
Cap Bon
Annaba
Tabarka
Menzel Bourguiba
Nefza
Mateur
Carthage
Kelibia
N
Béja
Bulla Regia
TUNIS
Korba
Jendouba
Thuburbo Majus
Nabeul
Hammamet
Dougga
Zaghouan
Le Kef
Gulf of Hammamet
Maktar
Sousse
Kalaa Khasba
Kairouan
Sebkha Sidi el Hani
Monastir
Mahdia
Djebel Shambi 1,544 m
Sbeitla
El Jem
Kasserine
Sfax
Gafsa
Kerkennah Islands
Chott el Rharsa
Gulf of Gabès
Tozeur
Chott Fejej
Isle Of Djerba
Nefta
Chott el Djerid (Salt Lake)
Kebili
Gabès
Djorf
Douz
Zarzis
Sabria
Medenine
To Tripoli
ALGERIA
Remada
LIBYA

0   100
km

1,270 km facing E to the central Mediterranean Sea. The Gulf of Tunis is included in the N zone while to the S, forming part of the E facing coast, are the Gulfs of Hammamet and Gabès, the latter lying between the islands of Djerba in the S and Kerkennah in the N.

Borders
Tunisia has a long land border with Algeria, with a multiplicity of crossing points. It has a short land border will Libya, the crossing point at Ras Jedir being well used at present. The Tunisia/Libya offshore boundary dispute over the Bouri oilfield in the Gulf of Gabès was arbitrated in favour of Libya. Tunisia and Libya are, however, contemplating joint development of other oilfields lying across their offshore boundary. The creation of the United Maghreb Association has made other potential border disputes with neighbours less likely in the short term. Travel between UMA states also helps all UMA and other Arab travellers and tends to make it slightly easier for non-Arab tourists to get through border crossings in Tunisia and other N African countries.

Main regions
Traditionally, Tunisians relate to their tribal or hometown areas which often do not coincide with the country's physical regions. The Tunis metropolitan area is regarded as the principal region, with the Medjerda valley, the Sahel, the interior plateau and the S also being differentiated.

Three physical regions can be distinguished. **Northern Tunisia** is the economically dominant area. In the extreme N forming a rugged coastline – an extension of the mainly sandstone Algerian Atlas – rises a distinctive range known as the Northern Tell. In places these uplands with altitudes exceeding 1,000m are covered with cork oak and pine. The S flanks of the Tell in the Béja region are lower, more open and more fertile. To the E are the rich alluvial plains around Bizerte. The Oued Medjerda, Tunisia's only major perennial flow, cuts a wide fertile valley to the S of these ranges flowing NE to enter the sea in the Gulf of Tunis. This is the major agricultural region noted particularly for cereals. Further S, aligned SW-NE, is an extension of the higher, broader and mainly limestone Saharan Atlas. This forms the distinctive Dorsal/High Tell region with its harsher climate and sparser vegetation. The Dorsal range, which boasts Tunisia's highest point, Djebel Shambi at 1,544m, ends in the NE at the peninsula of Cap Bon. This peninsula is Tunisia's richest region, with a mild climate, fertile soils and a dense population.

Central Tunisia is a lower central plateau of semi-arid steppe land. Its harsh environment renders the area bleak and barren, especially in the W. Only the lower, E steppe offers opportunities for stock raising and cereal cultivation. The Sahel, a low-lying and flat westward extension of the coastal plain, has seasonal salt lakes and sandy soils with a widespread, dense cover of olive groves which are supported by light rainfall, heavy dews and the tempering influence of the Mediterranean Sea.

Southern Tunisia, lying S of the steppes and stretching from the Algerian border to the sea, is an area of low-lying salt lakes or *chotts*, some below sea level, which are flooded during the winter and which dry to give extensive seasonal salt flats. Other depressions, where the water table is exposed or very close to the surface, produce the spectacular green oases of date palms. The depressions in the N and the level summits of the Djebel Dahar to the E give way S to the sand dunes and rocky wastes of the Great Eastern Erg, the Sahara.

Relief/altitude
Tunisia is a country of low relief, less than 1% of the land being over 1,000m

and more than 65% being under 350m. The highest land lies to the N and W.

Rivers

The only major river in Tunisia is the Oued Medjerda, which runs in the N from the Souk Ahras area in Algeria to the Gulf of Tunis. It has been heavily engineered for irrigation purposes and carries only a moderate flow in its easterly reaches. Elsewhere the streams are short *oueds* which often drain internally into seasonal salt lakes, the largest complex being in the Chott el Djerid, S of Gafsa. *Oueds* in spate are dangerous and in recent years heavy floods in the S have carried away whole villages. Travellers should not attempt to cross *oueds* in flood and should certainly not camp in stream beds.

Climate

The climate of the N region is archetypically Mediterranean in character with hot dry summers and warm, wet, westerly winds in winter. To the S the influences of the Sahara increase and the aridity of the landscape intensifies. Rainfall is irregular and decreases progressively to the S with annual averages ranging from 1,000 mm in N regions to 200-400 mm on the central plateau and less than 200 mm in the S. Rainfall, nowhere reliable, is most regular in the N. Humidity is generally low, especially away from the coast and towards the S. High temperatures and high relative humidity are an unpleasant combination, especially in Jun-Jul.

The prevailing wind is from the W, though in summer NE winds also occur. A fierce, hot sirocco-type wind from the Sahara, the *ghibli*, takes temperatures into the mid 40°C range, relative humidity to 10% and has serious effects on human and plant life. Temperatures are influenced by proximity to the coast. Average temperatures increase to the S and extremes of temperature between day and night occur in the desert. For the visitor, summers can be hot by day

and over warm at night on the coast and unbearably hot (45°C) by day and surprisingly cool (10°C) by night inland. Winters are pleasantly mild in the N in the lowlands but temperatures fall quickly with altitude giving snow-blocked passes, while high daytime desert temperatures plummet at night making it 'too cold to sleep'.

The natural vegetation and farm crops are strongly influenced by the climate. The cork oak and pine forests of the wetter cooler N give way to thin pastures and esparto grass cover and eventually to desert in the S where the oases, supplied by natural springs, contrast sharply with the surrounding barren sands.

Flora and fauna

The variety and quantity of vegetation is controlled by climatic conditions. Cork oaks clothe the mountain slopes in the N, esparto grass covers vast areas of the plains further S while the separate oases offer a wide selection. In spring the semi-desert in bloom is a sight to behold. The number of large wild mammals is declining but wild boar still roam in the cork forests of the N and gazelle bound across the scrub land in the S.

Lake Ichkeul and the surrounding reed beds in the N and the temporary lakes in the S provide resting places for migratory birds such as storks and flamingoes, bee eaters and hoopoes. There are many birds of prey at all times of the year. Other less attractive creatures such as snakes which are rarely seen, and scorpions, also to be treated with great respect, are natives of Tunisia. See page 49, section on wildlife of N Africa.

Agriculture

Land use

This is recorded as arable and orchards 31%, meadow and pasture 20%, forest and woodland 4% and non agricultural 45%. Yields are generally low as a consequence of the unreliable precipitation, small dispersed plots of land, outdated methods of farming and lack of investment by absentee landlords. Due to poor investment in vital water supplies, 75% of farm output comes from non-irrigated plots.

Land tenure

Currently nearly 65% of Tunisia's farms are under 10 ha, 31% are between 10 and 50 ha and only 5% are over 50 ha. Few farmers own their land, most is owned by absentee landlords. Tenants rarely have legal protection. The farms, already too small to be economically viable due to division for inheritance, are made up of geographically separate plots often some distance apart. A government move to consolidate plots

---

SCORPIONS – THE ORIGINAL STING IN THE TAIL

Scorpions really deserve a better press. They are fascinating creatures, provided they no not lurk in your shoe or shelter in your clothes.

Scorpions are not insects. They belong to the class Arachnida as do spiders and daddy longlegs. There are about 750 different kinds of scorpions. The average size is a cosy 6 cms but the largest, *Pandinus imperator*, the black Emperor scorpion of West Africa, is a terrifying 20 cm long. The good news is that only a few are really dangerous. The bad news is that some of these are found in North Africa.

They really are remarkable creatures with the ability to endure the hottest desert climates, revive after being frozen in ice, and survive for over a year without food or water. They have a remarkable resistance to nuclear radiation, a characteristic yet to be proved of great use.

Scorpions are nocturnal. They shelter during the heat of the day and to keep cool wave their legs in the air. They feed on insects and spiders, grasping their prey with their large claw-like pincers, tearing it apart and sucking the juices. Larger scorpions can devour lizards and small mammals.

Their shiny appearance is due to an impervious wax coating over their hard outer shell which protects them from any water loss. They have very small eyes and depend on their better developed senses of touch and smell. The sensitive bristles on the legs point in all directions and pick up vibrations of movements of potential prey or enemies. This sensitivity gives them ample warning to avoid being seen by heavy-footed humans.

The oft reported 'courtship dance' before mating is merely repeated instinctive actions. The grasping of claws and the jerky 'dance' movements from side to side are a prelude to copulation during which the male produces spermatozoa in a drop of sticky fluid to which the female is led so that they may enter her body. The male departs speedily after the 'dance' to avoid being attacked and devoured.

Scorpions bear live young. After hatching, the young crawl on to the female's back and are carried there for two or three weeks until their first moult. They gradually drop off after that time and have to fend for themselves.

Most scorpions retreat rather than attack. They sting in self-defence. The sting is a hard spine and the poison is made in the swelling at the base. The sole of the bare foot, not surprisingly, is most often the site of a sting, and the advice in the section on Health (see page 20) is not to be ignored. The African **fat-tailed scorpion** (we do not recommend measuring the size) is described as aggressive and quick-tempered. It is responsible for most of the reported stings to humans and most of the human fatalities in North Africa. The beautifully named *Buthus occitanus*, the small **Mediterranean yellow scorpion** and *Leirus quinquestriatus*, the **African golden scorpion**, also have neurotoxic stings that can be fatal.

through land reform was not popular. Some 220 co-operative farms exist, mainly in the northern region and are mainly concerned with cereal growing.

Potential

The economic potential of Tunisia is considerable. There are large areas that could be brought under irrigation. Improved land tenure would also benefit farm output. Even in the Medjerda Valley the modern irrigation schemes are not fully and effectively used because of poor rural leadership and lack of incentives for farmers. Tunisia is rich in natural resources – phosphates, iron, zinc and lead – all of which offer the basis for further industrialization. The full extent of the country's petroleum resources is not yet known but good yields of both oil and natural gas are already contributing to foreign exchange earnings, while the country's position as a transit zone for an increasing volume of natural gas moving by pipeline from Algeria to Italy is an added bonus. Tourism has continuing potential for improvement, not just in the desert S where current efforts are concentrated, but in rehabilitation of the coastal areas of mass tourism, where age and poor management can be corrected to the advantage of the country's foreign exchange earnings. As with other states of N Africa, the potential will only be revealed if political stability can be maintained.

Culture

Ethnic origins

Tunisia is populated over the fertile plains and valleys by mainly Arab stock of the Beni Hillal and Beni Sulaim. As much as 98% of the population is Arab. The original Berber population and mixed Berber-Arab groups are found in the remoter inland areas and in the hills of the S. Pure Berber stock accounts for a mere 1% of the total population and are found in the Matmata region. There is a 3% residual element of the European colonists, of which more than half is French and the remainder Italian in origin. After Arabic, French is an important second language in the larger towns. Orthodox Islam is the main religion but revivalist Islam is increasingly prevalent among younger Tunisians.

Population density

Tunisia's estimated population in 1992 was 8.5 million, growing at a rate of slightly over 1.9% annually. The population distribution is biased heavily towards the N and the coasts. Greater Tunis now includes almost 2 million people. The capital, the Medjerda Valley and the coastal strip as far S as Sfax account for over 60% of the population. Kairouan province with 0.5 million and Gafsa with 0.25 million people are the only important population centres away from the N and E coasts. Migration from the land to the towns is increasing. Population densities in Tunis run at 2,000/sq km against less than 10 in the deserts of the S. Tunisia has a youthful population with some 37% under 15 years of age.

Quality of life

Tunisia is attempting to improve the quality of its labour force and its educational system is struggling to lift standards. By 1990 approximately 63% of the population over 10 was literate (74% of males and 52% of females). Tunis has centres of academic excellence in its university institutes of higher studies.

Income/head is calculated at US$1,500. This is gradually improving but only erratically. Slumps in tourism, trade and remittance income from workers abroad have depressed levels in recent years. There is great variation in income levels between the better off people in Tunis and the poor semi-nomads of the deserts. The labour force is diversified including, among others, 23.0% in farming, 1.6% in mining, 17.9% in manufacturing industry and 12.5% in construction. Under-employment and unemployment remain a problem and many Tunisians emigrate to Libya or Europe for work.

History since Independence

For the history of this region before Tunisia gained Independence see The History of N Africa, page 24. For information on the Desert Campaign of WW2, see page 548.

Tunisia's Independence from the French Protectorate administration was achieved on 20 Mar 1956. The transformation from self-government to Independence was managed by **Habib Bourguiba**, head of Tunisia's national liberation movement, the **Neo-Destour**, and later president. The new state had three basic, interconnected problems to resolve: its relations with France, the crucial issue of economic development, and its future political structures.

Relations with France began badly. In 1958 French aircraft bombed the Tunisian border village of Sakiet Sidi Youssef, apparently in retaliation for Tunisian support for Algerian Independence. In response, Tunisia demanded that French forces should abandon the naval base in Bizerte granted at NATO request. French refusal led to fighting and over a thousand Tunisians died before France withdrew.

In 1959 land belonging to European (mainly French) settlers in Tunisia was expropriated. The French left, taking their capital, a development which had an adverse effect on the Tunisian economy. Subsequently relations with France normalized and Tunisia became noted for its cautious, pro-western attitudes in international diplomacy, President Bourguiba becoming a well-known independent voice in Arab affairs.

Economy After Independence the Tuni-

sian Government concentrated on state-directed economic development, the collectivization of agriculture and government control of major industrial enterprises. By 1969, popular resistance and economic stagnation convinced the president of this policy's failure and a free market economy was instituted.

One consequence of this was a growing disparity between rich and poor which, by the 1980s, caused a rift between the governing **Destourian Socialist Party** on the one hand and the **UGTT**, formerly part of the Destourian Socialist Party, on the other. Severe riots during a general strike in Jan 1978 ushered in a period of social tension. Countrywide riots followed in Jan 1984 when the IMF, concerned over Tunisia's growing foreign debt, insisted the government remove food subsidies. A programme was introduced in 1987 to revive the economy, together with a wide-ranging programme of privatization. Tunisia, with Europe its major market, faces the negative implications of the new Single European Market.

Social and political affairs The need for economic development had social and political effects. Firstly, as part of the process of modernization and development, monogamy was introduced into the legal code. Then, in 1963, President Bourguiba attempted to abolish fasting during Ramadan in the interests of economic efficiency. Popular resistance undermined this initiative but, overall, Tunisia underwent a process of secularization and social modernization during the first two decades of Independence.

Secondly Bourguiba introduced a single-party system, in which his now renamed Destourian Socialist Party became the sole official party. The Communist Party was banned, re-emerging in the early 1980s, and leading members of the UGTT which, after the Jan 1978 'Black Thursday' riots found itself in opposition to government throughout the 1980s, were frequently imprisoned.

Islamic fundamentalism became a significant political movement in the early 1970s. By the 1980s its influence was widespread through Tunisian society. An organized Islamicist political movement, the **Mouvement de Tendence Islamique** (MTI), appeared. Though initially tolerated it was soon seen as a major threat and its leaders were imprisoned, while its frustrated supporters turned to urban violence in response.

The collapse of the Bourguiba régime
The repression of the MTI was symbolic of events in Tunisia during the 1980s. As economic difficulties increased so, too, did the alienation of the Bourguiba régime from the population at large. The promise of political liberalization was replaced by repression and Tunisia acquired an unhappy reputation over human rights abuses. In foreign affairs Tunisia and Libya, but for a brief period in 1974, have not seen eye to eye. A friendship treaty with Algeria, conversely, worsened relations with both Libya and Morocco.

After 1984 President Bourguiba began increasingly to interfere with government, relying on a small group of advisers, particularly **Zine El-Abidine Ben Ali**, whom he appointed Interior Minister in 1986 and Premier in 1987. Within a week of being appointed, the new premier seized power in a 'legal' palace coup – legal because constitutional niceties were observed – and President Bourguiba, then in his eighties, was declared mentally incompetent to discharge his duties.

Tunisia today The removal of President Bourguiba reduced political and social tension, whereas the execution of the MTI leadership, which he had demanded and which had precipitated the coup, would have led to serious unrest. The new president proposed political liberalization with a multi-party system.

Political prisoners were released, new political parties were permitted and political consensus was sought around a National Charter. Economic reform was pushed ahead and foreign confidence in Tunisia was restored. However the new régime could not bring itself to legalize the Islamicist movements, thus thwarting full political liberalization. In legislative elections in 1994 the majority of seats was won by the **Rassemblement Constitutionnel Démocratique**, demonstrating its reluctance to abandon power, although allowing five permitted opposition parties a minor role in the Assembly.

President Ben Ali is being forced back on policies similar to those of his predecessor. The major domestic crisis, the relationship between government and the Islamicist movement, became increasingly bitter in the 1990s. Tunisia's future social and political scene will, however, depend largely on successful economic reforms and on improvements in its relationships with its N African and European neighbours. In Feb 1989 Tunisia joined neighbouring states in the **Maghreb Arab Union**. Within the wider Muslim world, Tunisia was increasingly isolated for its opposition to the UN-authorized war to force Iraq out of Kuwait in 1991. In recent years Tunisia has mended its political fences with the Gulf States and the moderate Arab governments.

Modern Tunisia

Government

The republic
Tunisia is a republic headed by a president with a 5-year term and considerable powers over the armed forces and the cabinet. The current president is Zine El-Abdine Ben Ali who constitutionally unseated Habib Bourguiba, Tunisia's president since Independence, in 1987. Ben Ali is a former army general and

diplomat, chosen to change and protect the ruling party. There is an executive cabinet appointed by the president reporting to a single 141-member, 5-year elected legislative chamber. All Tunisians over 20 years of age are eligible to vote in elections. The socialist Democratic Constitutional Rally party has ruled since Independence (see History, page 367) under various names. Some secular, but generally innocuous, political opposition is permitted but radical Islamic groups are vigorously suppressed.

Domestic policy

Central government policies are concerned with maintaining political stability in a climate of contained Islamic revivalism. The cabinet's last major reshuffle in Oct 1991, leant towards the hard line in attitudes towards the fundamentalist Islamic groups. The government is also greatly concerned with keeping the economy developing to cope with a growing population and the pressures of worldwide recession.

Foreign policy

In foreign policy Tunisia has moved towards a slightly more Arab stance. Tunis was, until recently, the site of the PLO headquarters, and the Arab League has offices there. Tunisia is seeking better relations with its Maghreb allies but also needs US and European aid together with foreign visitors for its principal industry, tourism. Moderation thus tends to dominate foreign relations.

Regional government

This is through 23 *wilayat* (governorates) and sub-districts, while regional political representation is managed through delegations which have access to the higher levels of central government.

Economy

Tunisia has a more diversified economy than surrounding countries. Its modest endowment with oil has been an advantage in providing funding for non-oil development but has never been sufficient to encourage reliance on petroleum. There is, nevertheless, deep vulnerability to external economic pressures including the vagaries of international trade, foreign aid flows, variation in tourist numbers and access to the EU bloc for Tunisia's trade and labour. A youthful and fairly fast-growing population creates an added need for economic growth.

Agriculture

Is the basis of the economy, employs 23% of the labour force and produces about 18% by value of all national output. Chief crops are cereals, citrus fruit, olives, dates and grapes. Approximately 20% of the value of agricultural production comes from cereals. Olive oil is an important export accounting for 4% of the total but suffers heavy competition from Spain and Italy in the main European market. The Sahel is a monoculture of olives over much of its area. Irrigation is vital to ensure reliable cropping but large areas of the country with low rainfall lack provision of supplementary water supplies. Fishing and sponge gathering are important in the coastal ports, notably in the Gulf of Gabès. Fishing provides about 6% of the country's food supply with a catch of 95,000 tonnes/annum. Tuna fishing is declining as stocks in the Mediterranean dwindle. Esparto grass is collected to export for paper making and the oak forests of the N provide timber and cork.

Industry

Tunisia remains a large producer and exporter of phosphates with annual production running at some 7 million tonnes/annum from the Gafsa region. The main mines are at Djebel Mdilla, Redeyef, Metlaoui, and Phillippe Thomas. Phosphate and its products of phosphoric acid and fertilizer provide about 8% of all exports. Industrialization based on phosphates is developing slowly with plants to produce superphosphates and sulphuric acid. Other mineral resources being worked include lead and zinc at Laghouat and Djebel Hallouf and iron at Djerissa.

Manufacturing

Tunisia has made remarkable steps in effective industrialization, most of it small scale and private sector. Manufacturing now accounts for 18% of the work force and 17% of national production. The main products, principally from the N are cement, flour, steel, textiles, and beverages. The textile industry is most remarkable with piece-goods being made up in Tunisia for re-export back to manufacturers in Western Europe. In recent years this trade has provided 30% of Tunisia's total export earnings. There is a long established handicraft industry which has benefited through the tourist trade. Nabeul pottery, Kairouan carpets, decorative ironwork, leather goods, regional brass and hand-crafted textile wares are all world famous and find a steady market among tourists.

Energy

Tunisia's oil industry by no means compares with that of Libya or Algeria, with proved reserves of only 1,700 million barrels of crude oil (0.2% of the world total) and production of approximately 95,000 barrels/day with natural gas output of 304 million cubic metres/annum. Production comes from the El Borma field in the S, Sbeitla field in the S Atlas and the Itayem fields close to Sfax, all of which feed to a refinery and export complex at Sekhira. The Ashtart field offshore in the Gulf of Gabès is also productive and recent discoveries have been made both offshore and in the Cap Bon areas. It is hoped that oilfields lying across the offshore boundary line with Libya will eventually be exploited jointly. Crude and products sales account for 13% of exports.

Miskar gas field in the Gulf of Gabès was brought on stream by British Gas in

1995 enabling Tunisia to export more oil and to use less Algerian gas.

Tourism

Is a major employer and foreign exchange earner. Considerable investment in new hotels has come partially from abroad. The number of tourists rose from a mere 56,000 in 1961 to 3.7 million in 1993. Receipts from tourism are estimated annually at US$1,133mn. The industry is developing from bases in Tunis/Sidi Bou Said along the E coast/Sahel to the S where desert tours are of increasing popularity and serve to spread the benefits of foreign tourists. Tunisians are aware of the negative social effects of tourism and deal fairly and sensibly with foreigners so that the country retains a good name and visitors return. Efforts are being made to provide high class hotels in the main coastal resorts to attract higher spending tourists, especially from Germany and France. Depression in Western Europe and political problems in Tunisia have tended in recent years to depress tourist numbers.

Trends

Economic trends have not favoured Tunisia recently. Rainfall has been irregular, falling for short periods unfavourable to farming but causing severe damage through flooding. The world depression has reduced the flow of foreign tourists and led to falling oil

GROSS DOMESTIC PRODUCT 1991		
	Value (TD000,000)	Share (%)
Agriculture	2,135.2	17.8
Mining	765.8	6.4
Manufacturing	2,049.4	17.1
Construction	459.8	3.9
Electricity/gas/utilities	237.2	2.0
Transport/communications	832.2	7.0
Trade	2,840.3	23.7
Other services	1,591.4	13.3
Total	11,970.4	100.0

Source: *Encyclopaedia Britannica*

prices. The coming of the EU single market has adversely hit the Tunisian export trade, 70% of which has traditionally gone to Western European states. Fewer Tunisian workers, who annually sent back US$560mn in 1991 are now being accepted in Europe. The problem was clearly seen in the balance of merchandise trade where the deficit rose to US$2,410mn in 1993. Membership of the United Maghreb Association (UMA), has so far failed to open up markets for Tunisia other than for migrant labour, though access to Libya has improved trade in recent years and encouraged Libyan tourism.

Gross National Domestic Product has run at about US$14,800mn/annum.

Tunisia has an increasing foreign debt, which stood at US$9,200mn by 1993 and has since worsened. Imports regularly outstrip exports in value and rising imports for defence and security are adding to the deficit. Inflation, officially put at 4% annually, is rather higher in Tunis and other urban centres. Expenditures in a roughly balanced state budget ran at TD2,966 million in 1991, of which the main areas were education, health, security, defence and agriculture.

ECONOMIC INDICATORS

	1992	1993
Exports (TD mn)	3,567	3,803
Imports (TD mn)	5,689	6,213
Balance of trade (TD mn)	-945	-811
Inflation index (1985=100)	157.8	164.1
Foreign debt (US$ mn)	8,500	9,200

Sources: IMF, EIU, *Encyclopaedia Britannica*

TUNIS

CONTENTS

Tunis	372
Places of interest	374
Local information	384
Around Tunis	389

MAPS

Tunis Region	373
Bardo Museum	375
Tunis Medina	380
Tunis Centre	382
Tunis Metro	387
Tunis and surroundings	389
Carthage	391
Thuburbo Majus	395

The history of the city, so close to Carthage, goes back to Punic times but it was not until the Arab invasion in the 7th century and the final destruction of Carthage that the city of Tunis flourished. The medina grew in importance with the Great Mosque Ez-Zitouna, the intellectual and religious centre, as its heart. The souks, commercial and crafts centres, developed around the Mosque. Tunis then became the second city in Afriqiya (a province of the Arab Empire) after Kairouan.

Pop 1,200,000; *Alt* 3m.

ACCESS Air The airport is situated 7 km outside the city. To reach the centre either take bus No 35 (cost TD0.75) that stops on Ave Bourguiba by Tunis Air. The airport bus normally runs every 30 mins day and night, but from 2400 to 0600 there is only one every hour. Cost 600 mills. Otherwise take a taxi – this should not cost more than TD3, with baggage may be more. Beware of the unofficial taxis without meters. If you can't wait for an official one, be sure to agree on the price before getting in. **Train** The main train station is very central, just three streets S of Ave Bourguiba, between Ave de Carthage and the medina.

The suburban station TGM is 1 km away at the port end of Ave Bourguiba. **Road** There are two bus stations. Buses from Algeria and places S arrive at place Mongi Bali by the main train station. Buses from the N arrive at Bab Saadoun. Bus No 3 will take you to the town centre from here. The main louage terminus is 500m to the S of the train station but louages from Sousse, Medenine, Tozeur and Tataouine drop passengers by the medina walls 200m W of the train station and louages from Sfax at the station itself. From the port trains run every 10-15 mins to the TGM station and taxis are available to the town centre.

History

For a short time Tunis became the capital of the **Aghlabids** (894-905) but it was under the rule of the **Hafsid Dynasty** (1230-1574) that Tunis blossomed, with more than 100,000 inhabitants within its walls. The geographer and philosopher Ibn Khaldoun (1232-1406) was born during this period in Tunis when the intellectual and cultural importance of the city was at its peak.

Between 1534 and 1574 the town went through a period of turbulence.

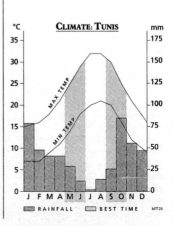

CLIMATE: TUNIS

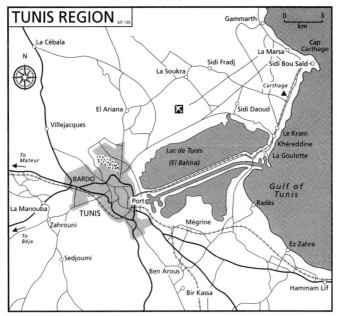

First attacked by Kherredine Pasha, better known as the pirate **Barbarossa**, from Turkey, then captured by the Algerians and subsequently by Don Juan of Austria. It was only with the Turkish invasion, in 1574, that a period of calm returned. The influx of 80,000 Moors from Spain at the start of the 17th century gave a renewed vitality to the city and its surroundings. Craftsmen trained in techniques unknown in Tunis made their appearance, including the makers of the important *chechias* (little red hats that were exported throughout the Mediterranean for over three centuries) (see page 379).

The Husseinite Dynasty lasted until the French colonization in 1881, but not without internal rivalries and chronic clashes with the Algerians over supremacy in the Maghreb region. This period was highly prolific in terms of the construction of palaces, *medressa* and

mosques and greatly contributed to the shaping of the old medina as we know it today. The Husseinite Dynasty, highly in debt, finally fell, giving way to French colonization. With the arrival of the French, large urban works were undertaken, giving rise to the new town built between the medina and the lake, with Ave de la Marine (today Ave Bourguiba) as its central point linking the city to the sea. The ville nouvelle became the centre of the modern town giving it a distinctly European air. (See History of N Africa, page 24.)

Tunis was occupied by the Germans for 6 months during WW2. Today it is a modern city and the centre of all the country's activities. Since Independence the population has increased dramatically from 400,000 to 1,200,000 resulting in overcrowding and the need for constant expansion. The city holds an interesting mixture of European and

N African cultures, although in the ville nouvelle life has definitely been influenced by Europe, but enter the medina and you will be in another world. Indeed the medina is a good place to start your journey.

The town is situated on the shores of a lake linked to the sea at La Goulette. The new city, with Ave Bourguiba as its centre, is laid out in a quasi-geometric fashion. The medina, in contrast, is full of small, confusing, winding streets. The medina is no longer walled, as the French replaced the old walls with large boulevards all around the old city. However, no cars can penetrate into the medina, making a welcome change from the overcrowded and noisy streets of the new town. La Goulette, the link between the sea and the lake, is the first of the coastal resorts and is linked to Tunis by train (the TGM) and road, both of which cross the lake over a causeway. The train goes on to the other coastal resorts of Sidi Bou Saïd, La Marsa and Gammarth, the smarter suburbs of Tunis full of luxurious villas. The first nice beaches are also situated here, and on summer weekends La Marsa is full of day-trippers from Tunis.

Climate

The climate is typically Mediterranean, but with a slight wind from the sea. The hottest season is obviously summer while the period from Nov to Feb is mild and sometimes rainy. The best seasons for a visit are late spring and autumn.

Places of interest

Around the city

The **Ville Nouvelle** with few specific things to see, is the centre of the city's life. Walk in the late afternoon on Ave Bourguiba and the surrounding streets to see the city coming to life and the cafés filling up. Drink at the *Café de Paris* and watch people go by. Here you will find shops selling European newspapers (generally only a day late). The parks are pleasant all the year round (see Parks, page 384). Most of the monuments are in the old part of town.

Dar ben Abdallah Palace is off rue des Teinturiers along rue Sidi Kacem. The museum is located in a most beautiful traditional late 18th/early 19th century Tunisian mansion. The **Museum of Popular Arts and Traditions**, T 256195, is housed here. The building, with its sculptured and painted wood, its carved plaster work and marble tiles is as interesting as the collection it holds. The museum is organized around the central courtyard. The exhibits retrace traditional life throughout the 19th and 20th century in the medina showing everyday scenes covering everything from housekeeping skills to cooking implements, clothes and furniture. In the *hammam* (bath) there is an interesting map of the medina indicating the location of all the Moorish *hammam* throughout the old city. A very well kept and presented museum. Open daily 0930-1630 except Sun. Entrance TD1.

The Bardo National Museum officially known as **The Alaoui National Museum**, lies to the W of town, T 513842. Take bus No 3 from the TGM station or Place du 7 Novembre, Ave Habib Bourguiba and Ave de Paris.

This museum, considered to be the most important in the Maghreb, is clearly signed once in the Bardo area of town, entrance on rue Mongi Slim, W border of park. The no-entry sign on the big iron gates is obviously ignored by all and cars with blue tourist plates and huge buses are parked there. Some park outside on the road. Walk in past the guarded National Assembly building. The museum is very crowded especially early morning when it opens as tour groups 'do' this first. During the day the heat builds up and the upstairs rooms can be very uncomfortable. Purchase tickets to right of main door, entrance

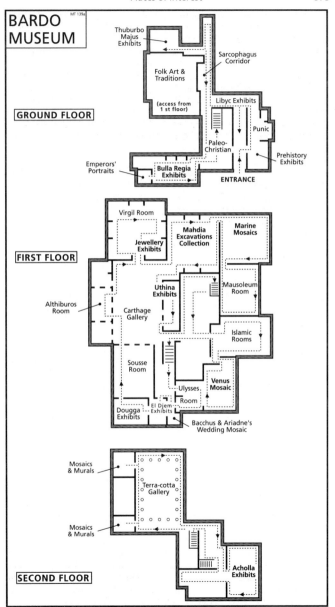

BARDO MUSEUM MT 139a

GROUND FLOOR

Thuburbo Majus Exhibits

Folk Art & Traditions

(access from 1st floor)

Sarcophagus Corridor

Libyc Exhibits

Punic

Paleo-Christian

Prehistory Exhibits

Emperors' Portraits

Bulla Regia Exhibits

ENTRANCE

FIRST FLOOR

Virgil Room

Jewellery Exhibits

Mahdia Excavations Collection

Marine Mosaics

Uthina Exhibits

Mausoleum Room

Althiburos Room

Carthage Gallery

Islamic Rooms

Sousse Room

Ulysses Room

Venus Mosaic

Dougga Exhibits

El Djem Exhibits

Bacchus & Ariadne's Wedding Mosaic

SECOND FLOOR

Mosaics & Murals

Terra-cotta Gallery

Mosaics & Murals

Acholla Exhibits

TD3 and photography TD1, open summer 0830-1730 and winter 0930-1630, closed Mon, toilets. The shop has very little information, guide books are rare. In the building take note of your position and route as there are no *sortie* signs until the exit is reached, making a quick departure in an emergency very difficult.

The **museum** situated in a park just 3 km W of the centre of Tunis, is set in a former Bey's palace. This historical monument from the mid-19th century is a masterpiece of Spanish-Moorish architecture. Its many attractive features include its actual proportions, its decorated wooden and stucco ceilings, and the walls covered with ornamental tiles. The exhibits illustrate the main civilizations that developed in Tunisia and the museum is noted for its vast collection of mosaics which give a picture of the daily life, pastimes and beliefs of the Roman populations in Africa. The extensive collection is best attempted in more than one visit. Plan shows recommended route with indication of main rooms and important features worth noting, place of origin of artifacts indicated in brackets.

Ground floor

Go through the **Entrance hall**, ticket office and shop to the **Prehistory** section, a collection of flint blades, bones, costume ornaments and engraved stones from the Acheulean, Mousterian, Ibero-Moorish, Capsian and Neolithic eras.

The **Punic** rooms have 1st century, small terracotta statue of the god Baal-Hammon (Thinissut, Cap Bon); a 4th century group of three divinities, Pluto, Demeter and Kore (carrying a piglet); 4th century stele of Priest and Child (Carthage), the child being carried ready for sacrifice. In the second room is a collection of masks made of glass paste or pottery generally placed in tombs with expressions designed to frighten evil spirits; personal decorations, necklaces, etc, and a Punic tomb reconstruction in a smaller adjoining room with arrangement of funeral objects (Cap Bon).

Libyc exhibits include bas-reliefs showing gods; funeral monuments with bilingual inscriptions in Libyc/Punic or Libyc/Latin. The **Sarcophagus corridor** has two 2nd century marble sarcophagi, one representing the nine Muses (Porto Farina), the other the four seasons; 3rd century Roman funeral effigy of a Romano/African citizen (Borj el Amri) and the Boglio stele, also 3rd century Roman, from a series dedicated to Saturn.

The **Thuburbo Majus** corridor and room have inscriptions, statues, marble wall panels, geometric and floral mosaics; a small bas-relief representing Maenads from 1st century while the **Paleo-Christian** corridor and room display a collection of tomb mosaics and church pavements. See particularly the 4th century "Ecclesia Mater" tomb mosaic (Tabarka) showing the section of a church with candles on the altar; tomb mosaic with two figures and seven crowns inscribed with the names of the seven martyrs; limestone font (Gightis) in centre of room; tiles showing Biblical scenes.

In the **Bulla Regia** room from the Temple of Apollo, 2nd century BC, stands a very languid god (Bulla Regia). A gallery of portraits of Roman emperors completes the ground floor rooms.

On a staircase leading to the first floor is a series of mosaics 4th-6th centuries from funeral monuments of the Christian era (Tabarka), some giving age and occupation of the deceased; a statue of Apollo (Carthage).

First floor

The **Ulysses** room is named after the famous Ulysses mosaic (Dougga) on display here. He is depicted bound to the ship's mast to prevent him following the sirens, on the right, playing musical instruments. Ulysses' companions have stopped their ears with wax (not visible) and are looking in the opposite direction to avoid the same fate.

Other mosaics include the very large late 3rd/early 4th century (Utica) Neptune and Amphitrite in a chariot drawn by sea horses with two nereids seated on sea tigers, with three boats each with a bejewelled lady surrounded by cupids; the self crowning of a semi nude/bejewelled Venus 4th century (Carthage); Marsyas the satyr and Apollo making music while Minerva looks on (judges?) and the surrounds depict the four seasons, 3rd century (El Djem). At one end of the room is a fountain (Thuburbo Majus), normally found in the largest room in a villa, has the head of Oceanus depicted on the exterior and the interior decorated with nereids and sea monsters.

In the corridor is **Bacchus and Ariadne**'s wedding mosaic from the 4th century (Thuburbo Majus).

The **El Djem** room holds intricate *xenia* (still life) mosaics related to food and hospitality (such as men playing dice), animals (fish, duck) and musical instruments often found in dining rooms of wealthy villa owners, from 3rd century; a 3rd century mosaic – hunting, horses, hounds and a hiding hare; on the floor Bacchus rides his triumphal chariot drawn by tigers lead by Pan.

In the **Dougga** room (don't miss the magnificent painted ceiling) are two ancient models of the city, one of the Square of the Capital and the other of the theatre. On the walls and floor are mosaics (La Chebba, Carthage and Thuburbo Majus). Neptune, placed centrally, is magnificent in his chariot with hunting and seasonal agricultural scenes around, 2nd century (La Chebba, Sfax). Opposite are three dark skinned giants working the forge of Vulcan, found in the Cyclops' thermae, 4th century (Dougga); also Cup bearers serving guests (Dougga).

The huge **Sousse** room houses a large collection of mosaics from Sousse, Carthage and Tabarka; the head and feet of a colossal statue of Jupiter (Thuburbo Majus); Punic, Greek and Roman lamps, ceramics (El Aouja near Kairouan); on the floor a 3rd century mosaic of Neptune surrounded by sea creatures (Sousse); "Lord Julius" mosaic early 5th century (Carthage) – the life of Julius, a wealthy personage – a central imposing villa and pictures of the cycle of the seasons and rural life; three big pavings from apses from private villas (Tabarka) probably of the same age as the Carthage mosaic; mosaics illustrating a circus 3rd century (Carthage) and chariot races 6th century (Gafsa).

An imposing gallery, colonnade and high ornamented ceiling houses sculpture, mainly from **Carthage**. In the centre is an altar dedicated to the "Gens Augusta" with bas-reliefs on all four sides dated between 1st century AD and 1st century BC; on the floor are two famous 3rd century mosaic pavements (Uthina/Oudhna), the first of Bacchus surrounded by cupids among the vines and a second showing agricultural activities and hunting scenes. There are statues of Roman gods and an imposing statue of Emperor Hadrian.

To the side in the **Althiburos** room are mosaics (Althiburos and Carthage), on the floor a 4th century mosaic of Roman boats, all correctly titled, also a 4th century banqueting scene with guests seated on benches rather than reclining on couches; a mosaic of hunting scenes, a temple containing Apollo and Diana and a crane being sacrificed 5th-7th centuries AD (Carthage-Salammbo) indicating a survival of pagan practices into the Christian era.

The **Virgil** room is octagonal with a magnificent dome of carved plaster work. Here the 3rd century mosaic showing a seated Virgil in meditation between the muses of history and tragedy (Sousse) is the only portrait of the poet; in the centre of the floor the 3rd century mosaic has medallions with the signs of the zodiac surrounding god-heads of the days of the week (Bir Chana near Zaghouan).

The ornamentation in the **Jewellery** room is mainly Punic, some from as long ago as the 7th century BC, mainly from Carthage but also Utica and Kerkouane. There are matching necklaces and earrings of tiny ceramic/ivory figures/objects, rings, seals etc, solid gold jewellery and gold plate on bronze.

The excavations from **Mahdia** were discovered by sponge divers early this century, the cargo of a Greek ship which sank off the Tunisian coast. The display includes Helenistic bronze and marble, furniture, pieces of the wrecked ship, and marble statues of Aphrodite 2nd-1st century BC which look a little worse for wear after their long immersion.

Marine mosaics are sections of a huge mosaic of a seascape including dolphins, nereids and sea monsters (Carthage) while central in the **Mausoleum** room is displayed a mausoleum of a Carthaginian with carved reliefs on all four sides. On the walls are mosaics, in particular one of animals' heads (Thuburbo Majus).

The **Uthina (Oudhna)** room, originally the dining room, has many mosaics of hunting or mythology. Of particular interest are *emblemata* made from tiny tesserae embedded in terracotta. Two here show the remains of a meal. Also a large paving of a headless Orpheus with his lyre charming the wild animals.

At this point it is necessary to go downstairs to see the **Folk art and traditions room** before ascending to view the **Islamic rooms** situated in the smaller, older (1831) building set around a patio. The huge hall displays artifacts from the 9th-13th centuries, musical instruments, weapons, household objects; jewellery in particular gold necklaces,

bracelets and earrings; traditional costumes, furniture; parchments, manuscripts, verses of the Koran, most of the documents from the great mosque of Kairouan, in particular pages from the Blue Koran; *tiraz* fabrics with Koranic inscriptions; astrolobes, sundials and compasses; ceramics.

The last room on this floor has 4th century paving of an apse called Hunting the Wild Boar, showing three stages of the hunt; **Venus** being crowned by two female centaurs; a splendid peacock with a spread tail.

The main staircase leads to the **2nd floor** where the **gallery** overlooking the Carthage room contains terracotta statuettes of protective gods such as Venus and Mercury from temples and tombs. Here also are objects from necropoli of the 1st-3rd centuries, glasses, bowls, dishes from tombs, funeral urns and statuettes. Don't miss the surgeons kit with lancets, scalpels and forceps.

The corridors and rooms around the stairhead have yet more mosaics, 4th century depicting Theseus slaying the Minotaur in a large maze of brown on cream, while the border depicts the walls and gates of a city (Thuburbo Majus); two mosaics on the theme of animal sports with a haloed Bacchus (El Djem) and a 4th century example from Thelepte/Feriana; a 2nd century paving (Thuburbo Majus), depicts a meditating poet seated on a column shaft, a mosaic in praise of intellect. In a separate room is a 3rd century Diana the Huntress on a deer, the medallions portray animals of the hunt, boars, gazelle etc (Thuburbo Majus); and Venus on a rock, 3rd century (Utica).

The items in the **Acholla** room (N of Sfax) were collected from private houses, large fragments from the Trajan thermae representing groin vault decoration; two panels of identical background showing busts of the four seasons and *xenia* with baskets of fruit; and two T-shaped mosaics (the blank sides being hidden by benches) one of *xenia* with birds and animals and the other relating to the Labours of Hercules. The final item, a fountain, is decorated with shoals of fish.

The **Medina** of Tunis, with its typical layout and interesting architectural styles has been designated by UNESCO as part of mankind's cultural heritage. The mosque and many other monuments here are not open to the public. The admission times of those which are accessible are given in the text. **NB** It is important to dress correctly when visiting a mosque. The following route visits the areas of interest within the medina.

Start from Place de la Victoire, inside **Bab Bhar** (21) by the British Embassy. Walk up rue Jamaa Zitouna which is the centre for tourist shops selling a mixture of goods from all around Tunisia, but the best deals are not to be had here. Going up the street, the **Bibliothèque Nationale** (18) is on the right and straight ahead is the **Great Mosque Ez-Zitouna** (1). Round the mosque to the right is the **Souk el Attarine**, which specializes in perfumes. Traditionally each perfume has a particular significance. For example, orange will be used for marriages. Although today the souk sells a wider range of goods it is still possible to buy concentrates of perfume essences very cheaply.

The **Tourbet Aziza Othmana** (16) lies behind the souk up a small street. Follow the N side of the Great Mosque to its entrance by the minaret then turn right towards the **Hammouda Pasha Mosque** (6) and rue de la Kasbah.

Turn W (left) up rue de la Kasbah through one of the oldest souks in the medina specializing in the round red felt *chechias*, the traditional men's headwear more likely associated with older Morocco (see page 373), to the **Sidi Youssef Mosque** (2), the place du Gouvernement, and another entrance to the medina. Continuing the tour turn back into the medina and take the narrow

street to the right, rue Sidi Ben Ziad to the **Dar el Bey** (11). Keep this building on your right and walk ahead to the Souk el Leffa, a small covered street, specializing in carpets, though these can be bought more cheaply in Kairouan. Some of the carpet shops here have terraces with impressive views over the medina but walking through three storeys of carpets and not buying takes some nerve.

Continue down the Souk el Leffa to the back of the Great Mosque and go right between this and the **Medersa Mouradia** (9) along the Souk des Femmes. A little street, the Souk des Orfèvres, on the right at the start of the Souk des Femmes sells lovely jewellery. A detour to the right at Souk el Kachachine leads first to the **Dar Hussein** (13) and then the **Dar el Haddad** (14).

Souk des Femmes becomes rue Tourbet el Bey. Follow this until you come to **Torbet el Bey** (15). Turn left in front of the building and right down its E side and turn left into rue Sidi Kassem which has the **Dar Ben Abdallah** (12) palace on the right and further down on the left on the corner of rue de Teinturiers is the **Mosque des Teinturiers** (3). The **Dar Othman** (10) stands opposite.

On either side along the rue des Teinturiers are small streets with dyers working using techniques that have hardly changed throughout the centuries. Go down one of these streets and take a close look. The dyers are accustomed to tourists 'peeping in' but it is better not to take pictures too conspicuously. Follow the rue des Teinturiers, which becomes the Souk el Belat, back towards the rue Jamma Zitouna, passing on the left, on the corner of rue du Trésor, a small mosque with a beautiful 14th century minaret.

At the street after this mosque turn left to the **Three Medressa Complex** (17) which includes **Medersa Slimania, Medersa Bachia** and **Medersa of the Palm Tree**.

Now you have seen the main sights it is time to wander in the small streets and perhaps find areas not frequented by tourists towards the Bab al Jazira, along the rue des Teinturiers, or towards Bab Souika to the N. It is interesting to look at the different houses and perhaps peep inside. The exterior of the houses are generally quite similar and do not give any idea of the hidden splendour. All the houses have large wooden doors, simply decorated with nails. The rooms are generally organized around a central courtyard with no external windows in order to ensure privacy. The houses are generally quite large as the entire family lives there, including married sons. Each house has its own well.

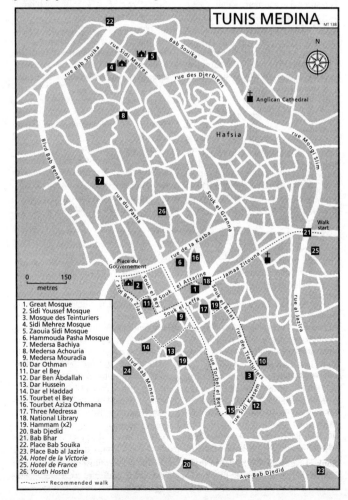

TUNIS MEDINA

MT 138

1. Great Mosque
2. Sidi Youssef Mosque
3. Mosque des Teinturiers
4. Sidi Mehrez Mosque
5. Zaouia Sidi Mosque
6. Hammouda Pasha Mosque
7. Medersa Bachiya
8. Medersa Achouria
9. Medersa Mouradia
10. Dar Othman
11. Dar el Bey
12. Dar Ben Abdallah
13. Dar Hussein
14. Dar el Haddad
15. Tourbet el Bey
16. Tourbet Aziza Othmana
17. Three Medressa
18. National Library
19. Hammam (x2)
20. Bab Djedid
21. Bab Bhar
22. Place Bab Souika
23. Place Bab al Jazira
24. *Hotel de la Victorie*
25. *Hotel de France*
26. *Youth Hostel*

---------- Recommended walk

National monuments

The **Bibliothèque Nationale**, on rue Jamaa Zitouna is a very beautiful building with a spacious courtyard. It was originally built as a barracks in 1813 by Hammouda Husseinite and has now been converted into the National Library. Most books are in Arabic. Access is restricted to serious students.

Great Mosque Ez-Zitouna (The Olive Tree), rue Jamaa Zitouna is the largest and most venerable mosque in Tunis, built in 732 but some reports date it back to the foundation of the Islamic city in 698. The 44m high minaret was placed there in 1834. The mosque is the centre of the medina and the old city expanded and developed around it, the most noble merchants being situated closer to the mosque (as for example the perfume sellers in the Souk el Attarine) whereas the less noble trades such as the dyers were relegated to the areas nearer the walls. All of the 184 columns surrounding the courtyard were brought from buildings in Carthage, giving an interesting architectural ensemble. The prayer room has antique columns and a finely sculpted stucco ceiling, unfortunately, though, this part cannot be visited. Courtyard open to non-Muslims from 0930-1200 all year, closed Fri and Sun, entrance TD3. Students with card free.

Souk el Attarine Traditionally each perfume has a particular significance. For example, orange will be used at weddings. Although today this souk sells a wider range of goods, it is still possible to buy concentrates or perfume essences very cheaply. Other items for sale include candles and quilted baskets, traditional presents from the fiancé to his future bride. Note the intricate carvings found on the wooden counters and shelves which indicate the wealth of this souk.

Souk el Kumach (cloth) lies to the W side of the Great Mosque. Two rows of stone columns divide the souk into a wider central lane for traffic and pedestrians with the shops located on each side. There is a door at each end of the market. That to the N has impressive columns.

Souk el Birka at the S end of Souk el Bey was built in the early 17th century and is now occupied by the Jeweller's guild. It is almost square with a central dome. The wooden block used for the auction of slaves used to stand in the centre, while purchasers sat on surrounding benches.

Tourbet Aziza Othmana is at 9 Impasse Ech-Chammaia, off rue El Jelloud which leads towards the Great Mosque coming from rue de la Kasbah. Built c 1655, this is the tomb of the princess renowned for her generosity. Before dying she let her slaves go free and established a fund for a hospital, for poor girls who could not afford to marry and to provide fresh flowers for her tomb every day. Today the Tourbet is a private house and cannot be visited.

Tourbet and Mosque of Hammouda Pasha, rue Sidi Ben Arrous. The style of the mosque, built c 1655, shows a strong Italian influence, which is not surprising as Hammouda Pasha's father was Italian and converted to Islam in order to promote his career. The style is highly original and at the time was very innovative. This mosque influenced the style of the Bourguiba Mosque in Monastir.

Sidi Youssef Mosque is in Souk el Bey, just behind place du Gouvernement. An interesting mosque built in the 17th century by the Turks for the local Turkish merchants. It was architecturally innovative because it was the first mosque to have an octagonal minaret, setting the style for many future Turkish mosques.

Dar el Bey, place du Gouvernement. Built in 1795 this old royal guesthouse has been converted since Independence into the prime minister's office. It is an interesting building, particularly with regard to its Andalusian influences.

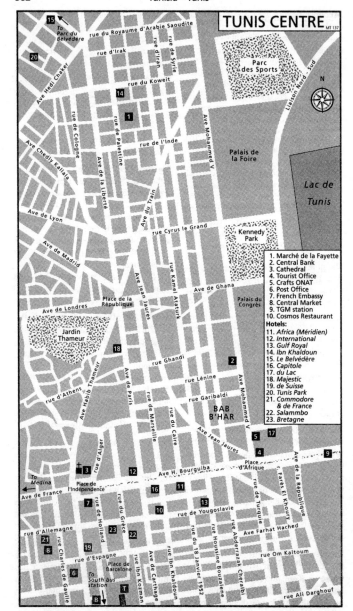

TUNIS CENTRE MT 137

To Parc du Belvédère

rue du Royaume d'Arabie Saoudite

rue d'Irak

rue d'Iran

rue de Syrie

Parc des Sports

Ave Hedi Chaker

rue du Koweit

rue de Cologne

rue de Palestine

rue de l'Inde

Ave Mohammed V

Palais de la Foire

N

Ave Chedly Kallala

rue de la Liberté

rue du Train

Lac de Tunis

Ave de Lyon

Ave de Madrid

rue Cyrus le Grand

Kennedy Park

Ave de Londres

Place de la République

rue Kamel Ataturk

Ave de Ghana

Palais du Congrès

Jardin Thameur

rue Jean Jaures

rue Ghandi

2

rue Lénine

rue d'Athens

Ave Habib Thameur

Ave de Paris

rue de Marseille

rue du Caire

rue Garibaldi

BAB B'HAR

Ave Mohammed V

Ave Jean Jaures

5

17

rue d'Alger

4

Place d'Afrique

9

Ave de la République

To Medina

3

12

Ave H. Bourguiba

rue Fares El Khoury

Place de l'Indépendance

16

11

Ave de France

7

rue du Grèce

10

13

rue de Yougoslavie

rue de Turquie

rue d'Allemagne

23

22

rue Houssine Bouziane

Ave Farhat Hached

21

8

19

rue d'Espagne

Place de Barcelone

Ave de Carthage

rue Ibn Khaldoun

rue du 18 Janvier 1952

rue Abderrazak Cheraibi

rue Om Kaltoum

rue Charles de Gaulle

6

To South bus station

Ave Ibn Kozman

B

rue Ali Darghout

1. Marché de la Fayette
2. Central Bank
3. Cathedral
4. Tourist Office
5. Crafts ONAT
6. Post Office
7. French Embassy
8. Central Market
9. TGM station
10. Cosmos Restaurant

Hotels:
11. *Africa (Méridien)*
12. *International*
13. *Gulf Royal*
14. *Ibn Khaldoun*
15. *Le Belvédère*
16. *Capitole*
17. *du Lac*
18. *Majestic*
19. *de Suisse*
20. *Tunis Park*
21. *Commodore & de France*
22. *Salammbo*
23. *Bretagne*

Medersa Mouradia College built in cloth market by Mourad II, son of Hammouda Pasha, in 1673. The huge studded door in a wide marble surround leads into a paved courtyard. Upstairs are the old narrow-doored students' rooms and prayer chamber. Young apprentices learn their crafts here today. Open 0930-1630 except Sun, entrance TD3.

Dar Hussein, place du Château. Built by Ismail Kahia (1758-1781) this is a beautiful mansion which was used by the French as their army headquarters while in Tunisia. With the coming of Independence it became the National Art and Archaeology Institute and houses beautiful manuscripts of the Koran, glassware from Kairouan and ceramics from Rakkada as well as valuable objects from other Islamic countries.

Dar el Haddad, Impasse de l'Artillerie. Built in the 16th century it is one of the oldest palaces in the medina and was once owned by a rich Andalusian, Said El Haddad El Andalousi. Over time it has been inhabited by many different families and left to fall into decay. It was bought by the city of Tunis in 1966 and declared a National Monument.

Tourbet el Bey, rue Tourbet el Bey. Built by Ali Pasha II (1758-1782), this mausoleum houses the tombs of the members of the royal family. Over the centuries, it has been extended many times with little regard to the overall harmony. The most prominent style is Italian and it is interesting to note the domes covered in green, scale shaped tiles. The previous leaders of the dynasty had been buried in the Tourbet Sidi Kacem, rue Sidi Kacem. An interesting building which can normally be visited 0930-1600 except Sun, entrance TD3.

Dar Ben Abdallah, built in 1796, houses the Centre of Popular Arts and Traditions where the collection of objects recreates bourgeois life in Tunis in the 19th century. There is a selection of gold embroidered/jewel encrusted costumes and unusually fine everyday objects. Open 0930-1630 except Sun, entrance TD3.

Dar Othman Othman Dey 1544-1610 used the spoils of his piracy to build this beautiful palace at a distance from the kasbah, the Janissaries and other unrest. The palace looks out on to rue M'Bazaa. The majestic façade of black and white marble has a huge door surmounted by two carved lintels separated by a pointed arch of alternate coloured stones.

Mosque des Teinturiers (Dyers), rue des Teinturiers. Built by Hussein Ben Ali Tourki, the founder of the Husseinite dynasty, in 1716. No expenses seemed to have been spared, the ceramics coming from Turkey and the marble from Italy. Clearly influenced by the Sidi Youssef mosque with its octagonal minaret, it nevertheless has the novelty of sharing the central courtyard with a *medersa*.

Three Medressa These contain students' cells opening onto three sides of the courtyard with the mosque on the fourth side. The cloister round courtyard of **Medersa of the Palm Tree** (1714) is supported by horseshoe arches on stone columns with Turkish capitals. This surrounds a garden but the palm tree no longer exists. Black marble columns with white marble capitals support the arches in **Medersa Bachia** (1752). A stone fountain is incorporated in the design. The building is now a school for apprentice craftsmen. **Medersa Slimania** (1754) was built by Ali Pasha in memory of his son Suleimane who was poisoned by his brother. The entrance and courtyard are very beautiful and decorated with wonderful ceramics. It has now been converted into a cultural centre. Open 0930-1630 all year, closed Sun, entrance TD3.

Beaches

Tunis city has no beaches as it is on a highly polluted lake, but there are beaches nearby. The coast N from La

Goulette is just one long beach. The preferred beaches tend to be further along at La Marsa and Gammarth. It is easy to reach them by taking the TGM to La Marsa which is probably better but gets crowded at weekends.

Parks

Belvédère Park is to the N of the city. To get there take the bus No 5 from place de l'Indépendence and get off at place Pasteur or Metro line No 2 from Place de Barcelona to Palestine station. It is then a short walk to this very large park which is pleasantly cool in summer. There is also a well established zoo, the only one we can recommend in Tunisia (entrance under 9, 100 mills, over 9, 800 mills, photography 100 mills) and a museum of interesting contemporary Tunisian art. Tunis' other park, Jardin Thameur, in the centre of town, is attractive, well used and consequently crowded.

Local information

In town Around the ville nouvelle and Ave Bourguiba towards the medina you will find most of the cheap hotels, the shopping streets and the post office. On Ave Bourguiba are branches of most main banks and the large travel agencies and the tourist information office. To the S you will find the train station and the main bus and louages station for the S of the country.

● **Accommodation**

Price guide:			
AL	US$90+	**D**	US$20-40
A	US$75-90	**E**	US$10-20
B	US$60-75	**F**	under US$10
C	US$40-60		

Few of the cheaper hotels in the centre of Tunis have any character, and some prefer to cater for Tunisians rather than foreign travellers. Consider staying in pleasanter surroundings in Sidi Bou Saïd and visiting Tunis using the TGM.

AL *Africa Méridien Hotel*, 50 Ave Bourguiba, T 347477, 170 rm, a/c, 3 restaurants, 3 bars, movie theatre, pool, hairdresser, car rental, conference facilities.

A *Hotel des Ambassadeurs*, rue Hedi Chaker, T 288011, rooms facing the Belvédère

Park, a/c, restaurant; **A** *International Hotel*, 49 Ave Bourguiba, T 254855, 228 rm, central, good restaurants; **A** *Mechtel Hotel*, T 783200, Ave Taieb Mehiri, Belvédère Park, 450 rm, pool.

B *Hotel Capitole*, 60 Ave Bourguiba, T 244997, clean, some rm with bath, bit expensive, noisy; **B** *Hotel Gulf Royal*, Ave de la Yougoslavie, T 342422, expensive, poor value for money; **B** *Hotel Ibn Khaldoun*, rue de Palestine, by the Marché Lafayette, T 783211, good, a/c, restaurant, organized entertainment; **B** *Hotel Le Belvédère*, rue des Etats-Unis, T 783133, quiet, close to the Belvédère Park, a/c, restaurant.

C *Hotel du Lac*, Ave Bourguiba, central, T 258322, restaurant, 208 rm all a/c; **C** *Hotel Excel*, 35 Ave Bourguiba, T 355088, F 341929, central position, TV, no breakfast; **C** *Hotel St. George*, 16 rue de Cologne, behind Ave de la Liberté, T 282937, 36 rm, 26 with bath, very good, clean hotel, a/c, restaurant, parking available; **C** *Hotel Tej*, 14 rue Lt. Aziz Tej, T 344899, clean, overpriced, a/c.

D *Hotel Carlton*, 31 Ave Bourguiba, T 258167, clean, 40 rm with bath, a/c, slightly noisy position on main road, currently undergoing refurbishment; **D** *Hotel Dar Masmoudi*, 18 rue du Maroc, off rue d'Algerie, T 342428, very close to medina, very quiet, most rm with bath; **D** *Hotel de Suisse*, 5 rue de Suisse, T 243821, 23 rm, most with bath, clean, quiet, parking; **D** *Hotel Maison Dorée*, 6 rue de Hollande, just off Ave de la Yougoslavie behind the French Embassy, T 240632, has seen better days, good condition, spotlessly clean, good service, quite quiet, 54 rm with bath, breakfast incl, restaurant; **D** *Hotel Majestic*, Ave de Paris, T 242848, old-fashioned, 100 rm, 40 with a/c, large terrace, central, restaurant; **D** *Hotel Ritza*, 35 Ave Thameur, T 245428, close to the Thameur park, 30 rm, communal shower; **D** *Hotel Transatlantique*, 106 Ave de Yougoslavie, T 240680, relatively quiet for a central hotel, most rm with bath, breakfast incl; **D** *Tunis Park Hotel*, 7 rue de Damas off Ave Taieb Mehiri by the Belvédère Park, T 286696, 28 rm, good, very quiet, restaurant.

E *Hotel de France*, 8 rue Mustapha M'Barek, T 245876, very close to the *Hotel Commodore* and the medina, clean, 49 rm with bath, good value; **E** *Hotel Salammbo*, 6 rue de Grèce, off Ave Bourguiba, T 337498, clean hotel, 52 rm, most with bath.

F *Gare Hotel*, rue de Gare, rec; F *Hotel Cirta*, 42 Ave Charles de Gaulle, T 241582, communal pay showers, very cheap; F *Hotel Commodore*, 17 rue d'Allemagne opp the central market, T 244941, clean, quiet hotel just by the entrance to the medina, 48 rm, most have bath, no breakfast, very cheap; F *Hotel Continental*, 5 rue de Marseille, T 259834, very quiet and cheap, communal shower; F *Hotel Crystal*, Ave de Carthage, quiet, clean, communal shower; F *Hotel de Bretagne*, 7 Ave de Grèce, T 242146, 25 rm, quite clean and quiet; F *Hotel de l'Agriculture*, 25 Ave Charles de Gaulle, T 246394, opp *Hotel Cirta*, very quiet situation, clean; F *Hotel de la Victoire*, 7 Bab el Menara, T 26, 20 rm (those on front are noisy), communal shower, clean, best of this category; F *Hotel Rex*, 65 rue de Yougoslavie, T 257397, 29 rm, communal pay shower, rather depressing; F *Nouvelle Hotel*, T 243379, 3 place Mongi Bali, next to the station, could be cleaner, communal showers, noisy.

Youth hostels: 1) Radès, 10 km SW of Tunis, T 483631, 120 beds, meals provided, take the train from the main station, a 10 min walk from Radès station; 2) In the medina, 25 rue Saida Ajoula, T 567850, 70 beds, 500m from place du Gouvernement la kasbah, 1.5 km from central station; 3) *Centre d'hébergement Jelili ez Zahra*, Oued Meliane Ezzahara, BP1140, T 481547, 72 beds, kitchen, meals provided, take bus No 26A from place Barcelone; 4) Possibility of staying in the Bardo University campus in the summer, contact T 784241, rue du Mali, Tunis.

Camping: *Le Moulin Bleu*, Hammam Plage, 20 km S of Tunis.

● **Places to eat**

> **Price guide:**
> ♦♦♦Expensive; ♦♦average; ♦cheap.

NB it is better not to eat fish on Mon as the fresh fish market is closed on Sun.

♦♦♦ *Bagdad*, Ave Bourguiba, very good Tunisian food, rec; *Chez Nous*, rue de Marseille, French cooking with some Tunisian specialities, alcohol; *Chez Slah*, 14 rue Pierre de Coubertin, T 258588, perhaps the best restaurant in Tunis, highly rec but the bill will be large, good idea to book; *Cosmos*, rue Ibn Khaldoun, very good food, especially the fish, service slow; *Dar Jeld*, rue Dar Jeld in the medina, off place du Gouvernement, very good traditional Tunisian cooking set in an old house, a great night out

with entertainment provided most evenings, closed Sun, booking rec; *L'Etable*, Ave Bourguiba, nr place de l'Afrique, Tunisian specialities, alcohol; *Le Poisson Doré*, rue Ibn Khaldoun, specializes in seafood; *La Trattoria*, 44 Ave Bourguiba, beside *Africa Hotel*.

♦♦ *Café Zitouna*, Jamaa Zitouna in medina, Tunisian food served amid beautiful tiled decorations; *La Mama*, rue de Marseille, mixture of French, Italian and traditional Tunisian cooking, alcohol.

♦ *Abdelaziz Elleuch*, 6 rue de Cair, T 257701, couscous and fish; *Cafè Africa*, beside *Africa Hotel* for mint tea and an opportunity to watch the crowds; *Le Carcassonne*, Ave de Carthage, very clean, cheap and good; *Le Roi d'Espagne*, rue de Lénine, off rue de France, good food in a very simple setting, alcohol; *Le Prince*, place de Barcelone, opp the train station, self-service, clean, cheap, very good typical Tunisian food; *Restaurant Novelty*, rue de Paris, self-service, very good, a warm welcome, cheap food, no alcohol, try the coucha; *Restaurant Zitouna*, Ave de Carthage/rue d'Espagne, Turkish food, no alcohol.

● **Banks & money changers**
American Express, c/o Carthage Tour, 59 Ave Bourguiba, T 254820, open 0800-1900, Sun 0900-1200; **BIAT**, Ave Bourguiba (American Express); **BT**; **STB**, Ave Bourguiba, by the *Africa Hotel*, open daily 0700-1900; **UBCI**, Ave Bourguiba.

● **Embassies & consulates**
Algeria, 136 Ave de la Liberté, T 280082; **Canada** (and Australian affairs), 3 rue Didon, T 286577; **Egypt**, 16 rue Essayouti, T 230004; **France**, Place de l'Indépendance, T 245700; **Germany**, 18 Ave Challaye, T 281246; **Italy**, rue de Russie, T 361811 (open 0930-1130); **Ivory Coast**, 6 rue Ibn Charaf, T 283878; **Jordan**, 4 rue Didon, T 288401; **Libya**, 48 bis rue du 1 Juin, T 283936; **Morocco**, 39 rue du 1 Juin, T 288063; **Netherlands**, 6 rue Meycen, T 287455; **Norway**, 7 Ave Bourguiba, T 245933; **Senegal**, 122 Ave de la Liberté, T 282393; **Sweden**, 87 Ave Taieb Mehri, T 283433; **Switzerland**, 10 rue ech-Chenkiti, 1002 Belvédère, T 795957; **UK**, 5 place de la Victoire, T 245100; **USA**, 144 Ave de la Liberté, T 282566.

● **Entertainment**
Discotheques/Nightclubs: most nightclubs are outside Tunis centre along the N coast.

However, most large 4-star hotels in town have nightclubs. At Sidi Bou Said: *La Barraka*. At La Marsa: *Le Galaxy* by the *Hotel Tour Blanche*. This would appear to be the club most in fashion. In Tunis centre there are also a few cabarets: *Monseigneur*, 2 rue de Marseille; *La Potinière*, 11 rue de Hollande.

Hammams: Turkish baths, are an institution in Tunisia. Everybody goes there once a week. It is a revitalizing experience and well worth a visit. The morning is reserved for men and the afternoon (until 1800 after which the men can return) for women. Rue du Maroc, next to *Hotel Dar Masmoudi*, rue de Marseille, level with No 42, just off Ave Bourguiba. There are also many older ones in the medina (see map 379) and a few on rue du Pasha.

● **Hospitals & medical services**
Chemists: all night, 43 Ave Bourguiba, opp *Africa Hotel*; 20 Ave de la Liberté, by Ave de Madrid; 44 Ave Bab Djedid.
Hospitals: Hôpital Principal Aziza Othmana, place du Gouvernement, T 633655; Hôpital Charles Nicolle, T 663000.

● **Post & telecommuncations**
Area code: 01.
Post Office: main PTT rue Charles de Gaulle, open Mon-Thur 0730-1230 and 1700-1900, Fri-Sat 0730-1330, Sun 0900-1100. A 24-hour telephone centre is off rue Gamal Abdul Nasser.

● **Shopping**
Bookshops: there are many bookshops in rue de France, but most books are in Arabic or French. The only English books can be found in the *Africa Hotel* and they are generally not very good. If you read Arabic or French go to Librairie Clairefontaine, 4 rue d'Alger. There is also an interesting book shop, Librarie Alif, which often puts on small exhibitions at 3 rue de Hollande (behind the French Embassy).

Handicrafts: Tunisian craftsmanship can be excellent and it is possible (after a bit of bargaining) to get a very good deal. Leather goods and brass objects are plentiful and of very good quality. The best place to go, at least to find out the official prices and have an overall idea of crafts produced, is the *Office National de l'Artisanat (ONAT)* on Ave Mohammed V, just beyond the Tourist Office, off place de l'Afrique has a showroom of local crafts and arts from around Tunisia. It is interesting to go there before leaving Tunis, as you will see the local diversities and specialities. It is also worth see-

ing the prices before entering the souks. They also have a list of the official prices for carpets according to the quality. You will find many of these, among lots of less interesting goods, in the medina in rue Jemaa Zitouna. Be selective.

By the Great Mosque, the **Souk Del Attarine** specializes in perfumes and precious stones. Amber is generally well worked but watch out for plastic imitations (amber resists the heat of a match). **Jewellery** can be found in the *Souk des Orfèvres*, and *Souk el-Berka*. For carpets and blankets go to *Souk el Leffa*, but carpets are generally cheaper in Kairouan. If you get a carpet be sure you have the receipt and that there is a quality stamp on the back. For leather, go to the *Souk el-Sekkajine*, but be warned that the quality is sometimes mediocre.

Many of the market stalls which scattered the streets selling 'necessities' like toothpaste, fly-spray and ladies' stockings and most of the cheap eating stalls have been moved away to rue Moncef Bey, visited by buses Nos 2 and 100.

If you are not looking for souvenirs, the best place to go is Ave Charles de Gaulle in the new city where you will find supermarkets (*Monoprix*), chemists, and camera shops.

Hairdresser: Coiffeur pour hommes, rue Gamal Abdel Nasser, nr telephone office.

● **Sports**
Diving: the Centre Nautique International de Tunisie, 22 rue de Medine, T 282209, for information about diving and fishing.

Gliding and Flying: at the Federal Centre at Djebel Ressas SW of Tunis.

Golf: there is an 18 hole course at La Soukra (close to the airport), T 765919, 4,432m, par 66.

Riding: at La Soukra and Ksar Said. Race meetings every Sun at Ksar Said.

Shooting: (pigeons) in Forest of Radès S of Tunis.

Swimming pools: at El Menza (Cité Olympique) and the piscine municipale in Belvédère Park, by place Pasteur. You can also try the large 4-star hotels, *Hotel Africa* has a pool on the 3rd flr.

Tennis: in the Belvédère Park and Park des Sports, Ave Mohammed V. Tunis 'Open' in Mar.

● **Tour companies & travel agents**
La Maison du Voyage, Ave Gamal Abdul

Nasser, beside the Post Office; *Sedec Tour*, rue de Marseille; *Tourafrica*, Ave Bourguiba, next to *Africa Hotel*; *Tunisian Travel Service*, 19 Ave Bourguiba, T 348100.

● **Tourist offices**

The tourist information offices are: **Tunisian National Tourist Office**, 1 Ave Mohammed V (place de l'Afrique), T 341077, F 350997, open 0730-1330 in summer, 0830-1200 and 1500-1800 in winter, closed Sun and public holidays; **ONTT**, branches at train station and airport, also at 51 Ave de la Liberté; **Regional Tourist Office for Tunis**, 29 rue Hatem Ettai (corner of rue de la Palestine), T 289403/288720, Tx 15347.

● **Useful addresses**

Ambulance: T 491286

Doctor: T 341250, T 346767.

Fire station and **Police**: T 197.

● **Transport**

Local Bus: you will probably not need to use more than a few routes during your stay in Tunis. For more information go to the bus station in front of the train station on place de Barcelone. Bus No 3 leaves from Ave Bourguiba in front of Tunis Air, or from Ave de Paris in front of the *Hotel Majestic* and goes to the Bardo Museum and S bus station. Bus No 5 leaves from place de l'Indépendance and goes to place Pasteur by Belvédère Park. Bus No 35 leaves from Ave Bourguiba for a 30 mins ride to the airport. **Car hire**: many firms have an agent at airport. **Avis**, Ave Bourguiba, in the *Africa Hotel* lobby, Ave Bourguiba, T 341249; **Ben Jemaa**, Excelsior Garage, 53 Ave de Paris, T 240060; **Budget**, 14 Ave de Carthage, T 256806; **Carthage Tours**, 59 Ave Bourguiba, T 254605; **Chartago Rent**, 3 Ave Bourguiba, T 349168; **Europacar**, 17 Ave Bourguiba, T 340303; **Garage selection**, 65 Ave Hedi Chaker, T 284698; **Hertz**, 29 Ave Bourguiba, T 248559; **Topcar**, 23 Ave Bourguiba, T 344121. **Metro**: there is a brand new tramway system in Tunis which is rapidly expanding. At present there are five lines but many more are under construction. The tramway is the city's answer to severe congestion and has so far been successful. The central tram station is at the train station and another large station is on place de la République. **Taxis**: are

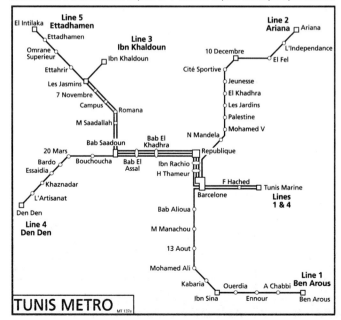

TUNIS METRO

quite cheap but may be difficult to find, particularly at rush hour. The maximum you should have to pay is about TD4-5 and that is for a long trip to La Marsa. All taxis have meters and use them, so make sure they have switched it on. The best place to find a taxi is in front of the main train station. Most taxis are painted yellow, but this is a recent decision and some older taxis are different colours.

Air To get to the airport either take a taxi or bus No 35 from Ave Bourguiba, opp *Africa Hotel*, 30 min. **Airline information** Aeroflot, 24 Ave Thameur, T 340845; Air Algérie, 28 Ave de Paris, T 341590; Air France, 1 rue d'Athènes, T 341577; GB Air, 17 Ave Bourguiba, T 244261; Egypt Air, 49 Ave Bourguiba, T 341182 in the *International Hotel*; KLM, 50 rue Lucy Faure, T 341309; Lufthansa, Ave Ouled Haffouz, close to the Belvédère Park, in the *Mechtel Hotel*; Royal Air Maroc, 45 Ave Bourguiba T 249016, in the Le Colisée building, B stairs, 3rd flr; Tunis Air, 48 Ave Bourguiba, T 259189, central office 133 Ave de la Liberté, T 288100. **Internal flights**: (Airport T 235000, 236000) by Tunisair to **Djerba** daily at 1530 (1 hr), costs US$50; **Monastir** Wed, Thur, Sat; **Sfax** daily except Mon, **Tozeur** Mon, Fri, Sat, Sun; **Tabarka** Fri, Sun 1310. Tunis Air subsidiary Tunisavia have introduced more flights using small 72 seater planes. In summer it is important to book well in advance as places are hard to come by. **International flights** T 754000/755000, winter schedule (there are additional flights in summer): **Algiers** Tues, Wed, Thur, Fri at 0825, 1550 or 1750; **Brussels** Mon, Tues, Thur, Sat at 0850 or 0915; **Cairo** Mon 1540, Wed 2100; **Casablanca** daily except Fri at 0700 or 1900; **London** daily at 1335 or 1415; **Paris** daily at 0820 or 1400.

Train TGM: the TGM (Tunis-La Goulette-La Marsa) is the train linking Tunis to the coastal resorts and suburbs. The station is at the end of Ave Bourguiba, beyond place de l'Afrique. It is open 24 hrs a day with trains every 10-15 mins during the day and every hour at night. The service goes to La Goulette, Carthage, Sidi Bou Said and La Marsa. The main train station is in the centre of the new city on place de Barcelone. Information on T 244440/427. **National departures**: **Bizerte** 0550, 1130, 1600, 1830; **Bir Bou Rekba** and **Sousse** 0710 (on to El Djem, Sfax and Gabès); 0900, 1840 (on to Monastir) 1205, 1535 (on to Monastir and Mahdia); 1305, 1730 (on to El Djem and Sfax); 2120 (on to El Djem, Sfax, Gabès, Gafsa

and Metlaoui); Nabeul 1805. **To Algeria**: only one train goes on to Algiers, all the others stop at the border. **Algiers** 1255; **Ghardimaou** (border) 0635, 1200, 1425, 1620, 1750. All trains go via Béja and Djendouba (except the 1425). Sample fare: Tunis to Sfax 2nd class TD7.5, bicycle TD6.5.

Road Bus: there are two bus stations in Tunis. The **N bus station** is situated at Bab Saadoun. To get there take the bus No 3 from Ave Bourguiba by *Hotel Africa Méridien*. Get off just after Bab Saadoun, the bus station is on the right. Buses from here go to the N coast. For information about buses to the N, T 562299/562532. Departures from here to Bizerte; Raf Raf and Ras el Djebel; Medjez el Bab and Béja, change here for Aïn Draham, Jenbouba and Tabarka; Mateur and Tabarka; Medjez el Bab, Teboursouk and Le Kef, change here for Thala. The **S bus station** is at Bab El Fellah and has buses to all other places including Algeria and Libya. To reach the station walk from the main train station, a distance of 800m. Take the rue de La Gare on the right of the station, at the end of the street the station is on the other side of the road. For information about buses to the S, T 495255/490391. Departures from here to Hammamet and Nabeul; to Kairouan via Enfida or El Fahs and on to Gafsa (change here for Tozeur and Nefta) or Kasserine; Sousse (change here for El Djem), Sfax and Gabès, change for Tataouine, Medenine, Ben Gardane, Zarzis and Matmata. **Buses to Algeria, Libya and Morocco**: Algeria (Annaba) daily at 0700; **Libya** (Tripoli) Mon, Wed, Fri and Sun at 1700 cost TD25 plus TD2/piece of luggage, takes 8-10 hrs; **Morocco** (Casablanca) Sat at 0630. **NB** During the summer it can be difficult to get a seat on a bus. You may have to put up a bit of a fight at the ticket office. The best thing is to book. This service is available for most lines, but it is best to check. **Louages**: are large taxis that take five people and go from one city to another. The city names shown do not necessarily indicate where the car is going, but only where it is licensed. The louage stations are sited next to bus stations, at the front of the N station and to the left of the S station. If going S during the summer you will find that most louages go in the evening or at night, as it is cooler.

● **Sea Ferry**: for information, see page 481.

AROUND TUNIS

The area to the NE of Tunis encompasses the important historical sites, the most expensive suburbs and the nearest beaches. Take the dual carriageway W from place de l'Afrique.

La Goulette

ACCESS from Tunis is very easy by the TGM or the road that runs alongside it on the causeway, a very interesting ride. There is a very practical, free ferry service between La Goulette and Radès which enables travellers going S to bypass Tunis. The service runs 24 hrs a day. The harbour has berths for 60 yachts, min-max draft, 3-6m.

La Goulette (The Gullet) is at the narrow entrance to the Lake of Tunis and is the main harbour of Tunis with ferries to Europe. It is dominated by a fortress built by Charles V of Spain in 1535, when he assisted the Hafsids fight against Barbarossa. It functions as a harbour, an important naval base, a dormitory for Tunis and also as a highly industrialized area. Nevertheless in summer it is a very pleasant place to go for a meal of fresh fish or just to stroll. The main street, with restaurants and bars everywhere, comes to life in the evening.

From the **Fortress of Karraka** enjoy a splendid view over the harbour and the Gulf of Tunis. The fortress was a prison and has a gruesome history. Entrance TD1, photography TD3.

● **Places to eat** The best grilled fish restaurants are situated by the port. Try *La Petite Etoile*, *Café Vert* and *L'An 2000*. Cheaper restaurants can be found on the side roads.

Carthage

ACCESS From Tunis drive along the causeway and through La Goulette or take the TGM from the end of Ave Bourguiba. The stations are strategically situated for visiting the sites or, as an alternative,

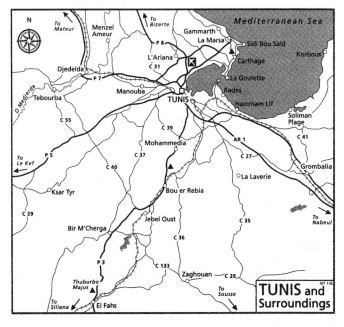

TUNIS and Surroundings

calèches are available at Carthage Hannibal station. Taxi from airport costs TD6.

Carthage is now one of the smart suburbs of Tunis, well placed close to the sea. The remains of the old city of Carthage can be visited at various locations in the area, but there is little left of the grandeur. Nevertheless, the old Roman and Punic ruins are well worth seeing, to give an idea of past splendours.

History
According to Virgil, Carthage was founded in 814 BC by the Princess Dido (Didon). She was the one with the initiative and a sharp knife who wangled a piece of land large enough to build a new city – **Kart Hadascht**. It soon became a major power and trade centre, attempting to rival both the Greeks and the Romans by setting its sights, unsuccessfully, on Sicily. Everybody knows the extraordinary story of **Hannibal** (see box, page 392), who crossed the Alps with 40,000 men and 38 elephants to attack Rome. Unfortunately, the Romans eventually took revenge and Scipio's armies won a decisive battle in Zama in 202 BC. Carthage was subjected to a siege lasting 3 years and was eventually seized and razed to the ground in 146 BC to the delight of Cato who had had this in mind for some time.

However this was not to be the end of Carthage as the Romans, under Caesar Augustus in 44 BC, returned to make it the capital of the Roman Province of Afrique, the cultural and intellectual centre. At this time Carthage was known as Rome's bread basket due to its highly fertile hinterland. It later collapsed as a significant power after the successive invasions of the Vandals, Byzantines and Arabs. After the Arab invasion, Carthage was mainly used as a source of building material for Islamic monuments and the expanding city of Tunis (see History of N Africa, page 24).

Places of interest
All sites here open 0700-1900 summer,

0830-1730 winter, closed Sun. Entrance TD4, photography TD4 covers all sites.

Local information
● Accommodation
A *Hotel Elyssa Didon*, on Byrsa Hill, T 275344, close to the museum, 22 rm, expensive, very quiet, overlooking the sea, excellent restaurant.

Tophet, Oceanographic Museum and the Punic Ports

Get off at the TGM station at Carthage Salammbo and walk down towards the sea. First is the Tophet (crematorium) and then along the road, on the right, the Oceanographic Museum and the Punic Ports. It is then only a short walk up to the TGM station Carthage Byrsa.

At **Tophet** are the remains of the sanctuary of the Carthaginian divinities Tanit and Baal. There is not much left to see. According to legend the Carthaginians brought their children here to be ritually sacrificed and urns containing ashes and remains of many children have in fact been found. Whether sacrifices actually occurred and how frequently is still unknown, but opinion tends to confirm that they did take place, along with a much more important form of animal sacrifice. The **Oceanographic Museum** is of most interest to those who are keen on fish and fishing.

The **Punic Ports** The main harbour used to be the very heart of Carthaginian prosperity. The N basin boasting safe anchorage for 220 vessels was the naval base and the S base was for merchant ships.

The museum, amphitheatre, theatre and Roman Villas Alight at TGM station Carthage Hannibal. Walk up Ave de l'Amphithéatre to the summit of Mt Byrsa which was the Acropolis of Punic and Roman Carthage, an ideal view point. Here is the large cathedral and seminary (now the museum) constructed by the French during the Protectorate. On the southern slope are the remains of the Punic residential quarter (2nd century BC), built in a regular rectangular grid, houses, water tanks, drains, plastered walls, tiled floors. Down the other side of the hill the amphitheatre is on one side of the road and a collection of cisterns on the other. Returning towards the sea down Ave 7th Novembre on the left is the theatre behind which lie the Ro-

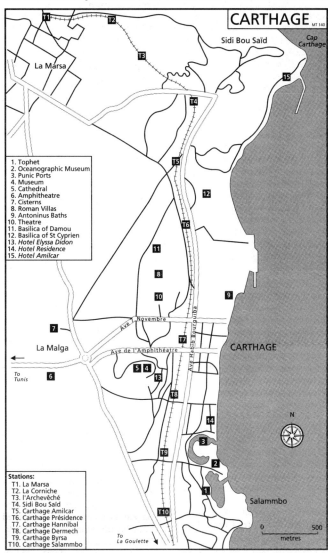

CARTHAGE MT 140

Sidi Bou Saïd

Cap Carthage

La Marsa

1. Tophet
2. Oceanographic Museum
3. Punic Ports
4. Museum
5. Cathedral
6. Amphitheatre
7. Cisterns
8. Roman Villas
9. Antoninus Baths
10. Theatre
11. Basilica of Damou
12. Basilica of St Cyprien
13. *Hotel Elyssa Didon*
14. *Hotel Residence*
15. *Hotel Amilcar*

Ave Novembre

La Malga

To Tunis

Ave de l'Amphithéatre

Ave Habib Bourguiba

CARTHAGE

N

Salammbo

Stations:
T1. La Marsa
T2. La Corniche
T3. l'Archevéché
T4. Sidi Bou Saïd
T5. Carthage Amilcar
T6. Carthage Présidence
T7. Carthage Hannibal
T8. Carthage Dermech
T9. Carthage Byrsa
T10. Carthage Salammbo

To La Goulette

0   500
metres

HANNIBAL: JUMBOS IN THE PASSES AND CARNAGE BY CARTHAGE

Hannibal, unfortunately recalled by many only as the man who crossed the Alps with a herd of elephants, deserves far greater acclaim.

He was one of the greatest army commanders of ancient times, recognized for his innovative military strategies and his charismatic leadership.

He was born in Carthage in 247 BC, the son of the military leader Hamilcar Barca. He spent much of his early life in regions of Spain then controlled by Carthage, fighting wayward Spanish tribes and consolidating Carthaginian power. He made such an impression that at the age of 26 he was promoted to Commander-in-Chief of the Carthaginian army. His expansionist policies upset the Romans and led to the Second Punic War with Hannibal commanding the Carthaginian side. In a bold manoeuvre he advanced on Roman Italy, crossing the Pyrenees, the Rhône in France and the Alps. He started this incredible military exercise leaving Spain with some 40,000 troops, numerous horses and 38 elephants to use as battering rams. He lost men by desertion, guerrilla warfare by the Gauls and natural causes, but gained supporters on the way. His arrival in the Po Basin, most probably via the Mt Cenis Pass, with 20,000 infantry, 6,000 cavalry and a handful of elephants showed conclusively Hannibal's considerable ability to organize and command. It was surely a glorious feat.

The first encounter between Hannibal's troops and Scipio's Roman forces sent N to meet them, was on the plains W of the Ticino River. Here Hannibal's numerically inadequate cavalry gained the upper hand. Their second meeting, known as the Battle of Trebia river, also went in Hannibal's favour. The Battle of Trasimene in the spring of 217 BC left thousands of Romans dead and Hannibal triumphant. Hannibal had one further impressive victory at Cannae where despite

---

man Villas. If you visit the Basilicas of Damou and St Cyprien next then backtrack to the Baths of Antoninus you will have visited all the major sites and be back at the TGM station.

In the **amphitheatre** early Christians were thrown to the lions and gladiators as entertainment for the audience. Unfortunately there is very little to see since only limited excavation work has been carried out.

The **cisterns** were the main reservoirs for the Carthage water supply. Today they are in a bad state.

The **theatre** has been completely restored and is currently used for the annual Carthage Festival. The building is not very interesting in itself as it is not very true to the original, but the festival receives great praise. The **Roman Villas** have also been restored badly.

The **Antoninus Baths**, once the biggest baths in N Africa were truly enormous. They are in a splendid position by the sea and are one of the best preserved sites in Carthage. Even though there are only a few pieces of building still standing they give a good idea of the grandeur that was.

The **museum**, T 730036, situated behind the cathedral has a new reception area. The redesigned exhibition galleries have better lighting and better information panels. The three large wings on the ground floor are devoted to Punic, Roman, Christian and Islamic periods while the four galleries above attempt to recreate the history of the Carthaginian city state. It is a worthwhile stop but is somewhat overshadowed by the magnificent collection in the Bardo museum.

Sidi Bou Saïd

Sidi Bou Said station is 10 mins walk from the centre. The village is beautiful,

being far outnumbered, his troops encircled and trapped the Romans, and by attacking from the rear slaughtered about 50,000 enemy troops in one day. Hannibal's leadership and military tactics thus brought about the worst defeat ever suffered by the Roman army.

Hannibal did not take the opportunity to march on Rome but remained in Italy and, despite suffering from extended supply lines, a lack of naval support and allies who gave greater consideration to affairs of their own, continued to harass the Romans. His fighting strength gradually weakened and the Roman strategy of avoiding direct confrontation allowed him only minor victories.

Meanwhile the Carthaginians were forced out of Spain by Scipio, the Roman general who went on to invade Africa in 204 BC. Hannibal at this point abandoned his campaign in Italy and rushed home to protect his country. Despite the peace proposals agreed between Scipio and the Carthaginian army, Hannibal broke the armistice and concentrated the remaining forces on present day Sousse. Details differ on the campaign which followed that culminated in the Battle of Zama, but in essence Hannibal's troops were defeated, over 20,000 men died and Hannibal fled. A treaty was signed between Rome and Carthage in 201 BC, a disappointing end for Hannibal to his military career.

Carthage was allowed a deal of self government by the Romans, with Hannibal a leading figure. While Carthage recovered rapidly under his hands he was not universally popular and it is understood that his speedy removal to Ephesus was to avoid arrest. He outstayed his welcome in Ephesus, his advice to King Antiochus on how to conduct his war against Rome was not heeded and when Syria lost the war in 190 BC, part of the price was Hannibal's surrender. Accounts vary on what followed but eventually by 183 BC, the Romans were in a position to demand his surrender. To avoid arrest, at the age of 64, Hannibal committed suicide.

a pleasant place to stay in contrast to Tunis. It is built on a cliff facing the Mediterranean, all the white painted houses having blue doors. The buildings go all the way down to the sea, ending by the small port. The narrow, winding streets follow the curves of the hill, and provide a most interesting walk. The architecture is superb and the houses have been very well preserved. There is an excellent view from the top of the hill where there is a small cemetery on the right. A steep climb, consider taking a taxi.

For refreshments try the picturesque but very expensive Moorish *Café des Nattes* in the cobbled square in the centre of the village. Another place to have a drink, particularly at sunset, is the *Café Sidi Chabaane*, situated at the end of the village. Coffee here TD1. The view from here over the sea is quite exceptional.

Follow the walk down to the harbour and along the path which continues back up the hill at the end of the Cap. Being on every tourist's itinerary Sidi Bou Saïd can get very crowded, especially in summer, but most people tend to congregate in the main streets and it is possible to find some peace in the small back streets.

The elegant white painted (sometimes natural olive wood) bird cages with distinctive domes are made here by hand.

● **Accommodation B** *Hotel Amilcar*, at the foot of Sidi Bou Saïd cliff, T 270788, all rm have a view over the Gulf looking towards the Cap Bon peninsula, private beach, pool; **C** *Hotel Residence*, 16 rue Hannibal, Salammbo, T 731072, 8 rm with heating and shower, no a/c, clean, attractive, restaurant, 10 mins from beach, excellent position for visiting Carthage; **D** *Hotel Dar Zarrouk*, T 740215, F 336908, 100 yr old building, beautiful mosaic walls, once housed the harem, 12 rm with high dome ceilings, bath, heating but no a/c, very very attractive, rm with sea view, TD2 extra, breakfast, other meals in restaurant adjacent to hotel; **D** *Sidi Bou Said*, on a hill slightly out of the village, T 740411, 34 rm, good standard, pool, unfortunately no sea view; **E** *Hotel Boufares*, central, T 740091, 8 rm centred around a shaded patio in a typical house, very clean and cheap, cold in winter, excellent breakfast, no restaurant, it is vital to book in the summer season, ask manager to play his lute.

● **Places to eat** There is not much choice here. ◆◆◆*Restaurant Pirates*, by the harbour at the bottom of the cliff specializes in fish and sea-food, expensive but worth it as the food is excellent. ◆◆*Restaurant La Bagatelle*, at the bottom of the hill before the village, good setting, good food, very popular. ◆*Restaurant Chergui* on the main street, on the right of *Café des Nattes*, large terrace with a fantastic view, food is good value. There are lots of stalls selling nuts and sticky sweets.

● **Banks & money changers** UBCI, in the new town at the bottom of the hill, on the road to La Goulette.

● **Hospitals & medical services Chemist**: all night chemist next to the bank.

● **Useful addresses Hammam**: nr the bank, clean, rec. **Harbour**: has berths for 380 yachts, min-max draft 2-4m.

La Marsa

This town lies at the TGM terminus (or catch bus No 20) and is relaxed and quiet, full of luxurious villas. It has a beautiful beach lined with palm trees, far away from the bustle of Tunis and therefore popular at weekends, especially in summer. There is little to do apart from sit on the beach, in a restaurant or in a café. Accommodation is expensive along the coast, most of the hotels being three or four star. **D** *Hotel Plaza*, rue du Maroc, 5 mins from TGM station, beautiful surroundings. Have a drink at the *Café Safsaf*, and try some of their pastries or Tunisian cooking.

Gammarth

Here, there is a long line of expensive villas, luxury hotels and restaurants strung along the coast. However it is possible to reach the beach to the N beyond the hotels (most of them are right on the beach). The beach is good, but crowded in summer, when it can be noisy and the litter builds up.

● **Accommodation AL** *Abou Nawas*, T 741444, F 740400, 45 apartments, 127 rm with a/c, pool in summer, good beach, 6 restaurants/bars, excellent food, all sport activities are organized; **B** *Megara*, on Blvd Taieb Mehiri, T 270366, Moorish decor, 77 rm, large pool, lovely gardens; **C** *La Tour Blanche*, T 271697, is situated a little way up from the coast and therefore has a view, pool, *The Galaxy* – the trendiest nightclub in Tunis – is attached.

● **Places to eat** These are generally expensive. ◆◆◆*Les Dunes hotel*, Baie des Singes, *Le Pêcheur*, beyond *Les Dunes*.

The road continues NW to Raoud through the sand dunes and reaches Tunis via the P8. The coastal area is being developed as another tourist complex.

Zaghouan

Lying 60 km S of Tunis, Zaghouan has a regular bus service from Tunis and louages from Tunis and Hammamet. It is an interesting journey travelling inland and gaining in altitude. A complex system of cisterns and aqueducts once carried fresh water over 132 km, following the contours to Carthage. Parts of the aqueduct can still be seen on the road from Tunis. Zaghouan is dominated by the towering 1,300m high Djebel Zaghouan. The spring and the beginning of the aqueduct can be visited, about 2 km out of town. A few reservoirs can still be seen, but the real interest is the beauty of the site.

● **Accommodation C** *Djebel el Oust*, T 679740, Complex Thermal, Djebel el Oust, bungalows, a/c in public rooms, views towards mountains; **C** *Les Nymphes*, T 675094, Zaghouan 1100, PO Box 11, 1.5 km out of town towards Roman aqueduct. **Youth hostel**: *Maison des Jeunes*, Zaghouan, 85 beds, meals available, T 675265.

● **Post & telecommunications Area code**: 02.

Jebel Oust, 30 km SW from Tunis is one of Tunisia's three main health spas.

Bou Kornine National Park, 18 km SE from Tunis, near Hammam Lif, is home of the Bonelli's and short-toed eagle, a popular place for picnics. Reached by a minor road off the P1 in the centre of Hammam Lif.

At **Oudna**, 20 km S of Tunis, are the remains of Roman **Uthina** built by Octavius Augustus in 2nd century AD. There is an amphitheatre, a theatre, 2 baths, some cisterns, an aqueduct, a capitol, a temple, a basilica and some houses.

Thuburbo Majus

This is 55 km S along the P3 from Tunis. Access by bus or louage from Tunis. Get off at Fahs and walk or get a taxi. If coming from Tunis, ask the driver to stop at Thuburbo Majus (before you get to El Fahs) from which it is a short walk to the site. It is better not to follow the signposts, but to cut across between the two hills, just behind the signpost.

History

Thuburbo Majus was originally a Punic city, but when the Romans conquered Carthage they agreed to pay dues to Rome and so survived. In 27 BC the Emperor Augustus founded a colony of veterans in order to control the strategic situation of the city. Thuburbo Majus was placed in a central position, between the fertile lands of central Tunisia and the coast. The Punic heritage mixed well with the Roman presence and it was at this time that most of the major monuments were constructed, such as the Capitol and the Baths.

Places of interest

The **Forum** and the **Capitol** dominate the ruins. The forum is well preserved and a statue of Jupiter from the Capitol has been taken to the Bardo Museum. There is evidence that some of the buildings behind the Capitol were converted

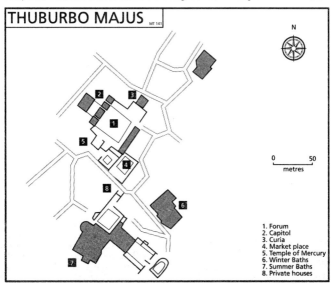

THUBURBO MAJUS _{MT 141}

N

0   50
metres

1. Forum
2. Capitol
3. Curia
4. Market place
5. Temple of Mercury
6. Winter Baths
7. Summer Baths
8. Private houses

into olive oil presses. Olive oil was an important product exported from Thuburbo Majus. The **Temple of Mercury** is an example of the refined architecture of the time, while the existence of baths and gymnasia shows that the town must have been wealthy. The site is interesting and the view over the surrounding area towards Djebel Zaghouan is impressive. Open 0800-1200 and 1500-1900 in summer and 0930-1630 in winter, closed Mon, entrance TD2.

Local information
● **Accommodation**

There is no accommodation at or nr the site. Thuburbo Majus makes a good day trip from Tunis, returning via Zaghouan. The nearest **youth hostel** is in Zaghouan convenient for travellers going E to Enfida and Sousse.

To the E lies **Radès**. **Youth hostel**, Banlieu Sud, T 483631, 10 km from Tunis, 10 mins from Radès station, 56 beds, meals available, ring to book as it takes groups and can get full.

Further E, **Borj Cedria** has a good beach used by people from Tunis at weekends and in summer. Many of them come out by train. The German cemetery commemorating all who fell in the Tunisian campaign between Nov 1942 and May 1943 is down a small signposted road, opposite the station and to the left of the café.

● **Accommodation** **C** *Dar*, T 290188, 144 beach bungalows; **C** *Salwa*, T 290764, 116 rm, pool.

Massicault with **Commonwealth WW2 cemetery** at Borj el Amri (1,576 graves), 28 km SW of Tunis beside the P5. Open 0730-1430 Sat-Thur. Bus No 23a from Tunis. Hotel Magreb and restaurant on S side of road.

CAP BON PENINSULA

CONTENTS

Tunis to Hammamet   397
North to Cap Bon   399
Cap Bon South to Tunis   403

MAPS

Hammamet   398
Cap Bon   400
Nabeul   401

This region, protruding like a thumb into the Mediterranean, was an essential part of the Roman Empire for food supplies. Today it is the source of fresh fruit and early vegetables for much of Europe and of Tunisian wine from its 33,000 ha of vineyards. Furthermore, with the growth of the all year holiday hotels built along the beautiful sandy beaches, it is the Tunisia of the package tourist.

TUNIS TO HAMMAMET

Hammamet

ACCESS Frequent buses and trains come from Tunis and a train runs from Monastir airport. Buses and taxis stop near the medina. The station is a short walk away, or share a taxi.

Hammamet, 65 km SE from Tunis, is probably one of the best known resorts in Tunisia. A once small, sleepy village adjoining a beautiful beach, it now has a population of 30,000 and welcomes tourists in their thousands. The change has been very carefully executed, with attention to the preservation of the site, no hotel permitted higher than a palm tree! The development of the town started in the 1920s, when Rumanian millionaire, **George Sebastian**, built a beautiful villa and invited many of his artistic friends such as Paul Klee, André Gide and Frank Lloyd Wright to visit. In 1959, George Sebastian's house was bought by the state and made into an International Cultural Centre. An open air theatre was built in the extensive grounds 4 years later. A very interesting **international festival** is held here annually in Jul/Aug, with dance, theatre and music (ranging from jazz to classical). During most of the year the house and gardens can be visited.

The town has kept some of its charm, even though a commercial centre (find the banks and a supermarket here) was recently constructed. Equally the medina, surrounded by its walls and lying adjacent to the sea, has kept its attraction. Escape from the tourist shops and walk around the small back streets. Ignore the museum in the kasbah but visit the small café at the top of the walls, with the view of the sea and the fishermen sorting nets near their colourful boats. The fishermen work at night, attracting the fish by means of powerful lamps.

Places of interest
The **Medina** is the main landmark in Hammamet, built right on the beach. Originally constructed in 904, frequently damaged and restored, the walls protect the **Great Mosque**, the baths and the narrow, winding streets containing numerous stalls intent on attracting the tourists and the fresh food stalls of the daily market. Weekly market Thur morning.

The **Kasbah** was originally built in the 12th century and has now been restored. It is more impressive as a setting than as a place to visit.

Local information
● **Accommodation**
As there are lots of expensive hotels along the coast to the N and to the S of the town, it is easy to find somewhere to stay. These same rooms, however, are much cheaper if booked as part of a package.

A *Hotel Club-Hammamet*, route Touristique,

T 281882, 337 rm on 2 flrs, a/c, very good, beach, indoor pool complex, outdoor Olympic size pool, many activities, good food, large rm facing the sea; **A** *Hotel Manar*, route Touristique, T 281333, 200 rm, 6 flrs, a/c, 2 pools, tennis, golf.

B *Hotel Kacem Centre*, Ave Habib Bourguiba, nr train station, T 279580, F 279588, 67 rm with 2 ring hob and fridge, crockery and utensils, 2 pools, roof top terrace with BBQ, a/c, 800m to private beach shared with *Yasmina*, restaurant, fitness centre; **B** *Hotel la Residence*, 72 Ave Habib Bourguiba, T 280406, F 280396, Moorish style, 184 rm with 2 ring hob, fridge, utensils and crockery, roof top pool heated in winter, full a/c, restaurant, 10 mins from beach, 4 km to golf.

D *Hotel Alya*, rue Ali Belhouane, T 280218, central, very clean, half the rm look over the medina, the others over a street, roof terrace, bar, 300m from beach; **D** *Hotel Bellevue*, Blvd Ibn el Fourat, T 281121, beach, central, clean

rm, most with view; **D** *Hotel Sahbi*, in town centre, T 280807, central, 200m from beach, pleasant large rm, some with views; **D** *Les Citronniers*, route des Hotels, by *Hotel Bennila*, T 281650, modern, very close to beach, no views, barbecue, drinks, food on the beach.

E *Hotel Bennila*, route des Hotels, from the centre take the road to Sousse and turn left by the UIB bank, T 280356, clean, pleasant rm, pool, quite cheap.

Youth hostel: T 280440, 100 beds, meals, central location, beside *Hotel Bellevue*.

Camping: *Ideal Camping*, 34 Ave de la République, T 280302, adequate, restaurant, electric hook-ups, shaded area, book in summer, tent TD2.5, car TD2.5, person TD1.5/night.

● **Places to eat**

◆◆◆*La Coupola*, T 281138, Ave du Koweit; *La Pergola*, T 280993, Shopping Centre, central.

HAMMAMET MT 144

1. Kasbah
2. Police
3. Tourist Office
4. Post Office
5. Shopping Centre
6. Dispensary
Hotels:
7. Alya
8. Bellevue
9. Sahbi
10. Yasmina
11. Olympia
12. Kacem Centre
13. Camping
14. Youth Hostel

To Hotel Bennila & Les Citronniers

Ave du Koweit

Ave Taleb Mehiri

Ave du Président Habib Bourguiba

Avenue Hedi Ouali

Oued el Gaïd

rue de la Corniche

t. Farhat Hached

Avenue Habib Thameur

Avenue Mongi Slim

Avenue de la République

Avenue de la Libération

To Hotel Manar & Club Hammamet

rue Sidi Bou Ali

route touristique

rue Taleb el Azzbi

rue des Jasmins

rue de la Stade

Blvd Ibn el Fourat

rue Ali Belhouane

Medina

Cemetery

Mediterranean Sea

TIPPED OFF

The all too numerous feral cats found scavenging around the hotel areas although appealing are best not handled. The Society for the Protection of Animals in Tunisia along with the London based Society for the Protection of Animals in North Africa are working to control the numbers. The cats are caught, neutered and marked by the removal of the tip of the left ear and released to continue an active, but thereafter, unproductive life.

♦♦*Restaurant Achour*, T 280140, central, rue Ali Belhouane, reputedly the best fish restaurant in Hammamet, terrace; *Restaurant Barberousse*, in the medina, wonderful terrace, pleasant decor, very touristy.

♦*Pizzeria* T 80825, Shopping Centre, central; *Restaurant de la Poste*, central square, opp the medina, terrace has a great view over the medina and the golf course, good food, quite cheap.

● Banks & money changers
Money can be changed in the big hotels or the banks in the centre of town. **BDS**, Ave du Koweit; **BT**, Ave Bourguiba; **STB**, Ave du Koweit; **UIB**, Ave des Nations Unies, an exension of Ave du Koweit.

● Entertainment
Nightclubs: mainly to the S of Hammamet, on the road to Sousse, in the direction of the route des Hotels. *Ranch Club*, *La Tortue*, *Manhatten*, *Calypso*, and *Mexico* all in Hammamet Sud. *Bedouina*, T 280095, Ave des Nations Unies, an extension of Ave du Koweit.

Theatre: Centre Culturel, T 280656, Ave des Nations Unies.

● Hospitals & medical services
Chemist: open nights, two on Ave de la République, T 280876 or T 280257.

● Post & telecommunications
Area code: 02.
Post Office: Ave de la République, Mon-Sat 0730-1230 and 1700-1900 in summer, winter 0800-1200 and 1500-1800. Sun always 0900-1100.

● Sports
All watersports are available, also horse (and camel!) riding, golf, tennis, and go-karting. Ask at any hotel. Yasmin Golf Course, T 282722, has 18 holes, 6,114m and par 72. Cytrus Golf Course, 2 courses of 6,175m at par 72, fees TD 28-30/day. Hot air ballooning. Leisure Centre, T 280656, Ave Bourguiba.

● Tour companies & travel agents
Carthage Tours, rue Dag Hammarskjold, T 280513; *Hammamet Travel Service*, rue Dag Hammarskjold, T 280193; *Tourafrica*, rue Dag Hammarskjold, T 280446; *Tunisian Travel Service*, Ave des Nations Unies, T 280040.

● Tourist offices
The tourist information office is at 32 Ave Bourguiba, by the new shopping complex in town centre, T 280423.

● Useful addresses
Police: Av Habib Bourguiba, T 280079.

● Transport
Local Car hire: Avis, Route de la Gare, T 280164; **Europacar**, Ave des Nations Unies, T 280146; **Hertz**, Ave des Hotels, opp *Hotel Miramar*, T 280187; **Intercar**, Ave des Nations Unies, T 280423; **Topcar**, Ave des Nations Unies, T 281247. **Cycle hire**: TD2/hr or TD10/day from *Hotel Kacem* Centre. **Taxi**: can be hired from in front of the medina. Some attempt is made at destination colour coding, but check.

Train The nearest trains are at Bir Bou Rebka reached by bus or louage. Information T 280174.

Road Bus: the bus station is front of the medina. Frequent departures for **Tunis**, **Sousse** and **Nabeul**.

NORTH TO CAP BON

Nabeul

ACCESS The bus station on Ave Habib Thameur. Taxi rank by hospital on Ave Farhat Hached.

Nabeul, Roman Neapolis, 65 km SE from Tunis, with a population of 40,000, is considered the capital of tourism in Tunisia, though it is difficult to know why.

El Haouaria · Cap Bon
Zembra
Zembretta
Sidi Daoud
Kerkouane
Tazoghrane
C 45
Kelibia · C 27
Gulf of
Tunis
C 26
Korbous · Sidi Aissa
Menzel Temime
Menzel
Bou Zelfa · C 43
Mediterranean
Sea
Potinville · Soliman
C 44
Korba
Grombalia
To
Tunis
Bou Argoub
C 27
To
Zaghouan
Bir Bou Rekba
Nabeul
Hammamet
To
Sousse
0   10
km
C 35
Bou Ficha
Gulf of
Hammamet

CAP BON

MT 142

The centre of the town is only a collection of shops and services for tourists.

Places of interest

Museum, 44 Ave Bourguiba displays local remains. Worth looking in but do not go out of your way, open winter 0930-1630, summer 0800-1200 and 1500-1900, entrance 600 mills, closed Mon.

Nabeul's speciality is **pottery**, its largest industry after tourism. The art of polychrome ceramics was introduced in the 15th century by the Andalusians. Try and visit a workshop to see how the various shapes are achieved. Other local crafts are **straw products**, **ironwork** and **sandstone** carved into intricate patterns (particularly in the village of **Dar Chaabane** 2 km N). In Dar Chaabane the mosque has an interesting, finely-sculpted doorway. Otherwise the town has little charm. On Fri a large market is held, but this is simply a tourist attraction. Busloads of tourists arrive and prices and quality respectively go up and down. Further S you can visit more authentic markets.

The beach, 20 mins walk, has fine sand but promenade has no seats, no shade, no cafés. Neighbouring Hammamet is much more attractive.

Local information
● **Accommodation**

A *Hotel Kheops*, outskirts of Nabeul, T 286555, good restaurant, Olympic size pool, indoor pool, 300 rm, a/c, bath, TV, phone,

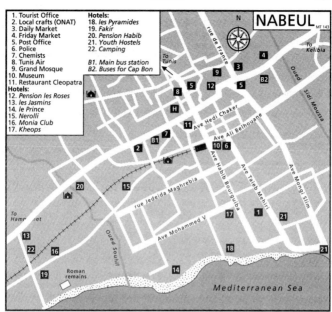

1. Tourist Office
2. Local crafts (ONAT)
3. Daily Market
4. Friday Market
5. Post Office
6. Police
7. Chemists
8. Tunis Air
9. Grand Mosque
10. Museum
11. Restaurant Cleopatra

Hotels:
12. Pension les Roses
13. les Jasmins
14. le Prince
15. Nerolli
16. Monia Club
17. Kheops

Hotels:
18. les Pyramides
19. Fakir
20. Pension Habib
21. Youth Hostels
22. Camping

B1. Main bus station
B2. Buses for Cap Bon

NABEUL MT 143

terrace, watersports, tennis, disco.

B *Hotel Les Pyramides*, E end of Ave Bourguiba, T 285444, large hotel with accommodation in 350 bungalows, beach, pool, organized activities.

C *Hotel les Jasmins*, Ave Habib Thameur, T 280222, 188 beds, an older hotel, comfortable, not central.

D *Hotel Fakir*, opp the Roman remains of Neapolis, T 285477, brand new, small, pleasant rm, 200m from beach, very welcoming owner prefers individual travellers to groups.

F *Pension el Habib*, Ave Habib Thameur, T 287190 outskirts of Nabeul coming from Hammamet, beach, very clean, communal bath/toilets, all rm with handbasin, roof terrace, main road is slightly noisy; **F** *Pension Les Roses*, rue Farhat Hached, T 285570, clean, well kept, central, communal bath/toilets.

Youth hostels: 2 km from town centre at the end of Ave Mongi Slim, by the beach, T 285547, 56 beds, closed all Feb. Also *Centre de Séjour et de Vacances 'La Gazelle'*, T 221366, 70 beds, meals available. Also *Maison des Jeunes*, Ave Taieb Mehiri,

T 86689, 80 beds, clean, meals available, don't expect hot water.

Camping: *Hotel les Jasmins*, on the road to Hammamet, 1 km out of town, hot/cold water, shop, restaurant, outdoor theatre in an extensive orange grove.

● **Places to eat**
◆◆*Les Oliviers*, T 286613, Ave Hedi Chaker.

◆*Cleopatra*, Ave Habib Bourguiba, small, clean; *Karim* snack bar in central square; *La Rotonde*, T 285782, Ave Taieb Mehiri. Also restaurants down by the beach.

● **Banks & money changers**
Most banks are on Ave Bourguiba and Ave Farhat Hached, in the town centre.

● **Entertainment**
Nightclub: *Monia Club*, T 285713, route de l'Hotel Neapolis.

Theatre: *Maison de la Culture*, T 286817, Ave Farhat Hached.

● **Post & telecommunications**
Area code: 02.
Post Office: main office, Ave Bourguiba, open Mon-Sat 0800-1800, also Ave Mongi Slim.

● **Shopping**

Crafts are the best buys. Visit *ONAT* on Ave Thameur to see the local products and check the prices without having to buy them. The traditional green/yellow pottery is a good buy. The wrought iron, like the stone carvings, are very weighty items to fit in your suitcase!

● **Tourist offices**

The tourist information office stands back from road on Ave Taieb Mehiri, T 286737. Towards the beach, from town centre. Bus and train times are normally posted outside the office. Closed in winter.

● **Useful addresses**

Police: Ave Habib Bourguiba, T 285474; Garde National, Ave Taieb Mehri, T 286153.

● **Transport**

Local Car hire: Avis, *Hotel Kheops*, T 286555; **Hertz**, Ave Thameur, T 285327; **Europcar**, Ave Farhat Hached, T 287085; **Rent a Car**, Ave Thameur, T 286679; **Matei**, Ave Bourguiba, T 285967; **Nova Rent**, Ave Habib Bourguiba, T 222072.

Train The nearest trains are at Bir Bou Rebka reached by bus or louage. Information T 285054.

Road The bus station is on Ave Thameur. Information on T 285261. Frequent buses to **Hammamet** starting at 0530, **Tunis** (every half hour), **Kelibia**, **Zaghouan** 8 each day, **Sousse** starting at 0645, **Mahdia** starting at 0730 and **Kairouan** (direct at 0600, 0800 and 1215).

Korba

14 km N of Nabeul, is a small village on Oued Bou Eddine used by *Club Mediterrané*. Its remains of a Roman aqueduct are worth a visit. A rough road inland leads up to a reservoir. **Youth hostel**, 100 beds, meals provided, family rm, T 289296.

Menzel Temime, 27 km N of Korba, has a **Youth hostel**, 40 beds, T 298116.

Kelibia

This is a small, pleasantly authentic, modern fishing village dominated by an impressive 7th century Byzantine fortress sitting on the hill. The village offers the visitor peace and quiet, particularly welcome if coming from Nabeul. The best beaches are situated 2-3 km N of Kelibia at the NE corner of Cap Bon.

Places of interest

The Byzantine fort is much restored. Turn right off main road N of the village for a magnificent view. Entrance TD3, free for students. Excavations in vicinity of Fort are of Roman Clupea. Alternate years in Jul an international amateur film festival is held here. Watch fishermen at night using power lamps to catch sardines, anchovies and mackerel.

Local information

● **Accommodation**

D *Ennassim*, by the sea, T 296245, rm around a small courtyard.

E *Florida*, by the sea, T 296248, small hotel next door to *Ennassim*, most rm with sea view, shaded terrace.

Youth hostel: T 296105, 80 beds, on the road to Mansoura, by the sea.

● **Places to eat**

The restaurants in both the hotels are good, as is *Café Sidi el Bahri* by the port where it is pleasant to have a drink in the afternoon and watch the fishing boats return. Try the fish, it should be fresh!

♦♦♦*El Mansoura*, T 296321, and *Cluppea*, T 296296, both on the beach, in very good setting, fish dishes rec.

♦♦*Le Relais*, T 296173, route de la Plage. Kelibia is noted for its dry wine. Try in particular the Muscat sec de Kelibia.

● **Sports**

Some watersports are available but the resort is not really set up for this. Harbour has berths for 20 yachts, min-max draft 2-5m.

● **Transport**

Road Buses leave every hour in the morning to El Haouaria and there are frequent departures to Nabeul. Bus from Tunis leaves from Bab Aliona.

Sea An interesting hydrofoil link with Trapani in Sicily is advertised during the summer, taking 4 hrs and carrying up to 180 passengers.

Kerkouane

About 12 km N from Kelibia and halfway between Kelibia and El Haouaria a small signposted road goes down towards the sea and the site. This remarkable example of the only purely Punic town, still well preserved, is thought to have been built in 6th century BC and abandoned following the fall of Carthage to the Romans. It was never inhabited after that time, which accounts for its good state. The street layout and house foundations are clearly visible, with all the houses following the same pattern of rooms round a central courtyard. All the houses had baths, saying something about the sophistication of Punic civilization. The main economic activity seems to have been the manufacture of an expensive purple dye from decomposed shell fish. Perhaps this explains the baths! Open 0830-1730 except Mon. Entrance TD1, photography TD1.

El Haouaria

ACCESS The louages and bus station are on Ave Bourguiba in the town centre.

12 km NE from Kerkouane, is El Haouaria, a small village famous for its falconry festival and its position at the end of the Cap Bon peninsula. The village itself is of little interest, but the surrounding countryside and beaches are delightful.

Places of interest
The **Falconry Festival** is held each May. 3 km from the village on the shore near the extremity of the Cap are the **Ghar el Kebirk Caves**. It is thought that the rock quarried from here was used to build parts of Carthage. You are advised to let the official guide show you round as he knows more than the unofficial ones! The mountains along the coast and behind the villages offer interesting walks.

Towards the end of the Cap Bon peninsula there is a beautiful little beach, **Ras Ed Drak**, which is quite secluded and still relatively unknown. It is 4 km from the village along a road leading to the end of the peninsula. The view from

the end of **Cap Bon** is superb. It is said that on a clear night the lights of Sicily, 140 km away, can be seen.

Local information
● **Accommodation**
D *De l'Eperrier*, Ave Bourguiba, T 297017, F 297258, 10 rm, with bath, very good restaurant.

● **Places to eat**
Restaurant in *De l'Eperrier* (English spoken) rec. Try *Les Grottes*, T 297296, Grottes Romaines, and cheaper *Fruits de la Mer*, Ave Hedi Chaker, with fresh fish.

● **Banks & money changers**
BNA and STB on Ave Bourguiba nr the Post Office.

● **Post & telecommunications**
Post Office: At the start of Ave Bourguiba, by the louages and bus station.

● **Sports**
Hunting, enquire at the Association de Chasseurs de Tunis for details of quail, woodcock, partridge and hare hunting.

● **Transport**
Road There is an irregular bus service, either via the N coast from Tunis (but this takes a while because the bus stops everywhere) or via Kelibia. **Louage**: taking a louage is much faster.

CAP BON SOUTH TO TUNIS

Sidi Daoud

This small fishing village along the coast road to Korbous has a large and obtrusive fish canning plant. It hosts a traditional Fishing Festival in late May/early Jun each year. This festival, known as the *Matanza*, is quite violent, as the large tuna fish are caught in nets, dragged towards the shore and then harpooned, filling the sea with blood. Pacifists might prefer the splendid view from the village towards the island of Zembra. Bus from Bab el Fellah in Tunis.

Korbous

ACCESS From Sidi Daoud the road turns inland. Just beyond Sidi Aïssa at Bir Meroua you should turn right and go towards Korbous. This is a very scenic road which circles the hill and, on reaching the coast, follows the cliff with the sea literally below. The view towards La Goulette and Sidi Bou Saïd is very impressive. Worth the detour even if you have no intention of stopping at Korbous. The *Restaurant Dhrib* serves very good, cheap meals. There is only one café, down by the sea, with a large terrace.

A small thermal spa resort five springs, with prospects of expansion, overlooking the sea, Korbous was first discovered and used by the Romans. On the hilltop is a beautiful villa, previously used by Bourguiba as one of his summer resorts. The thermal institute and its baths which could be cleaner, can be visited and used. Strange atmosphere as many visitors have come for health reasons.

At **Aïn Atrous** the spring of heated sulphurous water (50°C) goes straight into the sea.

Local information
● **Accommodation**
Most of the hotels are expensive and used by the people undergoing treatment at the spa.

A *Aïn Oktor*, T 294552, 4 km along the road to Soliman, 30 rm, overlooking the sea, no beach, thermal cures; **A** *Chiraz*, Route de Korbous, T 293230; **A** *Les Sources*, T 294533, large terrace overlooking the sea, 140 rm, thermal cures, pool;

● **Places to eat**
Chez Korbsi in town centre and *La Brise* at Sidi Rair.

Excursions
Grombalia and **Menzel Bou Zelfa**, about 40 km SE of Tunis are inland villages worth visiting. At Grombalia in Sep there is a Wine Festival, while Menzel Bou Zelfa has an Orange Festival in Apr-May. Menzel Bou Zelfa, 44 km from Tunis on the C43, can be reached via Soliman and Grombalia, 41 km from Tunis, is on the main P1 from Tunis to Hammamet and the main railway line from Tunis.

Zembra and Zembretta are small islands off the end of Cap Bon with steep cliffs making access difficult. The sea for 1.5 nautical miles beyond low tide is designated as a *nature reserve* with no fishing allowed. Grey puffins nest here.

<table>
<tr><td colspan="2">**CONTENTS**</td></tr>
</table>

Tunis to Bizerte   405
From Bizerte to Tabarka   411
Tabarka to Ain Draham
  and Le Kef   414
Le Kef to Teboursouk and Tunis   419

MAPS

Bizerte   407
Northern Tunisia   410
Tabarka   413
Bulla Regia   416
Dougga   420

The N of Tunisia has so far escaped the mass tourism of elsewhere in the country, but this may not be for long as there are many impressive Roman sites to visit and the landscape is exceedingly attractive. In summer the temperature is high but more bearable than in the S, with the mountains and thickly wooded areas behind the coast being most welcoming. The coast between Bizerte and the Algerian border offers steep cliffs, small bays and many secluded beaches, well off the main routes. The towns of Bizerte, Tabarka and Le Kef have much to interest the traveller and the Roman remains in Dougga are not to be missed.

Small villages permit sights of pink pinafored school girls, boys in blue smocks and seasonal farm produce on sale on road side – melons, grapes, live chickens.

TUNIS TO BIZERTE

Bizerte

ACCESS Bizerte is 64 km from Tunis, bus Nos 44 and 62, 1 hr by taxi, a pleasant, slightly hilly, journey through fairly fertile farmland with large areas of olive and citrus. Leave Tunis on the P8 heading NNW for Bizerte. The road crosses the wide flood plain of the Oued Medjerda, the only permanently flowing river in the country and the river responsible for the alluvial deposits which silted up the bay and reduced important trading ports to insignificance.

History
(*Pop* 400,000; *Alt* 5m) Bizerte is the biggest town on the N coast and the fourth largest town in Tunisia. Its history goes back to Punic times when the natural harbour attracted the Phoenician sailors. The town was destroyed with the fall of Carthage, but later rebuilt by Caesar. Conquered by the Arabs in 661, Bizerte expanded during the Hafsid Dynasty. The arrival of the Moors from Spain in the 17th century, as in other cities in Tunisia, gave it a new lease of life and guaranteed its fortune. The opening of the Suez Canal in 1869, and the arrival, in 1882, of the French who appreciated its strategically important position and turned the town into a naval arsenal, were other important factors in Bizerte's development.

Since Independence the industrial sector has expanded. There is an oil refinery and a large ironworks. Bizerte lies N of the swing bridge over the 8 km long canal which joins the inland Lake of Bizerte (111 sq km and noted for its oysters and mussels) to the open sea. The road from the bridge leads into the regular grid pattern of streets, a legacy of the French, beyond which lies the well preserved medina and the old port. The town is currently undergoing an expan-

406 Tunisia – The North

sion of the tourist infrastructure.

Places of interest

The old harbour is charming with its blue and white houses overlooking the fishing boats and in the evening it has a different but equally pleasant atmosphere. From there you can penetrate into the **kasbah**, the old fortified town. The labyrinth of little streets with painted walls is fascinating to walk through and, leaving the old town, you can wander into the newer medina, peeping into doorways where craftsmen can be seen at work using techniques that are centuries old. The new city is of little interest except for the bustling life and cafés. **Local markets** are held. The main market is behind the old harbour and there is another on Ave Taieb Mehiri, before the town hall. Bizerte has an **Oceanographic Museum** which is not as impressive as it sounds. There are some good **beaches** on either side of the town, but the most popular one is at Remel, over the bridge to the S. North of town the Corniche with hotels and restaurants leads to Cap Blanc, an old fort and scrubland used for picnics.

Festival of Sidi el Béchir, 1st Thur in Sep; Festival of Bizerte Jul/Aug; International Festival of Mediterranean music alternate years.

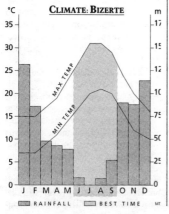

CLIMATE: BIZERTE

Excursions

Utica is an old Roman city of which little remains. The museum on the site contains a few small items of interest. Worth a visit if transport is available but a long walk on a hot day for little reward. It is 2.5 km E from the new town of **Utique**, on the main road. The site is clearly signposted. The museum is on the left, shade for parking and picnics, and the site itself is another 500m down the road. Open winter 0800-1700, summer 0800-1800, closed Mon and public holidays. Entrance TD1 and TD1 photography charge.

Like many ancient cities in Tunisia, Utica founded in 1101 BC was first a Punic city, later taken over by the Romans. It was, at one stage, the first capital of the Roman province of Africa and, as such, rich in public monuments. The city used to be by the sea, exporting agricultural produce from its rich farmlands. Utica's collapse, like that of other Roman cities, came with the invasions by the Vandals and the Byzantines. The final fall was the Arab conquest.

The Roman site is not extensive and has only been partially excavated. It is a beautiful position. The most visible monuments are the pool and wells in the **House of the Cascades**, centred around a patio. Some mosaics depicting fishing scenes are still well preserved under wooden covers. Look out for the Chemtou marble as well as white and green marble from Greece. The Punic necropolis can be seen next to the pool.

The **Museum** is very small, divided into two rooms. The Punic room has some gold brooches and earrings of 4th-3rd centuries BC, oil lamps from 7th-1st centuries BC, vases from Greece and Italy indicating trade and small sarcophagi for the bones and ashes of children who, according to legend, were sacrificed here. The Roman room has statues, an inscription from 1st-2nd centuries AD, a mosaic of a hunting scene and an interesting diagram of the excavations of the House of Cascades. There is no accommodation at Utica.

Kalaat el Andalous village stands on what was a headland before the sea retreated, an agricultural area, mainly vines. Houses are part of Medjerda development project sponsored by World Bank. Market day, Wed. Beside main mosque are post office, bank, petrol and Haj Ali café. The views S and E to **Sidi Bou Saïd** and **Cap Bon** are well worth the walk.

Also worth a visit is **Cap Blanc**, a rocky headland just 10 km N of Bizerte. This is the most N tip of Africa and is very beautiful.

Local information
● **Accommodation**

Most of the large hotels are situated on the Corniche which is about 3 km out of the town.

C *Corniche*, route de la Corniche, T 431844, F 431830, 4 km out of town, low season prices acceptable, beach, 87 rm with sea view, fly screens, no a/c, pool, many organized activi-

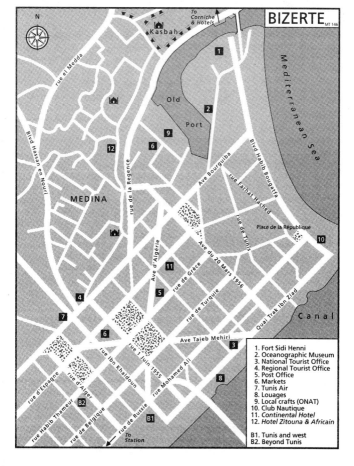

1. Fort Sidi Henni
2. Oceanographic Museum
3. National Tourist Office
4. Regional Tourist Office
5. Post Office
6. Markets
7. Tunis Air
8. Louages
9. Local crafts (ONAT)
10. Club Nautique
11. *Continental Hotel*
12. *Hotel Zitouna & Africain*

B1. Tunis and west
B2. Beyond Tunis

ties, large nightclub, fully booked in summer; **C** *Nador*, T 431846, next to *Corniche* and very similar, 105 rm, beach, pool, no disco, tennis, fully booked in summer.

D *Petit Mousse*, route de la Corniche, T 432185, very pleasant, 12 rm, good atmosphere, beach across the road, excellent restaurant, eat outside in summer.

F *Continental*, rue d'Istambul, T 431436, probably one of the best deals if you want a cold shower and a clean, cheap bed, but don't expect much else; **F** *Hotel Africain*, next to and similar to *Zitouna*, on edge of medina, T 434412; **F** *Zitouna*, place Slaheddine Bouchoucha, T 431447, edge of the medina, very noisy external rooms, no showers.

Youth hostels: 1 km N of city centre up Blvd Hassan en Nouri, beyond the medina on route de la Corniche, kitchen, meals provided, 100 beds, T 431608. Also *Remel Plage*, 3 km from city centre, any bus going S of the canal will stop at the turn off, 50 beds, closed Feb, T 440804.

Camping: camping is permitted at Remel Plage hostel.

● **Places to eat**
◆◆*Belle Plage*, Corniche, T 431817; *L'Eden* on Corniche, T 439023 for seafood; *Le Petit Mousse*, in *Hotel Petit Mousse*, excellent food and fresh fish, not cheap but worth the price.

◆*La Mamma*, T 433695, rue Ibn Khaldoun, sells pizzas and pancakes; *Restaurant de la Liberté*, next door to *Hotel Continental*, good, cheap food.

● **Banks & money changers**
The banks arrange a rota so one always stays open later. **BNT**, rue 1er Juin; **STB**, rue Farhat Hached, there is also another branch behind the ONAT, by the old harbour; **CFCT**, Ave Bourguiba which takes Eurocheque and Visa.

● **Hospital & medical services**
Chemist: all night, 18 rue Ali Belhaoane, T 432461.

Hospital: on rue du 3 Août, T 431422.

● **Post & telecommunications**
Area code: 02.
Post Office: main office, 6 Ave d'Algérie, takes parcels as well. Around the back of main building is the telecommunications office, also on rue el Medina and place Pasteur.

● **Shopping**
Visit the *ONAT* office just by the old harbour.

They have a good selection of regional art. Bizerte specializes in ironwork, woodwork, pottery, carpets and embroidery.

● **Sports**
Club Nautique, T 432262, on the right of the main beach in town, hires out surfboards and does various other watersports. Sub-aqua fishing is very popular. Otherwise try one of the hotels on the Corniche. The *Corniche* hotel organizes water skiing and rents surfboards. Horse riding is offered at some of the hotels. Some of the big hotels and small enterprises hire out bicycles, which is a cheap way of getting to the beach. Municipal swimming pool (heated) on Blvd Hassan en Nouri. Marina for 100 boats.

● **Tour companies & travel agents**
Tourafrica, Ave Bourguiba, T 432315; *Transtour*, rue d'Alger, T 432174; *Via Bizerte*, rue 1er Mai, T 432901.

● **Tourist offices**
National Tourist Office (ONTT), 1 rue d'Istambul, T 432703/432897. The office is hard to find. It is situated by the canal, about 100m before the bridge, towards the sea. Will provide a map of Tunisia, a map of Bizerte and information about places to stay in the region.

● **Useful addresses**
Police: T 431200, rue du 20 Mars 1956

● **Transport**
Local Bicycles & Motorbike hire: Ben Othman, Ave Bourguiba; **Ben Kilani**, Ave Bourguiba, T 431622 and **Ben Aleya**, rue Sassi Bahri. **Car hire**: Avis, 7 rue d'Alger, T 433076; **Budget**, 7 rue d'Alger, T 432174; **Europcar**, 52 Ave d'Algérie, T 439018; **Hertz**, Place des Martyrs, T 433679; **Inter Rent**, 19 rue Mohammed Rejiba, T 431455. **Shipping Co**. **Navitour**, 29 Ave d'Algérie, T 431440.

Air The nearest airport is Tunis. Information from Tunis Air, 76 Ave Bourguiba, T 432201.

Train The station is approx 15 mins walk SW along canal out of town. Information on T 431317. To Tunis 0540, 0810, 1350, 1835.

Road Bus: the main bus station is by the bridge over the canal. A short walk N up Ave d'Algérie to the town centre. Information on T 431222/431317. Bus station for places W is on rue d'Alger. Frequent buses to **Tunis** and **Ras Djebel**; change at Ras Djebel for **Raf Raf** and **Ghar el Melh**; **Aïn Draham** (via Tabarka) leaves early morning. **Louages**: leave by the canal under the bridge to all destinations, but some are harder to obtain if the demand is low. Louages terminate on the Quai Trak Ibn Ziad under the bridge or at the N end of Ave d'Algérie. Sometimes available at the station.

Sea Navitour, 29 Ave d'Algérie, T 431440.

Ras Djebel

This is a large modern settlement on the coast E of Bizerte on the road to the beaches of Raf Raf. The town has a café, a patisserie called FSRD and *Hotel Okba* but not much else of interest. By contrast the surrounding area is very beautiful. The beach at Ras Djebel is very crowded in the summer and as most people prefer to camp near the town, anywhere further W is better. To the N, Cap Zebib offers magnificent views and the road from Bizerte to Ras Djebel is very scenic with a panoramic view over the coast by Bizerte. On the beach is a tiny marina with fishing boats. Drive with care as the road stops dead 1m from cliff edge...those in the know turn left.

Raf Raf

ACCESS The buses from Bizerte, Ras Djebel and Tunis stop just by the beach. Bus No 1B from Tunis.

The town of Raf Raf at the top of the hill which houses the well-to-do of Tunis in attractive villas is not particularly special. Take the steep (10%) road to Raf Raf plage which is very beautiful. The white sand backed by dunes and the settlement extending virtually to the beach makes it a unique setting. Unfortunately there is little accommodation. It makes a pleasant day excursion from either Tunis or Bizerte. Consequently in the summer, on Fri market and especially at weekends, Raf Raf gets very crowded with trippers and the approach roads become jammed with cars. Raf Raf produces the best table grapes in Tunisia, on sale, in season, all along the road.

The Ile Pilau just off the coast, looks just like a fortress and makes an interesting photographic subject.

Local information
● Accommodation

It is possible to stay in straw huts on the beaches which can be rented overnight for about TD10, but you will have to bring everything you need.

C *Hotel Dalia*, small, only 22 rm, about half have sea view, very clean, close to beach, open all year, expensive due to location.

● Places to eat

The restaurant in the *Hotel Dalia* is good, clean and cheap. There are a few other restaurants along the beach, try *Restaurant Andalous*, but they tend to be overpriced.

Locals are occupied making traditional bird cages to sell to tourists.

● Transport

Road Bus: departures for Bizerte and Ras Djebel. Three daily to Tunis. **Louages**: also available, but in summer towards the end of the day it can be quite crowded as everybody is leaving. Hitching may take time as most cars are already full.

Ghar el Melh

ACCESS Ghar el Melh via Aousdja is served by buses Nos 5 and 3A from Tunis and Bizerte. There are no buses E to Sidi Ali el-Mekki.

This is a clean, S facing fishing village by a shallow salt lagoon with a notorious past of piracy and smuggling. Very busy in season, quality restaurants. The road continues past the village and on 6 km to the splendid beach of **Ras Sidi Ali el Mekki** with a small café/shop and straw cubicles for camping, rented at TD5/day. At the end of the peninsula, built partially into the cliff is the *marabout* of Sidi Ali el Mekki, a place of pilgrimage. This is an attractive and secluded spot.

Sounine

Further N, has rocky beach, expensive villas, show huts for rent on beach, café Budan on corner, also *Café l'Escale* for coffee and snacks. In spring every electricity pylon has a storks' nest. In autumn the fields are full of tall white squills.

Metline

This is a small town built into the hillside. Take the road round it to the W for a splendid view. **El Alia**, built on the crossroads, is a splendid example of the settlements built by returnees from Andalucía. Here thistles are grown for the felting of *chechias* (see page 379). The road SW from here towards Menzel Bourguiba has been upgraded and is very busy. Once across the P8 it skirts the lake shore. Good views as no buildings beside lake.

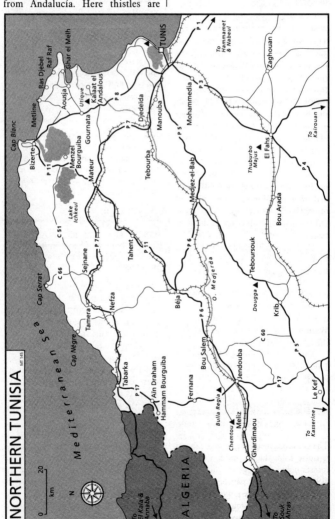

NORTHERN TUNISIA MT 145

Menzel Bourguiba

A large provincial town on the W side of Lake Bizerte with nothing particular to attract visitors. The pollution it produces is most unpleasant. Menzel Bourguiba does make a good base from which to visit Lake Ichkeul.

Lake Ichkeul

This animal sanctuary of 12,600 ha, 1m-3m deep, is 25 km away and is arguably the most interesting of Tunisia's six National Parks. Access off P11 S of Menzel Bourguiba just after the railway crossing. Water birds and waders are among the thousands of over-wintering migrants found here and 75 species of mammal such as water buffalo, wild boar, porcupine, otter and jackal and around 500 species of reptile live in this protected marsh/lake/mountain habitat. Expeditions to watch the 180 species of bird (best Mar, Apr and Nov) are offered by some tour agents. The Tourist Office in Bizerte arranges visits to the reserve.

There is a small Ecological museum high above a car park overlooking the lake. Minor road beyond the museum is closed to traffic but walkers are welcome on the circular route round Djebel Ichkeul. The numerous tracks across the dry lake floor are not recommended. **Warning** The minor road marked S of the lake to the C51 does not exist.

Water flows from Lake Ichkeul into Lake of Bizerte via Oued Tindja which is only 5 km long.

FROM BIZERTE TO TABARKA

The coast between Bizerte and Tabarka is quite wild, the sea hidden by thick forests noted as refuge for the last lion (1925) and the last panther (1932) in Tunisia. The coastline is worth trying to reach, especially if you like deserted beaches, although access is difficult. By car from Bizerte to Tabarka take the road W towards Menzel Bourguiba and turn right 5 km after Bizerte on the C51, in the direction of **Sejnane**. This road, running in a valley for much of the way, is very beautiful. At Sejnane the route rejoins the main road to **Nefza** and **Tabarka**.

Sejnane

This is a pretty mountain village rich in metal ores and producing unusually decorated pottery, animals and statuettes, in Berber style. Packed with donkeys, Peugeot trucks and women in colourful tribal dress on market day, Thur. It is a good base from which to visit these attractive and very secluded N beaches, though you will need to have your own transport or be very lucky with lifts. Don't set off for any of these out of the way coastal spots without plenty of provisions.

On the C51, 11 km from Sejnane turn right at the cross roads (signposted) to **Cap Serrat**. This is a headland with a lighthouse and a good, often deserted, beach. It may be possible to buy food at the kiosk on the beach – but don't rely on it.

At Tamera, 10 km before Nefza on the Bizerte road, turn right and follow the winding track signed 'plage' for about 10 km. At the end there is a small fishing village, **Sidi Mechrig**, overlooked by a Roman fortress, and, of course, a beautiful beach. People set up camp here for the summer. There is a hotel. Leaving Tamera, branching from the Sidi Mechrig track, there is a rough scenic ride to the coast at **Cap Negro**, an area once known for its coral fishing.

The closest beach to Tabarka is **Zouara** beach, only 20 km before the town. Turn right off the Bizerte road before Aïn Sebna (a sign indicates the way) and follow a fairly easy track for 5 km. This is a beautiful beach with fine sand, but again there is no infrastructure whatsoever.

Tabarka

ACCESS The louage station is on the main street Ave Bourguiba. From the long distance bus station on rue du Peuple turn left down the hill to the central square. The local bus station is about 50m up the hill from the main square. The airport lies 9km E of town at Ras Rajel.

A minor seaside resort, 175 km W from Tunis, situated where the forested slopes of the Khroumirie range meet the sea. It is a magnificent setting and although this small resort is being enlarged the new hotel complex, good quality and well designed, is situated to the E of town and does not intrude. By the seafront, in town, Porto Corallo has been sympathetically developed with a new hotel, marina and restaurant. The wrecks in the bay add a gruesome interest.

The origins of the town can be traced back to Haron (5th century BC) who is said to have established a trading post here. The Phoenician town was called *Thabraca* meaning 'place in the shade'. As a 3rd century Roman town it was noted for its trade in 'big cats', export of wood for building, lead and iron from its mines and the yellow marble (see Chemtou page 416).

Thabraca played an important role in developments associated with luxurious buildings – painters, decorators, sculptors and ceramic artists made it the town of 'arts'. Mosaic artists founded a school here whose prestige won wide renown abroad for 3 centuries.

The town prospered with the spread of Christianity in the 5th century and especially during the reign of the Fatmides in the 10th century. In the 16th century it regained its status as a strategic harbour for merchant shipping. More than once the Genoese took possession of it, only to lose it again. It was taken by Tunisia in the 18th century and acted as a fortress in WW2 under the French Protectorate.

Places of interest

Tabarka is the centre for diving on the N coast and the diving centre in the Yachting club on the seafront is open all year. The club also organizes other watersport activities including underwater photography. In autumn, hunting, especially of wild boars, is an expanding tourist industry. Archaeological museum open 0830-1730 winter, 0900-1300 and 1500-1900 summer, closed Mon, entrance TD1.

From the town walk along the coast past the old fort built by the Genoese to the **Aiguilles** (needles), carved out of the rock by sea and wind. The view from the top of the old fort is impressive and worth the effort of walking up. An 18 hole golf course has recently been opened along Route Touristique. The course overlooking the sea is in 100 ha of pine and oak forest. Coral jewellery is on sale and there is a **coral festival** in Jul with street fairs and markets when the town is certainly more lively. Market Fri. There is a **WW2 cemetery** with 500 graves 15 km E of town on the P7, open 0730-1430, Sat-Thur.

La Galite is a small archipelago of seven islands (Gallo, Plastro, Ganton and Galite are the largest) in the Mediterranean about 60 km from Tabarka. A few fishermen, wine producers and their families live here. There are remains of Roman tombs and Punic relics. Contact the Tourist Office in Tabarka from a visit here. It is a restricted area for fishing and a classified **nature reserve** with colonies of walrus.

Local information
● **Accommodation**
The new A/B grade hotels along Route Touristique have increased the number of beds available but in summer booking is essential.

A *Abou Nawas Montazah*, T 644532/508, F 644530, 306 rm with balcony, phone, heating, no a/c, no fly screens, Olympic size pool, beach site, tennis, windsurfing, scuba diving tuition, exercise rm and sauna, minimal carpeting so noise echoes through hotel at every step.

Look out for **A** *Grande Hotel* currently under construction in the Porto Corallo complex in the marina.

B *Iberotel Mehari*, T 644088, F 644505, 200 rm, much quieter than Montazah, good restaurant, pool, beach site, tennis; **B** *Morjane*, on the road behind the sand dunes, T 644453, 160 rm, the first hotel built on the beach, very convenient.

C *Les Mimosas*, on the left as you enter the town, T 644376, on top of a hill overlooking the bay, pool, 70 rm with sea view.

E *De France*, Ave Bourguiba, T 644577, 38 beds, restaurant, old fashioned charm, probably the best of the cheap hotels but has certainly known better days; **E** *Hotel Corail*, 76 Ave Bourguiba, 50 beds, cheap, but only rec if funds are low or everything else is full; **E** *Hotel de la Plage*, rue des Pecheurs, T 644039, 14 beds; **E** *Hotel Novelty*, Ave

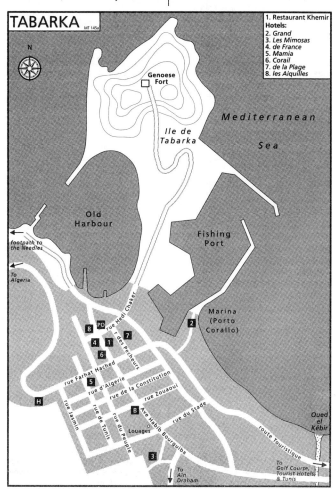

Bourguiba, brand new, central, very clean.

● **Places to eat**
All on Ave Habib Bourguiba.

◆◆*Hotel de France*, good food at very decent prices.

◆*Hotel Corail*; *Les Agriculteurs*, T 644585, good, cheap, very filling food; *Novelty 66*, T 644367.

● **Banks & money changers**
BNT and UIB on Ave Bourguiba; BNA on rue de Peuple.

● **Hospital and medical services**
Hospital: on rue de Calle, T 644023.

● **Post & telecommunications**
Area code: 08.
Post Office: Ave Hedi Chaker, T 644417. Mon-Fri 0830-1230 and 1500-1800, Sat 0830-1330.

● **Shopping**
Handicrafts: include olive wood carvings, basket work, carpets, Berber pottery and Tabarka briar pipes.

● **Sport**
Deep sea diving: Scuba Diving Club, Port de Tabarka, T 644478, the first sub-aqua sports centre in Tunisia, open all year, best season Apr-Oct. Dive sites only 15 mins by boat.

Golf: 18 hole course, 6,400m, par 72, fees TD30-35/day.

Horse riding: can be arranged at the hotels.

Hunting: Hunting Club, Route d'Aïn Draham, T 644417.

Sailing: the marina has 50 moorings with planned extension to 280 berths.

Tennis: at the hotels.

● **Tourist office**
32 Ave Bourguiba, T 644491, open 0900-1200 and 1600-1900, after the main square on the right. Only basic information.

● **Useful addresses**
Police station: on rue du Peuple, T644021; Maritime police, Port de Tabarka; Border police, Melloula, T 644317.

● **Transport**
Local Car hire: Hertz, Port Corallo, T 644570.

Air Internal flights to Tunis Fri 1600, Sun 1830 take 40 mins. From Tunis Fri 1450, Sun 1730.

Road Tuf tuf: from tourist hotels to ma-

rina/old harbour along tourist road. Leaves on the hour from old harbour. The long distance bus station is in rue du Peuple (1st street on the right going uphill from the central square). Information on T 444048. Departures Tunis (via Mateur) 0400, 0500, 0730, 0900, 1545; Tunis (via Béja) 0600, 1000, 1300. The local bus station is 50m uphill from the central square. Frequent departures to Aïn Draham and Jendouba. Two buses a day to Bizerte. Information on T 644097. Louages: the station is at the beginning of Ave Bourguiba. Departures for Jendouba, Aïn Draham, Le Kef and sometimes Tunis.

TABARKA TO AIN DRAHAM AND LE KEF

The road from Tabarka S to Aïn Draham is a typical mountain road and very scenic, with a wonderful view towards the coast. At Babouch there is a turning W to Hammam Bourguiba, 17 km, a thermal spa greatly prized by the Romans. Ruins here of vaulted arches, high rendered brick walls and columns with ornamental capitals. There are two springs the lower emerging at 38.5°C and the higher at 50°C with different chemical properties said to relieve respiratory conditions. **E** *Hotel Hammam Bourguiba*, T (086) 32517, F (086) 32497 open all year, has 40 rm and 20 bungalows and is used by Tunisians taking treatment. This road also leads to the Algerian border but the crossing in this area has about 10 km between control posts, a walk not to be undertaken lightly. Border post at Babouch, T 647150.

Aïn Draham

Aïn Draham, which means 'silver spring', lies 175 km W of Tunis and 26 km S of Tabarka. It is known as a spa town. It is a very picturesque village surrounded by thick cork-oak forests way up at 1,000m in the mountains. It is an ideal place in summer away from the unpleasant heat, but can be quite chilly in winter when snow is common. Aïn

Draham is also the heart of the wild boar hunting region and it can be difficult to find places in hotels during the season from Oct to Mar. It is a quaint little town with one steep, central street (one way), and is important as a market town for the region. Housing has spread to other side of valley.

Places of interest

The Association du Patrimoine Populaire et Historique Aïn Draham is found in a small office where products of the regional arts are displayed. It is interesting and the people are very welcoming.

Just N of Aïn Draham, to the W of the road, is Col de Ruines. This small detour has splendid views as does the terrace of *Hotel Nour el Aïn*.

Benir Metir is a spectacular detour off the main road S of Aïn Draham. It is one of Tunisia's largest reservoirs on a tributary of the Oued Medjerda.

Local information
● Accommodation
B *Hammam Bourguiba*, in Hammam Bourguiba, T 647217.

C *Hotel Nour el Aïn*, T 655000, F 655185, 60 rm, open all year, covered heated pool, health club, international menu, busiest in hunting season.

D *Beau Séjour*, Ave Bourguiba, T 647005, 30 rm, an old hunting lodge, restaurant, central, book in summer; **D** *Les Chênes*, T 647211, 32 rm, out of town, 7 km towards Jendouba, looking very worn, good, food, rather secluded, set in the middle of the forest; **D** *Rehana*, T 647391, at the S end of the village on the road to Jendouba, 75 rm, comfortable hotel with a very memorable view overlooking the valley, within walking distance of the village, book in summer.

Youth hostel: is at the top of the hill, kitchen, 150 beds, T 647087.

● Places to eat
◆◆*Grand Maghreb* is good but expensive.

◆*Café de la Republique*, on Av 7 Novembre is rec.

● Banks & money changers
Are all on Ave Bourguiba. **BNT**, **STB** are opp Association du Patrimoine, and **BNA** is beyond the Tourist Office.

● Hospitals & medical services
Hospital: is on route de l'Hôpital, T 647047.

● Post & telecommunications
Area code: 08.
Post Office: Ave Bourguiba, T 647118, further up the road after the Association du Patrimoine.

● Sport
Wild boar hunting and woodcock shooting are advertised for this region in winter. Huge new sports complex 6 km S of town.

● Tourist office
Syndicat D'Initiative, Ave Bourguiba, towards the top, T 647115.

● Useful addresses
Police: Ave Bourguiba, T 647150.

● Transport
Road The bus station is at the bottom of Ave Bourguiba, on the right, by the cemetery. Frequent buses to **Tunis**, **Jendouba** and **Tabarka**. **Louages**: the station is situated at the top of Ave Bourguiba, on the square. Main routes are to <F85MJendouba and **Tabarka**.

Bulla Regia

ACCESS Bulla Regia lies 3 km E of the Aïn Draham-Jendouba road. Take a bus from Jendouba and ask to get off at Bulla Regia. The intersection is 6 km N of Jendouba and is signed only to Bou Salem. You will have to walk or hitch the remaining 3 km. There is no accommodation at the site. Open summer 0800-1900 and 0830-1730 winter, closed Mon, entrance TD1, photography fee TD1. Visit the museum first (café and toilets) where you may be able to buy a guide book.

History In 2 BC, Bulla Regia was the capital of one of the three small Roman kingdoms in Numidia, but prosperity came under the rule of Hadrian, when the town was annexed to the Empire.

Places of interest The ruins are laid out on terraces on the steep slopes of Djebel Rebia (647m) overlooking a large plain, which is particularly hot in summer and cold in winter and there is no doubt that it was to escape the unpleasant extremes of this climate that the houses were built

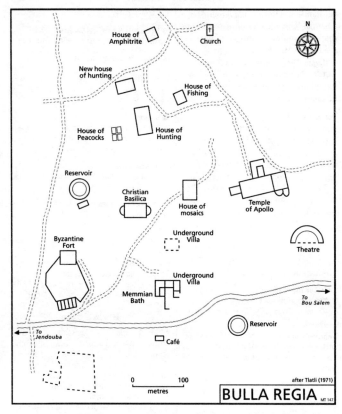

House of
Amphitrite

† Church

N

New house
of hunting

House of
Fishing

House of
Peacocks

House of
Hunting

Reservoir

Christian
Basilica

House of
mosaics

Temple
of Apollo

Byzantine
Fort

Underground
Villa

Theatre

Underground
Villa

Memmian
Bath

*To
Bou Salem*

*To
Jendouba*

Reservoir

Café

0   100
metres

after Tlatli (1971)

BULLA REGIA MT 147

partly underground, as they are at Mat-mata (see page 466). These **underground villas** are the main attraction here. Despite earthquake damage to the surface features, due to the unusual architecture, many of the villas are well preserved. The general style was to have the eating and sleeping rooms centred around a large underground courtyard. Judging from the luxurious decoration, most of them belonged to rich inhabitants. Notice the ceilings are arched. Most of the better mosaics have been taken to the Bardo museum (see Tunis page 374), but in the **House of Fishing** and the **House of Amphitrite** some magnificent mosaics are

still in place. Above ground structures which are still visible include the **Theatre** complete with stage, the **Memmian Baths** near the entrance, the **Forum**, the **Temple of Apollo**, and a Christian Basilica. There is a festival here each Sep.

Return from Bulla Regia W across the P17 towards **Chemtou**. Look out for the abrupt change of surface after the village. The rough track continues W then turns S to the ruins of what was a Numidian town and then a Roman colony founded under Augustus 27 BC-14 AD and famed for its yellow marble quarried until Byzantine times. The settlement had a theatre, part of which is still standing, a Forum and a Sanctuary to Saturn. The remains of the bridge on which was a water-driven cornmill stand beside the Oued Medjerda. The blocks of marble from the nearby quarry were each marked with name of the reigning Emperor, the proconsul for Africa and the quarry manager. The stone was an important export, and a road 60 km long and 5.1m wide was constructed to the port at Tabarka.

The track across the river bed leading S to the P6 requires a 4WD vehicle.

The track directly W from Chemtou leads to Thuburnica, a visit for the really dedicated.

Jendouba

Jendouba, 44 km S of Tabarka and 154 km W of Tunis, is an important crossroads and administrative centre. This town provides easy access to Bulla Regia and the Algerian border. There are branches of all the main banks here.

● **Accommodation D** *Similthu*, on the right, by the roundabout when arriving from Bulla Regia, T 631695, new hotel, 26 rm, restaurant, on the main road, not very appealing. **E** *Atlas*, rue du 1er Juin 1955, T 630566, behind the police station, probably the only decent hotel in town. **Youth hostel**: 60 beds, meals, T 631292.

● **Transport Train** The train station is off the main square, by the police station. Departures **Tunis** 0554, 1033, 1240, 1515, 1653; **Algeria** (Annaba/Algiers) 1539. **Road Bus**: the bus station is to W of town, past the railway lines. Information on T 630411. Frequent local buses to **Tunis**, **Le Kef**, **Tabarka** and **Aïn Draham**, also buses to the border at Ghardimaou. They do not cross the border so you will have to cross on foot. **Louages**: for **Ghardimaou** they leave from the station on Blvd Sakiet Sidi Sousse. For Tunis they leave from rue 1 Juin 1955.

Excursions

Ghardimaou, 34 km W of Jendouba, is on the way out towards Algeria. It is not worth a visit on its own account. There is the E *Hotel Thubernic* if you wish to stay on the way to **El Feidja**, one of Tunisia's six National Parks, in the hills near the Algerian frontier, set up to protect the Barbary deer. The nearest town is Aïn Soltane. Take the P6 out of Jendouba and turn N just before the frontier post. Border at Ghardimaou T 645004.

Before proceeding S to Le Kef, visitors are recommended to find time to make a journey NE to **Béja**, either by road or railway. For the first 22 km to Bou Salem, both are alongside the Oued Medjerda, the only river in Tunisia which flows all year round. The road, which never seems to be free of roadworks, crosses the two main tributaries, the Oued Mellègue and Oued Tessa which can be spectacular in flood and very disappointing at other times, while the railway line from Jendouba to Béja runs along the far side of the main valley. Bou Salem is a large successful market town dealing with the agricultural produce, mainly cereals but some grapes and some livestock, of this fertile valley. It is possible to see in this journey the area that the Romans used as their 'bread basket'. From Bou Salem the road climbs up the wooded slopes to Béja providing panoramic views back towards the route travelled, while the railway crosses and recrosses the main river before turning N to Béja.

Béja

ACCESS The bus and train stations are at the bottom of the main street with frequent connections to/from Tunis and Jendouba.

(*Pop* 35,000;*Alt* 234m) This town has had an eventful history, marked by various unfriendly visitors over the centuries razing it to the ground! Today, fortunately for the residents, there is less excitement but it is worth a wander round the medina and up the keep in the kasbah for a fine view. Béja has an attractive location, surrounded by excellent agricultural land with hills to the NW and is very busy as it commands the junction of six important roads.

Places of interest

Trajan's Bridge, once part of the Roman E-W road network lies on the minor road C76 about 13 km SW of Béja. The road leaves Béja beside the station and crosses the railway before crossing the Oued Béja. This Roman bridge, which seemingly has nothing to do with Trajan at all, is still in splendid condition. Its 70m span is a monument to the workmanship from the time of Tiberius. Barrage Kasseb lies 16 km W.

There are **WW2 cemeteries** in the area. One is just outside the N limits of the town with 396 graves and another with 99 graves about 800m N of Thibar village which lies on the C75 between Béja and Teboursouk, adjacent to the agricultural college. Both open 0730-1430 Sat-Thur.

Local information
● Accommodation
There are two small hotels.

D *Hotel Vaga*, T 450818, with 36 beds.

F *Hotel Phoenix*, T 450188, with 30 beds.

Youth hostel: T 450621, opp the bus station, 80 beds, meals available.

● Tour companies & travel agents
Vaga Tours, Ave 18 Janvier, T 451805.

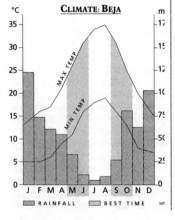

Climate: Béja chart showing °C (left axis, 0–35), m (right axis), MAX TEMP and MIN TEMP curves, months J F M A M J J A S O N D, with RAINFALL and BEST TIME legend.

Le Kef

Le Kef (The Rock) 58 km S of Jendouba is perched 750m up on a rocky hill. It is a very beautiful little town with a long history, mainly military in nature due to its important strategic position. It became a Roman colony in the 2nd century because of its situation. When the French entered Tunisia, they captured Le Kef in 1881 and made it an important military centre. During WW2 it became the provisional capital of the still free Tunisia. Today the town is an important economic and cultural regional centre. It is an interesting place to visit and remains authentic and relatively untouched by tourism. Also, due to its long history, it is rich in monuments.

Places of interest

If you want to visit the town, it is a good idea to stop off at the Association de Sauvegarde de la Medina, on place de l'Indépendance. They have a charming little office and are very helpful. The best way to visit the medina is to walk around with no fixed itinerary. Some parts are as beautiful as Sidi Bou Saïd, with the advantage that here there are no crowds.

The **Regional Museum of Popular Arts and Traditions** is on the square at the top of the town. An interesting museum set in the old and very beautiful Zaraouia Sidi Ali Ben Aissa. There are four rooms, the most interesting presents elements of the everyday nomadic life, including a large tent. Open winter 0930-1630 and summer 0900-1300 and 1500-1900, closed Mon, entrance TD1.

The **kasbah** is an old Turkish fort built in 1601 with an impressive view. Entrance TD1. In summer the Bou Makhlouf festival takes place in the courtyard.

The **Mosque of Sidi Bou Makhlouf**, a reminder of the Andalasian presence so widespread in the area, is just behind the kasbah. This is a very beautiful mosque with interesting domes and an octagonal minaret. The inside is highly decorated with ceramics and stucco. Also worth a visit is **Dar el Kous** behind Ave Bourguiba. This is a 4th century Christian basilica dedicated to St Peter.

A minor road, the C72, climbs N to the side of the 1,500 ha lake held back by the Nebeur Dam. The lake is an impressive 18 km long. A better view is obtained from the dam on the Oued Mellègue by turning off the road to Jendouba after the steep winding road passes Nebeur.

Local information
● Accommodation
D *Hotel Sicca Veneria*, place de l'Indépendence, T 221561, ugly, 34 rm, central, relatively cheap, restaurant.

E *Hotel Chez Venus*, Ave Bourguiba, T 224695, 20 rm with bath, good value, helpful owner.

F *La Medina*, 18 rue Farhat Hached, T 220214, simple, new, fairly clean and welcoming; **F** *La Source*, place de la Source, T 221397, 9 rm, central, set around a patio next to the Muezzin's loudspeaker, not very clean, slightly shabby.

● Places to eat
♦♦*Restaurant Chez Venus*, Ave Bourguiba, very pleasant atmosphere, probably the best food in town, a bit more expensive than the others.

♦*Restaurant l'Auberge*, Ave Bourguiba, good, cheap Tunisian food; *Restaurant Ed Dyr*, Ave Hedi Chaker, good value.

● Banks & money changers
STB, place de l'Indépendence; **BT**, Ave Hedi Chaker.

● Post & telecommunications
Post Office: Ave Hedi Chaker.

● Tour companies & travel agents
Nord Ouest Voyages, rue Essour, T 221839.

● Transport
Road The bus station is a 20 mins walk downhill from Place de l'Indépendence. Information on T 20105. Frequent buses to **Tunis** and **Jendouba**, connections also to Sfax; Kairouan; Nabeul; Gafsa; Sousse; and Bizerte. **Louages**: the louages station is by the bus station.

Excursions
Hammam Mellègue, a thermal spa 4 km SW of Le Kef, turn right off P5. **Kalaat Es Senam** and **Table de Jugurtha**, turn right off P17 29 km S from Le Kef, before the railway and after 14 km bear left and S. Table de Jugurtha is 1,271 m and for the energetic there are views over to Algeria!

LE KEF TO TEBOURSOUK AND TUNIS

The P5 from Le Kef NW towards Tunis, passes through an interesting mixture of small present day Tunisian towns and ancient remains of Roman and Byzantine origin. This is a rich agricultural area of pasture, cereals and wooded hills.

Just N of the small town of Krib, on the left at Km 119, are the ruins of the triumphal arch and several other remains of the Roman settlement of **Musti**. The site is entered through a green gate. Just 10 km further along what remains of a Byzantine fort stands on a hill to N of road. This is the site of the ancient settlement of **Agbia**. There is no sign, just take the track across a field. Immediately beyond, on the left is a turn to **Dougga**. This is a very rough route and a long walk – best approach is from Teboursouk.

On towards Tunis the older part of **Teboursouk**, on a hillside, overlooks the P5 while the modern part of town lies along the main road. **Aïn Tounga** immediately to the E of the road contains an imposing Byzantine fortress and remains of Roman Thignica, while **Testour** still reflects its Andalusian origins, home of the Moors driven from Spain in the 15th century. WW2 cemetery to N of road at Km 61 post.

Dougga

ACCESS Take a bus or louages to the new settlement of Dougga (set up to house the folk who were dwelling on the site) and

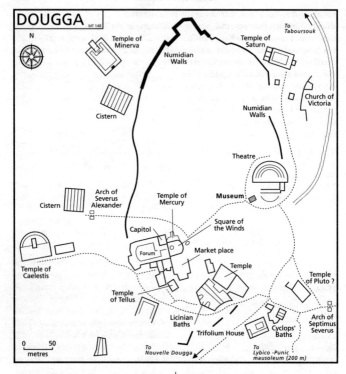

DOUGGA MT 148

N

Temple of Minerva

Numidian Walls

To Taboursouk

Temple of Saturn

Church of Victoria

Cistern

Numidian Walls

Theatre

Museum

Cistern

Arch of Severus Alexander

Temple of Mercury

Square of the Winds

Capitol

Forum

Market place

Temple

Temple of Caelestis

Temple of Pluto ?

Temple of Tellus

Licinian Baths

Trifolium House

Cyclops' Baths

Arch of Septimus Severus

0   50
metres

To Nouvelle Dougga

To Lybico -Punic mausoleum (200 m)

walk up a track behind the village. The ruins are 3 km further on along a track. The easiest way is to go from Teboursouk and take a taxi or louages.

History

The Roman ruins of Dougga which cover over 25 ha are 7 km S from the town of Teboursouk and very clearly signed. It was originally a Punic town allied to Rome against Carthage. As a consequence, after the downfall of Carthage, the town was granted a certain degree of independence. Romanization only started towards 150 AD, after 2 centuries of coexistence. By the time Carthage had been rebuilt by the Romans, Dougga had become the economic and administrative centre of the whole region, enjoying great prosperity.

Having become a Roman colony by the end of the 2nd century, the town reached the height of its wealth under the rule of Septimus Severus. Its downfall in the 4th century was caused by the heavy dues paid to the Romans and religious quarrels. When the Vandals invaded, most of the population had moved to Teboursouk. Today the ruins of Dougga spreading over 25 ha still give a very good idea of the everyday life in the ancient city.

Places of interest

Dougga is the largest of the Roman sites in Tunisia and is considered the most dramatic. This is the one site not to be missed. The ruins are on the slope of a small hill and the view and situation are beautiful. It is possible to do a superficial visit in an hour or so, but it is really worthwhile spending a great deal more time. On arrival, one of the 'guides' hanging round the entrance will no doubt want to show you around. Most of these guides are not official and do not hold a card issued by the Tourist Office. If you are in a hurry, it can be a good idea to take one, but be careful to agree on the price beforehand. Café and toilets at entrance.

The Monuments are open 0830-1730 winter and 0700-1900 summer, closed Mon, entrance fee TD1, photography TD1. The much restored **Theatre** originally built in 168/9 AD, is a typical example of a Roman theatre. It is quite modest in size, but could nevertheless seat 3,500 people in its 19 tiers cut into the hill slope. Each summer there is a festival here at which theatre groups from around the world perform.

Down the track to the W is the main section of the site including **The Capitol**, with its impressive steps and six huge fluted columns. It was built in 166 AD and dedicated to the gods Jupiter, Juno and Minerva. The open space to the W is the **Forum**. Few of the original 35 columns (red veined marble from Chemtou with white capitals and bases) remains. This section also contains the **Temple of Mercury,** which faces on to the **Square of the Winds** named after a compass based inscription naming 12 winds; the **market place** lying further S and a **temple** (261 AD) dedicated to Tellus, goddess of crop fertility.

To the W, through what was the Numidian perimeter wall, stands the remains of **Arch of Severus Alexander** (an undistinguished emperor 222-235 AD). The arch spanned a road, paved in herringbone style, which eventually lead to Carthage. In the olive trees the **Temple of Caelestis** (Juno), also constructed during the reign of Severus Alexander, has a rectangular sanctuary set in a semicircular courtyard. Definite Greco-Ro-man influences here. A number of columns still remain.

Lower down the slope, below the main section, stand the 3rd century **Licinian Baths**, a very complicated building. The fireplace which heated the water, the hot room with the pipes visible in the walls, the cold room and 'exercise' room remain.

The House of Trifolium, the brothel, named after the clover leaf shape of one of the rooms, dates from the 3rd century and is the best conserved and largest house yet discovered on the site. It is built on two levels with the entrance at street level and the rooms one floor lower. **The Baths of the Cyclops**, associated with the House of Trifolium, are named after the magnificent mosaic showing three giants, the Cyclops, working on the forge of Vulcan, the god of Hell. (This mosaic is now in the Dougga room of the Bardo Museum.) They are not in a very good state, except for the communal latrine!

The Libyo-Punic **Mausoleum**, dates back to the 2nd century BC. It was virtually destroyed by the British Consul in Tunis in the 1840s, who took stones bearing bilingual inscriptions in Punic and Libyan back to the British Museum.

To the far N of the site are temples dedicated to Minerva, constructed 138-161 AD but now in ruins; and to Saturn (195 AD) into the cliff, the four columns overlooking the valley towards Teboursouk. This temple has three sections, a vestibule behind the four columns, a large central area and to the NW three chambers once housing statues and objects of worship. The early Christian Church of Victoria, 4th/5th century, is built of pieces taken from the Theatre and the Temple of Saturn. There is a central nave and two unequally sized side-aisles. Outside is a Christian cemetery.

Local information

● **Accommodation**

It is best to stay overnight in **Teboursouk**, although there is only one hotel there.

D *Hotel Thugga*, on the main road to Tunis, T 465713, 66 beds, has obviously seen better days, rather poor quality.

Youth hostel: in Teboursouk, T 465095, 40 beds.

● **Transport**

Road There is an hourly bus to **Le Kef** and **Tunis** and many links to **Béja** and **Jendouba**. Information on T 465016.

Medjez-el-Bab

This is a market town and an important crossing point of the Oued Medjerda. New bypass and bridge have been constructed. The British First and Eighth armies played an important part here in WW2 (see The Desert War, page 548). It has two WW2 cemeteries. One is 3 km SW of town on the P5 with 2,900 graves and a memorial to soldiers who died in Tunisia and Algeria and have no known grave. The other has 240 graves and is 17 km W of town on the P6 beside the church in the old town of Oued Zarga. Both open 0730-1430 Sat-Thur.

● **Accommodation** **E** *Hotel Membressa*, small, 14 rm, communal shower.

CENTRAL TUNISIA

CONTENTS

The Gulf of Hammamet	423
Kairouan	435
Sfax, The Kerkennah Islands and El Djem	442

MAPS

Central Tunisia	424
Sousse	427
Monastir	431
Mahdia	434
Kairouan Mosque	437
Kairouan	438
Maktar	440
Sbeitla	441
Sfax	444
Kerkennah Islands	446
El Djem	449

Central Tunisia contains a diversity of interesting sights. It includes the Sahel bristling with olive trees; the busy coastal resort area accessed from Monastir airport; the holy city of Kairouan; Sbeitla and El Djem, the best preserved and most important Roman remains in the county; the busy city of Sfax and the peaceful Islands of Kerkennah. These are separated by long distances and the route we have devised takes in all these places and returns you, eventually, to the coast at Sousse.

The Sahel, or shoreland, is the low-lying E coastal plain of Tunisia extending from the Gulf of Hammamet to the Gulf of Gabès, and inland some 50 km, reaching a maximum altitude of around 275m. The region has a long history, going back to the Carthaginians and the Romans, with the amphitheatre in **El Djem** (Thysdrus) being one of the most important

remains in N Africa. The cultivation of olive trees, introduced by the Romans, continues today with **olive oil** making an important contribution to the region's prosperity. The Sahel region was greatly influenced, both culturally and architecturally, by the Arab invasions and the founding of **Kairouan** which became the fourth holy city of Islam. The medinas in most of the coastal towns have been preserved as well as monuments dating back to the 7th and 8th centuries. The Sahel, because of its good beaches and pleasant climate which is tempered in summer by cool sea breezes, has become an important tourist area centred on Sousse and Monastir. Nevertheless, there are many areas where few tourists visit, such as the charming town of Mahdia and the quiet Kerkennah Islands.

THE GULF OF HAMMAMET

Sousse

ACCESS Buses come here from all the major cities to one of the two bus stations, either on Bab el Djedid or by place Farhat Hached, the main square. The train station is very convenient, right in the middle of the town on Blvd Hassouna Ayachi. Taxis and louages arrive by Bab el Djedid on Ave Mohammed Ali. The nearest airport is Skanes/Monastir.

(*Pop* 300,000; *Alt* 6m) Sousse is the third largest city in Tunisia. It is highly industrialized but the town centre is still very pleasant. It is a city of many facets making it an interesting place to visit. Situated by the sea on the Gulf of Hammamet, with the harbour right by the main square, it has long beaches and an elegant promenade. The walled medina, looking down towards the sea, contains narrow, winding streets.

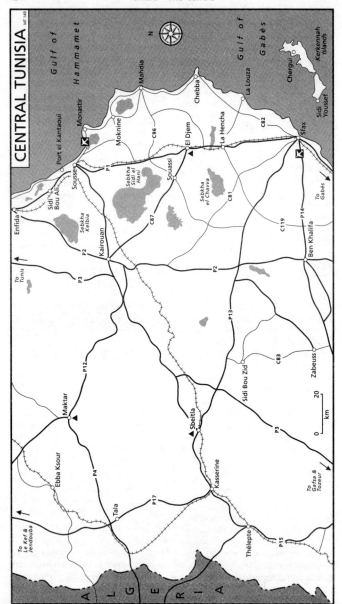

History

Founded in the 9th century BC by the Phoenicians, Sousse is one of the oldest ports in the Mediterranean. In the 4th century BC, Carthage became the leading city, and Sousse entered into its sphere of influence. During the second Punic-Roman war, Hannibal used Sousse as his base, but was beaten in 202 BC. During the third Punic-Roman war, Sousse changed its allegiance to the Romans thereby avoiding destruction and gaining the status of free town. Unfortunately, with the victory of Caesar over the armies of Pompeii in Thapsus (46 BC), Sousse was again in the position of having chosen the wrong side and Caesar imposed heavy taxation on the town. Nevertheless under the rule of Trajan (98-117 AD) the city became an important commercial centre.

Sousse managed to survive the many invasions that followed until the Arab invasion in the 7th century when it was destroyed. In the 9th century, with the coming of the Aghlabite Dynasty to Kairouan, it again prospered, as that inland city's port, but it was conquered again in the 12th century by the Normans and in the 16th century by Spain. During WW2 it was again seriously damaged.

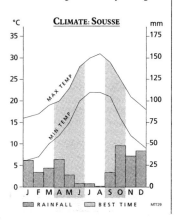

CLIMATE: SOUSSE

Places of interest

The old **Medina** is still surrounded by the original walls, built in 859 and restored in 1205. The way to enter the medina is either via Bab el Djedid, or through the place des Martyrs beside the central square which leads to the Great Mosque. The breach in the walls was the result of bombardments during 1943.

The **Great Mosque** is by a large esplanade leading towards the ribat. Built in the 9th century by the Aghlabite Emir Abou Abbas Mohammed, it was probably a conversion of a kasbah built a few years earlier. Further renovations and restorations have taken place. On two corners, large, round towers dominate the marble floored courtyard and make it look like the fortress it may originally have been. Overall the monument is very simple, the courtyard being decorated solely by inscriptions around its sides. Only the courtyard can be visited. Open 0800-1300, closed Fri. Entrance tickets TD1 can be bought opposite the mosque and at the local ONTT.

The **Ribat** is a type of fortified monastery. It formed part of a chain of forts built by the Arab Aghlabids along the coast which functioned as religious centres and a means of protection for the Muslim population against potential invaders. They communicated by smoke signals, since they were all in sight of one another. The ribat at Sousse was built in 820, using some materials from older sites, as can be seen at the entrance where antique columns are placed on either side of the door. The interior is very plain. On the 1st floor a large prayer room takes up all the S side. Go to the top of the watch tower, up the narrow stairway, where the view over the city and the sea is fantastic. Open 0800-1900 in summer, 0930-1200 and 1400-1800 in winter, closed Mon. Entrance TD1, photo fee TD1.

The **Zaouia Zakkak** is a beautiful building dominated by a small Turkish octagonal minaret. You cannot visit the inside, but from the outside it is splendid.

The **museum** is set in the **kasbah**, at the SW end of the medina. The kasbah was built in the 11th century and extended in the 16th, around an old signal tower (the Khalef) dating back to 859. The museum contains mainly mosaics which are well presented and well preserved. Though less numerous and interesting than the Bardo's collection in Tunis, Sousse has its share of masterpieces. The majority of the mosaics are from the 3rd and 4th centuries, the central theme being the sea. Particularly worth seeing is the 3rd century *'Bacchus' Triumph'* in room 8. This mosaic, found in Sousse, illustrates the victory of a young god over the forces of evil. Another mosaic nearby portrays Zeus and Ganymède. See also the *'Lion and the Dog catching a Hare'* in room 14 dating from the end of the 2nd century. Entrance is via Blvd Maréchal Tito. Open 0800-1200 and 1500-1900 in summer, 0930-1200 and 1400-1800 in winter. Closed Mon, entrance fee TD1, photo fee TD1.

The **Souks** are mainly situated around the N end of the rue d'Angleterre. On the W is Souk el Reba, where material and perfume are sold. Again on the right is the Kalaout el Koubba, a building whose original function is unknown but which was probably built in the 19th century. Continue up the Souk el Reba and go out by Bab el Gharbi and turn left along the walls to come to the kasbah and the museum. After visiting the museum re-enter the medina by following the walls to the Bab el Khabli. Following the rue el Hadjira will bring you back to the rue d'Angleterre. Shopping in the tourist shops on rue d'Angleterre can be expensive. Either drive a hard bargain or buy your souvenirs elsewhere. **Markets** are held each Sun, slightly out of town on the Sfax road.

The **Catacombs** are to the W of Sousse, consisting of more than 250 galleries containing up to 15,000 tombs over a distance of 5 km. They were built and used between the 2nd and 4th centuries and are rather a disappointment. Currently closed for repairs which may take some years.

The **beach** starts in front of the Corniche, but it is much nicer, and less crowded further N. Surfboards can be rented all along the beach.

Local information
● Accommodation

There are more than 40 hotels in Sousse, some with over 1,000 beds. Most are fully booked in summer.

A *Hotel Chems el Hana*, T 226900, F 226076, elegant, 243 rm with bath, a/c, phone, TV, terrace, 2 restaurants, 2 pools, fitness centre, tennis, golf, wheel chair access.

B *Nour Justina*, on Corniche, T 226382, 422 beds, seafront, food and service is reputedly not quite up to scratch.

C *Hotel Fares*, Blvd Hassouna Ayachi, just off place Farhat Hached, T 227800, 180 beds, central, private beach 200m away, a/c, high rm with view; **C** *Le Claridge*, Ave Bourguiba, T 224759, 60 beds, centre of new town, very noisy, very clean; **C** *Le Printemps*, Blvd de la Corniche, T 229335, F 224055, 69 rm for 2/4 persons, with hob, fridge and utensils, restaurant, 5 mins walk from town centre.

D *Hotel Ahla*, place de la Grande Mosquée, T 220570, 100 rm, clean, pleasant, very quiet; **D** *Hotel Hadrumete*, place Assed Ibn el Fourat, by port, 35 rm with bath, clean, good restaurant, pool, enclosed terrace café, 2 mins to sea – better value for money than *Azur*; **D** *Sousse Azur*, 5 rue Amilcar, off Ave Habib Bourguiba, T 226960, F 228145, 20 rm, restaurant, coffee lounge, 10 mins from town centre.

E *Hotel de Paris*, 15 rue des Rempart, by the walls close to place Farhat Hached, T 220564, very clean, some rm on the roof, close to the medina and the new town; **E** *Hotel Medina*, behind the Great Mosque on rue de Paris, T 221722, very clean, some rm with bath, roof terrace, restaurant/bar, no phone bookings, so arrive early in summer; **E** *The Hotel Amira*, 52 rue de France, nr Bab Djedid in the medina, T 226325, clean, half rm have bath, some with view, panoramic roof terrace.

F *Hotel de Gabès*, 12 rue de Paris, T 226977,

best of the cheap hotels, very clean, some rm on roof, good views from terrace, only 14 rm so book in summer; **F** *Hotel Ezzouhour*, 48 rue de Paris, T 228729, in the medina, very

simple, some rms with bath, otherwise communal shower, very cheap, pleasant manager; **F** *Hotel Perles*, 71 rue de Paris, T 224609, in the medina, very small, could be cleaner, com-

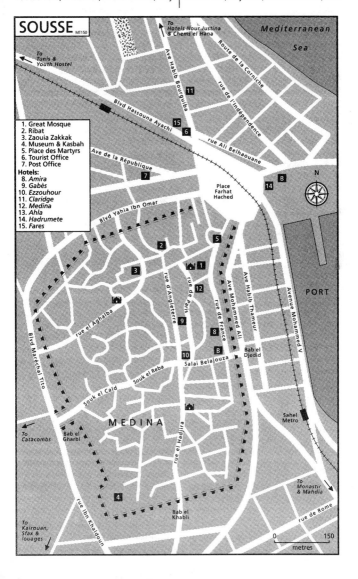

SOUSSE MT150

1. Great Mosque
2. Ribat
3. Zaouia Zakkak
4. Museum & Kasbah
5. Place des Martyrs
6. Tourist Office
7. Post Office

Hotels:
8. Amira
9. Gabès
10. Ezzouhour
11. Claridge
12. Medina
13. Ahla
14. Hadrumete
15. Fares

To Hotels Nour Justina & Chems el Hana

Mediterranean Sea

To Tunis & Youth Hostel

Ave Habib Bourguiba

Route de la Corniche

rue de l'Independence

Blvd Hassouna Ayachi

rue Ali Belhaouane

Ave de la République

Place Farhat Hached

N

PORT

Blvd Yahia Ibn Omar

rue d'Angleterre

rue de Paris

rue de France

Ave Mohammed Ali

Ave Habib Thameur

Avenue Mohammed V

Blvd Maréchal Tito

rue el Aghalba

Bab el Djedid

Sahel Metro

Salai Belajouza

Souk el Reba

Souk el Caid

MEDINA

Bab el Gharbi

To Catacombs

rue el Hadjira

To Monastir & Mahdia

rue Ibn Khaldoun

Bab el Khabli

rue de Rome

To Kairouan, Sfax & louages

0   150
metres

munal shower, cheapest hotel in Sousse.

Youth hostel: T 227548, 3 km out along Tunis road, at Plage Boujaafar, 2 km from station, kitchen, meals available, 90 beds.

● **Places to eat**

Good choice available on Route de la Corniche and Ave Habib Bourguiba. Most restaurants cater for tourists, menus in many languages. Some cafés in the medina advertise only in Arabic.

♦♦♦*Le Bonheur*, T 225742, place Farhat Hached, good grilled meat and fish, large terrace on the street; *Restaurant Cherif*, by the harbour, specializes in fish and seafood; *Restaurant des Remparts*, T 226326, rue de l'Eglise, by medina walls close to place Farhat Hached, more expensive because it serves alcohol; *Restaurant Mahlouf*, T 226508, place Farhat Hached, excellent food, particularly the fish, large terrace.

♦♦*Restaurant le Golfe*, Ave Habib Bourguiba in Boujaafar complex, clean, good choice.

♦*Restaurant Ben Henda*, rue de Paris, in the medina, simple but tasty food; *Restaurant Hassoumi*, rue de Rabat, just off the Corniche, very cheap, good Tunisian food, clean; *Restaurant Populaire*, rue de France, typical medina restaurant; *Restaurant Tunisien*, rue Ali Belhaouane, nice setting, some dishes a bit more expensive, very good fish.

● **Banks & money changers**

BDS and STB on Ave Bourguiba; UIB, Ave Habib Thameur; BT, rue Ali Belhaouane; BNT, rue de l'Indépendence. Money can also be changed in any of the large hotels.

● **Entertainment**

Casino: *El Hana Palace Hotel.*

● **Hospital & medical services**

Chemist: open nights, 38 Ave de la République, T 224795; 45 route de la Corniche; Ave H. Thameur. Chemists display names of those open late.

Hospital: Ave Farhat Hached, rue Ibn el Jattar, T 221411.

● **Post & telecommunications**

Area code: 03.

Post Office: Ave de la République, just off place Farhat Hached.

● **Shopping**

Fixed price articles, good selection at Socopa in *Hotel Abou Nawas Boujaafar* and the larger Soula Centre off place Farhat Hached.

● **Sports**

Harbour: the harbour has berths for 10 yachts, min-max draft 3-9m.

● **Tour companies & travel agents**

Carthage Tour, Ave Bourguiba, T 227954; *Tourafrica*, rue Khaled Ibn Walid, T 224277; *Tunisian Travel Service*, route de la Corniche, T 227599.

● **Tourist office**

The tourist information offices are at Regional ONTT, 1 Ave Bourguiba, by place Farhat Hached, T 225157, open 0730-1930 most days. The local office is opp, T 220431.

● **Useful addresses**

Toilets: Train station, Tourist Office, Medina in rue el Achalba.

● **Transport**

Local Car hire: Avis, route de la Corniche, T 225901; Budget, 63 Ave Bourguiba, T 224041; Europcar, route de la Corniche, T 226252; Hertz, Ave Bourguiba, T 225428; Inter Rent, route de la Corniche, T 227562; Top Car, rue Ahmed Zaatir, T 226060.

Air Tunis Air, Ave Bourguiba, T 227955 for details of flights from Skanes/Monastir airport.

Train 'Sahel Metro' is one line which goes all the way to **Mahdia** along the coast stopping at all the resorts, small towns and Monastir international airport (TD0.6 single). Hourly from 0600-2000. The trip **Sousse-Mahdia** takes just under 1½ hrs (TD3.75 return). The station is at the S end of Ave Mohammed V, 100m down from the Bab Djedid towards the harbour, T 225321.

For Tunis: The station is on Blvd Hassouna Ayachi, up the road from place Farhat Hached. Information on T 221955. Departures to **Tunis** 0348, 0530, 0650, 0757, 1310, 1418, 1527, 1830, 2012; **Gabès** (via El Djem/Sfax) 0918, 1509, 1618, 1935, 2324; **Gafsa/Metlaoui** 2324. For **Hammamet** and **Nabeul** get off at Sidi Bou Rekba and continue journey by bus or louage. 'Noddy' road trains between Sousse and Port el Kantaoui leaves place Boujaafar in Sousse on the hour 0900-1800 in winter 0900-2300 in summer, returning at half past the hour. There is a blue train and a yellow train, tickets cannot be transferred.

Road There are 2 bus stations. The first is on place Sidi Yahya by the Bab Djedid, the second by place Farhat Hached, on the place du Port. Information on T 224202. Departures from Bab Djedid to **Kairouan** (1½ hrs, TD2.39);

Hammamet (2 hrs, TD2.99); **Nabeul** (2¾ hrs, TD3.45); **Gabès** (5 hrs, TD9.27) and **Sfax** (2½ hrs, TD4.96); **Djerba** (via Zarzis); **Kebili** (7¼ hrs, TD12.96); **Douz** (7¼ hrs, TD13.9); **Medenine**; **Matmata** (7 hrs, TD10.74); **Tataouine** (9 hrs, TD13.11; **Port el Kantaoui** (30 mins, TD0.45). Departures from place du Port to **Tunis** and **Bizerte**. **Louages**: the louage station has moved from Bab Djedid, on rue Mohammed Ali to Souk el Ahad, nr camel market on route de Sfax. Take a taxi as it's a 30 mins walk. **Taxi**: yellow taxis have meters.

Sea CTN (Compagnie de Transport Maritime) T 224861, F 224844.

EXCURSIONS FROM SOUSSE

Port el Kantaoui

10 km N of Sousse, Port el Kantaoui was developed as a tourist town. It has been created with a certain amount of good taste with many restaurants and cafés and lots of 4-star hotels. In addition, it boasts a 340 berth marina, yacht basin and golf courses. The overall impression is, fortunately, not too overpowering. Offering every imaginable facility, Port el Kantaoui is geared, unashamedly, towards mass charter tourism.

● **Accommodation AL** *Diar el Andalous* T 246200, F 246348, luxurious, 300 rm, beach, a/c, indoor and outdoor pools, tennis, disco, free watersports; **AL** *Marhaba Palace* T 243633/240200, just like a palace, 250 splendid rm, indoor and outdoor pools, tennis, garden; **C** *Hotel Salem*, Ave Bourguiba, 261 rm, no a/c, pool, disco, no credit cards. **NB** Don't look for cheap hotels in this area.

● **Places to eat** are all expensive. All hotel restaurants provide good (pricey) meals as do ◆◆◆*Le Beach Club*, T 241799, *Le Yacht Club*, T 241799 and *Le Club House*, T 241756. ◆◆*Neptune VI*, floating restaurant, T 241799, giant prawns special. For cheap meals go into Sousse.

● **Sport Diving**: Port el Kantoui International Diving Centre, Port de Plaisance, T 241799. **Fitness club**: Beach club nr swimming pool at N end of harbour, T 241799, TD4/session, offers many sporting and health activities. **Golf**: International 'Open' each Apr. El Kantaoui

T 231755 has a 27 hole tournament golf course, par 108, 9,576m where green fees are TD30-TD40/round and lessons are available. Palm Links Golf Course and Monastir Golf Course, shaded by olive trees, are both 18 hole, par 72, 6,140m. **Sailing & fishing**: Yachts and catamarans can be hired from the yacht basin or you can take a trip in an ancient sailing boat. Aquascope trips available to view underwater life. Harbour has berths for 300 yachts, min-max draft 2-4m. Organized at quayside are: Sailing trip, daily weather permitting at 1000 and 1430, 3 hr, TD20 – with an hour for swimming and fishing. Catamaran trip, daily 1000, 1200, 1400 and 1600, 2 hrs, TD15. Fishing day trip 1000-1800, TD80, winter half day for TD40, eat what you catch or take it home. Aquascope, 3 vessels operating daily 0700-1800, an hour for TD12-15, goes down to 25m – but as sea bed is featureless and the water murky not worth it. **Scuba diving**: with tuition and equipment.

● **Tourist offices** The tourist information office is on the left as you enter through archway into the port, manager Mohammed Lakhdar very helpful.

Enfida (Enfidaville)

43 km N of Sousse, Enfida is an administrative centre of little touristic interest, situated where the P2 to Kairouan leaves the main P1 route from Tunis to Sousse. Train station is 10 mins walk E of town centre. Buses run from Sousse hourly on the half hour. Everything on the main road – bus station, police, museum, market. No hotels, no restaurants, no taxis. Tourist information by talking to museum curator.

Places of interest

The **Museum** in the old French church on the main street contains a mixture of old tombstones and mosaics. It is interesting as it demonstrates the diversity of Tunisia's cultural and religious past. Entrance 600 mills, photography TD1, open 0930-1630, closed Mon. Each Sun a highly colourful **market**, where all the farmers and bedouins from the surrounding areas meet, is held at the S end of town on the road to Sousse and Kairouan. Many things, including material and clothes, are much cheaper here than in Tunis. Covered vegetable/fruit market open daily.

A WW2 cemetery lies to the W of town containing graves of 1,551 soldiers from Britain and the Commonwealth who died in 1943 during the Eighth Army's advance across N Africa.

Roman remains at Gheguernia, called Henchir Fraga, about 7 km N of town; also at Aïn M'Deker 16 km NW on C113. Spa at Aïn Garci 16 km W.

Takrouna

A small Berber village perched 195m high on an outcrop, Takrouna has an amazing view. It is reached by leaving Enfida on the C133 to Zaghouan and taking the signposted 2nd turning on the left after 5 km. The village is noted for its honey.

S from Enfida the P1 cuts through the salt water marsh and lakes to Sousse. The road to **Hergla**, on the left 17 km from Enfida, offers an alternative, more scenic, route to Sousse and the opportunity to view the surrounding area.

Monastir

ACCESS The 'Sahel Metro' runs from the airport, 9 km away, to town. The bus, train and louage stations are on Ave de la République just 5 mins walk to the town centre.

Lying on the coast about 25 km S of Sousse on a headland at the S point of the Gulf of Hammamet, Monastir is an attractive fishing port with an elegant promenade along the bay.

History

Habib Bourguiba was born here in 1903, and this has largely contributed to the development of the town. It is now part of a large tourist complex which continues N to Skanes and Sousse. Monastir's history goes back to Phoenician times, later becoming a major military base for Caesar. During the 7th century, with the construction of the ribat, it became part of the coastal defence system. Then, after the fall of Kairouan in the 11th century, Monastir became the religious capital. The Turks made it into a stronghold and it was not until 3 Aug 1903, when Bourguiba put in an appearance, that Monastir made it back onto the map.

Places of interest

The **Ribat** was built in 796 by Harthama Ibnou Ayyoun, as part of the coastal look out system. One of the oldest and largest of the military structures built by the Arabs in N Africa, it was later refortified and surrounded by an additional wall during the 9th and 11th centuries, which gives the whole edifice an interesting mixture of contrasting styles and shapes. The view over the sea from the top of the Nador (watch tower) is recommended, especially at sunset. The ribat holds a small, interesting Islamic Museum mostly containing old manuscripts and miniatures and a unique Arab astrolabe (for measuring altitude) dating back to the 10th century. Open 0800-1900 in summer, 0900-1200 and 1400-1800 in winter. Closed Mon, entrance TD3, photo fee TD2.

The style of the **Great Mosque** is simple, in contrast with that of the ribat. Built in the 9th century, it was later extended in the 11th century. Notice that some of the pillars have capitals of an earlier date.

The **Bourguiba Mausoleum**, where ex-President Bourguiba is buried, was built in 1963 at the same time as the **Bourguiba Mosque**. The mosque is in the old town and was built following the richly decorated traditional style of architecture. The mosque cannot be visited by non-Muslims.

The **medina** is over clean and sanitized and has been so extensively restored that it has lost its original character and much of its interest.

There is a weekly Sat **market** in Souk Essabt on place Guedir El Foul and the

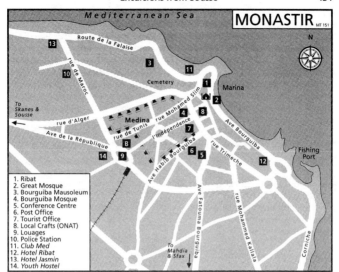

MONASTIR MT 151

1. Ribat
2. Great Mosque
3. Bourguiba Mausoleum
4. Bourguiba Mosque
5. Conference Centre
6. Post Office
7. Tourist Office
8. Local Crafts (ONAT)
9. Louages
10. Police Station
11. *Club Med*
12. *Hotel Ribat*
13. *Hotel Jasmin*
14. *Youth Hostel*

rue Salem B'Chir. Local **handicrafts** can be seen at the ONAT in quartier Chraga in the centre of Monastir.

Local information
● Accommodation
Most of the hotels are very expensive, mainly uninspiring tower blocks and many are closed in winter. You are advised to go back to Sousse or on to Mahdia for the night.

E *Hotel Jasmin*, route de la Falaise T 462511, very pleasant, 16 rm, cheap, welcoming, with a beach across road and a very good restaurant frequented by locals.

Youth hostel: on rue de Maroc, town centre, T 461216, 60 beds.

● Places to eat
♦♦*de Tunisie*, Ave Ali Belhouane, behind *Hotel Hadrumete*, Dutch owned, Tunisian and Indian food; *El Medina*, place de l'Independence, corner of Ave de l'Independence, opp medina wall, small, clean, pavement tables, friendly staff; *Le Grill* on marina, T 460923.

♦*La Pizzeria*, T 460923, Port de Plaisance, on marina. Good snack bar at airport.

● Banks & money changers
STB and UIB, Ave Bourguiba; BT, place de l'Indépendence. Money can also be changed

in large hotels.

● Hospitals & medical services
Chemist: *Charhine* on Ave Bourguiba and *Karoui* on Ave de la République.
Hospital: *Hôpital Fattouma Bourguiba*, Ave Fattouma Bourguiba, T 461141.

● Post & telecommunications
Area code: 03.
Post Office: Ave Bourguiba, by the Palais des Congrès (conference centre).

● Shopping
Monoprix, rue de Tunis, opp medina wall.

● Sports
Golf: there is a golf course, T 461120, 10 km out of town, on road to Sfax and Kairouan, 6,140m, par 72, green fees TD26-30.

Horse riding: available, ask at any large hotel for details. Horse racing each Sun.

Watersports: including scuba diving and sailing, at the Cap Monastir. Ask at *Hotel Marina* T 462066. Underwater diving school, T 461156. Monastir Yacht club has 386 berths. Marina T 462305/462509.

● Tour companies & travel agents
Tourafrica, Ave Bourguiba, T 461381; *Carthage Tours*, in *Hotel Habib* on Corniche, T 461847.

● **Tourist offices**

The tourist information office is at ONTT, Quartier Chraga, in front of the Bourguiba Mosque, T 461960. Also in front of the airport, T 461205.

● **Useful addresses**

Garage: there are 3 garages on Ave Bourguiba.

Police: on rue de Libye, T 461432.

● **Transport**

Local Car hire: Avis, airport, T 463031; **Europcar**, airport, T 461314; **Hertz**, Ave Bourguiba, T 461404, and at airport, T 461314; **Inter rent**, airport, T 461314; **Nova Rent**, Av Habib Bourguiba, T 467826.

Air *Tunis Air* at airport, T 460300 and in Monastir close to *Hotel Ribat*, T 462550, *Air Liberté*, airport, T 460300. Flight information

THE OLIVE – A SYMBOL OF PEACE AND HARMONY

In the 2nd and 3rd centuries AD, while under Roman rule, the cultivation of the olive tree (*oleo europeae sylvestris*) spread through North Africa – from Morocco to Libya. In **Volubilis (see page 148)** 55 olive presses were found. Today crossing this region by air the chequer-board pattern of olive cultivation is very distinctive. On the ground the endless hectares of olives are even more impressive.

The most important olive producers are in the Mediterranean Basin, Spain, Italy, Greece and **Tunisia**. The olive is a sub-tropical, broad-leaved, evergreen tree, both fire and drought resistant. It grows 3-12m high and many trees are said to be between 50-100 years old. The leathery, lance shaped leaves, growing in pairs are dark green above and silvery underneath. From the tiny white flowers the green olives develop.

The olive branch, synonymous with peace, was Noah's first indication of the receding flood.

In modern olive cultivation on the plains the trees are planted 10m x 10m apart, leaving room for machinery and yields reach 50 kg per tree. Traditional methods produce 15-20 kg per tree.

The method of harvesting and production has not essentially changed. Removal of the fruits must be done with care. Tunisians are forbidden to hit trees with sticks to remove the olives. Reminders are given on TV at the harvest season. It damages the tree and bruises the olives which lets in the air and allows oxidization which reduces the quality. The berries are washed in tepid water then crushed. The oil is separated from the water by centrifuge, filtered, kept at a regulated temperature in airtight steel vats, then bottled. The older method incorporates rotating stone grinders, the resulting paste being fashioned into rings on esparto grass mats which are then squeezed by an animal turning the screw tighter and tighter. The resulting oils, dark and thick, are then purified.

Olive oil is classified as:

Extra virgin oil: oil with no flaws – is produced from olives which are picked ripe and processed immediately. Acidity must not be above 1%. It adds flavour and aromatic fragrance to dishes. Like good wine it is rich and delicious.

Virgin olive oil: from olives not bruised, damaged or subjected to adverse temperatures or too much air. Can only be blended with other virgin oils. Acidity maximum 1.5%.

Pure olive oil: lacks the quality of the above, being more acidic and cheaper. Read the labels on the bottle with care.

Olive oil is one of the easiest oils to digest. It is healthy, containing no cholesterol. It is safe for frying, heating up to 210°C without igniting. It is also very handy for anointing passing royalty.

Skanes/Monastir airport on T 461313. Departures to **Djerba** Tues 1620; **Tunis** Thur 0720. **Scheduled international flights**, Amsterdam Tues 1530; **Brussels** Sun 0830; **Frankfurt** Tues 0910; **Lyon** Fri 1055; **Nice** Thur 0720; **Paris** Thur 0820, Fri 1045, Sat 1430; **Rome** Mon 1505.

Train Opposite the bus station. Information on T 460755. **Tunis** (via Sousse) 0610, 1238, 1758 (TD5). 'Sahel Metro' goes to the airport and to **Sousse** and **Mahdia** along the coast every hour from 0600-2000.

Road Bus: the bus station is at the S end of Ave de la République. Information on T 461059. Departures to **Tunis** 0445; **Sfax** 0500, 0600, 1100. There are also frequent buses to **Sousse** (TD6). **Louages:** leave from in front of the bus station. **Taxi**: some taxi drivers take advantage of tourists – check there is a meter or agree a price.

Sea Cruises: to Kuriat Island in Gulf of Hammamet T 461156.

Mahdia

ACCESS Bus station by the market and the harbour. The train station and louage station are nearby.

Mahdia, 60 km S of Sousse, is a charming little town which has to some extent escaped the tourist mania of the rest of the coast. Situated on the headland of Cap d'Afrique the town is surrounded by sea on three sides.

The traditional olive cultivation around the town and especially N of Mahdia has been taken over by extensive market gardening – plastic covered, tunnel shaped, head high greenhouses – growing tomatoes, pepper, melons, fennel etc.

History

The history of Mahdia is closely linked with the Shi'ite branch of Islam. The Shi'ites believe that the Caliph must descend from Ali and Fatima (the prophet's daughter) and that the Sunnis are usurpers and heretics. After a 7 year war with the Aghlabids, Obaid Allah, known as **El Mehdi** (the Saviour), the founder of the Fatimid Dynasty (followers of Fatima) finally secured victory and sought to establish his own capital. Mahdia was founded in 912 on an easily defended site and El Mehdi settled down in the still unfinished town in 921 in order to reinforce his power and protect himself. However his cruelty and his enemies' hatred made peace short-lived. In 944 the city was kept under siege for 8 months by the army of Abou Yazid. The siege was unsuccessful. The new dynasty moved to a city closer to Kairouan, Sabra el-Mansouriyya. The inhabitants of the abandoned capital concentrated on the sea for their welfare with the profits from fishing, commerce and piracy bringing a period of prosperity.

However reprisals followed, with first an unsuccessful Christian expedition to dislodge the pirates in 1088, then the occupation by Roger of Sicily in 1148. Later various other attempts were made to rid the town of the pirates, by a joint French-Genoan force in 1390 and in 1550 by Charles V of Spain. The Spanish were finally successful in 1554. As a result, the inhabitants were forced to revert to more traditional ways of life, such as olive cultivation and the production and weaving of silk. Today Mahdia is one of the largest fishing ports in Tunisia. The industry specializes in 'blue fish' such as mackerel and sardines, shining bright lamps at night to attract the fish.

Places of interest

The **medina** is beautiful even though there are not many specific things to see. Stroll around on the marble paved streets and peep into the doorway of one of the numerous weaving workshops producing high quality silk and cotton material for wedding dresses. At night, walk towards the main square in the medina, place du Caire, and have a drink in the café under the arcades. This is the local social centre and has a lot of atmosphere. There is a walk to the end of **Cap Afrique**, through the old ceme-

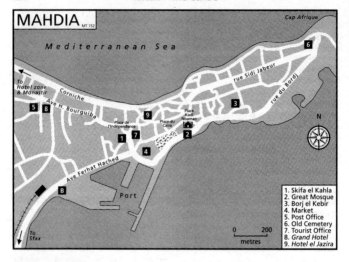

MAHDIA MT 152

Cap Afrique

Mediterranean Sea

To Hotel zone & Monastir

Corniche

Ave H. Bourguiba

rue Sidi Jabeur

rue du Bordj

N

Place de l'Independence

Place Kadi Noaman

Place du Caire

Ave Ferhat Hached

Port

To Sfax

1. Skifa el Kahla
2. Great Mosque
3. Borj el Kebir
4. Market
5. Post Office
6. Old Cemetery
7. Tourist Office
8. Grand Hotel
9. Hotel el Jazira

0   200
metres

tery to the lighthouse.

Good spot to watch the sunrise is S shore near Grande Mosque, just you, the sun and all the fishermen.

Skifa el Kahla (Obscure Gateway), is the main gate into the town. The tip of the Cap and the medina used to be behind a large wall and only 'safe' people were permitted to enter. At the time of El Mehdi only troops and a few, privileged people lived within the walls in order to minimise the risk of rebellion. The people lived outside, but within the walls were their shops and workshops. This meant that starting a rebellion during the day could jeopardize the life of their families outside, while to do so during the night would lead to the loss of their livelihood. The present gate was built in 1554, after El Mehdi's time, following the departure of the Spanish.

The **Great Mosque** is on place Kadi Noaman, at the top of the main street. The mosque was totally rebuilt in 1963 following the original 10th century Fatmid plans. The work was done with great skill and faithfulness to the original.

Unfortunately the mosque can only be entered by Muslims.

The **Bordj el Kebir** was built around the same period as the Skifa el Kahla. The Bordj is an impressive fortress built on the highest point of the headland overlooking the sea. The view from the top is good, but a visit to the Bordj is of limited interest. Open 0800-1200 and 1500-1900, closed Mon, entrance TD1. Festival here evenings Jul and Aug.

Beaches

Mahdia has very beautiful beaches. By the village the shore is rocky, but the water is very clear. Further N along the Corniche, towards the hotels, the beaches are excellent. 'A Zone Touristique' is being built N of Mahdia reducing the area's attraction.

Local information

● **Accommodation**

B *Club Cap Mahdia*, along route Touristique, T 681725, F 680405, 250 rm, beautiful, newly built, beach, quality service, pool, nightclub, tennis, horse-riding and all watersports, closed Nov and Dec, value for money.

D *Corniche*, Ave 7 Novembre, T 694201, F 694190, 16 rm with bath, small, cheap, clean, good restaurant, 2 km from town, not on beach side; **D** *Sables d'Or*, 3km N out of town, along the Corniche, T 681137, by the sea, beach, 68 rm are individual bungalows, sea view, most watersports.

E *Hotel Rand*, 20 Ave Taieb M'Hiri, T 680525, 22 rm with bath, breakfast incl, no restaurant, central, clean, pleasant staff and owner, hairdresser.

F *Hotel el Jazira*, rue Ibn el Fourat, close to Skifa el Kahla, T 681629, only hotel in the medina, very simple, clean, communal bath/ toilet rather antiquated, uninviting, some rm with sea view.

Youth hostel: in Mahdia, T 681559, 60 beds, meals available, family rms, very clean, good view from roof, signposted from train station, about 5 mins walk. Another at Chebba, T 683815, 37 km from Mahdia, 60 beds, convenient for those taking the coast road C82 S to Sfax.

Camping: El Asfour, close to *Sables d'Or*, large, well organized site.

● **Places to eat**

◆◆*Neptune*, Ave 7 Novembre, start of *Corniche*, T 681927, clean, tidy, fish dishes sold by weight before cooking, seats 40; *Restaurant le Lido*, by harbour, very good fish.

◆*L' Espadon* nr *Hotel Corniche*, T 681476, small, pleasant decor, close to beach, cheap, seats 26; *Restaurant el Moez*, between main gate and market, very cheap, good food, typical local restaurant, no alcohol.

● **Banks & money changers**

BNT on place de l'Indépendence; BT and STB on Ave Bourguiba.

● **Post & telecommunications**

Post Office: in the new part of town on Ave Bourguiba.

● **Shopping**

Market: on E side of port sells fish daily and other fresh produce and general goods on Fri.

● **Sports**

Harbour: 20 yacht berths, min-max draft 3-6m.

Health & Fitness Club: *Hotel Ahu Nawas* in hotel zone.

● **Tourist offices**

The tourist information office is inside the medina's main gate, Skifa el Kahla, on the right, T 681098, friendly but uninformative.

● **Useful addresses**

Police: Ave Bourguiba, nr supermarket.

● **Transport**

Train 'Sahel metro' train every hour 0500-1800 to **Monastir, Skanes/Monastir airport** and **Sousse**. Train station is down the street from the bus station, by the harbour. **Tunis** (via Sousse) 0500, 1130, 1645. Takes 4 hrs (TD1.5).

Road Bus: the bus station is by the harbour. Frequent buses to **Sousse** and **Monastir**. Less frequent buses to **Tunis, Sfax, Gabès** and **Kairouan. Louages**: by the harbour, beyond the bus station, destinations El Djem, Kairouan, Monastir, Sfax and Sousse.

KAIROUAN

ACCESS The bus station is SE of Bab ech Chouhada, 15 mins walk from the centre. Louages from Tunis arrive at Bab ech Chouhada. All others arrive outside the Post Office.

(*Pop* 100,000; *Alt* 60m) The recommended route goes inland now to Kairouan, situated 65 km SW from Sousse along the P12 in the middle of a large plain and visible for miles around. The spiritual and religious capital of Tunisia, the city was the first base for the conquering Arab, and Muslim armies from the E. Still surrounded by the original walls, the town has a particular charm. The early morning or evening light over its ochre buildings is especially beautiful. Kairouan is also the capital of traditional carpet manufacture and the market town for Tunisia's main fruit growing area. It has a healthy climate thanks to its altitude. It stands at the junction of roads to Tunis, Sousse and Gafsa.

History

The city was founded in 671 by Aqbar ibn Naffi as an outpost for the conquest of the Maghreb. He chose the site for its strategic value, being both far enough away from the coast where Byzantine fleets still threatened, and from the Berbers in the mountains who were strongly opposed to the new invaders. The town was attacked by the Berbers who won two significant victories, the more important in 688. The hostilities did not last long, however, with the Berbers soon converting to Islam. During the 9th century and the rule of the Aghlabids, the town found prosperity, and independence from Baghdad.

With the arrival of the Fatimids in N Africa in 909 a break occurred within Kairouan, an established centre for Sunnism, and the new Shi'ite leadership. As a result, El Medhi founded Madhia and moved his capital there. After the rebellion of Abou Yazid, in 953, the new Fatimid Caliph El-Mansor moved the capital back to a new city, Sabra el-Mansouriyya, just 2 km away from Kairouan. This meant the older settlement was bypassed commercially, most trade being done in the new city.

The real decline came with the invasion from Egypt in 1057, when Kairouan changed its allegiance from the Fatimids in Cairo to the Abbasids in Baghdad. The city was ransacked and it was not until the Hafsids were in control of Kairouan in the 13th century that the city redeveloped. Finally, under the Husseinite Dynasty in the 18th century, the city regained some of its past glory. Today Kairouan is a very important re-

ligious centre, the primary holy city in the Maghreb region, preceded in status only by Mecca, Medina and Jerusalem.

Places of interest

If time is short there are numerous guided tours of the town which take in the main sights. These leave from the Tourist Office.

Kairouan is a most confusing town. Street names are frequently changed, some have two names and the locals you ask will recognize neither. Accept this as a challenge which adds to the charm of the place.

Buy your ticket first at the tourist office. It costs TD2 for seven sites. Mosquée Okba – the Great Mosque; Mausolée Abi Zomaâ – Zaouia Sidi Sahab or Barber's Mosque; Bassins Aghlabites – Aghlabide Pools; Mausolée Sidi Abid – Zaouia of Sidi Abid el Ghariani; Musée Rakkada – National Museum of Islamic Art; Mausolée Sidi Abada – Zaouia of Sidi Amor Abbada; Barrouta – Bir Barouta.

Photo fee TD1 at each site. Official guide TD7 for all the sites, for a group about TD10.

The **medina** is still surrounded by its original walls and is an interesting place to walk around, particularly in the early morning when shops are opening and the sun is coming up. The medina is centred around the main street, Ave Bourguiba. Walking up here from Bab ech Chouhada, on the right after the Bir Barouta, there is a small covered souk. Further up, again on the right following the signs for the *Hotel Marhala*, is a small busy market. The medina gets very lively in the morning towards the Bab de Tounes, at the N end of Ave Bourguiba.

The **Great Mosque**, built by Aqbar ibn Naffi, dates from the founding of the city in 671, and was built to be the centre of the new town. As such it is the oldest western mosque. It was severely damaged by the Berbers in 688, was virtually rebuilt in the 9th century and later en-

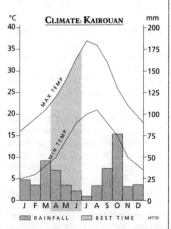

CLIMATE: KAIROUAN

°C / mm

MAX TEMP

MIN TEMP

J F M A M J J A S O N D

RAINFALL   BEST TIME   MTT30

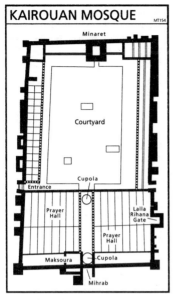

KAIROUAN MOSQUE

MT154

Minaret

Courtyard

Cupola

Entrance

Prayer Hall

Lalla Rihana Gate

Prayer Hall

Maksoura

Cupola

Mihrab

larged, but nevertheless has kept its original style. The courtyard is very large, paved in white marble with an interesting sundial in the middle indicating the times of the five daily prayers. Close to the sundial the rain water was collected in a cistern for use in ritual ablutions. The minaret is thought to date from 836. The door leading up to the top is built of materials from older sites. Enquire if it is possible to climb up the 128 steps for a superb view. The prayer hall is filled with numerous imposing granite and marble columns brought from older sites in other parts of the country. Unfortunately non-Muslims are unable to view the woodcarving on the pulpit or the 9th century tiles from Baghdad in the niche which faces Mecca. Open daily 0800-1800 except Fri and during prayers.

The **Aghlabide Pools** to the N of the town were built by Abou Ibrahim Ahmed in the 9th century. One is large, 128m in diameter, while the other is much smaller. They were part of a much more elaborate water system. An aqueduct carried water from a nearby river and the smaller pool was used to settle the silt carried in the water. Open 0830-1730 winter, 0800-1200 and 1500-1900 summer.

Zaouia Sidi Sahab (also known as the Barber's Mosque) is the burial place of one of the Prophet's companions, Abou Djama El Balaoui. The Zaouia is known as the Barber's Mosque because Abou El Balaoui carried about with him three hairs from the Prophet's beard, from which he would never be parted! The present building dates back to the 17th century. It is beautifully decorated with Andalusian style ceramics. To get to the mausoleum, you first enter into a small room and continue along an open air corridor, richly decorated in multi-coloured ceramics. The next small room with a finely worked plaster ceiling opens on to the main courtyard, with the mausoleum. Access is reserved to Muslims. Notice the painted wooden ceilings under the arcade surrounding the courtyard. On Fri when circumcision ceremonies take place and during the Mouled (the Prophet's birthday), there are numerous pilgrims.

Mosque of the Three Doors, on the E side of Bir Barouta, built in 866 by a holy man from Córdoba, is one of the oldest mosques in Kairouan which takes its name from the three large doors leading inside. There are interesting inscriptions above the doorway.

To reach the **Zaouia of Sidi Abid el Ghariani**, in the medina, take the 2nd road on the right after the main gate. This burial place of Sidi Abid, a 13th century saint, was constructed in the 14th century. Of particular interest is the room with the mausoleum. The ceiling is extremely finely worked wood, with fine plasterwork all around. The building in itself is very beautiful, based around three courtyards. Today it houses the office of the Association de Sauveguard de la Medina (an organization dedicated to helping to preserve the medina) and the regional office of the National Art and Archaeology Institute. Open during office hours.

Bir Barouta, in the centre of the medina, is an old well which functions by the movement of a camel going round in circles. Not an essential visit!!

Zaouia of Sidi Amor Abbada was built by a 19th century blacksmith who designed huge objects, deemed to be useless, such as huge anchors to held

Tunisia on to the land, huge swords, giant guns etc many of which are on display in his tomb with seven domes.

National Museum of Islamic Art, 8 km S of Kairouan, open daily 0900-1430, closed Mon.

Visits could also include demonstrations of how 'Makrouth' the famous sweet unique to Kairouan is made, as well as carpet weaving, and copper beating.

Local information
● Accommodation
Don't worry about the address, all the hotels

KAIROUAN MT153

To Enfida & Tunis

N

Avenue de la République

rue des Aglabites

Boulevard Est

To el Fahs, Tunis & bus station

Route du Bathen

Place de Tunis

Kasbah

rue de la Kasbah

Great Mosque

To Sousse

Bab el Khoukha

MEDINA

rue el Farabi

Blvd Sadikia

Ave Habib Bourguiba

Blvd Idris Snoussi

rue Zouagha

To Sousse

To Sbeitla à Gafsa

Avenue de la République

Blvd H. Chaker

Blvd H. Bourguiba

Ave Farhat Hached

To Sfax

0   200
metres

1. Bab de Tounes
2. Bab ech Chouhada
3. Place des Martyrs
4. Bir Barouta
5. Mosque of Three Doors
6. Zaouia Sidi Sahab
7. Zaouia of Sidi Abid el Ghariani
8. Zaouia Sidi Amor Abbada
9. Police Station
10. Post Office
11. Tourist Office
12. ONAT (Crafts)
13. Aghlabid Pools
14. *Hotel Splendid*
15. *Hotel Sabra*
16. *Marhala*
17. *Hotel Continental*
18. *Hotel Amina*
19. *Hotel Tunisia*
20. *Youth Hostel*

are all clearly signposted in English.

B *Hotel Continental*, T 220607, to the N by the Aghlabide pools, 175 rm, a/c, large pool, garden.

C *Hotel Amina*, route de Tunis, T 226555, F 225411, 60 rm, heating, a/c, pool.

D *Le Splendid*, T 220522, rue du 9 Avril, 28 rm with bath, a/c, clean, basic, bar and busy restaurant, slightly over-priced; **D** *Tunisia*, T 221855, Ave Farhat Hached, 44 rm with bath, breakfast, no restaurant, comfortable, very clean, no a/c but fans on ceiling.

F *Hotel Marhala*, T 220736, 35 Souk El Bey in the medina nr Bir Barouta, 30 rm with bath, very pleasant, real Tunisia, well run, small, view from top rm, roof terrace; **F** *Hotel Sabra*, T 220260, rue Ali Belhaouane, by place des Martyrs, clean, pleasant, friendly staff, roof terrace, 30 rm, rm at back are quieter, hammam next door, rec.

Youth hostel: Ave de Fés, T 220309, in the new town, kitchen, 70 beds, reports say noisy and not clean.

● **Places to eat**
♦*Restaurant des Sportifs*, Place de la Victoire, couscous speciality; *Restaurant El Karawan*, rue Soukeina Ben El-Houssein, behind *Tunisia Hotel*, typical Tunisian cooking, family run; *Restaurant Fairouz*, signposted off Ave Bourguiba in the medina, good food, cheap; *Restaurant Sabra*, Ave Farhat Hached, an excellent, cheap place to eat typical Tunisian food; *Roi du Couscous*, place du 7 Novembre, Tunisian food at cheap prices, closes in late afternoon, best for lunch or early dinner.

● **Banks & money changers**
BDS, UIB and BT on place de l'Indépendence.

● **Hospitals & medical services**
Hospital: by the Aghlabide pools, T 220036.

● **Post & telecommunications**
Area code: 07.
Post Office: Place du 7 Novembre, rue Farhat Hached.

● **Shopping**
Bargains: Kairouan is one of the major centres for **carpets** in the country. Visit first the display of old and new carpets at the ONAT on Ave Ali Zouaoui, to get an idea of real prices even though carpets can be cheaper elsewhere. Be careful when walking around, the 'Musées de Tapis' (carpet museums) are really shops which have their own carpets on display.

● **Tourist offices**
The tourist information office is opp *Hotel Continental*, nr Aghlabide pools. There are 2 offices, turn left for information and right to buy tickets for the monuments. Welcoming, competent staff will organize you a tour or an official guide if requested. Open 0800-1730 daily except Sun 0800-1200, T 220452/221797.

● **Useful addresses**
Police: T 220577.

● **Transport**
Local Car hire: Budget, Ave de la République, T 220528; Hertz, Ave Ibn el Jazzar, T 224529.

Road Bus: the station is on the road to Sousse. For information T 220125. Departures to Tunis; Kebili/Douz; Gafsa; Tozeur; Djerba; Zarzis; Medenine and Nefta. **Louages**: departures for Tunis are from Bab ech Chouahada. All other destinations leave from the Post Office. To El Djem possible by louage, requires changes and patience.

Around Kairouan

Kelbia Lake is halfway between Kairouan and Sousse. It lies to the SW of the P2, the main road from Nabeul to Kairouan just after the intersection with the MC48 road to Sousse. The best way to view the lake is to walk around the shore, but clear paths and viewing points are rare as the water level of the lake changes during the year. In summer it is dry. It is an important **Wildlife Reserve**, with a wide variety of birds. During the summer you may spot squacco herons, purple gallinules or the fantailed warbler. In the winter, migrating birds such as flamingo pass through.

Maktar

Maktar, population 7,500, lies 114 km W of Kairouan along the scenic P12. The Roman city of Mactaris which dates from around AD 200 was built on the site of an earlier Numidian defensive position. The ruins are entered by the museum through the Roman gate. Open winter 0830-1730, summer 0800-1200 and 1500-1900, entrance TD1, photography TD1. The remains of the amphitheatre lie to the left and further left, across the Roman road are the remains of a **temple** dedicated to the Carthaginian god Hathor Miskar. The central section of the site contains the former forum and the remains of Trajan's Arch, looking less triumphal than in its heyday of 115 AD. Beyond are the foundations of the 5th century Basilica of Hildeguns and after another 100m are the **Baths** which are considered the best preserved thermal baths in Africa. Much of the splendour is in its mosaics.

To the W lies the **Schola Juvenum**, claimed as one of the prettiest ruins in Tunisia, once an educational establishment for young people and in the area around this is a temple dedicated to Bacchus, an open space that was the Forum, a cemetery and yet more baths.

Maktar town lies to the N of the site and at an altitude of over 900m is refreshingly cool. The town is built on the hillside and the buses stop at the lower end of the town while the louages stop higher up the main street.

• **Accommodation** C *Mactaris*, T 876014, 20 rms, reasonable standard.

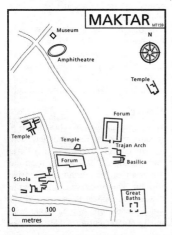

Sbeitla

ACCESS The bus station is in the centre of the new town and the louages are next to it. Many buses come here from Kasserine, Gafsa, Tunis and Kairouan. The train station is on rue Habib Thameur to S of town.

The 75 km journey S from Maktar to Sbeitla is along winding minor roads through the Dorsal region. Within 2 km of leaving Maktar, there is a magnificent view N to the mountains and as the P4 climbs through the Djebel Skarna (1076m), the Tunisia seen by the visitor here is in sharp contrast to the level plains of the Sahel. As the road descends, the ruins of the ancient settlement of Sufes at Sbiba lie to the left. 40 km beyond is Sbeitla.

The new city is of no special interest, but the old Roman ruins are really worth a visit, being considered one of the best preserved sites in Tunisia. Enter opposite the museum into the Byzantine quarter where there are three forts/dwellings constructed of materials taken from older buildings and with fortifications necessary at those unsettled times; a **church** dedicated to Saints Gervais, Protais and Tryphon; **baths** badly damaged and partially rebuilt with a mosaic of fish and crustaceans and an oil press (originally there were two presses and a windmill). The **Arch of Diocletian** forms part of the old walls to the S of the site.

In the central area is a large **cistern** which supplied water to the city, the rainwater being perhaps supplemented by an underground canal. Close by are the remains of a large public **baths**, with hot and cold rooms and a geometric mosaic decorating the room dedicated to exercise. The **fountain** is one of three public fountains dating from the 4th century.

Turn right here to the **theatre**, a shadow of its glorious past. The tiers are in ruins but the orchestra pit is clearly visible as are the colonnades round the stage. Worth the detour if only for the magnificent view over the Oued Sbeitla. The **Church of St Severus** was built in the courtyard of a Roman temple, now only four columns of stone mark the corners of the building. Turn left along the street originally with shops on either side to the magnificent **capitol** entered through the **Arch of Antonius Pius**. This gateway, dated 138-161 AD was built in the style of a triumphal arch and formed part of the ancient walls. The three massive **temples** which stand side by side opposite this gate, across the vast square, paved **Forum** are dedicated (from right to left) to Juno, Jupiter and Minerva. The central temple was more opulent in decoration. The columns of the temple of Minerva are especially delicate. Close to the Forum is another church constructed on the site of an older building. This is in poor condition but visible are the central aisle and the two smaller side aisles separated by a double colonnade.

The group of buildings to the NE comprises two churches, a baptistery, a chapel and small baths. The **Basilica Bellator** named after a fragment of inscription found there measures 34m by 15m, has a central nave and two side aisles. The mosaic floor in the choir still remains. The baptistery was converted into a chapel dedicated to Bishop Juncundus (5th century) who is believed to have been martyred by the vandals. The adjacent **Basilica Vitalis** measures 50m by 25m. A marble table decorated with biblical themes found here is now in the Bardo museum. The museum on the site has only a photograph.

If time permits explore the NW of the site through the houses and unidentified temple to the amphitheatre and across to the much restored bridge.

The Roman town, originally known as Sufetula, was probably built in the year 3 BC, but little is known about it until the period under the rule of Emperor Vespasian (69-79 AD). The town

was very prosperous during the 2nd and 3rd centuries, judging by the remains of the public buildings. During the Byzantine period, the town was briefly made capital of the province then, in 646, the Governor Gregory declared himself independent from Constantinople called himself Emperor and moved his administration from Carthage to Sufetula, which he considered to be a better centre from which to defend the country against the Arabs. This proved not to be the case when Gregory was killed defending Sufetula in 647 and the town was taken by the Arabs.

The best time to visit this impressive ruined town is early in the morning or in the evening when the soft sunlight is particularly beautiful on the stones of the temples and one is less likely to have to share the experience with a bus-load of tourists. Open 0830-1730 winter and 0600-2000 in summer. Closed Mon, entrance TD1, photo fee TD1. Most of the site is accessible in a wheelchair.

Opposite the ruins (adjacent to the Coca-cola stall and coach park) is a museum containing artefacts and photographs of Sbeitla divided into five

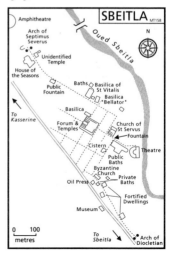

SBEITLA MT158

ESPARTO GRASS – PAPER IN THE DESERT

Esparto grass, also called *Alfa* or *Halfa*, is a needlegrass (*Stipa tenacissima*) indigenous to northern Africa and southern Spain. It is very common on the infertile, dry, sandy soils of interior Tunisia and Algeria where nothing else will thrive. The plants grow in clumps maybe 2m across with the cylindrical stems reaching 1m in height. The young grass can be used as animal fodder but later becomes too tough even for camels to chew.

This grass has been used over the centuries to make ropes, mats, storage utensils, baskets and sandals. Today it is harvested for the manufacture of paper by a process developed in the UK in 1856. Esparto has a very high cellulose content. The fibres are strong and flexible, and standard in size and shape and make a better paper than either wood pulp or rags. The resulting paper is of high quality being uniform in texture, opaque and very smooth.

sections covering prehistory, Roman sculptures, ceramics, Christian/Byzantine and Muslim periods. A visit to the museum first may make the site visit more valuable. Open daily 0600-2000. Entrance included in fee for ruins. There are toilets beside the museum.

Local information
● **Accommodation**
C *Hotel Sufetula*, just before the ruins en route from Kasserine, T 465074, pleasant, clean hotel, pool, a/c, it is the only good hotel in Sbeitla and charges accordingly.

Youth hostels: in **Kasserine**, 67 km from Sbeitla, 3 km from Kasserine centre, T 470053, 92 beds, meals available; **Siliana**, 35 km N of Maktar, T 08870871, 70 beds.

Excursion to Kasserine
Kasserine lies 38 km SW of Sbeitla. Behind it to the W stands Djebel Chambi (1,544m) the highest peak in Tunisia providing an interesting dimension to the spectacular sunsets. **Chambi National Park** protects the last of the mountain gazelles. Take the P17 N from Kasserine and before the Oued Hatab turn left/W on the P13. 5 km after crossing the railway look for a track road to the left which skirts Djebel Chambi and returns to the P17. Kasserine depends on esparto grass for its livelihood (see above), and little else grows here. The town is dominated by the huge cellulose processing factory. The remains of the **Mausoleum of the Flavii** adjacent to the

main road are more attractive. This is a three storey funeral tower of Roman origin and is the best preserved of its kind.

The bus to Kasserine from Sbeitla stops right in front of the ruins. To get a seat in a louage go into town to the terminal. There is no direct bus to Gafsa from Sbeitla. Taking louages to **Gafsa** requires changes at Kasserine, Fériana and Mejel Ben Abbès each leg costing about TD1.5. If you get stuck in Fériana try **E** *Hotel Mabrouk* near bus and louage stop.

SFAX, THE KERKENNAH ISLANDS AND EL DJEM

Sfax

ACCESS The main bus station is at the E side of Ave Bourguiba, in front of the train station. There is another bus station at the other end of Ave Bourguiba at Ibn Chabat, beyond the market for services to Gabès and all destinations S. Louages stop on place de la République. The airport 6 km to the SW, T 241700, handles international package tours and internal flights.

(*Pop* 400,000; *Alt* 21m) Sfax is the second largest city in Tunisia. It is highly industrialized, but the centre of the city has retained a lot of its charm. Sfax is a thriving city with two distinct parts: the new town, built to a geometric pattern, and the medina, still surrounded by its original walls. It is a delight for tired visitors for the site is absolutely flat.

History

Nothing remains of the ancient town of Taparura, but its commercial tradition is still well in place. In the 7th century the town was already a trade centre, exporting olive oil to Italy. By the 10th century, Sfax declared itself an independent state, only to be conquered by Roger of Sicily in 1148. It later put up a valiant resistance to the Venetians in 1785 and surrendered to the French in 1881 only after fierce attacks. Bombardment during WW2 destroyed a large part of the town. Today, its main activity is centred around phosphate exports, but olive oil continues to be a major industry.

Places of interest

The **Archaeological Museum**, T 229744, is in place Hedi Chaker (in the new town), off Ave Bourguiba. This small museum of seven rooms displays Islamic, early Christian and Roman exhibits, mostly mosaics, manuscripts and pottery. There is a 3rd century Roman painted funeral artefact. Open 0900-1200 and 1500-1830 in summer, 1400-1730 in winter, closed Sun, entrance TD3.

The **medina** is one of the best preserved and most authentic in Tunisia. Unlike the souks of Tunis and Sousse, it is primarily aimed at the locals, who do most of their shopping there. Many artisans and craftsmen still work here and earn a living in a traditional way. This all makes the medina very interesting for visitors, particularly as its walls are still intact and the difference in atmosphere between the old and new cities is clear.

Dar Jellouli, T 221186, houses the **Regional Museum of Popular Arts and Traditions** at 5 rue Sidi Ali Nour, off rue de la Driba. Set in a beautiful 17th century palace, the museum is extremely interesting and enables one to have a very good idea of life in Tunisia in the last century. On the ground floor the rooms are organized around a small courtyard. Each contains well-explained lifesize pictures of traditional Tunisian living. In one room is a kitchen complete with implements, in another living rooms with all the furniture and so on. On the 1st floor is a display of the traditional clothes and jewellery of each social class. A visit is definitely worthwhile and the setting is superb. Open 0930-1630, except Mon and public holidays, entrance TD3.

The **Great Mosque** was built in the 10th century, and from the outside the minaret, made of three superimposed towers in the same style as the Great Mosque of Kairouan, can be seen. Unfortunately, the interior is closed to visitors.

An interesting itinerary is to enter the medina by the main gate, **Bab Diwan**, and go up the road on the left, leading to the **Great Mosque**. Passing by, only glimpses of its interior, reputed to be very beautiful, can be seen since it is closed to visitors. Continue down rue des Teinturiers and enter the **souk**. Within the souks, one can find everything from clothes and meat to saddles for donkeys. At the end of this street are the city walls

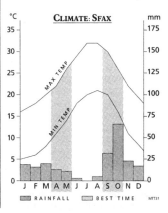

CLIMATE: SFAX

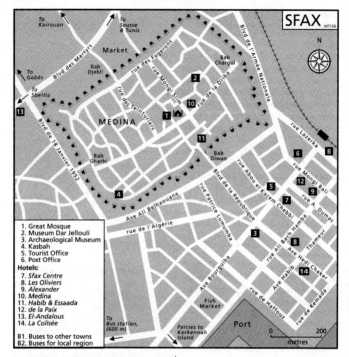

SFAX MT156

To Kairouan
To Sousse & Tunis
Blvd de l'Armée Nationale
Market
Blvd des Martyrs
Bab Djebli
rue des Forgerons
Bab Chargui
To Gabès
To Sbeitla
rue Mongi Slim
rue de la Driba
rue des Teinturiers
13
MEDINA
2
10
1
rue Lazerka
B
11
Bab Gharbi
Bab Diwan
6
rue Mongi Bali
4
rue Abou el Kacem Chebbi
5
12
9
rue A. Dumas
Ave Ali Belhaouane
Blvd de la République
7
rue de l'Algérie
Blvd de 18 Janvier 1952
rue Patrice Lumumba
3
rue Ali Bach Hamba
8
Ave Hedi Chaker
Thameur
Ave Bourguiba
14
Ave Habib
rue de Haffouz
rue de Remada
Fish Market

To Bus station, (600 m)
Ferries to Kerkennah Island
Port
0   200
metres

1. Great Mosque
2. Museum Dar Jellouli
3. Archaeological Museum
4. Kasbah
5. Tourist Office
6. Post Office
Hotels:
7. Sfax Centre
8. Les Oliviers
9. Alexander
10. Medina
11. Habib & Essaada
12. de la Paix
13. El-Andalous
14. La Colisée

B1. Buses to other towns
B2. Buses for local region

and the rue des Forgerons (blacksmiths). Opposite is the **Bab Djebli**, a gate looking over a recently built market, where food is generally sold. This can be worth a visit. In the rue des Forgerons, artisans work in little workshops doubtless in the same way as they have for centuries. Go right up rue Mongi Slim. Again, this is the heart of the souks. Some buildings have superb façades. Follow rue de la Driba and on the left is the **Dar Jellouli Museum**. Without doubt, the best way to see the medina is to spend a few hours walking around, particularly as this is really one of the few authentic medinas left. Also of note is place de la Kasbah, to the W of Bab Diwan. The **kasbah** itself is of no great interest, but there is a beautiful private building on the square. In the streets leading into the medina

from here notice the iron grilles on the first floors of most houses. Also notable is a beautiful 17th century private house on place Barberousse.

Local information
● Accommodation

A Hotel Sfax Centre, Ave Bourguiba, T 225700, F 225521, 115 rm, 8 suites, brand new, very little character, all mod cons.

B Syphax Novotel, Route Soukra, T 243333, F 245226, 127 rm, rec to all travel agents.

C Hotel el-Andalous, Blvd des Martyrs, T 299100, F 299425, 90 a/c rm, bar, 2 restaurants, on busy street but quiet inside and in rear rooms, free underground parking; **C** Hotel Les Oliviers, Ave Habib Thameur, new town centre, T 225188, charming, 50 rm, old style, good condition, pool.

D Hotel Alexander, rue Alexandre Dumas, T 221911, in new town, extremely well kept, 30 rm, clean, very good restaurant; **D** La

Colisée, rue Taieb M'Hiri, T 277800, F 299350, 40 rm with bath, a/c, heating, restaurant.

F *Hotel de la Paix*, rue Alexandre Dumas, T 221436, in new town, 30 rm, pay showers, very clean; **F** *Hotel El Habib*, rue Borj Ennar, T 221373, in medina, 22 rm, clean, communal showers; **F** *Hotel Essaada*, rue Borj Ennar, T 220892, opp *El Habib*, 43 beds, small, clean, communal showers; **F** *Hotel Medina*, 53 rue Mongi Slim, T 220354, 32 beds, in medina (not surprisingly!), small, clean, pay shower.

Youth hostel: on the road to the airport, T 243207, 126 beds, train station 1 km.

● **Places to eat**
◆◆*Chez Nous*, rue Patrice Lumumba, good choice at a good price; *Le Baghdad*, Ave Farhat Hached, very good restaurant, nice decor, but a bit expensive; *Le Corail*, T 227301, Ave Habib Maazoun, very comfortable restaurant, excellent seafood, expensive, fixed menu is value for money; restaurant in *Hotel Alexander*.

◆*La Renaissance*, 77 Ave Hedi Chaker, T 220439, choice of fish and meat dishes, clean; *Restaurant Tunisien*, just inside Bab Diwan on the right, cheap, good food.

For a **drink** go to place de l'Indépendence and the surrounding streets, or to the medina. Try *Café Diwan*, on the left after the main gates following the walls.

● **Banks & money changers**
STB and UIB, Ave Hedi Chaker; **BIAT**, rue Salem Harzallah; **BT**, Ave Bourguiba; **BNT**, rue Taieb Mehiri; **UBCI**, rue Abou el Kacem Chebbi.

● **Hospitals & medical services**
Chemist: all night, *Rekik*, *Polyclinique Ettaoufik*, T 241105, 25 rue Alexandre Dumas; *Kilani*, Ave Habib Bourguiba, T 220740.
Hospital: *Hôpital Hedi Chaker*, route d'El Aïn, T 244422.

● **Post & telecommunications**
Area code: 04.
Post Office: large building at E end of Ave Bourguiba.

● **Shopping**
Markets: Central Market on Ave Habib Bourguiba; Fish market Bab Jedid to SW of town; also route de Gabès/Ave Farhat Hached. Monoprix, 12 rue Abou el Kacem, open daily 0800-1900.

● **Sports**
Fitness centre: Samorail, route Sidi Monsour, nr beach.

● **Tour companies & travel agents**
General Voyage, Ave Hedi Chaker, T 221067; *Tourafrica*, Ave Hedi Chaker, T 229089; *Univers Tours*, Ave Bourguiba, T 222029.

● **Tourist offices**
The tourist information office is at Place de l'Indépendence, in a little kiosk, T 224606.

● **Useful addresses**
Police: rue Victor Hugo T 229710; Garde National T 227688; Customs, rue Mongi Bali, T 229184.

● **Transport**
Local Car hire: Avis, rue Tahar Sfar, T 224605; **Europacar**, 40 rue Tahar Sfar, T 226680; **Hertz**, 47 Ave Bourguiba, T 228626; **Locar**, rue Habib Maazoun, T 223738; **Rent a Car**, rue Habib Maazoun, T 227738; **Solvos**, rue Habib Maazoun, T 229882.

Air *Tunis Air*, 4 Ave de l'Armée, opp the Post Office, T 228628; *Air France*, rue Taieb Mehiri, T 224847; *Tunisavia*, rue Habib Maazoun, T 222736. The airport is about 4 km SW on the road to Gafsa. Flights to **Tunis** Mon-Fri at 0700-0820, Tues-Sat 1920.

Train Information on T 21999. Departures for **Tunis** (via Sousse) 0555, 1225, 1325, 1825, 0145; **Gabès** 1128, 0210; **Metlaoui** (via Gafsa) 0143. 2nd class return Sousse TD7 plus 650 mills fee each way. Takes 2 hrs.

Road Bus: services for **Gabès, Djerba, Zarzis, Tataouine, Ben Ghardane** and **Tunis** leave from the bus station on Ave Bourguiba, by the train station. Information on T 22355. All other destinations are served from the bus station at the other end of Ave Bourguiba. **Louages**: leave from place de la République.

Sea Ferry: to the Kerkennah islands in summer (Jul-Aug), departures every 2 hrs 0600-2000. Winter 4 boats/day 0700-1700. Foot passengers free. The price for cars is TD3.5 a0nd the crossing lasts just over 1 hr. For further information contact Sonatrak, Ave Hedi Khefacha, T 222216.

Mahrès to S of Sfax has **C** *Tamaras*, 60 beds and **E** *Younga*, T 290334, 20 beds.

The Kerkennah Islands

ACCESS Daily crossings from Sfax, six in summer, four in winter. Crossings take just over 1 hr. For information contact Sonatrak, Ave Hedi Khefacha, Sfax, T 222216. Most hotels in Sfax have time-tables available. In Kerkennah the ferry lands at Sidi Youssef, on the island of Gharbi, about 20 km from the hotel zone. The islands are linked by a Roman cause-way. A minibus service is provided and will meet the incoming ferries, though this costs more than the service bus. A bus will go directly to the hotels, so be sure to take the right one! All buses go to Remla. For El Attaya, there are a few buses a day, but they tend to stop early, so check the times. Buses for the ferries leave about an hour before ferry departure time. Times can be checked at the bus station in Remla, beside *Hotel el Jazira*. All other hotels should have this information. Otherwise, rent a bike, particularly as the islands are flat!

There are seven islands in the group with a total area of 15,000 ha made up of 6,000 ha of agriculture, 4,000 ha of palm trees and the rest uncultivated salt flats. The two large inhabited islands, Gharbi to the W and Chergui to the E, lie 20 km from the mainland. They are very beautiful, with wonderful, almost deserted, gently sloping sandy beaches, ideal for small children. The islands are almost flat (maximum altitude 13m) and covered in palm trees and with many lagoons. His-torically they have been a place of exile, from Hannibal to Bourguiba. At the mo-ment tourism is just developing with most of the hotels concentrated around the *zone des hôtels* in Sidi Frej, with a few in Remla.

The rest of the island is almost un-touched, making it quite easy to 'get away from it all'. A good way to get around is to rent a bicycle from *Hotel Farhat*. Some of the beaches are difficult to get to without transport as the buses only go through the main villages. The inhabitants have the reputation of being the most hospitable in Tunisia. The peo-ple live largely off fishing and now tour-ism. The fishing is indeed an interesting event to watch as very unusual tech-niques are used. The traditional tech-nique, known as *'sautade'*, resembles a hunt rather than fishing. The fishermen

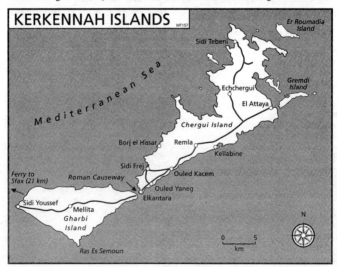

KERKENNAH ISLANDS MT157

Er Roumadia Island

Sidi Tebeni

Mediterranean Sea

Echchergui

Gremdi Island

El Attaya

Chergui Island

Borj el Hissar   Remla

Kellabine

Sidi Frej

Ouled Kacem

Ferry to Sfax (21 km)   Roman Causeway

Ouled Yaneg

Elkantara

Sidi Youssef   Mellita
Gharbi Island

N

0   5
km

Ras Es Semoun

place baskets, made out of palm leaves, on the seabed and stand in the shallow waters surrounding the island, hitting the sea with palm tree fronds. The fish (mullet in this case) hide in the baskets and are consequently trapped. This is truly an interesting sight and can be viewed at very close range since many fishermen, for a small fee, will take a passenger with them. It is also possible to rent a *felouka* (traditional fishing boat) with a captain and go either for a day trip round part of the island and probably a quiet lunch out at sea, or for a week and a total tour of the island. Information for these trips at either El Attaya, a small fishing village in the N of the island, or at one of the two larger hotels, the *Grand Hotel* and the *Hotel Farhat*, in Sidi Frej.

Otherwise activity is restricted to lying on the beach and taking life easy! In Remla it is possible to visit a carpet factory, without the anxiety of sales pressure as here they don't sell, but ship them to the mainland for retail.

Places of interest

Visit the museum in **Résidence du Salud du President Bourguiba** beyond El Attaya on the NE of Chergui. It commemorates Bourguiba's escape by boat into Libya in 1945 and contains the shack he hid in and some photographs. From Remla ½-day island tour TD13 or 'sea picnic' for TD20.

Local information
● Accommodation

Many hotels are closed in winter and those that remain open are often poorly heated.

C *Grand Hotel*, Sidi Frej, T 281266, F 281485, large hotel, 114 rm on 2 flrs, half with sea view, a/c dining room, pool, tennis, organized watersports, cycle hire, nightclub, beach restaurant, open all year; **C** *Hotel Farhat*, Sidi Frej, T 281240, F 281237, next to *Grand Hotel*, 308 beds, well decorated, pleasant, pool, tennis, beach virtually non-existent.

E *Hotel Cercina*, Sidi Frej, T 281228, F 281262, very good, beach, 70 beds, half rm have bath, most rm are bungalows, some have

sea view, restaurant has typical Kerkennian fish specialities.

F *Hotel el Jazira*, Remla, T 281058, well kept, small, 24 rm, communal bath/toilet, bar, good restaurant open all year but cold in winter.

Youth hostel: Remla, just behind the stadium, T 281148, 80 beds, meals available, family rm.

Camping: in El Attaya.

● Places to eat

◆◆*Restaurant La Sirène* by the bank in Remla, very good fish and seafood, alcohol available, shaded terrace.

◆*Le Régal*, El Attaya, N of Remla, by the harbour, very good simple, cheap food, welcoming owner. Try the special Kerkennah sauce of tomato and garlic which is excellent on shellfish.

● Bank & money changers

UIB is in centre of Remla, beside *Hotel el Jazira*.

● Hospital & medical services

Chemist: *Behiri* in centre of Remla, T 281074.

Hospital: Remla, T 281052.

● Post & telecommunications

Area code: 04.

Post Office: T 281000, Centre of Remla. There are a few other branches, the closest to the hotel zone being in Ouled Kacem.

● Shopping

Best buys are olive oil and saffron.

● Sports

All watersports including windsurfing and octopus fishing, horse and camel riding and tennis.

Harbour: El Attaya has berths for 10 yachts, min-max draft 3-4m.

Useful addresses

Police: T 281053. Maritime police, Mellita, T 223615.

● Transport

Sea Ferry: office on Hedi Khefacha, frequent ferries summer 0600-2000 about every 2 hrs and winter 0700-1700 4 return journeys. Car TD3.5, passengers free.

El Djem (El Jem)

ACCESS The train station on main Tunis-Sousse-Sfax line is 10 mins E of the amphitheatre and the bus station is by the museum, 500m from the amphitheatre. In summer the buses are full and it is difficult to find a place. The louages terminate in a street by the station.

This is a small town of around 10,000 people in the middle of a plain full of olive trees that would be of little interest if it were not for its imposing Roman amphitheatre.

History

The ancient town of Thysdrus was probably founded by the Punics, but it was only under the Romans, in particular the rule of Hadrian (117-138), that the town prospered. Hadrian encouraged the continued cultivation of olive trees and the town became an important centre for the manufacture and export of olive oil. By the 3rd century the town reached its peak, as the ruins of luxurious villas testify. But, due to political rivalries within the Empire, El Djem's fortunes gradually decreased, and were finally brought to an end during the Arab invasion, when the olive groves were set on fire, definitively ending El Djem's commercial prosperity.

Places of interest

The huge **Amphitheatre**, 148 m long by 122 m wide, has a perimeter of over 425 m. With seating for 35,000 it was the third largest amphitheatre in the Roman Empire. Construction, which is attributed to Emperor Gordien I (a keen follower of the kind of live (dead?) entertainment provided here), began in the 2nd century and when one considers that the nearest quarries were over 30 km away the task must have been enormous. It was never completed due to lack of funds and political instability. The stone was too soft for fine sculpture – hence the simplicity of the decoration.

Two smaller **amphitheatres** can be found on the other side of the road to Sfax. The older one from the 1st century

was simply cut into the rock and the second one was built on top of it. Some 30 **Roman villas** have been excavated here, all of which indicate a considerable wealth. The dwellings, built round an inner courtyard and surrounded by a colonnaded gallery, were paved with colourful mosaics depicting mythological themes (most now in the nearby museum).

It was used throughout the centuries as a fortress or stronghold. In 1695, Mohammed Bey ordered a hole to be made in the amphitheatre's walls to prevent its use during any further uprisings. The theatre was thereafter used as a convenient supply of building stones by the inhabitants of the town. Nevertheless much of the original building remains and is very well preserved; it is a truly impressive sight. Open daily from dawn till dusk. Entrance TD2. Photography permit TD1 includes visit to museum.

The **Museum** is 500m from the amphitheatre on the road to Sfax, set in a replica of a Roman villa. It is very interesting, with magnificent mosaics. In the main room is the famous mosaic '*Orpheus and the animals*' while, particularly notable in the end room, are two mosaics, '*Lion devouring a boar*' and next to it '*Tiger attacking two wild asses*'. These were found in a villa which once stood beside the museum. Open 0700-1900 in summer and 0730-1730 in winter, entrance included with ticket to amphitheatre. Clean toilets here and at the site.

International Music Festival Jul 15-Aug 7 in Amphitheatre. Details from Sousse Tourist Office (no office in El Djem).

Local information

● Accommodation

C *Hotel Club el Ksar*, 5 km from El Djem on route de Sousse, 35 rm, bar, restaurant, 3 pools, nearing completion.

E *Relais Julius*, off the main square by train station and nr bus stop, T 03 690044, simple, clean, cheap, 15 rm with bath round the courtyard, restaurant.

● **Places to eat**

The cafés in front of the amphitheatre are expensive, prices reduce with distance from site. Café Bacchus (no alcohol despite name) opp site, distinctive blue and white décor, shaded terrace, good coffee, mint tea, basic toilet.

A meal at ◆◆*Relais Julius* is better value for money.

Shopping

Supermarket: on Ave Habib Bourguiba. Mar- ket day Mon, opp train station.

● **Transport**

Train Departures for **Tunis** (via Sousse) 0649, 1316, 1416, 1825, 0145; **Sfax** 1020, 1620, 1726, 2043, 0035; **Gabès** (via Sfax) 1020, 0035; **Metlaoui** 0035.

Road Bus: the bus station is by the museum. Frequent buses run to **Sfax, Sousse, Gabès** and **Tunis**. **Louages**: by the train station, 5 mins E of the amphitheatre.

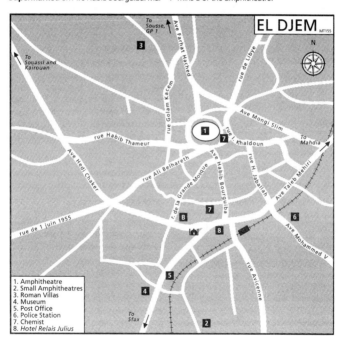

EL DJEM MT155

1. Amphitheatre
2. Small Amphitheatres
3. Roman Villas
4. Museum
5. Post Office
6. Police Station
7. Chemist
8. *Hotel Relais Julius*

CONTENTS

Gafsa to Tozeur   450
Tozeur and the Road to Algeria   456
Tozeur to Kebili and Douz   459

MAPS

Gafsa   451
The Djerid   452
Tozeur   454
Nefta   457

The Chott el Djerid gives its name to this low-lying region of salt lakes stretching from the Algerian border to the sea. Most of the oases lie on its perimeter. The Chott covers approximately 5,000 sq km, twice the size of Luxembourg and is mainly dry lake covered with a crust of salt. It is an impressive sight, especially from the P16 which links Tozeur and Kebili where mirages are frequent. The area has more on offer, however, than just the Chott. The oases, situated on the very edge of the desert to the W and E, are magnificent. Nefta and Douz, the doorways to the Sahara, are easily accessible and have a distinctive charm. The whole area abounds with fascinating landscapes and oasis villages and time should be spent here in order to explore thoroughly. In summer the temperatures reach 45°C and moving around becomes a slower and less comfortable process. The best periods to visit are spring and Nov when temperatures are more agreeable, the dates are being harvested and many festivals are held.

GAFSA TO TOZEUR

Gafsa

ACCESS The train station is 3 km E of town in the new suburb of Gafsa Gare. Buses and louages terminate in the main square, in front of *Hotel Gafsa*.

(*Pop* 60,000; *Alt* 313m) Gafsa (Roman Capsa) is the capital of the region, the largest and most important oasis town in the Djerid. It stands at the junction of the P3, P14 and P15, the crossroads between the deep S and the N. This pink-walled town is built in a mixture of styles from both N and S. The large boulevards and modern buildings are reminiscent of the N, while the narrow streets close to the Piscines Romaines have a definite echo of the S.

Gafsa made the headlines in 1980 when a commando troop of 300 exiled Tunisians came from Libya and captured the city. It took the army 3 days to dislodge them. The reasons behind the seizure of the town remain something of a mystery.

The industrial basis of the town is phosphates and sections near the rail-

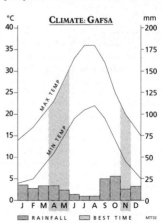

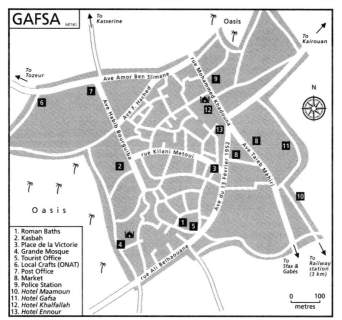

```
GAFSA  MT161
```

To Kasserine
Oasis
To Kairouan
To Tozeur
Ave Amor Ben Slimane
Ave Mohammed Khadouna
Ave Habib Bourguiba
Ave F. Hached
rue Kilani Metoui
Ave du 13 Février 1952
Ave Taieb Mehiri
rue Ali Belhaouane
N
Oasis
To Sfax & Gabès
To Railway station (3 km)

1. Roman Baths
2. Kasbah
3. Place de la Victorie
4. Grande Mosque
5. Tourist Office
6. Local Crafts (ONAT)
7. Post Office
8. Market
9. Police Station
10. *Hotel Maamoun*
11. *Hotel Gafsa*
12. *Hotel Khalfallah*
13. *Hotel Ennour*

0   100
metres

way to the SE are to be avoided for that reason. Gafsa sees many tourists but pays attention to them only as a source of income and offers no real welcome. As a gateway to the S Gafsa is best passed through quickly.

Places of interest

The **Piscines Romaines** (Roman baths) are at the end of Ave Bourguiba and consist of two deep rectangular pools which overflow into a *hammam*. Open 0800-1200 and 1500-1900 in summer, 1930-1630 in winter, closed Mon, fee TD1. In the summer, youths jump from their side or from the top of a palm tree into the pools. Fun to watch but they will expect a tip! The surrounding square has recently been carefully redeveloped and has a small café. The tourist information office is also here.

On the same street is the **kasbah**. From a distance the kasbah looks like a splendid pink fortress. It was built by

the Hafsids and has been restored recently. A visit is of limited interest. The **oasis** starts just behind it, containing over 100,000 palm trees and numerous citrus trees. The main products are oranges and lemons which are better quality than the dates. For a typical oasis visit **Lalla** along the P15 SW to Gabès, turning left after crossing the railway at Gafsa Gare.

Local information

● Accommodation

B *Hotel Maamoun*, Ave Taieb Mehiri, T 222740, central, modern, relatively nondescript building, 46 a/c rm, restaurant used by tour buses, not very clean, indifferent service but all modcons.

C *Hotel Jugurtha*, 4 km W of town at oasis of Sidi Ahmed Zarroug, T 221467, impressive site, 78 rm, pool, tennis, its age is starting to show.

D *Hotel Gafsa*, on the main square in town centre, T 222676, modern, soulless, a/c.

E *Khalfallah*, rue Mohammed Khadouma, by police station, T 221468, clean, on a noisy road, rather expensive for what is provided. **F** *Ennour*, Ave du 13 Février 1952, T 220620, very cheap, outside showers; **F** *Hotel de la République*, Ave Ali Belhouane, T 221807, quite new, clean, 20 rm, probably the best of the cheap hotels.

Youth hostel: 2 km from station, T 220268, kitchen, meals provided, 56 beds.

● **Places to eat**
◆◆*Restaurant Semiramis*, rue Ahmed Senoussi, T 221009, by *Hotel Gafsa*, one of the best places in town for French and Tunisian cooking, a bit expensive.

◆*Restaurant de Carthage* on the main square, good, cheap, typical Tunisian food.

● **Banks & money changers**
BDS is on the main square, under *Hotel Gafsa*; STB nearby.

● **Post & telecommunications**
Post Office: Ave Bourguiba N of the kasbah.

● **Shopping**
Handicrafts: the craft centre is clearly signposted at the N end of Ave Bourguiba. This is a school set up by the ONAT to train people in the art of carpet making. Make a visit to the workshops. The best buys are the striped and geometrically patterned woollen blankets and woollen rugs and shawls.

● **Tourist offices**
The tourist information office is by Piscines Romaines at the end of Ave Bourguiba, T 221644.

● **Transport**
Train The station is rather inconveniently situated outside the town in the suburb of Gafsa Gare, along the road to Gabès. One train daily at 2026 goes on to **Tunis** (via Sfax and Sousse).

Road Bus: the bus station is by the main square. Information on T 221587. Frequent departures to **Tozeur** and **Nefta**, also buses to **Kairouan**, **Sfax**, **Sousse**, **Gabès** and **Sbeitla**. Tunis 0730, 1030, 1230 (TD4). **Louages**: on the main square in front of *Hotel Gafsa*.

Around Gafsa are **Metlaoui** and, adjacent to it, **Phillippe Thomas**, named after the discoverer of the phosphate deposits which are mined here. The only real interest is the situation by the Seldja Gorge. Access by train, bus or louages all of which arrive in the centre of the town.

● **Transport Train** The station is in the town centre, one train daily to **Tunis**, (via Gafsa and Sfax) at 1915; **Redeyef** at 1555; **Moulares** at 1505.

Bou Hedma National Park, is an area of pre-desert steppe, where there has been a re-introduction of Dorcas gazelles, Addax antelopes and ostriches. It is 83 km E of Gafsa on the C124.

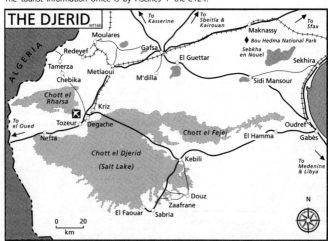

Seldja Gorges

These amazing gorges with 200m high sandstone cliffs are best seen from the train to Redeyef which departs daily from Metlaoui. This is a tourist train, the Red Lizard, and was once used to transport the Bey. It comes complete with the original furniture and fittings which have seen better days. It does the journey in about 2 hrs and leaves daily at 1100. A fascinating trip, but some days full of tourists, which is only to be expected. Alternatively, take an ordinary train which is advertised to leave at 1500 to Moulares and 1555 to Redeyef. This is much cheaper but less appealing. Both trains return to Metlaoui at 1830. To travel the 5 km to the Gorges by car, take the track on the right at the end of Metlaoui going towards Tozeur. At the end of the track there are two tunnels. Walk through into the Gorges. It is best to do this in the morning before the temperature gets too high.

Redeyef is another phosphate mining town and is really very unpleasant. The oases of Tamerza, Chebika and Midès are well worth a visit from Redeyef or from Tozeur and could be combined with a visit to the Seldja Gorges making a circular tour.

Tozeur

ACCESS The airport is 4 km out of town. The bus station on Ave Farhat Hached is used by buses from Tunis, Nefta, Gafsa and Kebili. The louage station is opposite.

The town is famous for its oasis and more particularly its 200,000 or so palm trees. The oasis is a splendid place to walk, or take a swim in one of the tepid springs. The atmosphere is fresh, the vegetation is surprisingly dense and the area is large enough to be able to absorb the crowds. The old town is very beautiful and still untouched. Nevertheless, Tozeur is the well established political and commercial centre of the Djerid and with its new international airport is starting to develop an significant tourist industry. Tourism is still a relative newcomer, but many hotels are being built.

Places of interest

The old town is fascinating. Go down Ave Bourguiba, turn left before the market into Ave Ibn Chabbat. Down this street on the right, follow rue de Kairouan (signposted to the museum) which passes under an arch. This is the oldest part of the town with many archways and intriguing side streets. Some of the houses date back to the 14th century. They are wonderfully decorated with inscriptions from the Koran or with floral and geometric patterns, most of them built out of earthen bricks in an elaborate decorative style particular to this region. Notice that few houses have windows on to the street. They are organized in the traditional style with the rooms set round a central courtyard. The doors are also interesting, decorated with nails and bearing three door knockers. The one on the left is for women, on the right for men and the lowest for children. Each knocker emits a different sound, eg deeper for men, enabling residents to recognize who is at the door.

The small **Museum of Popular Arts and Traditions** in rue de Kairouan is very interesting, and clearly displayed, set in the old Mosque (Sidi Aissa). Everyday objects are on view giving a good insight into the daily life of people in Tozeur. The rooms contain such diverse objects as traditional clothes for celebrations, jewellery, oil lamps, cooking implements and weapons. Also on display are manuscripts written by Ibn Chabbat in the 14th century, setting out the complex water distribution system in the oasis. In the courtyard you can see one of the doors with the three knockers. This is a worthwhile visit, due to the simple charm of the museum and its setting. Open 0900-1200 and 1500-1800 in summer, closes 1700 in winter. Closed Mon.

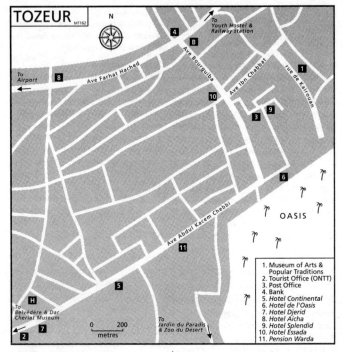

TOZEUR MT162

N

To
Youth Hostel &
Railway station

Ave Bourguiba

Ave Ibn Chabbat

rue de Kairouan

To
Airport

Ave Farhat Hached

OASIS

Ave Abdul Kacem Chebbi

To
Belvédère & Dar
Cheriat Museum

0   200
metres

To
Jardin du Paradis
& Zoo du Désert

1. Museum of Arts &
   Popular Traditions
2. Tourist Office (ONTT)
3. Post Office
4. Bank
5. *Hotel Continental*
6. *Hotel de l'Oasis*
7. *Hotel Djerid*
8. *Hotel Aicha*
9. *Hotel Splendid*
10. *Hotel Essada*
11. *Pension Warda*

The Oasis is the very reason for the existence of the town. It is beautifully fresh in summer, due to the large number of irrigation canals fed by more than 200 springs. Get there by following the signposts to the 'Jardin du Paradis' or take the road leading to the Belvédère, on the left after the Tourist Office. If the peace of the oasis is to be appreciated the well advertised tour by *calèche* is to be avoided. Problems with water supply and neglect have resulted in the loss of some of the palm trees. While the people of Tozeur turn to tourism for their income they would do well not to ignore the oasis which attracts the visitors.

The Belvédère is a large cliff by the side of the oasis where many of the springs emerge. Bathing in the hot springs has been recommended. The road to the Belvédère (3 km) goes through one of the most picturesque parts of the oasis. It is a long, but nevertheless very pleasant, walk starting on the left along Ave Abul Kacem Chebbi, beyond the Tourist Office, and following the river. From the top of the Belvédère the view over the Chott and the oasis despite the dead palm trees is most impressive, particularly in the late afternoon.

Le Jardin du Paradis and **Zoo du Désert** are through the oasis (about 3 km), following the well signposted road which starts just before the *Hotel Continental*. It is a superb garden, with amazing trees and plants, particularly impressive in the spring time, and pleasantly fresh in the summer. Try the special, very refreshing drink, reputedly unique to the Jardin, with natural pistachio, banana, violet, rose or pomegranate flavourings. Next to the Jardin is the Desert Zoo with examples of many desert animals and reptiles including snakes and scorpions. A sorry place with many of the animals trapped in minute cages. Not recommended. Open daily from 0700 until dusk. Entrance TD1.

The **Dar Cheraït Museum** past the Tourist Office is brand new, located in an imitation bourgeois Tunis house. The collection is, as usual, the reconstruction of traditional life in the previous century with rooms set up as kitchens, living rooms and even *hammams*. There are also many exhibits devoted to the life of the Beys and some of their weapons (more works of art than instruments of death), ceremonial clothes, jewellery and furniture including the Bey's bed. An interesting museum, perhaps a little too flashy, but nevertheless an impressive collection of many authentic works of art from recent Tunisian history. Open 0800-2400. Entrance TD2.5. Photography fee TD1.5. In addition to the museum, the Dar Cheraït has a garden, no charge, with palm trees and amazing lighting, 2 restaurants (one with a floor show), good food and a Moorish café. Try their hot chocolate.

Local information
● Accommodation

B *El Hafsi*, on route Touristique, past the Tourist Office, T 450966, very pleasant, modern, restaurant, pool, 62 rm, being extended.

C *Hotel Continental*, Ave Abdul Kacem Chebbi, T 450411, conveniently situated adjacent to oasis, 150 rm, slightly rundown, pool, less expensive than *l'Oasis*; **C** *Hotel de l'Oasis*, on Ave Bourguiba, T 450522, 125 a/c rm, modern, tasteful, pool, garden.

D *Hotel Dar Ghaour*, rue de Kairouan, T 452782, beside *Hotel Splendid*, opened 1993; **D** *Hotel El Djerid*, Ave Abdul Kacem Chebbi, T 450488, has definitely known better days, pool, 50 rm, clean, slightly over-priced.

E *Hotel Aicha*, rue Farhat Hached, T 450988, some rm with bath and a/c; **E** *Hotel Splendid*, opp the Post Office, T 450053, faded charm, requires some attention, clean, most rm with bath, pool, restaurant.

F *Hotel Essada*, Ave Bourguiba, opp the market, T 450097, very simple, noisy, communal bath/toilets, TD1 for a hot shower; **F** *Pension Warda*, off Ave Abdul Kacem Chebbi, just before road to oasis, T 450597, very cheap, simple, very clean rm, very welcoming, dry your laundry on the roof.

Youth hostel: Ave de la République, close to the station, T 06 450235, 47 beds. Reported to be very dirty.

Camping: at Degache, 10 km N of Tozeur on the C106. *Bedouin Camping*, down the track opp the piscine municipale, clean facilities, food available, shady sites. TD5 for 2 people, 1 car and 1 tent – rates pro rata.

● Places to eat
Are all on or around Ave Bourguiba.

◆◆*Restaurant Le Petit Prince*, Ave Bourguiba, set in pleasant surroundings, very good, more expensive than the others.

◆*Restaurant de la République*, Ave Bourguiba, similar to *Paradis*, particularly good couscous; *Restaurant du Paradis*, by the *Hotel Essaada*, off Ave Bourguiba, very good, cheap, a few pleasant tables outside, rec; *Restaurant du Soleil*, Ave Abdul Kacem Chebbi, good atmosphere; *Restaurant El Faouiz*, Ave Bourguiba, very good, simple Tunisian food, cheap.

● Banks & money changers
STB and BDS on Ave Bourguiba, BNT and BIAT on Ave Farhat Hached.

Entertainment
Hammam: 1 min from *Hotel Essada*.

● Hospital & medical services
Hospital: Hôpital Régional de Tozeur, Cité de l'Hôpital, T 450400.

● Post & telecommunications
Post Office: on the main square off Ave Bourguiba.

● Shopping
Bargains: there are many shops in Tozeur, but it is important to sort out the cheap imitations from the real bargains. Carpets and blankets are a very good buy, but be careful. In season the fresh dates are excellent.

● Sports
Hot air ballooning.

● Tour companies & travel agents
Rapide Voyages, T 450203; *Cartours*, T 450547; *Tunisie Voyages*; *Mehari Voyages* – all on Ave Farhat Hached.

● **Tourist offices**

The tourist information office is **ONTT**, Ave Abdul Kacem Chebbi, close to *Hotel Djerid*, T 450503. Organizes camel trips from Tozeur. There is an official price list for all excursions. *Pension Warda* and *Hotel de l'Oasis* offer 4WD tours to Nefta, Tamerza and Seldja Gorge.

● **Useful addresses**

Police: T 450126, 1 km down route de Gafsa.

● **Transport**

Car hire: Avis, 3 Ave Farhat Hached, T 453547; **Europacar**, Ave Abdul Kacem Chebbi, T 450119; **Hertz**, Ave Habib Bourguiba, T/F 450214.

Air *Tunis Air*, Ave Farhat Hached, T 452127; at the airport, T 450388. The airport is 4 km along the road to Nefta. Flights to **Tunis** Mon 0600 and 1055, Tues, Sat and Sun 0600; **Djerba** (TD27), Thur 1455; **Paris**, Fri 1805 and **Lyon**, Thur 0845. There are seasonal changes, always check.

Road Bus: frequent buses to **Tunis**, **Nefta**, **Gafsa** and **Kebili**. A few buses a day to **Gabès**, **Kairouan** and the N. Information on T 451557. **Louages**: opp the bus station. Louages have destinations marked only in Arabic, ask for your destination. Be early at the stop and be sharp as Tunisians with less luggage slip quickly into the seats. Six a day to Kebili, none direct to Chebika, go via Redeyef (or hitchhike).

Around Tozeur

For those with transport there are three wonderful oases not to be missed, Chebika, Temerza and Midès, some 70 km NW from Tozeur. Take the track on the left after El-Hamma du Djerid. After 60 km of easy track Chebika is reached and Temerza is 15 km further along a very beautiful road. From Temerza it is 5 km to Midès. Return via Metlaoui to see the Seldja Gorges. A splendid ½ day excursion.

Chebika is a small oasis of palms and vegetables in a narrow gorge. It is very beautiful with an amazing landscape. The old, abandoned village appears to be hanging to the rocks while its residents have moved out to the new village. Walk up the gorge by the river to the small waterfall. Be prepared for some climbing. Above is the source of the river and further to the left there is a good view of Chebika.

Temerza is another beautiful village built along the top of the mountain. The old village has been abandoned but is worth a visit for the view. The new village is of no real interest, but a walk along the river bank is interesting. The area's only hotels are here, A *Temerza Palace*, T 448562, F 445214, probably the most beautiful of the new hotels, stunning views from terrace and pool overlooking old village, good restaurant; D *L'Hotel des Cascades*, T 445365, 50 individual bungalows, outdoor restaurant, pool, beautiful location, excellent views at sunset, rec. A cheaper and more pleasant alternative is to rent a tent from the locals at the entrance to the village (TD5 pp) and spend the night in the oasis by the river. This is not an official camping area.

Midès is 6 km from Temerza along a rough but negotiable road. The landscape is amazing, with canyons and an oasis. Driving through at sunset is unforgettable. Surrounded by canyons on three sides, the village looks as though it is suspended in mid-air.

TOZEUR AND THE ROAD TO ALGERIA

Nefta

ACCESS The bus station is on the N side of the main street, Ave Bourguiba. The louages stop opposite.

Nefta is a small oasis town 23 km W of Tozeur at the edge of the Sahara. The real desert is encountered just along the P3 towards the Algerian border only 36 km away. The oasis in Nefta has about 400,000 palm trees which produce some of the best dates in Tunisia and has the advantage of being visited by fewer tourists than Tozeur. The Corbeille, a wide, deep basin which originally had springs flowing from its sides, must be seen as well as the old town.

Nefta is known as the home of Sufism, an Islamic sect formed by ascetics who were concerned with trying to achieve communion with God by means of spiritual development rather than the study of the Koran. The participants are called *faqirs* or dervishes and only a few ever reach the end of the path, ie unity with God, at which stage they can be called a Sufi. Sufism was rejected by orthodox Islam but became quite popular due to the open-minded view it promoted, and the incorporation of local rites and traditions.

One of the visible peculiarities of Sufism in Tunisia is the importance of saints and their shrines. This partly accounts for the large number of *marabouts* in the S and in Nefta. In many cases, as with the *marabout* of Sidi Bou Ali, they became places of worship. According to legend, Sidi Bou Ali was the creator of Nefta and of Sufism. There are over 120 *marabouts* in Nefta! Every year, 3 days after the *Id el Kebir* (end of Ramadan) a large celebration takes place, attracting people from all over Tunisia. Many activities in-

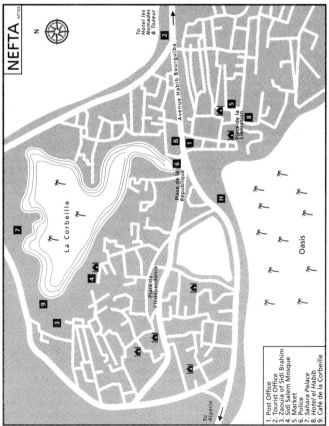

NEFTA

To Hotels les Nomades & Tozeur

Avenue Habib Bourguiba

Place de la Libération

La Corbeille

Place de la République

Oasis

Place de l'Indépendance

To Algeria

1. Post Office
2. Tourist Office
3. Zaouia of Sidi Brahim
4. Sidi Salem Mosque
5. Market
6. Police
7. Sahara Palace
8. Hotel el Habib
9. Café de la Corbeille

cluding music and dance take place in the courtyard of Sidi Bou Ali's *marabout* and in Nefta's main street. It is nevertheless basically a religious festival.

Places of interest
The **Corbeille** is a large depression situated to the N of Ave Bourguiba and from the ridge surrounding it there is an excellent view over the **oasis** below and towards the Chott el Djerid in the distance to the E. The best view is from the *Café de la Corbeille* which is reached by taking the road N from the Tourist Office or by foot through the old town N of the place de la République. Walk down into the oasis. Notice the numerous *marabouts* which are particularly beautiful at sunset. Children will want to act as guides but this is not necessary. The Tourist Office provides guides who are both competent and friendly.

The **old part of town** on the W side with its maze of narrow arcades is easily accessible from the Corbeille. It is recorded as having 24 mosques. The old town continues on the other side of the Ave Bourguiba and this is well worth strolling around, particularly as not that many tourists make the effort.

The **Zaouia of Sidi Brahim** (his tomb) is at the head of the Corbeille adjacent to *Café de la Corbeille*. Sidi Salem's Mosque, also known as the Great Mosque, is on the ridge above the Corbeille.

Local information
● **Accommodation**
A *Sahara Palace*, just behind the Corbeille, T 457046, 100 a/c rm and 9 suites, large, luxurious, Olympic size pool, disco, well situated overlooking the oasis.

D *Hotel Marhala*, T 457027, brand new hotel, pool, restaurant, tasteful decorations.

E *Hotel Les Nomades*, at the entrance to town on the left, T 457052, typical rm with beds on the flr, all rm have bath, original, very welcoming staff, pool, currently being renovated.

F *Hotel El Habib*, well situated in the centre of the old town, signposted, T 457497, clean and very basic, some rm with bath, rooftop restaurant.

● **Places to eat**
Restaurant du Sud, Ave Bourguiba, good, cheap Tunisian food; *Restaurant la Source*, by the Tourist Office on Ave Bourguiba, Tunisian specialities.

● **Banks & money changers**
BDS and **UIB** on Ave Bourguiba.

● **Hospitals & medical services**
Hospital: Hôpital Local de Nefta, rue des Martyrs, T 457193.

● **Post & telecommunications**
Post Office: Ave Bourguiba, 150m beyond the Tourist Office.

● **Shopping**
Best buys: Desert Sand Roses, found a few metres under the desert surface, are unusual and attractive objects. They are formed due to evaporation from the mineral barites and are created in beautiful patterns. They make an excellent buy, particularly as they are not well known in Europe. The only problem might be transport as they come in all sizes, the biggest being really big. The market is about 10 km beyond Nefta on the road to Algeria. It is necessary to bargain as prices generally start three or four times higher than the actual value. The market is by the Chott and is very beautiful in the late afternoon or early morning light. You are also less likely to meet a bus load of tourists whose arrival would have the inevitable effect of increasing prices.

● **Tourist offices**
The main tourist information office is on Ave Bourguiba, on the right as you enter the town, T 457184. It organizes *calèches* and camel rides round the oasis. They also organize excursions into the desert and the dunes. Guides are available. Open daily 0800-1800.

● **Useful addresses**
Police: T 457134.

Repairs & fuel: *El Kaoui* and *Chkoba* both on Ave Bourguiba.

● **Transport**
Road Bus: departures to **Tunis** (takes 8 hrs); Sfax; Kairouan; Gafsa; Hazoua and the Algerian border. Buses do not cross the border but taxis do, otherwise you are faced with a 5 km stretch of no-man's land to get to the Algerian border post. From the other side, it is an 80 km stretch to the first town, El Oued, but louages are available. **Louages**: depart frequently to **Tozeur** (takes 20 min). There is

a service to **Hazoua** and the Algerian border.

Excursion Algeria is only 35 km W of Nefta and El Oued (see page 335) another 64 km. An interesting excursion for those with a visa, in more settled times, but not to be considered at present.

TOZEUR TO KEBILI AND DOUZ

This is a worthwhile route to follow. It goes via the small oases of Degache and Kriz right through the centre of the massive salt lake, Chott El Djerid. It is a most impressive sight, a single black line of road cutting through the white salt deposits. Mirages and interesting optical illusions are frequent. Just after the Chott el Djerid, at Zaouia, 20 km before Kebili, is C *L'Hotel des Dunes*, T 05 99211, excellent, very well decorated, pool, entertainment includes *mecheoui* under tents with traditional dancing and music! **Menchia** has cafés for a rest en route. **Telmine** is another compact oasis reached before **Kebili.**

Kebili

ACCESS The bus station is in the main street (the road to Douz) with buses to Douz, Gabès and Tozeur. The louages station is by the old military compound.

This is a small regional town of military importance just W of the main road at the E end of the Chott el Djerid. One of the few interesting sights is the hot baths 4 km out of town towards Douz. There are two pools, one for the men and another further up the stream for women. An early morning bathe is very refreshing.

Local information
● **Accommodation**
C *Fort des Autruches*, signposted off the road to Douz, T 90233, 60 rm in an old fort, recently renovated, pool, bar on a terrace overlooking the oasis and the Chott, clean, a good place as stopover, but in summer it is advisable to book.

F *Ben Said*, Ave Habib Bourguiba, T 491573, on left of road to Douz, nr centre of town and louage

stop, clean rm, shared bathroom, highly rec.

Youth hostel: T 490635, 60 beds, bathrooms awful, meals available, catch bus in town centre towards Tozeur to Total petrol station.

Djemma is noted for the water in the public fountain which, unlike most water in the area, is not brackish.

Douz

This really is the gate to the desert, where the oasis meets the sand dunes! Unfortunately the new hotels have not been positioned with consideration for anyone else's view. The village is compactly built with narrow streets in order to protect against the summer heat and keep the sand at bay. The fight against the sand is incessant and women sweep the sand away from the doorstep, only to repeat the process a few hours later. Douz is also the meeting point between the nomads and sedentary population. An increasing number of nomads are settling down. By the large hotels lies a small, modern village inhabited mainly by settled nomads. The desert is all around Douz and after a few km out of town the road is hemmed in by dunes. Douz makes a good centre from which to study the oases.

Places of interest
The **Ofra Sand Dune**, one of the largest easily accessible sand dunes. Take the road towards the hotels and park by one of them or, alternatively, hire a camel by the Tourist Office. The official prices are posted in the Tourist Office. Particularly attractive at sunset. Small museum on way to dunes.

Festival du Sahara is a 4 day festival including exhibitions on traditional ways of life, Arabic poetry, plays, and many competitions such as camel races, jumping and fights. The Festival takes place every year at the end of Dec. Check exact dates with the Tourist Office. At this popular period be sure to have booked a hotel room.

There is a **market** each Thur attended by many nomads. There is also an animal market which sometimes has camels. Get there early if you want to buy one!

Douz is an important point of departure for many **desert trips**. One of the most interesting is a week's camping trip through the desert to Ksar Guilane by camel. For the less adventurous, trips in 4WD vehicles are a good way of seeing the desert. Remember that in summer the desert gets much too hot for these trips. If interested, contact Agence Abdel Moulah Voyage in Douz, 150m from the Tourist Office, T 495484, F 495366.

Excursions

Zaafrane is accessible by bus, louage or hitchhiking from Douz. Zaafrane really is a village in the desert. The old village has been abandoned and is slowly being covered by the sand. The surrounding landscape of endless dunes and sand with the occasional palm tree is very impressive. **E** *Hotel Zaafrane*, small, cheap hotel, clean and very simple, café. Excursions by camel are available TD25/day, following a circuit around the water holes and eating biscuits cooked in the sand. A superb walk from Zaafrane back to Douz (3-4 hrs) via the sand sea. Navigate using Douz Post Office tower which is visible from the top of the dunes. Real desert environment including animal tracks in the sand. If a storm comes head N to the oasis and back to the road. Carry plenty of liquid and a compass. Sabria between Zaafrane and El Faouar has little to see except more dunes and an old cemetery with two marabouts.

El Faouar is also accessible by bus, louage or hitchhiking. This is the last village on the road. Try and see the **market** on Thur when any nomads and locals assemble. It is at its most interesting when dates are in season. Go early in the morning as many goods have disappeared by 1000. **D** *Hotel El Faour*, is virtually built in the desert with pool, a/c, restaurant. The hotel organizes camel trips (2-3 hrs) in the desert and you can learn dune skiing! There is a direct route for 4WD vehicles from El Faouar to Kebili (54 km) via Blidet and Touiba.

Local information
● Accommodation

C *Mehari*, at the end of route Touristique, by the Ofra dune, T 495145, 125 rm, luxury with a/c, nightclub, 2 pools, a tower block provides excellent views for guests but spoils the view for everyone else; Three new hotels also by Ofra dune are **C** *Caravanserail*, T 470123; **C** *Touareg*, T 470057, F 470313; **C** *Sahara Douz*.

D *Hotel Saharien*, on route Touristique, T 495337/9, accommodation in over 100 bungalows most with bath, very clean, pool, rec.

E *Hotel Rose du Sable*, route Touristique, T 495336, 45 rm, not quite as nice as *Saharien* but cheaper, all rm with bath, nearly all with a/c, being renovated, check they have finished before you book.

F *Hotel Bel Habib*, in place des Souk, T 495309, newly opened, clean, very cheap, welcoming owners, communal bath/toilet, large breakfast, interesting views from terrace over fruit and vegetable market. Owner will organize lifts – eg Ksar Guilane in 4WD for TD5; **F** *Hotel de la Tente* next to louage station, dormitories, bath with hot water, sleep on the roof in a bedouin tent for 2TD, manager very kind, rec; **F** *Hotel Splendid* in town has been rec.

● Places to eat

El Khods, 100m from Tourist Office, good simple food, cheap; *Restaurant Ali Baba*, in town, on the left on the road to Kebili, serves the 'best couscous on Tunisia'.

● Post & telecommunications
Post Office: in the centre of the town.

● Tourist offices

The tourist information office **ONTT**, route de Zaafrane, T 495350, is in the same building as the local tourist office. They are separated by a café. Local office, T 495341, open every day, all day. They organize excursions into the desert on camels.

● Transport

Road Bus: from the station at the roundabout by the cemetery there are frequent buses to **Kebili**; **Tunis** 0600 (via Kairouan) and 2030 (via Gabès and Sfax); **Gabès** 0700, 1000, 1430; **Tozeur** 0630; **El Faour** (via Zaafrane) 0645, 0800, 0900. **Louages**: are based opp the bus station in the centre of town. Louages to Kebili TD1.5, to Gabès TD6.

CONTENTS	
Gabes to Matmata and the Mountain Villages	461
Matmata to Douz via the Desert Track	467
Medenine and South to Tataouine	468
Zarzis and the Island of Djerba	470

MAPS	
Southern Tunisia	462
Gabès	464
Matmata	466
Djerba Island	473
Houmt Souk	475

This is where the N fringe of the Sahara begins. The architecture and landscape change noticeably as one goes S. There are few sites of historical acclaim but a great many interesting places to visit such as the unusual troglodyte dwellings in Matmata and the beautiful *ksour* of Medenine. The Sahara is the main attraction for visitors who want to see white desert sand dunes and palm tree filled oases, so the number of tourist centres is increasing with alarming speed but the distances are such that it is possible to avoid the crowds.

GABES TO MATMATA AND THE MOUNTAIN VILLAGES

Gabès

ACCESS The bus station is on the main street, Ave Farhat Hached, at the W end, after the roundabout, towards the oasis. Walk E to the town centre. Trains from Tunis and the coastal resorts, Gafsa and Metlaoui arrive at the station on Ave 1 Juin, in the centre of town. The louages station is also on Ave Farhat Hached.

(*Pop* 94,000; *Alt* 4m; *Best seasons* spring and autumn) Gabès, 138 km S of Sfax, with its characteristic ochre buildings, is the first town along the route which gives a feel of 'the South'. It extends along the Oued Gabès which feeds the oasis and provides the harbour. The main attraction is the oasis which comes right down to the sea.

Gabès is a relatively new city, much of it having been rebuilt after WW2 and the serious flood in 1962. Despite the long beaches and fine sand, the coast is not very appealing. A major industrialization programme in the area over the last 15 years means the sea is probably polluted, but it is nevertheless worth a stop to enjoy the coolness of the oasis. Gabès is also an excellent centre for visits to the surrounding villages of Chenini (do not confuse this with village of same name near Tataouine), and Matmata and a good stop over on the way to Kebili, Medenine and Djerba.

History

Thought to be of Phoenician origins, by 161 BC Gabès was part of Carthage, and a trading link with the S. It later came under Roman influence and was destroyed during the Arab invasion. The

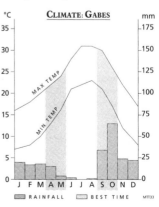

CLIMATE: GABES

RAINFALL   BEST TIME

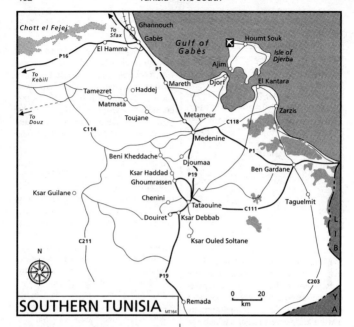

SOUTHERN TUNISIA

Chott el Fejej · To Sfax · Ghannouch · Gabès · Gulf of Gabès · Houmt Souk · Isle of Djerba · El Hamma · P16 · To Kebili · P1 · Ajim · Mareth · Djorf · El Kantara · Tamezret · Haddej · Matmata · Metameur · Zarzis · To Douz · Toujane · C118 · C114 · Medenine · P1 · Beni Kheddache · Djoumaa · Ben Gardane · Ksar Haddad · P19 · Ghoumrassen · Ksar Guilane · Chenini · Taguelmit · Tataouine · Douiret · Ksar Debbab · C111 · Ksar Ouled Soltane · C211 · N · P19 · C203 · Remada · LIBYA · 0 20 km · MT164

rebirth of the town is linked to the arrival of Sidi Boulbaba, the Prophet's companion, in the 7th century. He is now revered as the town's patron saint. Gabès later became a *fondouk*, or halt on the way S. During WW2 the Afrika korps settled in Gabès, using it as a strategic point on their supply lines to Libya. The town was finally liberated in Mar 1943 by British and French troops, but only after extensive damage had been done. Today, apart from traditional industries such as fishing and agriculture based on fruit from the oasis and the 200,000 palm trees, Gabès has become highly industrialized with a massive cement and brick factory, an oil refinery, harbour and projects for petro-chemical industries. Oil and gas wells have been drilled offshore in the Gulf of Gabès. Fortunately, though, the industries are dispersed over the surrounding suburbs, making them less conspicuous.

Places of interest

The **Great Mosque** at the junction of Ave de la République and Ave Bechir Dzir was built in 1938 and in itself is of little interest, but the surrounding area has a souk and many shops selling handicrafts made of plaited palm fronds – everything from hats to baskets and mats. Shops also sell jewellery, food and spices, giving the whole market a colourful touch and interesting aroma. Both spices and plaited items are very good buys.

The **Oasis** is very large, covering 10 sq km, and has more than 300,000 palm trees which shelter hundreds of olive and fruit trees in addition to numerous vegetable gardens. To get to the more attractive parts of the oasis you can go by car towards the village of Chenini by taking the main road towards Sfax, turning left in the direction of Kebili, then left again, signposted Chenini. Alternatively go on foot from the other end of the oasis, by the bus station, crossing the little bridge. Following the road it is 7 km to Chenini, but it is not necessary to go that far since there are pleasant walks along the small, shaded paths between the palm trees, especially in summer. A more picturesque way to see the oasis is to take a *calèche* from the end of Ave Farhat Hached. The price, TD7, is set by the Tourist Office. These are a tourist trap, strictly for the undiscerning as is the zoo complete with crocodiles and scorpions. Neither is recommended. At the end of the oasis, towards the source of the river, are located the **Sidi Ali el Bahoul Mausoleum** and a very small, but refreshing, waterfall. The region attracts a very high proportion of tourists but the oasis is large, and it is easy to get away from the crowds.

Mosque Sidi Boulbaba, one of the most important religious monuments in the area, is on the road towards Matmata, down the continuation of Ave de la République. This is the burial place of Sidi Boulbaba, who was the Prophet's barber after he came from Kairouan. The building is very elegant, with beautiful arcades. Only the inner courtyard is open to visitors.

The **Museum of Popular Arts and Traditions** is next to the Sidi Boulbaba mosque, set in an old *medersa* dating from the 17th century which has a simple but appealing architectural style. The museum has a collection of everyday objects demonstrating the traditional way of life in Gabès. The material is well displayed but unfortunately there is a disappointing lack of information. One very interesting room displays tools used within the oasis and behind there is a small garden with typical fruit trees. Open daily 0800-1200 and 1500-1900 in summer, 0930-1630 in winter. Closed Mon, entrance TD1, T 271111.

Local information
● Accommodation
C *Hotel Chems*, end of Ave Habib Thameur on the right after the railway, T 270547, beach, over 200 rm, most parts tastefully decorated, each with a small terrace, some with sea view;

C *Hotel de l'Oasis*, at the end of Ave Habib Thameur, T 270782, on the right after the railway, 82 rm, no pool, beach, the best and most expensive hotel in town; **C** *Hotel Nejib*, corner of Ave Bourguiba and Ave Farhat Hached, T 271686, 56 rm, all modcons, a/c, noisy due to main streets on both sides, slightly over-priced but very comfortable and convenient.

D *Chelah Club* (Village de Vacation), in Chenini in the oasis, T 270442, clearly signposted, accommodation in small wooden chalets, good situation, pool; **D** *Régina*, 135 Ave Bourguiba, T 272095, only 14 rm with bath, arranged around central courtyard, clean, restaurant, in summer dinner is served on the patio, best of the cheap hotels.

E *Hotel Atlantic*, 4 Ave Bourguiba, T 270034, old hotel retains some charm but needs decorating, clean, all 48 rm have bath, restaurant, good value, rec.

F *Ben Nejima*, 68 rue Ali Djemel, nr train station, T 271591, clean and very simple, hot communal showers, rooms at front rather noisy, good restaurant; **F** *Hotel de la Poste*, 116 Ave Bourguiba, T 270718, very cheap but not really very clean, communal bath and toilets.

Youth hostel: Rue de l'Oasis, T 270271, in quarter called 'Petite Jara' N of the souk, small rm, 80 beds, breakfast TD0.7, bathrooms unpleasant.

Camping: on main road, follow sign opp Agil petrol station. Cheap and adequate, also at Youth Hostel, TD2 pp.

● Places to eat
◆◆*Restaurant Chez Amori*, 82 Ave Bourguiba, has good, simple Tunisian food, choose the fish before it is cooked, very friendly; *Restaurant l'Oasis*, 15-17 Ave Farhat Hached, T 270098, a very popular restaurant especially for locals at lunch time, evenings are quieter, more expensive than the others. Restaurant in *Hotel Ben Nejima* has good, well presented food.

◆*Le Pacha*, Ave Farhat Hached, good, filling food, served by welcoming people; *Restaurant à La Bonne Table*, Ave Bourguiba, good, cheap food. There are also several very small, very cheap restaurants beside the daily vegetable market off Ave Farhat Hached which serve Tunisian food.

● Banks & money changers
BIAT, Ave Farhat Hached; BT, UIB and BDS on Ave Bourguiba (0800-1200 and 1400-1700).

● **Hospitals & medical services**
Chemist: all night, two in Ave Habib Bourguiba.
Hospital: Hôpital Universitaire, Cité M'Torrech, T 272700.

● **Post & telecommunications**
Area code: 05.

Commercial Centre: Ave Bechir Jaz'iri, direct mail to Europe.
Post Office: T 270544, Ave Bourguiba, opp *Hotel Régina*.

● **Shopping**
Bargains: ONAT on Blvd Farhat Hached has a range of quality goods. Open 0900-1300 and

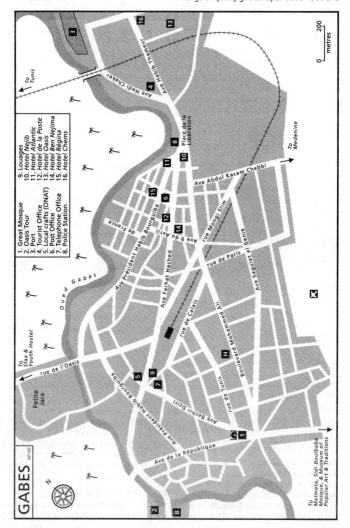

1. Great Mosque
2. Oasis Tour
3. Port
4. Tourist Office
5. Local crafts (ONAT)
6. Post Office
7. Telephone Office
8. Police Station
9. Louages
10. Hotel Nejib
11. Hotel Atlantic
12. Hotel de la Poste
13. Hotel Oasis
14. Hotel Ben Nejima
15. Hotel Régina
16. Hotel Chems

GABES

To Tunis

To Medenine

To Sfax & Youth Hostel

Petite Jara

To Matmata, Sidi Boulbaba Mosque, & Museum of Popular Art & Traditions

Oued Gabès

Ave Habib Thameur

Ave Hedi Chaker

Place de la Libération

Ave Abdul Kacem Chebbi

Ave President Habib Bourguiba

Ave de France

Ave 9 du Avril

rue Mongi Slim

Ave Farhat Hached

rue de Paris

Ave Saguiet el Genie

rue de Calais

rue de l'Oasis

Ave President Habib Bourguiba

Ave Bechir Dziri

rue de Tunis

Boulevard Mohammed Ali

Ave de la République

200 metres

N

1600-1900 in summer; 0830-1230 and 1500-1800 in winter. Gabès is well known for its straw work which can be bought in the souk or the markets. Also rec is the Berber jewellery. Gabès is the last town where you can buy a European newspaper, although it will probably be several days old. The daily **vegetable market** gives a good insight into Tunisian life.

Crafts: The ONAT school/workshop is worth a visit to see all the local handicrafts on display, closed afternoons on Fri and Sat. This is where the various craft techniques are taught. The course lasts 2-3 years for jewellery making, the majority of the young artisans opening their own shops on completing the course. There are courses, too, on palm frond weaving and carpet making and the demonstrations show how these skills are taught.

● **Sports**
Harbour: 20 yacht berths min-max draft 2-4.5m.

Sponge fishing, fishing for tuna fish, king shrimps, octopus.

● **Tour companies & travel agents**
Sahara Tours, Ave Farhat Hached, T 270930; *Gabès Voyage*, Ave Farhat Hached, T 270797; *Carthage Tours*, Ave Bourguiba, T 270840.

● **Tourist offices**
The tourist information office is at Place de la Libération, T 220254.

● **Transport**
Local Car hire: Avis, rue du 9 Avril, T 270210; **Budget**, 57 Ave Farhat Hached, T 270930; **Europcar**, 12 Ave Farhat Hached, T 274720; **Hertz**, 30 rue Ibn el Jazzar, T 270525. **Cycle hire**: enquire at the Youth hostel or at *Hotel de la Poste*.

Air (nearest airport is Sfax 137 km N or Houmt-Souk on Djerba 106 km E) **Tunis Air**, Ave Bourguiba, T 270697; **Tunis Avia**, route de Sfax, T 272501.

Train The train station is off rue Farhat Hached. Information on T 270944. Departures as follows: **Tunis** (via Sfax) 1525, 2242. For **Metlaoui or Gafsa** take the 2242 and change at Sfax for the 0140.

Road The bus station is at the end of Ave Farhat Hached, by the entrance to the oasis. Information on T 270008. Departures to: **Matmata** (takes 1 hr, TD2); **Ben Gardane; Chenini** from the corner of rue de la République and rue Haj Jilani Lahbib; **Djerba; Gafsa; Kebili;** **Sfax; Sousse; Tunis. Louages**: the louage station is opp the ONAT on Ave Farhat Hached. It is possible to get a round trip visiting all the villages and the area surrounding Gabès. Tour operators offer a variety of options, including travel by 4WD vehicle with a group of 5-10 people (see Travel agents).

Matmata

ACCESS Ensure the buses from Gabès or the daily bus from Tunis drop you in the original Matmata, not Matmata Nouvelle which is 15 km down the road. A minibus runs between Matmata Nouvelle and Matmata costing 700 mills. It leaves when it is full.

Matmata is an amazing **troglodyte** village set in the mountains. The scenery round about is like a lunar landscape, with the houses being dug into the ground. See box, page 526. The only visible signs above ground are the TV aerials! There are also many very beautiful *marabouts* scattered over the mountainside. The village is inhabited by 3,500 people, but about half of them leave to work in the N or in Europe at some point in their lives, often setting up as bakers. Some who return, having earned sufficient money, build themselves a 'real' house in Matmata Nouvelle, 15 km down the road to Gabès. A section of the population still live in the underground dwellings, but their number is slowly decreasing. If you want to see the inside of one of the underground houses it isn't really necessary to take a guide, but doing so is one way of obtaining entry. The fee should be negotiated but is generally very reasonable, in the region of TD1-2.

The Berbers, known as the Matmata, have been living in these houses for over 700 years. They originally constructed their homes underground in the soft rock to protect themselves from possible attacks and from the harsh climate. Habits are only now starting to change due to the exodus of the young people who set off to the large cities in the hope of finding work and an easier life.

There is little scope for agriculture in Matmata due to the harsh climate and the lack of water, which explains the tendency to migrate. However there is still some work to be found in the village, particularly in the ever-expanding tourist sector, and many locals make their money from the tourists who flock here during the day. Indeed it is worth staying overnight in Matmata in order to appreciate the village once the crowds have left and drive out to Zeraoua and Tamezret to see the sunset. Doing so, especially in one of the underground hotels, is quite an experience.

Places of interest

Underground dwellings On arriving in Matmata it is unclear where to go since nothing is visible, but walking around will reveal one of the 700 underground houses. Many of these can be visited in return for a small payment at the end of the tour. Take the opportunity to see the unusual living conditions. Even if you are not planning to spend a night in Matmata, go and visit a hotel, access being free, and see the labyrinth of tunnels leading from one courtyard to another. For further detail, see page 526.

Overlooking the village is a small fort which, unfortunately, cannot be visited since it is in a military zone.

Excursions

Matmata Nouvelle, 15 km away, is often ignored but a visit here will help explain the reasons why the villagers moved and give also some insight into the process of settlement of the nomads. There is a variety of places to visit. Going SE towards Médenine, take the track which goes via Toujane. This is shorter, but not necessarily quicker, and a very picturesque route (See Toujane, see page 467). If you are travelling to Douz or Kebili or feeling adventurous, take the track to Tamezret. (See Tamezret below).

Local information
● Accommodation

C *Hotel les Troglodytes*, T 230062, F 230173, 1 km down road to Tamezret on left, above ground, pool, a/c rooms, opened 1992.

D *Hotel Matmata*, T 30066, small, above ground (so no troglodyte charm), all rm have bath, a/c, comfortable, clean, pool, restaurant.

E *Hotel Marhala*, T 230015, slightly out of the village, up the road towards the fort, probably the best of the 3 underground hotels, government owned, very clean, very basic (bed, door without lock, light bulb!), communal bath/toilet, quiet, good traditional restaurant, book in summer.

F *Hotel Berbers*, T 230024, most recent and smallest underground hotel, communal bath/toilet, restaurant, book in season, a curious experience; **F** *Hotel Sidi Driss*, T 230005, largest and most touristy, endless corridors and courtyards, communal bath/toilet.

Youth hostel: 'Berber City' grottoes, Old Matmata, 6070, 50 beds.

● Places to eat

For a decent meal it is best to eat in the hotels, although there are a few restaurants in the market place. *Café Restaurant Ouled Aziz*, at the entrance to Matmata has good traditional Tunisian food and is quite cheap. *Café de la Victoire* has been rec.

MATMATA
Rough Sketch   MT168

To Gabès

N

To Toujane

To Tamezret

1. Police Station
2. Post Office
3. Tourist Office
4. Chemist
5. Restaurant
Hotels:
6. *Marhala*
7. *Matmata*
8. *Kousseila*
9. *Sidi Driss*
10. *Les Berbères*
11. *Les Troglodytes*

● **Banks & money changers**
Banks are situated in Matmata Nouvelle, 15 km along the road to Gabès.

● **Post & telecommunications**
Post Office: in the centre of town.

● **Tourist offices**
The tourist information office is next to the Post Office.

● **Transport**
Road Bus: Tunis 2030; Sousse 2215; **Gabès** 0530, 0730, 0900, 1100, 1230, 1330, 1400, 1600, 1730, 2000; **Tamezret** 1400.

Haddej

To get to this village (Haddège on Michelin map), 6 km N of Matmata on the road to Gabès take the track to the right where the tourist shop and café are situated. Track not suitable for vehicles therefore very peaceful. Takes 1 hr to walk. Access is difficult without your own transport. Haddej is a very traditional village similar to Matmata but less involved with tourism. It is possible to see what Matmata must have been like before the tourist influx.

Tamezret

This beautiful Berber village lies 13 km W of Matmata. The road here from Matmata is black top and amazingly good. The scenery is quite extraordinary, a mixture of the moon and the Grand Canyon! The village is built on the side of a mountain. The houses built of dried earth blend in perfectly with the scenery. Stroll around the narrow, winding streets and walk up to the top of the village from where there is a marvellous view across the desert, particularly at sunset.

Toujane

No buses go along this road but it is possible to get a lift. By car it is a very worthwhile trip, mostly along a very easy track (be sure to have a spare tyre). Go S in the direction of Tèchine and turn left after 6 km where there is a large white boulder indicating Toujane-Médenine. The track is steep and narrow and winds up to a fantastic view over the plain below and E towards the sea. On a bright and clear day it is possible to see Djerba! At the end of the track, go left and start the descent to Toujane which will suddenly appear, apparently clinging to the mountain side. It is a beautiful village on an exceptional site. Wander around and look at the carpets and the *kilims*, small smooth woven carpets with traditional designs originally used as prayer mats and in tents. They are all made locally and are cheaper here than in the main towns. Purchases can be made at Chez Laroussi on the road.

Towards Medenine
Continue on the road through the village. The first few km are black top and although the rest, about 30 km, is unsurfaced, it is neither difficult nor dangerous.

MATMATA TO DOUZ VIA THE DESERT TRACK

This journey can be done in a car which does not have 4WD (but don't tell the hire agency your plans!!!). It is an exciting experience and 60 km shorter than the route via El Hamma-Kebili, although not necessarily faster. Don't forget to take water and do not travel after rain as the vehicle will sink. (See Travel and Survival in the desert, page 45.) Take the black top road to Tamezret and follow the track W. Turn left at the junction after the pipeline, and about 2½ km further is the small *Café Djelili* where the food is excellent. Another 10 km will bring you to the *Café Sahara Centre* offering food, accommodation and selling 'Arab' headgear to tourists. Here you can sleep out in the open under an incredible star-studded sky. The road from here on is more or less a straight 43 km to Douz.

MEDENINE AND SOUTH TO TATAOUINE

Medenine

ACCESS The bus station is on rue du 18 Janvier and the louages stop in a small street opposite.

This is an important crossroads town. However it holds little interest for the visitor, having been extensively modernized with few traces of its past remaining. Medenine is at the centre of the **ksour** area. A *ksar* (plural *ksour*) is a fortified village built in a characteristic style with curved, whitewashed houses and the typical *ghorfas* (granaries). Originally the villages were not fortified, but with the Arab invasion and other dangers the Berbers were obliged to build defences. The *ksour* were generally built on the top of a hill, in an easily defensible position, out of dried earth which blends in with the colour of the landscape. Medenine is a good place for the start of excursions towards Metameur and the surrounding area where some *ksour* have been better preserved than in Medenine. This region is a frontier between two cultures, the nomads and the settled people. Once the area was totally controlled by nomads but today the tents have been replaced by small concrete houses and the camel by a Peugeot truck.

Increasing tourism has made some souvenir sellers more aggressive.

Local information
● **Accommodation**
D *Hotel Sahara*, Ave Bourguiba, T 640007, 20 rm, is a bit better than the others, fairly central, too pricey for what it offers.

F *Hotel Essaada* and **F** *Hotel Hana*, T 640690, both in Ave Bourguiba, quite noisy, but well placed, central.

Youth hostel: on the road to Djorf, T 640338, 60 beds.

● **Place to eat**
Restaurant in *Hotel Sahara*.

● **Banks & money changers**
On Ave Bourguiba Bank in the town centre.

● **Post & telecommunications**
Post Office: Ave Bourguiba.

● **Useful addresses**
Police: T 640033.

● **Transport**
Road Bus: information on T 640427. Buses to Tunis; Djerba, Tataouine, Zarzis, Ben Gardane, Gabès, Gafsa and Sfax.

Around Medenine

Metameur can be reached by louage, hitchhiking or a bus to the junction. Take the road to Gabès, turning left after 6 km to the village which is 1 km further up the road. Metameur is a beautiful village with *ghorfas*, which are still in relatively good condition, on the small hill.

● **Accommodation** **D** *Hotel El Ghorfa*, T 640294, 35 rm, a charming little hotel built in the ghorfas, a wonderful place if you want to get away from everything for a few days.

Gightis on the coast 27 km N of Medenine has remains of Romano-African style buildings, Capitol, Forum, Temples, Baths and is an interesting excursion.

Djoumaa is situated 36 km SW of Medenine on the C113 to Beni Kheddache. There are buses here from Medenine at 0815 and 1000, returning at 1000 and 1400. It is worth a trip to this most attractive hill top village with splendid views. The *ksar* has only recently been abandoned.

Beni Kheddache, beyond Djoumaa, can be reached by the same buses from Medenine at 0815 and 1000. The village is of little interest in itself, but from here you can take the desert track S to Ksar Haddad and on to Tataouine.

Medenine to Ben Gardane

This 77 km of road is very busy as goods go into Libya this way. Getting a lift is easy. There are 3-4 buses daily. Stay in Ben Gardane at **E** *Hotel de l'Algerie*, rue 20 Mars, T 665279 or **F** *Baghdad*, rue de Zarzis, T 666123, next to bus station, clean, shared toilet facilities. A very good unofficial exchange rate for Libyan dinars is available here.

Medenine to Tataouine

With your own transport the most interesting route is via Beni Kheddache and S via Ghoumrassen. The track is not difficult and the landscape is fantastic. This is the area inhabited by the Haouia. Without transport, the quickest and easiest way is to do the 49 km by bus. For the more determined there is a bus from Medenine to Beni Kheddache and a bus from Ghoumrassen to Tataouine and it is possible to hitch a ride between the two villages.

Tataouine

ACCESS Buses from Medenine, Zarzis, Houmt Souk, Ghoumrassen and Tunis arrive at the bus station on rue du 1 Juin 1955. The louages station is on the same street.

The major town in the *ksour* area, Tataouine is a good place to start a circuit round the *ksour*. It is not a very interesting town, but more charming than Medenine. Especially lively and interesting is the market on Mon and Thur.

Places of interest

A very colourful **market** is held Mon and Thur on Ave Farhat Hached. There is a possibility of finding a bargain in the carpets, jewellery, straw goods, and particularly the materials from the bedouin women.

Local information
● **Accommodation**
The choice is very limited.
B *Sangho*, T 860124, F 862177, 62 rm, 9 km S at the Douiret/Remada intersection turn right towards Ghoumrassen el Bled, clearly signed, spotlessly clean, tastefully decorated, pool, tennis, restaurant, opened Jul 1993.

D *La Gazelle*, Ave Bourguiba, T 860009, a/c, all 23 rm have bath, could be better looked after and cleaner, decent restaurant, 62 rm, definitely over-priced and not very welcoming, but unfortunately one of the few suitable hotels in town.

F *Hotel Medina*, rue Habib Mestaoui, T 860999, hot showers, restaurant, breakfast TD1; *Hotel Ennour*, Ave Bourguiba, T 860131, by the main road to Remeda, not very clean and quite noisy.

● **Transport**
Road Bus: information on T 862138. Buses to **Medenine**; **Gabès**; **Djerba**; **Tunis** and **Sousse**.

Around Tataouine

Ksar Ouled Soltane is one of the best preserved *ksour* in Tunisia and has virtually no tourists. Take the road directly S of Tataouine, to the left of the main road to Remada, in the direction of Maztouria to the *ksar* of Ben Barka. From the terrace at the top there is a splendid view. 8 km after Maztouria turn left and the village is 2 km further on.

Ksar Ouled Debbab is about 10 km along the P19 on the road S to Remada. This beautiful hilltop *ksar*, now abandoned and falling into ruin, blends into the surrounding landscape. The people now live in the new town at the foot of the hill.

Douiret The road for Douiret, 9 km through land cultivated after the winter rains but barren in the summer, is W from the centre of Ksar Ouled Debbab. The old, almost abandoned village is perched on the hillside 2 km further along the track. It is very impressive, quite eerie, the place has a mystical touch. The white mosque attracts attention while the earth coloured houses tone in with the hillside. There is a small *marabout* on the left on the way into the village. Watch out for dogs. Notice the inscriptionless tomb stones. Douiret has the privilege of having so far escaped the tourists.

Roads from Douiret to Chenini

A possible route on to Chenini is via a scenic track N through the mountains. Take the usual precautions regarding water and spare tyres. It can be done in a Peugeot 205 or Citroen AX. Cross the new village of Douiret and take the track on to the W. It is best to check with one of the villagers to make sure the route is not closed by floods. The other road to

Chenini is S of Tataouine, turn right after 2 km on the C207 to Ghoumrassen el Bled and 3 km further on keep straight ahead when the main route swings right. Total distance 10 km. There is no need to stop in the new town, rather follow the road round the hill to the only restaurant which serves excellent couscous.

Good news for walkers. Chenini is only 5½ km from Douiret over the top past the highest houses. Seek a guide as the only people en route will be girls herding goats.

Chenini

(Do not confuse with village of same name near Gabès, page 461). This is an amazing Berber village built on either side of a rock crest. The houses which are built into the rock have a small courtyard, where animals are kept. There are some *ghorfas* at the top of the village, but only a few are still in use. Chenini men are traditionally known as newspaper sellers. Visit the underground mosque with its particularly intriguing long tomb stones. Chenini has become part of the tourist route but, despite the crowds climbing up and down the village, it is worth seeing for the extraordinary setting. The streets here are just ledges, scarcely wide enough for two people to pass! The restaurant at the bottom of the hill has good, reasonably-priced food. At lunch service can be slow since many groups call in here. With a packed lunch and a drink you will have more time for seeing the sights.

Guermessa

About 4 km along the road to Tataouine, after the new town of Chenini, take a dirt track on the left. Follow the telephone poles. After 2-3 km the track forks, keep left still following the poles. At the end of this road you will come to the village of Guermessa. The new village is of no interest but behind, along a dirt track to the W, is the old village. It is similar to Chenini, but without the tourists. From

the top (½ hr climb) the panorama of the surrounding area is breathtaking.

Ghoumrassen el Bled

Ghoumrassen is only 8 km further on to the W from Guermessa. The most interesting part is towards the centre of the town. Behind the town, to the N, you can see the old abandoned village clinging to the cliff topped by a small mosque, as if watching over the inhabitants. If you have the energy, it is worthwhile going up to the mosque. From here you will see the old *ghorfas* and the rest of the old town. This is a good example of how the inhabited area changes as circumstances alter.

Ksar Haddad

A quiet little village 5 km N along the road after Ghoumrassen el Bled. The only *ghorfas* left have been beautifully conserved and transformed into a hotel. The E *Hotel Ksar Haddad* is very cheap, simple rms, with bath/toilets which could be cleaner, restaurant serving good, traditional meals at reasonable prices. Even if the comforts are limited, a night in the hotel is an experience not to be missed.

Ksar Guilane

A very beautiful village, it is only accessible from Chenini with a 4WD vehicle, though it is preferable to take a guide. From Douz a normal car will do. This is a magnificent oasis in the middle of the desert and no opportunity to visit it should be allowed to slip by. It is quite out of this world! Unfortunately some tour agencies have 'found' this area and it is not now so peaceful.

ZARZIS AND THE ISLAND OF DJERBA

Zarzis

ACCESS Buses arrive some 100m from central square, by the Esso garage, and the louage station is next to the nearby Shell garage.

The town has long been associated with Djerba as a tourist resort, and is not without certain similarities. The architecture is quite similar and the landscape, with large olive groves and long, white beaches is indeed very reminiscent of Djerba. The town, originally the market town for the area, is highly developed for tourism and generally well organized. The main point of interest in the town, apart from the market on Mon and Fri is the Sponge Festival (from 15 Jul to 15 Aug) which is celebrated with traditional dances and music, fishing boat competitions and, of course, sponge fishing. Zarzis is the road access to Djerba, across the causeway which was originally built by the Carthaginians and later rebuilt by the Romans. The road as it stands today was rebuilt in 1953. The only other access to Djerba is by the Djorf ferry.

Local information
● Accommodation
D *Zita*, T 680246, 600 rm, a/c, adequate restaurant, coffee shop, an old building.

F *Hotel l'Olivier*, close to the bus station, T 680637, 20 beds, simple, clean, probably the best of the cheap hotels. All the others, used by package tours, are very similar, spread out along the beach to the N of the town, are expensive with at least 3 stars, and generally very big.

Youth hostel: 40 beds, T 681599.

Camping: Sonia site rec.

● Banks & money changers
STB, town centre; **BNT**, rue de Palestine; **BT**, rue de Palestine and rue d'Algérie; **BDS**, town centre. There are also bureaux de change along route Touristique, 100m beyond the Tourist office. One takes VISA and Eurocheques.

● Hospital & medical services
Hospital: in town centre, T 680302.

● Post & telecommunications
Area code: 05.

Post Office: is in rue Mohammed V. There is another Post Office/ telephone centre in the hotel zone, about 1 km N of the Tourist Office.

● Sports
Zarzis is a typical resort town with provision for watersports such as swimming, windsurfing and water skiing at all the large hotels along the beach. **Harbour** has 60 yacht berths, minmax draft 2-4.5m. Sponge fishing is advertised.

● Tour companies & travel agents
Agency Globus, T/F 668288; *Zarzis Travel Service*, route de Djerba, T 681072; *Zarzis Voyage*, route de Ben Gardane, T 680654.

● Tourist offices
The tourist information office is at Route des Hotels, route du Port, close to the *Hotel Zarzis*, T 680445.

● Transport
Car hire: Avis, T 681706; Europcar, T 680562 and Hertz, T 680284, all on route des Hotels; **Express**, in *Hotel Oamarit*, T 680770; **Mattei**, next to *Hotel Sangho*, T 680124.

Road Bus: Tunis 2100; Sousse 1300 (via Medenine); there are about 4 buses a day to **Medenine** and **Ben Gardane**, more frequent departures towards Djerba. Information on T 680661.

Beyond Zarzis The C109 follows the coast, skirts the salt lakes and reaches Ben Gardane 46 km away. You are now just 33 km from the Libyan border.

Island of Djerba

Djerba, with an area of 614 sq km, is a virtually flat island. Altitude reaches only 55m in the centre and it measures 29 km E-W and 28 km N-S. The island is surrounded by 130 km of white beaches, while the centre is covered by olive groves and palm trees. Djerba has a long history of independence and the architectural style, unique to the island, testifies to this. The number of settlements is small as, in general, the houses are spread around the countryside and Houmt Souk in the N is the only significant town. Unfortunately Djerba is well established in the tourist circuit and can be very crowded in summer. Nevertheless, the tourists tend to congregate in Houmt Souk or stay in their hotels. The centre of the island is relatively quiet, is less well adapted to tourism and has only the basic facilities.

History

Djerbian history began with Ulysses in the Odyssey. Homer wrote that Ulysses landed in Djerba and had great difficulty in leaving again, not least because of the attractions of the lotus flower he found on the island. The island then became in turn Phoenician, Carthaginian and Roman. Known at the time as 'Menix' it went through a period of turbulence, as did most of Tunisia, due to the decadence of the Roman Empire and successive invasions. Djerba was finally conquered by the Arabs in 667, but was later involved in the rivalries between the Kharejite sect and the orthodox Muslims.

By the 15th century Djerba had become a den of pirates and various efforts were made to dislodge them, the most fateful being in 1560 when an attempt was made to fight off the pirate Dragut (see page 506). This failed and Dragut built a tower with the skulls of the slain Christians. The tower was fortunately demolished in 1848! Since then, Djerbian history has been marked by French colonization. The Djerbians were actually quite happy to see the French come, fearing attacks from rebellious inland tribes.

Today Djerba's main resources are agriculture, fishing, handicrafts and, most importantly, tourism. Agriculture is difficult on the island due to the lack of water. There are many palm trees but they produce poor quality dates, due to the high salt content of the water. Olive trees are more successful and olive oil is an important industry. Over 80 varieties of fish inhabit the sea around Djerba including shark, skate, and swordfish, but fishing is an occupation that is slowly declining, due to the continued use of traditional fishing methods and the preference for employment in hotels, usually for a bigger salary. Crafts are still important, particularly catering for the large tourist market.

The people

Those living on Djerba have always been quite isolated from the mainland. The effect has been the development of a unique style of life and architecture. The population is now mostly Berber in origin but, until recently, there was also a significant Jewish population on the island, one of the oldest communities in the world, dating back to 566 BC and the fall of Jerusalem to Nebuchadnezzar. Now there are only about 1,000 Jewish people left here, a large number having emigrated to Israel. The Arab population, numbering over 100,000, belong to the Ibadite sect which derives from the rigorous and austere Kharejite sect, established shortly after the Arab invasion. It is said the Djerbians followed this branch of Islam so as to keep some independence from the mainstream Islam preached by the Arab invaders.

Today, the population is faced with the new problems of tourism and the influence of western culture. Having lived for so long in isolation, they were perhaps less well equipped than other places for the large influx of tourists. The industry is having an adverse effect on the island's population and way of life since many of the traditional occupations such as agriculture and fishing are being abandoned for easier and better paid jobs in the tourist industry. Other residents have been forced to change jobs or leave due to the ever increasing cost of living, making Djerba an island with a very high emigration rate. In Tunisia and the Mediterranean region the word Djerba is synonymous with trader and grocer.

Architecture

Djerba is well known for its particular style of architecture. Houses, or *menzels* are found randomly scattered around the countryside, with no real village centres. The houses were organized in this way against the danger of attack and depending on the location of wells.

Houmt Souk (the quarter of the souks) was until recently the only town and, in effect, the market place for Djerba. The striking white-painted, often single-storey houses are organized around central courtyards, with no external windows. They resemble small forts since each has at least one tower. Each house has a cistern to collect the precious rain water. There are also many small, fortified mosques (as many as 200) which add to the attraction of the scenery. Driving or cycling round the centre of the island is a discovery and a delight.

Houmt Souk

ACCESS By road is either from Zarzis across the 6 km causeway, or via the ferry from Djorf to Ajim. Coming from Gabès, the ferry saves a lot of time but in summer be prepared to queue. The crossing only takes 15 mins. The ferry runs every 30 mins until 2000 when it is hourly through the night. Free for foot passengers and motorbikes, TD1 for cars by day and TD1.5 at night. All buses arrive at the bus station in the centre of Houmt Souk. Djerba has its own international airport to the W of Houmt Souk receiving scheduled flights from Frankfurt, Lyon, Geneva, Zürich, Brussels and Paris, as well as regular internal flights from Tunis and Tozeur.

This is the only real town (40,000 inhabitants) on the island and therefore its capital. It has a certain charm when not taken over by tourists. Notice some of the houses are old *fondouks* where nomads rested for the night. Some have been transformed into hotels just as some houses in the small squares have been converted into cafés and restaurants. The town has nevertheless preserved a careful balance and has not been totally destroyed by tourism.

DJERBA ISLAND

Places of interest

The **souk** is in the centre of the town. The main souk, not to be missed, is covered and has many small shops selling mainly silver, brass, leather goods, shoes, material and clothes. Prices tend to be high, shop around for the best price. Don't forget to bargain! Djerba is noted for its straw mats, blankets, jewellery (most still made by the Jews) and pottery, particularly from Guellala. The typical Djerbian pottery has a special white colour obtained by the addition of sea water. The market is held around the souk every Mon and Thur. The pottery and straw mats are sold on the main square, by Ave Bourguiba. Get there early.

Walking around the town will not take very long as it is quite small. Little streets lead on to charming squares with cafés. Notice the large doorways indicating an old *fondouk*.

The **Zaouia of Sidi Brahim**, built in 1674, is particularly interesting with its multiple arches. Across the road is the **Mosque of the Stranger**, remarkable for the large number of small domes around the main one. The **Mosque of the Turks,** further N, is interesting due to its splendid Turkish minaret. Unfortunately, all these monuments are closed to non-Muslims.

The **Bordj el Kebir** (the Great Tower) by the harbour is a 15th century Arab fort which was later reinforced by the pirate Dragut. Inside it is possible to see the ruins of an earlier fort built in the 13th century, though the site goes back further to Roman occupation. Open 0800-1200 and 1500-1900 summer, 0830-1730 winter, closed Fri. Entrance TD3. From the top of the fort is a wonderful view over the sea and harbour. There is the **market** by the harbour held every Mon and Thur. The fish auction is particularly interesting.

The **Museum of Popular Arts and Tradition** on Ave Abdelhamid el Cadhi is set in an old *zaouia* dedicated to Sidi Zitouni who used to come here and heal the mentally ill. The collection is very interesting and well labelled. The first room displays the traditional Djerbian costumes and jewellery and explains the history of the island. Another room shows a pottery workshop, the instruments used and the fabrication process. The last room is particularly special, as it was once a place of pilgrimage. This room is known as *quoubet el khyal* (the Ghost's Dome). Open 0800-1200 and 1500-1900 in summer, 0830-1630 in winter, closed Fri, entrance TD2.

Beaches

Close to Houmt Souk the beaches are not very pleasant. The nearest to be recommended is 6 km E along the road towards the hotels. Turn left along a track just before the *Hotel Ulysses*. There are other good beaches further along the coast, but the litter problem is increasing.

Local information
● **Accommodation**

There are over 50 hotels on the island.

A *Hotel Ulysses*, T 657422, 300 rm all a/c, on beach, pool, restaurant, nightclub, sports activities, 10 km from Houmt Souk.

B *Aquarius Club*, T 657790, 600 beds and *Meridiana*, 400 beds, both beach hotels at Taguermes 28 km from Houmt Souk; **B** *Djerba Orient*, T 657440, opp *Hotel Ulysses*, 56 beds, 10 km from Houmt Souk, not on beach.

D *Dar Faiza*, rue Ulysses, T 650083, pool, tennis, restaurant; **D** *Hotel Sables d'Or*, rue Mohammed Ferjani, T 650423, charming old house transformed into a small hotel, some rm rather dark.

E *Hotel Le Hadji*, off the main square, T 650630, modern, very clean hotel, all rm with bath; **E** *Hotel Erryadh*, off place Hedi Chaker in rue Mohammed Ferjani, T 650756, an old *fondouk*, Berber style rm with bath arranged around a central courtyard, very clean, lots of charm, important to book in season; **E** *Hotel Marhala*, beyond place Hedi Chaker on rue Moncef Bey, T 650146, small, beautifully decorated, clean and cheap, rm around attractive central courtyard, communal bath/toilets, rec.

F *Hotel Arischa*, on the street on the right opp ONAT, at the bottom on the left, T 650384,

converted *fondouk* with a central patio, clean;
F *Hotel Sindbad*, place Mongi Bali, T 650047,
in town centre, opp the Post Office, old *fondouk* with simple, clean rm, communal
bath/toilet, one of the cheapest in Houmt
Souk; **F** *Hotel Essalem* nr market, rec as
cheap, clean and friendly.

Youth hostels: 11 rue Moncef Bey, T 650619,
120 beds, very basic, pay a bit more and go to
a hotel.

● **Places to eat**
◆◆◆*Restaurant La Princesse d'Haroun*,
T 650488, by the harbour, specializes in fish,

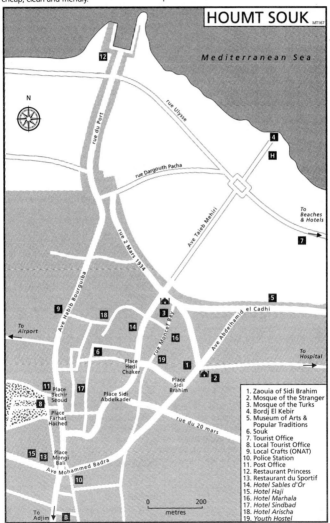

1. Zaouia of Sidi Brahim
2. Mosque of the Stranger
3. Mosque of the Turks
4. Bordj El Kebir
5. Museum of Arts &
Popular Traditions
6. Souk
7. Tourist Office
8. Local Tourist Office
9. Local Crafts (ONAT)
10. Police Station
11. Post Office
12. Restaurant Princess
13. Restaurant du Sportif
14. *Hotel Sables d'Or*
15. *Hotel Haji*
16. *Hotel Marhala*
17. *Hotel Sindbad*
18. *Hotel Arischa*
19. *Youth Hostel*

cosy atmosphere and decor.

Cheaper restaurants are: ♦♦*Le Mediter-*
ranéen, 5 rue Moncef Bey, seafood and Tunisian food; *Restaurant du Sud*, place Hedi
Chaker, a bit touristy but the food is good.

♦*Restaurant Berbère*, place Farhat Hached,
small, typical, good couscous; *Restaurant*
Central, Ave Bourguiba, good, cheap food;
Restaurant du Sportif, Ave Bourguiba, very
good, cheap Tunisian food.

● **Banks & money changers**
STB, place Farhat Hached; BNT, place Ben
Daamech; BT, rue du 20 Mars; BDS, Ave Bourguiba. There are also many bureau de change
offices around the town which accept credit
cards and are open more flexible hours.

● **Hospitals & medical services**
Hospital: main hospital on Ave Bourguiba,
T 650018. Private hospital 'El Yasmin' on Ave
Mohammed Badra.

● **Post & telecommunications**
Area code: 05.
International exchange: on the side of the
Post Office.
Post Office: Ave Bourguiba, after the main
square.

● **Shopping**
Handicrafts: the main ONAT craft shop is on
Ave Bourguiba, where the workshops and
training centre are open for viewing.

● **Sports**
Harbour: 10 yacht berths, min-max draft 1-3m.

● **Tour companies & travel agents**
Carthage Tours, centre of town, T 650308;
Djerba Voyage, Ave Bourguiba, T 650071;
Malik Voyagec, rue Habib Thameur,
T 650235; *Sahara Tours*, Ave Taleb Mehiri,
T 652646; *Tourafricac*, centre of town,
T 650104.

● **Tourist offices**
The local information office is on Ave Bourguiba, just before the Post Office, T 650157.
Main office at the start of route Touristique,
slightly out of town, T 650016, Tx 651956.
Closed on Sat afternoon, Fri, Sun and public
holidays.

● **Transport**
Local Bus: Djerba has a good public bus
service to most parts of the island. There is
a bus link with most major Tunisian towns. The
bus station, through which all buses pass, is in
the centre of Houmt Souk. Information on
T 650076. Buses No 10 and 11 go hourly round
the island, along the coast past the major
hotels; No 12 goes to Ajim and the Djorf ferry;
No 13 to Beni Maquel; No 14 to Guellala and
No 16 to Sedouikech. Car hire: although cars
can be rented they are expensive and there is
a minimum 24 hour rental. However it is a good
idea if you intend to go down to the S. Be
careful in Houmt Souk when you park, as the
Police have clamps (same problem as in Tunis:
the difficulty is not the fine but finding the
person with the keys to come and remove the
clamp!). Avis, Ave Mohammed Badra,
T 650151; Budget, rue du 20 Mars 1934,
T 650185; Europacar, Ave Abdelhamid el
Cadhi, T 650357; Hertz, Ave Abdelhamid el
Cadhi, T/F 650039, highly rec; Topcar, rue du
20 Mars 1934, T 650536. Cycle hire: the
island is small and flat making bicycles, which
can be rented at most large hotels and in
Houmt Souk, an attractive means of transport.
Moped: from Location Cycles, Ave Abdelhamid el Cadhi, TD15-20/day. Taxis: are a
good way of getting around but can be hard
to find, particularly at night, on market day or
away from main routes. Taxi to airport costs
TD3. Taxis from airport to Tripoli, Libya take 4-5
hrs.

Air Tunis Air, Ave Bourguiba, T 650586; Air
France, Ave Abdelhamid el Cadhi, T 650461.
The airport is 8 km from Houmt Souk, served
by a bus from town, but be sure to check the
times beforehand. Flight information on
T 650233. In the summer there are many more
flights in addition to those listed below. Scheduled international flights: Frankfurt Tues
0715; Lyon Thur 0705 or 1600; Geneva/Zu-
rich Sat 0835; Brussels Sat 0815 and Tues
0700; Paris Sat 1725 and Sun at 1055. There
is a daily flight to Tunis at 0615 (1 hr), cost
US$50.

Road Bus: the bus station is in the centre of
Houmt Souk. Information T 652239. Departures to: Sfax; Gabès; Medenine; Tataouine
(2½ hrs); Zarzis and Tunis. Louages: by the
bus station.
Sea Ferries: Ajim to Djorf run by CTN.

Excursions

Taxi tour of the island takes 2 hrs.

Midoun is the island's second largest
town. A large black community, descendants of slaves brought from Sudan, ex-

ists here. It has a particularly good weekly market each Fri. To see an interesting olive press over 300 years old take the road towards Houmt Souk and turn right at the crossroads, rue Salah Ben Youssef. It is about 400m on the left by the well and hidden by an olive tree. A mule or camel was used to turn the stone roller to crush the olives which were then transferred to a sieve where a large palm tree trunk squeezed out the oil into a jar underneath. All around are chambers once used for stocking olives.

Ajim is the island's main harbour and the departure point for ferries to Djorf on the mainland. It was once an important sponge fishing harbour. This activity is now virtually abandoned, due to the difficulties and dangers of the job. Today, Ajim is an important fishing port. The village itself is of minimal interest, but there are a few cafés and restaurants with large terraces.

El May has a typical Djerbian mosque with thick walls and a low, rounded minaret, resembling a fort. On Sat morning, a small local market takes place here.

Er Riadh In the village a signposted road on the left leads to the **El Griba Synagogue**. The original synagogue is said to have been built at the time of the first Jewish settlement in 586 BC. The present building was constructed in the 1920s and has become a spiritual centre for the study of the Torah. It is an interesting stop in an Islamic country. Inside the synagogue heads will have to be covered (head covers provided). In the first room, old men recite the Torah. The second room holds what is said to be one of the oldest Torahs in the world. Open 0700-1800 except Sat. A small contribution is appreciated.

Guellala is renowned for its pottery, particularly the typical Djerbian white coloured ware. The clay for the pottery comes from the small hill nearby, on the road to Sedouikech. Guellala has over 500 artisans making pottery, now mostly selling to the tourists. Indeed it has shops from one end of the village to the other. Fabrication de Poiterie in the main street will provide details on how the pottery is made.

Mahboubine has an interesting mosque, a picturesque and peaceful village square and provides an opportunity to become acquainted with the real people of Djerba. Don't spoil it by taking photographs. The taxi driver said "At Mahboubine there is nothing" – nothing more enjoyable than this visit.

The West coast is still untouched by tourism and is ideal for walks, or a trip along the coast. Unfortunately the coast is mainly rocky, but there are a few beaches. To get there, take the road to the airport and continue straight on towards Borj Jellij, until the road goes right. Here you should take the track to the left and follow it S, all the way to Ajim. A few km along the track, on the right, there are a few beautiful houses and a mosque by the sea. Allow ½ day to Borj Jellij and all day to Ajim. Make sure the taxi driver knows exactly where to meet you.

The Northeast coast Here you will find the tourists and all the large hotels. There are lovely beaches kept clean near the hotels, but not elsewhere, with white sand but they get very crowded in summer. Surfboards can be rented and various other watersports are organized in all the major hotels. If you want some peace, go to the W coast!

The East coast There is an excellent walk, takes 3 hrs, from Aghir to Borj Kastil which is a fort falling into ruin. There are interesting views, especially S across the mainland and the causeway. A very primitive overnight stop, if necessary, is available at the fisherman's cottage at the end of the walk.

INFORMATION FOR VISITORS

CONTENTS

Before you go	478
Entry requirements	478
When to go	479
Health	479
Money	479
Getting there	480
Air; train; road; sea; customs.	
When you arrive	481
Conduct; electricity; hours of business; official time; photography; safety; shopping; tipping; weights and measures; worship.	
Where to stay	482
Food and drink	483
Getting around	484
Air; train; road.	
Communications	486
Language; postal services; telephone services.	
Entertainment	487
Media; sport.	
Holidays and festivals	487
Further reading	488

Before you go

Entry requirements

● Visas

Passports Check all passport and visa requirements with your nearest Tunisian Embassy. For stays of over 6 months (US citizens 4 months) a residence visa is required. Tourist visas are not needed by nationals of EU, USA, Canada or Japan. At passport control you will be asked your hotel name. If you are undecided, give the name of any hotel in the town you plan to visit to avoid unnecessary questions.

For a private car you will need a driving licence, registration document (log book), and a Green Card valid for Tunisia. Stays of over 3 months are expensive as extension of vehicle permits is costly.

● Representation overseas

Algeria, 11 Rue de Bois de Boulogne, Algiers, T 601388; **Austria**, Chegastr 3, 1030 Vienna, T 786552; **Belgium**, 278 Ave de Tervuesen, 1150 Brussels, T 7621448; **Canada**, 515 O'Connor St, Ottawa, T 2370330, Tx 534161; **Egypt**, 26 Rue el Jazirah, Zamalek, Cairo, T 3412379; **France**, 27 Rue Barbet de Jouy, 75007 Paris, T 45559598; **Germany**, Godesberger Allee 103, 53 Bonn 2, T 228 376981; **Italy**, 7 Via Asmara, Rome, T 8390748; **Japan**, 292 Ichibabcho, Chiyoda-Ku, Tokyo 102, T 3534111, Tx 27146; **Jordan**, Ave el Aska, 4th Circle, Amman, T 674307; **Libya**, Rue Bèchir el Ibrahimi, Tripoli, T 30331; **Mauritania**, BP 681, Nouakchott, T 52871; **Morocco**, Corner of 6 Ave du Fes & 1 Rue d'Ifrane, Rabat, T 30576; **Senegal**, Rue el Hadj Seydou, Nourou Tall, Dakar, T 31261; **Spain**, Plaza Alonzo-Martinez 3, Madrid, T 4473508; **Sudan**, Rue No 18, Baladia St, Khartoum, T 0024811/76538; **Syria**, 6 Jaddet al-Chaffi, Damascus, T 660356; **Switzerland**, 58 Rue de Moillebeau, 1029 Geneva, T 333023; **UK**, 29 Princes Gate, London SW7, T 0171 584 8117; **USA**, 1515 Massachusetts Ave NW, Washington DC 20005, T 202 8621850, Tx 248377.

● Tourist Information

Tourist offices in Tunisia are open Mon-Thur 0830-1745, Fri-Sat 0830-1330, Sun and public hols 0900-1200. They are open longer in summer.

Tunisian National Tourist Offices Overseas: **Canada**, 1125 Blvd de Maisonneuve Ouest, Montreal, T 514 985 2586; **France**, 32 Ave de l'Opera, Paris, T 75002; **Germany**, Dusseldorf Steinstrasse 23, 4000 Dusseldorf, T 84218; **Italy**, via Sardegna No 17, 00187 Rome, T 4821934; **Netherlands**, Muntplein 2111, 1012 WR Amsterdam, T 020224971; **Saudi Arabia**, BP 13582-Jeddah 21414, T 6534981, F 6534612; **Spain**, Plaza de Espana 18, Plaza de Madrid, Madrid 28008, T 2481435; **Sweden**, Engelbrektsgaten 19, 11432 Stockholm, T 00468 206773; **UK**, 77A Wigmore St, London W1H 9LJ, T 0171 224 5561; **USA**, contact embassy in Washington, T 2346644.

● Tunisian Hotel Associates

Is at 304 Old Brompton Rd, London, SW5 9JF, T 0171 373 4412.

● Specialist tour companies

Martin Randall Travel, 10 Barley Mow Passage, Chiswick, London W4 4PH, T 0181 994 6477 – Roman and Islamic Cities; *Branta Holidays*, 7 Wingfield St, London SE15 4LN T 0171 634 4812 – birdwatching winter visitors on Lake Ichkeul and Tozeur; *Andante Travel*, Grange Cottage, Winterbourne Dauntsey, Salisbury, Wilts, SP4 6ER, T 01980 610555 – Art and Archaeology; *Explore Worldwide*, 1 Frederick St, Aldershot, Hants, T 01252 319448, offer interesting excursions to the ancient sites and into the mountains; *Prospect Music and Art Tours*, 454 Chiswick High Rd, London W4 5TT, T 0181 995 2151; *Discovery Cruises*, 47 St Johns Wood High St, London NW8 7NJ, T 0171 586 7191 – sailing from Athens; *Medward Travel*, 304 Old Brompton Rd, London, SW5 9JF, T 0171 373 4411, F 0171 244 8174 for individual requirements; *Regency Cruises*, 2 Telfords Yard, 6 The Highway, London E1 9BQ, T 01473 292222 – sailing from Nice.

When to go

● **Best time to visit**
The best season to visit is spring when the N is still green after the winter rains, the S is not yet too hot and the summer tourists have not arrived. The second best time is autumn when it is cooler, but tends to be very dusty. Summer can be extremely hot. Even in Tunis the summer temperatures can reach a maximum of 40°C while the S is even hotter. Despite this, it is the most popular time of the year for visitors. Winters are cold, very cold at some altitudes, and it can be damp in the N.

● **Climate**
There are considerable differences between the N and the S. Spring is a good period but it sometimes rains in the N. The summer is very hot, particularly inland and in the desert areas. On the coast the heat is made bearable by a light sea breeze. Autumn is the best period to visit the S and the oases. It is still warm, but can get very cold at night. Swimming in the sea is possible until Oct. In Nov it rains over most of the country, but never for very long. Winter is the ideal period for excursions in the Sahara, even though the nights are very cold the days are warm and the sky is blue.

● **Clothing**
Requirements depend on the time of year and the place. In summer it is necessary to be protected from the sun and to dress with consideration for the heat, bearing in mind that temperatures can fall very sharply at night

in the desert. From Nov to Mar a warm coat is recommended and from Oct to May an umbrella or raincoat may be needed in the N.

Health

● **Staying healthy**
No vaccinations are necessary but a tetanus injection could make you feel more secure. The tap water in Tunis and most tourist centres is fit to drink but bottled water is easily available and may be better in the long run. Protection from the sun is essential. Most proprietary drugs are available over the counter from chemist shops in the main streets of even the smallest towns. Chemists can generally give advice on small problems. See regional sections for hospitals and chemists. Rabies is not to be lightly dismissed. While commonly associated with dogs, too many trusting tourists have been bitten by stray cats and had to undergo a series of very unpleasant injections.

The Society for the Protection of Animals in N Africa, 15 Buckingham Gate, London SW1E is working with the Society for the Protection of Animals (SPA) of Tunisia to control the number of feral cats which are found scavenging especially near hotels (see box, page 399).

● **Further health information**
Read the section on Health, see page 15.

Money

● **Cost of living**
It is much cheaper to live in Tunisia than Europe with a hotel costing as little as TD10-25 a night and food TD7-10 a day. Transport is cheap, too, making it therefore quite possible to live well on TD120 a week. Sample prices: bottle of water TD0.45; litre of milk TD0.45; bread TD0.30; cup of tea/coffee TD1/TD0.80; glass of beer TD1.80; haircut TD3-4.

● **Credit cards**
Cards of various types are accepted by most banks. STB and BT accept Visa and most of their branches accept Mastercard. American Express is accepted in certain travel agencies and bureaux de change and in some branches of the BIAT. Obtaining money with a credit card is generally easy and the wait very short, just the length of a phone call. Credit cards can be used in all major hotels, restaurants and tourist shops. For all money changes a passport is necessary.

Most hotels of 2 stars and over and most good restaurants accept Visa, Diners Club,

American Express and Mastercard. Some shops in the souk will accept credit cards. AmEx office in Tunis is at Carthage Tours, 59 Ave Habib Bourguiba.

Credit cards are required for deposit when hiring cars.

● **Currency**

The monetary unit is the dinar TD1 = 1,000 millimes. Exchange rates are fixed daily by the Central Bank. For rates for Jul 1995 see table, page 7. The exchange rate is fixed, with no black market price, and no need to shop around. Notes in circulation 5, 10, and 20 dinars. Coins in circulation 5, 10, 20, 50, and 100 millimes $\frac{1}{2}$ and 1 dinar. Often prices over a dinar are still given in millimes which can be confusing. A taxi meter from the airport to central Tunis may say 3000 which is TD3. Be careful.

Tunisian dinars can only be obtained in Tunisia. You can take in as much foreign currency as you like. If you are carrying over £300 in foreign currency, complete a currency declaration so you can take it out again. No dinars can be taken out of the country. At the end of your stay you may change back up to 30% of the total value of foreign currency converted during the trip up to a maximum of TD100 dinars – so don't change more than you need at any one time and save all paperwork associated with financial transactions.

Crossing into Algeria it is mandatory to change some money (about AD1200). Sometimes they accept TCs. Be sure to save all the transaction slips as these may be checked.

Money can be changed at all border crossings. Eurocheques and TCs in European currencies and US dollars and are accepted at all banks and post offices.

Tunisian dinars are not accepted beyond customs control at the airport.

● **Taxes**

There are no direct taxes levied on visitors. Indirect taxes are included in prices.

Getting there

● **General note**

There are no problems getting into Tunisia. Tourists are encouraged and visitors are made very welcome. Package holidays and tours are probably the cheapest way of seeing the country in some comfort. Individual travellers will find this the easiest country to move around within N Africa.

● **Air**

From Europe There are six international airports in Tunisia: Tunis, Djerba, Monastir, Sfax, Tabarka and Tozeur. In summer there are numerous charter flights from Europe, mostly to Djerba and Monastir. These can be very cheap, but generally have restrictions regarding length of stay and legally must include accommodation. In summer, book well in advance. For information on charter flights, contact the Tunisia National Tourist Office, 77a Wigmore St, London, W1H 9LJ, enquiries, T 0171 224 5561.

Tunisair, GB Airways, and Air France (via Paris or Marseille) have scheduled flights to Tunis from London. All major European airlines fly to Tunis.

From the USA There are no direct flights. The best and cheapest way is to fly to London and get a charter or cheap scheduled flight from a bucket shop.

From North Africa Tunisair, Royal Air Maroc, Air Algérie and Egyptair fly into Tunis. Prices are generally reasonable and there are many scheduled flights. In summer finding places can be difficult.

Airfares Economy fares on scheduled flights, generally quite cheap, are more expensive in summer. Cheaper tickets can be purchased at bucket shops.

Best deals are with charter flights and tour operators who fly into airports further S, contact the Tunisian Tourist Office (**see above**). Air fares from adjacent N African countries are generally cheaper. Return fares – Casablanca to Tunis TD325 (3 hrs), Algiers to Tunis TD197 (1 hr). Airport tax of TD2 is payable in Tunisia, but this is generally included in the ticket price.

● **Train**

There is a daily train from Algeria at 1900 entering Tunisia via Ghardimaou, return journey leaves Tunis at 1255. One way 2nd class fare TD20 for a 24 hrs journey.

● **Road**

There are many road crossings to Algeria, the largest in the N at Ghardimaou and Barbouch are reached by local buses and louages. There are regular buses from Algeria and a daily bus to Annaba from Tunis at 0700 returning at 1700 and to Casablanca each Sat at 0630 returning at 2100. The main crossing in the S is at Hazoua beyond Nefta on the P3. Road crossings into Libya are at Ras Jedir on the coast and at Ghadames. The bus for Libya leaves

Tunis on Mon, Wed, Fri and Sun at 0700. Where the bus service fails there is generally a taxi service to the border.

● Sea

There are regular car/passenger ferries from Marseille (France) 24 hrs, Genoa (Italy) 24 hrs and to Tunis. From Marseille every 3 days in winter, daily in summer (takes 24 hrs). Contact Southern Ferries in London T 0171 491 4968 who are agents for SNCM and CTN lines. Genoa: From Ponte Colombo Sat at 1700, 24 hrs crossing. For information, contact Paris T 149242424. (No UK office). Trapani: Mon (Tues in Ramadan) at 0900, crossing takes 7-8 hrs, passenger single TD53/63, medium car single TD100/118, on Tirrenia line who also run to Cagliari. Their agent in UK is Serena Holidays, T 0171 373 6548. In summer there is a jetfoil service between Trapani and Kelibia.

Sea travel from Marseille is very pleasant but can be expensive. Adult return economy fare TD260 (FF1,510), students and under 25's TD220 (FF1,340). Return rate for cars around TD560 (FF3,300) depending on vehicle length.

● Customs

Customs at the airport are slow as most bags (particularly those belonging to Tunisians) are searched. Be patient. Leaving Tunisia the customs officials are rarely in evidence.

Duty free allowances You may take into Tunisia 2 cameras of different types, 20 films, cassette player, 2 tapes, video camera (which will go down on your passport), portable typewriter, portable radio, binoculars, child's pushchair, sports equipment, 1 litre of spirits, 2 litres of wine, 400 cigarettes or 100 cigars or 500gm tobacco, 1/4 litre of perfume, 1 litre of toilet water and gifts to value of £30.

Duty free goods to take out of Tunisia such as perfume, cigarettes, wine, spirits and gifts are available in varying quantity and quality in airport departure louages, note Tunisian money is not accepted beyond passport control.

Import/export bans Weapons may not be taken in or out of Tunisia. Permits can be obtained for hunting weapons on organized visits. Possession of underwater weapons is a serious offence. The Tunisians are, understandably, strongly opposed to people exporting genuine pieces of their archaeological heritage.

Registration Other than the usual embarkation card filled in on arrival at a port or airport, no other formalities are necessary. Hotels register their guests. Informal visitors will need to register themselves with the nearest police station.

When you arrive

● Conduct

Clothing It is as well to remember that this is a Muslim country and you should dress casually but decently. There are strict rules for acceptable clothing for visiting a mosque. See the chapter on travelling in a Muslim country, (page 37).

Hammams Modest behaviour is expected in the hammam so cover yourself somehow.

● Electricity

The current is 220V on 2 pin plugs. Take an international adaptor plug. In the far S you may encounter 110V.

● Hours of business

Vary in summer, winter and Ramadan. These are minimum times: **Shops** between 0800-1230 and 1430-1800, Sat 0800-1300 but they open earlier in summer with one session 0730-1300. Shops in tourist areas are always open!!

Banks 0800-1100 and 1400-1700 Mon-Thur, 0800-1100 and 1300-1500 Fri. Closed afternoons in summer. Ramadan 0800-1230. In Tunis, some banks are open outside these hours, and in most tourist resorts, money can be changed in large hotels at the aiports and in bureau de change establishments.

Government and Public Services 15 Jul-15 Sep 0730-1330. 16 Sep-14 Jul 0830-1330 and 1500-1745. Fri-Sat 0830-1330. During Ramadan opening hours are different and everything is generally closed in the afternoon.

● Official time

Tunisia is on Central European Time which is one hour ahead of GMT.

● Photography

Taking photographs is no problem in Tunisia, but be aware that some people object to being photographed and taking pictures of women is best avoided without their permission. However children love to be photographed – again and again! Avoid photographing military installations or risk losing your film, your camera or even gaining some hospitality in a police station. Film is readily available throughout the country, check the sell-by date. Bring your own specialist and video films.

● **Safety**

There is no threat to personal security in Tunisia. Normal vigilance is recommended against petty crime and basic common sense used with respect to personal property, especially money and passports.

● **Shopping**

A good range of crafts is available in Tunisia. You have the choice of buying them in tourist shops, the souks or in the Office National de l'Artisanat Tunisien (ONAT). It is a good idea to go to the ONAT first where the official prices are listed. Even though the prices are higher here than in the streets, the quality is guaranteed. The best place for shopping is undoubtedly the souk in the medinas. The prices are generally lower and bargaining is part of the fun. No prices are fixed and, as a general rule, the real price is 50% less than the price first given (but could be 90% less).

Carpets are made throughout Tunisia but best bought in Kairouan where the quality is superior and the prices cheaper. All carpets should have a sealed quality certificate. There are three main types – the *Alloucha*, made with natural long wool; the *Zerbia* again with long wool but coloured (the colours used are generally artificial and not all natural as claimed) and the *Mergoum* made of short wool or silk. Don't forget to bargain. For advice on types and official prices go to ONAT.

Copper and brass goods vary in quality and price. The most common items are beaten copper plates, in different sizes. Some are still handmade, but most are mass produced.

Hammams open for women in afternoons, men either before or after. Modesty essential, nudity not acceptable. TD1, massage TD5.

Jewellery is either Berber or Arab in origin and sometimes is a mixture of both. When buying gold or silver, be sure it has the official stamp on it: a horse head for 18 carat gold and a scorpion for 9 carat. A grape cluster is used for silver of 900 mills/gram. Anything without the stamps should be treated with care. Prices vary with the degree of craftsmanship and some items can be very expensive. A traditional design is the Hand of Fatima (the daughter of the Prophet). See page 58.

Leather goods are of very good quality but not always cheap. Be sure to check the sewing as it is often of poor quality and the item may soon fall to pieces.

Perfumes many different types are available

in various quantities, but the 'staying' qualities cannot be guaranteed.

Pottery is produced in large quantities, but good quality ware is found in both Nabeul and Guellala on the island of Djerba.

Straw goods are actually woven palm leaf fronds, mostly from Gabès and Djerba. They are cheap and range from simple baskets to touristy camels.

● **Tipping**

Service is included on bills in restaurants and hotels. If you intend to stay for a while at a café, or return to a hotel it pays to leave something. Tips of 5-10% are the norm in restaurants.

● **Weights and measures**

The metric system is used throughout. See conversion table on page 14.

● **Worship**

Anglican services in St Georges' Church, place Bab Carthage, Tunis each Sun at 1000, also each Sun in Sousse, at 0930, 16, rue de Malte. **French Protestant service** in Eglise Réformée, rue Charles de Gaulle, Tunis, each Sun at 1000. **French Catholic mass** in Jeanne d'Arc Chapel, Tunis and daily in the Cathédral Saint-Vincent-de-Paul 0815 and 1830, Sat 1800, Sun 0900 and 1100.

Where to stay

● **Hotels**

Hotels and hostels in Tunisia are all controlled by the Tourist Board, and divided into five categories. The top is 4-star luxury, the lowest one star. Each year the Tourist Board checks the hotels and renews their ranking, but it is often hard to understand their criteria as it is perfectly possible to find an unclassified (NC) hotel far cleaner and more pleasant than a 3-star one. The ranking also fails to take into account the level of service. The best way of judging a hotel is not to rely on the ranking, but to **ask to see a room**. The differences can be enormous. It must also be said that some hotels are really dirty with decrepit furniture. In this guide, we have tried to cover a range of hotels, all of them clean (well, fairly clean), but with a difference in comfort levels. It is also impossible to give a totally accurate description of a hotel as managements can change. Equally, you will be very surprised to find excellent, very clean small hotels in the medinas, with very friendly management. Quite a few hotels, which are gen-

HOTEL CLASSIFICATIONS

AL US$90+. International class luxury hotel. All facilities for business and leisure travellers are of the highest international standard.

A US$75-90. International hotel with air conditioned rooms with WC, bath/shower, TV, phone, mini-bar, daily clean linen. Choice of restaurants, coffee shop, shops, bank, travel agent, swimming pool, some sport and business facilities.

B US$60-75. As **A** but without the luxury, reduced number of restaurants, smaller rooms, limited range of shops and sport.

C US$40-60. Best rooms have air conditioning, own bath/shower and WC. Usually comfortable, bank, shop, pool.

D US$20-40. Best rooms may have own WC and bath/shower. Depending on management will have room service and choice of cuisine in restaurant.

E US$10-20. Simple provision. Perhaps fan cooler. May not have restaurant. Shared WC and showers with hot water (when available).

F under US$10. Very basic, shared toilet facilities, variable in cleanliness, noise, often in dubious locations.

erally still clean, have a distinctly 'past-it' look and urgently need refurbishment. All prices are posted in the reception and can be consulted. All official prices are per person and not per room. In all classified hotels, and even some unclassified ones, breakfast is included in the price. It may be a good idea to request half board, as the difference in price is often very small. If travelling out of season check heating (some hotels have none) and number of blankets.

● **Youth hostels**

Tunisian hostels are part of the International Federation and accept YHA cards. In all there are 35 hostels. Hostels are located at Aïn Draham, Béja, Bizerte (2), Chebba, Gabès, Gafsa, Djerba, Hammamet, Jendouba, Kairouan, Kasserine, Kebili, Kelibia, Korba, Mahdia, Matmata, Médenine, Menzel Temime, Monastir, Nabeul (2), Nasrallah, Remla, Siliana, Sfax, Sousse, Teboursouk, Tozeur, Tunis (3), Zaghouan and Zarzis. Minimum age for unaccompanied children is 15, no maximum but priority

is given to younger members. Open 0700-2300. Some close in middle of day. Price/night TD3-4. Hire of bed linen and sleeping bags possible at all hostels for 500 mills/night. Use of kitchen 300 mills. Breakfast 700 mills, lunch and dinner TD3.

● **Camping**

Organized sites with full facilities are relatively few and far between but clearly signed when provided. Always ask permission of the landowner and/or local police before attempting 'casual' camping. None is allowed on tourist beaches. Camping is permitted at the Youth Hostels at Nabeul and Remel (Bizerte). The major camp sites are at Hammam Plage, Nabeul, Hammamet and Zarzis.

Food and drink

RESTAURANT CLASSIFICATIONS

Given the variations in price of food on any menu our restaurants are divided where possible into three simple grades:
♦♦♦ expensive, ♦♦ average and ♦ cheap.

● **Food**

In Tunisia food is very good, quite varied and generally cheap. The small restaurants which do not serve alcohol are cheaper. Restaurants with alcohol are more expensive, even though the quality of the food and service is not necessarily better. Most local products are fresh and good quality. Food is cooked with spices but is never too hot. Along the coast and on the islands, fish is the main dish, and this is always fresh. Fish prices are often by weight, and you can have a nasty surprise if you haven't had it weighed before eating it. In most main towns you will find a large number of French restaurants which can generally be relied on for quality and price. Prices are not always indicated on the menu. Be sure to check before you order.

Specialities – Starters

Chorba – flavoured soup with lots of pepper.

Brik – deep-fried pastry containing egg and tuna, minced beef, lamb or vegetables, usually spinach, very popular.

Salade Michouia – cubed, mixed cooked vegetables with tuna and egg, can be very spicy, served cold.

Salade Tunisienne – Salade Nicoise with tomatoes, onions, tuna and egg.

Main Dishes

Keftaji – seasoned meat balls served with peppers.

Chakchouka – ratatouille with chick peas, tomatoes, peppers, garlic and onions, containing pieces of veal and served with a poached egg.

Couscous – steamed coarse semolina or millet served with vegetables and meat or fish. Typical dish eaten throughout the Maghreb.

Mechoui – grilled meat (usually lamb), very good.

Tajine – solid cheese quiche, with meat and vegetables, cooked in the oven.

Coucha – roast lamb with potatoes and peppers cooked in the oven, excellent.

Merguez – small spicy mutton or beef sausages, generally grilled.

Mermiz – stewed mutton with beans.

Soboku – steamed mutton with tomato sauce.

Fish: the best are the *Rouget* (red mullet), *Mulet* (mullet), *Merou* (grouper), *Lou de Mer* (perch) and sole; seafood is also very good.

Desserts

Like all Mediterranean countries, Tunisia has many varieties, all very sweet!

Baklava – puff pastry with lots of honey.

Makroud – semolina cake with crushed dates, baked in oil and dipped in honey.

Halva – very sweet cake made from sesame seeds.

Loukoum – Turkish delight.

Bjaouia – almonds, pistachio nuts and puffed rice in a cake mixture.

Fruit

Dates – the season for fresh dates is Oct. There are over 100 types but the best, the deglet nur, come from the desert oases, particularly Tozeur and Nefta.

Pastèque – watermelon, particularly refreshing in summer.

Grenade – pomegranates, served with sugar and sprinkled with jasmine flavoured water.

● Drink

The national drink is tea, generally mint tea. Try not to refuse if you are offered some as this may be seen as insulting! Tea is also served black with lots of sugar, or green tea TD1/cup. Coffee is also widely drunk TD1/cup. Two types are served, expresso and cappuccino. (In local bars coffee and tea is only TD0.5.) The most common and cheapest beer is Celtia (a Tunisian make) but Tunisian made Tuborg and Stella, as well as imported beers, can be found.

Wine The Tunisians have been making wine for over 2,000 years. Wines sold under certificate are under the strict control of the state. The **red wines** are more acidic than western palates are used to and vary in quality. It is difficult to recommend any particular wine but for experience try one from the medium-priced *Magon Rouge* to the cheaper *Vieux Thibar*. The **rosé** is by far the best bet. It can be drunk with anything and is rarely awful. Recommended are *Haut Mornag* and *Sidi Rais* and the more expensive *Château Mornag*. The **white wines** are generally dry – try *Sidi Rais*. Also considered worth a try are *Blanc de Blanc* and *Muscat sec de Kelibia*. Tunisian *vins gris* (untranslateable!) include *Gris de Tunisie* and *Gris de Bizerte*.

Other alcohol Tunisia also produces three types of very strong alcohol. **Boukha** is made from distilled figs, **Laghmi** is palm tree sap drunk immediately after it is collected and **Thibarine** is palm sap left to ferment for a while. Most imported alcohols are available generally in hotels and rarely in bars, but they are very expensive. Take your own alcohol to 'dry' restaurants.

Soft drinks are widely available. Bottled water is very good and is offered, but not free, with all meals. The larger 1.5 litre bottle costs about $1/2$ TD. The smaller, resealable plastic bottles are just right for taking on short journeys.

Cafés are an interesting experience. They are generally packed with men (no women) and intensely smokey and noisy! A good way to make contact with the locals is to try a Shisha. They are water pipes, but the tobacco is slightly different from cigarette tobacco, and flavoured with honey or sometimes apples. Stronger than cigarettes (but not the local Crystal cigarettes) it is nevertheless a good way to start up a conversation as somebody will invariably ask you if you like it.

Getting around

● Air

Flights: Tun Inter (reservations via Tunis Air) run regular internal flights between Tunis, Tabarka, Monastir, Djerba and Tozeur. They are generally arranged so that travellers from other towns can spend the day in Tunis. Flights are not expensive but places are scarce. Tunisavia are flying smaller 72 seater planes on internal flights and have small planes for hire.

● Train

This is a good way of travelling in the main areas. The trains travel quite slowly so there is ample opportunity to see the scenery. From Tunis the lines go N to Bizerte (1 hr 50 mins) and Tabarka, W to Jendouba (3 hr) and Algeria and S as the 'Sahel Metro' to Hammamet (1½ hr), Sousse (2¼ hr), Sfax (4½ hr) and Gabès (7 hr) through all the coastal resorts. The TGM runs frequently from Tunis to Carthage and La Marsa stopping in all the suburbs. The only line inland goes diesel-electric to Metlaoui (11 hr), via Gafsa (10 hr). The service is quite efficient, nearly all trains leaving on time. First class trains with modern rolling stock, adjustable seats and refreshments are good but lack the atmosphere, interest and cheapness of the 2nd class. On a return ticket, 25% reduction cards can be obtained, valid 8 days. Timetables available from any station and most tourist offices in Tunisia and abroad. In addition to the return ticket an extra 'admission' fee is charged to enter the return train, about 350 mills, most unusual. The names of smaller stations are not always clearly marked on the platform and the public address system is not always used for smaller stations either.

● Road

Bicycles and motorbikes: are a good way to see the country, depending on the terrain. Mountain bikes are recommended. Summer heat may make progress difficult, autumn or spring being a better choice. Bring essential spare parts, though if a problem occurs help is easily available as all towns and villages have mechanics. Spare parts for motorcycles may prove harder to find. Cyclists are advised to wear bright colours. **Bus**: is the cheapest means of transport, and therefore the most popular. Virtually all towns and villages are on a bus route. Local buses can be a very interesting experience, as everything from fruit to chickens is transported. The inter-city lines are generally fast and comfortable. On most lines there are slightly more expensive a/c buses available, vital in summer, check the different companies for facilities available. Times available from bus stations and tourist offices. Advance booking is possible on most inter-city lines, very useful during summer. Arrive in advance, as buses are more likely to depart early than late. **Car hire**: is probably one of the best ways of seeing the country, but prices are quite high as cars are expensive here. Expect

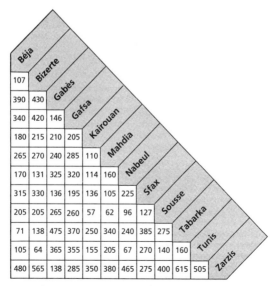

	Béja	Bizerte	Gabès	Gafsa	Kairouan	Mahdia	Nabeul	Sfax	Sousse	Tabarka	Tunis
Bizerte	107										
Gabès	390	430									
Gafsa	340	420	146								
Kairouan	180	215	210	205							
Mahdia	265	270	240	285	110						
Nabeul	170	131	325	320	114	160					
Sfax	315	330	136	195	136	105	225				
Sousse	205	205	265	260	57	62	96	127			
Tabarka	71	138	475	370	250	340	240	385	275		
Tunis	105	64	365	355	155	205	67	270	140	160	
Zarzis	480	565	138	285	350	380	465	275	400	615	505

Tunisia: distances by road between major cities (Km)

to pay TD370-500/week with unlimited mileage. There are a many agencies, everything from the large internationals (which tend to be the most expensive) to smaller local companies. The standard cars are generally Peugeot 205 and Citroen AX. Shop around as prices can differ and when comparing prices check the 17% VAT is included. It can also be cheaper to buy a package including flight and car in London or Paris. International driving licences are normally required but a current European licence is usually sufficient. Be warned that insurance is unlikely to include the tyres, the wheels or the windows and replacement can be extortionate. Read the small print on the contract and check on the excess charge. Consider bringing your own car. Balance the hire charges against the ferry charge and greater flexibility.

Car breakdown You may be rescued by a patrolling Garde Nationale. Failing that, hitch to the nearest village for a mechanic or to ring the hire firm. Travellers intending to drive in the S are advised to read the section on travelling in the desert (see page 45).

Driving in Tunisia is on the right. The roads are generally good but the number of cars on the road far exceeds the number of competent drivers. Be particularly careful when driving through villages, as children and animals have little road sense. Be very careful, too, of Peugeot pickups, which are more than likely to turn suddenly or stop without indicating. In town, the real danger is the pedestrians. Obey the speed limits, a strict 50 km in towns and 90 km on the main roads. There are numerous police controls, particularly by speed limit signs. Infringement of traffic regulations can cost up to TD500. If you are stopped, smile. It will make things easier. Safety belts are compulsory. Petrol is very cheap and there is no shortage of petrol stations. Avoid no parking zones in cities as illegally parked cars are clamped (TD7) or towed away which is tedious rather than expensive. Roads signs are French/International with Arabic translations.

Hitchhiking is easy, particularly going along the coast. Inland can be more difficult but is generally not a problem. Normally the ride is not free except in an emergency. Shared taxis are found on many routes and private cars and pickups will act in the same capacity, expecting payment as a matter of course. Foreign travellers may get a free ride. Remember drivers have a choice and may not choose heavily laden, unkempt passengers, especially not for a free ride. While the editors appreciate that hitch-hiking may be the only way to reach a given destination, travellers do so always at their own risk.

Louages, large taxis taking up to five or six people, are a very popular mode of transport and often the fastest. They leave as soon as they are full and have a station in virtually every town. They are excellent transport for a group or large family even though all children count full fare. Be sure to settle the price before leaving. They are generally a little more expensive than the train. The town indicated in the window of the louage does not indicate where it is going, but only where it is licensed! Be warned that some of the cars are old and slow, but some are brand new and travel fast (often too fast). In summer, it can be a good idea to travel in the evening, or at night, when it is considerably cooler.

Taxis should have meters and the meter should be turned on. If you hire a taxi for yourself, charges run at 200 mills plus 120 mills/km with an extra charge for luggage (sometimes for each piece of luggage). Higher fares after 2100.

● **Boat**
Ferry services ply to Djerba and the Kerkennah Islands.

● **Walking**
Is not usual but with a good map, adequate supplies and stout footwear it is possible. French series 1:50,000 maps, now out of date, are available in some parts of Tunisia, via France. Dogs can be a problem. Take a stout stick or an umbrella which can double as a sun shade!

Communications

● **Language**
Arabic is the first language but virtually everyone has some French. In the tourist areas shop keepers and hotel staff speak 3 or 4 European languages, (see page 59).

● **Postal services**
Stamps are available from post offices, some shops, some kiosks and most hotels. Post offices open Mon-Thur 0800-1200 and 1400-1700, Fri-Sat 0800-1230. Summer opening 0730-1200 except Sun. During Ramadan Mon-Thur 0800-1400, Fri-Sat 0800-1200. Postcard reaches the UK in one week, USA 2

weeks. Postcard to Europe costs 350 mills, to USA 400 mills. Letters 450/500 mills. Parcels about TD25 for 10 kg.

● Telephone services

The telephone system is quite efficient and once you can get hold of a phone getting through should present no problems. Pay phones only take dinars. It costs TD1.2/min to UK. Collect calls are possible but harder to make. Local calls are cheaper after 2200.

National calls can be more difficult, although, again, the real problem is getting hold of a telephone. Public call boxes are generally in, or adjacent to, post offices. Queues can be huge and enough to deter all but the very determined. Calls from hotels are much more expensive with a minimum charge for 3 mins of TD5-10, but much more comfortable.

Taxi phones, black lettering on a yellow background are kiosks, with attendants, with direct dial facility. They are **not** just for taxis.

International code 216.

Local codes

- **01** Carthage, La Marsa, Tunis
- **02** Bizerte, Hammamet, Zaghouan and Nabeul
- **03** Monastir, Mahdia and Sousse
- **04** Sfax and Kerkennah
- **05** Gabès, Djerba, Medenine, Tataouine, Kebili and Zarzis.
- **06** Tozeur, Gafsa and Sidi Bouzid
- **07** Kairouan and Kasserine
- **08** Tabarka, Le Kef, Aïn Draham, Jendouba, Siliana and Béja.
- **09** All car phones.

Entertainment

● Media

There are three daily newspapers in French, Le Temps, La Presse and L'Action. All international papers can be found in the main towns – usually the next day. Radio and TV is mostly in Arabic except for Antenne 2 (French) and RAI1 (Italian). There are no English programmes. BBC World Service can be picked up easily. For frequencies, see page 13.

Cinema in French and Arabic, costs TD1.5.

● Sport

Tunisia offers a variety of sports including:
Hunting and shooting of various game birds and wild boar. It is necessary to be part of an organized party for firearm permits during official hunting seasons.

Golf El Kantaoui Golf Course, Port El Kan-

taoui, T 03 31755, F 03 40506; Monastir Golf Course, Route de Ouardanine, T 03 61120; Hammamet Golf Course, Bir Bou Rekba, T 02 82722; Tabarka Golf Course, Montazah Tabarka, T 08 44321; Soukra Golf Course, nr Tunis, route de la Soukra, T 765919. Average green fees TD30; Djerba Golf Course.

Riding on horses and camels: Horse racing at Kassar Saïd 10 km W of Tunis.

Tennis: at most large tourist complexes.

Watersports: including sailing, skiing, windsurfing, snorkelling, scuba diving, fishing and underwater fishing. Contact Centre Nautique International de Tunisie, 22 rue de Medine, Tunis.

There are 26 ports and anchorages varying from 5 to 380 berths. The main pleasure ports are Port el Kantaoui, Monastir, Sidi Bou Said and Tabarka.

Holidays and festivals

1 Jan:	New Year's Day
18 Jan:	Anniversary of the Revolution
20 Mar:	Independence Day
21 Mar:	Youth Day
9 Apr:	Martyr's Day
1 May:	Labour Day
1 Jun:	Victory Day
25 Jul:	Republic Day
13 Aug:	Women's Day
3 Sep:	Anniversary of PSD
15 Oct:	Evacuation of Bizerte
7 Nov:	New Era Day

● Local festivals

Many towns have festivals, some more interesting than others and some invented for the tourists. Interesting ones are mentioned in the text. Major ones include:

Apr *Ksar Festival* in Tataouine – Berber folklore and tradition; Nefta; Nabeul Fair, display of agricultural products; *Orange Festival* in Menzel Bou Zelfa (close to Hammamet), orange picking and folklore.

May *Sparrow Hawk Festival* in El Haouaria, hunting scenes and hawk displays; *Tunis fair* – alternate years.

Jun *Ulysses Festival* in Djerba, folklore of the island and simulation of Ulysses' arrival; *Dougga Festival* at Roman theatre; *Malouf Festival* in Testour – Andalusian folklore with Spanish performers.

Jul Carthage – events at Roman theatre; Monastir and Sousse both have *International*

Festivals of music, dance and theatre.

Aug Sousse *Baba Aoussou Festival*; Hammamet *International Festival* of music, dance and theatre; Carthage – cinema of the developing countries; *El Djem Festival* of folklore and theatre in Roman Colosseum; *Béja* – wheat festival.

Sep *Wine Festival* at Grombalia – between Tunis and Nabeul; *Cavalry Festival* in Kairouan – Traditional Arab horse display.

Oct Carthage film festival alternate years.

Nov Tozeur *Sahara Festival* – oasis tradition and folklore.

Dec Douz *Sahara Festival*: Sahara folklore, camel races, cavalry and music – the best of the oasis festivals.

● **Religious feast/fast days**

These change every year as they follow the lunar calendar. Approximate dates for 1996:

    21 Jan: Beginning of Ramadan (see page 40).

    22 Feb: Aïd Esseghir celebrated by parties, music in the streets

    29 Apr: Aïd el Kebir

    20 May: Ras el Am Hejri (New Year 1417)

    29 Jul: Mouled of the Prophet

    23 Sep: Jewish feast of forgiveness in Djerba

● **Market days**

In every town there is a market, some of limited interest, particularly in the main tourist areas. However the genuine markets are both interesting and colourful.

Mon Tataouine, Houmet Essouq, Kairouan, Aïn Draham, Mareth, Maktar, Kelibia, Mahres.

Tues Ghardimaou, Kasserine, Béja, Bizerte, Haffouz, Krib.

Wed Sbeitla, Nefta, Moknine, Sers and Jendouba.

Thur Gafsa, Teboursouk, Le Kef, Djerba, Bou Salem and Douz.

Fri Mahdia, Zaghouan, Tabarka, Mateur, Sfax, Nabeul, Zarzis.

Sat El Fahs, Ben Gardane, El Alia, Thibar.

Sun Sousse, Hammam Lif, El Djem, Enfida, Fernana.

Further reading

● **Books**

Anon, *Les Mosquées de Tunisie*, Tunis, 1973; Brett, M. (ed), *Northern Africa, Islam and modernisation*, Cass, London, 1973; Brown, LC, *The Tunisia of Ahmed Bey*, University Press, Princeton, 1974; Douglas, N, *Fountains in the Sand*, 1985; Hopkins, M, *Tunisia to 1993*, London, 1989; Hopwood, D, *Habib Bourguiba of Tunisia – The tragedy of Longevity*, Macmillan, £45; Kassab, A, *Etudes Rurales en Tunisie*, Tunis, 1980; Knapp, W, *Tunisia*, Thames & Hudson, 1970; Latham, JD, *Towards a study of Andalusian immigration and its place in Tunisian history*, Cahiers de Tunisie, 1957; Lloyd, C, *English Corsairs on the Barbary Coast*, London, 1981; Messenger, C, *The Tunisian Campaign*, 1982; Sladen, D, *Carthage and Tunis*, London, 1906; Woodford, JS, *The City of Tunis*, Menas Press Ltd, Wisbech, 1990.

● **Guidebooks and Maps**

Guide du Routard Tunisie, Algérie et Sahara edited by Hachette; *Guide Bleu Tunisie* edited by Hachette; *Stay Alive in the Desert*, KEM Melville, edited Roger Lascelles.

    The best map by far is Michelin 972, price £5. Map of Tunisia by Kümmerly and Frey, price £5, scale 1: million gives geomorphological details and a pictorial view worth studying before the visit. The Tourist Office will give you their free map which is good enough to pinpoint the main places but lacks detail.

We wish to acknowledge the work done by Derek Alderton in the updating of this chapter, Emma Kay at the Tunisian National Tourist Office, and contributions from Thomas Tolk of Bonn, Ivan de Jonge of Meerbeke, Jens Roth of Garbsen, and Bob Kuehn of New Orleans.

LIBYA

INTRODUCTION

L ibya, the fourth largest state in Africa lies between latitudes 33°N and approximately 20°N and longitudes 20°E and 25°E. It lies in a transitional climatic zone between the Mediterranean and the Sahara Desert, having only a narrow cultivated strip in the N and more than 90% of its territory in the arid zone. The two northern coastlands of Tripolitania and Cyrenaica have been associated throughout history with Mediterranean civilizations, notably the North African provinces of Rome and Byzantium. The Muslim invasion attached Libya to the Muslim and Arab worlds of the east, diversifying and complicating its affiliation to Mediterranean society and southern Europe. Libya came under the Ottomans and semi-independent local Turkish rulers or *bashaws* until the initial occupation of the country by Italy in 1911. Libya gained its Independence in 1951 as a monarchy under King Idris Senussi I. In 1969 a revolution saw the creation of a 'Jamahiriyah', or country of the masses, by Colonel Ghadhafi. Libya became increasingly an oil-based economy but after 1976 its economic and political relationships with other countries deteriorated, culminating in the severance of its worldwide air connections in 1992.

CONTENTS

Introduction	489
Land and life	489
Culture	493
History	495
Modern Libya	496
Tripoli	502
Benghazi	534
Fezzan	550
Al-Khalij	559
Information for Visitors	569

Basics

OFFICIAL NAME al-Jamahiriyah al-Arabiyah al-Libiyah ash-Shabiyah al-Ishtirakiyah (Socialist People's Libyan Arab Jamahiriyah)

NATIONAL FLAG Green.

OFFICIAL LANGUAGE Arabic.

OFFICIAL RELIGION Islam.

INDICATORS *Population* 5,225,000 (1994); *Urban* 82%; *Religion* Sunni Muslim 97%; *Birth rate* 43 per 1,000 *Death rate* 8.2 per 1,000, *Life expectancy* 62 men, 65 women; *GNP per capita* US$6,600.

Land and life

Geography

The state of Libya has an area of 1,759,540 sq km, three times the surface area of France. It has a 1,750 km seaboard with the Mediterranean stretching from Zuwarah in the W to Al-Bardia in the E. Most people live and work along the N coast. Elsewhere the country fades immediately inland into semi, then full desert S into the deep Sahara. The desert regions are lightly populated and support major routes often over 1,000 km in length where N to S transport tracks pass from oasis to oasis, ultimately linking with Chad, Sudan and

Niger in Central Africa. For all its extent, therefore, Libya is a country where the ambitious traveller can see much of what exists simply by following the few key lines of communication.

Libya and North Africa

Libya is a cultural and geographic bridge firstly between Egypt and the Arabian lands to the E, the *mashreq* and the territory of the extreme Arab W, the *maghreb*. Secondly, Libya acts as a link between the Mediterranean/Europe and Saharan Africa. The Arabic spoken in Libya is generally different from the Berberized and French-influenced Arabic of the Maghreb with its quite separate accent and dialect from the Arabic of the Nile valley. The coming of oil wealth profoundly affected the attitudes

of small groups of an often bedouin population, barely 1 million in all, with their Libyan attitudes, way of life, and political structure. Apparently less culturally stable and profound, it is immediately different to the great Nilotic civilizations to the E, and to the more Mediterranean and French influenced societies to the W.

Libya and Europe

Although Libya was colonized by the Italians for a brief period (1911-1943) as its 'Fourth Shore' and was politically allied to Europe under the Senussi monarchy until 1969, since that time the country has become detached from European values. In contrast to the Maghreb, Libya will seem to be alien to the traveller from the W. Management and administrative systems are generally slow except in the new, small but flourishing private sector. The role of the state is much greater and impinges much further on people's private lives than in West Europe.

Borders

Libya is bounded to the W by Tunisia and Algeria. In the extreme SW, the border is not fully agreed and travellers are advised to keep to the main roads. In the E, the Libyan frontier with Egypt is for the most part agreed. Libya shares a border with Sudan in the SE. The entire S border is subject to dispute with Chad. The Uzu strip was bitterly fought over until 1990 when it was agreed to settle the matter by reference to the International Court of Justice.

Regions

Traditionally Libya was divided into three provinces – Tripolitania, Cyrenaica and Fezzan. Indeed, until recently, Libya was a united kingdom of these three provinces and Libyans still identify with these historic divisions. Recent political changes brought four new administrative districts including Tripoli, Benghazi, Sabha and Al-Khalij or 'Gulf'. Tribal territories are still observed in the popular culture of some districts.

Relief

A set of geographical districts naturally defined by relief features is recognized locally, the principal natural zones being the densely settled regions of the Jefara Plain, the Jabal Nafusa, Sirt, the Benghazi Plain, the Jabal Al-Akhdar, Fezzan and Al-Kufrah. In the centre and S very large scale features dominate. In the W the Hammadah Al-Hamra is a vast stony plain with no settlements and few lines of communication. Adjacent to the E of the Hammadah is the Jabal As-Sawda, the black mountains, a desolate and topographically broken area. In the S, Fezzan, is the great sand sea of Murzuq through which travel is feasible only via

the few great *wadi* systems which traverse it. In the E, the settled zone of the Jabal Al-Akhdar is followed to the S by the Dahar, an extensive area of enormous sand seas, of which Calanscio is possibly the greatest. It is dangerous to travel off the few highways which link the small oases. Water holes are few and population numbers very thin. In the deepest SE lie the Tibesti Mountains, the land of the Tibu tribes, where security is unreliable and the traveller is advised to enter only when accompanied by an official courier.

Rivers

Libya has only one permanently flowing river, the Wadi Ki'am, in the W province between Al-Khums and Zliten. This is a tiny stream of no more than 2 km running from a spring source to a reservoir impounded in a lagoon adjacent to the seashore. Elsewhere the *wadis* run in spate after heavy rains but are dry for the rest of the year. *Wadis* in flood can fill at a dangerous speed. Among the major *wadis* of Libya are the Mejennin which runs through the W suburbs of Tripoli city. It is now mainly controlled through dams and diversion works in its upper reaches. The Wadi Soffejin drains much of S Tripolitania to the Gulf of Sirte, partly feeding the enormous natural salt marshes at Tauorga, located to the S of Misratah. In Cyrenaica the Wadi Derna is a rich area, its stream running for much of the year and providing irrigation water for a fertile oasis adjacent to the port. The generally waterless Wadi Al-Kuf runs through the hills of the Jabal Al-Akhdar in a steep, scenic gorge.

Climate

The Libyan climate is very varied. The Mediterranean coast has warm winters with an unreliable rainfall, though on average over 200 mm. Extended periods of poor rainfall are experienced even in this coastal zone. Summers are hot and often humid. Relative humidity in Jul can reach an uncomfortable 80+% for days on end especially in Tripolitania. The mountains of the Jabal Al-Akhdar attract considerably more reliable rainfall in winter and early spring, while in summer the heights are cooler than the surrounding plains. Further S the climate becomes increasingly Saharan. Low temperatures and occasional random rainfall are experienced in winter with a large daily temperature range from 15-20°C during the day to sub-zero at night. Cold nights also occur in early and late summer. Summers are hot and very dry in the S with highs of over 50°C but one can also feel cold in the night when a sweater is welcome. Al-Aziziyah, inland on the Jefara Plain behind Tripoli, has one of the world's highest recorded temperatures, 55°C.

The *ghibli* wind blows hot air from the Sahara across N Libya and carries a large amount of dust which severely reduces visibility. Relative humidity drops immediately at the onset of the *ghibli* to less than 15% and air temperatures rise rapidly. The wind is most noticeable in W Libya and is often associated with the spring solstice.

Flora and fauna

Outside the coastal plains, the Jabal Nafusah and the Jabal Al-Akhdar, the natural vegetation is dominated by tamarind, palm and fig trees. The acacia arabica, alfalfa grass, salt bush and a range of grasses grow thinly except after rain in the semi-desert. Other plants include the asfodel and wild pistachio. The dromedary was the principal animal of the region but is declining rapidly in importance. There is still a residual belief that the region was formerly, perhaps in Roman times, very rich and climatically more favoured than at present. Wall and cave paintings and graffiti of leopards, elephants, wolves and other animals of the Savanna suggest that this was so. There are antelope, gazelle and porcupine. Falcons, eagles,

and other birds of prey are present in small numbers. During the period of bird migrations, many small migrant birds get blown into the Sahara and even the occasional exotic species strays into the oases. There are snakes, few dangerous, and scorpions which are to be carefully avoided. See also the introduction to North Africa, page 50.

Agriculture

Agriculture remains the main occupation of the Libyans despite the protracted existence and economic dominance of the oil industry. In good years rainfall turns the countryside green and the semi-desert blooms with a profusion of flowers, the Jefara Plain being particularly attractive at such times. Poor rainfall means thin crops from rainfed farming and a reliance on underground water resources lifted by diesel and electric pumps. A series of dry years causes the water table to fall dramatically and leads to the excessive use of pumps. Around Tripoli, salt water from the sea has been drawn into deep aquifers more than 20 km inland from the coast. Water for both agriculture and human use has become increasingly salty over the years.

The Jabal Al-Akhdar of Cyrenaica has a generally reliable rainfall of more than 300 mm per year but has only limited underground water resources. Here agriculture is rainfed and is mainly concerned with grain production. In the S areas of the country farming activity is limited to small oases where underground water occurs naturally in see pages for traditional farming or can be pumped in modern development projects. The traditional farms have successfully resisted extinction as the economy has been modernized, though many modern reclamation schemes, as at Al-Kufrah, have been abandoned as costs have risen and environmental limitations taken their toll.

In much of the broad zone of N Libya,

including the semi-arid steppes and the inland *wadi* catchments, various forms of pastoral nomadism were important in the past. Tribal territories spread S from the coast to enable seasonal migrations of the nomads. In the central Jefara of Tripolitania, the fringes of the Gulf of Sirte and much of the S slopes of the Jabal Al-Akhdar, forms of full nomadism were practised. Other parts of the N were under types of semi-nomadism (family herding movement) or seasonal transhumance (movements of flocks by shepherds). The coming of the oil era, the imposition of firm boundaries between North African states and other processes of modernization brought much of the nomadic activity to a halt. Some semi-nomadic shepherding of large flocks of sheep and goats still goes on in traditional pasture areas but on a minor scale, involving only small numbers of people.

Agricultural land use in Libya is concentrated on the coastal strip. Only 1% of the country is cultivated with a further 7.6% as pasture, rough grazing or forest. The only natural woodland, mainly evergreen scrub, occurs on the Jabal Al-Akdar, though this has been much reduced by clearances for agriculture. Total forested land is claimed at 0.4% of the land surface area.

The **land tenure** situation in Libya has evolved rapidly through the last 100 years. Communal, tribal land ownership was generally practised in Libya except in the settled oases. The Italian colonial period saw a great expansion of state-controlled lands which eventually devolved to the government of the independent state of Libya in 1951-61. Government intervention in all forms of ownership, ostensibly to socialize fixed assets in the country after the introduction of the Green Book decrees of 1973/75, led to more de facto nationalization of land. Small farmers are again being encouraged to remain in private ownership. In certain circumstances, individuals are also allowed to own more than one house. Some communal properties, mainly in the semi-arid steppes, are held by tribal groups. A gradual reassertion of private rights in land and other property began with the human rights decrees of 1977 and were reinforced by the privatization programmes implemented from 1989.

Economic potential

Libyan economic potential is greatly limited by the constraints of a harsh environment. No more than a fragment of the land receives rainfall adequate to support agriculture; underground water reserves are slight and declining. Even the costly movement of water from the S to the N by the Great Manmade River (GMR) projects inaugurated in late 1991 do little to mitigate the problem of water shortage. Other natural resources are scant. Oil, gas and some small chemical deposits occur. There is some potential for the development of the SW where yellow cake (low grade uranium) is found. Overall, however, the country is poorly endowed and its physical resources inevitably must restrict its future development.

Culture

People

The **population** of Libya was estimated at 5,225,000 in 1994, 4.1% above the preceding year. There is great racial diversity. The original Berber population of W Libya gradually mixed with incoming Arab tribes after the 8th century BC, though some small groups of more or less pure Berbers from the Jabal Nafusa area of Tripolitania still exist. The peoples of E Libya are proud to be mainly Arab. Intermixture through marriage with slaves and other peoples of negro origin such as the Tibu from the Tibesti mountains of S Libya gives a further dimension to the racial variety. The coastal cities originally contained populations of Jewish, foreign Arab, Maltese, Greek and many others.

Tribal traditions are strong. Outside Tripoli the country was economically and socially structured on *qabila* (tribal) lines with *lahmah* (clans) and extended family sub-clans. Each tribe had a defined territory and a specific history of alliances and friction with adjacent groups. During Italian colonial rule, the legal and economic basis of society was changed, partly through systematic removal of Arabs from the land but also by the economic upheaval that came with colonial occupation and warfare.

Nonetheless, tribal affiliation has social importance in marriage, kinship and status, especially outside the major urban centres.

Some 95% of people are found in the narrow N coastal strip, with 82% of all Libyans crowded into urban areas. Many of those registered as rural in fact commute to work in nearby towns. Tripoli attracts long-distance daily commuters and there are few areas of the NW not dominated economically by the capital despite recent attempts to decentralize. There is an average of three persons per sq km, though in the coastal

THE TRIBES OF LIBYA

Libya remains a tribal society despite an attempt to undermine the system by the Italian colonial authorities, and strong forces for modernization since Independence especially since 1969. Perhaps the growth of an apparently all-powerful state control over the lives of ordinary people gave the tribal system the fillip it needed to survive. Caught up in a political regime many neither understood nor cared for, they turned to their traditional roots, the family, the extended family and the tribe. The genesis of the tribal system and its genealogies are all-important in giving strength to the tribes of the present day.

The tribes of Tripolitania are often of mixed Arab and Berber descent but might identify exclusively with one aspect of their ethnic origin. Geographically the tribes of different racial origin are in small areas so that there are few large confederations made up of a single ethnic source. In N Cyrenaica the tribes are exclusively Arab from the Obeidat of the Ulad Ali in the E to the Al-Magarba of Ajdabiyah and Sirt. All the tribes claim an individual or family as a common origin and it is not unusual for the pure Arab and Berber tribes to be able to establish long family trees. There are formerly saintly clans grouped around a *marabout* as a common ancestor. Some tribes claim their origins in a member of the family of the Prophet Mohammed. Other tribes have family trees which are suspect but which, nevertheless, serve to unite and bond the tribe. The still-practised custom of marriage between cousins brings a sense of closeness to those families involved.

Each tribe is made up of at least four different levels of organization, the nuclear family, the extended family, the large family group or sub-tribe and the tribe. The family and extended families are represented by the eldest male. The sub-tribe and tribe have a chosen or acknowledged head. Formerly the head or shaikh would act for his group in dealings with tribes or clans of a similar kind and with the outside world. This latter formality is less visible in modern society for, since 1969, the government has not given recognition to the tribal units. An element of social support and economic backing comes from the tribe together with a feeling of a shared territory. A person's identity originates powerfully in his tribal and family name, which declares ethnic origin, historical status and possibly current political strength.

strip the densities are much higher.

It is estimated that about 46% of the Libyan population is less than 15 years old, 26% between 15 and 29 and a mere 4.1% above 60 years of age, a profoundly youthful population even by Third World standards. The balance between males and females is reported as 52% male and 48% female.

Religion

Libya is almost uniformly Sunni Muslim. Practice of Islam is normal for most people though, with some notable exceptions, Islam is kept as a way of life rather than a political force, in contrast to Algeria. Within Sunni Islam there is variation in attachment to different schools of jurists. Most Libyans are of the Malekite school, though Berber minority groups of Kharejite thought are also found.

Literacy

Rates are much improved in Libya from a very poor base level at Independence. By 1990, 75% of males and 50% of females were literate. The educational system has been the subject of constant interference by the authorities, and standards, especially in higher education, have fallen in recent years. Even so there are 47,000 persons each year in higher education with university levels, except in medicine and some other limited areas, approximating in most cases to those of European secondary schools.

Income

As an oil economy Libya generates an apparently high income per head at US$6,600. This figure can be misleading in the sense that the government controls and spends the greatest portion of national income which benefits the population at large. There is poor distribution of income, the isolated rural regions of the country being much worse off in real terms than the coastal cities. Between individuals, however, there is less visible difference in income than in other Arab states. Libyan participation in the workforce is low at 25% of the total population with only 9% of women taking part in paid employment. By far the majority of Libyans work for the government or its agencies, leaving foreign labourers to work in industry and perform other menial tasks.

History since Independence

British and French military administrations withdrew in 1951 when the state became independent as a United Kingdom of Cyrenaica, Tripolitania and Fezzan under the first Senussi monarch. The king kept close links with the British and Americans, permitting the retention of British land forces and American and British airforce facilities. Libya was economically poor at this period, having one of the lowest standards of living in the world. Foreign aid supported the state until an increasing volume of oil company expenditures in Libya on goods and services for exploration activity gradually improved the economy. Severe strains affected the Libyan nation as Arab nationalist and anti-western ideology generated by Gamal Abdel Nasser in Egypt spread to Libya.

Oil was struck in commercial quantities in 1959 and oil exports began in 1961. Libya rapidly became financially independent and initiated sensible reforms in housing, health and education. Employment opportunities improved and a development programme for agriculture, industry and infrastructure was set in motion. Young Libyan technocrats were given scope to implement their policies and the country made rapid steps forward from a low economic base level. The king took little part in the management of the country. Politically the nation was concentrated in a United Kingdom of Libya in 1963, with a parliament of limited powers centred in

Tripoli. The Palestine question and the spread of Nasserite ideas made Libya politically unstable.

A coup d'état by a group of young army officers took place on September 1, 1969. The leader of the coup was Mu'amar Ghadhafi who was a disciple of Gamal Abdel Nasser, overtly anti-western and deeply convinced of the need to obtain full rights for the Palestinians. He banned alcohol and the use of foreign languages for official purposes. He closed down the remaining foreign military bases on Libyan soil. He abolished most private sector activities in the economy and promised a new Arab socialist society under the banner of the Socialist People's Libyan Jamahiriyah. He elaborated a set of philosophies encapsulated in his Green Book which set out his ideas on the nature of an Arab socialist state. He adopted the position of qa'ed (guide) and announced that democracy was untenable. Instead he set up people's committees in all administrative districts and work places as best representing the interests of the masses. Perhaps his greatest success was in threatening the assets of the foreign oil companies in Libya and in helping to force up oil prices in the early 1970s.

The Libyan role in favour of Arab unity and against western interests was pursued through the creation of a vast and expensive military establishment, political activities abroad designed to frustrate western interests and a solid pro-Palestinian stance. While oil revenues remained very high, Libya's international position gained some notoriety in Lebanon, Uganda and Chad. Military successes were denied the Libyan authorities and, as oil wealth declined first in the mid-1970s and then in the 1980s, Libyan foreign policy ceased to be significant in international affairs.

At home a series of economic plans promised rapid and integrated regional development of the country, but erratic implementation of projects, shortages of money and personnel and distraction abroad diluted the effort. Despite having a small indigenous population, Libya has never quite developed beyond oil as a productive and well-organized state with high personal incomes. In 1989 the socialist system of centralized national and economic management was abandoned piecemeal.

Political power is concentrated in the hands of Colonel Ghadhafi and, to a lesser extent, his close associates. An annual People's Congress permits some ventilation of other ideas and an apparent control system on spending of state revenues. In fact there have been few political changes to compare with the liberalization and privatization of the economy in recent years.

Despite official statements and propaganda images of Libya abroad, most Libyans are gentle and friendly, not least with foreign visitors who are clearly tourists and/or travellers. Travellers should, however, note that the security situation is slightly tense at the time of writing following harassment of foreigners in some southern locations.

Modern Libya

Government

The ideal of government was expressed in the Third Universal Theory, expounded by Colonel Ghadhafi in the early 1970s and enshrined in the **Green Book**, the first sections of which were published in 1976. Ghadhafi attempted to bring together strands of his own beliefs – Islam, freedom from foreign intervention, equality of people and the welfare of the greater Arab nation – within a unified philosophy. He was never taken entirely seriously in this ambition outside the country. Events were also to prove that Libya itself was resistant to his ideas. Despite the single minded expenditure of large sums on imposing socialism at home, including

COLONEL MU'AMAR GHADHAFI

Colonel Ghadhafi was born in the Gasr Bu Hadi area of Sirt on the coast of the Gulf of Sirte (Sidra) in 1942. His parents were from the Ghadhafa tribe, a mixed Arab-Berber group, which practised semi-nomadic herding of animals with some shifting grain cultivation in the arid steppelands surrounding the traditional tribal territories. He went to secondary school in Misratah before joining the army as an officer cadet. He graduated from the military academy and was eventually posted to Sabha in the Fezzan area. He briefly attended the University of Libya in Benghazi and undertook a short stay in the United Kingdom on a training course.

He rose to fame in Sep 1969 as the head of a group of revolutionary officers who overthrew the monarchy and set up an Arab republic ruled by a Revolutionary Command Council. The political programme introduced by Ghadhafi was simple and based mainly on the ideas of the Egyptian nationalist leader Gamal Abdel Nasser. Colonel Ghadhafi was anti-western, anti-Israel and in favour of a centrally controlled social and economic system within Libya. British and American military bases in Libya were closed down after the revolution. All public signs had to be written in Arabic and all foreigners, including any remaining Italian residents, were no longer made welcome.

Initially Colonel Ghadhafi was received by the Libyan people with acclaim. His simple creed of Arab nationalism fitted the mood of the day. In the early 1970s Libya became immensely rich in oil revenues as, aided by Libyan actions against the oil companies, the price of oil rose dramatically on the international market. At the same time, Colonel Ghadhafi issued his philosophy to guide the revolution, the so-called **Green Book**, preaching a form of Arab socialism. He also saw for himself a role as messianic leader of all the Arabs and a focus around which the Arab world could be united. At home, he entered into bold programmes for economic development, with expansion of agriculture, provision of state welfare schemes and investments in industry and infrastructure. Power was, at least in theory, devolved down to regional municipal assemblies which reported annually to a General People's Congress.

By the end of the 1970s Colonel Ghadhafi faced increasing difficulties. Abroad, Libya's attempts at Arab unity had failed. Libya had been unable to affect events in the Arab-Israel dispute despite a great deal of fiery rhetoric. Colonel Ghadhafi had also made an unsuccessful attempt to intervene in a war in Uganda to support the unpopular leader Idi Amin. Meanwhile Ghadhafi's political credentials were eroded by the rise of revolutionary Islamic movements in Iran and the Arab world. The collapse of oil prices after 1980 weakened the Libyan economy at a time when Colonel Ghadhafi became deeply embroiled in a territorial dispute with Chad over the Uzu strip, a band of desert lying between the two countries. Despite huge outlays in men and material, the war against Chad was lost and was taken to the International Court for arbitration. Suspicions that there was Libyan involvement in international terrorism came to a head in 1988 when responsibility for the destruction by a bomb of a Pan Am aircraft from UK to the USA at Lockerbie in Scotland was attributed to two Libyan officials. Libya eventually fell under a UN air transport embargo and was isolated from the international community as a pariah state.

In Libya, Colonel Ghadhafi lost some popularity as a result of these adverse changes but remained as the political guide of the country, defended by loyal echelons of the armed forces and without real rivals.

the devolution of bureaucratic powers to the four major regions – Tripoli, Sabha, Al-Khalij and Benghazi – and the removal of all private privileges of ownership of goods, property and even a fully private life, by 1987 the dream had to be abandoned. The structures he established persisted, however. A Basic People's Congress meets to manage the affairs of state, with Colonel Ghadhafi taking the position of 'guide' to the revolution. The congress acts officially through a series of appointed secretariats, which are now, for all practical purposes, ministries in the traditional mode. The revolutionary fervour, which characterized Libya in the 1970s and 1980s, has dimmed considerably and lives on only in the apparatus for security and military matters. Since he has these agents of political control in his hands, Colonel Ghadhafi effectively has the final say in decision-making in the country. There is no official opposition party and opponents of the régime have generally fled abroad.

The secretariats which look after day-to-day administration are spread out throughout the country as part of a deliberate policy of regionalizing management. Key ministries are in Sirt, though some scattered government offices also exist.

In foreign policy, Libya acted to harass the western powers at whose doors Colonel Ghadhafi laid many of the ills of Libya and the Arab nation. While he could play off the West against the USSR and had access to considerable oil revenues, he successfully worked against the USA and EU states in propaganda and support for their opponents. The demise of the USSR as a world power in 1991, a massive fall-off in oil revenues in the mid-1980s and the rise of the conservative states as leading elements within the Arab world left him vulnerable to foreign pressures to accept international legal norms for state activities. This was signalled in Libyan problems

in 1992 with US and British demands over the Lockerbie incident.

Economy

Libya is an oil-based economy. Oil was first exported commercially in 1961 and thereafter output rose rapidly so that at the end of the 1960s Libya was the fifth largest Opec producer of crude oil with more than 3 million barrels per day. This expansion was based geographically on the oilfields in the vast embayment of the Gulf of Sirte where small but prolific oilfields were found in the sedimentary rocks. While some oil was discovered by the major international oil companies such as Esso, Mobil and BP, there were also many small independent oil companies involved, for which Libya was the only source of traded crude oil. By the end of the 1960s a development of oilfields, pipelines and oil terminals had taken place in what had been a barren desert area lying between Tripoli and Benghazi. Following the revolution of 1969, economic policies were aligned towards making the country self sufficient.

Traditional agriculture

This was mainly self sufficient with small surpluses going to the many local occasional markets. The coastlands were comparatively rich agriculturally, favoured by adequate rainfall and available underground water for irrigation. Small fragmented farms were the rule on the coast, though many families had access to communal tribal lands for shifting cultivation and grazing animals to the S of the coastal oases.

Superimposed on this pattern of Arab farming and semi-nomadic herding is an Italian colonial structure established in the 1920s and 1930s but replicated since Independence by the Libyans themselves. The ex-colonial landscape is still a powerful feature of the country, especially in Tripolitania. Enormous areas of geometrically planted olive, almond and eucalypt plantations extend across the Jefara and parts of the Jabal Al-Nafusa, often in association with small colonial farmhouses. Although the Italian farmers have now gone, their legacy in the landscape, perpetuated by the local farmers who bought them out and by the government, remains and adds significantly to current output of olive oil and almonds.

The greatest single changes by Libyan farmers, though on a model mainly reminiscent of the Italians, is the introduction of citrus fruit orchards and the intensification of output through irrigation in what had originally been dryland or lightly irrigated Italian estates. The most important single field crop is fodder. Libyans prize their mutton enormously and sheep are kept by most farmers. There has also been an expansion of beef and dairy herding, which also requires abundant fodder production, mainly types of lucerne. On the Jabal Al-Nafusa, there is little irrigation and dryland crops are olives, figs and apricots. Grain of excellent quality is grown on the Jefara plain on lands owned by the Jabal tribes.

In E Libya, the Jabal Al-Akdar are used for dryland cereals, some fruit and a large area of fodder. In the S, Fezzan and Al-Khalij, oases survive using irrigation for intensive vegetable and fruit production. Libya's best dates come from the SW, the *deglet nur* being the most prized. (See also Algeria, page 288 and Tunisia, page 288).

Modern farming

Contemporary agriculture other than the private sector activities already noted has until recently been mainly state managed. Underground water resources in the deep SE at Al-Kufrah, Tizerbu and Serir were developed for agriculture and new agricultural production units created in the SW at Sabha, Murzuq and other sites. Expensive imported technology was employed in these schemes and imported labour from Sudan, Egypt and elsewhere since Libyans were generally not prepared to move to these inhospitable regions. Despite the investment of very large resources, the majority of agricultural schemes in the S were abandoned or run down when Libya's oil revenues declined during the mid-1980s.

Libya's biggest and most spectacular development, the Great Manmade River (GMR), will carry water in a large diameter pipeline from wellfields in Al-Kufrah, Serir and Tizerbu to the coast and thence to Benghazi in the E and Sirt in the W. A second pipeline, it is projected, will transport water from the Murzuq Basin in the SW to the Jefara Plain adjacent to Tripoli. The movement of water to the N is at the cost of the closure of most major irrigation schemes in the S. Although the government has promised that the new water will be used in the coastlands for agriculture in addition to supplying industrial and urban areas, high costs of the water delivered there make its use in irrigation questionable. The need for new water illustrates the other great problem for farming in Libya – the falling water tables and intrusion of sea water into aquifers in coastal areas.

Oasis economies

In the oases of the deep S and the small towns at a modest distance from the coast, there is little industry. Here life revolves around earnings from agriculture and remittance income from employment on the coast. Construction of private villas and other housing is the most pronounced area of economic activity in the countryside, though farming is still a way of life for many Libyans outside the major coastal towns and involvement in transportation also absorbs a great deal of energy in these areas.

Petroleum

Provides the government with its principal foreign exchange income, US$7,650mn in 1993, the main source of general revenues in the annual budget (90%) and the most important single commodity for export (99%). The two areas of production are around the W borderlands and the Gulf of Sirt, the latter with export terminals at Sidrah, Ras Lanuf, Al-Brayqah and Zuwetina. The main oilfields are linked by pipelines to coastal terminals. Serir oilfield and its associated installations in the extreme SE are tied in to a terminal at Marsa Hariga near Tobruk (Tubruq), while a small line runs on a NS axis in the W to Zaviyah oil refinery. An offshore field, Bouri, is sited on the Libyan continental shelf close to Tunisian waters in the NW. It was won from Tunisia in a judgment of the International Court of Justice in 1982. Libyan oil reserves are only moderate, rated at around 29,000 million barrels, which would last some 52 years at present rates of extraction. Libya produces approximately 1.5 million barrels per year and exports some three-quarters of its output, mainly to West Europe. The National Libyan Oil Co owns refineries in Italy and Germany. Domestic refineries are found at Zaviyah, Al-Brayqah and Ras Lanuf.

Economic plans

The comparatively short life expectancy of Libya as a major oil exporter has given emphasis to the need to develop alternative sources of exports for the future. A set of economic development plans has been adopted by the government, the latest being a programme for 1980-2000 with aims to bolster self-sufficiency, create new jobs and lay the foundations for a future non-oil economy. Some successes were won, including an improvement in the country's transport infrastructure. Excellent road systems serve all parts of the country. New hospitals, hotels and schools have been set up so that even the most isolated settlements can offer good housing, health and educational facilities. Grandiose plans for a rail system to replace the old Italian lines closed in the 1960s have been delayed. A North African link through Libya from Morocco and Algeria to Egypt is under consideration, while a mineral and general purpose line from Brak (Brach) to carry iron ore to the Misratah steel plant is under consideration. Air transport in Libya serves most major settlements but its growth has been impeded by USA sanctions against Libya which have limited the availability of new aircraft to Libyan Arab Airways, the national carrier.

Industry

Economic development outside transport and other infrastructure has been expensive and limited. Only petrochemicals, with large scale complexes set up at Ras Lanuf and Bu Kammash with a smaller operation planned at Sirt, have shown rapid growth, but they depend on the oil sector for raw materials, are highly polluting and employ few Libyans. The Misratah iron and steel mills began operations in 1989 and

ECONOMIC INDICATORS US$ BILLION			
	1989	**1991**	**1993**
Oil revenues	7.500	9,600	7,650
Exports	7.750		7,700
Imports	5.497		8,260
National income	19.500	21,100	32,000
Current account balance	+2.253		-560
Inflation (%)	15		15
Foreign debt			3,500
Source: Economist Intelligence Unit			

brought great prosperity to this old market town. How commercially viable the plants are remains to be seen. Elsewhere in industry the state agencies set up a variety of new concerns in food processing, soap making, aluminium and construction goods materials. As from the late 1980s, Libyan entrepreneurs were encouraged to begin work in industry on their own account, a move which saw the opening of many small scale workshops, stores and corner shop businesses.

Economic trends

The poor performance of the oil sector since the mid-1980s has dominated trends since that time. The late 1980s was a poor time for Libya and things have picked up only as better management of limited oil revenues and improved internal economic liberalisation has had an effect. The growth of private enterprise has been the main area of economic growth in the immediate past.

CONTENTS

Tripoli	502
The Capital	502
Tripoli District	511
Tripoli to Al-Khums and Misratah	511
Tripoli to Farwa and the Tunisian Frontier	516
Tripoli to the Jabal Nafusa at Gharyan	519
Sites to visit in Jefara Plain	520
Travel in the Jabal Nafusa	523
Jabal Nafusa – Gharyan to Nalut	525
Al-Khums to Tarhunah and Tripoli	532

MAPS

Tripoli Medina	503
Tripoli	504-505
East of Tripoli	513
West of Tripoli	517
Leptis Magna	521
Sabrata	523
The Jabal Nafusa	527
Ghadames house plan	530
Al-Khums to Tripoli	533

The climate of Tripoli is Mediterranean with hot dry summers, cool winters and some modest rainfall. Weather can be variable, influenced by the Sahara Desert and the Mediterranean Sea which moderates daily temperature ranges.

INDICATORS *Alt* Sea level. The population of Greater Tripolitania is 2,014,200. District populations are Tripoli 1,083,100, Gharyan 204,300, Nikat Al-Khums (Homs) 196,000, Zaviyah 326,500 and Jabal Nafusa 204,300. Growth of population is 4.5% per year. Literacy in Tripoli is higher than the national average though official figures of M 95% F 90% seem too good to be true. The labour force comprises Libyans 300,000 and immigrants 250,000. The average income per head is US$5,310, with inflation at 10%. Although the official language is Arabic, Berber is also common in the hill lands of Tripolitania, and English, French and Italian are also spoken.

The Capital

Tripoli, or Tarabalus Al-Gharb (Tripoli of the W in Arabic), is the major city and de facto capital of Libya. The removal of many government secretariats and faculties of the Tripoli, Al-Fatah, university has not changed the reality of Tripoli as the real political centre of Libya. The People's Congress meets in Tripoli and Colonel Ghadhafi is for the most part resident there. Plans continue to be talked about in government circles for the construction of yet another new capital which would be sited on neutral territory outside the two polarized traditional provinces of Tripolitania and Cyrenaica. Under King Idris Senussi, before the revolution of 1969, a new capital was set up at Al-Bayda in the Jabal Al-Akdar. It rooted itself well but

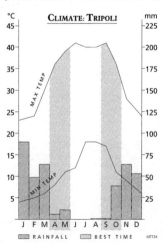

CLIMATE: TRIPOLI

RAINFALL   BEST TIME

MTT34

political changes took away its role as capital. Colonel Ghadhafi and foreign consultants have proposed a new site for the capital on the coast of the Gulf of Sirte to act as a point of unity between the W and E regions. The fact that Colonel Ghadhafi has his tribal and close family links in Sirt adds to the attraction of this proposal.

Places of interest

The old walled city of Tripoli, the **medina**, is one of the classical sites of the Mediterranean. The basic street plan was laid down in the Roman period when the walls were constructed on the landward sides against attacks from the interior of Tripolitania. The high walls survived many invasions, each conqueror restoring the damage done. In the 8th century the Muslim ruler built

a wall on the sea-facing side of the city. Three great gates gave access to the town, Bab Zanata on the W, Bab Hawara on the SE and Bab Al-Bahr in the N wall. Constant rebuilding means that few ancient commercial buildings remain and even the oldest mosque, Al-Naqah, was reconstructed in 1610. The **castle**, Al-Saraya Al-Hamra, occupies a site known to be pre-Roman in the E quadrant of the city and still dominates the skyline of Tripoli. The castle is made up of many distinct sections, formerly public and private quarters of the ruling family. The women were kept in a harem and a number of beautiful courtyards lie segregated from the alleyways which run through the castle. The upper walls afford a fine view to the sea and across the town.

The old city itself was made up of a

TRIPOLI MEDINA MT186

1. Al-Saraya Al-Hamra (castle)
2. Mosque of Al-Karamanli
3. Mosque of En-Naqah
4. Mosque of Mohammad Pasha
5. Mosque of Dragut
6. Medersa of Uthman Pasha
7. Mosque of Mahmud
8. Mosque of Gurgi
9. Mosque of Sidi Salem
10. Suq Al-Kebir
11. Suq Al-Najarah
12. Suq Al-Turk
13. Synogogue
14. Bab Al-Jedid
15. Aurelian Arch
16. Suq Al-Mushir
17. Castle Museum
18. Medina Museum

PORT

Reclaimed Area (Port)

Green Square

To Hotels Bab el Bahr & Bab el Medina

Corniche

Sh Hara Kebir

Sh Hara Seghin

Sh Homet Gharyan

Sh Kusset Sidi Omban

Sh Sidi Hamura

Sh Jama Al-Draghut

Sh Kusset Al-Seffar

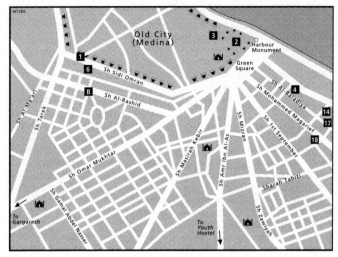

series of separate quarters, two major parts of which were Jewish (*hara* is the name designating the Jewish areas of Tripoli). Narrow streets criss-cross the old city off which run blind alleys. While the piece-meal development of the city gave rise to the impasses and randomness to the street pattern the blind alleys were often ways of sealing off areas controlled by single or extended families or ethnic groups so that attackers or casual passers-by would not intrude on family life, especially the lives of women. The through alleys in Tripoli old city are generally unroofed but with buttresses at intervals which help to hold up the walls on either side of the alley and provide some shelter from the sun. Walls facing the public alleys are for the most part plain with few windows, a device to increase privacy and deter curiosity. Doorways to houses and interior courtyards are remarkably ornate in contrast to the tall plain walls around them. Massive arches are used, displaying Roman or Islamic decorations while the doors themselves are often high, studded and provided with ancient locks.

Individual houses in the old city still display their great cloistered courtyards and ornate tile, wood and plaster work. There are also several grand *serais* or *funduqs*, where merchants lodged their goods and animals around large courtyards. Generally less decorated than private houses, nonetheless they played an important role in the life of the city when the large traders organized and managed trans-Saharan caravans. The manufacturing and retail *suqs* of old Tripoli were carefully run by guilds of craftsmen and capitalists producing craft products for daily use. Pottery, metalwork, traditional clothing and jewellery were made here. Some of the *suqs* still trade under vaulted brick ceilings, though very few goods are now manufactured in situ. Suq Al-Mushir is the popular tourist area of the old city situated immediately off Green Square adjacent to the castle. There are seven **mosques** in the old city, containing a wealth of indigenous architectural detail (see map, page 503).

There was an exodus of the traditional families from the old city after

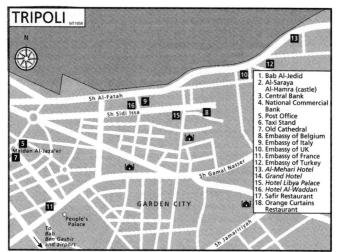

TRIPOLI MT185R

N

Sh Al-Fatah

Sh Sidi Issa

Maidan Al-Jaza'er

Sh Gamal Nasser

GARDEN CITY

People's Palace

To Bab Ben Gashir and airport

Sh Jamaririyah

1. Bab Al-Jedid
2. Al-Saraya Al-Hamra (castle)
3. Central Bank
4. National Commercial Bank
5. Post Office
6. Taxi Stand
7. Old Cathedral
8. Embassy of Belgium
9. Embassy of Italy
10. Embassy of UK
11. Embassy of France
12. Embassy of Turkey
13. Al-Mehari Hotel
14. Grand Hotel
15. Hotel Libya Palace
16. Hotel Al-Waddan
17. Safir Restaurant
18. Orange Curtains Restaurant

Independence in 1951. Families moved to occupy houses and apartments vacated by the departing Italians to take advantage of better sanitation, water supply and other facilities. By the mid 1970s the situation had deteriorated so badly that the majority of residents in the old city was immigrant workers from overseas. Neglect of the fragile buildings enabled damp to get into their fabric and many fell to ruin. The Libyan authorities determined to halt the rot and established a group to undertake restoration of key buildings and to write up the history of the city. In addition to the establishment of a research workshop and library in the old city, the main mosques, synagogues and consular houses have been restored in excellent taste.

Any tour of the old city should begin at the **castle**, entered from the land side near Suq Al-Mushir, entrance free, closes at 1400. It houses a library and a well organized museum and has excellent views over the city from the walls. This is one of the two principal **museums** in Tripoli, the other being in the medina, approximately 500m away. The **Castle Museum** is essentially concerned with the archaeology and ancient history of Libya. It covers the Phoenician, Greek and Roman periods well and has an expanding collection of materials on the Islamic period. The top floor is devoted to Libyan modern history. Open weekdays 0800-1400, closed Fri. Entrance LD0.50. The main route through the old city runs from the castle towards the sea, with the old French and British consulates, the Medina Museum and the Aurelian Arch all worthy of close attention. The old city walls are still standing. The **Harbour Monument** stands at the gates of the old city on the edge of the former corniche road adjacent to the castle. There are a number of restored houses, consulates and a synagogue in the narrow streets. The **Medina Museum**, easily found as a renovated building standing all alone in a cleared section to the NW of the medina, has a library with illustrated displays and helpful staff with a great knowledge of the medina area. Open weekdays 0800-1400, closed Fri. Entry is free and is from Bab Al-Jedid on the W side of the city walls not far from the taxi station. The main merchant quarter is entered from the gate at Suq Al-Mushir. There are many separate small *suqs* such as the Suq Al-Attar (medicinal drugs), Suq As-Siiaja (goldsmiths), the remnants of which still operate though without their former Jewish workers and owners.

There are a number of interesting mosques in the old town including the **Karamanli Mosque**, the **En-Naqah Mosque** and the **Gurgi Mosque**. The En-Naqah mosque, the oldest of the Tripoli mosques, is called the camel mosque because it is said that the citizens of Tripoli met the great Arab conqueror Amr Ibn Al-As with a camel-load of valuables to buy the survival of the city. Amr Ibn Al-As refused to accept this gift and instead asked that a mosque be built. The present mosque is of various dates, the last major rebuilding dating from 1610/11 when it was called the 'Great Mosque'. The plan of the mosque is slightly irregular and aligned on a NW axis. The sanctuary makes use of columns of varied sources, some Roman. There are 42 brick-built domes comprising the roof of the mosque. The *mihrab* (a niche in the wall indicating the direction of Mecca) is in the middle of the *qibla* wall. There is a *mimbar* (low pulpit). A square minaret has a spiral stairway of palm wood and plaster.

Another interesting mosque is that of **Dragut**, the well-known Islamic admiral and scourge of shipping in the Mediterranean. He died during the great siege of Malta and was returned and buried in Tripoli in the large Dragut mosque, which was damaged during WW2 but later restored. It has a square minaret and a small cemetery.

The **Al-Jami' Mosque**, the true 'Great Mosque' of Tripoli, contains interesting inscriptions to Othman Ra'is, who founded it in 1670 AD. The most magnificent mosque in Tripoli is the

Mosque of Ahmad Pasha Karamanli, Governor of Tripoli in 1711 and founder of the Karamanli Dynasty. It is located a few metres from the castle near the main entrance to the *suq*. The mosque has an adjacent *medersa* in the W corner of the grounds, tombs and a cemetery. The centre point is a sanctuary with 25 domes as a roof, the two domes over the fine *mihrab* being more elevated and carrying stucco work. The tombs of Ahmad Pasha and many of his family lie in a separate room with a large domed roof of spectacular design. The minaret is a very distinctive octagonal design in the Turkish style.

The best known of the Tripoli mosques is the **Gurgi Mosque** with its elegant architecture. It was built comparatively recently in 1833 by Yussef Gurgi (of Georgia in the Caucasus from which his family came) as an Islamic Hanifite establishment. It has a 16m square plan with nine columns and 16 small domes, of which four over the main structures such as the *mihrab* and the *mimbar* are elevated. There are many delicately decorated areas of the mosque, especially around the *mihrab*. The octagonal minaret with two balconies is the tallest of the old Tripoli mosques. If the traveller wishes to view just one of Tripoli's mosques, the Gurgi Mosque is the one to choose.

Modern Tripoli spilled out from the tight confines of the old city as early as the 18th century and possibly before that. It is known from the letters of the European consuls such as Tully, resident in Tripoli during Karamanli times, that a thriving community existed on the flat lands immediately outside the old city known as the Menshia. Here the troublesome members of the traditional military class lived with farmers, traders and other individuals. The entire area was redeveloped by the Italians in the first half of the 20th century as a colonial city for Italian residents. They created a set of administrative buildings, many of which stand today, together with official residences and general residential areas. The garden city is still the most affluent and pleasant area of Tripoli, situated adjacent to the People's Palace. Straight streets were constructed, radiating from Green Square in front of the castle, together with a cathedral and a financial district adjacent to the *suq*, along what is now Sharah Omar Mukhtar.

This pleasing colonial urban form was broken by the revolution of 1969. In an attempt to diminish the apparent colonial heritage and European influence, all street names were changed, the cathedral closed and signs not in Arabic removed. Far more influential in changing the character of Tripoli, there was massive population growth during the post-revolutionary years combined with an influx of Libyans to Tripoli. Tripoli City grew 5-fold in population size to stand at 600,000 by 1990. Extensive new suburbs grew up on all sides, many ill-planned so that Tripoli became a large metropolitan area in its own right spreading in all directions across the oases on its edge to reach out and encompass major satellite settlements such as Tajurah to the E and Zaviyah to the W.

The removal of some civil service personnel to other sites together with a fall in prosperity in the late 1980s eased some of the traffic congestion but expansion of the city continues, with people commuting 60-80 km into the city from outlying towns. At peak times, 0730-0900, 1330-1430 and 1800-1930, roads are choked and extra time must be allowed for travelling to appointments and particularly to the airport or bus station.

The main commercial streets lie in the centre. Most lead off Green Square in front of the castle. All street names are in Arabic but Libyans will assist in giving directions. The coast road, built over the former harbour area and adjacent to new wharves, is principally for

vehicular traffic moving E. There are no buildings. The inner coast road from Green Square, Sharah Al-Fatah (originally Adrian Pelt, named after the UN official who sponsored Libyan Independence in 1951) is built up on its inland side with a number of public buildings and the main hotels. It travels on E along the corniche passing the major embassies of Italy, UK (currently operating as a 'British interests' section of the Italian embassy), Turkey and others. The road is planted with ornamental palms and has cafés and gardens along it. Sharah Mohammed Magarief, one of the capital's two main streets, runs from Green Square to the former cathedral. At its S end 500m S of the former cathedral is the People's Palace, built for the late King Idris and now in the service of the popular committees and the political activists supporting Colonel Ghadhafi. The French embassy faces it and on its NW corner is one of the oil company offices. The National Oil Company office is on Sharah Gamal Nasser, to the W side of the palace. Travelling up the E side of the palace leads to the Sharah Ben Ashur in the centre of a high class residential district, the garden city to the E and new properties to the W.

Walking around Tripoli centre is straightforward, though beyond the main business and shopping precincts there is little to see and walking, especially in the heat, is not recommended. For a **tour of the modern city** on foot begin in Green Square and travel W along Sharah Omar Mukhtar to see the private business district. Turn round at the Tripoli Fair building and return to Green Square from which go SE down Sharah Mohammed Magarief towards the post office and former cathedral, now used as a mosque. The rooms above the post office display pictures of Tripoli during the Italian and British occupation. From the post office square (Maidan Al-Jaza'er) either turn directly right to Sharah Tahiti and thence right again into one of the commercial thorough-fares with small Arab lock-up shops or go on past the post office towards the People's Palace and thence left to the harbour front and back towards the Green Square. This itinerary effectively shows the best of the modern city.

The cemetery for British and Italian Christians – Al Magbarah al Masihi-yyah – lies between Sharah Gamal Nasser and Sharah Jamairiyah.

In Tripoli there are **war cemeteries** from WW2. The British and Common-wealth Cemetery is 2 km W of Tripoli and 364m S of the main road. There is also a British Military Cemetery.

Local information

● **Accommodation**

Price guide:			
AL	US$90+	D	US$20-40
A	US$75-90	E	US$10-20
B	US$60-75	F	under US$10
C	US$40-60		

Tripoli is moderately endowed with hotels, adequate for a country with little development of commercial tourism but a large immigrant worker population. Business visitors are fairly well catered for with five or so luxury hotels in Tripoli centre. Cheaper accommodation is difficult to find when arriving in the evening, for example off the Benghazi bus, so book ahead. The newest hotel is the **A** *Al-Mehari*, Sharah Al-Fatah, overlooking the harbour, T 33 34091/6, Tx 22090, pool, best service in Tripoli, US$215 double room, must be paid in US dollars, but not AL grade; **A** *Grand Hotel* (ask for *Funduq Al-Kebir*), also on Sharah Al-Fatah to the E, T 44 45940, F 45959 very close to the medina, central, two restaurants, good buffet, excellent café, car hire, tall building is good landmark, currently US$200 double room, must be in foreign exchange, but not AL grade, travel agency.

C *Bab al Bahr* and *Bab el Medina* side by side on sea front to W of medina, sea views, fair; *Al Waddan*, Sharah Sidi Issa at LD60 is not such a good deal as two mentioned above but better position in town.

D *Hotel Atlas*, top of Sharah Omar Mukhtar on a small square to the right, T 33 36815, simple but clean rooms with bath; **D** *Hotel Lula*, seafront to the E of the medina, T 33 31013, clean, many rooms with sea view, restaurant, café, room with bath, breakfast incl; **D** *Hotel White Sea*, off seafront E of the medina, T 606241, large, 200 rm, with bath, half a/c, roof terrace, clean but rather informal, breakfast incl; **D** *Libya Palace* (Qasr Libya), T 3331181, Sharah Sidi Issa, service and cleanliness of good standard, busy reception area, quiet rooms, travel agency, rec.

There are also small workers' hotels with shared facilities (category **E**) on the seafront beneath the walls of the medina, mainly clean but noisy. Outside Tripoli there are several tourist villages which can offer accommodation on request, but which are often very full in the vacation periods (see entries in Tripoli District section, pages 511).

● **Youth hostels**

Tripoli city for camping and dormitory accommodation, 69 Sharah Amr Ibn Al-As, T 44 45171, kitchen, 120 beds, breakfast available, family rm, 2 km from Green Square. *Gergarish*, Sharah Gergarish, 5 km S of Tripoli, open 0700-2400, 200 beds, meals, family room, laundry, airport 20 km, harbour 2 km, T 74755. Booking recommended at both hostels.

● **Places to eat**

The main restaurants for western visitors are in the principal hotels, all of which are open to non-residents. Some hotels such as the *Grand* and the *Al-Mehari* have more than one restaurant. They are all 'dry' but adequate. Popular eating places for the large numbers of non-Libyan Arabs are to be found in the city centre on or just off Sharah Omar Mukhtar and on the main roads immediately leading off to the S from the Green Square. They are cheap and offer Arab cuisine tending towards the rough and ready but generally hygienic. ♦♦♦*Gazala*, T 4441079, Maidan Gazala nr main post office, open 1230-1530 and 1930-2230, fixed price menu of LD15, eat plenty of appetizers and soup before the one big fish course; *Grand Hotel* has excellent buffet, eat as much as you want for LD15; ♦♦*Safir Restaurant*, just behind *Grand Hotel* on Sharah al-Baladiya, fixed price menu LD13, serves very good Moroccan and Tunisian food; *Badwen*, 110-112 Sharah al-Baladiya, T 33 39995, in front of the public gardens, recognized by brown door and short queue at entrance, Lebanese owned, rec for tasty soup and meat; ♦*Pizza Place* and patisserie, in front of the main post office, excellent pizza and wide choice of cakes and pastries, take away only, open 1100-1400 and 1600-2000; *Orange Curtains* another fast food take away round the corner from *Safir* and *Badwen* recognized by orange curtains, tuna sandwiches, hamburgers, yoghourt and milkshakes.

Best coffee in town served in *Hotel Kebir* and the *Circolo Italiana* in Italian Consulate.

● **Banks & money changers**
As money can be changed elsewhere to greater advantage a bank may not be necessary.

Generally open 0800-1400, in the central shopping zone, with one conveniently on the roundabout adjacent to Green Square and others on the S main roads leaving the square. Go early for shorter queues. **Al-Umma Bank**, Sharah Omar Mukhtar, T 33 34031; **Central Bank of Libya**, Sharah Gamal Nasser, T 33 33591; **Jamahiriya Bank**, Sharah Mohammed Magarief, T 33 33553; **Libyan National Arab Bank**, Sharah 1st September, T 20751-2; **National Commercial Bank**, Green Square, T 33 37191; **Sahara Bank**, Sharah 1st September, T 33 32771; **Wahhadah Bank**, T 33 34016.

● **Embassies**
Tripoli is the diplomatic capital. **UK** citizens, for whom there is no embassy, should address themselves to the Italian embassy/consulate for assistance where there is a British affairs desk T 33 31191. Nationals of the USA, Venezuela and other countries suffer from periodic interruptions in diplomatic relations. Travel agents will have information on the current and constantly changing situation.

Algeria, 12 Sharah Kairouan, T 44 40025; **Belgium**, 1 Sharah Abu Obeidat Ibn Al-Jerah, T 33 37797; **Chad**, 25 Sharah Mohammed Sadeqi, T 44 43955; **CIS**, Sharah Mostafa Kamel, T 33 30545/6; **Czechoslovakia**, Sharah Ahmad Lotfi Al-Said, T 33 34959; **France**, Sharah Ahmad Lotfi Al-Said, T 33 33526-7; **Germany**, Sharah Hassan Al-Masha'i, T 33 30554; **Greece**, 18 Sharah Jellal Beyar, Tx 20409; **India**, 16 Sharah Mahmud Sheltut, T 44 41835-6; **Iraq**, Sharah Gurgi, T 70856; **Italy**, Sharah Wahran, POB 219, T 33 30742; **Jordan**, Sharah Ibn Oof, T 33 32707; **Kuwait**, Sharah Amar Ibn Yasr, T 44 40281-2; **Lebanon**, Sharah Amar Ibn Yasr, T 33 33733; **Malta**, 13 Sharah Abu Bin Ka'ab, T 33 38081-4; **Mauritania**, Sharah Issa Wukuak, T 44 43646; **Morocco**, Sharah Bashir Al-Ibrahimi, T 44 41346; **Niger**, Sharah Tantawi Jowheri, T 44 43104; **Pakistan**, Sharah Khatabi, T 44

40072; **Saudi Arabia**, 2 Sharah Kairouan, T 33 30485-6; **Spain**, Sharah Al-Jaza'er, T 33 35462; **Syria**, 4 Sharah Mohammed Rashid Rida, T 33 371955; **Tunisia**, Sharah Bashir Al-Ibrahimi, T 33 31051-2; **Turkey**, 36 Sharah Gamal Abdel Nasser, T 46528/9; **UAE**, Sharah Aljaza'er, T 44 44146-8; **United Kingdom** c/o Italian Embassy, T 33 31191, when open Sharah Al-Fatah, T 33 31195.

● **Hospitals & medical services**
Chemists: in all shopping areas are normally marked with a red crescent or green cross sign. Chemists have a duty rota which is normally reliable, but travellers with special needs are advised to bring their own stores.

Hospitals: there are several large, well-equipped hospitals. The central civil unit is on the main road out to Sidi Mesri near the inner ring road. A secondary hospital is at Al-Khadra (the old military hospital).

● **Post & telecommunications**
Area code: 021.
Post office: this is found on Maidan Al-Jaza'er opposite the former cathedral and has telecommunications facilities.
Telephone: 5 digit numbers beginning with 3 place 33 in front, beginning with 4 place 44 in front.

● **Shopping**
Sharah 1st September and Sharah Mohammed Magarief have shops with clothes and other consumer goods, travel agents, and an abundance of cafés. Two more streets fan out from Green Square and the adjacent traffic island. Sharah Mizran and Sharah Amr Ibn Al-As carry small scale commercial activity, bakers, general goods shops, traders and others.

Joining these streets to Sharah 1st September and Al-Fatah area are cross links, the most important of which is Sharah Tahiti. Sharah Omar Mukhtar leads off Green Square directly to the SW. On the right is a red marble faced building, the Secretariat of Justice, with the rest of the street given over to trading houses, Arab restaurants, cafés and shops. On the right the street opens up on the site of the **Tripoli Fair ground** used for international exhibitions. Sharah Omar Mukhtar ultimately gives access to the main western suburbs such as **Gurgi** and the former European villa area of **Giorgim Poppoli** with its supermarkets, beach clubs and tourist centres. Sharah Ben Ashur has dry cleaning, a pharmacy, a bakery and grocery stores. Throughout the central business and inner residential districts there are excellent doctors' surgeries, chemist shops, food stores, general goods shops, bakeries and small cafés. There are some popular restaurants, though these are almost entirely confined to the streets off and adjacent to the streets fanning out of Green Square. The poorer residential suburbs have small scale facilities and often no doctors, though pharmacies are common. The larger suburbs with pre-existing commercial centres such as Gurgi have a full range of facilities.

Books: the main shop is *Fergiani's* nr the roundabout off Green Square on Sharah 1st September with a second shop in Sharah Al Jamaririyah nr Eliarmuk Square. Try also *Dar Al Hadara* close to *Fergiani's* at 90 Sharah 1st September, T 33 3975 for books in Arabic and English on scientific subjects. Books are otherwise available from official Libyan agencies which in the past acquired books exclusively by the state publishing organization. Most are in Arabic and/or are academic or somewhat propagandist.

● **Sports**

There is a state-sponsored football team and some local football played. Dates and times of games are advertised in the Arabic press. The main opening for sport for visitors to Tripoli is swimming, snorkelling and scuba-diving in the sea along the coastline. For medium to long stay travellers it is worth joining a beach club, most are on the Gurgi side of the city. Each club is marked with a large board which, though in Arabic, makes it quite clear that it is a sports centre. It is advised that enquiries are made personally at the gate, through a state agency or, most easily, through a travel agent.

● **Tour companies & travel agents**

These are in the shopping precincts in the main avenues leading from the Green Square. *Libyan Travel & Tourist Co* on Sharah 1st September headed by Salem Azzabi T 44 48005. Also *Libya Tours Co* in *Libya Palace Hotel*, T 33 31189, F 33 36688 where English and French are spoken. Ask for Mrs Hafida. *Libyan Arab Airlines* LAA main office opp Tripoli Fair ground, T 33 37500 open 0730-1630; best office is by *Hotel Kebir*.

● **Transport**

Local Bus: there are frequent, though in rush hour crowded, bus services across town on regular routes. The green/grey Tripoli service buses can be easily recognized with a destination board in Arabic but also a route number.

The service can be rather erratic and breakdowns are common but the system is cheap. Buses run through the main bus terminal and other stops are clearly marked. There are no printed time tables and it is best to ask at your hotel before proceeding. **Taxis**: are very expensive with a price of LD5 for the shortest trips but in the heat might be attractive to those with some distance to travel. Outlying parts of Tripoli can be reached by shared taxis at very reasonable rates. Otherwise, most travellers will be able to walk from point to point in the central area since the places to visit are concentrated around the city centre. Taxis leave from stands between Sharah Omar Mukhtar and the sea. They ply for hire on a shared basis but, with haggling over the price, can be hired by an individual or private group.

Air The main airport at Ben Ghashir/Suani Ben Yadim is some 24 km from the centre of Tripoli. A bus service is available to/from the main hotels and the bus station. Passengers with a deal of luggage are advised to face a charge of some LD25 for a private taxi rather than try the alternative. Uncertainties over transport to and from the airport are such that travellers should check well before the date of their flight with the airline, hotel or travel agent. Note must be taken of difficulties caused by the UN embargo on international flights to Libya. It is now only possible to enter Libya by land and sea until the embargo is lifted. Most access under the embargo is by ferry from Malta or overland through Tunisia. The Libyan Airlines central office is located on Sharah Haiti.

Internal flights to **Benghazi**, 3 daily flights at 1000, 1700 and 2200 with extra flights most days at 1300 or 1800. Takes 1 hr and costs LD28, LD56 rtn; to **Ghadames** alternate Tues at 1230, cost LD20; to **Sabha** Wed/Sat 1300, takes 1¼ hrs; to **Tobruk** flights on 5 days each week, takes 1¾ hrs, costs LD44.

Travellers are reminded that due to the shortage of spare parts caused by the embargo air journeys in Libya are not recommended.

Road Bus: the terminal is in the street adjacent to the international departure station approximately 1 km W from the medina. For international links (see page 572). Domestic timetables are very flexible. Departures from Tripoli leave early in the morning and passengers for small or distant Libyan settlements should be at the bus station not later than 0630 to be sure of a seat. Buses for the 12 hrs journey to **Benghazi** cost LD10 for the public service and LD15 for the private service leaving daily at 0830 using air conditioned coaches. Internal bus routes cover all towns and cities. Small 10 seater private buses do the journey from/to **Ghadames**, leaving when full in the late afternoon. Cost LD7, with several stops for refreshment and police checks. Try the agency round the corner from the government ticket office, T 622090 or T501088.

TRIPOLI DISTRICT

Tripoli outside the city traditionally comprises the greater province and in this Handbook, the area defined by the Jefara Plain. The present administrative district of Tripoli is made up of the whole of the old province of Tripolitania taking in the Jabal Nafusa, Sirt and parts as far S as Jufra, Mizdah and Ghadames. The Great Jefara Plain covers the coastal lowlands from the Tunisian frontier in the W at Zuwarah to Misratah in the E and is bounded to the S by the line of the Jabal Nafusa as far as Al-Khums and thereafter as the 'Small Jefara' to Misratah in the E by a low range of hills. The district is a fertile and generally well watered zone except for the central area from Al-Assa to the S of Ajailat which is very arid. Rainfall comes in the winter months and causes flash flooding in the many *wadis*. Most water courses are now well controlled but it is wise to stay out of *wadi* beds in winter. Individuals may be carried away and drowned in flash floods.

The cultivated zone along the coastal strip is a narrow belt of palm oases. Cultivation here is very dense with multiple cropping in the spring and summer seasons. In its most sophisticated form, intercropping gives olives immediately below the palm canopy and other taller fruit trees, themselves standing clear of lower varieties such as pomegranates and apricot. Below the trees are tall vegetables such as peppers or maize and a final undercrop of wheat, barley or a vegetable such as broad beans. Cropping of this kind was labour-intensive

but enabled a self-sufficient agriculture based on irrigation from shallow wells.

Animal herding is important on the Jefara Plain. Few black tents of the true nomads are now to be seen. Even the Sian nomads of the extreme W adjacent to Tunisia have become sedentary, but sheep and goats can be seen throughout Libya particularly in the Jefara where herds are exceptionally dense. The sheep are Barbary fat-tailed varieties for the most part, with an ability to survive heat and short periods of drought. The animals are very valuable, being much prized for eating by the Libyans, each sheep fetching US$300 or more, depending on the animal and the season. Most herds are looked after by a hired shepherd.

The Jefara Plain drops from the foot of the Jabal very evenly and gradually to reach the coast in an often rocky and shallow shelf though there are excellent beaches well away from Tripoli city. Zuwarah and the W coasts are open, sandy and generally deserted except on Fri when they are crowded with people from Tripoli. Inland from the Arab oases are the former Italian farms with their regularly laid out orchards spreading deep into the interior. The Jefara Plain narrows considerably E until the Jabal reaches the coast in a low ridge at Al-Khums, separating the main Jefara from the limited coastal plain between Al-Khums and Misratah. The roads on the Jefara are wide, black topped and generally in good condition.

TRIPOLI TO AL-KHUMS AND MISRATAH

The main coastal highway runs from Tripoli to the E via Al-Khums and Misratah. The road links all the major coastal towns and passes through one of the richest agricultural zones of the country. The highlight of the route is Leptis Magna, the most imposing Roman ruin in North Africa.

This trip takes at least 1 hr. There is a choice of routes in the environs of Tripoli of either the old coast road or the modern highway. Buses and taxis leave Tripoli on the coastal main highway. A dual carriageway leaves Tripoli city via Bab Ben Ghashir and travels through dense developments of villas and small houses, mainly expensive properties built on former oasis gardens. Architecturally the housing is very mixed – old square, single storey, whitewashed farmsteads interspersed with very modern villas of a slightly inferior finish. Occasional whitewashed small domed shrines, the tombs of *marabouts* or Islamic holy men, are visible, their titles being used for regional or topographical place names. **Accommodation E** *Madinah Siahiah Tajurah (Tajurah tourist village)* is located approximately 32 km E of Tripoli. Its surrounding beach is popular with Libyans on Fri but is otherwise clear for other tourists. Km 32 is its local name. The tourist village is an old development and open to all-comers.

Gasr Garabouli Km 60 from Tripoli lies on the old coast road and is now by-passed. Take the spur into town for petrol, police, shops and other services. There are small and mixed developments of shops, cafés and market places. The town area remains lightly wooded with some ex-Italian farms to be seen among dense, recent Libyan housing.

East from Gasr Garabouli there is open country with orchards and olives and almond plantations. At Gasr Khiar there are roadside shops on the main highway, cafés and petrol. Al-Khums is way-marked at Km 41. Along the main road other than in the smaller settlements there are plenty of roadside cafés. Small shacks of modern origin cater for

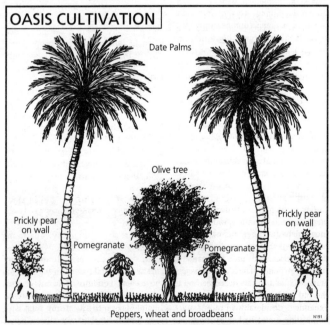

OASIS CULTIVATION

Date Palms

Olive tree

Prickly pear on wall

Prickly pear on wall

Pomegranate

Pomegranate

Peppers, wheat and broadbeans

N191

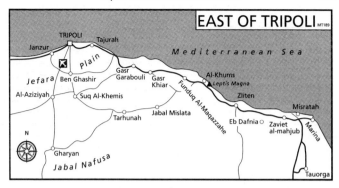

travellers, especially on Fri and public holidays.

Telathin (literally Km 30 mark) is a tiny settlement providing chiefly a mosque, but with a shop and café adjacent. There is a fine area for swimming at the coast just N of the road. This is a highly recommended road in springtime when almond trees are flowering. In season succulent oranges are on sale at the roadside. A good black top road runs to it then goes on to a rocky seashore 2 km below. Al-Khums then lies approximately 20 km to the E over the forested ridge. **Accommodation D** *Funduq & Mat'am Al-Naqazzah*, clean, 15 beds, restaurant and café, cooler in summer than the surrounding plains, hotel and restaurant of good contemporary design but now run down, situated in an area of conifer trees just to the N of the main road.

Al-Khums

Al-Khums from the outside is not a very pretty sight. It contains low quality and incomplete dwellings in an apparently poor state of repair. The area has a very drab exterior with much accumulated rubbish around. The Al-Khums Fri market is held in the street leading to the old harbour. The main town has expanded considerably in recent years. Some Italian and British military and civilian landmarks are still to be found, with the army barracks as they were. The old market place next to the barracks is now the town taxi stand with transport available on a trip or day basis in private or shared taxi. There is an Arabic language cinema on the left of the street opposite the taxi ranks. Old Turkish houses have been demolished and replaced by a ghastly town council building just below the cinema.

ACCESS Care is needed when driving at all times and especially on the outskirts of Al-Khums where slow moving vehicular and pedestrian traffic makes the main highway dangerous. Buses stop in the town centre near the taxi rank and on the main road at the *Al-Khums Hotel*.

● **Accommodation** At the junction of the main coastal highway and the first black top road after the *Naqazzah Hotel*, turn off to the **E** *Khums Hotel*, cheap but noisy from close-passing traffic; the town's original hotel is still open for business as **E** *Funduq Al-Khums Siahiah*, it is fairly run down but offers 18 rm, public telephone on site, restaurant and dingy café open 0600-2400. **Youth hostel** *Sports City*, 3 km SW of centre, T (23) 20888, 160 beds, meals, kitchen, laundry, family rooms.

There is a vast extension to the town from the army barracks E along the coast towards Wadi Lebda and between the coast and the by-pass built up solidly with mainly poor quality housing areas with few services for the traveller. Chalets

THE DELU WELL –
TRADITIONAL WELL OF LIBYA AND NORTH AFRICA

Water was always essential to life in North Africa. Given the scarcity of surface water, it was necessary for survival to lift water from underground. In traditional Libya – more or less until the 1960s – water was lifted from a shallow water table along the coast or from depressions in the desert by means of a device called a *delu*. The name is taken from the word for a goatskin, which is made into a bag, dipped into a well and drawn up full of water for both household and irrigation purposes.

The mechanism is simple and effective. A shallow one or 2m diameter well is hand dug to about 2 or 3m below the water table and lined with stone work or cement. Above ground an often ornate gantry is made of two upright stone or wooden pillars rising from the side of the wellhead. A cross beam between the top of the two pillars acts as an axle to a small pulley wheel which carries a rope tied to the mouth of the goatskin bag. The rope is drawn up or let down by the ingenious use of a ramp to ease the task of lifting water to the surface. An animal travels down the ramp when pulling up the goatskin from the bottom of the well and moves up the ramp to return the bag into the bottom of the well. Most *delu* wells have a secondary rope attached to the bottom of the goatskin bag which can be used when the full bag is at the top of the gantry to upend it and tip out the water.

The rate of water lifting by the *delu* method is obviously limited. The capacity of the bag is about 20 litres. Working from dawn to dusk, however, enough water could be raised to irrigate up to 3 or 4 ha of land – enough to feed a family and leave a small surplus for sale in the market. Most wells were equipped with a storage basin adjacent to the wellhead so that water could be raised and stored for household use and to give a reserve of water for irrigation.

The creak of the wooden pulley wheel of the *delu* was one of the characteristic sounds of the North African oases until the 1960s. After that time diesel and electric power pumps became available and the *delu* system fell into disuse. A few *delu* gantries remain as museum pieces and only the observant traveller in the deepest S of the Saharan oases will come across this splendid and environmentally friendly technology in day-to-day operation.

have been built along the sea shore towards Leptis Magna. The modern port is located on the W of the town. There is some industry including a cement plant. Shared taxi from Tripoli costs LD5 to Al-Khums and LD1 to the site, takes about 1½ hr.

Leptis Magna

Open daily 0800-1730, 250 mills adult, 100 mills child. Shared taxi from Tripoli costs LD5 to Al-Khums and LD1 to the site. With museum, café and telephone this is a busy site. There are warnings

that the ruins must not be touched nor artefacts taken away. These must be taken very seriously since successful prosecution can lead to imprisonment. The few sellers of items to be found on the site are operating illegally and should not be approached. There are guides available for a fee (LD5 seems to be a minimum) who speak the main European languages. Although Leptis Magna, designated by UNESCO as a World Heritage site, is an important archaeological site it is not complex since the best elements date from a fairly

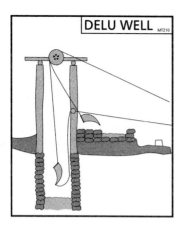

DELU WELL MT210

specific period. The information in this guide should enable most travellers to get a good overall view of the site. For specialists, an extended guided tour of the sites and the museum at Leptis Magna is recommended (see page 520). Guidebooks, maps and postcards of this site and others in Libya are available here.

ACCESS Travelling E from Al-Khums and Leptis Magna take the old road through the palm oases. The road is a single black top carriageway, often built up above the adjacent gardens. Beware of local traffic emerging abruptly from side roads and of the road surface in wet weather when the black top becomes notoriously slippery and vehicles can slide off into the palmeries. For cyclists the steep road embankment through this narrow route also has its hazards since two cars can pass only with difficulty. The old single track road has constant small scale road works. Children walk on the road and there is much local traffic from side roads. Motorists and others wishing to avoid the oasis route can take the new road which passes 1 km further inland between the palmeries and the main area of the former Italian La Valdagno agricultural estate to Wadi Ki'am. Buildings come right up to the new road.

For those with time the oasis route is to be preferred. After Leptis, the oasis, here called the Sahel Al-Ahmad, has dense mainly modern farmhouses. Farming continues in *suani* (small walled irrigated traditional gardens) but little effort is put into farming at present. The principal spring field crops in the gardens are wheat, barley and broad beans. The crops are mainly thin but the palm canopy remains for most part in good trim, providing welcome shade.

At **Wadi Ki'am**, Tripolitania's only flowing river, the long-established agricultural estate spreads out on both sides of the road. The original farm was a mere 120 ha of 2 ha plots fed by irrigation from the impounded stream of a spring source in the Wadi Ki'am. There is now an extension of reclaimed land under orchards and trees from Wadi Ki'am W to join up with old Sahel Al-Ahmad oasis and ex-La Valdagno.

Zliten

Zliten (37 km E of Al-Khums) is a thriving administrative and academic centre. Turn left into town for all main services. Zliten is surrounded by *marabout* tombs famous for their qualities of improving fertility, so inspiring pilgrimages. These tombs are best visited with a local inhabitant. Visit the *zawia* shrine of Sidi Abdesselam and the cemetery of his descendants. There is one hotel, *Des Gazelles*. **Accommodation Youth hostel** *Kashr House*, Zliten, 20 beds, breakfast, shop, kitchen.

Misratah

The highway E from Zliten passes through poor grade lands with a slightly less reliable rainfall than areas further W. The coastal strip was thinly populated in the past and had only small and very discontinuous Arab oases. The Italians seized much of the coastal strip to set up estates for Italian farmers. The largest was Ed-Dafnia where the orchard groves of olives and almonds cover what was originally a mainly thin pastureland. The Italian effort at land settlement was added to by the Libyan Government after Independence with new areas reclaimed and ex-Italian estates taken over by Libyan farmers. Close to Misratah in the Zaviet Al-Mahjub district, a former private estate developed by the pre-Fascist Governor of Tripolitania, General Volpi, can be seen forming a fine garden and farmed area. However, the Italian farming estates which were so much the characteristic of Misratah oases have been reduced in importance by occupation by townsfolk who treat their holdings as amenity areas rather than as working farms.

The expansion of **Misratah** as an urban centre has also been prodigious. Population growth within the town has been much increased by mass migration from the rural areas. Misratah is the administrative and educational capital of E Tripolitania with most ministries having local offices. Schools, hospitals and colleges are located in the new town. Its layout is well organized and mainly rectangular. There seems to be less riotous self-build construction in progress than elsewhere.

Two events have strengthened the city. First, the construction of the two iron and steel mills in the settlement which have created employment and demand for local services so that there is a real sense in Misratah of growth and development. The power of the steel mill authorities is considerable and has helped to give a sense of unity to the town. Second, the old marina has been extensively redeveloped to take shipping coming to service the industrial plant with raw materials and other goods. The central business district provides a multitude of traditional shops, cafés and restaurants. A large number of immigrant managers and labourers live in the town and this is reflected in a fairly cosmopolitan atmosphere in the cafés. Many foreigners are housed on the steel mill residential site.

Places of interest The most interesting items are the sand dunes on the W side of the town, some of the tallest sea dunes in the world. There is also the steel mill and the port.

● **Accommodation** *Hotel Misratah* is large, modern and generally as well run as the larger hotels in Tripoli; booking is advised, rates as for those in the capital, large restaurant and other facilities. **Youth hostel** 4 km W of centre, T 24855, open 0700-2300, 120 beds, family rooms, meals, kitchen, laundry, bus 400m, reservations rec May-Sep.

● **Places to eat** You can eat in Arab cafés in the central business district. For a western type menu use *Hotel Misratah*.

Tauorga, some 40 km S of Misratah, is situated in the middle of a swamp formed by the great Tauorga salt lake and was reputed to be a refuge for escaping slaves. The town is located on a set of springs which provides water for agriculture, including a modern farm settlement set up by the government. Travellers would be better basing themselves in Al-Khums so that they can more easily get access to Leptis Magna and the beautiful mountain countryside of the Jabal Mislata to its hinterland.

TRIPOLI TO FARWA AND THE TUNISIAN FRONTIER

W from Tripoli is the coastal road to Tunisia. Although heavily built-up with modern housing for many km on the fringes of Tripoli city, it eventually becomes open olive-growing country with many interesting tourist sites and the magnificent Roman ruins of Sabrata.

Leave Tripoli through Sharah Omar Mukhtar and Gurgi taking the main coastal highway W. The new highway is fast except during the rush hours and

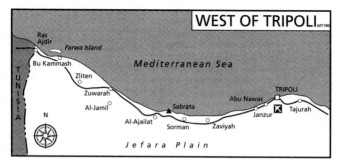

can be dangerous at major junctions. The dual carriageway road runs through palmeries and orchards as far as Zaviyah, thereafter its single track is more dangerous in an area subject to fog in spring. Undisciplined coastal traffic moves along this route to and from Tunisia. The main highway bypasses most of the coastal sites, however, and is recommended for car, caravan and motorcycle travellers. It ends at Zuwarah and the Farwa crossing point into Tunisia. Given a considerable flow of commercial traffic between the two countries now that there are only the barest of formalities for Arabs belonging to members of the United Maghreb Association, there can be long queues of cars and trucks at the frontier.

ACCESS Buses from Zaviyah and Zuwarah can be picked up or a shared taxi hired inside Libyan territory for those coming in from Tunisia. From Zuwarah both express luxury buses and ordinary interurban service buses can be caught to finish the journey to Tripoli. The border post has few facilities other than a petrol station and a small café on the Libyan side. **Youth hostel** *Zaviyah*, 40 km W of Tripoli, T 24019, 80 beds, breakfast incl, other meals available, family rooms.

Sabrata

This is a 2-part town, one a modern residential centre and the other the archaeological site. There is a café and other services, including shops and cold drinks available at many main roadside shops. Sabrata town is rapidly expanding and some new industry has been set up. Many large villas extend down from the old coastal road towards the ruins. A new Faculty of Arts of Zaviyah University has been set up here. Shared taxi to Sabrata LD2. Taxi from town to ruins LD1.

Places of interest
The Sabrata ruins (see page 522) are open all week. Entry for adults is 250 mills and children 100 mills. The main **Sabrata Museum** and new **Punic Museum** are open Wed-Mon 0800-1700. A café and shop are located outside the complex. The site is clean and well run.

Beach
At Telil there is a good sandy area with shallow water. It is popular with Libyan families. The beach is served by black top dual carriageway from the main road from junction W of Sabrata city.

Local information
● **Youth hostel**
160 beds, kitchen, meals, family rooms, laundry, open 0700-2400, 1 km NW of town, T (24) 2821, booking rec May-Aug.

● **Camp sites**
Camping is banned in the woodlands around the archaeological site.

● **Places to eat**
There is a major restaurant at the ruins at the side of the large car park immediately outside the archaeological compound, which is open 0800-2200 winter and summer. The restau-

rant caters for Libyan and foreign visitors including large groups. The area offers a café and billiards.

● **Useful addresses**
Petrol: there is a petrol station in the town and another at the road junction at Ajailat.

Zuwarah

This is an expanding town on the extreme W of the Tripolitanian coastal belt, approximately 100 km from Tripoli and 60 km from the border with Tunisia. The main employer is the petrochemical complex at Bu Kammash. Most commercial and municipal activity is concentrated in the centre of the town on the old road 1 km to the N of the new dual carriageway coastal highway. The town extends to the seashore. New villas mostly take up the coastal block.

Local information
● **Accommodation**
E *Zuwarah Esterah Siahiah* (*Zuwarah Tourist Resthouse*) in the middle of the town adjacent to the square, a cheap, small hotel used by Libyans.

● **Camp sites**
No camping facilities are reported, though along the coast there are plenty of good camping sites in woodlands or on the coast. Ask permission if possible before setting up camp.

● **Places to eat**
Zuwarah Esterah Siahiah (*Zuwarah Tourist Resthouse*) is the best restaurant and café and is in the middle of the town adjacent to the square.

● **Hospitals & medical services**
First aid: the Red Crescent clinic is on the old road.

● **Post & telecommunications**
Post Office: this is near the clinic on the old road.

● **Useful addresses**
Petrol: there are two petrol stations to the E and W of town on the main highway.

● **Transport**
Road The shared taxi/bus services to E and W along the coast road are very frequent. Costs LD7 Zuwarah to Tunis. LD10 Tripoli to Tunis. Express buses with a/c on Tripoli to Tunis run can be stopped in Zuwarah.

Janzur is on the old road as is the **D** *Janzur Tourist Village*, right on the coast, mainly new, with a wide range of accommodation – bungalows and apartments, excellent facilities, sailing, tennis, cinema, well equipped children's play room, shops, clinic, signposted in Arabic as *Medina Siahiah Janzur*; **D** *Abu Nawas Village*, another beach village in the Giorgim Poppoli area, old but cheap and open to all-comers at LD7 per night, close to shops, chemists and restaurants sited on the main street of N Gurgi; **E** *Old Janzur Tourist Village*, is further in towards the Tripoli boundary, comparatively run down, but convenient for shopping and facilities of what was Giorgim Poppoli estate.

Booking at these tourist villages is not easy from a distance since they are run by state organizations and are not essentially commercial in design. Persistence in seeing the on-site manager might be the best way to get accommodation. Their big disadvantage is their isolation from the city when bus or shared taxi transport is available on the old coast road 500m S of the beach club sites. Charges per night vary with the season and the quality of the complex between LD5 and LD20.

The old coast road into Tripoli is very crowded with shopping traffic and local people and should be avoided in the rush hours. Tripoli centre is only 5 km away but it can take 30 mins or more to complete the journey across the Wadi Mejennin bridge and then via Sharah Omar Mukhtar.

Farwa Island

The island of Farwa lies just offshore adjacent to the coast at the border post. Access to the departure point for Farwa Island is by road, though there is an airstrip nearby that could be used if upgraded. The island is approached either by a rough causeway built at the time of the construction of the nearby Bu Kammash petrochemical/refinery complex, or by ferry from a pier at Bu Kammash village to the W of the plant. The ferry, run by local fishermen, is an occasional rather than a regular service. There are sea police and customs officials at both the pier and the causeway to control movement and those at the pier can be helpful in retaining a boatman.

Places of interest

The island, 12 km long and 2 km at its widest, is basically flat with dunes giving a slight elevation. Some 4,000 palm trees exist and have been tidied up in the central section of the island to look attractive. There is to be a tourist complex built on the island. The sand is fine grained and silver coloured. Other than the view of the petrochemical plant, the site is absolutely first class.

Travelling back to Tripoli, take the old road and travel into the main settlements along the coast. The road is slower than the main highway and often crowded, especially in the Tripoli suburb of Gurgi.

TRIPOLI TO THE JABAL NAFUSA AT GHARYAN

Directly S of Tripoli is the Gefara Plain, itself abutting the hills of the Jabal Nafusa. The Tripoli-Gharyan route gives an ideal cross-section of lands and climates through the Plain and the Jabal foothills.

Take the road S to Gharyan which now leads not only to the Jabal Nafusa but also from there to the deep SW at Ghadames and Ghat. The road is heavily built up in the long tentacles of the Tripoli suburbs. There are then dense farmstead settlements out to the Suani Ben Yadim turn off. The road is dual carriageway and busy with traffic, mostly local. After the Suani Ben Yadim and Ben Ghashir towns/oases, the highway runs through a countryside of trees

and orchards. It is very green in spring, with uncultivated places forming rich pasture. The 2-lane highway is very fast from Suani Ben Yadim to Az-Zahra and onward to the main town of Al-Aziziyah.

Aziziyah has a petrol station, post office, hospital and several banks all situated on the main street or immediately adjacent in the few principal side roads. It is 221 km from Aziziyah to Nalut on the W end of Jabal Nafusa via the Wadi Hayyah route on the plain, via a single carriageway which is straight and fast.

Aziziyah to Gharyan

There are roadside stalls selling oranges in season. The wooded landscape thins rapidly with travel S. The road remains dual carriageway. The first sightings of the Jabal peaks can be had as the road approaches the scarp slope of the Jabal Nafusa. A few km S of Al-Aziziyah the landscape becomes open with very few trees. This is prime cereal-growing country in years of good rainfall. There is a large grain silo at Km 29 to Gharyan indicating this zone as a major contributor to Libyan wheat and barley production. At Km 25, the road begins the rise towards the Jabal. It is a slow climb through wooded terrain. There is a quarry for tile making materials on the right as the main road climbs into the scarp face, then at Km 18 the sharp rise into the scarp face begins. There is a café at its foot on the left hand side of the road. On climbing the scarp the old Italian road to the left can be seen. Though it is no longer maintained it is a good alternative route for walkers and the more adventurous cyclists. At the top of the slope the roadside is built up increasingly with houses. There are olive trees mainly around the Guassem area of Gharyan, 11 km from the town itself. Approximately an hour from Tripoli centre you arrive at Gharyan. (For travel in the Jabal (see page 523) – Jabal Nafusa and Ghadames.)

SITES TO VISIT IN THE JEFARA PLAIN

Leptis Magna

Leptis Magna is among the most complete and magnificent of the three towns (tripolis) of North Africa. It began as a Phoenician port of call on the trading route across the region, though it was ultimately administered in the 6th century BC, it is thought, from Carthage. The city grew up at the mouth of the Wadi Lebda where a small port was developed over the years, exporting important volumes of grain and olives. It joined Rome in 111 BC and enjoyed full rights as a *colonia* to Roman citizenship under the Emperor Trajan (98-117 AD).

The early Roman period saw the construction of basic harbour works and a forum close by the original Punic settlement. The city flourished under the rule and patronage of Septimus Severus (193-211 AD) who was born in Leptis Magna. Most of the major buildings at Leptis date from his time. The city spread W along the coast and inland. All the important buildings can be reached adjacent to or just off the main paved monumental road from the present entrance through the new parts of the site. A full inspection of the wealth of monuments requires at least a full day and rather longer for visitors with a specialist interest since Leptis Magna is well preserved and has an unequalled range of buildings from the classical period. In summer the site is very hot and justice can be done only by a series of visits when the heat is less oppressive.

A minimum tour begins at the **harbour** at the original Punic site and the adjacent ruins of the **Old Forum**. The newer harbour works undertaken during the reign as Emperor of Septimus Severus are also on view in this same area. The **triumphal arch** together with the new quarter along the 410m monumental road also date from this period.

In the new quarter the key sites are the Colonnaded Street, the semi circular **Nymphaeum**, the **Forum** and **Basilica**. Other areas to be seen include the magnificent **Amphitheatre** dating from 56 AD, among the most photogenic sites in North Africa, and the **baths** constructed during the time of the Emperor Hadrian.

Leptis Magna – an extended tour

Leptis Magna is a Roman city of great grandeur situated at the mouth of the Wadi Lebda immediately to the E of the town of Al-Khums. The origins of the town are not known with certainty. It is probable that a Berber settlement first existed at the site which was developed by Levantine trading groups from Tyre and Sidon that made use of the small natural harbour. Greeks also appear to have been at the site. In Carthaginian times the people at Lebda paid tribute of one talent per day, reflecting a certain prosperity based on a trading hinterland stretching deep into Tripolitania and Surt. By the time of the 3rd Punic War there were approximately 10,000-15,000 inhabitants in the city. In 107 AD Leptis set up formal relations with Rome and, despite the disruption caused by attacks from tribes from the desert interior, the city continued to develop.

The fortunes of Leptis Magna were greatly improved in 193 AD when Septimus Severus was made Emperor of Rome. He had been born at Leptis on Apr 11, 146 AD. He created a basilica at Leptis together with a great imperial forum. The prosperity of the city was considerable and the population grew to 60,000-80,000 people. Leptis suffered later from a decline in the Saharan trade and the silting of the mouth of the river. Attacks from Asturian groups beginning in 363 AD brought great problems for the city. In 455 AD the Vandals arrived and took Leptis, leaving it eventually in the hands of the Berber Zenata tribe until 533 when the Byzantines un-

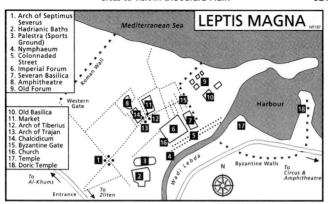

1. Arch of Septimus Severus
2. Hadrianic Baths
3. Palestra (Sports Ground)
4. Nymphaeum
5. Colonnaded Street
6. Imperial Forum
7. Severan Basilica
8. Amphitheatre
9. Old Forum
10. Old Basilica
11. Market
12. Arch of Tiberius
13. Arch of Trajan
14. Chalcidicum
15. Byzantine Gate
16. Church
17. Temple
18. Doric Temple

der Belasarius restored Roman rule. The Byzantines were put under heavy pressure from all sides and in Libya from attacks by the Zenata and finally the Arab invasions of 643-644 AD. The later incursions of the Beni Hillal and Beni Sulaim led to the completed abandonment of Leptis Magna in the 11th century. Coastal sand dunes overwhelmed the site, preserving it from destruction during the succeeding centuries hence the site is below the present ground level with access via a steep flight of steps.

The first of the antiquities at the site is the **Arch of Septimus Severus** (1) which lies on the left at the end of a short avenue leading from the entrance. It has four facias. To the E of the arch is the **Hadrianic Baths** (2) (terme), an enormous construction covering with its ancilliary buildings approximately 3 ha and amongst the largest bath houses built outside Rome itself. The baths were put in place in 123-127 AD and improved and extended at various later dates. Excavations at the baths were begun in 1920 by Dr P Romanelli. The baths are best approached through the **Palaestra** (3), which is made up of a rectangular base with circular ends surrounded by a portico of 72 columns. There are five doorways into the baths, two on the N aspect leading from the

Palestra. To the S two more doorways open onto a Corridor of 74.8m parallel to the fascia. Behind lies the Frigidarium a room of 30.35 x 15.40m. In the centre of the Frigidarium is a small monument dedicated to Septimus Severus, possibly commemorating the grant of full Roman rights to the city by that emperor. At the E and W sides of the Frigidarium are two highly decorated pools still showing their facings of black granite. Immediately S of the Frigidarium are two anterooms and connecting corridors together with a Tepidarium and its lateral pools. Further S lies the Calidarium in a room 22.15m x 19.90m. This room leads on by two doors to heated rooms, the Stufe or Sudatorium. Along the E and W sides of this blocks of rooms are parallel salons which give access to the main baths.

The Severan **Nymphaeum** (4), high walls semicircular in shape and containing a fountain basin stands at the S end of the **Colonnaded Street** (5) which connects the Hadrianic Baths with the harbour. The street lies between the **Imperial Forum** (6) and the **Severan Basilica** (7) and the harbour. It has a broad, central section on either side of which stood covered porticoes. The supporting columns which carried arches stood on square raised pedestals. The

Imperial Forum lies at the heart of Severan Leptis Magna. The Forum was constructed as a great wall of 92m backing on to the Basilica, with an inset arc. There is an entrance from the street on the SW side. It is a spectacular sight despite the ravages of time and looters. It abuts onto the Basilica in the N and forms a great trapezoidal shape with maximum dimensions of 132m x 87m.

The **Old Basilica** (10) is 38m x 92m and built as a rectangle on the E side of the **Old Forum** (9). It has two semicircular recesses at its narrow ends. There are three lines of columns running the length of the church. The Basilica is surrounded by side galleries. Various dedications in Latin are found in the Basilica including an ornate inscription to Emperor Caesar Lucius Septimus. There is a great variety of sculptures and reliefs of mythical figures and animals.

The **amphitheatre** (8) at Leptis Magna is in excellent condition and commands views in all directions from the W side of the city. The theatre has a diameter of 70m and faces to the NE, heavily columned and with the stage and its entrances still clearly visible.

There is another set of baths at the site located close to the sea in the waterfront area of the city to the W of the Old Forum. These baths were never finished and are thought to have been under construction at the time of the Vandal invasions. The new baths are best approached from the E through a hexagonal domed hall, named by the British archaeologist Richard Goodchild the New Calidarium. Adjacent and to the N of the New Calidarium is a building of similar size which was used as an Apodyterium for an earlier bath system but later became disused. West again of these buildings is the New Frigidarium, which was constructed to be a vaulted hall with a plunge bath at each corner but which was not completed.

The **harbour** at Leptis is in the form of a basin open to the E and fed with water from the Wadi Lebda. There is a small **Doric temple** (18) at the site in Hellenistic style and a tower. The harbour has been studied by underwater archaeologists and some of the finds are shown in the main museum near the main site entrance. There are clear signs of severe silting, yet the historical record shows that Leptis port handled many thousands of tonnes of olive oil and food grain every year over many centuries as the centre of Rome's North African granary.

The **Circus** is on the extreme E side of the site, shaped as a great narrow horse shoe of 450m in length and 100m wide aligned parallel to the coastline. It is as yet not fully excavated but the starting gates are clearly to be seen at the city end, while the monumental arch and the circular terminus is at the E end. There are two tunnels at ground level carved apparently through solid rock. There are tiers of seats rising from the base around the arena. The **amphitheatre**, which lies immediately S of the Circus in the same complex, is thought to date from 56 AD and has been well excavated by Italian archaeologists. It is slightly elliptical in shape with circumferences of 100m x 80m.

Shortly after the time of Septimus Severus, the Roman Empire had increasing difficulties in maintaining law and order in its domains in North Africa. In 263 AD Leptis was overrun by the Asturians and, despite some attempts at reconstruction under Byzantium rule, it never again flourished. The Arab invaders of the 7th century brought a final extinction of urban life to the site. Most of the excavations at Leptis were undertaken in the Italian period when the monuments, preserved from damage by encroaching sands, were unearthed.

Sabrata ruins

Like Leptis Magna, Sabrata began as a settlement to service the coastal trade of

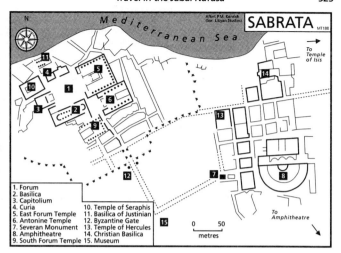

After: P.M. Kenrick
(Soc. Libyan Studies)

SABRATA MT188

N

M e d i t e r r a n e a n   S e a

To Temple of Isis

1. Forum
2. Basilica
3. Capitolium
4. Curia
5. East Forum Temple
6. Antonine Temple
7. Severan Monument
8. Amphitheatre
9. South Forum Temple
10. Temple of Seraphis
11. Basilica of Justinian
12. Byzantine Gate
13. Temple of Hercules
14. Christian Basilica
15. Museum

To Amphitheatre

0   50
metres

the Carthaginians. It was developed as a permanent site in the 4th century BC to act as a terminal for the trans-Saharan trade since it had a natural harbour on an otherwise long and unindented coastline. The site was later to become part of the three cities with Leptis and Oea (Tripoli). It was never favoured as much as Leptis Magna and has nothing to match its range and richness of buildings. Its coastal site is nonetheless impressive and Italian excavations and some reconstruction have made it well worth a visit. Access is from the main road in the new town towards the sea down a splendid avenue of old cypress trees. From Tripoli takes 50 mins in a black/white taxi, costs LD40.

The entrance is by the **museum** (15). Walk NW along the main thoroughfare, through the **Byzantine Gate** (12) in the walls down into the site. On the left is the **South Forum Temple** (9), 2nd century AD before the piazza is reached. This wider area has the **Antonine Temple** (5) up five steps on the right and the **Basilica** (2) on the left. The remains of the Basilica show that it has been much changed since the original building of

the 1st century AD. The main monument is the **Amphitheatre** (8), used today as a theatre and concert hall. There is a variety of public baths, temples and fountains, with many first class **mosaics** both on site and in the adjacent **museum**. Some Byzantine remains are on show to exemplify the revival after the Vandal invasions. The site was finally abandoned in the mid-7th century at the time of the Arab invasions. There appear to be no guides available but there are publications and artifacts on show at the museum. Entrance LD0.25, open from 0900-sunset daily, museums closed Tues. It is best to avoid visiting on Fri, other days are less crowded.

TRAVEL IN THE JABAL NAFUSA

The Jabal Nafusa, geologically complex, is a long plateau which runs in broken foothills from Al-Khums on the coast in the E to the start of the Jabal proper at Al-Qusbat, some 20 km to the SW of Al-Khums and then further W into S Tunisia. It forms a scarp slope between 600m and 900m above the Jefara Plain.

It drops in altitude only gradually to the S into a set of rough basins, the largest of which lies around the town of Mizdah reputed to be the home of sorcerers, weavers of spells and holy men. The Hammadah Al-Hamra, a vast level-topped plateau, is reached after climbing another scarp to the S of Mizdah.

The Jabal has a climate quite different from the Jefara. Rains are slightly less reliable than the northern plains and diminish rapidly from the crest of the scarp to the S. Most places have over 250 mm of rain per year. Winters are quite cold and snow and frost can be experienced. Air temperatures throughout the year are lower than on the Jefara. Both winter dress and sleeping bags need to be heavier and windproof. The evenings and nights in the summer are far more comfortable than in the plains. **Gharyan** is the main town of the Jabal Nafusa.

The Jabal economy has proved remarkably versatile. Agriculture survives in most areas though it has become increasingly concentrated on growing cereals and rainfed orchard crops. Figs and apricots are famous on the Jabal and it is often the Berber groups who farm the rich grain land of the Jefara under the shadow of their mountain homes. The greatest source of funds for the Jabal groups is, however, remittance income from members of the family living elsewhere, usually in Tripoli or in other coastal towns. Even permanent residents of Tripoli have houses in their tribal territories and a great deal of investment flows back to the Jabal villages in this way.

Berber history and culture

The culture of the Jabal Nafusa is for the most part Berber, though Arab tribes are interspersed within the main groups. Historically, the Berbers held the lands of the Jefara Plain with their main centre at Sabrata but they were driven back into the hills by the Arab invaders. The relative isolation of the Berber communities has meant not only a survival of their language and close kinship ties but also quite distinct urban forms and housing styles. In religion the Berbers are Muslim but follow the Ibadite branch of Islam, regarded by many Sunni Muslims as a heresy. The Berbers were aggressively separate from the Arabs on the Jabal Nafusa however much they intermarried with the Arab tribes elsewhere in Libya. The Berbers of the Jabal Nafusa participated in the revolts against Arab rule, the most ferocious of which took place in 896 AD.

More recently, the Berbers looked for the creation of a semi-autonomous Berber province. They had been a favoured group under the Italian occupation, making up important parts of the police forces in Tripolitania. On Independence it was hoped that Berber cultural separateness would be acknowledged and their language given equal status with Arabic. The rise of Arab nationalism at this time forestalled any chance that the small numbers of Berbers, less than an estimated 150,000 in all at that time, could make their voice heard. The revolution of 1969 set back Berber aspirations and for some time the government in Tripoli refused to admit there was any such group as the Berbers.

Despite the rapid economic changes that have taken place in Libya as a result of the spending of oil wealth, the Berbers still keep a sense of cultural separateness and even superiority.

Berber architecture

A distinctive feature of the Jabal Nafusa is troglodyte architecture. Buildings are excavated into the earth and rock to give only a slight external built up area. Both houses and mosques were constructed in this fashion which made them warm in the often bitter winters experienced on the Jabal and cool in the heat of summer. At Mizdah the troglodyte way of life was pursued until the 1970s so that families could escape the extremes of heat experienced in ordinary houses.

There is a doubt about the origins of some of the great ruined **castles** on the Jabal such as those at **Sharwas** and **Wighu**. They were the centres of the original Berber societies which were set up after the Berbers were driven into the hills by the Arabs and became the focus of revolt against the invaders during the bitter struggles of the 9th century. There is evidence that internecine strife between powerful Berber clans at Sharwas and Wighu in the 11th century resulted in extensive damage to their fortresses. The castles were eventually abandoned, Sharwas as late as the 16th century, but stand as bleak but recognizable ruins on the peaks of the Jabal E of Yafran.

The castles are quite different from the fortified granaries seen, for example at Nalut, Kabao and elsewhere in which small cells were created in the rock or built up one on top of another to accommodate stored grain and other items. These now mainly ruined buildings were surrounded by walls for reasons of defence. A third phase of abandoned dwellings can now be seen comprising the houses and quarters occupied until very recently in towns such as Jadu. The houses were built of loosely assembled stone with limited mortaring between joints and were clustered in tribal quarters and extended family dwellings incorporating areas for living, cooking and keeping the animals in safety at night. Prosperity in recent years has led many residents of the towns of the Jabal to move into private housing of the villa style situated in the open fields around the old settlements. The old quarters have been abandoned in many cases and are crumbling into ruin. This situation is causing rapid deterioration in towns such as Jadu.

JABAL NAFUSA – GHARYAN TO NALUT

The Jabal Nafusa road is narrow and slow but offers the prospect of visits to a variety of Berber centres. There are apricot and fig orchards as well as traditional terraced farmland to be seen as the highway carries the traveller W and S along the top of the scarp slope.

Gharyan

(*Pop* 100,000; *Alt* 900m) The centre of Gharyan shows signs of intensive rebuilding, reflecting the site's importance as a regional administrative centre. On climbing the scarp and traversing the olive groves where the road comes on to the summit of the Jabal, turn off right for Gharyan town, marked clearly but in Arabic script. Ask for '*al-markaz al-medinah*', the centre of the town. Note that the climate of Jabal is much cooler than the plain and even in spring can be several degrees colder on the ridge than on the Jefara. Petrol available here.

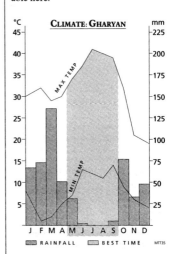

CLIMATE: GHARYAN

DOWNSTAIRS ONLY – THE TROGLODYTE TENDENCY

Underground living, has certain advantages. The soft rock permits easy construction of the intitial dwelling and allows extensions when necessary. The ground insulates the dwelling keeping it a constant 17°C, cool in summer and cosy in winter and insulates against noisy neighbours too.

The plans are very similar, a large circular depression or *hush* (pl *hiyash*) some 7-8m deep and about 10m in diameter entered by one steep slope or tunnel. From this courtyard seven or eight rooms are cut into the surrounding earth, as stables, stores, sleeping and living accommodation. Rooms are comfortably appointed, walls are whitewashed, shelves are cut for goods, extra holes make cupboards and today electricity replaces the oil lamps. Small animals joined their owners in this establishment. Holes in the ceiling were used to drop fodder to the animals and into the grain stores. Water was collected in cisterns.

In large establishments, for extended families or like those now used as hotels in Matmata, Tunisia (see page 466) one or two courtyards are linked together.

In particular the Gharyan region of Tripolitania, Libya, (see page 524) is noted for it cave dwellings excavated in the regions' sandy-clay soils.

• **Accommodation** A *Hotel Rabta*, brand new, in excellent condition, clean, run in a business-like way, working lifts, 68 rm, for the business traveller there are suites costing LD35 for single and LD45 for double, restaurant serves lunches and dinners at LD7.500 pp, modern café facing onto the street, film theatre, most modern facilities, owned by the Libyan Social Security Organization; D *Funduq Gharyan Siahiah (Gharyan Tourist Hotel)*, T 041 30105, very run down and seedy, 44 rm in use, modest price for Libya, small restaurant and café, open all the year. **Youth hostel** 120 beds, breakfast incl, family rooms, meals, laundry, kitchen and **camping** facilities in Gharyan at T (41) 31491, open 0700-2300, booking rec. Information at the City Hall.

Leave Gharyan and travel W via the dual carriageway, passing through olive groves in rolling uplands. Shortly there is a road on the left to **Tigrinnah**, a former tobacco-growing area and now with fairly dense villa housing straddling it. Good views are to be had to the SW over broken country. The Jabal top is lightly wooded with olives and figs. After Tigrinnah, at a small settlement called Abuzeyan, the road divides with Mizdah 82 km and Sabha 700 km by road to the left.

After Tigrinnah the road on the top of the Jabal becomes a single carriageway. It passes through Assabah village

with villas dispersed in farmlands. The village centre has a petrol station. Travel on 95 km to **Jadu**. The road traverses increasingly arid countryside with a light scrub covering to the hills. There are small occasional groups of houses such as Al-Gualith at Km 91 and Km 79. At Km 77 there is a mosque, a café and a petrol station. At Km 76 a turn to the right leads to **Kikla** 12 km away. On the main road, a green area under cultivation at Km 75-73 is an agricultural project run by the government. There are good places for picnics on sections of the old road visible from the new highway.

Turn right for **Yafran** off the main highway. This is classic old Berber town perched on the Jabal top and now much modernized but worth a visit. At Km 21 the black top road passes through fairly dense trees and cultivation. Note the good mainly reddish soils around Yafran. Reliable and heavy rains in late autumn and winter give the basis for a sound agriculture. There are fine views across the top of Jabal from the road towards Yafran. Also note the house decorations even on modern units, with complex ironwork doors, plaster work symbols such as butterflies and aircraft on house sides. Several small straggling

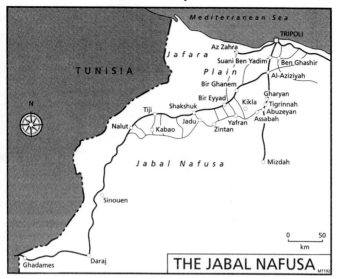

THE JABAL NAFUSA

villages lie along the roadside. A petrol station is located at **Qalah**, a village just before Yafran.

Yafran has been modernized. The old town and fortified grain storage towers and other ruins are still visible on the hilltops in the town. The new town spreads along the black top road. Cultivation is still undertaken sporadically on terraces and scarp-top fields. The town is very scattered around a one-way traffic system through narrow streets. A hotel is under construction but no hotel is currently in use. The town has all services, almost all clustered in the main square and the streets immediately adjacent to it. There is a **Youth hostel** in the city centre, T 0421 2394, 45 beds, meals available.

Leave Yafran and continue to **Al-Awenia** and **Aïn Rumia**. This road gives wide views across from the Jabal to the Jefara below. Some terraces cut into the Jabal face are still used for agriculture but many effectively have been abandoned. At Aïn Rumia there is a café open only in summer. The spring at the site is no longer running since the water is being used for the water supply to the town. But the gardens there are flourishing with palm trees in the cultivated valley. This spot can be crowded on Fri and public holidays. Return to the main road where a signpost at the junction gives 66 km to **Nalut** and 24 km to **Zintan**. Travel on the Zintan road to return to Tripoli. Otherwise continue W along the top of the Jabal scarp. Pass through a further red soil zone with fruit tree cultivation. **Accommodation Youth hostel** *Zintan*, T (44) 2191, 30 beds, breakfast provided, shop, central position.

Towards **Jadu** the rainfall decreases and the landscape is very arid, with few trees and little cultivation. At Km 10 turn right to Jadu. Arrive at Jadu passing through many new villas on the outskirts. The town gives the impression of a physical shambles since older communal and family stone constructed dwellings have been abandoned and new villas are randomly scattered across the landscape. In many ways Jadu has lost its old fashioned charm but is an important Berber town with notable tribes such as the Qabila Mizu there still. Berber is the main language in the households of the town. There is no hotel but petrol is available here. **Transport Road Bus**: services to both local and inter urban destinations run from just outside the town centre. **Taxi**: the taxi station is sited on the side of the main road at the entry to town.

Leave Jadu to head for **Shakshuk** at the foot of the scarp. There are two roads down the scarp, the newer one is better surfaced and better maintained. Both offer a breathtaking view N from the escarpment across the Jafara plain. Shakshuk is a small settlement with animal pens and houses sited a short distance off the road. At the junction with the Jefara highway from Nalut there is a petrol station and small general shop which sells drinks and grocery items.

The traveller can either go on the fast road along the Jefara W or return to the mountain road which leads on a winding route to Nalut. The mountain road passes through arid landscapes and enables rewarding visits to the Berber settlements at Tmizda, Kabao (petrol available here), Wighu, Sharwas and other sites. Those keen to see indigenous Berber architecture should perhaps take the slow road on the scarp. Those not prepared to accept the very considerable Berber charms of Nalut would find the Jefara road far quicker.

Nalut is a small town with all public services near the centre. Work is proceeding to provide it with proper hotel facilities including a basic rest house for people coming up from Farwa on a desert tour. It is well provided with bus, taxi and other transport facilities, being the take off point for Ghadames and Ghat. It has petrol, car repair shops and garages. Expect work to be done slowly and at some considerable cost.

From Nalut and Jadu, as noted, there is access down the scarp to the Jefara

single carriageway black top road returning to Tripoli. Roads off to the right lead back to the Jabal settlements at Kabao, Zintan, Yafran and most other settlements. There is a petrol station at Bir Eyyad and a roadside police control station. The control is not interested in tourists but have your passports ready in any case. At Bir Ghanem, the old stopping place on the Tripoli road, there is petrol, a café and shops. Carry on to the N passing through Sahel Jefara, again with a café and a small market. Another road to the left immediately after Sahel Jefara leads to Zaviyah, 78 km distant. Thereafter there is a slight increase in woodlands within government run agricultural projects and ex-Italian roadside trees. Some shifting grain cultivation is visible on the plain in spring. Increasingly dense cultivation indicates that **Al-Aziziyah** is being approached. Turn left at Al-Aziziyah (petrol available here) and Tripoli lies 38 km to the N.

Ghadames

(*Pop* estimated 7,500; *Alt* 500m; *Rainfall* under 25 mm annually) Ghadames is a very beautiful small oasis town located where the international frontiers of Libya, Algeria and Tunisia join. The residential area is divided into the old and new towns. The old town is situated within the oasis whereas the new town has been built on the dry slopes above the oasis. Since 1986 all but one family have moved out of the old town. The old traditional houses are not easily adapted to the fast-changing contemporary lifestyles of the people of Ghadames. Fortunately, the old town has not been simply abandoned and still plays an important role in the life of the inhabitants. In effect, the old town is surrounded by small plots of farming land, still highly cultivated. In the high temperatures of the summer, the inhabitants of the new city return to their original town in search of coolness and protection. The old town with its Saharan architecture and great beauty is a uniquely preserved example of its kind.

History

The history of Ghadames is interesting. Paleolithic and Neolithic tools have been found in the surrounding region, but the first real documented information about Ghadames comes from the Romans who in 19 BC set up a garrison in what was then named Cydaus. Under the Byzantines, the town was set up to be an episcopate, under the tenure of a bishop, and some ruins from this period can be seen in the surrounding area. The Arab invasion in 667, led by Uqba Ibn Nefi, visited Ghadames before the Muslim forces continued on into Tunisia. By the 8th century, Ghadames was an important desert port of call for caravans and pilgrims but was also able to preserve its Independence. Until 1860, Ghadames was paying taxes to the Bey of Tunis. The second Turkish occupation of Libya in 1835 forced the town to recognize the authority of the Turkish Bey in Tripoli. When the Italians landed in Tripoli in 1911 it took them 3 years to reach Ghadames and even then their

stay was of short duration. The Italians eventually returned on a permanent basis in 1924. They were great admirers of Ghadames and the area was treated sympathetically. New gardens were built and administrative offices set up there together with a small but pleasant hotel.

During WW2, Ghadames was occupied by the Free French Army led by General Leclerc and held under the Tunisian Protectorate until it was given up reluctantly at Libyan Independence in 1951. The last French troops left in 1955.

Ghadames suffered considerably with the development of less traditional sea-borne trade routes from West Africa. Situated in a very hostile environment even though there was water, trans-Saharan trade had been the main economic activity of the oasis. The people of Ghadames were trading and resident as far S as Timbuktu and on the Moroccan coast. The main trade consisted of caravans from the S bringing slaves, gold, leather and ivory in exchange for cotton, sugar and various products manufactured in Europe. By the start of the 19th century, trade had started to fall off due to the abolition of slavery. The decline was erratic and did not really end altogether until around 1910. Today, the inhabitants' only local sources of income are camel breeding and farming, the latter being very limited due to the lack of irrigation water and cultivable land, which is estimated at a mere 75 ha.

Architecture

The remarkable thing about Ghadames is the manner in which the people have been able to use all the resources available in a poor environment, together with their own traditions and architecture, to create perfect living conditions within this particular climate. The houses are built with mud, lime, palm tree trunks and fronds, the only available building materials. The result is impressive. Not only are the houses very elegant and beautiful, fitting perfectly

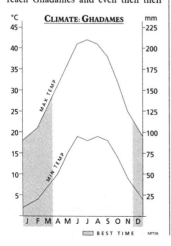

CLIMATE: GHADAMES

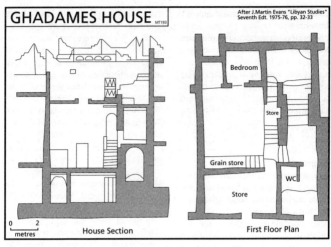

GHADAMES HOUSE MT193

After J.Martin Evans "Libyan Studies"
Seventh Edt. 1975-76, pp. 32-33

Bedroom

Store

Grain store

WC

Store

0   2
metres

House Section

First Floor Plan

into the environment, but they are also very practical. Built on two storeys, they have a central room on the first floor acting as a kind of courtyard with all the rooms leading out from it. The rooms are lit by an ingenious hole in the high ceiling, letting in sunlight that reflects off the white walls and provides quite sufficient illumination. The walls are made of mud and the upper floors are supported by palm tree trunks covered with fronds and mud. The interior of the house is decorated by the wife and tradition has it that this must be completed before the day of the marriage. The husband-to-be gives the key to his bride and she decorates their new home without his interference. The decorations are very simple, generally red patterns painted directly onto the white walls, with the addition of mirrors and a few small cabinets.

The roof is the domain of the women, the kitchen being on the roof. By tradition and due to the separation of sexes, the women were only permitted into the streets, either just after sunrise or just before sunset when the men are absent at the mosque for communal prayers.

Otherwise in the old town they were confined to the house, especially the upper floors. However rather than hamper communication and freedom, this facilitated it, as most roofs touch and the women could easily move around from one roof to another. This is another remarkable feature of the architecture in Ghadames, possible because of the close intertwining of houses. All dwellings are physically linked together, to give shade from the sun and thus increasing the coolness of the settlement in the summer.

Within the houses there are some interesting features. One small room called the *koubba* is only used twice during the lifetime of the owners. First during the wedding ceremonies and second, if the husband dies, it is used by the widow to receive relatives and friends. The store room also has a clever system for preserving food. Due to climatic and other uncertainties, keeping a large stock of food was very important. Wheat would be stocked and a wall built with a small hole remaining open. A torch would be inserted in order to burn the oxygen and the hole quickly filled enabling wheat to be stored for years. When it was needed the walls would simply be demolished.

The streets also have charming characteristics. Small winding streets have covers for the most part, giving them a tunnel-like appearance and providing coolness with a few light wells between houses to illuminate the otherwise semi-dark streets. The roads lead to small public squares, some of which are covered. Most streets are lined with benches for the men to sit on.

Irrigation

An interesting feature of the oasis is the integration of the vegetation and cultivable land with the residential part of the town. The gardens are about 5m below normal street level in order to be closer to the water table. Within the village there are two artesian wells operating in addition to Aïn Fares, the spring of the horses. Aïn Fares is said to have been discovered by Oqba Ibn Nefi, but this seems unlikely since the oasis predates the Muslim invasion by a very considerable period. The sense of coolness given by the running water and the shade of the palm trees makes the heat bearable in the summer months.

Places of interest

In the old town there is nothing specific to see because the beauty of the site is in the total harmony of the buildings and the small winding streets. In the old town situated behind the *Aïn Fares Hotel* there is a **House Museum**, a preserved Ghadames house. The interior is richly decorated with all the traditional furniture and implements of the oasis people. This is particularly interesting as it gives an insight into the traditional way of life in Ghadames earlier this century.

There is another 'Popular' **museum** at the entrance to the new town with a collection covering the popular and traditional aspects of life throughout the region, with clothes, weapons, tools and even desert animals. On the main square of the new town there is a large **market**

every Tues and a small market every other day.

Local information
● Accommodation
C *Hotel Luaha*, T (0484) 2569/70, 1 km or 10 mins walk from town centre, currently clean and everything works, bargain at LD25 for double with sitting room, breakfast LD3 each.

The **D** *Aïn Fares Hotel* used to be an old Italian colonial style hotel, wonderful location right by the old town but neglected and dirty and not very welcoming, at LD20 not a bargain.

● Youth hostel
T 2023, 1 km SE of town centre, 120 beds, breakfast incl, family room, shop, laundry, open 0700-2300, booking rec Dec-Apr, kitchen. Its café is the young people's meeting point and gets very lively in the evenings.

● Tour companies & travel agents
The recently opened *Ghadames Travel and Tourism*, Sharah Saydi Aqba, T/F (0484) 2533 or *Cidamos Tours and Travel*, T/F (0484) 2596, Sharah Sidi Okba, manager Mr Bashir Hammoud will organize any trip in the surrounding area, including complete guided tours of the old town of Ghadames and trips into the desert down towards Ghadames.

The best guide is Mr Ahmed Gassem Aoui, mayor of Ghadames for 40 years who delights in showing the old town and explaining the socio-economic system. If you ask for him by name you can avoid the Tourist agency upgrade of his fee.

● Transport
Air Flights to **Tripoli** every other Tues at 1230, costs LD20. Departure times change at short notice and travellers should check daily on the situation.

Road Bus: there are two buses a day to **Tripoli**. Officially they leave at 0700 and 1000, but in reality they leave when full. Be at the terminal at least 90 mins before the official time as this is when the bus is likely to leave. All buses to Tripoli go via **Nalut**. Small 10 seater private buses do the journey from/to Tripoli. Cost LD7, with several stops for refreshment and police checks. **Car**: the road surface from Ghadames to Nalut is good but attention must be given to the occasional small sand dunes across the road which can be dangerous even at moderate speeds.

To the W of the town, the small village of

Tunine is very similar and still inhabited, though it is much smaller and less attractive. Some very primitive forms of water lifting *delu* systems are still standing (see box, page 514). Further along the road after Tunine there is a large number of sand dunes. It is particularly satisfying to walk up to the top of the dunes and watch the desert sunset.

To Algeria: in more settled times this is a border crossing to Algeria, currently **not** recommended.

AL-KHUMS TO TARHUNAH AND TRIPOLI

The Jabal road back to Tripoli is well worth taking. The highway is occasionally narrow but this disadvantage is offset by a route through hill agriculture and breathtaking plantations of almond and olives.

The alternative to a direct route back to Tripoli from **Al-Khums** and **Leptis Magna** is to follow the road through the Jabal Nafusa via Tarhunah which takes about 2 hrs. From Al-Khums travel W on the main highway to Tripoli but take the Tarhunah road at the first left hand junction. It is 67 km to Tarhunah from this junction. The road follows more or less the line of old road but is a good width of carriageway now. Take care on this road as it is dangerous, with mixed traffic and many curves as the road rises towards the town of **Al-Qusbat**.

Al-Qusbat is the central place of the Jabal Mislata (a sub-region of the Jabal Nafusa) and has been much extended in an undistinguished way, spoiling the former charm of the place. There are most facilities including a post office, clinic, petrol station and regional council office. A large hospital is being built. There is no hotel and travellers interested in walking across Mislata should stay in Al-Khums.

From Al-Qusbat take the road to Tarhunah. The road passes through scenic country in open landscape with ex-Italian olive and almond plantations at Al-Khadra and Qasr Dawn. Qasr Dawn has a hospital, police, school and shops.

At **Tarhunah** is the Faculty of Law of Al-Nasser University N of the town towards Shershara. Cinema, shops, Libyan Arab Airlines, an old hospital and a new one under construction are among the range of facilities in the town. This once beautiful town is now modernized to the detriment of its character. There was a hotel under construction but a dispute with the Turkish building firm has meant that it has been abandoned. The famous *Lady of Gharyan*, a wall painting on the barracks wall in the town painted by a US soldier in WW2, has sadly disappeared. Tarhunah's excellent wines are also no longer to be found on the open market. Leave Tarhunah towards Shershara. **Youth hostel**, c/o Education Department, Tarhunah, T 3379, 20 beds, breakfast available, kitchen.

Shershara The much-visited spring at Shershara has now stopped flowing as water has been diverted away and the local water table has fallen. A small stream now comes in through a narrow upper valley with dense trees. It flows under the road which acts as an Irish bridge and there is a tiny fall of water on rocks below the roadway. The lower valley is green but very dirty with plastic and other rubbish. What was a very beautiful area is now very disappointing. **Places to eat** The hotel at Shershara, *Funduq Shershara*, is in a poor state: the rooms are not now used, but it has a restaurant and café. The staff do their best but the general effect is not very good. The hotel has no water from time to time. Arabic tea and a selection of cold soft drinks are available. Open 0800 to 2100.

Take the main road from Tarhunah out to the NW. A dual carriageway leads down to Tripoli. An alternative road leads W to Gharyan. The Tripoli road is

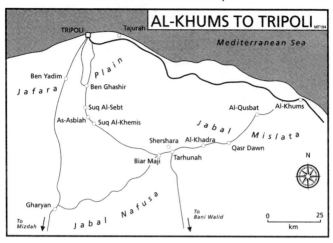

fast but winding. There is a junction slightly N of Tarhunah which permits a direct link from the petrol station at Biar Maji to Bani Walid approximately 85 km to the S, and a second junction to Qatamah, 32 km from Biar Maji. **Youth hostel** in former *Bani Walid hotel*, T (322) 2415, 30 beds, meals available, shop. It is a single carriageway road but good quality. Travellers can go directly via Mizdah to Sebha on black top without touching Tarhunah town. The road to Tripoli goes on to **Suq Al-Khemis**. Here there is a large roadside market, post office, police, shops and other basic facilities. At **As-Asbiah** is a junction with hospital, hospital-related housing but little else. Reaching **Suq Al-Sebt** there are more roadside shops, a petrol station and other services.

At **Ben Ghashir** the road leads off at a junction to the international airport link. Also from this point there is a dual carriageway to Tripoli. It is rather slow with lots of traffic. Roadside orange sellers are found in the spring season. Farm tractors and vehicles are plentiful on this dangerous road, mixing with fast airport and through traffic. Travellers can take the Tripoli-airport road with greater safety and speed.

BENGHAZI

CONTENTS

Benghazi	534
Travel in the Jabal Al-Akhdar	537

MAPS

Benghazi	535
The Jabal Al-Akhdar	538
Tolmeita	540
Cyrene	542
Apollonia	546
Wadi Derna	547

Benghazi is the second largest town in Libya after Tripoli and as such is an important economic and administrative centre. The town acts as the main port for the E of Libya and has a number of food processing and packaging plants as well as other small and medium sized industries.

(*Pop* 500,000 (estimated 1992); *Alt* Sea level; *Maximum recorded temperature* 40.1°C) The city has little to offer to the visitor as many of the older monuments have been destroyed, some during WW2 but most through contemporary 'development' of the city. The present town is therefore relatively modern and charmless, except for areas in the old town and around the *funduq* market. Benghazi is nevertheless a good stopover point for trips to the E and into the Jabal Al-Akhdar.

The city enjoys a thoroughly Mediterranean climate with hot dry summers and warm winters with some rainfall. The Jabal Al-Akhdar region behind and to the E of Benghazi has a markedly heavier and more reliable winter rainfall of over 300 mm, with the scarp top attracting the larger rainfall total.

History

The town of Benghazi was probably founded around 515 BC, but no real information exists as to the precise date. The first settlers were most probably Greeks from Cyrene who had come down to the coastal plain. It is known that the first settlement was called Euesperides and was situated much further inland than the present city. In 249 BC, Ptolemy III of Egypt subjected Cyrenaica to Egyptian rule and married Berenice, the heiress to the Cyrenaican Kingdom. A new site was found for the town of Euesperides, closer to the sea, probably because the old harbour had silted up, and the town was renamed Berenice. The situation of the ancient city is virtually identical to the present old town of Benghazi. The town then became part of the Roman Empire but once again little is known of its role. In the 6th century AD, the Byzantine Emperor Justinian made a number of repairs to the city after it had suffered an attack by the Vandals.

In 643 AD, the Arabs invaded, led by Omar Ibn el As, but they had little interest in Berenice. The two main cities at the time were Ajdabiyah and Al-Marj, due to their closer proximity to the main

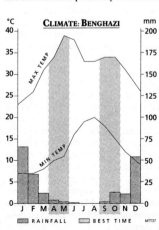

CLIMATE: BENGHAZI

RAINFALL   BEST TIME

MT37

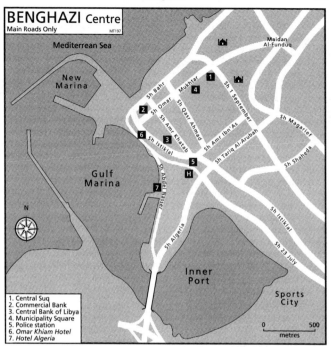

BENGHAZI Centre
Main Roads Only   MT197

Mediterrean Sea

New Marina

Gulf Marina

Maidan Al-Funduq

Sh Bahr
Sh Omar
Mukhtar
Sh Qasr Ahmad
Sh Amr Khateb
Sh Istiklal
Sh 1 September
Sh Amr Ibn As
Sh Tariq Al-Arubah
Sh Magarief
Sh Shaheda
Sh Abdel Naser
Sh Algeria
Sh Istiklal
Sh 23 July

N

Inner Port

Sports City

1. Central Suq
2. Commercial Bank
3. Central Bank of Libya
4. Municipality Square
5. Police station
6. *Omar Khiam Hotel*
7. *Hotel Algeria*

0   500
metres

trans-African caravan routes. Very little is known of Berenice until the 15th century, when local tradition has it that merchants from Misrath and Zliten once again started using Berenice as a trading place. In 1579 the town was given the name Ibn Ghazi after a holy man of the city at that period. In 1648 the Turks, having previously settled in Tripolitania, advanced on Cyrenaica. By 1650 they held a position of strength in Ibn Ghazi, having built a fort. The town became the main centre for tax collecting. Because of this, few travellers or merchants came near it! In 1711, the Ottoman régime in Libya was interrupted by the Karamanli takeover and this once again plunged Benghazi into a period of stagnation. It was only under the second Ottoman occupation, beginning in 1835, that Benghazi again prospered.

In 1911, Benghazi was subjected to a siege by the Italian Navy, the city only surrendering after bombardment from the sea. The Italians then created a stronghold out of the city, building large walls encircling the centre. It took 20 years for the Italians to gain control of the surrounding areas, and only after 1931 were they in a position to start building up the city. The Italians poured large sums into urbanization projects and virtually managed to recreate an Italian city in North Africa. The real disaster for the town came during WW2 when the city changed hands five times and was incessantly bombed by the Allies or the Axis. When General Montgomery finally liberated the city in November 1942, there was little left. Subsequently, due to the uncertainties as to the future of Libya, no major reconstruction works were carried out by the British Military Administration.

With Independence in 1951, the city gained in importance as the regional capital and as the seat of the Federal Government, but developments were slow, particularly due to the government's lack of funds. In 1959, oil was found in the area around Sirt and the town became an important centre in the oil trade, particularly with the arrival of a large number of Europeans and Americans working in the oil fields. BP established its main office in Benghazi rather than Tripoli. Throughout the 1960s and 1970s, as oil revenues increased, the town developed rapidly. In the early 1980s the harbour was redeveloped in order to cater for large cargo vessels, new roads were built and small industries started to appear.

SOCIAL INDICATORS Benghazi is similar to Tripoli in per capita income (US$5,410), literacy (M 67%, F 50%) and life expectancy (61/65 years).

ACCESS There are frequent flights from Tripoli and other Libyan cities and, in normal circumstances, a few international flights. There is a bus service between the airport and central Benghazi (32 km). Taxis run into the town centre but make sure to agree a price before departure.

Places of interest

Benghazi has few sites of any touristic value, but it is interesting to walk around the old town and see the myriads of small shops selling every imaginable type of merchandise. Particularly interesting is the **funduq**, a large market that mainly sells vegetables and fresh products. The atmosphere is typical of any Middle Eastern market and a worthwhile experience. The surrounding area is filled with stalls, particularly on Fri when traffic comes to a standstill. You will see trucks full of goods from Egypt, especially furniture, as well as a labour market where painters, electricians, carpenters, and so on stand by the side of the road waiting for an employer.

There are some **Roman remains** by the Regional Administration building on the seafront, but they are small and of only specialized interest. Otherwise there is the beach, either N or S along the coast. There are a number of good beach clubs, with restaurants and snack facilities.

The **Commonwealth Cemetery** in Benghazi is sited 6 km SSE of Benghazi on the inner ring road and in town there is a **Military Cemetery** containing 311 British war dead.

Local information
● Accommodation

A *Tibesti Hotel*, T 97178, 274 rm, largest and newest, luxurious, *hammam*, impersonal.

B *Uzu Hotel*, very clean, modern, half the room overlooking inner harbour.

D *Hotel Al-Anis*, T 93147, rec, very simple, clean, good restaurant, welcoming, very cheap, best in this category; **D** *Hotel Atlas*, Sharah Abdel Nasser, T 92314, not marvellous, acceptable for 1 night; **D** *Ghordabeia Hotel*, Sharah Abdel Nasser, T 97342/5, room with shower, small hotel, friendly proprietor; **D** *Hotel Omar Khiam*, Sharah Abdel Nasser, T 95102, 200 rm, once one of the best in Benghazi, has since become neglected, welcoming, cheap, central; *Tourist Village Garians*, T 96350, very cheap with good recreational facilities, closed in winter.

● Youth hostel

Sports City, 1 km SW of town centre, T 95961, 200 beds, breakfast incl, kitchen, meals, family rooms, laundry, booking rec May-Oct.

● Places to eat

Restaurant Al-Shallal, Sharah Abdel Nasser, by the *Hotel Atlas*, mainly Turkish food; *Restaurant Ali Ayamama* Sharah Abdel Nasser, behind the *Tibesti Hotel*; *Ghordabeia Hotel* restaurant has a Kentucky Fried Chicken licence!! *Restaurant 23 July*, in the gardens by the inner harbour just before reaching the *Uzu Hotel*. Food and snacks are available at the various beach clubs nr the city. Café in *Tibesti Hotel* open all day for snacks around LD5. Good *patisserie* nr car hire Bab Almadena in Sharah Abdel Nasser.

● Banks & money changers

Both the *Tibesti* and the *Uzu Hotels* have banking facilities. Otherwise the main banks are as follows: **Central Bank of Libya**, Sharah Abdel Nasser, T 91165; **Jamahiriya Bank**, Sharah Abdel Nasser; **National Commercial Bank**, Sharah Omar Mukhtar; **Sahara Bank**, Sharah Abdel Nasser, T 92766; **Umma Bank**, Sharah Omar Mukhtar, T 93377; **Wahhadah Bank**, Sharah Abdel Nasser, T 94527.

● **Consulates**
Most embassies and consulates are located in Tripoli to which ultimate reference for assistance must be made (see page 509). Among countries with consulates in Benghazi are: **Czechoslovakia**, T 92149; **France**, T 27566; **Greece**, Sharah Gamal Abdel Nasser, T 93064; **Italy**, Sharah Amr Ibn'As, T 98077; **Poland**, Sharah Gamal Abdel Nasser, T 98363/92867; **Saudi Arabia**, Fuehat, T 20815.

● **Hospitals & medical services**
Chemists: Sharah Gamal Abdel Nasser.

Hospitals: Benghazi has central hospital facilities and a modern complex on the outskirts of the town. While the air embargo remains in force, bear in mind that it is not easy to be repatriated from Libya in the event of an emergency.

● **Post & telecommunications**
Post Office: Sharah Omar Mukhtar. There is a smaller post office behind the *Tibesti Hotel* on Sharah Gamal Abdel Nasser.
Telephone Local code 061.

● **Shopping**
These are concentrated in the main street and the road leading from the centre W, Sharah Gamal Abdel Nasser, to the so-called Christmas Tree area. Some of the older suburbs have grocery and Arab lock-up shops selling a range of produce.

Markets: the *funduq* offers an abundance of reasonably priced vegetables and other perishable products.

● **Sports**
There are several beach clubs not far from the city centre on the Ghar Yunis road towards the university campus. The bigger hotels, such as the *Tibesti*, have Arab baths. The *Tourist Village Garians*, T 6350, 5 km to the S of the town, has a pool, tennis, bowling, snooker and other sports/recreational activities, facilities can be used by non-residents for a small entrance fee. Only open in summer.

● **Tour companies & travel agents**
Libyan Travel and Tourism Company is located at the start of Sharah Gamal Abdel

Nasser, towards the harbour. This is a new agency specializing in organized tours. It can provide guides and transport. The company also issues tickets for all major airlines, T 93009. *Libyan Arab Airways* have an office on Sharah Gamal Abdel Nasser, behind the *Tibesti Hotel*. Both the *Tibesti* and the *Uzu Hotels* have travel agents that can issue tickets for all major airlines.

● **Transport**
Air Internal: to **Tripoli** daily at 0800, 1900 and 2000 with extra flights most days at 1500 or 1600. Takes 1 hr, costs LD28; flights per week **Ghadames** (3), **Ghat** (3), **Hun** (4), **Al-Kufrah** (1), **Misratah** (5), **Sabha** (5), **Sirt** (4), **Tobruk** (3).

Road Bus: Faltco company. The bus station is after the *funduq* on the right. Be sure to be there well in advance as buses tend to leave earlier rather than later than officially stated. Daily: **Tripoli** (4), **Cairo** (2), **Damascus** Wed and Sun 0800. General Transport company. Brand new bus station right next to the Funduq market. Daily: **Tripoli** 0730 (2 buses); **Al-Khums** 0700; **Misratah** 0800; **Al-Kufrah** 0730; **Sabha** Tues, Fri and Sun 0700; **Tobruk** 0730, 1100; **Derna** 0800. **Car hire**: Tibesti Car Service is in the foyer of the *Tibesti Hotel*, T 92030, prices for 24 hrs start at LD2; **Bab Almadena** T 99855, PO Box 7268, Sharah Abdel Nasser, nr *Hotel Algeria*. Local taxis are available for short or day-hire at expensive rates. **Taxi**: all the intercity taxis leave from the *funduq* area. They are all grouped by destination and leave when full. Slightly more expensive than the bus. Sample fare to Al-Bayda LD5.

TRAVEL IN THE JABAL AL-AKHDAR

The Jabal Al-Akhdar or Green Mountain range runs from Tocra to Derna. The highest point is close to Al-Bayda and reaches 880m. The Jabal is one of the few places where rainfall (about 300 mm per annum) is enough to sustain farming. The beauty of the landscape, the relative coolness in the summer as well as the important Greek and Roman remains make it an important part of any tour within Libya.

During the Greek Pentapolis period, the Jabal was reputed to be virtually the

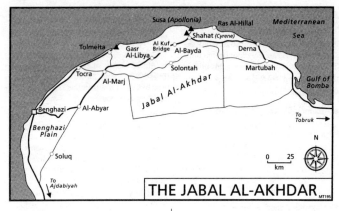

THE JABAL AL-AKHDAR

granary for mainland Greece and ever since has been seen, not entirely correctly, as a very fertile area. Recently, great efforts have been made to develop intensive farming using modern techniques and irrigation. An important underground water supply has made intensive irrigation farming a reality, particularly on the Al-Marj plateau. Production is still low and concentrated on fruits and vegetables, but some progress is being made. There are many new problems, particularly linked with overpumping and declining water tables, which are limiting development.

The Jabal peoples are historically independently minded and this area is not one that conforms easily with norms set by Tripoli. There was, for many years, difficulty with travel and access to certain areas within the Jabal. Given the ability of the local tribes to feed themselves and to sustain long periods of warfare, the region has been regarded with apprehension by outside groups. The Jabal Al-Akhdar has played a singular role in the history of Libya. It was the stronghold of anti-colonial rule and insurrection, giving great trouble to all would-be colonial rulers. Under the Senussi and Omar Mukhtar, the Cyrenaican tribes sustained many years of modern warfare in a one-sided struggle against the Italians. Today the Jabal is a major trade route to Egypt as well as having significant tourist potential.

Through Jabal Al-Akhdar

Tocra is a small town about 60 km from Benghazi. The new town is of little interest but the old part of town and the small central square with its **market** is worth a look around. Tocra has well-researched Roman ruins, though not all the workings are totally uncovered. Nevertheless, they are interesting and the small **Turkish fort** provides a good view over the plain towards the Jabal.

History

Teuchira, the original Greek name for Tocra, was founded around 510 BC. It became part of the Pentapolis. It changed names more than once and was called Arsinoe after the wife of Ptolemy II, and was briefly known as Cleopatris, the name of the daughter of Cleopatra and Mark Antony. There are still some surrounding walls built by the Byzantine Emperor Justinian in the 6th century and the Turkish fort, most probably built over the site of the Greek acropolis. From the ruins that have been excavated it is possible to deduce that the community at Tocra was poorer than the inhabitants of the other Pentapolis towns.

Al-Marj

The present Al-Marj is virtually a new city, the old town having been completely destroyed during an earthquake in 1963. The inhabitants were then relocated in the new town with a gigantic modern mosque that dominates the sky-line.

● **Accommodation** There is one hotel at Al-Marj which can be used as a good stop-over point. **D** *Al-Marj Hotel*, T (67) 2700, is situated nr the centre of the new town, seems to have known better days, but is nevertheless clean, with a restaurant and cafeteria. **Youth hostels** T (67) 3669, 60 beds, breakfast incl, meals, kitchen, family rooms, bus 600m.

● **Transport Road** The bus and taxi station is about 500m in front of the mosque. There are no fixed times for buses, as they are only passing through, but they stop in Al-Marj in the morning between 0800 and 1000. Best to be there early. Otherwise there are shared taxis leaving throughout the day for destinations E and W.

Tolmeita (Ptolemais)

This site is of real interest for the Graeco-Roman ruins of the port of Ptolemais. The village itself is very small, but the situation on the coastal plain is magnificent. The scenery along the road from Al-Marj is very beautiful, particularly when driving down through the mountains towards the sea. The ruins are extensive and cover an area larger than in Cyrene, but remain largely unexcavated. Nevertheless, the site is worth a visit. Tolmeita is literally at the end of the road, for after early morning there are no buses. Transport back to Al-Marj or on to Tocra is by taxi if you can find one. The site surveyor (whose English is excellent) and the Chief of Police routinely ask visitors questions as Ghadhafi has a rest house down the coast. If relying on public transport visit Tolmeita then Tocra.

History

The ancient city of Ptolemais was named after Ptolemy II Philadelphus in the 3rd century BC. The town was actu-ally founded earlier but only became of importance under the Ptolemy's rule as part of the Pentapolis. Ptolemais was originally the harbour for the inland city of Barce (Al-Marj), but later was of importance in its own right. After the Roman occupation the city was altered and buildings constructed, proving its continuing role as an important centre. From the 3rd century, both Apollonia and Ptolemais became the main cities in Cyrenaica. In the 4th century, Ptolemais became the seat of the bishop and the capital of a province and fortifications were increased against raids by Berber tribes, but were insufficient to prevent the Vandals in the 5th century from taking the city. Ptolemais fell into decay with the Arab invasion and its only use was in providing building material for the new village. The site was rediscovered in 1935 by the Italians who started excavations there and set up the museum.

Places of interest

On the site there are several monuments that should not be missed. The **Street of the Monuments** is from the Roman period and was clearly an important place within the city, lined with porticoes, fountains, statues of people and deities, and inscriptions. The **Hellenistic Palace** is probably the largest and most interesting of excavated monuments dating back to the 1st century BC and altered in the 2nd century. From its size and elaborate decorations, it was clearly the house of a person of note. The house included large reception rooms with mosaic floors and traces of marble-panelled walls. There are two courtyards, one with an ornamental water tank, the other with Corinthian columns and traces of marble and mosaic floors. The house had two storeys, the basement presumably reserved for the servants. To the N of the building, one can see signs of the existence of private baths. On the N side, ie on the street, there is evidence

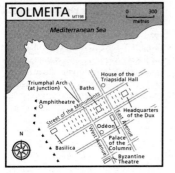

TOLMEITA MT198

0 ____ 300
metres

Mediterranean Sea

House of the
Triapsidal Hall

Triumphal Arch
(at junction)   Baths

Amphitheatre

Street of the Monuments

Headquarters
of the Dux

Odéon

N   West Avenue   Palace
                         of the
        Basilica   Columns

                         Byzantine
                         Theatre

that the front of the house had shops in it, a usual practice for private houses.

Not far from the palace, to the S, lies the **Forum**. This was rebuilt in the 1st century BC on the site of the Hellenistic Agora. The Romans built a large vaulted roof, a technique unknown to the Greeks. The entire structure covers 14 large reservoirs that were almost certainly fed by an aqueduct, traces of which can be seen by the Roman bridge that crosses over the *wadi* to the E of the site. The **Headquarters of the Dux** (Caserne d'Anastase) is a massive fortified building which presumably housed the garrison. Excavations of the **House of the Triapsidal Hall** indicate urban life continued here after the Islamic Conquest.

There are other worthwhile monuments to see but the excavations have not yet fully exposed the ruins and are thus not so immediately interesting as those mentioned above. To the W, remains of the walls that protected the city can still be seen. Close to the walls, a fully excavated **Basilica** dating back to the 5th century AD is well preserved. The church is original in that it was not an older converted building, a common practice during this period, and was built with defences. Vaults and arches replace the usual columns, but the nave was still roofed in wood. To the N of the basilica lies the **Amphitheatre**. Built by

the Romans in the 1st century BC it was mostly used for gladiator fights and wild animal shows. Unfortunately today there is little to see. The **Odéon** was used both as a theatre and as a council chamber. The **Palace** has a dozen columns standing. To the S, in the hillside, is the Greek theatre, probably built in the 2nd century BC. Once again little is visible. Finally, the ancient harbour was at the same place as the modern one. Some traces of buildings and their foundations can still be seen on the E side of the harbour, as can the location of some of the jetties.

There is a small museum located at the end of the road which passes through the village, by the harbour. The collection is small but interesting and mostly holds mosaics and sculptures from the Roman period. Some of the mosaics are very well preserved and are particularly of value, not for their great quality, but as an insight into life in Ptolemais, such as scenes with various wild animals, including lions and tigers.

Gasr Al-Libya

This small town is located on the road from Al-Marj to Al-Bayda. In itself it does not necessitate a visit but a fine old **Byzantine Fort** stands nearby. Coming from Al-Marj, take the road that goes to the left on entering the village. The site is 2 km down the road. The ruins date back to the 6th century and contain a well preserved **Byzantine Church**. The church was most probably fortified. The walls are still in perfect condition but the roof, originally made of wood, has been replaced. In the centre of the nave lies a large mosaic, which is in good condition. There is also a small museum that contains a set of mosaics. All the mosaics have been cut out of the floor of another building further down the hill. They are interesting because they give an account of what was clearly an important Christian community at the start of the 6th century. The rest of the ruins are dominated by a small **Turkish Fort** built as a stronghold and lookout over the surrounding countryside: it was later used by the Italians during their attempts to subdue the region. From the top of the fort there is a wonderful view.

Wadi Al-Kuf

On the road to Al-Bayda, there is an impressive new bridge crossing a deep gorge at Wadi Al-Kuf. The bridge is over 500m above the gorge and the view is breathtaking, definitely worth a stop. It is possible to take the road that goes along the bottom of the gorge. The cliffs in the side of the gorge are filled with small caves and quaint rock formations.

Al-Bayda

This is an important administrative regional centre. Once briefly the administrative capital of Libya in 1964, it is now the site of an important Islamic university. This is no coincidence since in 1843 Mohammed Ben Ali Al-Senussi established his radical Islamic movement in Al-Bayda, a movement that was to spread throughout Cyrenaica. In the 19th century the Turks had problems with the Senussi hold on the population and the leaders of the movement had to settle for safety in Jaghbub and Al-Kufrah. The Senussi led the rebellion against the Italians, finally leading Idris Al-Senussi to the throne and Libyan Independence in 1951. Today, Al-Bayda is a good stopover point and is very close to the major archaeological site of Cyrene.

● **Accommodation** There is one good hotel in the main street. The **D** *Bayda Palace Hotel*, T 084 23455, run down, clean, rooms with a/c.

● **Transport Road Bus**: there is a bus station on the main street, by the telecom tower. There are frequent buses to **Shahat** (Cyrene) every hour from 0800-1700. Other main line buses stop here, but there are no fixed timetables, except that the majority of the buses pass here in the morning.

Cyrene

Shahat (Cyrene) The modern city of Shahat is of little visual interest but the archaeological remains of Cyrene are very impressive and possibly the most worthwhile site in Libya after Leptis Magna. The situation of Shahat on the upper slopes of the Jabal Al-Akhdar is extremely fine, overlooking a high plateau leading to the sea. The site is as impressive as the actual remains of what must have been a very large city, but the combination of the two make it an absolute must for the traveller along the Cyrenaican shore. There is an hourly bus here from Al-Bayda. The last bus returns at 1700. Closed Mon and Fri. There is **no** public transport of any kind around the town so car-less travellers will need to rely on lifts from townspeople to reach the site in bad weather.

History

Cyrene goes back to the first half of the 7th century BC. The first settlers came from the island of Thera (Santorini) and the most plausible explanation is the over-population of the island and the necessity of finding an alternative outlet for settlement. The story has it that a young man named Battus went to Del-

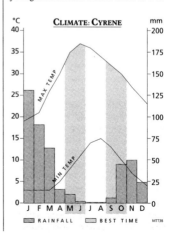

CLIMATE: CYRENE

RAINFALL   BEST TIME

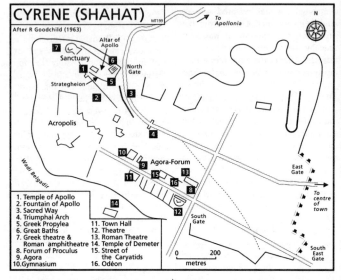

CYRENE (SHAHAT)   MT199   To
After R Goodchild (1963)   Apollonia   N

Altar of
Apollo
7   Sanctuary   6
1   North
Strategheion   5   Gate
2   3

Acropolis   4

10   Agora-Forum   East
9   Gate
11   15   13
16   To
8   centre
12   of
14   South   town
Gate
South
East
0   200   Gate
metres

1. Temple of Apollo
2. Fountain of Apollo
3. Sacred Way
4. Triumphal Arch
5. Greek Propylea   11. Town Hall
6. Great Baths   12. Theatre
7. Greek theatre &   13. Roman Theatre
   Roman amphitheatre   14. Temple of Demeter
8. Forum of Proculus   15. Street of
9. Agora   the Caryatids
10.Gymnasium   16. Odéon

phi to consult the Oracle, who told him to go and settle in Libya. He then left with an expedition, only to land on an offshore island. He later returned to see the Oracle, who told him he had not been to Libya yet. He made another attempt and landed on the mainland, but not yet at the original site of Cyrene. It was only after a 6 year period that the colonists moved to the site of Cyrene and founded what was by the 5th century BC one of the largest cities in Africa.

Relations between the Libyans and the Greeks were friendly, both civilizations gaining from each other, and intermarriage between the two communities being permitted. When the city flourished, large numbers of Greeks came and settled in Cyrene: this gave rise to tensions and a small revolt by the Libyans in the 6th century BC. The city was ruled by Battus and his family until 331 BC and the coming of Alexander the Great. The Golden Age, from 450 BC until about 300 BC, saw Cyrene's prosperity increase. Due to the large number of crops obtained every year

(up to 3), Cyrene was able to relieve famines in Greece and feed its own growing population.

The city also exported very valuable goods such as the silphium plant, now extinct, which was used as a laxative and an antiseptic. It was so important that the plant was depicted on the coins of the country for many centuries. Cyrene became part of the Pentapolis (Cyrene, Barka, Berenice, Tocra, Apollonia), a federation of five cities with agreements on trade, and joint coinage. This type of federation was quite common within Greek colonies until Alexander the Great attempted to unify all the cities.

On his death, the Greek Empire was split up and Cyrenaica came into the hands of the Ptolemy in Egypt. Cyrenaica passed into Roman hands when the illegitimate son of Ptolemy XI, who had inherited the Pentapolis, gave up his holding. In 75 BC, Cyrenaica was incorporated into the Roman Empire but, due to internal rivalries within the empire, the Pentapolis was neglected.

Emperor Augustus restored stability and gave a new span of life and prosperity to Cyrene. Various revolts broke out, the most serious by the Jewish community. In 115 AD Emperor Trajan ruthlessly suppressed the revolts but they brought about the inevitable decline of the city. Emperor Hadrian undertook large reconstruction works but the city never really recovered. By the 4th century AD the city was largely deserted and falling into decay. It was never again inhabited, except periodically by nomads.

Until the 19th century, very little attention was paid to Cyrene. One of the first expeditions was in 1838 by a British group and a few other outsiders followed in 1861 and 1864, but it was not until the Italian occupation that major excavation work was carried out. No real work on the site has been undertaken since the Italians and their successor under the British Military Administration, Professor Goodchild, left and much work still needs to be done.

Places of interest

The site which is large and complicated to view, as much is obscured by more recent buildings and agricultural land use, can be divided into two main parts, the **Sanctuary of Apollo** and the **Agora-Forum Area**. The sanctuary is situated below the main part of the town, and contains the **Temple of Apollo** (1) and the **Fountain of Apollo (Sacred Fountain)** (2). The main approach down the **Sacred Way** (3) was through an arch which still stands. Pilgrims came from all over the African world of Greece to attend the ritual ablutions in the purifying waters of the sacred fountain and to venerate Apollo. Worship continued into Roman times, with the addition of the **Great Baths** (6) built by the Emperor Trajan in the 2nd century. Once in the sanctuary, the pilgrims would congregate on the upper terrace and approach the temple through the **Greek Propylea** (5), four lofty pillars. These still stand and are of Doric style dating back to the Hellenistic period. Close by stands the **Strategheion**, built in honour of Apollo to celebrate the victory of three generals in the 4th century BC. It has since been restored and roofed.

The **Temple of Apollo** is certainly one of the oldest buildings in Cyrene, the rest of the sanctuary developing around it. The foundations of the original 7th century BC temple can still be seen, but it was later rebuilt and enlarged in the 4th century BC. Traces of blue paint still exist on the old Greek parts of the temple clearly showing that all buildings were painted, and often in bright colours. As a result of the Jewish revolts, the temple was burnt down and the Romans rebuilt a copy of the original Greek Doric temple. Later, during the Byzantine period, the temple was converted into a Christian chapel. Notice on either side of the entrance the inscriptions with the names of the Roman priests of Apollo, some being important Roman officials. In front of the temple to the SE stands the **Altar of Apollo** where the ceremonies took place. Traces of the channels which drained away the blood of the sacrificed animals can be seen, as can, between the altar and the temple, fragments of the metal ring to which the animals were tethered.

The **Fountain of Apollo** is situated by the cliff behind the Temple of Apollo. The water was used for purification and was said to have curative properties. Notice the seating inside the tank for people undergoing purification. This is one of the largest buildings in the **Great Baths**. The original building by Trajan in 98 AD was destroyed during the Jewish revolt and rebuilt by Hadrian in 119 AD. It is highly decorated, with marbled floors and walls and the baths looking, in their original form, quite superb. Most rooms had vaulted roofs and mosaic decoration. The **Calidarium**, or hot rooms, had raised floors and pipes in the walls for the passage of hot air from the furnace. In the **Great Hall**, a large cold bath is still in very good condition and fed by pipes coming from the Apollo fountain. The baths had more than just a hygienic role and were also highly important as a kind of social club, where all citizens would come and meet. Interestingly, before the reconstruction by Hadrian, mixed bathing was common, but a new law forbade this and two baths had to be built.

The **Theatre**, to the W of the site, is in fact a Roman theatre and not Greek as the building technique would suggest. The Greeks built theatres in hillsides, whereas the Romans generally built them on flat ground. In effect the theatre in the sanctuary is an amphitheatre, that is to say with a circular stage. Due to the sharp fall on one side of the building, seats were provided only on the hill side. Nevertheless, the Roman amphitheatre was probably built on the site of an earlier Greek theatre.

The **Agora-Forum** area is the real centre of the city and had all the conveniences of a metropolis. There were shops, theatres, baths, law courts and temples. The city had as its centre the **Agora**, equivalent to the Roman forum. Most of the main civic buildings were situated here. In the principal square is the **Tomb of Battus**, the founder of the city. This was a very special honour, as generally no tombs were allowed within the city walls. Close by are the remains of the supposed **Gymnasium**, the school for the elite youth where intellectual work was as important as physical exercise. In the square is the **Naval Monument**, probably erected in the 3rd century BC to commemorate a victory at sea. On the S of the square is the **Prytaneum**, or Town Hall. This building was the administrative centre of the town. The building resembled the plan of a private house, built around a central courtyard, with a sacred fire held in a niche to the E side symbolizing the communal home of the people. The officers of the Town Hall lived and worked within the building and invited privileged citizens and visitors to eat there. The Town Hall dates back to the Hellenistic period with only a few additions during the Roman times. The building was used until the Imperial officials from Rome took over the governing of the city.

On the E side of the Town Hall lies the **Capitolium**. The building dates to the end of the Hellenistic period and was converted by the Romans into the temple where Jupiter, Juno and Minerva were worshipped, symbolizing the empire. The front has four white marble Doric columns and by the entrance are Greek inscriptions commemorating the gratitude of the city for the help Emperor Hadrian gave for the reconstruction of the town after the Jewish revolt.

To the E, going from the agora to the **Forum of Proculus** (8), is the **Street of Caryatids** (15). The road was originally lined on the N side with figures standing on pedestals (Caryatids) but they have all fallen over and are very damaged. On the S of the road is one of the most elegant houses in Cyrene, once belonging to Jason Magnus, a priest of Apollo. Built around the 2nd century BC by joining two houses, it is richly decorated, with mosaic floors, some well preserved. The larger of the two houses (on the higher level to the W) held the reception rooms. In the largest of the reception rooms remains of the magnificent marble floor can be seen. On the N, three small temples were incorporated into the house. One of the temples was the owner's private chapel. Both houses were built around a central courtyard. The second smaller house held the family's apartments.

Further E, the remains of a theatre are visible. This was probably built in the 3rd century BC and it is suggested that it was built as a replacement for the theatre in the sanctuary that had been converted into an amphitheatre. To the N of the Street of Caryatids, stands the impressive Forum of Proculus, probably built during the Hellenistic period, but later rebuilt by the Romans. The large central courtyard is lined with Doric colonnades, and in the centre lie the remains of an earlier temple, probably dedicated to Dionysius. Various fortifications were added to the forum during the 4th and 5th centuries when Cyrene was in constant fear of Berber attacks. To the NW of the forum lies a small **Roman Theatre**, which has been renovated and is sometimes used for performances. On the N side of the forum stands a **Basilica** built in the 6th century AD. Such buildings were used as an exchange for merchants or as law courts. The site extends for more than 3 km and this description has tried to give an account of the most interesting monuments, many of the others being in a poor state or still in need of excavation.

Particularly interesting is the **Necropolis** all around the site, making up an estimated 50 sq km. Tombs were not allowed inside the city walls and all tombs were thus situated on the surrounding lands and in particular in the side of the hill in front of the sanctuary. The tombs were dug out of the rock and formed small caves, often done in conjunction with quarrying, and the bodies placed directly into coffins carved out of the rock. The doorway was then sealed with a large stone. Due to the stones being movable, most of the tombs were broken into and even sometimes inhabited by nomads. It is strange that virtually all the bodies were actually placed within the tomb as, until the Christian period, cremation was commonly practised. Only a few lead urns containing ashes have been found. No clear explanation seems to have been found as to why interment was systematically practised. The shrine tomb was also a widely-used burial chamber. The tombs resembled small mausoleums or tem-

ples. These mostly date back to the Hellenistic period. The number of tombs may at first seem impressive, but one must remember that the period of occupation stretched from 700 BC to 400 AD. **Accommodation Youth hostel** Former *Shahat Tourist Hotel*, open 0600-1000 and 1400-2400, 200 beds, kitchen, meals, laundry, family rooms, T (851) 2102, booking rec Jun-Sep.

Susa (Apollonia)

This is a tiny settlement by the coast about 20 km from Shahat. The old town is very beautiful but falling into decay. The real interest of the town is the ruins of Apollonia, Cyrene's harbour. The site is by the sea, but a large part of the town and harbour have been submerged due to landslides. Susa can be reached by a road coming from Shahat, highly recommended because of the fine view over the coast and Susa itself.

Apollonia was founded at the same time as Cyrene and was named after the city's principal god. The harbour was at first a dependency of Cyrene, but later in the 2nd and 3rd centuries it gradually increased in stature, as the mother city declined, and finally became the capital of Upper Libya.

Approaching the site from the W, drive through the town square heading towards Derna and look for the track to the left leading up to the ramparts which leads to parking space on the beach. The first important monument encountered is the **Extra-Mural Church** (1). The **City Walls**, from which huge quantities of stone have fallen, continue up the Acropolis hill and turn N to the **Theatre** and the sea. Within the walls the **Cisterns** and the **Chambers** were both used for storage. The **Eastern Church** (4) dating from the 5th century contains green marble columns from an earlier Roman building. The **Baths** (6) to the left of **Main Street** now lie close to the sea, while on the hill top to the S are the

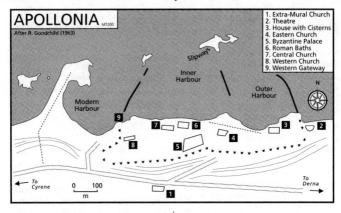

APOLLONIA MT200
After R. Goodchild (1963)

1. Extra-Mural Church
2. Theatre
3. House with Cisterns
4. Eastern Church
5. Byzantine Palace
6. Roman Baths
7. Central Church
8. Western Church
9. Western Gateway

Slipways

Inner Harbour

Outer Harbour

N

Modern Harbour

To Cyrene

0   100
m

To Derna

extensive remains of the **Byzantine Palace** (5). The **Central Church** (7) and **Western Church** (8) are beyond to the W, the latter built up against the ramparts, making use of the wall in its structure. The **Western Gateway** (9), threatened by the encroaching sea, leads nowhere. Further remains lie submerged.

Even though there is nothing of any specific value, the site nevertheless gives an impression of life within the ancient port. Apollonia is also wonderfully situated and a walk around the site is worthwhile.

The **Museum** is situated in the centre of the old town. It is small with a collection of mainly Byzantine mosaics and sculpture. There are also a few Roman and Greek exhibits. The collection is not very rich, reflecting the small amount of work put into excavations at the site. Even so, there is an interesting room on traditional clothes, tools and crafts that provides an insight into the traditional way of life in this part of Libya.

The road from Susa to Derna

This is a very beautiful road following the coast, with the Jabal Al-Akhdar to the right. The coast is mostly rocky but the occasional beach provides a good spot to stop for a swim or a picnic.

Ras Al-Hillal (Crescent Headland) is a small but picturesque village by a rocky cape from which it takes its name. There are few small beaches along the coast from the town. In the town right on the beach there is a hotel, currently being refurbished. The hotel is more of a holiday village, with rooms and bungalows to rent.

Derna

Derna is an important town on the E side of the Jabal. Beautifully situated surrounded by the last hills of the Jabal with the *wadi* lying in the centre, Derna is a delightful town. The E part of the town is mostly new, but the old centre on the W side of the *wadi* is still very pleasing to the eye. From the central square, the covered *suq* goes N with many small streets leading to it. To the W of the *suq* lies the old town with its small streets occasionally leading to tiny squares, still very authentic because still inhabited. The new town has expanded around the old centre and not to the latter's detriment. All the shopping and activity still takes place within the *suqs* and old town. A good time to witness the thriving activity is on a Thur evening, when the entire population seems to congregate in the centre. This is an occasion to have a coffee in the café in the

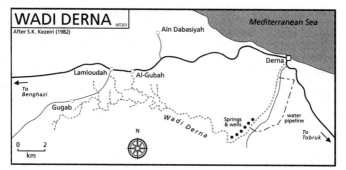

WADI DERNA MT201
After S.K. Kezeiri (1982)

Aïn Dabasiyah

Mediterranean Sea

Derna

Lamloudah
Al-Gubah

To
Benghazi

Gugab

Wadi Derna

Springs
& wells

water
pipeline

To
Tobruk

N

0   2
km

middle of the central square. Also on the square is the *Jabal Al-Akhdar Hotel.*

History

Derna was founded by the Greeks at the time of the Pentapolis. It was not an important town and never became part of the Pentapolis but did develop during the Ptolemaic period. In 96 BC it became part of the Roman Empire, and during the Byzantine period was the episcopate for the region. In 693 AD the Greeks attempted to land and take the region but were pushed back by an army led by Abu Shaddad Zuhayr, who was killed in the fighting and subsequently made a town hero.

Under the Arabs, Derna fell into decay. The harbour was less good than others in the region and situated too far N from the main caravan and trade routes that passed about 90 km S. It was only in the 15th century AD that Derna re-emerged with the arrival of Andalusians, mostly migrating from other North African countries where they had already settled. During this period, Derna was involved in rivalries with Benghazi over trade.

During the Turkish occupation, the Dernawis did not like being ruled from Tripoli, and in 1656 an expedition was sent to quell the inhabitants, resulting in large scale destruction of the town and its population. Under the auspices of the Governor Mohammed Ibn Mahmud in

the 17th century, the town grew with the building of a Great Mosque and the initiation of irrigation works. In 1805, Derna was the scene of a curious event. The town was bombarded by the American Navy in an attempt to prevent pirate attacks against American ships. The Americans had already tried attacking Tripoli but had failed. An overland expedition left from Egypt heading for Tripoli, but never got further than Derna, when an agreement was finally made. During the second Turkish occupation, beginning in 1835, Derna was an important base for controlling the hinterland. Finally, during Italian colonization, the town was expanded and cleaned up, attracting many tourists. During WW2, the town changed hands a number of times and suffered from heavy bombing. Today, Derna is an important economic centre with an expanded harbour. It is also at the centre of an important irrigation project. Two dams have been built 2 km and 15 km upstream on the Wadi Derna and water is transported as far as Tobruk.

Places of interest

In the town there is a small organization called *Haila* run by Mohammed Ahneid that concentrates on preserving the cultural heritage of the town. They have an interesting **museum** with rooms recreating the traditional homes which gives a very good insight into the traditional

THE DESERT WAR 1940-1943

Italy, the colonial power in Libya at the outbreak of WW2, invaded Egypt in the closing weeks of 1940 thus beginning a long period of fighting between the Axis powers and Great Britain in North Africa. Italian and later German strategic plans were the displacement of Britain from Egypt, destruction of Britain's imperial communications links through Suez and the opening up of the Middle East oilfields to Axis penetration. The local Arab and Berber peoples of North Africa played a remarkably small role in events, though royalist Libyan troops joined the British in the final liberation of their country. The damage and disruption of the war were considerable and their negative effects persisted long after the end of hostilities.

The Italians were soon expelled from Egypt and much of eastern Libya but were powerfully reinforced in Tripolitania in Feb 1941 by the arrival of German troops and armour which rapidly drove the British back to the Egyptian frontier by Apr. The German formations were led by Rommel with skill and audacity. Air power favoured the joint German-Italian armies in the earlier part of the campaign. Rommel's eastward advance was slowed by the protracted resistance of the garrisons, first Australian then British and Polish, at Tobruk. Meanwhile, the main armies fought pitched battles around the Libyan-Egyptian border until Rommel withdrew temporarily in Dec 1941. He used his improved lines of communications in the W to prepare a counter attack and pushed E again as far as Gazala, near Derna, in Jan and Feb 1942 and, after a pause, into Tobruk and deep into Egypt in Jun though his advance was finally held at El-Alamein after a fierce battle. Rommel made a final attempt at Alam Halfa, E of El-Alamein, to push aside British and Commonwealth forces and break through to the Nile Valley in Aug 1942 but failed in the face of a strong defensive effort and his own growing losses of men and equipment.

The balance in the desert war was changing in mid-1942 as the Allies gradually won superiority in the air and had more freedom of movement at sea. The Germans and Italians began increasingly to suffer from shortages of equipment, while the health of Field Marshal Rommel gave rise to concern. On the Allied side General Montgomery took over leadership and began a build-up of the Eighth Army sufficient to overwhelm the well trained and experienced Afrika Korps. Montgomery opened his attack at El-Alamein on 23 October 1942 and after 11 days of hard fighting the Axis army was beaten back and retreated by rapid stages to the W to make a last stand in Tunisian territory.

The German attempt to hold on in North Africa was made difficult by sea and airborne landings by Allied, including American, troops in Morocco and Algeria in Nov 1942. These two countries were liberated with ease when French Vichy units, formerly collaborating with the Germans, were brought round to supporting the invasion. German and Italian reinforcements were rushed to Tunis and a battle began to stop the advance of allied units from the W as they fought their way in from Algeria and from the S through Libya. German attacks in the Battle of Kasserine in the hills N of Gafsa during Jan and Feb 1943 almost succeeded in halting Allied progress but when Rommel's final assault on Montgomery's advancing Eighth Army arriving from Libya failed in early Mar, the Axis forces retreated northwards behind the Mareth Line on the Gulf of Gabès before being outflanked and being forced to withdraw by Montgomery's troops. A final set of battles in northern Tunisia saw the Allies push through the Medjerda Valley to Tunis and Bizerte in May 1943, effectively ending Axis resistance in North Africa.

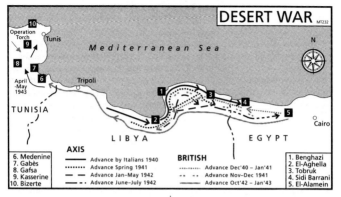

way of life. The organization will also arrange tours of the town and its principal sights as well as the surrounding area. There are a few excellent beaches E of Derna as well as caves in the cliff once inhabited by Christians seeking to escape persecution.

The centre of the town is the most interesting area. Walk around the old town and the *suqs*. The valley of the Wadi Derna is very beautiful. Take the road that follows the river. The road follows an impressive valley, green at the bottom, dry and rocky on the sides. The first of the dams is at the outskirts of the town, the second about 15 km upstream. About 8 km after the first dam, water can be seen pouring out of the rock from an important spring. Continuing up the valley brings you to the last dam, where the landscape begins to look much less cultivable but the panorama definitely gains in beauty.

WW2 Military cemeteries The intensive fighting in the period 1940-43 in North Africa left large numbers of war dead on all sides. There are two Commonwealth war cemeteries, commemorating 6,124 souls, one 7 km E of Tobruk on the Alexandria/El-Adem road and the other, the Knightsbridge War Cemetery, Acroma, 24 km W of Tobruk on the S of the coast road. German war dead, numbering some 6,026,

are interred near Tobruk at El-Adem S of the crossroads in a fort-like structure. The Italian war cemetery of the WW2 period is across the border in Egypt at El-Alamein.

Local information
● **Accommodation**
D/E *Jabal Al-Akhdar Hotel*, T 081 22303, very beautiful entrance with mosaic tiled floor, the rest is awful.

E *Hotel Al-Bahr*, on the seafront, basic, clean, cheap, shared bath, good restaurant.

● **Youth hostel**
5 km W of centre, 200 beds, meals, kitchen, family rooms, laundry.

● **Transport**
Air Tobruk to Tripoli Tues, Thur, Fri, Sat at 1015 and Mon at 1430. Takes 1¼ hrs and costs LD44.

Road Bus: there are frequent buses to towns all around the country. There are few fixed timetables, but most buses leave early in the morning. The General Transport Company has a bus to **Benghazi** at 0800. The bus from Benghazi to Derna leaves at the same time.

To Egypt

From Derna, the road E leads to Solum and the Egyptian border. Formalities at the Egyptian border are few but it is busy and can be very hot. There are few reliable facilities there so travellers should be prepared to be self-sufficient until they reach Marsa Matruh in Egypt.

FEZZAN

CONTENTS	
Fezzan	550
MAPS	
Fezzan	551

The third of the great historic provinces of Libya is Fezzan, a region spreading over some 684,280 sq km of desert lands in the SW of the country. The bulk of Fezzan is made up of uninhabited sand seas and deserts interspersed with gravel and stone plains. In the N and the E of Fezzan there are extensive areas of stone desert called *hammada*. Sabha, the capital, is the hub of the transport system in Fezzan and travellers can move to all key sites from there.

Sabha

Within the desert areas are a number of great *wadis* which give human access and have a modest availability of underground water. The two main dry *wadi* beds are the Al-Shatti and the Al-Ajal (Al-Hayyah). A shallow topographic basin around Murzuq also gives access to sub-surface water at shallow depths.

There are dry salt lakes or *sabkhas* throughout the region, the greatest number being found in the Wadi Shatti and the Hofra-Sharqiya zone. The highest part of Fezzan lies in the Tibesti Mountain area, a huge uplifted massif in the Uzu region running to altitudes of 3,376m in the extreme SE of the system. Deeply incised *wadi* valleys are clearly vegetated and rich in animal and plant life. Lower elevations are reached in Jabal As-Soda, 840m and 1200m in the Jabal Al-Haruj Al-Aswad.

Climate

The climate of Fezzan is hot and dry. Everywhere is arid and desertic. Rainfall is slight and irregular at 8.3 mm per year, often falling as an occasional heavy downpour. Heavy rain storms bring chaos to transport and can lead to extensive damage to property with flash floods and disintegrating walls of traditional buildings. Temperatures are high during the day with no cloud cover, allowing rapid cooling at night. Daily ranges in temperature of 40°C are possible. Temperatures are higher in the summer with the Jun mean monthly temperature at 30.6°C in the regional capital, Sabha. Spring and particularly Jan is a better time to travel when average temperatures fall to 11.6°C. Winds can be severe in the desert, with westerlies dominating the winter and easterly/northerlies the summer. Fezzan experiences the *ghibli* wind in the form of a very hot, dry and uncomfortable blast of several days' duration. Transport can be disrupted during the *ghibli*.

Population

Human settlement was possible only

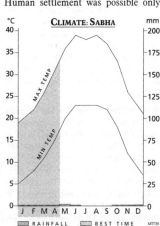

FEZZAN MT202

where water could be reached easily by primitive technology in the Wadis Ajal and Shatti and in the Murzuq basin. Even here the densities of human populations were thin and villages widely scattered. Recent economic development has, despite enormous expenditures of cash and effort, made little difference to this underlying pattern. In 1980 the population was estimated at 190,265 of which only 165,245 were Libyan nationals. The population was growing at 5.1% annually, mainly through inward migration by foreigners from countries such as Chad and Sudan. Non-Libyans represented 13% of the population of Fezzan at that time, a figure which has since gone up by at least 50%.

The indigenous peoples are dark-skinned but of Arab extraction. The Tibu and the Tuareg tribes have some Arab characteristics but are otherwise of separate origin. The Tuareg have their own, Berber-related, language of Tamashek. In recent years some have settled in towns. The Fezzanese are known as friendly and hospitable people. Only the Tibu, a tall and very dark group from the Tibesti, are unreliable in their treatment of strangers. A number of Europeans have been taken hostage in the Tibesti, though never within Libyan Tibesti. *Great care* is needed in travelling in Tibesti since it is isolated, difficult of access, bleakly inhospitable in its climate and unpoliced over very large areas.

Economy

The economy of Fezzan was traditionally dependent on oasis agriculture, some pastoral herding among the Tuareg and trans-Saharan trade. In recent years this has entirely changed as a result of oil revenues and the growing influence of the central authorities in Tripoli. Employment now depends on the state more than on traditional activities. No less than 80% of people rely on government generated services for a living. Agriculture employs a mere 7% and trade another 10%. Perhaps as much as 90% of all regional income comes from the government. The cause of the skew in the economy is directly related to the nature of oil income which is spent by the government. Investment by the government ran at US$7,000 per head of population in the region in the late 1970s and early 1980s, though it has since fallen significantly. Libyans have tended to give up active involvement in farming and employ foreigners. In services and construction foreigners make up over 80% of the work force.

Agriculture

This is known to have been practised in this region since the 5th century BC when the Garamantes used a form of irrigation in areas adjacent to Ghat. Agriculture was largely self-sufficient but was also designed to provide surpluses to feed passing caravan traffic. The main crops have always been barley and wheat in the winter and millet, sorghum and maize in the summer, together with vegetables and fruits in great variety. Forage crops were vital both for keeping animals on the farm and for providing food for the passing caravan trade. Farms are generally tiny and fragmented into small parcels. Including unused and unirrigated lands, average farm sizes at 7 ha were less than half of that for the rest of the country. Each irrigated plot is carefully levelled, provided with water and sheltered from the wind with palm frond hedges or mud walls. The main commercial field crops are tomatoes and onions, both of which are exported to the N. Fezzan produces more than two thirds of all dates in Libya

at 86,523 tonnes per year from no less than 4,649,936 trees. Olives, grapes, figs and oranges are also grown among a vast range of fruits. Sheep and goats are the main animals kept, the richest grazing zone being the Wadi Shatti. The number of camels (dromedaries) is falling rapidly as they are no longer used for transport or ploughing. Some development of cattle herding for milk production is underway.

Modern agricultural estates have sprung up throughout the region and are easily recognized by their straight boundaries and regularly laid out facilities. The biggest projects include those at Maknusa and Wadi Aril which are principally designed to produce grain and fodder. They are basically agribusinesses run with large amounts of capital but few employees. Occasionally they have attracted local herders who make use of the fodder for their livestock. A second category of development estates is the settlement farm where small farms are set up within large estates run initially by government agencies. Farmers are recruited to take over the farms. There has been friction from time to time as locals have resented incoming farmers. The presence of estates means fresh water, electricity and telephones but not necessarily accommodation for the traveller.

Industry

By definition, industry in Fezzan is poorly developed. The resource base is weak but there are some oil and natural gas deposits in the extreme W and some iron ores in the Wadi Shatti. But these resources are most easily used in the N and at best will represent primary exports. Small workshops have grown up in Fezzan but they are mainly concerned with servicing government activities and construction, with mechanical workshops, building materials and food processing jobs dominating the sector. For the traveller it will be worthwhile looking out for the *local glass making plant* at Brak, the *handicraft centre* at Ghat and the *leather factory* at Traghan.

Access and travel in the province

Access to Fezzan is limited by the few international entry points. Most travellers will have to come through Tripoli, though there is the chance to enter directly from Niger and Algeria. Similarly, the internal access points are either via the airports at Sabha and Ghat or along the main roads to Sabha from the N of the country.

There are two main lines of road entry to Fezzan. The first is the traditional route from the coast at Bu Grayn via the Jufra region to Sabha and the second is the new road from just outside Gharyan via Mizdah. Significant resources have been expended in Libya to improve the road system and the main highways are by and large in good condition and constantly being supplemented by new spurs. The road system in Fezzan (see below) covers the main economic and strategic axes.

Road system of the Fezzan

Key Routes	Journey Length (km)	time (min)
Sabha – Traghan	128	100
Sabha – Obari	200	150
Edri – Brak – Ashkida	147	120
Murzuq – Zuwaylah	136	105
Obari – Ghat	370	300
Umm Al-Araneb – Qatrun	150	125

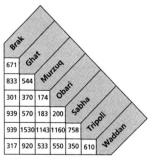

Fezzan: distances by road between major cities (Km)

The main road system is fast and served by buses and taxis on regular scheduled/on demand routes. The buses are cheap but taxis can be expensive over long distances. The driving at times can be careless and even harrowing. Travel at cool times of day and use a/c buses when available. At present only the key routes between Sabha and Tripoli are served by super-express services. The bus services are important because the air link is crowded, infrequent and inconvenient. Buses give a cheap and easy way to continue a journey rather than put up with long stays in oasis towns.

The bus station in Sabha, the main transport hub for the area, is in the Jabeya district. Its facilities are very basic. Almost all long distance bus services run from Sabha usually on a once-a-day basis for major routes and alternate days or a lesser frequency for other services. The inter-urban taxi services are always available and are normally on, or adjacent to, the main street of each town.

Since travellers in Fezzan will find their lives dominated by the transport facilities, a distance matrix of main centres in the region is given below. The distances between centres are considerable and, even on the bus or in a taxi, you should take enough food, drink and clothing to manage through very hot and very cold conditions. A breakdown can cause long waits for which travellers should be well prepared, especially on some of the long inter-settlement roads in the S.

Places of interest

Topography Fezzan offers endless but varied desert landscapes. A good relief map is essential to make the best of this experience. Secondly, there are a few small sites to visit, some living oases, others archaeological monuments or remains. The oases are best grouped into areas for visiting. The smaller ones should be visited with a guide if unwelcome attention or suspicion is not to be aroused especially by male groups. In the Wadi Al-Ajal (Al-Hayyah) there are still comparatively unspoiled villages such as Bent Bayah to the W where magnificent forms of traditional architecture are still in use. In Ghat there are still strings of small traditional settlements worthy of a half day visit with a translator. Similar villages exist as populated or recently abandoned sites throughout the province. The further they are from the developed centres, the more interesting the villages become, though some, like Umm Al-Araneb, have undergone a total population change in recent times.

The **architecture** in Fezzan is highly individualistic. Houses are built of sun-dried mud bricks in most regions, though near rocky outcrops flat natural stone can be incorporated into the buildings with mud rendering on both sides. Most houses are single-storey. The flat roofs are constructed with palm wood cross members covered with palm fronds sealed with a beaten mud coating. Ornamentation is provided on the roof corners by a triangular motif in which two flat bricks are leaned against each other above a horizontal brick or stone. This emblem is used in a variety of forms either as a single unit or in combination along the top of a wall. Doorways can be highly decorated, often with calligraphic or symbolic representations above the main door to the house. Some houses carry horn-shaped fixtures above their entrances, thought to be against the effects of the evil eye. Painting is rare except to highlight a doorway and it is usually the religious buildings which carry white or blue washes. Variations of style are noticeable throughout Fezzan.

The minarets of mosques in Fezzan are also distinctive and worth looking out for. They are often square-shaped and only slightly raised above the level of single-storeyed mosques, usually painted white. A complex and beautiful three-tiered mosque of this kind exists at Obari. Other fine mosques can be found, and **Zuwaylah** is worth calling at to see its **mosque**, the ruins of an associated **fort** and the 12th century tombs of Beni El-Khattab, square constructions of mud bricks faced with stone. Some of the Turkish stone forts survive and the Murzuq fort can be seen in the centre of the new town.

The archaeological sites
Fezzan is rich in pre-historic sites where well-preserved cave paintings can be viewed. The main sites are: (1) **Akakus** and **Tashinat** where there are excellent wall carvings; (2) in the **Wadi Fuet** close to Ghat there are a number of coloured wall paintings; (3) **Zinkekra** in the W Garma area where there are rock carvings; (4) **Wadi Buzna**. The artwork depicting antelope, elephant and giraffe-like animals and human hunters dates from 6000-3000 BC.

Libya is famous for the **Garamantian** civilization of the Wadi Al-Ajal. The centre was **Garma**, established about 2000 BC, and only rediscovered in the 1960s. A series of ruins and sites are open for visitors to the Wadi Al-Ajal. The city of Germa is a clear attraction, lying close to Obari just off the Sabha road. Nearby are the tombs of Saniat Jebril and Ben Howaidi. Other tombs and cemeteries include the tombs of Ahramat Al-Hatiyah, the royal cemetery to the S of Jarma, the cemeteries at Bent Bayah and Budrinnah, and Al-Khareyk, the latter W of Garagra. There are the remains of forts at Al-Abiad and Al-Gullah. The full range of urban life is not yet known since excavations at the site have not been finished.

All Libyan monuments are open 0800-1700 and are normally closed on Tues. In Fezzan there is a certain informality over working hours and even the guardianship of sites. Local guides will see that you review the full extent of the known ruins but often travellers will be on their own. Care is needed to treat the sites well and not to take artifacts. Urban monuments, especially mosques, need a low key approach with permission asked before entering. Again, having a local Fezzanese with you can make a great deal of difference to your reception. Housing of interest will either be a prepared tourist site without a family in residence as at Bent Bayah or must be approached with care if there are women resident. There are rarely facilities of any kind at the Fezzanese archaeological sites.

Obari lakes

A strange site, signposted off the only main road to the N and well worth travelling a short distance to see is that of the Obari lakes. About 13 small lakes exist in the Obari sand sea sited between the great dunes of the system. The main lakes are **Mandara** 200-300m diameter, lake **Umm Al-Ma'**, which usually has water throughout the year, **Bahar Al-Daud** 300m diameter, **Tademsha, Umm Al-Hassan**, **Neshnusha**, **Bahar Al-Trunia, Frejia** and **Oudnei**. They are fed by ground water from the sand sea when the water table builds up in the dune systems. Most are very shallow, less than a metre, and many dry up during the summer. The water is very brackish in the lakes but water drawn from the dunes can be used in irrigation and for human consumption. There is a myth in Libya that the lakes area was populated by people who were 'worm-eaters', a belief arising from the local custom of eating shrimps taken from the lakes. Not surprisingly, local people do not take kindly to the 'worm-eating' story!

Excursions

A first approach to an area as widespread but thinly populated as Fezzan is to take the major geographical axes along the excellent road system. The main elements can be taken in using the following routes: **(1) Brak – Edri** along the Wadi Al-Shatti giving access to the old town of Brak, the S rim of the Hammadah Al-Hamra and the small traditional settlements of the valley; **(2) Sabha to Obari** along the line of the Wadi Al-Ajal taking in the traditional villages and the Garamantian sites; **(3)** the **Murzuq – Zuwaylah** road with more Garamantian remains, the fort at Murzuq, the mosque at Zuwaylah and the old and new towns at Umm Al-Araneb and **(4)** either by road or air, a visit to **Ghat and the SW corner of Libya**, one of the most unspoiled and rewarding areas of the country for the traveller.

In addition to this overall travel scheme, some specific **organized excursions** are available through the travel agencies, the most active for Fezzan as a whole being in the *Akakus Tours*, see page 556.

Fezzan tour includes trips to the old villages of *Ghat* and down to the *Wadi Ayadar* and to *Takhakhori*. The visitor travels through the desert of the *Msak Mallat* and *Msak Satafet* to look at the country and some ancient sites and also crosses one of the world's great sand seas, *Erg Murzuq*. The caravan then goes to the *Wadi Matkhandus* to look at wall engravings and to the *Wadi Berjuj* before arriving at *Murzuq city. Zuwaylah* and the sand dune lakes are visited. There is also a full scale visit to the ruins of *Garma* before returning via Al-Awenat to Ghat. The visit can be tailored to individual or group requirements to run between 7 nights to 13 nights under bivouac.

Teshuinat tour This takes the traveller in 4WD vehicles and under canvas through the *Akakus mountains*, and the immediately surrounding sand seas, to look in at *Ghat*, *Al-Awenat* and the extreme SW corner of Fezzan. The circuit lasts for between 3 and 5 nights and includes a visit to the cave painting sites of that region.

Discover Libya tour offers a very varied set of packages of as short as 3 nights and as long as 17 nights. Again, travel is in 4WD vehicles and accommodation mainly in tents. It begins in *Tripoli* then moves along the Mediterranean coast through *Leptis Magna* and then *Sabrata* to the W borders to track down through *Nalut* on the western Jabal to *Ghadames*, a long cross-desert run to *Sabha* and on to the principal sites in *Fezzan*.

Central Saharan expeditions Akakus have arranged with the authorities in Algeria and Niger to take visitors across the international border to visit all the major central *Saharan cave painting sites*. The excursion is imaginative and unusual, taking in *Ghat* and *Tumu* in Libya, *Djanet* in Algeria and *Madama* and *Bilma* and *Agadez* in Niger. This is an exciting chance to see this previously difficult region in a 21 night tour which enters via Libya and leaves via Niger or vice versa. A more limited route through Libya and Algeria to the sites in those two countries takes between 7 and 17 nights depending on how many sites are taken into the itinerary.

Given the costs and administrative difficulties of setting up desert visits to this part of the world, *Akakus Tours* offer of desert expeditions is extremely attractive. Other tour operators are being set up. The largest in Tripoli is the *Libyan Travel & Tourism Company*, T 21 48005/48011 F 21 43455. Their desert tours in Fezzan include a 15 day desert visit from Tripoli to the S flying from Tripoli to Sabha and thereafter by 4WD vehicle to Gabroun and Mandara sand dune lakes, and on to Garma and Wadi Berjuj. The itinerary goes to the Matkhandus prehistoric painting sites and then across the Murzuq sand sea to Gassi Ohabran, the Wadi Selfoufet in the Akakus and finally to Ghat, returning to Tripoli via Sabha by air.

Privately organized groups in 4WD vehicles or on desert motor cycles enjoy travelling this area. The more common itineraries are from Ghadames E to Darj, SE on the desert tracks to Idri and on to Brak perhaps returning N from here to the coast or else travelling S to Sabha then W to Obari and Ghat. From here the route is N adjacent to the Algerian border back to Ghadames. This last leg 450 km across the Hamadat al Hamrah plateau, windy, bleak and with extremes of temperature (-15°C at night) is not well defined and not to be undertaken lightly.

Local information
● Accommodation
The tourist potential of Fezzan has been neglected almost entirely. The obvious attractions of desert travel, of the unique nature of the less 'developed' oases and of the archaeological sites were overlooked. Few hotel facilities exist in general, and very few have been constructed with travellers from overseas in mind. There are only 400 or less hotel beds of a satisfactory kind available in the whole of Fezzan. The main hotels are in Sabha and include a new Social Insurance Tourist Centre, **B** *Hotel Al-Fatah*.

The **E** *Al-Galah Hotel*, rather run down, 57 rm, 114 beds; **E** *Mountain Hotel*, small, 19 rm, 38 beds. There are also rest houses in Sabha owned by official organizations to which access can only normally be obtained with the help of official letters of introduction from Tripoli. Other hotels include the new Hotel at Hun, where the old *Tourist Hotel* still functions, though parts of it seem to have been given over to foreign labourers. An 11-year-old hotel exists at Ghat and rest house facilities are available if not already occupied – ask for information at the Municipality building. It is best to telephone for a booking before arrival in Ghat to *Akakus Tours*, though they normally accommodate their guests in bivouacs. Small guest houses exist at Ghat, Traghan, Hun, Hammera and Garma but their facilities are limited and cannot be guaranteed to be available.

● Youth hostels
1) *Sabha*, Gamal Abdel Nasser St, 3 km E of town centre, T 27337, 160 beds, family rooms, laundry, meals, kitchen, open 0700-2300. 2) *Ghat*, 40 beds, kitchen, meals, T (72) 32360. 3) *Hun*, 50 beds, kitchen, T (57) 3379. 4) *Waddan*, T (580) 2310, 160 beds, meals available, laundry, family rooms, booking rec

Sep-Nov;. **5) Murzuq**, T 62, former *Murzuq Tourist Hotel*, 30 beds, with breakfast, kitchen. **6) Umm Al-Araneb**, T (72) 62228, 120 km from Sabha, 90 km from Murzuq, 30 beds, with breakfast, kitchen. **7) Fejeaj**, People's Housing Project, 60 km from Sabha, 40 beds, meals, kitchen, T (71) 28323.

● **Camping**
Is unlimited in the desert, though the security services do not look kindly on wild camping by foreigners unless supervised by a Libyan agency. Individual campers should either be discreet in their overnight stops, providing all their needs from their own resources, or ask permission from tourist agencies/local authority *baladiyah* offices in the nearest town. Often school or college facilities can be used by travellers.

There is a growth industry in camping in the S though this is under official auspices. In the SW, *Akakus Tours*, T 0724 2804/2318, Tx 2938 Ghat, (General Manager, A Younis, home T 0724 2938) offers visits to the major archaeological sites of the region, especially Garma, under canvas. They will reserve travel to and from Libya, make hotel reservations in Libya, assist travel groups with handling arrangements on site. They offer a number of separate trips, one to Murzuq, Ghat, Obari, Al-Awenat over 8-13 nights, another through Teshuinat in the extreme SE of Ghat over 3-6 nights and another to a 21-night visit through the Libyan-Niger borderlands. These desert circuits are designed for fairly rich and very fit Europeans and are an excellent introduction to parts of the Sahara which have been virtually closed to all but a few specialists for the last 20 years.

● **Places to eat**
Eating out in Fezzan is a rather limited experience because local Fezzanese rarely eat outside their own homes. Restaurants and cafeterias do exist adjacent to the hotels and guest houses. In Sabha, Brak and Obari, the range of facilities is acceptable, with two or three eating places available. Cooking is basic and to local or Arab tastes with either rice or macaroni as its basis except in the few new hotels where forms of international cuisine can be found. In the summer heat, cooking is scarcely worthwhile and there is cold or tinned food available from the small private shops at a comparatively high price. The tourist agencies normally provide their clients with food cooked by their own staff. Eating in private homes is to be encouraged where invitations are received. Here the food is varied, wholesome and often interesting.

● **Banks & money changers**
Few banking points in Fezzan deal with foreign exchange, especially any slightly unusual currency or TCs. Use the main banks in Sabha on the main street or, as a second and not always reliable best, the big hotels which usually have a small branch of a bank in-house.

● **Entertainment**
In Fezzan is limited to visiting friends' houses and having the occasional formal civic reception. Otherwise there are a few cafés and restaurants which stay open while customers remain. Most towns have a cinema with films in Arabic. Sports centres, nightclubs and other tourist attractions are altogether absent. For sport, the younger locals play volleyball and football.

● **Hospitals & medical services**
Chemists: most small settlements have pharmacies, but it is wise in Fezzan to travel with a comprehensive first aid kit and any personal medical drugs needed. Chemists shops are to be found in all centres and even small villages will have clinics of sorts with some medical drugs available. As elsewhere in Libya, people with special needs should ensure that they carry adequate supplies.

Hospitals: Fezzan is well served by health centres, clinics and dispensaries. Hospital facilities are spread thinly, not surprising in a landscape of very distant settlements and low population densities. There are principal hospitals at Murzuq, Obari, Sabha, Al-Shatti and Sawkenah, that is in each district. Some of the smaller hospitals have limited staffing and facilities. On average Fezzan has half the health provision that other parts of the country enjoy. The traveller is warned that, together with a road accident rate far higher than the rest of the country, the overall record of which is very bad in any case, health repatriation insurance is more than usually important.

● **Shopping**
In the Fezzan can be much more rewarding than in all other parts of Libya other than Ghadames. The leatherwork of the region, especially at Ghat, is excellent if at times quaintly crude in finish. The main traditional items are leather handled and sheathed knives, short spears/arrows and Arab slippers of ornate design. Woven date palm fronds are used to

make a variety of matting products from fruit basins and rice trays to place mats. Tuareg and other ladies' ornaments are interesting and there is some glasswork. An attempt to resurrect the carpet industry is underway and some patterns are plain but effective.

● **Tour companies & travel agents**
There are many **LAA** offices in Tripoli for travelling to Fezzan. The head office at Sharah Haiti, POB 2555, Tripoli, Sales T 606833/36. In Fezzan, LAA has offices at Sabha T 071 23876, at Ghat T 0724 2035 and at Hun T 057 2456. In Ghat, **Akakus Tours**, T 0724 2804.

● **Transport**
Local Bus: within the larger towns access can either be by bus or taxi. Distances are very short since no town is large except Sabha. All the town centres or hotels and the airports are served by bus. **Car hire**: self-drive car hire is difficult though this can occasionally be arranged through a travel agent. More normally arrange for a car, preferably a 4WD vehicle if you are visiting sites off the road, with a driver. This can be expensive and rentals of LD100-LD200 per day are not uncommon. There are many mechanical workshops in the main towns which can repair and service vehicles.

Some of the work is rough and ready but most makes of vehicle can be handled. Fuel is available in the main towns and most small villages. Drivers should always set off with a full tank and adequate spare fuel to reach the next large town rather than the next petrol station. Shortages of fuel do occur at individual stations from time to time. **Cycle hire**: hire of cycles and motorcycles is not normal though some repair shops will lease them, but not cheaply or readily. **Taxi**: this can be expensive and prices should be negotiated in advance where possible. (See also Access and travel, page 553.)

Air There are regional airports at **Sabha, Ghat, Hun** and **Uzu**, though only Sabha has facilities for international flights. The airport is on the fringe of the town next to the old Turkish fort area. It has been rebuilt as a regional/international airport. The passenger reception facilities are fair. Scheduled international air services to Sabha, when permitted, include flights from Accra, Alexandria, Casablanca, Damascus, Khartoum, and Ndjemena. Flights into **Sabha** are mainly by Libyan Arab Airlines. To **Tripoli** Wed and Sat at 1500, takes 1 1/4 hrs. Booking well in advance is essential.

AL-KHALIJ

CONTENTS	
Al-Khalij	559
MAPS	
Al-Khalij	560
Al-Jaghbub	563

Al-Khalij (the Gulf) takes its name from the Gulf of Sirte. The province is an artificial creation of recent years and includes the Sirtican coastal embayment together with the routes to and from the entire SE quadrant of the country down to the Egyptian border S of 28°N and the Sudanese border E of 16°30'E. The area of the province is estimated at 730,960 sq km. The province was intended in the period after the coup d'état of 1969 to unite the centre of the country and give a political bloc strong enough to offset the traditional domination of Tripolitania and Cyrenaica. In fact, it has remained as an enormous no man's land around the Gulf of Sirte with a long tail S into the desert, the oases of which retain their individuality from the coastlands to which they were attached.

Climate

In this region the climate is in general Saharan. There are still inadequate data to give precise definitions of microclimate over this very large region. Extreme temperatures run at well over 50°C and lows of well below freezing are experienced, especially at night. Rain is very rare but can come occasionally in downpours inducing flash floods and surface erosion over limited areas. The coast, especially around Sirt, gets a rainfall of more than 100 mm, though this is very erratic and rare wet years are followed by many years of drought.

Land

The Libyan Desert covers the territory between the 18° and 29° parallels N and the 18° and 28° meridians E. Its N limits are marked by the marginal settlement at Siwa in Egypt and Al-Jaghbub and Gialo in Libya. It comprises a vast sedimentary depression formed of limestones and marine origin clays. The area forms a flat platform with the strata tilted slightly to the N. The only high relief is in the Jabal Al-Awenat in the extreme SE where heights of 1,908m are attained at the Libyan-Egyptian-Suda-

CLIMATE: AL-KHALIJ

	Sirt	Ajdabiyah	Gialo	Al-Kufrah
Mean annual minimum °C	8.6	7.3	6.3	4.8
Extreme minimum °C	2.4	0.0	-2.0	-3.3
Mean annual maximum °C	31.0	33.7	37.8	38.9
Extreme maximum °C	46.7	46.7	49.1	46.0
Relative humidity %	51-84	45-82	26-61	11-61
Mean annual rainfall mm	180.8	126.9	9.2	1.9
Maximum monthly rainfall mm	215.7	102.6	26.2	11.2
Maximum annual rainfall mm	429.5	227.6	50.3	11.9
Minimum annual rainfall mm	6.7	3.4	1.0	0.0

Source: *Speerplan*

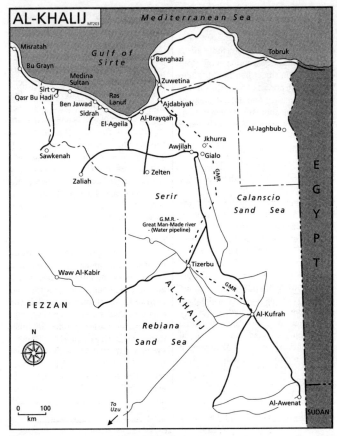

nese border tripoint. The visible topography of the desert is dominated by sand, mainly in the form of dunes in the Jaghbub sand sea and elsewhere gravel desert such as the Serir Calanscio. Al-Khalij includes two other major sand seas, those of Calanscio, to the W of Serir Calanscio, and Rebiana, in the SW of Al-Khalij. The coast is also a desert, the Sirt desert made up of a low broken plateau.

The N coastlands are open to access from the sea and the sides. Southern Al-Khalij on the contrary has histori- cally been, and still remains, difficult of entry from outside. Until the 1980s there was no permanent all-weather highway between the main settlement of the S, Al-Kufrah, and the N coast. Even now a single black top road acts as the link between the two very separate sections of the province, traversing 876 km from Ajdabiyah to Al-Kufrah.

Population

The Libyan population of Al-Khalij is very small, at best 175,000 and possibly as low as 165,000 in 1990 with a further

40,000-45,000 foreign migrant workers. These estimates are very imprecise. Growth rates for the area have generally fallen according to UN data to about 3% per year, with the exception of the main coastal urban site at Ben Jawad, where 5.5% growth prevails. Overall, it appears that the country and inland areas of Al-Khalij are approximately maintaining their population size while losing many of their younger people to the coast and to the cities outside the region. The populations of the coastal sub-regions are very concentrated in the urban settlements. In the S the population is also clustered in small villages for security, except on modern farm estates where, incongruously, farms are laid out geometrically across the desert landscape in the teeth of regional social traditions.

Industry

The main towns of the province are the centres of the oil industry at Al-Brayqah, Ras Lanuf and Zuwetina. The only exceptions are Ajdabiyah and Sirt. The former is a route centre where the road from the S joins the coast. Ajdabiyah district contains approximately half the population of the Al-Khalij region, about 100,000 persons, by far the majority in the town area itself. Inland, the main towns are Al-Kufrah, Gialo-Awjilah and Tizerbu, all very small. The new coastal towns and the modern extensions to the S oases are dispersed and reliant on motor transport for communication between the different parts of the town. On the coast, the oil towns are well planned and the residential districts are made up of two areas, first the concentrated bungalow towns set up by foreign oil companies for their employees and second, modern towns built by the Libyan authorities at great expense for civil servants and other services. The oil towns are strung along and adjacent to the coastal highway.

The local economy

In Al-Khalij, this comprises agriculture and government services. Approximately 25% of the work force is employed in agricultural pursuits and perhaps 30% in government services. Agriculture is, for Libyans, a part-time activity. The males in Al-Khalij work with a government agency and also labour or manage their own farms in their, often generous, spare time. There are 42,500 ha under cultivation, of which about 11,000 ha is irrigated. Most dryland cultivation and livestock herding is concentrated along the coast, where the rainfall is slightly better and more reliable than the interior.

Inland farming is oasis-based in small fields with associated palmeries. Modern sector large settlement projects have been developed at great expense, the Al-Kufrah project running into several billions of US$. The units are capital intensive, based on water lifted from deep within the Nubian sandstones. The deep wells fed 100 x 100 ha circles of land with water through an automated mobile-rotating arm sprinkler system. They were used first for growing fodder for sheep. The costs were unsupportable and the project was turned over to grain production. Technical and economic problems continued and the units were eventually run down and many abandoned with water switched to supply the Great Manmade River Scheme (GMR).

A settlement scheme was also devised for Al-Kufrah, comprising 5,500 ha of hexagons each made up of 16 farms. The history of the settlement scheme is sad and expensive. Libyans by and large ignored the project and costs ran out of control against a small return in agricultural produce. Other production projects of a comparable kind were put in hand further N at Serir and were also beset by environmental and economic problems. Settlement schemes at Gialo and Tizerbu were also attempted. The residual areas of cultivation can still be seen in these various sites.

Private sector commerce was always important in the province, tied into participation in trans-Saharan caravan traffic. In the period since liberalization of the economy there has been a return by Libyans to shopkeeping, commerce and small-scale manufacturing.

However it is **oil** and **natural gas** which dominate the economy of Al-Khalij. Oil and gas fields are located in the N section of the province, the materials being pumped to the coast where they are exported as crude hydrocarbons or refined. There are many oil-related industries in the region. There is a gas processing plant and oil refinery at Al-Brayqah and another old small refinery at Zuwetina. New refinery capacity has been added at Ras Lanuf, while petrochemical units have been set up at Al-Brayqah, Ras Lanuf and Marada. Installations associated with the oil industry spread deep into the Sirtican embayment towards Waha, Mejid and Serir oilfields.

Al-Khalij's **water resources** are from three sources, groundwater, surface *wadi* flow and seawater desalination plants. The coastal zone has a limited and much depleted shallow aquifer. In the S there are very large deep aquifers in the Old Nubian sandstones within the 2 million sq km of the Al-Kufrah basin. The strength of these S reserves is uncertain and it is likely that extraction at present rates will be sustained for only 50 years or so. In the early 1980s it was decided to transfer water from the Al-Kufrah Basin to the N coastlands through a large diameter concrete pipeline, the Great Manmade River, costing some US$7bn or more. The GMR runs from the S water fields to the coast near to Ajdabiyah and from there along the coast towards Benghazi and Sirt. The object of the line is advertised as principally for agriculture but it is thought by many experts that the bulk of water will only be utilized economically in urban water supply and for industrial end use. The GMR has been the largest development project in Libya for the last decade and the future of Libyan agriculture will rest on how the water is put to use.

Zuwetina is a small, formerly agricultural, centre now overwhelmed by the growth of the oil industry in its vicinity and the influx of foreign workers. The old settlement is sited off the highway to the N, where there are still farmed gardens and some fishing.

The **oases of the S** were never heavily populated. They acted as stopover points for the trans-Saharan caravans. Al-Kufrah was in fact a set of scattered palm grove villages in a large low plain in which water seepages occurred. Recent changes have resulted in considerable building activity both for new agricultural estates on the perimeter of the settlements and administrative, military and other buildings, often rather unsympathetic in architecture.

Tizerbu (see also page 566), has recently been developed, formerly being no more than a fuelling and water point on the route from the S and W Sahara to Al-Kufrah and Ajdabiyah. It now has most services including garages, fuel and a chemist together with urban services such as telephones, piped water, clinics and electricity. It is of little other merit. The **Gialo group of oases** are scattered around water holes some 250 km from Ajdabiyah. Originally very pretty with traditional farms and well laid out palm groves, Gialo-Awjilah had some development of settlement farms and administrative services. It has fuel, water and limited urban facilities and is well worth a visit (see Places of interest, page 565).

ACCESS Al-Khalij is reached mainly from adjacent provinces, though there are direct links in from Chad and Sudan, controlled by the military and not recommended both for that reason and because of the problem of finding safe transport overland. **Air** In normal times

AL-JAGHBUB

Mediterranean Sea

Derna
Al-Bayda
Al-Marj
Benghazi
Tobruk
Jabal Al-Akhdar
Ajdabiyah
Al-Jaghbub
N
0   100
km
Awjilah
MT196

international flights come to Al-Khalij, mainly via Tripoli or Benghazi, although lateral entry is possible direct from Algiers or via Sabha or other airports when there are external links open for the entry of foreigners. On internal airlines, Sirt links directly with Tripoli, Benghazi and Sabha, while Al-Kufrah links directly with Benghazi only. **Road** Access is from the N and still principally via the coastal highway coming in from Tripoli to the W and Cyrenaica to the E. Ajdabiyah is then the gateway S to Al-Kufrah. New roads have been built across the Sirtican embayment to support the oil industry, some pasture-land developments and military/strategic objectives by providing a second land link between the two main parts of the country and reducing reliance of the exposed coast road. The main artery to the W comes in from Bu Grayn via Waddan and Zella through Marada eventually reaching Al-Brayqah and Gialo. A continuation of this road project continues E to Al-Jaghbub, hugging the N edge of the Libyan sand desert and thence leading N to Tobruk. A second road leads from Tobruk to the S of the Jabal Al-Akhdar the 400 km to Ajdabiyah via Bir Ghiymah. The traveller should be aware that there are a number of roads leading S from the coastal highway at Sidrah, Ras Lanuf and through Bir Zelten. These are private roads run by the oil companies for servicing their oil fields and facilities. They should not be used except with specific permission as trespass might be misinterpreted as a threat to the security of the oil fields. **Sea** Theoretically, passengers from ships docking in the ports

of Al-Khalij could enter by that route but, other than for sailors taking rare and limited shore leave, this is not open for most travellers.

Places of interest

The great deserts of Al-Khalij have an attraction of their own, though they are at least over large areas heavily visited by commercial activities connected with oil and water developments. Even the extreme S is no longer terra incognita in that a major war between Libya and Chad was fought across this region in the period 1980-90. The very light human settlement of the province in past centuries has meant that there is little of human interest by way of monuments to see. Rather, there is a limited number of small oasis sites with a certain charm. Only the dedicated and highly inquisitive traveller can be encouraged to traverse vast distances in Al-Khalij to visit them.

Local information
● Accommodation

Facilities for travellers and tourists in Al-Khalij are minimal. This, after all, is the country's oil producing area and there are deemed to be few sights that a bona fide tourist would wish to see. Even the official tours run by semi-state agencies steer clear of this area. Provisions are for oil workers, workers in the water industry and for service personnel. Most accommodation, transport and entertainment is dedicated to a specific company workforce. There are some hotels but very few that cater for travellers. Ajdabiyah has a number of rest houses and cheap hotels for migrant Arab workers. They are basic but can be serviceable. The traveller to Al-Khalij must be adaptable and willing to accept hospitality where he/she can find it or get official hospitality from a secretariat or other official agency before entering the region. The modest privatization of the economy is opening up better prospects for the availability of accommodation but the easiest way for travellers is to ask at the *baladiyah* (local council) offices for a room in the school dormitory or the youth hostel.

● Youth hostel

Sirt on Sharah Sawadah, 2 km N of town centre, open 0700-2300, 120 beds, kitchen, meals provided, laundry, family groups, bus 1 km, airport 30 mins, T 2867, booking rec Mar-Apr.

● **Camping**

Camping is possible but in the oilfield area this should be done discreetly and preferably with the permission of the owner or the authorities. Elsewhere, camping in the oases can only be undertaken with permission but this is unlikely to be withheld.

● **Places to eat**

Eating out is difficult except in Ajdabiyah and Sirt where there are local cafeterias or restaurants providing often a limited service in range of meals and opening hours. Elsewhere, the coastal highway has small routestop cafés and cold drink stands where electricity is available. Catering is generally for institutions or households and the eating places are few and far between. Travellers should always have spare food and water, especially on the long inter-centre routes.

Sirt – the western entry to Al-Khalij

This small staging post on the coast road was used by the Italians as an administrative centre. It gained new life following the change of régime in 1969 since Colonel Ghadhafi came from the Ghadafha tribal area close by. Sirt was built up as a military centre and bastion for the government. Developments in communications, industry and agriculture there were given priority. The population of the town and its immediate hinterland is estimated at over 50,000. Development of the garrison and administrative centre has meant the emergence of a completely new, if not entirely well-integrated, town with all services but little of note for the visitor to see. Spreading from the town are a series of valleys and low hills where attempts have been made to develop agriculture, mainly orchards. Sirt has been connected by road to the Al-Jufra oases to the S by a good new 227 km black top road. Sirt has cafeterias, restaurants and hotel accommodation, *Hotel Mahari*, five star, T 60100, in addition to all services such as fuel, workshops, garages,

PTT and medical facilities. Travellers should be careful when taking photographs not to include military installations.

Places of interest

Close by Sirt is the unmarked battlefield of **Qasr Bu Hadi** where in WW1 the Italians were beaten by the Libyans in a pitched battle. Along the coast is the site of **Medina Sultan** where the remains of a large mosque and Fatimid city have been discovered and partially excavated. Medina Sultan was set up at the point where a trans-Saharan route met the coast at a sheltered anchorage on the Gulf of Sirte coast. Fragments of pottery and inscriptions can be seen on the site.

● **Transport Air** Air services support the government central administration in the S and there are two daily flights from **Tripoli**. Departures from **Benghazi** to Sirt are Mon, Wed, Fri 1745, Sat. Sirt also advertises direct flights internally to **Sabha** Tues, Thur and Sat. A direct flight to **Algiers** runs when the embargo is not in force. **Road** By shared taxi or bus along the coast road.

Ajdabiyah and the road to Gialo and Al-Kufrah

Originally a small Arab town, Ajdabiyah has now been developed to the S of the coastal highway as a residential centre for foreign workers and some Libyan staff associated with the oil industry and government services in the Al-Khalij district. It is mainly new but badly maintained with little sense of civic pride. Its utilities including water, telephone, fuel and electricity are good but other services such as hospitals and clinics leave a lot to be desired by modern standards. The concentration of low paid temporary foreign workers, mainly Sudanese, Egyptian and undenominated central Africans has done nothing to enhance the position of the town and, compared with Ras Lanuf new town and Al Brayqah, it has little to recommend it. Shops, mosques and fuel are all available close to the coastal highway and the road is now dangerous for driving given the unplanned, encroaching shops and housing built close to it.

Places of interest

At Ajdabiyah there are a number of monuments worthy of a visit. A **10th century Fatimid mosque** existed here, highly regarded because of its external staircase and square block base originally carrying an octagonal minaret. The site is now in ruins. The mosque's courtyard is still visible. The sanctuary façade is composed of a series of niches and there is a single arcade surrounding the courtyard. There are small Roman remains in the form of rock-cut inscriptions, indicating that Ajdabiyah was a significant site long before the Arab invasion. Clearly, however, the Fatimid period was the one in which the city flourished.

● **Transport Road Bus**: There is an excellent de-luxe and a regular bus service from **Tripoli** and **Benghazi** as well as intermediate points on the coast road. Buses start their runs early in the morning covering 161 km from Benghazi and 863 km from Tripoli. **Taxi**: Shared taxis run very frequently from Benghazi. Passengers from Tripoli can find their way to Misratah after having visited other Tripolitanian sites before catching the taxi or bus for the long run to Sirt (463 km from Tripoli and 561 km from Benghazi) and Ajdabiyah.

Gialo

History

Gialo is a centre in the Gialo-Awjilah groups of oases with Jkhurra, Leskerre and Bir Buattifel. The site is some 30m above sea level and lies in a shallow 30 km depression in the desert. Water is available from wells and in Awjilah there was formerly an important spring source. Awjilah was the main trading oasis taking advantage of the routes S and to the coast. It had the largest and most productive palmeries with some 50,000 trees. Gialo has in recent times tended to be the main town of the group because of its prominence on the main

N-S routeway and its central position within the oasis cluster. Gialo consists of a number of smaller villages, the main ones being Lebba and Al-Areg. Gialo is renowned for the quality of its dates.

Places of interest

Outside Gialo itself, the area is thinly populated and consists mainly of palmeries owned by people living in Gialo, Awjilah or absentee from the district. The rural population of the groups of oases at Gialo is some 20,000, of which about 3,000 are non-Libyans. The Libyan population is almost entirely of Berber origin. There is a unique **mosque** at Awjilah, **Al-Jami Al-Atiq**, built of a series of beehive domes of clay bricks and mud. The building measures approximately 30m x 21m and has been abandoned as an active place of prayer. The minaret has collapsed. On the minaret gallery below there is an inscription in Arabic, 'The witness is here deposited till judgment day, I testify that there are no gods other than God and that Mohammed is His Prophet. May the blessing of God be upon him by Abd Allah Ibn Abdulahmid Al-Qadi 1178 H (1764 AD)'.

● **Transport Road Buses** and **shared taxi**: services run regularly to Gialo from the main station on the edge of Ajdabiyah or from the junction of the coast road with the S road to Al-Kufrah. The road to Al-Kufrah leaves on a clearly signposted road from the coastal highway at Ajdabiyah and cuts across the coastal hills and through a series of *wadis* and internal drainage basins to the settlement at Sahabi to Gialo at Km 250.

Al-Kufrah

Al-Kufrah is a group of oases long isolated in the Libyan desert by its very distance from the N and lack of wells on the formidable route to it. The site is made up of five major clusters, the main one originally Busaimah, in an enormous elliptical desert depression around the Wadi Al-Kufrah. The basin is on a 50 km axis NE to SW, and a 20 km axis NW to SE. The centre of the oasis is at 475m above sea level. The main oases are Al-Jawf, with 5 km x 3 km of cultivated land in gardens and palmeries. To the E of Al-Jawf is Busaimah made up of two small oases and Ez-Zurgh a former slave settlement.

History

Al-Kufrah was a quiet and rarely visited Tibu settlement until 1840 when it was overwhelmed by the Zuwaya tribe from Awjilah who converted the people to follow the Senussiya movement. Al-Kufrah became the centre of the Senussiya when Sayyid Mohammed Ali Al-Senussi moved there in 1894 to escape the influence of the Turkish governor of Cyrenaica. The Senussi thrived at Al-Kufrah and spread their influence deep into the Sahara, developing trade and communications links as they went. Al-Kufrah took on a considerable prosperity. The site was unvisited by non-Muslims until the Saharan explorer Rohlfs called there in 1879. The period from 1911 when the Italians invaded N Libya to their occupation of Al-Kufrah in 1931 was a difficult one. Al-Kufrah's trading base was cut off and the war in the N depleted the resources of the Senussi.

In the modern period, the Italians made a rough motor road link between the oasis and the N and provided landing strips along its route. Al-Kufrah was a staging post within the Italian colonial system linking with its East African possessions. Modern facilities were set up including an airbase, a garrison, a school, hospital and other facilities. WW2 delivered a severe blow to Al-Kufrah. It was a base in early years for the Italians and then for the British Long Range Desert Group. The colonial subsidy was withdrawn. Trade never recovered and the place relapsed into a backwater until oil exploration began. The oil industry attracted the people of Al-Kufrah to act as guides and drivers

in the desert and eventually a promise was made by Occidental Oil to assist in the development of the underground water at Al-Kufrah. Thus started a series of upheavals which entirely changed the oasis into a form of temporary boom town, overwhelmed local agriculture as a way of life and converted the site into a centre for military and civil government offices.

Places of interest

The settlement and production agricultural complexes are still there and can be visited with 4WD vehicles. The water gathering systems for the Great Manmade River are also visible. Otherwise there is nothing of lasting architectural and historical interest to see. Travel around the outlying oases is interesting and some fragments of the original economy remain to be seen. **Al-Jawf** has all services, including guest houses. Hospitality is best gained from the town council offices if the traveller has not organized a family or official reservation in advance.

● **Transport Air** There are internal flights to Al-Kufrah from Benghazi on Mon at 1200 and the return same day at 1430 connects to Tripoli. **Road Bus:** the road to Al-Kufrah leaves directly S from Gialo as a well maintained black top highway some 625 km in length. Shared taxis and buses run from Ajdabiyah to Gialo regularly. Visits further S can be arranged but there are less frequent departures. For those travelling from Ajdabiyah to Al-Kufrah via the Gialo-Awjilah groups of oases it might be easier to pick up transport in Gialo for Al-Kufrah. An express bus service is promised on the Benghazi-Ajdabiyah-Al-Kufrah route.

Other desert oases

In the S **Tizerbu** (see page 562), a palm grove oasis 600 km NW of Al-Kufrah is now served by black top road. Tizerbu is an elongated palmery almost 30 km long. It formerly had a tiny Tibu population the remains of whose fort, **Qasr Giranghedi**, can still be seen. Tizerbu has been modernized to manage agricul-

THE LONG RANGE DESERT GROUP

During WW1 the British army in Egypt developed a light car patrol system using Model T Fords and Rolls Royce armoured cars to penetrate the Libyan desert to protect their western flanks against attacks from Senussi armed groups. This activity was the direct military predecessor of the Long Range Desert Group (LRDG) established in Jun 1940 as the Long Range Patrols attached to the British army command in Cairo. The organization was the brainchild of R A Bagnold, who gathered an initial team made up of men with great experience of pre-war travel in the desert to harry the Axis forces behind their lines in the Saharan regions of Libya. Early recruits to the team were taken from the New Zealand Command and it was New Zealanders who remained an essential part of the LRDG.

Each patrol was originally made up of two officers and some 30 men supported by 11 trucks, with heavy machine and anti-aircraft guns, though this complement was later halved. The basic skills of the men of the LRDG were in signalling, navigation and intelligence-gathering. Map-making and the determining of routes through the desert were also important activities for the men of the LRDG. The LRDG patrols went out from Siwa in Egypt to Al-Kufrah in Libya, usually in the early days of the war to bring information of enemy movements in Uwainat, Jalu, Agheila and Ain Dua. On 1 March, 1941, the Free French General Leclerc captured Al-Kufrah from the Italians and the LRDG thereafter used this oasis as their base for the war in Libya.

During 1942 the LRDG was used in association with Major David Stirling's parachute raiders and other commando groups to attack Axis airfields and aircraft behind enemy lines. Its personnel were important in monitoring General Rommel's troop movements in the period leading up to the battle of El-Alamein in late 1942. After the defeat of the Axis army in Egypt at El-Alamein, the LRGD was engaged in attempts to cut off German forces retreating to Tunisia. Once the North African campaign moved into central Tunisia in 1943, the role of the LRDG came to an end.

tural development programmes in the oases and some settlement of Sudanese and others has proceeded in recent years.

Al-Awenat lies in the extreme SE of Libya, 325 km from Al-Kufrah, to be distinguished from Al-Awenat in the SW. The town is small and a security point for the Libyan authorities on the frontier with Sudan and Egypt. A new road into Sudan is under debate but nothing has thus far been accomplished. The town has basic telephone, health and other services. Visitors to Al-Kufrah by air should ensure that they have return bookings though there is an LAA sales office in the town, T 28701. Flights elsewhere in the S of Al-Khalij are for oil company purposes and are normally available only to company personnel.

Al-Jaghbub

An oasis lying 230 km inland from Tobruk, Al-Jaghbub is also connected by a new road from Gialo, 310 km away.

History

The oasis was important during the Senussi movement as a centre of resistance to the British and later the Italians. A large *zawia* or religious school was set up there, and the town flourished until the Senussi were forced to go further S to Al-Kufrah in 1895. The town is set in a large basin around Wadi Jaghbub and parts are below sea level forming closed sub-basins. Three main depressions exist, including the W one which is some 25 km in length, a central basin and an E basin. The traditional oasis gardens grow a wide range of irrigated crops such as peppers, tomatoes, potatoes and grain between palm trees. Natural vegetation is sparse with sage bush, and seasonal flora after rain. There is a rich variety of wildlife of the smaller rodents, mammals and gazelle.

Places of interest

The town is small, its traditional, often 2-storey, houses made of natural rock and palm trunks. The main **mosque** contains the tombs of the Senussi leaders, Mohammed Ben Ali Al-Senussi, Al-Shattabi   Al-Hasini   Al-Idrisi el-Majiajhiri. The site of a small **traditional koranic school** can be found, part of the teaching establishment which at one stage in the 19th century made Jaghbub the second most active and famous Islamic religious centre in North Africa. Cars with drivers can be arranged to visit the more distant oases. The area remains slightly run down but still tranquil.

• **Accommodation** Accommodation is difficult though there is provision for travellers at a rest house and the *baladiyah* will be helpful for short-stay guests.

• **Transport Road Buses and shared taxis**: come from the central public transport stand at Tobruk. Buses seem to run on a twice daily but irregular basis while fairly cheap, shared taxis are always available.

Warning: travel in Al-Khalij

Other than the detail given above on access and travel facilities in each of the small towns of the region, it must be emphasized that Al-Khalij is generally neutral or hostile to travellers and tourists. The desert is unforgiving to incompetence and bad planning. Very great distances separate the few settlements. The climate is increasingly extreme with travel S. Travellers should at all times stick to the black top roads. Off road travel is only for those with several all-terrain vehicles accompanied by a guide and with radio communication. Plenty of warm clothing, water and food should be carried. Travel in public transport during the cool but light hours of the day.

Al-Khalij is not tourist-friendly in other ways. As an oilfield and water source province of the country, it is run by either large commercial organizations, Libyan administrations or the military. The province is not structured for the normal traveller in either its transport or accommodation systems. To get round this, travellers should make arrangements to have their trip made 'official' by co-opting the help of the oil companies or a Libyan authority before arrival. If Libyan tourist companies offer passages through the area this should be used even by the hardened traveller since it will provide basic services from official sources. Local people can be friendly in this area and hospitality may be expected from the regional or town councils or individuals for a limited time.

There are very limited tourist facilities and guides to the area are few.

INFORMATION FOR VISITORS

CONTENTS

Before you go	569
Entry requirements	569
When to go	570
Health	570
Money	570
Getting there	571
Air; Train; Road; Sea; Customs	
When you arrive	573
Airport information; Clothing; Electricity; Hours of business; Official time; Photography; Safety; Shopping; Tipping; Weights and measures	
Where to stay	574
Food and drink	575
Getting around	576
Air; Road; Boat; Walking	
Communications	577
Language; Postal services; Telephone services	
Entertainment	578
Media; Sport	
Holidays and festivals	578
Further reading	579

● **General note**

Getting to Libya is not easy. Visa allocation is carefully controlled and mainly confined to those with bona fide jobs in the country. An invitation from a Libyan official agency or individual will perhaps assist the granting of a visa. Tourism is growing in importance for economic reasons, however, and there is a gradual relaxation of controls on this score. To take maximum advantage of this trend, travellers must take up a package from an officially recognized Libyan travel agency. Private visits to Libya can be made but access at frontier posts, for example, cannot be guaranteed except for residents of the Union of Maghreb States (Algeria, Morocco, Tunisia and Mauritania). The UN air embargo on international flights to Libya has added to the difficulties of all travellers.

Before you go

Entry requirements

● **Visas**

Travellers to Libya need a visa, normally issued at the People's Bureau, embassy or consulate overseas. Cost around US$50 (£20 for UK nationals), valid for 3 months, must be used within 45 days of issue. Applications with a translation of passport details in Arabic, should be given 10 to 14 days in advance of travel since it is usual for the Libyan authorities overseas to check details with Tripoli before a visa is issued. It is possible to get a visa at the port of entry, though this carries risks of long delays or capricious acts by border officials. Those with Arab passports normally do not require visas. Non-Arabic passports must be stamped with an official Arabic translation of the personal details of the individual's passport. In the UK the Passport Office 7-78 Petty France, London SW1, T 0171 279 3434 will do this as a matter of routine on presentation of the passport. Libyan embassy in Malta also provides visa and Arabic translation.

Visa extensions For extensions beyond the normal visa period, the immigration police should be informed and the fact noted in the passport.

Registration Immigration and sometimes currency declaration forms are needed on arrival. The forms themselves are in Arabic but English translations are available from the airlines. Only the Arabic question form should be filled in with answers in English or French. Copies of the forms should be carefully retained since they will be requested on exit. Normally hotels register guests on arrival. If visitors are not staying in an official hotel, they should register themselves with the police otherwise they can be stopped and held. Worse, they can be delayed on departure, even missing flights if officials are convinced that malpractice rather than ignorance is the cause of the problem.

Departure Passengers leaving Libya should check that they have a Departure Date Tax Stamp (LD3) available from a marked kiosk in the departure hall and a completed immigration form which is available from the airline desk. At airports all luggage has to be identified by its owner before it is cleared by customs and placed on board the aircraft. There is also sometimes a currency control. Only small amounts of Libyan currency may be exported, preferably less than LD10. Any excess Libyan dinars should be changed back into hard currency before passing through the departure gate. Passports and boarding cards should be readily available since police and airline checks can be made up to a few minutes before departure.

Insurance For those travellers not already equipped with travel or other insurance, there are facilities available in Libya directly through the Libyan Insurance Co or the Libya Travel and Tourist Co shop in Tripoli, T 36222.

● Representation overseas
Belgium, 28 Ave Victoria, 1050 Brussels, T 02 6492113; **France**, Paris, T 45534070; **Germany**, Bonn, T 0228 820090; **Italy**, Rome, T 06 8414518; **Malta**, Dar Jamaharia Notabile Rd, Balzan, BZN 01, T 010 356 486347; **Spain**, Madrid, T 01 4571368; **Tunisia**, Tunis 48 bis rue du 1 Juin, T 283936; **UK**, London T 0171 486 8250/071 486 8387, F 071 224 6349.

● Tourist information
Libya is only now awakening to the potential of tourism. Facilities are few and far between. Local tourist offices exist but are generally understaffed and ill-informed. They rarely have useful information, maps or guides. At present the best sources of help and information are the new private travel agencies springing up across the country. They have enterprise and initiative and understand the needs of foreign travellers. In Tripoli contact the Libyan Travel and Tourist Co T 36222 which has an office in Sharah Mizran close by the LAA head office. Other area offices are mentioned in the regional sections within the Handbook.

Be warned that while private travel agencies can provide some information and perhaps transport some may imply that without the 'official' guides' which only they can provide, there may be problems with the police. Certainly this is not true.

● Specialist tour companies
Arab Tours Ltd, 60 Marylebone Lane, London, WlM 5FF, T 0171 9353273, F 0171 4864237, offer a 9-day tour of Libya's classical cities, via Tunisia, at £897 pp.

When to go

● Best time to visit
The two coastal strips of Libya around Tripoli and N Cyrenaica together with the Jabal Nafusah and Jabal Al-Akhdar are all blessed with a Mediterranean climate which makes them pleasant in most seasons. The outstanding times to visit are in the spring after the rains when the ground is covered with flowers and other vegetation and the almond blossom is out. Autumn, too, can be most mild and attractive on the coast after the summer heat.

The ideal time to travel in the S is the period from Oct to Mar, when it is cooler. The summer in the S is absolutely to be avoided.

Health

● Staying healthy
Certified vaccinations against smallpox are no longer required, but prudence demands that anti-cholera and tetanus injections are received before entry. Travellers expecting to travel into the Libyan S might feel that a voluntary, yellow fever injection is worthwhile. Walkers and cyclists would also be wise to take up any anti-rabies protection that is safely available.

● Medical facilities
Libyan hospitals are fairly well equipped but are under-resourced in some critical areas. Travellers must take into account that, with a UN air embargo in place, it is difficult to be airlifted out in case of emergency. There are hospitals and clinics in most towns of over 25,000 population and emergency para-medical services exist to service the main motor traffic routes. In theory treatment is free for all in public hospitals and clinics. In practice it is better to find private assistance if ill.

Most proprietary drugs are available over the counter in Libya and chemist shops are to be found in the main streets of all but the smallest of towns (see Chemist and Hospital sections for each of the regions).

● Further health information
See page 15, main health section.

Money

● Credit cards
Cards can be used only in a small number of big hotels and in some of the larger travel agents. Cash is the normal medium of exchange and most shops are not equipped to handle credit cards of any kind. Credit cards at

hotels are best if not of US origin, though generics such as Visa and Mastercard are normally suitable.

● Cost of living

Libya is an oil economy and it mainly imports its necessities from abroad. Prices tend to be high reflecting this external reliance, some inefficiency in the distribution system and the high level of mark-up by the merchants. Specialist western foods and commodities like Libyan mutton are very expensive. Eating out is also far from cheap even in the small popular cafés if a full meal is taken. Otherwise fresh vegetables and fruit are moderately priced. Bread is very cheap and tasty. Pharmaceuticals, medical goods and imported high-tech items can be expensive. Personal services from plumbers to dry cleaners are expensive. Travel is comparatively cheap by air as well as land but hotels are few and the even fewer good quality hotels are very expensive. In general, assume that most things will be more expensive than in the USA or Western Europe, though this is offset by the generosity of the Libyans in rural areas in finding accommodation for visitors in public buildings.

● Currency

The Libyan dinar is the standard currency which is divided into 1,000 dirhams. Notes in circulation are LD10, 5, 1, 0.50; coins LD0.25, 0.10, 0.05 and 0.01. There are banks at Tripoli and Benghazi airports. Principal banks will exchange TCs and currency notes at the official rate of exchange. There is also a black market in foreign currency in which a very variable rate is available. The black market is however best avoided.

All travellers should have US$500 in foreign exchange on entry. This regulation is rarely enforced. The Libyan Dinar is only convertible at the official rate inside Libya by official institutions. Travellers may have to fill in a currency form on arrival (cash and TCs) and present it together with receipts of monies exchanged on departure. The system is not watertight nor fully implemented but is perhaps best observed. Keep receipts from the banks. A sensible procedure is to make sure that you do not leave the country with either more than a few Libyan Dinars or more foreign currency than you arrived with.

For exchange rates at Jul 1995, see table on page 7.

● Taxes

Provided that travellers do not accept official employment in Libya, there are no direct taxes other than the LD3 exit tax payable at the airport before entering the departure gate. Indirect taxes are included in payments as you go.

Getting there

● Air

Libyan Arab Airlines is the main carrier. Air services to and from Tripoli, the main entry port for the entire country, have been difficult for some years. An embargo on the transfer of arms and strategic materials to Libya by the USA for its alleged involvement in state terrorism in the early 1980s led to a depletion in the Libyan aircraft fleet, which is ageing and inefficient. A number of foreign airlines do not visit Tripoli for political or commercial reasons. In Apr 1992, the UN Security Council introduced a ban on air traffic to Libya as part of a campaign to bring to book alleged perpetrators of the Lockerbie air disaster of 1988. In normal conditions foreign visitors by air are advised to have reserved firm flights for departure since it is not always easy to get return flights booked inside Libya. It is advised that all entries to Libya while the embargo remains in force should be by land frontier or by sea.

International flights In normal circumstances flights to Tripoli via LAA or other regular scheduled services from Europe arrive from Amsterdam, Athens, Belgrade, Brussels, Budapest, Frankfurt, Larnaca, Madrid, Malta, Moscow, Paris, Prague, Rome, Sofia, Vienna, Warsaw and Zurich. Most of the above are only on a 1 day a week basis. Alitalia, Lufthansa, Malta Airlines and Swissair are among the most frequent carriers to Libya. There are no direct flights to Libya from the USA, Canada or UK at the present time even when the UN embargo is not operative. Flights to Libya from African points of origin include Accra, Alexandria, Algiers, Cairo, Casablanca, Khartoum, Ndjamena, Niamey, Nouakchott and Tunis. Most Middle Eastern airlines have flights to Tripoli with the main scheduled flights in from Amman, Damascus, Dubai, Istanbul and Jeddah. The other incoming flight in normal times is from Karachi.

Fares The fare structure for flights, when they are in operation, is polarized. Swissair, for example, runs business class only flights to Libya. LAA is also expensive and not easy to get discounts for. Cheapest access by air is via Air Malta. Air Malta or airlines serving the Tunisian S such as Liberté to Monastir or Tunis Air/UK Air to Sfax are amongst the cheapest carriers during the embargo.

● **Train**

Libya's railways were gradually dismantled after WW2 and there are no services within Libya. Libya can be approached by train from the Egyptian frontier as far as Marsa Matruh. On the Tunisian side there are trains from Tunis and the N as far S as Gabès from which travellers can go by bus or shared taxi to the Libyan frontier 188 km distant. Fares on both Tunisian railways CFT and Egyptian Railways are moderate (see page 485 for Tunisia).

● **Road**

Bus These run from Cairo and Alexandria in Egypt and from Tunis and all major E coast towns in Tunisia to the Libyan frontiers. Buses from further afield include direct services from Algiers, Casablanca and Amman. Passengers should cross the frontier on foot and then take advantage of Libyan domestic bus services (see Tunisia, page 480 for details of arrival at the Libyan border posts). Once in Libya, there are two main bus transport companies, one engaged principally in long-distance international services and the other plying between Libyan cities and towns.

When leaving Libya the traveller can use the Libyan International Bus Company which has an office behind the Tripoli medina off Sharah Omar Mukhtar to the W of the old citadel, in an area now being cleared of buildings and reconstructed. Buses tend to leave Tripoli very early in the morning, not later than 0800. Passengers should be at the bus station by at least 0700. The buses fill up rapidly, particularly while the air embargo is in operation and buses can leave as soon as all seats are taken. There are five main destinations, Tunis, Benghazi, Alexandria, Cairo and Damascus. Fares are low. It costs LD10 to Benghazi, LD47 to Alexandria, LD52 to Cairo and LD78 to Damascus and equivalents in Egyptian or Syrian currency on return. Most services are run on a daily basis except for Damascus which leaves Tripoli on Tues and Sat only. The coaches used on international runs are of good quality, with a/c and all services provided. Coming into Libya, bookings can be made on Libyan bus lines in Cairo through travel agents. Times of departures can be variable. Otherwise it is as convenient and cheaper, if not so comfortable, to use internal Libyan services once through the international border.

Taxis Both local and international transport is as much in the hands of taxi drivers as the bus companies. In Tripoli, the taxis leave from large stands between Sharah Omar Mukhtar and the sea. They ply for hire normally on a shared basis but can be had for an individual or private group with suitable haggling over the price. On a shared basis they are normally cheaper than the luxury buses and far more frequent in their departures. Driving standards are variable among taxi drivers and good nerves are required of passengers! Travellers entering via land borders are advised that taking a shared taxi is easier and quicker than waiting for the bus. If a bus is preferred, take a shared taxi to the nearest town (Zuara in the W and Solum in the E) and take the bus from there in conditions of comfort.

Taxis to Djerba (Tunisia) leave from Sharah Al-Rashid nr the bus station, cost LD25-40 depending on number of passengers, takes 4-5 hrs, depending on border controls.

● **Sea**

Air travellers can bypass the UN air embargo on Libya by flying to an adjacent country – Malta, Tunisia or Egypt and continuing their journeys by land, using buses or shared taxis or by sea on the regular ferry run from Malta.

Shipping services The overnight ferry from Valetta in Malta uses modern vessels, usually the *MV Garnata* of 3,672 dwt, with other passenger vessels, the *MV Toletela* of 3,671 dwt and the *MV Garyounis* of 3,423 dwt. Sailing times change monthly and travellers should check with the General National Maritime Transport Co, Sharah Al-Baladiya, T 33 34865 or via Seamalta in Malta on T 00356 25994212, Tx 1210 1321. Currently boat departs 1900 from Valletta and costs US$200 one-way, or 1800 from Tripoli in front of *Hotel Al-Mehari* costs LD63 one-way, LD102 return. Journey takes 12 hrs. There are agents for GNMTC in Tunisia, Morocco, Turkey, Italy, Germany, Belgium and Holland. Regular sailings run between Libyan ports and Alexandria and Izmir. Fares vary seasonally and annually and current levels can be checked with GNMTC agents.

● **Customs**

Duty free goods are available at the main airport departure lounge at Tripoli airport for foreign currencies only. A range of cigarettes, cigars, perfumes, watches and travel goods can be found. No other tourist facilities of this kind are available and offers elsewhere of duty free goods should be avoided as not worth the hassle.

Import-export bans Libya has a stringent ban on the import of alcohol of any kind. It is a pointless risk taking in beer, spirits, or indeed drugs. Severe penalties can be imposed and at the very least passengers can be incarcerated pending deportation. It is rather easier to carry books and newspapers into the country than formerly, though sensitivities remain and it is best not to carry literature which might be misunderstood or thought to be anti-Libyan. Firearms cannot be imported without special permission. Radio transmitters and electronic means of printing will attract official attention and should clearly be for personal use only.

On leaving Libya make sure that you have no antiquities. The Libyan authorities take unkindly to the illegal export of their ancient monuments and penalties for infringement can be ferocious.

When you arrive

● **Airport tax**

Is LD3 is payable on leaving Libya. Only Libyan currency is accepted. At Tripoli airport, from which the majority of flights leave Libya, there is a special counter for buying the exit stamp before passing through to the passport and customs formalities. Without a stamp you will be sent back to start the entire process again. (See Documents, page 569).

● **Clothing**

For general guidance, refer to the section on Travelling in Islamic countries on page 37.

There are three imperatives on clothing in Libya:

❏ Do not offend Muslim sentiment by wearing scanty clothing.

❏ Wear clothes which prevent sunstroke and sunburn;

❏ Wear clothes that enable you to keep your key documents on your person.

Libyan traditional workday dress, the *barakan*, is a vestige of the Roman toga made up in woven wool material of 5m length by 2m width which wraps round the head and body. This in a country with the world's highest recorded temperature! Scanty clothing is not regarded as sensible on grounds of either re-

ligion or practicality. Women should be careful not to leave arms and legs overly exposed. In a country where women dress well in public in both traditional and modern costume, to wear less could be seen as provocative or indicating moral slackness. In any case, outside the main hotels or private transport the need is to be sheltered from the sun, the sand and the glare. Desiccation problems effecting exposed areas of skin can come on quickly and harshly in the summer months for those who fail to look after themselves.

● **Electricity**

Libyan electricity services use a standard 240V system for power. Take an international adaptor plug as socket sizes can vary. Electric power is available in all but the most isolated of settlements.

● **Hours of business**

Working hours vary from summer 0700-1400 to winter 0800-1300 and 1600-1830 in private offices. Official agencies run on a basic day of 0800-1400, though it is always better to start communications with official offices and banks before 0900 since they can become busy or officials can be in meetings at later times. Shops open from approximately 0900-1400 and again from 1630-2030, depending on area and trade.

● **Official time**

GMT -1.

● **Photography**

The large sand deserts, arid rock formations and fine ruins of classical antiquity make photography in the excellent light conditions of Libya a great pleasure. Do not photograph military installations, and take care in photographing women: preferably if male do not photograph women at all. The camera still carries the feeling of intrusion and/or the evil eye in some areas. Film is generally available for 35 mm cameras and most other types of film can also be found in Libya. Kodak and Fuji brands are readily available in the capital. Check the 'sell by date'. For specialist and video film try to bring reserves from outside. Beyond Tripoli and Benghazi film supplies cannot be guaranteed.

● **Safety**

This is very good in Libya. Occasional violence causes more noise than damage and walking through the streets is generally safer than in Europe. After dark, and indeed at all times everywhere, in Libya foreign nationals are advised to carry their passports. Libyans are used to foreigners in their midst but their visitors are almost exclusively male. European females need, therefore, to follow a sensible dress code and to act with suitable decorum, especially in Tripoli, to avoid arousing undue interest.

Women A woman travelling alone in Libya must appreciate that this is a totally segregated society, women sit apart and eat apart or after the men. On long distance buses the driver will organize space for the women. As no-one is prepared to speak it can be very lonely. The biggest problem is getting a room in a hotel without a male companion. The bus driver may feel obliged to introduce you to the hotel receptionist thereby giving some respectability, otherwise only the expensive hotels will accept women alone: take this into account when budgeting for a trip. One advantage of a woman being of no significance is the lack of problems at check points and compared with Egypt the lack of hassle. Travel alone in Libya by experienced female travellers can be recommended with the proviso that eventually the sheer masculinity of society and the feeling of isolation caused by the lack of communication makes leaving a welcome relief.

A special warning is necessary to travellers in the S Fezzan. This zone in the Uzu strip and to the S was a war zone until recently and its ownership is still unsettled. There are risks off the road in Uzu of offending the Libyan security officials. Travel in this area should only be with official knowledge. Any abandoned or scattered armament or ammunition should not be touched.

● **Shopping**
Best buys Libya is more of a consumer society than a producer of goods for export other than petroleum. In the SW of the country, especially in Ghadames and Ghat, craft goods of value are available. Leatherwork, woven palm frond articles and small rugs all have an individual charm. Stamp collectors will find a vast range of interesting stamps available from the main post offices in Tripoli and Benghazi where some small attempt is made to cater for the philatelist.

● **Tipping**
Is not widespread in Libya and is only expected by those giving personal services in hotels, cafés and restaurants. The normal rate is 10%. For small services in hotels use quarter and half

dinar notes. At the airport only use porters if you are heavily weighed down with luggage then tip at half a dinar per heavy bag. Taxi drivers should, unless there is actually a working meter and then perhaps in any case, give a price before starting the journey. Tips for Libyan drivers are not the rule but will be accepted. Foreign drivers in Libyan employ tend to be more demanding of tips. Do not get drawn into bribing officials at any level since it is a sure way of bringing increasing difficulties and possibly severe delays.

● **Weights and measures**
Libya uses the metric system. See conversion table on page 14.

Where to stay

● **Hotels**
Libya is thinly provided with hotels, even in the populated N coastal area. This is mainly a result of years of state control when tourism was discouraged. The slow re-establishment of the

HOTEL CLASSIFICATIONS

AL	US$90+. International class luxury hotel. All facilities for business and leisure travellers are of the highest international standard.
A	US$75-90. International hotel with air conditioned rooms with WC, bath/shower, TV, phone, mini-bar, daily clean linen. Choice of restaurants, coffee shop, shops, bank, travel agent, swimming pool, some sport and business facilities.
B	US$60-75. As **A** but without the luxury, reduced number of restaurants, smaller rooms, limited range of shops and sport.
C	US$40-60. Best rooms have air conditioning, own bath/shower and WC. Usually comfortable, bank, shop, pool.
D	US$20-40. Best rooms may have own WC and bath/shower. Depending on management will have room service and choice of cuisine in restaurant.
E	US$10-20. Simple provision. Perhaps fan cooler. May not have restaurant. Shared WC and showers with hot water (when available).
F	under US$10. Very basic, shared toilet facilities, variable in cleanliness, noise, often in dubious locations.

private sector is making for a revival in the hotel trade at the bottom end of the market. Tripoli, the national capital, can boast few top quality international hotels (*Al-Mahari*, *Funduq Al-Kebir*, and *Waddan*) which despite their charges are not AL grade. Elsewhere standards are entirely variable and the regional comments on hotels should be read with care before setting out from the capital.

On the coast there are a number of often well-provisioned beach clubs with residential facilities. They are designed to cater for groups of officially approved visitors but can in certain circumstances be open to all travellers. They are best approached through a Libyan travel agent or a Libyan state organization for sports, youth or scouts.

● **Youth hostels**

Libya has a remarkable number of youth hostel facilities. They are basic but often available when hotels are not! The locations, numbers of beds and telephone numbers of Libyan youth hostels are given in all regional sections. Opening hours 0600-1000 and 1400-2300 unless otherwise stated. In all there are 25 youth hostels in Libya. The minimum age is 14. Overnight fees for members are LD1,000-2,000 including sheets, breakfast LD500, lunch LD2,500 and dinner LD2,000. The Libyan Youth Hostel Association is at 69 Amr Ibn Al-As St POB 8886, Tripoli, T 45171, Tx 20420 LYHA. Additionally, it is possible to stay in the dormitories of secondary boarding schools during holiday periods. This is best arranged officially in advance, otherwise through the local *baladiyah* (municipality offices).

● **Camping**

Is moderately popular in Libya, though as a mass organized venture through the state. Private camping is less usual except near bathing places on the Mediterranean shore. Here there are picnic sites which double as camping areas. They are crowded on public holidays but otherwise little used. Certain areas near to military camps and oil company installations are closed to all camping and any indications to this end are best complied with. Do not camp close to private farms or housing without an invitation to do so. Whenever possible seek permission from local farmers or land owners before setting up camp.

RESTAURANT CLASSIFICATIONS

Given the variations in price of food on any menu our restaurants are divided where possible into three simple grades:
♦♦♦ expensive, ♦♦ average and ♦ cheap.

● **Food**

Outside the capital, eating is confined to the main hotel restaurants, their cafés or to popular eating houses which can be found near the centres of most provincial towns. Outside Tripoli, restaurant and popular café opening hours are limited. In the evening eat before 2100 or risk finding them closed. As Libyans prefer to eat at home, restaurants tend to be for foreigners and travellers. The exception is in the use of cafés in the towns where males, mainly younger males, gather for social purposes. On Fri and holidays, Libyans picnic and buy food from beachside stalls. Libyan cuisine is a Mediterranean mixture with a strong legacy of the Italian period with pastas very popular, particularly macaroni. Local dishes include *couscous*, with a bowl of boiled cereal as a base carrying large pieces of mutton and some potatoes. The best traditional forms of *couscous* in Libya use millet as a cereal though now most meals come with wheat. *Bazin* is a Libyan speciality – hard, paste-like food made of water, salt and barley and is really not recommended except to the gastronomically hardy. '*Aish* is a similar food from the same ingredients but slightly softer and prepared differently. *Sherba* (Libyan soup) is delicious but highly spiced. For the rest, the range of meals is quite sophisticated as in Tunisia, with Italian influences being greatest in Tripolitania and rather more Arab dishes (less macaroni!) in Cyrenaica (see Tunisia, Information for Visitors, page 483). Family life is kept separate from public acquaintances, and invitations to dine in a Libyan home are rarely given. Any foreigner invited to a Libyan home should thus feel very favoured.

The offerings in cafés and restaurants will be very limited and mainly made up of various hot meat, chicken and vegetable stews either with potatoes or macaroni. In the main hotels, cuisine is 'international' and very bland.

Good dates and excellent oranges can be bought cheaply. There are olives of a slightly sour taste, apricots, figs and almonds in season, all of which are good value. The smaller varieties of banana are available at increasingly competitive prices.

● **Drink**

It should be emphasized that alcoholic drinks are banned in Libya. Offers of illegal liquor should be avoided even in private houses unless its provenance is beyond doubt. Local brews or 'flash' can be of questionable quality while traditional brews of *bokha* (a form of arak), or *laghbi* (beer), made from the date palm are illegal and lead to abuse of the date palm. Otherwise, Libyans drink local bottled mineral waters, most of which are not always reliable copies of lemonades, colas and orange drinks available worldwide. In season, real orange juice can be bought from stalls on the streets. These drinks are cheap and widely available. Take a bottle opener since most drinks are in glass bottles. The local tap water throughout much of Libya is slightly brackish. For personal use, buy bottled water such as *moyyat Ben Ghashir* (Ben Ghashir water).

Beverages include Libyan tea, which is heavy boiled thick tea, often with mint or peanuts in a small glass. If ordinary tea is wanted ask for *shay kees* (tea from a teabag) *bil leben* (with milk). Coffees include Nescafé (ask for Nescafé) with or without milk and Turkish (sometimes called Arabic) coffee. With the latter, specify whether you want it *bil sukar* (sweet) or *bedoon sukar* (unsweetened).

Getting around

● **Air**

There are connecting flights to the main cities – easiest access is from Tripoli. See separate towns for details. Book in advance as all flights are very busy – overbooking is common so arrive early. **NB** The UK Foreign Office has advised travellers to Libya **not** to use internal airlines as a lack of spare parts prevents satisfactory safety standards.

● **Road**

Bus The bus service is excellent including good quality air-conditioned intercity services and more interesting crowded local buses – see individual town entries.

Car hire Car hire for self-drive in Libya is not reliable. Vehicles on offer are often old and in only moderate condition. Whilst they are suitable for use in town, they should not be taken on long journeys without thorough pre-travel checks. Among the best hire locations are the main hotels, where agents have desks in the foyer. Hire rates for cars are high and variable, especially outside of Tripoli.

Cycling Travel by bicycle is unusual. Off the main track, cycling is extremely difficult in stony and sandy, albeit flat terrain. Cyclists are advised to be well marked in brightly coloured clothing. Puncture repair shops exist in the towns alongside the main roads at the point of entry, though they mainly deal with cars and light motorcycles rather than bicycles. In the countryside, repair of cycles will be difficult but the profusion of small pick-up trucks means that it is very easy to get a lift with a cycle into a settlement where repairs can be effected.

Hitchhiking Is used in Libya but not normally for a free ride except in emergencies. There are many shared taxis travelling the road and travellers usually make use of these on a paid basis. Private cars or pick-up trucks will act in the same capacity but will expect a small payment in the normal course. Foreign travellers might find themselves picked up for free for curiosity. In general hitchhiking is not to be encouraged since travellers in the S in particular will not be able to hitch reliably. Carry water and other safety supplies.

Motoring Great effort has gone into creating the road system and very few areas of the country are now inaccessible. Drive on the right of the road. Drivers are supposed to wear seat belts and these are checked by the police on entering and leaving Benghazi and Tripoli. Driving in Libya is poorly regulated and standards of driver training are very variable. The accident rate is high by international standards. Visitors should drive defensively for their own safety and to ensure that they are not involved in accidents, especially those involving injury to humans, for which they might be deemed culpable. Drivers can be held in jail for long periods and the settlement of law suits against drivers guilty of dangerous driving leading to death or injury of a third party can be protracted and difficult.

Care is needed in **off-road driving** since there are difficult sand dune areas and other regions where soft sand can quickly bog down other than 4WD vehicles. Even in far-flung parts of the Jefara Plain, the traffic is quite regular and people are never far away. In the central Jefara there are large areas of military installations which are best avoided. Petrol stations are fairly well distributed but only on the main through roads. Any off road travel

Communications 577

should only be undertaken with a full tank and a spare petrol supply. Good practice is never to leave the black top road unless there are two vehicles available to the party. A reliable and generous water supply should also be taken. This is especially important in summer when exhaustion and dehydration can be major problems if vehicles need digging out of sand.

Fuel distribution is a monopoly of a state agency and there are petrol stations in every town and at most key road junctions. But, as noted in the regional sections of this Handbook, motorists should ensure that they fill up regularly rather than rely on stretching their fuel supply, since occasionally a station might be out of use for lack of deliveries or a cut in the electricity supply. Travel in the Saharan regions requires special precautions since running out of fuel can be fatal. There is no equivalent of Automobile Club services in Libya but passing motorists are normally very helpful. Drivers should always be aware of the enormous distances between settlements in S Libya and take defensive action to ensure fuel, water, food and clothing reserves at all times (see Surviving in the Desert, page 45). International driving licences are normally required though, in most cases, easily understood (English or Italian) foreign licences might be accepted.

Taxis Individual taxis are more expensive, more flexible and generally more comfortable over the same distance than the local bus. The taxis do have meters but these may not be in use. **Shared taxis** (larger) are a very popular mode of travel, leaving for a particular destination as soon as they are full. Be sure you have settled the price in advance. If in doubt check with the other passengers. These taxis look quite decrepit but generally get to their destination.

● **Walking**
In Libya other than for point to point travel, walking is not normal. Hiking is to be approached, therefore, in the knowledge that it may attract curiosity and possibly disbelief. Maps of good scale for walking eg better than 1:50,000 are very rare and thus travel has to be by sight lines, compass work and common sense. In many areas of the Jefara sighting to topographic markers on the Jabal can be used or lines on the taller minarets in the small towns are distinctive guides. Dogs are not a general problem in Tripolitania except near large farms where they are used for security purposes. Carry a stout stick and have some stones for

throwing at approaching aggressive dogs, which is how the Libyans deal with this problem.

● **Boat**
There are no rental facilities for boats and only a limited few individuals own boats for pleasure purposes. There are small boat marinas at Tripoli and Benghazi for sailors bringing their own boats into port. It is occasionally possible to hire small fishing boats with their owners for the hour or day. Visits to Farwa, for example, near Zuara are only feasible by this means. The opening of new watersport tourist sites for foreign tourists such as at Farwa Island will make boat hire easier in the future.

Communications

● **Language**
Arabic is the official language throughout Libya. Given the Arab nationalist leanings of the government under Colonel Ghadhafi, Arabic is regarded with some pride as a cultural emblem. Immediately after the 1969 revolution or coup d'état, all foreign language signs were removed, including street names, shop names, signposts and indications on official buildings. The result is that it is difficult for non-Arabic speakers to make use of written signs. In normal circumstances Libyans are most helpful to foreigners and will point out routes and other destinations. Unfortunately, however, it is only the older generation who have colloquial English, French or Italian since the educational system is less good than formerly in teaching foreign languages and fewer Libyans travel abroad than previously. Tripoli City is the least difficult for the non-Arabic speaker followed by Benghazi. The answer to this problem, other than learning the Arabic script and some vocabulary before travelling, is to be very patient asking your way until help is volunteered by a source you can comprehend.

The private commercial sector is likely to be best aware of **English** and **Italian** since companies trade abroad so that calling in offices or agencies can locate assistance in an emergency. **French** is understood widely by the older generation in the SW of country in the areas of Ghadames and Ghat. Italian is still a used language in the Tripoli area. English is probably best used in Benghazi, Al-Khalij and the E where there are many oil industry workers who have rubbed shoulders with English speaking personnel. Language difficulties should not put off potential travellers in Libya since the Libyans themselves are helpful and patient. A few words or phrases in Arabic will ease the way considerably. (See key words and phrases, page 59.)

Berber is spoken as a first language in some rural areas, especially the Jabal Nafusah. Tamashek, related to Berber, is spoken by the few Tuaregs in the region of Ghadames. In the deep S around the Tibesti Mountains, the Tibu language is the lingua franca.

● **Postal services**

Independent Libya inherited a good postal system. Poste restante and post office box facilities are available in the main cities at the respective central post offices. The service to and from Europe, costing LD 350 for a letter, takes about 7 to 10 days in normal circumstances but, bearing in mind the international air embargo, long land transit for mail makes this a much longer and riskier process. Internal mail is cheap, and for in-city letters, fairly fast and efficient. Libya produces a great range of collectors' stamps and there is a philatelic counter in Tripoli main post office.

● **Telephone services**

PTT facilities exist in all towns and most villages. Internal calls are straightforward, though there can be some waiting time for a public line at the PTT office. International calls from all points can be difficult since there are restricted numbers of lines. The PTT offices in Tripoli and Benghazi are still quicker than trying international calls from private telephones. In-coming international calls, by contrast, are comparatively easy to get through. The **international code** for Libya is 218. Libya internal area codes are **Benghazi** 61, **Benina** 63, **Derna** 81, **Ghadames** 484, **Sabrata** 24, **Tobruk** 87, **Tripoli** 21, **Tripoli Int Airport** 22, **Zawiya** 23, **Zuarah** 25. Rates for calls are at standard international levels.

Fax and telex facilities are available from luxury hotels and the main PTT offices which are advertised as being open 24 hrs a day but suffer from the constraint on telephone lines. Late night automatic fax facilities in private offices are useful if available through friends of friends.

Entertainment

● **Media**

Until very recently the Libyan media were powerfully controlled from the centre. This situation is changing only very slowly so that the media reflect the wishes of the régime. This does not make for good entertainment. Other than programmes in Arabic, which technically and in content leave so much to be desired that most Libyans watch videos or foreign stations via satellite especially CNN, not the regular local television, there is a news broadcast in French and English each evening for approximately half an hour each. There is an occasional sports programme, either Arab or international, shown on TV which is culturally neutral. The radio channel carries programmes of western music from time to time. The state produces daily broadsheets in French and English together with Arabic language newspapers. Foreign newspapers can be bought though they are often very out of date even when the air system is working normally. BBC World Service news and programmes can be picked up easily in Libya (see frequency chart, 13).

● **Sport**

Libya participates in the various Arab League sports tournaments but facilities for individuals are still very limited. Health centres exist for travellers at a few of the main hotels. Swimming is universally available in the Mediterranean or in the pools attached to the beach clubs in the main cities. Libyans themselves play volleyball for which there are plenty of facilities and football. Horse riding and trotting are also generally enjoyed. There is often a Tripoli Horse Show with international interest, now suspended. A Secretariat (ministry) of Sport exists but its activities are not given priority. The beach clubs near Tripoli and Benghazi have first class facilities for tennis, table tennis and canoeing and other sports. In the smaller towns the schools tend to be centres for sports while in industrial towns some of the companies have their own clubs with squash and tennis courts, for example.

Holidays and festivals

Libya, as Muslim country, observes all the main Islamic festivals as holidays (see page 40 for details on Ramadan). Fridays are days of rest. In addition there are several national holidays.

2 Mar:	Declaration of the People's Authority
11 Jun:	Evacuation of foreign military bases
1 Sep:	Anniversary of the 1969 Revolution

Approximate dates for 1996:

12 Jan:	Beginning of Ramadan
21 Feb:	Aïd al-Fitr (End of Ramadan)
29 Apr:	Aïd al-Aladah
20 May:	Islamic New Year 1417
29 Jul:	Prophet's Birthday

Further reading

● Books and maps

The best available maps are Michelin Carte Routière et Touristique, *Afrique Nord et Ouest* at 1/4,000,000 and Cartographia *Libya* at 1/2,000,000. Libyan maps of 1/50,000 are available for the main settled areas but are difficult to find except in the university library and the Secretariat of Planning. There are few contemporary guidebooks to Libya. A very useful book is the Arabic/English language *Atlas of Libya*, available at the Fergiani Book Stores, Sharah 1st September, Tripoli. The *Antiquities of Tripolitania* by DEL Hayes, pub Dept Antiquities, Tripoli 1981; *Cyrene and Apollonia an Historical guide*, by Richard Goodchild, Dept Antiquities, Tripoli 1963.

There are a few books on Libya which are not essentially political. Of these the best are J Davis's (1987) book *Libyan Politics: Tribe & Revolution*. On history J Wright's (1982) *Libya: A Modern History* is a good review while JA Allan's (1981) *Libya: The Experience of Oil* deals with oil and agricultural development. On the disputed areas of S Libya books include M Alawar, (1983) *Bibliography of Chad and the Libyan Borderlands* and J Wright, (1989) *Libya, Chad and the Central Sahara*.

We wish to thank Stephano Chiarli for updating this chapter on Libya. He travelled many, many km on bus, taxi and plane to check the public transport sections and on foot to check the town details.

GLOSSARY

GLOSSARY

A

Agora	Market/meeting place
Aïd/Eïd	Festival
Aïn	Spring
Affanes	Woollen slipper used by nomads
Abbasids	Muslim Dynasty ruled from Baghdad 750-1258
Aghlabids	Orthodox Muslim Dynasty in Tunisia and eastern Algeria 800-909
Alaouite	Present rulers of Morocco since 1666
Alcázar	Royal Palace
Alcazaba	Fortress
Almohads	Islamic Empire in North Africa 1130-1269
Almoravids	Islamic Empire in northwestern Africa 1054-1147
Andalucía	Moorish Spain
Arabesque	Geometric pattern with flowers and foliage used in Islamic designs

B

Bab	City gate
Bâches	Converted pick-up truck
Bahri	North/northern
Baladiyah	Municipality
Baksheesh	Money as alms, tip or bribe
Baraka	Blessing
Barakan	Woollen wrap 5m by 2m to cover entire body
Barbary	Name of North Africa 16th-19th centuries
Barboushe	Soft, flat leather slipper
Basha	see Pasha
Basilica	Imposing Roman building, with aisles, later used for worship
Bazaar	Market
Bedouin	Nomadic desert Arab
Beni	Sons of (tribe)
Berber	Indigenous tribe of North Africa
Bey	Governor (Ottoman)
Bidonville	Shanty town
Borj	Fort

B (continued)

Bour	Depressions in sand down to water table for cultivation
Burnous	Man's cloak with hood – tradional wear

C

Caid	Official
Calèche	Horse drawn carriage
Calidarium	Hot room
Capital	Top section of a column
Caravanserai	Lodgings for travellers and animals around a courtyard
Chaouia	Berbers of the Aurés
Chechia	Man's small red felt hat
Chotts	Low-lying salt lakes
Couscous	Steamed semolina with lamb

D

Dar	House
Darj w ktaf	Carved geometric motif of intersecting arcs with superimposed rectangles
Dechra	Earth coloured terraced hamlets topped by fortress silos
Deglet Nur	High quality translucent date
Delu	Water lifting device at head of well
Dey	Commander (of janissaries)
Djebel	Mountain
Djemma	Main or Friday mosque
Dour	Village settlement

E

Eïd	see Aïd
Erg	Sand dune desert

F

Faqirs	Muslim who has taken a vow of poverty
Fassi	A person or item from Fes
Fatimids	Muslim dynasty 909-1171AD claiming descent from Mohammed's daughter Fatimah

Foggara	Underground water channel
Fondouk/ Funduq	Lodgings for goods and animals around a courtyard
Forum	Central open space in Roman town
Ful/Fuul	Beans

G

Gare Routière	Bus station
Garrigue	Mediterranean scrubland – poor quality
Ghibli	Hot dry wind from south
Ghorfa	Granary or storehouse/ room/temporary dwelling
Ginan	Small garden or tree embayment
Gymnasium	Roman school for mind and body

H

Habous	Religiously endowed land in Morocco
Hafsids	Berber dynasty 13th-16th century in present day Tunisia and Algeria
Hamada	Stone desert
Hammam	Bath house
Hara	Jewish quarter in Tripoli
Harem	Women's quarters
Harira	Soup
Harmattan	Mauritanian hot dry wind from east that raises temperatures and reduces humidity
Hassi	Well

I

Idrissid	Dynasty founded by Moulay Idriss I 788AD
Imam	Muslim religious leader

J

Jabal	see Djebel
Jallabah	Outer garment with sleeves and a hood – often striped
Jami'	Mosque
Janissaries	Elite Ottoman soldiery
Jebel	see Djebel
Jihad	Holy war by Muslims against non-believers

K

Kasbah	Castle/Fort
Kilim	Woven carpet
Kif	Hashish
Kissaria	Covered market
Koubba	Dome on tomb of holy man, also special room in houses in Ghadames
Ksar (pl Ksour)	Fortified village

L

Levanter	Strong easterly wind
Liwan	Vaulted arcade

M

Mahboub	Coins worn as jewellery
Maghreb	Western Arab world – Morocco, Algeria and Tunisia
Malekite	Section of Sunni Islam
Maquis	Mediterranean scrubland – often aromatic
Marabout	Muslim holy man/his tomb
Marinids	Berber dynasty 13th-15th centuries, strongest in Morocco
Maristan	Hospital
Mashrabia	Wooden screen
Mashreq	Eastern Arab world
Mastaba	Tomb
Mausoleum	Large tomb building
Mecheoui	Moroccan meat dish (mutton)
Medersa (pl Medressa)	School usually attached to a mosque
Medina	Old walled town, residential quarter
Mellah	Jewish quarter of old town
Menzel	House
Mihrab	Recess in wall of mosque indicating direction of Mecca
Mimbar	Pulpit in a mosque
Minaret	Slender tower of mosque from which the muezzin calls the faithful to prayer
Mosque	Muslim place of worship
Moulid/ Mouloud	Religious festival – Prophet's birthday
Moussem	Religious gathering
Muezzin	Priest who calls the faithful to prayer
Mullah	Muslim religious teacher
Murabtin	Dependent tribe

N

Necropolis	Cemetery

O

Oasis	Watered desert gardens
Obelisk	Tapering monolithic shaft of stone with pyramidal apex
Ottoman	Major Muslim Empire based in Turkey 13th-20th centuries
Oued	see Wadi
Ouled	Tribe
Outrepassé	Horse-shoe shaped arch

P

Pasha	Governor
Phoenicians	Important trading nation based in eastern Mediterranean from 1100 BC
Piscine	Pool
Pisé	Sun-baked clay used for building
Piste	Unsurfaced road

Q

Qibla	Mosque wall in direction of Mecca
Qasr	see Ksar

R

Rabbi	Head of Jewish community
Ramadan	Muslim month of fasting
Reconquista	Christian campaigns to recapture Iberian territory from Muslims
Reg	Rock desert
Ribat	Fortified monastery

S

Saadian	Moroccan dynasty from 1541
Sabil	Public water fountain
Sabkha	Dry salt lake
Saggia	Water channel
Sahn	Courtyard
Sarcophagus	Decorated stone coffin
Sahel	Coast/ coastal plain
Salat	Worship
Sebkha	see Sabkha
Serais	Lodging for men and animals
Serir	Sand desert
Shahada	Profession of faith
Shergui	Hot, dry desert wind
Sidi	Mr/Saint
Souq	Traditional market
Stele	Inscribed pillar used as gravestone
Suani	Small walled irrigated traditional garden
Sufi	Muslim mystic
Suq	see Souq
Sunni	Orthodox Muslims

T

Tagine/Tajine	Stew
Taifa	Sub-tribe
Tamashek	Language of Touareg
Tariqa	Brotherhood/Order
Tizi	Mountain pass
Touareg	Nomadic Saharan dwellers, noted for men's blue face covering
Troglodyte	Underground dweller

V

Vandals	Empire in North Africa 429-534 AD
Visir	Governor

W

Wadi	Water course – usually dry
Wikala	Merchants' hostel
Wilaya/Wilayat	Governorate/district

Z

Zaouia/Zawia	Shrine/Sennusi centre
Zayyanids	Berber dynasty NW Algeria in 13th century
Zellij	Geometrical mosaic pattern made from pieces of glazed tiles
Zeriba	House of straw/grass

TINTED BOXES

The practice of Islam: living by the
  Prophet   38
Economic indicators – Morocco   75
Neatly shod   178
Handmade carpets   190
Bottled up   195
The argane tree – the tree of the
  flying goats   208
Blooming trees   222
Caveat emptor – the art of
  bargaining   232
Economic indicators – Mauritania   250
Mirages – illusions in the desert   259
Camels – ships of the desert   262
Fundamentalism   284
Economic indicators – Algeria   290
Asses, Donkeys and Mules   306
The French Foreign Legion   332
The Mozabites   345

Scorpions – the original sting in
  the tail   365
Economic indicators – Tunisia   371
Hannibal: jumbos in the passes and
  carnage by Carthage   392
Tipped Off   399
Esparto Grass – paper in the desert   442
The Olive - a symbol of peace and
  harmony   432
The tribes of Libya   494
Colonel Mu'amar Ghadhafi   497
Economic indicators – Libya   500
The delu well – traditional well of
  Libya and North Africa   514
Downstairs only – the Troglodyte
  tendency   526
The Desert War 1940-1943   548
The Long Range Desert Group   567

INDEX

A

Adrar   259, 342
Afourgan Dayat   197
Agadir   198
Agard Oudad   222
Agdz   212
Aguelmane Azigza   195-196
Aïn Atrous   404
Aïn Draham   414
Aïn El Hammam   307
Aïn Leuh   196
Aïn Rumia   527
Aïn Sefra   338
Aïn Tagourit   301
Aïn Taya   308
Aïn-Témouchent   329
Aioun-El-Atrouss   266
Aït Arbi   215
Aït Benhaddou   212
Ajdabiyah   564
Ajim   477
Akjoujt   260
Akka   209
Al Hoceima   112
Al-Awenat   567
Al-Awenia   527
Al-Aziziyah   492
Al-Bayda   541
Al-Brayqah   500
Al-Jaghbub   567
Al-Jawf   566
Al-Khalij   559
Al-Khums   513
Al-Kuf   491
Al-Kufrah   565
Al-Marj   539
Al-Qusbat   532
Aleg   265
ALGERIA   278-360
    Before you go   354
    Communications   359
    Entertainment   359
    Entry requirements   354
    Food and drink   358
    Further reading   359
    Getting around   358
    Getting there   355
    Holidays & festivals   359
    Money   355
    When to go   355
    When you arrive   356
    Where to stay   357
Algiers   291

Amazrou   213
Ameln Valley   221
Amizmiz   188
Amogjar   261
Amorgar   261
Amsel   350
Ancient Cotta   102
Annaba   317
Aoua Dayat   197
Apollonia   545
Arris   322
As-Asbiah   533
Asilah   118
Asni   188
Assekrem   350
Atar   260
Aurés Mountains   319
Azaza   307
Azilal   194
Aziziyah   519
Azougui   261
Azrou   195
Azzefoun   308
Azzemour   131

B

Badriane   341
Batna   320
Béchar   338
Béja   417
Bejaïa   308
Ben Ghashir   533
Benghazi   534
Beni Abbès   340
Beni Bahdel lake   333
Beni Isquen   346
Beni Kheddache   468
Beni Mellal   193
Beni Yenni   307
Beni-Saf   329
Bhalil   165
Bin El Ouidane dam   194
Bir-Moghrein   264
Biskra   323
Bizerte   405
Blida   303
Bogué   269
Borj Cedria   396
Bou Hamed   108
Bou Izakarn   209
Bouarfa   219
Boujad   194
Boujdour   225

Boumalne   215
Boutilimit   265
Brak   500
Bulla Regia   415

C

Cabo Negro   108
Calanscio   491
Cansado   258
Cap Afrique   433
Cap Blanc   407
Cap Bon   403
Cap Bon Peninsula   397
Cap Carbon   309
Cap de Garde   319
Cap Falcon   329
Cap Malabata   102
Cap Nègre   411
Cap Rosa   319
Cap Serrat   411
Cap Spartel   102
Cap Tafarit   257
Carthage   389
Casablanca   124
Cascades d'El Ourit   333
Cascades d'Ouzoud   194
Cascades de Ras
    El Oued   169
Caves of Hercules   102
Ceuta   103
Chaouen   108
Chebika   456
Chefchaouen   108
Chenini   462, 470
Cherchell   324
Chetaïbi   319
Chichaoua   188
Chinguetti   261
Choum   264
Chréa   303
Col du Kerdous   221
Constantine   314
Cuicul   312
Cyrenaica   491
Cyrene   541

D

Dades Valley   214
Dahar   491
Dakhla   225
Dar Caid Ourika   192
Dar Chaabane   400

Dar M'Ter   108
Dayat Chiker   169
Dellys   308
Derna   546
Djanet   352
Djebel Shambi   363
Djebel Tahat   350
Djemaa El Fna,
    Marrakech   176
Djemila   312
Djemma   459
Djerba   471
Djoumaa   468
Djurdjura National Park   307
Djurdjura Range   306
Dougga   419
Douiret   469
Douz   459
Draa Valley   212

E

El Alia   410
El Ateuf   347
El Djem   448
El Eubbab   332
El Faouar   460
El Goléa   342
El Haouaria   403
El Jadida   132
El Jebha   108
El Jem   448
El Kala   319
El Kantara   323
El Kef Gabsa   341
El Kelaa des M'Gouna   215
El Ksiba   195
El May   477
El Oued   335
El-Dar-el-Beida   124
Enfida   429
Er Rachidia   196, 217
Er Riadh   477
Erfoud   218
Erg Chebbi   219
Essaouira   136

F

Farwa Island   518
Fes (Fez)   151
Fezzan   491, 550
Figuig   219
Fort Trinquet   264
Foum El Hassan   209
Foum-Zguid   209

G

Gabès   461
Gafsa   450
Gammarth   394
Gasr Al-Libya   540
Gasr Garabouli   512
Ghadames   528
Ghar el Kebirk Caves   403
Ghar el Melh   409
Ghardaïa   343
Ghardimaou   417
Gharyan   525
Ghoumrassen el Bled   470
Gialo   565
Gialo oases   562
Gorges du Dades   215
Gorges du Todra   216
Gouffre du Friouato   169
Goulimine   222
Goulmima   217
Goulmin lake   307
Grand Erg Oriental   334
Grande Kabylie   304
Grombalia   404
Grotte du Chameau   115
Guellala   477
Guémar   336
Guermessa   470
Gulf of Sirte   491

H

Haddej (Haddège)   467
Hammadah   491
Hammam Bourguiba   414
Hammamet   397
Hannibal   392
Hassi Messaoud   337
Hergla   430
Hippo Regius   319
Hirafok   350
Hoggar mountains   347
Houmt Souk   473

I

Ifrah Dayat   197
Ifrane   197
Ifrane de l'Anti Atlas   209
Iharen   350
Illizi   352
Imeleoulaouene   350
Imlil   188
Immouzer de Kandar   197
Immouzer des Ida
    Outanane   204
In Aménas   351
In Salah   348

Inezgane   204
Irherm   209
Islam   38
Islas Chafarinas   115
Isles des Purpuraires   138
Italian   498
Iwik   256
Izgzer   341

J

Jabal Al-Akhdar   491
Jabal As-Sawda   491
Jabal Nafusa   523
Jabbaren   353
Jadu   526
Janzur   518
Jardins Exotiques   91
Jefara Plain   511
Jendouba   417
Jijel   310

K

Kabila   108
Kabylia   304
Kaedi   269
Kairouan   435
Kalaat el Andalous   407
Kasbah Tadla   194
Kasbah Telouet   193
Kasserine   442
Kebili   459
Kediel Aj-Jill   242
Kelbia Lake   439
Kelibia   402
Kenitra   122
Kerkennah Islands   446
Kerkouane   402
Kerzaz   340
Ketama   111
Keur Massène   268
Khenifra   195
Kherrata gorges   310
Khounbga   194
Kiffa   265
Kikla   526
Korba   402
Korbous   403
Koumbi Saleh   266
Ksar el Kebir   121
Ksar es Seghir   102
Ksar Guilane   470
Ksar Haddad   470
Ksar Ouled Debbab   469
Ksar Ouled Soltane   469

L

L'Arbaa-Nath-Iraten   306
La Gouèra   258
La Goulette   389
La Marsa   394
Laayoune   224
Lake Ichkeul   411
Larache   120
Le Kef   418
Leptis Magna   514-520
Les Andalouses   327
LIBYA   489-579
   before you go   569
   communications   577
   entertainment   578
   entry requirements   569
   food and drink   575
   further reading   579
   getting around   576
   getting there   571
   health   570
   holidays & festivals   578
   money   570
   when to go   570
   when you arrive   573
   where to stay   574
Lixus   121

M

M'Hamid   214
M'Zab   342
Maghnia   333
Mahdia   433
Maktar   439
Mamora Forest   91
Mandara Lake   555
Mansourah   332
Marrakech   172
Martil   108
Massif de Edough   319
Matmata   465
MAURITANIA   240-277
   before you go   270
   communications   276
   entertainment   276
   entry requirements   270
   food and drink   274
   further reading   276
   getting around   274
   getting there   272
   health   271
   holidays & festivals   276
   money   271
   when to go   271
   when you arrive   273
   where to stay   274
Mderdra   268

Medenine   468
Medjerda, Oued   364
Medjez-el-Bab   422
Mehdiya   123
Mejennin   491
Meknes   140
Melika   346
Melilla   114
Menzel Bou Zelfa   404
Menzel Bourguiba   411
Menzel Temime   402
Mers El Kebir   329
Merzouga   219
Meski   217
Metameur   468
Metlaoui   452
Metline   410
Midelt   196
Midès   456
Midoun   476
Mischliffen   197
Misratah   515
Mohammedia   123
Monastir   430
Moretti   300
MOROCCO   65-239
   before you go   226
   communications   237
   entertainment   237
   entry requirements   226
   food and drink   233
   further reading   239
   getting around   235
   getting there   228
   health   227
   holidays & festivals   238
   money   227
   when to go   227
   when you arrive   230
   where to stay   232
Mostaganem   326
Moulay Abdellah (Tit)   134
Moulay Bousselham   122
Moulay Idriss   148
Mrirt   195
Murzuq   491

N

Nabeul   399
Nador   113
Nakhla   336
Nalut   528
Nédroma   333
Nefta   456
Nema   266
Nouadhibou   257
Nouakchott   251

O

Obari lakes   555
Ofra Sand Dune   459
Oran   326
Ouadane   262
Oualata   266
Oualidia   134
Ouargla   337
Ouarzazate   209
Oued Laou   108
Oued Zem   194
Ouezzane   116
Ouirgane   189
Oujda   169
Oujeft   260
Oukaimeden   191
Ouled Said   341
Oulmes-Tarmilate   195
Oumesnate   221
Ourika Valley   192

P

Parc National du
   Banc d'Arguin   256
Petite Kabylie   304
Phillippe Thomas   452
Plage des Nations   91
Plage des Pêcheurs   255
Port el Kantaoui   429

Q

Qalah   527

R

Rabat   76
Rachid   267
Radès   396
Raf Raf   409
Ras Al-Hillal   546
Ras Djebel   409
Ras Ed Drak   403
Ras Lanuf   500
Ras Sidi Ali el Mekki   409
Redeyef   453
Restinga Smir   108
Rhoufi   322
Rissani   218
Robbah   336
Rosso   268

S

Sabha   550
Sabrata   517, 522
Safi   134

588

Sahel 363
Saïdia 115
Sale 89
Sbeitla 440
Sefrou 165
Sejnane 411
Seldja Gorges 453
Selibaby 269
Senussi 490
Seraidi 319
Serir 499
Sétif 310
Setti Fatma 192
Sfax 442
Shahat 541
Shakshuk 528
Shershara 532
Sidi Bou Saïd 392
Sidi Daoud 403
Sidi Fredj 300
Sidi Harazem 165
Sidi Ifni 222
Sidi Mechrig 411
Sidi Moussa d'Aglou 221
Sidi-Bel-Abbès 333
Sidrah 500
Sijilmassa 218
Sirt 564
Skhirat 91
Skoura oasis 214
Smara 225
Soffejin 491
Souk Ahras 319
Sousse 423
Steha 108
Suq Al-Khemis 533
Suq Al-Sebt 533
Susa 545

T

Tabarka 412
Tafilalt 218
Tafraoute 221
Tagant 267
Tagdawst 265
Taghit 339
Tahanaoute 188
Takouatz Guerrisséne
    glacier 307
Takrouna 430
Tala Guilef 306
Tamanrasset 348
Tamchaket 265
Tamegroute 213
Tamekrest 350
Tamelhat 337
Tamezret 467

Tamrit 352
Tan Zoumaitak 353
Tan-Tan 223
Tanger 92
Tarfaya 223
Targa 108
Tarhazoute 204
Tarhunah 532
Taroudant 205
Tassili N'Ajjer 350
Tassili National Park 352
Tata 209
Tataouine 469
Tauorga 516
Taza 167
Tazrouk 350
Teboursouk 419
Telathin 513
Temacine 337
Temara 91
Temerza 456
Temples
    Bulla Regia 415
    Cyrene 541
    Dougga 419
    Leptis Magna 514
    Sabrata 517
    Sbeitla 440
    Thuburbo Majus 395
    Volubilis 148
Ténès 326
Terjit 260
Tetouan 104
Thamugadi 321
The Grand Erg
    Occidental 338
The Souf 334
Thuburbo Majus 395
Tibesti 491
Tichi 309
Tichit 267
Tiddis 316
Tigzirt 308
Tikjda 307
Timbedra 266
Timenzouzine 353
Timgad 321
Timimoun 341
Timoulay Izder 209
Tin Mal 189
Tinejdad 217
Tinerhir 216
Tinlabbé 263
Tipasa 301
Tissint 209
Tizerbu 562, 566
Tizi Ouzou 304
Tizi-n-Test 191

Tizi-n-Tichka 192
Tiznit 220
Tlemcen 329
Tobruk 500
Tocra 538
Tolmeita 539
Tophet 390
Toubkal National Park 188
Touggourt 336
Toujane 467
Tozeur 453
Trajan's Bridge 418
Tripoli 502
Tripolitania 491
Tunis 372
TUNISIA 361-488
    before you go 478
    communications 486
    entertainment 487
    entry requirements 478
    food and drink 483
    further reading 488
    getting around 484
    getting there 480
    health 479
    holidays & festivals 487
    money 479
    when to go 479
    when you arrive 481
    where to stay 482

U

Utica 406
Utique 406
Uzu 491

V

Volubilis 148

W

Wadi Al-Kuf 541
Wadi Ki'am 515

Y

Yafran 526, 527
Yakouren 307

Z

Z'Goum 336
Zaafrane 460
Zaghouan 394
Zagora 213
Zarzis 470
Zaviyah 500

Zegzel Gorges 115
Zembra 404
Zembretta 404
Zeralda 301

Ziz Gorge 197
Zliten 515
Zouara 411
Zouerate 264

Zuwarah 518
Zuwaylah 554
Zuwetina 562

590

INDEX OF MAPS

Agadir 201
Al-Khalij 560
Al-Khums to Tripoli 533
Algeria 280-281
Algiers 292-293
Algiers and
  surroundings 301
Algiers Kasbah 296
Annaba 317
Apollonia 546
Assekrem Circuit 350
Aurés 320
Bardo Museum 375
Benghazi 535
Bizerte 407
Bulla Regia 416
Cap Bon 400
Carthage 391
Casablanca 125
Casablanca Centre 128
Casablanca Medina 126
Central Morocco 139
Central Tunisia 424
Chaouen 109
Constantine 315
Constantine and
  surroundings 311
Cyrene 542
Desert War 549
Djemila 313
Djerba Island 473
Djerid 452
Dougga 420
East of Tripoli 513
El Djem 449
El Jadida 133
Essaouira 137
Ferry routes 9
Fes 153

Fes El Bali 155
Fes El Jedid 161
Fes Ville Nouvelle 162
Fezzan 551
Gabès 464
Gafsa 451
Ghadames house plan 530
Ghardaïa 344
Grand Erg Occidental 339
Grand Erg Oriental 335
Hammamet 398
High and Middle Atlas 189
Hoggar 347
Houmt Souk 475
Important historical sites 25
Jabal Al-Akhdar 538
Jabal Nafusa 527
Jaghbub 563
Kabylia 305
Kairouan 438
Kairouan Mosque 437
Kerkennah Islands 446
Leptis Magna 521
Libya 490
Mahdia 434
Maktar 440
Marrakech 175
Marrakech Medina 181
Marrakech Souqs 179
Matmata 466
Mauritania 241
Mediterranean Coast and
  The Rif (Morocco) 102
Meknes 144
Meknes Medina 145
Monastir 431
Morocco 66
Nabeul 401
Nefta 457

Northern & Central Atlantic
  Coast (Morocco) 118
Northern Tunisia 410
Northwest Algeria 325
Nouakchott 252
Oran 328
Ouarzazate 211
Rabat and Sale 78-79
Rabat Medina 83
Sabrata 523
Sbeitla 441
Sfax 444
Souqs of Marrakech 179
Sousse 427
Southern Morocco 199
Southern Tunisia 462
Tabarka 413
Tanger Medina 96
Tanger 94
Taroudant 206
Tassili N'Ajjer 351
Tetouan 105
Thuburbo Majus 395
Timgad 321
Tipasa 302
Tlemcen 330
Tolmeita 540
Tozeur 454
Tripoli 504-505
Tripoli Medina 503
Tunis Centre 382
Tunis Medina 380
Tunis Metro 387
Tunis Region 373
Tunis surroundings 389
Tunisia 362
Volubilis 149
Wadi Derna 547
West of Tripoli 517

TRADE & TRAVEL
Handbooks

1996

Trade & Travel *Handbooks* are available worldwide in good bookshops. They can also be obtained by mail order directly from us in Bath (see below for address). Please contact us if you have difficulty finding a title.

South American Handbook

Mexico & Central American Handbook

Caribbean Islands Handbook

India Handbook

Thailand & Burma Handbook

Vietnam, Laos & Cambodia Handbook

Indonesia, Malaysia & Singapore Handbook

Morocco & Tunisia Handbook
with Algeria, Libya and Mauritania

East African Handbook
with Kenya, Tanzania, Uganda and Ethiopia

New in January 1996:
Egypt Handbook
Nepal & Tibet Handbook
Sri Lanka Handbook
Pakistan Handbook

Keep in touch. If you would like a catalogue or more information about the new titles please contact us at :

Trade & Travel, 6 Riverside Court, Lower Bristol Road, Bath BA2 3DZ. England

Tel 01225 469141   Fax 01225 469461   Email 100660.1250@compuserve.com

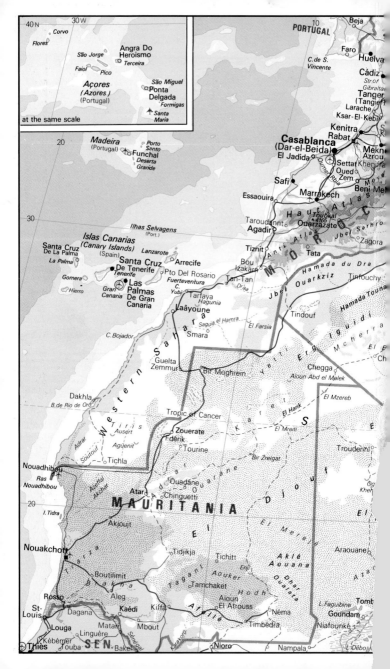

40 N
30 W
Corvo
Flores
São Jorge   Angra Do
Faiol   Heroismo
            Terceira
Pico
Açores
(Azores)
(Portugal)
São Miguel
Ponta
Delgada
Formigas
Santa
Maria
at the same scale

10
PORTUGAL   Beja
                  Faro   Huelva
         C. de S.
         Vincente   Cádiz
                    Str of
                    Gibraltar
                         Tanger
                         (Tangier)
                    Larache
                    Ksar-El-Kebir
                  Kenitra
                  Rabat   Mekn
Casablanca   Azrou
(Dar-el-Beida)   Khenifra
El Jadida   Settat
         Oued
         Zem   Beni Mel
Safi   Marrakech

Madeira
(Portugal)
Porto
Santo
Funchal
Deserta
Grande

20

30
Ilhas Selvagens
(Port.)

Essaouira
                Marrakech
Taroudannt   Haut Atlas
              Toubkal
              4165
Agadir   Ouarzazate
                        Jbel Sarhro
Tiznit   Anti Atlas   Zagora
                 Tata
Bou
Izakarn   Hamada du Dra
Tan-Tan
         Jbel Ouarkziz   Tinfouchy
C. Yubi Tarfaya   Hamada Touna
      Hagunia
Laâyoune Dràa
         Saguia el Hamra   Yetti
         El Farsia
Smara

Islas Canarias
(Canary Islands)
(Spain)   Lanzarote
Santa Cruz   Arrecife
De La Palma
La Palma Santa Cruz
         Tenerife
Gomera   Pto Del Rosario
Hierro   Fuerteventura
    Gran   Las
    Canaria Palmas
         De Gran
         Canaria

C.Bojador
                Guelta
                Zemmur   Bir Moghrein

Dakhla
B. de Rio de Oro

Adrar
Soutouf
Tichla
Aguenit
            Tropic of Cancer
            Zouerate
            Fdérik
Tiris   Tourine
Ausert
                        Bir Zreigat

Erg   Iguidi
Mcherra
El F
Ch

Chegga
Aioun Abd el Malek

Kaet
El Hank
El Mreiti
Troudenni

Og
Kheh

Nouadhibou
Ras
Nouadhibou
Azefal
Akchar

Ouadane
Chinguetti
Atar

MAURITANIA

I. Tidra

Akjoujt

Nouakchott

Trarza

Tidjikja

Boutilimit
Aleg
Rosso   Kaédi   Kiffa
St-
Louis Dagana
Louga   Matam Mbout
Linguère
Kébémer
Touba Bakel
SEN.

El   Djouf

El Merbid

Aklé
Aouana

Tichitt
Enji
Tamchaket   Hodh
Aioun   Oualata
El Atrouss

El

Araouane

Azac
L. Faguibine Tomb
Goundam
Néma   Timbédra Niafounké
Nioro   Nampala L. Débo

Tagant
Tamourt
Aouker

Dhar

Afollé
Aoutef